Management

EIGHTH EDITION

Management

EIGHTH EDITION

Stephen P. Robbins

San Diego State University

Mary Coulter

Southwest Missouri State University

PEARSON

Prentice
Hall

Upper Saddle River, NJ 07458

Library of Congress Cataloging-in-Publication Data
Robbins, Stephen P.
    Management/Stephen P. Robbins, Mary Coulter.—8th ed.
        p. cm.
    Includes bibliographical references and index.
    ISBN 0-13-143994-4
    1. Management.   I. Coulter, Mary K.   II. Title.
HD31.R5647   2005
658—dc22   2003066351

Acquisitions Editor: Michael Ablassmeir
Editor-in-Chief: Jeff Shelstad
Assistant Editors: Melanie Olsen, Ashley Keim
Media Project Manager: Jessica Sabloff
Executive Marketing Manager: Shannon Moore
Marketing Assistant: Patrick Danzuso
Senior Managing Editor (Production): Judy Leale
Production Assistant: Joe DeProspero
Permissions Supervisor: Suzanne Grappi
Manufacturing Buyer: Diane Peirano
Design Manager: Maria Lange
Designer: Steve Frim
Interior Design: Wanda Espana
Cover Design: Robin Hoffmann
Cover Photography: NilsWalter Studio
Illustrator (Interior): Bruce Killmer
Photo Researcher: Melinda Alexander
Image Permission Coordinator: Debbie Latronica
Manager, Print Production: Christy Mahon
Composition/Full-Service Project Management: Preparé, Inc.
Printer/Binder: Von Hoffmann

Credits and acknowledgments borrowed from other sources and reproduced, with permission, in this textbook appear on the appropriate page within text; photo credits appear on page 576.

Pearson Prentice Hall™ is a trademark of Pearson Education, Inc.
Pearson® is a registered trademark of Pearson plc
Prentice Hall® is a registered trademark of Pearson Education, Inc.

Pearson Education LTD.
Pearson Education Singapore, Pte. Ltd
Pearson Education, Canada, Ltd
Pearson Education—Japan

Pearson Education Australia PTY, Limited
Pearson Education North Asia Ltd
Pearson Educación de Mexico, S.A. de C.V.
Pearson Education Malaysia, Pte. Ltd

10 9 8 7 6 5 4 3 2 1
ISBN 0-13-143994-4

● ● ● ● About the Authors

Stephen P. Robbins received his Ph.D. from the University of Arizona and has taught at the University of Nebraska at Omaha, Concordia University in Montreal, the University of Baltimore, Southern Illinois University at Edwardsville, and San Diego State University. Dr. Robbins' research interests have focused on conflict, power, and politics in organizations, behavioral decision making, and the development of effective interpersonal skills. His articles on these and other topics have appeared in journals such as *Business Horizons*, the *California Management Review, Business and Economic Perspectives, International Management, Management Review, Canadian Personnel and Industrial Relations*, and *The Journal of Management Education.*

Dr. Robbins is the world's best-selling textbook author in the areas of management and organizational behavior. His most recent textbooks include *Organizational Behavior, 10th ed.* (Prentice Hall, 2003), *Essentials of Organizational Behavior, 7th ed.* (Prentice Hall, 2003), *Fundamentals of Management, 4th ed.* with David DeCenzo (Prentice Hall, 2004), and *Supervision Today! 4th ed.* with David DeCenzo (Prentice Hall, 2004). In addition, Dr. Robbins is the author of the global best-sellers *The Truth About Managing People … and Nothing But the Truth* (Financial Times Press, 2002) and *Decide & Conquer* (Financial Times Press, 2004).

An avid participant in masters' track and field competition, Dr. Robbins has set numerous indoor and outdoor age-group world sprint records since turning 50 in 1993. He has won more than a dozen indoor and outdoor U.S. national titles at 60, 100, 200, and 400 meters, and has won seven gold medals at the World Masters Championships.

Mary Coulter received her Ph.D. in Management from the University of Arkansas in Fayetteville. Before completing her graduate work, she held different jobs including high school teacher, legal assistant, and government program planner. She has taught at Drury University, the University of Arkansas, Trinity University, and since 1983, at Southwest Missouri State University. Dr. Coulter's research interests have focused on competitive strategies for not-for-profit arts organizations and the use of new media in the educational process. Her research on these and other topics has appeared in such journals as *International Journal of Business Disciplines, Journal of Business Strategies, Journal of Business Research, Journal of Nonprofit and Public Sector Marketing*, and *Case Research Journal*. In addition to *Management*, Dr. Coulter has published other books with Prentice Hall including *Strategic Management in Action*, now in its third edition, and *Entrepreneurship in Action*, which is in its second edition. When she's not busy teaching or writing, she enjoys puttering around in her flower gardens, playing the piano, reading all different types of books, and enjoying many different activities with husband Ron and daughters Sarah and Katie.

●●●Brief Contents

Contents

Management
EIGHTH EDITION

PREFACE

This book is the number-one selling basic management textbook in the United States and the world! It has been translated into Spanish, Russian, Dutch, Thai, Bahasa Indonesian, Czech, and Chinese, and reprinted in English in the Philippines and China, with special adapted editions for Canada, Australia, and India. If there's such a thing as a "global" management textbook, this book probably has earned that distinction.

There's no doubt that the world managers confront has changed, is changing, and will continue to change. The dynamic nature of today's organizations means both rewards *and* challenges for those individuals who will be managing those organizations. Management is a dynamic discipline and a textbook on the subject should reflect those changes to help prepare you to manage under those conditions. Thus, we've written this eighth edition of *Management* to provide you with the best possible understanding of what it means to be a manager confronting these changes.

HALLMARK FEATURES

Adopters continually praise this book for its strong applications orientation. This is not a book that just describes management theories. In addition to including explanatory examples (which most other textbooks do), we go out and talk with real managers. Then we bring their experiences to our readers. No other textbook has so successfully blended management theory with management practice. We're confident that this new edition will continue to make management concepts meaningful and to excite readers about the possibilities for careers in management. We'd like to describe some of the features we have retained in this edition.

"A Manager's Dilemma" and "Managers Respond to a Manager's Dilemma"

Each chapter opens with a dilemma that a real-life manager is facing. These managers come from an array of companies such as Mattel Toys, Zara, Okemo Mountain Resort, Svenska Handelsbanken, Panera Bread, BMW, and Haier Group. Each dilemma ends with the statement "What would you do?", providing students a glimpse into the decision-making process. Then, we close the chapter with a section titled "Managers Respond to a Manager's Dilemma" where two real, practicing managers provide a short discussion of what they'd do if they were faced with the opening dilemma, drawing on the management concepts and tools presented in the chapter.

A Manager's Dilemma

As one of the world's most respected financial institutions, UBS AG is Switzerland's largest bank and a major player in international financial circles. The Zurich- and Basel-based company has assets of more than $834 billion and has positioned itself so that each of its business groups (UBS Wealth Management and Business Banking, UBS Warburg Ltd., UBS Global Asset Management, and UBS PaineWebber) is in the top rankings of its core business. Dr. Gabriela Payer, Fruithof (pictured here), managing director and head of marketing technology for UBS AG, is playing a key role in the company's choice of future directions.

Fruithof has been the driving force behind many of the company's Internet strategies and solutions. Like many financial institutions in the United States and around the globe, UBS has made a major commitment to online services. Customers can get information on their accounts using personal computers, personal digital assistants, and phones. They can pay bills, conduct transactions, trade stocks, or view their holdings and activities. In addition, a secure e-mail feature lets customers send messages and attachments without using the public Internet. Since the bank also owns two mutual fund and brokerage firms with thousands of customers, Fruithof led the development of a customer-relationship management program that included customized call centers and interactive voice response systems with built-in speech recognition. In many instances, the company can prioritize and route incoming calls based on a customer's relationship and standing with the bank. For example, customers who use a wide range of bank services and provide high profits will have their calls taken immediately, while low-profit customers have to wait for an available service representative.

The company's multichannel approach to online banking has been quite successful. Internal performance studies indicate that overall work productivity has improved by 30 percent at call centers. Also, more than 70 percent of incoming inquiries are handled by electronic systems.

Fruithof says, "The Internet doesn't change the rules of business; it's just another way to conduct business. When you understand your core values and goals, you have the knowledge to make the right moves at the right time." Put yourself in her shoes. Now that the online banking initiative has been implemented, what types of plans might she need to guide the use of the Internet in other additional marketing activities?

What would _you_ do?

Managers Respond to a **Manager's** Dilemma

Sandra M. Steiner
Executive Vice President, Business Development, Westminster, Colorado

Brett is fortunate he has so many employees using the current site. From that base of users, he could ask them to complete a questionnaire regarding the items they find most useful and ask the managers within the Australian group how they use the site when working with their employees. This would give him information about the real usefulness of the information provided, identify additional items that could be introduced in an upgrade, and give him good knowledge of the strengths offered by the current site. When considering offering the site to new locations, he should allow for some new content tailored to local needs. Brett could invite a representative group of employees and managers to view the current site and get their feedback. Before expanding the program, it's critical that he knows the reasons employees find it to be of value and then build on that knowledge.

David Jolliffe
Manager, New Media & Editorial Services, Pearson Canada, Toronto, Ontario, Canada

Extending an employee intranet to other units poses a number of challenges. The first concerns the content and structure of the portal itself. To be well received, the site needs to reflect the practices, policies, issues and events of each local business unit so these employees feel the resource belongs to them as much as it does the head office. It also needs to integrate local content so it's easy to find; ensure the local materials are of the same high quality as other information; and treat employees as well-rounded people by including personal items such as carpool postings, weather reports, or trade/sell services. In other words, the site needs to have obvious value for local employees. Initially, this utility will need to be demonstrated through advertising, site search contests, and employee presentations. As with all change, people have to be convinced of the added value of the innovation.

"Managers Speak Out"

In selected chapters, you'll find this theme box in which real managers are interviewed and answer a broad range of questions. Some of these managers include Pearson Education's Marjorie Scardino and Jack Stack, CEO of SRC Holdings Corporation. The information in these interviews provides a diverse perspective of managers and managerial philosophies and reinforces that this textbook truly links management theory and practice.

MANAGERS SPEAK OUT

Marjorie Scardino, CEO
Pearson PLC
London, England

Describe your job.
I am the CEO of a media company that publishes books, newspapers and magazines, and educational materials—both textbooks and online programs. We're all about "education" in the broadest sense of the word: education for a five-year-old learning to read, a CEO understanding the way his (or her) industry is heading, an investor picking a stock, or a college student studying a course like the one you're in now. The company has total sales of about $6 billion, employs 30,000 people, has headquarters in London and New York, and makes about 70 percent of its sales in the United States.

My job has three main parts:

1. _Strategy:_ It's my responsibility to figure out what the company should do to become more valuable and to produce returns for shareholders, as well as to add something to the world. To do this, we have to look at our assets and our markets and the relevant economic, political, and social trends and decide on the most promising combination of those factors. Then, we have to create a plan for shaping the business into that combination and making sure that our products, sales, and operations are all consistent with that plan.

2. _Execution:_ No matter how good our strategy, we won't get very far if we can't carry out our plan. That involves innovative product design, ingenious marketing strategy, irresistible sales skills, and efficient and engaging customer service. It involves judicious attention to the costs of conceiving, making, selling, and delivering our products, and keeping the right balance between growth and costs. It involves making the pursuit of the plan a process that we can measure and monitor and constantly adjust. It involves knowing when to take a risk.

3. _Culture and people._ Finally, and possibly most importantly, my job is to set the tone for a company environment and way of behaving in which we can all be most productive and to exemplify that culture myself. The ingredients in culture include everything from pay and benefits to communicating with each other to how we deal with outsiders and how we treat each other inside. A company's culture is important in determining whether we can attract and keep the best people and whether, when situations are confusing, our employees know how they must behave.

Why are managers important to organizations?
Managers set the goals, the agenda, the measures of achievement, and the standards of behavior. In the most successful organizations, they do all that by setting an example, inspiring and orchestrating in a democratic rather than an autocratic way.

What skills do managers need to be effective in today's environment?
The ability to see the bigger picture, concentration, parallel thinking, ability to see connections, listening, sense of humor, risk taking, humility, and generosity.

Skill-Building Modules

In this section of the textbook, you will have the opportunity to learn about, practice, and reinforce specific management skills. We have included 21 skills that encompass the 4 functions of management: planning, organizing, leading, and controlling. (See the matrix that follows.)

For each of the skills, we provide the following: (1) A short introduction discusses some basic facts about the skill and defines it, if necessary. (2) A section called "Learning About" describes the suggested behaviors for doing that skill. These behaviors are presented in numbered lists in order to illustrate the specific actions associated with that skill. (3) A section entitled "Practice" presents a short scenario designed to provide you with an opportunity to practice the behaviors associated with the skill. Your professor may have you do different things with the practice scenarios. (4) A section entitled "Reinforcement" is designed to present additional activities that you could do to practice and reinforce the behaviors associated with the skill.

Management Skills and Management Functions Matrix

Skill	Planning	Organizing	Leading	Controlling
Acquiring power		✓	✓	✓
Active listening			✓	
Budgeting	✓		✓	
Choosing an effective leadership style			✓	
Coaching		✓	✓	
Creating effective teams		✓	✓	
Delegating (empowerment)		✓	✓	✓
Designing motivating jobs			✓	
Developing trust		✓	✓	✓
Disciplining			✓	✓
Interviewing		✓	✓	
Managing Conflict			✓	
Managing resistance to change			✓	✓
Mentoring			✓	
Negotiating		✓	✓	
Providing feedback			✓	
Reading an organization's culture	✓		✓	
Scanning the environment	✓			✓
Setting goals	✓	✓		✓
Solving problems creatively	✓	✓		
Valuing Diversity				

1 • ACQUIRING POWER

Power is a natural process in any group or organization, and to perform their jobs effectively, managers need to know how to acquire and use power—the capacity of a leader to influence work actions or decisions. We discussed the concept of power in Chapter 17 and identified five different sources of power for leaders including legitimate, coercive, reward, expert, and referent. Why is having power important? Because power makes you less dependent on others. When a manager has power, he or she is not as dependent on others for critical resources. And if the resources a manager controls are important, scarce, and nonsubstitutable, her power will increase because others will be more dependent on her for those resources.

Skills Modules

Management students need to learn how *to do* management tasks as well as to learn *about* management. Today, the "hows" of being a manager have become just as important as the "whats." To reflect the importance being placed on skills, we retained our in-book Skills Modules. The 21 key skills found in the Skills Modules section following Chapter 19 encompass the four management functions.

Managing Entrepreneurial Ventures

The Global Entrepreneurship Monitor (GEM) Report shows that entrepreneurship plays an increasingly important role in economies around the world. Effective management is just as important in small or new entrepreneurial ventures as it is in large. This material is found in five separate sections and can be easily located by the tinted pages after Parts Two, Three, Four, Five, and Six.

Writing Style

This revision continues both authors' commitment to present management concepts in a lively and conversational style. Our goal is to present chapter material in an interesting and relevant manner without oversimplifying the discussion. We think you'll find our writing style and numerous examples make our book very readable.

NEW TO THIS EDITION

We are very excited about the innovations incorporated into *Management 8e*! This is truly a textbook for students in today's changing world. We think one of the reasons this book is the market leader is that it has developed a reputation for continually introducing new content. Some of our new cutting-edge topics include:

- Customer service management (Chapters 1 and 2)
- Customer responsive cultures (Chapter 3)
- Innovative cultures (Chapter 3)
- GLOBE (Global Leadership and Organizational Behavior Effectiveness) cross-cultural studies (Chapter 4)
- Ethical leadership (Chapter 5)
- Social impact management (Chapter 5)
- Decision-making biases and errors (Chapter 6)
- Highly reliable organizations (Chapter 6)
- Strategic "rule of three" (Chapter 8)
- First movers (Chapter 8)
- Virtual/network/modular organizations
- Managing Internet gripe sites (Chapter 11)
- Communities of practice (Chapter 11)
- Politically correct communication (Chapter 11)
- The influence of job satisfaction on customer satisfaction (Chapter 14)
- Social loafing (Chapter 15)
- Employee recognition programs (Chapter 16)
- Stock option programs (Chapter 16)
- Moral leadership (Chapter 17)
- Online leadership
- The heroic leader (Chapter 17)
- Managing earnings (Chapter 18)
- Controlling customer interactions (Chapter 18)
- Corporate governance (Chapter 18)
- Mass customization (Chapter 19)

management
eighth edition
STEPHEN P. ROBBINS / MARY COULTER

Integrative Topics

In addition to this new material, we chose to highlight five integrative topics in this new edition. These topics are **globalization, ethics, diversity, customer service**, and **innovation**. (See Exhibit P-1.) Other than customer service (which, we're sure you'll agree, is critical to an organization's success but which is a topic not covered by other basic management texts), these topics aren't new to management textbooks. So why did we choose to highlight these? Because managers in twenty-first century organizations have to effectively and efficiently manage each if they want their organizations to be successful. We think our integrative approach helps students better understand how these issues permeate the management process.

Chapter	Globalization and Cross-Cultural Differences	Diversity	Ethics	Customer Service	Innovation
1			8	15	15-16
2	37	39	38; 42	43-44	41-42
3	69	58	60-61; 74-75	61-62; 64-65	60-61
4	77-97		87; 95-96		
5	105; 114-115		108; 110-122; 125		
6		149	144; 154-155		
7			165; 175		171-172
8			184; 201-202	197-198	198-199
9	208		208; 224-225		
10	247-248		235; 252-253		248-249
11	264	263-264; 275-276	270; 278-279	273; 274-275	273-274
12		301-302; 303-304	297; 307		
13		323	325; 332-333		327-330
14	354	354	363; 366-367	346	
15	373; 376; 377; 378	374	377; 388-389		379-380
16	407-408	409; 410	413; 418-419		
17	443-444	444-445	438; 449-450		
18	475-476	466	473; 481-483; 486	479-481	473-474
19	491		497; 508-509	494-495; 505-506	502-504
Part-ending material	127-128; 129-130 226-227; 334-335; 452; 510		127; 130-131; 226; 334; 452; 510	229	227-228; 338-339

Better Presentation of Material on Controlling

In order to streamline the presentation, reduce redundancy, and better integrate the concepts on the controlling function, we chose to combine material from Chapter 20 and Chapter 18. This newly integrated chapter provides an insightful and contemporary overview of the controlling function that managers perform.

"Becoming a Manager"

To reinforce our already strong applications orientation, we have added a new, boxed theme in every chapter that provides suggestions for students on activities and actions they can do right now to help them in preparing to become a manager.

Integration of Text and Technology

Innovative, integrated, interactive . . .
A learning package for today's management student!

We think one of the most important innovations we've made in the eighth edition is the integration of the text with our technology. Color-coded chapter callouts link the text material to our material on our Robbins Online Learning System (R.O.L.L.S.) Web site (www.prenhall.com/robbins), which now features six elements:

We have integrated many exercises from the **R**obbins **O**nline **L**earning **S**ystem (R.O.L.L.S.), found on **www.prenhall.com/robbins**, throughout this text. These exercises are called out by a color that is keyed to a particular section of the R.O.L.L.S. Web site. When you see the color bar, go to **www.prenhall.com/robbins, then to R.O.L.L.S.** to find an exercise that relates to the topic being discussed.

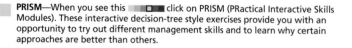

Diversity—When you see this ▬▬◻ click on "You Be the Manager: Diversity in Action" to find an exercise that puts you in the role of a manager making a decision about diversity.

S.A.L. (Self-Assessment Library)—When you see this ▬▬◻ click on S.A.L. and complete the suggested self-assessment exercise. These exercises will help you discover things about yourself, your attitudes, and your personal strengths and weaknesses.

Q & A—When you see this ◼◻▬ click on Q & A, your 24/7 educational assistant. These video clips and written material presented by your authors address questions that we have found students frequently ask.

Passport—When you see this ◼◻▬ click on Passport to find information about nine different countries. You'll use this information to complete the Passport case scenarios found at the end of Parts Two–Six.

Ethics—When you see this ◼◻▬ click on "You Be the Manager: Putting Ethics into Action" to find an interactive exercise that puts you in the role of a manager making decisions about ethical issues.

PRISM—When you see this ▬◻◼ click on PRISM (PRactical Interactive Skills Modules). These interactive decision-tree style exercises provide you with an opportunity to try out different management skills and to learn why certain approaches are better than others.

Self-Assessment Library (S.A.L)

Help students create a portfolio of skills. The Self-Assessment Library is a self-contained, interactive library of 49 behavioral questionnaires that help students discover things about themselves, their attitudes, and their personal strengths and weaknesses.

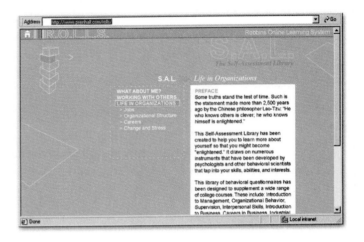

Early management thinkers such as Taylor, Fayol, and Weber gave us principles of management that they generally assumed to be universally applicable. Later research found exceptions to many of their principles. For example, division of labor is valuable and widely used, but jobs can become *too* specialized. Bureaucracy is desirable in many situations, but in other circumstances, other structural designs are *more* effective. Management is not (and cannot be) based on simplistic principles to be applied in all situations. Different and changing situations require managers to use different approaches and techniques. The **contingency approach** (sometimes called the situational approach) says that organizations are different, face different situations (contingencies), and require different ways of managing. (▬▬▬◻▣ Go to the Web and check out S.A.L. #47—How Well Do I Respond to Turbulent Change?)

Practical Interactive Skills Modules (PRISM)

Show students how to manage! This feature consists of 12 interactive decision-tree style skills exercises that provide students with an opportunity to try out different management skills and to learn why certain approaches are better than others.

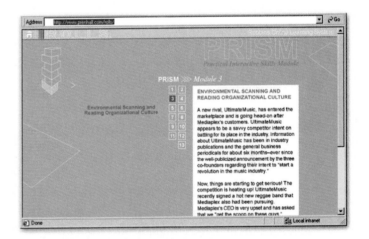

Environmental Scanning

How can managers become aware of significant environmental changes such as a new law in Germany permitting shopping for "tourist items" on Sunday? Or retailer Toys "R" Us deciding to partner with Amazon.com in response to other toy retailers' major Internet portals? Or the precipitous decline in the working-age populations in Japan, Germany, Italy, and Russia? Managers in both small and large organizations use **environmental scanning**, which is the screening of large amounts of information to anticipate and interpret changes in the environment. Extensive environmental scanning is likely to reveal issues and concerns that could affect an organization's current or planned activities. (▬▬▬◻▣ Go to the Web and check out PRISM #3—Environmental Scanning.) Research has shown that companies with advanced environmental scanning systems have increased their profits and revenue growth.[5]

Passport: Managing in a Global Environment

We wanted to make globalization come alive for students! And *Passport*, our interactive multimedia approach, does that by teaching students about the globalization challenges that managers face. *Passport* consists of two different global case scenarios at the end of Parts Two, Three, Four, Five, and Six, and nine different country profiles on R.O.L.L.S. In order to come up with appropriate suggestions and solutions for these case scenarios, students need to research information about the countries described in the case scenarios. Students will find a map and click on a desired country to get the facts on that country. The nine country profiles provide written and video information including a general overview of the country's background, economy, population, and workforce; specific information about the country's national culture; and detailed information about doing business in that country including management practices and organizational characteristics. Using this information, students will make decisions about the most appropriate ways to handle the managerial problems described in the case scenarios.

How is quality achieved? That's the issue managers must address. A good way to address quality initiatives is to think in terms of the management functions—planning, organizing and leading, and controlling—that need to take place. (▮▮▮▮ Check out Passport Scenario 2 on p. 510)

Planning for Quality Managers must have quality improvement goals and strategies and plans formulated to achieve those goals. Goals can help focus everyone's attention toward some objective quality standard. For instance, at the Rockwell Collins avionics plant based in Decorah, Iowa (where Rockwell International's communications and navigation equipment are made), a quality goal being pursued by employees over the next four years is a 30 percent reduction in defects.[32] Although this goal is

You're the Manager: Putting Ethics into Action

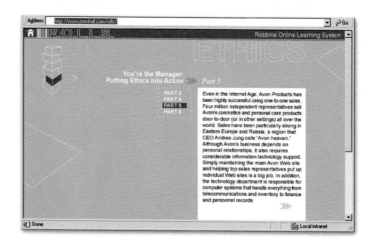

Help students understand the ethical challenges they'll face as managers! In these interactive exercises, students are put in the role of a manager making decisions about current ethical issues.

Information Controls

Information is critical to monitoring and measuring an organization's performance. Managers need the right information at the right time and in the right amount. Inaccurate, incomplete, excessive, or delayed information will seriously impede performance. How can managers use information for control? (▮▮▮▮ Check out You're the Manager: Putting Ethics into Action on p. 510.)

You're the Manager: Diversity in Action

Managing a changing workforce. These interactive exercises put students in the role of a manager making decisions related to age, gender, or ethnic diversity.

What Is a Group?

A **group** is defined as two or more interacting and interdependent individuals who come together to achieve particular goals. Groups can be either formal or informal. *Formal groups* are work groups defined by the organization's structure that have designated work assignments and specific tasks. In formal groups, appropriate behaviors are established by and directed toward organizational goals. Exhibit 15–1 provides some examples of different types of formal groups in today's organizations. (▉▉▉▉ Go to the Web and check out You're the Manager: Diversity in Action #3.)

In contrast, *informal groups* are social. These groups occur naturally in the workplace in response to the need for social contact. For example, three employees from different departments who regularly eat lunch together are an informal group. Informal groups tend to form around friendships and common interests.

Q&A

We designed Q&A to be students' 24/7 tutorial. Arranged in chapter order, these video clips and written material prepared and presented by your authors address those questions that we have found are most frequently asked by students.

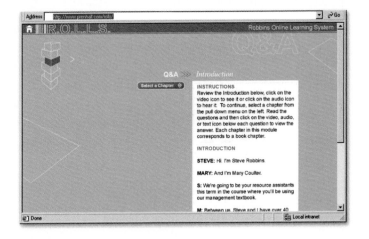

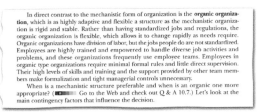

In direct contrast to the mechanistic form of organization is the **organic organization**, which is as highly adaptive and flexible a structure as the mechanistic organization is rigid and stable. Rather than having standardized jobs and regulations, the organic organization is flexible, which allows it to change rapidly as needs require. Organic organizations have division of labor, but the jobs people do are not standardized. Employees are highly trained and empowered to handle diverse job activities and problems, and these organizations frequently use employee teams. Employees in organic type organizations require minimal formal rules and little direct supervision. Their high levels of skills and training and the support provided by other team members make formalization and tight managerial controls unnecessary.

When is a mechanistic structure preferable and when is an organic one more appropriate? (▉▉▉▉ Go to the Web and check out Q & A 10.7.) Let's look at the main contingency factors that influence the decision.

IN-TEXT LEARNING AIDS

A good textbook should teach as well as present ideas. To that end, we've tried to make this book an effective learning tool. We'd like to point out some specific pedagogical features that we designed to help readers better assimilate the material presented.

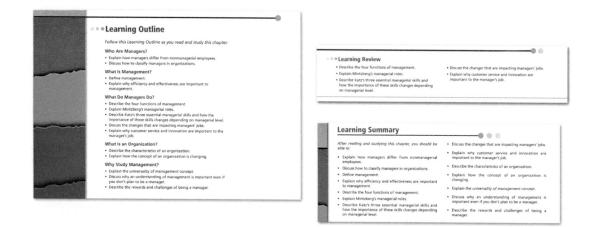

Learning Outline, Learning Review, and Learning Summary

While most textbooks have learning objectives and a chapter summary, there's no clear link between these and the chapter material. So here is a solution. The chapter-opening Learning Outline combines a chapter outline and the learning objectives so students see what material they're going to be covering in the chapter. Then, at the end of each major chapter section, students will find a Learning Review, in which they review the material they just read. Finally, at the end of the chapter, the Learning Summary summarizes the important chapter material. This approach helps students focus their attention on the major issues within each chapter.

Thinking Critically About Ethics

Being able to think critically about issues is important for managers. In the body of every chapter, you'll find a "Thinking Critically About Ethics" box. This learning aid provides material that stresses the ethical values in managerial decisions.

Ethics Exercise

The highly publicized corporate scandals of recent years have reemphasized the importance of managerial and organizational ethics. Thus, in addition to our "Thinking Critically About Ethics" boxes found in each chapter, we've added end-of-chapter ethics exercises that introduce students to current ethical dilemmas faced by managers.

Thinking About Management Issues

At the end of every chapter you'll find questions that are designed to get you to think about management issues. These questions require you to demonstrate that you not only know the key facts in the chapter but also can apply those facts in dealing with more complex issues.

Working Together: Team-Based Exercise

The pervasiveness of teamwork in organizations led us to design a team-based exercise at the end of every chapter that explores and builds on concepts or theories presented in the chapter.

Case Application and Questions

Each chapter includes a case application and questions for analysis. A case is simply a description of a real-life situation. By reading and analyzing the case and answering the questions at the end of the case, you can see if you understand and can apply the management concepts discussed in the chapter.

Key Terms

Every chapter highlights a number of key terms that you'll need to know. These terms are highlighted in bold print when they first appear and are defined at that time in the adjoining margin.

SUPPLEMENTS

The eighth edition supplements package has been designed to help you understand all the wonderful tools that are available and how best to integrate the media, technology, and test questions for your classroom needs.

• AIME (Annotated Instructor's Media Edition)

Recognizing that not everyone teaches the basic Management course the same way, AIME is designed to provide a fully integrated, flexible teaching resource for the instructor. Videos, skills exercises, team exercises, and online resources have been selected by chapter, allowing instructors the ability to shape and customize their course to best meet their specific goals.

• Instructor's Manual

• Test Item File

Contains more than 2,500 questions, including true/false, multiple-choice, essay questions, and scenario-based questions.

• Instructor's Resource CD-ROM

Contains the electronic testing software, PowerPoints, instructor's manual, and Test Item File.

• Test Gen EQ Test Generating Software

• Overhead Color Transparencies

• Study Guide

• R.O.L.L.S. (Robbins OnLine Learning System) Internet site (www.prenhall.com/robbins)

Features (1) Self-Assessment Library, (2) Q&A, (3) PRISM, (4) Passport, (5) You're the Manager: Putting Ethics into Action, and (6) You're the Manager: Diversity in Action.

• Companion Website

Featuring *In the News* articles and an interactive study guide for students, and supplement files for download for the professor.

• OneKey *Online Resources*

OneKey gives you access to the best teaching and learning resources all in one place. OneKey for *Robbins/Coulter Management, Eighth Edition* is all your students need for anywhere – anytime access to your course materials.
- OneKey is all you need to plan and administer your course.
- All your instructor resources are in one place to simplify your course preparation.
- OneKey for convenience, simplicity, and success . . . for you and your students.
For more information, visit http://www.prenhall.com/robbins.

• Online Courses

WebCT and Blackboard courses are available with this text.

Real results. In real time.

Put student results at your fingertips.

Assess your students' progress with the **Prentice Hall Personal Response System** (PRS)—a wireless polling system that enables you to pose questions, record results, and display those results instantly in your classroom.

The PRS enables each student to respond privately to questions posed, giving you immediate feedback that will provide valuable insight into student learning. Over 200 universities and colleges are already using the Personal Response System. Join the movement to interactive classrooms and real-time feedback.

How does it work?

- Each student gets a cell-phone-sized transmitter which they bring to class. You have a receiver (portable or mounted) connected to your computer. The number of receivers in the classroom depends on class size.

- You ask multiple-choice, numerical-answer, or matching questions during class, and students answer using their transmitters.

- The receiver, connected to your computer, tabulates the answers and displays them graphically in class.

- You can record the results for grading, or simply use them as a discussion point.

How much does it cost?

Students need only purchase the transmitter once for just *$15 net** with a Prentice Hall text. Once purchased there is no additional cost, and students can use the transmitter in any relevant class.

Plus, for every 40 transmitters ordered by your bookstore, Prentice Hall will give adopting institutions one free receiver—a $250 value—and the software needed to run the system.

IMAGINE THE POSSIBILITIES.

Increased Interactivity

Immediate Insight

Higher Attendance

100% Participation

Just-In-Time Teaching Potential

In-class Surveys & Polls

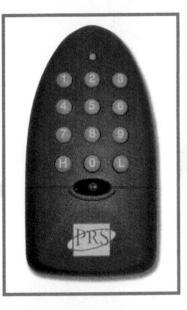

Interested?

For more information on using the Prentice Hall PRS in your courses, just contact your Prentice Hall representative. You can find the name of your local representative via our website at **www.prenhall.com**.

*Prices effective September 2003 and subject to change without notice.

NEW VIDEO PACKAGE

Prentice Hall is committed to providing you with the most up-to-date, exciting, new principles of management video library! Not only are these videos tied to the most pertinent topics in management today—highlighting cutting-edge companies, not-for-profits, and entrepreneurial enterprises—but they also include footage from top news sources such as ABC News, CNBC, CNN, NBC, and PBS!

Our goal is to provide you with new video segments *annually* that highlight relevant issues in the news illustrating how people lead, manage, and work effectively.

Following are the descriptions of some of the exciting segments included in this new video library:

Massachusetts General Hospital. All you have to do is catch one episode of *ER* to know that a hospital is a hectic place. In the high-stakes world of medicine, a simple error can mean life or death. At Boston's renowned Massachusetts General Hospital, they're trying to change all that. Through the use of a wireless network, barcode scanners, desktop stations, and an intranet database of patient information, Mass General and its affiliates are able to have all the patient info electronically at their fingertips. No more handwritten charts, insurance nightmares, or medicine mix-ups. You can even have your medical records zapped directly to a new doctor when it matters most—in an emergency.

American Apparel. One look at American Apparel and anyone can see it's not your average garment factory. Nestled among the sewing machines are happy workers enjoying an afternoon massage. In the distance you can hear the roar of a crowd. No, they're not grumbling about wages or staging a walkout. It's actually a pep rally led by American Apparel's fearless and somewhat eccentric leader, Dov. At this T-shirt manufacturer, every employee's well-being is valued—whether you're a product designer or moving boxes in the warehouse. All this attention to people makes it possible for American Apparel to be innovative and risk taking. And, it allows it to make some of best shirts on the planet.

Ernst & Young. Work's a drag, but that's life in the big city. At Ernst & Young, life just got a little bit better for its 160,000 employees around the world. By putting "people first," Ernst and Young has been able to improve the lives of its employees both on the job and off. Providing flexible work schedules allows Ernst & Young's employees to spend a little more time in the business of life without sacrificing service to their clients.

WNBA. Ever hear the old expression, "There are no small parts, just small actors?" Spend a day with the WNBA's Connecticut Sun and you'll be a believer. In basketball and business alike, it's a team game—whether you're making that 3-point shot at the buzzer, icing down an ankle at halftime, or arranging travel. On this team, everyone shines.

JetBlue. CEO David Neeleman refers to JetBlue as a service company, not an airline. Launched in February 2000 with a $130 million investment from Weston Presidio Capital, Chase Capital, and George Soros, JetBlue turned a profit within the first six months. Accustomed to the cut-throat environment of low-cost carriers, Neeleman based his business model on doing more with fewer employees, buying brand-new planes that cost less to maintain, leather seats that "cost twice as much but last twice as long," and providing 24 channels of free live satellite TV at every seat.

American Red Cross. The American Red Cross was founded to aid the victims of war. Since that time the role of the Red Cross has been expanded to aid victims of natural disasters as well as victims of manmade disasters such as nuclear attacks and the terrorist attacks of September 11, 2001. With more than 1,000 local chapters, how does this organization maintain its high moral ideals? Get the answer to this question in this segment.

Patagonia. Yvon Chouinard founded Patagonia more than 20 years ago, making climbing gear by hand for his friends. In addition to its commitment to customers, "serious users who rely on the product in extreme conditions," the firm also is responsible to its employees, providing a family-friendly workplace, and to the environment, donating millions of dollars to grassroots environmentalist groups in the United States and abroad.

Golf Network. Unlike other Internet companies, Golf Network is driven by the basic bricks-and-mortar business economics, where managing expenses and delivering profits are priorities. Established in 1993, Golf Network has become the premier golf portal on the Internet.

Dr. Martens. Dr. Martens makes shoes that say something about the wearer. Whether they're old or young, fans of the 40-year-old firm are proud to own distinctive footwear that speaks to the rebellious spirit in them and proclaims them as out of the ordinary. Dr. Martens' management feels a strong responsibility to its workforce and believes that developing employees is good for individuals *and* for the firm. Listen as Howard Johnstone, group administration director and company secretary, discusses values, attitudes, and motivation at this popular footwear company.

Body Glove. This well-known maker of wetsuits has expanded to other products ranging from cell phone covers to resort hotels. How did it get there? Interviews with Scott Daley (vice president of marketing) and Russ Lesser (president) explain how the company came up with its product ideas, where it found the materials used in many of its products, and how services (like diving cruises) fit into the whole picture.

ACKNOWLEDGMENTS

Every author relies on the comments of reviewers, and ours were particularly helpful. We want to thank the following people for their insightful and helpful comments and suggestions for the eighth edition of *Management*:

Louis Firenze, Northwood University

Les Ledger, Central Texas College

Henry C. Bohleke, San Juan College

Henry Jackson, Delaware County Community College

Michele Fritz, DeAnza College

Barbara Foltz, Clemson University

Wendy Wysocki, Monroe Community College

Corey Moore, Angelo State University

Jacqueline H. Bull, Immaculata University

Kathleen Jones, University of North Dakota

Phillip Flamm, Angelo State University

James C. Hayton, Utah State University

Clint Relyea, Arkansas State University

James Salvucci, Curry College

Bobbie Chan, Open University of Hong Kong

William H. Kirchman, Fayetteville Technical Community College

Ellis L. Langston, Texas Tech University

Susan D. Looney, Delaware Technical and Community College

Patrick Rogers, North Carolina A&T University

Rhonda Palladi, Georgia State University

Michelle Reavis, University of Alabama Huntsville

Don C. Mosley, Jr., University of South Alabama

Marvin Karlins, University of South Florida

Allen D. Engle, Sr., Eastern Kentucky University

Wei He, Indiana State University

Jay Christensen-Szalanski, University of Iowa

Robert W. Hanna, California State University, Northridge

Charles Stubbart, Southern Illinois University

Sandy J. Miles, Murray State University

James F. Cashman, The University of Alabama

H. Gregg Hamby, University of Houston

Frank Hamilton, University of South Florida

Dena M. Stephenson, Calhoun Community College

Tan Eng, Ngee Ann Polytechnic

In addition, we would like to thank the reviewers of previous editions. Their contributions are appreciated.

Seventh Edition

W.L. Loh, Mohawk Valley Community College

Lavelle Mills, West Texas A&M University

Elliot M. Ser, Barry University

Anne C. Cowden, California State University, Sacramento

Russell Kent, Georgia Southern University

Roy Cook, Fort Lewis College

Judson C. Faurer, Metro State College

Phyllis G. Holland, Valdosta State College

Diane L. Ferry, University of Delaware

Aline Arnold, Eastern Illinois University

Janice Feldbauer, Austin Community College

Donald Conlon, University of Delaware

Gary L. Whaley, Norfolk State University

James Spee, The Claremont Graduate School

Joseph F. Michlitsch, Southern Illinois University-Edwardsville

John L. Kmetz, University of Delaware

Suhail Abboushi, Duquesne State

Philip M. VanAuken, Baylor University

Augustus B. Colangelo, Penn State

Dale M. Feinauer, University of Wisconsin, Oshkosh

Sixth Edition

Daniel Cochran, Mississippi State University

Ram Subramanian, Grand Valley State University

Gary Kohut, University of North Carolina at Charlotte

Thomas Deckleman, Owens Community College

Victor Preisser, Golden Gate University

Robb Bay, Community College of Southern Nevada

Claudia Daumer, California State University – Chico

Anne M. O'Leary-Kelly, Texas A&M University

Frank Tomassi, Johnson & Wales University

James McElroy, Iowa State University

Ernest Bourgeois, Castleton State College

Sharon Clinebell, University of N. Colorado

Thomas Clark, Xavier University

Fifth Edition

June Freund, Pittsburgh State University

James Robinson, The College of New Jersey

Rick Moron, University of California, Berkeley

Bill Walsh, University of Illinois

Andy Kein, Keller Graduate School of Management

Daivd Kennedy, Berkeley School of Business

Jim Jones, University of Nebraska, Omaha

Rick Castaldi, San Francisco State University

Fourth Edition

Isaiah O. Ugboro, North Carolina A&T State University

Emilia S. Westney, Texas Tech University

Shelia Pechinski, University of Maine

Tracy Huneycutt Sigler, Western Washington University

Thomas G. Thompson, University of Maryland, University College

Gary M. Lande, Montana State University

Charles V. Goodman, Texas A&M University

Bobbie Williams, Georgia Southern University

Joseph Atallah, Devry Institute of Technology

Roger R. Stanton, California State University

Regardless of how good the manuscript is that we turn in, it's only a few computer disks until our friends at Prentice Hall swing into action. Then PH's crack team of editors, production experts, technology whizzes, designers, marketing specialists, and sales representatives turn those digital characters into a bound textbook and see that it gets into faculty and students' hands. Our thanks on making this book "go" include Michael Ablassmeir, Shannon Moore, Jill Wasiowich, Jessica Sabloff, Melanie Olsen, Melissa Yu, Judy Leale, Steve Frim, Elisa Adams, Melinda Alexander, and Jeff Shelstad. In addition, we would like to thank Carol Harvey of Assumption College and June Allard of Worcester State College, who are diversity experts and authors of *Understanding and Managing Diversity: Readings, Cases, and Exercises,* second edition (Prentice Hall, 2002), for taking our ideas for the interactive diversity exercises on R.O.L.L.S. and making them the outstanding feature they are. Also, we want to thank Marian Wood for developing and writing the wonderful end-of-chapter ethics exercises and interactive ethics exercises on R.O.L.L.S.

A special Thank You! goes to Rebecca Rast (who graduated from Southwest Missouri State University in 2002 and is now working for American Property and Casualty Company). She coordinated the responses coming from our "real-life" managers. We also appreciate and thank all of those managers who so graciously gave of their time to either be part of the "Managers Speak Out" feature or the "Managers Respond" feature. Without their contributions, our belief in showing managers as real people would be hard to do.

Finally, Steve would like to thank his wife Laura for her encouragement and support. Mary would like to acknowledge and thank her extremely understanding and tolerant husband, Ron, and their beautiful and talented daughters, Sarah and Katie.

Part ONE
Introduction

Introduction to Management and Organizations

····· A **Manager's** *Dilemma*

"Take care of yourself and treat others fairly. It makes better people who do good things. Better people translate into better business."[1] That's the simple management philosophy of Tom Gegax (pictured), founder and CEO of Tires Plus, a tire retailer with over 150 stores scattered across 12 states and revenues approaching $200 million. In an industry with extremely aggressive competitors, including retail-ing giants Wal-Mart and Goodyear, Tires Plus hopes to expand nationally and double in size in the next five years. And Tom's simple philosophy likely will play an important role in whether or not that goal is achieved.

Tom's managerial philosophy resulted from his having to deal with three significant personal crises (a divorce, cancer, and a million-dollar business deficit) in a single eight-month period. He said, "As long as our lives seem to be going OK, we don't get on the path for personal growth. It often takes a wake-up call." Forced to change his life for his own personal well-being and for the survival of his business, Tom recognized that he had to put some balance in his personal and work lives. Making those changes wasn't easy, but now he's a firm believer that balanced people are happier, healthier, and more confident, all of which benefits their employers as well.

For Tires Plus, this new philosophy resulted in several changes, including a new employee fitness center at the company's Minneapolis headquarters and adopting the language and culture of sports as a pattern for the company's structure—for instance, store managers are coaches, salespeople and mechanics are teammates, and the company's operations manual is known as the playbook. Ultimately, Tom believed that these changes would help employees to take better care of themselves and then take better care of customers. Since customer service is critical in this industry, employees must provide exceptional customer service if the company is going to reach its goals.

Now put yourself in Tom's shoes. What managerial skills should he encourage his coaches (store managers) to use to ensure that all the company's teammates (employees) do what it takes to please customers and help his firm reach its goal of doubling revenue in five years?

············**What** would *you* do **?**

om Gegax is a good example of what today's successful managers are like and the skills they must have in dealing with the problems and challenges of managing in the twenty-first century. These managers may not be who or what you might expect! They can be found from under age 18 to over 80. They run large corporations as well as entrepreneurial start-ups. They're found in government departments, hospitals, small businesses, not-for-profit agencies, museums, schools, and even such nontraditional organizations as political campaigns and consumer cooperatives. Managers can also be found doing managerial work in every country on the globe. In addition, some managers are top-level managers while others are first-line managers, and today they are just as likely to be women as they are men. Although women are well represented in the lower and middle levels of management, the number in top executive positions remains low. Data collected by Catalyst, a nonprofit research group, found that only 15.7 percent of corporate officers in *Fortune* 500 companies are women. That figure drops to 7.9 percent if you look at only the elite top-level managerial jobs of chairman, president, chief executive officer, chief operating officer, and executive vice president. A number of organizations, including Southwest Airlines, Ikon Office Solutions, Nordstrom, Avon, Hewlett-Packard, Kraft Foods, Xerox, and Golden West Financial, have taken significant steps to attract and promote women executives.[2] But no matter where managers are found or what gender they are, the fact is that they have exciting and challenging jobs! And organizations need managers more than ever in these uncertain, complex, and chaotic times. *Managers do matter!* How do we know that managers matter to organizations? A Gallup Organization study based on interviews with 2 million workers at 700 companies found that the single most important variable in employee productivity and loyalty wasn't pay or benefits or workplace environment; it was the quality of the relationship between employees and their direct supervisors.[3] In addition, Watson Wyatt Worldwide, a global consulting firm, found in its WorkUSA 2002 study that the way a company manages its people can significantly affect its financial performance. As that report concluded, "There's no question that it pays to manage people right."[4]

This book is about the important managerial work that Tom Gegax and the millions of other managers like him do. It recognizes the reality facing today's managers—that the world has changed and thus is redefining how work is done in organizations and the relationships between workers and managers. In workplaces of all types—factories, offices, restaurants, retail stores, and the like—new technologies and new ways of organizing work are altering old approaches. Today's successful managers must be able to blend tried-and-true management approaches with new approaches. In this chapter, we introduce you to managers and management by looking at who managers are, what management is, what managers do, and what an organization is. Finally, we'll wrap up the chapter by discussing why it's important to study management.

WHO ARE MANAGERS?

It used to be fairly simple to define who managers were: They were the organizational members who told others what to do and how to do it. It was easy to differentiate *managers* from *nonmanagerial employees*; the latter term described those organizational members who worked directly on a job or task and had no one reporting to them. But it isn't quite that simple anymore! The changing nature of organizations and work has, in

Key for Robbins Online Learning System (R.O.L.L.S.) Web Site Integration

We have integrated many exercises from the **R**obbins **O**nline **L**earning **S**ystem (R.O.L.L.S.), found on *www.prenhall.com/robbins*, throughout this text. These exercises are called out by a color that is keyed to a particular section of the R.O.L.L.S. Web site. When you see the color bar, go to *www.prenhall.com/robbins, then to R.O.L.L.S.* to find an exercise that relates to the topic being discussed.

Diversity—When you see this ▪▪▪▪▫▪ click on "You Be the Manager: Diversity in Action" to find an exercise that puts you in the role of a manager making a decision about diversity.

S.A.L. (Self-Assessment Library)—When you see this ▪▪▪▪▫▪ click on S.A.L. and complete the suggested self-assessment exercise. These exercises will help you discover things about yourself, your attitudes, and your personal strengths and weaknesses.

Q & A—When you see this ▪▫▪▪▪▪ click on Q & A, your 24/7 educational assistant. These video clips and written material presented by your authors address questions that we have found students frequently ask.

Passport—When you see this ▪▪▫▪▪▪ click on Passport to find information about nine different countries. You'll use this information to complete the Passport case scenarios found at the end of Parts Two–Six.

Ethics—When you see this ▪▪▪▪▪▪ click on "You Be the Manager: Putting Ethics into Action" to find an interactive exercise that puts you in the role of a manager making decisions about ethical issues.

PRISM—When you see this ▪▪▪▪▫▪ click on PRISM (PRactical Interactive Skills Modules). These interactive decision-tree style exercises provide you with an opportunity to try out different management skills and to learn why certain approaches are better than others.

▪ **Q & A**
Whenever you see this green square, go to the R.O.L.L.S. Web site (*www.prenhall.com/robbins*) to the Q & A, your 24/7 educational assistant. These video clips and written material presented by your authors address questions that we have found students frequently ask.

• • • **manager**
Someone who works with and through other people by coordinating their work activities in order to accomplish organizational goals.

• • • **first-line managers**
Managers at the lowest level of the organization who manage the work of nonmanagerial employees who are directly involved with the production or creation of the organization's products.

many organizations, blurred the clear lines of distinction between managers and non-managerial employees. Many traditional nonmanagerial jobs now include managerial activities.[5] (▪▪▪▪▫▪ Go to the Web and check out Q & A 1.1.) For example, employees at Medtronic, Inc., a leading global manufacturer of implantable biomedical devices, are blending managerial and nonmanagerial activities.[6] Whether it's on one of its assembly lines in Mexico where work is clearly separated as managerial and nonmanagerial or on a marketing team at corporate headquarters in Minneapolis where managerial responsibilities are shared by a manager and team members, they get the work done.

How *do* we define who managers are? A **manager** is someone who works with and through other people by coordinating their work activities in order to accomplish organizational goals. A manager's job is not about *personal* achievement—it's about helping *others* do their work and achieve. That may mean coordinating the work of a departmental group, or it might mean supervising a single person. It could involve coordinating the work activities of a team composed of people from several different departments or even people outside the organization, such as temporary employees or employees who work for the organization's suppliers. Keep in mind, also, that managers may have other work duties not related to coordinating and integrating the work of others. For example, an insurance claims supervisor may also process claims in addition to coordinating the work activities of other claims clerks.

Is there some way to classify managers in organizations? In traditionally structured organizations (often pictured as being shaped like a pyramid where the number of employees is greater at the bottom than at the top), managers are often described as first-line, middle, or top. (See Exhibit 1–1 on p. 6.) (▪▪▪▫▪▪ Go to the Web and check out Q & A 1.2.) Identifying exactly who the managers are in these organizations isn't difficult, although they may have a variety of titles. **First-line managers** are at the lowest level of management and manage the work of nonmanagerial employees who are directly or indirectly involved with the production or creation of the organization's products. They're often called *supervisors* but may also be called shift managers, district managers,

Exhibit 1–1

Managerial Levels

Top Managers

Middle Managers

First-Line Managers

Nonmanagerial Employees

●● **middle managers**
Managers between the first-line level and the top level of the organization who manage the work of first-line managers.

●●● **top managers**
Managers at or near the top level of the organization who are responsible for making organization-wide decisions and establishing the goals and plans that affect the entire organization.

department managers, office managers, or even foremen. **Middle managers** include all levels of management between the first-line level and the top level of the organization. These managers manage the work of first-line managers and may have titles such as regional manager, project leader, plant manager, or division manager. At or near the top of the organization are the **top managers**, who are responsible for making organization-wide decisions and establishing the plans and goals that affect the entire organization. These individuals typically have titles such as executive vice president, president, managing director, chief operating officer, chief executive officer, or chairman of the board. In the chapter-opening case, Tom Gegax is a top-level manager. He holds the title of CEO (Chief Executive Officer). Marjorie Scardino, profiled in the "Managers Speak Out" box, is also a top-level manager. Both are involved in creating and implementing broad and comprehensive changes that affect the entire organization.

Not all organizations get work done using this traditional pyramidal form, however. Some organizations, for example, are more flexible and loosely configured with work being done by ever-changing teams of employees who move from one project to another as work demands arise. Although it's not as easy to tell who the managers are in these organizations, we do know that someone must fulfill that role—that is, there must be someone who works with and through other people by coordinating their work to accomplish organizational goals.

●●● Learning Review

- Explain how managers differ from nonmanagerial employees.

- Discuss how to classify managers in organizations.

Donna Rodrigues, principal of the University Park Campus School in Worcester, Massachusetts, has used her management skills to help raise standards among her teachers and students. She improved the curriculum, outlawed swearing and fighting, sent teachers to the homes of students who were absent too often, and promised parents that all their children would go to college. Rodrigues, a middle manager within the school district hierarchy, believes that treating the students like adults helped motivate them to perform at their best.

Marjorie Scardino, CEO
Pearson PLC
London, England

Describe your job.

I am the CEO of a media company that publishes books, newspapers and magazines, and educational materials—both textbooks and online programs. We're all about "education" in the broadest sense of the word: education for a five-year-old learning to read, a CEO understanding the way his or her industry is heading, an investor picking a stock, or a college student studying a course like the one you're in now. The company has total sales of about $6 billion, employs 30,000 people, has headquarters in London and New York, and makes about 70 percent of its sales in the United States.

My job has three main parts:

1. *Strategy:* It's my responsibility to figure out what the company should do to become more valuable and to produce returns for shareholders, as well as to add something to the world. To do this, we have to look at our assets and our markets and the relevant economic, political, and social trends and decide on the most promising combination of those factors. Then, we have to create a plan for shaping the business into that combination and making sure that our products, sales, and operations are all consistent with that plan.

2. *Execution:* No matter how good our strategy, we won't get very far if we can't carry out our plan. That involves innovative product design, ingenious

marketing strategy, irresistible sales skills, and efficient and engaging customer service. It involves judicious attention to the costs of conceiving, making, selling, and delivering our products, and keeping the right balance between growth and costs. It involves making the pursuit of the plan a process that we can measure and monitor and constantly adjust. It involves knowing when to take a risk.

3. *Culture and people.* Finally, and possibly most importantly, my job is to set the tone for a company environment and way of behaving in which we can all be most productive and to exemplify that culture myself. The ingredients in culture include everything from pay and benefits to communicating with each other to how we deal with outsiders and how we treat each other inside. A company's culture is important in determining whether we can attract and keep the best people and whether, when situations are confusing, our employees know how they must behave.

Why are managers important to organizations?

Managers set the goals, the agenda, the measures of achievement, and the standards of behavior. In the most successful organizations, they do all that by setting an example, inspiring and orchestrating in a democratic rather than an autocratic way.

What skills do managers need to be effective in today's environment?

The ability to see the bigger picture, concentration, parallel thinking, ability to see connections, listening, sense of humor, risk taking, humility, and generosity.

WHAT IS MANAGEMENT?

●●● **management**
Coordinating work activities so that they are completed efficiently and effectively with and through other people.

●●● **efficiency**
Getting the most output from the least amount of inputs; referred to as "doing things right."

Simply speaking, management is what managers do. But that simple statement doesn't tell us much, does it? A more thorough explanation is that **management** is coordinating work activities so that they are completed efficiently and effectively with and through other people. We already know that coordinating the work of others is what distinguishes a managerial position from a nonmanagerial one. However, this doesn't mean that managers can do what they want anytime, anywhere, or in any way. Instead, management involves the efficient and effective completion of organizational work activities, or at least that's what managers aspire to do.

Efficiency refers to getting the most output from the least amount of inputs. Because managers deal with scarce inputs—including resources such as people, money, and equipment—they're concerned with the efficient use of those resources.

THINKING CRITICALLY ABOUT ETHICS

How far should a manager go to achieve efficiency or effectiveness? Suppose that you're the catering manager at a local country club and you're asked by the club manager to lie about information you have on your work group's efficiency. Suppose that by lying you'll save an employee's job. Is that okay? Is lying always wrong, or might it be acceptable under certain circumstances? What, if any, would those circumstances be? What about simply misrepresenting information that you have? Is that always wrong, or might it be acceptable under certain circumstances? When does "misrepresenting" become "lying?"

● ● ● **effectiveness**
Completing activities so that organizational goals are attained; referred to as "doing the right things."

For instance, at the Siemens AG factory in Forchheim, Germany, where employees make X-ray equipment, efficient manufacturing techniques were implemented by doing things such as cutting inventory levels, decreasing the amount of time to manufacture products, and lowering product reject rates. These efficient work practices paid off as the plant was named one of *Industry Week*'s best plants for 2002.[7] From this perspective, efficiency is often referred to as "doing things right"—that is, not wasting resources. However, it's not enough just to be efficient. Management is also concerned with being effective, completing activities so that organizational goals are attained. **Effectiveness** is often described as "doing the right things"—that is, those work activities that will help the organization reach its goals. For instance, at the Siemens factory, goals included reducing equipment installation time for customers and cutting costs. Through various work programs, these goals were pursued *and* achieved. Whereas efficiency is concerned with the means of getting things done, effectiveness is concerned with the ends, or attainment of organizational goals (see Exhibit 1–2). Management is concerned, then, not only with getting activities completed and meeting organizational goals (effectiveness) but also with doing so as efficiently as possible. In successful organizations, high efficiency and high effectiveness typically go hand in hand. (▇▇▇▇ Go to the Web and check out Q & A 1.3.) Poor management is most often due to both inefficiency and ineffectiveness or to effectiveness achieved through inefficiency.

● ● ●Learning Review

- Define management.

- Explain why efficiency and effectiveness are important to management.

Exhibit 1–2

Efficiency and Effectiveness in Management

WHAT DO MANAGERS DO?

Describing what managers do isn't easy or simple. Just as no two organizations are alike, no two managers' jobs are alike! Despite this fact, management researchers have, after many years of study, developed three specific categorization schemes to describe what managers do: functions, roles, and skills. In this section, we'll examine each of these approaches and take a look at how the manager's job is changing.

Management Functions

According to the functions approach, managers perform certain activities or duties as they efficiently and effectively coordinate the work of others. What are these activities or functions? In the early part of the twentieth century, a French industrialist named Henri Fayol first proposed that all managers perform five functions: planning, organizing, commanding, coordinating, and controlling.[8] In the mid-1950s, a management textbook first used the functions of planning, organizing, staffing, directing, and controlling as a framework. Today, most management textbooks (and this one is no exception) still continue to be organized around the management functions, although they have been condensed to four basic and very important ones: planning, organizing, leading, and controlling (see Exhibit 1–3). Let's briefly define what each of these management functions encompasses.

If you have no particular destination in mind, then you can take any road. However, if you have someplace in particular you want to go, you've got to plan the best way to get there. Because organizations exist to achieve some particular purpose, someone must clearly define that purpose and the means for its achievement. Management is that someone. Managers performing the **planning** function define goals, establish strategies for achieving those goals, and develop plans to integrate and coordinate activities.

Managers are also responsible for arranging work to accomplish the organization's goals. We call this function **organizing**. When managers organize, they determine what tasks are to be done, who is to do them, how the tasks are to be grouped, who reports to whom, and where decisions are to be made.

Every organization includes people, and a manager's job is to work with and through people to accomplish organizational goals. This is the **leading** function. When managers motivate subordinates, influence individuals or teams as they work, select the most effective communication channel, or deal in any way with employee behavior issues, they are leading.

The final management function is **controlling**. After the goals are set (planning), the plans formulated (planning), the structural arrangements determined (organizing), and the people hired, trained, and motivated (leading), there has to be some evaluation of whether things are going as planned. To ensure that work is going as it should, managers must monitor and evaluate performance. Actual performance must be compared with the previously set goals. If there are any significant deviations, it's management's job to get work performance back on track. This process of monitoring, comparing, and correcting is what we mean by the controlling function.

• • • planning
Management function that involves defining goals, establishing strategies for achieving those goals, and developing plans to integrate and coordinate activities.

• • • organizing
Management function that involves determining what tasks are to be done, who is to do them, how the tasks are to be grouped, who reports to whom, and where decisions are to be made.

• • • leading
Management function that involves motivating subordinates, influencing individuals or teams as they work, selecting the most effective communication channels, or dealing in any way with employee behavior issues.

• • • controlling
Management function that involves monitoring actual performance, comparing actual to standard, and taking action, if necessary.

Exhibit 1–3

Management Functions

Planning	Organizing	Leading	Controlling	
Defining goals, establishing strategy, and developing subplans to coordinate activities	Determining what needs to be done, how it will be done, and who is to do it	Directing and motivating all involved parties and resolving conflicts	Monitoring activities to ensure that they are accomplished as planned	Lead to → Achieving the organization's stated purpose

Just how well does the functions approach describe what managers do? Do managers always plan, organize, lead, and then control? In reality, what a manager does may not always happen in this logical and sequential order. But that doesn't negate the importance of the basic functions that managers perform. Regardless of the "order" in which the functions are performed, the fact is that managers do plan, organize, lead, and control as they manage. To illustrate, look back at the chapter-opening case. How was Tom Gegax involved in planning, organizing, leading, and controlling? Planning can be seen in the company's goal of doubling its size in five years. An example of organizing can be seen in the change of the company's structure to reflect the culture and language of sports. Providing employees with ways to balance their personal and work lives was a good example of leading; and Tom was controlling as he looked for ways to ensure that exceptional customer service was being provided.

The continued popularity of the functional approach to describe what managers do is a tribute to its clarity and simplicity. But some have argued that this approach isn't appropriate or relevant.[9] So let's look at another perspective.

Management Roles

Henry Mintzberg, a prominent management researcher, studied actual managers at work. He says that what managers do can best be described by looking at the roles they play at work. His studies allowed him to conclude that managers perform 10 different but highly interrelated management roles.[10] The term **management roles** refers to specific categories of managerial behavior. (Think of the different roles you play and the different behaviors you're expected to perform in these roles as a student, a sibling, an employee, a volunteer, and so forth.) As shown in Exhibit 1–4, Mintzberg's 10 management roles are grouped around interpersonal relationships, the transfer of information, and decision making.

The **interpersonal roles** are roles that involve people (subordinates and persons outside the organization) and other duties that are ceremonial and symbolic in nature. The three interpersonal roles include being a figurehead, leader, and liaison. The **informational roles** involve receiving, collecting, and disseminating information. The three informational roles include monitor, disseminator, and spokesperson. Finally, the **decisional roles** revolve around making choices. The four decisional roles include entrepreneur, disturbance handler, resource allocator, and negotiator.

As managers "play" these different roles, Mintzberg concluded that their actual work activities involved interacting with others, with the organization itself, and with the context outside the organization. He also proposed that a manager's activities in these roles fall somewhere between reflection (thoughtful thinking) and action (practical doing).[11] When managers reflect, they're thinking, pondering, and contemplating. When managers act, they're doing something; they're performing; they're actively engaged. We can see an example of both reflection and action in our chapter opener. Reflection is shown in the way Tom dealt with three personal crises in a short period of time by developing a new managerial philosophy. Action is shown in the changes Tom implemented as a result of his new philosophy.

A number of follow-up studies have tested the validity of Mintzberg's role categories among different types of organizations and at different levels within given organizations.[12] The evidence generally supports the idea that managers—regardless of the type of organization or level in the organization—perform similar roles. However, the emphasis that managers give to the various roles seems to change with their orga-

Jada and Brett Holcomb have built a successful business around their jewelry cart in an Atlanta mall. To reach $300,000 in annual revenues, the Holcombs have relied on the management skill of planning. Brett explains how planning avoids one pitfall of the vending cart business: "One critical mistake a lot of people make is they try to go into a [shopping] center for Christmas, the highest-cost leasing months, with an unproven product. . . . It's not always the case that just because it's the holidays you make a lot of money." The Holcombs' future plans include staying in the mall but moving into the wholesaling end of the business as well.

● ● ● **management roles**
Specific categories of managerial behavior.

● ● ● **interpersonal roles**
Managerial roles that involve people and other duties that are ceremonial and symbolic in nature.

● ● ● **informational roles**
Managerial roles that involve receiving, collecting, and disseminating information.

● ● ● **decisional roles**
Managerial roles that revolve around making choices.

Exhibit 1–4

Mintzberg's Managerial Roles

Role	Description	Examples of Identifiable Activities
Interpersonal		
Figurehead	Symbolic head; obliged to perform a number of routine duties of a legal or social nature	Greeting visitors; signing legal documents
Leader	Responsible for the motivation of subordinates; responsible for staffing, training, and associated duties	Performing virtually all activities that involve subordinates
Liaison	Maintains self-developed network of outside contacts and informers who provide favors and information	Acknowledging mail: doing external board work; performing other activities that involve outsiders
Informational		
Monitor	Seeks and receives wide variety of internal and external information to develop thorough understanding of organization and environment	Reading periodicals and reports; maintaining personal contacts
Disseminator	Transmits information received from outsiders or from subordinates to members of the organization	Holding informational meetings; making phone calls to relay information
Spokesperson	Transmits information to outsiders on organization's plans, policies, actions, results, etc.	Holding board meetings; giving information to the media
Decisional		
Entrepreneur	Searches organization and its environment for opportunities and initiates "improvement projects" to bring about changes	Organizing strategy and review sessions to develop new programs
Disturbance handler	Responsible for corrective action when organization faces important, unexpected disturbances	Organizing strategy and review sessions that involve disturbances and crises
Resource allocator	Responsible for the allocation of organizational resources of all kinds—making or approving all significant organizational decisions	Scheduling; requesting authorization; performing any activity that involves budgeting and the programming of subordinates' work
Negotiator	Responsible for representing the organization at major negotiations	Participating in union contract negotiations

Source: H. Mintzberg, *The Nature of Managerial Work* (New York: Harper & Row, 1973), pp. 93–94. Copyright © 1973 by Henry Mintzberg. Reprinted by permission of Harper & Row, Publishers, Inc.

nizational level.[13] Specifically, the roles of disseminator, figurehead, negotiator, liaison, and spokesperson are more important at the higher levels of the organization; while the leader role (as Mintzberg defined it) is more important for lower-level managers than it is for either middle- or top-level managers.

So which approach to describing what managers do is correct—functions or roles? Each has merit. However, the functions approach still represents the most useful way of conceptualizing the manager's job. "The classical functions provide clear and discrete methods of classifying the thousands of activities that managers carry out and the techniques they use in terms of the functions they perform for the achievement of goals."[14] Many of Mintzberg's roles align well with one or more of the functions. For instance, resource allocation is part of planning, as is the entrepreneurial role, and all three of the interpersonal roles are part of the leading function. Although most of the other roles fit into one or more of the four functions, not all of them do. The difference can be explained by the fact that all managers do some work that isn't purely managerial.[15] Our decision to use the management functions to describe what

Most of the 100 people who work for Atiq Raza, CEO of high-tech firm Raza Foundries, are both technically brilliant and difficult to manage. While his staff embodies a high level of technical skill, Raza, with physics and engineering degrees of his own, has developed his human skills so well that his employees are almost fanatically devoted to him. "Managing these people isn't for everybody," he says. "But they're powerful engines. If you harness their energy and creativity, you have a Ferrari on your hands."

●●● **technical skills**
Knowledge of and proficiency in a specialized field.

●●● **human skills**
The ability to work well with other people individually and in a group.

●●● **conceptual skills**
The ability to think and to conceptualize about abstract and complex situations.

managers do doesn't mean that Mintzberg's role categories are invalid, as he clearly offered important insights into managers' work.

Management Skills

As you can see from the preceding discussion, a manager's job is varied and complex. Managers need certain skills to perform the duties and activities associated with being a manager. What types of skills does a manager need? Research by Robert L. Katz found that managers needed three essential skills.[16] **Technical skills** include knowledge of and proficiency in a certain specialized field, such as engineering, computers, accounting, or manufacturing. These skills are more important at lower levels of management since these managers are dealing directly with employees doing the organization's work. **Human skills** involve the ability to work well with other people both individually and in a group. Because managers deal directly with people, this skill is crucial! Managers with good human skills are able to get the best out of their people. They know how to communicate, motivate, lead, and inspire enthusiasm and trust. (Go to the Web and check out S.A.L. #20—What's My Emotional Intelligence Score?) These skills are equally important at all levels of management. Finally, **conceptual skills** are the skills managers must have to think and to conceptualize about abstract and complex situations. Using these skills, managers must be able to see the organization as a whole, understand the relationships among various subunits, and visualize how the organization fits into its broader environment. These skills are most important at the top management levels. Exhibit 1–5 shows the relationship of these skills and the levels of management.

A professional association of practicing managers, the American Management Association, has also identified important skills for managers that encompass conceptual, communication, effectiveness, and interpersonal aspects. See a complete list of these skills in Exhibit 1–6.[17]

In today's demanding and dynamic workplace, employees who are invaluable to an organization must be willing to constantly upgrade their skills and take on extra work outside their own specific job areas. There's no doubt that skills will continue to be an important way of describing what a manager does. In fact, understanding and developing management skills are so important that we've incorporated a condensed skills feature in the text. At the end of this book and on our R.O.L.L.S. Web site (*www.prenhall.com/robbins*), you'll find material on skill building, including our interactive skills exercises. The skills we've chosen to feature in these skill-building modules reflect a broad cross section of managerial activities that we and most experts believe are important elements of the four management functions. A matrix showing the relationship between these skills and the management functions is shown in Exhibit 1–7. Note that many of the skills are important to more than one function.

●●●━

Exhibit 1–5

Skills Needed at Different Management Levels

Exhibit 1–6

Managerial Skills

Conceptual Skills
- Ability to use information to solve business problems
- Identification of opportunities for innovation
- Recognizing problem areas and implementing solutions
- Selecting critical information from masses of data
- Understanding of business uses of technology
- Understanding of organization's business model

Communication Skills
- Ability to transform ideas into words and actions
- Credibility among colleagues, peers, and subordinates
- Listening and asking questions
- Presentation skills; spoken format
- Presentation skills; written and/or graphic formats

Effectiveness Skills
- Contributing to corporate mission/departmental objectives
- Customer focus
- Multitasking: working at multiple tasks in parallel
- Negotiating skills
- Project management
- Reviewing operations and implementing improvements
- Setting and maintaining performance standards internally and externally
- Setting priorities for attention and activity
- Time management

Interpersonal Skills
- Coaching and mentoring skills
- Diversity skills: working with diverse people and cultures
- Networking within the organization
- Networking outside the organization
- Working in teams; cooperation and commitment

Based on American Management Association Survey of Managerial Skills and Competencies, March/April 2000, found on AMA Web site (**www.ama.org**), October 30, 2002.

Exhibit 1–7

Management Skills and Management Functions Matrix

Skill	Function			
	Planning	Organizing	Leading	Controlling
Acquiring power		✓	✓	
Active listening			✓	✓
Budgeting	✓			✓
Choosing an effective leadership style			✓	
Coaching			✓	
Creating effective teams		✓	✓	
Delegating (empowerment)		✓	✓	
Designing motivating jobs		✓	✓	
Developing trust			✓	
Disciplining			✓	✓
Interviewing		✓	✓	
Managing conflict			✓	✓
Managing resistance to change		✓	✓	✓
Mentoring			✓	
Negotiating			✓	
Providing feedback			✓	✓
Reading an organization's culture		✓	✓	
Scanning the environment	✓			✓
Setting goals	✓			✓
Solving problems creatively	✓	✓	✓	✓
Valuing diversity	✓	✓	✓	✓

As you study the management functions in more depth in later chapters of this book, you'll have the opportunity to practice some of the key skills that are part of doing what a manager does. Although no skill-building exercise can make you an instant expert in a certain area, these modules can provide you with an introductory understanding and appreciation of some of the skills you'll need to master in order to be an effective manager.

How the Manager's Job Is Changing

Managers have always had to deal with changes taking place inside and outside their organization. (▮▮▮▮▮ Go to the Web and check out S.A.L. #7—How Well Do I Handle Ambiguity?) In today's world where managers everywhere are dealing with the continued aftermaths of 9/11 and corporate ethics scandals, global economic and political uncertainties, and technological advancements, change is a constant. For example, Ronnie Antebi, manager of A&R Welding in Atlanta, had to find ways to keep his welders employed as customer demand fluctuated. His solution: Form special crews of welders who are sent out of state when local demand falls.[18] Or consider the management challenges faced by Thomas Michaud, John G. Duffy, and Andy Senchak, top executives at Keefe, Bruyette, & Woods Inc., a financial services firm that was headquartered in 2 World Trade Center. Sixty-seven employees, almost one-third of its workforce, died in the collapse of the buildings on 9/11. Not only did these managers have to deal with the painful emotional losses, they had to get the business up and running and keep it going for the surviving employees. Although most managers are not likely to have to manage under such terrible circumstances, the fact is that *how* managers manage is changing. Exhibit 1–8 illustrates some of the most important changes facing managers. Throughout the rest of this book, we'll be discussing these

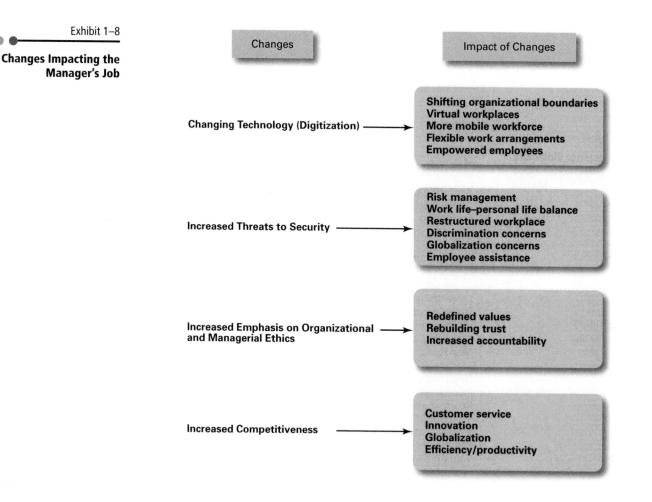

Exhibit 1–8

Changes Impacting the Manager's Job

Changes	Impact of Changes
Changing Technology (Digitization)	Shifting organizational boundaries Virtual workplaces More mobile workforce Flexible work arrangements Empowered employees
Increased Threats to Security	Risk management Work life–personal life balance Restructured workplace Discrimination concerns Globalization concerns Employee assistance
Increased Emphasis on Organizational and Managerial Ethics	Redefined values Rebuilding trust Increased accountability
Increased Competitiveness	Customer service Innovation Globalization Efficiency/productivity

changes and their impact on the way managers plan, organize, lead, and control. We want to highlight two of these changes that appear to be having a significant impact on managers' jobs: the increasing importance of customers and innovation.

Importance of Customers to the Manager's Job. Every workday John Chambers, CEO of Cisco Systems, listens to 15 to 20 voice mails that have been forwarded to him from dissatisfied Cisco customers. He says, "E-mail would be more efficient, but I want to hear the emotion, I want to hear the frustration, I want to hear the caller's level of comfort with the strategy we're employing. I can't get that through e-mail."[19] Here's a manager who recognizes the importance of customers. Every organization needs customers. Without customers, most organizations would cease to exist. Yet, focusing on the customer has long been thought to be the responsibility of marketing types. "Let the marketers worry about the customers" is how many managers felt. We're discovering, however, that employee attitudes and behaviors play a big role in customer satisfaction. For instance, an analysis of a Qantas Airways' passenger survey confirms this. Passengers were asked to rate their "essential needs" in air travel. Almost every factor listed by passengers was directly influenced by the actions of Qantas' employees—from prompt baggage delivery, to courteous and efficient cabin crews, to assistance with connections, to quick and friendly check-ins.[20] Managers everywhere are beginning to understand that delivering consistent high-quality service is essential for success and survival in today's competitive environment and that employees are an important part of that equation.[21] The implication is clear—they must create a customer-responsive organization where employees are friendly and courteous, accessible, knowledgeable, prompt in responding to customer needs, and willing to do what's necessary to please the customer.[22] We'll examine customer service management and its importance to planning, organizing, leading, and controlling in several chapters.

Importance of Innovation to the Manager's Job. "Nothing is more risky than not innovating."[23] Innovation means doing things differently, exploring new territory, and taking risks. And innovation isn't just for high-tech and technologically advanced organizations. Examples of successful innovation can be found in organizations you might not expect. For instance, for over 25 years, CSX Transportation (the railroad company) had transported Tropicana's orange juice products from the processing plants to market.[24] Mistrust between the two organizations had built up over the years, and the relationship was often adversarial. It affected all aspects of the way employees in both organizations did their jobs. One day a CSX rail inspector proposed the idea of inspecting the rail cars on the Tropicana property rather than bringing them all the way to the CSX rail yard many miles away, as had been done for years. After all, this

What mixes diesel fuel with U.S.-made soybean extract, burns cleaner than other fuels, and doesn't require any engine modifications? Biodiesel, or B20, is the innovative fuel product sold primarily by World Energy Alternatives of Massachusetts. Its U.S. market has grown to 15 million gallons in just a few years, and although that's not much compared to the 136 billion gallons of gas Americans consume each year, CEO Gene Gebolys says his firm is ready to "write the rules of the industry." Such innovation could play a role in reducing U.S. dependence on foreign oil supplies.

back-and-forth transport of rail cars simply for inspection was costly and time-consuming. Granted, the idea wasn't a technological breakthrough, but it was innovative—a way of doing things differently. It was also valuable for both parties. What role did managers play? Someone had to create and maintain an environment in which employees felt free to innovate. And someone had to act on the idea. That someone was the managers. In today's world, organizational managers—at all levels and in all areas—need to encourage their employees to be on the lookout for new ideas and new approaches, not just in the products or services the organization provides, but in everything that's done. We'll examine innovation and its importance to planning, organizing, leading, and controlling in several chapters.

•••Learning Review

- Describe the four functions of management.
- Explain Mintzberg's managerial roles.
- Describe Katz's three essential managerial skills and how the importance of these skills changes depending on managerial level.

- Discuss the changes that are impacting managers' jobs.
- Explain why customer service and innovation are important to the manager's job.

WHAT IS AN ORGANIZATION?

••• organization
A deliberate arrangement of people to accomplish some specific purpose.

Managers work in organizations. But what is an organization? An **organization** is a deliberate arrangement of people to accomplish some specific purpose. Your college or university is an organization; so are fraternities and sororities, government departments, churches, Amazon.com, your neighborhood video store, the United Way, the Colorado Rockies baseball team, and the Mayo Clinic. These are all organizations because they have three common characteristics as shown in Exhibit 1–9.

First, each organization has a distinct purpose. This purpose is typically expressed in terms of a goal or a set of goals that the organization hopes to accomplish. Second, each organization is composed of people. One person working alone is not an organization, and it takes people to perform the work that's necessary for the organization to achieve its goals. Third, all organizations develop some deliberate structure so that their members can do their work. That structure may be open and flexible, with no clear and precise delineations of job duties or strict adherence to any explicit job arrangements—in other words, it may be a simple network of loose relationship. Or the structure may be more traditional, with clearly defined rules, regulations, and job descriptions and some members identified as "bosses" who have authority over other members. But no matter what type of structural arrangement an organization uses, it does require some deliberate structure so members' work relationships are clarified. In summary, the term *organization* refers to an entity that has a distinct purpose, includes people or members, and has some type of deliberate structure.

Although these three characteristics are important to our definition of *what* an organization is, the concept of an organization is changing. It's no longer appropriate

••• Exhibit 1–9

Characteristics of Organizations

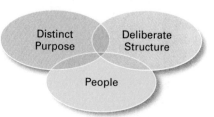

Exhibit 1–10

**The Changing
Organization**

Traditional Organization	New Organization
• Stable	• Dynamic
• Inflexible	• Flexible
• Job-focused	• Skills-focused
• Work is defined by job positions	• Work is defined in terms of tasks to be done
• Individual-oriented	• Team-oriented
• Permanent jobs	• Temporary jobs
• Command-oriented	• Involvement-oriented
• Managers always make decisions	• Employees participate in decision making
• Rule-oriented	• Customer-oriented
• Relatively homogeneous workforce	• Diverse workforce
• Workdays defined as 9 to 5	• Workdays have no time boundaries
• Hierarchical relationships	• Lateral and networked relationships
• Work at organizational facility during specific hours	• Work anywhere, anytime

to assume that all organizations are going to be structured like Procter & Gamble, ExxonMobil, or General Motors, with clearly identifiable divisions, departments, and work units. In fact, one of GM's subsidiaries, Saturn Corporation, may be more characteristic of what contemporary organizations look like, with its flexible work arrangements, employee work teams, open communication systems, and supplier alliances. Just how is the concept of an organization changing? Exhibit 1–10 lists some differences between traditional organizations and new organizations. As these lists show, today's organizations are becoming more open, flexible, and responsive to changes.[25]

Why are organizations changing? Because the world around them has changed and continues to change. Societal, economic, political, global, and technological changes have created an environment in which successful organizations (those that consistently attain their goals) must embrace new ways of getting work done. As we stated earlier, even though the concept of organizations may be changing, managers and management continue to be important to organizations.

• • • Learning Review

- Describe the characteristics of an organization.
- Explain how the concept of an organization is changing.

WHY STUDY MANAGEMENT?

You may be wondering why you need to study management. (▮▮▯▯▯ Go to the Web and check out Q & A 1.4.) If you're an accounting major, a marketing major, or any major other than management, you may not understand how studying management is going to help you in your career. We can explain the value of studying management by looking at the universality of management, the reality of work, and the rewards and challenges of being a manager.

The Universality of Management

Just how universal is the need for management in organizations? We can say with absolute certainty that management is needed in all types and sizes of organizations, at all organizational levels and in all organizational work areas, and in all organizations,

Career Opportunities in Management

Agilent Technologies cuts an additional 4,000 jobs! SAS Group, the Scandinavian airline company, cuts 13 percent of its workforce! McDonald's eliminates 300 administrative positions![26]

Are management jobs disappearing? You might think so based on news reports showing widespread layoffs. The truth is: There are abundant management jobs and the future looks bright![27]

The U.S. Bureau of Labor Statistics estimates a 10 percent to 20 percent growth in all executive, administrative, and managerial jobs through the year 2008. These jobs, however, may not be in the organizations or fields that you'd expect. The demand for managers in traditional, *Fortune* 500 organizations and particularly in the area of traditional manufacturing is not going to be as strong as the demand for managers in small and medium-sized organizations in the services field, particularly information and health care services. And do keep in mind that a good place to land a management position can be a smaller organization.

● ● ● **universality of management**
The reality that management is needed in all types and sizes of organizations, at all organizational levels, in all organizational areas, and in organizations in all countries around the globe.

no matter what country they're located in. This is known as the **universality of management.** (See Exhibit 1–11.) Managers in all these settings will plan, organize, lead, and control. However, this is not to say that management is done the same way. The differences in what a supervisor in a software applications testing facility at Microsoft does versus what the CEO of Microsoft does are a matter of degree and emphasis, not of function. Because both are managers, both will plan, organize, lead, and control, but how they do so will differ.

Since management is universally needed in all organizations, we have a vested interest in improving the way organizations are managed. Why? We interact with organizations every single day of our lives. Does it frustrate you when you have to spend three hours in a department of motor vehicles office to get your driver's license renewed? Are you irritated when none of the salespeople in a department store seems interested in helping you? Do you get annoyed when you call an airline three times and their sales representatives quote you three different prices for the same trip? These are all examples of problems created by poor management. Organizations that are well managed—and we'll share many examples of these throughout the text—develop a loyal customer base, grow, and prosper. Those that are poorly managed find themselves with a declining customer base and reduced revenues. By studying management, you'll be able to recognize poor management and work to get it corrected. In addition, you'll be able to recognize good management and encourage it, whether it's in an organization with which you're simply interacting or whether it's in an organization in which you're employed.

● ● ● Exhibit 1–11

Universal Need for Management

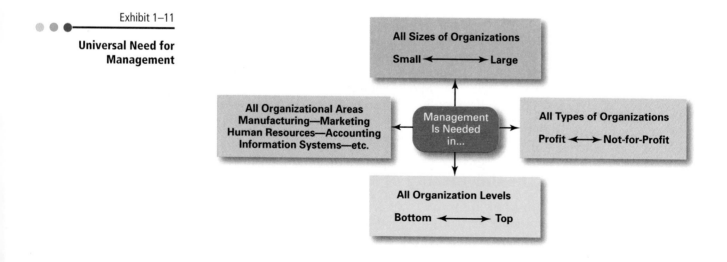

Becoming a Manager

- ◆ *Keep up with the current business news.*
- ◆ *Read books about good and bad examples of managing.*
- ◆ *Observe managers and how they handle people and situations.*
- ◆ *Talk to actual managers about their experiences—good and bad.*
- ◆ *Get experience in managing by taking on leadership roles in student organizations.*
- ◆ *Start thinking about whether or not you'd enjoy being a manager.*
- ◆ ▬▬□■ *Go to the Web and complete any of these exercises from the Self-Assessment Library (S.A.L.) found on R.O.L.L.S. #7—How Well Do I Handle Ambiguity?, #12—What's My Attitude Toward Achievement?, #20—What's My Emotional Intelligence Score?, and #45—How Motivated Am I to Manage?*

The Reality of Work

Another reason for studying management is the reality that for most of you, once you graduate from college and begin your career, you will either manage or be managed. For those who plan on management careers, an understanding of the management process forms the foundation upon which to build your management skills. For those of you who don't see yourself in a management position, you're still likely to have to work with managers. Also, assuming that you will have to work for a living and recognizing that you are very likely to work in an organization, you'll probably have some managerial responsibilities even if you're not a manager. Our experience tells us that you can gain a great deal of insight into the way your boss behaves and the internal workings of organizations by studying management. Our point is that you don't have to aspire to be a manager to gain something valuable from a course in management.

Rewards and Challenges of Being a Manager

We can't leave our discussion of the value of studying management without looking at the rewards and challenges of being a manager. (See Exhibit 1–12.) What *does* it mean to be a manager?

● ● ● ●
Exhibit 1–12

Rewards and Challenges of Being a Manager

Rewards	Challenges
• Create a work environment in which organizational members can work to the best of their ability	• Do hard work
• Have opportunities to think creatively and use imagination	• Have to deal with a variety of personalities
• Help others find meaning and fulfillment in work	• Often have to make do with limited resources
• Support, coach, and nurture others	• Motivate workers in chaotic and uncertain situations
• Work with a variety of people	• Successfully blend knowledge, skills, ambitions, and experiences of a diverse work group
• Receive recognition and status in organization and community	• Success depends on others' work performance
• Play a role in influencing organizational outcomes	
• Receive appropriate compensation in form of salaries, bonuses, and stock options	
• Good managers are needed by organizations	

Being a manager in today's dynamic workplace provides many challenges. (▮▮▮ Go to the Web and check out S.A.L. #45—How Motivated Am I to Manage?) It can be a tough and often thankless job. You may have to deal with a variety of personalities and many times have to make do with limited resources. It can be a challenge to motivate workers in the face of uncertainty and chaos. And managers may find it difficult to effectively blend the knowledge, skills, ambitions, and experiences of a diverse group of employees. Finally, as a manager, you're not in full control of your destiny. Your success typically is dependent upon others' work performance.

Despite these challenges, being a manager *can be* very rewarding. You're responsible for creating a work environment in which organizational members can do their work to the best of their ability and help the organization achieve its goals. In addition, as a manager, you often have the opportunity to think creatively and use your imagination. You help others find meaning and fulfillment in their work. You get to support, coach, and nurture others and help them make good decisions. You'll get to meet and work with a variety of people—both inside and outside the organization. Other rewards of being a manager may include receiving recognition and status in the organization and in the community, playing a role in influencing organizational outcomes, and receiving attractive compensation in the form of salaries, bonuses, and stock options. Finally, organizations need good managers. Nothing great ever happens by itself! It's through the combined efforts of motivated and passionate people that organizations accomplish their goals. As a manager, you can get satisfaction from knowing that your efforts, skills, and abilities are needed.

• • •Learning Review

- Explain the universality of management concept.
- Discuss why an understanding of management is important even if you don't plan to be a manager.

- Describe the rewards and challenges of being a manager.

Managers **Respond** to a **Manager's** Dilemma

···**Rita Warner**

**Director of Training and Marketing in Customer Service,
Pearson Education, Old Tappan, New Jersey**

Tom Gegax has the passion, vision, and energy to get Tires Plus on the road to exceptional customer service and to double in size and revenue in five years. While Tom's management philosophy is admirably idealistic, he may need some additional strategies to accomplish his goals including setting realistic goals by being aware of the company's current financial situation, surveying his competitors, determining whether his current organization can support the planned expansion, sharing his vision with employees, motivating managers and employees by letting them know how they're going to benefit from the plan, providing training to employees, and implementing a recognition program to communicate milestones and to celebrate and reward achievements. As long as Tom plans well, organizes his approach, and evaluates and adjusts his business plan as needed, he'll be on his way to success.

Lucy Kawaihalau

**President/Owner, Kauai Vacation Rentals and Real Estate, Inc.,
Lihue, Kauai, Hawaii**

First, Tom Gegax has a great idea in adopting sports as a pattern for his company's structure. To achieve his goal, I think Tom should start by creating a mission statement for the company as a whole. Then, the coaches and teammates can co-create mission statements that support the company's mission statement. All players must agree and be clear about what exceptional service really means. It's important that there be a service standard, defined in the play book, so that all employees know what it is and so that customers (fans) have something on which to rely. In addition, to achieve the five-year goal, I think the coaches and teammates should write down personal goals and plan and take actions that will help them achieve these goals. Success would be achieved when everyone is enjoying their work; are happy, healthy, and confident; and, as a result, continue to attract fans.

Learning Summary

After reading and studying this chapter, you should be able to:

- Explain how managers differ from nonmanagerial employees.

- Discuss how to classify managers in organizations.

- Define management.

- Explain why efficiency and effectiveness are important to management.

- Describe the four functions of management.

- Explain Mintzberg's managerial roles.

- Describe Katz's three essential managerial skills and how the importance of these skills changes depending on managerial level.

- Discuss the changes that are impacting managers' jobs.

- Explain why customer service and innovation are important to the manager's job.

- Describe the characteristics of an organization.

- Explain how the concept of an organization is changing.

- Explain the universality of management concept.

- Discuss why an understanding of management is important even if you don't plan to be a manager.

- Describe the rewards and challenges of being a manager.

Thinking About Management Issues

1. Is your course instructor a manager? Discuss in terms of managerial functions, managerial roles, and skills.

2. "The manager's most basic responsibility is to focus people toward performance of work activities to achieve desired outcomes." What's your interpretation of this statement? Do you agree with this statement? Why or why not?

3. Why do you think the skills of job candidates have become so important to employers? What are the implications for (a) managers in general, and (b) you personally?

4. Is there one best "style" of management? Why or why not?

5. What characteristics of new organizations appeal to you? Why? Which do not? Why?

6. In today's environment, which is more important to organizations—efficiency or effectiveness? Explain your choice.

7. Can you think of situations where management doesn't matter to organizations? Explain.

Working Together: Team-Based Exercise

By this time in your life, all of you have had to work with individuals in managerial positions (or maybe *you* were the manager), either through work experiences or through other organizational experiences (social, hobby/interest, religious, and so forth). What do you think makes some managers better than others? Are there certain characteristics that distinguish good managers? Form small groups of 3–4 with other class members. Discuss your experiences with managers—good and bad. Draw up a list of the characteristics of those individuals you felt were good managers. For each item, indicate which management function you think it falls under. As a group, be prepared to share your list with the class and to explain your choice of management function.

Case Application

Lipschultz, Levin & Gray

You might be surprised to find the passionate emphasis placed on people at a CPA firm. Yet, at Lipschultz, Levin & Gray (*www.thethinkers.com*), self-described "head bean counter" Steven P. Siegel recognizes that his people make the organization. He describes his primary responsibility as assuring that LLG's clients have the best professionals working for them. And the best way to do this, Siegel feels, is by developing the creativity, talent, and diversity of its staff so that new knowledge can be acquired and shared without getting hung up on formal organizational relationships or having employees shut away in corner offices.

The commitment to its people starts with the company's mission, which says, "LLG's goal is to be the pre-eminent provider of the highest quality accounting, tax and consulting services. LLG accomplishes this goal by leaving no stone unturned in exploring new and superior alternatives of supplying our services, and developing such methods on a global basis. Our environment promotes creativity, individual development, group interchange, diversity, good humor, family and community, all for the purpose of assisting in our clients' growth." To further demonstrate that commitment, Siegel has implemented several significant changes at LLG. Because he's convinced that people do their best intellectual work in nontraditional settings, every telltale sign of what most people consider boring, dull CPA work has been eliminated. None of the firm's employees or partners has an office or desk to call his or her own. Instead, everyone is part of a nomadic arrangement where stuff (files, phones, laptops) is wheeled to a new spot every day. Everywhere you look in the company's office, you see versatility, comfort, and eccentricity. For instance, a miniature golf course is located in the middle of everything. The motivation behind this open office design is to create opportunities for professionals to gather—on purpose or by accident—without walls, cubicles, or offices to get in the way.

Visitors to LLG realize that the firm is different as soon as they walk in the door. A giant, wall-mounted abacus (remember the image of bean counters) decorates the interior. And visitors are greeted by a "Welcome Wall" with a big-screen television that flashes a continuous slide show of one-liners about business, life, and innovation. The setting may be fun and lighthearted, but the LLG team is seriously committed to servicing its clients. So serious in fact, that they state: "We have one goal. To 'Delight' you. Good, even great, is not enough any more. We will 'Dazzle' you and we will guarantee it; We will deliver our service with integrity, honesty and openness in everything we do for you and with you; We will absolutely respect the confidentiality of our working relationship; We will return your phone calls, facsimiles and e-mails within 24 hours; We will always provide exceptional service, designed to help you add significant value to your business; We will meet the deadlines we set together with you; We will communicate with you frequently, building a win–win relationship with you; and You will always know in advance our fee arrangement for any service."

DISCUSSION QUESTIONS

1. Keeping professionals excited about work that can be routine and standardized is a major challenge for Siegel. How could he use technical, human, and conceptual skills to maintain an environment that encourages innovation and professionalism in his CPA firm?

2. What management roles would Steven be playing as he (a) made a presentation to potential clients, (b) assessed the feasibility of adding a new consulting service, (c) kept employees focused on the company's commitments to customers?

3. What can you tell about LLG's emphasis on customer service and innovation? In what ways does the organization support its employees in servicing customers and in being innovative?

4. Would LLG's approach work for all CPA firms? Why or why not? What could other managers learn from Steven Siegel?

Steven P. Siegel, self-described "head bean counter" at Lipschultz, Levin & Gray.

Sources: Information from company Web site (*www.thethinkers.com*), March 15, 2003; and N. K. Austin, "Tear Down the Walls," *Inc.*, April 1999, pp. 66–76.

• • • Learning Outline

Follow this Learning Outline as you read and study this chapter.

Historical Background of Management
- Explain why studying management history is important.
- Describe some early evidences of management practice.

Scientific Management
- Describe the important contributions made by Frederick W. Taylor and Frank and Lillian Gilbreth.
- Explain how today's managers use scientific management.

General Administrative Theorists
- Discuss Fayol's 14 management principles.
- Describe Max Weber's contributions to the general administrative theory of management.
- Explain how today's managers use general administrative theories of management.

Quantitative Approach to Management
- Explain what the quantitative approach has contributed to the field of management.
- Discuss how today's managers use the quantitative approach.

Toward Understanding Organizational Behavior
- Describe the contributions of the early advocates of OB.
- Explain the contributions of the Hawthorne Studies to the field of management.
- Discuss how today's managers use the behavioral approach.

The Systems Approach
- Describe an organization using the systems approach.
- Discuss how the systems approach is appropriate for understanding management.

The Contingency Approach
- Explain how the contingency approach differs from the early theories of management.
- Discuss how the contingency approach is appropriate for studying management.

Current Trends and Issues
- Explain why we need to look at the current trends and issues facing managers.
- Describe the current trends and issues facing managers.

Chapter

2

Management Yesterday and Today

A **Manager's** *Dilemma*

"You rarely see anything original anymore in this industry. Usually, everybody copies everybody else's ideas." This harsh assessment of the toy industry by an industry analyst might surprise you. Yet, when Ivy Ross (pictured below), senior vice president of worldwide girls' design at Mattel Toys, needed a new hit toy, *she* was determined to do something original.[1]

Mattel's most popular products include Barbies for girls and Hot Wheels for boys. When Ivy and Adrienne Fontanella (president of the girls' division) wanted to develop a new hit in a new market, they didn't want just another doll. They knew from market research that sewing and jewelry kits were popular with girls, but that "Legolike construction sets" were more popular with boys. They also knew that the reason wasn't that girls didn't like to build things; it was that girls build differently from boys. The challenge was to innovate a building toy that would appeal to girls.

To inspire innovative thinking, Ross put together a team from various departments to collaborate on this new product. Outside experts and Mattel's own child psychology expert schooled the team in architecture and play patterns. The team also watched groups of girls play. Ivy dubbed the team's innovation process

Project Platypus. She said, "Why a platypus? When I looked up the definition, it said an uncommon mix of different species." And, that's a good description of what it takes to be innovative.

One of the hardest adjustments for the team initially was the lack of structure. Ivy let the team organize itself and encouraged members to align themselves with whatever tasks they were passionate about—toy design, package design, marketing, and so forth. What did the platypi come up with? A toy for 5- to 10-year-old girls called the Ello Creation System that consisted of colorful, easy-to-use plastic pieces and reusable stickers designed for the open-ended, creative way girls play—an innovative toy developed in an innovative way. (You can see it at *www.mattel.com*.)

Put yourself in Ivy's position. What can she learn from Project Platypus to help her better manage innovation throughout her division?

What would *you* do **?**

attel's push to come up with something innovative for the marketplace isn't all that unusual today. Many organizations both large and small have made similar commitments to pursuing innovation with all its challenges and rewards. Why? Global competition and general competitive pressures reflect today's reality: Innovate or lose. Although Ivy Ross was innovative in how she inspired her employees in thinking about this new toy, she recognized that it's not always easy to implement new ideas. In fact, the history of management is filled with evolutions and revolutions in implementing new ideas.

Looking at management history can help us understand today's management theory and practice. It can help us see what worked and what didn't work. In this chapter, we'll introduce you to the origins of many contemporary management concepts and show how they have evolved to reflect the changing needs of organizations and society as a whole. We'll also introduce important trends and issues that managers currently face, in order to link the past with the future and demonstrate that the field of management is still evolving. (■□■ Go to the Web and check out Q & A 2.1.)

■ **Q & A**
Whenever you see this green square, go to the R.O.L.L.S. Web site (*www.prenhall.com/robbins*) to the Q & A, your 24/7 educational assistant. These video clips and written material presented by your authors address questions that we have found students frequently ask.

HISTORICAL BACKGROUND OF MANAGEMENT

Organized endeavors directed by people responsible for planning, organizing, leading, and controlling activities have existed for thousands of years. The Egyptian pyramids and the Great Wall of China, for instance, are tangible evidence that projects of tremendous scope, employing tens of thousands of people, were undertaken well before modern times. The pyramids are a particularly interesting example. The construction of a single pyramid occupied more than 100,000 workers for 20 years.[2] Who told each worker what to do? Who ensured that there would be enough stones at the site to keep workers busy? The answer to such questions is *managers*. Regardless of what managers were called at the time, someone had to plan what was to be done, organize people and materials to do it, lead and direct the workers, and impose some controls to ensure that everything was done as planned.

Another example of early management can be seen during the 1400s in the city of Venice, Italy, a major economic and trade center. The Venetians developed an early form of business enterprise and engaged in many activities common to today's organizations. For instance, at the arsenal of Venice, warships were floated along the canals, and at each stop materials and riggings were added to the ship. Doesn't that sound a lot like a car "floating" along an automobile assembly line while components are added to it? In addition to this assembly line, the Venetians also used warehouse and inventory systems to keep track of materials, human resource management functions to manage the labor force, and an accounting system to keep track of revenues and costs.[3]

These examples demonstrate that organizations and managers have been around for thousands of years. However, two pre-twentieth-century events are particularly significant to the study of management.

First, in 1776, Adam Smith published *The Wealth of Nations*, in which he argued for the economic advantages that organizations and society would gain from the **division of labor**, the breakdown of jobs into narrow and repetitive tasks. Using the pin industry as an example, Smith claimed that 10 individuals, each doing a specialized task, could together produce about 48,000 pins a day. However, if each person worked alone performing each task separately, it would be quite an accomplishment to produce even 10 pins a day! Smith concluded that division of labor increased productivity by increasing each worker's skill and dexterity, by saving time lost in changing tasks, and by creating labor-saving inventions and machinery. The continued popularity of job specialization—for example, specific tasks performed by members of a hospital

●●● **division of labor**
The breakdown of jobs into narrow and repetitive tasks.

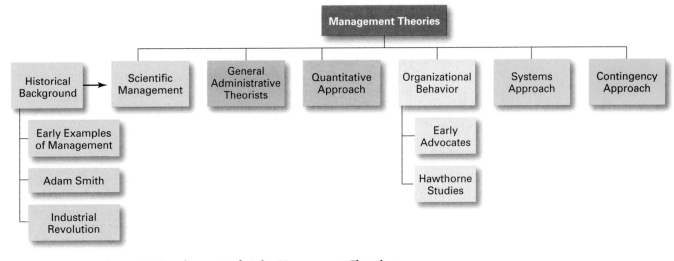

Exhibit 2–1 **Development of Major Management Theories**

surgery team, specific meal preparation tasks done by workers in restaurant kitchens, or specific positions played by players on a football team—is undoubtedly due to the economic advantages cited by Adam Smith.

The second important pre-twentieth-century influence on management is the **Industrial Revolution**. Starting in the eighteenth century in Great Britain, the revolution had crossed the Atlantic to America by the end of the Civil War. What the Industrial Revolution did was substitute machine power for human power, which, in turn, made it more economical to manufacture goods in factories rather than at home. These large, efficient factories required managerial skills. Why? Managers were needed to forecast demand, ensure that enough material was on hand to make products, assign tasks to people, direct daily activities, and so forth. The need for a formal theory to guide managers in running these large organizations had arrived. However, it wasn't until the early 1900s that the first major step toward developing such a theory was taken.

In the next sections we present the six major approaches to management: scientific management, general administrative theory, quantitative, organizational behavior, systems, and contingency. (See Exhibit 2–1.) Keep in mind that each approach is concerned with the same "animal"; the differences reflect the backgrounds and interests of the writer. A relevant analogy is the classic story of the blind men and the elephant, in which each man declares the elephant to be like the part he is feeling: The first man touching the side declares that the elephant is like a wall; the second touches the trunk and says the elephant is like a snake; the third feels one of the elephant's tusks and believes it to be like a spear; the fourth grabs a leg and says an elephant is like a tree; and the fifth touches the elephant's tail and concludes that the animal is like a rope. Each is encountering the same elephant, but what each observes depends on where he stands. Similarly, each of the six perspectives is correct and contributes to our overall understanding of management. However, each is also a limited view of a larger animal. We'll begin our journey into management's past by looking at the first major theory of management—scientific management.

●●● **Industrial Revolution**
The advent of machine power, mass production, and efficient transportation.

Learning Review

- Explain why studying management history is important.

- Describe some early evidences of management practice.

SCIENTIFIC MANAGEMENT

If you had to pinpoint the year modern management theory was born, 1911 might be a logical choice. That was the year Frederick Winslow Taylor's *Principles of Scientific Management* was published. Its contents became widely accepted by managers around the world. The book described the theory of **scientific management**: the use of scientific methods to define the "one best way" for a job to be done.

●●● **scientific management**
The use of the scientific method to determine the "one best way" for a job to be done.

Important Contributions

Important contributions to scientific management theory were made by Frederick W. Taylor and Frank and Lillian Gilbreth. Let's look at what they did.

Frederick W. Taylor Taylor did most of his work at the Midvale and Bethlehem Steel Companies in Pennsylvania. As a mechanical engineer with a Quaker and Puritan background, he was continually appalled by workers' inefficiencies. Employees used vastly different techniques to do the same job. They were inclined to "take it easy" on the job, and Taylor believed that worker output was only about one-third of what was possible. Virtually no work standards existed. Workers were placed in jobs with little or no concern for matching their abilities and aptitudes with the tasks they were required to do. Taylor set out to correct the situation by applying the scientific method to shop-floor jobs and spent more than two decades passionately pursuing the "one best way" for each job to be done.

Taylor's experiences at Midvale led him to define clear guidelines for improving production efficiency. He argued that these four principles of management (see Exhibit 2–2) would result in prosperity for both workers and managers.[4] How did these scientific principles really work? Let's look at an example.

Probably the best known example of Taylor's scientific management was the pig iron experiment. Workers loaded "pigs" of iron (each weighing 92 lbs) onto rail cars. Their daily average output was 12.5 tons. However, Taylor believed that by scientifically analyzing the job to determine the "one best way" to load pig iron, output could be increased to 47 or 48 tons per day. After scientifically applying different combinations of procedures, techniques, and tools, Taylor succeeded in getting that level of productivity. How? He put the right person on the job with the correct tools and equipment, had the worker follow his instructions exactly, and motivated the worker with an economic incentive of a significantly higher daily wage. (■■■■■ Go to the Web and check out Q & A 2.2.) Using similar approaches to other jobs, Taylor was able to define the "one best way" to do each job. Overall, Taylor achieved consistent productivity improvements in the range of 200 percent or more. Through his groundbreaking studies of manual work using scientific principles, Taylor became known as the "father" of scientific management. His ideas spread in the United States, France, Germany, Russia, and Japan, and inspired others to study and develop methods of scientific management. His most prominent followers were Frank and Lillian Gilbreth.

Frederick W. Taylor (1856–1915) was the father of scientific management. Working at Midvale Steel Company, Taylor witnessed many inefficiencies. He sought to create a mental revolution among both workers and managers by defining clear guidelines for improving production efficiency.

●●●——— Exhibit 2–2

Taylor's Four Principles of Management

1. Develop a science for each element of an individual's work, which will replace the old rule-of-thumb method.
2. Scientifically select and then train, teach, and develop the worker.
3. Heartily cooperate with the workers so as to ensure that all work is done in accordance with the principles of the science that has been developed.
4. Divide work and responsibility almost equally between management and workers. Management takes over all work for which it is better fitted than the workers.

Frank and Lillian Gilbreth, parents of 12 children, ran their household using scientific management principles and techniques. Two of their children wrote a book, Cheaper by the Dozen, *that described life with the two masters of efficiency.*

●●● **therbligs**
A classification scheme for labeling 17 basic hand motions

Frank and Lillian Gilbreth A construction contractor by trade, Frank Gilbreth gave up that career to study scientific management after hearing Taylor speak at a professional meeting. Frank and his wife Lillian, a psychologist, studied work to eliminate wasteful hand-and-body motions. The Gilbreths also experimented with the design and use of the proper tools and equipment for optimizing work performance.[5]

Frank is probably best known for his experiments in bricklaying. By carefully analyzing the bricklayer's job, he reduced the number of motions in laying exterior brick from 18 to about 5, and on laying interior brick the motions were reduced from 18 to 2. Using Gilbreth's techniques, the bricklayer could be more productive and less fatigued at the end of the day.

The Gilbreths were among the first researchers to use motion pictures to study hand-and-body motions. They invented a device called a microchronometer, which recorded a worker's motions and the amount of time spent doing each motion. Wasted motions missed by the naked eye could be identified and eliminated. The Gilbreths also devised a classification scheme to label 17 basic hand motions (such as search, grasp, hold) which they called **therbligs** (Gilbreth spelled backward with the *th* transposed). This scheme allowed the Gilbreths a more precise way of analyzing a worker's exact hand movements.

How Do Today's Managers Use Scientific Management?

The guidelines that Taylor and others devised for improving production efficiency are still used in organizations today.[6] When managers analyze the basic work tasks that must be performed, use time-and-motion study to eliminate wasted motions, hire the best qualified workers for a job, and design incentive systems based on output, they're using the principles of scientific management. (■□■■■ Go to the Web and check out Q & A 2.3.) But current management practice isn't restricted to scientific management. In fact, we can see ideas from the next major approach—general administrative theory—being used as well.

●●● **Learning Review**

• Describe the important contributions made by Frederick W. Taylor and Frank and Lillian Gilbreth.

• Explain how today's managers use scientific management.

GENERAL ADMINISTRATIVE THEORISTS

●●● **general administrative theorists**
Writers who developed general theories of what managers do and what constitutes good management practice.

Another group of writers looked at the subject of management but focused on the entire organization. These were the **general administrative theorists** who developed more general theories of what managers do and what constituted good management practice. Let's look at some important contributions that grew out of this perspective.

Important Contributions

The two most prominent theorists behind the general administrative approach were Henri Fayol and Max Weber.

Henri Fayol   We mentioned Fayol in Chapter 1 because he described management as a universal set of functions that included planning, organizing, commanding, coordinating, and controlling. Because his ideas were important, let's look more closely at what he had to say.[7]

Fayol wrote during the same time period as Taylor. While Taylor was concerned with first-line managers and the scientific method, Fayol's attention was directed at the activities of *all* managers. He wrote from personal experience as he was the managing director of a large French coal-mining firm.

• • • **principles of management**
Fundamental rules of management that could be taught in schools and applied in all organizational situations.

Fayol described the practice of management as something distinct from accounting, finance, production, distribution, and other typical business functions. His belief that management was an activity common to all human endeavors in business, government, and even in the home led him to develop 14 **principles of management**—fundamental rules of management that could be taught in schools and applied in all organizational situations. These principles are shown in Exhibit 2–3. (■□■■■■ Go to the Web and check out Q & A 2.4.)

Max Weber   Weber (pronounced VAY-ber) was a German sociologist who studied organizational activity. Writing in the early 1900s, he developed a theory of authority structures and relations.[8] Weber described an ideal type of organization which he called a **bureaucracy**—a form of organization characterized by division of labor, a clearly defined hierarchy, detailed rules and regulations, and impersonal relationships. Weber recognized that this "ideal bureaucracy" didn't exist in reality. Instead he intended it as a basis for theorizing about how work could be done in large groups. His theory became the model structural design for many of today's large organizations. The features of Weber's ideal bureaucratic structure are outlined in Exhibit 2–4.

• • • **bureaucracy**
A form of organization characterized by division of labor, a clearly defined hierarchy, detailed rules and regulations, and impersonal relationships.

Bureaucracy, as described by Weber, is a lot like scientific management in its ideology. Both emphasize rationality, predictability, impersonality, technical competence, and authoritarianism. Although Weber's writings were less operational than Taylor's, the fact that his "ideal type" still describes many contemporary organizations attests to the importance of his work.

How Do Today's Managers Use General Administrative Theories?

Some of our current management ideas and practices can be directly traced to the contributions of the general administrative theorists. For instance, the functional view of the manager's job can be attributed to Fayol. In addition, his 14 principles serve as a frame of reference from which many current management concepts have evolved.

Exhibit 2–3

• • •————————

Fayol's 14 Principles of Management

1. *Division of work.* Specialization increases output by making employees more efficient.
2. *Authority.* Managers must be able to give orders and authority gives them this right.
3. *Discipline.* Employees must obey and respect the rules that govern the organization.
4. *Unity of command.* Every employee should receive orders from only one superior.
5. *Unity of direction.* The organization should have a single plan of action to guide managers and workers.
6. *Subordination of individual interests to the general interest.* The interests of any one employee or group of employees should not take precedence over the interests of the organization as a whole.
7. *Remuneration.* Workers must be paid a fair wage for their services.
8. *Centralization.* This term refers to the degree to which subordinates are involved in decision making.
9. *Scalar chain.* The line of authority from top management to the lowest ranks is the scalar chain.
10. *Order.* People and materials should be in the right place at the right time.
11. *Equity.* Managers should be kind and fair to their subordinates.
12. *Stability of tenure of personnel.* Management should provide orderly personnel planning and ensure that replacements are available to fill vacancies.
13. *Initiative.* Employees who are allowed to originate and carry out plans will exert high levels of effort.
14. *Esprit de corps.* Promoting team spirit will build harmony and unity within the organization.

Exhibit 2–4

Weber's Ideal Bureaucracy

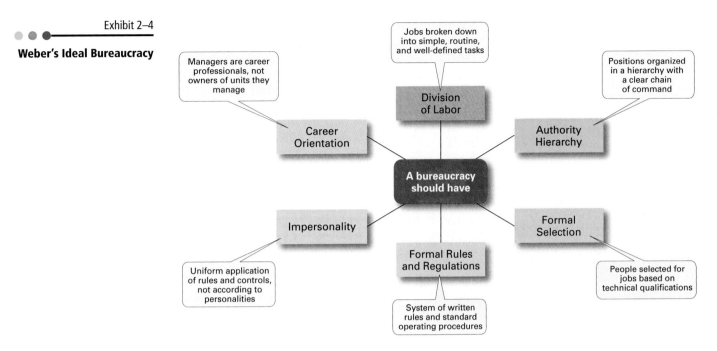

Weber's bureaucracy was an attempt to formulate an ideal prototype for organizations. Although many characteristics of Weber's bureaucracy are still evident in large organizations, his model isn't as popular today as it was in the twentieth century. Many contemporary managers feel that bureaucracy's emphasis on strict division of labor, adherence to formal rules and regulations, and impersonal application of rules and controls takes away the individual employee's creativity and the organization's ability to respond quickly to an increasingly dynamic environment. However, even in highly flexible organizations of talented professionals—such as Mattel, General Electric, or Cisco Systems—some bureaucratic mechanisms are necessary to ensure that resources are used efficiently and effectively.

●●●●Learning Review

- Discuss Fayol's 14 management principles.
- Describe Max Weber's contributions to the general administrative theory of management.
- Explain how today's managers use general administrative theories of management.

QUANTITATIVE APPROACH TO MANAGEMENT

●●● **quantitative approach**
The use of quantitative techniques to improve decision making.

The **quantitative approach** involves the use of quantitative techniques to improve decision making. This approach also has been called *operations research* or *management science*.

Important Contributions

The quantitative approach evolved out of the development of mathematical and statistical solutions to military problems during World War II. After the war was over, many of the techniques that had been used to solve military problems were applied to businesses. One group of military officers, nicknamed the Whiz Kids, joined Ford Motor Company in the mid-1940s and immediately began using statistical methods and quantitative models to improve decision making. Two of these individuals whose names you might recognize are Robert McNamara (who went on to become president

Quantitative methods employ computer applications among other tools in the management process. The software to produce a type of 3D animation called "previz" has been around for over 30 years, and visual-effects artists have been planning movie explosions with it since the 1990s. Then Colin Green realized that previz could also be an innovative project management tool for movie crews. His 13-employee firm, Pixel Liberation Front, creates shot-by-shot rough drafts of scenes from films like The Matrix Reloaded *and* The Matrix Revolutions—*simulations that help filmmakers set budgets and schedules. "I knew ahead of time what I was going to do in extremely accurate ways," says director David Fincher of PLF's work on* Fight Club *and* Panic Room, *"and that helped me make a better end product."*

of Ford, U.S. Secretary of Defense, and head of the World Bank) and Charles "Tex" Thornton (who founded Litton Industries).

What exactly does the quantitative approach do? It involves applications of statistics, optimization models, information models, and computer simulations to management activities. Linear programming, for instance, is a technique that managers use to improve resource allocation decisions. Work scheduling can be more efficient as a result of critical-path scheduling analysis. The economic order quantity model helps managers determine optimum inventory levels. Each of these is an example of quantitative techniques being applied to improve managerial decision making.

How Do Today's Managers Use the Quantitative Approach?

At Circuit City's some 626 locations, everything from the clothes the floor salespeople wear to how long zero percent financing should be offered has been studied by statisticians. They found, for instance, that flat commissions worked better than the product-based commission that had been used for 48-plus years. This and other findings from two studies in early 2000 and 2001 led to company changes that contributed an estimated $300 million in sales for 2002.

The quantitative approach contributes directly to management decision making in the areas of planning and control. For instance, when managers make budgeting, scheduling, quality control, and similar decisions, they typically rely on quantitative techniques. The availability of software programs has made the use of quantitative techniques somewhat less intimidating for managers, although they must still be able to interpret the results. We cover some of the more important quantitative techniques in Chapters 9 and 18.

The quantitative approach hasn't influenced management practice as much as the next one we're going to discuss—organizational behavior—for a number of reasons. These include the fact that many managers are unfamiliar with and intimidated by the quantitative tools, behavioral problems are more widespread and visible, and it is easier for most students and managers to relate to real, day-to-day people problems than to the more abstract activity of constructing quantitative models.

● ● ● Learning Review

- Explain what the quantitative approach has contributed to the field of management.

- Discuss how today's managers use the quantitative approach.

TOWARD UNDERSTANDING ORGANIZATIONAL BEHAVIOR

● ● ● **organizational behavior (OB)**
The field of study concerned with the actions (behavior) of people at work.

As we know, managers get things done by working with people. This explains why some writers have chosen to look at management by focusing on the organization's human resources. The field of study concerned with the actions (behavior) of people at work is called **organizational behavior (OB)**. Much of what currently makes up the field of human resource management, as well as contemporary views on motivation, leadership, trust, teamwork, and conflict management, has come out of organizational behavior research.

Early Advocates

Although a number of people in the late 1800s and early 1900s recognized the importance of the human factor to an organization's success, four stand out as early advocates of the OB approach: Robert Owen, Hugo Munsterberg, Mary Parker Follett, and Chester Barnard. The contributions of these individuals were varied and distinct, yet they all believed that people were the most important asset of the organization and should be managed accordingly. Their ideas provided the foundation for such management practices as employee selection procedures, employee motivation programs, employee work teams, and organization-environment management techniques. Exhibit 2–5 summarizes the most important ideas of these early advocates.

The Hawthorne Studies

Without question, the most important contribution to the developing OB field came out of the **Hawthorne Studies**, a series of studies conducted at the Western Electric Company Works in Cicero, Illinois. These studies, which started in 1924, were initially designed by Western Electric industrial engineers as a scientific management experiment. They wanted to examine the effect of various illumination levels on worker productivity. Like any good scientific experiment, control and experimental groups were set up with the experimental group being exposed to various lighting intensities, and the control group working under a constant intensity. If you were the industrial engineers in charge of this experiment, what would you have expected to happen? It's logical to think that individual output in the experimental group would be directly related to the intensity of the light. However, they found that as the level of light was increased in the experimental group, output for both groups increased. Then, much

• • • **Hawthorne Studies**
A series of studies during the 1920s and 1930s that provided new insights into individual and group behavior.

Exhibit 2–5 **Early Advocates of OB**

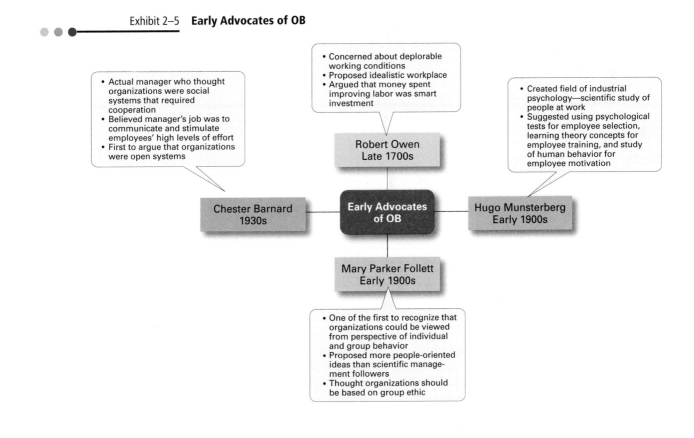

to the surprise of the engineers, as the light level was decreased in the experimental group, productivity continued to increase in both groups. In fact, a productivity decrease was observed in the experimental group *only* when the level of light was reduced to that of a moonlit night. What would explain these unexpected results? The engineers weren't sure, but concluded that illumination intensity was not directly related to group productivity, and that something else must have contributed to the results. They weren't able to pinpoint what that "something else" was, though.

In 1927, the Western Electric engineers asked Harvard professor Elton Mayo and his associates to join the study as consultants. Thus began a relationship that would last through 1932 and encompass numerous experiments in the redesign of jobs, changes in workday and workweek length, introduction of rest periods, and individual versus group wage plans.[9] For example, one experiment was designed to evaluate the effect of a group piecework incentive pay system on group productivity. The results indicated that the incentive plan had less effect on a worker's output than did group pressure, acceptance, and security. The researchers concluded that social norms or group standards were the key determinants of individual work behavior.

Scholars generally agree that the Hawthorne Studies had a dramatic impact on management beliefs about the role of human behavior in organizations. Mayo concluded that behavior and attitudes are closely related, that group influences significantly affect individual behavior, that group standards establish individual worker output, and that money is less a factor in determining output than are group standards, group attitudes, and security. These conclusions led to a new emphasis on the human behavior factor in the management of organizations and the attainment of goals.

However, these conclusions were criticized. Critics attacked the research procedures, analyses of findings, and conclusions.[10] From a historical standpoint, it's of little importance whether the studies were academically sound or their conclusions justified. What *is* important is that they stimulated an interest in human behavior in organizations. (■□■▨▨ Go to the Web and check out Q & A 2.5.)

How Do Today's Managers Use the Behavioral Approach?

The behavioral approach has largely shaped today's organizations. From the way managers design motivating jobs to the way they work with employee teams to the way they use open communication, we can see elements of the behavioral approach. Much of what the early OB advocates proposed and the conclusions from the Hawthorne Studies provided the foundation for our current theories of motivation, leadership, group behavior and development, and numerous other behavioral topics which we'll address fully in later chapters.

● ● ● Learning Review

- Describe the contributions of the early advocates of OB.
- Explain the contributions of the Hawthorne Studies to the field of management.

- Discuss how today's managers use the behavioral approach.

● ● ● **system**
A set of interrelated and interdependent parts arranged in a manner that produces a unified whole.

● ● ● **closed systems**
Systems that are not influenced by or do not interact with their environment.

● ● ● **open systems**
Systems that dynamically interact with their environment.

THE SYSTEMS APPROACH

During the 1960s, researchers began to analyze organizations from a systems perspective, a concept taken from the physical sciences. A **system** is a set of interrelated and interdependent parts arranged in a manner that produces a unified whole. The two basic types of systems are closed and open. **Closed systems** are not influenced by and do not interact with their environment. In contrast, **open systems** dynamically interact with their environment. Today, when we describe organizations as systems, we mean open systems. Exhibit 2–6 shows a diagram of an organization from an open systems perspective. As you can see, an organization takes in inputs (resources) from the envi-

Exhibit 2–6

The Organization as an Open System

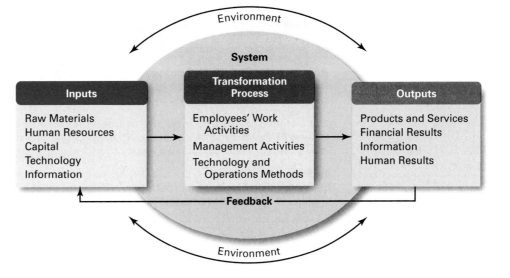

ronment and transforms or processes these resources into outputs that are distributed into the environment. The organization is "open" to its environment and interacts with that environment.

The Systems Approach and Managers

How does the systems approach contribute to our understanding of management thinking? Systems researchers envisioned an organization as being made up of "interdependent factors, including individuals, groups, attitudes, motives, formal structure, interactions, goals, status, and authority."[11] What this means is that managers coordinate the work activities of the various parts of the organization and ensure that all the interdependent parts of the organization are working together so that the organization's goals can be achieved. For example, the systems approach would recognize that, no matter how efficient the production department might be, if the marketing department doesn't anticipate changes in customer tastes and work with the product development department in creating products customers want, the organization's overall performance will suffer.

In addition, the systems approach implies that decisions and actions taken in one organizational area will affect others and vice versa. For example, if the purchasing department doesn't acquire the right quantity and quality of inputs, the production department will not be able to do its job effectively.

Finally, the systems approach recognizes that organizations are not self-contained. They rely on their environments for essential inputs and as sources to absorb their outputs. No organization can survive for long if it ignores government regulations, supplier relations, or the varied external constituencies upon which it depends. (We'll cover these external forces in Chapter 3.)

How relevant is the systems approach to management? Quite relevant. Think, for example, of a day-shift manager at a local Wendy's restaurant who every day must coordinate the work of employees filling customer orders at the front counter and the drive-through windows, direct the delivery and unloading of food supplies, and address any customer concerns that come up. This manager "manages" all parts of the "system" so that the restaurant meets its daily sales goals. (■□■■■ Go to the Web and check out Q & A 2.6.)

⬤ ⬤ ⬤ Learning Review

- Describe an organization using the systems approach.

- Discuss how the systems approach is appropriate for understanding management.

Exhibit 2–7

**Popular Contingency
Variables**

Organization Size. As size increases, so do the problems of coordination. For instance, the type of organization structure appropriate for an organization of 50,000 employees is likely to be inefficient for an organization of 50 employees.

Routineness of Task Technology. To achieve its purpose, an organization uses technology. Routine technologies require organizational structures, leadership styles, and control systems that differ from those required by customized or nonroutine technologies.

Environmental Uncertainty. The degree of uncertainty caused by environmental changes influences the management process. What works best in a stable and predictable environment may be totally inappropriate in a rapidly changing and unpredictable environment.

Individual Differences. Individuals differ in terms of their desire for growth, autonomy, tolerance of ambiguity, and expectations. These and other individual differences are particularly important when managers select motivation techniques, leadership styles, and job designs.

THE CONTINGENCY APPROACH

Early management thinkers such as Taylor, Fayol, and Weber gave us principles of management that they generally assumed to be universally applicable. Later research found exceptions to many of their principles. For example, division of labor is valuable and widely used, but jobs can become *too* specialized. Bureaucracy is desirable in many situations, but in other circumstances, other structural designs are *more* effective. Management is not (and cannot be) based on simplistic principles to be applied in all situations. Different and changing situations require managers to use different approaches and techniques. The **contingency approach** (sometimes called the situational approach) says that organizations are different, face different situations (contingencies), and require different ways of managing. (▮▮▮▮▮ Go to the Web and check out S.A.L. #47—How Well Do I Respond to Turbulent Change?)

● ● ● **contingency
approach**
An approach that says that organizations are different, face different situations (contingencies), and require different ways of managing.

The Contingency Approach and Managers

A contingency approach to management is intuitively logical because organizations and even units within the same organization are diverse—in size, goals, work, and the like. It would be surprising to find universally applicable management rules that would work in *all* situations. But, of course, it's one thing to say that the method of managing "depends on the situation" and another to say what the situation is. Management researchers have been working to identify these "what" variables. Exhibit 2–7 describes four popular contingency variables. The list is by no means comprehensive—more than 100 different "what" variables have been identified—but it represents those most widely used and gives you an idea of what we mean by the term *contingency variable*. As you can see, the contingency variables can have a significant impact on managers. The primary value of the contingency approach is that it stresses there are no simplistic or universal rules for managers to follow. (▮▮▮▮▮ Go to the Web and check out Q & A 2.7.)

● ● ● **Learning Review**

- Explain how the contingency approach differs from the early theories of management.

- Discuss how the contingency approach is appropriate for studying management.

CURRENT TRENDS AND ISSUES

Where are we today? What current management concepts and practices are shaping "tomorrow's history"? In this section, we'll attempt to answer those questions by introducing several trends and issues that we believe are changing the way managers do their jobs. We introduced you to two important trends in Chapter 1—customer service management and innovation. In this chapter, we'll examine others including globalization, ethics, workforce diversity, entrepreneurship, e-business, knowledge management and learning organizations, and quality management. (■□■■■ Go to the Web and check out Q & A 2.8.) Throughout the text we focus more closely on these issues in various boxes, examples, and exercises included in each chapter.

Globalization

Management is no longer constrained by national borders. BMW, a German firm, builds cars in South Carolina. McDonald's, a U.S. firm, sells hamburgers in China. Toyota, a Japanese firm, makes cars in Kentucky. Australia's leading real estate company, Lend Lease Corporation, built the Bluewater shopping complex in Kent, England, and has contracts with Coca-Cola to build all the soft-drink maker's bottling plants in Southeast Asia. Swiss company ABB Ltd. has constructed power generating plants in Malaysia, South Korea, China, and Indonesia. There are significant opportunities from globalization, and the world has definitely become a global village! Yet, globalization can be controversial. After the terrorist attacks on the United States on 9/11, some have questioned whether the "openness" of globalization has made countries more vulnerable to conflicts over political and cultural differences. Regardless of the controversy, managers in organizations of all sizes and types around the world have to confront the challenges of operating in a global market.[12] Globalization is such an important topic that we devote one chapter to it (Chapter 4) and integrate discussion of its impact on the various management functions throughout the text. A number of our chapter-opening manager dilemmas, end-of-chapter cases, and chapter examples feature global managers and organizations. And to reinforce the importance of your need to "think globally," we've included background data on nine countries and opportunities for you to apply a global perspective in a number of case scenarios at the end of Parts Two–Six and on our Web site (*www.prenhall.com/robbins*).

McDonald's has plans to expand throughout India with fast-food menus that bear little resemblance to those served in the United States. Flavored with Indian spices to cater to local tastes and featuring many vegetarian dishes, the food is also free of beef and beef products in deference to Hindu beliefs. A McDonald's was attacked a few years ago because it was thought to be using beef tallow in its cooking processes.

Ethics

$299,150,992. That's the value of the stock cashed in by now-resigned or fired top managers Ken Lay of Enron, Sam Waksal of ImClone, Gary Winnick of Global Crossing, and Dennis Kozlowski of Tyco International as they sold shares at close to the firms' peak stock price.[13] The tragedy is that while these executives walked away with nearly $300 million, their companies lay in ruins and the jobs and retirement savings of thousands of their employees had vanished.

During the summer of 2002, it seemed as if every day brought to light another case of corporate lying, misrepresentations, and financial manipulations. What happened to managerial ethics? This important aspect of managerial behavior seems to have been forgotten or ignored as these managers put their self-interest ahead of others who might be affected by their decisions. Take, for example, the "Enron Three" (former chairman Ken Lay, former CEO Jeff Skilling, and former CFO Andy Fastow). All behaved as if the laws and accounting rules didn't apply to them. They used greed, manipulation, and collusion to deceive their board of directors, employees, stockholders, and others about Enron's worsening financial condition. Because of these managers' unethical actions, thousands of Enron employees lost their jobs and the company stock set aside in their retirement savings became worthless. Although Enron seemed to be the pivotal event in this corporate ethics crisis, executives at a number of other large companies were engaging in similar kinds of unethical acts.

What would you have done had you been a manager in these organizations? How would you have reacted? One thing we know is that ethical issues aren't simple or easy! Make one decision and someone will be affected; make another, and someone else is likely to be affected. In today's changing workplace, managers need an approach to deal with the complexities and uncertainties associated with the ethical dilemmas that arise. We propose a process as outlined in Exhibit 2–8. What does this process entail? First, managers need to make sure they understand the ethical dilemma they're facing. They need to step back and think about what issue (or issues) is at stake here. Next, it's important to identify the stakeholders that would be affected by the decision. What individuals or groups are likely to be impacted by my decision? Third, managers should identify the factors that are important to the decision. These include personal, organizational, and possibly external factors. We'll cover these factors in Chapter 5. Next, managers should identify and evaluate possible courses of action, keeping in mind that each alternative will impact affected stakeholders differently. Then, it's time to make a decision and act. As today's managers manage, they can use this process to help them assess those ethical dilemmas they face and to develop appropriate courses of action.

While most managers continue to behave in a highly ethical manner, the ethical abuses that were so widely publicized indicated a need to "upgrade" ethical standards. This is being addressed at two levels. First, ethics education is being widely emphasized in college curriculums. Second, organizations themselves are taking a more active role in creating *and using* codes of ethics, providing ethics training programs, and hiring ethics officers. We want to prepare you to deal with the ethics dilemmas you're likely to face. Therefore, we've included a "Thinking Critically about Ethics" box and an end-of-chapter ethics exercise in almost every chapter. In addition, we've included five comprehensive integrative and interactive ethics scenarios that you'll find on our R.O.L.L.S. Web site (*www.prenhall.com/robbins*). You'll have numerous opportunities to experience what it's like to deal with ethical issues and dilemmas!

Exhibit 2–8

● ● ●────

A Process for Addressing Ethical Dilemmas

Step 1: What is the **ethical dilemma?**
Step 2: Who are the **affected stakeholders?**
Step 3: What **personal, organizational,** and **external factors** are important to my decision?
Step 4: What are **possible alternatives?**
Step 5: Make a **decision** and act on it.

Workforce Diversity

●●● **workforce diversity**
A workforce that's more
heterogeneous in terms of
gender, race, ethnicity, age,
and other characteristics
that reflect differences.

Another issue facing managers in the twenty-first century is coordinating work efforts of diverse organizational members in accomplishing organizational goals. Today's organizations are characterized by **workforce diversity**—a workforce that's more heterogeneous in terms of gender, race, ethnicity, age, and other characteristics that reflect differences. How diverse is the workforce? A report on work and workers in the twenty-first century, called *Workforce 2020*, stated that the U.S. labor force would continue its ethnic diversification, although at a fairly slow pace.[14] Throughout the early years of the twenty-first century, minorities will account for slightly more than one-half of net new entrants to the U.S. workforce. The fastest growth will be Asian and Hispanic workers. In fact, Hispanics have now surpassed African Americans as the largest minority group in the United States.[15] However, this report also stated that a more significant demographic force affecting workforce diversity during the next decade will be the aging of the population. This trend is likely to affect the U.S. workforce in three ways. First, aging individuals will choose to work full-time, work part-time, or retire completely. Because of the negative performance of the stock market and its effect on many retirement investment accounts, many older employees may be forced to continue working. Think of the implications for an organization when older workers can't afford to retire and block career opportunities for younger employees, or if longtime employees with their vast wealth of knowledge, experience, and skills do choose to retire. Second, aging individuals typically begin to receive public entitlements. Having sufficient tax rates to sustain these programs has serious implications for organizations and younger workers since there will be more individuals demanding entitlements and a smaller base of workers contributing dollars to the program budgets. Finally, the aging population will become a powerful consumer force driving demand for certain types of products and services. Organizations in industries of potentially high market demand (such as entertainment, travel, specialized health care, financial planning, etc.) will require larger workforces to meet that demand while organizations in industries where market demand faces potential declines (such as singles bars, ski resorts, etc.) may have to make adjustments in their workforces through layoffs and downsizing.

Workforce diversity isn't a managerial issue only in the United States. It's an issue facing managers of organizations in Japan, Australia, Germany, Italy, and other developed countries. For instance, as the level of immigration increases in Italy, the number of women entering the workforce rises in Japan, and the population ages in Germany, managers are finding they need to effectively manage diversity.[16]

Does the fact that workforce diversity is an issue today mean that organizations weren't diverse before? No. They were, but diverse individuals made up a small percentage of the workforce, and organizations, for the most part, ignored the issue. Before the early 1980s, people took a "melting pot" approach to differences in organizations. We assumed that people who were "different" would want to assimilate. But we now recognize that employees don't set aside their cultural values and lifestyle preferences when they come to work. The challenge for managers, therefore, is to make their organizations more accommodating to diverse groups of people by addressing different lifestyles, family needs, and work styles. The melting pot assumption has been replaced by the recognition and celebration of differences.[17] Smart managers recognize that diversity can be an asset because it brings a broad range of viewpoints and problem-solving skills to a company, and additionally helps organizations better understand a diverse customer base. Many companies such as Levi Strauss, Advantica, McDonald's, Dole Food, Avis Rent A Car, SBC Communications, Avon Products, and Xerox have strong diversity management programs.[18] We'll highlight many diversity-related issues and how companies are responding to those issues throughout this text in our "Managing Workforce Diversity" boxes. In addition, you'll find diversity exercises on our R.O.L.L.S. Web site (*www.prenhall.com/robbins*).

A sudden layoff from his job in an airline catering firm after 30 years in the business caused Jack Goguen to assess his resources and then start his one-man firm, J R Home Remodeling. He had considerable skill in remodeling tasks, $20,000 for construction equipment and an SUV to haul it, and a plan to spread the word about his new business through realtors and mortgage brokers. After one year in business, he is making almost as much as he did in his previous job and reaping great satisfaction from working to his own standards. "A sole practitioner must perform every day," he says, "in order to survive and grow."

●●● **entrepreneurship**
The process whereby an individual or group of individuals uses organized efforts to pursue opportunities to create value and grow by fulfilling wants and needs through innovation and uniqueness, no matter what resources the entrepreneur currently has.

Entrepreneurship

Entrepreneurship is a growing activity.[19] But what exactly is **entrepreneurship**? It's the process whereby an individual or group of individuals uses organized efforts to pursue opportunities to create value and grow by fulfilling wants and needs through innovation and uniqueness, no matter what resources the entrepreneur currently has. It involves the discovery of opportunities and the resources to exploit them. Three important themes can be seen in this definition of entrepreneurship. First is the pursuit of opportunities. Entrepreneurship is about pursuing environmental trends and changes that no one else has seen or paid attention to. For example, Jeff Bezos, founder of Amazon.com, was a successful programmer at an investment firm on Wall Street in the mid-1990s. However, statistics on the explosive growth in the use of the Internet and World Wide Web (at that time, it was growing about 2,300% a month) kept nagging at him. He decided to quit his job and pursue what he felt were going to be enormous retailing opportunities on the Internet. Today, Amazon sells books, music, cars, furniture, jewelry, and numerous other items from its Web site.

The second important theme in entrepreneurship is innovation. Entrepreneurship involves changing, revolutionizing, transforming, or introducing new products or services or new ways of doing business. Dineh Mohajer is a prime example. As a fashion-conscious young woman, she hated the brilliant and bright nail polishes sold in stores. The bright colors clashed with her trendy pastel-colored clothing. She wanted pastel nail colors that would match what she was wearing. When she couldn't find them, Mohajer decided to mix her own. When her friends raved over her homemade colors, she decided to take samples of her nail polish to exclusive stores in Los Angeles. They were an instant hit! Today, her company, Hard Candy, sells a complete line of cosmetics in trendy stores across the United States—all the result of Mohajer's innovative ideas.

The final important theme in entrepreneurship is growth. Entrepreneurs pursue growth. They are not content for their organizations to stay small or to stay the same size. Entrepreneurs want their businesses to grow and work very hard to pursue growth as they continually look for trends and continue to innovate new products and new approaches.

We think an understanding of entrepreneurship is important and have included at the end of each major section in this book a special entrepreneurship module that looks at the management topics presented in that section from the perspective of entrepreneurs. (███ Go to the Web and check out S.A.L. #23—Am I Likely to Become an Entrepreneur?)

Managing in an E-Business World

Do you use e-mail to communicate? Can you find an advertisement that doesn't have a Web address in it somewhere? Today's managers function in an e-business world. In fact, as a student, your learning may increasingly be taking place in an electronic environment. While critics have questioned the viability of Internet-based companies (dotcoms), especially after the high-tech implosion in 2000 and 2001, e-business is here for the long term. E-business offers many advantages to organizations—small to large, profit or not-for-profit, global and domestic, and in all industries.[20]

●●● **e-business (electronic business)**
A comprehensive term describing the way an organization does its work by using electronic (Internet-based) linkages with its key constituencies in order to efficiently and effectively achieve its goals.

E-business (electronic business) is a comprehensive term describing the way an organization does its work by using electronic (Internet-based) linkages with its key constituencies (employees, managers, customers, clients, suppliers, and partners) in

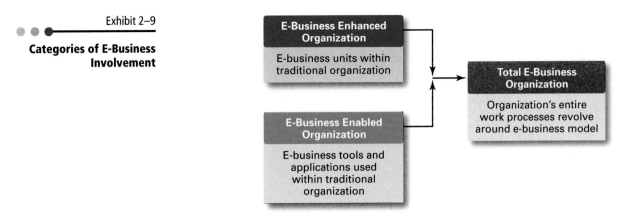

●●● **e-commerce (electronic commerce)**
The sales and marketing component of e-business.

order to efficiently and effectively achieve its goals. It includes **e-commerce**, which is essentially the sales and marketing component of e-business.[21] Firms such as Dell (computers) and Varsitybooks (textbooks) are engaged in e-commerce because they sell items over the Internet.

Not every organization is, or needs to be, a total e-business. Exhibit 2–9 illustrates three categories of e-business involvement.[22] The first type is an e-business *enhanced* organization, a traditional organization that sets up e-business capabilities, usually e-commerce, while maintaining its traditional structure. Many *Fortune* 500–type organizations have evolved into e-businesses using this approach. They use the Internet to *enhance* (not to replace) their traditional ways of doing business. For instance, the Internet division of Sears, a traditional bricks-and-mortar retailer with thousands of physical stores worldwide, is intended to expand, not replace, the company's main source of revenue.

Another category of e-business involvement is an e-business *enabled* organization, which uses the Internet to perform its traditional business functions better, but not to sell anything. In other words, the Internet *enables* organizational members to do their work more efficiently and effectively. Numerous organizations use electronic linkages to communicate with employees, customers, or suppliers, and to support them with information. For instance, Levi Strauss uses its Web site to interact with customers, providing them the latest information about the company and its products, but not to sell the jeans. It also uses an **intranet**, an internal organizational communication system that uses Internet technology and is accessible only to organizational employees, to communicate with its global workforce.

●●● **intranet**
An internal organizational communication system that uses Internet technology and is accessible only by organizational employees.

The last category of e-business involvement is when an organization becomes a total e-business. Organizations such as Amazon.com, Yahoo!, E*TRADE, and eBay are total e-business organizations. Their whole existence revolves around the Internet. Other organizations, like Charles Schwab & Company, have evolved into e-business organizations that seamlessly integrate traditional and e-business functions. When an organization becomes a total e-business, there's a complete transformation in the way it does its work. For instance, when managers at Schwab decided to merge its traditional and e-business operations, it had to reprice its core products, retrain all of its employees, and renovate all of its systems.[23]

Knowledge Management and Learning Organizations

Today's managers confront an environment in which change takes place at an unprecedented rate. As a result, many past management approaches and principles—created for a world that was more stable and predictable—no longer apply.

●●● **learning organization**
An organization that has developed the capacity to continuously learn, adapt, and change.

Organizations of the twenty-first century must be able to learn and respond quickly. These organizations will be led by managers who can effectively challenge conventional wisdom, manage the organization's knowledge base, and make needed changes. These organizations will need to be **learning organizations**—that is, ones that

Exhibit 2–10

**Learning Organization
Versus Traditional
Organization**

	Traditional Organization	Learning Organization
Attitude toward change	If it's working, don't change it.	If you aren't changing, it won't be working for long.
Attitude toward new ideas	If it wasn't invented here, reject it.	If it was invented or reinvented here, reject it.
Who's responsible for innovation?	Traditional areas such as R & D	Everyone in organization
Main fear	Making mistakes	Not learning; not adapting
Competitive advantage	Products and service	Ability to learn, knowledge and expertise
Manager's job	Control others	Enable others

have developed the capacity to continuously learn, adapt, and change. Exhibit 2–10 clarifies how a learning organization is different from a traditional organization.

Part of a manager's responsibility is to create learning capabilities throughout the organization—from lowest level to highest level and in all areas. How? An important step is understanding the value of knowledge as an important resource, just like cash, raw materials, or office equipment. To illustrate the value of knowledge, think about how you register for college classes. Do you talk to others who have had a certain professor? Do you listen to their experiences with this individual and make your decision based on what they have to say (their knowledge about the situation)? If you do, you're tapping into the value of knowledge. But in an organization, just recognizing the value of accumulated knowledge or wisdom isn't enough. Managers must deliberately manage that base of knowledge. **Knowledge management** involves cultivating a learning culture where organizational members systematically gather knowledge and share it with others in the organization so as to achieve better performance.[24] For instance, accountants and consultants at Ernst & Young, a professional-services firm, document best practices they have developed, unusual problems they have dealt with, and other work information. This "knowledge" is then shared with all employees through computer-based applications and through COIN (community of interest) teams that meet regularly throughout the company. Many other organizations—General Electric, Toyota, Hewlett-Packard, Buckman Laboratories—have recognized the importance of knowledge management to being a learning organization.

• • • knowledge management
Cultivating a learning culture where organizational members systematically gather knowledge and share it with others in the organization so as to achieve better performance.

THINKING CRITICALLY ABOUT ETHICS

Information is power—those who have information have power. Because information gives them power, it's human nature to want to keep that information, not share it. Knowledge hoarding is a business habit that's hard to break. In fact, it's an attitude that still characterizes many businesses. In a learning organization, however, we're asking people to share information.

Getting people to share information may turn out to be one of the key challenges facing managers. Is it ethical to ask people to share information that they've worked hard to obtain? What if performance evaluations are based on how well individuals do their jobs, and how well they do their jobs is dependent on the special knowledge that they have? Is it ethical to ask them to share that information? What ethical implications are inherent in creating an organizational environment that promotes learning and knowledge sharing?

Becoming a Manager

♦ *In other classes you take, see what ideas and concepts potentially relate to being a good manager.*

♦ *Pay attention to current business stories and how they relate to any of the six approaches to management.*

♦ *If you're working, try to note which of the six approaches to management you're using and how they're helping you do your job.*

♦ *As you make decisions, resolve problems, or just live your daily life, see if any of the six approaches to management might help you be more effective or efficient.*

♦ *Stay informed about the current trends and issues facing managers.*

♦ ▪▪▪▫▪ *Go to the Web and complete any of these exercises from the Self-Assessment Library (S.A.L.) found on R.O.L.L.S. #23—Am I Likely to Become an Entrepreneur? or #47—How Well Do I Respond to Turbulent Change?*

Quality Management

A quality revolution swept through both the business and public sectors during the 1980s and 1990s.[25] The generic term used to describe this revolution was total quality management, or TQM. It was inspired by a small group of quality experts, the most famous of whom were W. Edwards Deming and Joseph M. Juran. The ideas and techniques espoused by these two men in the 1950s had few supporters in the United States but were enthusiastically embraced by Japanese organizations. As Japanese manufacturers began beating out U.S. competitors in quality comparisons, Western managers soon took a more serious look at TQM. Deming's and Juran's ideas became the basis for today's quality management programs.

●●● **quality management**
A philosophy of management that is driven by continual improvement and responding to customer needs and expectations.

Quality management is a philosophy of management driven by continual improvement and responding to customer needs and expectations. (See Exhibit 2–11.) The term *customer* has expanded beyond the original definition of the purchaser outside the organization to include anyone who interacts with the organization's product or services internally or externally. It encompasses employees and suppliers as well as the people who purchase the organization's goods or services. The objective is to create an organization committed to continuous improvement in work processes.

Exhibit 2–11

●●●——

What Is Quality Management?

1. Intense focus on the *customer*. The customer includes not only outsiders who buy the organization's products or services but also internal customers who interact with and serve others in the organization.
2. Concern for *continual improvement*. Quality management is a commitment to never being satisfied. "Very good" is not good enough. Quality can always be improved.
3. *Process-focused*. Quality management focuses on work processes as the quality of goods and services is continually improved.
4. Improvement in the *quality of everything* the organization does. Quality management uses a very broad definition of quality. It relates not only to the final product but also to how the organization handles deliveries, how rapidly it responds to complaints, how politely the phones are answered, and the like.
5. *Accurate measurement*. Quality management uses statistical techniques to measure every critical variable in the organization's operations. These are compared against standards or benchmarks to identify problems, trace them to their roots, and eliminate their causes.
6. *Empowerment of employees*. Quality management involves the people on the line in the improvement process. Teams are widely used in quality management programs as empowerment vehicles for finding and solving problems.

Steinway pianos are made to rigorous quality standards that must be upheld throughout the eight months it takes to produce each instrument. Here workers at the firm's New York City factory force the wood of the cabinet into the proper curve, in the first of many production steps for manufacturing a 9-foot concert grand. Despite the fact that all Steinways are made the same way, one of the things musicians prize the pianos for is their individual "personality."

Quality management is a departure from earlier management theories that were based on the belief that low costs were the only road to increased productivity. The U.S. car industry is often used as a classic example of what can go wrong when managers focus solely on trying to keep costs down. In the late 1970s, GM, Ford, and Chrysler built products that many consumers rejected. Your second author remembers vividly purchasing a new Pontiac Grand Prix in 1978, driving it off the lot, pulling up to a gas pump, filling the gas tank, and watching gas pour out on the ground because of a hole in the car's gas tank! When you consider the costs of rejects, repairing shoddy work, product recalls, and expensive controls to identify quality problems, U.S. manufacturers actually were *less* productive than many foreign competitors. The Japanese demonstrated that it *was* possible for the highest-quality manufacturers to be among the lowest-cost producers. American manufacturers in the car and other industries soon realized the importance of quality management and implemented many of its basic components. Quality management is important, and we'll discuss it throughout this book.

● ● ●Learning Review

- Explain why we need to look at the current trends and issues facing managers.

- Describe the current trends and issues facing managers.

Managers **Respond** to a **Manager's** Dilemma

····Jan Coughtrey

**Vice President/Director Creative Services, Pearson Canada,
Don Mills, Ontario, Canada**

The ability of Ivy Ross's team to conceptualize and implement its goals quickly was, in part, due to its flexibility in developing new ideas and its empirical background research. However, for future innovation efforts, she might want to think about using a more structured team with clearly defined roles. This more structured team approach could help better guide and direct marketing strategies as it would give more focus to capturing not only a new customer base (in this case parents and daughters) but appealing to the existing customer base of girls. Not only would such a team be able to innovate products, it would help to ensure a successful product launch into the marketplace.

Martin Shova

**Associate Director, Creative Services, Kraft Foods,
East Hanover, New Jersey**

I'm a firm believer in "lead user research," which is finding out what your users are doing with your product. Big ideas usually come from technical innovation or quality research and must leverage the company's core strengths. It's also important to realize that you can make small but profitable innovations with current products as long as these innovations satisfy meaningful customer needs. If I were Ivy, I would approach innovation the same way. Gather data from lead users—kids—and apply this learning to existing and future product offerings. Her new product teams should be flexible, throw out old norms, and encourage discussion of *all* ideas. These teams should also include a diverse range of industry experience, have the necessary resources to complete the task, and most importantly, not be penalized should a project fail to meet its goals.

Learning Summary

● ● ●

After reading and studying this chapter, you should be able to:

- Explain why studying management history is important.
- Describe some early evidences of management practice.
- Describe the important contributions made by Frederick W. Taylor and Frank and Lillian Gilbreth.
- Explain how today's managers use scientific management.
- Discuss Fayol's 14 management principles.
- Describe Max Weber's contributions to the general administrative theory of management.
- Explain how today's managers use general administrative theories of management.
- Explain what the quantitative approach has contributed to the field of management.
- Discuss how today's managers use the quantitative approach.

- Describe the contributions of the early advocates of OB.
- Explain the contributions of the Hawthorne Studies to the field of management.
- Discuss how today's managers use the behavioral approach.
- Describe an organization using the systems approach.
- Discuss how the systems approach is appropriate for understanding management.
- Explain how the contingency approach differs from the early theories of management.
- Discuss how the contingency approach is appropriate for studying management.
- Explain why we need to look at the current trends and issues facing managers.
- Describe the current trends and issues facing managers.

Thinking About Management Issues

● ● ●

1. What kind of workplace would Henri Fayol create? How about Mary Parker Follett? How about Frederick W. Taylor?

2. Can a mathematical (quantitative) technique help a manager solve a "people" problem such as how to motivate employees or how to distribute work equitably? Explain.

3. Is globalization an issue for e-businesses? Explain.

4. "Entrepreneurship is only for small, start-up businesses." Do you agree or disagree with this statement? Explain.

5. How do societal trends influence the practice of management? What are the implications for someone studying management?

6. Would you feel more comfortable in a learning organization or in a traditional organization? Why?

Working Together: Team-Based Exercise

● ● ●

Building a base of knowledge that others in an organization can tap into and use to help do their jobs better is a bottom-line goal of knowledge management. Form groups of three or four class members. Your task is to do some preliminary work on creating a knowledge base for your college. Think about what organizational members could learn from each other in this organization. What common tasks might they perform that would help them learn from each other about how best to do those tasks?

What unique tasks do they perform that others might learn something from? After discussing these issues, come up with an outline of major areas of important knowledge for this organization. (Here are a couple of hints that might help you get started—using technology in classrooms, keeping in touch with former students and alumni.) As a group, be prepared to share your outline with the class and to explain your choices.

Case Application

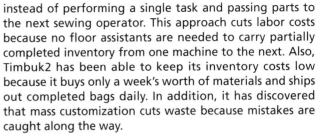

Timbuk2

There is a job that few have the stamina or agility to do, especially in cities with a lot of hills like San Francisco. However, bicycle messengers perform an important service, hauling bulky loads swiftly from location to location. Their bags have to be tough, waterproof, light-weight, and functional—and it's nice if they look great, too! Rob Honeycutt knows well what bike knapsacks need to be—he was a messenger once himself. Today, his company, Timbuk2 Designs, manufactures bags that appeal to the "hip, young, wacky nuts on bikes."

Honeycutt started the company in 1989 and its annual revenues are around $3.5 million. The company has grown in spurts—for instance, one year it was 10 percent and another year it was 70 percent. Such erratic growth has created definite management challenges for Honeycutt. But one thing that hasn't been a challenge is the company's commitment to making the best possible products.

Many bike messenger services claim that Timbuk2 bags are the best and most popular. The company offers what none of its competitors do: a three-panel construction design that allows customers to custom choose from 13 colors, giving them 2,197 possible color combinations. And Timbuk2's bags cost no more than the mass-produced ones. Honeycutt wanted to do what Toyota Motor Corporation did with cars—mass customize or make cars to customers' orders. He thought it might work because manufacturing bags is much simpler than making cars. However, things didn't quite work out until workers began experimenting with something Honeycutt had seen at a trade show demonstration. That something was the Toyota Sewing System, which calls for each sewing operator to move down a row of task-specific sewing machines

instead of performing a single task and passing parts to the next sewing operator. This approach cuts labor costs because no floor assistants are needed to carry partially completed inventory from one machine to the next. Also, Timbuk2 has been able to keep its inventory costs low because it buys only a week's worth of materials and ships out completed bags daily. In addition, it has discovered that mass customization cuts waste because mistakes are caught along the way.

Work begins early—6:00 A.M.—at Timbuk2. A dozen women, most of them Chinese immigrants, sew colorful strips of canvas together and add snaps and shoulder straps. By the end of each workweek, the workers will have finished a total of 400 bags. The company pays its employees more than other apparel makers and offers full medical benefits. When the company needed financing, it turned to Silicon Valley Community Ventures (SVCV), a funding source with a unique twist. SVCV invested money in Timbuk2 with the understanding that it would pay a living wage of at least $11 an hour and develop a pay incentive program that rewarded employees for learning new skills. This investment in employees seems to be paying off.

Although there are many things the company is doing right, Timbuk2 continues to refine its system, relying heavily on employee suggestions and ideas. In 1993 it took 144 minutes (almost 2-1/2 hours) to make one bag. Today, using employees' suggestions and automated machines, it has reduced that time to 12 minutes. Labor costs are about 16 percent of total costs and the goal is whittling that down to 12 percent.

In early 2000, Honeycutt decided to create an online buying process. Timbuk2 hired 15 people to create a Web site and to add to production. The Web site turned out to be a good decision, especially as the economy took a downturn. It started generating sales in October 2000 and today brings in almost half of Timbuk2's revenues.

Rob Honeycutt (on left in picture) of Timbuk2 Designs.

DISCUSSION QUESTIONS

1. Would principles of scientific management be useful to Timbuk2? Explain how.

2. How might knowledge of organizational behavior help Rob in managing his workforce of manual laborers and knowledge workers?

3. Using Exhibit 2–6, describe Timbuk2 as a system.

4. What characteristics and management practices does this company exhibit that might be important for successful organizations in the twenty-first century?

Sources: Information from company Web site (*www.timbuk2.com*), March 16, 2003; E. Corcoran, "The Dual Bottom Line," *Forbes*, November 25, 2002, pp. 130–132; and R. Furchgott, "Success Could Be in the Bag," *Business Week Enterprise*, December 16, 1996, pp. ENT8–ENT9.

Part TWO
Defining the Manager's Terrain

• • • Learning Outline

Follow this Learning Outline as you read and study this chapter.

The Manager: Omnipotent or Symbolic
- Contrast the actions of managers according to the omnipotent and symbolic views.
- Explain the parameters of managerial discretion.

The Organization's Culture
- Describe the seven dimensions of organizational culture.
- Discuss the impact of a strong culture on organizations and managers.
- Explain the source of an organization's culture and how that culture continues.
- Describe how culture is transmitted to employees.

Current Organizational Culture Issues Facing Managers
- Describe the characteristics of an ethical culture, an innovative culture, and a customer-responsive culture.
- Discuss why workplace spirituality seems to be an important concern.
- Describe the characteristics of a spiritual organization.

The Environment
- Describe the components of the specific and general environments.
- Discuss the two dimensions of environmental uncertainty.
- Identify the most common organizational stakeholders.
- Explain the four steps in managing external stakeholder relationships.

Chapter
3

Organizational Culture and the Environment: The Constraints

 It's unusual to find an organization that has essentially no employee turnover. But that's the case at Athleta Corporation.[1] The sports apparel company, based in Petaluma, California, has employee turnover of less than 1 percent a year. Meanwhile, employee productivity keeps increasing. To CEO Scott Kerslake (pictured), employee retention is a daily priority. He goes out of his way to make sure his 60 employees put their personal lives ahead of their jobs.

Athleta's employees are a diverse team. They come in all shapes and sizes with varying attitudes and abilities. They include soccer players, runners, cyclists, surfers, skiers, hikers, snowboarders, yoga enthusiasts, dancers, and skateboarders. Also, the employees have opinions and aren't afraid to share them with each other and with the company's managers. Despite their differences, they all share a fundamental passion—to offer active women the best products and advice on the planet through their catalog and online store. That passion for health, fitness, and life characterizes Athleta's employees, who also enjoy their fun, fast-paced, and semi-chaotic workplace. The company's unique work environment is about enjoying what they do and offering support to each and every team member.

And that extends to the canine members of the Athleta team! Sam, Hazel, Mac, Jake, Pete, Abby, Hanna, Stella, The Salad, and Bear are excellent running companions and are ready at a moment's notice to help their humans reduce stress by wrestling or fetching thrown objects.

Scott's approach to keeping his employees committed is simple—cultivate a culture of trust that allows them to set their own schedules and handle personal matters during the workday. Employees who need to attend to family problems or who have personal appointments know that they can take care of those things and not get in trouble. They know they're trusted to make up the time. Also, employees are cross-trained in each others' work areas and fill in for one another as needed.

Now, put yourself in Scott's position. As his company continues to grow and add employees, how can he maintain the employee-friendly culture he's created?

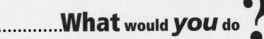
What would *you* do**?**

S cott Kerslake recognizes how important organizational culture is to his organization! He has formed a culture where employees enjoy being with each other and supporting each other. He also recognizes the challenges his organization faces in trying to manage its internal culture, especially as the organization grows. But how much actual impact does a manager like Scott have on an organization's success or failure? In the following section, we explore this important question.

THE MANAGER: OMNIPOTENT OR SYMBOLIC?

The dominant view in management theory and society in general is that managers are directly responsible for an organization's success or failure. We'll call this perspective the **omnipotent view of management**. In contrast, some observers have argued that much of an organization's success or failure is due to external forces outside managers' control. This perspective has been labeled the **symbolic view of management**. Let's look more closely at each of these perspectives so we can try to clarify just how much credit or blame managers should receive for their organization's performance.

The Omnipotent View

In Chapter 1 we discussed the importance of managers to organizations. This view reflects a dominant assumption in management theory: The quality of an organization's managers determines the quality of the organization itself. It's assumed that differences in an organization's effectiveness or efficiency are due to the decisions and actions of its managers. Good managers anticipate change, exploit opportunities, correct poor performance, and lead their organizations toward their goals, which may be changed if necessary. When profits are up, managers take the credit and reward themselves with bonuses, stock options, and the like. When profits are down, top managers are often fired in the belief that "new blood" will bring improved results. For instance, it only took nine months for the board of directors at Lands' End to replace its top manager when operating income declined and holiday sales fell far short of expectations.

The view of managers as omnipotent is consistent with the stereotypical picture of the take-charge business executive who can overcome any obstacle in carrying out the organization's goals. (■□■ Go to the Web and check out Q & A 3.1.) This omnipotent view, of course, isn't limited to business organizations. We can also use it to help explain the high turnover among college and professional sports coaches, who can be considered the "managers" of their teams. Coaches who lose more games than they win are seen as ineffective. They are fired and replaced by new coaches who, it is hoped, will correct the inadequate performance.

In the omnipotent view, when organizations perform poorly, someone has to be held accountable regardless of the reasons, and in our society, that "someone" is the manager. Of course, when things go well, we need someone to praise. So managers also get the credit—even if they had little to do with achieving positive outcomes.

The Symbolic View

Winn-Dixie Stores operates 1,070 grocery stores across a 12-state southern U.S. region. When the company decided to close 10 percent of its stores and cut 11,000 jobs, competitor Kroger found its business volume and revenues increasing. Was the sales increase for Kroger the result of managers' decisions and actions, or was it beyond their control? The symbolic view would suggest the latter.

The symbolic view says that a manager's ability to affect outcomes is influenced and constrained by external factors.[2] In this view, it's unreasonable to expect managers to significantly affect an organization's performance. Instead, an organization's results are influenced by factors outside the control of managers. These factors

---

● ● ● omnipotent view of management
The view that managers are directly responsible for an organization's success or failure.

● ● ● symbolic view of management
The view that managers have only a limited effect on substantive organizational outcomes because of the large number of factors outside their control.

■ Q & A
Whenever you see this green square, go to the R.O.L.L.S. Web site (*www.prenhall.com/robbins*) to the Q & A, your 24/7 educational assistant. These video clips and written material presented by your authors address questions that we have found students frequently ask.

Exhibit 3–1

Parameters of Managerial Discretion

| Organizational Environment | **Managerial Discretion** | Organizational Culture |

include, for example, the economy, customers, governmental policies, competitors' actions, industry conditions, control over proprietary technology, and decisions made by previous managers.

According to the symbolic view, managers symbolize control and influence.[3] How? They create meaning out of randomness, confusion, and ambiguity or try to innovate and adapt. Because they have a limited effect on organizational outcomes, a manager's actions involve developing plans, making decisions, and engaging in other managerial activities which they do for the benefit of stockholders, customers, employees, and the public. However, the part that managers actually play in organizational success or failure is minimal.

Reality Suggests a Synthesis

In reality, managers are neither helpless nor all powerful. (▬▭▬ Go to the Web and check out Q & A 3.2.) Internal and external constraints that restrict a manager's decision options exist within every organization. Internal constraints arise from the organization's culture and external constraints come from the organization's environment.

Exhibit 3–1 shows managers as operating within the constraints imposed by the organization's culture and environment. Yet, despite these constraints, managers are not powerless. They can still influence an organization's performance. In the remainder of this chapter, we'll discuss organizational culture and environment as constraints. However, as we'll see in other chapters, these constraints don't mean that a manager's hands are tied. As Scott, in our chapter-opening dilemma, recognized, managers can and do influence their culture and environment.

● ● ● Learning Review

- Contrast the actions of managers according to the omnipotent and symbolic views.

- Explain the parameters of managerial discretion.

THE ORGANIZATION'S CULTURE

We know that every person has a unique personality—a set of relatively permanent and stable traits that influence the way we act and interact with others. When we describe someone as warm, open, relaxed, shy, or aggressive, we're describing personality traits. An organization, too, has a personality, which we call its *culture*.

What Is Organizational Culture?

Payless Shoe Source, headquartered in Topeka, Kansas, understands what organizational culture is. As the world's largest footwear retailer, it's quite vulnerable to competitive attacks by the dynamic duo of retailing—Wal-Mart and Target. To be prepared, Payless's managers knew they were going to have to change the company's culture to become more aggressive, creative, and risk taking. One thing they did at the company's annual sales meeting was to send all the district managers out into the community on a scavenger hunt to find certain "treasures" including, among other things, a hook-and-ladder fire truck (which one team actually did find and bring back), hospital scrubs, and a Federal Express truck. Teams also had to photograph themselves next to certain items while carrying rubber chickens. And all this had to be accomplished within two hours. Why? To prove to the managers that they could work together to come up with creative solutions even under pressure-packed conditions. Although one scavenger hunt couldn't, by itself, bring about such a culture, it was a step toward the type of thinking that would be crucial if Payless was to continue growing.[4]

••• organizational culture
A system of shared meaning and beliefs held by organizational members that determines, in large degree, how employees act.

What is **organizational culture**? It's a system of shared meaning and beliefs held by organizational members that determines, in large degree, how they act toward each other and outsiders. (■□■■■■ Go to the Web and check out Q & A 3.3.) It represents a common perception held by an organization's members that influences how they behave. In every organization, there are values, symbols, rituals, myths, and practices that have evolved over time.[5] These shared values and experiences determine, in large degree, what employees perceive and how they respond to their world.[6] When confronted with problems or issues, the organizational culture—the "way we do things around here"—influences what employees can do and how they conceptualize, define, analyze, and resolve issues. (■□■■■■ Go to the Web and check out Q & A 3.4.)

Our definition of culture implies three things. First, culture is a *perception*. Individuals perceive the organizational culture on the basis of what they see, hear, or experience within the organization. Second, even though individuals may have different backgrounds or work at different organizational levels, they tend to describe the organization's culture in similar terms. That's the *shared* aspect of culture. Finally, organizational culture is a *descriptive* term. It's concerned with how members perceive the organization, not with whether they like it. It describes rather than evaluates.

Research suggests that there are seven dimensions that capture the essence of an organization's culture.[7] These dimensions are described in Exhibit 3–2. Each dimension ranges from low to high, which simply is a way of saying that it's not very typical of the culture (low) or is very typical of the culture (high). Appraising an organization on these seven dimensions gives a composite picture of the organization's culture. (■□■■■■ Go to the Web and check out Q & A 3.5.) In many organizations, one of these cultural dimensions often is emphasized more than the others and essentially shapes the organization's personality and the way organizational members work. For instance, at

Exhibit 3–2 **Dimensions of Organizational Culture**

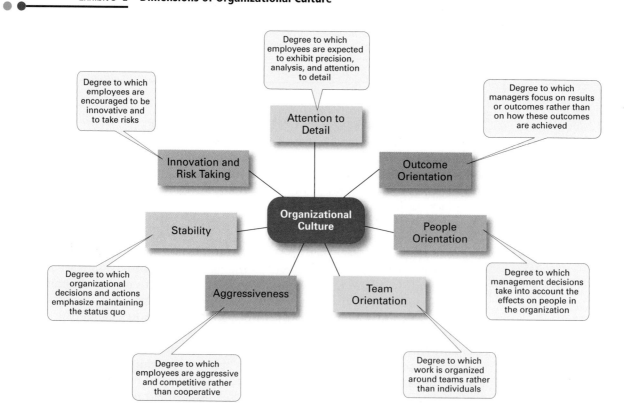

Exhibit 3–3

Contrasting Organizational Cultures

Organization A

This organization is a manufacturing firm. Managers are expected to fully document all decisions, and "good managers" are those who can provide detailed data to support their recommendations. Creative decisions that incur significant change or risk are not encouraged. Because managers of failed projects are openly criticized and penalized, managers try not to implement ideas that deviate much from the status quo. One lower-level manager quoted an often-used phrase in the company: "If it ain't broke, don't fix it."

Employees are required to follow extensive rules and regulations in this firm. Managers supervise employees closely to ensure that there are no deviations. Management is concerned with high productivity, regardless of the impact on employee morale or turnover.

Work activities are designed around individuals. There are distinct departments and lines of authority, and employees are expected to minimize formal contact with other employees outside their functional area or line of command. Performance evaluations and rewards emphasize individual effort, although seniority tends to be the primary factor in the determination of pay raises and promotions.

Organization B

This organization is also a manufacturing firm. Here, however, management encourages and rewards risk taking and change. Decisions based on intuition are valued as much as those that are well rationalized. Management prides itself on its history of experimenting with new technologies and its success in regularly introducing innovative products. Managers or employees who have a good idea are encouraged to "run with it," and failures are treated as "learning experiences." The company prides itself on being market driven and rapidly responsive to the changing needs of its customers.

There are few rules and regulations for employees to follow, and supervision is loose because management believes that its employees are hardworking and trustworthy. Management is concerned with high productivity but believes that this comes through treating its people right. The company is proud of its reputation as being a good place to work.

Job activities are designed around work teams, and team members are encouraged to interact with people across functions and authority levels. Employees talk positively about the competition between teams. Individuals and teams have goals, and bonuses are based on achievement of outcomes. Employees are given considerable autonomy in choosing the means by which the goals are attained.

Sony Corporation the focus is on product innovation. The company "lives and breathes" new-product development (outcome orientation), and employees' work decisions, behaviors, and actions support that goal. In contrast, Southwest Airlines has made its employees a central part of its culture (people orientation). Exhibit 3–3 describes how the dimensions can be combined to create significantly different organizations.

Strong Versus Weak Cultures

> • • • **strong cultures**
> Organizations in which the key values are intensely held and widely shared.

Although all organizations have cultures, not all cultures have an equal impact on employees' behaviors and actions. **Strong cultures**—cultures in which the key values are deeply held and widely shared—have a greater influence on employees than do weak cultures. The more employees accept the organization's key values and the greater their commitment to those values, the stronger the culture is. (▮▯▯▯▯ Go to the Web and check out Q & A 3.6.)

Whether an organization's culture is strong, weak, or somewhere in between depends on factors such as the size of the organization, how long it has been around, how much turnover there has been among employees, and the intensity with which the culture was originated. Some organizations do not make clear what is important and what is not, and this lack of clarity is a characteristic of weak cultures. In such organizations, culture is unlikely to greatly influence managers. Most organizations, however, have moderate to strong cultures. There is relatively high agreement on what's important, what defines "good" employee behavior, what it takes to get ahead, and so forth.

What impact does a strong culture have on an organization? One study found that employees in organizations with strong cultures were more committed to their organization than were employees in organizations with weak cultures. The organizations

At Stacy's Pita Chip Co., the environment is spotless but utilitarian, the equipment is used, and everything goes back into the business. Mark and Stacy Andrus have bootstrapped their low-fat snack chip business to reach sales of over $1.3 million in 37 states. The low-cost, hard-driving culture they've developed retains a sense of humor too, as is evident in the company's "dress code" shown here.

with strong cultures also used their recruitment efforts and socialization practices to build employee commitment.[8] And an increasing body of evidence suggests that strong cultures are associated with high organizational performance.[9] It's easy to understand why a strong culture enhances performance. After all, when values are clear and widely accepted, employees know what they're supposed to do and what's expected of them, so they can act quickly to take care of problems, thus preventing any potential performance decline. However, the drawback is that the same strong culture also might prevent employees from trying new approaches, especially during periods of rapid change.[10] (▮◻▮▮▮ Go to the Web and check out Q & A 3.7.)

What are the implications for the way managers manage? As an organization's culture becomes stronger, it has an increasing impact on what managers do.[11]

The Source of Culture

An organization's current customs, traditions, and general way of doing things are largely due to what it has done before and the degree of success it has had with those endeavors. The original source of an organization's culture usually reflects the vision or mission of the organization's founders. Their focus might be aggressiveness or it might be treating employees as family. The founders establish the early culture by projecting an image of what the organization should be. They're not constrained by previous customs or approaches. And the small size of most new organizations helps the founders instill their vision in all organizational members.

For example, Yvon Chouinard, the founder of the outdoor gear company Patagonia, Inc., was an avid "extreme adventurer." He approached the business in a laid-back, casual manner. For instance, he hired employees not on the basis of any specific business skills, but because he had climbed, fished, or surfed with them. Employees were friends, and work was treated as something that was fun to do. In a speech Chouinard gave a few years ago, he is said to have uttered the line, "Let my people go surfing!" Although the company (now called Lost Arrow) has more than 900 employees and revenues of $220 million (2002), its culture still reflects Chouinard's values and philosophy. To keep employees happy, it offers child care and yoga classes at work and donates one percent of its sales to green causes. And if the surf is good, employees are free to go enjoy it!

The impact of a founder on an organization's culture isn't unique to the United States. At Hyundai Corporation, the giant Korean conglomerate, the culture reflects the fierce, competitive style of its founder, Chung Ju Yung. Other well-known contemporary examples of founders from the United States and other countries who have had an enormous impact on their organization's culture include Bill Gates at Microsoft, Herb Kelleher at Southwest Airlines, Fred Smith at Federal Express, Sam Walton at Wal-Mart, Akio Morita at Sony, Ingvar Kamprad at IKEA, and Richard Branson at the Virgin Group.

How an Organization's Culture Continues

Once a culture is in place, certain organizational practices help maintain it. For instance, during the employee selection process, managers typically judge job candidates not only on the requirements of the job, but also on how well they might fit into the organization. At the same time, job candidates find out information about the organization and determine whether or not they are comfortable with what they see.

Find a Culture That Fits

Richard D'Ambrosio thought he had found the perfect job at an accounting firm. It had all the trappings of a good workplace—employee recognition awards and managers with "politically correct" answers to work-life questions. Yet, as soon as he signed on, he found himself in a culture that prized working long hours just for the sake of working long hours and where junior accountants were expected to be at the beck and call of the partners. If it was your wedding anniversary, too bad. If it was a holiday, too bad. It only took a few months before he quit. How can you avoid the same problem? How can you find a culture that fits?[12] Here are some suggestions.

First, figure out what suits you. For instance, do you like working in teams or on your own? Do you like to go out after work with colleagues or go straight home? Are you comfortable in a more formal or a more casual environment? Then, narrow your job search to those kinds of employers.

Once you've gotten through the initial job screening process and you start interviewing, the real detective work begins. And it involves more than investigating the "official" information provided by the employer. Try to uncover the values that drive the organization. Ask questions such as what are its proudest accomplishments? or how did it respond to past emergencies and crises? Ask, "If I have an idea, how do I make it happen?" Ask if you can talk to someone who's on the "fast track" to promotions and find out what they're doing and why they're being rewarded. Ask how you'll be evaluated—after all, if you're going to be in the game, shouldn't you know how the score is kept? Also, look for nonverbal clues. What do people have at their desks—family pictures or only work stuff? Are office doors closed or open? Are there doors? How does the physical climate feel? Is it relaxed and casual or more formal? Do people seem to be helping each other as they work? Are the bathrooms dirty? This might indicate a low value placed on anything to do with employees. Look at the material symbols and who seems to have access to them. And finally, during your investigation, do pay particular attention to the specific department or unit where you'd work. After all, this would be where you'd spend the majority of your working hours. Can you see yourself being happy there?

(▮▮▯▮▮ Go to the Web and check out PRISM #3— Reading an Organization's Culture. Also, see the "Managing Your Career" box above.)

The actions of top executives also have a major impact on the organization's culture. Through what they say and how they behave, top-level managers establish norms that filter down through the organization. This can have a positive effect on employees' willingness to take risks or to provide exceptional customer service, for instance. IBM's CEO Sam Palmisano wanted employees to value teamwork so he chose to take several million dollars from his 2003 bonus and give it to his top executives based on teamwork. He said, "If you say you're about a team, you have to be a team. You've got to walk the talk, right?"[13] Or, it also can have the opposite effect if top managers' behavior is self-serving, as we saw in the corporate ethics scandals of 2002.

• • • **socialization**
The process that adapts employees to the organization's culture.

Finally, an organization must help employees adapt to its culture through a process called **socialization**. Through the socialization process, new employees learn the organization's way of doing things. For instance, all new employees at Starbucks, the global specialty coffee retailer, go through 24 hours of training. Classes are offered on everything necessary to turn new employees into brewing consultants. They learn the Starbucks philosophy, the company jargon, and even how to help customers make decisions about beans, grind, and espresso machines. The result is employees who understand Starbucks' culture and who project an enthusiastic and knowledgeable interface with customers.[14]

Another benefit of socialization is that because new employees are unfamiliar with the organization's culture, there is the possibility that they might disrupt the beliefs and customs that are in place. The socialization process can minimize the chance of this happening.

Exhibit 3–4 on p. 56 summarizes how an organization's culture is established and maintained. (▮▮▯▮▮ Go to the Web and check out S.A.L. #42—What's the Right Organizational Culture for Me?) The original culture is derived from the founder's

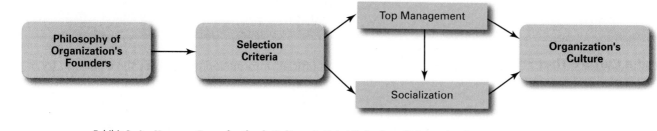

Exhibit 3–4 **How an Organization's Culture Is Established and Maintained**

philosophy. This, in turn, strongly influences the criteria used in hiring. The actions of the current top managers set the general expectations as to what is acceptable behavior and what is not. Socialization processes, if successful, will match new employees' values to those of the organization during the selection process and provide support during that critical time when employees have joined the organization and are learning the ropes.

How Employees Learn Culture

Culture is transmitted to employees in a number of ways. The most significant are stories, rituals, material symbols, and language.

Stories Organizational "stories" typically contain a narrative of significant events or people, including such things as the organization's founders, rule breaking, reactions to past mistakes, and so forth.[15] For instance, managers at Nike feel that stories told about the company's past help shape the future. Whenever possible, corporate "storytellers" (senior executives) explain the company's heritage and tell stories that celebrate people getting things done. When they tell the story of how co-founder Bill Bowerman went to his workshop and poured rubber into his wife's waffle iron to create a better running shoe, they're celebrating and promoting Nike's spirit of innovation. These company stories provide examples from which people can learn.[16] And at the 3M Company, the product-innovation stories are legendary. There's the story about the 3M scientist who spilled chemicals on her tennis shoe and came up with Scotchgard. Then there's the story about Art Fry, a researcher who wanted a better way

The corporate culture of Keefe, Bruyette & Woods Inc., a research, trading, and consulting firm in the financial industry, now includes as one of its "stories" a memorial to its 67 employees who were killed in the collapse of the World Trade Center on September 11, 2001. This painting of the U.S. flag, which hangs in the company's new midtown New York City offices, is made up of the names of all those who died. The company also paid $40 million to the lost employees' families.

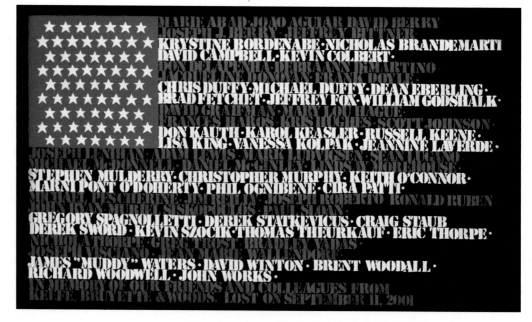

to mark the pages of his church hymnal and invented the Post-It Note. These stories reflect what made 3M great and what it will take to continue that success.[17] To help employees learn the culture, organizational stories anchor the present in the past, provide explanations and legitimacy for current practices, and exemplify what is important to the organization.[18]

Rituals Corporate rituals are repetitive sequences of activities that express and reinforce the values of the organization, what goals are most important, and which people are important.[19] One of the best-known corporate rituals is Mary Kay Cosmetics' annual awards ceremony for its sales representatives.[20] Looking like a cross between a circus and a Miss America pageant, the ceremony takes place in a large auditorium, on a stage in front of a large, cheering audience, with all the participants dressed in glamorous evening clothes. Salespeople are rewarded for their success in achieving sales goals with an array of flashy gifts including gold and diamond pins, furs, and pink Cadillacs. This "show" acts as a motivator by publicly acknowledging outstanding sales performance. In addition, the ritual aspect reinforces late founder Mary Kay's determination and optimism, which enabled her to overcome personal hardships, start her own company, and achieve material success. It conveys to salespeople that reaching their sales goals is important, and through hard work and encouragement they too can achieve success. Your second author had the experience of being on a flight out of Dallas one year with a planeload of Mary Kay sales representatives headed home from the annual awards meeting. Their contagious enthusiasm and excitement made it obvious that this annual "ritual" played a significant role in establishing desired levels of motivation and behavioral expectations, which, after all, is what an organization's culture should do.

Material Symbols When you walk into different businesses, do you get a "feel" for the place—formal, casual, fun, serious, and so forth? These feelings you get demonstrate the power of material symbols in creating an organization's personality. The layout of an organization's facilities, how employees dress, the types of automobiles provided to top executives, and the availability of corporate aircraft are examples of material symbols. Others include the size of offices, the elegance of furnishings, executive "perks" (extra "goodies" provided to managers such as health club memberships, use of company-owned resort facilities, and so forth), the existence of employee lounges or on-site dining facilities, and reserved parking spaces for certain employees. At WorldNow, a provider of Internet technology to local broadcast companies, an important material symbol is an old, dented drill that the founders purchased for $2 at a thrift store. The drill symbolizes the company's culture of "drilling down to solve problems." Every month, an employee is presented with the drill in recognition of outstanding work. The monthly winner is expected to personalize the drill in some way and devise a new rule for caring for it. One employee installed a Bart Simpson trigger; another made the drill wireless by adding an antenna. The company's "icon" carries on the culture even as the organization evolves and changes.[21]

Material symbols convey to employees who is important, the degree of equality desired by top management, and the kinds of behavior (for example, risk-taking, conservative, authoritarian, participative, individualistic, and so forth) that are expected and appropriate.

Language Many organizations and units within organizations use language as a way to identify members of a culture. By learning this language, members attest to their acceptance of the culture and their willingness to help preserve it. For instance, Microsoft employees have their own unique vocabulary: *work judo* (the art of deflecting a work assignment to someone else without making it appear that you're avoiding it); *eating your own dog food* (a strategy of using your own software programs or products in the early stages as a way of testing it even if the process is disagreeable); *flat food* (goodies from the vending machine that can be slipped under the door to a colleague who's working feverishly on deadline); *facemail* (actually talking to someone face-to-face, which is considered a technologically backward means of communicating); *death march* (the countdown to shipping a new product), and so on.[22] And employees at AOL soon learn that *cliff-hangers* refers to links on an AOL screen that tempt you to click to find out what's next; that *SpIMming* is the instant-messaging version of spamming, and that *the one-beat test* refers to the interval between two hand claps which is how long you have to command someone's attention on an AOL screen.[23]

Over time, organizations often develop unique terms to describe equipment, key personnel, suppliers, customers, processes, or products related to their business. New employees are frequently overwhelmed with acronyms and jargon that, after a short period of time, become a natural part of their language. Once learned, this language acts as a common denominator that unites members of a given culture.

How Culture Affects Managers

Because it constrains what they can and cannot do, an organization's culture is particularly relevant to managers. These constraints are rarely explicit. They're not written down. It's unlikely that they'll even be spoken. But they're there, and all managers quickly learn what to do and what not to do in their organization. (■□▨▨ Go to the Web and check out Q & A 3.9.) For instance, you won't find the following values written down anywhere, but each comes from a real organization.

- Look busy even if you're not.
- If you take risks and fail around here, you'll pay dearly for it.

MANAGING WORKFORCE DIVERSITY

Creating an Inclusive Workplace Culture

We know from our discussion in Chapter 2 that managing a diverse workforce is an important issue facing today's managers. As the composition of the workforce changes, managers must take a long hard look at their organizational culture to see if the shared meaning and beliefs that were appropriate for a more homogeneous workforce will support diverse views. How can managers create a workplace culture that advocates and encourages diversity?[24]

Diversity efforts by organizations are no longer driven by federal mandate. Instead, organizations have recognized that inclusive workplaces are good for business. Among other things, diversity contributes to more creative solutions to problems and enhances employee morale. Creating a workplace culture that supports and encourages the inclusion of all diverse individuals and views is a major organizational effort. Managers throughout the organization must value diversity and show that they do by their decisions and actions. An organization that truly wants to promote inclusiveness must shape its culture to allow diversity to flourish. One way to do this is for managers to assimilate diverse perspectives while performing the managerial functions. For example, at the Marriott Marquis Hotel in New York's Times Square, managers are taught in required diversity training classes that the best way to cope with diversity-related conflict is to focus narrowly on performance and never to define problems in terms of gender, culture, or race. And at Prudential, the annual planning process includes key diversity performance goals that are measured and tied to managers' compensation.

Beyond the day-to-day managerial activities, organizations should consider developing ways to reinforce employee behaviors that exemplify inclusiveness. Some suggestions include encouraging individuals to value and defend diverse views, creating traditions and ceremonies that celebrate diversity, rewarding appropriate "heroes" and "heroines" who accept and promote inclusiveness, and communicating formally and informally about employees who champion diversity issues.

Developing an organizational culture that supports diversity and inclusiveness may be challenging but offers high potential benefits. Organizations that allow diversity to prosper and thrive see cultural or environmental changes not as constraints, but as opportunities to bring out the best in all of their members.

Exhibit 3–5

**Managerial Decisions
Affected by Culture**

Planning

- The degree of risk that plans should contain
- Whether plans should be developed by individuals or teams
- The degree of environmental scanning in which management will engage

Organizing

- How much autonomy should be designed into employees' jobs
- Whether tasks should be done by individuals or in teams
- The degree to which department managers interact with each other

Leading

- The degree to which managers are concerned with increasing employee job satisfaction
- What leadership styles are appropriate
- Whether all disagreements—even constructive ones—should be eliminated

Controlling

- Whether to impose external controls or to allow employees to control their own actions
- What criteria should be emphasized in employee performance evaluations
- What repercussions will occur from exceeding one's budget

- Before you make a decision, run it by your boss so that he or she is never surprised.
- We make our product only as good as the competition forces us to.
- What made us successful in the past will make us successful in the future.
- If you want to get to the top here, you have to be a team player.

The link between values such as these and managerial behavior is fairly straightforward. (▉▉▢▢▢ Check out Passport Scenario 1 on page 127). If an organization's culture supports the belief that profits can be increased by cost cutting and that the company's best interests are served by achieving slow but steady increases in quarterly earnings, managers are unlikely to pursue programs that are innovative, risky, long term, or expansionary. For organizations that value and encourage workforce diversity, the organizational culture, and thus managers' decisions and actions, will be supportive of diversity efforts. (See the "Managing Workforce Diversity" box for more information on creating an inclusive workplace.) In an organization whose culture conveys a basic distrust of employees, managers are more likely to use an authoritarian leadership style than a democratic one. Why? The culture establishes for managers what is appropriate behavior. For instance, at St. Luke's advertising agency in London, a culture shaped by the value placed on freedom of expression, a lack of coercion and fear, and a determination to make work fun influences the way employees work and the way that managers plan, organize, lead, and control. The organization's culture is reinforced even by the office environment which is open, versatile, and creative.[25]

An organization's culture, especially a strong one, constrains a manager's decision-making options in all management functions. As shown in Exhibit 3–5, the major areas of a manager's job are influenced by the culture in which he or she operates.

●●●●**Learning Review**

- Describe the seven dimensions of organizational culture.
- Discuss the impact of a strong culture on organizations and managers.

- Explain the source of an organization's culture and how that culture continues.
- Describe how culture is transmitted to employees.

CURRENT ORGANIZATIONAL CULTURE ISSUES FACING MANAGERS

Nordstrom, the specialty retail chain, is renowned for its attention to customers. Nike's innovations in running shoe technology are legendary. Tom's of Maine is known for its commitment to doing things ethically and spiritually. How have these organizations achieved such reputations? Their organizational cultures have played a crucial role. Let's look at four current cultural issues managers should consider: creating an ethical culture, creating an innovative culture, creating a customer-responsive culture, and promoting workplace spirituality.

Creating an Ethical Culture

Andrew Fastow, former chief financial officer of Enron Corporation, had a Lucite cube on his desk that laid out the company's values. It included the following inscription: "When Enron says it's going to rip your face off, it will rip your face off."[26] Other Enron employees described a culture in which personal ambition was valued over teamwork, youth over wisdom, and earnings growth at any cost.[27]

The content and strength of an organization's culture influences its ethical climate and ethical behavior of its members.[28] A strong organizational culture will exert more influence on employees than a weak one. If the culture is strong and supports high ethical standards, it should have a very powerful and positive influence on employee behavior. For example, Alfred P. West, founder and CEO of financial services firm SEI Investments Company, spends a lot of time emphasizing to employees his vision for the company—an open culture of integrity, ownership, and accountability. He says, "We tell our employees a lot about where the company is going. We over-communicate the vision and strategy and continually reinforce the culture."[29]

An organizational culture most likely to shape high ethical standards is one that's high in risk tolerance, low to moderate in aggressiveness, and focuses on means as well as outcomes. Managers in such a culture are supported for taking risks and innovating, are discouraged from engaging in uncontrolled competition, and will pay attention to *how* goals are achieved as well as to *what* goals are achieved.

What can managers do to create a more ethical culture? Exhibit 3–6 outlines some suggestions.

Creating an Innovative Culture

You may not recognize IDEO's name, but you've probably used a number of its products. IDEO is a product design firm. It takes the product ideas that corporations bring it and turns those ideas into reality. Some of its creations range from the first commercial mouse (for Apple Computer) to the first standup toothpaste tube (for Procter & Gamble) to the handheld personal organizer (for Palm). It's critical that IDEO's culture support creativity and innovation.[30] Cirque du Soleil, the Montreal-based creator of circus theater, is another innovative organization. Its managers state that the organization's culture is based on involvement, communication, creativity, and diver-

---

Exhibit 3–6

● ● ●——————

Suggestions for Managers: Creating a More Ethical Culture

- Be a *visible role model.*
- Communicate *ethical expectations.*
- Provide *ethics training.*
- Visibly *reward ethical acts and punish unethical ones.*
- Provide *protective mechanisms* so employees can discuss ethical dilemmas and report unethical behavior without fear.

> **THINKING CRITICALLY ABOUT ETHICS**
>
> Do you think it's possible for a manager with high ethical standards to live by the values in an organizational culture that tolerates, or even encourages, unethical practices? How could a manager deal with such situations?

sity (which they see as a key to innovation).[31] Although these two companies are in industries where continual innovations are crucial to success (product design and entertainment), the fact is that successful organizations in all types of industries will need cultures that support innovation.

What does an innovative culture look like? According to Swedish researcher Goran Ekvall, it would be characterized by the following:

- *Challenge and involvement*—how much employees are involved in, motivated by, and committed to the long-term goals and success of the organization.
- *Freedom*—the degree to which employees can independently define their work, exercise discretion, and take initiative in their day-to-day activities.
- *Trust and openness*—the degree to which employees are supportive and respectful to each other.
- *Idea time*—the amount of time individuals have to elaborate on new ideas before taking action.
- *Playfulness/humor*—how much spontaneity, fun, and ease there is in the workplace.
- *Conflict resolution*—the degree to which individuals make decisions and resolve issues based on the good of the organization versus personal interest.
- *Debates*—how much employees are allowed to express their opinions and put forth their ideas for consideration and review.
- *Risk-taking*—how much managers tolerate uncertainty and ambiguity and whether employees are rewarded for taking risks.[32]

Creating a Customer-Responsive Culture

Harrah's Entertainment, the Las Vegas-based national gaming company, is fanatical about customer service, and for good reason. Company research showed that customers who were satisfied with the service they received at a Harrah's casino increased their gaming expenditures by 10 percent and those who were extremely satisfied increased their gaming expenditures by 24 percent. When customer service translates into these types of results, of course managers would want to create a customer-responsive culture![33]

But what does a customer-responsive culture look like? Research shows that six characteristics are routinely present.[34] First is the type of employees themselves. Successful, service-oriented organizations hire employees who are outgoing and friendly. Second is few rigid rules, procedures, and regulations. Service employees need to have the freedom to meet changing customer service requirements. Third is the widespread use of empowerment. Empowered employees have the decision discretion to do what's necessary to please the customer. Fourth are good listening skills. Employees in customer-responsive cultures have the ability to listen to and understand messages sent by the customer. Fifth is role clarity. Service employees act as links between the organization and its customers, which can create considerable ambiguity and conflict. This reduces employees' job satisfaction and can hinder employee

Schneider National, led by Chris Lofgren, is a transportation and logistics firm with a particularly customer-oriented culture. The focus isn't on getting fancy titles, or bigger offices, or more expensive furniture and other trappings. "If we're guilty of anything," says Lofgren, "sometimes we're too hard on ourselves." He believes that every day the company must earn the right to do business with its customers tomorrow.

● ● ● **workplace spirituality**
The recognition that people have an inner life that nourishes and is nourished by meaningful work that takes place in the context of community.

service performance. Successful customer-responsive cultures reduce employees' uncertainty about their roles and the best way to perform their jobs. (▮▮▮▯ Go to the Web and check out S.A.L. #44—Am I Experiencing Work-Family Conflict?) Finally, customer-responsive cultures have employees who are conscientious in their desire to please the customer. They're willing to take the initiative, even when it's outside their normal job requirements, to satisfy a customer's needs. Based on these characteristics, what can managers do to make their cultures more customer-responsive? Exhibit 3–7 lists some managerial actions.

Spirituality and Organizational Culture

What do Southwest Airlines, Ben & Jerry's, Blistex, Hewlett-Packard, and Tom's of Maine have in common? They're among a growing number of organizations that have embraced workplace spirituality. What is **workplace spirituality**? It's the recognition that people have an inner life that nourishes and is nourished by meaningful work that takes place in the context of community.[35] Organizations that promote a spiritual culture recognize that people have a mind and a spirit, seek to find meaning and purpose in their work, and desire to connect with other human beings and be part of a community.

Workplace spirituality seems to be important now for a number of reasons. Employees are looking for ways to counterbalance the stresses and pressures of a turbulent pace of life. Contemporary lifestyles—single-parent families, geographic mobility, the temporary nature of jobs, new technologies that create distance between people—underscore the lack of community that many people feel. People are looking for involvement and connection. In addition, aging baby boomers are reaching mid-life and looking for something meaningful in their lives, something beyond the job. Others desire to integrate their personal life values with their professional lives. For others, formalized religion hasn't worked and they continue to look for anchors to replace a lack of faith and to fill a growing sense of emptiness. What type of organizational culture can meet such demands? What differentiates spiritual organizations from their nonspiritual counterparts? Although research on this question is preliminary, five cultural characteristics tend to be evident in spiritual organizations.[36]

Strong Sense of Purpose Spiritual organizations build their cultures around a meaningful purpose. While profits are important, they're not the primary values of the organization. Southwest Airlines, for example, is strongly committed to providing the lowest airfares, on-time service, and a pleasant experience for customers. Tom's of Maine strives to sell personal care products that are made from natural ingredients and are environmentally friendly.

● ● ●　Exhibit 3–7

Suggestions for Managers: Creating a More Customer-Responsive Culture

- Hire service-contact people with the personality and attitudes consistent with customer service— friendliness, enthusiasm, attentiveness, patience, concern about others, and listening skills.
- Train customer service people continuously by focusing on improving product knowledge, active listening, showing patience, and displaying emotions.
- Socialize new service-contact people to the organization's goals and values.
- Design customer-service jobs so that employees have as much control as necessary to satisfy customers.
- Empower service-contact employees with the discretion to make day-to-day decisions on job-related activities.
- As the leader, convey a customer-focused vision and demonstrate through decisions and actions the commitment to customers.

Focus on Individual Development Spiritual organizations recognize the worth and value of individuals. They aren't just providing jobs; they seek to create cultures in which employees can continually grow and learn.

Trust and Openness Spiritual organizations are characterized by mutual trust, honesty, and openness. Managers aren't afraid to admit mistakes. And they tend to be extremely up front with employees, customers, and suppliers. The president of Wetherill Associates, a highly successful auto parts distributor, says, "We don't tell lies here, and everyone knows it. We are specific and honest about quality and suitability of the product for our customers' needs, even if we know they might not be able to detect any problems."[37]

Employee Empowerment The high-trust climate in spiritual organizations, when combined with the desire to promote learning and growth, leads to managers empowering employees to make most work-related decisions. Managers trust employees to make thoughtful and conscientious decisions. For instance, at Southwest Airlines, employees—including flight attendants, baggage handlers, gate agents, and customer service representatives—are encouraged to take whatever action they deem necessary to meet customer needs or help fellow workers, even if it means not following company policies.

Toleration of Employee Expression The final characteristic that differentiates spiritually based organizations is that they don't stifle employee emotions. They allow people to be themselves—to express their moods and feelings without guilt or fear of reprimand.

Although a number of organizations have created cultures that promote spirituality, critics of the spirituality movement in organizations have focused on two issues. First is the question of legitimacy. Do organizations have the right to impose spiritual values on their employees? Second is the question of economics—that is, are spirituality and profits compatible?

As far as the first question is concerned, an emphasis on spirituality clearly has the potential to make some employees uneasy. Critics might argue that secular institutions, especially businesses, have no business imposing spiritual values on employees. This criticism is probably valid when spirituality is defined as bringing religion and God into the workplace.[38] However, the criticism is less valid when the goal of a more spiritual organization is helping employees find meaning in their work. If the concerns about today's lifestyles and pressures discussed earlier truly characterize a growing number of workers, then maybe it is time for organizations to help employees find meaning and purpose in their work and to use the workplace as a sense of community.

The issue of whether spirituality and profits are compatible is certainly relevant for business managers and investors. The evidence, although limited, suggests that the two may be compatible. A study by a major consulting firm found that companies that introduced spiritually based techniques improved productivity and significantly reduced turnover.[39] Another study found that organizations that provided their employees with opportunities for spiritual development outperformed those that didn't.[40] Other studies also report that spirituality in organizations is positively related to creativity, employee satisfaction, team performance, and organizational commitment.[41]

● ● ● ● Learning Review

- Describe the characteristics of an ethical culture, an innovative culture, and a customer-responsive culture.
- Discuss why workplace spirituality seems to be an important concern.

- Describe the characteristics of a spiritual organization.

THE ENVIRONMENT

In Chapter 2 our discussion of an organization as an open system explained that an organization interacts with its environment as it takes in inputs and distributes outputs. Anyone who questions the impact of the external environment on managing should consider the following:

- The Cadillac Division of General Motors has watched its buyers grow silver haired. Its average new car buyer is now over 55 years old. To counteract this demographic trend, the company's managers are trying to attract a new generation of buyers.
- Duct tape manufacturers had to quintuple production in spring 2003 to meet demand from a nervous U.S. public intent on protecting homes from possible terrorist attacks.

As these two examples show, there are forces in the environment that play a major role in shaping managers' actions. In this section, we'll identify some of the critical environmental forces that affect managers and show how they constrain managerial discretion.

Defining the External Environment

● ● ● **external environment**
Outside institutions or forces that potentially affect an organization's performance.

The term **external environment** refers to forces and institutions outside the organization that potentially can affect the organization's performance. The external environment is made up of two components, the specific environment and the general environment, as shown in Exhibit 3–8.

● ● ● **specific environment**
The part of the environment that is directly relevant to the achievement of an organization's goals.

The Specific Environment
The **specific environment** includes those external forces that have a direct and immediate impact on managers' decisions and actions and are directly relevant to the achievement of the organization's goals. Each organization's specific environment is unique and changes with conditions. For instance, Timex and Rolex both make watches, but their specific environments differ because they operate in distinctly different market niches. What forces make up the specific environment? The main ones are customers, suppliers, competitors, and pressure groups.

CUSTOMERS As we've said a number of times, organizations exist to meet the needs of customers. It's the customer or client who absorbs the organization's output. This is true even for governmental organizations and other not-for-profits.

Exhibit 3–8

● ● ● **The External Environment**

Customers obviously represent potential uncertainty to an organization. Their tastes can change or they can become dissatisfied with the organization's products or service. Of course, some organizations face considerably more uncertainty as a result of their customers than do others. For example, what comes to mind when you think of Club Med? Club Med's image was traditionally one of carefree singles having fun in the sun at exotic locales. Club Med found, however, that as their target customers married and had children, these same individuals were looking for family-oriented vacation resorts where they could bring the kids. Although Club Med responded to the changing demands of its customers by offering different types of vacation experiences, including family-oriented ones, the company found it hard to change its image.

SUPPLIERS When you think of an organization's suppliers, you typically think in terms of organizations that provide materials and equipment. For Walt Disney World resorts in Florida, that includes organizations that sell soft drinks, computers, food, flowers and other nursery stock, concrete, and paper products. But the term *suppliers* also includes providers of financial and labor inputs. Stockholders, banks, insurance companies, pension funds, and other similar organizations are needed to ensure a continuous supply of money. Labor unions, colleges and universities, occupational associations, trade schools, and local labor markets are sources of employees. When the sources of employees dry up, it can constrain managers' decisions and actions. For example, a lack of qualified nurses, a serious problem plaguing the health care industry, is making it difficult for health care providers to meet demand and keep service levels high.

Managers seek to ensure a steady flow of needed inputs at the lowest price available. Because these inputs represent uncertainties—that is, their unavailability or delay can significantly reduce the organization's effectiveness—managers typically go to great lengths to ensure a steady, reliable flow. The application of e-business techniques is changing the way that organizations deal with suppliers. For example, Toyota Motor Corporation established electronic linkages with suppliers to ensure that it has the right materials at the right time and in the right place. Although these linkages might help managers manage uncertainty, they certainly don't eliminate it.

COMPETITORS All organizations have one or more competitors. Even though it's a monopoly, the U.S. Postal Service competes with FedEx, UPS, and other forms of communication

Newell Rubbermaid has come up with an effective strategy to fight the competition its household products meet at Wal-Mart, Home Depot, Lowe's, and other retail stores. It has hired 573 recent college graduates and trained them in its "Phoenix" program, with techniques that might be described as a combination of guerrilla marketing, management training, corporate culture overhaul, and introduction to retail. The students were chosen because of their high-achieving, super-motivated profiles, and one Rubbermaid manager says they have "put the fear of God into other salesmen."

such as the telephone, e-mail, and fax. Nike competes against Reebok, Adidas, and Fila, among others. Coca-Cola competes against Pepsi and other soft drink companies. Not-for-profit organizations such as the Metropolitan Museum of Art and Girl Scouts USA also compete for dollars, volunteers, and customers.

Managers cannot afford to ignore the competition. When they do, they suffer. For instance, until the 1980s, the three major broadcast networks—ABC, CBS, and NBC—virtually controlled what you watched on television. Now, with digital cable, satellite, DVD players and VCRs, and the Web, customers have a much broader choice of what to watch. As technological capabilities continue to expand, the number of viewing options will provide even more competition for the broadcast networks. The Internet is also having an impact on determining an organization's competitors because it has virtually eliminated the geographic boundaries. Through the power of Internet marketing, a small maple syrup maker in Vermont can compete with the likes of Pillsbury, Quaker Oats, and Smucker's.

These examples illustrate that competitors—in terms of pricing, new products developed, services offered, and the like—represent an environmental force that managers must monitor and to which they must be prepared to respond.

PRESSURE GROUPS Managers must recognize the special-interest groups that attempt to influence the actions of organizations. For instance, PETA's (People for the Ethical Treatment of Animals) pressure on McDonald's Corporation over its handling of animals during the slaughter process led McDonald's to stop buying beef from one of its suppliers until it met its standards for processing cattle. And it would be an unusual week if we didn't read about environmental or human rights activists picketing, boycotting, or threatening some organization in order to get managers to change some decision or action.

As social and political attitudes change, so too does the power of pressure groups. For example, through their persistent efforts, groups such as MADD (Mothers Against Drunk Driving) and SADD (Students Against Destructive Decisions) have managed to make changes in the alcoholic beverage and restaurant and bar industries and raised public awareness about the problem of drunk drivers.

●●● **general environment**
Broad external conditions that may affect the organization.

The General Environment The **general environment** includes the broad economic, political/legal, sociocultural, demographic, technological, and global conditions that *may* affect the organization. Changes in any of these areas usually do not have as large an impact as changes in the specific environment do, but managers must consider them as they plan, organize, lead, and control.

ECONOMIC CONDITIONS Interest rates, inflation, changes in disposable income, stock market fluctuations, and the stage of the general business cycle are some of the economic factors that can affect management practices in an organization. For example, many specialty retailers such as IKEA, The Limited, and Williams-Sonoma are acutely aware of the impact consumer disposable income has on their sales. When consumers' incomes fall or when their confidence about job security declines, they will postpone purchasing anything that isn't a necessity. Even charitable organizations such as the United Way or the Muscular Dystrophy Association feel the impact of economic factors. During economic downturns, not only does the demand for their services increase, their contributions typically decrease.

POLITICAL/LEGAL CONDITIONS Federal, state, and local governments influence what organizations can and cannot do. Some federal legislation has significant implications. For example, the Americans with Disabilities Act of 1990 (ADA) was designed to make jobs and facilities more accessible to people with disabilities, whether as customers or as employees. Exhibit 3–9 lists other significant legislation affecting businesses.

Organizations spend a great deal of time and money to meet governmental regulations, but the effects of these regulations go beyond time and money.[42] They also reduce managerial discretion by limiting the choices available to managers. Consider the decision to dismiss an employee.[43] Historically, employees were free to quit an organization at any time and employers had the right to fire an employee at any time

Exhibit 3–9

Selected U.S. Legislation Affecting Business

Legislation	Purpose
Occupational Safety and Health Act of 1970	Requires employer to provide a working environment free from hazards to health.
Consumer Product Safety Act of 1972	Sets standards on selected products, requires warning labels, and orders product recalls.
Equal Employment Opportunity Act of 1972	Forbids discrimination in all areas of employer–employee relations.
Worker Adjustment and Retraining Notification Act of 1988	Requires employers with 100 or more employees to provide 60 days' notice before a facility closing or mass layoff.
Americans with Disabilities Act of 1990	Prohibits employers from discriminating against individuals with physical or mental disabilities or the chronically ill; also requires organizations to reasonably accommodate these individuals.
Civil Rights Act of 1991	Reaffirms and tightens prohibition of discrimination; permits individuals to sue for punitive damages in cases of intentional discrimination.
Family and Medical Leave Act of 1993	Grants 12 weeks of unpaid leave each year to employees for the birth or adoption of a child or the care of a spouse, child, or parent with a serious health condition; covers organizations with 50 or more employees.
Child Safety Protection Act of 1994	Provides for labelling requirements on certain toys that contain parts or packaging that could harm children and requires manufacturers of such toys to report any serious accidents or deaths of children to the Consumer Product Safety Commission.
U.S. Economic Espionage Act of 1996	Makes theft or misappropriation of trade secrets a federal crime.
Electronic Signatures in Global and National Commerce Act of 2000	Gives online contracts (those signed by computer) the same legal force as equivalent paper contracts.
Sarbanes-Oxley Act of 2002	Holds businesses to higher standards of disclosure and corporate governance.

with or without cause. Laws and court decisions, however, have put increasing limits on what employers may do. Employers are increasingly expected to deal with employees by following the principles of good faith and fair dealing. Employees who feel that they've been wrongfully discharged often take their case to court. Juries are increasingly deciding what is or is not "fair." This trend has made it more difficult for managers to fire poor performers or to dismiss employees for off-duty conduct.

Other aspects of the political/legal sector are political conditions and the general stability of a country where an organization operates and the attitudes that elected governmental officials hold toward business. In the United States, for example, organizations have generally operated in a stable political environment. However, management is a global activity. Managers should be aware of major political changes in countries in which they operate because these political conditions can influence decisions and actions.

SOCIOCULTURAL CONDITIONS Rocco Papalia, chief of research and development at Frito Lay, the snack-food unit of PepsiCo Inc., is overseeing a move to make its snacks healthier. One of its test products is broccoli potato crisps. Why is Frito Lay looking at such a different product? Because health officials and consumers are increasingly anxious about the dangers of obesity and poor diet.[44] Managers must adapt their practices to the changing expectations of the society in which they operate. As societal values, customs, and tastes change, managers also must change. For instance, as workers have begun seeking more balance in their lives, organizations have had to adjust by offering family leave policies, more flexible work hours, and even on-site child care facilities. Other sociocultural trends in the United States include an increasing fear of violence and crime; more acceptance of gambling and gaming activities; more emphasis on religion and spiritual activities; pursuit of healthy lifestyles; and increasing dependence on technology. Each of these trends may pose a potential constraint to managers' decisions and actions. If an organization does business in other countries, managers need to be familiar with those countries' values and cultures and manage in ways that recognize and embrace those specific sociocultural aspects.

DEMOGRAPHIC CONDITIONS The demographic conditions encompass trends in the physical characteristics of a population such as gender, age, level of education, geographic location, income, family composition, and so forth. Changes in these characteristics may constrain how managers plan, organize, lead, and control.

One population group that we all have heard a lot about is the "baby boomers," a group that encompasses individuals born between the years 1946 and 1964. The reason you hear so much about the baby boomers is that there are so many of them. Through every life stage they've entered, they've had an enormous impact because of their sheer numbers. Other age cohorts besides boomers that have been identified include the Depression group (born 1912–1921), the World War II group (born 1922–1927), the Postwar group (born 1928–1945), Generation X (born 1965–1977), and Generation Y (born 1978–1994). Although each of these groups has its own unique characteristics, this last group is of particular interest because they're thinking, learning, creating, shopping, and playing in fundamentally different ways that are likely to greatly impact managers and organizations.

TECHNOLOGICAL In terms of the general environment, the most rapid changes have occurred in technology. We live in a time of continuous technological change. For instance, the human genetic code has been cracked. Just think of the implications of such an incredible breakthrough! Information gadgets are getting smaller and more powerful. We have automated offices, electronic meetings, robotic manufacturing, lasers, integrated circuits, faster and more powerful microprocessors, synthetic fuels, and entirely new models of doing business in an electronic age. Companies that capitalize on technology, such as General Electric, eBay, and Google, prosper. In addition, many successful retailers such as Wal-Mart and Limited Brands use sophisticated information systems to keep on top of current sales trends. Other organizations such as Prime Trucking Inc. and Amazon.com use information as a competitive advantage

Generation Y, which includes people born between 1978 and 1994, is one of the many demographic groups that managers watch for trends as they manage their firms. Such groups can create important market opportunities, such as the baby boomers' coming need for health care and retirement services, and short-term fads, such as the music and fashions that attract the Gen-Y shoppers.

and have adopted technologically advanced systems to stay ahead of their competitors. Similarly, hospitals, universities, airports, police departments, and even military organizations that adapt to major technological advances have a competitive edge over those that do not. The whole area of technology is radically changing the fundamental ways that organizations are structured and the way that managers manage.

GLOBAL By the end of this decade, Nigeria will have a larger population than Russia. Ethiopia will have more people than Germany, and Morocco will be more populous than Canada.[45] Do these facts surprise you? They shouldn't. They simply reflect what we said in Chapter 2—that globalization is one of the major factors affecting managers and organizations. Managers of both large and small organizations are challenged by an increasing number of global competitors and markets as part of the external environment. We'll cover this component of the external environment in detail in the next chapter.

How the Environment Affects Managers

Knowing *what* the various components of the environment are is important to managers. However, understanding *how* the environment affects managers is equally as important. (▢ Go to the Web and check out PRISM #3—Environmental Scanning.) The environment affects managers through the degree of environmental uncertainty that is present and through the various stakeholder relationships that exist between the organization and its external constituencies.

Assessing Environmental Uncertainty
Not all environments are the same. They differ by what we call their degree of **environmental uncertainty**, which is the degree of change and degree of complexity in an organization's environment. (See Exhibit 3–10.)

> ●●● **environmental uncertainty**
> The degree of change and degree of complexity in an organization's environment.

The first of these dimensions is the degree of change. If the components in an organization's environment change frequently, we call it a *dynamic* environment. If change is minimal, we call it a *stable* one. A stable environment might be one in which there are no new competitors, few technological breakthroughs by current competitors, little activity by pressure groups to influence the organization, and so forth. For instance, Zippo Manufacturing, best known for its Zippo lighters, faces a relatively stable environment. There are few competitors and little technological change. Probably the main environmental concern for the company is the declining trend in tobacco smokers, although the company's lighters have other uses and global markets remain attractive.

Exhibit 3–10

●●——

Environmental Uncertainty Matrix

Degree of Complexity	Degree of Change	
	Stable	**Dynamic**
Simple	**Cell 1** Stable and predictable environment Few components in environment Components are somewhat similar and remain basically the same Minimal need for sophisticated knowledge of components	**Cell 2** Dynamic and unpredictable environment Few components in environment Components are somewhat similar but are in continual process of change Minimal need for sophisticated knowledge of components
Complex	**Cell 3** Stable and predictable environment Many components in environment Components are not similar to one another and remain basically the same High need for sophisticated knowledge of components	**Cell 4** Dynamic and unpredictable environment Many components in environment Components are not similar to one another and are in continual process of change High need for sophisticated knowledge of components

In contrast, the recorded music industry faces a highly uncertain and unpredictable environment. Digital formats like MP3 and music-swapping Internet services like KaZaa have turned the industry upside down. Although music companies traditionally earned revenues by selling physical commodities such as LP records, cassettes, and CDs, the digital future represents chaos and uncertainty. This environment can definitely be described as dynamic.

What about rapid change that's predictable? Is that considered a dynamic environment? Bricks-and-mortar retail department stores provide a good example. They typically make one-quarter to one-third of their sales in December. The drop-off from December to January is significant. However, because the change is predictable, we don't consider the environment to be dynamic. When we talk about degree of change, we mean change that is unpredictable. If change can be accurately anticipated, it's not an uncertainty that managers must confront.

The other dimension of uncertainty describes the degree of **environmental complexity**. The degree of complexity refers to the number of components in an organization's environment and the extent of the knowledge that the organization has about those components. For example, Hasbro Toy Company, the second-largest toy manufacturer (behind Mattel) has simplified its environment by acquiring many of its competitors such as Tiger Electronics, Wizards of the Coast, Kenner Toys, Parker Brothers, and Tonka Toys. The fewer competitors, customers, suppliers, government agencies, and so forth that an organization must deal with, the less complexity and, therefore, the less uncertainty there is in its environment.

Complexity is also measured in terms of the knowledge an organization needs to have about its environment. For instance, managers at the online brokerage E*TRADE must know a great deal about their Internet service provider's operations if they want to ensure that their Web site is available, reliable, and secure for their stock-trading customers. On the other hand, managers of grocery stores have a minimal need for sophisticated knowledge about their suppliers.

How does the concept of environmental uncertainty influence managers? Looking again at Exhibit 3–10, each of the four cells represents different combinations of degree of complexity and degree of change. Cell 1 (an environment that is stable and simple) represents the lowest level of environmental uncertainty. Cell 4 (an environment that is dynamic and complex) is the highest. Not surprisingly, managers' influence on organizational outcomes is greatest in cell 1 and least in cell 4.

Because uncertainty is a threat to an organization's effectiveness, managers try to minimize it. Given a choice, managers would prefer to operate in environments such as those

•••• **environmental complexity**
The number of components in an organization's environment and the extent of the organization's knowledge about those components.

Protestors in the Mexican colonial city of Oaxaca want to prevent McDonald's from opening a fast-food store in the city's historic central square because they believe it will change the atmosphere of the square and destroy local heritage. McDonald's has responded to these stakeholders by saying that it wants "to be another option for the consuming public and thus form part of their community." How might this conflict be resolved?

in cell 1. However, they rarely have full control over that choice. In addition, most industries today are facing more dynamic change, making their environments more uncertain.

Managing Stakeholder Relationships What made VH1 *the* TV channel for music-loving baby boomers? One reason was that then-President John Sykes knew the importance of building relationships with the organization's various external stakeholders: the viewers, the music celebrities, advertisers, the affiliate TV stations, public service groups, and others. The nature of external stakeholder relationships is another way in which the environment influences managers. The more obvious and secure these relationships become, the more influence managers will have over organizational outcomes.

Who are **stakeholders**? We define them as any constituencies in the organization's external environment that are affected by the organization's decisions and actions. These groups have a stake in or are significantly influenced by what the organization does. (Check out You're the Manager: Putting Ethics into Action on page 127.) In turn, these groups can influence the organization. For example, think of the groups that might be affected by the decisions and actions of Starbucks—coffee bean farmers, employees, specialty coffee competitors, local communities, and so forth. Some of these stakeholders also may impact decisions and actions of Starbucks' managers. The idea that organizations have stakeholders is now widely accepted by both management academics and practicing managers.[46]

With what types of stakeholders might an organization have to deal? Exhibit 3–11 identifies some of the most common. (■◻■■■ Go to the Web and check out Q & A 3.9.) Note that these stakeholders do include internal and external groups. Why? Because both can affect what an organization does and how it operates. However, we're primarily interested in the external groups and their impact on managers' discretion in planning, organizing, leading, and controlling. This doesn't mean that the internal stakeholders aren't important, but we explain these relationships, primarily with employees, throughout the rest of the book.

Why is stakeholder-relationship management important? Why should managers even care about managing stakeholder relationships?[47] One reason is that it can lead to other organizational outcomes such as improved predictability of environmental changes, more successful innovations, greater degree of trust among stakeholders, and greater organizational flexibility to reduce the impact of change. But, does it affect organizational performance? The answer is yes! Management researchers who have looked at this issue are finding that managers of high-performing companies tend to consider the interests of all major stakeholder groups as they make decisions.[48]

Another reason given for managing external stakeholder relationships is that it's the "right" thing to do. What does this mean? It means that an organization depends

Exhibit 3–11

Organizational Stakeholders

Becoming a Manager

♦ *When you read current business or general news stories, see if omnipotent or symbolic views of management are being described.*

♦ *Notice aspects of organizational culture as you interact with different organizations.*

♦ *Read books about different organizations and entrepreneurs to better understand how an organization's culture forms and how it's maintained.*

♦ *Start thinking about the type of organizational culture in which you're going to be most comfortable.*

♦ *If you belong to a student organization, evaluate its culture. What does the culture look like? How do new members learn the culture? How is the culture maintained?*

♦ *When you evaluate companies for class assignments (this class and others you may be enrolled in), get in the habit of looking at the stakeholders that might be impacted by these companies' decisions and actions.*

♦ *Practice defining the general and specific environments of different organizations and notice how they're similar and different.*

♦ ▪▪▪▪▪ *Go to the Web and complete any of these exercises from the Self-Assessment Library (S.A.L.) found on ROLLS: #42—What's the Right Organizational Culture for Me?, or #44—Am I Experiencing Work–Family Conflict?*

on these external groups as sources of inputs (resources) and as outlets for outputs (goods and services), and managers should consider their interests as they make decisions and take actions. We'll address this issue in more detail in Chapter 5 as we look at the concepts of managerial ethics and corporate social responsibility.

How can these relationships be managed? (▪▪▪▪▪ Check out Passport Scenario 2 on page 127.) There are four steps. The first is identifying the organization's stakeholders. Which of the various groups might be impacted by decisions that managers make and which groups might influence those decisions? Those groups that are likely to be influenced by and to influence organizational decisions are the organization's stakeholders. The second step is for managers to determine what particular interests or concerns these stakeholders might have—product quality, financial issues, safe working conditions, environmental protection, and so forth. Next, managers must decide how critical each stakeholder is to the organization's decisions and actions. In other words, how critical is it to consider this stakeholder's concerns as managers plan, organize, lead, and control? The very idea of a stakeholder—a group that has a "stake" in what the organization does—means that it is important. But some stakeholders are more critical to the organization's decisions and actions than others. For instance, a critical stakeholder of a publicly supported state university would be the state legislature since it controls how much budget money the university gets each year. On the other hand, the university's computer hardware and software suppliers are important but not critical. Once managers have determined these things, the final step is determining how to manage the external stakeholder relationships. This decision depends on how critical the external stakeholder is to the organization and how uncertain the environment is.[49] The more critical the stakeholder and the more uncertain the environment, the more managers need to rely on establishing explicit stakeholder partnerships rather than just acknowledging their existence.

• • • •Learning Review

• Describe the components of the specific and general environments.

• Discuss the two dimensions of environmental uncertainty.

• Identify the most common organizational stakeholders.

• Explain the four steps in managing external stakeholder relationships.

Managers **Respond** to a **Manager's** Dilemma

Dana Murray
Director of Marketing, Bookman's Used Books, Music & Software, Tucson, Arizona

As Athleta Corporation grows, Scott will be challenged to maintain the culture he has worked hard to create. I believe there are several areas worth emphasizing in an effort to preserve this culture. First, *hiring*. Scott needs to be selective in his hiring in order to find new staff members that will embrace the culture and fit into the existing group. Second, *training*. Integrating new employees into the Athleta "way" is paramount. Selecting peers as training coaches will help showcase the company culture, provide support, and encourage communication. Finally, *management*. Company managers need to set employee goals that are conducive to the culture and encourage behavior that the company enjoys today.

Ann M. Kelly
Partner, Lake Partners Strategy Consultants, Seattle, Washington

The key is to formally institutionalize Athleta's unique culture. Scott is currently able to directly manage each employee's satisfaction because the size of the firm is still relatively small. However, as the organization grows, Scott will need to ensure that managers below him will be able to play the role of cultural czar just as effectively. Some specific actions for Scott include: (1) Recruit, screen, and hire employees who can do the job *and* share the same cultural values; (2) Be personally involved in new employee orientation; (3) Train the next level of management on how to make employee retention and work-life balance a priority; (4) Integrate cultural measurements into performance reviews; (5) Take frequent "temperature checks" to measure the current culture against the actual culture and make adjustments as necessary; (6) Continue to lead by example; and (7) Recognize that external factors may require some cultural adjustments.

Learning Summary

After reading and studying this chapter, you should be able to:

- Contrast the actions of managers according to the omnipotent and symbolic views.
- Explain the parameters of managerial discretion.
- Describe the seven dimensions of organizational culture.
- Discuss the impact of a strong culture on organizations and managers.
- Explain the source of an organization's culture and how that culture continues.
- Describe how culture is transmitted to employees.

- Describe the characteristics of an ethical culture, an innovative culture, and a customer-responsive culture.
- Discuss why workplace spirituality seems to be an important concern.
- Describe the characteristics of a spiritual organization.
- Describe the components of the specific and general environments.
- Discuss the two dimensions of environmental uncertainty.
- Identify the most common organizational stakeholders.
- Explain the four steps in managing external stakeholder relationships.

Thinking About Management Issues

1. Refer to Exhibit 3–3. How would a first-line manager's job differ in these two organizations? How about a top-level manager's job?
2. Describe an effective culture for (a) a relatively stable environment and (b) a dynamic environment. Explain your choices.
3. Classrooms have cultures. Describe your classroom culture using the seven dimensions of organizational culture. Does the culture constrain your instructor? How?
4. Can culture be a liability to an organization? Explain.
5. Why is it important for managers to understand the external forces that are acting on them and their organizations?
6. "Businesses are built on relationships." What do you think this statement means? What are the implications for managing the external environment?
7. What would be the drawbacks in managing stakeholder relationships?

Working Together: Team-Based Exercise

Although all organizations face environmental constraints, the forces in their specific and general environments differ. Get into a small group with three to four other class members and choose two organizations in different industries. Describe the specific and general external factors for each organization. How are your descriptions different for the two organizations? How are they similar? Now, using the same two organizations, see if you can identify the important stakeholders for these organizations. Also indicate whether these stakeholders are critical for the organization and why they are or are not. As a group, be prepared to share your information with the class and to explain your choices.

Ethical Dilemma Exercise

Just a few years ago, Enron was a thriving energy company, trading and delivering natural gas, oil, and electricity to customers around the world. At its peak, the company reported annual sales in excess of $100 billion. Under the surface, however, a highly aggressive, win-at-any-cost culture put managers under intense pressure to continually improve sales figures—even as Enron was plunging deeper into debt. Reports of ever-higher revenues attracted more investors, boosted the stock price, and enabled senior managers to reap huge bonuses.

Ultimately, Enron was forced into bankruptcy and several senior managers were indicted after the company's questionable financial dealings came to light. A board member who led the internal ethics investigation later commented: "This is a cultural issue as much as an accounting issue. This is a matter of corporate character and virtue."*

Imagine this is your second day at work as a manager supervising a team of Enron's financial analysts in the months before any questionable dealings are uncovered. Your boss, a senior executive, calls you in and asks you to have your team find "creative" ways of improving sales figures. Look back at the framework in Exhibit 2–8 and think about the potential consequences as you decide which of the following options you will choose—and why.

Option A: Call a meeting of your analyst team and present the boss's request as a hypothetical challenge designed to sharpen their skills.

Option B: Work by yourself to dream up three or four outlandish, impractical ideas so you can avoid being seen as someone who is not committed to Enron's success.

Option C: Privately discuss the situation with the human resources manager who hired you and explain why you are concerned about your boss's request.

* Situation adapted from information in: Wendy Zellner, "An Insider's Tale of Enron's Toxic Culture," *Business Week*, March 31, 2003, p. 16; Kristen Hays, "Enron Schemes Reflect Culture, Report's Author Says," *Los Angeles Times*, February 10, 2003, p. C-3.

Case Application

United States Air Force Academy

In the shadow of the towering peaks of the Rocky Mountains outside Colorado Springs, another menacing and troubling shadow is emerging. And it's likely to force drastic changes in an organization that is rich in tradition—the United States Air Force Academy. The shadow is a sexual assault scandal that may eventually prove to encompass much more than the 56 cases of rape and sexual assault already reported over the last 10 years. Investigators are working to uncover the details, which hasn't been easy because of the hierarchical, tightly controlled atmosphere that characterizes this and other military institutions. But Air Force Secretary James Roche is dealing with a tougher problem: What does it take to change a culture that seems hostile to women, where sexual predators sometimes escape punishment, and where victims themselves face career-threatening reprisals if they report the crimes? In testimony before a U.S. Senate panel, Roche said, "It's a climate problem, you're absolutely right. How we manage the place, how we lead the place has to change."

In the military's defense, in some respects it has done a better job than many organizations in dealing with racial and ethnic discrimination and in providing equal opportunity. Yet, that's not true for gender and sexual issues. The U.S. Navy's Tailhook scandal in 1991 was the first public indication of the problems that existed in the military. However, the uproar from this scandal led to the Navy instituting a series of changes that included clearer definitions of appropriate conduct, procedures for anonymous reporting, and a complaint resolution system. But the most important change for the Navy was a renewed emphasis on values. "We felt that we could control behav-

ior through regulations and discipline. But to make a lasting impact on the individuals and to begin to change attitudes, we needed to invest time and energy re-establishing basic values," said Barbara Spyridon Pope, former Assistant Navy Secretary, the person who oversaw the changes.

The Air Force Academy is hardly the only organization dealing with sexual assaults. Harvard University reported 50 forcible sex offenses on campus during a recent three-year period. The U.S. Military Academy at West Point investigated 15 cases during the same time period. And the Naval Academy in Annapolis, Maryland, had 11 accusations of indecent assault. Yet, critics point out a couple of disturbing facts about the incidents at the Air Force Academy. First is the sheer number of cases being uncovered. But more alarming and potentially more serious is the way the institution and its leaders are dealing with the complaints. Female cadets who have been sexually assaulted describe an intimidating atmosphere and say they felt victimized by the academy's procedures for investigating assaults and punishing offenders.

The culture at military institutions revolves around readiness, preparation, and adherence to rules. Cadets at the Air Force Academy are expected to strongly identify with their squadron or class and group norms play a crucial role in controlling behavior. Yet, that climate of group loyalty, rather than organizational loyalty, may be part of the problem. Secretary Roche understands that cultural change will not be easy. "Climate is something you work to change over a long period of time. Climate is how people think."

DISCUSSION QUESTIONS

1. Using Exhibit 3–2, describe the culture at military institutions such as the U.S. Air Force Academy. Why is that type of culture important to these organizations? On the other hand, what are the drawbacks of such a culture?

2. Describe how you think new cadets at the Air Force Academy "learn" the culture.

3. What challenges face Secretary Roche in changing the climate at the U.S. Air Force Academy? How might he address those challenges?

4. What role might stakeholders play in this situation? In answering this question, be sure to identify what stakeholders there are and what concerns each might have.

5. As this scandal is resolved, what types of cultural changes were implemented? (You will have to search for this information.)

U.S. Air Force Secretary James Roche.

Source: T. Kenworthy and P. O'Driscoll, "Climate Has to Change, Air Force Leader Says," *USA Today*, March 13, 2003, p. 4A. The Associated Press, "Air Force may punish chiefs at academy," *USA Today,* May 29, 2003, p. 4A.

● ● ●**Learning Outline**

Follow this Learning Outline as you read and study this chapter.

What's Your Global Perspective?

- Contrast ethnocentric, polycentric, and geocentric attitudes toward global business.
- Explain why it's important for managers to be sensitive to global differences.

Understanding the Global Environment

- Describe the current status of the European Union.
- Discuss the North American Free Trade Agreement and other regional trade alliances in Latin America.
- Tell about the Association of Southeast Asian Nations.
- Explain the interdependence that globalization involves.
- Discuss the role of the WTO.

Doing Business Globally

- Contrast MNCs, TNCs, and borderless organizations.
- Describe the three stages organizations go through as they go global.
- Define exporting, importing, licensing, and franchising.
- Describe global strategic alliances, joint ventures, and foreign subsidiaries.

Managing in a Global Environment

- Explain how the global legal-political and economic environments affect managers.
- Discuss Hofstede's five dimensions for assessing cultures.
- Explain the nine GLOBE dimensions for assessing cultures.
- Discuss the challenges of doing business globally in today's world.

Chapter

4

Managing in a Global Environment

Zara, the European clothing retailer, has been at various times described as having more style than GAP, faster growth than Target, and logistical expertise that rivals Wal-Mart's.[1] Although the company isn't well known in North America, Zara's managers have positioned the company for continued global success. That success is based on a simple principle—in fashion, nothing is as important as time to market.

Zara's store managers (around 530 worldwide) offer suggestions every day on cuts, fabrics, and even new lines. After reviewing the ideas, a team at headquarters in La Coruna, Spain, decides what to make. Designers draw up the ideas on their computers and send them over the company's intranet to nearby factories. Within days, the cutting, dyeing, sewing, and assembling commences. In three weeks, the clothes will be in stores from Barcelona to Berlin to Beirut. That isn't just a *bit* faster than rivals—it's 12 times faster. Zara has a twice-a-week delivery schedule that restocks old styles and brings in new designs. Rivals tend to get new designs once or twice a season. An important piece of this incredible operation is a warehouse run by Lorena Alba (pictured here), Zara's director of logistics.

Lorena runs the four-story, five-million-square-foot building (about the size of 90 football fields) with clockwork efficiency. To her, the warehouse isn't a place to store clothes, but a place to move them. The warehouse is connected to 14 Zara factories through a maze of tunnels with rails. Along the rails, cables carry merchandise bundles that are "addressed" with a metal bar so they end up exactly where they're supposed to. In the warehouse, each Zara store has its own "staging" area where its specific merchandise is packed. From there, the merchandise is sent to a loading dock and packed on a truck with other shipments in order of delivery.

As Zara continues to open new stores worldwide, Lorena will have to work closely with suppliers and in-store personnel from different cultures. Put yourself in her shoes. What cross-cultural problems might she face and how might cultural awareness help her deal with those problems?

What would **you** do **?**

T he Zara example illustrates that the global marketplace presents opportunities and challenges for managers. With the entire world as a market and national borders becoming increasingly irrelevant, the potential for organizations such as Zara to grow expands dramatically. A study of 1,250 highly diverse American manufacturing firms found that companies that operated in multiple countries had twice the sales growth and significantly higher profitability than strictly domestic firms.[2] The global opportunities are there for managers to exploit. (▮▮▮ Go to the Web and check out S.A.L. #46—Am I Well-Suited for a Career as a Global Manager?)

However, as our opening dilemma also implies, even large, successful organizations with talented managers face challenges in managing in the global environment. New competitors can suddenly appear at any time from anyplace on the globe. And, most importantly, managers must deal with cultural, economic, and political differences. The cultural and political differences have taken on added significance since 9/11, creating increased challenges for managers in global organizations as they deal with uncertainty, fear, and anxiety. Managers who don't closely monitor changes in their global environment or who don't take the specific characteristics of their location into consideration as they plan, organize, lead, and control are likely to find limited global success. In this chapter, we're going to discuss the issues managers have to face in managing in a global environment. (▮▮▮ Go to the Web and check out Q & A 4.1.)

WHO OWNS WHAT?

One way to grasp the nature of the global environment is to consider the country of ownership origin for some familiar products and companies. You might be surprised to find that many products you thought were made by U.S. companies aren't! Take the following quiz[3] and then check your answers at the end of the chapter on p. 97.

1. Ben and Jerry's Ice Cream is owned by a company based in:
   a. Mexico   b. Saudi Arabia   c. United Kingdom d. United States

2. The Bic Pen Company is based in:
   a. Japan   b. United Kingdom c. United States   d. France

3. PowerBar nutrition energy bars are products of a company based in:
   a. Brazil   b. Switzerland   c. United States   d. Germany

4. RCA television sets are produced by a company based in:
   a. France   b. United States   c. Malaysia   d. Taiwan

5. Skippy peanut butter is a product of a company based in:
   a. United States   b. Canada   c. Venezuela   d. United Kingdom

6. The owners of Godiva chocolate are based in:
   a. United States   b. Switzerland   c. France   d. Sweden

■ **Self-Assessment Library**
Whenever you see this orange square, go to the R.O.L.L.S. Web site (*www.prenhall.com/robbins*) to the Self-Assessment Library (S.A.L.) and complete the suggested self-assessment exercise. These exercises will help you discover things about yourself, your attitudes, and your personal strengths and weaknesses.

7. The company that produces Boboli pizza crust is based in:
   a. United States   b. Mexico   c. Italy   d. Spain

8. The parent company of Braun electric shavers is located in:
   a. Switzerland   b. Germany   c. United States   d. Japan

9. Greyhound Bus Lines is owned by a company located in:
   a. Mexico   b. United States   c. Canada   d. France

10. Seagram's mixers are a product of a company based in:
    a. United States   b. Canada   c. France   d. Russia

11. Hot Pockets frozen sandwiches are made by a company based in:
    a. Germany   b. United States   c. Switzerland   d. Brazil

12. Dr Pepper and 7-Up are products of a company based in:
    a. United States   b. Japan   c. Canada   d. United Kingdom

13. The company that markets Lipton tea is based in:
    a. China   b. United Kingdom   c. Japan   d. United States

14. Häagen-Dazs ice cream is a product of a company based in:
    a. Germany   b. France   c. United States   d. Switzerland

15. Wella hair care products are marketed by a company based in:
    a. United States   b. Switzerland   c. France   d. Germany

How well did you score? Were you aware of how many products we use every day that are made by companies *not* based in the United States? Most of us don't fully understand or appreciate the truly global nature of today's marketplace. And as you can see, these companies represent a broad cross section of products, markets, and industries.

WHAT'S YOUR GLOBAL PERSPECTIVE?

It's not unusual for Germans, Italians, or Indonesians to speak three or four languages. Most Japanese schoolchildren begin studying English in the early elementary grades. On the other hand, most U.S. children study only English in school. Americans tend to think of English as the only international business language and don't see a need to study other languages.

Monolingualism is just one of the signs that a nation suffers from **parochialism**, which is viewing the world solely through its own eyes and perspectives.[4] People with a parochial attitude do not recognize that others have different ways of living and working. Parochialism is a significant obstacle for managers working in a global business world. If managers fall into the trap of ignoring others' values and customs and rigidly applying an attitude of "ours is better than theirs" to foreign cultures, they will find it difficult to compete with other managers and organizations around the world that *are* seeking to understand foreign customs and market differences. (Go to the Web and check out Q & A 4.2.) This type of selfish, parochialistic attitude is one approach

The British Broadcasting Company's balanced and unbiased reporting on the war in Iraq, led by newspeople such as Rageh Omaar, demonstrates the geocentric view this British-based international firm brings to its product, the news. The BBC's U.S. ratings were up 28 percent during the conflict. "BBC doesn't just have a British view," says the firm's director of World Service and Global News. "It has a worldview for the world."

Exhibit 4–1

**Key Information About
Three Global Attitudes**

Orientation	Ethnocentric Home Country	Polycentric Host Country	Geocentric World
Advantages	• Simpler structure • More tightly controlled	• Extensive knowledge of foreign market and workplace • More support from host government • Committed local managers with high morale	• Forces understanding of global issues • Balanced local and global objectives • Best people and work approaches used regardless of origin
Drawbacks	• More ineffective management • Inflexibility • Social and political backlash	• Duplication of work • Reduced efficiency • Difficult to maintain global objectives because of intense focus on local traditions	• Difficult to achieve • Managers must have both local and global knowledge

••• parochialism
A narrow view of the world; an inability to recognize differences between people.

••• ethnocentric attitude
The parochialistic belief that the best work approaches and practices are those of the home country.

••• polycentric attitude
The view that the managers in the host country know the best work approaches and practices for running their business.

••• geocentric attitude
A world-oriented view that focuses on using the best approaches and people from around the globe.

that managers might take, but it's not the only one.[5] Exhibit 4–1 summarizes the key points about three possible global attitudes. Let's look at each more closely.

An **ethnocentric attitude** is the parochialistic belief that the best work approaches and practices are those of the *home* country (the country in which the company's headquarters are located). Managers with an ethnocentric attitude believe that people in foreign countries do not have the skills, expertise, knowledge, or experience that people in the home country do. They wouldn't trust foreign employees with key decisions or technology.

The **polycentric attitude** is the view that the managers in the *host* country (the foreign country in which the organization is doing business) know the best work approaches and practices for running their businesses. Managers with a polycentric attitude view every foreign operation as different and hard to understand. Thus, these managers are likely to leave their foreign facilities alone and let foreign employees figure out how best to do things.

The last type of global attitude that managers might have is the **geocentric attitude**, which is a *world-oriented* view that focuses on using the best approaches and people from around the globe. Managers with this type of attitude believe that it's important to have a global view both at the organization's headquarters in the home country *and* in the various foreign work facilities. For instance, the CEO of Home Décor (a disguised name), a fast-growing manufacturer of household accessories, is a Chinese immigrant who describes the company's strategy as "combining Chinese costs with Japanese quality, European design, and American marketing."[6] Using the geocentric view, major issues and decisions are viewed globally by looking for the best approaches and people regardless of origin.

Successful global management requires enhanced sensitivity to differences in national customs and practices. Management practices that work in Chicago might not be appropriate in Bangkok or Berlin. In Exhibit 4–2, read the examples of the cultural blunders that can happen when managers ignore foreign values and customs and rigidly apply their own. Later in this chapter and throughout the rest of the book, you'll see how a geocentric attitude toward managing requires eliminating parochial attitudes and carefully developing an understanding of cultural differences between countries.

••• Learning Review

• Contrast ethnocentric, polycentric, and geocentric attitudes toward global business.

• Explain why it's important for managers to be sensitive to global differences.

Exhibit 4–2

Examples of Cross-Cultural Blunders

- You're in Shanghai on business. Walking down the street one day, you pass a Chinese colleague. He asks you. "Have you eaten yet?" You answer, "No, not yet." He rushes off, looking embarrassed and uncomfortable. The phrase, "Have you eaten yet?" is a common greeting—just like "Hi, how are you?" in the United States. It's the Chinese way of saying "Is your belly full today?" or "Is life treating you well?"

- A U.S. manager transferred to Saudi Arabia successfully obtained a signature on a million-dollar contract from a Saudi manufacturer. The manufacturer's representative had arrived at the meeting several hours late, but the U.S. executive considered this tardiness unimportant. The American was certainly surprised and frustrated to learn later that the Saudi had no intention of abiding by the contract. He had signed it only to be polite after showing up late for the appointment.

- A U.S. executive visiting Germany for the first time was invited to the home of his largest customer. He decided to be a good guest and brought the hostess a bouquet of a dozen red roses. He later learned that in Germany it is bad luck to present an even number of flowers and that red roses are symbolic of a strong romantic interest.

- A U.S. executive based in Peru was viewed by Peruvian managers as cold and unworthy of trust because in face-to-face discussions he kept backing away. He didn't understand that in Peru and other Latin countries, the custom is to stand quite close to the person with whom you are speaking.

- The "thumbs up" gesture is considered offensive in the Middle East, rude in Australia, and a sign of "OK" in France.

- It's rude to cross your arms while facing someone in Turkey.

Source: See D.A. Ricks, M.Y.C. Fu, and J.S. Arpas, *International Business Blunders* (Columbus, OH: Grid, 1974); A. Bennett, "American Culture Is Often a Puzzle for Foreign Managers in the U.S." *Wall Street Journal*, February 12, 1986, p. 29; C.F. Valentine, "Blunders Abroad," *Nation's Business*, March 1989, p. 54; R.E. Axtell (ed.), *Do's and Taboos around the World*, 3rd ed. (New York: John Wiley & Sons, 1993); B. Pachter, "When in Japan, Don't Cross Your Legs," *Business Ethics*, March–April 1996, p. 50; and V. Frazee, "Keeping Up on Chinese Culture," *Global Workforce*, October 1996, pp. 16–17.

UNDERSTANDING THE GLOBAL ENVIRONMENT

As we discussed in Chapter 2, management is no longer constrained by national borders. Managers in all sizes and types of organizations are faced with the opportunities and challenges of managing in a global environment. What is the global environment like? An important feature is global trade. Global trade isn't new. Countries and organizations have been trading with each other for centuries. "Trade is central to human health, prosperity, and social welfare."[7] Examples of global trade abound, as we saw in the chapter-opening quiz. When trade is allowed to flow freely, countries benefit from economic growth and productivity gains because they specialize in producing the goods they're best at and importing goods that are more efficiently produced elsewhere. Global trade is being shaped by two forces: regional trading alliances and the agreements negotiated through the World Trade Organization.

Regional Trading Alliances

Just a few years ago, global competition was best described in terms of country against country—the United States versus Japan, France versus Germany, Mexico versus Canada. Now, global competition has been reshaped by the creation of regional trading agreements including the European Union (EU), North American Free Trade Agreement (NAFTA), the Association of Southeast Asian Nations (ASEAN), and others.

The European Union The signing of the Maastricht Treaty (named for the Dutch town where the treaty was signed) in February 1992 created the **European Union (EU)**, a unified economic and trade entity with 12 members—Belgium, Denmark, France, Greece, Ireland, Italy, Luxembourg, the Netherlands, Portugal, Spain, the United Kingdom, and Germany. Three other countries—Austria, Finland, and

● ● ● **European Union (EU)**
A union of 15 European nations created as a unified economic and trade entity.

 Exhibit 4–3   **European Union Countries**

Sweden—joined the group in 1995. (See Exhibit 4–3.) In 2004, the EU added 10 new members—Cyprus, Malta, the Czech Republic, Estonia, Hungary, Latvia, Lithuania, Poland, Slovakia, and Slovenia. Two other countries (Romania and Bulgaria) could join by 2007.[8] The economic power represented by the EU is considerable. The current EU membership covers a population base of 375 million people and the 25-member EU would encompass a population of 450 million.[9]

Before the creation of the EU, each nation had border controls, taxes, and subsidies; nationalistic policies; and protected industries. Now, as a single market, there are no barriers to travel, employment, investment, and trade. The EU took an enormous step toward full unification when 12 of the 15 countries became part of the Economic and Monetary Union, the formal system responsible for the development of the **euro**, a single European currency. As of this time, the United Kingdom, Denmark, and Sweden have chosen not to participate.[10]

The primary motivation for the joining of these European nations was to reassert their economic position against the strength of the United States and Japan. Working in separate countries with barriers against one another, European industries couldn't develop the efficiency of American and Japanese businesses. As the EU continues to evolve, it continues to assert its economic power in one of the world's richest markets. European businesses will continue to play an important role in the global economy. For instance, Unilever PLC of the United Kingdom is a powerful force in consumer products (look back at the "Who Owns What?" quiz), DaimlerChrysler AG of Germany is a solid competitor in automobiles, and Nokia of Finland is a dominant player in cell phones.

North American Free Trade Agreement (NAFTA) When agreements in key issues covered by the **North American Free Trade Agreement (NAFTA)** were reached by the Mexican, Canadian, and U.S. governments on August 12, 1992, a vast economic bloc was created. Between 1994, when NAFTA went into effect, and 2001 (the most recent year for complete statistics), Canada and Mexico have become the United States' numbers one and two trading partners, respectively, with Japan a distant

●●● **euro**
A single European currency used by 12 of the 15 EU members.

●●● **North American Free Trade Agreement (NAFTA)**
An agreement among the Mexican, Canadian, and U.S. governments in which barriers to free trade have been eliminated.

third.[11] Eliminating the barriers to free trade (tariffs, import licensing requirements, customs user fees) has resulted in a strengthening of the economic power of all three countries.

Other Latin American nations are moving to become part of free-trade blocs. Colombia, Mexico, and Venezuela led the way when all three signed an economic pact in 1994 eliminating import duties and tariffs. Now, 34 countries in the Caribbean region, South America, and Central America are negotiating a Free Trade Area of the Americas (FTAA) agreement, which is to be operational no later than 2005.[12] Already in existence is another free-trade bloc known as the Southern Cone Common Market or Mercosur. However, it's facing serious problems as many of those participating countries are becoming part of the larger, and potentially more powerful, FTAA.[13]

● ● ● **Association of Southeast Asian Nations (ASEAN)**
A trading alliance of ten Southeast Asian nations.

Association of Southeast Asian Nations (ASEAN) The **ASEAN** is a trading alliance of ten Southeast Asian nations. (See Exhibit 4–4.) During the years ahead, the Southeast Asian region promises to be one of the fastest-growing economic regions of the world. It will be an increasingly important regional economic and political alliance whose impact eventually could rival that of both NAFTA and the EU.

Other Trade Alliances Other regions around the world continue to look at creating regional trading alliances. For instance, the 53-nation African Union came into existence in July 2002.[14] Members of this alliance plan to create an economic development plan and work to achieve greater unity among Africa's nations. Like members of other trade alliances, these countries hope to gain economic, social, cultural, and trade benefits from their association.

The World Trade Organization

Global growth and trade among nations doesn't just happen on its own. Systems and mechanisms are needed so that efficient and effective trading relationships can develop. Indeed, one of the realities of globalization is that countries are interdependent—that is, what happens in one can impact others, whether it's positive or negative. For example, the severe Asian financial crisis in the late 1990s had the potential to totally disrupt economic growth around the globe and bring on worldwide recession. But it didn't. Why? Because there were mechanisms in place to prevent it from happening—mechanisms that encouraged global trade and averted the potential crisis. One of the most important of these mechanisms is the multilateral trading system called the **World Trade Organization (WTO)**.[15]

● ● ● **World Trade Organization (WTO)**
A global organization of 146 countries that deals with the rules of trade among nations.

Exhibit 4–4

● ● ● ━━━━

ASEAN Members

Source: Based on J. McClenahen and T. Clark, "ASEAN at Work," *IW.* May 19, 1997, p. 42.

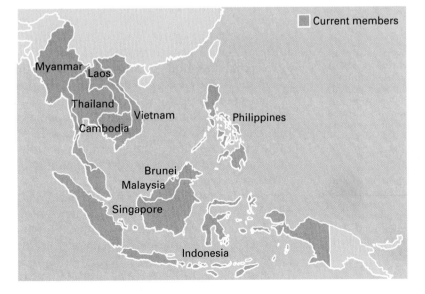

Current members

Myanmar
Laos
Thailand
Vietnam
Cambodia
Philippines
Brunei
Malaysia
Singapore
Indonesia

The WTO was formed in 1995 and evolved from the General Agreement on Tariffs and Trade (GATT), an agreement in effect since the end of World War II. Today, the WTO is the only *global* organization dealing with the rules of trade among nations. Its membership consists of 146 countries (as of April 4, 2003). At its core are the various trade agreements, negotiated and ratified by the vast majority of the world's trading nations. The goal of the WTO is to help businesses (importers and exporters) conduct their business. Although a number of vocal critics have staged visible protests and lambasted the WTO, claiming that it destroys jobs and the natural environment, the WTO appears to play an important role in monitoring and promoting global trade.

••• Learning Review

- Describe the current status of the European Union.
- Discuss the North American Free Trade Agreement and other regional trade alliances in Latin America.
- Tell about the Association of Southeast Asian Nations.
- Explain the interdependence that globalization involves.
- Discuss the role of the WTO.

DOING BUSINESS GLOBALLY

At 2:00 P.M. on a Saturday afternoon, north of Moscow, a hypermarket opened by French retail group Auchan is jam-packed with Russian shoppers. McDonald's Corporation says it's on track to continue expanding aggressively in China even though it already has more than 500 locations in 70 cities. Fabian Gomez, an audit partner for the Mexican branch of Deloitte Touche Tohmatsu, a global accounting and business-services organization, says, "A lot of our business is serving Mexican subsidiaries of international companies and the executives usually come from other places."[16] As you can see from these examples, organizations in different industries *and* from different countries are pursuing global opportunities. But how do organizations do business globally? That's what we want to look at in this section.

Different Types of Global Organizations

Organizations doing business globally aren't anything new. DuPont started doing business in China in 1863. H.J. Heinz Company was manufacturing food products in the United Kingdom in 1905. Ford Motor Company set up its first overseas sales branch in France in 1908. By the 1920s, other companies, including Fiat, Unilever, and Royal Dutch/Shell had gone multinational. But it wasn't until the mid-1960s that **multinational corporations (MNCs)** became commonplace. These organizations—which maintain significant operations in multiple countries but are managed from a base in the home country—inaugurated the rapid growth in international trade. With its focus on control from the home country, the MNC is characteristic of the ethnocentric attitude. Some examples of companies that can be considered MNCs include Sony, Deutsche Bank AG, and Merrill Lynch. Although these companies have considerable global holdings, management decisions with company-wide implications are made from headquarters in the home country.

Another type of global organization is the **transnational corporation (TNC)**—a company that maintains significant operations in more than one country but decentralizes management to the local country. This type of organization doesn't attempt to replicate its domestic successes by managing foreign operations from its home country. Instead, local employees typically are hired to manage the business and marketing strategies are tailored to that country's unique characteristics. This type of global organization reflects the polycentric attitude. For example, Switzerland-based Nestlé can

••• **multinational corporations (MNCs)**
A company that maintains significant operations in multiple countries but manages them from a base in the home country.

••• **transnational corporation (TNCs)**
A company that maintains significant operations in more than one country but decentralizes management to the local country.

be described as a transnational. With operations in almost every country on the globe, its managers match the company's products to its consumers. In parts of Europe, Nestlé sells products that are not available in the United States or Latin America. Another example of a transnational is Frito-Lay, a division of PepsiCo, which markets a Dorito chip in the British market that differs in both taste and texture from the U.S. and Canadian versions. Many consumer companies manage their global businesses as TNCs because they must adapt their products and services to meet the needs of the local markets.

Many companies are globalizing by eliminating structural divisions that impose artificial geographical barriers. This type of global organization is called a **borderless organization**. The borderless organization approaches global business with a geocentric attitude. For example, IBM dropped its organizational structure based on country and reorganized into industry groups. Bristol-Myers Squibb changed its consumer business to become more aggressive in international sales and created a management position responsible for worldwide consumer medicines such as Bufferin and Excedrin. And Spain's Telefonica eliminated the geographic divisions between Madrid headquarters and its widespread phone companies. The company will be organized, instead, along business lines such as Internet services, cellular phones, and media operations. Borderless management is an attempt by organizations to increase efficiency and effectiveness in a competitive global marketplace.[17]

> ● ● ● **borderless organization**
> A global type of organization in which artificial geographical barriers are eliminated.

How Organizations Go Global

Most organizations proceed through three stages as they go global. (See Exhibit 4–5.) Each successive stage requires more investment and thus entails more risk.

In Stage 1, managers make the first push toward going global merely by **exporting** the organization's products to other countries—that is, by making products at home and selling them overseas. In addition, an organization might choose initially to go global by **importing** products, selling products at home that are made overseas. Both exporting and importing are small steps toward being a global business and involve minimal investment and minimal risk. Most organizations start doing business globally this way. Many, especially small businesses, continue with exporting and importing as the way they do business globally. For instance, Haribhai's Spice Emporium, a small business in Durban, South Africa, exports spices and rice to customers all over Africa, Europe, and the United States. However, other organizations have built multimillion-dollar businesses by importing or exporting. For instance, that's what specialty retailer Pier 1 has done—importing exotic products for sale in its stores around the world.

In Stage II, managers make more of an investment by committing to sell products in foreign countries or to have them made in foreign factories, but still with no physical

> ● ● ● **exporting**
> An approach to going global that involves making products at home and selling them overseas.

> ● ● ● **importing**
> An approach to going global that involves selling products at home that are made overseas.

 Exhibit 4–5

How Organizations Go Global

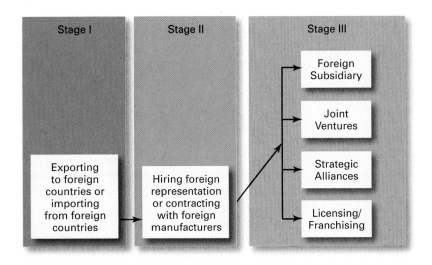

presence of company employees outside the company's home country. Instead, what is typically done on the sales side is to send domestic employees on regular business trips to meet foreign customers or to hire foreign agents or brokers to represent the organization's product line. Or, on the manufacturing side, managers will contract with a foreign firm to produce the organization's products.

Stage III represents the most serious commitment by managers to pursue global markets. As shown in Exhibit 4-5, managers can do this in different ways. **Licensing** and **franchising** are similar approaches since both involve an organization's giving another organization the right to use its brand name, technology, or product specifications in return for a lump-sum payment or a fee usually based on sales. The only difference is that licensing is primarily used by manufacturing organizations and franchising is used by service organizations. For example, Thai consumers can enjoy Bob's Big Boy hamburgers, Filipinos can dine on Shakey's Pizza, and Malaysians can consume Schlotzky's deli sandwiches—all because of franchises in these countries. And Anheuser-Busch chose to license the right to brew and market Budweiser beer to other brewers, such as Labatt in Canada, Modelo in Mexico, and Kirin in Japan. **Strategic alliances** are partnerships between an organization and a foreign company in which both share resources and knowledge in developing new products or building production facilities. The partners also share the risks and rewards of this alliance. For example, IBM of the United States, Toshiba of Japan, and Siemens of Germany formed a partnership to develop new generations of computer chips. A specific type of strategic alliance in which the partners agree to form a separate, independent organization for some business purpose is called a **joint venture**. For example, Hewlett-Packard has had numerous joint ventures with various suppliers around the globe to develop different components for its computer equipment. These partnerships provide a faster and more inexpensive way for companies to compete globally than doing it on their own. Finally, in Stage III, managers can make a direct investment in a foreign country by setting up a **foreign subsidiary**, a separate and independent production facility or office. This subsidiary can be managed as an MNC (domestic control), a TNC (foreign control), or as a borderless organization (global control). As you can probably guess, this arrangement involves the greatest commitment of resources and poses the greatest amount of risk. For instance, United Plastics Group of Westmont, Illinois, built three injection-molding facilities in Suzhou, China, and plans to build at least two more. Chuck Villa, the company's executive vice president for business development, says that level of investment is necessary because "it fulfills our mission of being a global supplier to our global accounts."[18]

••• licensing
An approach to going global by manufacturing organizations that involves giving other organizations the right to use your brand name, technology, or product specifications.

••• franchising
An approach to going global by service organizations that involves giving other organizations the right to your brand name, technology, or product specifications.

••• strategic alliances
An approach to going global that involves partnerships between an organization and a foreign company in which both share resources and knowledge in developing new products or building production facilities.

••• joint venture
An approach to going global that is a specific type of strategic alliance in which the partners agree to form a separate, independent organization for some business purpose.

••• foreign subsidiary
An approach to going global that involves a direct investment in a foreign country by setting up a separate and independent production facility or office.

••• Learning Review

- Contrast MNCs, TNCs, and borderless organizations.
- Describe the three stages organizations go through as they go global.

- Define exporting, importing, licensing, and franchising.
- Describe global strategic alliances, joint ventures, and foreign subsidiaries.

MANAGING IN A GLOBAL ENVIRONMENT

Assume for a moment that you're a manager going to work for a branch of a global organization in a foreign country. You know that your environment will differ from the one at home, but how? What should you be looking for? (▮▮▯▯▯ Go to the Web and check out Q & A 4.3.)

Any manager who finds himself or herself in a foreign country faces new challenges. In this section, we'll look at some of those challenges and offer guidelines for responding. Although our discussion is presented through the eyes of a U.S.

manager, our analytical framework could be used by any manager who has to manage in a foreign environment, regardless of national origin.

The Legal-Political Environment

U.S. managers are accustomed to stable legal and political systems. Changes are slow, and legal and political procedures are well established. Elections are held at regular intervals. Even changes in political parties after an election do not produce radical or quick transformations. The stability of laws governing the actions of individuals and institutions allows for accurate predictions. The same can't be said for all countries. Managers in a global organization must stay informed of the specific laws in countries where they do business.

Also, some countries have a history of unstable governments. Managers of businesses in these countries face dramatically greater uncertainty as a result of political instability. For instance, political interference is a fact of life in some Asian countries. Many large businesses have postponed doing business in China because the government controls what organizations do and how they do it. As Chinese consumers gain more power, however, that attitude is likely to change.

The legal-political environment doesn't have to be unstable or revolutionary to be a concern to managers. Just the fact that a country's laws and political system differ from those of the United States is important. Managers must recognize these differences if they hope to understand the constraints under which they operate and the opportunities that exist.

The Economic Environment

The global manager must be aware of economic issues when doing business in other countries. One of the first is understanding the type of economic system under which the country operates. The two major types are a market economy and a command economy. A **market economy** is one in which resources are primarily owned and controlled by the private sector. A **command economy** is one in which all economic decisions are planned by a central government. In actuality, no economy is purely market or command. For instance, the United States and the United Kingdom are two countries at the market end of the spectrum but they do have minimal governmental control. The economies of Vietnam and North Korea, however, would be more command-based. Then there's China, a country that's more command-based, but is moving to be more market-based. Why would

Victor Sassoon, pictured here at the Coffee Bean & Tea Leaf store on one of Singapore's most popular streets, hopes to rival Starbucks some day with his U.S.–based chain of coffee shops. With 222 outlets in 11 countries, Coffee Bean has a long way to go, and future plans include opening 280 new outlets in the United States, Spain, Germany, and Japan. For now, Sassoon is using a combination of business ownership models. The parent company owns all the American locations and franchises those outside the United States.

● ● ● market economy
An economic system in which resources are primarily owned and controlled by the private sector.

● ● ● command economy
An economic system in which all economic decisions are planned by a central government.

THINKING CRITICALLY ABOUT ETHICS

Foreign countries often have lax product-labeling laws. As a product manager for a U.S. pharmaceutical company, you're responsible for the profitability of a new drug whose side effects can be serious, although not fatal. Adding this information to the label or even putting an informational insert into the package will add to the product's cost, threatening profitability margins. What will you do? Why? What factors will influence your decision?

managers need to know about a country's economic system? Because it has the potential to constrain decisions and actions. Other economic issues a manager might need to understand include currency exchange rates, inflation rates, and diverse tax policies.

A global firm's profits can vary dramatically depending on the strength of its home currency and the currencies of the countries in which it operates. Any devaluation of a nation's currency significantly affects the level of a company's profits. The strength of a foreign nation's currency can also affect managers' decisions.

Inflation means that prices for products and services are going up. But it also affects interest rates, exchange rates, the cost of living, and the general confidence in a country's political and economic system. In most developing countries, consumer prices are rising more slowly than they were in the late 1990s, although inflation rates can, and do, vary widely.[19] Managers need to monitor inflation trends so they can make good decisions and anticipate any possible changes in a country's monetary policies.

Finally, diverse tax policies are a major worry for a global manager. Some host countries are more restrictive than the organization's home country. Others are far more lenient. About the only certainty is that tax rules differ from country to country. Managers need exact information on the various tax rules in countries in which they operate to minimize their business's overall tax obligation.

The Cultural Environment

A large global oil company found that employee productivity in one of its Mexican plants was off 20 percent and sent a U.S. manager to find out why. After talking to several employees, the manager discovered that the company used to have a monthly fiesta in the parking lot for all the employees and their families. Another U.S. manager had canceled the fiestas saying they were a waste of time and money. The message employees were getting was that the company didn't care about their families anymore. When the fiestas were reinstated, productivity and employee morale soared.

Union leader Yoo Jung Hwan and CEO Kim Seon Joong of Jinro consoled each other after their South Korean company was forced into bankruptcy by a group of foreign creditors. The move was controversial because South Korea has a strong cultural tradition against foreign ownership or control of Korean businesses. (Jinro, a distillery, produced the national drink, a rice liquor.) The court ruling in favor of the creditors is believed to be a first and will be immediately appealed.

At Hewlett-Packard, a cross-global team of U.S. and French engineers were assigned to work together on a software project. The U.S. engineers sent long, detailed e-mails to their counterparts in France. The French engineers viewed the lengthy e-mails as patronizing and replied with quick, concise e-mails. This made the U.S. engineers think that the French were hiding something from them. The situation spiraled out of control and had a negative effect on output until team members went through cultural training.[20]

●●● **national culture**
The values and attitudes shared by individuals from a specific country that shape their behavior and beliefs about what is important.

As we know from Chapter 3, organizations have different cultures. Countries have cultures too. **National culture** is the values and attitudes shared by individuals from a specific country that shape their behavior and their beliefs about what is important.[21]

Which is more important to a manager—national culture or organizational culture? For example, is an IBM facility in Germany more likely to reflect German culture or IBM's corporate culture? Research indicates that national culture has a greater effect on employees than does their organization's culture.[22] German employees at an IBM facility in Munich will be influenced more by German culture than by IBM's culture. This means that as influential as organizational culture may be on managerial practice, national culture is even more influential.

Legal, political, and economic differences among countries are fairly obvious. The Japanese manager who works in the United States or his or her American counterpart in Japan can get information about a country's laws or tax policies without too much difficulty. Getting information about a country's cultural differences isn't quite that easy! (■■■■ Go to the Web and check out Q & A 4.4.) The primary reason is that it's hard for natives to explain their country's unique cultural characteristics to someone else. For instance, if you're an American raised in the United States, how would you characterize U.S. culture? In other words, what are Americans like? Think about it for a moment and see how many of the characteristics in Exhibit 4–6 you identified.

Exhibit 4–6

●●●━━━━━━

What Are Americans Like?

- Americans are very *informal*. They tend to treat people alike even when there are great differences in age or social standing.

- Americans are *direct*. They don't talk around things. To some foreigners, this may appear as abrupt or even rude behavior.

- Americans are *competitive*. Some foreigners may find Americans assertive or overbearing.

- Americans are *achievers*. They like to keep score, whether at work or at play. They emphasize accomplishments.

- Americans are *independent* and *individualistic*. They place a high value on freedom and believe that individuals can shape and control their own destiny.

- Americans are *questioners*. They ask a lot of questions, even of someone they have just met. Many of these questions may seem pointless ("How ya' doin'?") or personal ("What kind of work do you do?").

- Americans *dislike silence*. They would rather talk about the weather than deal with silence in a conversation.

- Americans *value punctuality*. They keep appointment calendars and live according to schedules and clocks.

- Americans *value cleanliness*. They often seem obsessed with bathing, eliminating body odors, and wearing clean clothes.

Sources: Based on M. Ernest (ed.), *Predeparture Orientation Handbook: For Foreign Students and Scholars Planning to Study in the United States* (Washington, DC: U.S. Information Agency, Bureau of Cultural Affairs, 1984), pp. 103–05; A. Bennett, "American Culture Is Often a Puzzle for Foreign Managers in the U.S.," *Wall Street Journal*, February 12, 1986, p. 29; "Don't Think Our Way's the Only Way," *The Pryor Report*, February 1988, p. 9; and B.J. Wattenberg, "The Attitudes behind American Exceptionalism," *U.S. News & World Report*, August 7, 1989, p. 25.

Hofstede's Framework for Assessing Cultures One of the most widely referenced approaches to helping managers better understand differences between national cultures was developed by Geert Hofstede. (■□■■■ Go to the Web and check out Q & A 4.5.) His research found that managers and employees vary on five dimensions of national culture, which are as follows:

●●● **individualism**
The degree to which people in a country prefer to act as individuals.

●●● **collectivism**
A social framework in which people expect others in their group to look after them and to protect them.

- *Individualism versus Collectivism.* **Individualism** is the degree to which people in a country prefer to act as individuals. In an individualistic society, people are supposed to look after their own interests and those of their immediate family and do so because of the large amount of freedom that an individualistic society allows its citizens. The opposite is **collectivism**, which is characterized by a social framework in which people prefer to act as members of groups and expect others in groups of which they are a part (such as a family or an organization) to look after them and to protect them.

●●● **power distance**
A measure of the extent to which a society accepts the unequal distribution of power in institutions and organizations.

- *Power Distance.* Hofstede used the term **power distance** as a measure of the extent to which a society accepts the fact that power in institutions and organizations is distributed unequally. A high power distance society accepts wide differences in power in organizations. Employees show a great deal of respect for those in authority. Titles, rank, and status carry a lot of weight. In contrast, a low power distance society plays down inequalities as much as possible. Superiors still have authority, but employees are not afraid of or in awe of the boss.

●●● **uncertainty avoidance**
The degree to which people tolerate risk and prefer structured over unstructured situations.

- *Uncertainty Avoidance.* **Uncertainty avoidance** describes the degree to which people tolerate risk and prefer structured over unstructured situations. People in low uncertainty avoidance societies are relatively comfortable with risks. They're also relatively tolerant of behavior and opinions that differ from their own because they don't feel threatened by them. On the other hand, people in a society that's high in uncertainty avoidance feel threatened by uncertainty and ambiguity and experience high levels of anxiety, which manifests itself in nervousness, high stress, and aggressiveness.

●●● **quantity of life**
The degree to which values such as assertiveness, the acquisition of money and material goods, and competition prevail.

●●● **quality of life**
A national culture attribute that emphasizes relationships and concern for others.

- *Quantity versus Quality of Life.* The fourth cultural dimension, like individualism and collectivism, is a dichotomy. **Quantity of life** is the degree to which values such as assertiveness, the acquisition of money and material goods, and competition prevail. **Quality of life** is a national cultural attribute that emphasizes relationships and concern for others.[23]

●●● **long-term orientation**
A national culture attribute that emphasizes the future, thrift, and persistence.

●●● **short-term orientation**
A national culture attribute that emphasizes the past and present, respect for tradition, and fulfilling social obligations.

- *Long-term and Short-term Orientation.* Hofstede's final cultural attribute looked at a country's orientation toward life and work. People in **long-term orientation** cultures look to the future and value thrift and persistence. A **short-term orientation** values the past and present and emphasizes respect for tradition and fulfilling social obligations.

Although we don't have the space to review Hofstede's entire results for all the countries studied, we provide 12 examples in Exhibit 4–7.

The GLOBE Framework for Assessing Cultures Although Hofstede's cultural dimensions have been the main framework for differentiating among national cultures, the data on which it's based come from a single company and are almost 30 years old. In that time span, there have been a number of changes in the global environment, suggesting the need for an updated assessment of cultural dimensions, which the GLOBE project provides.[24]

The GLOBE (Global Leadership and Organizational Behavior Effectiveness) research program, which began in 1993, continues to investigate cross-cultural leadership behaviors. Using data from over 18,000 middle managers in 62 countries, the GLOBE research team identified nine dimensions on which national cultures differ:

Exhibit 4–7

Examples of Hofstede's Cultural Dimensions

Country	Individualism/ Collectivism	Power Distance	Uncertainty Avoidance	Quantity of Life[a]
Australia	Individual	Small	Moderate	Strong
Canada	Individual	Moderate	Low	Moderate
England	Individual	Small	Moderate	Strong
France	Individual	Large	High	Weak
Greece	Collective	Large	High	Moderate
Italy	Individual	Moderate	High	Strong
Japan	Collective	Moderate	High	Strong
Mexico	Collective	Large	High	Strong
Singapore	Collective	Large	Low	Moderate
Sweden	Individual	Small	Low	Weak
United States	Individual	Small	Low	Strong
Venezuela	Collective	Large	High	Strong

[a] A weak quantity score is equivalent to high quality of life.

Source: Based on G. Hofstede, "Motivation, Leadership, and Organization: Do American Theories Apply Abroad?" *Organizational Dynamics*, Summer 1980, pp. 42–63.

- *Assertiveness:* The extent to which a society encourages people to be tough, confrontational, assertive, and competitive versus modest and tender. This is essentially equivalent to Hofstede's quantity-of-life dimension.

- *Future orientation:* The extent to which a society encourages and rewards future-oriented behaviors such as planning, investing in the future, and delaying gratification. This is essentially equivalent to Hofstede's long-term/short-term orientation.

- *Gender differentiation:* The extent to which a society maximizes gender-role differences as measured by how much status and decision-making responsibilities women have.

- *Uncertainty avoidance:* Similar to Hofstede's description, the GLOBE team defined this dimension as a society's reliance on social norms and procedures to alleviate the unpredictability of future events.

- *Power distance:* As did Hofstede, the GLOBE team defined this as the degree to which members of a society expect power to be unequally shared.

- *Individualism/collectivism:* Again, this term was defined, as Hofstede did, as the degree to which individuals are encouraged by societal institutions to be integrated into groups within organizations and society.

- *In-group collectivsm:* In contrast to focusing on societal institutions, this dimension encompasses the extent to which members of a society take pride in membership in small groups, such as their family and circle of close friends, and the organizations in which they're employed.

- *Performance orientation:* This refers to the degree to which a society encourages and rewards group members for performance improvement and excellence.

- *Humane orientation:* This is defined as the degree to which a society encourages and rewards individuals for being fair, altruistic, generous, caring, and kind to others. This is similar to Hofstede's quality-of-life dimension.

How do different countries rank on these nine dimensions? Exhibit 4–8 on page 92 provides examples.

Exhibit 4–8

GLOBE Rankings

Dimension	Low	Medium	High
Assertiveness	Sweden New Zealand Switzerland Japan Kuwait	Egypt Ireland Philippines Ecuador France	Spain United States Greece Austria Germany
Future orientation	Russia Argentina Poland Italy Kuwait	Slovenia Egypt Ireland Australia India	Denmark Canada Netherlands Switzerland Singapore
Gender differentiation	Sweden Denmark Slovenia Poland Hungary	Italy Brazil Argentina Netherlands Venezuela	South Korea Egypt Morocco India China
Uncertainty avoidance	Russia Hungary Bolivia Greece Venezuela	Israel United States Mexico Kuwait Ireland	Austria Denmark Germany Sweden Switzerland
Power distance	Denmark Netherlands South Africa Israel Costa Rica	England France Brazil Italy Portugal	Russia Spain Thailand Argentina Morocco
In-group collectiveness	Denmark Sweden New Zealand Netherlands Finland	Japan Israel Qatar Austria Italy	Egypt China Morocco India Iran
Performance orientation	Russia Argentina Greece Venezuela Italy	Sweden Israel Spain England Japan	United States Taiwan New Zealand Hong Kong Singapore
Humane orientation	Germany Spain France Singapore Brazil	Hong Kong Sweden Taiwan United States New Zealand	Indonesia Egypt Malaysia Ireland Phillipines
Individualism/collectivism (with the first column indicating the most individualistic and the third column indicating the most collectivistic)	Greece Hungary Germany Argentina Italy	Hong Kong United States Egypt Poland Indonesia	Denmark Singapore Japan South Korea Sweden

Source: M. Javidan and R. J. House, "Cultural Acumen for the Global Manager: Lessons from Project GLOBE," *Organizational Dynamics*, Spring 2001, pp. 289–305.

The GLOBE project gives managers additional information to help them identify and manage cultural differences. It extended, not replaced, Hofstede's work. In fact, the GLOBE project confirms that Hofstede's five dimensions are still valid. But it also added some cultural dimensions and provides us with an updated description of national culture characteristics. (▬▢▬ Go to the Web and check out PRISM #6—Assessing Cross-Cultural Differences.)

Becoming a Manager

- ◆ *Learn as much as you can about other countries.*
- ◆ *Familiarize yourself with current global political, economic, and cultural issues.*
- ◆ *If given the opportunity, try to have your class projects or reports (in this class and other classes) cover global issues or global companies.*
- ◆ *Talk to professors or students who may be from other countries and ask them what the business world is like in their country.*
- ◆ *If you have the opportunity, travel to other countries.*
- ◆ *Go see a foreign film.*
- ◆ ■□■ *Go to the Web and complete Self-Assessment Exercise (S.A.L.) #46—Am I Well-Suited for a Career as a Global Manager? found on R.O.L.L.S.*

Global Management in Today's World

Like many organizations, following the terroristic attacks on September 11, 2001, Boeing Co., the Chicago-based aerospace company, laid off thousands of U.S. workers because of uncertainty over customer orders. Since then, as orders for planes have picked up, Boeing has decided that instead of hiring workers back, it will shift most of the work to lower-cost suppliers in the United States, as well as countries such as Russia and China. In Bangalore, India, General Electric has sunk more than $80 million into creating its largest research center outside the United States. The risks of such a move became alarmingly apparent when India and Pakistan nearly went to war in the summer of 2002.[25] Doing business globally today isn't easy! Managers face serious challenges—challenges arising from the openness associated with globalization and from significant cultural differences.

The push to go global has been widespread. Advocates praise the economic and social benefits that come from globalization. Yet, that very globalization has created challenges because of the openness that's necessary for it to work. What challenges? One is the increased threat of terrorism by a truly global terrorist network. Globalization is meant to open up trade and to break down the geographical barriers separating countries. Yet, opening up means just that—being open to the bad as well as the good. From the Philippines and the United Kingdom to Israel and Pakistan, organizations and employees face the risk of terrorist attacks. Another challenge from openness is the economic interdependence of trading countries. If one country's economy falters, it potentially could have a domino effect on other countries with which it does business. So far, however, that has not happened. The world economy has proved to be quite resilient. And there are mechanisms in place, such as the World Trade Organization, to isolate and address potential problems.

But it's not just simply the challenges from openness that managers must be prepared to face. The far more serious challenges come from the intense underlying and fundamental cultural differences—differences that encompass traditions, history, religious beliefs, and deep-seated values. Managing in such an environment will be extremely complicated! (■□■ Go to the Web and check out Q & A 4.6.) Although globalization has long been praised for its economic benefits, there are those who think that it is simply a euphemism for "Americanization"—that is, the way U.S. cultural values and U.S. business philosophy are said to be slowly taking over the world.[26] At its best, proponents of Americanization hope others will see how progressive, efficient, industrious, and free U.S. society and businesses are and want to emulate that way of doing things. However, critics claim that this attitude of the "almighty American dollar wanting to spread the American way to every single country" has created many problems.[27] Although history is filled with clashes between civilizations, what's unique about this period in time is the speed and ease with which misunderstandings and disagreements can erupt and escalate. The Internet, television and other media, and global air travel have brought the good and the bad of American entertainment, products, and behaviors to every corner of the globe. For those who don't like what Americans do, say, or believe, it can lead to resentment, dislike, distrust, and even outright hatred.

Successfully managing in today's global environment will require incredible sensitivity and understanding. Managers will need to be aware of how their decisions and actions will be viewed, not only by those who may agree, but more importantly, by those who may disagree. They will need to adjust their leadership styles and management approaches to accommodate these diverse views. Yet, as always, they will need to do this while still being as efficient and effective as possible in reaching the organization's goals.

•••• Learning Review

- Explain how the global legal-political and economic environments affect managers.
- Discuss Hofstede's five dimensions for assessing cultures.

- Explain the nine GLOBE dimensions for assessing cultures.
- Discuss the challenges of doing business globally in today's world.

Managers **Respond** to a **Manager's** Dilemma

····Stuart Silk

General Manager, Farnell-Newark InOne, Diadema, Brazil

There are probably three key areas where Lorena might encounter short- to medium-term cross-cultural issues. One is that as Zara continues to expand, it might have to open other distribution centers on other continents in order to ensure that the level of service is maintained. Language, culture, and work relations may vary significantly from the closely-managed operation currently in place in Spain.

Next, as more stores are opened in different countries, the company may run into more specific challenges in accommodating customers' requirements due to a lack of cultural sensitivity. (For instance, McDonald's only began making a profit in Portugal after it realized that it needed to open a small café within each store and serve espresso in cups and saucers.)

Last, Zara's expansion might mean either building manufacturing sites abroad and/or outsourcing some of the manufacturing to other countries. This may pose the challenge of moving from a more centralized management style to a more global style. To prevent these issues from becoming a problem, Lorena needs to ensure that she has a truly international (multilingual and multicultural) team in place; draw up a plan on how global logistics will support global expansion; start a succession plan and train new logistics managers who could be ready to take on overseas responsibilities; and encourage store managers to include suggestions on cultural specifics which may help in making the final product and brand expansion successful.

Learning Summary

After reading and studying this chapter, you should be able to:

- Contrast ethnocentric, polycentric, and geocentric attitudes toward global business.
- Explain why it's important for managers to be sensitive to global differences.
- Describe the current status of the European Union.
- Discuss the North American Free Trade Agreement and other regional trade alliances in Latin America.
- Tell about the Association of Southeast Asian Nations.
- Explain the interdependence that globalization involves.
- Discuss the role of the WTO.

- Contrast MNCs, TNCs, and borderless organizations.
- Describe the three stages organizations go through as they go global.
- Define exporting, importing, licensing, and franchising.
- Describe global strategic alliances, joint ventures, and foreign subsidiaries.
- Explain how the global legal-political and economic environments affect managers.
- Discuss Hofstede's five dimensions for assessing cultures.
- Explain the nine GLOBE dimensions for assessing cultures.
- Discuss the challenges of doing business globally in today's world.

Thinking About Management Issues

1. What are the managerial implications of a borderless organization?

2. Can the GLOBE framework presented in this chapter be used to guide managers in a Thai hospital or a government agency in Venezuela? Explain.

3. Compare the advantages and drawbacks of the various approaches to going global.

4. What challenges might confront a Mexican manager transferred to the United States to manage a manu-

facturing plant in Tucson, Arizona? Will these be the same for a U.S. manager transferred to Guadalajara? Explain.

5. In what ways do you think global factors have changed the way organizations select and train managers? What impact might the Internet have on this? Explain.

6. How might a continued war on terrorism impact U.S. managers and companies doing business globally?

Working Together: Team-Based Exercise

Moving to a foreign country isn't easy, no matter how many times you've done it or how receptive you are to new experiences. Successful global organizations are able to identify the best candidates for global assignments, and one of the ways they do this is through individual assessments prior to assigning people to global facilities. Form groups of three to five individuals. Your newly formed team, the Global Assignment Task Force, has been given the responsibility for developing a global aptitude assessment form for Zara (the company described in the chapter-

opening "Manager's Dilemma"). Because Zara is expanding its global operations significantly, it wants to make sure that it's sending the best possible people to the various global locations. Your team's assignment is to come up with a rough draft of a form to assess people's global aptitudes. Think about the characteristics, skills, attitudes, and so on, that you think a successful global employee would need. Your team's draft should be at least one-half page but not longer than one page. Be prepared to present your ideas to your classmates and professor.

Ethical Dilemma Exercise

Companies can go global in a number of ways. Known for its tires, the French firm Michelin licenses its brand to international manufacturers of related products such as snow chains and automotive breakdown kits. The U.S.-based sneaker firm New Balance has strategic alliances with overseas suppliers to manufacture and distribute its branded footwear around the world. Both approaches

to global business can lead to ethical questions. Should customers be informed that a branded product is made under license or by a strategic partner? Should companies be allowed to restrict how their licensees or partners use proprietary processes? And should partners be able to compete against partners in the international marketplace?

Consider New Balance's experience in China. For years the company contracted with local suppliers to make its branded sneakers for import to the United States and other countries. Eyeing the growing consumer market in China, it forged a strategic partnership with long-time local supplier Horace Chang to make and sell basic New Balance sneakers within China. A few years later, however, New Balance became worried that selling so many basic sneakers could hurt its image. Management told Chang to cut back production. Instead, he apparently kept making the sneakers and sold them through dealers in China, Japan, and elsewhere. New Balance quickly cut ties with Chang and went to court to stop his production. Chang fought back, showing an older document granting permission to make New Balance sneakers until the end of the contract. A company once considered a strategic partner had become a global competitor.[28]

Imagine you're a manager working under New Balance's vice president for international sales. You've just learned that basic sneakers made by Chang and bearing the New Balance brand are being sold for about $20 in Japanese discount stores. You want to protect your company's brand and reputation, yet you cannot stop Chang from selling shoes he's already produced. Review Exhibit 4-5 as you think about this global business dilemma and decide which of the following options to choose—and why.

Option A: Notify the Japanese discount stores to stop selling the basic sneakers because New Balance considers them counterfeits and doesn't want consumers to be deceived.

Option B: Alert consumers to the deception by placing ads in Japanese magazines and newspapers warning that New Balance considers the basic sneakers to be counterfeit.

Option C: Approach the Japanese discount stores with an offer to buy their remaining stock of New Balance sneakers and keep them off the market.

Case Application

National Basketball Association

Using an exceptionally well-executed game plan, the National Basketball Association (NBA) has emerged as the first truly global sports league. The transformation of a once-faltering domestic sport into a global commercial success reflects a keen understanding of managing in a global environment. And much of the credit should go to NBA commissioner David Stern, who has been consciously

building the NBA into a global brand. He says, "Basketball is a universal language, and it's about to bloom on a global basis."

Professional basketball sparked the interest of fans and players around the globe in the mid-1990s, and the NBA cashed in on the game's universal appeal. At one time, if you had asked someone in China what the most popular basketball team was, the answer would have been the "Red Oxen" from Chicago (the Bulls). Today, the NBA's center of attention *comes* from China. Yao Ming, the seven-foot-five-inch centerpiece of the Houston Rockets has a personality that appeals to fans around the world. But he's not the only global player in the league. Others include the Dallas Mavericks' Dirk Nowitzki, a seven-footer from Germany; Pau Gasol of the Memphis Grizzlies, a native of Spain and also seven feet tall; San Antonio Spurs' guard Tony Parker from France; Denver Nuggets' forward Nene Hilario from Brazil; and Orlando Magic guard Gordan Giricek from Croatia. And all eyes are focused on Darko Milicic, a seven-foot teenager from Serbia who was the second pick in the 2003 NBA draft. What started as a trickle in the 1980s with occasional foreign stars like Hakeem Olajuwon (Nigeria) and the late Drazen Petrovic (Croatia), has turned into a flood. A record 64 players from 34 countries and territories outside the United States are playing in the NBA.

The NBA is proving that the game can be played globally also. The league is putting the finishing touches on plans to hold several pre-season games in Europe, Latin America, and Asia. In addition, Stern predicts that there will be multiple teams in Europe by the end of the decade. Developers are starting to build modern arenas to help promote expansion of the game. But today's global appeal didn't come easily.

In the mid-1990s, the league wanted to be a global entertainment leader and had the resources and capabilities to make it happen. However, the 1998–1999 season almost brought it to a crashing end. A brutal contract

David Stern, Commissioner of the NBA.

negotiation with players forced the cancellation of more than one-third of the league's games. The lockout frustrated and angered fans. Stern found the league's many global business initiatives grinding to a halt. Then, there was the issue of the NBA's most celebrated and revered icon, Michael Jordan. His first retirement in 1999 took away one of the league's key draws, both as a player and as a celebrity. From its winning streak, the NBA was suddenly struggling. However, Stern wasn't throwing in the towel.

To address the challenges facing the NBA, Stern looked at what the league had to offer. What it had was consumer familiarity with basketball both domestically and globally, some talented young players, and a recognized image and track record. If those things could be exploited, the NBA might be able to get back in the game.

One of the actions that Stern took was to expand its network of offices globally. Why? The league hoped to re-ignite the NBA's popularity with global consumers by being visible. He explained, "The model is the rock concert. Sell lots of records. Tour occasionally."

Another thing that Stern did was enhance the league's Internet presence through its Web site. Today, some 40 percent of the visitors to the Web site (which includes sites in Spanish, Japanese, and Chinese) log on from outside the United States. The NBA pushes its games and merchandise to fans around the world via their computers.

The global appeal is filling the league's coffers. About 20 percent of all NBA merchandise is now sold outside the United States—an extra $430 million in annual revenue. Almost one million fans pay $10 a month to listen to streaming English or Spanish audio of almost any game on the league's Web site. The NBA is building an NBA City theme restaurant in the Dominican Republic and is thinking of opening NBA stores in Asia and Europe. Separate NBA boutiques can be found in big department stores such as El Corte Ingles in Spain. Then there's the television revenue. Nearly 15 percent of its $900 million in annual TV revenue comes from partners in 212 countries and territories outside the United States.

DISCUSSION QUESTIONS

1. What global attitude do you think the NBA and its member teams exhibit? Explain why this attitude has or hasn't contributed to the NBA's global success.

2. What legal-political, economic, and cultural differences might be significant to an NBA team recruiting a player from a foreign country? How would you deal with these differences? As NBA teams start playing in other countries, would these differences change? Explain.

3. How has the NBA exhibited effective and efficient managing in the global environment?

4. What could other organizations learn from the NBA's global experience?

Sources: D. Eisenberg, "The NBA's Global Game Plan," *Time*, March 17, 2003, pp. 59–63; J. Tyrangiel, "The Center of Attention," *Time*, February 10, 2003, pp. 56–60; "Spin Master Stern," *Latin Trade*, July 2000, p. 32; Information from NBA's Web page [*www.nba.com*], March 31, 2000; J. Tagliabue, "Hoop Dreams, Fiscal Realities," *New York Times*, March 4, 2000, pp. B1+; D. Roth, "The NBA's Next Shot," *Fortune*, February 21, 2000, pp. 207–16; A. Bianco, "Now It's NBA All-the-Time TV," *Business Week*, November 15, 1999, pp. 241–42; and D. McGraw and M. Tharp, "Going Out on Top," *U.S. News and World Report*, January 25, 1999, p. 55.

Answers to "Who Owns What" Quiz

1. c. United Kingdom
   Ben & Jerry's Ice Cream was purchased by Unilever, PLC in April 2000.
2. d. France
   Bic Pen Company is a part of Société BIC S.A.
3. b. Switzerland
   PowerBar was purchased by Swiss giant Nestlé in 2000.
4. a. France
   RCA television sets are produced by Thomson Multimedia SA, a French company.
5. d. United Kingdom
   Skippy peanut butter is a product of BestFoods which Unilever PLC purchased in 2000.
6. a. United States
   Godiva chocolates are a business division of Campbell Soup Company.
7. b. Mexico
   Grupo Bimbo, the world's third-largest bread maker, bought the rights to make and distribute Boboli pizza crusts in 2002.
8. c. United States
   Braun electric shavers are a part of the Gillette Company.

9. c. Canada
   Greyhound Bus Lines is a division of a Canadian company, Laidlaw Industries.
10. a. United States
    The Coca-Cola Company purchased the Seagram's line of mixers in 2002.
11. c. Switzerland
    Nestlé SA purchased the maker of Hot Pockets in 2002.
12. d. United Kingdom
    Cadbury Schweppes PLC owns the Dr Pepper/7-Up businesses.
13. b. United Kingdom
    Lipton tea is a product of BestFoods which Unilever PLC purchased in 2000.
14. d. Switzerland
    Häagen-Dazs ice cream is a product of Nestlé SA which took full control of the product in 2002.
15. a. United States
    Consumer products giant Procter & Gamble purchased a controlling stake in Wella in 2003.

● ● ● Learning Outline

Follow this Learning Outline as you read and study this chapter.

What Is Social Responsibility?

- Contrast the classical and socioeconomic views of social responsibility.
- Discuss the role that stakeholders play in the four stages of social responsibility.
- Differentiate between social obligation, social responsiveness, and social responsibility.

Social Responsibility and Economic Performance

- Explain what research studies have shown about the relationship between an organization's social involvement and its economic performance.
- Explain what conclusion can be reached regarding social responsibility and economic performance.

The Greening of Management

- Describe how organizations can go green.
- Relate the approaches to being green to the concepts of social obligation, social responsiveness, and social responsibility.

Values-Based Management

- Discuss what purposes shared values serve.
- Describe the relationship of values-based management to ethics.

Managerial Ethics

- Contrast the four views of ethics.
- Discuss the factors that affect ethical and unethical behavior.
- Discuss the six determinants of issue intensity.
- Explain what codes of ethics are and how their effectiveness can be improved.
- Describe the important roles managers play in encouraging ethical behavior.

Social Responsibility and Ethics in Today's World

- Explain why ethical leadership is important.
- Discuss how managers and organizations can protect employees who raise ethical issues or concerns.
- Describe social impact management.

Chapter

5

Social Responsibility and Managerial Ethics

A **Manager's** *Dilemma*

 Suppose that you've ordered a new mattress and arranged for it to be delivered. If that mattress was made by Coco-Mat and you lived in Kifisia, a suburb of Athens, Greece, your mattress might be delivered to you by a company van or even by horse and cart if that was the most economical way to do so. Although it may seem surprising that a successful business might actually use horses, Paul Efmorfidis, vice president and

co-founder of Coco-Mat, says that his company uses technology—old or new—if it helps the company live up to its values.[1]

Coco-Mat has been making mattresses since 1989 when Paul and his brother Michael invented a mattress of coconut fiber and natural latex and founded the company. Since that time, the business has grown. But Paul says, "Although we're very successful, we're more proud of our ethical values. What we're trying to do, in a way, is sell our ideas." And those ideas are based on a strong commitment to social responsibility.

As Coco-Mat manufactures its mattresses, almost no waste is produced. For instance, scrap mattress is used to stuff old-fashioned rag dolls and left-over latex is shredded for pillow stuffing. Also, Paul stresses that the raw materials must be sustainable. They use cotton rather than synthetic material to cover the mattresses, and seaweed and horsehair are

used in the mattresses as well. In addition to the sustainability it practices, Paul stresses employee involvement. Employees can earn incentive rewards (up to 40 percent of their pay) by attending quality management seminars and participating in company sporting events and other activities. Coco-Mat also makes a special effort to hire diverse people. For instance, at the company's factory in Xanthi, 15 nationalities are represented.

The company's socially responsible approach to doing business has brought it praise from the Greek Ministry of Development and the European Union. Its practices also won it first place in Cambridge University's Research, Business, and the Environment Program.

Put yourself in Paul's position. As he looks to branch out into other areas of furniture manufacturing, would it make more sense, from a long-term perspective, to be less socially responsible and more focused on profits?

What would **you** do **?**

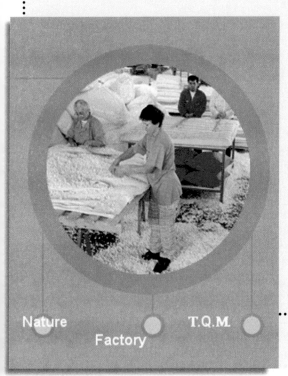

Nature

Factory

T.Q.M.

Deciding how much social responsibility is enough—for instance, when is it better to be focused on profits—is just one example of the complicated types of ethical and social responsibility issues that managers, such as Paul Efmorfidis, may have to cope with as they plan, organize, lead, and control. As managers go about their business, social factors can and do influence their actions. In this chapter, we'll introduce you to the issues surrounding social responsibility and managerial ethics. Our discussion of these topics is placed at this point in the text because both social responsibility and ethics are responses to a changing environment and are influenced by organizational culture (Chapter 3). Also, both social responsibility and ethics are important considerations when making decisions (Chapter 6).

WHAT IS SOCIAL RESPONSIBILITY?

Using digital formats like MP3 and Internet file-sharing sites such as Kazaa, music lovers all over the world obtain and share their favorite recordings free. Large global corporations want to lower their costs and be more competitive by locating in countries where human rights are not a high priority, and justify it by saying that they're bringing in jobs and helping to strengthen the local economies. Automobile manufacturers build gas-guzzling sport utility vehicles that have the potential to seriously injure people in smaller, more fuel-efficient vehicles because customers want them and are willing to pay the prices. Are these companies being socially responsible? What factors influenced managers' decisions in these situations? Managers regularly face decisions that have a dimension of social responsibility: Employee relations, philanthropy, pricing, resource conservation, product quality and safety, and doing business in countries that violate human rights are some of the more obvious. (■□■■■ Go to the Web and check out Q & A 5.1.) How do managers make such decisions? Let's begin by looking at two different perspectives.

Two Views of Social Responsibility

What does it mean for an organization to be socially responsible? Few concepts have been described in so many different ways. For instance, it's been called "profit making only," "going beyond profit making," "voluntary activities," "concern for the broader social system," and "social responsiveness."[2] A great deal of attention has been focused on the extremes. On one side, there's the classical—or purely economic—view, and on the other side is the socioeconomic position.

The Classical View   The **classical view** says that management's only social responsibility is to maximize profits. The most outspoken advocate of this approach is economist and Nobel laureate Milton Friedman.[3] He argues that managers' primary responsibility is to operate the business in the best interests of the stockholders (the owners of a corporation). What are those interests? Friedman contends that stockholders have a single concern: financial return. He also argues that anytime managers decide to spend the organization's resources for "social good," they're adding to the costs of doing business. These costs have to be passed on to consumers either through higher prices or absorbed by stockholders through a smaller profit returned as dividends. Do understand that Friedman isn't saying that organizations should *not* be socially responsible; he thinks they should. But the extent of that responsibility is to maximize organizational profits for stockholders.

The Socioeconomic View   The **socioeconomic view** is the view that management's social responsibility goes beyond making profits to include protecting and improving society's welfare. This position is based on the belief that corporations are *not* independent entities responsible only to stockholders. They also have a responsi-

■ **Q & A**
Whenever you see this green square, go to the R.O.L.L.S. Web site (*www.prenhall.com/robbins*) to the Q & A, your 24/7 educational assistant. These video clips and written material presented by your authors address questions that we have found students frequently ask.

●●● **classical view**
The view that management's only social responsibility is to maximize profits.

●●● **socioeconomic view**
The view that management's social responsibility goes beyond making profits to include protecting and improving society's welfare.

The socioeconomic view of social responsibility goes beyond profit to include improving society's welfare. Making the highest possible profit is not, in fact, the goal of City Fresh Foods, a Massachusetts firm founded by Glynn Lloyd (left) to combine his two passions, selling healthy food and helping people in low-income areas. Now run by Glynn and his brother Sheldon (right), City Fresh is a $2 million business that supplies Meals on Wheels and senior centers and is looking at big expansion opportunities. Says Glynn of his firm, "It's a vehicle for people to be employed, gain wealth, and at the same time provide a service to the neighborhood."

bility to the larger society that endorses their creation through various laws and regulations and supports them by purchasing their products and services. In addition, proponents of this view believe that business organizations are not just merely economic institutions. Society expects and even encourages businesses to become involved in social, political, and legal issues. For example, proponents of the socioeconomic view would say that Avon Products Inc., was being socially responsible when it initiated its Breast Cancer Crusade to provide women with breast cancer education and early detection screening services, and which, after 10 years, has raised more than $250 million worldwide.[4]

And they would say that the educational programs implemented by Brazilian cosmetics manufacturer Natura Cosmeticos SA in public primary schools in São Paulo, to improve children's literacy and decision-making skills, were socially responsible.[5] Why? Through these programs, the managers were protecting and improving society's welfare. More and more organizations around the world are taking their social responsibilities seriously, especially in Europe, where the view that businesses need to focus on more than just profits has a stronger tradition than in the United States.[6]

Comparing the Two Views The key differences between these two perspectives are easier to understand if we think in terms of the people to whom organizations are responsible. Classicists would say that stockholders or owners are the only legitimate concern. Others would respond that managers are responsible to any group affected by the organization's decisions and actions—that is, the stakeholders.[7] Exhibit 5–1 shows a four-stage model of the progression of an organization's social responsibility.[8]

A Stage 1 manager is following the classical view of social responsibility and pursues stockholders' interests while following all laws and regulations. At Stage 2, managers expand their responsibilities to another important stakeholder group—employees. Because they'll want to attract, keep, and motivate good employees, Stage 2 managers will improve working conditions, expand employee rights, increase job security, and focus on human resource concerns.

At Stage 3, managers expand their responsibilities to other stakeholders in the specific environment, primarily customers and suppliers. Social responsibility goals for these stakeholders might include fair prices, high-quality products and services, safe products, good supplier relations, and similar actions. Their philosophy is that they can meet their responsibilities to stockholders only by meeting the needs of these other stakeholders.

Finally, Stage 4 characterizes the highest socioeconomic commitment. At this stage, managers feel a responsibility to society as a whole. They view their business as a public entity and feel a responsibility to advance the public good. The acceptance of such responsibility means that managers actively promote social justice, preserve the environment, and support social and cultural activities. They do these things even if such actions may negatively affect profits.

Exhibit 5–1

To Whom Is Management Responsible?

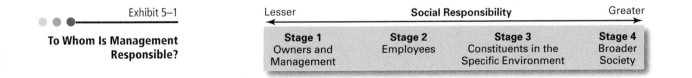

Lesser		Social Responsibility		Greater
Stage 1 Owners and Management	**Stage 2** Employees	**Stage 3** Constituents in the Specific Environment	**Stage 4** Broader Society

Exhibit 5–2

● ● ●━━━━━

Arguments For and Against Social Responsibility

For	Against
Public expectations Public opinion now supports businesses pursuing economic and social goals.	*Violation of profit maximization* Business is being socially responsible only when it pursues its economic interests.
Long-run profits Socially responsible companies tend to have more secure long-run profits.	*Dilution of purpose* Pursuing social goals dilutes business's primary purpose—economic productivity.
Ethical obligation Businesses should be socially responsible because responsible actions are the right thing to do.	*Costs* Many socially responsible actions do not cover their costs and someone must pay those costs.
Public image Businesses can create a favorable public image by pursuing social goals.	*Too much power* Businesses have a lot of power already and if they pursue social goals they will have even more.
Better environment Business involvement can help solve difficult social problems.	*Lack of skills* Business leaders lack the necessary skills to address social issues.
Discouragement of further governmental regulation By becoming socially responsible, businesses can expect less government regulation.	*Lack of accountability* There are no direct lines of accountability for social actions.
Balance of responsibility and power Businesses have a lot of power and an equally large amount of responsibility is needed to balance against that power.	
Stockholder interests Social responsibility will improve a business's stock price in the long run.	
Possession of resources Businesses have the resources to support public and charitable projects that need assistance.	
Superiority of prevention over cures Businesses should address social problems before they become serious and costly to correct.	

Arguments For and Against Social Responsibility

Another way to understand whether organizations should be socially responsible is by looking at the arguments for it and against it. Exhibit 5–2 outlines the major points that have been presented.[9]

How much and what type of social responsibility businesses should pursue continues to be a topic of interest and heated debate. (■◻■■■■ Go to the Web and check out Q & A 5.2.) Now is probably a good time to define what we mean by the term *social responsibility*.

From Obligations to Responsiveness to Responsibility

We can better understand social responsibility if we first compare it to two similar concepts: social obligation and social responsiveness.[10] **Social obligation** is the obligation of a business to meet its economic and legal responsibilities. The organization does only what it's obligated to do and reflects the classical view of social responsibility. In contrast to social obligation, however, both social responsibility and social responsiveness go beyond merely meeting basic economic and legal standards.

Social responsiveness refers to the capacity of a firm to adapt to changing societal conditions. The idea of social responsiveness stresses that managers make practical decisions about the societal actions in which they engage.[11] A socially responsive organization is guided by social norms and acts the way it does because of its desire to sat-

● ● ● **social obligation**
The obligation of a business to meet its economic and legal responsibilities.

● ● ● **social responsiveness**
The capacity of a firm to adapt to changing social conditions.

isfy some popular social need. For instance, managers at American Express Company identified three themes—community service, cultural heritage, and economic independence—to serve as guides for deciding which worldwide projects and organizations to support.[12] By making these choices, managers were "responding" to what they felt were important social needs.

A socially responsible organization views things a little differently, and goes beyond what it must do by law or chooses to do because it makes economic sense, to do what it can to help improve society because it's the right, or ethical, thing to do. We define **social responsibility** as a business's obligation, beyond that required by law and economics, to pursue long-term goals that are good for society.[13] Note that this definition assumes that a business obeys laws and pursues economic interests. But also note that this definition views business as a moral agent. That is, in its effort to do good for society, it must differentiate between right and wrong.

Social responsibility adds an ethical imperative to do those things that make society better and not to do those that could make it worse. As Exhibit 5–3 shows, social responsibility requires business to determine what is right or wrong and to make ethical decisions and engage in ethical business activities. A socially responsible organization does what is right because it feels it has a responsibility to act that way. For example, when Aspen Skiing Company completed one of the first certified "green" (environmentally sustainable) buildings in the United States, CEO Pat O'Donnell said, in response to reporters' questions about whether the decision made economic sense, "We did this because it was the right thing to do. It cost us hundreds of thousands of dollars more, but management and ownership agreed that this is part of our guiding principles and part of our values-based business."[14] That's the attitude of a socially responsible manager and organization.

How should we view an organization's social actions? In the United States, a company that meets pollution control standards established by the federal government or that does not discriminate against employees over the age of 40 in promotion decisions is meeting its social obligation and nothing more because there are laws mandating these actions. However, when it provides on-site child care facilities for employees, packages products in 100 percent recycled paper, or announces that it will not purchase, process, or sell any tuna caught with dolphins, it is being socially responsive. Why? Working parents and environmentalists have demanded such actions.

Many U.S. companies practice social responsiveness. Advocates believe that the concept replaces philosophical talk with practical action. They see it as a more tangible and achievable goal than social responsibility.[15] (▮◻▮▮ Go to the Web and check out Q & A 5.3.) Rather than assessing what's good for society in the long term and making moral judgments, managers in a socially responsive organization identify the prevailing social norms and then change their social involvement to respond to changing societal conditions. For instance, environmental stewardship seems to be an important social norm at present and many companies are looking at ways to be environmentally responsible. Alcoa of Australia developed a novel way to recycle the used linings of aluminum smelting pots and Japanese auto parts manufacturer Denso generates its own electricity and steam at many of its facilities. Other organizations are addressing other popular social issues. For instance, media companies such as Prentice Hall, McGraw-Hill, the *New York Times*, and the *Washington Post* are involved in efforts to increase literacy. These are examples of socially responsive actions for today. (▮◻▮▮ Go to the Web and check out Q & A 5.4.)

••• social responsibility
A business's obligation, beyond that required by law and economics, to pursue long-term goals that are good for society.

Exhibit 5–3

Social Responsibility Versus Social Responsiveness

	Social Responsibility	Social Responsiveness
Major consideration	Ethical	Pragmatic
Focus	Ends	Means
Emphasis	Obligation	Responses
Decision framework	Long term	Medium and short term

Source: Adapted from S.L. Wartick and P.L. Cochran, "The Evolution of the Corporate Social Performance Model," *Academy of Management Review*, October 1985, p. 766.

• • • **Learning Review**

- Contrast the classical and socioeconomic views of social responsibility.
- Discuss the role that stakeholders play in the four stages of social responsibility.

- Differentiate between social obligation, social responsiveness, and social responsibility.

SOCIAL RESPONSIBILITY AND ECONOMIC PERFORMANCE

In this section, we want to look at the question: How do socially responsible activities affect a company's economic performance? Findings from a number of research studies can help us answer this question.[16]

The relationship between social involvement and economic performance of the firm can be complicated, but there is little question that disregard for social issues is costly. Repeated and allegedly avoidable environmental disasters laid at the door of Massey Energy, the nation's sixth-largest coal-mining company, have cost millions of dollars worth of damage to neighboring communities. The firm has also missed its earnings estimates in eight recent fiscal quarters, lost $33 million, and seen its stock slide from $28 to less than $11 per share. Don Blankenship, CEO, says one accident that spilled 20 times as much crude oil as the Exxon Valdez and killed fish and plants for 36 miles along a tributary of the Big Sandy River, "could have happened to anyone."

The majority of these studies showed a positive relationship between social involvement and economic performance. For instance, one study found that firms' corporate social performance was positively associated with both *prior* and *future* financial performance.[17] But we should be cautious about making any compelling assumptions from these findings because of methodological questions associated with trying to measure "social responsibility" and "economic performance."[18] Most of these studies determined a company's social performance by analyzing the content of annual reports, citations of social actions in news articles on the company, or "reputation" indexes based on public perception. Such criteria certainly have drawbacks as reliable measures of social responsibility. Although measures of economic performance (such as net income, return on equity, or per share stock prices) are more objective, they are generally used to indicate only short-term economic performance. It may well be that the impact of social responsibility on a firm's profits—positive or negative—takes a number of years to appear. If there's a time lag, studies that use short-term financial measures are not likely to show valid results. There's also the issue of causation. If, for example, evidence showed that social involvement and economic performance were positively related, this wouldn't necessarily mean that social involvement *caused* higher economic performance. It very well could be the opposite. That is, it might mean that high profits afforded companies the luxury of being socially involved.[19] These methodological concerns shouldn't be taken lightly. In fact, one study found that if the flawed empirical analyses in these studies were "corrected," social responsibility had a neutral impact on a company's financial performance.[20] And one study found that participating in social issues not related to the organization's primary stakeholders was negatively associated with shareholder value.[21]

Another way to look at the issue of social responsibility and economic performance is by evaluating socially responsible mutual stock funds. These mutual funds provide a way for individual investors to support socially responsible companies. (For a list of such funds, go to *www.socialfunds.com.*) Typically, these funds use some type of **social screening**, that is, applying social criteria to investment decisions. For instance, these funds usually will not invest in companies that are involved in liquor, gambling, tobacco, nuclear power, weapons, price fixing, or fraud. Although many of these social funds (equity, bond, and money market) have outperformed the market average in the long run, the last few years have not been good for stock funds of any type.[22] However, the average social fund fell only 21.5 percent versus a 22.4 percent decline for the average U.S. diversified stock fund.[23]

What conclusion can we draw from all of this? The most meaningful one is that there is little evidence to say that a company's social actions hurt its long-term economic performance. Given political and societal pressures on business to be socially involved, managers would be wise to take social goals into consideration as they plan, organize, lead, and control.

• • • **social screening**
Applying social criteria (screens) to investment decisions.

- Explain what research studies have shown about the relationship between an organization's social involvement and its economic performance.

- Explain what conclusion can be reached regarding social responsibility and economic performance.

THE GREENING OF MANAGEMENT

Until the late 1960s, few people (and organizations) paid attention to the environmental consequences of their decisions and actions.[24] Although there were some groups concerned with conserving the land and its natural resources, about the only popular reference to saving the environment you would have seen was the ubiquitous printed request "Please Do Not Litter." A number of highly visible ecological problems and environmental disasters (*Exxon Valdez* oil spill, mercury poisoning in Japan, and Three Mile Island and Chernobyl nuclear power plant accidents) brought about a new spirit of environmentalism among individuals, groups, and organizations. Increasingly, managers began to confront questions about an organization's impact on the natural environment. This recognition of the close link between an organization's decisions and activities and its impact on the natural environment is referred to as the **greening of management**. Let's look at some green issues managers may have to address.

> ● ● ● **greening of management**
> The recognition of the close link between an organization's decisions and activities and its impact on the natural environment.

Global Environmental Problems

Americans spend more on trash bags to throw away waste than 90 other countries spend on all consumed products. The average mass-produced water bottle contains small amounts of a heavy toxic metal known to cause cancer. The rubber soles on a pair of shoes are loaded with lead that can last decades after the shoes are thrown away. The Business Roundtable, an organization that represents some of America's largest companies and has long challenged the science behind global warming, appeared to significantly change its stance when it announced it was asking all members to measure their current levels of greenhouse-gas emissions and then pledge to reduce them by a specific amount over time.[25] Have we got your attention yet? Managers are going to have to be informed about green issues. To do so, however, they first must understand the nature of global environmental problems.

The list of global environmental problems is long. Some of the more serious ones include natural resource depletion, global warming, pollution (air, water, and soil), industrial accidents, and toxic wastes. How did these problems occur? Much of the blame can be placed on industrial activities in developed (economically affluent) countries over the last half century.[26] Various reports have shown that affluent societies account for more than 75 percent of the world's energy and resource consumption and create most of the industrial, toxic, and consumer waste.[27] An equally disturbing picture is that as the world population continues to grow and as emerging countries become more market oriented and affluent, global environmental problems can be expected to worsen.[28] However, many organizations around the world have embraced their responsibility to respect and protect the natural environment. What role *can* organizations play in addressing global environmental problems? In other words, how can they go green?

How Organizations Go Green

There are many things managers and organizations can do to protect and preserve the natural environment.[29] Some do no more than what is required by law—that is, they fulfill their social obligation; others have made radical changes to make their products and production processes cleaner. For instance, the 3M Corporation has been a leader

Exhibit 5–4

Approaches to Being Green

Source: Based on R.E. Freeman. J. Pierce, and R. Dodd. *Shades of Green: Business Ethics and the Environment* (New York: Oxford University Press, 1995).

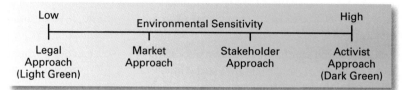

in waste-reduction efforts with its 3 Ps Program (Pollution Prevention Pays). Hangers Cleaners uses a pollution-free process to clean clothes. Whirlpool won an industry competition and a $30 million prize for developing a CFC-free, high-efficiency refrigerator. (CFCs, an abbreviation for chlorofluorocarbons, have been linked to the degradation of the ozone layer surrounding the earth.) And IBM, DaimlerChrysler, Toyota, IKEA, and Canon have focused their environmental programs on preventing pollution, not just on cleaning it up. Although these examples are interesting, they don't tell us much about how organizations go green. One model of environmental responsibility uses the term *shades of green* to describe the different approaches that organizations may take.[30] (See Exhibit 5–4.)

The first approach is the *legal* (or *light green*) *approach*—that is, simply doing what is required legally. Under this approach, organizations exhibit little environmental sensitivity. They obey laws, rules, and regulations willingly and without legal challenge and may even try to use the law to their own advantage, but that's the extent of their being green. For example, many durable product manufacturers and oil refiners have taken the legal approach and comply with the relevant environmental laws and regulations, but go no further. This approach is a good illustration of social obligation—these organizations simply follow their legal obligations to prevent pollution and protect the environment.

As an organization becomes more sensitive to environmental issues, it may adopt the *market approach*, where it responds to the environmental preferences of its customers. Whatever customers demand in terms of environmentally friendly products will be what the organization provides. For example, DuPont developed a new type of herbicide that helped farmers around the world reduce their annual use of chemicals by more than 45 million pounds. By developing this product, the company was responding to the demands of its customers (farmers) who wanted to minimize the use of chemicals on their crops.

Under the next approach, the *stakeholder approach*, the organization works to meet the environmental demands of multiple stakeholders such as employees, suppliers, or the community. (■▨▨▨▨ Check out You're the Manager: Putting Ethics into Action on page 127.) For instance, Hewlett-Packard Corporation has several corporate environmental programs in place for its supply chain (suppliers), product design and product recycling (customers and society), and work operations (employees and community). Both the market approach and the stakeholder approach are good illustrations of social responsiveness.

Finally, if an organization pursues an *activist* (also called a *dark green*) *approach*, it looks for ways to respect and preserve the earth and its natural resources. The activist approach exhibits the highest degree of environmental sensitivity and is a good illustration of social responsibility. For example, Ecover, a Belgian company that produces cleaning products from natural soaps and renewable raw materials, operates a near-zero-emissions factory. This green factory is an environmentally sound engineering marvel with a huge grass roof that keeps the factory cool in summer and warm in winter and a water treatment system that runs on wind and solar energy. The company chose to build this type of facility because of its deep commitment to protecting and preserving the environment.

As president of the Ms. Foundation for Women, Marie C. Wilson exemplifies the stakeholder approach to social responsibility. Her organization is a strong supporter of paid family leave for all employees who need to care for aging parents or newborn children. "By letting your employees know you support paid family leave," she says, "you can send the message to your employees that their family lives and personal growth matter to you." Wilson includes males in the Ms. Foundation's stakeholders too. She recently changed "Take Our Daughters to Work Day" to "Take Our Daughters and Sons to Work Day."

● ● ●**Learning Review**

- Describe how organizations can go green.
- Relate the approaches to being green to the concepts of social obligation, social responsiveness, and social responsibility.

VALUES-BASED MANAGEMENT

●●● **values-based management**
An approach to managing in which managers establish and uphold an organization's shared values.

Patagonia, a maker of outdoor sports clothing and gear, passionately pursues environmental preservation. Its strong environmental commitment influences employees' actions and decisions in areas from product design to marketing to shipping. In addition, the company gives 10 percent of its profits to environmental causes and actively seeks to educate its customers and suppliers about environmental issues. Patagonia is an example of a company that practices values-based management. **Values-based management** is an approach to managing in which managers establish and uphold an organization's shared values. An organization's values reflect what it stands for and what it believes in. As we discussed in Chapter 3, the shared organizational values form the organization's culture and serve many purposes.[31] (███████ Go to the Web and check out Q & A 5.5.)

Purposes of Shared Values

Exhibit 5–5 shows the four purposes of shared values. The first is serving as guideposts for managerial decisions and actions.[32] For instance, at Tom's of Maine, a manufacturer of all-natural personal care products, the corporate Statement of Beliefs guides managers as they plan, organize, lead, and control. One of the eight beliefs states, "We believe that different people bring different gifts and perspectives to the team and that a strong team is founded on a variety of gifts."[33] This statement expresses to managers the value of diversity—diversity of opinions, diversity of abilities—and serves as a guide for managing teams of people. Another belief states, "We believe in products that are safe, effective, and made of natural ingredients." Again, think how this statement might influence and guide company managers.

Another purpose is shaping employee behavior and communicating what the organization expects of its members. For example, employees at Herman Miller, which manufactures office, residential, and health care furniture, follow the company's values as they design, manufacture, and ship furniture around the world. What are those values? Here's what their Web site says, "Our people and the designers we work with are concerned with larger issues of humanity and equality and bettering the world we work in. What arrives on a truck is furniture. What went into that truck was

Exhibit 5–5   **Purposes of Shared Values**

THINKING CRITICALLY ABOUT ETHICS

In an effort to be (or at least appear to be) socially responsible, many organizations donate money to philanthropic and charitable causes. In addition, many organizations ask their employees to make individual donations to these causes. Suppose you're the manager of a work team, and you know that several of your employees can't afford to pledge money right now because of various personal and financial problems. You've also been told by your supervisor that the CEO has been known to check the list of individual contributors to see who is and is not "supporting these very important causes." What would you do? What ethical guidelines might you suggest for individual and organizational contributions to philanthropic and charitable causes?

an amalgam of what we believe in: innovation, design, operational excellence, smart application of technology, and social responsibility." As employees do their jobs, they know what behaviors are expected of them because of these shared values.[34]

Shared corporate values also influence marketing efforts. For example, we previously mentioned Avon's commitment to educating women about breast cancer. Its managers decided to support this program after the company asked women what their number-one health concern is and breast cancer was the answer. How does Avon's commitment to women's health influence its marketing efforts? The company's global sales force of more than 3.9 million independent representatives educates women about the disease by bringing brochures on their sales visits. The director of the Breast Cancer Awareness Crusade says, "All of the interaction that happens with an Avon rep on something as important as breast cancer should improve customer relations and make for easier sales." Avon has found a way to link its business to an important social concern and to improve its marketing efforts all at the same time.

Finally, shared values are a way to build team spirit in organizations.[35] When employees embrace the stated corporate values, they develop a deeper personal commitment to their work and feel obligated to take responsibility for their actions. Because the shared values influence the way work is done, employees become more enthusiastic about working together as a team to support the values they believe in. At companies such as Tom's of Maine, Avon, Herman Miller, and numerous others, employees know what is expected of them on the job. The shared corporate values not only guide the way they work, but serve to unite them in a common quest. (Check out Passport Scenario 1 on p. 127.)

The Bottom Line on Shared Corporate Values

An organization's managers are responsible for establishing and upholding the corporate values they want employees to embrace. A 2002 survey on corporate values by the American Management Association showed that managers at a number of organizations have made a commitment to a set of core values and are holding their employees accountable for them.[36] Almost 86 percent of the respondents said the corporate values of their organization were specifically written or stated. A listing of these stated values is provided in Exhibit 5–6.

However, this survey also showed that these organizations didn't just state their values—64 percent said that their corporate values were linked to performance evaluations and compensation. In these organizations, the shared values served as a powerful incentive to employee behavior—good or bad, ethical or unethical. Just how do shared values affect behavior? Let's look at two different organizations, both transformed by circumstances, whose shared values affected the way employees behaved.

Exhibit 5–6

Survey of Stated Values of Organizations

Core Value	Percentage of Respondents That Stated Core Value
Customer satisfaction	77%
Ethics/integrity	76%
Accountability	61%
Respect for others	59%
Open communication	51%
Profitability	49%
Teamwork	47%
Innovation/change	47%
Continuous learning	43%
Positive work environment	42%
Diversity	41%
Community service	38%
Trust	37%
Social responsibility	33%
Security/safety	33%
Empowerment	32%
Employee job satisfaction	31%
Have fun	24%

Source: "AMA Corporate Values Survey," (www.amanet.org), October 30, 2002.

The first is Empire Blue Cross and Blue Shield, which had offices in New York's World Trade Center. The company's mid-level managers took the initiative to act independently and get the business up and running as soon as possible after the initial shock of the 9/11 attacks had passed. One communications manager who fled the collapsing building worked around the clock in temporary offices to get phone lines and voice mail working again. Other managers formed informal work teams at various locations to keep departments operating. CEO Michael Stocker said that his past efforts to instill values of risk-taking and entrepreneurial thinking "where you can make mistakes and don't always have to ask someone above you if you can try something" definitely contributed to employees' willingness to step in and do whatever it took.[37] The company's values as reinforced by the stories, rituals, and material awards (including the "giraffe award," which was given to employees willing to "stick their necks out") emphasized to employees what was important and influenced how employees responded in this crisis.

Contrast Empire's shared "get-it-done" values with Enron, which also emphasized risk-taking and entrepreneurial thinking. However, Enron carried these values to the extreme. It "valued personal ambition over teamwork, youth over wisdom, and earnings growth at any cost."[38] One former employee described corporate values in which family time and quality of life were seen as weaknesses. "Anybody who did not embrace the 'elbows-out' culture didn't get it. They were 'damaged goods' and 'shipwrecks,' likely to be fired by their bosses at blistering annual job reviews known as rank-and-yank sessions."[39] Top-level executives embraced the values of taking risks, making deals, and pushing the limits. Employees behaved according to the expectations and beliefs embodied in Enron's shared values. They focused exclusively on the ends and didn't worry about means.

As these examples show, an organization's values are reflected in the decisions and actions of employees. In the next section, we're going to look at managerial ethics and the things that influence whether employees choose to behave ethically or unethically.

Learning Review

- Discuss what purposes shared values serve.
- Describe the relationship of values-based management to ethics.

MANAGERIAL ETHICS

When you see top managers like those formerly at Enron, Worldcom, Tyco International, and Imclone being greedy and using financial manipulations, lying, and group pressure to deceive others, you may conclude that corporate America has no ethics. Although that is by no means true, what *is* true is that managers—at all levels, in all areas, in all sizes, and in all kinds of organizations—will face ethical issues and dilemmas. (■□■■■ Go to the Web and check out Q & A 5.6.) For instance, is it ethical for a sales representative to offer a bribe to a purchasing agent as an inducement to buy? Would it make any difference if the bribe came out of the sales rep's commission? Is it ethical for someone to use a company car for private use? How about using company e-mail for personal correspondence or using the company phone to make personal phone calls? How would you handle these situations? As managers plan, organize, lead, and control, they must consider ethical dimensions.

What do we mean by ethics? The term **ethics** refers to rules and principles that define right and wrong conduct.[40] In this section, we examine the ethical dimensions of managerial decisions. Many decisions that managers make require them to consider who may be affected—in terms of the result as well as the process.[41] To better understand the complicated issues involved in managerial ethics, we'll look at four different views of ethics and the factors that influence a person's ethics, and offer some suggestions for what organizations can do to improve the ethical behavior of employees.

Four Views of Ethics

The four perspectives on ethics include the utilitarian view, rights view, theory of justice view, and integrative social contracts theory.[42] The **utilitarian view of ethics** says that ethical decisions are made solely on the basis of their outcomes or consequences. Utilitarian theory uses a quantitative method for making ethical decisions by looking at how to provide the greatest good for the greatest number. Following the utilitarian view, a manager might conclude that laying off 20 percent of the workforce in her plant is justified because it will increase the plant's profitability, improve job security for the remaining 80 percent, and be in the best interests of stockholders. Utilitarianism encourages efficiency and productivity and is consistent with the goal of profit maximization. However, it can result in biased allocations of resources, especially when some of those affected by the decision lack representation or a voice in the decision. Utilitarianism can also result in the rights of some stakeholders being ignored.

Another ethical perspective is the **rights view of ethics**, which is concerned with respecting and protecting individual liberties and privileges such as the rights to privacy, freedom of conscience, free speech, life and safety, and due process. This would include, for example, protecting the free speech rights of employees who report legal violations by their employers. The positive side of the rights perspective is that it protects individuals' basic rights, but the drawback is that it can hinder productivity and efficiency by creating a work climate that's more concerned with protecting individuals' rights than with getting the job done.

The next view is the **theory of justice view of ethics**. Under this approach, managers impose and enforce rules fairly and impartially and do so by following all legal rules and regulations. A manager using the theory of justice perspective would decide to provide the same rate of pay to individuals who are similar in their levels of skills, performance, or responsibility and not base that decision on arbitrary differences such as gender, personality, race, or personal favorites. Using standards of justice also has pluses and minuses. It protects the interests of those stakeholders who may be underrepresented or lack power, but it can encourage a sense of entitlement that might make employees reduce risk-taking, innovation, and productivity.

The final ethics perspective, the **integrative social contracts theory**, proposes that ethical decisions be based on existing ethical norms in industries and communities in order to determine what constitutes right and wrong. This view of ethics is based on the inte-

⁕⁕• ethics
Rules and principles that define right and wrong conduct.

⁕⁕• utilitarian view of ethics
A view of ethics that says that ethical decisions are made solely on the basis of their outcomes or consequences.

⁕⁕• rights view of ethics
A view of ethics that's concerned with respecting and protecting individual liberties and privileges.

⁕⁕• theory of justice view of ethics
A view of ethics in which managers impose and enforce rules fairly and impartially and do so by following all legal rules and regulations.

⁕⁕• integrative social contracts theory
A view of ethics that proposes that ethical decisions be based on existing ethical norms in industries and communities in order to determine what constitutes right and wrong.

When management at the New York Times discovered that one of its reporters, Jayson Blair, had falsified details large and small in dozens of stories he filed over a period of years, it took swift action to both make amends for the errors and restore the newspaper's long-standing reputation for responsible reporting. Blair resigned, and the Times promptly published an unusually long and detailed story about the case to which no less than 10 writers and editors contributed. It also ran corrections to Blair's flawed reports over the years that covered several pages. Apologizing to its readers, the Times itself admitted that Blair's "widespread fabrication and plagiarism represent a profound betrayal of trust and a low point in the 152-year history of the newspaper."

gration of two "contracts": the general social contract that allows businesses to operate and defines the acceptable ground rules, and a more specific contract among members of a community that addresses acceptable ways of behaving. For instance, in deciding what wage to pay workers in a new factory in Ciudad Juarez, Mexico, managers following the integrative social contracts theory would base the decision on existing wage levels in the community. Although this theory focuses on looking at existing practices, the problem is that some of these practices may be unethical.[43]

Which approach to ethics do most businesspeople follow? Not surprisingly, most follow the utilitarian approach.[44] Why? It's consistent with such business goals as efficiency, productivity, and profits. However, that perspective needs to change because of the changing world facing managers. Trends toward individual rights, social justice, and community standards mean that managers need ethical standards based on nonutilitarian criteria. This is an obvious challenge for managers because making decisions on such criteria involves far more ambiguities than using utilitarian criteria such as efficiency and profits. The result, of course, is that managers increasingly find themselves struggling with the question of the right thing to do.

Factors That Affect Employee Ethics

Whether a person acts ethically or unethically when faced with an ethical dilemma is the result of complex interactions between the stage of moral development and several moderating variables including individual characteristics, the organization's structural design, the organization's culture, and the intensity of the ethical issue. (See Exhibit 5–7.) People who lack a strong moral sense are much less likely to do the wrong things if they're constrained by rules, policies, job descriptions, or strong cultural norms that disapprove of such behaviors. Conversely, intensely moral individuals can be corrupted by an organizational structure and culture that permits or encourages unethical practices. Let's look more closely at the factors that influence whether individuals will behave ethically or unethically.

Stage of Moral Development Research confirms the existence of three levels of moral development, each composed of two stages.[45] At each successive stage, an individual's moral judgment becomes less and less dependent on outside influences. The three levels and six stages are described in Exhibit 5–8 on p. 112.

The first level is labeled *preconventional*. At this level, a person's choice between right or wrong is based on personal consequences involved, such as physical punishment, reward, or exchange of favors. Ethical reasoning at the *conventional* level

Exhibit 5–7

Factors That Affect Ethical and Unethical Behavior

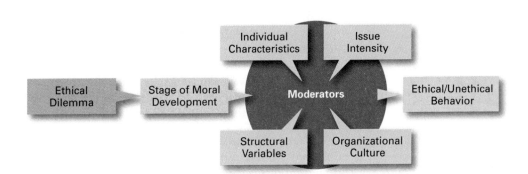

Exhibit 5–8

Stages of Moral Development

Source: Based on L. Kohlberg, "Moral Stages and Moralization: The Cognitive-Development Approach," in T. Lickona (ed.). *Moral Development and Behavior: Theory, Research, and Social Issues* (New York: Holt, Rinehart & Winston, 1976), pp. 34–35.

Level	Description of Stage
Principled	6. Following self-chosen ethical principles even if they violate the law
	5. Valuing rights of others and upholding absolute values and rights regardless of the majority's opinion
Conventional	4. Maintaining conventional order by fulfilling obligations to which you have agreed
	3. Living up to what is expected by people close to you
Preconventional	2. Following rules only when doing so is in your immediate interest
	1. Sticking to rules to avoid physical punishment

indicates that moral values reside in maintaining expected standards and living up to the expectations of others. At the *principled* level, individuals make a clear effort to define moral principles apart from the authority of the groups to which they belong or society in general.

We can draw some conclusions from research on the levels and stages of moral development.[46] First, people proceed through the six stages sequentially. They move up the moral ladder, stage by stage. Second, there is no guarantee of continued moral development. An individual's moral development can stop at any stage. Third, the majority of adults are at Stage 4. They are limited to obeying the rules and will be inclined to behave ethically, although for different reasons. For instance, a manager at Stage 3 is likely to make decisions that will receive peer approval; a manager at Stage 4 will try to be a "good corporate citizen" by making decisions that respect the organization's rules and procedures; and a Stage 5 manager is likely to challenge organizational practices that he or she believes to be wrong.

Individual Characteristics Every person joins an organization with a relatively entrenched set of **values**. Our values—developed at a young age from parents, teachers, friends, and others—represent basic convictions about what is right and wrong. (▨▨▨ Go to the Web and check out S.A.L. #9—What Do I Value?) Thus, managers in the same organization often possess very different personal values.[47] Although *values* and *stage of moral development* may seem similar, they're not. Values are broad and cover a wide range of issues; the stage of moral development specifically is a measure of independence from outside influences.

Two personality variables also have been found to influence an individual's actions according to his or her beliefs about what is right or wrong: ego strength and locus of control. **Ego strength** is a personality measure of the strength of a person's convictions. People who score high on ego strength are likely to resist impulses to act unethically and instead follow their convictions. That is, individuals high in ego strength are more likely to do what they think is right. We would expect employees with high ego strength to be more consistent in their moral judgments and moral actions than those with low ego strength.

Locus of control is a personality attribute that reflects the degree to which people believe they control their own fate. People with an *internal* locus of control believe that they control their own destinies; those with an *external* locus believe that what happens to them is due to luck or chance. How does this influence a person's decision to act ethically or unethically? Externals are less likely to take personal responsibility for the consequences of their behavior and are more likely to rely on external forces. Internals, on the other hand, are more likely to take responsibility for consequences and rely on their own internal standards of right and wrong to guide their behavior.[48] Also, employees with an internal locus of control are likely to be more consistent in their moral judgments and actions than those with an external locus of control.

Structural Variables An organization's structural design influences whether employees behave ethically. Some structures provide strong guidance, whereas others create ambiguity and uncertainty. Structural designs that minimize ambiguity and

values
Basic convictions about what is right and wrong.

ego strength
A personality measure of the strength of a person's convictions.

locus of control
A personality attribute that reflects the degree to which people believe they control their own fate.

Patrice Tanaka is the co-founder of a $5 million marketing agency in New York City that helps corporations develop programs to benefit women, such as Avon's Breast Cancer Crusade and Liz Claiborne's program to raise awareness of domestic violence. The culture of her firm is suggested by her motives in founding the company: "If you are fortunate to achieve success, you have an obligation to help other women and girls do the same. . . . We find it inexcusable for a person or a business to behave irresponsibly as a citizen of our community."

uncertainty through formal rules and regulations and those that continuously remind employees of what is ethical are more likely to encourage ethical behavior.

Other organizational mechanisms that influence ethics include performance appraisal systems and reward allocation procedures. Some organizational performance appraisal systems focus exclusively on outcomes. Others evaluate means as well as ends. When employees are evaluated only on outcomes, they may be pressured to do "whatever is necessary" to look good on the outcome variables, and not be concerned with how they got those results. Recent research suggests that "success may serve to excuse unethical behaviors."[49] Just think of the impact of this type of thinking. The danger is that if managers take a more lenient view of unethical behaviors for successful employees, other employees will model their behavior on what they see. Closely associated with the appraisal system is the way rewards are allocated. (▮▮▮▮ Go to the Web and check out S.A.L. #14—What Rewards Do I Value Most?) The more that rewards or punishment depend on specific goal outcomes, the more pressure there is on employees to do whatever they must to reach those goals and perhaps compromise their ethical standards. Although these structural factors are important influences on employees, they're not the most important. What *is* the most important?

Research continues to show that the behavior of managers is the single most important influence on an individual's decision to act ethically or unethically.[50] People look to see what those in authority are doing and use that as a benchmark for acceptable practices and expectations.

Organization's Culture The content and strength of an organization's culture also influence ethical behavior.[51] (▮▮▮▮ Go to the Web and check out S.A.L. #42—What's the Right Organizational Culture for Me?) An organizational culture most likely to encourage high ethical standards is one that's high in risk tolerance, control, and conflict tolerance. Employees in such a culture are encouraged to be aggressive and innovative, are aware that unethical practices will be discovered, and feel free to openly challenge expectations they consider to be unrealistic or personally undesirable.

As we discussed in Chapter 3, a strong culture will exert more influence on employees than a weak one. If the culture is strong and supports high ethical standards, it has a very powerful and positive influence on their decision to act ethically or

The Boeing Company's imaginative poster series reinforces the core values of integrity and ethical behavior for its employees.

unethically. (■□■■■ Go to the Web and check out Q & A 5.7.) The Boeing Company, for example, has a strong culture that has long stressed ethical dealings with customers, employees, the community, and stockholders. To reinforce the importance of ethical behaviors, the company developed a series of serious and thought-provoking posters designed to get employees to recognize that their individual decisions and actions are important to the way the organization is viewed. (See some examples on page 113.)

Issue Intensity A student who would never consider breaking into an instructor's office to steal an accounting exam doesn't think twice about asking a friend who took the same course from the same instructor last semester what questions were on the exam. Similarly, a manager might think nothing about taking home a few office supplies yet be highly concerned about the possible embezzlement of company funds.

These examples illustrate the final factor that affects a manager's ethical behavior: the intensity of the ethical issue itself.[52] As Exhibit 5–9 shows, six characteristics determine issue intensity: greatness of harm, consensus of wrong, probability of harm, immediacy of consequences, proximity to victim(s), and concentration of effect.[53] These six factors determine how important an ethical issue is to an individual. According to these guidelines, the larger the number of people harmed, the more agreement that the action is wrong, the greater the likelihood that the action will cause harm, the more immediately that the consequences of the action will be felt, the closer the person feels to the victim(s), and the more concentrated the effect of the action on the victim(s), the greater the issue intensity. When an ethical issue is important—that is, the more intense it is—the more we should expect employees to behave ethically.

Ethics in an International Context

Are ethical standards universal? Hardly! Social and cultural differences between countries are important factors that determine ethical and unethical behavior. (■□■■■ Go to the Web and check out Q & A 5.8.) For example, the manager of a Mexican firm bribes several high-ranking government officials in Mexico City to secure a profitable government contract. Such a practice would be seen as unethical, if not illegal, in the United States, but is standard business practice in Mexico.

Should Coca-Cola employees in Saudi Arabia adhere to U.S. ethical standards, or should they follow local standards of acceptable behavior? If Airbus (a European company) pays a "broker's fee" to a middleman to get a major contract with a Middle

Exhibit 5–9 **Determinants of Issue Intensity**

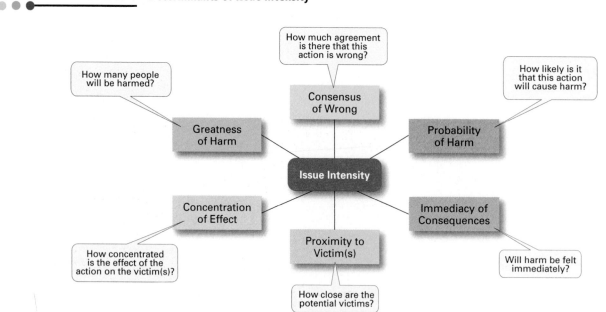

Eastern airline, should the Boeing Company be restricted from doing the same because such practices are considered improper in the United States?

In the case of payments to influence foreign officials or politicians, there is a law to guide U.S. managers. The Foreign Corrupt Practices Act makes it illegal for U.S. firms to knowingly corrupt a foreign official. However, even this law doesn't always reduce ethical dilemmas to black or white. In some Latin American countries, for example, government bureaucrats are paid ridiculously low salaries because custom dictates that they receive small payments from those they serve. Payoffs to these bureaucrats "grease the machinery" of government and ensure that things get done. The Foreign Corrupt Practices Act does not expressly prohibit small payoffs to foreign government employees whose duties are primarily administrative or clerical *when* such payoffs are an accepted part of doing business in that country.

It's important for individual managers working in foreign cultures to recognize the various social, cultural, and political and legal influences on what is appropriate and acceptable behavior.[54] And global organizations must clarify their ethical guidelines so that employees know what is expected of them while working in a foreign location, which adds another dimension to making ethical judgments.

At the World Economic Forum in 1999, the United Nations secretary general challenged world business leaders to "embrace and enact" The Global Compact, a document outlining nine principles for doing business globally in the areas of human rights, labor, and the environment.[55] These nine principles are listed in Exhibit 5–10. Global organizations have been asked to incorporate these guidelines into their business activities. The goal: a more sustainable and inclusive global economy. Today, hundreds of companies and international labor organizations from all regions of the world are engaged in The Global Compact. Organizations making this commitment are doing so because they believe that the world business community plays a significant role in improving economic and social conditions.

Improving Ethical Behavior

Managers can do a number of things if they're serious about reducing unethical behaviors in their organizations. They can seek to hire individuals with high ethical standards, establish codes of ethics and decision rules, lead by example, delineate job goals and performance appraisal mechanisms, provide ethics training, conduct social audits, and provide support to individuals facing ethical dilemmas. (■■■ Go to

Exhibit 5–10

The Global Compact

Human Rights

Principle 1: Support and respect the protection of international human rights within their sphere of influence.

Principle 2: Make sure business corporations are not complicit in human rights abuses.

Labor Standards

Principle 3: Freedom of association and the effective recognition of the right to collective bargaining.

Principle 4: The elimination of all forms of forced and compulsory labor.

Principle 5: The effective abolition of child labor.

Principle 6: The elimination of discrimination in respect of employment and occupation.

Environment

Principle 7: Support a precautionary approach to environmental challenges.

Principle 8: Undertake initiatives to promote greater environmental responsibility.

Principle 9: Encourage the development and diffusion of environmentally friendly technologies.

Source: The Global Compact Web site (www.unglobalcompact.org), August 14, 2000.

the Web and check out S.A.L. #19—How Do My Ethics Rate?) Taken individually, these actions will probably not have much impact. But when all or most of them are implemented as part of a comprehensive ethics program, they have the potential to significantly improve an organization's ethical climate. The key term here, however, is *potential.* There are no guarantees that a well-designed ethics program will lead to the desired outcome. Sometimes corporate ethics programs can be little more than public relations gestures, having minimal influence on managers and employees. For instance, retailer Sears has a long history of encouraging ethical business practices and, in fact, has a corporate Office of Ethics and Business Practices. However, the company's ethics programs didn't stop managers from illegally trying to collect payments from bankrupt charge account holders or from routinely deceiving automotive service center customers into thinking they needed unnecessary repairs. Even Enron's 2000 annual report outlined values that most would consider ethical—communication, respect, integrity, and excellence—yet the way top managers behaved didn't reflect those values at all.[56]

Employee Selection Given that individuals are at different stages of moral development and possess different personal value systems and personalities, the selection process—interviews, tests, background checks, and so forth—could be used to eliminate ethically questionable applicants. The selection process should be viewed as an opportunity to learn about an individual's level of moral development, personal values, ego strength, and locus of control.[57] But it isn't easy! Even under the best circumstances, individuals with questionable standards of right and wrong will be hired. However, this shouldn't be a problem if other ethics controls are in place.

Codes of Ethics and Decision Rules George David, CEO and chairman of Hartford, Connecticut-based United Technologies Corporation, believes in the power of a code of ethics. The company has a detailed, 16-page code of ethics, including 35 standards of conduct. Employees know the behavioral expectations, especially when it comes to ethics.[58] However, that's not the way it is in all organizations.

● ● ● **code of ethics**
A formal statement of an organization's primary values and the ethical rules it expects its employees to follow.

Ambiguity about what is and is not ethical can be a problem for employees. A **code of ethics**, a formal statement of an organization's primary values and the ethical rules it expects its employees to follow, is a popular choice for reducing that ambiguity. Nearly 95 percent of *Fortune* 500 companies now have codes of conduct. And, codes of ethics are becoming more popular globally. A survey of business organizations in 22 countries found that 78 percent have formally stated ethics standards and codes of ethics.[59]

What should a code of ethics look like? It's been suggested that codes should be specific enough to show employees the spirit in which they're supposed to do things yet loose enough to allow for freedom of judgment.[60] A survey of companies' codes of ethics found their content tended to fall into three categories: (1) Be a dependable organizational citizen; (2) don't do anything unlawful or improper that will harm the organization; and (3) be good to customers.[61] Exhibit 5–11 lists the variables included in each of these clusters.

How well do codes of ethics work? The reality is they're not always effective in encouraging ethical behavior in organizations. A survey of employees in U.S. businesses with ethics codes found that 75 percent of those surveyed had observed ethical or legal violations in the previous 12 months, including such things as deceptive sales practices, unsafe working conditions, sexual harassment, conflicts of interest, and environmental violations.[62] Does this mean that codes of ethics shouldn't be developed? No. But there are some suggestions managers can follow. First, ethics codes should be developed and then communicated regularly to employees. Second, all levels of management should continually reaffirm the importance of the ethics code and the organization's commitment to it, and consistently discipline those who break it. When managers consider the code of ethics to be important, regularly affirm its content, and publicly reprimand rule breakers, ethics codes can supply a strong founda-

Exhibit 5–11

Clusters of Variables Found in 83 Corporate Codes of Business Ethics

Cluster 1. Be a Dependable Organizational Citizen

1. Comply with safety, health, and security regulations.
2. Demonstrate courtesy, respect, honesty, and fairness.
3. Illegal drugs and alcohol at work are prohibited.
4. Manage personal finances well.
5. Exhibit good attendance and punctuality.
6. Follow directives of supervisors.
7. Do not use abusive language.
8. Dress in business attire.
9. Firearms at work are prohibited.

Cluster 2. Do Not Do Anything Unlawful or Improper That Will Harm the Organization

1. Conduct business in compliance with all laws.
2. Payments for unlawful purposes are prohibited.
3. Bribes are prohibited.
4. Avoid outside activities that impair duties.
5. Maintain confidentiality of records.
6. Comply with all antitrust and trade regulations.
7. Comply with all accounting rules and controls.
8. Do not use company property for personal benefit.
9. Employees are personally accountable for company funds.
10. Do not propagate false or misleading information.
11. Make decisions without regard for personal gain.

Cluster 3. Be Good to Customers

1. Convey true claims in product advertisements.
2. Perform assigned duties to the best of your ability.
3. Provide products and services of the highest quality.

Source: F.R. David, "An Empirical Study of Codes of Business Ethics: A Strategic Perspective," paper presented at the 48th Annual Academy of Management Conference, Anaheim, California, August 1988.

tion for an effective corporate ethics program.[63] Finally, an organization's code of ethics might be designed around the 12 questions listed in Exhibit 5–12 (on p. 118) that can be used as decision rules in guiding managers as they handle ethical dilemmas in decision making.[64]

Top Management's Leadership Doing business ethically requires a commitment from top managers. Why? Because it's the top managers who uphold the shared values and set the cultural tone. (▪▪□▪▪ Go to the Web and check out PRISM #4—Developing Trust.) They're role models in terms of both words and actions, though what they *do* is far more important than what they *say*. If top managers, for example, take company resources for their personal use, inflate their expense accounts, or give favored treatment to friends, they imply that such behavior is acceptable for all employees.

Top managers also set the cultural tone by their reward and punishment practices. The choices of whom and what are rewarded with pay increases and promotions send a strong signal to employees. As we said earlier, when an employee is rewarded for achieving impressive results in an ethically questionable manner, it indicates to others that those ways are acceptable. When wrongdoing is uncovered, managers who want to emphasize their commitment to doing business ethically must punish the offender and publicize the fact by making the outcome visible to everyone in the organization. This practice sends a message that doing wrong has a price and it's not in employees' best interests to act unethically!

Exhibit 5–12

12 Questions for Examining the Ethics of a Business Decision

1. Have you defined the problem accurately?
2. How would you define the problem if you stood on the other side of the fence?
3. How did this situation occur in the first place?
4. To whom and to what do you give your loyalty as a person and as a member of the corporation?
5. What is your intention in making this decision?
6. How does this intention compare with the probable results?
7. Whom could your decision or action injure?
8. Can you discuss the problem with the affected parties before you make the decision?
9. Are you confident that your position will be as valid over a long period of time as it seems now?
10. Could you disclose without qualm your decision or action to your boss, your chief executive officer, the board of directors, your family, society as a whole?
11. What is the symbolic potential of your action if understood? If misunderstood?
12. Under what conditions would you allow exceptions to your stand?

Source: Reprinted by permission of *Harvard Business Review.* An exhibit from "Ethics without the Sermon" by L.L. Nash. November-December 1981, p. 81. Copyright © 1981 by the President and Fellows of Harvard College All rights reserved.

Job Goals and Performance Appraisal Employees in three Internal Revenue Service offices were found in the bathrooms flushing tax returns and other related documents down the toilets. When questioned, they openly admitted doing it, but offered an interesting explanation for their behavior. The employees' supervisors had been putting increasing pressure on them to complete more work in less time. If the piles of tax returns weren't processed and moved off their desks more quickly, they were told that their performance reviews and salary raises would be adversely affected. Frustrated by few resources and an overworked computer system, the employees decided to "flush away" the paperwork on their desks. Although these employees knew what they did was wrong, it illustrates the impact of unrealistic goals and performance appraisals on behavior.[65] Under the stress of unrealistic goals, otherwise ethical employees may feel they have no choice but to do whatever is necessary to meet those goals.

Whether an individual achieves his or her goals is usually a key issue in performance appraisal. Keep in mind, though, that if performance appraisals focus only on economic goals, ends will begin to justify means. If an organization wants its employees to uphold high ethical standards, the performance appraisal process should include this dimension. For example, a manager's annual review of employees might include a point-by-point evaluation of how their decisions measured up against the company's code of ethics as well as how well goals were met.

Ethics Training More and more organizations are setting up seminars, workshops, and similar ethics training programs to encourage ethical behavior. (▮◼▮▮ Go to the Web and check out Q & A 5.9.) Ethics researchers estimate that over 40 percent of U.S. companies provide some form of ethics training.[66] But these training programs aren't without controversy. The primary debate is whether you can actually teach ethics. Critics, for instance, stress that the effort is pointless because people establish their individual value systems when they're young. Proponents, however, note that several studies have found that values can be learned after early childhood. In addition, they cite evidence that shows that teaching ethical problem solving can make an actual difference in ethical behaviors;[67] that training has increased individuals' level of moral development;[68] and that, if it does nothing else, ethics training increases awareness of ethical issues in business.[69]

How do you teach ethics? Let's look at how it's done at the Boeing Company.[70] Its training program, called "Questions of Integrity: The Ethics Challenge," consists of 54 different ethics situations and four possible ways of dealing with each. In work group discussions, supervisors discuss each situation, then ask their employees to choose the best outcome by holding up cards marked A, B, C, or D. For instance, one of the situations asks employees, "When walking through the halls, you constantly hear one of your male co-workers call any female employee 'babe.' What do you do?" Possible answers include:

a. "Speak to your co-worker in a nonconfrontational manner about the sexist comment."

b. "Tell his manager that the employee should be fired for sexual harassment."

c. "Nothing. Calling a woman 'babe' is a form of endearment."

d. "Tell your supervisor that you feel this is demeaning in the workplace."

The "ethically correct" answers are A and D. Other examples of the realistic ethical scenarios used in the training include selling Amway products at work, wearing a pro-choice T-shirt, and staying at a supplier's beach house. Boeing's ethics training program was designed to make ethics more relevant to employees' everyday workplace behaviors.

Ethics training sessions can provide a number of benefits.[71] They reinforce the organization's standards of conduct. They're a reminder that top managers want employees to consider ethical issues in making decisions. They clarify what practices are and are not acceptable. Finally, when employees discuss common concerns among themselves, they get reassurance they're not alone in facing ethical dilemmas, which can strengthen their confidence when they have to take unpopular but ethically correct stances.

Independent Social Audits An important element of deterring unethical behavior is the fear of being caught. Independent social audits, which evaluate decisions and management practices in terms of the organization's code of ethics, increase the likelihood of detection. These audits can be routine evaluations, performed on a regular basis just as financial audits are, or they can occur randomly with no prior announcement. An effective ethical program should probably have both. To maintain integrity, auditors should be responsible to the company's board of directors and present their findings directly to the board. This arrangement gives the auditors clout and lessens the opportunity for retaliation from those being audited.

Formal Protective Mechanisms Our last recommendation is for organizations to provide formal mechanisms to protect employees who face ethical dilemmas so that they can do what's right without fear of reprimand. (▮▯▮▮ Go to the Web and check out Q & A 5.10.) An organization might designate ethical counselors. When employees face an ethics dilemma, they could go to these advisers for guidance. As a sounding board, the ethical counselor would let employees openly verbalize their ethical problem, the problem's cause, and their own options. After the options are clear, the adviser might take on the role of advocate who champions the ethically "right" alternatives. Other organizations have appointed ethics officers who design, direct, and modify the organization's ethics programs as needed. The Ethics Officer Association reported that it gained more than 100 new members in 2002, as a result of the publicity on the corporate scandals, bringing its total membership to almost 900 major companies.[72] In addition, an organization might create a special appeals process that employees could use to raise ethical issues.[73]

● ● ● ● Learning Review

- Contrast the four views of ethics.
- Discuss the factors that affect ethical and unethical behavior.
- Discuss the six determinants of issue intensity.
- Explain what codes of ethics are and how their effectiveness can be improved.
- Describe the important roles managers play in encouraging ethical behavior.

SOCIAL RESPONSIBILITY AND ETHICS IN TODAY'S WORLD

News headlines seem to abound with stories of irresponsible and ethically questionable practices at large and well-known companies: Pepsico acknowledged its role in putting Coca-Cola under inquiry by the European Commission because it believed Coke was abusing its dominant position in the European market; Dutch company Royal Ahold, the world's third-largest food retailer, admitted to overstating earnings; Prudential Insurance is accused of sales fraud and forgery; and Bausch and Lomb is accused of using deceptive accounting principles and practices in order to meet strict numbers-oriented performance goals. Then, of course, there's the list of high-profile U.S. companies embroiled in financial controversies including, among others, Adelphia Communications, Arthur Andersen, Dynegy, Enron, ImClone, Qwest, and WorldCom. What's going on? Has business forgotten about ethics and social responsibility?

A survey of employees shows that workplace pressures are leading more and more of them to consider acting unethically or illegally on the job.[74] The results indicated that 56 percent of those surveyed felt pressure to act unethically or illegally on the job, with 48 percent saying they have actually committed such activities. Here's a sampling of these types of unethical business activities reported:

- Cut corners on quality control (16 percent)
- Covered up incidents (14 percent)
- Abused or lied about sick days (11 percent)
- Lied to or deceived customers (9 percent)
- Put inappropriate pressure on others (7 percent)
- Falsified numbers or reports (6 percent)
- Lied to or deceived superiors on serious matters (5 percent)
- Withheld important information (5 percent)
- Misused or stole company property (4 percent)
- Took credit for someone's work or idea (4 percent)
- Engaged in copyright or software infringement (3 percent)

Unfortunately, it's not just at work that we see these behaviors. Irresponsible and unethical behaviors are prevalent across our society. A 2002 study of high school students showed that the number who said they had cheated on an exam at least once in the last year jumped to 74 percent.[75] College students, although somewhat better, exhibited similar behavior. A survey conducted by Students in Free Enterprise (SIFE) reported that some 59 percent admitted cheating on a test. And although that statistic is troubling by itself, the more alarming statistic was that only 19 percent said they would report a classmate who cheated.[76] What does this say about what managers and organizations may have to deal with in the future? It's not too far-fetched to say that organizations may have difficulty upholding high ethical standards when their future employees—these students—so readily accept unethical behavior.

What are the implications for managers? We think they must focus on three issues: ethical leadership, protection for those who report wrongdoing, and social impact management.

Ethical Leadership

Managers must provide ethical leadership. As we said earlier, the examples set by managers have a strong influence on employees' decisions to behave ethically or not. When managers cheat, lie, steal, manipulate, take advantage of situations or people, or treat others unfairly, what kind of signal are they sending to employees (or other stakeholders)? Probably not the one they want to send. What can managers do to provide ethical leadership?

The best thing managers can do is to be a *good role model*. Be ethical and honest. Unfortunately, in a national poll, only 54 percent of employees say they believe most corporate executives are honest and ethical.[77] Yet, employees crave honesty more than any other quality of leadership. Given a list of 28 attributes, one employee survey said honesty was by far the most important, followed by integrity/morals/ethics.[78] What does it mean to be honest? It means telling the truth. It means not hiding or manipulating information. Even bad news is more tolerable when people know they're being told the truth. Because workplace honesty can't be regulated or legislated, it has to be encouraged by leaders who themselves are honest and willing to admit their failures.[79]

Other things ethical leaders should do include *sharing their values*—that is, regularly communicating to employees what they believe about ethics and values; *stressing important shared values* through visible organizational culture manifestations such as symbols, stories, ceremonies, and slogans; and *using the reward system* to hold everyone accountable to the values, which means paying attention to which employee behaviors are rewarded and which are punished. (■□ Check out Passport Scenario 2 on page 127.)

Protecting Employees Who Raise Ethical Issues

What would you do if you saw other employees doing something illegal, immoral, or unethical? Although the high-profile corporate scandals in 2002 made all of us more aware of the devastation that corporate wrongdoing can cause, would you step forward? Many of us may be reluctant because of the perceived risks. However, it's important that managers assure employees who raise ethical concerns or issues to others inside or outside the organization that they will face no personal or career risks. These individuals, often called **whistleblowers**, can be a key part of any company's ethics program because they're willing to step forward and expose unethical behavior, no matter what the cost professionally or personally. For example, in August 2001, Sherron Watkins, a vice president at Enron, blew the whistle in a letter she wrote to chairman Ken Lay where she clearly outlined her concerns about the company's accounting practices. Her statement that "I am incredibly nervous that we will implode in a wave of accounting scandals" couldn't have been more prophetic.[80] Then in May 2002, Coleen Rowley blew the whistle on her employer, the FBI, when she accused her bosses of ignoring clear warnings of the 9/11 terrorist attacks. Because of their actions, Watkins, Rowley, and another whistleblower, Cynthia Cooper of WorldCom, were named *Time* magazine's persons of the year in 2002.[81] Despite the accolades given to these women, research has shown that most observers of wrongdoing don't report it.[82] That's the attitude managers have to address. What can they do to protect employees so they're willing to step up if they see bad things occurring?

Many companies have set up toll-free ethics hotlines and are encouraging whistleblowers to come forward. For instance, Dell has an ethics hotline that employees can call anonymously to report infractions that the company will then investigate. At Charlotte-based Duke Energy, employees can call a toll-free ethics hotline run by an outside organization and leave their names or remain anonymous.[83] In addition, managers need to encourage a culture where bad news can be heard and acted on before it's too late. Michael Josephson, founder of the Josephson Institute of Ethics (*www.josephsoninstitute.org*) says, "It is absolutely and unequivocally important to establish a culture where it is possible for employees to complain

●●● whistleblower
Individuals who raise ethical concerns or issues to others inside or outside the organization.

Sherron Watkins, formerly a vice president at the now defunct energy firm Enron Inc., risked her job and her career in order to draw attention to corporate wrongdoing in her organization. Though whistleblowers such as Watkins now have some legal protections, raising ethical issues from within is still a difficult task.

Becoming a Manager

♦ *Try to clarify your own personal views on how much social responsibility you think an organization should have*

♦ *Research different companies' codes of ethics.*

♦ *Think about the organizational values that will be important to you.*

♦ *When faced with an ethical dilemma, use the 12 questions in Exhibit 5-12 to help you make a decision.*

♦ *Work through the Thinking Critically about Ethics dilemmas found in each chapter.*

♦ ▮▮▯▯ *Go to the Web and complete S.A.L. #19—How Do My Ethics Rate? found in the Self-Assessment Library on R.O.L.L.S.*

and protest and to get heard."[84] Even if some whistleblowers do have a personal agenda, it's imperative that a whistleblower's information be taken seriously. Finally, there is some legal protection. Under the Sarbanes-Oxley Act of 2002, the law enacted to crack down on business wrongdoing in publicly traded companies, whistleblowers in the United States who report suspected corporate violations of laws now have broad protection from reprisals and retaliation. And there's a stiff penalty attached for a manager who retaliates—a 10-year jail sentence.[85]

Social Impact Management

● ● ● **social impact management**
The field of inquiry at the intersection of business practice and wider societal concerns that reflects and respects the complex interdependency between those two realities.

As stakeholders continue to pressure organizations to respond to societal issues, managers are expected to be responsible in the way they do business. Some experts have suggested that managers address their social responsibilities from the perspective of the impacts they have on society. This new line of thought called **social impact management** has been defined as the "field of inquiry at the intersection of business practice and wider societal concerns that reflects and respects the complex interdependency between those two realities."[86] This concept, developed by associates at the Aspen Institute, an international not-for-profit organization dedicated to informed dialogue and inquiry on issues of global concern, attempts to get businesspeople to understand the interdependency between business needs and wider societal concerns. Thus, as managers plan, organize, lead, and control, they would ask, "How does this work when we think about the social context within which business operates?"[87] At the least, if managers think about managing social impacts, just as they manage risk or strategy, they will be more aware of whether they're being responsible in their decisions and actions.

Doing the right thing—that is, managing responsibly and ethically—isn't always easy. However, because society's expectations of its institutions are regularly changing, managers must continually monitor those expectations. What is acceptable today may be a poor guide for the future.

● ● ● **Learning Review**

• Explain why ethical leadership is important.

• Discuss how managers and organizations can protect employees who raise ethical issues or concerns.

• Describe social impact management.

Managers **Respond** to a **Manager's** Dilemma

Amanda Ferguson
Sales Representative, Eli Lilly and Company, St. Louis, Missouri

Paul absolutely should continue Coco-Mat's socially responsible approach to doing business as he considers branching into other areas of furniture manufacturing. Coco-Mat's emphasis on values has earned praise and the company has enjoyed past performance success. Even though social responsibility hasn't been shown to increase profits, it doesn't seem to hurt companies because the public expects social responsibility. This focus on ethical values has definitely given Coco-Mat a favorable public image, which in turn can impact long-run profits and stockholder interests. In order to continue the company's commitment to ethical values, Paul should keep rewarding employee involvement through incentive programs and maintain hiring for diversity. In addition, he might consider employee ethics training. Above all, Paul should strive to strengthen the shared values that Coco-Mat has established.

Steve Literati
Vice President of Corporate Finance, Pearson PLC, Upper Saddle River, New Jersey

Paul is presumably both an owner and manager of his company. In most corporate settings, the manager has the responsibility to operate from the viewpoint of *a manager*, not *owner*. The company's shareholders—the real owners—pay managers to manage certain aspects of the company's operations. I've always viewed my primary objective as a manager to be maximizing shareholder value. In seeking to achieve this objective, I must work within the law and within my own ethical and religious values. Paul must search his own mind and soul for what to do. I admire his sense of ethics and social responsibility. If those values are more important to him than material success, he should pursue his existing current strategy. But he should also realize that profits are generally necessary to sustain a company's operations so some attention should be placed on expanding *profitably*.

Learning Summary

After reading and studying this chapter, you should be able to:

- Contrast the classical and socioeconomic views of social responsibility.

- Discuss the role that stakeholders play in the four stages of social responsibility.

- Differentiate between social obligation, social responsiveness, and social responsibility.

- Explain what research studies have shown about the relationship between an organization's social involvement and its economic performance.

- Explain what conclusion can be reached regarding social responsibility and economic performance.

- Describe how organizations can go green.

- Relate the approaches to being green to the concepts of social obligation, social responsiveness, and social responsibility.

- Discuss what purposes shared values serve.

- Describe the relationship of values-based management to ethics.

- Contrast the four views of ethics.

- Discuss the factors that affect ethical and unethical behavior.

- Discuss the six determinants of issue intensity.

- Explain what codes of ethics are and how their effectiveness can be improved.

- Describe the important roles managers play in encouraging ethical behavior.

- Explain why ethical leadership is important.

- Discuss how managers and organizations can protect employees who raise ethical issues or concerns.

- Describe social impact management.

Thinking About Management Issues

1. What does social responsibility mean to you personally? Do *you* think business organizations should be socially responsible? Explain.

2. Do you think values-based management is just a "do-gooder" ploy? Explain your answer.

3. Internet file-sharing programs (such as Kazaa) are popular among college students. These programs work by allowing nonorganizational users to access any local network where desired files are located. Because these types of file-sharing programs tend to clog bandwidth, local users' ability to access and use a local network is

reduced. What ethical and social responsibilities does a university have in this situation? To whom does it have a responsibility? What guidelines might you suggest for university decision makers?

4. What are some problems that could be associated with employee whistle-blowing for (a) the whistle-blower and (b) the organization?

5. Describe the characteristics and behaviors of someone you consider to be an ethical person. How could the types of decisions and actions this person engages in be encouraged in a workplace?

Working Together: Team-Based Exercise

You have obviously already faced many ethical dilemmas in your life—at school, in social settings, and even at work. Form groups of three to five individuals. Appoint a spokesperson to present your group's findings to the class. Each member of the group is to think of some unethical behaviors he or she has observed in organizations. The incidents could be something experienced as an employee, customer, client, or an action observed informally.

Once everyone has identified some examples of ethically questionable behaviors, the group should identify three important criteria that could be used to determine

whether a particular action is ethical. Think carefully about these criteria. They should differentiate between ethical and unethical behavior. Write your choices down. Use these criteria to assess the examples of unethical behavior described by group members.

When asked by your instructor, the spokesperson should be ready to describe several of the incidents of unethical behavior witnessed by group members, your criteria for differentiating between ethical and unethical behavior, and how you used these criteria for assessing these incidents.

Ethical Dilemma Exercise

Should all merchandise licensed by a not-for-profit environmental activist organization be "dark green" products? The Sierra Club lobbies for stricter antipollution regulations, pushes companies to use more ecofriendly products and techniques, and leads wilderness trips to promote appreciation for nature. In short, the Sierra Club goes well beyond bare-minimum legal requirements by pursuing an activist approach to preserving the earth for future generations.

To raise money for its mission, the not-for-profit recently began licensing its name for a broad array of products, including jackets, coffee, and toys. The organization receives royalties of 5 percent to 20 percent of each product's retail price, and the manufacturers must include environmental advocacy information with every item. "We can raise money even as we promote environmentally conscious consumption," explained the executive director.[88]

Imagine you're a manager reporting to Johanna O'Kelley, the director of licensing, who wants to put the club's name on environmentally friendly products. A manufacturer has just proposed a Sierra Club bed cover containing organically grown cotton and colored with vegetable dyes. However, the cover will have to contain some synthetic fibers to keep threads of the filler from working their way through the top. Review Exhibit 5-9 as you think about this dilemma and decide which of the following options you will choose—and why.

Option A: Ask the manufacturer to minimize synthetic content without sacrificing product quality and to clearly label all content.

Option B: Reject the proposal because the product will not be completely organic.

Option C: Release a statement to the media explaining the reason for mixing synthetic and organic content in this licensed product.

Case Application

Arthur Andersen

"Think straight. Talk straight." You probably can't find much more explicit language than this! Yet, at Arthur Andersen, these words, as found in its corporate motto, obviously weren't clear enough, because in June 2002, the company was found guilty of obstruction of justice for its role in shredding Enron-related documents. This conviction was the final blow to the once-proud firm. The guilty verdict forced Andersen to cease providing audit services for publicly owned companies—in essence, the death sentence for the organization. The sad part is that if the company had stood by the ethics championed by its founder, Arthur E. Andersen, it would be thriving today and setting an example for the profession's highest standards instead of being remembered for the lowest. The story of what went wrong at Andersen isn't just about some botched audits, although it was a part of some of the biggest ones ever. Instead, it was about a fundamental change in the company's culture and the values of an industry that once prided itself on protecting investors in publicly owned firms.

Andersen was founded in 1918 by accountant Arthur E. Andersen. The company grew rapidly during the 1920s and, in addition to providing accounting services to businesses, began conducting financial investigations, which was the start of its consulting practice. By 1979, management consulting accounted for about 20 percent of the firm's revenues. However, after the flood of corporate reorganizations during the 1980s, consulting fees rose to 40 percent of revenues. The accountants and the consultants began a power struggle that escalated as the rev-

Joe Berardino, former CEO of Arthur Andersen.

enues brought in by the consultants grew. Tensions between the two groups increased until 1989, when, in an attempt to cater to both, Andersen Worldwide was formed as an umbrella organization. However, even that new structural arrangement didn't resolve the power issue. The consultants were angry about having to share their fast-growing profits with the audit partners. (The consultancy's portion of revenues was up to 56 percent by the mid-1990s.) Yet, from the accountants' perspective, they felt they had subsidized the consulting business for a number of years, and often used audit services as a loss leader just to win a company's consulting business. As consulting grew in importance, the auditing practice was no longer the "soul of the firm." By 1997, the rift between the two groups was so strong that Andersen Consulting's partners voted to break away. After three years of acrimonious arbitration, the consultancy agreed to pay its former parent $1 billion (whose accounting partners had been expecting as much as $15 billion) for its independence. The consulting group changed its name to Accenture and, unlike its former parent, continues doing business today.

The split between the accountants and the consultants left Andersen—the accounting firm—smaller, weaker, and less profitable. With a significant source of revenues gone, the company focused on gaining them back—no matter what. The pursuit of revenues became the highest priority. Employees were strongly encouraged to drive up billings and were compensated on how much revenue they generated. This intense pressure to get clients and keep them happy may have compromised the "straight talk." There's no better example of "keeping the customer happy" than Enron Corporation, which was paying Andersen about $1 million a week in fees by the late 1990s. Enron was exactly the kind of client that Andersen was seeking—fast-growing and risk-taking, but an organization that paid its billings without question. However, an evaluation done in 2001 that assessed the riskiness of each of Andersen's 2,500 audit clients, not surprisingly placed Enron (and some 50 other clients) on the "maximum risk" list. Another 700 clients were considered "high risk." These precarious client risk levels, coupled with the push to generate revenues, was a formula for disaster. And on top of that, if a lower-level employee saw something questionable, there was widespread fear about speaking up.

In Andersen's defense, it wasn't the only accounting firm that had nurtured these cozy relationships between auditors, analysts, and clients. In 1998, Securities and Exchange Commission chairman Arthur Levitt Jr. said, "Accounting is being perverted. Auditors and analysts are participants in a game of nods and winks." He urged new rules to restrict the ability of the accounting firms to consult for the same companies they audited. The person who brokered a compromise with the SEC in 2000 was Joe Berardino, head of Andersen's U.S. audit practice. The compromise: A deal whereby accounting firms had to publicly disclose audit and consulting fees, but were not expressly prohibited from signing consulting contracts with audit clients. Berardino's handling of this situation helped him get elected as chief executive of Andersen in 2001, garnering 90 percent of the partners' votes. The former chief accountant of the SEC, Lynn Turner, said, "It was the dumbest reason to elect a person CEO. They should have elected someone who realized that their customer was the investing public and who could deliver high quality audits." Under Berardino's turn at the firm's helm, the long-held beliefs, known as the "four cornerstones, which were provide good client service, produce quality audits, manage staff well, and produce profits," became the "three pebbles and the boulder." And guess which was the boulder?

As Enron collapsed and as Andersen's role in the situation became clearer, Joe Berardino resigned in March 2002 as CEO of Andersen. "His emphasis on growth over audit quality, his reluctance to walk away from big clients with questionable accounting, and a stunning ignorance of potentially crippling issues all contributed to the firm's undoing." Even today, Berardino seems able to accept only limited responsibility for the catastrophe. Although he says that he bore his responsibility by stepping down, he also blames forces outside Andersen for the accounting scandals, points to stockholders who invested in companies without thoroughly examining their filings, and criticizes corporate board members who didn't do their due diligence and ask the right questions.

DISCUSSION QUESTIONS

1. What factors do you think contributed to how employees at Andersen behaved?

2. Identify the main stakeholders involved in this situation. What concerns might each stakeholder have had? Were any of the stakeholders' concerns in conflict with each other? Explain. What impact might this have had on employees?

3. Using Exhibit 5-9, analyze the intensity of the ethical dilemmas facing Andersen's employees as they were pressured to grow revenues. How might the other factors that affect ethical and unethical behavior be involved? (See Exhibit 5-7.)

4. Evaluate Joe Berardino's ethical leadership. What recommendations would you have made to him?

5. Is there anything that could have prevented the downfall of Andersen? If no, why not? If so, what?

Sources: Company information on Andersen and Accenture from Hoover's Online (*www.hoovers.com*), April 13, 2003; B.L. Toffler, *Final Accounting: Ambition, Greed, and the Downfall of Arthur Andersen* (New York: Broadway Books, 2003); J. Weber, "How Andersen Turned to the Dark Side," *BusinessWeek*, March 17, 2003, p. 26; J.A. Byrne, "Fall From Grace," *BusinessWeek*, August 12, 2002, pp. 50–56; I.J. Dugan, D. Berman, and A. Barrionuevo, "On Camera, People at Andersen, Enron Tell How Close They Were," *Wall Street Journal*, April 15, 2002, pp. A1+; M. McNamee, A. Borrus, and C. Palmeri, "Out of Control at Andersen," *BusinessWeek*, April 8, 2002, pp. 32–33; K. Brown and others, "Called to Account," *Wall Street Journal*, March 15, 2002, pp. A1+; A. Berenson and J.D. Glater, "A Tattered Anderson Fights for Its Future," *New York Times*, January 13, 2002, pp. BU1+; and J. Weber and others, "Arthur Andersen: How Bad Will It Get?" *BusinessWeek*, December 24, 2001, pp. 30–31.

Part 2
You're the Manager: Putting Ethics into Action

As a manager, you'll often face decisions involving ethical questions. How can you learn to identify an ethical dilemma, keep stakeholders in mind, think through the alternatives, and foresee the consequences of your decisions? This unique interactive feature, positioned at the end of Parts Two, Three, Four, Five, and Six, casts you in the role of a manager dealing with hypothetical yet realistic ethical issues. To begin, read the preview paragraph below. Then log on to www.prenhall.com/robbins and go to the R.O.L.L.S. Web site to consider the decisions you would make in the role of manager.

Managers at the nonprofit Sierra Club are dedicated to keeping the earth green. On the one hand, these managers are accountable to the 700,000 members who donate money to fund environmental protection and education programs. On the other hand, many other stakeholder groups are affected by management's decisions and actions, including government officials, legislators and regulators, businesses, students, and the community at large. In this hypothetical scenario, you'll play the role of a manager reporting to the Sierra Club's director of licensing. You face some difficult decisions about developing suitable guidelines for mutual funds bearing the Sierra Club name. The organization's credibility—and your own—are at stake. What will you do? Log onto **www.prenhall.com/robbins** to put ethics into action!

Passport

Scenario 1

Making sure every Java World customer has a pleasant and memorable experience every time he or she comes into any one of the company's 230 U.S. outlets isn't an easy task. Yet, it's a task that both Java World and Paula Seeger take seriously. As the company's vice president of customer relations, Paula is responsible for helping store managers keep customers satisfied. The company is fanatical about pleasing customers, and that strategy has paid off. Java World has seen its same-store revenues and profits steadily increase each year for the last five years.

Paula's first job with Java World was working part time at one of the seven Houston stores while attending business school at the University of Houston. It was during that time that she began to understand the importance of customer service. The store's regular customers sought her out because they knew she would get their order right, get it to them quick, and make it fun! Java World's employees were encouraged to create fun for the customers and to not just meet, but exceed their service expectations.

Although Paula had never thought about pursuing a full-time career with Java World, the company was expanding so rapidly that it always needed energetic and talented college graduates. After graduating from the University of Houston with a marketing degree, Paula joined Java World's corporate customer relations department. Now, six years later, she is facing what is probably her biggest management challenge—the opening of the company's first non-U.S. stores in Mexico City and Singapore. These stores will be expected to provide the same type of customer experience and the same high level of customer service as the U.S. stores. Each new employee needs to understand how important these strategies are to the company's future and the company's expectations about customer service. It's Paula's job to help the new store managers instill and reinforce these values. Next week, she leaves for Mexico City to meet with Sam Quinones, the store manager for the Mexico City facility and goes from there to Singapore to meet with Josephine Wee, the store manager for Singapore. What might work best in each location? Should the approach be the same? What cross-cultural problems might Sam and Josephine face in stressing the importance of Java World's beliefs about customer service to their new employees, and how could they best deal with them?

To answer these questions, you'll have to do some research on the countries. Go to www.prenhall.com/robbins, to the R.O.L.L.S. Web site, and click on Passport. When the map appears, click on the countries you need to research. You'll find background information on the country and general information about the country's economy, population, and workforce. In addition, you'll find specific information on the country's culture and the unique qualities associated with doing business there.

Scenario 2

Every time his office phone rings, Charles Mathidi's stomach clenches. As the plant manager for the South African subsidiary of Quality Scientific Instruments (QSI) AG, he's besieged weekly by customers calling to complain about late delivery. They want to know where their product orders are. QSI products are well known for their reliability and durability, which is important in the sometimes harsh conditions in which the company's instruments are used. And Charles's plant has upheld those high quality standards in the equipment it manufactures. Yet, that quality reputation can only go so far. When customers have been promised by the company's sales representatives that their desired delivery date is "no problem," they expect to receive their equipment orders on or before that date.

Charles has tried unsuccessfully to discuss the issue of unrealistic delivery dates with the sales manager, Geoff Hall, who transferred six months ago to the South African subsidiary from a similar position in the company's United Kingdom office. Geoff had been extremely successful in building QSI's market share in the UK, and that's why the company's executive vice president for sales, Detlef Erhard, had recommended that Geoff move to Durban. After all, there was an enormous and growing market in South Africa and the entire African continent that QSI wanted to exploit. And so far, Geoff's team of sales reps had been quite successful at bringing in new business.

Yet, Charles felt that if they didn't start being more honest with customers about realistic order delivery dates that the issue would only get worse and might eventually have a negative impact on sales. Next week, Detlef was coming to Durban for his monthly visit from headquarters in Stuttgart. Charles had asked to meet with him and Geoff. What cross-cultural problems might Charles

encounter in discussing this situation with Geoff and Detlef? What ethical issues might he need to bring up? What stakeholders are impacted by QSI's actions? Can the three executives ethically meet the demands of all important stakeholders? How?

To answer these questions, you'll have to do some research on the countries. **Go to www.prenhall.com/robbins, the R.O.L.L.S. Web site, and click on Passport.** *When the map appears, click on the countries you need to research. You'll find background information on the country and general information about the country's economy, population, and workforce. In addition, you'll find specific information on the country's culture and the unique qualities associated with doing business there.*

Managing Entrepreneurial Ventures

The Context of Entrepreneurship

Russell Simmons is an entrepreneur.[1] He co-founded Def Jam Records because the emerging group of New York hip-hop artists needed a record company and the big record companies refused to take a chance on the unknown artists. Then, he co-founded the men's clothing line Phat Farm to market the increasingly popular hip-hop fashions. Today, Simmons' businesses have annual revenues of more than $260 million and Simmons' net worth is estimated to be over $200 million.

In this module on entrepreneurship, we're going to look at the activities that entrepreneurs like Russell Simmons engage in. We'll start by describing what entrepreneurship is and why it's important. Then, we'll discuss the entrepreneurial process, what entrepreneurs do, and social responsibility and ethical issues affecting entrepreneurs.

What Is Entrepreneurship?

Entrepreneurship is the process where an individual or group of individuals, through organized efforts, risk time and money in pursuit of opportunities to create value and grow through innovation, regardless of the resources they currently control. The three important themes in this definition are (1) the pursuit of opportunities, (2) innovation, and (3) growth. Entrepreneurs are pursuing opportunities to grow a business by changing, revolutionizing, transforming, or introducing new products or services. For example, Hong Liang Lu of UTStarcom knew that less than 10 percent of the Chinese population was served by a land-line phone system and that service was very poor.[2] He decided that wireless technology might be the answer. Now, his company's inexpensive cell phone service is a hit in China with over 12 million subscribers and growing fast. Looking to continue his success, Lu's company is preparing to move into other markets including India, Vietnam, and Panama.

Many people think that entrepreneurial ventures and small businesses are one and the same, but they're not. There are some key differences between the two. Entrepreneurs

create **entrepreneurial ventures**—organizations that are pursuing opportunities, are characterized by innovative practices, and have growth and profitability as their main goals. A **small business**, on the other hand is one that is independently owned, operated, and financed; has fewer than 100 employees; doesn't necessarily engage in any new or innovative practices; and has relatively little impact on its industry.[3] A small business isn't necessarily entrepreneurial because it's small. Being entrepreneurial means being innovative and seeking out new opportunities. Even though entrepreneurial ventures may start small, they pursue growth. Some new small firms may grow, but many remain small businesses, by choice or by default.

Why Is Entrepreneurship Important?

Entrepreneurship is, and continues to be, important to every industry sector in the United States and in most advanced countries.[4] Its importance in the United States can be shown in three areas: innovation, number of new start-ups, and job creation.

Innovation Innovating is a process of changing, experimenting, transforming, and revolutionizing, and a key aspect of entrepreneurial activity. The "creative destruction" process that characterizes innovation leads to technological changes and employment growth. Entrepreneurial firms act as "agents of change" by providing an essential source of new and unique ideas that might otherwise go untapped.[5] Statistics back this up. New small organizations generate 24 times more innovations per research and development dollar spent than do *Fortune* 500 organizations, and they account for over 95 percent of new and "radical" product developments.[6] And a report recently released by the U.S. Small Business Administration documented that patent applications by small business were more likely to be cited in subsequent patent applications than were patent applications of larger firms.[7] This is important because research has shown that highly cited patents represent economically and technologically significant inventions. This is further proof of how important small business is to innovation in America.

Number of New Start-Ups   Because all businesses—whether they fit the definition of entrepreneurial or not—were new start-ups at one point in time, the most convenient measure we have of the role that entrepreneurship plays in the number of new start-ups is to look at the number of new firms over a period of time. Data collected by the U.S. Small Business Administration show that the number of new start-ups increased after a decline in 2001, although the increase in 2002 was only 0.9 percent, which experts said was likely due to the slow economy during that year.[8] If we assume that some of these new businesses engage in innovative practices and pursue profitability and growth, then entrepreneurship has contributed to the overall creation of new firms.

Job Creation   We know that job creation is important to the overall long-term economic health of communities, regions, and nations. The latest figures show that small businesses provide approximately 75 percent of the net new jobs added to the U.S. economy.[9] Small organizations have been creating jobs at a fast pace even as many of the world's well-known and largest global corporations continued to downsize. These numbers reflect the importance of entrepreneurial firms as job creators.

But what about entrepreneurial activity outside the United States? What kind of impact has it had? A landmark annual assessment of global entrepreneurship called the Global Entrepreneurship Monitor (GEM) studied the impact of entrepreneurial activity on economic growth in various countries. The GEM 2002 report covered 37 countries that were divided into five global regions based on levels of entrepreneurial activity. (See Exhibit P2–1.)

What did the researchers find? The highest levels of entrepreneurial activity were in the developing Asian countries (Thailand, India, Korea, and China) and Latin American countries (Chile, Argentina, Brazil, and Mexico); and the lowest levels were in the developed Asian countries (Japan, Hong Kong, Chinese Taipei, and Singapore) and Eastern European counties (Russia, Croatia, Poland, Slovenia, and Hungary). The remaining regions had medium levels of entrepreneurial activity. The GEM report concludes that "Evidence continues to accumulate that

Exhibit P2–1

Level of Entrepreneurial Activity by Global Region

Highest Levels	*Developing Asia*	Thailand
		India
		Korea
		China
	Latin America	Chile
		Argentina
		Brazil
		Mexico
Medium Levels	*Former British Empire (Anglo)*	New Zealand
		United States
		Canada
		Australia
		South Africa
	European Union + 4	Iceland
		Ireland
		Norway
		Switzerland
		Israel
		Denmark
		Italy
		United Kingdom
		Germany
		Spain
		The Netherlands
		Finland
		Sweden
		France
		Belgium
Lowest Levels	*Eastern Europe*	Hungary
		Slovenia
		Poland
		Croatia
		Russia
	Developed Asia	Singapore
		Chinese Taipei
		Hong Kong
		Japan

Source: Based on GEM 2002 Executive Summary, p. 7.

the national level of entrepreneurial activity has a statistically significant association with subsequent levels of economic growth."[10] From a global perspective, therefore, we also can conclude that entrepreneurship plays an important role in a country's economic growth.

The Entrepreneurial Process

What's involved in the entrepreneurial process? There are four key steps that entrepreneurs must address as they start and manage their entrepreneurial ventures. The first is *exploring the entrepreneurial context*. The context includes the realities of today's economic, political/legal, social, and work environment. It's important to look at each of these aspects of the entrepreneurial context because they determine the "rules" of the game and what decisions and actions are likely to meet with success. Also, it's through exploring the context that entrepreneurs confront that next critically important step in the entrepreneurial process—*identifying opportunities and possible competitive advantages*. We know from our definition of entrepreneurship that the pursuit of opportunities is an important aspect. Once entrepreneurs have explored the entrepreneurial context and identified opportunities and possible competitive advantages, they must look at the issues involved with actually bringing their entrepreneurial venture to life. Therefore, the next step in the entrepreneurial process is *starting the venture*. Included in this phase are researching the feasibility of the venture, planning the venture, organizing the venture, and launching the venture. Finally, once the entrepreneurial venture is up and running, the last step in the entrepreneurial process is *managing the venture* which an entrepreneur does by managing processes, managing people, and managing growth. We'll explore each of these important steps in the entrepreneurial process in the entrepreneurship modules at the end of Parts 3, 4, 5, and 6.

What Do Entrepreneurs Do?

Describing what entrepreneurs do isn't an easy or simple task! No two entrepreneurs' work activities are exactly alike. In a general sense, entrepreneurs are creating something new, something different. They're searching for change, responding to it, and exploiting it.[11]

Initially, an entrepreneur is engaged in assessing the potential for the entrepreneurial venture and then dealing with start-up issues. In exploring the entrepreneurial context, entrepreneurs are gathering information, identifying potential opportunities, and pinpointing possible competitive advantage(s). Then, armed with this information, the entrepreneur begins researching the venture's feasibility—uncovering business ideas, looking at competitors, and exploring financing options. After looking at the potential of the proposed venture and assessing the likelihood of pursuing it successfully, the entrepreneur proceeds to planning the venture. This includes such activities as developing a viable organizational mission, exploring organizational culture issues, and creating a well-thought-out business plan. Once these planning issues have been resolved, the entrepreneur must look at organizing the venture, which involves choosing a legal form of business organization, addressing other legal issues such as patent

or copyright searches, and coming up with an appropriate organizational design for structuring how work is going to be done. After these start-up activities have been completed, the entrepreneur is ready to actually launch the venture. This involves setting goals and strategies, and establishing the technology-operations methods, marketing plans, information systems, financial-accounting systems, and cash flow management systems.

Once the entrepreneurial venture is up and running, the entrepreneur's attention switches to managing it. What's involved with actually managing the entrepreneurial venture? An important activity is managing the various processes that are part of every business: making decisions, establishing action plans, analyzing external and internal environments, measuring and evaluating performance, and making needed changes. Also, the entrepreneur must perform activities associated with managing people, including selecting and hiring, appraising and training, motivating, managing conflict, delegating tasks, and being an effective leader. Finally, the entrepreneur must manage the venture's growth, which includes such activities as developing and designing growth strategies, dealing with crises, exploring various avenues for financing growth, placing a value on the venture, and perhaps even eventually exiting the venture.

Social Responsibility and Ethics Issues Facing Entrepreneurs

As they launch and manage their ventures, entrepreneurs are faced with the often difficult issues of social responsibility and ethics. Just how important are these issues to entrepreneurs? An overwhelming majority of respondents (95 percent) in a study of small companies believed that developing a positive reputation and relationship in communities where they do business is important for achieving business goals.[12] However, despite the importance these individuals placed on corporate citizenship, more than half lacked formal programs for connecting with their communities. In fact, some 70 percent of the respondents admitted that they failed to consider community goals in their business plans. Yet, there are some entrepreneurs who take their social responsibilities seriously. For example, Josie Ippolito, president of La Canasta Mexican Food Products, Inc., in Phoenix, manages a factory that turns out one million tortillas daily and is located in the middle of an inner-city neighborhood.[13] The company is committed to the economic well-being of its neighborhood and employs about 100 workers from the local area. La Canasta is growing and rather than abandoning the neighborhood, Josie added an expansion to her current facility that will double capacity. She says, "Where are these people going to get jobs?"

Other entrepreneurs have pursued opportunities with products and services that protect the global environment. For example, Univenture Inc., of Columbus, Ohio, makes recyclable sleeves and packaging for disc media. Its products are better for the environment as compared to the traditional jewel boxes most compact discs are packaged in. Ross Youngs, president and CEO, says, "Our products won't break. If someone throws it away, it's because they don't want it. Hopefully they will end up in the recycle bin because our products are recyclable."[14]

Ethical considerations also play a role in decisions and actions of entrepreneurs. Entrepreneurs do need to be aware of the ethical consequences of what they do, especially in today's post-Enron climate where businesspeople are often viewed as unethical. The example they set, particularly if there are other employees, can be profoundly significant in influencing behavior.

If ethics are important, how do entrepreneurs stack up? Unfortunately, not too well! In a survey of employees from different sizes of businesses who were asked if they thought their organization was highly ethical, 20 percent of employees at companies with 99 or fewer employees disagreed. [15]

● ● ● Learning Summary

After reading and studying this material, you should be able to:

- Differentiate between entrepreneurial ventures and small businesses.

- Explain why entrepreneurship is important in the United States.

- Discuss the global importance of entrepreneurship.

- Describe the four key steps in the entrepreneurial process.

- Explain what entrepreneurs do.

- Discuss why social responsibility and ethics are important considerations for entrepreneurs.

Part THREE
Planning

●●● Learning Outline

Follow this Learning Outline as you read and study this chapter.

The Decision-Making Process
- Define decision and the decision-making process.
- Describe the eight steps in the decision-making process.

The Manager as Decision Maker
- Discuss the assumptions of rational decision making.
- Describe the concepts of bounded rationality, satisficing, and escalation of commitment.
- Explain what intuition is and how it affects decision making.
- Contrast programmed and nonprogrammed decisions.
- Contrast the three decision-making conditions.
- Explain maximax, maximin, and minimax decision choice approaches.
- Describe the four decision-making styles.
- Discuss the twelve decision-making biases managers may exhibit.
- Describe how managers can deal with the negative effects of decision errors and biases.
- Explain the managerial decision-making model.

Decision Making for Today's World
- Explain how managers can make effective decisions in today's world.
- List the six characteristics of an effective decision-making process.
- Describe the five habits of highly reliable organizations.

Chapter
6

Decision Making: The Essence of the Manager's Job

As the newly appointed first international president of a large real estate service company, Cecilia A. Mowatt (pictured here) is preparing for the challenges of managing the changes taking place within her organization.[1] The company Cecilia is managing was established in 1994 and is an international organization of real estate service providers in key markets in 20 countries. It operates in over 80 markets from Brussels to Glasgow to Munich to Moscow to St. Louis.

Through its structure of almost 3,000 professionals, the company works to meet the needs of its real estate clients anywhere in the world.

Cecilia brings a unique perspective to her management position. After obtaining her undergraduate degree at Standford University, she earned a combination law degree and M.B.A. from the University of California at Berkeley. She's fluent in three languages (Spanish, French, and English), which is an asset in communicating with company associates and customers worldwide. In addition, because Cecilia's parents immigrated to the United States (her mother from Colombia via Panama and her father from Jamaica), she has had significant exposure to people from other cultures. This experience allows her to easily "embrace people of different cultures." Through her previous work experiences as an attorney for the U.S. Securities and Exchange Commission, as administrator of a 200-property lease portfolio at Ameritech,

and as senior asset manager for McDonald's Corporation, Cecilia has gained a perspective on the business world *and* the challenges of managing real estate successfully and profitably. Cecilia describes her management style as very people oriented. "I'm quite the egalitarian when it comes to my fellow human beings. I hate to think that I'm making anybody uncomfortable." But, she also describes herself as very process and detail oriented.

During 2002, Cecilia's company developed new technologies to better benefit its clients and partners, including a revamped Web site. Now, as the company prepares to continue its global expansion in a business climate that is increasingly challenging, Cecilia needs to ensure that this decision to provide more information online to clients and to its partners continues to be effective.

Put yourself in Cecilia's position. How could she evaluate the effectiveness of the company's decision to revamp its Web site for clients and member firms? What decision criteria might she use for each?

What would *you* do **?**

L ike managers everywhere, Cecilia Mowatt needs to make good decisions as she manages. Making good decisions is something that every manager strives to do since the overall quality of managerial decisions has a major influence on organizational success or failure. In this chapter, we examine the concept of decision making and how managers make decisions.

THE DECISION-MAKING PROCESS

While watching a sports competition, have you ever felt that you could make better decisions than the coaches on the field or court? In the Helsinki suburb of Pukinmaki, the fans of PK-35, an amateur soccer team, get that chance![2] The coach doesn't make decisions about what to do on the field, but instead relies on 300 fans who text message their instructions via their cell phones. How's the shared decision making working? During the first season of the experiment, the team won first place in its division and was promoted to the next higher division. Although we're unlikely to see this type of wireless interactive decision making any time soon in organizations, it does illustrate that decisions, and maybe even how they're made, do play a role in performance.

Individuals at all levels and in all areas of organizations make **decisions**. That is, they make choices from two or more alternatives. For instance, top-level managers make decisions about their organization's goals, where to locate manufacturing facilities, what new markets to move into, and what products or services to offer. Middle- and lower-level managers make decisions about weekly or monthly production schedules, problems that arise, pay raises, and disciplining employees. But making decisions isn't something that only managers do. *All* organizational members make decisions that affect their jobs and the organization they work for. How do they make those decisions?

Although decision making is typically described as "choosing among alternatives," that view is too simplistic. Why? Because decision making is a comprehensive process, not just a simple act of choosing among alternatives.[3] Even for something as straightforward as deciding where to go for lunch, you do more than just choose burgers or pizza. Granted, you may not spend a lot of time contemplating a lunch decision, but you still go through the process when making that decision. What *does* the decision-making process involve?

Exhibit 6–1 illustrates the **decision-making process**, a set of eight steps that begins with identifying a problem and decision criteria and allocating weights to those criteria; then moves to developing, analyzing, and selecting an alternative that can resolve the problem; implements the alternative; and concludes with evaluating the decision's effectiveness. This process is as relevant to your personal decision about what movie to see on a Friday night as it is to a corporate action such as a decision to utilize technology in managing client relationships. The process also can be used to describe both individual and group decisions. Let's take a closer look at the process in order to understand what each step involves. We'll use an example—deciding what is the best franchise to purchase—to illustrate.

Step 1: Identifying a Problem

The decision-making process begins with the existence of a **problem** or, more specifically, a discrepancy between an existing and a desired state of affairs.[4] Take Joan, a laid-off sales manager, who's decided she wants to become an entrepreneur rather than return to a corporate job. For simplicity's sake, assume that Joan doesn't want to purchase an existing small business and instead has decided to look at possible franchises to purchase. Now we have a problem. There's a disparity between where Joan is now (unemployed) and where she wants to be (an entrepreneur and franchise owner). She has a decision to make about the best franchise to purchase.

• • • decision
A choice from two or more alternatives.

• • • decision-making process
A set of eight steps that include identifying a problem, selecting an alternative, and evaluating the decision's effectiveness.

• • • problem
A discrepancy between an existing and a desired state of affairs.

Exhibit 6–1

The Decision-Making Process

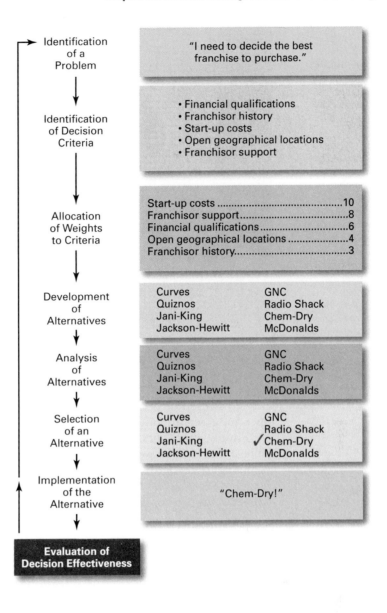

Identification of a Problem

"I need to decide the best franchise to purchase."

Identification of Decision Criteria

- Financial qualifications
- Franchisor history
- Start-up costs
- Open geographical locations
- Franchisor support

Allocation of Weights to Criteria

Start-up costs 10
Franchisor support 8
Financial qualifications 6
Open geographical locations 4
Franchisor history...3

Development of Alternatives

Curves	GNC
Quiznos	Radio Shack
Jani-King	Chem-Dry
Jackson-Hewitt	McDonalds

Analysis of Alternatives

Curves	GNC
Quiznos	Radio Shack
Jani-King	Chem-Dry
Jackson-Hewitt	McDonalds

Selection of an Alternative

Curves	GNC
Quiznos	Radio Shack
Jani-King	✓Chem-Dry
Jackson-Hewitt	McDonalds

Implementation of the Alternative

"Chem-Dry!"

Evaluation of Decision Effectiveness

One thing our example doesn't do is tell us how managers identify problems. In the real world, most problems don't come with neon signs flashing "problem." For example, if sales representatives complain to their manager that their computers are inadequate to do their jobs effectively, that might be a clear signal to the manager that something needs to be done, but few problems are that obvious. Managers also have to be careful not to confuse problems with the symptoms of the problem. Is a 5 percent drop in sales a problem? Or are declining sales merely a symptom of the real problem, such as unsatisfactory products, high prices, or poor advertising? Also, keep in mind that problem identification is subjective. What one manager considers a problem might not be considered a problem by another manager. Furthermore, a manager who mistakenly resolves the wrong problem perfectly is likely to perform just as poorly as the manager who doesn't identify the right problem and does nothing.

As you can see, effectively identifying problems isn't simple or trivial.[5] Managers can be better at it if they understand the three characteristics of problems: you have to be aware of them, be under pressure to act, and have the resources needed to take action.[6]

Managers become aware of a problem by seeing where things stand currently versus where they should be or where they want them to be. If they're not where they want them to be or if things aren't going as they should, then a discrepancy exists. But that's not enough to make it a problem.

For Russell Ziegler, pictured here with his family, the decision to delay a family move to Singapore, where he is to oversee his company's regional office for two years, hinged on criteria that included the progress of the SARS outbreak in Asia, its possible risk to the family's health, and the willingness of his employer, Macromedia, to allow him to wait a few weeks to see whether the disease would escalate. In the interim, Ziegler traveled to Singapore alone for a two-week trip during which he was impressed by the government's efforts to contain SARS. He returned home more confident and prepared to make the move with his wife and two children.

A discrepancy without pressure to act is a problem that can be postponed. To initiate the decision process, the problem must put pressure on the manager to act. Pressure might come from, for example, organizational policies, deadlines, financial crises, competitor actions, customer complaints, expectations from the boss, or an upcoming performance evaluation.

Finally, managers aren't likely to characterize something as a problem if they believe they don't have the authority, information, or resources necessary to act on it. If managers recognize a problem and are under pressure to act but feel they have inadequate resources, they usually describe the situation as one in which unrealistic expectations are being placed on them.

Step 2: Identifying Decision Criteria

● ● ● **decision criteria**
Criteria that define what's relevant in a decision.

Once a manager has identified a problem, the **decision criteria** important to resolving the problem must be identified. That is, managers must determine what's relevant in making a decision. Whether explicitly stated or not, every decision maker has criteria that guide his or her decisions. In our franchise purchase example, Joan has to assess what factors are relevant to her decision. These might include criteria such as start-up costs, financing availability, failure rate, growth potential, open geographical locations, franchisor history, financial qualifications, and franchisor support. After careful consideration, Joan decides that start-up costs, financial qualifications, franchisor history, open geographical locations, and franchisor support are the relevant criteria in her decision.

Step 3: Allocating Weights to the Criteria

If the criteria identified in Step 2 aren't equally important, the decision maker must weight the items in order to give them the correct priority in the decision. How do you weight criteria? (▮▯▮▮▮ Go to the Web and check out Q & A 6.1.) A simple approach is to give the most important criterion a weight of 10 and then assign weights to the rest against that standard. Thus, a criterion with a weight of 10 would be twice as important as one given a 5. Of course, you could use 100 or 1,000 or any number you select as the highest weight. The idea is to prioritize the criteria you identified in Step 2 by assigning a weight to each.

Exhibit 6–2 lists the criteria and weights that Joan developed for her franchise purchase decision. As you can see, start-up cost is the most important criterion in her decision, and franchisor history is the least important.

◼ **Q & A**
Whenever you see this green square, go to the R.O.L.L.S. Web site (*www.prenhall.com/robbins*) to the Q & A, your 24/7 educational assistant. These video clips and written material presented by your authors address questions that we have found students frequently ask.

Exhibit 6–2

Criteria and Weights for Franchise Decision

Criterion	Weight
Start-up costs	10
Franchisor support	8
Financial qualifications	6
Open geographical locations	4
Franchisor history	3

Step 4: Developing Alternatives

The fourth step requires the decision maker to list viable alternatives that could resolve the problem. (▮▯▮ Go to the Web and check out PRISM #12—Setting Goals and Solving Problems Creatively.) No attempt is made to evaluate the alternatives, only to list them. Using the Franchise 500® list developed by *Entrepreneur* magazine, Joan identified eight potential franchises as viable choices including Curves for Women, Quiznos Sandwiches, Jani-King Cleaning Service, Jackson-Hewitt Tax Service, GNC Vitamin and Nutritional Products Store, Radio Shack, Chem-Dry Carpet Cleaning, and McDonald's.

Step 5: Analyzing Alternatives

Once the alternatives have been identified, a decision maker must critically analyze each one. How? By appraising it against the criteria established in Steps 2 and 3. From this comparison, the strengths and weaknesses of each alternative become evident. Exhibit 6–3 shows the assessed values that Joan gave each of her eight alternatives after extensively studying the franchise opportunities and reading the latest information from business magazines.

Keep in mind that the ratings given the eight franchises are based on the personal assessment made by Joan. Some assessments can be done objectively. For instance, the start-up costs are the total investment required by the franchisor, and financial qualifications are the amounts set by the franchisor. However, the assessment of franchisor support is more of a personal judgment. The point is that most decisions by managers involve judgments—the criteria chosen in Step 2, the weights given to the criteria in Step 3, and the evaluation of alternatives in Step 5. This explains why two franchise buyers with the same amount of money may look at two totally different sets of alternatives or even rate the same alternatives differently.

Exhibit 6–3 represents only an assessment of the eight alternatives against the decision criteria. It doesn't reflect the weighting done in Step 3. If you multiply each alternative (Exhibit 6–3) by its weight (Exhibit 6–2), you get Exhibit 6–4 (see p. 138). The sum of these scores represents an evaluation of each alternative against both the established criteria and weights. There are times when a decision maker might not have to do this

Exhibit 6–3

Assessed Values of Franchise Opportunities Using Decision Criteria

	Start-Up Costs	Franchise Support	Financial Qualifications	Open Locations	Franchisor History
Franchise					
Curves for Women	10	3	10	8	5
Quiznos Sandwiches	8	7	7	8	7
Jani-King	8	5	7	10	10
Jackson-Hewitt Tax Service	8	7	7	8	7
GNC Vitamins and Nutritional Supplements	7	8	7	8	7
Radio Shack	8	3	6	10	8
Chem-Dry Carpet Cleaning	10	7	8	6	7
McDonald's	4	10	4	8	10

Exhibit 6–4

Franchise	Start-Up Costs	Franchise Support	Financial Qualifications	Open Locations	Franchisor History	Total
Curves for Women	100	24	60	32	15	231
Quiznos Sandwiches	80	56	42	32	21	231
Jani-King	80	40	42	40	30	232
Jackson-Hewitt Tax Service	80	56	42	32	21	231
GNC Vitamins and Nutritional Supplements	70	64	42	32	21	229
Radio Shack	80	24	36	40	24	204
Chem-Dry Carpet	100	56	48	24	21	249
McDonald's	40	80	24	32	30	206

step. If one choice had scored 10 on every criterion, you wouldn't need to consider the weights. Similarly, if the weights were all equal, you could evaluate each alternative merely by summing up the appropriate lines in Exhibit 6–3. In this instance, the score for Curves for Women would be 36 and Radio Shack's score would be 35.

Step 6: Selecting an Alternative

The sixth step is choosing the best alternative from among those considered. Once all the pertinent criteria in the decision have been weighted and viable alternatives analyzed, we merely choose the alternative that generated the highest total in Step 5. In our example (Exhibit 6–4), Joan would choose Chem-Dry Carpet Cleaning since it scored highest on the basis of the criteria identified, the weights given to the criteria, and her assessment of each franchise's ranking on the criteria. It's the "best" alternative and the one she should choose.

Step 7: Implementing the Alternative

Step 7 is concerned with putting the decision into action. This involves conveying the decision to those affected by it and getting their commitment to it. (■□■■■■ Go to the Web and check out Q & A 6.2.) If the people who must carry out a decision participate in the process, they're more likely to enthusiastically support the outcome than if you just tell them what to do. Parts Three through Five of this book discuss how decisions are implemented by effective planning, organizing, and leading. (■■□■■■ Check out Passport Scenario 1 on p. 226)

Step 8: Evaluating Decision Effectiveness

The last step in the decision-making process involves evaluating the outcome of the decision to see if the problem had been resolved. (■□■■■ Go to the Web and check out Q & A 6.3.) Did the alternative chosen in Step 6 and implemented in Step 7 accomplish the desired result? How to evaluate results is detailed in Part Six of this book, where we look at the control function.

What if this evaluation showed the problem still existed? The manager would need to assess what went wrong. Was the problem incorrectly defined? Were errors made in the evaluation of the various alternatives? Was the right alternative selected but poorly implemented? Answers to questions like these might send the manager back to one of the earlier steps. It might even require re-doing the whole decision process.

When Lloyd Graff, co-owner and president of Graff-Pinkert Inc., discovered that the company bookkeeper was systematically stealing from the firm, he and his brother Jim, vice president and treasurer, had several alternatives for getting the company's money back. (The bookkeeper was fired.) They lacked insurance covering employee theft, and the local police were not equipped to prosecute white-collar crime. They considered suing their bank and accountants for negligence in cashing sloppily forged checks, but they felt the case could drag on for years. They chose to work with the FBI, which could pursue the case because the fraudulent checks had crossed state lines, and under a plea bargain agreement they were able to recover a large proportion of the stolen funds.

● ● ● ●Learning Review

- Define decision and the decision-making process.
- Describe the eight steps in the decision-making process.

THE MANAGER AS DECISION MAKER

Everyone in an organization makes decisions, but decision making is particularly important in a manager's job. As Exhibit 6–5 shows, decision making is part of all four managerial functions. That's why managers—when they plan, organize, lead, and control—are frequently called *decision makers*. In fact, we can say that *decision making* is synonymous with *managing*.[7]

The fact that almost everything a manager does involves making decisions doesn't mean that decisions are always long, complex, or evident to an outside observer. Much of a manager's decision making is routine. Every day of the year you make a decision about when to eat dinner. It's no big deal. You've made the decision thousands of times before. It's a pretty simple decision and can usually be handled quickly. It's the type of decision you almost forget *is* a decision. Managers make dozens of these routine decisions every day. Keep in mind that even though a decision seems easy to make or has been faced by a manager a number of times before, it still is a decision.

We've made it pretty clear that managers make decisions, but we still don't know much about the manager as a decision maker and how decisions are actually made in organizations. How can we best describe the decision-making situation and the person who makes the decisions? We look at those issues in this section. We'll start by looking at three perspectives on how decisions are made.

Making Decisions: Rationality, Bounded Rationality, and Intuition

● ● ● **rational decision making**
Describes choices that are consistent and value-maximizing within specified constraints.

Managerial decision making is assumed to be **rational**. By that we mean that managers make consistent, value-maximizing choices within specified constraints.[8] What are the underlying assumptions of rationality, and how valid are those assumptions?

Exhibit 6–5

Decisions in the Management Functions

Planning	**Leading**
• What are the organization's long-term objectives?	• How do I handle employees who appear to be low in motivation?
• What strategies will best achieve those objectives?	• What is the most effective leadership style in a given situation?
• What should the organization's short-term objectives be?	• How will a specific change affect worker productivity?
• How difficult should individual goals be?	• When is the right time to stimulate conflict?
Organizing	**Controlling**
• How many employees should I have report directly to me?	• What activities in the organization need to be controlled?
• How much centralization should there be in the organization?	• How should those activities be controlled?
• How should jobs be designed?	• When is a performance deviation significant?
• When should the organization implement a different structure?	• What type of management information system should the organization have?

Exhibit 6–6

**Assumptions of
Rationality**

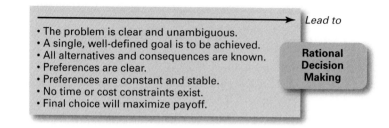

Lead to

- The problem is clear and unambiguous.
- A single, well-defined goal is to be achieved.
- All alternatives and consequences are known.
- Preferences are clear.
- Preferences are constant and stable.
- No time or cost constraints exist.
- Final choice will maximize payoff.

Rational Decision Making

Assumptions of Rationality A decision maker who was perfectly rational would be fully objective and logical. He or she would carefully define a problem and would have a clear and specific goal. Moreover, making decisions using rationality would consistently lead to selecting the alternative that maximizes the likelihood of achieving that goal. Exhibit 6–6 summarizes the assumptions of rationality.

The assumptions of rationality apply to any decision—personal or managerial. However, because we're concerned with managerial decision making, we need to add one further assumption. Rational managerial decision making assumes that decisions are made in the best interests of the organization. That is, the decision maker is assumed to be maximizing the organization's interests, not his or her own interests.

How realistic are these assumptions? Managerial decision making can be rational if the following conditions are met: The manager is faced with a simple problem in which the goals are clear and the alternatives limited, in which the time pressures are minimal and the cost of seeking out and evaluating alternatives is low, for which the organizational culture supports innovation and risk-taking, and in which the outcomes are relatively concrete and measurable.[9] But most decisions that managers face in the real world don't meet these requirements.[10] So how are most decisions in organizations usually made? The concept of bounded rationality can help answer that question.

Bounded Rationality Despite the limits to perfect rationality, managers are expected to be rational when making decisions.[11] Managers know that "good" decision makers are supposed to do certain things: identify problems, consider alternatives, gather information, and act decisively but prudently. Managers are expected to exhibit the correct decision-making behaviors. By doing so, they signal to others that they're competent and that their decisions are the result of intelligent deliberation. However, certain aspects of the decision-making process aren't realistic with respect to how managers actually make decisions. Managers tend to operate under assumptions of **bounded rationality**; that is, they make decisions rationally, but are limited (bounded) by their ability to process information.[12] Because they can't possibly analyze all information on all alternatives, managers **satisfice**, rather than maximize. That is, they accept solutions that are "good enough." (■□■■ Go to the Web and check out Q & A 6.4.) They're being rational within the limits (bounds) of their information-processing ability. Let's look at an example. Suppose that you're a finance major and upon graduation you want a job, preferably as a personal financial planner, with a minimum salary of $34,000 and within 100 miles of your hometown. You accept a job offer as a business credit analyst—not exactly a personal financial planner but still in the finance field—at a bank 50 miles from home at a starting salary of $35,000. A more comprehensive job search would have revealed a job in personal financial planning at a trust company only 25 miles from your hometown and starting at a salary of $38,000. Because the first job offer was satisfactory (or "good enough"), you behaved in a boundedly rational manner by accepting it, although according to the assumptions of perfect rationality, you didn't maximize your decision by searching all possible alternatives and then choosing the best. (■□■■ Go to the Web and check out Q & A 6.5.)

●●● **bounded rationality**
Decision-making behavior that's rational, but limited (bounded) by an individual's ability to process information.

●●● **satisficing**
Acceptance of solutions that are "good enough."

Intuition played a strong part in Barbara Choi's decision to locate her firm, a cosmetics and personal care products manufacturer, in Valley Springs Industrial Center in Los Angeles. In Chinese, the numbers of the building's address signify continued growth.

Most decisions that managers make don't fit the assumptions of perfect rationality and, instead, they make those decisions using a boundedly rational approach. That is, they make decisions based on alternatives that are satisfactory. However, keep in mind that their decision making also may be strongly influenced by the organization's culture, internal politics, power considerations, and by a phenomenon called **escalation of commitment**, which is an increased commitment to a previous decision despite evidence that it may have been wrong.[13] For example, studies of the events leading up to the *Challenger* space shuttle disaster point to an escalation of commitment by decision makers to launch the shuttle on that day even though the decision was questioned by certain individuals. Why would decision makers want to escalate commitment to a bad decision? Because they don't want to admit that their initial decision may have been flawed. Rather than search for new alternatives, they simply increase their commitment to the original solution.

Role of Intuition Rod Aissa, vice president for talent and development and casting at MTV says, "One day I was home with strep throat and I saw a rerun of MTV's *Cribs* that featured the Osbourne's house. They were such a dynamic family. I thought, 'They would make great TV.' So I set up a dinner with Sharon Osbourne, the kids, and two MTV executives. We just wanted to watch them interact... All of it hit us in the gut so strongly. We never tested the show. We just knew it would make great TV."[14] Like Rod Aissa, managers regularly use their intuition and it may actually help improve their decision making.[15] What is **intuitive decision making**? It's making decisions on the basis of experience, feelings, and accumulated judgment. Researchers studying managers' use of intuitive decision making identified five different aspects of intuition, which are described in Exhibit 6–7.

Making a decision on intuition or "gut feeling" doesn't necessarily happen independently of rational analysis; rather, the two complement each other. A manager who has had experience with a particular, or even similar, type of problem or situation

• • • **escalation of commitment**
An increased commitment to a previous decision despite evidence that it may have been wrong.

• • • **intuitive decision making**
Making decisions on the basis of experience, feelings, and accumulated judgment.

Exhibit 6–7   **What Is Intuition?**

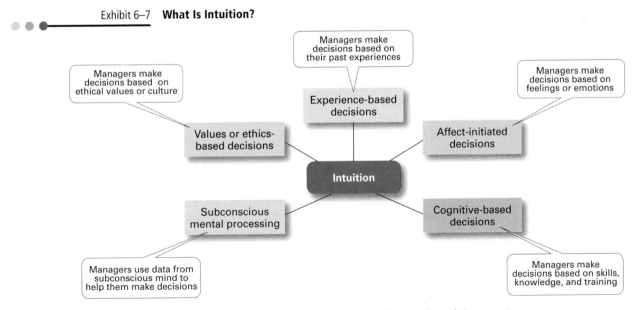

Source: Based on L.A. Burke and M.K. Miller. "Taking the Mystery Out of Intuitive Decision Making." *Academy of Management Executive.* October 1999, pp. 91–99.

often can act quickly with what appears to be limited information. Such a manager doesn't rely on a systematic and thorough analysis of the problem or identification and evaluation of alternatives but instead uses his or her experience and judgment to make a decision. (Go to the Web and check out Q & A 6.6.)

How common is intuitive decision making? (Go to the Web and check out S.A.L. #18—How Intuitive Am I?) One survey of managers and other organizational employees revealed that almost one-third of them emphasized "gut feeling" over cognitive problem solving and decision making.[16]

Types of Problems and Decisions

Managers at eating establishments in Springfield, Missouri, make decisions weekly about purchasing food supplies and scheduling employee work shifts. It's something they've done numerous times. But now they're facing a different kind of decision—one they've never encountered—how to adapt to a newly enacted no-smoking ordinance. And this situation isn't all that unusual. Managers in all kinds of organizations will face different types of problems and decisions as they do their jobs. Depending on the nature of the problem, the manager can use different types of decisions.

Structured Problems and Programmed Decisions Some problems are straightforward. The goal of the decision maker is clear, the problem is familiar, and information about the problem is easily defined and complete. Examples of these types of problems might include a customer's returning a purchase to a store, a supplier's being late with an important delivery, a news team's responding to a fast-breaking event, or a college's handling of a student wanting to drop a class. Such situations are called **structured problems**, which are straightforward, familiar, and easily defined problems. For instance, a server in a restaurant spills a drink on a customer's coat. The manager has an upset customer and something needs to be done. Because drinks are frequently spilled, there's probably some standardized routine for handling the problem. For example, the manager offers to have the coat cleaned at the restaurant's expense. This is what we call a **programmed decision**, a repetitive decision that can be handled by a routine approach. Because the problem is structured, the manager doesn't have to go to the trouble and expense of going through an involved decision process. The "develop-the-alternatives" stage of the decision-making process either doesn't exist or is given little attention. Why? Because once the structured problem is defined, its solution is usually self-evident or at least reduced to a few alternatives that are familiar and have proved successful in the past. The spilled drink on the customer's coat doesn't require the restaurant manager to identify and weight decision criteria or to develop a long list of possible solutions. Rather, the manager relies on a programmed decision, of which there are three types: a procedure, rule, or policy.

••• **structured problems**
Straightforward, familiar, and easily defined problems.

••• **programmed decision**
A repetitive decision that can be handled by a routine approach.

A **procedure** is a series of interrelated sequential steps that a manager can use to respond to a structured problem. The only real difficulty is in identifying the problem. Once it's clear, so is the procedure. For instance, a purchasing manager receives a request from a sales manager for 15 Palm handhelds for the company's sales reps. The purchasing manager knows how to make this decision—follow the established purchasing procedure.

••• **procedure**
A series of interrelated sequential steps that can be used to respond to a well-structured problem.

A **rule** is an explicit statement that tells a manager what he or she can or cannot do. Rules are frequently used because they're simple to follow and ensure consistency. For example, rules about lateness and absenteeism permit supervisors to make disciplinary decisions rapidly and fairly.

••• **rule**
An explicit statement that tells managers what they can or cannot do.

A third type of programmed decisions is a **policy**, which is a guideline for making a decision. In contrast to a rule, a policy establishes general parameters for the decision maker rather than specifically stating what should or should not be done. Policies typically contain an ambiguous term that leaves interpretation up to the decision

••• **policy**
A guideline for making decisions.

maker. (■□▬▬▬ Go to the Web and check out Q & A 6.7.) Here are some sample policy statements:

- The customer always comes first and should always be *satisfied*.
- We promote from within, *whenever possible*.
- Employee wages shall be *competitive* within community standards.

Notice that the terms *satisfied*, *whenever possible*, and *competitive* require interpretation. For instance, the policy of paying competitive wages doesn't tell a company's human resources manager the exact amount he or she should pay, but it does give direction to the decision he or she makes.

Unstructured Problems and Nonprogrammed Decisions Not all problems managers face are structured and solvable by a programmed decision. Many organizational situations involve **unstructured problems**, which are problems that are new or unusual and for which information is ambiguous or incomplete. Whether to build a new manufacturing facility in Beijing is an example of an unstructured problem. So too is the problem facing restaurant managers in Springfield deciding how to modify their facilities and operations to comply with the city's new no-smoking ordinance. When problems are unstructured, managers must rely on nonprogrammed decision making in order to develop unique solutions. **Nonprogrammed decisions** are unique and nonrecurring and require custom-made solutions. When a manager confronts an unstructured problem, there is no cut-and-dried solution. It requires a custom-made response through nonprogrammed decision making.

Integration Exhibit 6–8 (see p. 144) describes the relationship among problems, decisions, and organizational level. Because lower-level managers confront familiar and repetitive problems, they mostly rely on programmed decisions such as procedures, rules, and policies. The problems confronting managers usually become more unstructured as they move up the organizational hierarchy. Why? Because lower-level managers handle the routine decisions themselves and let upper-level managers deal with the decisions they find unusual or difficult. Similarly, higher-level managers delegate routine decisions to their subordinates so they can deal with more difficult issues. (■□▬▬▬ Go to the Web and check out Q & A 6.8.)

Few managerial decisions in the real world are either fully programmed or nonprogrammed. These are extremes, and most decisions fall somewhere in between.

•• • unstructured problems
Problems that are new or unusual and for which information is ambiguous or incomplete.

•• • nonprogrammed decisions
A unique decision that requires a custom-made solution.

Matthew Jay's innovative ski trail maps, printed on plastic and attached to the safety bars of chair lifts, presented the Forest Service with a nonprogrammed decision. The Aspen Skiing Company's four resorts had agreed to try the maps, but the Forest Service has jurisdiction over the White River National Forest, in which they operate and in which outdoor advertising is banned. The agency ordered the maps removed once, but Jay lobbied for another chance, and the Forest Service granted time to come up with a compromise.

Exhibit 6–8

Types of Problems, Types of Decisions, and Level in the Organization

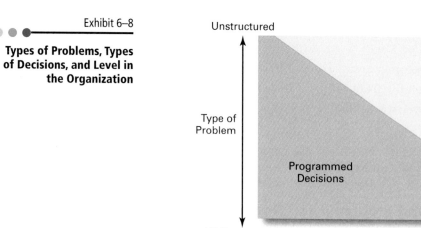

Few programmed decisions are designed to eliminate individual judgment completely. At the other extreme, even a unique situation requiring a nonprogrammed decision can be helped by programmed routines. It's best to think of decisions as *mainly* programmed or *mainly* nonprogrammed, rather than as completely one or the other.

One of the more challenging tasks facing managers as they make decisions is analyzing decision alternatives (Step 5 in the decision-making process). In the next section, we'll look at analyzing alternatives under different conditions.

Decision-Making Conditions

There are three conditions managers may face as they make decisions: certainty, risk, and uncertainty. What are the characteristics of each?

Certainty The ideal situation for making decisions is one of **certainty**, that is, a situation in which a manager can make accurate decisions because the outcome of every alternative is known. For example, when Idaho's state treasurer is deciding in which bank to deposit excess state funds, he knows the exact interest rate being offered by each bank and the amount that will be earned on the funds. He is certain about the outcomes of each alternative. As you might expect, most managerial decisions aren't like this.

Risk A far more common situation is one of **risk**, conditions in which the decision maker is able to estimate the likelihood of certain outcomes. The ability to assign probabilities to outcomes may be the result of personal experiences or secondary information. Under risk, managers have historical data that let them assign probabilities to different alternatives. Let's work through an example.

Suppose that you manage a ski resort in the Colorado Rockies. You're thinking about adding another lift to your current facility. Obviously, your decision will be influenced by

••• certainty
A situation in which a manager can make accurate decisions because all outcomes are known.

••• risk
A situation in which the decision maker is able to estimate the likelihood of certain outcomes.

THINKING CRITICALLY ABOUT ETHICS

You're in charge of hiring a new employee to work in your area of responsibility, and one of your friends from college needs a job. You think he's minimally qualified for the position, but you feel that you could find a better qualified and more experienced candidate if you kept looking. What will you do? What factors will influence your decision? What will you tell your friend?

MANAGING YOUR CAREER

Taking Risks

"IYAD-WYAD-YAG-WYAG: If you always do what you've always done, you'll always get what you've always got! So if your life is ever going to improve, you'll have to take chances." (Anonymous)[17]

How will you approach your various career moves in the time you spend working over the course of your lifetime? Will you want to do what you've always done? Or will you want to take chances, and how comfortable will you be taking chances? Taking career risks doesn't have to be a gamble. Responsible risk-taking can make outcomes more predictable. Here are some suggestions for being a responsible, effective risk-taker in career decisions. It's important to thoroughly evaluate the risk. Before committing to a career risk, consider what you could lose or who might be hurt. How important are those things or those people to you? Explore whether

you can reach your goal in another way, thus making the risk unnecessary. Find out everything you can about what's involved with taking this career risk—the timing; the people involved; the changes it will entail; and the potential gains and losses, both in the short run and the long run. Examine closely your feelings about taking this risk: Are you afraid? Are you ready to act now? Will you know if you have risked more than you can afford to lose? Finally, ensure your employability. The most important thing you can do is ensuring that you have choices by keeping your skills current and continually learning new skills.

As with any decision involving risk, the more information you have available, the better able you are to assess the risk. Then, armed with this information, you can make a more informed decision. And even though you won't be able to eliminate all the negatives associated with taking the risk, you can, at least, know about them.

---

the additional revenue that the new lift would generate and additional revenue will depend on snowfall. The decision is made somewhat clearer because you have fairly reliable weather data from the last 10 years on snowfall levels in your area—three years of heavy snowfall, five years of normal snowfall, and two years of light snow. Can you use this information to help you make your decision about adding the new lift? If you have good information on the amount of revenues generated during each level of snow, the answer is yes.

You can calculate expected value—the expected return from each possible outcome—by multiplying expected revenues by snowfall probabilities. The result is the average revenue you can expect over time if the given probabilities hold. As Exhibit 6–9 shows, the expected revenue from adding a new ski lift is $687,500. Of course, whether that justifies a decision to build or not depends on the costs involved in generating that revenue—such as the cost to build the lift, the additional annual operating expenses for another lift, the interest rate for borrowing money, and so forth.

Uncertainty What happens if you have a decision where you're not certain about the outcomes and can't even make reasonable probability estimates? We call such a condition **uncertainty**. Managers do face decision-making situations of uncertainty. Under these conditions, the choice of alternative is influenced by the limited amount of information available to the decision maker and by the psychological orientation of the decision maker. The optimistic manager will follow a *maximax* choice (maximizing the maximum possible payoff), the pessimist will follow a *maximin* choice (maximizing

• • • **uncertainty**
A situation in which a decision maker has neither certainty nor reasonable probability estimates available.

Exhibit 6–9

Expected Value for Revenues from the Addition of One Ski Lift

Event	Expected Revenues	× Probability	= Expected Value of Each Alternative
Heavy snowfall	$850,000	0.3	$255,000
Normal snowfall	725,000	0.5	362,500
Light snowfall	350,000	0.2	70,000
			$687,500

Exhibit 6–10

Payoff Matrix

(in millions of dollars) Visa Marketing Strategy	MasterCard's Response		
	CA_1	CA_2	CA_3
S_1	13	14	11
S_2	9	15	18
S_3	24	21	15
S_4	18	14	28

the minimum possible payoff), and the manager who desires to minimize his maximum "regret" will opt for a *minimax* choice. Let's look at these different choice approaches using an example.

A marketing manager at Visa International has determined four possible strategies (S_1, S_2, S_3, and S_4) for promoting the Visa card throughout the southeastern United States. The marketing manager also knows that major competitor MasterCard has three competitive actions (CA_1, CA_2, CA_3) it's using to promote its card in the same region. For this example, we'll assume that the Visa executive had no previous knowledge that would allow her to place probabilities on the success of any of the four strategies. She formulates the matrix shown in Exhibit 6–10 to show the various Visa strategies and the resulting profit to Visa depending on the competitive action used by MasterCard.

In this example, if our Visa manager is an optimist, she'll choose S_4 because that could produce the largest possible gain: $28 million. Note that this choice maximizes the maximum possible gain (maximax choice).

If our manager is a pessimist, she'll assume that only the worst can occur. The worst outcome for each strategy is as follows: S_1 = $11 million; S_2 = $9 million; S_3 = $15 million; S_4 = $14 million. These are the most pessimistic outcomes from each strategy. Following the *maximin* choice, she would maximize the minimum payoff; in other words, she'd select S_3 ($15 million is the largest of the minimum payoffs).

In the third approach, managers recognize that once a decision is made, it will not necessarily result in the most profitable payoff. There may be a regret of profits forgone (given up)—*regret* referring to the amount of money that could have been made had a different strategy been used. Managers calculate regret by subtracting all possible payoffs in each category from the maximum possible payoff for each given event, in this case for each competitive action. For our Visa manager, the highest payoff, given that MasterCard engages in CA_1, CA_2, or CA_3, is $24 million, $21 million, or $28 million, respectively (the highest number in each column). Subtracting the payoffs in Exhibit 6-10 from those figures produces the results shown in Exhibit 6–11.

The maximum regrets are S_1 = $17 million; S_2 = $15 million; S_3 = $13 million; and S_4 = $7 million. The *minimax* choice minimizes the maximum regret, so our Visa manager would choose S_4. By making this choice, she'll never have a regret of profits forgone of more than $7 million. This result contrasts, for example, with a regret of $15 million had she chosen S_2 and MasterCard had taken CA_1.

Exhibit 6–11

Regret Matrix

(in millions of dollars) Visa Marketing Strategy	MasterCard's Response		
	CA_1	CA_2	CA_3
S_1	11	7	17
S_2	15	6	10
S_3	0	0	13
S_4	6	7	0

Although managers will try to quantify a decision when possible by using payoff and regret matrices, uncertainty often forces them to rely more on intuition, creativity, hunches, and "gut feel." Regardless of the decision situation, each manager has his or her own style of making decisions.

Decision-Making Styles

Suppose that you were a new manager at Sony or at the local YMCA. How would you make decisions? Managers' decision-making styles differ along two dimensions.[18] The first is an individual's *way of thinking*. Some of us are more rational and logical in the way we process information. A rational type looks at information in order and makes sure that it's logical and consistent before making a decision. Others tend to be creative and intuitive. Intuitive types don't have to process information in a certain order but are comfortable looking at it as whole. (▬▬▭ Go to the Web and check out S.A.L. #4—How Flexible Am I?)

The other dimension describes an individual's *tolerance for ambiguity*. Again, some of us have a low tolerance for ambiguity. These types need consistency and order in the way they structure information so that ambiguity is minimized. On the other hand, some of us can tolerate high levels of ambiguity and are able to process many thoughts at the same time. (▬▭ Go to the Web and check out S.A.L. #7—How Well Do I Handle Ambiguity?) When we diagram these two dimensions, four decision-making styles are evident: directive, analytic, conceptual, and behavioral (see Exhibit 6–12). Let's look more closely at each style.

● ● ● **directive style**
A decision-making style characterized by low tolerance for ambiguity and a rational way of thinking.

● ● ● **analytic style**
A decision-making style characterized by a high tolerance for ambiguity and a rational way of thinking.

● ● ● **conceptual style**
A decision-making style characterized by a high tolerance for ambiguity and an intuitive way of thinking.

● ● ● **behavioral style**
A decision-making style characterized by a low tolerance for ambiguity and an intuitive way of thinking.

- *Directive style.* Decision makers using the **directive style** have low tolerance for ambiguity and are rational in their way of thinking. They're efficient and logical. Directive types make fast decisions and focus on the short run. Their efficiency and speed in making decisions often result in their making decisions with minimal information and assessing few alternatives.
- *Analytic style.* Decision makers with an **analytic style** have much greater tolerance for ambiguity than do directive types. They want more information before making a decision and consider more alternatives than a directive style decision maker does. Analytic decision makers are characterized as careful decision makers with the ability to adapt or cope with unique situations.
- *Conceptual style.* Individuals with a **conceptual style** tend to be very broad in their outlook and look at many alternatives. They focus on the long run and are very good at finding creative solutions to problems.
- *Behavioral style.* Decision makers with a **behavioral style** work well with others. They're concerned about the achievements of those around them and are receptive to suggestions from others. They often use meetings to communicate, although they try to avoid conflict. Acceptance by others is important to this decision-making style.

● ● ● ──●
Exhibit 6–12

Decision-Making Styles

Source: S.P. Robbins and D.A. DeCenzo, *Supervision Today.* 2nd ed. (Upper Saddle River, NJ: Prentice Hall, 1998). p. 166.

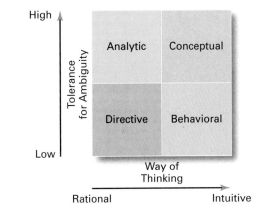

The choice of an advertising agency is often made by those with a conceptual approach to decision making. Marketing executives from Virgin Atlantic Airways saw presentations from five ad agencies before choosing Crispin Porter & Bogusky, a small firm whose inventive proposal showed how efficiently the airline's $15 million ad budget could be spent. The marketing team from Virgin allowed 10 weeks to make a decision; it took four days. The winning team is pictured here with the paper airplanes that played a part in their pitch.

● ● ● **heuristics**
Rules of thumb that managers use to simplify decision making.

Although these four decision-making styles are distinct, most managers have characteristics of more than one style. It's probably more realistic to think of a manager's dominant style and his or her alternate styles. (■□■■■■ Go to the Web and check out Q & A 6.9.) Look back at our chapter opener, for example. What style(s) does Cecilia appear to use? Although some managers will rely almost exclusively on their dominant style, others are more flexible and can shift their style depending on the situation.

Managers should also recognize that their employees may use different decision-making styles. (■□■■■■ Go to the Web and check out Q & A 6.10.) Some employees may take their time, carefully weighing alternatives and considering riskier options (analytic style), while other employees may be more concerned about getting suggestions from others before making decisions (behavioral style). This doesn't make one approach better than the other. It just means that their decision-making styles are different. (■■■□■ Go to the Web and check out S.A.L. #17—What's My Decision-Making Style?) The "Managing Workforce Diversity" box addresses some of the issues associated with valuing diversity in decision making.

Decision-Making Biases and Errors

When managers make decisions, not only do they use their own particular style, many use "rules of thumb" or **heuristics** to simplify their decision making. Rules of thumb can be useful to decision makers because they help make sense of complex, uncertain, and ambiguous information.[19] Even though managers may use rules of thumb, that doesn't mean those rules are reliable. Why? Because they may lead to errors and biases in processing and evaluating information. Exhibit 6–13 identifies 12 common decision errors and biases that managers make. Let's take a quick look at each.[20]

When decision makers tend to think they know more than they do or hold unrealistically positive views of themselves and their performance, they're exhibiting the *overconfidence bias*. The *immediate gratification bias* describes decision makers who tend to want immediate rewards and to avoid immediate costs. For these individuals, decision choices that provide quick payoffs are more appealing than those in the future. The *anchoring effect* describes when decision makers fixate on initial information as a starting

● ● ●— Exhibit 6–13

Common Decision-Making Errors and Biases

The Value of Diversity in Decision Making

Have you decided what your major is going to be? How did you decide? Do you feel your decision is a good one? Is there anything you could have done differently to make sure that your decision was the best one?[21]

Making good decisions is tough! Managers are continuously making decisions—for instance, developing new products, establishing weekly or monthly goals, implementing an advertising campaign, reassigning an employee to a different work group, resolving a customer's complaint, or purchasing new laptops for sales representatives. One important suggestion for making better decisions is to tap into the diversity of the work group. Drawing upon diverse employees can prove valuable to a manager's decision making. Why? Diverse employees can provide fresh perspectives on issues. They can offer differing interpretations on how a problem is defined and may be more open to trying new ideas. Diverse employees usually are more creative in generating alternatives and more flexible in resolving issues. And getting input from diverse sources increases the likelihood that creative and unique solutions will be generated.

Even though diversity in decision making can be valuable, there are drawbacks. The lack of a common perspective usually means that more time is spent discussing the issues. Communication may be a problem, particularly if language barriers are present. In addition, seeking out diverse opinions can make the decision-making process more complex, confusing, and ambiguous. And with multiple perspectives on the decision, it may be difficult to reach a single agreement or to agree on specific actions. Although these drawbacks are valid concerns, the value of diversity in decision making outweighs the potential disadvantages.

Now, about that decision on a major. Did you ask others for their opinions? Did you seek out advice from professors, family members, friends, or co-workers? Getting diverse perspectives on an important decision like this could help you make the best one! Managers also should consider the value to be gained from diversity in decision making.

point and then, once set, fail to adequately adjust for subsequent information. First impressions, ideas, prices, and estimates carry unwarranted weight relative to information received later. When decision makers selectively organize and interpret events based on their biased perceptions, they're using the *selective perception bias*. This influences the information they pay attention to, the problems they identify, and the alternatives they develop. Decision makers who seek out information that reaffirms their past choices and discount information that contradicts past judgments exhibit the *confirmation bias*. These people tend to accept at face value information that confirms their preconceived views and are critical and skeptical of information that challenges these views. The *framing bias* is when decision makers select and highlight certain aspects of a situation while excluding others. By drawing attention to specific aspects of a situation and highlighting them, while at the same time downplaying or omitting other aspects, they distort what they see and create incorrect reference points. The *availability bias* is when decisions makers tend to remember events that are the most recent and vivid in their memory. The result? It distorts their ability to recall events in an objective manner and results in distorted judgments and probability estimates. When decision makers assess the likelihood of an event based on how closely it resembles other events or sets of events, that's the *representation bias*. Managers exhibiting this bias draw analogies and see identical situations where they don't exist. The *randomness bias* is when decision makers try to create meaning out of random events. They do this because most decision makers have difficulty dealing with chance even though random events happen to everyone and there's nothing that can be done to predict them. The *sunk costs error* is when decision makers forget that current choices can't correct the past. They incorrectly fixate on past expenditures of time, money, or effort in assessing choices rather than on future consequences. Instead of ignoring sunk costs, they can't forget them. Decision makers who are quick to take credit for their successes and to blame failure on outside factors are exhibiting the *self-serving bias*. Finally, the *hindsight bias* is the tendency for decision makers to falsely believe that they would have accurately predicted the outcome of an event once that outcome is actually known.

How can managers avoid the negative effects of these decision errors and biases? The main thing is being aware of them and then trying not to exhibit them. Beyond

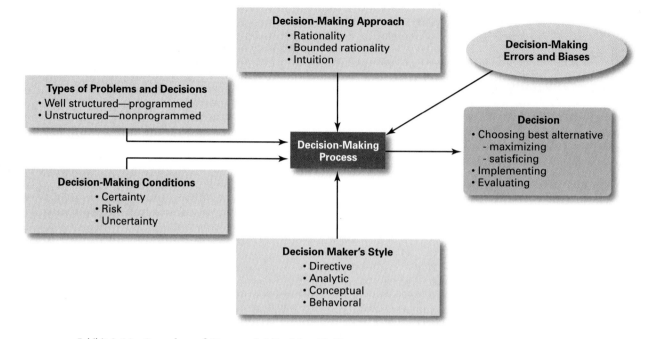

Exhibit 6–14   **Overview of Managerial Decision Making**

that, managers also should pay attention to "how" they make decisions and try to identify the heuristics they typically use and critically evaluate how appropriate those are. Finally, managers might want to ask those around them to help identify weaknesses in their decision-making style and try to improve on them.

Summing Up Managerial Decision Making

How can we best sum up managerial decision making? Exhibit 6–14 provides an overview. Because it's in their best interests, managers *want* to make good decisions—that is, choose the "best" alternative, implement it, and determine whether or not it takes care of the problem—the reason a decision was needed in the first place. Their decision-making process is affected by four factors including the decision-making approach being followed, the decision-making conditions, the type of problem being dealt with, and the decision maker's own style of decision making. In addition, certain decision-making errors and biases may impact the process. Each of these factors plays a role in determining how a manager makes a decision. So whether that decision involves addressing an employee's habitual tardiness, resolving a problem with product quality, or determining whether to enter a new market, remember that it has been shaped by a number of factors.

• • • Learning Review

- Discuss the assumptions of rational decision making.
- Describe the concepts of bounded rationality, satisficing, and escalation of commitment.
- Explain what intuition is and how it affects decision making.
- Contrast programmed and nonprogrammed decisions.
- Contrast the three decision-making conditions.

- Explain maximax, maximin, and minimax decision choice approaches.
- Describe the four decision-making styles.
- Discuss the twelve decision-making biases managers may exhibit.
- Describe how managers can avoid the negative effects of decision errors and biases.
- Explain the managerial decision-making model.

DECISION MAKING FOR TODAY'S WORLD

Per Carlsson, a product development manager at IKEA, "spends his days creating Volvo-style kitchens at Yugo prices." His job is to take the "problems" identified by the company's product-strategy council (a group of globe-trotting senior managers who monitor consumer trends and establish product priorities) and turn them into furniture that the entire world wants to buy. One "problem" recently identified by the council: The kitchen has replaced the living room as the social and entertainment center in the home. Customers are looking for kitchens that convey comfort and cleanliness while still allowing them to pursue their gourmet aspirations. Carlsson has to take this information and make things happen. There are a lot of decisions to make—programmed and nonprogrammed—and the fact that IKEA is a global company makes it even more challenging. Comfort in Asia means small, cozy appliances and spaces, while North American customers want oversized glassware and giant refrigerators. His ability to make good decisions quickly has significant implications for IKEA's success.[22]

Today's business world revolves around making decisions, often risky ones, usually with incomplete or inadequate information, and under intense time pressure. In a recent survey of managers, 77 percent said that the number of decisions made during a typical workday had increased and more than 43 percent said that the amount of time given to each decision had decreased.[23] Most managers are making one decision after another, and as if that weren't challenging enough, more is at stake than ever before. Bad decisions can cost millions. What do managers need to do to make effective decisions in today's fast-moving world? Here are some guidelines.

- *Know when it's time to call it quits.* When it's evident that a decision isn't working, don't be afraid to pull the plug. As we said earlier, many decision makers block or distort negative information because they don't want to believe that their decision was bad. They become so attached to the decision that they refuse to recognize when it's time to move on. In today's dynamic environment, this type of thinking simply won't work.

- *Practice the five whys.* When the environment is highly uncertain, one way to encourage good decision making is to get people to think more broadly and deeply about the issues. Because of the intense time pressure that managers face, it may be tempting to do just a superficial analysis. The "five whys" approach suggests that employees learn to ask "why" not just once, but five times.[24] Asking the first time "why" this is happening usually results in a superficial explanation for the problem; subsequent "whys" force decision makers to probe more deeply into the causes of the problem and possible solutions.

- *Be an effective decision maker.* An effective decision-making process has these six characteristics: "(1) It focuses on what's important; (2) It's logical and consistent; (3) It acknowledges both subjective and objective thinking and blends analytical with intuitive thinking; (4) It requires only as much information and analysis as is necessary to resolve a particular dilemma; (5) It encourages and guides the gathering of relevant information and informed opinion; and (6) It's straightforward, reliable, easy to use, and flexible."[25]

The remaining suggestions for making decisions in today's fast-moving world come from Karl Weick, an organizational psychologist who has made a career of studying organizations and how people work. He says that the best way for managers to respond to unpredictability and uncertainty is "by building an organization that expertly spots the unexpected when it crops up and then quickly adapts to the changed environment."[26] He calls these organizations *highly reliable organizations* (HROs) and says they share five habits. First, they're *not tricked by their success.* HROs are preoccupied with their failures. They're alert to the smallest deviations and react early and quickly to anything that doesn't fit with their expectations. He talks about Navy aviators who describe "leemers—a gut feeling that something isn't right."

Becoming a Manager

♦ *Pay close attention to decisions you make and how you make them.*

♦ *When you feel you haven't made a good decision, assess how you could have made a better one. Which step of the decision-making process could you have improved?*

♦ *Work at developing good decision-making skills.*

♦ *Read books about decision making.*

♦ *Ask people you admire for advice on how they make good decisions.*

♦ ▪▪▫▪ *Go to the Web and complete these Self-Assessment Exercises from the Self-Assessment Library (S.A.L.) on R.O.L.L.S.: #7—How Well Do I Handle Ambiguity?, #17—What's My Decision-Making Style?, #18—How Intuitive Am I?, and #47—How Well Do I Respond to Turbulent Change?*

Typically, these leemers turn out to be accurate. Something, in fact, is wrong. Organizations need to create climates where people feel safe trusting their leemers. Another characteristic of HROs is that they *defer to the experts on the front line.* Frontline workers—those who interact day in and day out with customers, products, suppliers, and so forth—have firsthand knowledge of what can and cannot be done, what will and will not work. Get their input. Let them make decisions. Next, HROs *let unexpected circumstances provide the solution.* One of Weick's better-known works is his study of the Mann Gulch fire in Montana that killed 13 smoke jumpers in 1949. The event was a massive, tragic organizational failure. However, the reaction of the foreman illustrates how effective decision makers respond to unexpected circumstances. When the fire was nearly on top of his men, he invented the escape fire—a small fire that consumed all the brush around the team, leaving an area where the larger fire couldn't burn. His action was contrary to everything firefighters are taught (that is, you don't start fires—you extinguish them), but at the time it was the best decision. The fourth habit of HROs is that they *embrace complexity.* This characteristic is similar to the five whys we discussed earlier. Because business is complex, these organizations recognize that it "takes complexity to sense complexity." Rather than simplifying data, which we instinctively try to do when faced with complexity, these organizations aim for deeper understanding of the situation. They tap into their complexity to help them adapt more effectively. Finally, HROs *anticipate, but also anticipate their limits.* These organizations do try to anticipate as much as possible, but they recognize that they can't anticipate everything. As Weick says, they don't "think, then act. They think by acting. By actually doing things, you'll find out what works and what doesn't."

Making decisions in today's fast-moving world isn't easy. Successful managers will need good decision-making skills to effectively and efficiently plan, organize, lead, and control.

● ● ●Learning Review

- Explain how managers can make effective decisions in today's world.

- List the six characteristics of an effective decision-making process.

- Describe the five habits of highly reliable organizations.

Managers **Respond** to a **Manager's** Dilemma

····**Jeffrey Sears**
Manager of Web Services, Pearson Education,
Bloomington, Minnesota

When delivering any solution to your customers, no matter how successful it may appear from your perspective, the solution needs to make an issue better. This is especially true with technology. A first step Cecilia might want to take is to offer a brief online survey to each site visitor. The questions would be simple, such as: Does this online survey make your job easier? If yes, does it save time, reduce cost, improve customer service, all of the above, other? If no, why not? Any general comments. Over time, more detailed questions could be added as customer needs become more sophisticated. The need for simple validation of proposed solutions must be done with an eye to constant, gradual improvements to customer service. It isn't your place to decide if it's successful—that lies with your customers.

Cindy Brewer
National Parts Sourcing Manager, Sears, Inc.,
Chicago, Illinois

Before committing any more resources to the continued development of the Web site, Cecilia obviously wants to evaluate the way it stands now to make sure it's meeting the needs of the targeted users—that is, the clients and member firms. Therefore, the main focus of her evaluation should be on these users. Given that we're evaluating a Web site and the fact that online surveys are quite common and easy to create, I would recommend a short, simple online survey that users could fill out and send back. The results of this survey could become one of Cecilia's criteria for evaluating the decision's effectiveness. Other possible criteria Cecilia might consider include the number of "hits" that the Web site generates, the number of service problems with the Web site that are reported, or even an objective Web site design evaluation by an outside expert or consultant.

Learning Summary

After reading and studying this chapter, you should be able to:

- Define decision and the decision-making process.
- Describe the eight steps in the decision-making process.
- Discuss the assumptions of rational decision making.
- Describe the concepts of bounded rationality, satisficing, and escalation of commitment.
- Explain what intuition is and how it affects decision making.
- Contrast programmed and nonprogrammed decisions.
- Contrast the three decision-making conditions.

- Explain maximax, maximin, and minimax decision choice approaches.
- Describe the four decision-making styles.
- Discuss the decision-making biases managers may exhibit.
- Explain the managerial decision-making model.
- Discuss the ways managers can make better decisions.
- Explain how managers can make effective decisions in today's world.
- List the six characteristics of an effective decision-making process.
- Describe the five habits of highly reliable organizations.

Thinking About Management Issues

1. Why is decision making often described as the essence of a manager's job?

2. How might an organization's culture influence the way managers make decisions?

3. All of us bring biases to the decisions we make. What would be the drawbacks of having biases? Could there be any advantages to having biases? Explain. What are the implications for decision making?

4. Would you call yourself a systematic or intuitive thinker? What are the decision-making implications of these labels? What are the implications for choosing an employer?

5. How can managers blend the guidelines for making effective decisions in today's world with the rationality and bounded rationality models of decision making, or can they? Explain.

6. Why do good managers sometimes make bad decisions? How can managers improve their decision-making skills?

Working Together: Team-Based Exercise

What is involved with being a good decision maker? Form groups of three to four students. Discuss your experiences making decisions—for example, buying a car, choosing classes and professors, making summer or spring break plans, and so forth. Share times when you felt you made good decisions. Analyze what happened during that decision-making process that contributed to it being a good decision. Then consider some decisions that you felt were bad. What happened to make them bad? What common characteristics, if any, did you identify among the good decisions? The bad decisions? Come up with a bulleted list of practical suggestions for making good decisions. Be prepared to share your list with the class.

Ethical Dilemma Exercise

Competitive problems are rarely well structured, as the managers at Charles Schwab & Company know. Over the years, the brokerage firm has successfully competed with well-established rivals such as Merrill Lynch by making nonprogrammed decisions. For example, management decided to charge customers less for trading stocks, bonds, and mutual funds and to implement technology giving customers more trading choices. Because the competitive environment is constantly changing, Schwab's advertising managers can never be certain about the outcome of decisions concerning how to promote the firm's competitive advantages.

Not long ago, some competing brokerage firms paid hefty fines to settle charges stemming from conflicts of interest involving their research and recommendations to customers. In the aftermath of these scandals, Schwab managers decided on an advertising campaign to stress that Schwab does things differently. One tongue-in-cheek commercial took viewers behind the scenes at a fictitious competitor's office, where brokers chanted "Buy, buy, buy." A broker looked at a restaurant take-out menu as he told a customer on the phone, "I have your portfolio right here, and I think you should buy." Some networks rejected these aggressive commercials. The ads also raised questions about potential conflicts of interest created by Schwab brokers steering business to in-house traders and mutual funds.[27]

Imagine you're an advertising manager at Schwab. Your advertising agency has suggested a newspaper ad in which a fictitious competing broker is quoted as saying, "My investment advice is perfectly objective, even though I work on commission." A Schwab broker is then quoted as saying, "I don't work on commission like other brokers do, so my investment advice is perfectly objective." Review

Exhibit 6-14 as you think about this dilemma and decide which of the following options to choose—and why.

Option A: Tell the agency to put an asterisk after the Schwab quote and explain in small print that Schwab brokers receive no commissions, but the firm profits from in-house transactions.

Option B: Tell the agency to change the Schwab broker's quote to: "I don't work on commission like other brokers do, so you won't be pressured to buy or sell."

Option C: Tell the agency to change the Schwab broker's quote to: "My investment advice is much more objective than the advice of any broker who works on commission."

Case Application

C.F. Martin Guitar Company

The Nazareth, Pennsylvania–based C.F. Martin Guitar Company has been producing acoustic instruments since 1833. A Martin guitar is among the best that money can buy. Current CEO Christian Frederick Martin IV—better known as Chris—continues to be committed to the guitar maker's craft. During 2002, the company sold about 77,000 instruments and hit a record $77 million in revenue. Despite this success, Chris is facing some serious issues.[28]

Martin Guitar Company is an interesting blend of old and new. Although the equipment and tools may have changed over the years, employees remain true to the principle of high standards of musical excellence. Building a guitar to meet these standards requires considerable attention and patience. In a 1904 catalog, a family member explained, "How to build a guitar to give this tone is not a secret. It takes care and patience." Now well over a century later, this statement is still an accurate reflection of the company's philosophy.

From the very beginning, quality has played an important role in everything that Martin Guitar does. Through dramatic changes in product design, distribution systems, and manufacturing methods, the company has remained committed to making quality products. Part of that quality approach includes a long-standing ecological policy. The company depends on natural-wood products to make its guitars, but a lot of the wood supply is vanishing. Chris has long embraced the responsible use of traditional wood materials, going so far as to encourage suppliers to find a sustainable-yield alternative species. Based on thorough customer research, Martin introduced guitars that used structurally sound woods with natural cosmetic defects that were once considered unacceptable. In addition, Martin follows the directives of CITES, the Convention on International Trade in Endangered Species of Wild Fauna and Flora (*www.cites.org*), even though it has the potential to affect its ability to produce the type of quality products it has in the past. This treaty barred the export of the much-desired Brazilian rosewood, which is considered endangered. A guitar built from the remaining supply of this popular wood has a hefty price tag—more than $9,500. Similar prices may be in line for the leading alternative, Honduras mahogany. Even ebony, used for fingerboards and bridges, is likely to be next. Chris says, "All of us who use wood for the tone (it makes) are scrambling. Options are limited."

Although the company is rooted in its past, Chris isn't afraid to take it in new directions. In the late 1990s, he decided to start selling guitars in the under-$800 segment, a segment that accounts for 65 percent of the acoustic guitar industry's sales. Although this model doesn't look, smell, or feel like the company's pricier models, customers claim it sounds better than most other instruments in that price range. Chris explained, "My fear was that if we didn't look at alternatives, we'd be the company making guitars for doctors and lawyers. If Martin just worships its past without trying anything new, there won't be a Martin left to worship."

DISCUSSION QUESTIONS

1. How do you think good decision making has contributed to the success of this business?

2. A decision to move into a new market as Chris did is a major decision. How could he have used the decision-making process to help make this decision?

3. What criteria do you think would be most important to Chris as he makes decisions about the company's future?

4. Would you characterize the conditions surrounding C.F. Martin Guitar Company as conditions of certainty, risk, or uncertainty? Explain your choice.

5. What could Chris learn from the concept of highly reliable organizations to help him be a better decision maker?

CEO Chris Martin.

● ● ●Learning Outline

Follow this Learning Outline as you read and study this chapter.

What Is Planning?
- Define planning.
- Differentiate between formal and informal planning.

Why Do Managers Plan?
- Describe the purposes of planning.
- Discuss the conclusions from studies of the relationship between planning and performance.

How Do Managers Plan?
- Define goals and plans.
- Describe the types of goals organizations might have.
- Explain why it's important to know an organization's stated and real goals.
- Describe each of the different types of plans.

Establishing Goals and Developing Plans
- Discuss how traditional goal setting works.
- Explain the concept of the means–end chain.
- Describe the management by objectives (MBO) approach.
- Describe the characteristics of well-designed goals.
- Explain the steps in setting goals.
- Discuss the contingency factors that affect planning.
- Describe the approaches to planning.

Contemporary Issues in Planning
- Explain the criticisms of planning and whether or not they're valid.
- Describe how managers can effectively plan in today's dynamic environment.

Chapter

7

Foundations of Planning

As one of the world's most respected financial institutions, UBS AG is Switzerland's largest bank and a major player in international financial circles.[1] The Zurich- and Basel-based company has assets of more than $834 billion and has positioned itself so that each of its business groups (UBS Wealth Management and Business Banking, UBS Warburg Ltd., UBS Global Asset Management, and UBS PaineWebber) is in the top rankings of its core business. Dr. Gabriela Payer Fruithof (pictured

here), managing director and head of marketing technology for UBS AG, is playing a key role in the company's choice of future directions.

Fruithof has been the driving force behind many of the company's Internet strategies and solutions. Like many financial institutions in the United States and around the globe, UBS has made a major commitment to online services. Customers can get information on their accounts using personal computers, personal digital assistants, and phones. They can pay bills, conduct transactions, trade stocks, or view their holdings and activities. In addition, a secure e-mail feature lets customers send messages and attachments without using the public Internet. Since the bank also owns two mutual fund and brokerage firms with thousands of customers, Fruithof led the development of a customer-relationship management program that included customized call centers and interactive voice response systems with built-in speech recognition. In many instances, the company

can prioritize and route incoming calls based on a customer's relationship and standing with the bank. For example, customers who use a wide range of bank services and provide high profits will have their calls taken immediately, while low-profit customers have to wait for an available service representative.

The company's multichannel approach to online banking has been quite successful. Internal performance studies indicate that overall work productivity has improved by 30 percent at call centers. Also, more than 70 percent of incoming inquiries are handled by electronic systems.

Fruithof says, "The Internet doesn't change the rules of business; it's just another way to conduct business. When you understand your core values and goals, you have the knowledge to make the right moves at the right time." Put yourself in her shoes. Now that the online banking initiative has been implemented, what types of plans might she need to guide the use of the Internet in other additional marketing activities?

What would *you* do **?**

L ike Gabriela Payer Fruithof, managers everywhere need to plan. In this chapter we present the basics of planning: what it is, why managers plan, and how they plan. Then we'll conclude by looking at some contemporary issues in planning.

Victoria Hale founded the nonprofit Institute for One World Health with an informal plan. Inspired by a conversation about pharmaceutical science with a New York City cab driver, Hale went back to an essay she'd written years earlier about diseases that would benefit from drug development efforts. Using that as her preliminary business plan, she incorporated the Institute the next day. The Institute's goal is to persuade companies with important but not profitable drugs to donate those to the Institute for tax and public relations benefits. The Institute then uses grants and donations to distribute the drugs to needy patients around the world.

WHAT IS PLANNING?

Harley-Davidson is known worldwide for its motorcycles—the Fat Boy, Electra Glide, Deuce, and Night Train are among its most popular models.[2] However, demand for Harley motorcycles exceeds supply, and customers face lengthy waits for the most popular models. Although that may seem a nice problem to have, what happens if customers get upset enough to buy from a competitor? Should the managers be doing a better job of planning?

As we stated in Chapter 1, **planning** involves defining the organization's goals, establishing an overall strategy for achieving those goals, and developing a comprehensive set of plans to integrate and coordinate organizational work. It's concerned with both ends (what's to be done) and means (how it's to be done).

Planning can either be formal or informal. All managers engage in some planning, but their planning might be informal. In informal planning, nothing is written down, and there is little or no sharing of goals with others in the organization. (▮▮▮▮ Go to the Web and check out S.A.L. #22—How Good Am I at Personal Planning?) This type of planning often is done in small businesses where the owner-manager has a vision of where he or she wants the business to go and how to get there. Informal planning is general and lacks continuity. Although it's more common in smaller organizations, informal planning does exist in some large organizations as well. And some small businesses may have very sophisticated planning processes and formal plans.

When we use the term *planning* in this book, we mean *formal* planning. In formal planning, specific goals covering a period of years are defined. These goals are written and shared with organizational members. Finally, specific action programs exist for the achievement of these goals; that is, managers clearly define the path they want to take to get the organization and the various work units from where they are to where they want them to be. (▮▮▮▮ Go to the Web and check out Q & A #7.1.)

● ● ● **Learning Review**

- Define planning.

- Differentiate between formal and informal planning.

WHY DO MANAGERS PLAN?

Setting goals, establishing strategies to achieve those goals, and developing a set of plans to integrate and coordinate activities seem pretty complicated. Given that fact, why should managers want to plan? Does planning impact performance?

Purposes of Planning

••• planning
A process that involves defining the organization's goals, establishing an overall strategy for achieving those goals, and developing a comprehensive set of plans to integrate and coordinate organizational work.

We can identify at least four reasons for planning. Planning provides direction, reduces uncertainty, minimizes waste and redundancy, and sets the standards used in controlling. Let's look at each of these purposes.

Planning provides direction to managers and nonmanagers alike. When employees know where the organization or work unit is going and what they must contribute to reach goals, they can coordinate their activities, cooperate with each other, and do what it takes to accomplish those goals. Without planning, departments and individuals might work at cross purposes, preventing the organization from moving efficiently toward its goals.

Planning reduces uncertainty by forcing managers to look ahead, anticipate change, consider the impact of change, and develop appropriate responses. Even though planning can't eliminate change or uncertainty, managers plan in order to anticipate change and develop the most effective response to it.

In addition, planning reduces overlapping and wasteful activities. When work activities are coordinated around established plans, redundancy can be minimized. Furthermore, when means and ends are made clear through planning, inefficiencies become obvious and can be corrected or eliminated.

Finally, planning establishes the goals or standards that are used in controlling. If we're unsure of what we're trying to accomplish, how can we determine whether we've actually achieved it? In planning, we develop the goals and the plans. Then, through controlling, we compare actual performance against the goals, identify any significant deviations, and take any necessary corrective action. Without planning, there would be no way to control.

Planning and Performance

■ Q & A
Whenever you see this green square, go to the R.O.L.L.S. Web site (*www.prenhall.com/robbins*) to the Q & A, your 24/7 educational assistant. These video clips and written material presented by your authors address questions that we have found students frequently ask.

Is planning worthwhile? Do managers and organizations that plan outperform those that don't? Intuitively, you would expect the answer to be a resounding yes. While studies of performance in organizations that plan are generally positive, we can't say that organizations that formally plan *always* outperform those that don't plan. (■■■■ Go to the Web and check out Q & A 7.2.)

Numerous studies have looked at the relationship between planning and performance.[3] We can draw the following conclusions from these studies. First, generally speaking, formal planning is associated with higher profits, higher return on assets, and other positive financial results. Second, the quality of the planning process and the appropriate implementation of the plans probably contribute more to high performance than does the extent of planning. Next, in those studies in which formal planning didn't lead to higher performance, the external environment often was the culprit. Governmental regulations, powerful labor unions, and other critical environmental forces constrain managers' options and reduce the impact of planning on an organization's performance. Finally, the planning/performance relationship is influenced by the planning time frame. Organizations need at least four years of systematic formal planning before performance is impacted.

••• Learning Review

- Describe the purposes of planning.
- Explain the conclusions from studies of the relationship between planning and performance.

HOW DO MANAGERS PLAN?

Planning is often called the primary management function because it establishes the basis for all the other functions that managers perform. Without planning, managers wouldn't know what to organize, lead, or control. In fact, without plans, there wouldn't *be* anything to organize, lead, or control! So how *do* managers plan? That's what we want to look at in this section.

The Role of Goals and Plans in Planning

••• **goals**
Desired outcomes for
individuals, groups, or entire
organizations.

••• **plans**
Documents that outline how
goals are going to be met
including resource
allocations, schedules, and
other necessary actions to
accomplish the goals.

Planning involves two important elements: goals and plans. **Goals** are desired outcomes for individuals, groups, or entire organizations.[4] Goals are objectives, and we use the two terms interchangeably. They provide the direction for all management decisions and form the criteria against which actual work accomplishments can be measured. That's why they're often called the foundation of planning. And you have to know the desired target or outcome before you can establish plans for reaching it. **Plans** are documents that outline how goals are going to be met and that typically describe resource allocations, schedules, and other necessary actions to accomplish the goals. As managers plan, they're developing both goals and plans.

Types of Goals At first glance, it might appear that organizations have a single objective: for business firms, to make a profit; for not-for-profit organizations, to meet the needs of some constituent group(s). In reality, all organizations have multiple objectives. Businesses also want to increase market share and keep employees enthused about the organization. A church provides a place for religious practices but also assists economically disadvantaged individuals in its community and acts as a social gathering place for church members. No single measure can be used to evaluate whether an organization is successful. (■□■■■ Go to the Web and check out Q & A 7.3.) Emphasis on one goal, such as profit, ignores other goals that must also be reached if long-term success is to be achieved. Also, as we discussed in Chapter 5, using a single objective such as profit can result in unethical practices because managers will ignore other important parts of their jobs in order to look good on that one measure.

Examples of both financial and strategic goals from some well-known U.S. corporations are shown in Exhibit 7–1. Financial goals are related to the financial perfor-

Goals are the outcomes we desire. At the Bronx Zoo, where Patrick Thomas, curator of mammals, recently gazed into the eyes of Siberian tiger "Taurus" through a sheet of inch-thick glass, "Our goal is to have animals engaged in normal behaviors." Thomas goes on to say of the new tiger habitat, "You want the exhibit to inspire visitors to care about saving tigers." The goal of the three-acre Tiger Mountain is particularly important; its six residents represent the mere 5,000 tigers left in the wild.

Exhibit 7–1

Stated Objectives from Large U.S. Companies

Financial Objectives	Strategic Objectives
• Faster revenue growth	• A bigger market share
• Faster earnings growth	• A higher, more secure industry rank
• Higher dividends	• Higher product quality
• Wider profit margins	• Lower costs relative to key competitors
• Higher returns on invested capital	• Broader or more attractive product line
• Stronger bond and credit ratings	• A stronger reputation with customers
• Bigger cash flows	• Superior customer service
• A rising stock price	• Recognition as a leader in technology and/or product innovation
• Recognition as a "blue chip" company	• Increased ability to compete in international markets
• A more diversified revenue base	• Expanded growth opportunities
• Stable earnings during recessionary periods	

Source: A.A. Thompson Jr. and A.J. Strickland III, *Strategic Management* 12th ed. (New York: McGraw-Hill/Irwin, 2001), p. 43.

mance of the organization while strategic goals are related to other areas of an organization's performance. Except for a few of the financial ones, these goals could apply to a not-for-profit organization as well. Note, too, that although survival isn't specifically mentioned as a goal, it's extremely important to all organizations. An organization must survive if other goals are to be achieved.

Another way to describe goals is in terms of whether they're real or stated. Exhibit 7–1 is a list of **stated goals**—official statements of what an organization says, and what it wants its stakeholders to believe, its goals are. However, stated goals—which can be found in an organization's charter, annual report, public relations announcements, or in public statements made by managers—are often conflicting and excessively influenced by what society believes organizations should do. (▮▮▮▮ Go to the Web and check out Q & A 7.4.)

•●● **stated goals**
Official statements of what an organization says, and what it wants its various stakeholders to believe, its goals are.

The conflict in stated goals exists because organizations respond to a variety of stakeholders. And these stakeholders frequently evaluate the organization by different criteria. For example, when Bill Ford Jr., chairman of Ford Motor Company, announced the goal of making its vehicles more fuel efficient and more environmentally friendly as a way to best serve its shareholders, environmentalists and Ford executives viewed it differently.[5] The company reached out to environmental groups by initiating discussions on fuel economy issues. It also released a corporate citizenship report that acknowledged "very real conflicts" between Ford's stated commitment to the environment and its continued marketing of gas-guzzling SUVs. Environmentalists, while encouraged by the company's concern, were wary of its ultimate intent. Ford executives who were well aware of the need to produce vehicles that the public demanded and that added dollars to the bottom line, had long been criticized by environmentalists, thus making them reluctant to cooperate in any collaborative discussions. Was the goal of being more environmentally friendly true and the goal of doing the best for its shareholders false? No. Both were true, but they did conflict.

Have you ever read an organization's goals as stated in its company literature? For instance, Claire's Stores' goal is "to continue expanding our brand strength and proven formula across North America, Europe, and Japan." Nike's goal is to "bring inspiration and innovation to every athlete." Winnebago's goal is "to continually improve products and services to meet or exceed the expectations of our customers." And Revlon Cosmetics says its goal is "to provide glamour, excitement, and innovation to consumers through high-quality products at affordable prices."[6] These types of statements are usually vague and are more likely to represent management's public relations skills than provide meaningful guides to what the organization is actually trying to accomplish. It shouldn't be surprising then to find that an organization's stated goals are often quite irrelevant to what actually goes on.[7] Such

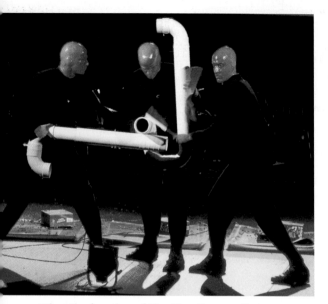

When the founders of Blue Man Group, a three-man band/performance troupe, decided they were ready to expand by hiring performers to do Blue Man shows around the country, they were anxious to keep the acts consistent with their original vision. They finally realized they needed a specific plan to guide the 38 new performers they were bringing on board, so they locked themselves in an apartment and talked through their creative vision in great detail. The result? A 132-page operating manual that tells the story of the Blue Man show and allows it to be reproduced by others. Ironically, by writing the plan, though it is a somewhat unorthodox one, the founders were able to express artistic ideals that had been understood among them but never stated before.

• • • **real goals**
Goals that an organization actually pursues, as defined by the actions of its members.

goals are substantially determined by what various stakeholders want to hear. If you want to know an organization's **real goals**—those goals that an organization actually pursues—observe what organizational members are doing. Actions define priorities. For example, universities that proclaim the goal of limiting class size, facilitating close student–faculty relations, and actively involving students in the learning process and then put them into lecture classes of 300 or more are pretty common! An awareness that real and stated objectives differ is important for understanding what might otherwise seem to be management inconsistencies.

Types of Plans The most popular ways to describe organizational plans are by their breadth (strategic versus operational), time frame (short term versus long term), specificity (directional versus specific), and frequency of use (single use versus standing). These planning classifications aren't independent. As Exhibit 7–2 illustrates, strategic plans are long term, directional, and single use. Operational plans are short term, specific, and standing. Let's describe each of these types of plans.

Strategic plans are plans that apply to the entire organization, establish the organization's overall goals, and seek to position the organization in terms of its environment. Plans that specify the details of how the overall goals are to be achieved are called **operational plans**. How do the two types of plans differ? Strategic plans tend to cover a longer time frame and a broader view of the organization. Strategic plans also include the formulation of goals whereas operational plans define ways to achieve the goals. Also, operational plans tend to cover short time periods—monthly, weekly, and day-to-day.

The difference in years between short term and long term has shortened considerably. It used to be that long term meant anything over seven years. Try to imagine what you'd like to be doing in seven years and you can begin to appreciate how difficult it was for managers to establish plans that far in the future. As organizational environments have become more uncertain, the definition of *long term* has changed. We define **long-term plans** as those with a time frame beyond three years.[8] We define **short-term plans** as those covering one year or less. The

Exhibit 7–2 **Types of Plans**

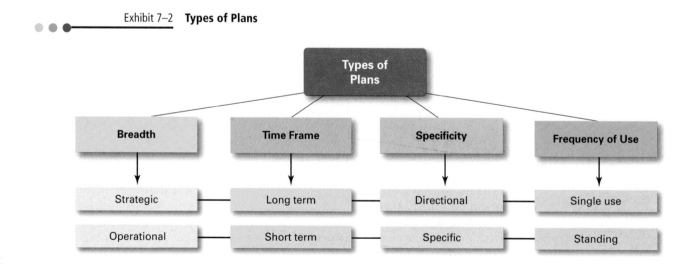

Exhibit 7–3

Specific Versus Directional Plans

Directional Plans   Specific Plans

strategic plans
Plans that apply to the entire organization, establish the organization's overall goals, and seek to position the organization in terms of its environment.

operational plans
Plans that specify the details of how the overall goals are to be achieved.

long-term plans
Plans with a time frame beyond three years.

short-term plans
Plans covering one year or less.

specific plans
Plans that are clearly defined and that leave no room for interpretation.

directional plans
Plans that are flexible and that set out general guidelines.

single-use plan
A one-time plan specifically designed to meet the needs of a unique situation.

standing plans
Ongoing plans that provide guidance for activities performed repeatedly.

intermediate term is any time period in between. Although these time classifications are fairly common, an organization can designate any time frame it wants for planning purposes.

Intuitively, it would seem that specific plans would be preferable to directional, or loosely guided, plans. **Specific plans** are plans that are clearly defined and which leave no room for interpretation. They have clearly defined objectives. There's no ambiguity and no problem with misunderstanding. For example, a manager who seeks to increase his or her unit's work output by 8 percent over a given 12-month period might establish specific procedures, budget allocations, and schedules of activities to reach that goal. The drawbacks of specific plans are that they require clarity and a sense of predictability that often do not exist.

When uncertainty is high and managers must be flexible in order to respond to unexpected changes, directional plans are preferable. **Directional plans** are flexible plans that set out general guidelines. (Exhibit 7–3 illustrates how specific and directional planning differ.) They provide focus but don't lock managers into specific goals or courses of action. Instead of detailing a specific plan to cut costs by 4 percent and increase revenues by 6 percent in the next six months, managers might formulate a directional plan for improving profits by 5 to 10 percent over the next six months. The flexibility inherent in directional plans must be weighed against the loss of clarity provided by specific plans.

Some plans that managers develop are ongoing while others are used only once. A **single-use plan** is a one-time plan specifically designed to meet the needs of a unique situation. For instance, when Charles Schwab introduced its online discount stock brokerage service, top-level executives used a single-use plan to guide the creation and implementation of the new service. In contrast, **standing plans** are ongoing plans that provide guidance for activities performed repeatedly. Standing plans include policies, rules, and procedures, which we defined in Chapter 6. (▮▯▯▯ Go to the Web and check out Q & A 7.5.) An example of a standing plan would be the sexual harassment policy developed by the University of Arizona. It provides guidance to university administrators, faculty, and staff as they perform their job duties.

Learning Review

- Define goals and plans.
- Describe the types of goals organizations might have.

- Explain why it's important to know an organization's stated and real goals.
- Describe each of the different types of plans.

ESTABLISHING GOALS AND DEVELOPING PLANS

Taylor has just been elected president of her business school's honorary fraternity. She wants the organization to be more actively involved in the business school than it has been in the past. Marcel graduated from the university with a degree in marketing and computers three years ago and went to work for a regional consulting services firm. He recently was promoted to manager of the eight-person e-business development team and hopes to strengthen the team's financial contributions to the firm. What should Taylor and Marcel do now? The first thing is to establish goals. How? That's what we're going to look at in this section.

Approaches to Establishing Goals

As we stated earlier, goals provide the direction for all management decisions and actions and form the criteria against which actual accomplishments are measured. Everything organizational members do should be oriented toward helping their work units and helping the organization achieve its goals. (■■■■■ Check out You're the Manager: Putting Ethics into Action on p. 226.) These goals can be established through a process of traditional goal setting or management by objectives.

● ● ● **traditional goal setting**
An approach to setting goals in which goals are set at the top level of the organization and then broken into subgoals for each level of the organization.

In **traditional goal setting**, goals are set at the top of the organization and then broken into subgoals for each organizational level. For example, the president of a manufacturing business tells the vice president of production what he expects manufacturing costs to be for the coming year and tells the marketing vice president what level he expects sales to reach for the year. These goals then are passed down to the next organizational level and written to reflect the work responsibilities of that level, passed down to the next level, and so forth. Then, at some later point, performance is evaluated to determine whether the assigned goals have been achieved. This traditional perspective assumes that top managers know what's best because they see the "big picture." Thus, the goals that are established and passed down to each succeeding level serve to direct, guide, and in some ways, constrain, individual employees' work behaviors. Employees work to meet the goals that have been assigned in their areas of responsibility.

One of the problems with this traditional approach is that if top managers define the organization's goals in broad terms—achieving "sufficient" profits or increasing "market leadership"—these ambiguous goals have to be made more specific as they flow down through the organization. At each level, managers define the goals, applying their own interpretations and biases as they make them more specific. However, what often happens is that goals lose clarity and unity as they make their way down from the top of the organization to lower levels. Exhibit 7–4 illustrates what can happen in this situation. (■■■■ Go to the Web and check out Q & A 7.6.)

● ● ● **means–ends chain**
An integrated network of goals in which the accomplishment of goals at one level serves as the means for achieving the goals, or ends, at the next level.

When the hierarchy of organizational goals *is* clearly defined, however, it forms an integrated network of goals, or a **means–ends chain**. This means that higher-level goals (or ends) are linked to lower-level goals, which serve as the means for their accom-

Exhibit 7–4

The Downside of Traditional Objective Setting

Exhibit 7–5

Steps in a Typical MBO Program

1. The organization's overall objectives and strategies are formulated.
2. Major objectives are allocated among divisional and departmental units.
3. Unit managers collaboratively set specific objectives for their units with their managers.
4. Specific objectives are collaboratively set with all department members.
5. Action plans, defining how objectives are to be achieved, are specified and agreed upon by managers and employees.
6. The action plans are implemented.
7. Progress toward objectives is periodically reviewed, and feedback is provided.
8. Successful achievement of objectives is reinforced by performance-based rewards.

••• **management by objectives (MBO)**
A management system in which specific performance goals are jointly determined by employees and their managers, progress toward accomplishing those goals is periodically reviewed, and rewards are allocated on the basis of this progress.

plishment. In other words, the achievement of goals at lower levels becomes the means to reach the goals at the next level (ends), and the accomplishment of goals at that level becomes the means to achieve the goals at the next level (ends), and so forth and so on, up through the different levels of the organization. That's how the traditional goal-setting approach is supposed to work.

Instead of traditional goal setting, many organizations use **management by objectives (MBO),** a management system in which specific performance goals are jointly determined by employees and their managers, progress toward accomplishing these goals is periodically reviewed, and rewards are allocated on the basis of this progress. Rather than using goals only as controls, MBO uses them to motivate employees as well.

Management by objectives consists of four elements: goal specificity, participative decision making, an explicit time period, and performance feedback.[9] Its appeal lies in its focus on the accomplishment of participatively set objectives as the reason for and motivation behind individuals' work efforts. Exhibit 7–5 lists the steps in a typical MBO program.

Do MBO programs work? Studies of actual MBO programs confirm that MBO increases employee performance and organizational productivity. A review of 70 programs, for example, found organizational productivity gains in 68 of them.[10] This same review also identified top management commitment and involvement as important conditions for MBO to succeed.

One problem of MBO programs is that they may not be as effective in times of dynamic environmental change. An MBO program needs some stability for employees to work toward accomplishing the set goals. If new goals must be set every few weeks, there's no time for employees to work on accomplishing the goals and measuring that accomplishment. Another problem of MBO programs is that an employee's overemphasis on accomplishing his or her goals without regard to others in the work unit can be counterproductive. A manager must work closely with all members of the work unit to assure that employees aren't working at cross purposes. Finally, if MBO is viewed simply as an annual exercise in filling out paperwork, employees won't be motivated to accomplish the goals. (■▯■■■ Go to the Web and check out Q & A 7.7.)

THINKING CRITICALLY ABOUT ETHICS

"I'm telling you. After my talk with my manager today about my work goals for the next quarter, I think our company's MBO program actually stands for 'manipulating' by objectives, not management by objectives," Carlos complained to his friend Sabrina. He went on, "She came in and outlined what she thought I should be working on and then asked me what I thought of it. I guess that's her way of getting me to participate in the goal setting."

Is it unethical for a manager to enter a participative goal-setting session with a pre-established set of goals that he or she wants the employee to accept? Why or why not? Is it unethical for a manager to use his or her formal position to impose specific goals on an employee? Why or why not?

Exhibit 7–6

Characteristics of Well-Designed Goals

- Written in terms of outcomes rather than actions
- Measurable and quantifiable
- Clear as to a time frame
- Challenging yet attainable
- Written down
- Communicated to all necessary organizational members

Characteristics of Well-Designed Goals Goals are not all created equal! Some goals are better than others. How do you tell the difference? What makes a "well-designed" goal?[11] Exhibit 7–6 outlines the characteristics of well-designed goals.

A well-designed goal should be *written in terms of outcomes* rather than actions. The desired end result is the most important element of any goal and, therefore, the goal should be written to reflect this. Next, a goal should be *measurable and quantifiable*. It's much easier to determine if a goal has been met if it's measurable. For instance, suppose one of your goals is to "produce a high-quality product." What exactly do you mean by high quality? Because there are numerous ways to define quality, the goal should state specifically how you will measure whether or not the product is high quality. This means that even in areas where it may be difficult to quantify your intent, you should try to find some specific way or ways to measure whether that goal is accomplished. Otherwise, why have the goal if you can't measure whether it's been met? In addition to specifying a quantifiable measure of accomplishment, a well-designed goal should also be *clear as to a time frame*. Although open-ended goals may seem preferable because of their flexibility, in fact, goals without a time frame make an organization less flexible because you're never sure when the goal has been met or when you should call it quits because the goal will never be met regardless of how long you work at it. A well-designed goal will specify a time frame for accomplishment. Next, a well-designed goal should be *challenging but attainable*. Goals that are too easy to accomplish are not motivating and neither are goals that are not attainable even with exceptional effort. Next, well-designed goals should be *written down*. Although actually writing down goals may seem too time-consuming, the process of writing the goals forces people to think them through. In addition, the written goals become visible and tangible evidence of the importance of working toward something. Finally, well-designed goals are *communicated to all organizational members* who need to know the goals. Why? Making people aware of the goals ensures that they're all "on the same page" and working in ways to secure the accomplishment of the organizational goals.

Steps in Goal Setting What steps should managers follow in setting goals? The goal-setting process consists of five steps.

1. *Review the organization's* **mission**, the purpose of an organization. These broad statements of what the organization's purpose is and what it hopes to accomplish provide an overall guide to what organizational members think is important. (We'll look more closely at organizational mission in Chapter 8.) It's important to review these statements before writing goals because the goals should reflect what the mission statement says.

2. *Evaluate available resources.* You don't want to set goals that are impossible to achieve given your available resources. Even though goals should be challenging, they should be realistic. After all, if the resources you have to work with won't allow you to achieve a goal no matter how hard you try or how much effort is exerted, that goal shouldn't be

••• **mission**
The purpose of an organization.

Rosanne Haggerty is the founder and executive director of Common Ground Community, a nonprofit housing organization based in New York. She is putting her organization's goals—to create cheap, secure, short-term residences for the homeless—into quantifiable terms by first measuring the extent of the problem. "We're going to count and document the homeless," says Haggerty, who is shown here with a "before" picture of the newly renovated Times Square Hotel in which she stands. "We're going to establish a target for reducing that number... What's it going to take to get each one of these people who's now homeless into some type of stable accommodation?"

Rodney K. G. Goodwin
Executive Director of
Marketing and Regional
Head for Southern Africa
(retired)
HSBC Equator
Avon, Connecticut

Describe your job.

Although I retired in April 2003, I held the position of Executive Director of Marketing and Regional Head for Southern Africa for HSBC Equator, a member of the HSBC Group (Hong Kong and Shanghai Banking Corporation). My job was that of a business development and international marketing executive for a merchant banking organization focused exclusively on Sub-Saharan Africa. My primary responsibility was to generate revenue, lots of it, and as fast as possible. Some 20 years ago when I entered this business, it was a daunting task to head out to totally uncharted territory in Africa to identify, select, and implement projects. It was my assignment to fly 10,000 miles from the bank's headquarters in Connecticut to enter countries like Angola, Congo-Kinshasa, or Mozambique and do things such as set up African offices, establish key contacts in the government and private sectors, establish credit guidelines and systems, provide training, and so forth. At the close of my career in 2003, the marketing had become more sophisticated, the team that I managed had become more experienced, and the revenue targets much greater. However, Africa had not changed that much and many, if not all, of the responsibilities still applied.

How important are goals to what you do?

It is essential to set goals and targets. It is the only way to measure progress and track the business development that has taken place over a month, quarter, or year. As I set out on a given year, I needed to know my quantitative and qualitative objectives. Setting goals and parameters for each year permitted my subordinates and me to identify: the market on which to focus, the products to promote and sell, the clients to target, the quarterly and annual revenue goals, the budget with which to work in order to achieve revenue goals, and the team to be assembled to carry out the work identified. These goals are also key to tracking one's own performance and that of employees. For a manager it serves to avoid confusion and misunderstandings at year-end when job evaluations and bonuses are being awarded or not.

What skills do you think managers need to be effective?

Today's manager must be someone who knows himself or herself well, is confident in who he or she "is" and is not easily threatened or intimidated, is a good listener, understands human nature, is a good communicator both verbally and in writing, knows how to relate to superiors/peers/subordinates, uses his or her intuition and acts on it, is quick to address human resources problems, is willing to delegate, recognizes his or her limitations, sets high standards by example, is able to identify talent and expertise and enable it to grow and flourish, operates with integrity and impartiality, leads at all times and is an advocate for his or her team, earns respect from peers and subordinates through excellence in performance and knowledge of the business, treats subordinates with respect, has a positive outlook, has a "can do" attitude and approach, has a sense of urgency, and is a self-starter.

set. That would be like the person with a $50,000 annual income and no other financial resources setting a goal of building an investment portfolio worth $1 million in three years. No matter how hard he or she works at it, it's not going to happen.

3. *Determine the goals individually or with input from others.* These goals reflect desired outcomes and should be congruent with the organizational mission and goals in other organizational areas. These goals should be measurable, specific, and include a time frame for accomplishment.

4. *Write down the goals and communicate them to all who need to know* We've already explained the benefit of writing down and communicating goals.

5. *Review results and whether goals are being met.* Change, as needed.

Once the goals have been established, written down, and communicated, a manager is ready to develop plans for pursuing the goals.

Developing Plans

The process of developing plans is influenced by three contingency factors and by the planning approach followed.

Contingency Factors in Planning Look back at our chapter-opening "Manager's Dilemma." How will Gabriela know what types of plans to develop for guiding the use of the Internet in other marketing activities at UBS AG? Will strategic or operational plans be needed? How about specific or directional plans? In some situations, long-term plans make sense; in others they do not. What are these situations? Three contingency factors affect planning: level in the organization, degree of environmental uncertainty, and length of future commitments.[12]

Exhibit 7–7 shows the relationship between a manager's level in the organization and the type of planning done. For the most part, operational planning dominates managers' planning efforts at lower levels. At upper organizational levels, planning becomes more strategy oriented.

The second contingency factor that affects planning is environmental uncertainty. When environmental uncertainty is high, plans should be specific, but flexible. Managers must be prepared to amend plans as they're implemented. (Go to the Web and check out S.A.L. #7—How Well Do I Handle Ambiguity?) At times, managers may even have to abandon their plans.[13] For example, at Continental Airlines, CEO Gordon M. Bethune and his management team established a specific goal of focusing on what customers wanted most—on-time flights—to help the company become more competitive in the highly uncertain airline industry. Because of the high level of uncertainty, the management team identified a "destination, but not a flight plan," and changed plans as necessary to achieve that goal of on-time service. Also, it's important for managers to continue formal planning efforts through periods of environmental uncertainty because studies have shown that it takes at least four years of such efforts before any positive impact on organizational performance is seen.[14]

The last contingency factor affecting planning also is related to the time frame of plans. The more that current plans affect future commitments, the longer the time frame is for which managers should plan. This **commitment concept** means that plans should extend far enough to meet those commitments made when the plans were developed. Planning for too long or too short a time period is inefficient and ineffective. To see how important the commitment concept is to planning, just look to the streets of Queens, New York, where a gritty old industrial building has been transformed into a temporary home for the Museum of Modern Art as its original building goes through significant renovation. In the early 1990s, the museum's board decided to expand its midtown location to meet its goal of "being a vital forward-looking institution committed to the art of the present as well as to the great achievements of the modern tradition."[15] Initial plans were developed, but building cost estimates proved to be too low and then there was the devastating impact from 9/11. Despite the uncertainties, it wasn't feasible to back out of the project. Instead, construction proceeded, and the new and redesigned museum is scheduled to open in 2005. This illustrates the

• • **commitment concept**
Plans should extend far enough to meet those commitments made today.

Exhibit 7–7

Planning in the Hierarchy of Organizations

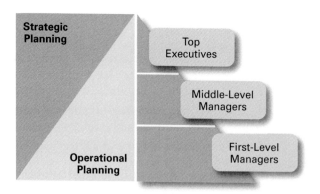

commitment concept because a decision made back in the early 1990s became a commitment for future actions and expenditures. Once the board decided to build a facility, it had to plan for the increased costs and construction delays due to 9/11. The future impact of the decision to build was that it committed the board to live with the decision and all its consequences, good and bad.

Approaches to Planning Federal, state, and local government officials are working together on a plan to boost populations of wild salmon in the northwestern United States. Managers in the Global Fleet Graphics division of the 3M Company are developing plans detailing innovative solutions for satisfying increasingly demanding customers and battling more aggressive competitors. Emilio Azcárraga Jean, chairman and president of Grupo Televisa, the Mexican broadcasting company, gets input from many different people before setting company goals and then turns over the planning for achieving the goals to various executives. In each of these situations, planning is done a little differently. (■■□■■ Check out Passport Scenario 2 on p. 226.) *How* an organization plans can best be understood by looking at *who* does the planning.

In the traditional approach, planning was done entirely by top-level managers who were often assisted by a **formal planning department**, a group of planning specialists whose sole responsibility was to help write the various organizational plans. Under this approach, plans developed by top-level managers flowed down through other organizational levels, much like the traditional approach to goal setting. As they flowed down through the organization, plans were tailored to the particular needs of each level. Although this approach helped make managerial planning thorough, systematic, and coordinated, all too often the focus was on developing "the plan," a thick binder (or binders) full of meaningless information, that was stuck away on a shelf and never used by anyone for guiding or coordinating work efforts. In fact, in a survey of managers about formal top-down organizational planning processes, over 75 percent said that their company's planning approach was unsatisfactory.[16] A common complaint was that "plans are documents that you prepare for the corporate planning staff and later forget." Although this traditional top-down approach to planning is still used by many organizations, it can be effective only if managers understand the importance of creating a workable, usable document that organizational members actually draw on for direction and guidance, not a document that looks impressive but is never used.

Another approach to planning is to involve more organizational members in the process. In this approach, plans aren't handed down from one level to the next, but instead are developed by organizational members at the various levels and in the various work units to meet their specific needs. For instance, at Dell's server manufacturing facility in Austin, Texas, employees from production, supply management, and channel management meet weekly to make plans based on current product demand and supply. In addition, work teams set their own daily schedules and track their progress against those schedules. If a team falls behind, team members develop "recovery" plans to try to get back on schedule.[17] When organizational members are more actively involved in planning, they see that the plans are more than just something written down on paper. They can actually see that the plans are used in directing and coordinating work.

● ● ● **formal planning department**
A group of planning specialists whose sole responsibility was helping to write various organizational plans.

● ● ● **Learning Review**

- Discuss how traditional goal setting works.
- Explain the concept of the means–end chain.
- Describe the management by objectives (MBO) approach.
- Describe the characteristics of well-designed goals.

- Explain the steps in setting goals.
- Discuss the contingency factors that affect planning.
- Describe the approaches to planning.

CONTEMPORARY ISSUES IN PLANNING

We conclude this chapter by addressing two contemporary issues in planning. Specifically, we're going to look at criticisms of planning, and then at how managers can plan effectively in dynamic environments.

Criticisms of Planning

Formalized organizational planning became popular in the 1960s and, for the most part, it still is today. It makes sense for an organization to establish some direction. But critics have challenged some of the basic assumptions underlying planning. What are the primary arguments directed at formal planning?

1. *Planning may create rigidity.*[18] Formal planning efforts can lock an organization into specific goals to be achieved within specific timetables. When these goals are set, the assumption may be that the environment won't change during the time period the goals cover. If that assumption is faulty, managers who follow a plan may face trouble. Rather than remaining flexible—and possibly throwing out the plan—managers who continue to do the things required to achieve the original goals may not be able to cope with the changed environment. Forcing a course of action when the environment is fluid can be a recipe for disaster.

2. *Plans can't be developed for a dynamic environment.*[19] Most organizations today face dynamic environments. If a basic assumption of making plans—that the environment won't change—is faulty, then how can you make plans at all? (■▢■■■■ Go to the Web and check out Q & A 7.8.) Today's business environment is often chaotic, at best. By definition, that means random and unpredictable. Managing under those conditions requires flexibility, and that may mean not being tied to formal plans.

3. *Formal plans can't replace intuition and creativity.*[20] Successful organizations are typically the result of someone's innovative vision. But visions have a tendency to become formalized as they evolve. Formal planning efforts typically involve a thorough investigation of the organization's capabilities and opportunities and a mechanical analysis that reduces the vision to some type of programmed routine. That approach can spell disaster for an organization. For example, the rapid growth of Apple Computer in the late 1970s and throughout the 1980s was attributed, in part, to the innovative and creative approaches of one of its co-founders, Steven Jobs. As the company grew, Jobs felt there was a need for more formalized management—something he was uncomfortable doing. He hired a CEO who ultimately ousted Jobs from his own company. With Jobs's departure came increased organizational formality, including detailed planning—the same things that Jobs despised so much because he felt that they hampered creativity. By the mid 1990s, Apple, once an industry leader, was struggling for survival. The situation became so bad that Jobs was brought back as CEO to get Apple back on track. However, the company's renewed focus on innovation led to the debut of the iMac in 1998, a radically new look for the iMac in 2002, and an online music store in 2003.

Terri Williamson put her backgrounds in chemistry and professional branding to good use when she decided to create a line of cosmetics under the brand name "Glow." She planned carefully, checking the Internet to be sure the product name was available, creating a distinctive look and feel for the packaging of her product line, hand-picking the Hollywood location of her store, and mixing and remixing essential oils and other ingredients in her home to come up with a distinctive sandalwood scent. Williamson's plans were coming to fruition in 2001 and 2002, with steadily rising sales among her celebrity clients, when everything changed. Jennifer Lopez unveiled her own new fragrance called "Glow by J.Lo," and Williamson's Glow Industries began a trademark infringement suit that is still pending.

4. *Planning focuses managers' attention on today's competition, not on tomorrow's survival.*[21] Formal planning has a tendency to focus on how to capitalize on existing business opportunities within an industry. It often doesn't allow managers to consider creating or reinventing an industry. Consequently, formal plans may result in costly blunders and high catch-up costs when other competitors take the lead. On the other hand, companies such as Intel, General Electric, Nokia, and Sony have found success forging into uncharted waters, spawning new industries as they go.

5. *Formal planning reinforces success, which may lead to failure.*[22] Success breeds success. That's an "American tradition." If it's not broken, don't fix it, right? (■□■■ Go to the Web and check out Q & A 7.9.) Well, maybe not! Success may, in fact, breed failure in an uncertain environment. It's hard to change or discard previously successful plans—to leave the comfort of what works for the anxiety of the unknown. Successful plans, however, may provide a false sense of security, generating more confidence in the formal plans than is warranted. Many managers will not face the unknown until they're forced to do so by environmental changes. By then, it may be too late!

How valid are these criticisms? Should managers forget about planning? No! Although the criticisms have merit when directed at rigid, inflexible planning, today's managers can be effective planners if they understand planning in dynamic, uncertain environments.

Effective Planning in Dynamic Environments

The external environment is continually changing. For instance, a wireless networking technology called Wi-Fi, a radio signal that beams Internet connections out 300 feet, is revolutionizing all kinds of industries from airlines to automobile manufacturing to consumer electronics. The power of the Internet also is being used by companies in new and unique ways including product design or logistics. Consumers continue to increase the amounts they spend on eating out instead of cooking at home. And the euro is now the official currency of a majority of countries in the European Union.

How can managers effectively plan when the external environment is continually changing? (■■□■ Go to the Web and check out S.A.L. #47—How Well Do I Respond to Turbulent Change?) We have already discussed uncertain environments as one of the main contingency factors that affect the types of plans managers develop. Because dynamic environments are more the norm than the exception for today's managers, let's revisit how to plan in an uncertain environment.

Becoming a Manager

- ◆ *Practice setting goals by doing so for various aspects of your personal life such as academic, career preparation, family, and so forth.*
- ◆ *Be prepared to change your goals as circumstances change.*
- ◆ *For goals that you've set, write out plans for achieving those goals.*
- ◆ *Write a personal mission statement.*
- ◆ *If you're employed, talk to your manager(s) about the types of planning they do. Ask them for suggestions on how to be a better planner.*
- ◆ ■■□■ *Go to the Web and complete any of the following exercises from the Self-Assessment Library (S.A.L.) found on R.O.L.L.S.: #4—How Flexible Am I?, #12—What's My Attitude Toward Achievement?, #21—What Time of Day Am I Most Productive?, and #22—How Good Am I at Personal Planning?*

In an uncertain environment, managers want to develop plans that are specific, but flexible. Although this may seem contradictory, it's not. To be useful, plans need some specificity, but the plans should not be cast in stone. Managers must recognize that planning is an ongoing process; the plans serve as a road map, although the destination may be changing constantly due to dynamic market conditions. They should be willing to change directions if environmental conditions warrant. This flexibility is particularly important as plans are implemented. Managers must stay alert to environmental changes that could impact the effective implementation of plans and make changes as needed. Keep in mind, also, that it's important to continue formal planning efforts, even when the environment is highly uncertain, in order to see any effect on organizational performance. It's the persistence in planning efforts that contributes to significant performance improvement. Why? It seems that, as with most activities, managers "learn to plan" and the quality of their planning improves when they continue to do it.[23]

Finally, effective planning in dynamic environments means flattening the organizational hierarchy as the responsibility for establishing goals and developing plans is pushed to lower organizational levels, since there's little time for goals and plans to flow down from the top. Managers must train their employees in setting goals and establishing plans and then trust that they will do so. And you need look no further than Bangalore, India, to find a company that effectively understands this. Just a short decade ago, Wipro Limited was "an anonymous conglomerate selling cooking oil and personal computers, mostly in India. Today, it is a $904 million-a-year global company, and most of its business comes from information-technology services."[24] Accenture, EDS, IBM, and the big U.S. accounting firms know all too well the competitive threat Wipro represents. Not only are Wipro's employees low cost, they're knowledgeable and skilled. And they play an important role in the company's planning. Since the information services industry is continually changing, employees are taught to analyze situations and to define the scale and scope of a client's problems in order to offer the best solutions. They're the ones on the front line with the clients and it's their responsibility to establish what to do and how to do it. It's an approach that has positioned Wipro for success no matter how the industry changes.

● ● ● ● Learning Review

- Explain the criticisms of planning and whether or not they're valid.

- Describe how managers can effectively plan in today's dynamic environment.

Managers **Respond** to a **Manager's** Dilemma

Steve Hidy

Director of Client Services, Corporate Information Systems, Pearson Education, Bloomington, MN

As Gabriela points out, the Internet is just another way to conduct business. To plan for expanding Internet use, she should look at all customer and vendor interactions and assess all the traditional marketing methods to identify those areas that will generate the greatest return on investment. For example, instead of road-show seminars, which are traditionally held in large hotels or convention center and incur travel expenses for both the customer and the vendor, Gabriela might consider Webcasts to deliver the company's message. Or she might decide to create audiovisual presentations that users can download from the Internet and view when they want and how they want. Through Gabriela's leadership, her company is well on its way to incorporating technology into their marketing strategies.

Daniel Borden

Senior Finance Manager, Europe and Southeast, International Network Services, Atlanta, Georgia

Gabriela has successfully leveraged technology to improve productivity. She may want to consider taking this technology to the next level by using it to analyze customers' profitability profiles for strategic marketing. How could she do this? One way is to market various financial products to customers based on their responses while on the company's Web site. Or she might consider using the current call routing system as a marketing tool based on responses customers provide as they make menu choices by playing recorded promotions while the customer waits or having customer service representatives pitch products. The goals of these approaches would be to increase sales of financial products to the existing customer base and to sell customers on products with higher profit margins. One caution—UBS should carefully evaluate these potential strategies in light of their customers' privacy rights.

Learning Summary

After reading and studying this chapter, you should be able to:

- Define planning.

- Differentiate between formal and informal planning.

- Describe the purposes of planning.

- Explain the conclusions from studies of the relationship between planning and performance.

- Define goals and plans.

- Describe the types of goals organizations might have.

- Explain why it's important to know an organization's stated and real goals.

- Describe each of the different types of plans.

- Discuss how traditional goal setting works.

- Explain the concept of the means–end chain.

- Describe the management by objectives (MBO) approach.

- Describe the characteristics of well-designed goals.

- Explain the steps in setting goals.

- Discuss the contingency factors that affect planning.

- Describe the approaches to planning.

- Explain the criticisms of planning and whether or not they're valid.

- Describe how managers can effectively plan in today's dynamic environment.

Thinking About Management Issues

1. Will planning become more or less important to managers in the future? Why?

2. If planning is so crucial, why do some managers choose not to do it? What would you tell these managers?

3. Explain how planning involves making decisions today that will have an impact later.

4. How might planning in a not-for-profit organization such as the American Cancer Society differ from planning in a for-profit organization such as Coca-Cola?

5. What types of planning do you do in your personal life? Describe these plans in terms of being (a) strategic or operational, (b) short or long term, and (c) specific or directional.

6. "Organizations that fail to plan are planning to fail." Do you agree or disagree with this statement? Explain your position.

7. Would manager ever use informal planning? Why or Why not?

Working Together: Team-Based Exercise

People Power[2], a training company that markets its human resource programs to corporations around the globe, has had several requests to design a training program to teach employees how to use the Internet for researching information. This training program will then be marketed to potential corporate customers. Your team is spearheading this important project. There are three stages to the project: (1) researching corporate customer needs, (2) researching the Internet for specific information sources and techniques that could be used in the training module, and (3) designing and writing a specific training module. The first thing your team has to do is identify at least three goals for each stage. As you proceed with this task, you don't need to come up with specifics about "how" to proceed with these activities; just think about "what" you want to accomplish in each stage.

Form small groups of three or four individuals. Complete your assigned work as described above. Be sure that your goals are well designed. Be prepared to share your team's goals with the rest of the class.

Ethical Dilemma Exercise

Some lower- and mid-level managers go to great lengths to achieve their goals rather than disrupt the means–ends chain that supports the accomplishment of higher-level goals. But how far is too far? Coca-Cola has admitted that some personnel acted improperly when they took steps to manipulate the results of a product test at Burger King restaurants in Richmond, Virginia. If the test succeeded, the product—Frozen Coke—would be introduced in more Burger King outlets. In turn, the prospect of higher sales was a milestone toward meeting Coca-Cola's overall revenue and profit goals.

Burger King executives and franchisees were not pleased when they found out about the manipulated test results. Coca-Cola's president sent a written apology to Burger King, noting: "These actions were wrong and inconsistent with the values of the Coca-Cola Company. Our relationships with Burger King and all our customers are of the utmost importance to us and should be firmly grounded in only the highest-integrity actions."[25] Did Coca-Cola managers feel too much pressure to deliver results?

Imagine that you're a district manager with Coca-Cola and you're being promoted to a new position at the end of the month. Your area's sales are an important component of the corporation's statewide and national sales goals. However, this month's sales are running below the planned level. What can you do to give sales a boost so you meet the target for your final month in this job?

Option A: Arrange an area-wide supermarket promotion in which consumers receive $1 off the purchase of any Coca-Cola six-pack when they make a total store purchase of $20 or more.

Option B: Arrange a special promotion in which any consumer who brings unopened cans or bottles of competing soft drinks to local supermarkets receives two equivalent Coca-Cola products.

Option C: Ask area supermarkets to double their current monthly order and promise that any unsold Coca-Cola products can be returned during the following month.

Case Application

Lend Lease Corporation

"Every project we take on starts with a question: How can we do what's never been done before?" That's the guiding philosophy of Australia's Lend Lease Corporation (**www.lendlease.com**). And it's done some pretty spectacular projects including building the foundations for the Sydney Opera House, the Newington Olympic Village for the 2000 Summer Olympics, and soundstages for *The Matrix* and *Mission: Impossible 2*. But building isn't the company's only business. It's also a market leader in terms of being a global, integrated real estate business with expertise in real estate investment, project management and construction, and property development. It currently has over $91 billion (Australian dollars) of global real estate assets that it manages.

Lend Lease is an Australian business success story and is seen as one of the most exciting companies to work for in Australia. How does Lend Lease manage to be consistently successful *and* persistently different? Managing Director and Chief Executive Officer Greg Clarke recognizes that effective managerial planning plays an important role. One of its projects, the Bluewater complex in Kent, England—one of Europe's largest retail and leisure destinations—illustrates how planning is done at Lend Lease.

In the mid-1990s, two Lend Lease executives—Stuart Hornery and director of special projects Malcolm Latham—stood at the edge of an abandoned limestone quarry about 20 miles outside of London, surveying the barren landscape. Instead of seeing what most people would—an industrial wasteland—they envisioned a

Lend Lease Corporation's Bluewater real estate project.

dramatic and unique civic space that would be a community gathering place in addition to being a popular retail shopping center. They made the decision to purchase the site from Blue Circle Industries, a British cement company that had been trying to develop it for more than eight years. Upon signing the deal, Lend Lease got a preapproved development plan that was in place for the site. However, company executives chose to abandon everything in this plan but the project's name: Bluewater. That's when the company's own planning efforts got serious.

Less than three weeks after that initial visit to the site, a team of Lend Lease employees, including Hornery and Latham and six of the company's best retail, property, and project-management experts, met with Eric Kuhne, a well-respected U.S. architect. The team's goal was to bring to life Hornery and Latham's vision for the Bluewater site. What they developed was an innovative, break-the-mold plan, simply titled, The Bluewater Factors. The team's plan outlined a shopping complex featuring a glowing white roofscape; 1.6 million square feet of retail space; a 13,000-car parking garage; and over 50 acres of parks, seven lakes, and more than 1 million trees and shrubs. The project's scale would prove to be an enormous undertaking. However, the company's planning would once again prove effective.

For such complex projects, Lend Lease uses project-control groups (PCG) to blend creativity and accountability. The project gets a PCG which plays a role similar to a corporate board of directors. Members of a PCG don't work on the project day-to-day, but are accountable for it. Project managers are challenged to assemble a PCG with the best possible diverse mix of skills, intuition, and experiences of people from both inside *and* outside the company. These PCGs can include as few as 3 people or as many as 15. They meet every six or seven weeks during the project's duration. And these meetings are serious. There's a precise agenda, a set of minutes, a financial review, and several other reports on the key aspects of the project. But these meetings aren't just about making sure that deadlines and budgets are being met. They're also an opportunity to engage in active questioning and exploration of ideas for better implementation. They're a cross between dreams and discipline. One project manager said, "We know that we have to make a case for why we are doing something in the first place. That means we're not afraid to stop things. We're brutal about pulling the plug and moving on, even when we've already spent a lot of time and money on a project."

The PCG for the Bluewater project included Hornery, Latham, Kuhne, the CEO of Lend Lease's European business, and the investment director of Prudential (one of Lend Lease's biggest investors). It also included a revolving group of architects; engineers; manufacturers; community advocates; local planning authorities; experts on construction, retail, and finance; *and* customers. Every five to six weeks, the PCG met to discuss budgets, agendas, and proposals for innovations. Did this commitment to effective planning work?

The time from initial idea to final leasing stage was just 1,628 days (a little under 4-1/2 years). The project came in two weeks ahead of schedule, on budget, and fully leased with more than 320 retailers from around the world. The Bluewater complex is a sprawling triangle with three two-story malls. Each mall's shopping streets connect with the surrounding landscape and each mall features a "leisure village" that integrates its shopping area with nearby recreational space. The complex features health clubs, restaurants, and a cinema complex. There are even "welcome" halls decorated like luxury hotels and staffed by full-time concierges. Since its grand opening in March 2000, an average of more than 75,000 people per day have visited Bluewater.

The complex features health clubs, restaurants, and a cinema.

DISCUSSION QUESTIONS

1. What role do you think goals play in planning done at Lend Lease? Explain.

2. How does Lend Lease illustrate effective planning in a dynamic environment?

3. What approach to developing plans does Lend Lease appear to follow? Explain.

4. Would Lend Lease's approach work in other organizations? Why or why not?

5. Lend Lease has a strong commitment to environmentally sustainable development. (Check out its Web site for information on its core values.) How might these core values affect planning efforts?

Sources: Information on company from Hoover's Online (*www.hoovers.com*), May 10, 2003, and from company's Web site (*www.lendlease.com*), May 10, 2003; P. LaBarre, "A Company without Limits," *Fast Company,* September 1999, pp. 160–186; and "Lend Lease Building on Its Success," *Business Asia,* March 15, 1999, p. 11.

•••Learning Outline

Follow this Learning Outline as you read and study this chapter.

The Importance of Strategic Management
- Explain why strategic management is important.
- Discuss what studies of the effectiveness of strategic management have shown.

The Strategic Management Process
- List the six steps in the strategic management process.
- Describe what managers do when they do external and internal analyses.
- Explain the role of resources, capabilities, and core competencies in the internal analysis.

Types of Organizational Strategies
- Explain the three growth strategies.
- Discuss the BCG matrix and how it's used.
- Define SBUs and business-level strategies.
- Describe the role of competitive advantage in business-level strategies.
- Explain Porter's five forces model.
- Describe the three generic competitive strategies.

Strategic Management in Today's Environment
- Discuss the implications of dynamic and uncertain environments on organizational strategy.
- Explain the rule of three and its significance for strategic management.
- Describe strategies applying e-business techniques.
- Explain what strategies organizations might use to become more customer oriented and to be more innovative.

Chapter

8

Strategic Management

Tim and Diane Mueller (in picture) run one of America's most admired independent ski areas—Okemo Mountain Resort in southern Vermont.[1] But the road they've traveled hasn't been easy. In 1982, they raised $600,000 by mortgaging their home and draining their savings to purchase a controlling stake in the ski area. And the early years were extremely rough. Uncooperative weather, dilapidated equipment, and demanding customers were a few of the problems they dealt with.

It's tough to make money in the ski industry. Ski areas are capital intensive and dependent on the weather. Even many large corporate operators with deep pockets have gone bankrupt trying to run a ski resort. When the Muellers purchased Okemo, not only did they have to cope with these realities, they had two additional challenges to overcome—a lack of resources and inexperience. Tim says, "We were young and naïve enough to think that we could make something happen. We never talked about what would happen if it didn't work." Because they didn't have the resources to focus on major improvements, they decided to emphasize quality and execution. They focused on delivering better service to customers and lavished time and attention on making snow and grooming the trails to perfection. The couple felt that these were the ways to deliver a better skiing experience. And even though they can now afford to make necessary equipment improvements, those two strategies continue to guide the company today.

Each fall, Diane indoctrinates the 1,200-plus seasonal employees with the importance of customer service. She tells them it's everyone's job to exceed the expectations of guests anytime and anywhere. And a lot of attention to detail goes into taking care of the mountain itself. Trails are groomed carefully year-round—a fact not missed by *Ski* magazine, which has ranked Okemo the best-groomed mountain in the East since 1999.

Put yourself in the Muellers' shoes. They're considering expanding their business by purchasing other ski areas. How could SWOT analysis help them make this decision?

What would *you* do **?**

he importance of having good strategies can be seen by what the Muellers have accomplished with Okemo Mountain Resort. By designing effective strategies to attract customers, they've built their resort into a prosperous, thriving organization. And as they ponder expansion plans, strategic management will once again play an important role. An underlying theme in this chapter is that effective strategies result in high organizational performance.

THE IMPORTANCE OF STRATEGIC MANAGEMENT

Effective managers around the world recognize the role that strategic management plays in their organization's performance. (■□■ Go to the Web and check out Q & A 8.1.) For instance, using well-designed strategies, Swedish company Electrolux is the world's number-one producer of household appliances and vacuum cleaners. It has "conquered" Europe and is looking to do the same in the U.S. market. Hindustan Lever Ltd. is India's largest consumer goods company and makes soaps, detergents, and food products. As a result of effective strategic management, it has achieved an average three-year total return to stockholders of 120 percent. And Millennium Pharmaceuticals of Cambridge, Massachusetts, wants to be *the* drug company for the new millennium. It's poised to exploit its scientific knowledge and capabilities in gene-based medicine and jump into the ranks of the world's top pharmaceutical companies. These companies illustrate the value of strategic management. In this section, we want to look at what strategic management is and why it's considered important to managers.

What Is Strategic Management?

To begin to understand the basics of strategy and strategic management you need look no further than at what's happened in the discount retail industry. The industry's two largest competitors—Wal-Mart and Kmart—have battled for market dominance since 1962, the year both companies were founded. The two chains have other striking similarities: store atmosphere, names, markets served, and organizational purpose. Yet, Wal-Mart's performance (financial and otherwise) has far surpassed that of Kmart. Wal-Mart is the world's largest and most successful retailer and Kmart is the largest retailer ever to seek Chapter 11 bankruptcy protection (from which it emerged in May 2003). Why the difference in performance? Organizations vary in how well they perform because of differences in their strategies and differences in competitive abilities.[2] Wal-Mart excels at strategic management, while Kmart struggles to find the right combination.

Strategic management is that set of managerial decisions and actions that determines the long-run performance of an organization.[3] It's an important task of managers and entails all of the basic management functions. We'll discuss in detail how strategic management takes place in an organization at a later point in the chapter.

●●● **strategic management**
That set of managerial decisions and actions that determines the long-run performance of an organization.

Why Is Strategic Management Important?

Stellar Blue is the newest color in H.J. Heinz Company's crazy-colored ketchup palette, which already includes green, purple, pink, orange, teal, and of course, the traditional red. Heinz's managers clearly understand the importance of strategic management because they know that every time a color is introduced the company's market share bumps up a little.

Why is strategic management so important? One of the most significant reasons is that it can make a difference in how well an organization performs. The most fundamental questions about strategy address why firms succeed or fail, and why, when faced with the same environmental conditions, they have varying levels of performance.

Studies of the factors that contribute to organizational performance have shown a positive relationship between strategic planning and performance.[4] In other words, it appears that organizations that use strategic management do have higher levels of performance. And that makes strategic management pretty important!

Another reason strategic management is important has to do with the fact that organizations of all types and sizes face continually changing situations. These changes may be minor or significant, but there's still change with which managers must cope. (▢ Go to the Web and check out S.A.L. #4—How Flexible Am I?) That's where strategic management comes in. By following the steps in the strategic management process, managers examine relevant variables in deciding what to do and how to do it. When managers use the strategic management process, they can better cope with the uncertain environments.

Strategic management is also important because of the nature of organizations. They're composed of diverse divisions, units, functions, and work activities—manufacturing, marketing, accounting, and so forth—that need to be coordinated and focused on achieving the organization's goals. (▢ Go to the Web and check out S.A.L. #7—How Well Do I Handle Ambiguity?) The strategic management process does this.

Finally, strategic management is important because it's involved in many of the decisions that managers make. Most of the significant current business events reported in the various business publications involve strategic management. For instance, recently, there were reports of Time Warner and Germany's Bertelsmann AG discussing a merger of their music operations; Talbot's retail chain opening its first men's store in Westport, Connecticut; and Volkswagen's CEO trying to find the right mix of strategic changes to revitalize his company. All are examples of managers making strategic decisions. How widespread is the use of strategic management? One survey of business owners found that 69 percent had strategic plans, and among those owners, 89 percent responded that they found their plans to be effective.[5] They stated, for example, that strategic planning gave them specific goals and provided their staff with a unified vision. Although a few management writers claim that strategic planning is "dead," most continue to emphasize its importance.[6]

Today, strategic management has moved beyond for-profit business organizations to include governmental agencies, hospitals, and other not-for-profit organizations. For instance, when the U.S. Postal Service found itself in intense competitive battles with overnight package delivery companies, electronic mail services, and private

NASCAR seems to be able to beat the slow economy, increase its fan base, and maybe even move into the mainstream. But costly rules adjustments, a pending antitrust lawsuit, lagging attendance at some tracks, and needed improvements at others present NASCAR's management with strategic decisions that will strongly affect its future. Says chief operating officer George Pyne, "We're really talking about managing success, and managing it in a way that is mindful of all the key ingredients that have made you successful—and also being mindful that the world is a changing place."

mailing facilities, its CEO (the U.S. Postmaster General) used strategic management to help pinpoint important issues and to design appropriate strategic responses, including the popular self-adhesive stamps and an electronic postmark used to certify e-mail messages. Although strategic management in not-for-profits hasn't been as well researched as that in for-profit organizations, we know it's important for these organizations as well.

• • • Learning Review

- Explain why strategic management is important.
- Discuss what studies of the effectiveness of strategic management have shown.

THE STRATEGIC MANAGEMENT PROCESS

• • • **strategic management process**
A six-step process that encompasses strategic planning, implementation, and evaluation.

The **strategic management process**, as illustrated in Exhibit 8–1, is a six-step process that encompasses strategic planning, implementation, and evaluation. Although the first four steps describe the planning that must take place, implementation and evaluation are just as important! Even the best strategies can fail if management doesn't implement or evaluate them properly. Let's examine the six steps in detail.

Step 1: Identifying the Organization's Current Mission, Objectives, and Strategies

Every organization needs a mission—a statement of the purpose of an organization. The mission answers the question: What is our reason for being in business? Defining the organization's mission forces managers to carefully identify the scope of its products or services. ( Go to the Web and check out Q & A 8.2.) For instance, the mission of Avon is "To be the company that best understands and satisfies the product, service, and self-fulfillment needs of women on a global level." The mission statement for the U.S. Federal Bureau of Prisons reads, "The Federal Bureau of Prisons protects society by confining offenders in the controlled environments of prisons and community-based facilities that are safe, humane, and appropriately secure, and which provide work and other self-improvement opportunities to assist offenders in becoming law-abiding citizens." The mission of eBay is "to build an online marketplace that enables practically

Exhibit 8–1 **The Strategic Management Process**

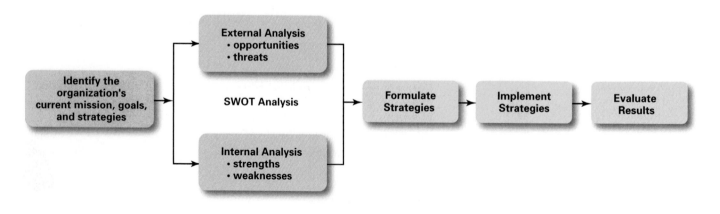

Exhibit 8–2

● ● ● ●━━━━━━

**Components of a Mission
Statement**

Customers: Who are the organization's customers?
We believe our first responsibility is to the doctors, nurses, and patients, to mothers and all others who use our products and services. (Johnson & Johnson)

Products or services: What are the organization's major products or services?
AMAX's main products are molybdenum, coal, iron ore, copper, lead, zinc, petroleum and natural gas, potash, phosphates, nickel, tungsten, silver, gold, and magnesium. (AMAX)

Markets: Where does the organization compete geographically?
Our emphasis is on North American markets, although global opportunities will be explored. (Blockway)

Technology: How technologically current is the organization?
The common technology in these areas is discrete particle coatings. (Nashua)

Concern for survival, growth, and profitability: Is the organization committed to growth and financial stability?
In this respect, the company will conduct its operations prudently, and will provide the profits and growth which will assure Hoover's ultimate success. (Hoover's Universal)

Philosophy: What are the organization's basic beliefs, values, aspirations, and ethical priorities?
It's all part of the Mary Kay philosophy—a philosophy based on the golden rule. A spirit of sharing and caring where people give cheerfully of their time, knowledge, and experience. (Mary Kay Cosmetics)

Self-concept: What is the organization's major competitive advantage and core competencies?
Crown Zellerbach is committed to leapfrogging competition within 1,000 days by unleashing the constructive and creative abilities and energies of each of its employees. (Crown Zellerbach)

Concern for public image: How responsive is the organization to societal and environmental concerns?
To share the world's obligation for the protection of the environment. (Dow Chemical)

Concern for employees: Does the organization consider employees a valuable asset?
Bama seeks people who want to learn and contribute in a team environment. We provide a safe work environment, operate as an equal opportunity employer, focus on employee development and retention, develop mutual respect and trust for each other and support promotion from within. We value the voice of each employee. (The Bama Companies)

Source: Based on F. David, *Strategic Management*, 8th ed. (Upper Saddle River, NJ: Prentice Hall, 2001), pp. 65–66.

anyone to trade practically anything almost anywhere in the world." These statements provide clues to what these organizations see as their reason for being in business. Exhibit 8–2 provides a description of the typical components of mission statements.

It's also important for managers to identify the goals currently in place and the strategies currently being pursued. As we explained in Chapter 7, goals are the foundation of planning. A company's goals provide the measurable performance targets that employees strive to reach. Knowing the company's current goals gives managers a basis for assessing whether those goals need to be changed. For the same reasons, it's important for managers to identify the organization's current strategies.

Step 2: External Analysis

In Chapter 3, we described the external environment as an important constraint on a manager's actions. Analyzing that environment is a critical step in the strategy process. (▬▬□▬ Go to the Web and check out PRISM #3—Environmental Scanning.) Managers in every organization need to do an external analysis. They need to know, for instance, what the competition is doing, what pending legislation might affect the organization, or what the labor supply is like in locations where it operates. In analyzing the external environment, managers should examine both the specific and general environments to see what trends and changes are occurring. (▬□▬▬ Go to the Web and check out Q & A 8.3.) For example, managers in the sporting goods industry recognized that the industry was changing.[7]

Long dominated by the large traditional sporting goods companies such as Nike and Rawlings, smaller companies whose products were aimed at extreme sports enthusiasts—sports participants who value risk-taking and pushing themselves to the limits—were entering the industry. Many of these smaller companies credited their success to the X Games, the competition that features everything from skateboarding to sky surfing to street luge. Managers at both the traditional companies and these smaller companies want to stay on top of the changes in the external environment so they can develop appropriate strategies.

After analyzing the environment, managers need to assess what they have learned in terms of opportunities that the organization can exploit, and threats that it must counteract. **Opportunities** are positive trends in external environmental factors; **threats** are negative trends.

One last thing to understand about external analysis is that the same environment can present opportunities to one organization and pose threats to another in the same industry because of their different resources and capabilities. For example, Southwest Airlines has prospered in a turbulent industry, while others such as American and Delta have struggled.

Step 3: Internal Analysis

Now we move from looking outside the organization to looking inside. The internal analysis should lead to a clear assessment of the organization's resources (such as financial capital, technical expertise, skilled employees, experienced managers, and so forth) and capabilities in performing the different functional activities (such as marketing, manufacturing, information systems, human resource management, and so forth). Any activities the organization does well or any unique resources that it has are called **strengths**. **Weaknesses** are activities the organization does not do well or resources it needs but does not possess. This step forces managers to recognize that every organization, no matter how large or successful, is constrained by the resources and capabilities it has available.

The internal analysis provides important information about an organization's specific resources and capabilities. If any of these organizational capabilities or resources are exceptional or unique, they're called the organization's **core competencies**. The core competencies are the organization's major value-creating skills, capabilities, and resources that determine its competitive weapons.[8] (▮▯▮▮ Go to the Web and check out Q & A 8.4.) For instance, Fujio Cho, President of Toyota Motor Corporation, called the company's newest Prius "a giant leap into the future," but the car is simply one more example of the company's core competencies in product research and manufacturing. Toyota is renowned worldwide for its effectiveness and efficiency. Experts who have studied the company point to its ability to nourish and preserve employee creativity and flexibility in a work environment that's fairly rigid and controlled.[9]

An understanding of the organization's culture is a crucial part of Step 3 that's often overlooked.[10] Managers should be aware that strong and weak cultures have different effects on strategy and that the content of a culture has a major effect on strategies pursued. (▮▯▮▮ Go to the Web and check out Q & A 8.5.)

●●● **opportunities**
Positive trends in external environmental factors.

●●● **threats**
Negative trends in external environmental factors.

●●● **strengths**
Any activities the organization does well or any unique resources that it has.

●●● **weaknesses**
Activities the organization does not do well or resources it needs but does not possess.

●●● **core competencies**
The organization's major value-creating skills, capabilities, and resources that determine its competitive weapons.

THINKING CRITICALLY ABOUT ETHICS

Many company Web sites have an "About Us" link that provides information about the company and its products or services—past, present, and oftentimes, future. This information is available for anyone to read, even competitors. In an intensely competitive industry where it's difficult for a company to survive much less be successful, would it be wrong for managers to include misleading, or even false information? Why or why not? Suppose that the industry wasn't intensely competitive? Would you feel differently? Explain.

As we discussed in Chapter 3, an organization's culture is its personality. It reflects the shared values, beliefs, and valued behaviors that embody the "way things are done around here." In a strong culture, almost all employees have a clear understanding of what the organization is about. This clarity should make it easy for managers to convey to new employees the organization's core competencies and strengths. At Nordstrom, which has a very strong culture of customer service and satisfaction, managers can instill cultural values in new employees in a much shorter time than could a competitor with a weak culture. The negative side of a strong culture, of course, is that it's more difficult to change. A strong culture may act as a significant barrier to accepting any changes in the organization's strategies. Successful organizations with strong cultures may become prisoners of their own successes.

Organizational culture also can promote or hinder an organization's strategic actions. One study showed that firms with "strategically appropriate cultures" outperformed other corporations with less appropriate cultures.[11] What is a strategically appropriate culture? It's one that supports the firm's chosen strategy. For instance, Avis, the number-two U.S. car rental company, has for a number of years stood on top of its category in an annual survey of brand loyalty. By creating a culture where employees obsess over every step of the rental car experience, Avis has built an unmatched record for customer loyalty.[12]

> ● ● ● **SWOT analysis**
> An analysis of the organization's strengths, weaknesses, opportunities, and threats.

The combined external and internal analyses are called the **SWOT analysis** because it's an analysis of the organization's *s*trengths, *w*eaknesses, *o*pportunities, and *t*hreats. Based on the SWOT analysis, managers can identify a strategic niche that the organization might exploit. (See Exhibit 8–3.)

Step 4: Formulating Strategies

Once the SWOT analysis is complete, managers need to develop and evaluate strategic alternatives and then select strategies that capitalize on the organization's strengths and exploit environmental opportunities or that correct the organization's weaknesses and buffer against threats. (▣▪▪ Go to the Web and check out Q & A 8.6.) Strategies need to be established for the corporate, business, and functional levels of the organization, which we'll describe shortly. This step is complete when managers have developed a set of strategies that give the organization a relative advantage over its rivals. (▪▣▪ Go to the Web and check out S.A.L. #8—How Creative Am I?)

Step 5: Implementing Strategies

After strategies are formulated, they must be implemented. A strategy is only as good as its implementation. No matter how effectively an organization has planned its strategies, it can't succeed if the strategies aren't implemented properly. (▣▪▪ Go to the Web and check out Q & A 8.7.) The rest of the chapters in this book address a number of issues related to strategy implementation. For instance, in Chapter 10, we discuss the strategy–structure relationship. In Chapter 12, we show that if new strategies are to succeed, they often require hiring new people with different skills, transferring some current employees to new positions, or laying off some employees. Also, since more organizations are using teams, the ability to build and manage effective teams is an important part of implementing strategy. (We cover teams in Chapter 15.) Finally, top management leadership is a necessary ingredient

Exhibit 8–3

● ● ●———

Identifying the Organization's Opportunities

MANAGING YOUR CAREER

Doing a Personal SWOT Analysis

A SWOT analysis can be a useful tool for examining your own skills, abilities, career preferences, and career opportunities. Doing a personal SWOT analysis involves taking a hard look at what your individual strengths and weaknesses are and then assessing the opportunities and threats of various career paths that might interest you.[13]

Step 1: Assessing personal strengths and weaknesses. All of us have special skills, talents, and abilities. Each of us enjoys certain activities and not others. For example, some people hate sitting at a desk all day; others panic at the thought of having to interact with strangers. List the activities you enjoy and the things you're good at. Also, identify some things you don't enjoy and aren't so good at. It's important to recognize our weaknesses so that we can either try to correct them or stay away from careers in which those things would be important. List your important individual strengths and weaknesses and highlight those you think are particularly significant.

Step 2: Identifying career opportunities and threats. We know from this chapter and Chapter 3 that different industries face different external opportunities and threats. It's important to identify these external factors for the simple reason that your initial job offers and future career advancement can be significantly influenced by the opportunities and threats. A company that's in an industry where there are significant negative

trends will offer few job openings or career advancement opportunities. On the other hand, job prospects will be bright in industries that have significant positive external trends. List two or three industries you have an interest in and critically evaluate the opportunities and threats facing those industries.

Step 3: Outlining five-year career goals. Taking your SWOT assessments, list four or five career goals that you would like to accomplish within five years of graduation. These goals might include things such as type of job you'd like to have, how many people you might be managing, or the type of salary you'd like to be making. Keep in mind that ideally you should try to match your individual strengths with industry opportunities.

Step 4: Outlining a five-year career action plan. Now it's time to get specific! Write a specific career action plan for accomplishing each of the career goals you identified in the previous step. State exactly what you will do, and by when, in order to meet each goal. If you think you'll need special assistance, state what it is and how you will get it. For example, your SWOT analysis may indicate that in order to achieve your desired career goal, you need to take more courses in management. Your career action plan should indicate when you will take those courses. Your specific career action plan will provide you with guidance for making decisions, just as an organization's plans provide direction to managers.

in a successful strategy. So, too, is a motivated group of middle- and lower-level managers to carry out the organization's specific strategies. Chapters 16 and 17 discuss ways to motivate people and offer suggestions for improving leadership effectiveness.

Step 6: Evaluating Results

The final step in the strategic management process is evaluating results. How effective have the strategies been? What adjustments, if any, are necessary? (███□██ Go to the Web and check out Q & A 8.8.) Anne Mulcahy, chairman and CEO of Xerox Corporation, made strategic adjustments to improve her company's competitiveness in the information services industry. She did this after assessing the results of previous strategies and determining that changes were needed. We discuss this step in our coverage of the control process in Chapter 18.

• • •• Learning Review

- List the six steps in the strategic management process.
- Describe what managers do when they do external and internal analyses.

- Explain the role of resources, capabilities, and core competencies in the internal analysis.

TYPES OF ORGANIZATIONAL STRATEGIES

Organizational strategies include strategies at the corporate level, business level, and functional level. (See Exhibit 8–4.) Managers at the top level of the organization typically are responsible for corporate-level strategies. Managers at the middle level typically are responsible for business-level strategies. And managers at the lower levels of the organization typically are responsible for the functional-level strategies. Let's look at each.

Corporate-Level Strategy

● ● ● **corporate-level strategy**
An organizational strategy that seeks to determine what businesses a company should be in or wants to be in.

A **corporate-level strategy** seeks to determine what businesses a company should be in or wants to be in. It reflects the direction in which the organization is going and the roles that each business unit in the organization will play in pursuing that direction. For instance, PepsiCo's corporate-level strategy integrates the strategies of its various business units—North American Soft Drinks, Pepsi International, Frito-Lay, Quaker Oats, Gatorade/Tropicana North America, and South Beach (SOBE) Beverage. PepsiCo had a restaurant division that included Taco Bell, Pizza Hut, and KFC, but because of intense competitive pressures in the fast-food industry and the restaurant division's inability to contribute to corporate growth, PepsiCo chose to concentrate on its soda and food divisions. It spun off the restaurant division as a separate and independent business entity now called YUM! Brands, Inc. What types of corporate strategies do organizations such as PepsiCo use?

There are three main corporate strategies: growth, stability, and renewal. To illustrate, Kellogg, Wal-Mart, and Apple are companies that seem to be going in different directions. Kellogg's managers are content to maintain the status quo and focus on the food industry. Wal-Mart, on the other hand is rapidly expanding its operations and developing new business and retailing concepts. It's also pursuing global opportunities. Meanwhile, sluggish sales and an uncertain outlook in the computer industry have prompted Apple to try a different direction as it launched an online music service called the iTunes Music Store. Each of these organizations is pursuing a different type of corporate strategy. Let's take a closer look at each type.

● ● ● **growth strategy**
A corporate-level strategy that seeks to increase the organization's operations by expanding the number of products offered or markets served.

Growth The **growth strategy** is a corporate-level strategy that seeks to increase the organization's business by expanding the number of products offered or markets served. By pursuing a growth strategy, the organization may increase sales revenues, number of employees, market share, or other quantitative measures. How can organizations grow? Through concentration, vertical integration, horizontal integration, or diversification.

Growth through concentration is achieved when an organization concentrates on its primary line of business and increases the number of products offered or markets served in this primary business. No other firms are acquired or merged with; instead the company chooses to grow by increasing its own business operations. For

Exhibit 8–4 **Levels of Organizational Strategy**

3M's new CEO, W. James McNerney, plans to follow a growth strategy that will reposition the company as a health care firm. He wants to expand the company's current offerings of low-tech medical products and medical-industry business software to include more medical treatments. So 3M scientists are working on treatments for respiratory, cardiovascular, skin, and sex-related diseases. Says McNerney of the new growth strategy, "We don't have a broken business equation here. We just need to learn to do things faster."

instance, Beckman Coulter, Inc., a Fullerton, California-based organization with annual revenues of over $2 billion, has successfully used the concentration strategy to become one of the world's largest medical diagnostics and research equipment companies. Another example is Bose Corporation of Framingham, Massachusetts. The company's focus on developing innovative audio products has helped make it the world's number-one stereo speaker manufacturer with sales of more than $1.3 billion.

A company also might choose to grow by vertical integration, which is an attempt to gain control of inputs (backward vertical integration), outputs (forward vertical integration), or both. In backward vertical integration, the organization attempts to gain control of its inputs by becoming its own supplier. For instance, French hospitality giant Accor, which owns Motel 6, Red Roof Inns, and numerous other lodging properties, also owns a majority of Carlson Wagonlit Travel, one of the world's largest travel agencies. In forward vertical integration, the organization gains control of its outputs (products or services) by becoming its own distributor. For example, Gateway Computer's retail stores are an example of an organization controlling its distribution.

In horizontal integration, a company grows by combining with other organizations in the same industry—that is, combining operations with competitors. For instance, Vail Resorts Inc., the nation's largest ski area, grew by combining with other ski resorts in Breckenridge, Keystone, and Arapahoe Basin. Horizontal integration has been used frequently in the airline and oil industries in the last few years. Because combining with competitors might decrease the amount of competition in an industry, the U.S. Federal Trade Commission assesses the impact of such proposed growth actions and must approve any proposed horizontal integration strategy. Other countries have similar restrictions. For instance, managers at America Online Inc., and Time Warner Inc., had to make certain concessions before the European Commission, the "watchdog" for the European Union, allowed that merger to stand.

Finally, an organization can grow through diversification, either related or unrelated. **Related diversification** is when a company grows by merging with or acquiring firms in different, but related, industries. For example, American Standard Cos., based in Piscataway, New Jersey, is in a variety of businesses including bathroom fixtures, air conditioning and heating units, plumbing parts, and pneumatic brakes for trucks. The company's "strategic fit" in these diverse businesses is its exploitation of efficiency-oriented manufacturing techniques developed in its bathroom fixtures business and transferred to all its other businesses. **Unrelated diversification** is when a company grows by merging with or acquiring firms in different and unrelated industries. For instance, Lancaster Colony Corporation owns businesses that make salad dressing, car mats, and scented candles; businesses that are different *and* unrelated.

Many companies use a combination of these approaches to grow. For instance, McDonald's has grown using the concentration strategy by opening more than 30,000 units in 120 countries, of which about 30 percent are company owned. In addition, it's used horizontal integration by purchasing Boston Market, Chipotle Mexican Grill, and Donato's Pizza chains. It also has a 33 percent stake in the U.K.-based sandwich shops Pret A Manger.

● ● ● **related diversification**
When a company grows by merging with or acquiring firms in different, but related, industries.

● ● ● **unrelated diversification**
When a company grows by merging with or acquiring firms in different and unrelated industries.

● ● ● **stability strategy**
A corporate-level strategy characterized by an absence of significant change.

Stability A **stability strategy** is a corporate-level strategy characterized by an absence of significant change. Examples of this strategy include continuing to serve the same clients by offering the same product or service, maintaining market share, and sustaining the organization's return-on-investment results.

Although it may seem strange that an organization might not want to grow, there are times when its resources, capabilities, and core competencies are stretched to their limits and expanding operations further might jeopardize its future success. When might managers decide that the stability strategy is the most appropriate choice? One situation might be that the industry is in a period of rapid upheaval with external forces drastically changing and making the future uncertain. At times like these, managers might decide that the prudent course of action is to sit tight and wait to see what happens.

Another situation where the stability strategy might be appropriate is if the industry is facing slow- or no-growth opportunities. In this instance, managers might decide to keep the organization operating at its current levels before making any strategic moves. This period of stability would allow them time to analyze their strategic options. For instance, the grocery industry is one that's growing very slowly. This fact, plus the all-out assault of Wal-Mart on grocery retailing, led managers at grocery chain A&P to follow a stability strategy. The company has consolidated certain locations and even sold off some poorer-performing divisions.

Finally, owners and managers of small businesses often purposefully choose to follow a stability strategy. Why? They may feel that their business is successful enough just as it is, that it adequately meets their personal goals, and that they don't want the hassles of a growing business.

Renewal The popular business periodicals frequently report stories of organizations that aren't meeting their goals or whose performance is declining. When an organization is in trouble, something needs to be done. Managers need to develop strategies that address organizational weaknesses that are leading to performance declines. These strategies are called **renewal strategies**. There are two main types of renewal strategies. A **retrenchment strategy** is a short-run renewal strategy used in situations when performance problems aren't as serious. There's no shortage of companies that have pursued a retrenchment strategy. A partial list includes some big corporate names: Procter & Gamble, AT&T, Kodak, Reebok, IBM, and Union Carbide. When an organization is facing minor performance setbacks, a retrenchment strategy helps it stabilize operations, revitalize organizational resources and capabilities, and prepare to compete once again.

However, what happens if the organization's problems are more serious? What if the organization's profits aren't just declining, but instead there aren't any profits at all, just losses? This type of situation calls for a more drastic strategy. The **turnaround strategy** is a renewal strategy for times when the organization's performance problems are more critical. Some well-known companies that have used a turnaround strategy include Sears, DaimlerChrysler, Apple, Continental Airlines, and Mitsubishi.

For both renewal strategies, managers cut costs and restructure organizational operations. However, a turnaround strategy typically involves a more extensive use of these measures than does a retrenchment strategy.

Corporate Portfolio Analysis When an organization's corporate strategy involves a number of businesses, managers can manage this collection, or portfolio, of businesses using a corporate portfolio matrix.[14] The first portfolio matrix—the **BCG matrix**—developed by the Boston Consulting Group, introduced the idea that an organization's businesses could be evaluated and plotted using a 2×2 matrix (see

●●● **renewal strategy**
A corporate-level strategy designed to address organizational weaknesses that are leading to performance declines.

●●● **retrenchment strategy**
A short-run renewal strategy.

●●● **turnaround strategy**
A renewal strategy for situations in which the organization's performance problems are more serious.

●●● **BCG matrix**
A strategy tool that guides resource allocation decisions on the basis of market share and growth rate of SBUs.

When A.G. Lafley took over as CEO, his renewal strategy for Procter & Gamble was surprisingly simple. Despite falling earnings and a drop in its stock price, the company didn't need radical change, Lafley felt. Instead, it needed to sell more of the products its customers had wanted all along. Downplaying the push for new products, Lafley chose the company's 10 best-selling brands and made them the firm's top priorities. "It's a basic strategy that worked for me in the Navy," where he served as supplies officer, he says. "The trick was to find the few things that were really going to sell well, and sell as many of them as you could." The strategy has brought the company's financial performance to new highs in just two years.

Exhibit 8–5

The BCG Matrix

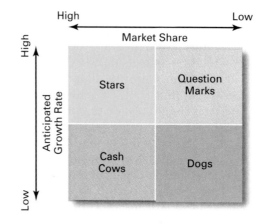

Exhibit 8–5) to identify which ones offered high potential and which were a drain on organizational resources.[15] The horizontal axis represents market share, which was evaluated as either low or high; and the vertical axis indicates anticipated market growth, which also was evaluated as either low or high. Based on its evaluation, the business was placed in one of four categories:

- *Cash cows* (low growth, high market share). Businesses in this category generate large amounts of cash, but their prospects for future growth are limited.
- *Stars* (high growth, high market share). These businesses are in a fast-growing market, and hold a dominant share of that market. Their contribution to cash flow depends on their need for resources.
- *Question marks* (high growth, low market share). These businesses are in an attractive industry but hold a small market share percentage.
- *Dogs* (low growth, low market share). Businesses in this category do not produce, or consume, much cash. However, they hold no promise for improved performance.

What are the strategic implications of the BCG matrix? Managers should "milk" cash cows for as much as they can, limit any new investment in them, and use the large amounts of cash generated to invest in stars and question marks with strong potential to improve market share. Heavy investment in stars will help take advantage of the market's growth and help maintain high market share. The stars, of course, will eventually develop into cash cows as their markets mature and sales growth slows. The hardest decision for managers is related to the question marks. After careful analysis, some will be sold off and others turned into stars. The dogs should be sold off or liquidated as they have low market share in markets with low growth potential.

A corporate portfolio matrix, such as the BCG matrix, can be a useful strategic management tool. It provides a framework for understanding diverse businesses and helps managers establish priorities for making resource allocation decisions.

Business-Level Strategy

• • • **business-level strategy**
An organizational strategy that seeks to determine how an organization should compete in each of its businesses.

Now we move to the business level. A **business-level strategy** seeks to determine how an organization should compete in each of its businesses. For a small organization in only one line of business or the large organization that has not diversified into different products or markets, the business-level strategy typically overlaps with the organization's corporate strategy. For organizations in multiple businesses, however, each division will have its own strategy that defines the products or services it will offer, the customers it wants to reach, and the like. For example, the French company LVMH-Moet Hennessy Louis Vuitton SA has different business-level strategies for its divisions such as Donna Karan fashions, Louis Vuitton leather goods, Guerlain perfume, TAG Heuer watches, Dom Perignon champagne, and other luxury products. Each division has developed its own unique approach for competing. When an organization is in several different businesses, these single businesses that are independent and formulate their own strategies are often called **strategic business units** or SBUs.

●●● **strategic business units (SBUs)**
Single businesses of an organization in several different businesses that are independent and formulate their own strategies.

●●● **competitive advantage**
What sets an organization apart; its distinct edge.

The Role of Competitive Advantage Developing an effective business-level competitive strategy requires an understanding of competitive advantage, a key concept in strategic management.[16] **Competitive advantage** is what sets an organization apart; that is, its distinct edge. That distinct edge comes from the organization's core competencies which, as we know from earlier in this chapter, might be in the form of organizational capabilities—the organization does something that others cannot do or does it better than others can do it. For example, Dell has developed a competitive advantage in its ability to create a direct selling channel that's highly responsive to customers. And Southwest Airlines has a competitive advantage because of its skills at giving passengers what they want—quick, convenient, and fun service. Or those core competencies that lead to competitive advantage also can come from organizational assets or resources—the organization has something that its competitors do not have. For instance, Wal-Mart's state-of-the-art information system allows it to monitor and control inventories and supplier relations more efficiently than its competitors, which Wal-Mart has turned into a cost advantage. And Harley-Davidson, Nike, and Coca-Cola all have well-known global trademarks that they use to get premium prices for their products.

Quality as a Competitive Advantage If implemented properly, quality can be a way for an organization to create a sustainable competitive advantage.[17] That's why many organizations apply quality management concepts to their operations in an attempt to set themselves apart from competitors.

As we first discussed in Chapter 2, quality management focuses on customers and continuous improvement. To the degree that an organization can satisfy a customer's need for quality, it can differentiate itself from competitors and attract a loyal customer base. Moreover, constant improvement in the quality and reliability of an organization's products or services may result in a competitive advantage that can't be taken away.[18] Let's look at how two very different companies use quality management to gain competitive advantage.

At Granite Rock Company of Watsonville, California, continuous improvement is an important strategic tool. What types of strategic quality innovations does the company use? It found through numerous customer surveys that on-time delivery was its customers' highest priority. Granite Rock set about establishing standards for achieving on-time performance. It studied Domino's Pizza outlets, which guarantee fast, accurate delivery. From that study, Granite Rock instituted a program in which customers simply drive up in their trucks, insert a card, and tell the machine how much of which material is needed—a process similar to using a bank ATM. The truck is loaded automatically and a bill sent to the customer later. The company's Granite Xpress is open 24 hours a day, seven days a week to meet customer needs.

LM Ericsson, the Swedish company, is the world's leading maker of wireless telecommunications infrastructure equipment. The company builds its products to meet all major wireless

Royal Caribbean International, which operates a fleet of 25 cruise ships, has chosen quality as its competitive advantage. As Maria Sastre, vice president of total guest satisfaction, says, "The Latin client . . . likes the latest and the greatest," and that means brand-new ships; multiple cabins to accommodate families that might include children, grandparents, or both; carefully selected menus and wine lists; and late-evening dining and entertainment featuring groups like the popular Gipsy Kings.

standards and continues to be a leader in upgrading carriers' networks to the 3G (third generation) standard. Its competitive advantage comes from the fact that its products are well known for their high quality and innovativeness, a source of pride for the company.

Sustaining Competitive Advantage Given the fact that every organization has resources and capabilities, what makes some organizations more successful than others? Why do some professional baseball teams consistently win championships or draw large crowds? Why do some organizations have consistent and continuous growth in revenues and profits? Why do some colleges, universities, or departments experience continually increasing enrollments? Why do some companies consistently appear at the top of lists ranking the "best," or the "most admired," or the "most profitable"? Although every organization has resources and work methods to do whatever it's in business to do, not every one is able to effectively exploit its resources or capabilities and to develop the core competencies that can provide it with a competitive advantage. And it's not enough for an organization simply to create a competitive advantage; it must be able to sustain it. That is, a sustainable competitive advantage enables the organization to keep its edge despite competitors' actions or evolutionary changes in the industry.

Competitive Strategies Many important ideas in strategic management have come from the work of Michael Porter.[19] His competitive strategies framework identifies three generic strategies from which managers can choose. Success depends on selecting the right strategy—one that fits the competitive strengths (resources and capabilities) of the organization and the industry it's in. Porter's major contribution has been to explain how managers can create and sustain a competitive advantage that will give a company above-average profitability. An important element in doing this is an industry analysis.

Porter proposes that some industries are inherently more profitable (and, therefore, more attractive to enter and remain in) than others. For example, the pharmaceutical industry is one with historically high profit margins, and the airline industry has notoriously low ones. But a company can still make a lot of money in a "dull" industry and lose money in a "glamorous" industry. The key is to exploit a competitive advantage.

In any industry, five competitive forces dictate the rules of competition. Together, these five forces (see Exhibit 8–6) determine industry attractiveness and profitability. Managers assess an industry's attractiveness using these five factors:

Exhibit 8–6

Forces in the Industry Analysis

Source: Based on M.E. Porter, *Competitive Strategy: Techniques for Analyzing Industries and Competitors* (New York: The Free Press, 1980).

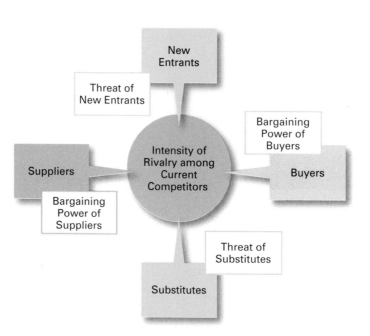

1. *Threat of new entrants.* Factors such as economies of scale, brand loyalty, and capital requirements determine how easy or hard it is for new competitors to enter an industry.
2. *Threat of substitutes.* Factors such as switching costs and buyer loyalty determine the degree to which customers are likely to buy a substitute product.
3. *Bargaining power of buyers.* Factors such as number of customers in the market, customer information, and the availability of substitutes determine the amount of influence that buyers have in an industry.
4. *Bargaining power of suppliers.* Factors such as the degree of supplier concentration and availability of substitute inputs determine the amount of power that suppliers have over firms in the industry.
5. *Current rivalry.* Factors such as industry growth rate, increasing or falling demand, and product differences determine how intense the competitive rivalry will be among firms currently in the industry.

Once managers have assessed the five forces and determined what threats and opportunities exist, they're ready to select an appropriate competitive strategy. According to Porter, no firm can be successful by trying to be all things to all people. He proposes that managers select a strategy that will give the organization a competitive advantage, which he says arises out of either having lower costs than all other industry competitors or by being significantly different from competitors. On that basis, managers can choose one of three strategies: cost leadership, differentiation, or focus. Which one managers select depends on the organization's strengths and core competencies and its competitors' weaknesses. (See Exhibit 8–7.)

When an organization sets out to be the lowest-cost producer in its industry, it's following a **cost leadership strategy**. A low-cost leader aggressively searches out efficiencies in production, marketing, and other areas of operation. Overhead is kept to a minimum, and the firm does everything it can to cut costs. You won't find expensive art or interior décor at offices of low-cost leaders. For example, at Wal-Mart's headquarters in Bentonville, Arkansas, office furnishings are sparse and drab but functional.

●●● **cost leadership strategy**
A business-level strategy in which the organization is the lowest-cost producer in its industry.

Exhibit 8–7

●●●——————

Requirements for Successfully Pursuing Porter's Competitive Strategies

Generic Strategy	Commonly Required Skills and Resources	Common Organizational Requirements
Overall cost leadership	Sustained capital investment and access to capital Process engineering skills Intense supervision of labor Products designed for ease in manufacture Low-cost distribution system	Tight cost control Frequent, detailed control reports Structured organization and responsibilities Incentives based on meeting strict quantitative targets
Differentiation	Strong marketing abilities Product engineering Creative flair Strong capability in basic research Corporate reputation for quality or technological leadership Long tradition in the industry or unique combination of skills drawn from other businesses Strong cooperation from channels	Strong coordination among functions in R&D, product development, and marketing Subjective measurement and incentives instead of quantitative measures Amenities to attract highly skilled labor, scientists, or creative people
Focus	Combination of the foregoing skills and resources directed at the particular strategic target	Combination of the foregoing organizational requirements directed at the particular strategic target

Source: Reprinted from M.E. Porter, *Competitive Strategy: Techniques for Analyzing Industries and Competitors* (New York: Free Press, 1980), pp. 40–41.

● ● **differentiation strategy**
A business-level strategy in which a company offers unique products that are widely valued by customers.

● ● ● **focus strategy**
A business-level strategy in which a company pursues a cost or differentiation advantage in a narrow industry segment.

● ● ● **stuck in the middle**
A situation where an organization hasn't been able to develop either a low cost or a differentiation competitive advantage.

● ● ● **functional-level strategy**
An organizational strategy that supports the business-level strategy.

Although low-cost leaders don't place a lot of emphasis on "frills," the product or service being sold must be perceived as comparable in quality to that offered by rivals or at least be acceptable to buyers. Examples of companies that have used the low-cost leader strategy include Wal-Mart, Hyundai, and Southwest Airlines.

The company that seeks to offer unique products that are widely valued by customers is following a **differentiation strategy**. Sources of differentiation might be exceptionally high quality, extraordinary service, innovative design, technological capability, or an unusually positive brand image. The key to this competitive strategy is that whatever product or service attribute is chosen for differentiating must set the firm apart from its competitors and be significant enough to justify a price premium that exceeds the cost of differentiating.

Practically any successful consumer product or service can be identified as an example of the differentiation strategy: Nordstrom (customer service); Sony (reputation for quality and innovative design); Coach handbags (design and brand image); and Kimberly-Clark's Huggies Pull-Ups (product design).

The first two of Porter's competitive strategies seek a competitive advantage in the broad marketplace. However, the **focus strategy** involves a cost advantage (cost focus) or a differentiation advantage (differentiation focus) in a narrow segment. That is, managers select a market segment in an industry and attempt to exploit it rather than serve the broad market. Segments can be based on product variety, type of end buyer, distribution channel, or geographical location of buyers. For example, at Compania Chilena de Fosforos SA, a large Chilean wood products manufacturer, Vice Chairman Gustavo Romero Zapata devised a focus strategy to sell chopsticks in Japan. Competitors, and even other company managers, thought he was crazy. However, by focusing on this segment, Romero's strategy managed to create more demand for his company's chopsticks than it had mature trees with which to make the products. Whether a focus strategy is feasible depends on the size of the segment and whether the organization can support the additional cost of focusing. Research suggests that the focus strategy may be the most effective choice for small businesses because they typically do not have the economies of scale or internal resources to successfully pursue one of the other two strategies.[20]

What happens if an organization is unable to develop a cost or differentiation advantage? Porter uses the term **stuck in the middle** to describe those organizations, which find it very difficult to achieve long-term success. Porter goes on to note that successful organizations frequently get into trouble by reaching beyond their competitive advantage and ending up stuck in the middle.

However, we now realize organizations *can* successfully pursue a low cost and a differentiation advantage, as studies have shown that such a dual emphasis can result in high performance.[21] To successfully pursue both, however, an organization must be strongly committed to quality products or services, and consumers of those products or services must value quality. By providing high-quality products or services, an organization differentiates itself from its rivals. Consumers who value high quality will purchase more of the organization's products, and the increased demand will lead to economies of scale and lower per-unit costs. For example, companies such as Anheuser-Busch, FedEx, Intel, and Coca-Cola differentiate their products while at the same time maintaining low-cost operations.

In its deal with Latina superstar Thalia to create a line of branded apparel and accessories, Kmart is using a focus strategy. The retail chain wants to become the favorite mass merchant of the Latino customer. "The Hispanic market is very important to us," says a company spokesperson. "This is really our effort to provide products for that customer."

Functional-Level Strategy

Functional-level strategies support the business-level strategy. For organizations that have traditional functional departments such as manufacturing, marketing, human resources, research and development, and finance, these strategies need to support the business-level strategy. For example, when R.R. Donnelley & Sons Company, a Chicago-based printer, made a business-level strategy decision to invest significant dollars in high-tech digital printing methods, its marketing department had to develop new sales plans and promotional pieces, the production department had to incorporate the digital equipment in the printing plants, and the human resources department had to update its employee selection and training programs. We don't cover specific functional strategies in this book as they are the content of other business courses you take.

● ● ● ● Learning Review

- Explain the three growth strategies.
- Discuss the BCG matrix and how it's used.
- Define SBUs and business-level strategies.
- Describe the role of competitive advantage in business-level strategies.

- Explain Porter's five forces model.
- Describe the three generic competitive strategies.

STRATEGIC MANAGEMENT IN TODAY'S ENVIRONMENT

There's no better example of the strategic challenges faced by managers in today's market environment than the recorded music industry. Global music sales tumbled 7.2 percent in 2002—the third drop in a row—and industry executives braced for more declines. Rampant global piracy, economic uncertainty, and intense competition from other forms of entertainment have devastated the music industry. Its very nature continues to change, and managers are struggling to find strategies that will help their organizations succeed in such an environment.[22] But the music industry isn't the only industry dealing with such enormous strategic challenges. Managers in all kinds of organizations face increasingly intense global competition and the increased demands of higher performance expectations by investors and customers. How have managers responded to these new realities? (▇▇ ▇□▇ Go to the Web and check out S.A.L. #47—How Well Do I Respond to Turbulent Change?) In this section we want to look at some new directions in strategy including the rule of three and its significance for strategic management, and at how managers are designing strategies to emphasize e-business, customer service, and innovation.

The Rule of Three

Fast food—McDonald's, Wendy's, Burger King. Credit cards—VISA, MasterCard, American Express. U.S. automakers—General Motors, Ford, DaimlerChrysler. Japanese automakers—Toyota, Honda, Nissan. Broadcast networks—NBC, ABC, CBS. South Korean chip makers—Goldstar, Hyundai, Samsung. Beer—Anheuser-Busch, Coors, Miller. Cruise lines—Carnival, Royal Caribbean, Star Cruises. Athletic shoes—Nike, Adidas, Reebok. Global food products—Nestlé, Unilever, Kraft Foods. What do these industry lists have in common? A phenomenon called the **rule of three**, which argues that competitive forces in an industry, if kept relatively free of government interference or other special circumstances, will inevitably create a situation where three companies dominate any given market.[23]

The premise of the rule of three is that each industry has three large, dominant players—that is, three "full-line generalists" that dominate and hold most of the industry market share. Although there are exceptions (for example, the soft-drink industry with Coca-Cola and Pepsi), the rule of three seems to hold true across many different industries. And why three? It seems that two companies tend to lead to monopolistic

● ● ● **rule of three**
Competitive forces in an industry, if kept relatively free of government interference or other special circumstances, will inevitably create a situation where three companies dominate any given market.

pricing or mutual destruction, while four encourages continual price wars, which can be detrimental. In addition to the big three, there are other firms in the industry that want to be successful. They play the role of "super niche players" by specializing either through product or market segmentation. Finally, there are ditch dwellers—a competitive position held by organizations that are not one of the highly efficient generalist "big three" or one of the highly focused niche players. These firms end up stuck "in the ditch" where competitive position and financial performance is weakest. Just as Porter pointed out with his stuck-in-the-middle strategy, in the ditch is where managers don't want their organizations to end up! This arrangement of generalist firms, specialists, and weak performers has been found to be fairly common across all kinds of industries around the world. For instance, take the discount retail industry. The big three include Wal-Mart, Costco, and Target. The super niche players include Kohl's, TJX (T.J. Maxx and Marshall's), and Walgreen's. In the ditch are Kmart and Mervyn's. In the airline industry, we have the big three (United, American, and Delta), the super niche players (Southwest and Jet Blue), and in the ditch (U.S. Air and Midwest Airlines).

Based on the rule of three, we can draw several strategic generalizations about companies and industries. These generalizations are summarized in Exhibit 8–8.

Since the rule of three says that most markets evolve in a cyclical fashion and describes how that evolution occurs, managers must understand where their industry is in that evolutionary process. This means strategizing for longer time frames—perhaps decades or more. Why? Because this type of planning forces managers to think beyond the temporary disruptions and competitive forces taking place. When focusing on the ultra long term, managers must determine the major drivers behind market restructuring, which includes radically different (even disruptive) technologies and intense regulatory and market shifts. Using the generalizations summarized in Exhibit 8.8, managers should be able to formulate strategies that are relevant to their company in light of its particular industry position. But they also must recognize the early warning signs of a pending industry shakeout. That way they can take advantage of product or market opportunities that appear and, most importantly, stay out of the ditch.

Exhibit 8–8

Selected Strategic Generalizations from the Rule of Three

- An industry starts out in an unorganized way, organizes through consolidation and standardization, and eventually ends up with companies that are full-line generalists (the three) and product/market specialists.
- The number of full-line generalists is three and their combined market share is generally between 70 and 90 percent.
- The financial performance of the three improves with increased market share up to a point, usually about 40 percent, at which time inefficiencies set in and government regulators impose more scrutiny.
- If one full-line generalist has 70 percent or more market share, there is usually no room for another one. If the market leader has between 50 and 70 percent market share, there's usually room for only one more generalist. And, if the market leader has considerably less than 40 percent share, there may be room (temporarily) for a fourth generalist.
- A market share of 10 percent is the minimum necessary level to be a viable full-line generalist.
- When an industry is going through a downturn, a fight for market share between numbers one and two will often send number three into the ditch. If this happens, however, a new number three player always emerges.
- The number one company is usually the least innovative although it may have the largest research and development budget; the number three company is usually the most innovative although its innovations are usually copied by the number one company unless it can protect them, which is becoming more difficult.
- Out-of-control growth can send specialists into the ditch.
- Ditch companies have the worst financial performance and have little chance of surviving.
- Ditch companies can become big players by merging with each other, but only if there's no viable number three, or they may seek a merger with a successful full-line generalist.

Source: Adapted from J.N. Sheth and R.S. Sisodia, "Competitive Markets and The Rule of Three," *Ivey Business Journal,* September/October 2002, pp. 1–4.

New Directions in Organizational Strategies

At FedEx's Memphis facility, employees don't get a paycheck or a deposit receipt, they get a Visa payroll card, a new form of debit card.[24] Each pay period, employees' Visa cards are credited with their earnings, which they're then free to "spend" just as if they had a check or cash. The paperless arrangement benefits all parties—employers save the cost of printing paper checks, banks save the cost of processing them, and employees avoid the hassle of having to go to the bank to cash their checks. And Visa, of course, is strategically exploiting another market opportunity; it is an example of an organization whose managers are effectively designing strategies for today's environment. What do strategies for today's environment encompass? We see three important aspects: e-business techniques, customer service, and innovation.

Strategies for Applying e-Business Techniques As we discussed in Chapter 2, e-business techniques offer many advantages to organizations, whether it's simply through e-commerce efforts or through being a total e-business.

There's no doubt that Internet technology has changed, and is changing, the way organizations do business. Using the Internet, companies have, for instance, (1) created knowledge bases that employees can tap into anytime, anywhere; (2) turned customers into collaborative partners who help design, test, and launch new products; (3) become virtually paperless in specific tasks such as purchasing and filing expense reports; (4) managed logistics in real time; and (5) changed the nature of numerous work tasks throughout the organization.

Managers can formulate strategies using e-business techniques that contribute to the development of a sustainable competitive advantage.[25] A cost leader can use e-business techniques to reduce costs in a variety of ways. It might use online bidding and order processing to eliminate the need for sales calls and to decrease sales force expenses; it could use Web-based inventory control systems that reduce storage costs; or it might use online testing and evaluation of job applicants. For example, General Electric applied e-business techniques as it initiated several Internet-based purchasing activities in order to reduce costs.

A differentiator needs to offer products or services that customers perceive and value as unique. How could e-business techniques contribute? The differentiator might use Internet-based knowledge systems to shorten customer response times; provide rapid online responses to service requests; or automate purchasing and payment systems so that customers have detailed status reports and purchasing histories. Dell Computer is an excellent example of a company that has exploited the differentiation advantage made possible by e-business techniques.

Finally, since the focuser targets a narrow market segment with customized products, it might provide chat rooms or discussion boards for customers to interact with others who have common interests; design niche Web sites that target specific groups with specific interests; or use Web sites to perform standardized office functions such as payroll or budgeting. One focuser that has capitalized on Internet technology is SalvageSale, a unique Web business that specializes in quick liquidation of commercial salvage goods. Its efficient use of e-business techniques allows it to keep costs low *and* appeal to a specific customer group, primarily insurance and transportation companies.

Today's Internet-enriched environment provides managers with many opportunities to design strategies that can help their organizations get a sustainable competitive advantage. At their disposal is a variety of e-business tools and techniques. The key challenge for managers is to know which ones to use, where, and when. But, as organizations such as General Electric, SalvageSale, and Dell demonstrate, well-chosen e-business strategies can help an organization succeed.

Customer Service Strategies Companies that emphasize customer service need strategies that cultivate that atmosphere from top to bottom. What kinds of strategies does that take? It takes giving customers what they want, communicating effectively with them, and providing employees with customer service training. Let's look first at the strategy of giving customers what they want.

New Balance Athletic Shoes does something that Nike and Reebok do not. It gives customers a truly unique product: shoes in varying widths. No other athletic shoe manufacturer has shoes for narrow or wide feet.[26] Also, look back at our chapter-opening dilemma at how the Muellers approached customers in giving them a memorable ski experience. It should come as no surprise that an important customer service strategy is giving customers what they want, a major aspect of an organization's overall marketing strategy.

Another important customer service strategy involves communication. Hot Topic is a fast-growing retail specialist that's fanatical about customer feedback, which it gets in the form of shopper "report cards." The company's CEO, Betsy McLaughlin, pores over more than 1,000 of them each week.[27] Managers should know what's going on with customers. They need to find out what customers liked and didn't like about their purchase encounter—from their interactions with employees to their experience with the actual product or service. But communication isn't a one-way street. It's also important to let customers know what's going on with the organization that might affect future purchase decisions. Having an effective customer communication system is an important customer service strategy.

Finally, we've discussed previously the importance of an organization's culture in emphasizing customer service. And this requires that employees be trained to provide exceptional customer service. For example, the 2002 Winter Olympic Games in Salt Lake City were memorable for the remarkable athletic accomplishments, but also for the outstanding customer service provided by the volunteers who served as parking lot attendants, ushers, ticket takers, and cleanup crews.[28] Achieving those high service-performance levels resulted from a huge investment in people training—training in key customer service skills such as listening, communication, and problem solving. In addition, the volunteers were encouraged to remember CHARGE, an acronym for Committed, Helpful, Adaptable, Respectful, Gracious, and Enjoy. After the initial training task of getting the volunteers to understand the overall mission of the Olympic games, managers had to show each individual how his or her contribution fit into the big picture and then demonstrate the skill to deliver it. The investment in training was an important element in the success of the games' customer service strategy, and is a good example of what managers must do if customer service is an important organizational goal.

Innovation Strategies When Procter & Gamble purchased the Iams pet-food business, it did what it always does—it used its renowned research division to look for ways to transfer technology from its other divisions to make new products.[29] One of the outcomes of this cross-divisional combination: a new tartar-fighting ingredient from toothpaste that's included in all of its dry adult pet foods.

Becoming a Manager

- ◆ As you keep up with the current business news, pay attention to organizational strategies that managers are using. What types of strategies are the successful organizations using?

- ◆ Use SWOT analysis when you apply for jobs—after all, why would you want to work for some organization that has a lot of weaknesses or is facing significant threats?

- ◆ Talk to managers about strategy. Ask them how they know when it's time to try a different strategy.

- ◆ As described in the "Managing Your Career" box, do a personal SWOT analysis.

- ◆ ▪▪▫▪ Go to the Web and complete any of the following exercises from the Self Assessment Library (S.A.L.) found on R.O.L.L.S.: #4—How Flexible Am I?, #7—How Well Do I Handle Ambiguity?, #8—How Creative Am I?, and #47—How Well Do I Respond to Turbulent Change?

Exhibit 8–9

● ● ●
**First-Mover Advantages—
Disadvantages**

Advantages	Disadvantages
• Reputation for being innovative and industry leader • Cost and learning benefits • Control over scarce resources and keeping competitors from having access to them • Opportunity to begin building customer relationships and customer loyalty	• Uncertainty over exact direction technology and market will go • Risk of competitors imitating innovations • Financial and strategic risks • High development costs

As this example shows, innovation strategies aren't necessarily focused on just the radical, breakthrough products. They can include the application of existing technology to new uses. And organizations of all kinds and sizes have successfully used both approaches. What types of innovation strategies do organizations need in today's environment? Those strategies should reflect their philosophy about innovation, which is shaped by two strategic decisions: innovation emphasis and innovation timing.

Managers must first decide where the emphasis of their innovation effort will be. Is the organization's focus going to be basic scientific research, product development, or process improvement? Basic scientific research requires the heaviest commitment in terms of resources because it involves the nuts-and-bolts activities and work of scientific research. In numerous industries (for instance, genetics engineering, information technology, or pharmaceuticals), an organization's expertise in basic research is the key to a sustainable competitive advantage. However, not every organization requires this extensive commitment to scientific research to achieve high performance levels. Instead, many depend on product development strategies. Although this strategy also requires a significant resource investment, it's not in the areas associated with scientific research. Instead, the organization takes existing technology and improves on it or applies it in new ways, just as Procter & Gamble did when it applied tartar-fighting knowledge to pet-food products. Both of these first two strategic approaches to innovation (basic scientific research and product development) can help an organization achieve high levels of differentiation, which is a significant source of competitive advantage.

Finally, the last strategic approach to innovation emphasis is a focus on process development. Using this strategy, an organization looks for ways to improve and enhance its work processes. The organization innovates new and improved ways for employees to do their work in all organizational areas. This innovation strategy can lead to an organization's lowering costs which, as we know, can be a significant source of competitive advantage.

Once managers have determined the focus of their innovation efforts, they must decide on their innovation timing strategy. Some organizations want to be the first with innovations whereas others are content to follow or mimic the innovations. An organization that's first to bring a product innovation to the market or to use a new process innovation is called a **first mover**. Being a first mover has certain strategic advantages and disadvantages as shown in Exhibit 8–9. Some organizations pursue this route, hoping to develop a sustainable competitive advantage. Others have successfully developed a sustainable competitive advantage by being the followers in the industry. They let the first movers pioneer the innovations and then mimic their products or processes. Which approach managers choose depends on their organization's innovation philosophy and specific resources and capabilities.

● ● ● **first mover**
An organization that's first to bring a product innovation to the market or to use a new process innovation.

● ● ● **Learning Review**

• Discuss the implications of dynamic and uncertain environments on organizational strategy.

• Explain the rule of three and its significance for strategic management.

• Describe strategies for applying e-business techniques.

• Explain what strategies organizations might use to become more customer oriented and to be more innovative.

Managers **Respond** to a **Manager's** Dilemma

···**Amit Shah**

Product Line Director, Advanced Placement, Pearson Prentice Hall, Somerville, Massachusetts

The Muellers have an excellent template in SWOT analysis to use as they evaluate their expansion decision. They clearly need to leverage, capitalize, and differentiate their product in a highly competitive and capital-intensive industry. Using a basic SWOT analysis, they could evaluate the following: Strengths—customer service and quality of trails; Weaknesses—lack of resources and undercapitalization; Opportunities—strategic expansion with multiple pricing models for facilities that can capitalize on the "small is good" approach; and Threats—not differentiated from large competitors who do not lack resources and have capital reserves to weather downturns. After completing the SWOT analysis, it's important that the Muellers use what the analysis showed them to come up with appropriate future strategies.

Pat Gray

Business Development Manager, Minol-MGT, L.P., Addison, Texas

It's essential to use a tool such as SWOT to weigh professional or personal decisions. The application of SWOT will better enable the Muellers to determine whether or not to expand their business by purchasing additional ski areas. Only by performing SWOT can managers weigh and analyze the factors that go into a sound business decision. It forces managers to examine the situation and provides them with a framework to support a strategic business decision. A SWOT analysis might show the Muellers the following: Strengths—exceptional customer service, best-groomed mountain, skilled workers; Weaknesses—possible lack of additional personnel to deliver quality service; Opportunities—minimize competition, diversify into new sports; and Threats—weather, new entrants into market, and continuance of quality customer service.

Learning Summary

After reading and studying this chapter, you should be able to:

- Explain why strategic management is important.

- Discuss what studies of the effectiveness of strategic management have shown.

- List the six steps in the strategic management process.

- Describe what managers do when they do external and internal analyses.

- Explain the role of resources, capabilities, and core competencies in the internal analysis.

- Explain the three growth strategies.

- Discuss the BCG matrix and how it's used.

- Define SBUs and business-level strategies.

- Describe the role of competitive advantage in business-level strategies.

- Explain Porter's five forces model.

- Describe the three generic competitive strategies.

- Discuss the implications of dynamic and uncertain environments on organizational strategy.

- Explain the rule of three and its significance for strategic management.

- Describe strategies for applying e-business techniques.

- Explain what strategies organizations might use to become more customer oriented and to be more innovative.

Thinking About Management Issues

1. Perform a SWOT analysis on a local business you think you know well. What, if any, competitive advantage does this organization have?

2. How might the process of strategy formulation, implementation, and evaluation differ for (a) large businesses, (b) small businesses, (c) not-for-profit organizations, and (d) global businesses?

3. "The concept of competitive advantage is as important for not-for-profit organizations as it is for for-profit organizations." Do you agree or disagree with this statement? Explain, using examples to make your case.

4. Should ethical considerations be included in analyses of an organization's internal and external environments? Why or why not?

5. How could the Internet be helpful to managers as they follow the steps in the strategic management process?

6. Find examples of five different organizational mission statements. Using the mission statements, describe what types of corporate-level and business-level strategies each organization might use to fulfill that mission statement. Explain your rationale for choosing each strategy.

Working Together: Team-Based Exercise

Examples of organizational strategies are found everywhere in business and general news periodicals. You should be able to recognize the different types of strategies from these news stories.

Form groups of three or four individuals. Using materials that your instructor provides you, find examples of five different organizational strategies. Determine whether the examples are corporate level, business level, or functional level and explain why your group made that choice. Be prepared to share your examples with the class.

Ethical Dilemma Exercise

What happens when a new entrant shakes up an entire industry and changes the competitive situation? Book retailing is a good example. In Japan, the Bookoff chain stirred up controversy by maneuvering around the country's law forbidding discounts on new books. Instead, Bookoff buys used books from customers, cleans them up, and sells them for half the original price. Even as Bookoff has expanded to 700 stores, competitors are upset because they cannot legally cut their prices to compete. Moreover, the Japan Booksellers Federation complains

that teenagers could be shoplifting books from other stores to sell to Bookoff.

In the United States, Amazon.com has used the Internet to successfully compete against long-established store chains such as Barnes & Noble. Amazon also allows dealers and individuals to sell used books alongside the new books posted on its online system, a practice that has drawn some protests. The Author's Guild wants its members to boycott Amazon because authors receive no royalties from sales of used books, only sales of new books.

Even though people buy and sell used books (and other items) through auctions on eBay—sales from which authors receive no royalties—Amazon is primarily a retailer competing with other retailers on and off the Web.[30]

Imagine you're an Amazon manager with responsibility for expanding revenues by broadening the range of products offered on the site. Recently several consignment shops opened in your area, specializing in used children's clothing. This makes you wonder whether Amazon should invite sellers to list branded used children's apparel in good condition alongside the new branded children's apparel you sell, made by Oshkosh B'Gosh, Lands' End, and other suppliers. Review 8–6 as you think about this challenge and decide which of the following options to choose—and why.

> **Option A:** You decide to invite the Salvation Army to list used children's clothing on your site; this will link Amazon with a good cause and give you time to field any complaints.

> **Option B:** You decide that selling used clothing would not be a good strategy, because of quality concerns and the potential conflict with suppliers.

> **Option C:** You decide to list only used baby clothing made by the suppliers of your current line of baby clothing; this will give price-conscious customers more options.

Case Application

Joe Boxer Corporation

Nicholas Graham is the king of underwear and the self-proclaimed "Chief Underpants Officer" of Joe Boxer Corporation. Graham loves to create a spectacle. From the time he put up the world's largest e-mail message center for Joe Boxer on a billboard in New York's Times Square to the time he dressed up as the Queen of England, suspended himself by a crane 100 feet above Times Square, and tossed boxer shorts attached to bagels down to the gathered crowd, Graham believes in promoting his company whenever, wherever, and however he can. There's no doubt that Graham's strength is branding. He says, "The brand is the amusement park. The product is the souvenir." And Graham's odd, and sometimes wacky, strategies reflect his philosophy. What he really loves is creating experiences for customers that provide a respite from the hubbub of the modern world—a single moment that makes them stop, do a double-take, and laugh. But things at Joe Boxer Corporation haven't always been so laughable.

From the company's beginning in 1985, Joe Boxer enjoyed phenomenal growth. Today it has one of the most recognized fashion brands. Among target customers aged 15 to 30, Joe Boxer has 87 percent brand awareness. However, over the years as the company grew, Graham found himself having to deal with the managerial complexities of running a major fashion company. Although he brought in executives to help with the details, the company rapidly lost cash and racked up $18 million in debt. Many of the financial problems stemmed from Graham's publicity stunts and cost overruns such as paying too much for manufacturing products. By 2001, the company was in such bad shape that a lawsuit filed by a licensee in which Joe Boxer was ordered to pay $3.15 million had Graham filling out bankruptcy papers. In fact, the press release announcing the company's bankruptcy had been written and was about to be sent when Bill Sweedler, CEO of Windsong Allegiance Group, LLC, came knocking on the company's door.

Windsong licenses designer labels and distributes branded underwear, so the Joe Boxer brand had significant appeal. Windsong acquired the resources of Joe Boxer in April 2001 in exchange for assuming all its debt. Not long after, Sweedler was able to sign an agreement with Kmart Corporation, who wanted exclusive rights to the valuable Joe Boxer name to help it appeal to teenagers and college students. Although the specific

Nicholas Graham, founder of Joe Boxer.

details of the agreement are not known, Windsong did receive a lump-sum payment that Sweedler will only say is "significantly higher than the $24 million that Target paid designer Mossimo." In addition, Windsong gets royalties on each dollar of Joe Boxer sales (projected to be $1 billion in its first year alone). And Kmart is responsible for all the manufacturing of Joe Boxer's products. Even if struggling Kmart closes down, Sweedler expects the Joe Boxer brand to be picked up by another retailer—Target, which has had a strategy of investing heavily in famous brands. But he believes that the Joe Boxer brand could actually turn out to be a better brand for Kmart than the Martha Stewart line, which has suffered as that line's namesake faced legal problems. Considering the risks of having a brand tied so closely to one person, Sweedler recognizes the importance of promoting Joe Boxer, not Nicholas Graham. But Graham hasn't been pushed aside. Although Sweedler is the man in charge, Graham continues to do what he does best for the company—serve as brand adviser and chief promoter.

DISCUSSION QUESTIONS

1. What competitive advantage(s) do you think Joe Boxer has? What competitive strategy does the company appear to be following? Explain your choices.

2. What might a SWOT analysis have shown Bill Sweedler of Windsong as he was evaluating Joe Boxer?

3. How could Sweedler use strategic management concepts to help him continue managing Joe Boxer for successful performance?

4. What might other organizations learn about strategic management from Graham's and Sweedler's experiences?

Sources: Information from company Web site (www.joeboxer.com), May 18, 2003, and Windsong Allegiance Web site (www.windsongallegiance.com), May 18, 2003; and P. Keegan, "The Rise and Fall (and Rise Again) of Joe Boxer," *Business 2.0,* December 2002/January 2003, pp. 76–82.

• • •Learning Outline

Follow this Learning Outline as you read and study this chapter.

Techniques for Assessing the Environment
- List the different approaches to environmental scanning.
- Explain what competitor intelligence is and ways that managers can do it legally and ethically.
- Describe how managers can improve the effectiveness of forecasting.
- Explain the steps in the benchmarking process.

Techniques for Allocating Resources
- List the four techniques for allocating resources.
- Describe the different types of budgets.
- Explain what a Gantt chart does.
- Explain a load chart.
- Describe how PERT network analysis works.
- Compute a breakeven point.
- Describe how managers can use linear programming.

Contemporary Planning Techniques
- Explain why flexibility is so important to today's planning techniques.
- Describe project management.
- List the steps in the project planning process.
- Discuss why scenario planning has become an important planning tool for managers.

Chapter

9

Planning Tools and Techniques

A **Manager's** *Dilemma*

To most people, China remains a country of mystery. However, with its acceptance into the World Trade Organization (WTO) and with its selection as the site for the 2008 Summer Olympics, China is poised to become a significant player in the global economy in the twenty-first century. Companies within China are positioning themselves to play a more active role in the global economy as well.

Junjie Li, president of Henan Electric Power Transmission and Transformation Construction Company (HETT), is one manager who is doing so. He has overseen the development and growth of one of China's most advanced companies.[1] HETT is based in the inland Henan Province, which is not one of China's richest or well-known regions. Yet, HETT has made a name for itself in China, the Middle East, southern Asia, and Africa by its ability to build major power plants quickly and efficiently. Junjie attributes part of his company's success to its early and broad embrace of an Internet business model for planning and managing projects beyond China's geographical borders. For example, when HETT was building power plants in Nigeria and Ethiopia, company engineers and managers used the Internet to collect and communicate a wide variety of information about quantity of work, equipment, materials, and human resources. The use of the Internet also extended from headquarters in Zhengzhou, where managers used remote finance monitoring systems to assure optimum utilization of resources. Junjie says, "Our profitability depends largely on how our different departments use the Internet to achieve our goals."

This focus on using the Internet has paid off. HETT's operating costs have decreased and the company's response time has shortened considerably, making it more efficient and effective in the competitive construction bidding process. Also, Internet applications have helped the company improve workplace safety and quality.

Junjie's next goal is to convince HETT vendors, partners, and customers to utilize the Internet. Put yourself in his position. What planning tools might Junjie use in accomplishing this goal?

What would **you** do **?**

In this chapter we'll discuss some basic planning tools and techniques that managers like Junjie Li or managers in any businesses—large or small—can use. (▪▪▪□▪ Go to the Web and check out S.A.L. #22—How Good Am I at Personal Planning?)We'll begin by looking at some techniques for assessing the environment. Then we'll review techniques for allocating resources. Finally, we'll discuss some contemporary planning techniques including project management and scenarios.

TECHNIQUES FOR ASSESSING THE ENVIRONMENT

Mark Hanson, vice president of marketing for Sony's Video Audio Integrated Operations (VAIO) division, is in charge of introducing the world's smallest laptop, code-named U, to the U.S. market. What will determine the product's success? Hansen says knowing the environment is a crucial factor.[2] In our description of the strategic management process in Chapter 8, we discussed the importance of assessing the organization's environment. In this section, we review three techniques to help managers do that: environmental scanning, forecasting, and benchmarking.

Environmental Scanning

How can managers become aware of significant environmental changes such as a new law in Germany permitting shopping for "tourist items" on Sunday? Or retailer Toys "R" Us deciding to partner with Amazon.com in response to other toy retailers' major Internet portals? Or the precipitous decline in the working-age populations in Japan, Germany, Italy, and Russia? Managers in both small and large organizations use **environmental scanning**, which is the screening of large amounts of information to anticipate and interpret changes in the environment. Extensive environmental scanning is likely to reveal issues and concerns that could affect an organization's current or planned activities. (▪▪▪□▪ Go to the Web and check out PRISM #3— Environmental Scanning.) Research has shown that companies with advanced environmental scanning systems have increased their profits and revenue growth.[3] Organizations that don't keep on top of environmental changes are likely to experience the opposite! For instance, Tupperware, the food-storage container company, enjoyed unprecedented success during the 1960s and 1970s, selling its products at

● ● ● **environmental scanning**
The screening of large amounts of information to anticipate and interpret changes in the environment.

Borders Group Inc. is the country's second-largest book retailer. In its efforts to boost sales at its U.S. stores, the firm has announced that it will now emphasize market research, a specialized form of environmental scanning. Relying less on "gut" reactions to new titles, the traditional strategy of the past, Borders will now aggressively seek input from focus groups, exit interviews, and customer polls, and it will call upon publishers to help it manage some 250 categories ranging from thrillers to cookbooks, determining what titles to carry, how many of each, and how the books will be displayed.

home-hostessed parties where housewives played games, socialized, and saw product demonstrations. However, as U.S. society changed—more women working full-time outside the home, an increasing divorce rate, and young adults waiting longer to marry—the popularity of Tupperware parties began to decline because no one had time to go to them. The company's North American market share fell from 60 percent to 40 percent while Rubbermaid, a competitor that marketed its plastic food-storage containers in retail outlets, increased its market share from 5 percent to 40 percent. By the early 1990s, most American women had no desire to go to a Tupperware party or knew how to find Tupperware products elsewhere. Yet, Tupperware's president, obviously clueless about the changed environment, predicted that before the end of the 1990s, the party concept would be popular once again.[4] This example shows how a once successful company can suffer by failing to recognize how the environment has changed.

●●● **competitor intelligence**
Environmental scanning activity that seeks to identify who competitors are, what they are doing, and how their actions will affect the organization.

One of the fastest-growing areas of environmental scanning is **competitor intelligence**.[5] It's a process by which organizations gather information about their competitors and get answers to questions such as: Who are they? What are they doing? How will what they're doing affect us? Let's look at an example of how one organization used competitor intelligence in its planning. Dun & Bradstreet (D&B), a leading provider of business credit, marketing, and purchasing information, has an active business intelligence division. The division manager received a call from an assistant vice president for sales in one of the company's geographic territories. This person had been on a sales call with a major customer and the customer happened to mention in passing that another company had visited and made a major presentation about its services. What was interesting was that, although D&B had plenty of competitors, this particular company wasn't one of them. The manager gathered together a team that sifted through dozens of sources (research services, Internet, personal contacts, and other external sources) and quickly became convinced that there was something to this; that this company was "aiming its guns right at us." Managers at D&B jumped into action to develop plans to counteract this competitive attack.[6]

Competitor intelligence experts suggest that 80 percent of what managers need to know about competitors can be found out from their own employees, suppliers, and customers.[7] Competitor intelligence doesn't have to involve spying. Advertisements, promotional materials, press releases, reports filed with government agencies, annual reports, want ads, newspaper reports, and industry studies are examples of readily accessible sources of information. Attending trade shows and debriefing the salesforce can be other good sources of competitor information. Many firms regularly buy competitors' products and have their own engineers study them (through a process called *reverse engineering*) to learn about new technical innovations. In addition, the Internet has opened up vast sources of competitor intelligence as many corporate Web pages include new-product information and other press releases. (▮◻▮▮▮▮ Go to the Web and check out Q & A 9.1.)

The concerns about competitor intelligence pertain to the ways in which competitor information is gathered. For instance, at Procter & Gamble, executives hired competitive intelligence firms to spy on its competitors in the hair care business. At least one of these firms misrepresented themselves to competitor Unilever's employees, trespassed at Unilever's hair care headquarters in Chicago, and went through trash dumpsters to gain information. When P&G's CEO found out, he immediately fired the individuals responsible and apologized to Unilever.[8] Competitor intelligence

In the first case brought under the new Economic Espionage Act, which was designed to discourage corporate spying, a waiter in MasterCard's corporate headquarters in Purchase, New York, was arrested for stealing volumes of confidential corporate information and trying to sell it to Visa. The waiter, whose name was Estrada, sent Visa an anonymous letter using a code name and offering to sell the credit card company information about a deal with Disney that its competitor was considering. Visa won praise for promptly contacting the FBI. "In the hands of a less scrupulous organization," said special agent Robert Cordier of the FBI, "they could have milked the situation for all it was worth."

becomes illegal corporate spying when it involves the theft of proprietary materials or trade secrets by any means. The Economic Espionage Act passed by Congress in 1996 makes it a crime in the United States to engage in economic espionage or to steal a trade secret.[9] The difficult decisions about competitive intelligence arise because often there's a fine line between what's considered *legal and ethical* and what's considered *legal but unethical.* Although the top manager at one competitive intelligence firm contends that 99.9 percent of intelligence gathering is legal, there's no question that some people or companies will go to any lengths—many unethical—to get information about competitors.[10]

One type of environmental scanning that's particularly important is global scanning. Because world markets are complex and dynamic, managers have expanded the scope of their scanning efforts to gain vital information on global forces that might affect their organizations.[11] The value of global scanning to managers, of course, is largely dependent on the extent of the organization's global activities. For a company that has significant global interests, global scanning can be quite valuable. For instance, Mitsubishi Corporation has elaborate information networks and computerized systems to monitor global changes.[12]

The sources that managers use for scanning the domestic environment are too limited for global scanning. Managers need to globalize their perspectives and information sources. For instance, they can subscribe to information clipping services that review world newspapers and business periodicals and provide summaries of desired information. Also, there are numerous electronic services that provide topic searches and automatic updates in global areas of special interest to managers.

Customers may be delighted at the heavy discounts retailers like Wal-Mart have offered in recent selling seasons. But the slashed prices may actually reflect flawed sales forecasts that left Wal-Mart, and many other retailers like Kmart and Target, with excess inventory they need to clear away with markdowns of up to 40 percent.

Forecasting

The second technique managers can use to assess the environment is forecasting. Forecasting is an important part of organizational planning and managers need forecasts that will allow them to predict future events effectively and in a timely manner. (▮▢▮▮▮▮ Go to the Web and check out Q & A 9.2.) Environmental

● ● ● **forecasts**
Predictions of outcomes.

scanning establishes the basis for **forecasts**, which are predictions of outcomes. Virtually any component in the organization's external environment can be forecasted. Let's look at how managers forecast and how effective forecasts are.

Forecasting Techniques Forecasting techniques fall into two categories: quantitative and qualitative. **Quantitative forecasting** applies a set of mathematical rules to a series of past data to predict outcomes. These techniques are preferred when managers have sufficient hard data that can be used. **Qualitative forecasting**, in contrast, uses the judgment and opinions of knowledgeable individuals to predict outcomes. Qualitative techniques typically are used when precise data are limited or hard to obtain. Exhibit 9–1 describes some popular forecasting techniques.

● ● ● **quantitative forecasting**
Forecasting that applies a set of mathematical rules to a series of past data to predict outcomes.

● ● ● **qualitative forecasting**
Forecasting that uses the judgment and opinions of knowledgeable individuals to predict outcomes.

Today, many organizations collaborate on forecasts by using Internet-based software known as CPFR, which stands for collaborative planning, forecasting, and replenishment.[13] CPFR offers a standardized way for retailers and manufacturers to use the Internet to exchange data. Each organization relies on its own data about past sales trends, promotion plans, and other factors to calculate a demand forecast for a particular product. If their respective forecasts differ by a certain amount (say 10 percent), the retailer and manufacturer use the Internet to exchange more data and written comments until they arrive at a single and more accurate forecast. This collaborative forecasting helps both organizations do a better job of planning.

Forecasting Effectiveness At *Fortune* 100 companies, it's not unusual to have 1,000 to 5,000 managers providing forecasting input. These businesses are finding that the more people they have involved in the process, the more they can improve the reliability of the outcomes.[14]

Exhibit 9–1

● ● ●━━━

Forecasting Techniques

Technique	Description	Application
Quantitative		
Time series analysis	Fits a trend line to a mathematical equation and projects into the future by means of this equation	Predicting next quarter's sales on the basis of four years of previous sales data
Regression models	Predicts one variable on the basis of known or assumed other variables	Seeking factors that will predict a certain level of sales (for example, price, advertising expenditures)
Econometric models	Uses a set of regression equations to simulate segments of the economy	Predicting change in car sales as a result of changes in tax laws
Economic indicators	Uses one or more economic indicators to predict a future state of the economy	Using change in GNP to predict discretionary income
Substitution effect	Uses a mathematical formula to predict how, when, and under what circumstances a new product or technology will replace an existing one	Predicting the effect of DVD players on the sale of VHS players
Qualitative		
Jury of opinion	Combines and averages the opinions of experts	Polling the company's human resource managers to predict next year's college recruitment needs
Salesforce composition	Combines estimates from field sales personnel of customers' expected purchases	Predicting next year's sales of industrial lasers
Customer evaluation	Combines estimates from established customers' purchases	Surveying major car dealers by a car manufacturer to determine types and quantities of products desired

The goal of forecasting is to provide managers with information that will facilitate decision making. Despite forecasting's importance to planning, managers have had mixed success with it.[15] Forecasting techniques are most accurate when the environment is not rapidly changing. The more dynamic the environment, the more likely managers are to forecast ineffectively. Also, forecasting is relatively ineffective in predicting nonseasonal events such as recessions, unusual occurrences, discontinued operations, and the actions or reactions of competitors.

Although forecasting has a mixed record, there are ways to improve its effectiveness.[16] (▮◻▮▮ Go to the Web and check out Q & A 9.3.) First, use simple forecasting methods. They tend to do as well as, and often better than, complex methods that may mistakenly confuse random data for meaningful information. For instance, at St. Louis-based Emerson Electric, chairman and former CEO Chuck Knight found that forecasts developed as part of the company's planning process were indicating that the competition wasn't just domestic anymore, but global. He didn't use any complex mathematical techniques to come to this conclusion but instead relied on the information already collected as part of his company's planning process. Next, compare every forecast with "no change." A no-change forecast is accurate approximately half the time. Third, don't rely on a single forecasting method. Make forecasts with several models and average them, especially when making long-range forecasts. Fourth, don't assume that you can accurately identify turning points in a trend. What is typically perceived as a significant turning point often turns out to be simply a random event. Fifth, shorten the length of forecasts to improve their accuracy because accuracy decreases as the period you're trying to predict increases. And, finally, remember that forecasting *is* a managerial skill and as such can be practiced and improved. Forecasting software has made the task somewhat less mathematically challenging, although the "number crunching" is only a small part of the activity. Interpreting the forecast and incorporating that information into planning decisions is the challenge facing managers.

Benchmarking

Suppose that you're a talented pianist or gymnast. To make yourself better, you want to learn from the best so you watch outstanding musicians or athletes for motions and techniques they use as they perform. That's what is involved in the final technique for assessing the environment we're going to discuss—**benchmarking**. This is the search for the best practices among competitors or noncompetitors that lead to their superior performance.[17] Does benchmarking work? Studies show that users have achieved 69 percent faster growth and 45 percent greater productivity.[18]

●●● **benchmarking**
The search for the best practices among competitors or noncompetitors that lead to their superior performance.

The basic idea behind benchmarking is that managers can improve performance by analyzing and then copying the methods of the leaders in various fields. (▮◻▮▮▮ Go to the Web and check out Q & A 9.4.) Today, companies such as Koch Industries, DuPont, Payless Shoe Source, and Volvo Construction Equipment use benchmarking as a standard tool in their quest for performance improvement. In fact, some companies have chosen some pretty unusual benchmarking partners! Southwest Airlines, for example, studied Indy 500 pit crews, who can change a race tire in under 15 seconds, to see how they could make gate turnarounds even faster. IBM studied Las Vegas casinos for ways to discourage employee theft. Many hospitals have benchmarked their admissions processes against Marriott Hotels. And Giordano Holdings Ltd., a Hong Kong-based manufacturer and retailer of mass-market casual wear borrowed its "good quality, good value" concept from Marks & Spencer, used Limited Brands to benchmark its point-of-sales computerized information system, and modeled its simplified product offerings on McDonald's menu. Even small companies have found that benchmarking can bring big benefits. For instance, Henkel Consumer Adhesives, a Cleveland-based producer of duct tape, benchmarks its processes against some big names—Wal-Mart, Rubbermaid, and PepsiCo. Why? To help it compete better against rival 3M Corporation.[19]

What does benchmarking involve? As shown in Exhibit 9–2, it typically follows four steps:

Exhibit 9–2

Steps in Benchmarking

Source: Based on Y.K. Shetty, "Aiming High: Competitive Benchmarking for Superior Performance," *Long Range Planning,* February 1993, p. 42.

1. A benchmarking planning team is formed. The team's initial task is to identify what is to be benchmarked, identify comparative organizations, and determine data collection methods.
2. The team collects internal data on its own work methods and external data from other organizations.
3. The data are analyzed to identify performance gaps and the cause of differences.
4. An action plan that will result in meeting or exceeding the standards of others is prepared and implemented.

How does a benchmarking team get data on other organizations?[20] First, you need to decide against whom you're going to benchmark. Use your network of contacts among customers, suppliers, and employees for organizations they think are best at the process you're trying to improve. Trade associations and industry experts often know what organizations have revolutionary practices. And watch for organizations that may have won local, regional, or national awards as potential benchmarking partners. Also, use the Internet. Competitors' Web sites can be rich sources of information. Many company Web sites describe new products or services being developed and often have financial information that can be analyzed. Experts also suggest that managers not overlook the possibility of developing partnerships with other organizations, even competitors, to share benchmarking data. Obviously, this will work only if you have something that others want. But if, for example, you're looking to improve your customer satisfaction process and you already have a great order system in place, you may be able to swap data with another organization that wants to know about your experience.

Learning Review

- List the different approaches to environmental scanning.
- Explain what competitor intelligence is and ways that managers can do it legally and ethically.

- Describe how managers can improve the effectiveness of forecasting.
- Describe what benchmarking is.
- Explain the steps in the benchmarking process.

TECHNIQUES FOR ALLOCATING RESOURCES

As we know from Chapter 7, once an organization's goals have been established, an important aspect of planning is determining how those goals are going to be accomplished. Before managers can organize and lead in order to implement the goals, they must have resources. **Resources** are the assets of the organization and include financial (debt, equity, retained earnings, and other financial holdings); physical (equipment, buildings, raw materials, or other tangible assets); human (experiences, skills, knowledge, and competencies of people); intangible (brand names, patents, reputation,

resources
The assets of the organization including financial, physical, human, intangible, and structural/cultural.

At the age of 26, Jason West, shown here with his running mates Rebecca Rotzler (left) and Julia Walsh, is the youngest mayor ever elected in the rural college town of New Paltz, New York. West will have his hands full as he undertakes his new duties. His campaign promises included using solar energy and finding alternative ways to handle the town's water treatment processes, but his constituents include many older residents who want the town's assets used in other ways. Finding a compromise that makes the best use of New Paltz's resources will be one of West's biggest challenges in his new job and will require him to make use of budgeting and scheduling techniques.

●●● **budget**
A numerical plan for allocating resources to specific activities.

trademarks, copyrights, registered designs, and databases); and structural/cultural (history, culture, work systems, working relationships, level of trust, policies, and structure) factors. How are these resources allocated effectively and efficiently so that organizational goals are met? (▢ Go to the Web and check out S.A.L. #21—What Time of Day Am I Most Productive?) That's what we want to look at in this section. Although managers can choose from a number of techniques for allocating resources (many of which are covered in courses on accounting, finance, human resources, and operations management), we'll discuss four techniques here: budgeting, scheduling, breakeven analysis, and linear programming.

Budgeting

Most of us have had some experience, as limited as it might be, with budgets. We probably learned at a very early age that unless we allocated our "revenues" carefully, our weekly allowance was spent on "expenses" before the week was half over.

A **budget** is a numerical plan for allocating resources to specific activities. Managers typically prepare budgets for revenues, expenses, and large capital expenditures such as equipment. It's not unusual, though, for budgets to be used for improving time, space, and use of material resources. These types of budgets substitute nondollar numbers for dollar amounts. Such items as person-hours, capacity utilization, or units of production can be budgeted for daily, weekly, or monthly activities. Exhibit 9–3 describes the different types of budgets that managers might use. (▢ Go to the Web and check out Q & A 9.5.)

Why are budgets so popular? Probably because they're applicable to a wide variety of organizations and work activities within organizations. We live in a world in which almost everything is expressed in monetary units. Dollars, pesos, euros, yen, and the like, are used as a common measuring unit within a country. It seems only logical, then, that monetary budgets would be a useful tool for allocating resources and guiding work in such diverse departments as manufacturing and marketing research or at various levels in an organization. Budgets are one planning technique that most managers, regardless of organizational level, use. It's an important managerial activity because it forces financial discipline and structure throughout the organization. However, many managers don't like preparing budgets because they feel the process is time-consuming, inflexible, inefficient, and ineffective.[21] How can the budgeting process be improved? Exhibit 9–4 provides some suggestions. Organizations such as

Exhibit 9–3

Types of Budgets

Source: Based on R.S. Russell and B.W. Taylor III. *Production and Operations Management* (Upper Saddle River, NJ: Prentice Hall, 1995), p. 287.

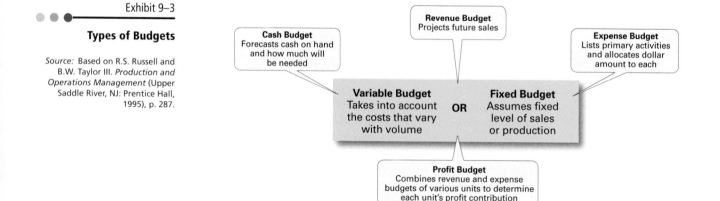

Cash Budget
Forecasts cash on hand and how much will be needed

Revenue Budget
Projects future sales

Expense Budget
Lists primary activities and allocates dollar amount to each

Variable Budget
Takes into account the costs that vary with volume

OR

Fixed Budget
Assumes fixed level of sales or production

Profit Budget
Combines revenue and expense budgets of various units to determine each unit's profit contribution

Exhibit 9–4

Suggestions for Improving Budgeting

- Be flexible.
- Goals should drive budgets—budgets should not determine goals.
- Coordinate budgeting throughout the organization.
- Use budgeting/planning software when appropriate.
- Remember that budgets are tools.
- Remember that profits result from smart management, not because you budgeted for them.

Texas Instruments, IKEA, Volvo, and Svenska Handelsbanken have incorporated several of these suggestions as they revamped their budgeting processes. (See the Budgeting Skills Module on p. 518 for an explanation of the mechanics of the budgeting process.)

Scheduling

Ann is a manager at an Express store in San Francisco. Every week she determines employees' work hours and the store area where each employee will be working. If you observed any group of supervisors or department managers for a few days, you would see them doing much the same—allocating resources by detailing what activities have to be done, the order in which they are to be completed, who is to do each, and when they are to be completed. These managers are **scheduling**. In this section, we'll review some useful scheduling devices including Gantt charts, load charts, and PERT network analysis.

Gantt Charts The **Gantt chart** was developed during the early 1900s by Henry Gantt, an associate of the scientific management expert Frederick Taylor. The idea behind a Gantt chart is simple. It's essentially a bar graph with time on the horizontal axis and the activities to be scheduled on the vertical axis. The bars show output, both planned and actual, over a period of time. The Gantt chart visually shows when tasks are supposed to be done and compares that with the actual progress on each. It's a simple but important device that lets managers detail easily what has yet to be done to complete a job or project and to assess whether an activity is ahead of, behind, or on schedule.

Exhibit 9–5 on page 214 depicts a simplified Gantt chart for book production developed by a manager in a publishing company. Time is expressed in months across the top

●●● scheduling
Detailing what activities have to be done, the order in which they are to be completed, who is to do each, and when they are to be completed.

●●● Gantt chart
A scheduling chart developed by Henry Gantt that shows actual and planned output over a period of time.

The trendy Zara clothing chain is expanding across Europe at the rate of one new store a week, its success relying heavily on its innovative product-delivery schedule. New goods are shipped from the warehouse to Zara's 600 stores every few days, instead of only once a season as its competitors do. Maintaining the marketing advantage of this carefully managed schedule will be Zara's big challenge as it continues its global expansion.

Exhibit 9–5

A Gantt Chart

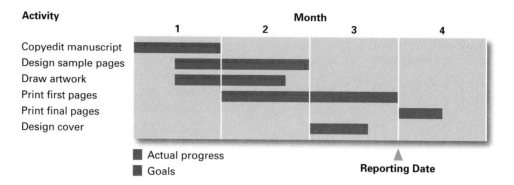

of the chart. The major work activities are listed down the left side. Planning involves deciding what activities need to be done to get the book finished, the order in which those activities need to be completed, and the time that should be allocated to each activity. Where a box sits within a time frame reflects its planned sequence. The shading represents actual progress. The chart also serves as a control tool because the manager can see deviations from the plan. In this example, both the design of the cover and the printing of first pages are running behind schedule. Cover design is about three weeks behind, and printing first pages is about two weeks behind schedule. Given this information, the manager might need to take some action to either make up for the two lost weeks or to ensure that no further delays will occur. At this point, the manager can expect that the book will be published at least two weeks later than planned if no action is taken.

Load Charts A **load chart** is a modified Gantt chart. Instead of listing activities on the vertical axis, load charts list either entire departments or specific resources. This arrangement allows managers to plan and control capacity utilization. In other words, load charts schedule capacity by work areas.

For example, Exhibit 9–6 shows a load chart for six production editors at the same publishing company. Each editor supervises the production and design of several books. By reviewing a load chart, the executive editor, who supervises the six production editors, can see who is free to take on a new book. If everyone is fully scheduled, the executive editor might decide not to accept any new projects, to accept new projects and delay others, to have the editors work overtime, or to employ more production editors. In Exhibit 9–6 only Antonio and Maurice are completely scheduled for the next six months. The other editors have some unassigned time and might be able to accept new projects or be available to help other editors who get behind.

PERT Network Analysis Gantt and load charts are useful as long as the activities being scheduled are few in number and independent of each other. But what if a manager had to plan a large project such as a departmental reorganization, the implementation of a cost-reduction program, or the development of a new product that required coordinating inputs from marketing, manufacturing, and product design? Such projects require coordinating hundreds and even thousands of activities, some of which must be done simultaneously and some of which can't begin until preceding activities have been completed. If you're constructing a building, you obviously can't start putting up the walls until

*•• **load chart***
A modified Gantt chart that schedules capacity by entire departments or specific resources.

Exhibit 9–6

A Load Chart

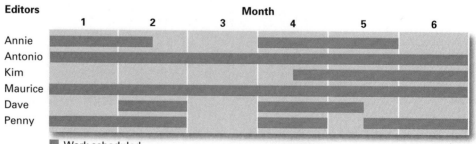

the foundation is laid. How can managers schedule such a complex project? The Program Evaluation and Review Technique (PERT) is highly appropriate for such projects.

A **PERT network** is a flowchart diagram that depicts the sequence of activities needed to complete a project and the time or costs associated with each activity. With a PERT network, a manager must think through what has to be done, determine which events depend on one another, and identify potential trouble spots. PERT also makes it easy to compare the effects alternative actions might have on scheduling and costs. Thus, PERT allows managers to monitor a project's progress, identify possible bottlenecks, and shift resources as necessary to keep the project on schedule.

To understand how to construct a PERT network, you need to know four terms. **Events** are end points that represent the completion of major activities. **Activities** represent the time or resources required to progress from one event to another. **Slack time** is the amount of time an individual activity can be delayed without delaying the whole project. The **critical path** is the longest or most time-consuming sequence of events and activities in a PERT network. Any delay in completing events on this path would delay completion of the entire project. In other words, activities on the critical path have zero slack time.

Developing a PERT network requires that a manager identify all key activities needed to complete a project, rank them in order of occurrence, and estimate each activity's completion time. Exhibit 9–7 explains the steps in this process.

Most PERT projects are complicated and include numerous activities. Such complicated computations can be done with specialized PERT software. However, let's work through a simple example. Assume that you're the superintendent at a construction company and have been assigned to oversee the construction of an office building. Because time really is money in your business, you must determine how long it will take to get the building completed. You've determined the specific activities and events. Exhibit 9–8 on page 216 outlines the major events in the construction project and your estimate of the expected time to complete each. Exhibit 9–9 on page 216 shows the actual PERT network based on the data in Exhibit 9–8. You've also calculated the length of time that each path of activities will take:

A-B-C-D-I-J-K (44 weeks)

A-B-C-D-G-H-J-K (50 weeks)

A-B-C-E-G-H-J-K (47 weeks)

A-B-C-F-G-H-J-K (47 weeks)

Your PERT network shows that if everything goes as planned, the total project completion time will be 50 weeks. This is calculated by tracing the project's critical path (the

---

• • • PERT network
A flowchart diagram showing the sequence of activities needed to complete a project and the time or cost associated with each.

• • • events
End points that represent the completion of major activities in a PERT network.

• • • activities
The time or resources needed to progress from one event to another in a PERT network.

• • • slack time
The amount of time an individual activity can be delayed without delaying the whole project.

• • • critical path
The longest sequence of activities in a PERT network.

Exhibit 9–7

• • ● ────────

Steps in Developing a PERT Network

1. *Identify every significant activity that must be achieved for a project to be completed.* The accomplishment of each activity results in a set of events or outcomes.

2. *Determine the order in which these events must be completed.*

3. *Diagram the flow of activities from start to finish, identifying each activity and its relationship to all other activities.* Use circles to indicate events and arrows to represent activities. This results in a flowchart diagram called a PERT network.

4. *Compute a time estimate for completing each activity.* This is done with a weighted average that uses an *optimistic* time estimate (t_o) of how long the activity would take under ideal conditions, a *most likely* estimate (t_m) of the time the activity normally should take, and a *pessimistic* estimate (t_p) that represents the time that an activity should take under the worst possible conditions. The formula for calculating the expected time (t_e) is then

$$t_e = \frac{t_o + 4t_m + t_p}{6}$$

5. *Using the network diagram that contains time estimates for each activity, determine a schedule for the start and finish dates of each activity and for the entire project.* Any delays that occur along the critical path require the most attention because they can delay the whole project.

Event	Description	Expected Time (in weeks)	Preceding Event
A	Approve design and get permits.	10	None
B	Dig subterranean garage.	6	A
C	Erect frame and siding.	14	B
D	Construct floor.	6	C
E	Install windows.	3	C
F	Put on roof.	3	C
G	Install internal wiring.	5	D, E, F
H	Install elevator.	5	G
I	Put in floor covering and paneling.	4	D
J	Put in doors and interior decorative trim.	3	I, H
K	Turn over to building management group.	1	J

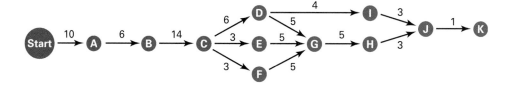

longest sequence of activities): A - B - C - D - G - H - J - K and adding up the times. You know that any delay in completing the events on this path would delay the completion of the entire project. Taking six weeks instead of four to put in the floor covering and paneling (Event I) would have no effect on the final completion date. Why? Because that event isn't on the critical path. However, taking seven weeks instead of six to dig the subterranean garage (Event B) would likely delay the total project. A manager who needed to get back on schedule or to cut the 50-week completion time would want to concentrate on those activities along the critical path that could be completed faster. How might the manager do this? He or she could look to see if any of the other activities *not* on the critical path had slack time in which resources could be transferred to activities that *were* on the critical path.

Breakeven Analysis

Managers at Glory Foods want to know how many units of their new seasoned canned vegetables must be sold in order to break even—that is, the point at which total revenue is just sufficient to cover total costs. **Breakeven analysis** is a widely used resource allocation technique to help managers determine breakeven point.[22]

Breakeven analysis is a simple calculation, yet it's valuable to managers because it points out the relationship between revenues, costs, and profits. To compute breakeven point (BE), a manager needs to know the unit price of the product being sold (P), the variable cost per unit (VC), and total fixed costs (TFC). An organization breaks even when its total revenue is just enough to equal its total costs. But total cost has two parts: fixed and variable. *Fixed costs* are expenses that do not change regardless of volume. Examples include insurance premiums, rent, and property taxes. *Variable costs* change in proportion to output and include raw materials, labor costs, and energy costs.

Breakeven point can be computed graphically or by using the following formula:

$$BE = \frac{TFC}{P - VC}$$

This formula tells us that (1) total revenue will equal total cost when we sell enough units at a price that covers all variable unit costs and (2) the difference between price and variable costs, when multiplied by the number of units sold, equals the fixed costs. Let's work through an example.

Exhibit 9–10

Breakeven Analysis

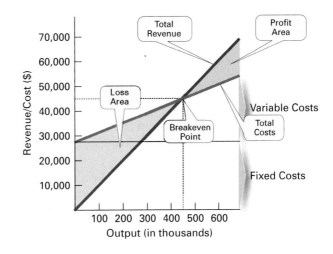

Assume that Miguel's Photocopying Service charges $0.10 per photocopy. If fixed costs are $27,000 a year and variable costs are $0.04 per copy, Miguel can compute his breakeven point as follows: $27,000 ÷ ($0.10 − $0.04) = 450,000 copies, or when annual revenues are $45,000 (450,000 copies × $0.10). This same relationship is shown graphically in Exhibit 9–10.

As a planning tool, breakeven analysis could help Miguel set his sales goal. For example, he could determine his profit goal and then calculate what sales level is needed to reach that goal. Breakeven analysis could also tell Miguel how much volume has to increase to break even if he's currently operating at a loss or how much volume he can afford to lose and still break even.

Linear Programming

Kamie Bousman manages a manufacturing plant that produces two kinds of cinnamon-scented home fragrance products: wax candles and a woodchip potpourri sold in bags. Business is good and she can sell all of the products she can produce. This is her problem: Given that the bags of potpourri and the wax candles are manufactured in the same facility, how many of each product should she produce to maximize profits? Kamie can use **linear programming** to solve her resource allocation problem.

●●● **linear programming**
A mathematical technique that solves resource allocation problems.

Although linear programming can be used here, it can't be applied to all resource allocation problems because it requires that there be limited resources, that the goal be outcome optimization, that there be alternative ways of combining resources to produce a number of output mixes, and that there be a linear relationship between variables (a change in one variable must be accompanied by an exactly proportional change in the other).[23] For Kamie's business, that last condition would be met if it took exactly twice the amount of raw materials and hours of labor to produce two of a given home fragrance product as it took to produce one.

What kinds of problems can be solved with linear programming? Some applications include selecting transportation routes that minimize shipping costs, allocating a limited advertising budget among various product brands, making the optimal assignment of people among projects, and determining how much of each product to make with a limited number of resources. Let's return to Kamie's problem and see how linear programming could help her solve it. Fortunately, her problem is relatively simple, so we can solve it rather quickly. For complex linear programming problems, managers can use computer software programs designed specifically to help develop optimizing solutions. (■□▨▨ Go to the Web and check out Q & A 9.6.)

First, we need to establish some facts about Kamie's business. She has computed the profit margins on her home fragrance products at $10 for a bag of potpourri and $18 for a scented candle. These numbers establish the basis for Kamie to be able to express her *objective function* as maximum profit = $10P + $18S, where P is the number of bags of potpourri produced and S is the number of scented candles produced. The

Exhibit 9–11

**Production Data for
Cinnamon-Scented
Products**

Department	Number of Hours Required (per unit)		Monthly Production Capacity (in hours)
	Potpourri Bags	Scented Candles	
Manufacturing	2	4	1,200
Assembly	2	2	900
Profit per unit	$10	$18	

objective function is simply a mathematical equation that can predict the outcome of all proposed alternatives. In addition, Kamie knows how much time each fragrance product must spend in production and the monthly production capacity (1,200 hours in manufacturing and 900 hours in assembly) for manufacturing and assembly. (See Exhibit 9–11.) The production capacity numbers act as *constraints* on her overall capacity. Now Kamie can establish her constraint equations:

$$2P + 4S \leq 1,200$$

$$2P + 2S \leq 900$$

Of course, Kamie can also state that: $P \geq 0$ and $S \geq 0$, because neither fragrance product can be produced in a volume less than zero.

Kamie has graphed her solution in Exhibit 9–12. The shaded area represents the options that don't exceed the capacity of either department. What does this mean? Well, let's look first at the manufacturing constraint line BE. We know that total manufacturing capacity is 1,200 hours, so if Kamie decides to produce all potpourri bags, the maximum she can produce is 600 (1,200 hours ÷ 2 hours required to produce a bag of potpourri). If she decides to produce all scented candles, the maximum she can produce is 300 (1,200 hours ÷ 4 hours required to produce a scented candle). The other constraint Kamie faces is that of assembly, shown by line DF. If Kamie decides to produce all potpourri bags, the maximum she can assemble is 450 (900 hours production capacity ÷ 2 hours required to assemble). Likewise, if Kamie decides to produce all scented candles, the maximum she can assemble is also 450 because the scented candles also take 2 hours to assemble. The constraints imposed by these capacity limits establish Kamie's *feasibility region*. Her optimal resource allocation will be defined at one of the corners within this feasibility region. Point C provides the maximum profits within the constraints stated. How do we know? At point A, profits would be 0 (no production of either potpourri bags or scented candles). At point B, profits would be $5,400 (300 scented candles × $18 profit and 0 potpourri bags produced = $5,400). At point D, profits would be $4,500 (450 potpourri bags produced × $10 profit and 0 scented candles produced = $4,500). At point C, however, profits would be $5,700 (150 scented candles produced × $18 profit and 300 potpourri bags produced × $10 profit = $5,700).

Exhibit 9–12

**Graphical Solution to
Linear Programming
Problem**

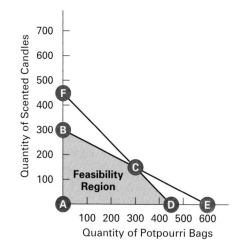

• • • Learning Review

- List the four techniques for allocating resources.
- Describe the different types of budgets.
- Explain what a Gantt chart does.
- Explain a load chart.

- Describe how PERT network analysis works.
- Compute breakeven point.
- Describe how managers can use linear programming.

CONTEMPORARY PLANNING TECHNIQUES

Wi-fi applications. SARS epidemics. HyperSonic Sound (HSS) technology. Anthrax scares. Deflation worries. Terrorist attacks. Changing competition. Today's managers face the challenges of planning in an environment that's both dynamic and complex. Two planning techniques that are appropriate for this type of environment are project management and scenarios. Both techniques emphasize *flexibility*, something that's important to making planning more effective and efficient in this type of organizational environment.

Project Management

• • • project
A one-time-only set of activities that has a definite beginning and ending point in time.

• • • project management
The task of getting a project's activities done on time, within budget, and according to specifications.

Different types of organizations, from manufacturers such as DaimlerChrysler and Boeing to software design firms such as Plumtree and Microsoft, use projects. A **project** is a one-time-only set of activities that has a definite beginning and ending point in time.[24] Projects vary in size and scope—from Boston's "big dig" downtown traffic tunnel to a sorority's holiday formal. **Project management** is the task of getting a project's activities done on time, within budget, and according to specifications.[25] (■□▨▨▨ Go to the Web and check out Q & A 9.7.)

More and more organizations are using project management because the approach fits well with the need for flexibility and rapid response to perceived market opportunities. When organizations undertake projects that are unique, have specific deadlines, contain complex interrelated tasks requiring specialized skills, and are temporary in nature, these projects often do not fit into the standardized planning procedures that guide an organization's other routine work activities. Instead, managers use project management techniques to effectively and efficiently accomplish the project's goals. What does the project management process involve?

Project Management Process In the typical project, work is done by a project team whose members are assigned from their respective work areas to the project and who report to a project manager. The project manager coordinates the project's activities with other departments. When the project team accomplishes its goals, it disbands and members move on to other projects or back to their permanent work areas.

The essential features of the project planning process are shown in Exhibit 9–13. The process begins by clearly defining the project's goals. This step is necessary

Exhibit 9–13　**Project Planning Process**

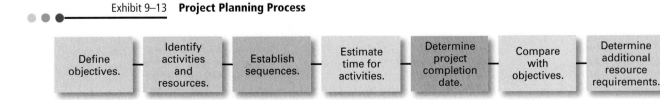

| Define objectives. | Identify activities and resources. | Establish sequences. | Estimate time for activities. | Determine project completion date. | Compare with objectives. | Determine additional resource requirements. |

Source: Based on R.S. Russell and B.W. Taylor III, *Production and Operations Management* (Upper Saddle River, NJ: Prentice Hall, 1995), p. 287.

because the manager and the team members need to know what's expected. All activities in the project and the resources needed to do them must then be identified. What materials and labor are needed to complete the project? This step may be time-consuming and complex, particularly if the project is unique and there is no history or experience with similar projects. Once the activities have been identified, the sequence of completion needs to be determined. What activities must be completed before others can begin? Which can be done simultaneously? This step often uses flowchart diagrams such as a Gantt chart, a load chart, or a PERT network. (■□■■■ Go to the Web and check out Q & A 9.8.) Next, the project activities need to be scheduled. Time estimates for each activity are done and these estimates are used to develop an overall project schedule and completion date. Then the project schedule is compared to the goals, and any necessary adjustments are made. If the project completion time is too long, the manager might assign more resources to critical activities so they can be completed faster.

Today, the project management process can take place online as a number of Internet-based project collaboration software packages are available. For instance, one package, OnProject.com, is described as an Internet workspace that allows users to share and manage information associated with projects. Suppliers and customers can even be part of the process.[26]

The Role of the Project Manager The temporary nature of projects makes managing them different from, say, overseeing a production line or preparing a weekly tally of costs on an ongoing basis. The one-shot nature of the work makes project managers the organizational equivalent of a hired gunman. There's a job to be done. It has to be defined—in detail. And the project manager is responsible for how it's done. For instance, Tom Kepper, senior manager of Intel's facilities and materials services group, monitors the company's construction projects around the world and is responsible for everything from resource procurement to invoice payment.[27]

Even with the availability of sophisticated computerized and online scheduling programs and other project management tools, the role of project manager remains difficult because he or she is managing people who typically are still linked to their permanent work areas. The only real influence project managers have is their communication skills and their power of persuasion. To make matters worse, team members seldom work on just one project. They're usually assigned to two or three at any given time. So project managers end up competing with each other to focus a worker's attention on his or her particular project.

Becoming a Manager

- ◆ Get in the habit of reading general news and business periodicals. Pay attention to events, trends, and changes that are written about.
- ◆ Practice competitor intelligence by using published sources about different companies when writing papers for class assignments.
- ◆ Take classes to learn about linear programming and forecasting techniques.
- ◆ Practice budgeting by applying it to your personal life.
- ◆ Try different scheduling tools when faced with class projects that need to be planned and managed.
- ◆ ■□■ Go to the Web and complete any of these exercises from the Self-Assessment Library (S.A.L.) found on R.O.L.L.S.: #21—What Time of Day Am I Most Productive?, #22—How Good Am I at Personal Planning?, or #47—How Well Do I Respond to Turbulent Change?

Scenario Planning

We already know how important it is that today's managers monitor and assess the external environment for trends and changes. As they assess the environment, issues and concerns that could affect their organization's current or planned operations are likely to be revealed. All of these won't be equally important, so it's usually necessary to focus on a limited set that are most important and to develop scenarios based on each.

A **scenario** is a consistent view of what the future is likely to be. Developing scenarios also can be described as *contingency planning;* that is, if this is what happens, then these are the actions we need to take. If, for instance, environmental scanning reveals increasing interest by the U.S. Congress in raising the national minimum wage, managers at Subway could create multiple scenarios to assess the possible consequences of such an action. What would be the implications for its labor costs if the minimum wage was raised to $8.00 an hour? How about $9.00 an hour? What effect would these changes have on the chain's bottom line? How might competitors respond? Different assumptions lead to different outcomes. The intent of scenario planning is not to try to predict the future but to reduce uncertainty by playing out potential situations under different specified conditions.[28] Subway could, for example, develop a set of scenarios ranging from optimistic to pessimistic in terms of the minimum wage issue. It would then be prepared to implement new strategies to get and keep a competitive advantage. An expert in scenario planning said, "Just the process of doing scenarios causes executives to rethink and clarify the essence of the business environment in ways they almost certainly have never done before."[29]

After the tragic events of September 11, 2001, many New York-area firms reexamined and revamped their contingency plans. Walter Hines, CFO of the New York Board of Trade, whose offices were destroyed with the World Trade Center, had to rebuild his company's financial records from scratch while filing insurance claims and looking for a new location. But Hines had a big advantage—the organization had a temporary backup facility from which its employees could work during the interim. As the company prepared to move back into downtown Manhattan, with a new backup location and a new chief information security officer, Hines realized that "the fact that things run smoothly today in our backup facilities doesn't mean we're back to normal. Things might never be back to normal."

• • • **scenario**
A consistent view of what the future is likely to be.

Although scenario planning is useful in anticipating events that *can be* anticipated, it's difficult to forecast random events—the major surprises and aberrations that can't be foreseen. For instance, an outbreak of deadly and devastating tornadoes in southwest Missouri on May 4, 2003, was a scenario that could be anticipated. The disaster recovery planning that took place after the storms was effective because this type of scenario had been experienced before. A response had already been planned and people knew what to do. But the planning challenge comes from the totally random and unexpected events. For instance, the 9/11 terrorist attacks in New York and Washington DC, were random, unexpected, and a total shock to numerous organizations. Scenario planning was of little use because no one could have envisioned this scenario. Another recent random event was the sudden spread of the SARS virus. However, as difficult as it may be for managers to anticipate and deal with these random events, they're not totally vulnerable to the consequences. (■□■■■ Go to the Web and check out Q & A 9.9.) Exhibit 9–14 lists some suggestions for preparing for unexpected events.

Planning tools and techniques can help managers prepare confidently for the future. (■■■□■ Go to the Web and check out S.A.L. #47—How Well Do I Respond to

Exhibit 9–14
• • •———
Preparing for Unexpected Events

- Identify potential unexpected events.
- Determine if any of these events would have early indicators.
- Set up an information-gathering system to identify early indicators.
- Have appropriate responses (plans) in place if these unexpected events occur.

Source: S. Caudron, "Frontview Mirror," *Business Finance*, December 1999, pp. 24–30.

Turbulent Change?) But they should remember that all the tools we've described in this chapter are just that—tools. They will never replace the manager's skills and capabilities in using the information gained to develop effective and efficient plans.

● ● ●Learning Review

- Explain why flexibility is so important to today's planning techniques.
- Describe project management.

- List the steps in the project planning process.
- Discuss why scenario planning has become an important planning tool for managers.

Managers **Respond** to a **Manager's** Dilemma

┄┄**Martha Barkman**

Project Manager, Harbor Properties, Inc., Seattle, Washington

Junjie has developed a successful tool for in-house use, but his obvious dilemma is how to combine this with outside companies' technology yet maintain security of sensitive information. First, he must meet with the information technology specialists from his major clients, designers, and contractors. Together they must determine the best software for their purpose and for compatibility. Junjie might insist his partners use his systems since he's already invested so much in them, however the partners might resist if they face a large capital cost due to incompatibility. The next step is a little harder, but Junjie needs to determine what information he really wants shared outside his company and with which outside vendor. He will have to be extremely careful in setting up system security to protect both his information and the various partners' information.

James A. Batchelder

Information Specialist, GMAC-RFC, Lakeville, Minnesota

I believe the best tools that Junjie could use to convince HETT's partners, customers, and vendors to use the Internet would be the use of charts and graphs displaying the advantages that the Internet has provided HETT over its competition. I would also show the improvement in HETT's operation before and after they started using the Internet. The first thing Junjie would have to do is collect historical operating data for HETT and its competitors. After collecting and organizing this information, Junjie could prepare charts and graphs to display the advantages and improved efficiencies that HETT has been able to realize.

Learning Summary

After reading and studying this chapter, you should be able to:

- List the different approaches to environmental scanning.
- Explain what competitor intelligence is and ways that managers can do it legally and ethically.
- Describe how managers can improve the effectiveness of forecasting.
- Explain the steps in the benchmarking process.
- List the four techniques for allocating resources.
- Describe the different types of budgets.
- Explain what a Gantt chart does.
- Explain a load chart.
- Describe how PERT network analysis works.
- Compute breakeven point.
- Describe how managers can use linear programming.
- Explain why flexibility is so important to today's planning techniques.
- Describe project management.
- List the steps in the project planning process.
- Discuss why scenario planning has become an important planning tool for managers.

Thinking About Management Issues

1. It's a waste of time and other resources to develop a set of sophisticated scenarios for situations that may never occur. Do you agree or disagree? Support your position.

2. Do intuition and creativity have any relevance in quantitative planning tools and techniques? Explain.

3. The *Wall Street Journal* and other business periodicals often carry reports of companies that have not met their sales or profit forecasts. What are some reasons a company might not meet its forecast? What suggestions could you make for improving the effectiveness of forecasting?

4. In what ways is managing a project different from managing a department or other structured work area? In what ways are they the same?

5. "People can use statistics to prove whatever it is they want to prove." What do you think? What are the implications for managers and how they plan?

Working Together: Team-Based Exercise

Benchmarking can be an important tool and source of information for managers. It also can be useful to students. Form small groups of three to four students. In your small group, discuss study habits that each of you has found to be effective from your years of being in school. As a group, come up with a bulleted list of at least eight suggestions in the time period allotted by your instructor. When the instructor calls time, each group should combine with one other group and share your ideas, again in the time allotted by your instructor. In this larger group, be sure to ask questions about suggestions that each respective small group had. Each small group should make sure that it understands the suggestions of the other small group it's working with. When the instructor calls time, each small group will then present and explain the study habit suggestions of the other small group it was working with. After all groups have presented, the class will come up with what it feels are the "best" study habits of all the ideas presented.

Ethical Dilemma Exercise

Managers rely on forecasts for predicting many future events, especially when planning revenues and profits. Forecasts are also important to financial analysts and investors assessing a company's investment potential and to bankers determining a company's ability to repay borrowed funds. For example, HealthSouth met many ambitious growth forecasts as it developed into a large chain of clinics and surgical centers with billions of dollars in annual revenues. Once its acquisitions slowed, however, HealthSouth had difficulty living up to lofty forecasts.

Then, according to a former chief financial officer, CEO Richard Scrushy pressured his managers: "If we weren't making the numbers, he'd say, 'Go figure it out.'" Even after repeatedly reassuring financial analysts that their estimates would be met, HealthSouth was forced to announce lower than expected results because of changes in government regulations. The stock price plummeted. Scrushy continued pushing his managers to find ways of avoiding disappointing results. During one high-level staff meeting, he reportedly told his executives, "I want each of the [divisional] presidents to e-mail all of their people who miss their budget. I don't care whether it's by a dollar." Two weeks later, with government investigators gathering evidence of fraud, HealthSouth fired Scrushy. Ultimately, 11 former managers pleaded guilty to fraud charges and Scrushy was named in a $1.4 billion fraud lawsuit.[30]

Imagine you're the financial manager of a HealthSouth clinic preparing revenue forecasts for the coming quarter. Too high a number will set unrealistic expectations for senior managers, analysts, investors, and bankers to use in decision-making; too low a number will make you and your facility look bad to upper management. Review Exhibit 9.1 as you think about this ethical challenge and decide which of the following options to choose—and why.

Option A: Use quantitative techniques to arrive at a preliminary estimate, ask for input from your facility's managers, and submit the most realistic figure you can.

Option B: Use the jury of opinion technique to involve your staff in estimating future revenue, then ask them to share responsibility by signing the forecast along with you.

Option C: Talk with your boss about the estimates submitted by other facilities, then use quantitative techniques to arrive at a forecast in a similar range.

Case Application

24/7 Gramercy Park

September 11, 2001, is one of those dates that people will always remember, even those who weren't directly affected by the events that occurred that day. But for those who *were* directly affected, the date was a turning point at which daily life changed in unimagined and unplanned ways. Wahday Washington and Tony Wilson were two people whose lives took an unexpected detour that day.

Washington and Wilson are co-owners of a workout facility called 24/7 Gramercy Park, a gym popular with hard-core and amateur body builders alike. The two purchased the facility (previously called Johnny Lats) in 1997. For four years they built their business into a success and felt it was time to expand. Washington said, "When we evaluated the growth we had at the first location and looked at the market, we knew 2001 was the year to expand." And the external trends seemed favorable. The health and fitness industry had its best year ever in 2000, a record number of Americans were exercising in health clubs, and, even more impressive, the New York region experienced the largest growth in health club memberships in the nation. The duo found a suitable building in the Tribeca area and took the plunge.

However, the second location in the 24/7 fitness empire turned out to be not exactly what they had expected. Washington and Wilson underestimated the amount of effort and resources it would take to make the building the fitness showcase they envisioned. The building was so old it had to be rewired with a totally new electric system, the sub-basement had to be excavated because of low ceiling clearance, and new lighting had to

be added. But they trudged onward because the location was so desirable. It was "within spitting distance" of the World Trade Center and New York's financial district, movie studios, and a growing shopping area.

At the same time the Tribeca construction was going on, another opportunity presented itself. One of the partners' main competitors offered to sell them his location that was near the original 24/7 facility. Washington and Wilson jumped at the offer, but they could do so only by bringing in a third partner who would own 50 percent of this location. Meanwhile, the remodeling wasn't going as quickly as planned at the Tribeca location. A planned opening in July 2001 didn't happen and the location still wasn't open by Labor Day. The expenses continued to mount and prepaid customers for the Tribeca location were upset over the delayed opening. Things were bad; then came September 11, 2001.

In the aftermath of the twin towers' collapse, lower Manhattan, including the Tribeca area, was shut down. Fortunately, the partner's 24/7 Tribeca building wasn't damaged structurally, but there was other damage to deal with. All businesses not related to the financial district were essentially closed because employees and customers couldn't get there. The contracting crews couldn't get in to complete renovations. And at least 20 percent of the gym's prepaid members had worked at the World Trade Center. To counteract some of the damage, Washington and Wilson received a $25,000 grant and a $25,000 loan from the Downtown Alliance. By December 2001, the Tribeca area became more accessible. When the 24/7 Tribeca location finally opened its doors on January 2, 2002, one year after it was purchased, it was six months later than scheduled and $150,000 over projected costs. Washington and Wilson described that time as a period of "growing pains." But that's behind them and they smile at the sight of all the customers working out at their three locations.

DISCUSSION QUESTIONS

1. What examples of effective and ineffective planning do you see in this case? How could Washington and Wilson have addressed their ineffective planning?

2. What planning tools and techniques might be most useful to Washington and Wilson as they continue to manage and grow their business? Be specific.

3. Given the unexpected and random nature of the attacks of September 11, 2001, what could Washington and Wilson have done differently to be better prepared?

Source: R. Barnes and D.R. Brown, "Surviving 9-11," *Black Enterprise*, September 2002, pp. 114–120.

Wahday Washington and Tony Wilson, of 24/7 Gramercy Park.

Part 3
You're the Manager: Putting Ethics into Action

●●●

As a manager, you'll often face decisions involving ethical questions. How can you learn to identify the ethical dilemma, keep stakeholders in mind, think through the alternatives, and foresee the consequences of your decisions? This unique interactive feature, positioned at the end of Parts Two, Three, Four, Five, and Six, casts you in the role of a manager dealing with hypothetical yet realistic ethical issues. To start, read the preview paragraph below. Then log onto www.prenhall.com/robbins and go to the R.O.L.L.S. Web site to consider the decisions you would make in the role of manager.

Despite a string of new products and new ad campaigns from Pepsi, its most aggressive competitor, Coca-Cola, has dominated the world soft-drink market for decades. In fact, Pepsi held the lucrative contract for supplying Burger King restaurants with soft drinks until Coca-Cola won the account in 1999. However, after Burger King learned that some Coca-Cola employees had rigged a market test of Frozen Coke, relations between the two companies became strained. In this hypothetical situation, you play the role of a Coca-Cola district manager looking for ways to bring sales up to forecast levels. How far can or should you go to meet your goals? Log onto www.prenhall.com/robbins to put ethics into action!

Passport

●●●

Scenario 1

As Luke Castillo, the quality control manager for Deere & Company's farm tractor division, waits for his flight from Chicago to Sao Paulo to depart, he jots down some notes about his meeting tomorrow with Ricardo Espinoza, manager of Deere's Brazilian plant. In his job, Luke travels a couple of weeks each month to the company's various manufacturing plants in the United States, Canada, Argentina, Brazil, and Mexico to assist them with quality control issues. Product quality is important in this industry and Luke is well versed in quality management techniques, having attended a number of quality certification programs and holding quality management positions in two other organizations. He's been in this particular position with Deere for three years and loves the challenge of getting the company's employees involved in resolving difficult product quality problems, although there are times when the job is more challenging. And this current trip to the Brazilian plant is likely to be one of those times!

Deere's Brazilian facility, located outside Sao Paulo, is managed by Ricardo Espinoza. Ricardo is new to the plant manager's position, although he has worked at the plant for 15 years. He started out on the assembly line and steadily moved up to positions with more responsibility. He is respected by his peers and by his regional manager. One of Ricardo's main goals for his plant is to improve the quality of the tractors made there, and he has asked for Luke's assistance. But Ricardo knows it will not be an easy task to implement a quality improvement program. Many of the plant's employees have worked there all their lives and are pretty set in their ways.

Employee involvement in planning and implementing this program will be essential to its success. What issues might Luke and Ricardo face as they prepare to introduce a quality improvement program in the plant? What will work best with Deere's Brazilian employees? How should Luke and Ricardo approach this project?

To answer these questions, you'll have to do some research on the countries. Go to www.prenhall.com/robbins, the R.O.L.L.S. Web site, and click on Passport. When the map appears, click on the countries you need to research. You'll find background information on the country and general information about the country's economy, population, and workforce. In addition, you'll find specific information on the country's culture and the unique qualities associated with doing business there.

Scenario 2

Yoko Sato is the merchandising manager for Toys "R" Us International in Tokyo, a position she has held for five years. After graduating from the University of Washington with a degree in marketing management, Yoko worked for a toy importer in Los Angeles for eight years—a job that provided numerous opportunities to learn about the toy business. When a new position with mega-retailer Toys "R" Us opened up back home in Japan, Yoko applied for the job and got it. Her educational training and years of work experience with the toy import industry were the deciding factors in her getting the job.

As merchandising manager for Japan, Yoko must ensure that all Toys "R" Us International stores located there have the correct mix of products they need, when they need them, and where they need them. She relies on several planning tools to get the product mix right. If she makes a bad decision, the stores either run out of popular selling toys or have a surplus of unsold toys. By doing a good job of planning, Yoko hopes to avoid those outcomes.

Tomorrow Yoko is meeting with a new toy importer, Wu Sihai, from Nanjing, China, to discuss a possible business deal. She has not done business with Wu before but is looking forward to discussing the possibilities. Keeping in mind that setting goals and planning are extremely important to Yoko's job performance, will there be any differences in how Yoko and Wu view the role of goal setting and planning? Explain. What might Yoko need to do to emphasize how important goals and planning are and yet still establish a business relationship with Wu?

To answer these questions, you'll have to do some research on the countries. Go to **www.prenhall.com/robbins**, the R.O.L.L.S. Web site, and click on Passport. When the map

appears, click on the countries you need to research. You'll find background information on the country and general information about the country's economy, population, and workforce. In addition, you'll find specific information on the country's culture and the unique qualities associated with doing business there.

Managing Entrepreneurial Ventures

Start-Up and Planning Issues

The first thing that entrepreneurs must do is identify opportunities and possible competitive advantages. Once they've done this, they're ready to start the venture by researching its feasibility and then planning for its launch. These start-up and planning issues are what we're going to look at in this second entrepreneurship module.

Identifying Environmental Opportunities and Competitive Advantage

How important is the ability to identify environmental opportunities? Consider the following: Over 4 million baby boomers turn 50 every year. J. Raymond Elliott, CEO of Zimmer Holdings, is well aware of that demographic trend. Why? His company, which makes orthopedic products, including reconstructive implants for hips, knees, shoulders, and elbows, sees definite marketing opportunities.[1] In 1994, when Jeff Bezos first saw that Internet usage was increasing by 2,300 percent a month, he knew that something dramatic was happening. "I hadn't seen growth that fast outside of a petri dish," he said. Bezos was determined to be a part of it. He quit his successful career as a stock market researcher and hedge fund manager on Wall Street and pursued his vision for online retailing, now the Amazon.com Web site.[2] What would you have done had you seen that type of number somewhere? Ignored it? Written it off as a fluke? The skyrocketing Internet usage that Bezos observed and the recognition of the baby boomer demographic by Elliott's Zimmer Holdings are prime examples of identifying environmental opportunities. Remember from Chapter 8 that opportunities are positive trends in external environmental factors. These trends provide unique and distinct possibilities for innovating and creating value. Entrepreneurs need to be able to pinpoint these pockets of opportunities that a changing context provides. After all, "organizations do not see opportunities, individuals do."[3] Peter Drucker, a well-known management author, identified seven potential sources of opportunity that entrepreneurs might look for in the external context.[4] These include the unexpected, the incongruous, the process need, industry and market structures, demographics, changes in perception, and new knowledge.

1. *The unexpected.* When situations and events are unanticipated, opportunities can be found. The event might be an unexpected success (positive news) or an unexpected failure (bad news). Either way, there can be opportunities for entrepreneurs to pursue. For instance, the threat of potential terrorist attacks after 9/11 proved to be a bonanza for security companies. And the SARS outbreak in 2003, while detrimental to many travel and tourism businesses, actually proved to be beneficial for medical products companies, especially those that made face masks. These events were unexpected and proved to be opportunities for entrepreneurial ventures.

2. *The incongruous.* When something is incongruous, there are inconsistencies and incompatibilities in the way it appears. Things "ought to be" a certain way, but aren't. When conventional wisdom about the way things should be no longer holds true, for whatever reason, there are opportunities to capture. Entrepreneurs who are willing to "think outside the box"—that is, to think beyond the traditional and conventional approaches—may find pockets of potential profitability. Sigi Rabinowicz, founder and president of Tefron, an Israeli firm, recognized incongruities in the way that women's lingerie was made. He knew that a better way was possible. His company has spent over a decade adapting a circular hosiery knitting machine to make women's underwear that is nearly seamless.[5] Another example of how the incongruous can be a potential source of entrepreneurial opportunity is Fred Smith, founder of FedEx, who recognized in the early 1970s the inefficiencies in the delivery of packages and documents. His approach was: Why not? Who says that overnight delivery is impossible? Smith's recognition of the incongruous led to the creation of FedEx, now a multibillion-dollar corporation.

3. *The process need.* What happens when technology doesn't immediately come up with the "big discovery" that's going to fundamentally change the very nature of some product or service? What happens is that there can be pockets of entrepreneurial opportunity in the various stages of the process as researchers and technicians continue to work for the monumental breakthrough. Because the full leap hasn't been possible, opportunities abound in the tiny steps. Take the medical products industry, for example. Although researchers haven't yet discovered a cure for cancer, there have been many successful entrepreneurial biotechnology ventures created as knowledge about a possible cure continues to grow. The "big breakthrough" hasn't happened, but there have been numerous entrepreneurial opportunities throughout the process of discovery.

4. *Industry and market structures.* When changes in technology change the structure of an industry and market, existing firms can become obsolete if they're not attuned to the changes or are unwilling to change. Even changes in social values and consumer tastes can shift the structures of industries and markets. These markets and industries become open targets for nimble and smart entrepreneurs. The whole Internet experience provides several good examples of existing industries and markets being challenged by upstart entrepreneurial ventures. For instance, eBay has prospered as an online middleman between buyers and sellers. And it's not just Beanie Babies or used books being bought and sold by individuals. Even businesses are getting in on the auction action. For example, Sun Microsystems lists up to 150 items per day on eBay, including servers that sell for more than $15,000. And the Disney Company uses the site to auction off authentic studio props from its movies. Meg Whitman, eBay's CEO, says that the company's job is connecting people, not selling them things. And connect them, they do! The online auction firm had 62 million registered users in 2003.[6]

5. *Demographics.* The characteristics of the world population are changing. These changes influence industries and markets by altering the types and quantities of products and services desired and customers' buying power. Although many of these changes are fairly predictable if you stay alert to demographic trends, others aren't as obvious. Either way, there can be significant entrepreneurial opportunities in anticipating and meeting the changing needs of the population. For example, Thay Thida is one of three partners in Khmer Internet Development Services (KIDS) in Phnom Penh, Cambodia. She and her co-founders saw the opportunities in bringing Internet service to Cambodians and have profited from their entrepreneurial venture.[7]

6. *Changes in perception.* Perception is one's view of reality. When changes in perception take place, the facts do not vary, but their meaning does. Changes in perception get at the heart of people's psychographic profiles—what they value, what they believe in, and what they care about. Changes in these attitudes and values create potential market opportunities for alert entrepreneurs. For example, think about your perception of healthy foods. As our perception of whether or not certain food groups are good for us has changed, there have been product and service opportunities for entrepreneurs to recognize and capture. For example, John Mackey started Whole Foods Market in Austin, Texas, as a place for customers to purchase food and other items free of pesticides, preservatives, sweeteners, and cruelty. Now, as the nation's number-one natural foods supermarket chain, Mackey's entrepreneurial venture consists of about 140 stores in more than 25 states.[8]

7. *New knowledge.* New knowledge is a significant source of entrepreneurial opportunity. Although not all knowledge-based innovations are significant, new knowledge ranks pretty high on the list of sources of entrepreneurial opportunity! It does take more than just having new knowledge, though. Entrepreneurs must be able to do something with that knowledge and to protect important proprietary information from competitors. For example, French scientists are using new knowledge about textiles to develop a wide array of innovative products that keep wearers healthy and smelling good. Neyret, the Parisian lingerie maker, innovated lingerie products woven with tiny perfume microcapsules that stay in the fabric through about 10 washings. Another French company, Francital, developed a fabric that is treated with chemicals to absorb perspiration and odors.[9]

Being alert to entrepreneurial opportunities is only part of an entrepreneur's initial efforts. He or she must also understand competitive advantage. As we discussed in Chapter 8, when an organization has a competitive advantage, it has something that other competitors don't; it does something better than other organizations do, or does something that others can't. Competitive advantage is a necessary ingredient for an entrepreneurial venture's long-term success and survival. Getting and keeping a competitive advantage is tough. However, it is something that entrepreneurs must consider as they begin researching the venture's feasibility.

Researching the Venture's Feasibility—Generating and Evaluating Ideas

It's important for entrepreneurs to research the venture's feasibility by generating and evaluating business ideas. Entrepreneurial ventures thrive on ideas. Generating ideas is an innovative, creative process. It's also one that will take time, not only in the beginning stages of the entrepreneurial venture, but throughout the life of the business. Where do ideas come from?

Generating Ideas. Studies of entrepreneurs have shown that the sources of their ideas are unique and varied. One survey found that "working in the same industry" was the major source (60 percent of respondents) of ideas for an entrepreneurial venture.[10] Other sources included personal interests or hobbies, looking at familiar and unfamiliar products and services, and opportunities in external environmental sectors (technological, sociocultural, demographics, economic, or legal-political).

What should entrepreneurs look for as they explore these idea sources? They should look for limitations of what's currently available, new and different approaches, advances and breakthroughs, unfilled niches, or trends and changes. For example, John C. Diebel, founder of Meade Instruments Corporation, the Irvine, California, telescope maker, came up with the idea of putting computerized attachments on the company's inexpensive consumer models so that amateur astronomers could enter on a keypad the coordinates of planets or stars they wanted to see. The telescope would then automatically locate and focus on the desired planetary bodies. It took the company's engineers two years to figure out how to do it, but Meade now controls more than half the amateur astronomy market.[11]

Exhibit P3–1

Evaluating Potential Ideas

Personal Considerations	Marketplace Considerations
• Do you have the capabilities to do what you've selected? • Are you ready to be an entrepreneur? • Are you prepared emotionally to deal with the stresses and challenges of being an entrepreneur? • Are you prepared to deal with rejection and failure? • Are you ready to work hard? • Do you have a realistic picture of the venture's potential? • Have you educated yourself about financing issues? • Are you willing and prepared to do continual financial and other types of analyses?	• Who are the potential customers for your idea: who, where, how many? • What similar or unique product features does your proposed idea have compared to what's currently on the market? • How and where will potential customers purchase your product? • Have you considered pricing issues and whether the price you'll be able to charge will allow your venture to survive and prosper? • Have you considered how you will need to promote and advertise your proposed entrepreneurial venture?

Evaluating Ideas. Evaluating entrepreneurial ideas revolves around personal and marketplace considerations. Each of these assessments will provide an entrepreneur with key information about the idea's potential. Exhibit P3–1 describes some questions that entrepreneurs might ask as they evaluate potential ideas.

A more structured evaluation approach that an entrepreneur might want to use is a **feasibility study**—an analysis of the various aspects of a proposed entrepreneurial venture designed to determine its feasibility. Not only is a well-prepared feasibility study an effective evaluation tool to determine whether an entrepreneurial idea is a potentially successful one; it can serve as a basis for the all-important business plan.

A feasibility study should give descriptions of the most important elements of the entrepreneurial venture and the entrepreneur's analysis of the viability of these elements. Exhibit P3–2 on page 230 provides an outline of a possible approach to a feasibility study. Yes, it covers a lot of territory and it takes a significant amount of time, energy, and effort to prepare. However, an entrepreneur's future success is worth that investment.

Researching the Venture's Feasibility—Researching Competitors

Part of researching the venture's feasibility is looking at the competitors. As we discussed in Chapter 9, researching the competition through competitor intelligence can be a powerful tool.

What would entrepreneurs like to know about their potential competitors? Here are some possible questions: What types of products or services are competitors offering? What are the major characteristics of these products or services? What are their products' strengths and weaknesses? How do they handle marketing, pricing, and distributing? What do they attempt to do differently from other competitors? Do they appear to be successful at it? Why or why not? What are they good at? What competitive advantage(s) do they appear to have? What are they not so good at? What competitive disadvantage(s) do they

appear to have? How large and profitable are these competitors?

For instance, Ezra Dabah, CEO of The Children's Place Retail Stores, carefully examined the competition as he expanded his chain of children's clothing stores nationwide. Although he faces stiff competition from the likes of GAPKids, JC Penney, and Gymboree, he feels that his company's approach to manufacturing and marketing will give it a competitive edge.[12]

Once an entrepreneur has this information, he or she should assess how the proposed entrepreneurial venture is going to "fit" into this competitive arena. Will the entrepreneurial venture be able to compete successfully? This type of competitor analysis becomes an important part of the feasibility study and the business plan. If, after all this analysis, the situation looks promising, the final part of researching the venture's feasibility is to look at the various financing options. This isn't the final determination of how much funding the venture will need or where this funding will come from, but is simply gathering information about various financing alternatives.

Researching the Venture's Feasibility—Researching Financing

Chances are that funds will be needed to start the entrepreneurial venture. A significant number of financing options are available to entrepreneurs. Exhibit P3–3 (see page 231) lists the various options.

Planning the Venture—Developing a Business Plan

Planning is also important to entrepreneurial ventures. Once the venture's feasibility has been thoroughly researched, the entrepreneur then must look at planning it. The most important thing that an entrepreneur does in planning the venture is develop a **business plan**—a written document that summarizes a business opportunity and defines and articulates how the identified opportunity is to be seized and exploited.

For many would-be entrepreneurs, developing and writing a business plan seems like a daunting task,

Exhibit P3–2

Feasibility Study

A. Introduction, historical background, description of product or service

1. Brief description of proposed entrepreneurial venture
2. Brief history of the industry
3. Information about the economy and important trends
4. Current status of the product or service
5. How you intend to produce the product or service
6. Complete list of goods or services to be provided
7. Strengths and weaknesses of the business
8. Ease of entry into the industry, including competitor analysis

B. Accounting considerations

1. Proforma balance sheet
2. Proforma profit and loss statement
3. Projected cash flow analysis

C. Management considerations

1. Personal expertise—strengths and weaknesses
2. Proposed organizational design
3. Potential staffing requirements
4. Inventory management methods
5. Production and operations management issues
6. Equipment needs

D. Marketing considerations

1. Detailed product description
2. Identify target market (who, where, how many)
3. Describe place product will be distributed (location, traffic, size, channels, etc.)
4. Price determination (competition, price lists, etc.)
5. Promotion plans (role of personal selling, advertising, sales promotion, etc.)

E. Financial considerations

1. Start-up costs
2. Working capital requirements
3. Equity requirements
4. Loans—amounts, type, conditions
5. Breakeven analysis
6. Collateral
7. Credit references
8. Equipment and building financing—costs and methods

F. Legal considerations

1. Proposed business structure (type; conditions, terms, liability, responsibility; insurance needs; buyout and succession issues)
2. Contracts, licenses, and other legal documents

G. Tax considerations (sales/property/employee; federal, state, and local)

H. Appendix (charts/graphs, diagrams, layouts, resumes, etc.)

indeed. However, a good business plan is valuable. It pulls together all the elements of the entrepreneur's vision into a single coherent document. The business plan requires careful planning and creative thinking, but if done well, it can be a convincing document that serves many functions. It serves as a blueprint and road map for operating the business. And the business plan is a "living" document that guides organizational decisions and actions throughout the life of the business, not just in the start-up stage.

If an entrepreneur has completed a feasibility study, much of the information included in it becomes the basis for the business plan. A good business plan covers six major areas: executive summary, analysis of opportunity, analysis of the context, description of the business, financial data and projections, and supporting documentation.

Exhibit P3–3

Possible Financing Options

- Entrepreneur's personal resources (personal savings, home equity, personal loans, credit cards, etc.)
- Financial institutions (banks, savings and loan institutions, government-guaranteed loan, credit unions, etc.)
- Venture capitalists—external equity financing provided by professionally managed pools of investor money
- Angel investors—a private investor who offers financial backing to an entrepreneurial venture in return for equity in the venture
- Initial public offering (IPO)—the first public registration and sale of a company's stock
- National, state, and local governmental business development programs
- Unusual sources (television shows, judged competitions, etc.)

Executive Summary. The executive summary summarizes the key points that the entrepreneur wants to make about the proposed entrepreneurial venture. These might include a brief mission statement; primary goals; brief history of entrepreneurial venture may be in the form of a time line; key people involved in the venture; nature of the business; concise product or service descriptions; brief explanations of market niche, competitors, and competitive advantage; proposed strategies; and selected key financial information.

Analysis of Opportunity. In this section of the business plan, an entrepreneur presents the details of the perceived opportunity. Essentially, this means (1) sizing up the market by describing the demographics of the target market, (2) describing and evaluating industry trends, and (3) identifying and evaluating competitors.

Analysis of the Context. Whereas the opportunity analysis focuses on the opportunity in a specific industry and market, the context analysis takes a much broader perspective. Here, the entrepreneur describes the broad external changes and trends taking place in the economic, political-legal, technological, and global environments.

Description of the Business. In this section, an entrepreneur describes how the entrepreneurial venture is going to be organized, launched, and managed. It includes a thorough description of the mission statement; a description of the desired organizational culture; marketing plans including overall marketing strategy, pricing, sales tactics, service-warranty policies, and advertising and promotion tactics; product development plans such as an explanation of development status, tasks, difficulties and risks, and anticipated costs; operational plans including a description of proposed geographic location, facilities and needed improvements, equipment, and work flow; human resource plans including a description of key management persons, composition of board of directors including their background experience and skills, current and future staffing needs, compensation and benefits, and training needs; and an overall schedule and timetable of events.

Financial Data and Projections. Every effective business plan contains financial data and projections. Although these calculations and interpretation may be difficult, they are absolutely critical. No business plan is complete without financial information. Financial plans should cover at least three years and contain projected income statements, pro forma cash flow analyses (monthly for the first year and quarterly for the next two), pro forma balance sheets, breakeven analyses, and cost controls. If major equipment or other capital purchases are expected, the items, costs, and available collateral should be listed. All financial projections and analyses should include explanatory notes, especially where the data seem contradictory or questionable.

Supporting Documentation. This *is* an important component of an effective business plan. The entrepreneur should back up descriptions with charts, graphs, tables, photographs, or other visual tools. In addition, it might be important to include information (personal and work related) about the key participants in the entrepreneurial venture.

Just as the idea for an entrepreneurial venture takes time to germinate, so does the writing of a good business plan. It's important for the entrepreneur to put serious thought and consideration into the plan. It's not an easy thing to do. However, the resulting document should be valuable to the entrepreneur in current and future planning efforts.

● ● ● Learning Summary

After reading and studying this material, you should be able to:

- Discuss how opportunities are important to entrepreneurial ventures.
- Describe each of the seven sources of potential opportunity.
- Explain why it's important for entrepreneurs to understand competitive advantage.
- List possible financing options for entrepreneurs.
- Describe the six major sections of a business plan.

Part **FOUR**

Organizing

Chapter

10

Organizational Structure and Design

Now over 130 years old, Svenska Handelsbanken, Sweden's premiere bank, is one of the largest banks in the Nordic region. Lars Grönstedt (pictured), president and group chief executive, oversees a business that is organized around a decentralized structure with a network of some 540 branches in Sweden, Denmark, Finland, and Norway, as well as in nine European countries and six countries outside Europe.[1] He believes that the bank's

30-plus years of developing its branch network has allowed it to consistently grow market share and achieve a return on equity above the average of its Nordic competitors. Now those competitors are starting to copy Handelsbanken's structural model. However, Lars says Handelsbanken's competitive advantage isn't just having *more* branches. It's the great degree of autonomy that branch managers are given that sets.

Handelsbanken's branch managers can choose their customers and product mix. They also set staffing numbers and decide salary levels. All customers, private and corporate, no matter what size, are the responsibility of a local branch. That means that even a large global customer such as Volvo is managed by a branch office. However, a branch office can "buy in" specialist services it may need in servicing important customers like Volvo. Each branch manager is also responsible for branch per-

formance, which is measured by a ratio of costs divided by revenues, and all the bank's branches are benchmarked against each other. If a branch starts underperforming, the regional office will offer advice and examples of what other branches have done. And, to stop predatory competition between its own branches, the company has set up strict geographical boundaries. Handelsbanken's number of centralized staff is a fraction of those of its competitors, and guidelines coming out of headquarters are few and far between. Handelsbanken's flat management structure and emphasis on personal responsibility and consensus approach is well suited to the Swedish culture.

Lars wants to continue to build the learning organization that they've started. He wants the bank to improve its capacity to continuously learn, adapt, and change. Put yourself in Lars's position. What could he do to make this happen?

What would **you** do **?**

233

Although Lars Grönstedt's desire to make Handelsbanken more of a learning organization might not be right for others, it does illustrate how important it is for managers to design an organizational structure that helps accomplish organizational goals and objectives. In this chapter, we'll present information about designing appropriate organizational structures. We'll look at the various elements of organizational structure and what contingency factors influence the design. We'll look at some traditional and contemporary organizational designs. And finally, we'll describe a learning organization and discuss what executives like Lars can do to continue to develop their companies as learning organizations.

DEFINING ORGANIZATIONAL STRUCTURE

Six miles south of McAlester, Oklahoma, employees in a vast factory complex make products that must be perfect. These people "are so good at what they do and have been doing it for so long that they have a 100 percent market share."[2] What do they make? Bombs for the U.S. military. And doing so requires a work environment that's an interesting mix of the mundane, structured, and disciplined, with high levels of risk and emotion. But the work gets done efficiently and effectively. Work also gets done effectively and efficiently at the Canadian Customs and Revenue Agency. Its workforce is more spread out and they rely on shared workspaces, mobile computing, and virtual private networks to get work done.[3] Both of these examples reflect the importance of organizing and organizational structure to get an organization's work done.

No other topic in management has undergone as much change in the past few years as that of organizing and organizational structure. Traditional approaches to organizing work are being questioned and reevaluated as managers search out structural designs that will best support and facilitate employees' doing the organization's work—ones that can achieve efficiency but also have the flexibility that's necessary for success in today's dynamic environment. Recall from Chapter 1 that **organizing** is defined as the process of creating an organization's structure. That process is important and serves many purposes. (See Exhibit 10–1.) The challenge for managers is to design an organizational structure that allows employees to effectively and efficiently do their work. (▮◻▮▮ Go to the Web and check out Q & A 10.1.)

Just what is **organizational structure**? It's the formal arrangement of jobs within an organization. When managers develop or change the structure, they're engaged in **organizational design**, a process that involves decisions about six key elements: work specialization, departmentalization, chain of command, span of control, centralization and decentralization, and formalization.[4]

Work Specialization

Remember our discussion of Adam Smith in Chapter 2, who first identified division of labor and concluded that it contributed to increased employee productivity. Early in the twentieth century, Henry Ford applied this concept in an assembly line where every Ford worker was assigned a specific, repetitive task.

••• organizing
The process of creating an organization's structure.

••• organizational structure
The formal arrangement of jobs within an organization.

••• organizational design
Developing or changing an organization's structure.

■ Q & A
Whenever you see this green square, go to the R.O.L.L.S. Web site (***www.prenhall.com/robbins***) to the Q & A, your 24/7 educational assistant. These video clips and written material presented by your authors address questions that we have found students frequently ask.

Exhibit 10–1

● ● ●━━━●

Purposes of Organizing

- Divides work to be done into specific jobs and departments.
- Assigns tasks and responsibilities associated with individual jobs.
- Coordinates diverse organizational tasks.
- Clusters jobs into units.
- Establishes relationships among individuals, groups, and departments.
- Establishes formal lines of authority.
- Allocates and deploys organizational resources.

Today we use the term **work specialization** to describe the degree to which activities in an organization are divided into separate jobs. The essence of work specialization is that an entire job is not done by one individual but instead is broken down into steps, and each step is completed by a different person. Individual employees specialize in doing part of an activity rather than the entire activity. (... Go to the Web and check out Q & A 10.2.)

During the first half of the twentieth century, managers viewed work specialization as an unending source of increased productivity. And for a time it was! Because it wasn't widely used, when work specialization *was* implemented, employee productivity rose. By the 1960s, however, it had become evident that a good thing could be carried too far. The point had been reached in some jobs where human diseconomies from work specialization—boredom, fatigue, stress, poor quality, increased absenteeism, and higher turnover—more than offset the economic advantages.

Most managers today see work specialization as an important organizing mechanism but not as a source of ever-increasing productivity. They recognize the economies it provides in certain types of jobs, but they also recognize the problems it creates when it's carried to extremes. McDonald's, for example, uses high work specialization to efficiently make and sell its products, and most employees in health care organizations are specialized. However, other organizations, such as Saturn Corporation, Hallmark, and Ford Australia have successfully broadened the scope of jobs and reduced work specialization.

Work specialization might make the job of answering phone calls all day monotonous to some, but not to Graciela Barreña (in front in picture), who works for the Argentine call center Indicom, in Buenos Aires. Her six-hour shift follows a pattern, with pager messages and calls about highway toll cards arriving in the early morning, and responses to free raffles and other toll-free calling services her employer offers filling much of the rest of the day. In between, Barreña provides customer service for a cheese factory and a diaper manufacturer.

• • • **work specialization**
The degree to which tasks in an organization are divided into separate jobs; also known as division of labor.

• • • **departmentalization**
The basis by which jobs are grouped together.

• • • **functional departmentalization**
Groups jobs by functions performed.

• • • **product departmentalization**
Groups jobs by product line.

Departmentalization

Does your college have an office of student affairs? A financial aid or student housing department? Once jobs have been divided up through work specialization, they have to be grouped back together so that common tasks can be coordinated. The basis by which jobs are grouped together is called **departmentalization**. Every organization will have its own specific way of classifying and grouping work activities. Exhibit 10–2 on page 236 shows the five common forms of departmentalization.

Functional departmentalization groups jobs by functions performed. This approach can be used in all types of organizations, although the functions change to reflect the organization's purpose and work. **Product departmentalization** groups jobs by product line. In this approach, each major product area is placed under the authority of a manager who's responsible for everything having to do with that product line.

THINKING CRITICALLY ABOUT ETHICS

Changes in technology have cut the shelf life of most employees' skills. A factory or clerical worker used to be able to learn one job and be reasonably sure that the skills acquired to do that job would be enough for most of his or her work years. That's no longer the case. What ethical obligation do organizations have to assist workers whose skills have become obsolete? What about employees? Do they have an obligation to keep their skills from becoming obsolete? What ethical guidelines might you suggest for dealing with employee skill obsolescence?

Exhibit 10–2   **The Five Common Forms of Departmentalization**

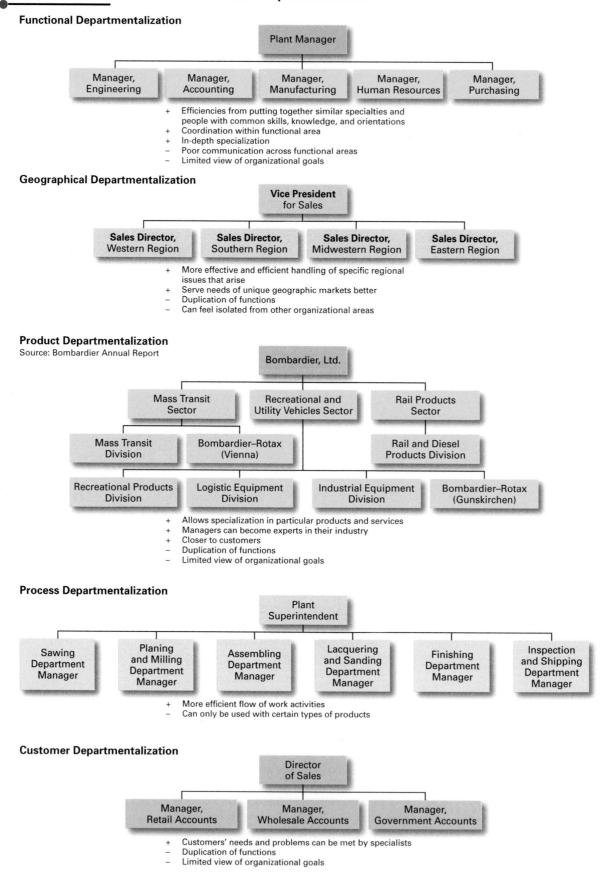

Functional Departmentalization

Plant Manager

- Manager, Engineering
- Manager, Accounting
- Manager, Manufacturing
- Manager, Human Resources
- Manager, Purchasing

+ Efficiencies from putting together similar specialties and people with common skills, knowledge, and orientations
+ Coordination within functional area
+ In-depth specialization
– Poor communication across functional areas
– Limited view of organizational goals

Geographical Departmentalization

Vice President for Sales

- Sales Director, Western Region
- Sales Director, Southern Region
- Sales Director, Midwestern Region
- Sales Director, Eastern Region

+ More effective and efficient handling of specific regional issues that arise
+ Serve needs of unique geographic markets better
– Duplication of functions
– Can feel isolated from other organizational areas

Product Departmentalization
Source: Bombardier Annual Report

Bombardier, Ltd.

- Mass Transit Sector
  - Mass Transit Division
  - Bombardier–Rotax (Vienna)
- Recreational and Utility Vehicles Sector
  - Recreational Products Division
  - Logistic Equipment Division
  - Industrial Equipment Division
  - Bombardier–Rotax (Gunskirchen)
- Rail Products Sector
  - Rail and Diesel Products Division

+ Allows specialization in particular products and services
+ Managers can become experts in their industry
+ Closer to customers
– Duplication of functions
– Limited view of organizational goals

Process Departmentalization

Plant Superintendent

- Sawing Department Manager
- Planing and Milling Department Manager
- Assembling Department Manager
- Lacquering and Sanding Department Manager
- Finishing Department Manager
- Inspection and Shipping Department Manager

+ More efficient flow of work activities
– Can only be used with certain types of products

Customer Departmentalization

Director of Sales

- Manager, Retail Accounts
- Manager, Wholesale Accounts
- Manager, Government Accounts

+ Customers' needs and problems can be met by specialists
– Duplication of functions
– Limited view of organizational goals

Geographical departmentalization groups jobs on the basis of territory or geography such as southern, midwestern, or northwestern regions or maybe U.S., European, Latin American, and Asian-Pacific regions. **Process departmentalization** groups jobs on the basis of product or customer flow. In this approach, work activities follow a natural processing flow of products or even of customers. Finally, **customer departmentalization** groups jobs on the basis of customers who have common needs or problems that can best be met by having specialists for each.

Large organizations often combine most or all of these forms of departmentalization. For example, a major Japanese electronics firm organizes each of its divisions along functional lines: its manufacturing units around processes, its sales units around seven geographic regions, and sales regions into four customer groupings.

Two popular trends in departmentalization are the increasing use of customer departmentalization and the use of cross-functional teams. Customer departmentalization is being used to monitor customers' needs and to respond to changes in those needs. For example, L.L. Bean is organized around a half-dozen customer groups. This structure allows the company to better understand its customers and to respond faster to their needs. Second, managers are using **cross-functional teams**, groups of individuals who are experts in various specialties and who work together. For instance, Joe Hinrich, executive director at Ford Motor Company's material planning and logistics division, believes in the use of cross-functional collaboration. He assembled a team of employees from Ford's finance, purchasing, engineering, quality control, and representatives from the company's outside logistics suppliers that has made several work improvement ideas.[5] We'll discuss the use of cross-functional teams more fully in Chapter 15.

Chain of Command

For many years, the chain-of-command concept was a cornerstone of organizational design. As you'll see, it has far less importance today. But contemporary managers still need to consider its implications when deciding how best to structure their organizations.

The **chain of command** is the continuous line of authority that extends from upper organizational levels to the lowest levels and clarifies who reports to whom. It helps employees answer questions such as "Who do I go to if I have a problem?" or "To whom am I responsible?"

You can't discuss the chain of command without discussing three other concepts: authority, responsibility, and unity of command. **Authority** refers to the rights inherent in a managerial position to tell people what to do and to expect them to do it.[6] To facilitate decision making and coordination, an organization's managers are part of the chain of command and are granted a certain degree of authority to meet their responsibilities. (■■■■■ Go to the Web and check out Q & A 10.3.) As managers coordinate and integrate the work of employees, those employees assume an obligation to perform any assigned duties. This obligation or expectation to perform is known as **responsibility**. Finally, the **unity of command** principle (one of Fayol's 14 principles of management) helps preserve the concept of a continuous line of authority. It states that a person should report to only one manager. Without unity of command, conflicting demands and priorities from multiple bosses can create problems. It did for Damian Birkel, a merchandising manager at Fuller Brush Company, who found himself reporting to two bosses—one in charge of the department store business and the other in charge of discount chains. Birkel tried to minimize the conflict by making a combined to-do list that he would update and change as work tasks changed.[7]

Early management theorists (Fayol, Weber, Taylor, and others) were enamored with the concepts of chain of command, authority, responsibility, and unity of command. However, times change and so have the basic tenets of organizational design. These concepts are considerably less relevant today because of things like information

---

• • • geographical departmentalization
Groups jobs on the basis of territory or geography.

• • • process departmentalization
Groups jobs on the basis of product or customer flow.

• • • customer departmentalization
Groups jobs on the basis of common customers.

• • • cross-functional teams
Groups of individuals who are experts in various specialties who work together.

• • • chain of command
The continuous line of authority that extends from upper organizational levels to the lowest levels and clarifies who reports to whom.

• • • authority
The rights inherent in a managerial position to tell people what to do and to expect them to do it.

• • • responsibility
The obligation to perform any assigned duties.

• • • unity of command
The management principle that each person should report to only one manager.

technology. Employees throughout the organization can access in a matter of a few seconds information that used to be available only to top managers. Also, with computers, employees communicate with anyone else anywhere in the organization without going through formal channels—that is, the chain of command. Moreover, as more organizations use self-managed and cross-functional teams and as new organizational designs with multiple bosses are implemented, the traditional concepts of authority, responsibility, and chain of command have become less relevant.

Span of Control

● ● ● **span of control**
The number of employees a manager can efficiently and effectively manage.

How many employees can a manager efficiently and effectively manage? This question of **span of control** is important because, to a large degree, it determines the number of levels and managers an organization has. All things being equal, the wider or larger the span, the more efficient the organization. An example can show why.

Assume that we have two organizations, both of which have approximately 4,100 employees. As Exhibit 10–3 shows, if one organization has a uniform span of four and the other a span of eight, the wider span will have two fewer levels and approximately 800 fewer managers. If the average manager made $42,000 a year, the organization with the wider span would save over $33 million a year in management salaries alone! Obviously, wider spans are more efficient in terms of cost. However, at some point, wider spans reduce effectiveness. When the span becomes too large, employee performance suffers because managers no longer have the time to provide the necessary leadership and support. (▮▯▮▮ Go to the Web and check out Q & A 10.4.)

The contemporary view of span of control recognizes that many factors influence the appropriate number of employees that a manager can efficiently *and* effectively manage. These factors include the skills and abilities of the manager and the employees, and characteristics of the work being done. For instance, the more training and experience employees have, the less direct supervision they'll need. Therefore, managers with well-trained and experienced employees can function quite well with a wider span. Other contingency variables that determine the appropriate span include similarity of employee tasks, the complexity of those tasks, the physical proximity of subordinates, the degree to which standardized procedures are in place, the sophistication of the organization's information system, the strength of the organization's culture, and the preferred style of the manager.[8]

The trend in recent years has been toward larger spans of control, which are consistent with managers' efforts to reduce costs, speed up decision making, increase flexibility, get closer to customers, and empower employees. (▮▮▯▮ Go to the Web and check out Q & A 10.5.) However, to ensure that performance doesn't suffer because of these wider spans, organizations are investing heavily in employee training. Managers recognize that they can handle a wider span when employees know their jobs well or can turn to co-workers if they have questions.

Exhibit 10–3

● ● ●

Contrasting Spans of Control

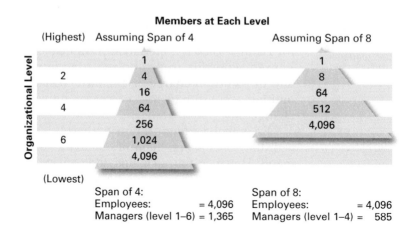

Members at Each Level

	Assuming Span of 4	Assuming Span of 8
(Highest)	1	1
2	4	8
	16	64
4	64	512
	256	4,096
6	1,024	
	4,096	
(Lowest)		

Organizational Level

Span of 4:
Employees: = 4,096
Managers (level 1–6) = 1,365

Span of 8:
Employees: = 4,096
Managers (level 1–4) =   585

Centralization and Decentralization

In some organizations, top managers make all the decisions and lower-level managers and employees simply carry out their orders. At the other extreme are organizations in which decision making is pushed down to the managers who are closest to the action. The former organizations are centralized, and the latter are decentralized.

Centralization describes the degree to which decision making is concentrated at a single point in the organization. If top managers make the organization's key decisions with little or no input from below, then the organization is centralized. In contrast, the more that lower-level employees provide input or actually make decisions, the more **decentralization** there is. Keep in mind that the concept of centralization–decentralization is relative, not absolute—that is, an organization is never completely centralized or decentralized. Few organizations could function effectively if all decisions were made by only a select group of top managers; nor could they function if all decisions were delegated to employees at the lowest levels. (▪▪▫▪▪ Go to the Web and check out PRISM #10—Delegating).

As organizations become more flexible and responsive, there's been a distinct trend toward decentralizing decision making. In large companies especially, lower-level managers are "closer to the action" and typically have more detailed knowledge about problems and how best to solve them than do top managers. For instance, when Interstate Bakeries Corporation purchased the Hostess and Wonder Bread brands from Ralston Purina Company, it immediately revived the lagging sales of familiar brands such as Twinkies, Ding Dongs, and HoHos—something that Ralston had not been able to do. How did Interstate accomplish what Ralston could not? Ralston was highly centralized and nearly all decisions were made by top managers. In contrast, Interstate pushed decision making down to individual plant and brand managers. They could react to local conditions in making decisions.[9] Another example can be seen at Honeywell of Australia and New Zealand, which moved from a hierarchical management structure to one that is much flatter and team-based. Before the change, nearly all decisions were made at headquarters, but since authority has been pushed down to individual plant and brand managers, the results have been increased revenues and a more intimate knowledge of the company's major customers.[10] Likewise, the Bank of Montreal's some 1,100 branches were organized into 236 "communities"—a group of branches within a limited geographical area. Each community is led by a community area manager, who typically works within a 20-minute drive of the other branches. This area manager can respond faster and more intelligently to problems in his or her community than could some senior executive in Toronto. As the company continues its southward expansion into the United States, it continues to use decentralization to successfully manage its various businesses in Chicago, Florida, and Seattle.[11]

●●● centralization
The degree to which decision making is concentrated at a single point in the organization.

●●● decentralization
The degree to which lower-level employees provide input or actually make decisions.

Bic Corporation has a thriving employee suggestion program, and a team of 15 employees who meet regularly to vote on the worth of their co-workers' ideas for improvements on the factory floor. Decentralized decision making gives the team, led by Charlie Tichy (with his back to the camera), the power to pass valued suggestions on to the appropriate supervisors, who have 10 days to act on them.

Exhibit 10–4

Factors That Influence the Amount of Centralization and Decentralization

More Centralization	More Decentralization
• Environment is stable.	• Environment is complex, uncertain.
• Lower-level managers are not as capable or experienced at making decisions as upper-level managers.	• Lower-level managers are capable and experienced at making decisions.
• Lower-level managers do not want to have a say in decisions.	• Lower-level managers want a voice in decisions.
• Decisions are significant.	• Decisions are relatively minor.
• Organization is facing a crisis or the risk of company failure.	• Corporate culture is open to allowing managers to have a say in what happens.
• Company is large.	• Company is geographically dispersed.
• Effective implementation of company strategies depends on managers retaining say over what happens.	• Effective implementation of company strategies depends on managers having involvement and flexibility to make decisions.

● ● ● **employee empowerment**
Increasing the decision-making discretion of employees.

Another term for increased decentralization is **employee empowerment**, which is increasing the decision-making discretion of employees. (▮▮▮▮ Go to the Web and check out S.A.L #40—How Willing Am I to Delegate?) We'll address empowerment more thoroughly in our discussion of leadership in Chapter 17.

What determines whether an organization will move toward more centralization or decentralization? Exhibit 10–4 lists some of the factors that have been identified as influencing the amount of centralization or decentralization an organization uses.[12]

Formalization

● ● ● **formalization**
The degree to which jobs within the organization are standardized and the extent to which employee behavior is guided by rules and procedures.

Formalization refers to the degree to which jobs within the organization are standardized and the extent to which employee behavior is guided by rules and procedures. If a job is highly formalized, then the person doing that job has little discretion as to what is to be done, when it's to be done, and how he or she does it. Employees can be expected to handle the same input in exactly the same way, resulting in consistent and uniform output. In organizations with high formalization, there are explicit job descriptions, numerous organizational rules, and clearly defined procedures covering work processes. (▮▮▮▮ Go to the Web and check out Q & A 10.6.) On the other hand, where formalization is low, job behaviors are relatively unstructured and employees have a great deal of freedom in how they do their work.

The degree of formalization varies widely between organizations and even within organizations. For instance, at a newspaper publisher, news reporters often have a great deal of discretion in their jobs. They may pick their news topics, find their own stories, research them the way they want, and write them up, usually within minimal guidelines. On the other hand, compositors and typesetters who lay out the newspaper pages don't have that type of freedom. They have constraints—both time and space—that standardize how they do their work.

● ● ● **Learning Review**

- Discuss the traditional and contemporary views of work specialization.
- Describe each of the five forms of departmentalization.
- Explain cross-functional teams.
- Differentiate chain of command, authority, responsibility, and unity of command.

- Discuss the traditional and contemporary views of chain of command.
- Discuss the traditional and contemporary views of span of control.
- Explain what factors influence the amount of centralization and decentralization.
- Explain how formalization is used in organizational design.

ORGANIZATIONAL DESIGN DECISIONS

Organizations don't have the same structures. A company with 30 employees isn't going to look like one with 30,000 employees. But even organizations of comparable size don't necessarily have similar structures. What works for one organization may not work for another. How do managers decide what organizational design to use? That decision depends upon certain contingency factors. In this section, we'll look at two generic models of organizational design and then at the contingency factors that favor each.

Mechanistic and Organic Organizations

●●● **mechanistic organization**
An organizational design that's rigid and tightly controlled.

Exhibit 10–5 describes two organizational forms.[13] A **mechanistic organization** is a rigid and tightly controlled structure. It's characterized by high specialization, rigid departmentalization, narrow spans of control, high formalization, a limited information network (mostly downward communication), and little participation in decision making by lower-level employees.

Mechanistic organizational structures tend to be efficiency machines and rely heavily on rules, regulations, standardized tasks, and similar controls. This organizational design tries to minimize the impact of differing personalities, judgments, and ambiguity because these human traits are seen as inefficient and inconsistent. Although there's no totally mechanistic organization, almost all large corporations and governmental agencies have some of these mechanistic characteristics.

●●● **organic organization**
An organizational design that's highly adaptive and flexible.

In direct contrast to the mechanistic form of organization is the **organic organization**, which is as highly adaptive and flexible a structure as the mechanistic organization is rigid and stable. Rather than having standardized jobs and regulations, the organic organization is flexible, which allows it to change rapidly as needs require. Organic organizations have division of labor, but the jobs people do are not standardized. Employees are highly trained and empowered to handle diverse job activities and problems, and these organizations frequently use employee teams. Employees in organic type organizations require minimal formal rules and little direct supervision. Their high levels of skills and training and the support provided by other team members make formalization and tight managerial controls unnecessary.

When is a mechanistic structure preferable and when is an organic one more appropriate? (▇▇▇▇▇ Go to the Web and check out Q & A 10.7.) Let's look at the main contingency factors that influence the decision.

Contingency Factors

Jim Mullen, CEO of Biogen, says, "The campfire culture doesn't work here anymore, with people sitting around telling each other what's going on. We need to be organized looking to the future. The complexity of this company was, and is, rapidly increasing. We need to motivate people to take risks, we need to look for innovation and creativity, and we need to demand results."[14] Top managers of most organizations typically put a great deal of thought into designing an appropriate structure. What that appropriate structure is depends on four contingency variables: the organization's strategy, size, technology, and degree of environmental uncertainty. (▇▇▇▇▇ Go to the Web and check out Q & A 10.8.)

Exhibit 10–5

Mechanistic Versus Organic Organization

Mechanistic	Organic
• High Specialization	• Cross-Functional Teams
• Rigid Departmentalization	• Cross-Hierarchical Teams
• Clear Chain of Command	• Free Flow of Information
• Narrow Spans of Control	• Wide Spans of Control
• Centralization	• Decentralization
• High Formalization	• Low Formalization

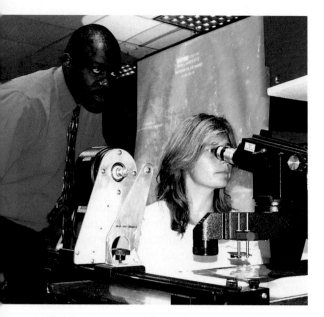

In 1996 Congress created the National Imagery and Mapping Agency (NIMA) by combining the capabilities of several agencies that were providing imagery intelligence, mapping, charting, and geodetic information to the Department of Defense and senior national policymakers. By combining organizations such as the Defense Mapping Agency (DMA) and the CIA's National Photographic Interpretation Center (NPIC) into one agency, NIMA now provides timely, relevant, and accurate geospatial intelligence information in support of national defense and security objectives. Geospatial intelligence is defined as the exploitation and analysis of imagery and geospatial information to describe, assess, and visually depict physical features and geographically referenced activities on Earth. Here, staff members at the National Geospatial Intelligence College send geospatial intelligence information to NIMA analysts.

Strategy and Structure An organization's structure should facilitate the achievement of goals. Because goals are influenced by the organization's strategies, it's only logical that strategy and structure should be closely linked. More specifically, structure should follow strategy. If managers significantly change the organization's strategy, they need to modify the structure to accommodate and support the change.

Alfred Chandler initially researched the strategy–structure relationship.[15] He studied several large U.S. companies and concluded that changes in corporate strategy led to changes in an organization's structure. He found that these organizations usually began with a single product or product line which required only a simple or loose form of organization. However, as they grew, their strategies became more ambitious and elaborate and the organization's structure changed to support the chosen strategy.

Most current strategy frameworks tend to focus on three dimensions: (1) innovation, which reflects the organization's pursuit of meaningful and unique innovations; (2) cost minimization, which reflects the organization's pursuit of tightly controlled costs; and (3) imitation, which reflects an organization's seeking to minimize risk and maximize profit opportunities by copying the market leaders. What structural design works best with each?[16] Innovators need the flexibility and free-flowing information of the organic structure, whereas cost minimizers seek the efficiency, stability, and tight controls of the mechanistic structure. Imitators use structural characteristics of both—the mechanistic structure to maintain tight controls and low costs and the organic structure to mimic the industry's innovative directions.

Size and Structure There's considerable evidence that an organization's size significantly affects its structure.[17] For instance, large organizations—those with 2,000 or more employees—tend to have more specialization, departmentalization, centralization, and rules and regulations than do small organizations. However, the relationship isn't linear. Rather, beyond a certain point, size becomes a less important influence on structure as an organization grows. Why? Essentially, once an organization has around 2,000 employees, it's already fairly mechanistic. Adding 500 employees to a firm with 2,000 employees won't have much of an impact. On the other hand, adding 500 employees to an organization that has only 300 members is likely to result in a shift toward a more mechanistic structure.

Technology and Structure Every organization has at least one form of technology to convert its inputs into outputs. For instance, workers at Maytag's Mexican facility build home appliances on a standardized assembly line. Employees at Kinko's Copies produce custom print jobs for individual customers. And employees at Bayer AG make aspirin and other pharmaceutical products using a continuous-flow production line. Each of these organizations uses a different type of technology.

The initial interest in technology as a determinant of structure can be traced to the work of British scholar Joan Woodward.[18] She studied several small manufacturing firms in southern England to determine the extent to which structural design elements were related to organizational success. Woodward was unable to find any consistent pattern until she segmented the firms into three categories based on the size of their production runs. The three categories, representing three distinct technologies, had increasing levels of complexity and sophistication. The first category, **unit production**, described the production of items in units or small batches. The second category, **mass production**, described large-batch manufacturing. Finally, the third and most technically complex group, **process production**, included continuous-process production. A summary of her findings is shown in Exhibit 10–6.

• • • **unit production**
The production of items in units or small batches.

• • • **mass production**
The production of items in large batches.

• • • **process production**
The production of items in continuous processes.

Exhibit 10–6

Woodward's Findings on Technology, Structure, and Effectiveness

	Unit Production	Mass Production	Process Production
Structural characteristics	Low vertical differentiation Low horizontal differentiation Low formalization	Moderate vertical differentiation High horizontal differentiation High formalization	High vertical differentiation Low horizontal differentiation Low formalization
Most effective structure	Organic	Mechanistic	Organic

Since Woodward's initial work, numerous studies have been done on the technology–structure relationship. These studies generally demonstrate that organizations adapt their structures to their technology.[19] The processes or methods that transform an organization's inputs into outputs differ by their degree of routineness or standardization. In general, the more routine the technology, the more mechanistic the structure can be. Organizations with more nonroutine technology are more likely to have organic structures.[20]

Environmental Uncertainty and Structure In Chapter 3 we introduced the organization's environment and the amount of uncertainty in that environment as constraints on managerial discretion. Why should an organization's structure be affected by its environment? Because of environmental uncertainty! Some organizations face relatively stable and simple environments; others face dynamic and complex environments. Because uncertainty threatens an organization's effectiveness, managers will try to minimize it. One way to reduce environmental uncertainty is through adjustments in the organization's structure.[21] The greater the uncertainty, the more an organization needs the flexibility offered by an organic design. On the other hand, in stable, simple environments, mechanistic designs tend to be most effective.

The evidence on the environment–structure relationship helps to explain why so many managers today are restructuring their organizations to be lean, fast, and flexible. Global competition, accelerated product innovation by competitors, and increased demands from customers for high quality and faster deliveries are examples of dynamic environmental forces. Mechanistic organizations are not equipped to respond to rapid environmental change and environmental uncertainty. As a result, we're seeing organizations designed to be more organic. (▪◼▪ Go to the Web and check out Q & A 10.9.)

Learning Review

- Contrast mechanistic and organic organizations.
- Explain the relationship between strategy and structure.
- Explain how organizational size affects organizational design.

- Discuss Woodward's findings on the relationship of technology and structure.
- Explain how environmental uncertainty affects organizational design.

COMMON ORGANIZATIONAL DESIGNS

What organizational designs do Ford, Toshiba, Nestlé, Procter & Gamble, and eBay have? In making organizational design decisions, managers have some common structural designs from which to choose. We'll first look at some traditional organizational designs and then at some that are more contemporary.

Traditional Organizational Designs

In designing a structure to support the efficient and effective accomplishment of organizational goals, managers may choose to follow more traditional organizational designs. These designs—the simple structure, functional structure, and divisional structure—tend to be more mechanistic. Exhibit 10–7 summarizes the strengths and weaknesses of each of these designs.

Simple Structure Most organizations start as entrepreneurial ventures with a simple structure consisting of owners and employees. A **simple structure** is an organizational design with low departmentalization, wide spans of control, authority centralized in a single person, and little formalization.[22] This structure is most commonly used by small businesses in which the owner and manager are one and the same.

Most organizations do not remain simple structures. As an organization grows, it generally reaches a point where it has to add employees. As the number of employees rises, the structure tends to become more specialized and formalized. Rules and regulations are introduced, work becomes specialized, departments are created, levels of management are added, and the organization becomes increasingly bureaucratic. (You can review Weber's concept of bureaucracy in Chapter 2.) (▮▮▮▮▮ Go to the Web and check out Q & A 10.10.) At this point, a manager might choose to organize around a functional structure or a divisional structure.

Functional Structure A **functional structure** is an organizational design that groups similar or related occupational specialties together. It's the functional approach to departmentalization applied to the entire organization. For instance, Revlon, Inc., is organized around the functions of operations, finance, human resources, and product research and development.

Divisional Structure The **divisional structure** is an organizational structure made up of separate business units or divisions.[23] In this design, each unit or division has relatively limited autonomy, with a division manager responsible for performance and who has strategic and operational authority over his or her unit. In divisional structures, however, the parent corporation typically acts as an external overseer to coordinate and control the various divisions, and it often provides support services such as financial and legal. Take Wal-Mart, for example. Its divisions include Wal-Mart Stores, Wal-Mart Realty, International, Specialty Stores, Sam's Clubs, Supercenters, and Wal-Mart Distribution Centers. Limited Brands is another example of an organization with a divisional structure. Its segments include Apparel (The Limited, Express, Henri Bendel, and Express Men's), Intimate Brands (Victoria's Secret, Bath and Body Works, and White Barn Candle Company), and Mast Industries (▮▮▮▮▮ Check out Passport Scenario 1 on p. 334).

●●● simple structure
An organizational design with, low departmentalization, wide spans of control, centralized authority, and little formalization.

●●● functional structure
An organizational design that groups similar or related occupational specialties together.

●●● divisional structure
An organizational structure made up of separate, semi-autonomous units or divisions.

Exhibit 10–7

●●●●

Strengths and Weaknesses of Common Traditional Organizational Designs

Simple Structure

- Strengths: Fast; flexible; inexpensive to maintain; clear accountability.
- Weaknesses: Not appropriate as organization grows; reliance on one person is risky.

Functional Structure

- Strengths: Cost-saving advantages from specialization (economies of scale, minimal duplication of people and equipment) and employees are grouped with others who have similar tasks.
- Weaknesses: Pursuit of functional goals can cause managers to lose sight of what's best for overall organization; functional specialists become insulated and have little understanding of what other units are doing.

Divisional Structure

- Strengths: Focuses on results—division managers are responsible for what happens to their products and services.
- Weaknesses: Duplication of activities and resources increases costs and reduces efficiency.

Contemporary Organizational Designs

As our chapter-opening "Manager's Dilemma" illustrated, managers in contemporary organizations are finding that these traditional hierarchical designs often aren't appropriate for the increasingly dynamic and complex environments they face. In response to marketplace demands for being lean, flexible, and innovative, managers are finding creative ways to structure and organize work and to make their organizations more responsive to the needs of customers, employees, and other organizational constituents.[24] Now, we want to introduce you to some of the newest concepts in organizational design. Exhibit 10–8 summarizes these contemporary designs.

Team Structures In a **team structure**, the entire organization is made up of work groups or teams that perform the organization's work.[25] (▮▭▬ Go to the Web and check out Q & A 10.11.) Needless to say, employee empowerment is crucial in a team structure because there is no line of managerial authority from top to bottom. Rather, employee teams are free to design work in the way they think is best. However, the teams are also held responsible for all work and performance results in their respective areas. Let's look at some examples of organizations that are organized around teams.

●●● **team structure**
An organizational structure in which the entire organization is made up of work groups or teams.

●●● Exhibit 10–8

Contemporary Organizational Designs

Team Structure

- What it is: A structure in which the entire organization is made up of work groups or teams.
- Advantages: Employees are more involved and empowered.
  Reduced barriers among functional areas.
- Disadvantages: No clear chain of command.
  Pressure on teams to perform.

Matrix-Project Structure

- What it is: Matrix is a structure that assigns specialists from different functional areas to work on projects but who return to their areas when the project is completed. Project is a structure in which employees continuously work on projects. As one project is completed, employees move on to the next project.
- Advantages: Fluid and flexible design that can respond to environmental changes.
  Faster decision making.
- Disadvantages: Complexity of assigning people to projects.
  Task and personality conflicts.

Boundaryless Structure

- What it is: A structure that is not defined by or limited to artificial horizontal, vertical, or external boundaries; includes *virtual, networked,* and *modular* types of organizations.
- Advantages: Highly flexible and responsive.
  Draws on talent wherever it's found.
- Disadvantages: Lack of control.
  Communication difficulties.

Learning Organization Structure

- What it is: A structure that supports an organization's capacity to continuously adapt and change.
- Advantages: Employees are continuously sharing and applying knowledge.
  Ability to learn can be a source of sustainable competitive advantage.
- Disadvantages: Getting employees to share what they know can be difficult.
  Collaboration conflicts can arise.

Acxiom Corporation, of Little Rock, Arkansas, needed a new organizational design in order to stay at the cutting edge of its field (data mining). So the company abandoned its old hierarchical structure and adopted a streamlined culture that focuses on teams, like the Global Data Development team shown here, which meets twice each month. Lee Parrish, leader of another Acxiom team, compared the firm's team structure to the hierarchy at his previous employer: "You had a job title. . . . Here, you have a role. Instead of a lot of wasted motion, you can reach out to people and spend your time working on proactive solutions to problems."

Whole Foods Market, Inc., the largest natural-foods grocer in the United States, is structured around teams.[26] Each Whole Foods store is an autonomous profit center composed of an average of 10 self-managed teams, each with a designated team leader. The team leaders in each store are a team; stores leaders in each region are a team; and the company's six regional presidents are a team. At Sun Life Assurance of Canada's U.S. office in Wellesley, Massachusetts, customer representatives work in eight-person teams trained to expedite all customer requests. Now, when customers call in, they're not switched from one specialist to another but to one of the teams who takes care of every aspect of the customer's request.

In large organizations, the team structure complements what is typically a functional or divisional structure. This allows the organization to have the efficiency of a bureaucracy while providing the flexibility that teams provide. To improve productivity at the operating level, for instance, companies such as Saturn, Motorola, and Xerox extensively use self-managed teams. And at Boeing, Baxter International, and Hewlett-Packard, cross-functional teams are used to design new products or coordinate major projects.

Matrix and Project Structures Other popular contemporary designs are the matrix and project structures. The **matrix structure** is an organizational structure that assigns specialists from different functional departments to work on one or more projects being led by project managers. Exhibit 10–9 shows an example of the matrix structure used in an aerospace firm. Along the top are the familiar organizational functions. The specific projects the firm is currently working on are listed along the left-hand side. Each project is managed by an individual who staffs his or her project with people from each of the functional departments. The addition of this vertical dimension to the traditional horizontal functional departments, in effect, "weaves together" elements of functional and product departmentalization, creating a matrix arrangement. (■□■■■ Go to the Web and check out Q & A 10.12.) One other unique aspect of this design is that it creates a *dual chain of command*. It explicitly violates the classical organizing principle of unity of command. How does a matrix structure work in reality?

Employees in a matrix organization have two managers: their functional department manager and their product or project manager, who share authority. The project managers have authority over the functional members who are part of their project team in areas relative to the project's goals. However, decisions such as promotions, salary recommendations, and annual reviews remain the functional manager's responsibility. To work effectively, project and functional managers have to communicate regularly, coordinate work demands on employees, and resolve conflicts together.

● ● ● **matrix structure**
An organizational structure that assigns specialists from different functional departments to work on one or more projects.

Design Engineering	Manufacturing	Contract Administration	Purchasing	Accounting	Human Resources (HR)
Alpha Project — Design Group	Manufacturing Group	Contract Group	Purchasing Group	Accounting Group	(HR) Group
Beta Project — Design Group	Manufacturing Group	Contract Group	Purchasing Group	Accounting Group	(HR) Group
Gamma Project — Design Group	Manufacturing Group	Contract Group	Purchasing Group	Accounting Group	(HR) Group
Omega Project — Design Group	Manufacturing Group	Contract Group	Purchasing Group	Accounting Group	(HR) Group

Exhibit 10–9 **A Matrix Organization in an Aerospace Firm**

● ● ● project structure
An organizational structure in which employees continuously work on projects.

Although the matrix structure continues to be an effective structural design choice for some organizations, many are using a more "advanced" type of **project structure**, in which employees continuously work on projects. Unlike the matrix structure, a project structure has no formal departments that employees return to at the completion of a project. Instead, employees take their specific skills, abilities, and experiences to other projects. In addition, all work in project structures is performed by teams of employees who become part of a project team because they have the appropriate work skills and abilities. For instance, at Oticon Holding A/S, a Danish hearing-aid manufacturer, there are no departments or employee job titles. All work is project based, and these project teams form, disband, and form again as the work requires. Employees "join" project teams because they bring needed skills and abilities to that project. Once the project is completed, however, they move on to the next one.[27]

Project structures tend to be fluid and flexible organizational designs. There's no departmentalization or rigid organizational hierarchy to slow down decision making or taking actions. In this type of structure, managers serve as facilitators, mentors, and coaches. They "serve" the project teams by eliminating or minimizing organizational obstacles and by ensuring that the teams have the resources they need to effectively and efficiently complete their work.

The Boundaryless Organization Another approach to contemporary organizational design is the concept of a **boundaryless organization**, an organization whose design is not defined by, or limited to, the horizontal, vertical, or external boundaries imposed by a predefined structure.[28] The term was coined by Jack Welch, former chairman of General Electric, who wanted to eliminate vertical and horizontal boundaries within GE and break down external barriers between the company and its customers and suppliers. This idea may sound odd, yet many of today's most successful organizations are finding that they can operate more effectively in today's environment by remaining flexible and *un*structured: that the ideal structure for them is *not* having a rigid, predefined structure. Instead, the boundaryless organization seeks to eliminate the chain of command, to have limitless spans of control, and to replace departments with empowered teams.[29] (■□■■■■ Go to the Web and check out Q & A 10.13.)

● ● ● boundaryless organization
An organization whose design is not defined by, or limited to, the horizontal, vertical, or external boundaries imposed by a predefined structure.

What do we mean by "boundaries"? There are internal boundaries—horizontal boundaries imposed by work specialization and departmentalization and vertical boundaries that separate employees into organizational levels and hierarchies. Then, there are external boundaries that separate the organization from its customers, suppliers, and other stakeholders. To minimize or eliminate these boundaries, managers might use virtual, network, or modular organizational structures.

● ● ● virtual organization
An organization that consists of a small core of full-time employees and that temporarily hires outside specialists to work on opportunities that arise.

A **virtual organization** is an organization that consists of a small core of full-time employees and that temporarily hires outside specialists to work on opportunities that arise.[30] An example of a virtual organization is StrawberryFrog, an international advertising

The Rolling Stones are a global business with budgets, profit and loss statements, and a virtual organization of accountants, bankers, lawyers, promoters, and others who manage their various revenue streams from ticket sales, album sales, royalties, merchandise, sponsorships, and other activities. All this is masterminded by Prince Rupert Zu Loewenstein, who has been the band's chief business advisor for more than 30 years. Speaking of the band's legendary leader, Keith Richards told Fortune *magazine, "Mick likes to run a pretty tight ship."*

● ● ● **network organization**
A small core organization that outsources major business functions.

● ● ● **modular organization**
A manufacturing organization that uses outside suppliers to provide product components or modules that are then assembled into final products.

● ● ● **learning organization**
An organization that has developed the capacity to continuously learn, adapt, and change.

agency based in Amsterdam. The small administrative staff accesses a network of about 50 people around the globe to complete advertising projects. By relying on this web of freelancers around the globe, the company enjoys a network of talent without all the unnecessary overhead and structural complexity. The inspiration for this structural approach comes from the film industry. If you look at the film industry, people are essentially "free agents" who move from project to project applying their skills—directing, talent search, costuming, makeup, set design—as needed.

Another structural option for managers wanting to minimize or eliminate organizational boundaries is the **network organization**, which is a small core organization that outsources major business functions.[31] This approach allows organizations to concentrate on what they do best and contract out other activities to companies that can do those activities best. Many large organizations use the network structure to outsource manufacturing. Companies like Nike, L.L. Bean, Reebok, and Cisco Systems have found that they can do hundreds of millions of dollars of business without owning manufacturing facilities. Cisco, for instance, is essentially a research and development company that uses outside suppliers and independent manufacturers to assemble the Internet routers its engineers design. Nike is essentially a product development and marketing company that contracts with outside organizations to manufacture its athletic footwear. And Sweden's Ericsson contracts its manufacturing and even some of its research and development to more cost-effective contractors in New Delhi, Singapore, California, and other global locations.[32]

The final boundaryless option for managers is similar to the network organization. It's a **modular organization**, which is a manufacturing organization that uses outside suppliers to provide product components or modules which are then assembled into final products.[33] An easy way to understand the modular structure is by using the analogy of building a home.[34] Just like a traditional organization structure with its fairly stable boundaries, a traditional home is a solid, stable object that takes a long time to build. It's built where it will remain and once it is built, it takes major effort to modify or add to it. On the other hand, the pieces of a modular home are assembled in an off-site location, broken apart, and reassembled on location to meet the owner's needs. Just like that modular home, a modular organization can quickly be redesigned as needed. Automobile manufacturers are leaders in this type of modular organizing. For instance, GM has a modular factory in Brazil where outside suppliers provide engineering and production of entire sections of the cars. The modules are delivered right to the assembly line where a small number of GM employees put them together into a finished automobile.[35]

The Learning Organization We first introduced the concept of a learning organization in Chapter 2 as we looked at some of the current issues facing managers. The concept of a learning organization doesn't involve a specific organizational design per se but instead describes an organizational mind-set or philosophy that has significant design implications. (▣▭▭▭ Go to the Web and check out Q & A 10.14.)

What is a **learning organization**? It's an organization that has developed the capacity to continuously learn, adapt, and change.[36] In a learning organization, employees practice knowledge management by continually acquiring and sharing new knowledge and are willing to apply that knowledge in making decisions or performing their work. Some organizational theorists even go so far as to say that an organization's ability to do this—that is, to learn and to apply that learning—may be the only sustainable source of competitive advantage.[37] Look back at the chapter-opening dilemma where the manager, Lars Gronstedt, wanted to continue to grow his organization as a learning organization. (▣▭▭▭ Go to the Web and check out Q & A 10.15.)

Exhibit 10–10

●●●○────

Characteristics of a Learning Organization

Source: Based on P.M. Senge, *The Fifth Discipline: The Art and Practice of Learning Organizations* (New York: Doubleday, 1990); and R.M. Hodgetts, F. Luthans, and S.M. Lee, "New Paradigm Organizations: From Total Quality to Learning to World Class," *Organizational Dynamics*, Winter 1994, pp. 4–19.

What would a learning organization look like? As you can see in Exhibit 10–10, the characteristics of a learning organization revolve around organizational design, information sharing, leadership, and culture.

In a learning organization, it's critical for members to share information and collaborate on work activities throughout the entire organization—across different functional specialties and even at different organizational levels. This can be done by minimizing or eliminating the existing structural and physical boundaries. In this boundaryless environment, employees are free to work together and collaborate in doing the organization's work the best way they can and to learn from each other. Because of this need to collaborate, teams also tend to be an important feature of a learning organization's structural design. Employees work in teams on whatever activities need to be done, and these employee teams are empowered to make decisions regarding their work or resolving issues. With empowered employees and teams, there's little need for "bosses" to direct and control. Instead, managers serve as facilitators, supporters, and advocates for employee teams.

Becoming a Manager

◆ *If you belong to a student organization or are employed, notice how various activities and events are organized through the use of work specialization, chain of command, authority, responsibility, and so forth.*

◆ *As you read current business periodicals, note what types of organizational structures businesses use and whether or not they're effective.*

◆ *Talk to managers about how they organize work and what they have found to be effective.*

◆ *Since delegating is part of decentralizing and is an important management skill, complete the Skill-Building Module on Delegating. Then practice delegating in various situations.*

◆ *Look for examples of **organizational charts** (a visual drawing of an organization's structure) and use it to try to determine what structural design the organization is using.*

◆ *▢▢ Go to the Web and complete the following exercises from the Self-Assessment Library (S.A.L.) Found on R.O.L.L.S.: #39—What Type of Organization Structure Do I Prefer?,—#40—How Willing Am I to Delegate?,—,#41—How Politically Oriented Am I?, and #7—How Well Do I Handle Ambiguity?*

●●● **organizational chart**
A visual drawing of an organization's structure.

Learning can't take place without information. For an organization to "learn," information must be shared among members. This means sharing information openly, in a timely manner, and in as accurate a form as possible. Because there are few structural and physical barriers in a learning organization, the environment is conducive to open communication and extensive information sharing.

Leadership also plays an important role as an organization becomes a learning organization. What should leaders in a learning organization do? One of their most important functions is facilitating the creation of a shared vision for the organization's future and then keeping organizational members working toward that vision. In addition, leaders should support and encourage the collaborative environment that's critical to learning. Without strong and committed leadership throughout the organization, it would be extremely difficult to be a learning organization.

Finally, the organizational culture is an important characteristic of a learning organization. In a learning organization, the culture is one in which everyone agrees on a shared vision and everyone recognizes the inherent interrelationships among the organization's processes, activities, functions, and external environment. There's a strong sense of community, caring for each other, and trust. In a learning organization, employees feel free to openly communicate, share, experiment, and learn without fear of criticism or punishment.

A Final Thought   No matter what structural design managers choose for their organizations, the design should help employees do their work in the best—most efficient and effective—way they can. The structure should aid and facilitate organizational members as they carry out the organization's work. After all, the structure is simply a means to an end. (▪▪▪◻▪ Go to the Web and check out S.A.L. #39—What Type of Organization Structure Do I Prefer?)

● ● ● ● Learning Review

- Contrast the three traditional organizational designs.
- Explain team-based, matrix, and project structure.
- Discuss the design of virtual, network, and modular organizations.
- Describe the characteristics of a learning organization.

Managers **Respond** to a **Manager's** Dilemma

⋯⋯Peter Crombie

Chief Executive, Crombie Corporation Pty. Limited, Manly, NSW, Australia

To continue to grow as a true learning organization, Lars will have to change the culture of his company. In the past, the organization has expanded with separate "cells" with an apparent lack of sharing of knowledge between those "cells." While there has been some knowledge transfer at branch level, that knowledge has not been passed on to other branches. The needed change in organizational mindset is likely to be fairly difficult for Lars because not only has it been imbedded as part of the company, it is well integrated into Swedish culture. To accomplish this, it will be necessary to set up an entirely new internal system to encourage the branches to share knowledge. Employees will need easy and direct access to this information. Most importantly, Lars will have to set a standard by sharing his knowledge and information.

Clare Carter

Pearson Education, Harlow, United Kingdom

Lars is right to believe that one of the ways to achieve his organization's competitive advantage is by ensuring that it continues to grow as a true learning organization. To do this, he might consider some of the following: setting up a branch mentoring system to encourage staff to develop and try new ideas; using discussion forums to share and develop best practices between branches; providing all branches access to a database so they can share key information; rotating staff so they can experience different practices and help introduce successful techniques they have used; ensuring that staff have the necessary skills to fully participate in a learning organization and to be able to adapt to any changes; developing appropriate training programs; and ensuring that all branch employees understand the shared vision of being a learning organization.

Learning Summary

After reading and studying this chapter, you should be able to:

- Discuss the traditional and contemporary views of work specialization.

- Describe each of the five forms of departmentalization.

- Explain cross-functional teams.

- Differentiate chain of command, authority, responsibility, and unity of command.

- Discuss the traditional and contemporary views of chain of command.

- Discuss the traditional and contemporary views of span of control.

- Explain what factors influence the amount of centralization and decentralization.

- Explain how formalization is used in organizational design.

- Contrast mechanistic and organic organizations.

- Explain the relationship between strategy and structure.

- Explain how organizational size affects organizational design.

- Discuss Woodward's findings on the relationship of technology and structure.

- Explain how environmental uncertainty affects organizational design.

- Contrast the three traditional organizational designs.

- Explain team-based, matrix, and project structures.

- Discuss the design of virtual, network, and modular organizations.

- Describe the characteristics of a learning organization.

Thinking About Management Issues

1. Can an organization's structure be changed quickly? Why or why not?

2. Would you rather work in a mechanistic or an organic organization? Why?

3. What types of skills would a manager need to effectively work in a project structure? In a boundaryless organization? In a learning organization?

4. The boundaryless organization has the potential to create a major shift in the way we work. Do you agree or disagree? Explain.

5. With the availability of advanced information technology that allows an organization's work to be done anywhere at any time, is organizing still an important managerial function? Why or why not?

Working Together: Team-Based Exercise

In relatively decentralized organizations, managers must delegate (assign or turn over) authority to another person to carry out specific duties. Read through the Skills Module on Delegating found on pp. 522–523. Form groups of three or four students. Your instructor will assign groups to either "effective delegating" or "ineffective delegating." Come up with a role-playing situation that illustrates what your group was assigned (effective or ineffective delegating), which you will present in class. Be prepared to explain how your situation was an example of effective or ineffective delegating.

Ethical Dilemma Exercise

Is a manager acting unethically by simply following orders within the chain of command? One recent survey of human resources managers found that 52 percent of the respondents felt some pressure to bend ethical rules, often because of orders from above or to achieve ambitious goals. This might happen in any organization. At WorldCom, for example, Betty Vinson was a senior manager when she and others received orders, through the chain of command, to slash expenses through improper accounting. She argued against the move. Her boss said he had also objected and was told this was a one-time "fix" to make WorldCom's finances look better. Vinson reluctantly agreed, but she felt guilty and told her boss she wanted to resign. A senior executive persuaded her to stay, and she continued following orders to fudge the accounting.

Soon Vinson realized that the figures would need fudging for some time. After investigators started to probe WorldCom's finances, she and others cooperated with regulators and prosecutors. Ultimately, the company was forced into bankruptcy. Some managers were indicted; some (including Vinson) pleaded guilty to conspiracy and fraud. Now WorldCom is working hard to change its image and reinforce ethical conduct. For example, the head of U.S. sales, marketing, and services has a zero-tolerance ethics policy and provides ethics training for the entire sales force.[38]

Imagine that you're a WorldCom salesperson. Your manager invites you to an expensive restaurant where she is entertaining several colleagues and their spouses. The boss orders you to put the meal on your expense account as a customer dinner. She says she'll approve the expense so you are reimbursed, and higher-level managers won't know that managers and their spouses were in attendance. Review this chapter's material on chain of command as you decide which of the following options to choose—and why.

Option A: You decide to put the meal on your expense account and ask her to approve it as quickly as possible so you can get repaid before anyone starts asking questions.

Option B: You decide to politely decline and suggest that one of the other attendees put the meal on his or her expense account, so you won't be involved.

Option C: You decide to put the meal on your expense account and immediately call WorldCom's independent ethics office to ask, anonymously, about the situation.

Case Application

Indigo Books & Music

Prior to 2001 there were two big-box bookstore chains in Canada—Chapters and Indigo. Indigo was formed in 1996 by Heather Reisman, who left her job as president of Cott Corporation, the beverage supplier, to found Indigo. It was the first book retail chain to add music, gifts, and licensed cafés to store locations. By 2000, the chain had expanded to 14 locations across Canada. The other large chain, Chapters, was formed in 1995 with the merger of Canada's then two largest bookstore chains—Cole's and SmithBooks. In 2001, Heather pulled a shocking coup when her company took over the much bigger Chapters chain. Chapters' losses were crippling the company, and its shareholders quickly approved the takeover bid.

What followed for Reisman was the task of merging the two organizations into one. Indigo and Chapters both had similar organizational structures—a functional-based design. Indigo's corporate structure, for instance, consisted of departments such as marketing, human resources, and retail. However, the new organization suddenly had 90 big-box stores and close to 7,000 employees. Moreover, with the takeover, Indigo gained control of the nationwide chain of 210 Cole's Books and SmithBooks stores, as well as a new Internet division, Chapters Online. The structure of the newly merged organization had to change in order to incorporate these new businesses.

The combined company, Indigo Books & Music, is now Canada's top bookseller. Its some 300 stores spread throughout the country's provinces sell books, magazines, CDs, and other items. Making the combined organization run efficiently has been a major challenge for Reisman. Indigo lost approximately $48 million in 2002 even as the number of employees grew by 26 percent. Results for 2003 were somewhat better as the company posted a small $1.4 million profit. So Reisman must continue to address the issue of keeping the company profitable in a challenging retail climate. Despite the challenges, most analysts don't doubt that Heather Reisman is up to resolving them.

Heather Reisman, CEO of Indigo Books & Music, pictured here with former South African President Nelson Mandela.

DISCUSSION QUESTIONS

1. When two organizations merge, what types of structural issues do you think might need to be addressed?

2. What role do you think organizational structure plays in an organization's efficiency and effectiveness? Explain.

3. Would a more mechanistic or a more organic structure be appropriate for Indigo? Why?

4. How might technology affect Indigo's organizational design?

Sources: Information on company from Company's Web site (*www.chapters.indigo.ca*) and Hoover's Online (*www.hoovers.com*), June 21, 2003; and H. Shaw, "Montreal's Steel Magnolia Won Canada's Book Battle," *Financial Post*, March 31, 2001, p. F3.

•••Learning Outline

Follow this Learning Outline as you read and study this chapter.

Understanding Communication

- Differentiate between interpersonal and organizational communication.
- Discuss the functions of communication.

The Process of Interpersonal Communication

- Explain all the components of the communication process.
- List the communication methods managers might use.
- Describe nonverbal communication and how it takes place.
- Explain the barriers to effective interpersonal communication and how to overcome them.

Organizational Communication

- Explain how communication can flow in an organization.
- Describe the three common communication networks.
- Discuss how managers should handle the grapevine.

Understanding Information Technology

- Describe how technology affects managerial communication.
- Define e-mail, instant messaging, voicemail, fax, EDI, teleconferencing, videoconferencing, intranet, and extranet.
- Explain how information technology affects organizations.

Communication Issues in Today's Organizations

- Discuss how Internet employee gripe sites affect communication.
- Explain how organizations can manage knowledge.
- Explain why communicating with customers is an important managerial issue.
- Describe how political correctness is affecting communication.

Chapter

11

Communication and Information Technology

Semifreddi's is an artisan-bread bakery (bakers of specialty bread and bread shaped in unusual and artistic ways) in Emeryville, California. Semifreddi is an Italian word meaning "half-cold" and refers to partially frozen desserts. Customers love the name *and* the hand-shaped specialty breads. Pictured in the center below, CEO Tom Frainier (a Berkeley M.B.A. who left the corporate world after seven successful years in manage-

ment) runs the company, whose annual revenues are over $7 million.[1] He describes himself as an "accessible, available, communicative guy." However, language barriers have been a challenge for Tom and his workers, most of whom are from Mexico, Laos, China, Peru, Cambodia, and Vietnam. Even though his workers have limited English-language skills, Tom feels that he communicates sufficiently well with his diverse workforce because no major problems have arisen—at least yet.

When customers began making comments about the lack of parking on one side of the bakery, Tom called an employee meeting, just as he did anytime there were issues to be discussed. He asked workers not to park in the spaces reserved for customers. Some employees misunderstood and thought he was telling them not to drive to work. Tom later said that his mistake was talking slowly and loudly and assuming that by doing so his

employees would understand him. However, the miscommunication over the parking issue was minor in comparison to another of his communication challenges.

Tom is a strong believer in open-book management, an approach in which the "books," or company financial statements, are shared with employees in order to help them better understand the business and make them feel more like a partner in it. To show his commitment to sharing information, he recently gathered together employees from different work shifts and shared a long list of financial numbers with them. When Tom asked them if they understood, all heads nodded in agreement. Tom said later, "I didn't realize that they were just being polite." His desire to involve his employees by sharing the financial results wasn't working.

Put yourself in Tom's position. What could he do to improve the effectiveness of his communications?

What would *you* do ?

om Frainier of Semifreddi's recognizes the importance of effectively communicating with his employees. Communication between managers and employees provides the information necessary to get work done effectively and efficiently in organizations. As such, there's no doubt that communication is fundamentally linked to managerial performance.[2] In this chapter, we'll present basic concepts in managerial communication. We'll explain the interpersonal communication process, methods of communicating, barriers to effective communication, and ways to overcome those barriers. We'll also look at organizational communication issues including communication flow and communication networks. And, because managerial communication is so greatly influenced by information technology, we'll look at it as well. Finally, we'll discuss several contemporary communication issues facing managers.

UNDERSTANDING COMMUNICATION

Unlike the character Bill Murray plays in *Groundhog Day*, Neal L. Patterson, CEO of Cerner Corporation, a health care software development company based in Kansas City, probably wishes he *could* do over one day. Upset with the fact that employees didn't seem to be putting in enough hours, he sent an angry and emotional e-mail to about 400 company managers that said, in part:

> We are getting less than 40 hours of work from a large number of our K.C.—based EMPLOYEES. The parking lot is sparsely used at 8 A.M.; likewise at 5 P.M. As managers, you either do not know what your EMPLOYEES are doing, or you do not CARE. You have created expectations on the work effort which allowed this to happen inside Cerner, creating a very unhealthy environment. In either case, you have a problem and you will fix it or I will replace you... I will hold you accountable. You have allowed things to get to this state. You have two weeks. Tick, tock.[3]

Although the e-mail was meant only for the company's managers, it was leaked and posted on a Yahoo! discussion site. The tone of the e-mail surprised industry analysts, investors, and of course, Cerner's managers and employees. The company's stock price dropped 22 percent over the next three days. Patterson apologized to his employees and acknowledged, "I lit a match and started a firestorm." This is a good example of why it's important for managers to understand the impact of communication.

The importance of effective communication for managers can't be overemphasized for one specific reason: Everything a manager does involves communicating. Not *some* things, but everything! A manager can't make a decision without information. That information has to be communicated. Once a decision is made, communication must again take place. Otherwise, no one would know that a decision was made. The best idea, the most creative suggestion, the best plan, or the most effective job redesign can't take shape without communication. Managers need effective communication skills. (▮▯▮ Go to the Web and check out Q & A 11.1.) We aren't suggesting that good communication skills alone make a successful manager. We can say, however, that ineffective communication skills can lead to a continuous stream of problems for the manager.

What Is Communication?

Communication is the transfer and understanding of meaning. The first thing to note about this definition is the emphasis on the *transfer* of meaning. This means that if no information or ideas have been conveyed, communication hasn't taken place. The speaker who isn't heard or the writer who isn't read hasn't communicated.

• • • **communication**
The transfer and understanding of meaning.

■ **Q & A**
Whenever you see this green square, go to the R.O.L.L.S. Web site (**www.prenhall.com/ robbins**) to the Q & A, your 24/7 educational assistant. These video clips and written material presented by your authors address questions that we have found students frequently ask.

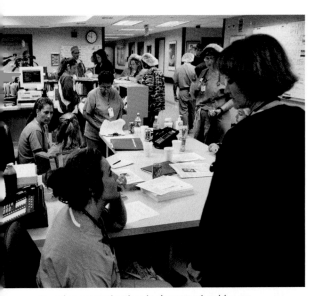

Good communication is characterized by an understanding of the sender's meaning, not necessarily by agreement between the parties. At Parkland Memorial Hospital, which delivers more babies than any other hospital in the country, 50 faculty members, 40 midwives, and 100 nurses communicate around the clock, and not just in person as they do at the nurse's station shown here. The charge nurses wear walkie-talkies to ensure that communication is ongoing no matter where they are.

More importantly, however, communication involves the *understanding* of meaning. For communication to be successful, the meaning must be imparted and understood. A letter written in Portuguese addressed to a person who doesn't read Portuguese can't be considered communication until it's translated into a language the person does read and understand. Perfect communication, if such a thing existed, would be when a transmitted thought or idea was perceived by the receiver exactly as it was envisioned by the sender.

Another point to keep in mind is that *good* communication is often erroneously defined by the communicator as *agreement* with the message instead of clearly understanding the message.[4] If someone disagrees with us, many of us assume that the person just didn't fully understand our position. In other words, many of us define good communication as having someone accept our views. But I can clearly understand what you mean and just *not* agree with what you say. In fact, many times when a conflict has gone on for a long time, people will say it's because the parties aren't communicating effectively. That assumption reflects the tendency to think that effective communication equals agreement. (▮◻▮▮▮ Go to the Web and check out Q & A 11.2.)

The final point we want to make about communication is that it encompasses both **interpersonal communication**—communication between two or more people—and **organizational communication**—all the patterns, networks, and systems of communication within an organization. Both these types of communication are important to managers in organizations.

●●● **interpersonal communication**
Communication between two or more people.

●●● **organizational communication**
All the patterns, networks, and systems of communication within an organization.

Functions of Communication

Why is communication important to managers and organizations? It serves four major functions: control, motivation, emotional expression, and information.[5]

Communication acts to *control* member behavior in several ways. As we know from Chapter 10, organizations have authority hierarchies and formal guidelines that employees are required to follow. For instance, when employees are required to communicate any job-related grievance first to their immediate manager, or to follow their job description, or to comply with company policies, communication is being used to control. But informal communication also controls behavior. When work groups tease or harass a member who's working too hard or producing too much (making the rest of the group look bad), they're informally controlling the member's behavior.

Communication encourages *motivation* by clarifying to employees what is to be done, how well they're doing, and what can be done to improve performance if it's not up to par. As employees set specific goals, work toward those goals, and receive feedback on progress toward goals, communication is required.

For many employees, their work group is a primary source of social interaction. The communication that takes place within the group is a fundamental mechanism by which members share frustrations and feelings of satisfaction. Communication, therefore, provides a release for *emotional expression* of feelings and for fulfillment of social needs.

Finally, individuals and groups need information to get things done in organizations. Communication provides that *information*.

No one of these four functions is more important than the others. For groups to work effectively, they need to maintain some form of control over members, motivate members to perform, provide a means for emotional expression, and make decisions. You can assume that almost every communication interaction that takes place in a group or organization is fulfilling one or more of these four functions.

●●●●**Learning Review**

- Explain why effective communication is important for managers.

- Define communication.

- Differentiate between interpersonal and organizational communication.

- Discuss the functions of communication.

INTERPERSONAL COMMUNICATION

●●● **message**
A purpose to be conveyed.

●●● **encoding**
Converting a message into symbols.

●●● **channel**
The medium a message travels along.

●●● **decoding**
Retranslating a sender's message.

●●● **communication process**
The seven elements involved in transferring meaning from one person to another.

●●● **noise**
Any disturbances that interfere with the transmission, receipt, or feedback of a message.

Before communication can take place, a purpose, expressed as a **message** to be conveyed, must exist. It passes between a source (the sender) and a receiver. The message is converted to symbolic form (called **encoding**) and passed by way of some medium (**channel**) to the receiver, who retranslates the sender's message (called **decoding**). The result is the transfer of meaning from one person to another.[6] Exhibit 11–1 illustrates the seven elements of the **communication process**: the communication source, the message, encoding, the channel, decoding, the receiver, and feedback. In addition, note that the entire process is susceptible to **noise**—disturbances that interfere with the transmission, receipt, or feedback of a message. Typical examples of noise include illegible print, phone static, inattention by the receiver, or background sounds of machinery or co-workers. Remember that anything that interferes with understanding can be noise, and noise can create distortion at any point in the communication process. Let's look at how distortions can happen with the sender, the message, the channel, the receiver, and the feedback loop.

A *sender* initiates a message by *encoding* a thought. Four conditions influence the effectiveness of that encoded message: the skills, attitudes, and knowledge of the sender, and the social-cultural system. How? We'll use ourselves, as your textbook authors, as an example. If we don't have the requisite skills, our message won't reach you, the reader, in the form desired. Our success in communicating to you depends on our writing skills. In addition, any preexisting ideas (attitudes) that we may have about numerous topics will affect how we communicate. For instance, our attitudes about managerial ethics or the importance of managers to organizations influence our writing. Next, the amount of knowledge we have about a subject affects the message(s) we are transferring. We can't communicate what we don't know; and if our knowledge is too extensive, it's possible that our writing won't be understood by the readers. Finally, the social-cultural system in which we live influences us as communication senders. Our beliefs and values (all part of culture) act to influence what and how we communicate. Think back to our chapter-opening "Manager's Dilemma" and how Tom Frainier wants to be an effective communicator. As he encodes his ideas into messages when communicating with employees, he needs to reflect on his skill, attitudes, knowledge, and the social-cultural system (of both the United States and his employees' countries of origin) in order to reduce any possible noise.

The *message* itself can distort the communication process, regardless of the kinds of supporting tools or technologies used to convey it. A message is the actual physical product encoded by the source. It can be the written document, the oral speech, and

●●—— Exhibit 11–1

The Interpersonal Communication Process

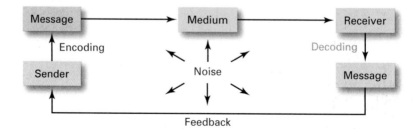

Communication channels have multiplied with the spread of new technologies like the high-speed Internet access known as Wi-Fi. At the 141 warehouse-type stores operated by BJ's Wholesale Club, for instance, managers have saved time and money by switching to Wi-Fi for their internal communications. The devices mean that managers like John Barrows can talk to customers, suppliers, or even the boss without having to hike across the aisles to the store's front-office telephone.

even the gestures and facial expressions we use. The message is affected by the symbols used to transfer meaning (words, pictures, numbers, etc.), the content of the message itself, and the decisions that the sender makes in selecting and arranging both the symbols and the content. Noise can distort the communication process in any of these areas.

The *channel* chosen to communicate the message also has the potential to be affected by noise. Whether it's a face-to-face conversation, an e-mail message, or a company-wide memorandum, distortions can, and do, occur. Managers need to recognize that certain channels are more appropriate for certain messages. (Think back to how Cerner's CEO chose to communicate his frustration with his managers by e-mail and whether that was an appropriate choice.) Obviously, if the office is on fire, a memo to convey the fact is inappropriate! And if something is important, such as an employee's performance appraisal, a manager might want to use multiple channels—perhaps an oral review followed by a written letter summarizing the points. This decreases the potential for distortion.

The *receiver* is the individual to whom the message is directed. Before the message can be received, however, the symbols in it must be translated into a form that the receiver can understand. This is the *decoding* of the message. Just as the sender was limited by his or her skills, attitudes, knowledge, and social-cultural system, so is the receiver. And just as the sender must be skillful in writing or speaking, the receiver must be skillful in reading or listening. A person's knowledge influences his or her ability to receive. Moreover, the receiver's attitudes and social-cultural background can distort the message.

The final link in the communication process is a *feedback loop*. Feedback returns the message to the sender and provides a check on whether understanding has been achieved. Because feedback can be transmitted along the same types of channels as the original message, it faces the same potential for distortion.

Methods of Communicating Interpersonally

You need to communicate to your employees the organization's new policy on sexual harassment; you want to compliment one of your workers on the extra hours she's put in to help your work group complete a customer's order; you must tell one of your employees about changes to her job; or you would like to get employees' feedback on your proposed budget for next year. In each of these instances, how would you communicate this information? Managers have a wide variety of communication methods from which to choose. (■□■■■ Go to the Web and check out Q & A 11.3.) These include face-to-face, telephone, group meetings, formal presentations, memos, traditional mail, fax machines, employee publications, bulletin boards, other company publications, audio- and videotapes, hotlines, electronic mail, computer conferencing, voice mail, teleconferences, and videoconferences. All of these communication channels include oral or written symbols, or both. How do you know which to use? Managers can use 12 questions to help them evaluate the various communication methods.[7]

1. *Feedback*—How quickly can the receiver respond to the message?

2. *Complexity capacity*—Can the method effectively process complex messages?

3. *Breadth potential*—How many different messages can be transmitted using this method?

4. *Confidentiality*—Can communicators be reasonably sure their messages are received only by those for whom they're intended?

5. *Encoding ease*—Can sender easily and quickly use this channel?

6. *Decoding ease*—Can receiver easily and quickly decode messages?

7. *Time-space constraint*—Do senders and receivers need to communicate at the same time and in the same space?

8. *Cost*—How much does it cost to use this method?

9. *Interpersonal warmth*—How well does this method convey interpersonal warmth?

10. *Formality*—Does this method have the needed amount of formality?

11. *Scanability*—Does this method allow the message to be easily browsed or scanned for relevant information?

12. *Time of consumption*—Does sender or receiver exercise the most control over when the message is dealt with?

Exhibit 11–2 provides a comparison of the various communication methods on these 12 criteria. Which method a manager ultimately chooses should reflect the needs of the sender, the attributes of the message, the attributes of the channel, and the needs of the receiver. For instance, if you need to communicate to an employee the changes being made in her job, face-to-face communication would be a better choice than a memo since you want to be able to address immediately any questions and concerns that she might have. (■■■□■ Go to the Web and check out S.A.L. #24—What's My Face-to-Face Communication Style?)

We can't leave the topic of interpersonal communication methods without looking at the role of **nonverbal communication**—that is, communication transmitted without words. Some of the most meaningful communications are neither spoken nor written. A loud siren or a red light at an intersection tells you something without words. When a college instructor is teaching a class, she doesn't need words to tell her that her students are bored when their eyes are glassed over or they begin to read the school newspaper in the middle of class. Similarly, when students start putting their papers, notebooks, and book away, the message is clear: Class time is about over. The size of a person's office or the clothes he or she wears also convey messages to others. These are all forms of nonverbal communication. The best-known types of nonverbal communication are body language and verbal intonation. (■■■■□ Go to the Web and check out You're the Manager: Diversity in Action #3.)

Body language refers to gestures, facial expressions, and other body movements that convey meaning. A person frowning "says" something different from one who's smiling. Hand motions, facial expressions, and other gestures can communicate emotions or temperaments such as aggression, fear, shyness, arrogance, joy, and anger. Knowing the meaning behind someone's body moves and learning how to put forth your best body language can help you personally and professionally.[8]

●●● **nonverbal communication**
Communication transmitted without words.

●●● **body language**
Gestures, facial configurations, and other movements of the body that convey meaning.

Exhibit 11–2 **Comparison of Communication Methods**

Channel	Feedback Potential	Complexity Capacity	Breadth Potential	Confidentiality	Encoding Ease	Time-Decoding Ease	Space Constraint	Cost	Personal Warmth	Formality	Scan-ability	Consumption Time
Face-to-face	1	1	1	1	1	1	1	2	1	4	4	S/R
Telephone	1	4	2	2	1	1	3	3	2	4	4	S/R
Group meetings	2	2	2	4	2	2	1	1	2	3	4	S/R
Formal presentations	4	2	2	4	3	2	1	1	3	3	5	Sender
Memos	4	4	2	3	4	3	5	3	5	2	1	Receiver
Postal mail	5	3	3	2	4	3	5	3	4	1	1	Receiver
Fax	3	4	2	4	3	3	5	3	3	3	1	Receiver
Publications	5	4	2	5	5	3	5	3	4	1	1	Receiver
Bulletin boards	4	5	1	5	3	2	2	4	5	3	1	Receiver
Audio/videotapes	4	4	3	5	4	2	3	2	3	3	5	Receiver
Hot lines	2	5	2	2	3	1	4	2	3	3	4	Receiver
E-mail	3	4	1	2	3	2	4	2	4	3	4	Receiver
Computer conference	1	2	2	4	3	2	3	2	3	3	4	S/R
Voice mail	2	4	2	1	2	1	5	3	2	4	4	Receiver
Tele-conference	2	3	2	5	2	2	2	2	3	3	5	S/R
Video-conference	3	3	2	4	2	2	2	1	2	3	5	S/R

Note: Ratings are on a 1–5 scale where 1 = high and 5 = low. Consumption time refers to who controls the reception of communication. S/R means the sender and receiver share control.

Source: P.G. Clampitt, *Communicating for Managerial Effectiveness* (Newbury Park, CA: Sage Publications, 1991), p. 136.

••• **verbal intonation**
An emphasis given to words
or phrases that conveys
meaning.

Verbal intonation refers to the emphasis someone gives to words or phrases that conveys meaning. To illustrate how intonations can change the meaning of a message, consider the student who asks the instructor a question. The instructor replies, "What do you mean by that?" The student's reaction will vary, depending on the tone of the instructor's response. A soft, smooth vocal tone conveys interest and creates a different meaning from one that is abrasive and puts a strong emphasis on saying the last word. Most of us would view the first intonation as coming from someone sincerely interested in clarifying the student's concern, whereas the second suggests that the person is defensive or aggressive.

The fact that every oral communication also has a nonverbal message can't be overemphasized. Why? Because the nonverbal component usually carries the greatest impact. "It's not *what* you said, but *how* you said it." People respond to *how* something is said as well as *what* is said. Managers should remember this as they communicate. (▮▯▮ Go to the Web and check out Q & A 11.4.)

Barriers to Effective Interpersonal Communication

In our discussion of the interpersonal communication process, we noted the continual potential for distortion. What causes distortion? In addition to the general distortions identified in the communication process, managers face other barriers to effective communication. (▮▯▮ Go to the Web and check out Q & A 11.5.)

••• **filtering**
The deliberate manipulation
of information to make it
appear more favorable
to the receiver.

Filtering **Filtering** is the deliberate manipulation of information to make it appear more favorable to the receiver. For example, when a person tells his or her manager what the manager wants to hear, that individual is filtering information. Does this happen much in organizations? Yes, it does! As information is communicated up through organizational levels, it's condensed and synthesized by senders so those on top don't become overloaded with information. Those doing the condensing filter communications through their personal interests and perceptions of what is important. (▮▯▮ Go to the Web and check out Q & A 11.6.)

The extent of filtering tends to be a function of the number of vertical levels in the organization and the organizational culture. The more vertical levels there are in an organization, the more opportunities there are for filtering. As organizations become less dependent on strict hierarchical arrangements and instead use more collaborative, cooperative work arrangements, information filtering may become less of a problem. In addition, the ever-increasing use of e-mail to communicate in organizations reduces filtering because communication is more direct as intermediaries are bypassed. Finally, the organizational culture encourages or discourages filtering by the type of behavior it rewards. The more that organizational rewards emphasize style and appearance, the more managers will be motivated to filter communications in their favor.

Emotions How a receiver feels when a message is received influences how he or she interprets it. You'll often interpret the same message differently, depending on whether you're happy or upset. Extreme emotions are most likely to hinder effective communication. In such instances, we often disregard our rational and objective thinking processes and substitute emotional judgments. It's best to avoid reacting to a message when you're upset because you're not likely to be thinking clearly.

Information Overload A marketing manager goes on a week-long sales trip to Spain where he doesn't have access to his e-mail and is faced with 1,000 messages on his return. It's not

Filtering, or shaping information to make it look good to the receiver, might not always be intentional. For John Seral, chief information officer of GE Plastics, the problem was that "when the CEO asked how the quarter was looking, he got a different answer depending on whom he asked." Seral solved the problem by building a continuously updated database of the company's most important financial information that gives not just the CEO but also 300 company managers instant access to sales and operating figures on their PCs and BlackBerrys. Instead of dozens of analysts compiling the information, the new systems require only six.

The Communication Styles of Men and Women

"You don't understand what I'm saying, and you never listen!" "You're making a big deal out of nothing." Have you said (or heard) these statements or ones like them to friends of the opposite sex? Most of us probably have! Research shows us that men and women tend to have different communication styles.[9] Let's look more closely at these differing styles and the problems that can arise, and try to suggest ways to minimize the barriers.

Deborah Tannen has studied the ways that men and women communicate, and reports some interesting differences. The essence of her research is that men use talk to emphasize status, while women use it to create connection. She states that communication between the sexes can be a continual balancing act of juggling our conflicting needs for intimacy, which suggests closeness and commonality, and independence, which emphasizes separateness and differences. It's no wonder, then, that communication problems arise! Women hear and speak a language of connection and intimacy. Men hear and speak a language of status and independence. For many men, conversations are merely a way to preserve independence and maintain status in a hierarchical social order. Yet for many women, conversations are negotiations for closeness and seeking out support and confirmation. Let's look at a few examples of what Tannen has described.

Men frequently complain that women talk on and on about their problems. Women, however, criticize men for not listening. What's happening is that when a man hears a woman talking about a problem, he frequently asserts his desire for independence and control by offering solutions. Many women, in contrast, view conversing about a problem as a way to promote closeness. The woman talks about a problem to gain support and connection, not to get the male's advice.

Here's another example: Men are often more direct than women in conversation. A man might say, "I think you're wrong on that point." A woman might say, "Have you looked at the marketing department's research report on that issue?" The implication in the woman's comment is that the report will point out the error. Men frequently misread women's indirectness as "covert" or "sneaky," but women aren't as concerned as men with the status and one-upmanship that directness often creates.

Finally, men often criticize women for seeming to apologize all the time. Men tend to see the phrase "I'm sorry" as a sign of weakness because they interpret the phrase to mean the woman is accepting blame, when he may know she's not to blame. The woman also knows she's not at fault. Yet she's typically using "I'm sorry" to express regret: "I know you must feel bad about this and I do, too."

Because effective communication among the sexes is important in *all* organizations, how can we manage these differences in communication styles? To keep gender differences from becoming persistent barriers to effective communication requires acceptance, understanding, and a commitment to communicate adaptively with each other. Both men and women need to acknowledge that there are differences in communication styles, that one style isn't better than the other, and that it takes real effort to "talk" with each other successfully.

••• **information
overload**
The information we have to
work with exceeds our
processing capacity.

possible to fully read and respond to each and every one of those messages without facing **information overload**—when the information we have to work with exceeds our processing capacity. Today's typical executive frequently complains of information overload. Statistics show that the average business e-mail user devotes 90 minutes a day to "organizing" e-mail. Other statistics show that employees send and receive an average of 204 e-mail messages every day.[10] The demands of keeping up with e-mail, phone calls, faxes, meetings, and professional reading create an onslaught of data that is nearly impossible to process and assimilate. What happens when individuals have more information than they can sort and use? They tend to select out, ignore, pass over, or forget information. Or, they may put off further processing until the overload situation is over. Regardless, the result is lost information and less effective communication.

Defensiveness When people feel that they're being threatened, they tend to react in ways that reduce their ability to achieve mutual understanding. That is, they become defensive—engaging in behaviors such as verbally attacking others, making sarcastic remarks, being overly judgmental, and questioning others' motives.[11] When individuals interpret another's message as threatening, they often respond in ways that hinder effective communication.

Language Words mean different things to different people. Age, education, and cultural background are three of the more obvious variables that influence the language a person uses and the definitions he or she gives to words. Author/journalist William F. Buckley Jr., and rap artist Nelly both speak English. But the language each uses is vastly different.

●●● **jargon**
Specialized terminology or technical language that members of a group use to communicate among themselves.

In an organization, employees typically come from diverse backgrounds (think back to our chapter-opening "Manager's Dilemma") and have different patterns of speech. Even employees who work for the same organization but in different departments often have different **jargon**—specialized terminology or technical language that members of a group use to communicate among themselves. (▭▬ Go to the Web and check out Q & A 11.7.)

Keep in mind that while we may speak the same language, our use of that language is far from uniform. Senders tend to assume that the words and phrases they use mean the same to the receiver as they do to them. This, of course, is incorrect and creates communication barriers. Knowing how each of us modifies the language would help minimize those barriers.

National Culture As the chapter-opening "Manager's Dilemma" pointed out, communication differences can also arise from the different languages that individuals use to communicate and the national culture they're part of. Interpersonal communication isn't conducted the same way around the world. For example, let's compare countries that place a high value on individualism (such as the United States) with countries where the emphasis is on collectivism (such as Japan).[12]

In the United States, communication patterns tend to be oriented to the individual and clearly spelled out. U.S. managers rely heavily on memoranda, announcements, position papers, and other formal forms of communication to state their positions on issues. U.S. supervisors may hoard information in an attempt to make themselves look good and as a way of persuading their employees to accept decisions and plans. And for their own protection, lower-level employees also often engage in this practice.

In collectivist countries, such as Japan, there's more interaction for its own sake and a more informal manner of interpersonal contact. The Japanese manager, in contrast to the U.S. manager, engages in extensive verbal consultation with subordinates over an issue first, and draws up a formal document later to outline the agreement that was made. The Japanese value decisions by consensus, and open communication is an inherent part of the work setting. Also, face-to-face communication is encouraged.

Cultural differences can affect the way a manager chooses to communicate. And these differences undoubtedly can be a barrier to effective communication if not recognized and taken into consideration.

Overcoming the Barriers

On average, an individual must hear new information seven times before he or she truly understands.[13] In light of this fact and the barriers to communication, what can managers do to overcome these barriers? The following suggestions should help make your interpersonal communication more effective.

Use Feedback Many communication problems can be directly attributed to misunderstanding and inaccuracies. These problems are less likely to occur if the manager uses the feedback loop in the communication process, either verbally or nonverbally.

If a manager asks a receiver, "Did you understand what I said?" the response represents feedback. Good feedback should include more than yes-and-no answers. The manager can ask a set of questions about a message to determine whether or not the message was received and understood as intended. Better yet, the manager can ask the receiver to restate the message in his or her own words. If the manager hears what was intended, understanding and accuracy should improve. Feedback includes subtler methods than directly asking questions or having the receiver summarize the message. General comments can give a manager a sense of the receiver's reaction to a message. (████ Go to the Web and check out S.A.L. #26—How Good Am I at Giving Feedback?)

Of course, feedback doesn't have to be conveyed in words. Actions *can* speak louder than words. A sales manager sends an e-mail to his or her staff describing a new monthly sales report that all sales representatives will need to complete. If some of them don't turn in the new report, the sales manager has received feedback. This feedback suggests that the sales manager needs to clarify further the initial communication. Similarly, when you're talking to people, you watch their eyes and look for other nonverbal clues to tell whether they're getting your message or not.

Simplify Language Because language can be a barrier, managers should choose words and structure their messages in ways that will make those messages clear and understandable to the receiver. Remember, effective communication is achieved when a message is both received and *understood*. Understanding is improved by simplifying the language used in relation to the audience intended. This means, for example, that a hospital administrator should always try to communicate in clear, easily understood terms and that the language used in messages to the surgical staff should be purposefully different from that used with office employees. Jargon can facilitate understanding when it's used within a group of those who know what it means, but it can cause many problems when used outside that group.

Listen Actively When someone talks, we hear. But too often we don't listen. Listening is an active search for meaning, whereas hearing is passive. In listening, two people are engaged in thinking: the sender *and* the receiver.

Many of us are poor listeners. (████ Go to the Web and check out S.A.L. #25—How Good Are My Listening Skills?) Why? Because it's difficult and usually more satisfying to be on the offensive. Listening, in fact, is often more tiring than talking. It demands intellectual effort. Unlike hearing, **active listening**, which is listening for full meaning without making premature judgments or interpretations, demands total concentration. The average person normally speaks at a rate of about 125 to 200 words per minute. However, the average listener can comprehend up to 400 words per minute.[14] The difference obviously leaves lots of idle time for the brain and opportunities for the mind to wander.

Active listening is enhanced by developing empathy with the sender—that is, by placing yourself in the sender's position. Because senders differ in attitudes, interests, needs, and expectations, empathy makes it easier to understand the actual content of a message. An empathetic listener reserves judgment on the message's content and carefully listens to what is being said. The goal is to improve your ability to receive the full meaning of a communication without having it distorted by premature judgments or interpretations. Other specific behaviors that active listeners demonstrate are listed in Exhibit 11–3. (████ Go to the Web and check out PRISM #11—Active Listening.)

• • **active listening**
Listening for full meaning without making premature judgments or interpretations.

Exhibit 11–3

Active Listening Behaviors

Source: Based on P.L. Hunsaker, *Training in Management Skills* (Upper Saddle River, NJ: Prentice Hall, 2001).

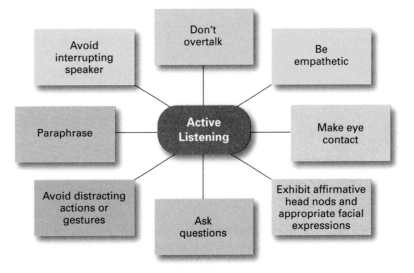

Constrain Emotions It would be naïve to assume that managers always communicate in a rational manner. We know that emotions can severely cloud and distort the transference of meaning. A manager who is emotionally upset over an issue is more likely to misconstrue incoming messages and fail to communicate his or her outgoing messages clearly and accurately. What can the manager do? The simplest answer is to refrain from communicating until he or she has regained composure.

Watch Nonverbal Cues If actions speak louder than words, then it's important to watch your actions to make sure they align with and reinforce the words that go along with them. The effective communicator watches his or her nonverbal cues to ensure that they convey the desired message.

● ● ● Learning Review

- Explain all the components of the communication process.
- List the communication methods managers might use.
- Discuss the criteria that help managers evaluate the various communication methods.
- Describe nonverbal communication and how it takes place.

- Explain the barriers to effective interpersonal communication.
- Discuss the ways to overcome the barriers.
- List the active listening behaviors.

ORGANIZATIONAL COMMUNICATION

An understanding of managerial communication isn't possible without looking at the fundamentals of organizational communication. In this section, we look at several important aspects of organizational communication including formal versus informal communication, the flow patterns of communication, and formal and informal communication networks.

Formal Versus Informal Communication

● ● ● **formal communication**
Communication that follows the official chain of command or is required to do one's job.

Communication within an organization is often described as formal or informal. **Formal communication** refers to communication that follows the official chain of command or is part of the communication required to do one's job. For example, when a manager asks an employee to complete a task, he or she is communicating formally. So is the employee who brings a problem to the attention of his or her manager. Any communication that takes place within prescribed organizational work arrangements would be classified as formal.

● ● ● **informal communication**
Communication that is not defined by the organization's structural hierarchy.

Informal communication is organizational communication that is not defined by the organization's structural hierarchy. When employees talk with each other in the lunch room, as they pass in hallways, or as they're working out at the company exercise facility, that's informal communication. Employees form friendships and communicate with each other. The informal communication system fulfills two purposes in organizations: (1) it permits employees to satisfy their need for social interaction, and (2) it can improve an organization's performance by creating alternative, and frequently faster and more efficient, channels of communication. (▬▬▬▬▭ Go to the Web and check out You're the Manager: Diversity in Action #1.)

Direction of Communication Flow

Organizational communication can flow downward, upward, laterally, or diagonally. Let's look at each.

● ● ● **downward communication**
Communication that flows downward from a manager to employees.

Downward Any communication that flows downward from a manager to employees is **downward communication**. Downward communication is used to inform, direct, coordinate, and evaluate employees. When managers assign goals to their employees,

When Paul and Peter Centenari pulled their cardboard box manufacturing company, Atlas, back from the brink of bankruptcy, they had a revelation. They decided that one key aspect of their new start would be opening the financial books of the firm to all 150 employees and discussing their significance at monthly meetings attended by the entire staff. Employees like Ranard Austin (pictured here) have been trained to understand Atlas's financial statements and now participate in decisions about everything from company policy to production-line improvements. For open-book management like this to work, the flow of downward communication has to be steady.

they're using downward communication. Managers are also using downward communication by providing employees with job descriptions, informing them of organizational policies and procedures, pointing out problems that need attention, or evaluating their performance. Downward communication can take place through any of the communication methods we described earlier.

Upward Communication Managers rely on their employees for information. Reports are given to managers to inform them of progress toward goals and any current problems. **Upward communication** is communication that flows upward from employees to managers. It keeps managers aware of how employees feel about their jobs, their co-workers, and the organization in general. Managers also rely on upward communication for ideas on how things can be improved. Some examples of upward communication include performance reports prepared by employees, suggestion boxes, employee attitude surveys, grievance procedures, manager–employee discussions, and informal group sessions in which employees have the opportunity to identify and discuss problems with their manager or even representatives of top-level management.

The extent of upward communication depends on the organizational culture. If managers have created a climate of trust and respect and use participative decision making or empowerment, there will be considerable upward communication as employ-

● ● ● **upward communication**
Communication that flows upward from employees to managers.

ees provide input to decisions. For example, FedEx CIO Robert Carter holds town hall meetings with his staff about every six weeks and sits down once a month with eight randomly selected employees to talk over issues and concerns. He has created an environment where employees want to share information and has found these communication encounters to be prime opportunities for finding out what's going on with his employees.[15] In a highly structured and authoritarian environment, however, upward communication still takes place, but will be limited in both style and content.

● ● ● **lateral communication**
Communication that takes place among any employees on the same organizational level.

Lateral Communication Communication that takes place among employees on the same organizational level is called **lateral communication**. In today's often chaotic and rapidly changing environment, horizontal communications are frequently needed to save time and facilitate coordination. Cross-functional teams, for instance, rely heavily on this form of communication interaction. However, it can create conflicts if employees don't keep their managers informed about decisions they've made or actions they've taken.

● ● ● **diagonal communication**
Communication that cuts across work areas and organizational levels.

Diagonal Communication **Diagonal communication** is communication that cuts across both work areas *and* organizational levels. When an analyst in the credit department communicates directly with a regional marketing manager—note the different department and different organizational level—about a customer problem, that's diagonal communication. In the interest of efficiency and speed, diagonal communication can be beneficial. And the increased use of e-mail facilitates diagonal communication. In many organizations, any employee can communicate by e-mail with any other employee, regardless of organizational work area or level. However, just as with lateral communication, diagonal communication has the potential to create problems if employees don't keep their managers informed.

Exhibit 11–4

**Three Common
Organizational
Communication Networks
and How They Rate on
Effectiveness Criteria**

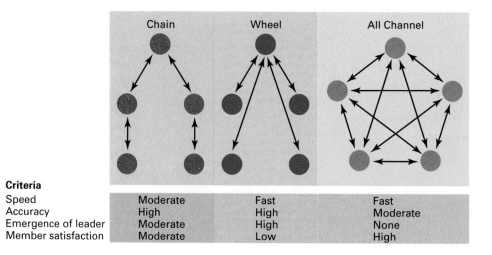

Criteria	Chain	Wheel	All Channel
Speed	Moderate	Fast	Fast
Accuracy	High	High	Moderate
Emergence of leader	Moderate	High	None
Member satisfaction	Moderate	Low	High

Organizational Communication Networks

The vertical and horizontal flows of organizational communication can be combined into a variety of patterns called **communication networks**. Exhibit 11–4 illustrates three common communication networks.

**●●● communication
networks**
The variety of patterns of
vertical and horizontal flows
of organizational
communication.

Types of Communication Networks In the *chain* network, communication flows according to the formal chain of command, both downward and upward. The *wheel* network represents communication flowing between a clearly identifiable and strong leader and others in a work group or team. The leader serves as the hub through whom all communication passes. Finally, in the *all-channel* network, communication flows freely among all members of a work team.

As a manager, which network should you use? The answer depends on your goal. Exhibit 11-4 also summarizes the effectiveness of the various networks according to four criteria: speed, accuracy, the probability that a leader will emerge, and the importance of member satisfaction. One observation is immediately apparent: No single network is best for all situations. If you're concerned with high member satisfaction, the all-channel network is best; if having a strong and identifiable leader is important, the wheel facilitates this; and if accuracy is most important, the chain and wheel networks work best.

●●● grapevine
The informal organizational
communication network.

The Grapevine We can't leave our discussion of communication networks without discussing the **grapevine**—the informal organizational communication network. The grapevine is active in almost every organization. Is it an important source of information? You bet! One survey reported that 75 percent of employees hear about matters first through rumors on the grapevine.[16]

What are the implications for managers? Certainly, the grapevine is an important part of any group or organization communication network and well worth understanding.[17] It identifies for managers those bewildering issues that employees consider important and anxiety producing. It acts as both a filter and a feedback mechanism, picking up on the issues employees consider relevant. More importantly, from a managerial point of view, it *is* possible to analyze what is happening on the grapevine—what information is being passed, how information seems to flow along the grapevine, and what individuals seem to be key conduits of information on the grapevine. By being aware of the grapevine's flow and patterns, managers can stay on top of issues that concern employees, and, in turn, can use the grapevine to disseminate important information. (▮◻▮▮▮ Go to the Web and check out Q & A 11.5.) Since the grapevine can't be eliminated, managers should "manage" it as an important information network.

Rumors that flow along the grapevine also can never be eliminated entirely. What managers can do, however, is minimize the negative consequences of rumors by limiting their range and impact. How? By communicating openly, fully, and honestly with employees, particularly in situations where employees may not like proposed or actual managerial decisions or actions. (■■■■■■ Go to the Web and check out Q & A 11.9.) Open and honest communication with employees can impact the organization in various ways. A study of employee attitudes by Watson Wyatt Worldwide concluded that open communication had a significant positive impact on employee attitudes, but only one out of three employees surveyed rated their company as favorable in this area. But for those companies that scored high on communication, this study showed that total returns to shareholders were three times higher than at companies that had poor communication.[18]. (■■■■■□ Go to the Web and check out You're the Manager: Diversity in Action #2.)

●●●●Learning Review

- Contrast formal and informal communication.
- Explain how communication can flow in an organization.

- Describe the three common communication networks.
- Discuss how managers should handle the grapevine.

UNDERSTANDING INFORMATION TECHNOLOGY

Technology is changing the way we live and work. Take the following four examples: Japanese employees and managers, housewives, and teens use wireless interactive Web phones to send e-mail, surf the Web, swap photos, and play computer games. At Postnet, the Swedish postal service's Internet subsidiary, employees work at tables with electrical and data-connection cables to plug in their laptop computers. Postnet's CEO spends her days walking around the office carrying her mobile phone which is connected to the postal system's main switchboard. Over 75 percent of IBM's 355,000 employees regularly use instant messaging software for communicating and for workplace collaboration. And at ChevronTexaco's worldwide headquarters in San Francisco, employees often meet to share information and to exchange ideas in "visualization centers" where data and graphics can be displayed on enormous screens.[19]

The world of communication isn't what it used to be! Managers are challenged to keep their organizations functioning smoothly while continually improving work operations *and* staying competitive even though both the organization and the environment are changing rapidly. Although changing technology has been a significant source of the environmental uncertainty facing organizations, these same technological advances have enabled managers to coordinate the work efforts of employees in ways that can lead to increased efficiency and effectiveness. Information technology now touches every aspect of almost every company's business. The implications for the ways managers communicate are profound. (■■■■■■ Go to the Web and check out Q & A 11.10.)

How Technology Affects Managerial Communication

Technology, and more specifically information technology, has radically changed the way organizational members communicate. For example, it has significantly improved a manager's ability to monitor individual or team performance, it has allowed employees to have more complete information to make faster decisions, and it has provided employees more opportunities to collaborate and share information. In addition, information technology has made it possible for people in organizations to be fully accessible, any time, regardless of where they are. Employees don't have to be at their desks with their computers on to communicate with others in the organization. Two developments in information technology seem to be having the most significant impact on current managerial communication: networked computer systems and wireless capabilities.

Pogo.com reported that in a single month over 1 million people at work visited its game site and the *average* workplace player spent more than 2 hours and 34 minutes per visit glued to a Pogo.com game. Funny stories, jokes, and pictures make their way from one employee's e-mail inbox to another's, to another's, and so forth. An elf bowling game sent by e-mail was a favorite diversion during the holiday season.

Although these may seem like fun and harmless activities, it's estimated that such Internet distractions cost businesses over $54 billion annually. While there's a high dollar cost associated with using the Internet at work for other than business reasons, is there a psychological benefit to be gained by letting employees do something to relieve the stress of pressure-packed jobs? What are the ethical issues associated with widely available Internet access at work for both employees and for organizations?[20]

Networked Computer Systems In a networked computer system, an organization links its computers creating an organizational network. Organizational members can then communicate with each other and tap into information whether they're down the hall, across town, or halfway across the world. Although we won't get into the mechanics of how a network system works, we will address some of its communication applications including e-mail, instant messaging, voice mail, fax, electronic data interchange, teleconferencing and videoconferencing, and intranets and extranets.

E-mail, the instantaneous transmission of written messages on linked computers, is a quick and convenient way for organizational members to share information and communicate.

Some organizational members who find e-mail slow and cumbersome are using **instant messaging (IM)**. This is interactive real-time communication that takes place among computer users who are logged onto the computer network at the same time. IM first became popular among teens and preteens who wanted to communicate online with their friends. Now, it's moving to the workplace. With IM, there's no waiting for a colleague to read e-mail. Whatever information needs to be communicated can be done so instantaneously. However, there are a couple of drawbacks to instant messaging. It requires users to be logged on to the organization's computer network at the same time. This leaves the network open to security breaches. Also, the most popular versions of IM software are currently incompatible with each other.[21] However, as new versions of IM software are created, these drawbacks are likely to be addressed.

A **voice-mail** system digitizes a spoken message, transmits it over the network, and stores the message for the receiver to retrieve later.[22] Voice mail allows information to be transmitted even though a receiver may not be physically present to take the information. Receivers can choose to save the message for future use, delete it, or route it to other parties.

Fax machines allow the transmission of documents containing both text and graphics over ordinary telephone lines. A sending fax machine scans and digitizes the document. A receiving fax machine reads the scanned information and reproduces it in hard copy form. Information that is best viewed in printed form can be easily and quickly shared by organizational members.

Electronic data interchange (EDI) is a way for organizations to exchange standard business transaction documents, such as invoices or purchase orders, using direct computer-to-computer networks. Organizations often use EDI with vendors, suppliers, and customers because it saves time and money. How? Information on transactions is transmitted from one organization's computer system to another through a telecommunications network. The printing and handling of paper documents at one organization are eliminated as is the inputting of data at the other organization.

e-mail
The instantaneous transmission of written messages on computers that are linked together.

instant messaging (IM)
Interactive real-time communication that takes place among computer users logged on the computer network at the same time.

voice mail
A communication system that digitizes a spoken message, transmits it over a network, and stores the message on disk for the receiver to retrieve later.

fax
Communication through machines that allow the transmission of documents containing both text and graphics over ordinary telephone lines.

electronic data interchange (EDI)
A way for organizations to exchange standard business transaction documents using direct computer-to-computer networks.

Meetings—one-on-one, team, divisional, or organization-wide—have always been one way to share information. The limitations of technology used to dictate that meetings take place among people in the same physical location, but that's no longer the case! **Teleconferencing** allows a group of people to confer simultaneously using telephone or e-mail group communications software. If meeting participants can see each other over video screens, the simultaneous conference is called **videoconferencing**. Work groups, large and small, that might be in different locations, can use these communication network tools to collaborate and share information. During the SARS virus outbreak, several companies used videoconferencing to communicate with customers and employees. Although videoconferencing allowed communication to continue, it still lacked that personal touch. For instance, Dale Fuller, CEO of Borland, who was scheduled to go to China to talk with officials about economic development and possible software sales, wondered whether not being there for the face-to-face meetings and having to communicate via videoconference instead would result in missed sales.[23]

Networked computer systems have allowed the development of organizational intranets and extranets. An **intranet** is an organizational communication network that uses Internet technology and is accessible only by employees. Many organizations are using intranets as ways for employees to share information and collaborate on documents and projects from different locations. For example, Buckman Laboratory, a manufacturer of specialty chemicals based in Memphis, Tennessee, uses an intranet so employees can easily find information about products, markets, and customers. Employees contribute information to and get information from this knowledge network known as K'Netix®. An **extranet** is an organizational communication network that uses Internet technology and allows authorized users inside the organization to communicate with certain outsiders such as customers or vendors. For instance, Harley-Davidson has developed an extranet that allows faster and more convenient communications with dealers.

Technology is the ruling force behind communication within British Petroleum's Digital Business division, where John Leggate is group vice president. Says Leggate, "We talk about 'living on the Web,' so that everything you want to see about the company can be found with a Web browser. We all have BlackBerrys, and all our offices have 802.11b (wireless connections). That conversation, however, is not about technology, but about being more productive... about being in touch with where things are going."

● ● ● **teleconferencing**
Communication system that allows a group of people to confer simultaneously using telephone or e-mail group communications software.

● ● ● **videoconferencing**
A simultaneous communication conference where participants can see each other.

● ● ● **intranet**
An organizational communication network that uses Internet technology and is accessible only by organizational employees.

● ● ● **extranet**
An organizational communication network that uses Internet technology and allows authorized users inside the organization to communicate with certain outsiders.

Wireless Capabilities At Seattle-based Starbucks Corporation, 600 district managers have been outfitted with mobile technology, allowing them to spend more time in the company's stores. Anne Saunders, vice president of Starbucks Interactive, says, "These are the most important people in the company. Each has between 8 and 10 stores that he or she services. And while their primary job is outside of the office—and in those stores—they still need to be connected."[24] While the communication possibilities for a manager in a networked world are exciting, the real potential is just beginning! Networked computer systems require organizations (and employees) to be connected by wires. Wireless communication depends on signals sent through air or space without any physical connection, using things such as microwave signals, satellites, radio waves and radio antennas, or infrared light rays. The latest twist in wireless capability is Internet access made possible by "hot spots," which are simply locations where users gain wireless access to the Internet. At the end of 2002 in the United States alone, there were about 4,000 of these hot spots, and projections for their number over the next couple of years ranged from 30,000 to the hundreds of thousands.[25] Since nearly 21 million U.S. workers are on the move on any given day, wireless smart phones, notebook computers, and other pocket communication devices have spawned a whole new way for managers to "keep in touch." And the number of worldwide mobile users keeps increasing. In the Asia-Pacific region alone, there are over 206 million mobile users.[26] Employees don't have to be at their desks with their phones or computers wired in and turned on to communicate with others in the organization. As technology continues to improve in this area, we'll see more and more organizational members using wireless communication as a way to collaborate and share information.

Technology need not always reduce face-to-face communication. To make contact easier between employees at its call center and in its information systems department, ASB, a New Zealand bank, adopted an open layout encompassing five areas on three different floors. There's a landscaped park area in the center, a café, a minigolf green, a TV room, and a barbecue area, all of which help bring people together. Since moving into the new design, bank managers have noted that the volume of interdepartmental e-mails has dropped, indicating that people are communicating in person more.

How Information Technology Affects Organizations

Employees—working in teams or as individuals—need information to make decisions and do their work. After describing the communications capabilities managers have at their disposal, it's clear that technology *can* significantly affect the way that organizational members communicate, share information, and do their work.

Communication and the exchange of information among organizational members are no longer constrained by geography or time. Collaborative work efforts among widely dispersed individuals and teams, sharing of information, and integration of decisions and work throughout an entire organization have the potential to increase organizational efficiency and effectiveness. And while the economic benefits of information technology are obvious, managers must not forget to address the psychological drawbacks.[27] For instance, what is the psychological cost of an employee always being accessible? Will there be increased pressure for employees to "check in" even during their off hours? How important is it for employees to separate their work lives and their personal lives? While there are no easy answers to these questions, these are issues that managers will have to face. In the next section, we're going to look at other important communication issues that managers in today's organizations must face.

● ● ●● Learning Review

- Describe how technology affects managerial communication.
- Define e-mail, instant messaging, voice mail, fax, EDI, teleconferencing, videoconferencing, intranet, and extranet.

- Explain how information technology affects organizations.

COMMUNICATION ISSUES IN TODAY'S ORGANIZATIONS

"Pulse lunches." That's what managers at Citibank's offices throughout Malaysia used to address pressing problems with declining customer loyalty and staff morale and increased employee turnover. By connecting with employees and listening to their concerns—that is, taking their "pulse"—during informal lunch settings, managers were able to make changes that boosted both customer loyalty and employee morale by over 50 percent and reduced employee turnover to nearly zero.[28]

Being an effective communicator in today's organizations means being connected—most importantly to employees and customers, but actually to any of the organization's stakeholders. In this section, we want to examine four communication issues that are of particular significance to today's managers, including managing Internet gripe sites, managing the organization's knowledge resources, communicating with customers, and using politically correct communication.

Managing Internet Gripe Sites

"Upper management was clueless." "I have never seen a finer example of the 'upward failure' model." "I saw people cry at work regularly." These were just a few of the messages posted anonymously on a discussion board at Vault.com by individuals identifying themselves as employees of Agency.com. After logging on and reading some of the gripes, Agency's co-founder and former CEO Kyle Shannon e-mailed his employees saying, "I can assure you that we take the messages on these boards very seriously." He apologized, acknowledged the company's growing pains, and promised he would "listen to the issues and address them as quickly as possible."[29]

In addition to employee gripe sites, other Internet gripe sites feature customers' complaints. Although our focus isn't on the customer gripe sites, many of them criticize organizations for alleged shortcomings such as lousy service or unreasonable policies—information that managers should make note of and evaluate as to what action needs to be taken.

A manager's first reaction to these public forum complaints about organizational decisions or actions is likely to be anger or denial. Yet, managers shouldn't be so fast to condemn these gripe sites. Instead, they should view them as a source of information. What can be learned from the information—accurate or inaccurate—that's posted on these sites?

A recent study of employee Internet gripe sites provided a "unique insight into the expression of employee and public grievances about companies."[30] The researchers concluded that company managers have been slow to recognize the value of this resource. What value would these sites have? In monitoring them, managers can instantly uncover employees' "hot-button" issues. As employees vent their frustration over perceived injustices, managers have the opportunity to tap into what they are feeling, even if employees' interpretations of situations may be inaccurate or incomplete. In addition, it's also a way for a manager to judge the mood of the workforce, especially in large, geographically dispersed organizations. In these organizations where employees may not have easy access to upper-level managers to discuss issues and concerns, the Internet gripe site can be viewed as another means of upward communication.

So what can managers do to "manage" these gripe sites? First, as we just discussed, recognize them as a source of valuable information. Then, just as he or she would do with information received in more traditional ways, a manager can either ignore it or respond to it. Some possible responses might include posting messages on the gripe site to clarify misinformation or taking actions to correct whatever problems have been written about. In addition, managers might set up an anonymous *internal* forum such as an intranet and encourage employees to post gripes there, rather than on the public Internet. Finally, managers should continue to monitor the Web sites. By keeping their fingers on the pulse of concerns important to employees, they can choose the best course of action.

Managing the Organization's Knowledge Resources

Kara Johnson is a materials expert at product design firm IDEO. To make finding the right materials easier, she's building a master library of samples linked to a database that explains their properties and manufacturing processes.[31] What Johnson is doing is managing knowledge and making it easier for others at IDEO to "learn" and benefit from her knowledge. That's what today's managers need to do with the organization's knowledge resources—make it easy for employees to communicate and share their

Tampa Bay head coach John Gruden is among the NFL coaches who have begun to move their strategizing and play making into the digital age. Although he still prefers an outdated Mac program for diagramming plays, Gruden has come a long way. He started out as a computer-phobic assistant coach for the San Francisco 49ers where he learned how to use SuperPaint 1.0, still his favorite tool, and later began using Microsoft Word for keeping notes about players, strategy, and coaching techniques. His files are only a couple of mouse clicks away, and with them he can recall every play he has ever called. Add to that an Avid video workstation that can break game tapes down into catalogs by type of play, and you have the technological basis for the painstaking preparation that can help a team be successful.

knowledge so they can learn from each other ways to do their jobs more effectively and efficiently. One way organizations can do this is to build online information databases that employees can access. For example, William Wrigley Jr. Co., recently launched an interactive Web site that allows sales agents to access marketing data and other product information. The sales agents can question company experts about products or search an online knowledge bank. In its first year, Wrigley estimates that the site has cut the research time of the sales force by 15,000 hours and made them more efficient and effective.[32] This is one example of how managers can use communication tools to manage this valuable organizational resource called knowledge.

• • • communities of practice
Groups of people who share a concern, a set of problems, or a passion about a topic, and who deepen their knowledge and expertise in that area by interacting on an ongoing basis.

In addition to online information databases for sharing knowledge, some knowledge management experts suggest that organizations create **communities of practice**, which are "groups of people who share a concern, a set of problems, or a passion about a topic, and who deepen their knowledge and expertise in that area by interacting on an ongoing basis."[33] The keys to this concept are that the group must actually meet in some fashion on a regular basis and use its information exchanges to improve in some way. For example, repair technicians at Xerox tell "war stories" to communicate their experiences and to help others solve difficult problems with repairing machines.[34] This isn't to say that communities of practice don't face challenges. They do. For instance, in large global organizations, keeping communities of practice going takes additional effort. To make these communities of practice work, it's important to maintain strong human interactions through communication. Interactive Web sites, e-mail, and video-conferencing are essential communication tools. In addition, these groups face the same communication problems that individuals face—filtering, emotions, defensiveness, overdocumentation, and so forth. However, groups can resolve these issues by focusing on the same suggestions we discussed earlier: using feedback, simplifying language, listening actively, constraining emotions, and watching for nonverbal cues.

The Role of Communication in Customer Service

You've been a customer many times; in fact, you probably find yourself in a customer service encounter several times a day. So what does this have to do with communication? As it turns out, a lot! *What* communication takes place and *how* it takes place can have a significant impact on a customer's satisfaction with the service and the likelihood of being a repeat customer. Managers in service organizations need to make sure that employees who interact with customers are communicating appropriately and effectively with those customers. How? By first recognizing the three components in any service delivery process: the customer, the service organization, and the individual service provider.[35] Each plays a role in whether or not communication is working. Obviously, managers don't have a lot of control over what or how the customer communicates, but they can influence the other two.

An organization with a strong service culture already values taking care of customers—finding out what their needs are, meeting those needs, and following up to make sure that their needs were met satisfactorily. Each of these activities involves communication, whether face-to-face, by phone or e-mail, or through other channels. In addition, communication is part of the specific customer service strategies the organization pursues. One strategy that many service organizations use is personalization. For instance, at Ritz-Carlton Hotels, customers are provided with more than a clean bed and room. Customers who have stayed at a location previously and indicated that certain items are important to them—such as extra pillows, hot chocolate, or a certain brand of shampoo—will find those items waiting in their room at arrival. The hotel's database allows service to be personalized to customers' expectations. In addition, all employees are asked to communicate information related to service provision. For instance, if a room attendant overhears guests talking about celebrating an anniversary, he or she is supposed to relay the information so something special can be done.[36] Communication plays an important role in the hotel's customer personalization strategy.

Communication also is important to the individual service provider or contact employee. The quality of the interpersonal interaction between the customer and that contact employee does influence customer satisfaction.[37] That's especially true when the service encounter isn't up to expectations. People on the front line involved with those "critical service encounters" are often the first to hear about or notice service failures or breakdowns. They must decide *how* and *what* to communicate during these instances. Their ability to listen actively and communicate appropriately with the customer goes a long way in whether or not the situation is resolved to the customer's satisfaction or spirals out of control. Another important communication concern for the individual service provider is making sure that he or she has the information needed to deal with customers efficiently and effectively. If the service provider doesn't personally have the information, there should be some way to get the information easily and promptly.[38]

"Politically Correct" Communication

Sears tells its employees to use phrases such as "person with a disability" instead of "disabled person" when writing or speaking about people with disabilities. It also suggests that when talking with a customer in a wheelchair for more than few minutes, employees place themselves at the customer's eye level by sitting down to make a more

Becoming a Manager

- ◆ *Practice being a good communicator—as a sender and a listener.*
- ◆ *When preparing to communicate, think about the most appropriate channel for your communication and why it may or may not be the most appropriate.*
- ◆ *Pay attention to your and others' nonverbal communication. Learn to notice the cues.*
- ◆ *Complete the Skill-Building Module on Active Listening found on p. 517.*
- ◆ *Go to the Web and complete the following exercises from the Self-Assessment Library (S.A.L.) on R.O.L.L.S.: #24—What's My Face-to-Face Communication Style?, #25—How Good Are My Listening Skills?, and #26—How Good Am I at Giving Feedback?*

comfortable atmosphere for everyone.[39] These suggestions, provided in an employee brochure that discusses assisting customers with disabilities, reflect the importance of politically correct communication. How you communicate with someone who isn't like you, what terms you use in addressing a customer, or what words you use to describe a colleague who is wheelchair-bound can mean the difference between losing a client, an employee, a lawsuit, a harassment claim, or a job.[40]

Most of us are acutely aware of how our vocabulary has been modified to reflect political correctness. For instance, most of us refrain from using words like *handicapped*, *blind*, and *elderly* and use instead terms like *physically challenged*, *visually impaired*, or *senior*. We must be sensitive to others' feelings. Certain words can and do stereotype, intimidate, and insult individuals. With an increasingly diverse workforce, we must be sensitive to how words might offend others. While it's complicating our vocabulary and making it more difficult for people to communicate, it is something managers can't ignore.

Words are the primary means by which people communicate. When we eliminate words from use because they're politically incorrect, we reduce our options for conveying messages in the clearest and most accurate form. For the most part, the larger the vocabulary used by a sender and a receiver, the greater the opportunity to accurately transmit messages. By removing certain words from our vocabulary, we make it harder to communicate accurately. When we further replace these words with new ones whose meanings are less well understood, we've reduced the likelihood that our messages will be received as we had intended them.

We must be sensitive to how our choice of words might offend others. But we need to acknowledge that politically correct language restricts communication clarity. Nothing suggests that this increased communication ambiguity is likely to be reduced anytime soon. This is just another communication challenge for managers.

● ● ● Learning Review

- Discuss how Internet gripe sites affect communication.

- Explain how organizations can manage knowledge.

- Explain why communicating with customers is an important managerial issue.

- Describe how political correctness is affecting communication.

Managers **Respond** to a **Manager's** Dilemma

····John Emerman
Owner, The Stone Oven Bakery, Cleveland, Ohio

As a bakery owner myself, I am well aware of the importance of clear communication with my employees. My employees have a diverse background in terms of culture, education, and their ability to assimilate information. Even though it is often easier to express ideas verbally, I have found that it is essential to use written communication for two reasons. First, it is virtually impossible to gather employees together at a single meeting. Second, my employees seem to absorb information more easily and take it more seriously when it is written. Written communication also allows me to be more specific about what I'm trying to express. Although written memos have helped me, it's important to follow up with your audience to make sure they get it. I also have one or two workers proofread any written communication to make sure it's clear and that my tone is right.

Chuck Pick
Owner, Chuck's Parking Service, Inc., Sherman Oaks, California

I have always said that assuming anything in business can be very dangerous. Tom is very lucky that in seven years he hasn't had any major employee-related issues. Tom needs to do away with his policy of open book management, which, although very thoughtful, is counterproductive. Instead of drawing his employees nearer to the business, he is probably pushing them farther away. Showing a low-wage-earning employee a multimillion-dollar balance sheet does not instill good feelings. Tom should spend more time getting to know his workforce. As an accessible and available manager, he should be more involved in the hiring process. He should identify each employee's communication strengths and weaknesses and use his more communicative employees to paraphrase the key points so their co-workers understand. The feedback he receives will let him know the exact level of understanding, thus improving the overall effectiveness of the communication.

Learning Summary

After reading and studying this chapter, you should be able to:

- Differentiate between interpersonal and organizational communication.
- Discuss the functions of communication.
- Explain all the components of the communication process.
- List the communication methods managers might use.
- Describe nonverbal communication and how it takes place.
- Explain the barriers to effective interpersonal communication and how to overcome them.
- Explain how communication can flow in an organization.
- Describe the three common communication networks.

- Discuss how managers should handle the grapevine.
- Describe how technology affects managerial communication.
- Define e-mail, instant messaging, voice mail, fax, EDI, teleconferencing, videoconferencing, intranet, and extranet.
- Explain how information technology affects organizations.
- Discuss how Internet employee gripe sites affect communication.
- Explain how organizations can manage knowledge.
- Explain why communicating with customers is an important managerial issue.
- Explain how political correctness is affecting communication.

Thinking About Management Issues

1. Why isn't effective communication synonymous with *agreement*?

2. Which do you think is more important for the manager: speaking accurately or listening actively? Why?

3. "Ineffective communication is the fault of the sender." Do you agree or disagree with this statement? Discuss.

4. How might managers use the grapevine for their benefit?

5. Is information technology helping managers to be more effective and efficient? Explain your answer.

Working Together: Team-Based Exercise

Form groups of five or six individuals. Each group should choose one person to remain in the room while the other members of each group leave the room. Your instructor will give you directions on what happens next.

After the exercise is over, each group should discuss where communication errors (both in sending and receiving information) occurred. You should also discuss what you learned about managerial communication from this exercise. Be prepared to share your important ideas with the class.

Ethical Dilemma Exercise

More and more organizational members are initiating messages through corporate blogs. Officially known as Weblogs, these are Web sites where an individual posts ideas, comments on contemporary issues, and offers other musings. Because anyone can visit the site and read the messages, companies have become concerned about messages that include sensitive data, criticize managers or competitors, use inflammatory language, or contain misrepresentations. Companies are also worried about the reaction of stakeholders who disagree with or are offended by blog postings. Corporate blogs are becoming so popular that companies such as Groove Networks have developed blog policies (see *www.ozzie.net/blog/2002/08/24.html*). In fact, CNN insisted that a reporter suspend a blog where he posted his conflicting thoughts about a career as a war correspondent, even though the reporter had a disclaimer saying the blog was "not affiliated with, endorsed by, or funded by CNN."

But what happens when a CEO sets up a blog? Alan Meckler, the CEO of Jupitermedia, started a blog as "a

diary of the ups and downs of trying to do something monumental"—create a new industry-wide technology conference. This event put Jupitermedia squarely in competition with a well-established event known as Comdex. In early blog entries, Meckler talked bluntly about the competing conference's management. Based on legal advice (and negative feedback from a few conference exhibitors), he softened his tone in later entries. Although he still blogs, Meckler notes, "I'm not stirring the pot anymore, which isn't my nature."[41] What is the most ethical way to deal with a corporate blog, especially one by a senior manager?

Imagine that you're Jupitermedia's public relations director. The CEO has just posted a blog message saying your conference was more financially successful than the competing conference. Because neither company releases profitability details, you know this statement can't be verified. You don't want Jupitermedia to look bad; you also know that your CEO likes to express himself. Review

Exhibit 11–1 as you think about the ethical challenge posed by this blog communication and decide which of the following options to choose—and why.

Option A: Meet with the CEO, explain your concerns, and suggest that he post a message stating honestly that he changed his message on the advice of the public relations department.

Option B: Leave the message but issue a press release reminding the public that the CEO's blog contains personal thoughts and does not represent the official views of Jupitermedia.

Option C: Contact your company's lawyers and ask them to force your CEO to remove this message from his blog before any conference exhibitors complain.

Case Application

Voyant Technologies

This is a story about a hallway conversation that cost $200,000 and four months of wasted effort. Talk about a communication blunder.

After a chance meeting in a headquarters hallway with his chief engineer, Bill Ernstrom, CEO of Voyant Technologies (a company that makes teleconferencing equipment), decided to have his engineers add streaming media to the company's flagship product. Now, Ernstrom wishes he had never had that conversation, especially after a product manager who had learned of the project produced a marketing report that showed most customers had little interest in streaming anything. That incident underscored a communication challenge that had been ignored for too long: The top engineers weren't listening to the product managers—and vice versa. Ernstrom says, "We got a long way down the road, built the code, got the engineers excited. Then we found out that we'd sell about ten units."

The communication barriers experienced by Voyant, based in Westminster, Colorado, aren't all that unusual in high-tech organizations. The cultural and language gap between computer "geeks" and the more market/business-oriented colleagues happens time and time again. In these types of organizations, the early stages of a new project belong to the engineers. It's crucial to get the technology right, but what they produce is "often elegant technology that has no market, is too complicated, or doesn't match customers' expectations." Ernstrom's challenge was to get the two competing groups to collaborate. His solution involved structural and communications changes.

The first structural change Ernstrom made was to hire managers to lead each of the company's four product lines. But this change wasn't enough as the engineers felt that these individuals knew little about the company's culture and even less about technology. To help the situation, Ernstrom decided that another new position was needed—a chief product officer. The person he hired, John Guillaume, had a strong telecommunications background in both engineering and marketing. Guillaume's first move was to raise the profile of the four product managers by giving them visible tasks, such as writing product definitions and presenting marketing research. Then, Guillaume took a riskier step and asked two of the star engineers to lead product groups, which they did reluctantly. With the structural changes in place, Ernstrom was ready to try some changes in communication.

Among these changes is that now when an employee has an idea for a new product, he or she submits a proposal through the company intranet. A team of engineers and product managers and the executive team assess the proposal. There's a lot more interaction between the "geeks" and the "suits." If the proposal is given the go-ahead, managers determine what content will be delivered at what time and the engineers get bonuses for meeting those goals.

By themselves, these changes might have accomplished little, but together they've done a lot to close the gap. Ernstrom firmly believes that the company's customers are happier than ever. As one engineer put it, "We're building stuff that people use."

DISCUSSION QUESTIONS

1. What barriers to communication were evident at Voyant? What other communication barriers likely existed? Explain.

2. What suggestions presented in this chapter might Voyant's employees have used to overcome communication barriers?

3. Why were the structural changes important to the success of the communication changes?

4. Why do you think Ernstrom believes that the company's customers are happier than ever before? What role do you think communication plays?

Bill Ernstrom (center) and managers Jeremy DuPont (right) and Warren Baxley (left) of Voyant Technologies.

Sources: Information on company from Hoover's Online (*www.hoovers.com*), May 29, 2003; and S. Clifford, "How to Get the Geeks and the Suits to Play Nice," *Business 2.0,* May 2002, pp. 92–93.

• • • Learning Outline

Follow this Learning Outline as you read and study this chapter.

Why Human Resource Management Is Important; The HRM Process

- Explain how an organization's human resources can be a significant source of competitive advantage.
- List the eight activities necessary for staffing the organization and sustaining high employee performance.
- Discuss the environmental factors that most directly affect the HRM process.

Human Resource Planning; Recruitment/Decruitment; Selection; Orientation; Training

- Contrast job analysis, job description, and job specification.
- Discuss the major sources of potential job candidates.
- Describe the different selection devices and which work best for different jobs.
- Describe what a realistic job preview is and why it's important.
- Explain why orientation is so important.
- Describe the different types of training and how that training can be provided.

Employee Performance Management; Compensation/Benefits; Career Development

- Describe the different performance appraisal methods.
- Discuss the factors that influence employee compensation and benefits.
- Describe skill-based pay systems.
- Describe career development for today's employees.

Current Issues in Human Resource Management

- Explain how managers can manage downsizing.
- Discuss how managers can manage workforce diversity.
- Explain what sexual harassment is and what managers need to know about it.
- Describe how organizations are dealing with work–life balance issues.

12

Human Resource Management

A **Manager's** *Dilemma*

National Australia Bank Limited (NAB), an international financial services group, provides a comprehensive and integrated range of financial products and services through almost 2,000 banking centers and branches located in Australia, New Zealand, Ireland, and Great Britain.[1] At the end of 2002, NAB had total assets of $377 billion, almost 8 million banking customers, and more than 2.8 million wealth management

customers. In addition, it was the largest financial services institution (by market capitalization) listed on the Australian Stock Exchange and was one of the world's top 50 financial services companies by revenues. To maintain its competitiveness in attracting and retaining top-notch talent to staff its growing global business, however, NAB was going to have to be more innovative, especially in its human resource practices.

NAB states that its biggest strength is its people. "We value our people, what they do, and how they do it." The company says its ultimate goals are to develop great people, create a great place to work, and encourage and reward winning performance. And NAB demonstrates its commitment to employees by investing significantly in their training and development—more than $55 million during 2002 alone.

Brett Ellison (pictured), head of NAB's Global eBusiness initia-

tive, was recently looking for ways to further enhance the company's human resource management system and at the same time make the company more cost-efficient and productive. After spending months surveying best practices at companies throughout the United States and Europe, Brett concluded that NAB needed an employee portal—an internal company Web site that would support various HRM activities. After convincing management to invest $11 million in the portal, it was up and running after only 84 days. The portal supports more than 100 different applications ranging from employee directories and online manuals to training materials and benefits information. More than 18,000 of its Australian employees use it.

Now, NAB is ready to extend the employee portal to its New Zealand and European branches. Put yourself in Brett's position. How should he introduce this program to these employees?

What would *you* do **?**

The challenge facing Brett Ellison in introducing a new technology—an Internet-based employee portal—to a large group of employees reflects only a small aspect of the types of human resource management (HRM) challenges facing today's managers. If an organization doesn't take its HRM responsibilities seriously, work performance and goal accomplishment may suffer. The quality of an organization is, to a large degree, merely the sum of the quality of people it hires and keeps. Getting and keeping competent employees are critical to the success of every organization, whether the organization is just starting or has been in business for years. Therefore, part of every manager's job in the organizing function is human resource management. (◼◻◻◻ Go to the Web and check out Q & A 12.1.)

■ **Q & A**

Whenever you see this green square, go to the R.O.L.L.S. Web site (*www.prenhall.com/robbins*) to the Q & A, your 24/7 educational assistant. These video clips and written material presented by your authors address questions that we have found students frequently ask.

● ● ● **high-performance work practices**
Work practices that lead to both high individual and and high organizational performance.

WHY HUMAN RESOURCE MANAGEMENT IS IMPORTANT

"Our people are our most important asset." Many organizations use this phrase, or something close to it, to acknowledge the important role that employees play in organizational success. These organizations also recognize that *all* managers must engage in some human resource management activities—even in large ones that have a separate HRM department. These managers interview job candidates, orient new employees, and evaluate their employees' work performance.

Can HRM be an important strategic tool? *Can* it help establish an organization's sustainable competitive advantage? The answer to these questions seems to be yes. Various studies have concluded that an organization's human resources can be a significant source of competitive advantage.[2] And that's true for organizations around the world, not just U.S. firms. The Human Capital Index, a comprehensive global study of over 2,000 firms conducted by consulting firm Watson Wyatt Worldwide, concluded that people-oriented HR can be a true source of competitive advantage.[3]

Achieving competitive success through people requires a fundamental change in how managers think about their employees and how they view the work relationship. It involves working with and through people and seeing them as partners, not just as costs to be minimized or avoided. That's what organizations such as Southwest Airlines, The Container Store, and Timberland are doing. In addition to their potential importance as part of organizational strategy and their contribution to competitive advantage, an organization's HRM practices have been found to have a significant impact on organizational performance.[4] For instance, one study reported that significantly improving an organization's HRM practices could increase its market value by as much as 30 percent.[5] The term used to describe these practices that lead to such results is **high-performance work practices**. High-performance work practices lead to both high individual and high organizational performance. Exhibit 12–1 lists examples of high-performance work practices. The common thread in these practices seems to be a commitment to improving the knowledge, skills, and abilities of an organization's employees; increasing their motivation; reducing loafing on the job; and enhancing the retention of quality employees while encouraging low performers to leave.

Whether an organization chooses to implement high-performance work practices or not, there are certain HRM

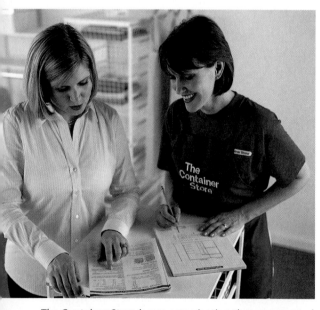

The Container Store is one organization that proves good human resource management can be a competitive advantage. With a corporate culture that strives to match employees' skills to the right job, focuses on talent rather than titles, and values "great" people as measurably more productive than merely "good" ones, this retailer of storage and organizing products has been on Fortune's list of the 100 best companies to work for four years in a row. According to the company Web site, "Customer service is The Container Store's core competency, so hiring people who are self-motivated and team-oriented with a passion for customer service is key."

Exhibit 12–1

Examples of High-Performance Work Practices

- Self-directed work teams
- Job rotation
- High levels of skills training
- Problem-solving groups
- Quality management procedures and processes
- Encouragement of innovative and creative behavior
- Extensive employee involvement and training

- Implementation of employee suggestions
- Contingent pay based on performance
- Coaching and mentoring
- Significant amounts of information sharing
- Use of employee attitude surveys
- Cross-functional integration
- Comprehensive employee recruitment and selection procedures

Sources: Based on M. Huselid, "The Impact of Human Resource Management Practices on Turnover, Productivity, and Corporate Financial Performance," *Academy of Management Journal,* June 1995, p. 635; and B. Becker and B. Gerhart, "The Impact of Human Resource Management on Organizational Performance: Progress and Prospects," *Academy of Management Journal,* August 1996, p. 785.

activities that must be completed in order to ensure that the organization has qualified people to perform the work that needs to be done—activities that comprise the human resource management process.

THE HUMAN RESOURCE MANAGEMENT PROCESS

••• human resource management process
Activities necessary for staffing the organization and sustaining high employee performance.

Exhibit 12–2 introduces the key components of an organization's **human resource management process**, which consists of eight activities necessary for staffing the organization and sustaining high employee performance. (■□■■■ Go to the Web and check out Q & A 12.2.) The first three activities ensure that competent employees are identified and selected; the next two activities involve providing employees with up-to-date knowledge and skills; and the final three activities entail making sure that the organization retains competent and high-performing employees who are capable of sustaining high performance.

Notice in Exhibit 12–2 that the entire HRM process is influenced by the external environment. We elaborated on the constraints that the environment puts on managers in Chapter 3, but let's briefly review those environmental factors that most

Exhibit 12–2   **The Human Resource Management Process**

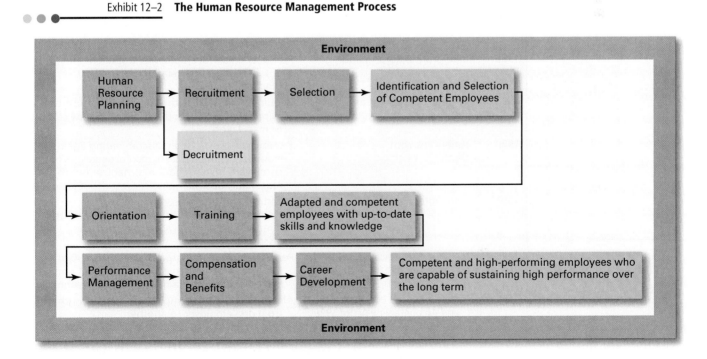

directly influence the HRM process—employee labor unions and governmental laws and regulations.

A **labor union** is an organization that represents workers and seeks to protect their interests through collective bargaining. (■□■■■ Go to the Web and check out Q & A 12.3.) In unionized organizations, many HRM decisions are regulated by the terms of collective agreements. These agreements usually define such things as recruitment sources; criteria for hiring, promotions, and layoffs; training eligibility; and disciplinary practices. Although only about 13.5 percent of the workforce in the United States is unionized, that percentage is higher in other countries. In Japan and Germany, respectively, 12.7 percent and 32.1 percent of the labor force belongs to a union. And in Mexico an estimated 20 percent of workers belong to a union.[6] Although labor unions can significantly affect an organization's HRM practices, no environmental constraint can match the influence of governmental laws and regulations, especially in North America.

The federal government has greatly expanded its influence over HRM by enacting a number of laws and regulations (see Exhibit 12–3 for examples). As a result, today's employers must ensure that equal employment opportunities exist for job applicants and current employees. Decisions regarding who will be hired, for instance, or which employees will be chosen for a management training program must be made without regard to race, sex, religion, age, color, national origin, or disability. Exceptions can occur only when special circumstances exist. For instance, a community fire depart-

Exhibit 12–3

●●●●—

**Major U.S. Federal Laws
and Regulations Related
to HRM**

Year	Law or Regulation	Description
1963	Equal Pay Act	Prohibits pay differences based on sex for equal work.
1964	Civil Rights Act, Title VII (amended in 1972)	Prohibits discrimination based on race, color, religion, national origin, or sex.
1967	Age Discrimination in Employment Act	Prohibits age discrimination against employees between 40 and 65 years of age.
1973	Vocational Rehabilitation Act	Prohibits discrimination on the basis of physical or mental disabilities.
1974	Privacy Act	Gives employees the legal right to examine personnel files and letters of reference concerning them.
1978	Mandatory Retirement Act	Prohibits the forced retirement of most employees before the age of 70; upper limit on age was removed in 1986.
1986	Immigration Reform and Control Act	Prohibits unlawful employment of aliens and unfair immigration-related employment practices.
1988	Worker Adjustment and Retraining Notification Act	Requires employers with 100 or more employees to provide 60 days notice before a facility closing or mass layoff.
1990	Americans with Disabilities Act	Prohibits employers from discriminating against individuals with physical or mental disabilities or the chronically ill: also requires organizations to reasonably accommodate these individuals.
1991	Civil Rights Act of 1991	Reaffirms and tightens prohibition of discrimination; permits individuals to sue for punitive damages in cases of intentional discrimination.
1993	Family and Medical Leave Act of 1993	Permits employees in organizations with 50 or more workers to take up to 12 weeks of unpaid leave each year for family or medical reasons.
1996	Health Insurance Portability and Accountability Act of 1996	Allows portability of employees' health insurance from one employer to another.

ment can deny employment to a firefighter applicant who is confined to a wheelchair, but if that same individual is applying for a desk job, such as fire department dispatcher, the disability cannot be used as a reason to deny employment. The issues involved, however, are rarely that clear-cut. For example, employment laws protect most employees whose religious beliefs require a specific style of dress—robes, long shirts, long hair, and the like. However, if the specific style of dress may be hazardous or unsafe in the work setting (e.g., when operating machinery), a company could refuse to hire a person who won't adopt a safer dress code.[7] (◼◻▬▬▬ Go to the Web and check out Q & A 12.4.)

● ● ● **affirmative action**
Programs that enhance the organizational status of members of protected groups.

Trying to balance the "shoulds and should-nots" of these laws often falls within the realm of **affirmative action**. Many organizations have affirmative action programs to ensure that decisions and practices enhance the employment, upgrading, and retention of members from protected groups such as minorities and females. That is, the organization not only refrains from discrimination but actively seeks to enhance the status of members from protected groups.

Managers are not completely free to choose whom they hire, promote, or fire. Although these laws and regulations have significantly helped to reduce employment discrimination and unfair employment practices, they have, at the same time, reduced managers' discretion over human resource decisions. (◼◻▬▬▬ Go to the Web and check out Q & A 12.5.) And because an increasing number of workplace lawsuits are targeting supervisors, as well as their organizations, managers need to be aware of what they can and cannot do by law.[8]

● ● ● Learning Review

- Explain how an organization's human resources can be a significant source of competitive advantage.
- List the eight activities necessary for staffing the organization and sustaining high employee performance.
- Discuss the environmental factors that most directly affect the HRM process.

HUMAN RESOURCE PLANNING

The United States will experience a shortage of 10 million workers over the next 10 years, according to the U.S. Bureau of Labor Statistics.[9] Aware of these predictions, managers at companies like John Deere Construction Equipment Company have plans in place to ensure that they have enough qualified technicians to fulfill their HR needs.[10]

● ● ● **human resource planning**
The process by which managers ensure that they have the right number and kinds of people in the right places, and at the right times, who are capable of effectively and efficiently performing assigned tasks.

Human resource planning is the process by which managers ensure that they have the right number and kinds of people in the right places, and at the right times, who are capable of effectively and efficiently performing assigned tasks. Through planning, organizations can avoid sudden talent shortages and surpluses.[11] HR planning can be condensed into two steps: (1) assessing current human resources and (2) assessing future human resource needs and developing a program to meet those future needs.

Current Assessment

Managers begin HR planning by reviewing the organization's current human resource status, usually through a *human resource inventory*. This information is taken from forms filled out by employees which include things such as name, education, training, prior employment, languages spoken, special capabilities, and specialized skills. The availability of sophisticated databases makes keeping and getting this information quite easy.

● ● ● **job analysis**
An assessment that defines jobs and the behaviors necessary to perform them.

Another part of the current assessment is the **job analysis,** which is an assessment that defines jobs and the behaviors necessary to perform them. For instance, what are the duties of a senior accountant who works for Boise Cascade? What minimal knowledge, skills, and abilities are necessary to be able to adequately perform this job? How do these requirements compare with those for a junior accountant or for an accounting manager? Information for a job analysis can be gathered by directly observing or filming individuals on the job, interviewing employees individually or in a group, having employees complete a structured questionnaire, having job "experts" (usually managers) identify a job's specific characteristics, or having employees record their daily activities in a diary or notebook.

With information from the job analysis, managers develop or revise job descriptions and job specifications. A **job description** is a written statement of what a jobholder does, how it is done, and why it is done. It typically describes job content, environment, and conditions of employment. A **job specification** states the minimum qualifications that a person must possess to perform a given job successfully. It identifies the knowledge, skills, and attitudes needed to do the job effectively. The job description and the job specification are both important documents when managers begin recruiting and selecting.

● ● ● **job description**
A written statement of what a jobholder does, how it is done, and why it is done.

● ● ● **job specification**
A statement of the minimum qualifications that a person must possess to perform a given job successfully.

Meeting Future Human Resource Needs

Future human resource needs are determined by the organization's mission, goals, and strategies. Demand for employees is a result of demand for the organization's products or services. On the basis of its estimate of total revenue, managers can attempt to establish the number and mix of employees needed to reach that revenue. In some cases, however, that situation may be reversed. When particular skills are necessary but in short supply, the availability of appropriate human resources determines revenues.

After they have assessed both current capabilities and future needs, managers are able to estimate HR shortages—both in number and in type—and to highlight areas in which the organization will be overstaffed. With this information, managers are ready to proceed to the next step in the HRM process.

RECRUITMENT AND DECRUITMENT

Once managers know their current human resource status and their future needs, they can begin to do something about any shortages or excesses. If one or more vacancies exist, they can use the information gathered through job analysis to guide them in **recruitment**—that is, the process of locating, identifying, and attracting capable applicants.[12] On the other hand, if HR planning shows a surplus of employees, management may want to reduce the organization's workforce through **decruitment**.[13]

● ● ● **recruitment**
The process of locating, identifying, and attracting capable applicants.

● ● ● **decruitment**
Techniques for reducing the labor supply within an organization.

Recruitment

At a job fair, a Southwest Airlines recruitment team distributed air sickness bags printed with the slogan "Sick of your job?"[14] A more conservative accounting firm, PricewaterhouseCoopers, recognized that attracting tomorrow's accountants who are mostly from the demographic group known as Generation Y meant using recruitment tools that appealed to them—in this case, an interactive Flash-animated Web site. (See illustraton on page 287.).[15] As these examples illustrate, potential job candidates can be found by using several sources.[16] Exhibit 12–4 explains these sources.

Web-based recruiting or e-recruiting has become a popular choice for organizations and applicants. For instance, when Yum! Brands, Inc., needed job applicants for management positions at its restaurants (Taco Bell, KFC, A&W, and Pizza Hut), they turned to online recruiter FlipDog.com. The results were so positive that they expanded their use of it.[17]

Although e-recruiting allows organizations to identify applicants cheaply and quickly, the quality of those applicants may not be as good as other sources. What recruiting sources have been found to produce superior candidates? The majority of

Exhibit 12–4

Major Sources of Potential Job Candidates

Source	Advantages	Disadvantages
Internet	Reaches large numbers of people; can get immediate feedback	Generates many unqualified candidates
Employee referrals	Knowledge about the organization provided by current employee; can generate strong candidates because a good referral reflects on the recommender	May not increase the diversity and mix of employees
Company Web site	Wide distribution; can be targeted to specific groups	Generates many unqualified candidates
College recruiting	Large centralized body of candidates	Limited to entry-level positions
Professional recruiting organizations	Good knowledge of industry challenges and requirements	Little commitment to specific organization

studies have found that employee referrals generally produce the best candidates.[18] The explanation is intuitively logical. First, applicants referred by current employees are prescreened by these employees. Because the recommenders know both the job and the person being recommended, they tend to refer applicants who are well qualified. Also, because current employees often feel that their reputation is at stake with a referral, they tend to refer others only when they're reasonably confident that the referral will not make them look bad.

Decruitment

The other approach to controlling labor supply is through decruitment, which is not a pleasant task for any manager. The decruitment options are shown in Exhibit 12–5 on page 288. Obviously people can be fired, but other choices may be more beneficial to the organization. Keep in mind that, regardless of the method used to reduce the number of employees in the organization, there is no easy way to do it, even though it may be absolutely necessary.

PricewaterhouseCoopers, one of the nation's largest accounting firms, has developed a Web site designed for recruiting a very specific group of people—the under-22 college market. Found at www.pwcglobal.com/lookhere, the interactive site with Flash animations includes videos of young interns and associates talking about their jobs and offers career advice and tips including topics like "Get Cool Assignments" and "Balance Work and Life." The firm is committed to recruiting in the college market right now, and its head of U.S. college recruiting says the Web was chosen as the medium for the recruiting campaign because for the target audience it is "radio, TV, newspaper, entertainment, and information all rolled up into one."

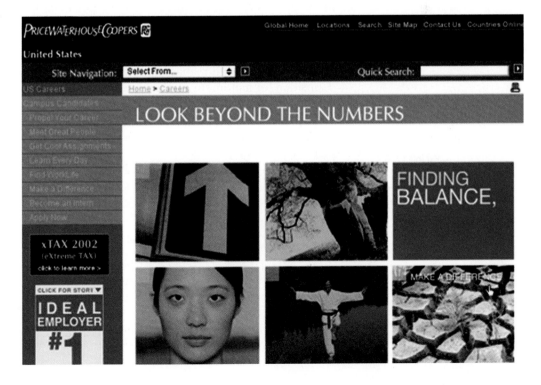

Exhibit 12–5

Decruitment Options

Option	Description
Firing	Permanent involuntary termination
Layoffs	Temporary involuntary termination; may last only a few days or extend to years
Attrition	Not filling openings created by voluntary resignations or normal retirements
Transfers	Moving employees either laterally or downward; usually does not reduce costs but can reduce intraorganizational supply-demand imbalances
Reduced workweeks	Having employees work fewer hours per week, share jobs, or perform their jobs on a part-time basis
Early retirements	Providing incentives to older and more senior employees for retiring before their normal retirement date
Job sharing	Having employees share one full-time position

SELECTION

selection process
The process of screening job applicants to ensure that the most appropriate candidates are hired.

Once the recruiting effort has developed a pool of candidates, the next step in the HRM process is to determine who is best qualified for the job. This step is called the **selection process**, the process of screening job applicants to ensure that the most appropriate candidates are hired. Errors in hiring can have far-reaching implications. The Athletic Department at the University of Notre Dame can attest to this. In December 2001, George O'Leary was hired as Notre Dame's football coach. Five days after he was hired, he resigned because of inaccuracies in his biographical materials—he lied about earning a master's degree in education from New York University and about lettering in football for three years at the University of New Hampshire. Not only was the hiring and subsequent resignation a personal embarrassment for O'Leary, it was an embarrassment for an organization that prides itself on integrity and credibility.[19]

What Is Selection?

Selection is an exercise in prediction. It seeks to predict which applicants will be successful if hired. Successful in this case means performing well on the criteria the organization uses to evaluate employees. In filling a sales position, for example, the selection process should be able to predict which applicants will generate a high volume of sales; for a position as a network administrator, it should predict which applicants will be able to effectively oversee and manage the organization's computer network.

Consider, for a moment, that any selection decision can result in four possible outcomes. As shown in Exhibit 12–6, two of these outcomes would be correct, and two would indicate errors.

Exhibit 12–6

Selection Decision Outcomes

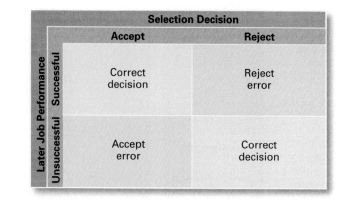

A decision is correct when the applicant was predicted to be successful and proved to be successful on the job, or when the applicant was predicted to be unsuccessful and would be so if hired. In the first case, we have successfully accepted; in the second case, we have successfully rejected.

Problems arise when errors are made in rejecting candidates who would have performed successfully on the job (reject errors) or accepting those who ultimately perform poorly (accept errors). These problems can be significant. Given today's HR laws and regulations, reject errors can cost more than the additional screening needed to find acceptable candidates. They can expose the organization to charges of discrimination, especially if applicants from protected groups are disproportionately rejected. The costs of accept errors include the cost of training the employee, the profits lost because of the employee's incompetence, the cost of severance, and the subsequent costs of further recruiting and screening. The major thrust of any selection activity should be to reduce the probability of making reject errors or accept errors while increasing the probability of making correct decisions. How do managers do this? By using selection procedures that are both valid and reliable.

Validity and Reliability

● ● ● **validity**
The proven relationship that exists between a selection device and some relevant job criterion.

Any selection device that a manager uses should demonstrate **validity**, a proven relationship between the selection device and some relevant criterion. For example, the law prohibits managers from using a test score as a selection device unless there is clear evidence that, once on the job, individuals with high scores on this test outperform individuals with low test scores. The burden is on managers to support that any selection device they use to differentiate applicants is related to job performance.

● ● ● **reliability**
The ability of a selection device to measure the same thing consistently.

In addition to being valid, a selection device must also demonstrate **reliability**, which indicates whether the device measures the same thing consistently. For example, if a test is reliable, any single individual's score should remain fairly consistent over time, assuming that the characteristics being measured are also stable. No selection device can be effective if it's low in reliability. Using such a device would be like weighing yourself every day on an erratic scale. If the scale is unreliable—randomly fluctuating, say 10 to 15 pounds every time you step on it—the results will not mean much. To be effective predictors, selection devices must possess an acceptable level of consistency.

Types of Selection Devices

Managers can use a number of selection devices to reduce accept and reject errors. The best-known include application forms, written and performance-simulation tests, interviews, background investigations, and in some cases, physical exams. Let's briefly review each of these devices. Exhibit 12–7 on page 290 lists the strengths and weaknesses of each of these devices.[20]

Application Forms Almost all organizations require job candidates to fill out an application. The application might be a form on which the person gives his or her name, address, and telephone number. Or it might be a comprehensive personal history profile, detailing the person's activities, skills, and accomplishments.

Written Tests Typical written tests include tests of intelligence, aptitude, ability, and interest. Such tests have been used for years, although their popularity tends to run in cycles. Today, personality, behavioral, and aptitude assessment tests are popular among businesses. Managers need to be careful regarding their use, however, since legal challenges against such tests have been successful when they're not job related or when they elicit information concerning sex, race, age, or other areas protected by equal employment opportunity laws.[21]

Managers know that poor hiring decisions are costly and that properly designed tests can reduce the likelihood of poor decisions. In addition, the cost of developing and validating a set of written tests for a specific job has decreased significantly.

Exhibit 12–7

● ● ●──────────

Selection Devices

Application Forms

Strengths:

- Relevant biographical data and facts that can be verified have been shown to be valid performance measures for some jobs.
- When items on the form have been weighted to reflect job relatedness, this device has proved to be a valid predictor for diverse groups.

Weaknesses:

- Usually only a couple of items on the form prove to be valid predictors of job performance and then only for a specific job.
- Weighted-item applications are difficult and expensive to create and maintain.

Written Tests

Strengths:

- Tests of intellectual ability, spatial and mechanical ability, perceptual accuracy, and motor ability are moderately valid predictors for many semiskilled and unskilled lower-level jobs in industrial organizations.
- Intelligence tests are reasonably good predictors for supervisory positions.

Weaknesses:

- Intelligence and other tested characteristics can be somewhat removed from actual job performance, thus reducing their validity.

Performance-Simulation Tests

Strengths:

- Based on job analysis data and easily meet the requirement of job relatedness.
- Have proven to be valid predictors of job performance.

Weaknesses:

- Expensive to create and administer.

Interviews

Strengths:

- Must be structured and well organized to be effective predictors.
- Interviewers must use common questioning to be effective predictors.

Weaknesses:

- Interviewers must be aware of legality of certain questions.
- Subject to potential biases, especially if interviews are not well structured and standardized.

Background Investigations

Strengths:

- Verifications of background data are valuable sources of information.

Weaknesses:

- Reference checks are essentially worthless as a selection tool.

Physical Examinations

Strengths:

- Has some validity for jobs with certain physical requirements.
- Done primarily for insurance purposes.

Weaknesses:

- Must be sure that physical requirements are job related and do not discriminate.

Performance-Simulation Tests What better way is there to find out whether an applicant for a technical writing position at Matsushita can write technical manuals than by having him or her do it? Performance-simulation tests are made up of actual job behaviors. The best-known performance-simulation tests are work sampling and assessment centers.

Exhibit 12–8

Suggestions for Interviewing

1. Structure a *fixed set of questions* for all applicants.
2. Have *detailed information about the job* for which applicants are interviewing.
3. *Minimize any prior knowledge* of applicants' background, experience, interests, test scores, or other characteristics.
4. *Ask behavioral questions* that require applicants to give detailed accounts of actual job behaviors.
5. Use a *standardized evaluation form.*
6. *Take notes* during the interview.
7. *Avoid short interviews* that encourage premature decision making.

Source: Based on D.A. DeCenzo and S.P. Robbins, *Human Resource Management,* 7th ed. (New York: Wiley, 2002, p. 200)

●●● **work sampling**
A selection device in which job applicants are presented with a miniature replica of a job and are asked to perform tasks that are central to it.

●●● **assessment centers**
Places in which job candidates undergo performance-simulation tests that evaluate managerial potential.

Work sampling involves presenting applicants with a miniature model of a job and having them perform a task or set of tasks that are central to it. Applicants demonstrate that they have the necessary skills and abilities by actually doing the tasks. This type of test is appropriate for jobs where work is routine or standardized.

Assessment centers are places in which job candidates undergo performance-simulation tests to evaluate managerial potential. In assessment centers, executives, supervisors, or trained psychologists evaluate candidates for managerial positions as they go through extensive exercises that simulate real problems they would confront on the job.[22] Activities might include interviews, in-basket problem-solving exercises, group discussions, and business decision games.

Interviews The interview, like the application form, is an almost universal selection device.[23] (▪▪▪▫▪ Go to the Web and check out PRISM #11—Interviewing) Not many of us have ever gotten a job without one or more interviews. Because there are so many variables that can impact interviewer judgment, the value of the interview as a selection device has been of considerable debate.[24] (▪▫▪▪▪ Go to the Web and check out Q & A 12.6.) Managers can make interviews more valid and reliable by following the suggestions listed in Exhibit 12–8.

Another important factor in interviewing job candidates is the legality of certain interview questions. Employment law attorneys warn managers to be extremely cautious in the types of questions they ask candidates. Exhibit 12–9 lists some examples of typical interview questions that managers *shouldn't* ask because they could expose the organization to lawsuits by job applicants. (▪▫▪▪▪ Go to the Web and check out Q & A 12.7.)

A new approach that some companies are using is *situational interviews* where candidates role play in mock scenarios. For instance, at a Wall Street bank, a prospective account representative might be asked to role play dealing with a customer who has an account discrepancy. The interviewers watch the candidate's reaction: how he or she processes the information, how he or she interacts with the "client," his or her body language, and which words he or she chooses.[25]

Exhibit 12–9

Examples of "Can't Ask and Can Ask" Interview Questions for Managers*

Can't Ask	Can Ask
• What's your birth date? or How old are you? • What's your marital status? or Do you plan to have a family? • What's your native language? • Have you ever been arrested?	• Are you over 18? • Would you relocate? • Are you authorized to work in the United States? • Have you ever been convicted of [fill in the blank]?—The crime must be reasonably related to the performance of the job.

* Managers should be aware that there are numerous other "can and can't ask" questions. Be sure to always check with your HR department for specific guidance.

Background Investigations If managers at Lucent Technologies had done a thorough background check, they might have discovered that the individual who eventually became director of recruitment (who is no longer with the company) was imprisoned for stealing money from student funds while a principal at a California high school and had lied about earning a doctorate at Stanford.[26]

Background investigations are of two types: verifications of application data and reference checks. The first type has proved to be a valuable source of selection information. For instance, managers at Krause Gentle Corporation, which operates more than 300 convenience stores in 12 states, perform background checks and drug and personality testing on new full-time hires. The result has been positive—lower employee turnover, which saves the company the headaches and additional costs of continually hiring.[27] The latter is essentially worthless as a selection tool because applicants' references tend to be almost universally positive. After all, a person isn't going to ask someone to write a reference if that person is likely to write a negative one.

Physical Examination This device would be useful only for a small number of jobs that have certain physical requirements. Instead, the physical examination is mostly used for insurance purposes as organizations want to be sure that new hires will not submit insurance claims for injuries or illnesses they had before being hired.

What Works Best and When?

Many selection devices are of limited value to managers in making selection decisions. Exhibit 12–10 summarizes the validity of these devices for particular types of jobs. Managers should use those devices that effectively predict for a given job.

In addition, managers who treat the recruiting and hiring of employees as if the applicants must be sold on the job and exposed only to an organization's positive characteristics are likely to have a workforce that is dissatisfied and prone to high turnover.[28]

During the hiring process, every job applicant develops a set of expectations about the company and about the job for which he or she is interviewing. When the information an applicant receives is excessively inflated, a number of things happen that have potentially negative effects on the company. First, mismatched applicants are less likely to withdraw from the selection process. Second, because inflated information builds unrealistic expectations, new employees are likely to become quickly dissatisfied and leave the organization. Third, new hires are prone to become disillusioned and less committed to the organization when they face the unexpected harsh realities of the job. In many cases, these individuals may feel that they were misled during the hiring process and may become problem employees.

Exhibit 12–10

Quality of Selection Devices as Predictors

Selection Device	Position			
	Senior Management	Middle and Lower Management	Complex Nonmanagerial	Routine Work
Application form	2	2	2	2
Written tests	1	1	2	3
Work samples	—	—	4	4
Assessment center	5	5	—	—
Interviews	4	3	2	2
Verification of application data	3	3	3	3
Reference checks	1	1	1	1
Physical exam	1	1	1	2

Note: Validity is measured on a scale from 5 (highest) to a1 (lowest). A dash means "not applicable."

●●● **realistic job preview (RJP)**
A preview of a job that provides both positive and negative information about the job and the company.

To increase job satisfaction among employees and reduce turnover, you should consider providing a **realistic job preview (RJP)**. An RJP includes both positive and negative information about the job and the company. For instance, in addition to the positive comments typically expressed during an interview, the job applicant might be told that there are limited opportunities to talk to co-workers during work hours, that promotional advancement is slim, or that work hours fluctuate so erratically that employees may be required to work during what are usually off hours (nights and weekends). Research indicates that applicants who have been given a realistic job preview hold lower and more realistic job expectations for the jobs they will be performing and are better able to cope with the frustrating elements of the job than are applicants who have been given only inflated information.

ORIENTATION

Did you participate in some type of organized "introduction to college life" when you started school? If so, you may have been told about your school's rules and regulations, the procedures for activities such as applying for financial aid, cashing a check, or registering for classes, and you were probably introduced to some of the college administrators. A person starting a new job needs the same type of introduction to his or her job and the organization. This introduction is called **orientation**.

●●● **orientation**
Introduction of a new employee to his or her job and the organization.

There are two types of orientation. *Work unit orientation* familiarizes the employee with the goals of the work unit, clarifies how his or her job contributes to the unit's goals, and includes an introduction to his or her new co-workers. *Organization orientation* informs the new employee about the organization's objectives, history, philosophy, procedures, and rules. This should include relevant human resource policies and benefits such as work hours, pay procedures, overtime requirements, and fringe benefits. In addition, a tour of the organization's work facilities is often part of the organization orientation.

Many organizations, particularly large ones, have formal orientation programs which might include a tour of the work facilities, a PowerPoint presentation describing the history of the organization, and a short discussion with representatives from the human resources department who describe the organization's benefit programs. Other organizations may use a more informal orientation program in which, for instance, the manager assigns the new employee to a senior member of the work group who introduces the new employee to immediate co-workers and shows him or her locations of the copy room, coffee machine, rest rooms, cafeteria, and the like. And then there are intense orientation programs like those at Trilogy, a software company based in Austin, Texas. It has a three-month total-immersion orientation called Trilogy University that introduces new hires to the company and its values, vision, goals, and strategy. In the first week of classes led by CEO Joe Liemandt and other Trilogy veterans, new Trilogians learn about programming languages, product plans, and marketing. The classes start at 8:00 A.M. and in the first month at least, don't end until midnight. After this, new employees work side-by-side with many of Trilogy's top performers on actual projects.[29]

Managers have an obligation to make the integration of the new employee into the organization as smooth and as free of anxiety as possible. They need to openly discuss employee beliefs regarding mutual obligations of the organization and the employee.[30] It's in the best interests of the organization and the new employee to get the person up and running in the job as soon as possible. Successful orientation, whether formal or informal, results in an outsider-insider transition that makes the new member feel comfortable and fairly well adjusted, lowers the likelihood of poor work performance, and reduces the probability of a surprise resignation by the new employee only a week or two into the job.

The 360-plus employees of Health Partners of Philadelphia, a not-for-profit health plan serving more than 145,000 Medicaid and Medicare members in southeastern Pennsylvania, rely on their HR department's Organizational Learning Center (OLC) for training. The three-person OLC team selects qualified employees who are subject-matter experts to serve as trainers. OLC breaks the training sessions into 45-minute classes that employees can fit easily into their workday, and can take and retake for reinforcement as needed. The training has helped increase productivity and reduce costs.

EMPLOYEE TRAINING

Everything that employees at Ruth's Chris Steak House restaurants need to know can be found on sets of 4 by $8\frac{1}{2}$ inch cards. Whether it's a recipe for caramelized banana cream pie or how to acknowledge customers, it's on the cards. And since the cards for all jobs are readily available, employees know the behaviors and skills it takes to get promoted. It's a unique approach to employee training, but it seems to work. Since the card system was implemented, employee turnover has decreased, something that's not easy to accomplish in the restaurant industry.[31]

Employee training is an important HRM activity. (Go to the Web and check out Q & A 12.8.) As job demands change, employee skills have to be altered and updated. It's been estimated that U.S. business firms spend over $54 billion on workforce development.[32] Managers, of course, are responsible for deciding what type of training employees need, when they need it, and what form that training should take.

Types of Training

Ranked as the top training organization in the United States for two years in a row, Pfizer Inc., obviously takes employee training seriously. It devotes 15 percent of its total payroll cost to employee training and uses different types of training ranging from sales to technical to leadership development. Jerry Godbehere, Pfizer's vice president of global learning and development, says, "Even though Pfizer has become the world's largest pharmaceutical company, I see individuals every day who have made an impact that is both helping patients and building the future of the company."[33] That outcome wouldn't be possible without a sincere organizational commitment to training.

When organizations invest in employee training, what are they offering? Exhibit 12–11 describes the major types of training that organizations provide.[34] Interpersonal skills training is a high priority for many organizations. For example, Shannon Washbrook, director of training and development for Vancouver-based Boston Pizza International, says that "Our people know the Boston Pizza concept; they

Exhibit 12–11

Types of Training

Type	Includes:
Interpersonal skills	Leadership, coaching, communication skills, conflict resolution, team building, customer service, diversity and cultural awareness, other interpersonal skills
Technical	Product training and knowledge, sales process, information technology, computer applications, other technical skills necessary to do a particular job
Business	Finance, marketing, lean manufacturing, quality, strategic planning, organizational culture
Mandatory	Safety, health, sexual harassment, and other legal compliance
Performance management	Any training to help an individual employee improve his or her work performance
Problem solving/Decision making	Defining problems, assessing causation, creativity in developing alternatives, analyzing alternatives, selecting solution
Personal	Career planning, time management, wellness, personal finance or money management, public speaking

Exhibit 12–12

Employee Training Methods

Traditional Training Methods

- *On-the-job*—Employees learn how to do tasks simply by performing them, usually after an initial introduction to the task.
- *Job rotation*—Employees work at different jobs in a particular area, getting exposure to a variety of tasks.
- *Mentoring and coaching*—Employees work with an experienced worker who provides information, support, and encouragement; also called an apprentice in certain industries.
- *Experiential exercises*—Employees participate in role playing, simulations, or other face-to-face types of training.
- *Workbooks/manuals*—Employees refer to training workbooks and manuals for information.
- *Classroom lectures*—Employees attend lectures designed to convey specific information.

Technology-Based Training Methods

- *CD-ROM/DVD/Videotapes/Audiotapes*—Employees listen to or watch selected media that convey information or demonstrate certain techniques.
- *Videoconferencing/teleconferencing/Satellite TV*—Employees listen to or participate as information is conveyed or techniques demonstrated.
- *E-learning*—Internet-based learning where employees participate in multimedia simulations or other interactive modules.

---

have all the hard skills. It's the soft skills they lack." To address that, Washbrook launched Boston Pizza College, a training initiative that uses hands-on, scenario-based learning about many interpersonal skills topics.[35]

Training Methods

Employee training can be delivered in traditional ways including on-the-job training, job rotation, mentoring and coaching, experiential exercises, workbooks and manuals, or classroom lectures. But many organizations are relying more on technology-based training methods because of their accessibility, lower cost, and ability to deliver information. For instance, a computer-based simulation called Virtual Leader by SimuLearn provides trainees with realistic leadership scenarios, including the following:

> "Be in the boardroom in 10 minutes," reads the e-mail from Senior Vice President Alan Young. The CEO is out on his boat, and a storm has knocked out all communication. Worse, there has been a massive fire in the call center in South America. We could lose billions, Young says. The board has given senior staff emergency powers. You're a top manager who has been called in to help. What do you do?"[36]

Exhibit 12–12 provides a description of the various traditional and technology-based training methods that managers might use. Of all these training methods, experts believe that organizations will increasingly rely on e-learning applications to deliver important information and to develop employees' skills.[37]

Learning Review

- Contrast job analysis, job description, and job specification.
- Discuss the major sources of potential job candidates.
- Describe the different selection devices and which work best for different jobs.

- Explain what a realistic job preview is and why it's important.
- Explain why orientation is so important.
- Describe the different types of training and how that training can be provided.

EMPLOYEE PERFORMANCE MANAGEMENT

Managers need to know whether their employees are performing their jobs efficiently and effectively or whether there is need for improvement. (▨▨▨▨ Go to the Web and check out S.A.L. #26—How Good Am I at Giving Feedback?) Evaluating employee performance is part of a **performance management system**, which is a process of establishing performance standards and appraising employee performance in order to arrive at objective human resource decisions as well as to provide documentation to support those decisions. Performance appraisal is a critical part of a performance management system. Let's look at some different methods of doing performance appraisal. (▨▨▨▨ Go to the Web and check out PRISM #8—Disciplining and Providing Feedback.)

Performance Appraisal Methods

Managers can choose from seven major performance appraisal methods. The advantages and disadvantages of each of these methods are shown in Exhibit 12–13.

Written Essays The **written essay** is a performance appraisal technique in which an evaluator writes out a description of an employee's strengths and weaknesses, past performance, and potential. The evaluator also makes suggestions for improvement.

Critical Incidents The use of **critical incidents** focuses the evaluator's attention on critical or key behaviors that separate effective from ineffective job performance. The appraiser writes down anecdotes that describe what an employee did that was especially effective or ineffective. The key here is that only specific behaviors, not vaguely defined personality traits, are cited.

Graphic Rating Scales One of the most popular performance appraisal methods is **graphic rating scales**. This method lists a set of performance factors such as quantity and quality of work, job knowledge, cooperation, loyalty, attendance, honesty, and initiative. The evaluator then goes down the list and rates the employee on each factor using an incremental scale, which usually specifies five points. For instance, a factor such as job knowledge might be rated from 1 ("poorly informed about work duties") to 5 ("has complete mastery of all phases of the job").

• • • **performance management system**
A process of establishing performance standards and evaluating performance in order to arrive at objective human resource decisions as well as to provide documentation to support those decisions.

• • • **written essay**
A performance appraisal technique in which an evaluator writes out a description of an employee's strengths and weaknesses, past performance, and potential.

• • • **critical incidents**
A performance appraisal technique in which the evaluator focuses on the critical behaviors that separate effective from ineffective job performance.

• • • **graphic rating scales**
A performance appraisal technique in which an employee is rated on a set of performance factors.

• • • **behaviorally anchored rating scales (BARS)**
A performance appraisal technique which appraises an employee on examples of actual job behavior.

Exhibit 12–13

Advantages and Disadvantages of Performance Appraisal Methods

Method	Advantage	Disadvantage
Written essays	Simple to use	More a measure of evaluator's writing ability than of employee's actual performance
Critical incidents	Rich examples; behaviorally based	Time consuming; lack quantification
Graphic rating scales	Provide quantitative data; less time-consuming than others	Do not provide depth of job behavior assessed
BARS	Focus on specific and measurable job behaviors	Time-consuming; difficult to develop
Multiperson comparisons	Compares employees with one another	Unwieldy with large number of employees; legal concerns
MBO	Focuses on end goals; results oriented	Time-consuming
360-degree appraisals	Thorough	Time-consuming

New Web-enabled software allows employers to track employee performance with greater precision than ever before. These British Airways reps are among those whose work time and personal time can be carefully differentiated by the software, which also tracks reps' handling of ticket sales and customer complaints, so managers can reward those whose performance is exemplary. Says Steven Pruneau, the manager in charge of the evaluation project, "We knew how many hours our planes were on the ground or in the air . . . But we didn't have a fraction of that kind of information about the productivity of our other assets—our human capital."

Behaviorally Anchored Rating Scales

Another popular approach is **behaviorally anchored rating scales (BARS)**. These scales combine major elements from the critical incident and graphic rating scale approaches. The appraiser rates an employee according to items along a numerical scale, but the items are examples of actual job behaviors rather than general descriptions or traits.

Multiperson Comparisons

Multiperson comparisons compare one individual's performance with that of others. This approach has received a lot of attention recently.[38] Made popular by former General Electric CEO Jack Welch, employees were rated as top performers (20 percent), middle performers (70 percent), or bottom performers (10 percent). For instance, Ford Motor Company evaluated managers in groups of 30 to 50. In each group, 10 percent had to get an A, 80 percent a B, and 10 percent a C. Although Ford has since chosen to drop its ranking system, the percentage of companies using these GE-style rankings rose to 33 percent in 2002. (▮▮▮▮▮ Check out out "You're the Manager: Putting Ethics into Action" on page 334.) [39]

Objectives

We previously introduced management by objectives (MBO) as we discussed planning in Chapter 7. MBO is also a mechanism for appraising performance. In fact, it's often used for assessing managers and professional employees.[40] With MBO, employees are evaluated by how well they accomplish specific goals that have been established by them and their manager.

• •● **multiperson comparisons**
Performance appraisal techniques that compare one individual's performance with that of others.

• ●● **360-degree feedback**
A performance appraisal method that utilizes feedback from supervisors, employees, and co-workers.

360-Degree Feedback

360-degree feedback is a method that utilizes feedback from supervisors, employees, and co-workers. In other words, this appraisal utilizes information from the full circle of people with whom the manager interacts. Some 32 percent of organizations surveyed by the Society for Human Resource Management use 360-degree feedback.[41] Companies such as Alcoa, Pitney Bowes, AT&T, DuPont, Levi Strauss, and UPS are using this approach. Users caution that, although it's effective for career coaching and helping a manager recognize his or her strengths and weaknesses, it's not appropriate for determining pay, promotions, or terminations.

THINKING CRITICALLY ABOUT ETHICS

At many specialty clothing companies, employees are expected to dress head-to-toe in the company's latest fashions. Yet, a growing number of retail employees, many of whom make low wages, are complaining that they can't afford it. In fact, three lawsuits filed in San Francisco against GAP, Abercrombie & Fitch, and Polo Ralph Lauren argue that the stores illegally force employees to buy these expensive clothes. They contend that by expecting employees to buy and wear a certain brand, the retailers are violating California labor laws as the state's labor code says that when a job requires a uniform, the employer must provide it. The companies say that the employees get a discount on any clothing that they purchase. What are the ethical implications of such demands for employees *and* the clothing companies? Is there an ethical solution? Explain.

COMPENSATION AND BENEFITS

Executives at Discovery Communications Inc., had an employee morale problem on their hands. Many of the company's top performers were making the same salaries as the poorer performers and the company's compensation program didn't allow for giving raises to people who stayed in the same position. The only way for managers to reward the top performers was to give them a bonus or promote them to another position. Executives were discovering that not only was that unfair, it was counterproductive. So they overhauled the program.[42]

Most of us expect to receive appropriate compensation from our employer. Developing an effective and appropriate compensation system is an important part of the HRM process.[43] Why? Because it can help attract and retain competent and talented individuals who help the organization accomplish its mission and goals. In addition, an organization's compensation system has been shown to have an impact on its strategic performance.[44] (Go to the Web and check out Q & A 12.9.)

Managers must develop a compensation system that reflects the changing nature of work and the workplace in order to keep people motivated. Organizational compensation can include many different types of rewards and benefits such as base wages and salaries, wage and salary add-ons, incentive payments, and other benefits and services.

How do managers determine who gets paid $9 an hour and who gets $350,000 a year? Several factors influence the differences in compensation and benefit packages for different employees. Exhibit 12–14 summarizes these factors, which are both job-based and business- or industry-based. Many organizations use an alternative approach to determining compensation called skill-based pay.

Because employees' skills tend to affect work efficiency and effectiveness, many organizations have implemented **skill-based pay** systems, which reward employees for the job skills and competencies they can demonstrate. In a skill-based pay system, an employee's job title doesn't define his or her pay category; skills do.[45] Skill-based pay systems seem to mesh nicely with the changing nature of jobs and today's work environment. As one expert noted, "Slowly, but surely, we're becoming a skill-based society where your market value is tied to what you can do and what your skill set is. In this new world where skills and knowledge are what really count, it doesn't make sense to treat people as jobholders. It makes sense to treat them as people with specific skills and to pay them for these skills."[46]

• • • **skill-based pay**
A pay system that rewards employees for the job skills they can demonstrate.

Exhibit 12–14

Factors That Influence Compensation and Benefits

Sources: Based on R.I. Henderson, *Compensation Management*, 6th ed. (Upper Saddle River, NJ: Prentice Hall, 1994), pp. 3–24; and A. Murray, "Mom, Apple Pie, and Small Business," *Wall Street Journal*, August 15, 1994, p. A1.

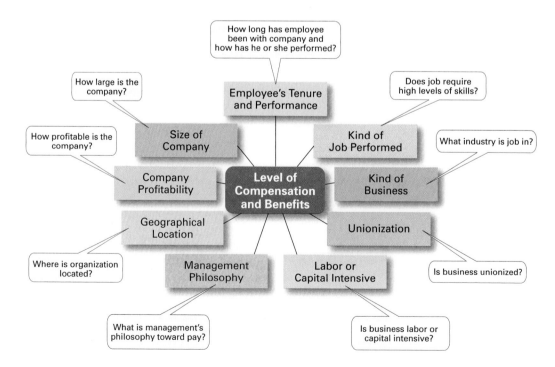

Although many factors influence the design of an organization's compensation system, flexibility is a key consideration. The traditional approach to paying people reflected a time of job stability when an employee's pay was largely determined by seniority and job level. Given the dynamic environments that many organizations face in which the skills that are absolutely critical to organizational success can change in a matter of months, the trend is to make pay systems more flexible and to reduce the number of pay levels. However, whatever approach managers take, they must establish a fair, equitable, and motivating compensation system that allows the organization to recruit and keep a productive workforce.

CAREER DEVELOPMENT

• • • **career**
A sequence of positions held by a person during his or her lifetime.

The term *career* has several meanings. In popular usage, it can mean advancement ("she is on a management career track"), a profession ("he has chosen a career in accounting"), or a lifelong sequence of jobs (his career has included 12 jobs in six organizations"). For our purposes, we define a **career** as the sequence of positions held by a person during his or her lifetime.[47] Using this definition, it's apparent that we all have, or will have, a career. Moreover, the concept is as relevant to unskilled laborers as it is to software designers or physicians. But career development isn't what it used to be![48]

The Way It Was

Although career development has been an important topic in management courses for years, we've witnessed some dramatic changes in the concept. Career development programs were typically designed by organizations to help employees advance their work lives within a specific organization. The focus of such programs was to provide the information, assessment, and training needed to help employees realize their career goals. Career development was also a way for organizations to attract and retain highly talented people. Those purposes have all but disappeared in today's workplace. Widespread organizational changes have led to uncertainty about the concept of a traditional organizational career. Downsizing, restructuring, and other organizational adjustments have brought us to one significant conclusion about career development: The individual—not the organization—is responsible for his or her own career! (▮▯▮▮▮ Go to the Web and check out Q & A 12.10.) You, therefore, must be prepared to do what is necessary to advance your career. You must take responsibility for designing, guiding, and developing your own career.[49] Both organizations and individuals are adjusting to the notion that organizational members have to look out for themselves and become more self-reliant.

You and Your Career Today

The idea of increased personal responsibility for one's career has been described as a *boundaryless career* in which individuals rather than organizations define career progression, organizational loyalty, important skills, and marketplace value.[50] The challenge for individuals is that there are no norms and few rules to guide them in these new circumstances. Instead, individuals assume primary responsibility for career planning, career goal setting, and education and training.[51] (▮▮▯▮ Go to the Web and check out S.A.L. #35—How Satisfied Am I with My Job?)

One of the first career decisions you have to make is career choice. The optimum career choice is one that offers the best match between what you want out of life and your interests, abilities, and market opportunities. Good career choice outcomes should result in a series of positions that give you an opportunity to be a good performer, make you want to maintain your commitment to your career, lead to highly satisfying work, and give you the proper balance between work and personal life. A good career match,

Exhibit 12–15

Top 10 Important Job Factors for College Graduates

(ranked in order of importance)

1. Enjoying what they do
2. Opportunity to use skills and abilities
3. Opportunity for personal development
4. Feeling what they do matters
5. Benefits

6. Recognition for good performance
7. Friendly co-workers
8. Job location
9. Lots of money
10. Working on teams

Source: Based on V. Frazee, "What's Important to College Grads in Their First Jobs?" *Personnel Journal*, July 1996, p. 21.

then, is one in which you are able to develop a positive self-concept, to do work that you think is important, and to lead the kind of life you desire.[52] Exhibit 12–15 provides the results of a survey of college graduates regarding what is important to them in their first jobs. How would you have ranked these items?

Once you've identified a career choice, it's time to initiate the job search. We aren't going to get into the specifics of job hunting, writing a résumé, or interviewing successfully, although those career actions are important. (■□■■ Go to the Web and check out Q & A 12.11.) Let's fast forward through all that and assume that your job search was successful. It's time to go to work! How do you survive and excel in your career? Exhibit 12–16 lists some suggestions for a successful management career.[53] By taking an active role in managing your career, your work life can be more exciting, enjoyable, and satisfying.

Exhibit 12–16

Some Suggestions for a Successful Management Career

Develop a Network
Continue Upgrading Your Skills
Consider Lateral Career Moves
Stay Mobile
Support Your Boss
Find a Mentor
Don't Stay Too Long in Your First Job
Stay Visible
Gain Control of Organizational Resources
Learn the Power Structure
Present the Right Image
Do Good Work
Select Your First Job Judiciously

●●● Learning Review

- Describe the different performance appraisal methods.
- Discuss the factors that influence employee compensation and benefits.

- Describe skill-based pay systems.
- Describe career development for today's employees.

CURRENT ISSUES IN HUMAN RESOURCE MANAGEMENT

We'll conclude this chapter by looking at some contemporary HR issues facing today's managers. These include managing downsizing, workforce diversity, sexual harassment, and work–life balance.

Managing Downsizing

•• • downsizing
The planned elimination of jobs in an organization.

Downsizing is the planned elimination of jobs in an organization. When an organization has too many employees—which can happen when it needs to cut costs, is faced with declining market share, or has grown too aggressively—one option for shoring up profits is by eliminating some of those excess workers. Well-known companies such as Boeing, McDonald's, Dell, J.P. Morgan Chase, and others have had to downsize in recent years.[54] How can managers best manage a downsized workplace? Expect disruptions in the workplace and in employees' personal lives. Stress, frustration, anxiety, and anger are typical reactions of both individuals being laid off and the job survivors. But are there things managers can do to lessen the pain? Yes.[55]

Open and honest communication is critical. Individuals who are being let go need to be informed as soon as possible. Survivors need to know the company's new goals and expectations, how their jobs might change, and what the future holds. Managers who have been through downsizing point out the importance of communicating openly and as soon as information is available.

In providing assistance to employees being downsized, many organizations offer some form of severance pay or benefits for a specified period of time. Managers want to be sure they're following any laws that might affect the length of time pay and benefits must be offered and the types of pay and benefits that must be provided. In addition, many organizations provide job search assistance.

Finally, studies find that downsizing is as stressful for the survivors as it is for the victims. Survivors often fear being the next to lose their jobs. Or they find their job responsibilities have increased in order to get all the work completed. To help survivors cope, managers might want to provide counselors for employees to talk to, hold group discussions, and communicate to them how important they are.

Managing Workforce Diversity

We've discussed the changing makeup of the workforce in several places throughout this book and provided insights in our "Managing Workforce Diversity" boxes in several chapters. In this section we'll show how workforce diversity is directly affected by basic HRM activities including recruitment, selection, and orientation and training.

Recruitment To improve workforce diversity, managers need to widen their recruiting net. For example, the popular practice of relying on employee referrals as a source of job applicants tends to produce candidates who are similar to present employees. However, some organizations, such as Exabyte, of Boulder, Colorado, have recruited and hired diverse individuals by relying on their current employees. The company's successful experience with a hearing-impaired employee led to hiring other hearing-impaired employees through employee referrals. But not every organization has the employee resources needed to achieve workforce diversity through employee referrals. So managers may have to look for job applicants in places where they might not have looked before. To increase diversity, managers are increasingly turning to nontraditional recruitment sources such as women's job networks, over-50 clubs, urban job banks, disabled people's training centers, ethnic newspapers, and gay rights organizations. This type of outreach should enable the organization to broaden its pool of diverse applicants.

Selection Once a diverse set of applicants exists, efforts must be made to ensure that the selection process does not discriminate. Moreover, applicants need to be made comfortable with the organization's culture and be made aware of management's

Efforts to adapt the workplace to the many different kinds of diversity among U.S. employees include laws to protect employees against discrimination and also laws requiring that physical modifications be made to offices and equipment. Xerox, for instance, provides its customers with kits to retrofit its copiers for use by workers with disabilities. This copier uses special software to assist the visually impaired.

desire to accommodate their needs. For instance, only a small percentage of women apply for Microsoft's technical jobs, but the company makes every effort to hire a high percentage of female applicants and strives to make sure that these women have a successful experience once they're on the job.[56]

Orientation and Training The outside-insider transition is often more challenging for women and minorities than for white males. Many organizations provide special workshops to raise diversity awareness issues. For example, at a Kraft manufacturing facility in Missouri, managers developed an ambitious diversity program reflecting the increased value the organization had placed on incorporating diverse perspectives. One thing they did was to reward "diversity champions," individual employees who supported and promoted the benefits of diversity. They also added diversity goals to employee evaluations, encouraged non-traditional promotions, sponsored six ethnic meal days annually, and trained over half of the plant's employees in diversity issues.[57]

Some organizations are aggressively pursuing diversity efforts. For instance, Advantica, the parent company of Denny's restaurants, was hit with a series of legal claims in the early 1990s. It responded with aggressive minority hiring and a supplier-diversity effort. The company has been ranked in the top three of the 50 best U.S. companies for minorities for three years straight. And Coca-Cola, which settled a class-action suit by black employees for $192 million in November 2000, has made strides in its diversity efforts including launching a formal mentoring program and required diversity training for employees.[58]

Sexual Harassment

Sexual harassment is a serious issue in both public and private sector organizations. During 2002, more than 14,000 complaints were filed with the Equal Employment Opportunity Commission (EEOC). Although most complaints are filed by women, with the exception of one year, the percentage of charges filed by males has risen every year since 1992.[59] Data also indicate that almost all *Fortune* 500 companies in the United States have had complaints lodged by employees, and about a third of them have been sued.[60] Not only were the settlements in these cases very costly for the companies in terms of litigation; it's estimated that sexual harassment costs a "typical *Fortune* 500 company $6.7 million per year in absenteeism, low productivity, and turnover."[61] And sexual harassment isn't a problem just in the United States. It's a global issue. For instance, sexual harassment charges have been filed against employers in such countries as Japan, Australia, the Netherlands, Belgium, New Zealand, Sweden, Ireland, and Mexico.[62]

Even though discussions of sexual harassment cases often focus on the large awards granted by a court, there are other concerns for employers. Sexual harassment creates an unpleasant work environment and undermines workers' ability to perform their jobs. (▮▮▮▮▮ Go to the Web and check out Q & A 12.12.)

• • • sexual harassment
Any unwanted activity of a sexual nature that affects an individual's employment.

Sexual harassment is defined as any unwanted activity of a sexual nature that affects an individual's employment. It can occur between members of the opposite sex or of the same sex. Although such activity is generally covered under employment discrimination laws, in recent years this problem has gained more recognition. By most accounts, prior to the mid-1980s this problem was generally viewed as an isolated incident, with the individual at fault being solely responsible (if at all) for his or her actions.[63]

Many problems associated with sexual harassment involve determining exactly what constitutes this illegal behavior. The EEOC defines sexual harassment as "unwelcome sexual advances, requests for sexual favors, and other verbal or physical conduct

Becoming a Manager

- ◆ *Using the Internet, research different companies that interest you and check out what they say about careers or their people.*
- ◆ *If you're working, note what types of HRM activities your managers do. What do they do that seems to be effective? Ineffective? What can you learn from this?*
- ◆ *Do career research in your chosen career by finding out what it's going to take to be successful in that career.*
- ◆ *Complete the Skill-Building Modules on Interviewing found on pp. 526–527 and Valuing Diversity found on pp. 537–538.*
- ◆ ■□■■ *Go to the Web and complete the following exercises from the Self-Assessment Library (S.A.L.) found on R.O.L.L.S.: #26—How Good Am I At Giving Feedback?, #35—How Satisfied Am I With My Job?, and #44—Am I Experiencing Work–Family Conflict?*

of a sexual nature when submission to or rejection of this conduct explicitly or implicitly affects an individual's employment, unreasonably interferes with an individual's work performance, or creates an intimidating, hostile or offensive work environment."[64] For many organizations, it's the offensive or hostile environment issue that is problematic. Managers must be aware of what constitutes such an environment. Another thing that managers must understand is that the victim doesn't necessarily have to be the person harassed but could be anyone affected by the offensive conduct.[65] The key is being attuned to what makes fellow employees uncomfortable—and if we don't know, we should ask![66]

What can an organization do to protect itself against sexual harassment claims?[67] The courts want to know two things: Did the organization know about, or should it have known about, the alleged behavior? and What did management do to stop it? With the number and dollar amounts of the awards against organizations increasing, there is a greater need for management to educate all employees on sexual harassment matters and have mechanisms available to monitor employees.

Work–Life Balance

What kinds of work–life balance issues can arise that might affect an employee's job performance? Here are some examples:

- Is it okay for someone to bring his baby to work because of an emergency crisis with normal child care arrangements?
- Is it okay to expect an employee to work 60 or more hours a week?
- Should an employee be given the day off to watch her child perform in a school event?

In the 1980s, organizations began to recognize that employees don't leave their families and personal lives behind when they walk into work. An organization hires a person who has a personal life outside the office, personal problems, and family commitments. Although managers can't be sympathetic with every detail of an employee's family life, we *are* seeing organizations more attuned to the fact that employees have sick children, elderly parents who need special care, and other family issues that may require special arrangements. In response, most major organizations have taken actions to make their workplaces more family-friendly by offering **family-friendly benefits**, which include a wide range of work and family programs to help employees.[68] They introduced programs such as on-site child care, summer day camps, flextime, job sharing, leaves for school functions, telecommuting, and part-time

●●● **family-friendly benefits**
Benefits which accommodate employees' needs for work–life balance.

Greg Strakosch, founder and CEO of interactive media company Tech Target of Needham, Massachusetts, has taken work–life policies further than many managers. He has made no policies requiring a set number of work hours for his 210 employees, nor has he limited sick days, personal days, or vacation days. "You're either sick one day or eight," he says, "but a set number of sick days strikes me as arbitrary and dumb." Although it's not for those who can't handle freedom, the company's "open leave" policy is "a competitive weapon," says Strakosch, and one that's contributed to a nearly 30 percent sales increase in 2003.

employment. Work–life conflicts are as relevant to male workers with children and women without children as they are for female employees with children. Heavy workloads and increased travel demands, for instance, are making it increasingly hard for many employees to meet both work and personal responsibilities. (▭ Go to the Web and check out S.A.L. #44—Am I Experiencing Work–Family Conflict?) A Harvard study, for example, found that 82 percent of men between the ages of 20 and 39 said that a "family-friendly" schedule was their most important job criterion.[69]

Today's progressive workplace is being modified to accommodate the varied needs of a diverse workforce. This includes providing a wide range of scheduling options and benefits that allow employees more flexibility at work and which allow them to better balance or integrate their work and personal lives. Despite these organizational efforts, work–life programs have room for improvement. Workplace surveys still show high levels of employee stress stemming from work–life conflicts. And large groups of women and minority workers remain unemployed or underemployed because of family responsibilities and bias in the workplace.[70] So what can managers do?

Recent research on work–life conflicts has provided new insights. For instance, evidence indicates that time pressures aren't the primary problem underlying the conflicts.[71] It's the psychological intrusion of work into the family domain and vice versa. People are worrying about personal problems at work and thinking about work problems at home. So Dad may physically make it home in time for dinner but his mind is elsewhere while he's at the dinner table. This suggests that organizations should devote less effort to helping employees with time-management issues and more effort to helping them clearly segment their lives. Keeping workloads reasonable, reducing work-related travel, and offering on-site quality child care are examples of HR practices that can help. Also, not surprisingly, people have been found to differ in their preferences for scheduling options and benefits.[72] Some people prefer organizational initiatives that better segment work from their personal lives. Others prefer programs that facilitate integration. For instance, flextime segments because it allows employees to schedule work hours that are less likely to conflict with personal responsibilities. On the other hand, on-site child care integrates by blurring the boundaries between work and family responsibilities. People who prefer segmentation are more likely to be satisfied and committed to their jobs when offered options such as flextime, job sharing, and part-time hours. People who prefer integration are more likely to respond positively to options such as on-site child care, gym facilities, and company-sponsored family picnics.

● ● ●Learning Review

- Explain how managers can manage downsizing.
- Discuss how managers can manage workforce diversity.
- Tell what sexual harassment is and what managers need to know about it.
- Describe how organizations are dealing with work–life balance issues.

Managers **Respond** to a **Manager's** Dilemma

·····Sandra M. Steiner
Executive Vice President, Business Development, Westminster, Colorado

Brett is fortunate he has so many employees using the current site. From that base of users, he could ask them to complete a questionnaire regarding the items they find most useful and ask the managers within the Australian group how they use the site when working with their employees. This would give him information about the real usefulness of the information provided, identify additional items that could be introduced in an upgrade, and give him good knowledge of the strengths offered by the current site. When considering offering the site to new locations, he should allow for some new content tailored to local needs. Brett could invite a representative group of employees and managers to view the current site and get their feedback. Before expanding the program, it's critical that he knows the reasons employees find it to be of value and then build on that knowledge.

David Jolliffe
Manager, New Media & Editorial Services, Pearson Canada, Toronto, Ontario, Canada

Extending an employee intranet to other units poses a number of challenges. The first concerns the content and structure of the portal itself. To be well received, the site needs to reflect the practices, policies, issues and events of each local business unit so these employees feel the resource belongs to them as much as it does the head office. It also needs to integrate local content so it's easy to find; ensure the local materials are of the same high quality as other information; and treat employees as well-rounded people by including personal items such as carpool postings, weather reports, or trade/sell services. In other words, the site needs to have obvious value for local employees. Initially, this utility will need to be demonstrated through advertising, site search contests, and employee presentations. As with all change, people have to be convinced of the added value of the innovation.

Learning Summary

● ● ●

After reading and studying this chapter, you should be able to:

- Explain how an organization's human resources can be a significant source of competitive advantage.
- List the eight activities necessary for staffing the organization and sustaining high employee performance.
- Discuss the environmental factors that most directly affect the HRM process.
- Contrast job analysis, job description, and job specification.
- Describe the difference between recruitment and decruitment.
- Discuss the major sources of potential job candidates.
- Describe the different selection devices and which work best for different jobs.
- Explain what a realistic job preview is and why it's important.

- Explain why orientation is so important.
- Describe the different types of training and how that training can be provided.
- Describe the different performance appraisal methods.
- Discuss the factors that influence employee compensation and benefits.
- Describe skill-based pay systems.
- Describe career development for today's employees.
- Explain how managers can manage downsizing.
- Discuss how managers can manage workforce diversity.
- Explain what sexual harassment is and what managers need to know about it.
- Describe how organizations are dealing with work–life balance issues.

Thinking About Management Issues

● ● ●

1. How does HRM affect all managers?.
2. Are there limits on how far a prospective employer should delve into an applicant's personal life by means of interviews or tests? Explain.
3. Should an employer have the right to choose employees without governmental interference? Support your conclusion.
4. Studies show that women's salaries still lag behind men's, and even with equal opportunity laws and regulations, women are paid about 73 percent of what men are paid. How would you design a compensation system that would address this issue?
5. What drawbacks, if any, do you see in implementing flexible benefits? (Consider this question from the perspective of both the organization and the employee.)
6. What are the benefits and drawbacks of realistic job previews? (Consider this question from the perspective of both the organization and the employee.)
7. What, in your view, constitutes sexual harassment? Describe how companies can minimize sexual harassment in the workplace.
8. Go to the Society for Human Resource Management Web site (www.shrm.org) and find the HR News section. Pick one of the News Stories to read and write a summary of the information. At the end of your summary, discuss the implications of the topic for managers.

Working Together: Team-Based Exercise

● ● ●

You work as director of human resources for a gift registry Web site based in St. Paul, Minnesota. Your company currently has 30 employees, but due to the popularity of its site, the company is growing rapidly. To handle customer demand, at least 30 additional employees are going to be needed in the next three months. In filling those positions, the company's CEO is committed to increasing employee diversity because she feels that this will add unique per-

spectives on the types of gift services provided by the company. She's asked you to head up a team to propose some specific practices for recruiting diverse individuals.

Form teams of three or four class members. Identify specific steps that your company can take to recruit diverse individuals. Be creative and be specific. Write down your proposed steps and be prepared to share your ideas with the class.

Ethical Dilemma Exercise

Everybody wants an A ranking; nobody wants a C ranking. Yet the multiperson ranking system used by Goodyear Tire and Rubber Company forced managers to rank 10 percent of the workforce as A performers, 80 percent as B performers, and 10 percent as C performers. Those ranked as A were rewarded with promotions; those ranked as C were told they could be demoted or fired for a second C rating. Goodyear abandoned its 10-80-10 system just before some C workers who had been fired filed a lawsuit claiming age discrimination. "It is very unfair to start with the assumption that a certain percentage of your employees are unsatisfactory," said one of the plaintiffs. "It was very subjective and designed to weed out the older people."

Like Goodyear, a growing number of companies have followed the lead of General Electric in regularly ranking employees. Many companies give poor performers an opportunity to improve before taking action. However, critics say the ranking system forces managers to penalize workers on poorly performing teams. They also say the ranking system can lead to age, gender, or race discrimination. In response, companies are training managers to use more objective measures for appraisals, such as monitoring progress toward preset goals.[73]

Imagine that you're a General Electric executive who must rank 20 percent of your subordinate managers as top performers, 70 percent as average, and 10 percent as needing improvement. Retaining incompetent or unmotivated managers is unfair to the rest of the staff and sends mixed signals. On the other hand, even if all your managers are competent, you must put 10 percent into the bottom category. Now it's appraisal time. Review Exhibit 12–13 as you consider this ethical challenge and decide which of the following options to choose—and why.

Option A: Before you submit the rankings, take the lowest-ranked performers aside and suggest that they immediately begin looking for new positions elsewhere to avoid being fired.

Option B: Draft a memo explaining that none of your subordinates is incompetent and deserves to be fired, then rank them all as top performers or average performers.

Option C: Apply the ranking as required and work individually with each of the lowest-ranked performers to develop plans for showing improvement within 90 days.

Case Application

Mitsubishi Motors North America

"We are a spirited, diverse workforce. We are a culture that looks for, and rewards, hard work and dedication. We are winners." Although similar sentiments are expressed by a lot of different types of organizations around the world, you might be surprised to discover that this is part of the mission statement at Mitsubishi Motors North America, Inc. (MMNA)—especially considering the company's history.

MMNA is one of the many businesses of the Japanese-based Mitsubishi Group. Although each member of the Mitsubishi Group is independent, they share the guiding principles of the Sankoryo, first announced in the 1930s by founder Mr. Koyata Iwasaki and revised to reflect today's realities:

- *Shoki Hoko:* Strive to enrich society, both materially and spiritually, while contributing toward the preservation of the environment.

- *Shoji Komei:* Maintain principles of transparency and openness, conducting business with integrity and fairness.

- *Ritsugyo Boeki:* Expand business, based on an all-encompassing global perspective.

These guiding principles serve as the foundation for how each Mitsubishi company is to conduct its business. And yet, conduct like this wasn't the way it used to be at MMNA's manufacturing facility in Normal, Illinois.

Opened in 1985 on the flat rolling farm land of central Illinois, MMNA's manufacturing facility was a technological marvel. It's considered the most complex factory in the United States and was designed to accommodate the production of several different models intermixed on one assembly line. When the Endeavor sport utility vehicle was added in January of 2003, workers were building six different cars and trucks, more than any other U.S. plant. And productivity at the plant had improved dramatically. Getting the facility to that level of performance took the guiding hand of plant manager Rich Gilligan, who took over as manager in 1998 at a time when the plant had two notorious distinctions: It was one of the most automated yet least productive plants in the industry, and it was known as the place sued by the U.S. government for the abusive

Rich Gilligan of Mitsubishi.

sexual harassment of its female workers. That lawsuit was what most people knew about Mitsubishi Motors.

The high-profile case told the story of a dismal workplace: "sexual graffiti written on fenders about to pass female line workers; pornographic pictures taped on walls; male workers taunting women with wrenches and air compressors; women asked by male workers to bare their breasts; other women fondled; and women who complained of being fired or passed over for promotion." Almost from the beginning, the plant had a bad reputation regarding the employment of women. People in the local community looked with suspicion at plant employees. One of the shift bosses said, "We had guys who had no bad marks asked to stop coaching girls' softball teams just because they worked at *that* plant." After numerous employee complaints, the EEOC entered the picture and filed suit on behalf of 500 female employees, charging the company with sexual harassment. The case dragged on for three years, further draining employee morale and damaging an already-distant relationship between American workers and Japanese managers. That's the environment that Gilligan inherited.

The first step in the turnaround was the June 1998 settlement of the EEOC lawsuit for $34 million—still the largest sexual harassment settlement in history. The money was distributed to more than 400 women, many of whom still work at the plant. The EEOC settlement also dictated a makeover of the work environment. Although Gilligan knew he needed to improve productivity and quality at the plant, he also knew that he needed his human resources to back whatever changes were made. But first he had to show his support for his employees. He backed their suggestions to put "respect"

at the top of a new mission statement and "quality" second. Then, he set up a new department to investigate all employee complaints and train new employees in racial and sexual discrimination cases. And employees go through a refresher course every two years. Gilligan said, "I hope the spirit of what we do goes well beyond what's written down." Also put in place was a *zero-tolerance policy*—unacceptable and detrimental behavior will not be tolerated under any circumstances.

The environment at the plant in Normal has improved significantly. During EEOC "monitoring from 1998 through 2001, 140 discrimination and harassment complaints were reported. In 52 of these, the zero-tolerance policy was violated, resulting in eight firings, 14 suspensions without pay, and 30 disciplinary actions." The EEOC said, in its final report written in 2001, that Mitsubishi's "handling of complaints was 'much stricter' than federal and state laws require."

In terms of the plant's performance, warranty costs are down from $38 per car to $15.19 per car. The number of hours to build a car has dropped from 37 worker hours to 21.8 hours; parts ruined in production are only $4.85 a car, down from $30. Mitsubishi announced in 2003 that it was investing $200 million to expand the capacity of its American subsidiary by 25 percent, creating 300 additional jobs at the Normal plant.

DISCUSSION QUESTIONS

1. What do you think Mitsubishi's philosophy might be regarding the role of strategic human resource management? Explain. Do Rich Gilligan's actions at the Normal plant fit the company's philosophy? Explain.

2. Is a zero-tolerance policy an appropriate response for combating sexual harassment? Why or why not?

3. You're in charge of orienting new employees at the Mitsubishi plant. Create a general outline of what your orientation program would include.

4. What could other companies learn from Mitsubishi's experiences?

Sources: Information on company from company Web site (*www.mitsubishicars.com*), June 1, 2003; "Mitsubishi Plans Big Boost to U.S. Production," *Industry Week* (*www.industryweek.com*), March 18, 2003; D. Kiley, "Workplace Woes Almost Eclipse Mitsubishi Plant," *USA Today,* October 21, 2002, pp. B1+; "EEOC Responds to Final Report of Mitsubishi Consent Decree Monitors," EEOC Web site (*www.eeoc.gov*), May 23, 2001; and S. Greengard, "Zero Tolerance: Making It Work," *Workforce,* May 1999, pp. 28–34.

Chapter

13 Managing Change and Innovation

Ron Daly (pictured), president of R.R. Donnelley Company's printing business, is facing some tough choices in changing his organization.[1] This Chicago-based company is a commercial printer with 52 plants located around the world. What does Donnelley print? In addition to popular publications such as *TV Guide* and *Sports Illustrated*, it also prints catalogs, retail inserts, phone directories, financial publications, and books (about half of

those found on the *New York Times* best-seller lists are printed by the company each year).

The first few years of the twenty-first century have been rough ones for Donnelley. The company was a consistently high performer during the 1970s and 1980s. But its managers fell asleep at the wheel and didn't make the investments in technology-driven efficiencies that their competitors were making during the 1990s. Never fully recovering from that error in judgment, the company continued to struggle. Revenues fell over $1 billion from $5.7 billion in 2000 to $4.7 billion in 2002 and profits per share were down more than 40 percent. Part of the problem seemed to be poor controls. The newly named CEO found no serious cost or process control systems in place. There also was no company-wide computer system for monitoring processes or inventory. Something had to

be done, and the CEO found that something in a someone—Ron Daly.

Daly, an engaging and personable guy who had been with the company for over 33 years, was president of Donnelley's directory-printing business. As measured by profitability and revenue growth, his plants were Donnelley's best. To achieve those results, he coaxed plant managers to develop standard colors, paper weights, and printing practices so that jobs could be completed at the printing plant where it was most efficient. Daly also directly dealt with employees who were tied to the old machines and methods. "If certain people got in the way," he said, "we found a way to get rid of them."

Put yourself in Ron Daly's position. You've now got to expand your change program and educate your employees about the importance and necessity of continuing the needed organizational change efforts. How would you go about it?

What would *you* do **?**

T he managerial challenges facing Ron Daly in educating his employees about the importance and necessity of continuing the company's change efforts are certainly not unique. Big companies and small businesses, universities and colleges, state and city governments, and even the military are being forced to significantly change the way they do things. Although change has always been a part of the manager's job, it has become even more important in recent years. We'll describe why change is important and how managers can manage change in this chapter. And since change is often closely tied to an organization's innovation efforts, we'll also discuss ways in which managers can nurture innovation and increase their organization's adaptability.

● ● ● **organizational change**
Any alterations in people, structure, or technology.

■ **Self-Assessment Library**
Whenever you see this orange square, go to the R.O.L.L.S. Web site (**www.prenhall.com/ robbins**) to the Self-Assessment Library (S.A.L.) and complete the suggested self-assessment exercise. These exercises will help you discover things about yourself, your attitudes, and your personal strengths and weaknesses.

WHAT IS CHANGE?

Jim Zawacki, president of GR Spring & Stamping Inc., a precision metal job shop supplier in Grand Rapids, Michigan, is like many managers today who are taking steps to make their workplaces more efficient and flexible. Why? In Zawacki's case, it's the threat of losing manufacturing jobs to low-wage nations like China.[2] Zawacki is doing what managers everywhere must do—change! If it weren't for **organizational change**—that is, any alterations in people, structure, or technology—the manager's job would be relatively easy. Planning would be simple because tomorrow would be no different from today. The issue of effective organizational design would also be solved because the environment would be free from uncertainty and there would be no need to adapt. Similarly, decision making would be dramatically streamlined because the outcome of each alternative could be predicted with almost certain accuracy. It would, indeed, simplify the manager's job if, for example, competitors did not introduce new products or services, if customers didn't demand new and improved products, if governmental regulations were never modified, or if employees' needs never changed. But that's not the way it is. Change is an organizational reality.[3] And managing change is an integral part of every manager's job. (▬▬□▬ Go to the Web and check out S.A.L. #4—How Flexible Am I?)

● ● ● **Learning Review**

• Define organizational change.

• Explain how managers are affected by change.

FORCES FOR CHANGE

In Chapter 3, we pointed out the external and internal forces that constrain managers. These same forces also bring about the need for change. Let's briefly look at these factors.

External Forces

The external forces that create the need for change come from various sources. In recent years, the *marketplace* has affected firms such as Yahoo! as competition from Google, LookSmart, AskJeeves, and AltaVista intensified. These companies constantly adapt to changing consumer desires as they develop new search capabilities.

Governmental laws and regulations are a frequent impetus for change. For example, the Sarbanes-Oxley Act of 2002 required U.S. companies to change the way they disclose financial information and enact corporate governance.

Changes in technology are evident everywhere and affect every aspect of our lives. Communication has been dramatically altered by advances in computer software, as Microsoft's Tammy Savage, shown here with her NetGen project team, can attest. Savage persuaded Microsoft executives to let her group develop "threedegrees," a new group chatware program for the 13 to 24 age group. The free application software uses cutting-edge technology to allow group instant messaging accompanied by photos and animation.

Technology also creates the need for change. For example, technological improvements in diagnostic equipment have created significant economies of scale for hospitals and medical centers. Assembly-line technology in other industries is changing dramatically as organizations replace human labor with robots. In the greeting card industry, e-mail and the Internet have changed the way people exchange greeting cards.

The fluctuation in *labor markets* also forces managers to change. Organizations that need certain kinds of employees must change their human resource management activities to attract and retain skilled employees in the areas of greatest need. For instance, health care organizations facing severe nursing shortages have had to change the way they schedule work hours.

Economic changes, of course, affect almost all organizations. For instance, global recessionary pressures force organizations to become more cost-efficient. But even in a strong economy, uncertainties about interest rates, federal budget deficits, and currency exchange rates create conditions that may force organizations to change.

Internal Forces

In addition to the external forces just described, internal forces also create the need for change. These internal forces tend to originate primarily from the internal operations of the organization or from the impact of external changes.

A redefinition or modification of an organization's *strategy* often introduces a host of changes. For instance, when Steve Bennett took over as CEO of the troubled Intuit Inc. (Quicken, QuickBooks, and TurboTax are its best-known products), he found a company still being run as haphazardly as a start-up venture. "The operation was a mess. It was losing money. Its technology was outdated. Execution was grindingly slow, and nothing was documented."[4] By orchestrating a series of well-planned and dramatic strategic changes, he turned it into a profitable company with extremely committed employees. In addition, an organization's *workforce* is rarely static. Its composition changes in terms of age, education, ethnic background, sex, and so forth. Take, for instance, an organization where a large number of seasoned executives, because of financial reasons, decide to continue working instead of retiring. There might be a need to restructure jobs in order to retain and motivate younger managers. Also, the compensation and benefits system might need to be adapted to reflect the needs of this older workforce.

The introduction of new *equipment* represents another internal force for change. Employees may have their jobs redesigned, need to undergo training on how to operate the new equipment, or be required to establish new interaction patterns within their work group.

Finally, *employee attitudes* such as job dissatisfaction may lead to increased absenteeism, more voluntary resignations, and even labor strikes. Such events often lead to changes in management policies and practices.

The Manager as Change Agent

• • • **change agents**
People who act as catalysts and assume the responsibility for managing the change process.

Organizational changes need a catalyst. People who act as catalysts and assume the responsibility for managing the change process are called **change agents**. Who can be change agents?

We assume that changes are initiated and coordinated by a manager within the organization. However, the change agent could be a nonmanager—for example, a change specialist from the human resources department or even an outside consultant whose expertise is in change implementation. For major systemwide changes, an organization often hires outside consultants to provide advice and assistance. Because they're from the outside, they can offer an objective perspective that insiders may lack. However, outside consultants are usually at a disadvantage because they have an extremely limited understanding of the organization's history, culture, operating procedures, and people. Outside consultants are also prone to initiate more drastic change than insiders would (which can be either a benefit or a disadvantage) because they don't have to live with the repercussions after the change is implemented. In contrast, internal managers who act as change agents may be more thoughtful, and possibly overcautious, because they must live with the consequences of their decisions.

• • • Learning Review

- Discuss the external and internal forces for change.
- Contrast using internal and external change agents.

TWO VIEWS OF THE CHANGE PROCESS

We can use two very different metaphors to describe the change process.[5] One metaphor envisions the organization as a large ship crossing a calm sea. The ship's captain and crew know exactly where they're going because they've made the trip many times before. Change comes in the form of an occasional storm, a brief distraction in an otherwise calm and predictable trip. In the other metaphor, the organization is seen as a small raft navigating a raging river with uninterrupted white-water rapids. Aboard the raft are half-a-dozen people who have never worked together before, who are totally unfamiliar with the river, who are unsure of their eventual destination, and who, as if things weren't bad enough, are traveling at night. In the white-water rapids metaphor, change is an expected and natural state, and managing change is a continual process. These two metaphors present very different approaches to understanding and responding to change. Let's take a closer look at each one.

The Calm Waters Metaphor

Up until the late 1980s, the calm waters metaphor was pretty descriptive of the situation that managers faced. It's best illustrated by Kurt Lewin's three-step description of the change process.[6] (See Exhibit 13–1.)

According to Lewin, successful change can be planned and requires *unfreezing* the status quo, *changing* to a new state, and *refreezing* to make the change permanent. The status quo can be considered an equilibrium state. To move from this equilibrium, unfreezing is necessary. Unfreezing can be thought of as preparing for the needed change. It can be achieved by increasing the driving forces, which are forces that drive change and direct behavior away from the status quo; decreasing the *restraining forces*, which are forces that resist change and push behavior toward the status quo; or combining the two approaches.

Exhibit 13–1

The Change Process

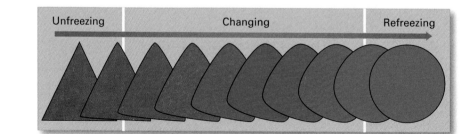

| Unfreezing | Changing | Refreezing |

Once unfreezing is done, the change itself can be implemented. However, merely introducing change doesn't ensure that the change will take hold. The new situation needs to be *refrozen* so that it can be sustained over time. Unless this last step is done, there's a strong chance that the change will be short lived as employees revert back to the old equilibrium state—that is, the old ways of doing things. The objective of refreezing, then, is to stabilize the new situation by reinforcing the new behaviors.

Note how Lewin's three-step process treats change simply as a break in the organization's equilibrium state. (▮▯▮ Go to the Web and check out Q & A 13.1.) The status quo has been disturbed and change is necessary to establish a new equilibrium state. However, a calm waters environment isn't what most managers face today.

White-Water Rapids Metaphor

The white-water rapids metaphor is consistent with our discussion of uncertain and dynamic environments in Chapters 3 and 8. It's also consistent with a world that's increasingly dominated by information, ideas, and knowledge.[7]

To get a feeling of what managing change might be like when you have to continually maneuver in uninterrupted and uncertain rapids, consider attending a college that had the following rules: Courses vary in length. Unfortunately, when you sign up, you don't know how long a course will run. It might go for two weeks or 30 weeks. Furthermore, the instructor can end a course any time he or she wants, with no prior warning. If that isn't bad enough, the length of the class changes each time it meets: Sometimes the class lasts 20 minutes; other times it runs for three hours. And the time of the next class meeting is set by the instructor during this class. There's one more thing. All exams are unannounced, so you have to be ready for a test at any time. To succeed in this type of environment, you'd have to be incredibly flexible and able to respond quickly to changing conditions. Students who are overly structured, "slow" to respond, or uncomfortable with change would not survive.

Growing numbers of managers are coming to accept that their job is much like what a student would face in such a college. The stability and predictability of the calm waters metaphor do not exist. Disruptions in the status quo are not occasional and temporary, and they are not followed by a return to calm waters. Many managers never get out of the rapids. They face constant change, bordering on chaos.

Is the white-water rapids metaphor an exaggeration? No! Although you'd expect this type of chaotic and dynamic environment in high-tech industries, even organizations in non-high-tech industries are faced with constant change. Take the case of Converse Inc., an athletic footwear manufacturer based in Massachusetts.[8] In this intensely competitive industry, a company has to be prepared for any possibility. Teens and preteens (a major target market) are no longer content with new sneaker styles every season. They want new and unique styles more often. Large megaretailers who sell the shoes are demanding more from manufacturers such as holding more inventory, replenishing supplies faster, and helping to find ways to sell more shoes. And competition is hot! Industry leaders Adidas, Reebok, and Nike keep the pressure on. The environmental demands were so overwhelming that Converse filed for Chapter 11 bankruptcy protection in

For a company in the midst of white-water rapids, look no further than Levi Strauss & Co., the venerable maker of jeans and jackets. Robert Hanson, president of the U.S. brand, and designer Caroline Calvin returned from assignment in Europe with a mission to turn the company's sagging fortunes around. With recent sales down 40 percent and six plants closing, the pair will be responsible for creating and implementing immediate changes throughout the firm. For example, here's how Hanson described the character of the new designs Levi's will unveil: "It has a bold, confident stature that doesn't say, Levi's is back. It says, 'Levi's is leading.'"

January 2001. However, managers at Converse who wanted to revitalize the brand knew that if they were to get the company out of bankruptcy and become profitable once again, they had to make changes. They decided to revive the once-popular Chuck Taylor line of canvas basketball shoes, make shoes for mountain biking and skateboarding, implement a company-wide quality management program, develop more athletic footwear for the women's and children's markets, and introduce a new collection of Converse brand apparel and accessories. Then, in July 2003, Converse managers announced another significant change. They had agreed to be acquired by Nike for $305 million. These significant changes were essential if Converse wanted to survive the white-water rapids environment in which it operated.

Putting the Two Views in Perspective

Does *every* manager face a world of constant and chaotic change? No, but the number who don't is dwindling. (▮▮▮▮ Go to the Web and check out S.A.L. #47—How Well Do I Respond to Turbulent Change?) Managers in such businesses as telecommunications, computer software, and women's clothing have long confronted a world of white-water rapids. These managers used to envy their counterparts in industries such as banking, utilities, oil exploration, publishing, and air transportation where the environment was historically more stable and predictable. However, those days of stability and predictability are long gone!

Today, any organization that treats change as the occasional disturbance in an otherwise calm and stable world runs a great risk. Too much is changing too fast for an organization or its managers to be complacent. It's no longer business as usual. And managers must be ready to efficiently and effectively manage the changes facing their organizations or their work areas. (▮▮▮▮ Go to the Web and check out Q & A 13.2.) How? That's what we'll discuss next.

● ● ● **Learning Review**

- Contrast the calm waters and white-water rapids metaphors of change.
- Explain Lewin's three-step model of the change process.
- Discuss the environment that managers face today.

MANAGING CHANGE

Managers at Hallmark, the world's largest greeting card company, knew that buyers of greeting cards were changing. Some of the emerging and evolving consumer trends they identified included peace of mind (success is measured by a person's sense of well-being), anxiety antidote (people are more involved with community and political activism), and make it easy (people want to minimize complexity in their lives).[9] To accommodate these trends, Hallmark's managers will look at changing the company's products, advertising, and perhaps even their human resource practices.

As change agents, managers should be motivated to initiate change because they are committed to improving their organization's performance. Initiating change involves identifying what organizational areas might need to be changed and putting the change process in motion. But that's not all there is to managing change. Managers must manage employee resistance to change. What we want to look at now are the types of change that managers can make and then at how they can deal with resistance to change.

Types of Change

What *can* a manager change? The manager's options fall into three categories: structure, technology, and people. (See Exhibit 13–2.) Changing *structure* includes any alteration in authority relations, coordination mechanisms, employee empowerment, job redesign, or similar structural variables. Changing *technology* encompasses modifications in the way work is performed or the methods and equipment that are used. Changing *people* refers to changes in employee attitudes, expectations, perceptions, and behavior.

Changing Structure We discussed structural issues in Chapter 10. Managers' organizing responsibilities include such activities as choosing the organization's formal design, allocating authority, and determining the degree of formalization. Once those structural decisions have been made, however, they aren't final. Changing conditions or changing strategies bring about the need to make structural changes.

What options does the manager have for changing structure? The manager has the same ones we introduced in our discussion of structure and design. A few examples should make this clearer. Recall from Chapter 10 that an organization's structure is defined in terms of work specialization, departmentalization, chain of command, span of control, centralization and decentralization, and formalization. Managers can alter one or more of these *structural components*. For instance, departmental responsibilities could be combined, organizational levels eliminated, or spans of control widened to make the organization flatter and less bureaucratic. Or more rules and procedures could be implemented to increase standardization. An increase in decentralization can be used to make decision making faster. Even downsizing involves changes in structure.

Another option would be to make major changes in the actual *structural design*. For instance, when Hewlett-Packard acquired Compaq Computer, several structural changes were made as product divisions were dropped, merged, or expanded. Or structural design changes might include a shift from a functional to a product structure or the creation of a project structure design. Avery-Dennis Corporation, for example, revamped its traditional functional structure to a new design that arranges work around cross-functional teams.

Changing Technology Managers can also change the technology used to convert inputs into outputs. Most early studies in management—such as the work of Taylor and the Gilbreths—dealt with efforts aimed at technological change. If you recall, scientific management sought to implement changes that would increase production efficiency based on time-and-motion studies. Today, major technological changes usually involve the introduction of new equipment, tools, or methods; automation; or computerization.

Exhibit 13–2

Three Categories of Change

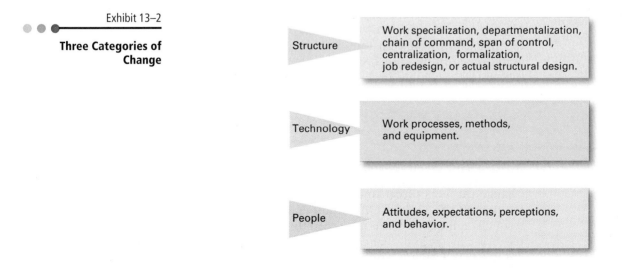

Structure	Work specialization, departmentalization, chain of command, span of control, centralization, formalization, job redesign, or actual structural design.
Technology	Work processes, methods, and equipment.
People	Attitudes, expectations, perceptions, and behavior.

Computerization has been the engine for all kinds of changes in the business environment, including employee training. Cisco's Internet Learning Solutions Group is charged with developing electronic training programs both for Cisco's own salesforce and channel partners and for the company's hundreds of thousands of customers. The team, whose leaders are pictured here, has developed tools ranging from virtual classrooms to video server technology and content development templates. "We really believe that our e-learning programs are a more effective way to grow skills in high volume in a shorter time than in the past," says the group's director.

Competitive factors or new innovations within an industry often require managers to introduce *new equipment, tools,* or *operating methods.* For example, coal mining companies in New South Wales updated operational methods, installed more efficient coal handling equipment, and made changes in work practices to be more productive. Even the U.S. Army applied sophisticated technology to its operations, including such advancements as three-dimensional shootout training devices and high-speed data links among troops on the battlefield.[10]

Automation is a technological change that replaces certain tasks done by people with machines. It began in the Industrial Revolution and continues today as one of a manager's options for structural change. Automation has been introduced (and sometimes resisted) in organizations such as the U.S. Postal Service, where automatic mail sorters are used, or in automobile assembly lines, where robots are programmed to do jobs that blue-collar workers used to perform.

Probably the most visible technological changes in recent years, though, have come through managers' efforts to expand *computerization.* Most organizations have sophisticated information systems. For instance, grocery stores and other retailers use scanners linked to computers that provide instant inventory information. Also, it's very uncommon for an office to not be computerized. At BP, employees had to learn how to deal with the personal visibility and accountability brought about by the implementation of an enterprise-wide information system. The integrative nature of this system meant that what any employee did on his or her computer automatically affected other computer systems on the internal network.[11] And the Benetton Group SpA uses computers to link together its manufacturing plants outside Treviso, Italy, with the company's various sales outlets and a highly automated warehouse.[12]

Changing People Changing people—that is, changing their attitudes, expectations, perceptions, and behaviors—isn't easy. Yet, for over 30 years now, academic researchers and actual managers have been interested in finding ways for individuals and groups within organizations to work together more effectively. The term **organizational development (OD)**, though occasionally referring to all types of change, essentially focuses on techniques or programs to change people and the nature and quality of interpersonal work relationships.[13] The most popular OD techniques are described in Exhibit 13–3. The common thread in these techniques is that each seeks to bring about changes in the organization's people. For example, executives at the Bank of Nova Scotia, Canada's second largest bank, knew that the success of a new customer sales and service strategy depended on changing employee attitudes and behaviors. Managers used different OD techniques during the strategic change including team building, survey feedback, and intergroup development. One indicator of how well these techniques worked in getting people to change was that every branch in Canada implemented the new strategy on or ahead of schedule.[14]

● ● ● **organizational development (OD)**
Techniques or programs to change people and the nature and quality of interpersonal work relationships.

Managing Resistance to Change

Change can be a threat to people in an organization. (▮▮▮▮▮▮ Go to the Web and check out Q & A 13.3.) Organizations can build up inertia that motivates people to resist changing their status quo, even though change might be beneficial. Why do people resist change and what can be done to minimize their resistance? (▮▮▮▮▮▮ Check out Passport Scenario 2 on page 334.)

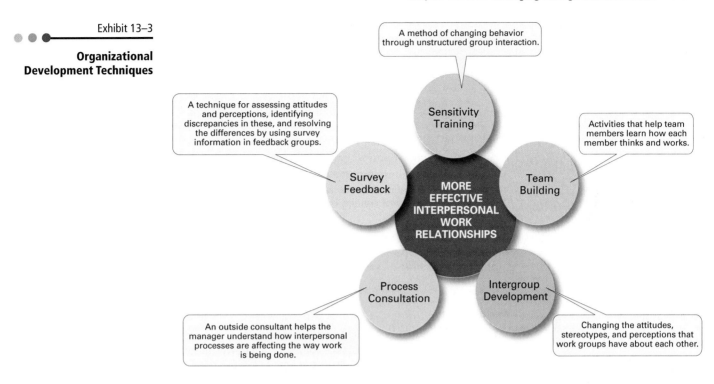

Exhibit 13–3

Organizational Development Techniques

Why People Resist Change It's often said that most people hate any change that doesn't jingle in their pockets. This resistance to change is well documented.[15] Why *do* people resist change? An individual is likely to resist change for the following reasons: uncertainty, habit, concern over personal loss, and the belief that the change is not in the organization's best interest.[16]

Change replaces the known with ambiguity and uncertainty. Regardless of how much you may dislike attending college, at least you know what's expected of you. When you leave college for the world of full-time employment, regardless of how eager you are to get out of college, you'll trade the known for the unknown. Employees in organizations are faced with similar uncertainty. For example, when quality control methods based on sophisticated statistical models are introduced into manufacturing plants, many quality control inspectors have to learn the new methods. Some inspectors may fear that they will be unable to do so and may, therefore, develop a negative attitude toward the change or behave poorly if required to use them.

Another cause of resistance is that we do things out of habit. Every day, when you go to school or work you probably go the same way. If you're like most people, you find a single route and use it regularly. As human beings, we're creatures of habit. Life is complex enough—we don't want to have to consider the full range of options for the hundreds of decisions we make every day. To cope with this complexity, we rely on habits or programmed responses. But when confronted with change, this tendency to respond in our accustomed ways becomes a source of resistance.

The third cause of resistance is the fear of losing something already possessed. Change threatens the investment you've already made in the status quo. The more that people have invested in the current system, the more they resist change. Why? They fear the loss of status, money, authority, friendships, personal convenience, or other economic benefits that they value. This helps explain why older workers tend to resist change more than younger workers. Older employees have generally invested more in the current system and thus have more to lose by changing.

A final cause of resistance is a person's belief that the change is incompatible with the goals and interests of the organization. For instance, an employee who believes that a proposed new job procedure will reduce product quality or productivity can be expected to resist the change. If the employee expresses his or her resistance positively, it can be beneficial to the organization.

Exhibit 13–4

Managerial Actions to Reduce Resistance to Change

Education and Communication

- Communicate with employees to help them see the logic of change.
- Educate employees through one-on-one discussions, memos, group meetings, or reports.
- Appropriate if source of resistance is either poor communication or misinformation.
- Must be mutual trust and credibility between managers and employees.

Participation

- Allows those who oppose a change to participate in the decision.
- Assumes that they have expertise to make meaningful contributions.
- Involvement can reduce resistance, obtain commitment to seeing change succeed, and increase quality of change decision.

Facilitation and Support

- Provide supportive efforts such as employee counseling or therapy, new skills training, or short, paid leave of absence.
- Can be time-consuming and expensive.

Negotiation

- Exchange something of value to reduce resistance.
- May be necessary when resistance comes from a powerful source.
- Potentially high costs and likelihood of having to negotiate with other resisters.

Manipulation and Co-optation

- Manipulation is covert attempts to influence such as twisting or distorting facts, withholding damaging information, or creating false rumors.
- Co-optation is a form of manipulation and participation.
- Inexpensive and easy ways to gain support of resisters.
- Can fail miserably if targets feel they've been tricked.

Coercion

- Using direct threats or force.
- Inexpensive and easy way to get support.
- May be illegal. Even legal coercion can be perceived as bullying.

Techniques for Reducing Resistance When managers see resistance to change as dysfunctional, they can use any of six actions to deal with it.[17] These six actions, described in Exhibit 13–4, include education and communication, participation, facilitation and support, negotiation, manipulation and co-optation, and coercion. Depending on the type and source of the resistance, managers might choose to use any of these. (▪▪▪◻▪▪ Go to the Web and check out PRISM #5—Managing Resistance to Change.)

• • • ● Learning Review

- Explain how managers might change structure, technology, and people.

- Explain why people resist change and how resistance might be managed.

Reinvent Yourself

Face it. The only constant thing about change is that it is constant. These days you don't have the luxury of dealing with change only once in a while. No, the workplace seems to change almost continuously. How can you reinvent yourself to deal with the demands of a constantly changing workplace?[18]

Being prepared isn't a credo just for the Boy Scouts; it should be your motto for dealing with a workplace that is constantly changing. Being prepared means taking the initiative and being responsible for your own personal career development. Rather than depending on your organization to provide you with career development and training opportunities, do it yourself. Take advantage of continuing education or graduate courses at local colleges. Sign up for workshops and seminars that can help you enhance your skills. Upgrading your skills to keep them current is one of the most important things you can do to reinvent yourself.

It's also important for you to be a positive force when faced with workplace changes. We don't mean that you should routinely accept any change that's being implemented. If you think that a proposed change won't work, speak up. Voice your concerns in a constructive manner. Being constructive may mean suggesting an alternative. However, if you feel that the change is beneficial, support it wholeheartedly and enthusiastically.

The changes that organizations make in response to a dynamic environment can be overwhelming and stressful. However, you can take advantage of these changes by reinventing yourself.

CONTEMPORARY ISSUES IN MANAGING CHANGE

Today's change issues—changing organizational cultures, handling employee stress, and making change happen successfully—are critical concerns for managers. What can managers do to change an organization's culture when that culture no longer supports the organization's mission? What can managers do to handle the stress created by today's dynamic and uncertain environment? And how can managers successfully manage the challenges of introducing and implementing change? These are the topics we'll be looking at in this section.

Changing Organizational Culture

When W. James McNerney Jr., took over as CEO of 3M Company, he brought with him managerial approaches from his old employer, General Electric. But he soon discovered that what was routine at GE was unheard of at 3M. For instance, he was the only one who showed up at meetings without a tie. And his blunt, matter-of-fact, and probing style of asking questions caught many 3M managers off guard. McNerney soon realized that he would first need to address the cultural issues before tackling any needed organizational changes.[19] The fact that an organization's culture is made up of relatively stable and permanent characteristics (see Chapter 3) tends to make that culture very resistant to change.[20] A culture takes a long time to form, and once established it tends to become entrenched. Strong cultures are particularly resistant to change because employees have become so committed to them. For instance, it didn't take long for Lou Gerstner, former CEO of IBM, to discover the power of a strong culture. Gerstner, the first outsider to lead IBM, needed to overhaul the ailing, tradition-bound company if it was going to regain its role as the dominant player in the computer industry. However, accomplishing that in an organization that prided itself on its long-standing culture was Gerstner's biggest challenge. He said, "I came to see in my decade at IBM that culture isn't just one aspect of the game—it *is* the game."[21] If, over time, a certain culture becomes inappropriate to an organization and a handicap to management, there might be little a manager can do to change it, especially in the short run. Even under the most favorable conditions, cultural changes have to be viewed in years, not weeks or even months.

To save United Airlines, UAL chairman and CEO Glenn Tilton will have to change a corporate culture that has been characterized in the past by friction between management and the unions, by disagreements among the employees, and by resistance to change. Tilton hopes to introduce flexibility, cooperation, teamwork, and commitment, along with cost savings and reorganization. Other CEOs have tried to transform the firm's culture and failed. The stakes are high; as one mechanic said, "Everybody's crossing their fingers and hoping this guy is the guy to do it, because he's all we've got right now."

Understanding the Situational Factors What "favorable conditions" might facilitate cultural change? (▉▉▉ ▉▉▉ Go to the Web and check out Q & A 13.4.) The evidence suggests that cultural change is most likely to take place when most or all of the following conditions exist:

- *A dramatic crisis occurs.* This can be the shock that weakens the status quo and makes people start thinking about the relevance of the current culture. Examples are a surprising financial setback, the loss of a major customer, or a dramatic technological innovation by a competitor.
- *Leadership changes hands.* New top leadership, who can provide an alternative set of key values, may be perceived as more capable of responding to the crisis than the old leaders were. Top leadership includes the organization's chief executive but might include all senior managers.
- *The organization is young and small.* The younger the organization, the less entrenched its culture. Similarly, it's easier for managers to communicate new values in a small organization than in a large one.
- *The culture is weak.* The more widely held the values and the higher the agreement among members on those values, the more difficult it will be to change. Conversely, weak cultures are more receptive to change than are strong ones.[22]

These situational factors help to explain why a company such as IBM faced challenges in reshaping its culture. For the most part, employees liked the old ways of doing things and didn't see the company's problems as critical.

How Can Cultural Change Be Accomplished? Now we ask the question: If conditions are right, how do managers go about changing culture? The challenge is to unfreeze the current culture, implement the new "ways of doing things," and reinforce those new values. No single action is likely to have the impact necessary to change something that's so ingrained and highly valued. Thus, there needs to be a comprehensive and coordinated strategy for managing cultural change, as shown in Exhibit 13–5.

As you can see, these suggestions focus on specific actions that managers can take to change the ineffective culture. Following these suggestions, however, is no guarantee that a manager's change efforts will succeed. Organizational members don't

Exhibit 13–5

The Road to Cultural Change

- Conduct a cultural analysis to identify cultural elements needing change.
- Make it clear to employees that the organization's survival is legitimately threatened if change is not forthcoming.
- Appoint new leadership with a new vision.
- Initiate a reorganization.
- Introduce new stories and rituals to convey the new vision.
- Change the selection and socialization processes and the evaluation and reward systems to support the new values.

quickly let go of values that they understand and that have worked well for them in the past. Managers must, therefore, be patient. Change, if it comes, will be slow. And managers must stay constantly alert to protect against any return to old, familiar practices and traditions.

Handling Employee Stress

As a student, you've probably experienced stress when finishing class assignments and projects, taking exams, or finding ways to pay rising college costs which may mean juggling a job and school. (░░▨▢ Go to the Web and check out S.A.L. #48—How Stressful Is My Life?) Then, there's the stress associated with getting a decent job after graduation. But, even after you've landed that job, your stress isn't likely to stop. For many employees, organizational change creates stress. A dynamic and uncertain environment characterized by mergers, restructurings, forced retirements, and downsizing has created a large number of employees who are overworked and stressed out.[24] In fact, 54 percent of U.S. employees in a national sample said they felt overworked and 55 percent said they were overwhelmed by their workload.[25] In this section, we review what stress is, what causes it, how to identify it, and what managers can do to reduce it.

stress
The physical and psychological tension an individual feels when he or she is facing or experiencing extraordinary demands, constraints, or opportunities and for which the outcome is perceived to be both uncertain and important.

What Is Stress? **Stress** is the physical and psychological tension an individual feels when he or she is facing or experiencing extraordinary demands, constraints, or opportunities and for which the outcome is perceived to be both uncertain and important.[26] Let's look more closely at what stress is.

Stress is not necessarily bad. Although it's often discussed in a negative context, stress does have a positive value, particularly when it offers a potential gain. Functional stress allows an athlete, stage performer, or employee to perform at his or her highest level in crucial situations. (▨▢░░ Go to the Web and check out Q & A 13.5.)

MANAGING WORKFORCE DIVERSITY

The Paradox of Diversity

When organizations bring diverse individuals in and socialize them into the culture, a paradox is created.[23] Managers want these new employees to accept the organization's core cultural values. Otherwise, the employees may have a difficult time fitting in or being accepted. At the same time, managers want to openly acknowledge, embrace, and support the diverse perspectives and ideas that these employees bring to the workplace.

Strong organizational cultures put considerable pressure on employees to conform, and the range of acceptable values and behaviors is limited. Therein lies the paradox. Organizations hire diverse individuals because of their unique strengths, yet their diverse behaviors and strengths are likely to diminish in strong cultures as people attempt to fit in.

A manager's challenge in this paradox of diversity is to balance two conflicting goals: to encourage employees to accept the organization's dominant values and to encourage employees to accept differences. When changes are made in the organization's culture, managers need to remember the importance of keeping diversity alive.

Exhibit 13–6

Causes of Stress

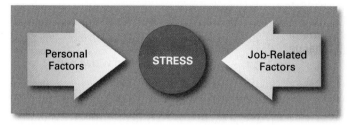

However, stress is more often associated with constraints and demands. A constraint prevents you from doing what you desire; demands refer to the loss of something desired. When you take a test at school or have your annual performance review at work, you feel stress because you confront opportunity, constraints, and demands. A good performance review may lead to a promotion, greater responsibilities, and a higher salary. But a poor review may keep you from getting the promotion. An extremely poor review might lead to your being fired.

Just because the conditions are right for stress to surface doesn't always mean it will. Two conditions are necessary for *potential* stress to become *actual* stress.[27] There must be uncertainty over the outcome, and the outcome must be important. Regardless of the conditions, stress exists only when there is doubt or uncertainty regarding whether the opportunity will be seized, whether the constraint will be removed, or whether the loss will be avoided. That is, stress is highest for individuals who are uncertain whether they will win or lose and lowest for individuals who think that winning or losing is a certainty. The importance of the outcome is also a critical factor. If winning or losing is unimportant, there is no stress. An employee who feels that keeping a job or earning a promotion is unimportant will experience no stress before a performance review.

Causes of Stress As shown in Exhibit 13–6, the causes of stress can be found in issues related to the organization or in personal factors that evolve out of the employee's private life. Clearly, change of any kind has the potential to cause stress. It can present opportunities, constraints, or demands. Moreover, changes are frequently created in a climate of uncertainty and around issues that are important to employees. It's not surprising, then, that change is a major stressor.

Symptoms of Stress What signs indicate that an employee's stress level might be too high? Stress shows itself in a number of ways. For instance, an employee who is experiencing high stress may become depressed, accident prone, or argumentative; may have difficulty making routine decisions; may be easily distracted, and so on. As Exhibit 13–7 shows, stress symptoms can be grouped under three general categories:

Exhibit 13–7

Symptoms of Stress

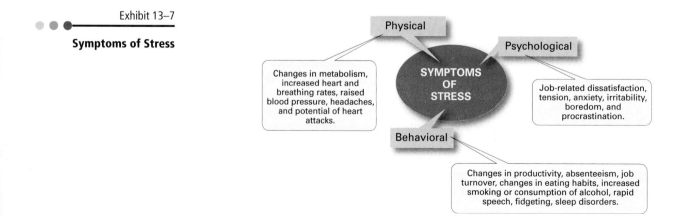

physical, psychological, and behavioral. Of these, the physical symptoms are least relevant to managers. Of greater importance are the psychological and behavioral symptoms since these directly affect an employee's work. (▬▬▯ Go to the Web and check out S.A.L. #49—Am I Burned Out?)

Reducing Stress As we mentioned earlier, not all stress is dysfunctional. Since stress can never be totally eliminated from a person's life, either off the job or on, managers are concerned with reducing the stress that leads to dysfunctional work behavior. How? Through controlling certain organizational factors to reduce organizational stress, and to a more limited extent, offering help for personal stress.

Things that managers can do in terms of organizational factors begin with employee selection. Managers need to make sure that an employee's abilities match the job requirements. When employees are in over their heads, their stress levels typically will be high. A realistic job preview during the selection process can also minimize stress by reducing ambiguity over job expectations. Improved organizational communications will keep ambiguity-induced stress to a minimum. Similarly, a performance planning program such as MBO will clarify job responsibilities, provide clear performance goals, and reduce ambiguity through feedback. Job redesign is also a way to reduce stress. If stress can be traced to boredom or to work overload, jobs should be redesigned to increase challenge or to reduce the workload. Redesigns that increase opportunities for employees to participate in decisions and to gain social support have also been found to reduce stress.[28]

Stress from an employee's personal life raises two problems. First, it's difficult for the manager to control directly. Second, there are ethical considerations. Specifically, does the manager have the right to intrude—even in the most subtle ways—in an employee's personal life? If a manager believes it's ethical and the employee is receptive, there are a few approaches the manager can consider. Employee *counseling* can provide stress relief. Employees often want to talk to someone about their problems, and the organization—through its managers, in-house human resource counselors, or free or low-cost outside professional help—can meet that need. Companies such as Citicorp, AT&T, and Johnson & Johnson provide extensive counseling services for their employees. A *time management program* can help employees whose personal lives suffer from a lack of planning that, in turn, creates stress may help them sort out their priorities.[29] Still another approach is organizationally sponsored *wellness programs*. For example, Coors Brewing Company of Golden, Colorado, offers employees a 30,000-square-foot fitness facility. SRA International of Fairfax, Virginia, provides employees with a nurse advocate program to help them remain healthy. At Lab Safety Supply Corporation, employees can take advantage of massage therapy and nutrition and fitness programs.[30] And at Eddie Bauer, busy or stressed executives can take naps in specially designated wellness rooms.[31]

THINKING CRITICALLY ABOUT ETHICS

Although numerous organizations provide stress reduction programs, many employees choose not to participate. Why? Many employees are reluctant to ask for help, especially if a major source of that stress is job insecurity. After all, there's still a stigma associated with stress. Employees don't want to be perceived as being unable to handle the demands of their job. Although they may need stress management now more than ever, few employees want to admit that they're stressed. What can be done about this paradox? Do organizations even *have* an ethical responsibility to help employees deal with stress?

The Ongoing Challenge of Making Change Happen Successfully

Organizational change isn't necessary only when strategies change or crises occur; it's an ongoing daily challenge facing managers in the United States *and* around the globe. In a global study of organizational changes in over 2,000 organizations in Europe, Japan, the United States, and the United Kingdom, 82 percent of the respondents had implemented major information systems changes, 74 percent had created horizontal sharing of services and information, 65 percent had implemented flexible human resource practices, and 62 percent had decentralized operational decisions.[32] Each of these major changes entailed numerous other changes in structure, technology, and people. When changes are needed, who makes them happen? Who manages them? Although you may think that it's the responsibility of top-level managers, actually managers at *all* organizational levels are involved in the change process.

Even with the involvement of all levels of managers in change efforts, change processes don't always work the way they should. In fact, a global study of organizational change concluded that "Hundreds of managers from scores of U.S. and European companies [are] satisfied with their operating prowess… [but] dissatisfied with their ability to implement change."[33] What can be done to address this shortcoming? How can managers make change happen successfully? Managers can increase the likelihood of making change happen successfully by focusing on making the organization ready for change, understanding their own role in the process, and increasing the role of individual employees. Let's look at each of these suggestions.

In an industry where growth is slowing and competitors are becoming stronger, United Parcel Service (UPS) prospers. How? By embracing change! Managers spent a decade creating new worldwide logistics businesses because they anticipated slowing domestic shipping demand. They continue change efforts in order to exploit new opportunities.[34] UPS is what we call a change-capable organization. What does it take to be a change-capable organization? Exhibit 13–8 summarizes the characteristics.

The second component of making change happen successfully is for managers to recognize their own important role in the process. Managers can, and do, act as change agents. But their role in the change process includes more than being catalysts for change. They also must be change leaders. When organizational members resist change, it's the manager's responsibility to lead the change effort. But even when there's no resistance to the change, someone has to assume leadership. That someone is the organization's managers.

What can a change leader do to make change happen successfully? Here are some suggestions: create a simple, compelling statement of the need for change; communicate constantly and honestly throughout the process; get as much employee participa-

---

Exhibit 13–8

● ● ●

Characteristics of Change-Capable Organizations

- *Link the present and the future.* Think of work as more than an extension of the past; think about future opportunities and issues and factor them into today's decisions.
- *Make learning a way of life.* Change-friendly organizations excel at knowledge sharing and management.
- *Actively support and encourage day-to-day improvements and changes.* Successful change can come from the small changes as well as the big ones.
- *Ensure diverse teams.* Diversity ensures that things won't be done like they're always done.
- *Encourage mavericks.* Since their ideas and approaches are outside the mainstream, mavericks can help bring about radical change.
- *Shelter breakthroughs.* Change-friendly organizations have found ways to protect those breakthrough ideas.
- *Integrate technology.* Use technology to implement changes.
- *Build and deepen trust.* People are more likely to support changes when the organization's culture is trusting and managers have credibility and integrity.

Source: Based on P.A. McLagan, "The Change-Capable Organization," *T&D*, January 2003, pp. 50–59.

tion as possible; respect employees' apprehension about the change but encourage them to be flexible; remove those who resist but only after all possible attempts have been made to get their commitment to the change (look back at the chapter-opening case and Ron Daly's recognition of the importance of doing this); aim for short-term change successes since large-scale change can be a long time coming; and set a positive example.[35]

The final aspect of making change happen successfully revolves around getting all organizational members involved. Successful organizational change is not a one-person job. Individual employees are a powerful resource in identifying and addressing change issues. "If you develop a program for change and simply hand it to your people, saying, 'Here, implement this,' it's unlikely to work. But when people help to build something, they will support it and make it work."[36] Managers need to encourage employees to be change agents—to look for those day-to-day improvements and changes that individuals and teams can make. For instance, a study of organizational change found that 77 percent of changes at the work-group level were reactions to a specific, current problem or to a suggestion from someone outside the work group; and 68 percent of those changes occurred in the course of employees' day-to-day work.[37]

● ● ● ● Learning Review

- Explain why changing organizational culture is so difficult and how managers can do it.

- Describe employee stress and how managers can help employees deal with stress.

- Discuss what it takes to make change happen successfully.

STIMULATING INNOVATION

"Winning in business today demands innovation."[38] Such is the stark reality facing today's managers. (▨◻▨▨ Go to the Web and check out Q & A 13.6.) In the dynamic, chaotic world of global competition, organizations must create new products and services and adopt state-of-the-art technology if they are to compete successfully.[39] Coors, for instance, has long been known for its technical innovations; it was the first beer company to use aluminum cans for packaging its products and was also the first to produce cold-filtered beer. However, the company isn't resting on its past successes. It continues to innovate products and processes.

What companies come to mind when you think of successful innovators? Maybe Sony Corporation, with its MiniDisks, PlayStations, Aibo robot pets, Cyber-Shot digital cameras, and MiniDV Handycam camcorders. Maybe 3M Corporation with its Post-It notes, Scotchgard protective coatings, and cellophane tape. Maybe Intel Corporation with its continual advancements in chip designs. What's the secret to the success of these innovator champions? What, if anything, can other managers do to make their organizations more innovative? In the following pages, we'll try to answer those questions as we discuss the factors behind innovation.

● ● ● creativity
The ability to combine ideas in a unique way or to make unusual associations between ideas.

● ● ● innovation
The process of taking a creative idea and turning it into a useful product, service, or method of operation.

Creativity Versus Innovation

Creativity refers to the ability to combine ideas in a unique way or to make unusual associations between ideas.[40] An organization that stimulates creativity develops unique ways to work or novel solutions to problems. But creativity by itself isn't enough. The outcomes of the creative process need to be turned into useful products, services, or work methods, which is defined as **innovation**. Thus, the innovative organization is characterized by its ability to channel creativity into useful outcomes. When managers talk about changing an organization to make it more creative, they usually

● ● ●
Exhibit 13–9

**Systems View of
Innovation**

Source: Adapted from R.W.
Woodman, J.E. Sawyer, and R.W.
Griffin, "Toward a Theory of
Organizational Creativity,"
Academy of Management Review,
April 1993, p. 309.

Inputs	Transformation	Outputs
Creative individuals, groups, organizations	Creative environment, process, situation	Innovative product(s), work methods

mean they want to stimulate and nurture innovation. Sony, 3M, and Intel are aptly described as innovative because they take novel ideas and turn them into profitable products and work methods.

Stimulating and Nurturing Innovation

Using the systems model we introduced in Chapter 2, we can better understand how organizations become more innovative.[41] (See Exhibit 13–9.) We see from this model that getting the desired outputs (innovative products) involves both the inputs and the transformation of those inputs. Inputs include creative people and groups within the organization. But having creative people isn't enough. It takes the right environment for the innovation process to take hold and prosper as the inputs are transformed. (■□■■ Go to the Web and check out Q & A 13.7.) What does this "right" environment—that is, an environment that stimulates innovation—look like? We've identified three sets of variables that have been found to stimulate innovation: the organization's structure, culture, and human resource practices. (See Exhibit 13–10.)

Are there innovative ways to be innovative? Scott Augustine seems to have found some. Augustine is CEO of Augustine Medical, a $64 million maker of medical devices like surgical warming blankets and heated tents for treating chronic wounds. Side-by-side with the engineers in the firm's research and development group, for instance, are prop builders from regional theater companies who put their imagination to work on the latest surgical materials and manufacturing processes. Augustine also requires every department in the firm to experiment all the time. "One thing that will get a senior manager in trouble fast is if I detect there's nothing new going on in their department," Augustine says. "I ask people constantly, 'What experiments have you done lately?'"

Structural Variables Research into the effect of structural variables on innovation shows five things.[42] First, organic structures positively influence innovation. Because this type of organization is low in formalization, centralization, and work specialization, organic structures facilitate the flexibility, adaptability, and cross-fertilization necessary in innovation. Second, the easy availability of plentiful resources provides a key building block for innovation. With an abundance of resources, managers can afford to purchase innovations, can afford the cost of instituting innovations, and can absorb failures. Third, frequent interunit communication helps break down barriers to innovation.[43] Cross-functional teams, task forces, and other such organizational designs facilitate interaction across departmental lines and are widely used in innovative organizations. Fourth, innovative organizations try to minimize extreme time pressures on creative activities despite the demands of white-water-type environments. Although time pressures may spur people to work harder and may make them feel more creative, studies show that it actually causes them to be less creative.[44] Finally, studies have shown that when an organization's structure provided explicit support for creativity from work and nonwork sources, an employee's creative performance was enhanced. What kinds of support were found to be beneficial? Things like encouragement, open communication, readiness to listen, and useful feedback.[45] 3M, for instance, is highly decentralized, takes on many of the characteristics of small, organic organizations, and supports its employees in their creative activities. The company also has the "deep pockets" needed to support its policy of allowing scientists and engineers to use a portion of their time on projects of their own choosing.[46]

Exhibit 13–10

Innovation Variables

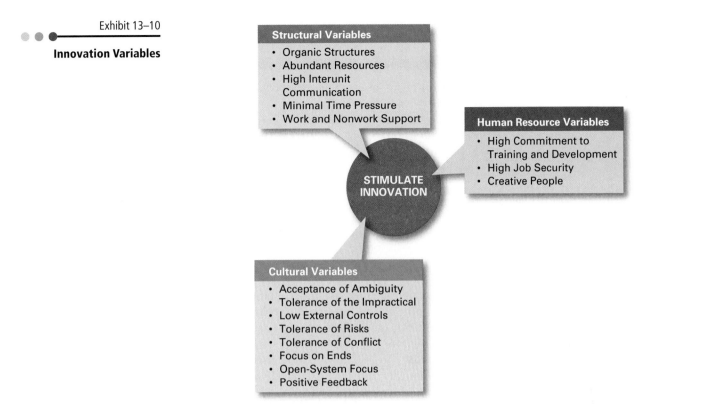

Structural Variables
- Organic Structures
- Abundant Resources
- High Interunit Communication
- Minimal Time Pressure
- Work and Nonwork Support

Human Resource Variables
- High Commitment to Training and Development
- High Job Security
- Creative People

STIMULATE INNOVATION

Cultural Variables
- Acceptance of Ambiguity
- Tolerance of the Impractical
- Low External Controls
- Tolerance of Risks
- Tolerance of Conflict
- Focus on Ends
- Open-System Focus
- Positive Feedback

Cultural Variables "Throw the bunny" is part of the lingo used by a project team at toy company Mattel. It refers to a juggling lesson where team members tried to learn to juggle two balls and a stuffed bunny. Most people easily learn to juggle two balls but can't let go of that third object. Creativity, like juggling, is learning to let go—that is, to "throw the bunny." And for Mattel, having a culture where people are encouraged to "throw the bunny" is important to its continued product innovations.[47]

Innovative organizations tend to have similar cultures.[48] They encourage experimentation, reward both successes and failures, and celebrate mistakes. An innovative culture is likely to have the following characteristics.

- *Acceptance of ambiguity.* Too much emphasis on objectivity and specificity constrains creativity. (▮▮▮▯▯ Go to the Web and check out S.A.L. #7—How Well Do I Handle Ambiguity?)
- *Tolerance of the impractical.* Individuals who offer impractical, even foolish, answers to what-if questions are not stifled. What at first seems impractical might lead to innovative solutions.
- *Low external controls.* Rules, regulations, policies, and similar organizational controls are kept to a minimum.
- *Tolerance of risk.* Employees are encouraged to experiment without fear of consequences should they fail. Mistakes are treated as learning opportunities.
- *Tolerance of conflict.* Diversity of opinions is encouraged. Harmony and agreement between individuals or units are *not* assumed to be evidence of high performance.
- *Focus on ends rather than means.* Goals are made clear, and individuals are encouraged to consider alternative routes toward meeting the goals. Focusing on ends suggests that there might be several right answers to any given problem.
- *Open-system focus.* Managers closely monitor the environment and respond to changes as they occur.
- *Positive feedback.* Managers provide positive feedback, encouragement, and support so employees feel that their creative ideas will receive attention.

Becoming a **Manager**

- *Pay attention to how you handle change. Figure out why you resist certain changes and not others.*
- *Practice using different approaches to managing resistance to change at work or in your personal life.*
- *Read material that's been written about how to be a more creative person.*
- *Find ways to be innovative and creative as you complete class projects or work projects.*
- ▪▪◻▪ *Go to the Web and complete these exercises from the Self-Assessment Library (S.A.L.) found on R.O.L.L.S: #4—How Flexible Am I?, #7—How Well Do I Handle Ambiguity?, #8—How Creative Am I?, #47—How Well Do I Respond to Turbulent Change?, #48—How Stressful Is My Life?, and #49—Am I Burned Out?*

Human Resource Variables In this category, we find that innovative organizations actively promote the training and development of their members so their knowledge remains current; offer their employees high job security to reduce the fear of getting fired for making mistakes; and encourage individuals to become "champions" of change. (▪▪◻▪ Go to the Web and check out S.A.L. #8—How Creative Am I?) **Idea champions** actively and enthusiastically support new ideas, build support, overcome resistance, and ensure that innovations are implemented. Research finds that these idea champions have common personality characteristics: extremely high self-confidence, persistence, energy, and a tendency toward risk-taking. Champions also display characteristics associated with dynamic leadership. They inspire and energize others with their vision of the potential of an innovation and through their strong personal conviction in their mission. They're also good at gaining the commitment of others to support their mission. In addition, champions have jobs that provide considerable decision-making discretion. This autonomy helps them introduce and implement innovations in organizations.[49] For instance, *Spirit* and *Opportunity*, two golf-cart-sized exploration rovers sent to explore the surface of Mars (scheduled to land on the planet in 2004) never would have been built had it not been for an idea champion by the name of Donna L. Shirley. As head of Mars exploration in the 1990s at NASA's Jet Propulsion Laboratory in Pasadena, California, Shirley had been working since the early 1980s on the idea of putting roving vehicles on Mars. Despite ongoing funding and management support problems, she continued to champion the idea until it was approved in the early 1990s.[50]

••• **idea champions**
Individuals who actively and enthusiastically support new ideas, build support, overcome resistance, and ensure that innovations are implemented.

●●●● **Learning Review**

- Explain why innovation isn't just creativity.
- Explain the systems view of innovation.
- Describe the structural, cultural, and human resource variables that are necessary for innovation.

- Explain what idea champions are and why they're important to innovation.

Managers **Respond** to a **Manager's** Dilemma

····Pauline Thomas

Secretary/Treasurer, Thomas Electric Inc., Glendale, Arizona

Ron should appoint a committee of local managers from all the company's plants to determine what changes need to be made in structure, technology, and people. Based on their findings, these changes should be put into effect by having the same local managers act as change agents. They should design and initiate an organizational development program to educate employees through communication, participation, facilitation, and support. Finally, Ron should have periodic meetings with the change agents to ensure that the changes are stabilized. In addition, he should continue to monitor the new systems as well as fluctuations in markets or other external factors to stay aware of new changes that may be required.

Learning Summary

After reading and studying this chapter, you should be able to:

- Define organizational change.
- Explain how managers are affected by change.
- Discuss the external and internal forces for change.
- Contrast using internal and external change agents.
- Contrast the calm waters and white-water rapids metaphors of change.
- Explain Lewin's three-step model of the change process.
- Discuss the environment that managers face today.
- Explain how managers might change structure, technology, and people.

- Explain why people resist change and how resistance might be managed.
- Explain why changing organizational culture is so difficult and how managers can do it.
- Describe employee stress and how managers can help employees deal with stress.
- Discuss what it takes to make change happen successfully.
- Explain why innovation isn't just creativity.
- Explain the systems view of innovation.
- Describe the structural, cultural, and human resource variables that are necessary for innovation.
- Explain what idea champions are and why they're important to innovation.

Thinking About Management Issues

1. Can a low-level employee be a change agent? Explain your answer.
2. Innovation requires allowing people to make mistakes. However, being wrong too many times can be fatal. Do you agree? Why or why not? What are the implications for nurturing innovation?
3. How are opportunities, constraints, and demands related to stress? Give an example of each.

4. Planned change is often thought to be the best approach to take in organizations. Can unplanned change ever be effective? Explain.
5. Organizations typically have limits to how much change they can absorb. As a manager, what signs would you look for that might suggest that your organization has exceeded its capacity to change?

Working Together: Team-Based Exercise

Stress is something that all of us face, and college students, particularly, may have extremely stressful lives. How do you recognize when you're under a lot of stress? What do you do to deal with that stress?

Form teams of three or four students. Each person in the group should describe how he or she knows when he or she is under a lot of stress. What symptoms does

each person show? Make a list of these symptoms and categorize them using Exhibit 13-7. Then, each person should also describe things that he or she has found to be particularly effective in dealing with stress. Make a list of these stress-handling techniques. Out of that list, identify your top three stress reducers and be prepared to share these with the class.

Ethical Dilemma Exercise

How can a city manager deal with barriers to change in an ethical way? Hisperia, California, with 65,000 residents, was badly in need of change. Its city council members publicly criticized each other as well as city employees, and some citizens talked of recalling city officials. Inefficiency was rampant, employee morale was low, management was disciplining more employees, and public trust was lacking. Although the city had been incorporated less than 20 years before, it already faced serious financial problems due to both growth and the effects of recession. However, coming to grips with the situation was difficult because of high turnover in the city's management and on the city council.

When Robb Quincey and Rod Foster became city manager and deputy city manager, they sought to instill constructive change so the government could function properly. Despite internal conflict, council disagreements, and public skepticism, the managers and elected officials agreed to restructure the city's organization, encourage innovation, and tackle contro-

versial issues. With public participation, they also defined a community vision as the basis for changes in financial reporting; changes to make policies and procedures consistent across departments; and changes to involve and inform the public. Following the philosophy that "it was far better to do our jobs than to keep our jobs," city managers and employees began to take risks. Just as important, they resolved to finish what they started. Ultimately the changes helped improve the city's financial position, boost productivity, attract new jobs and residents, and facilitate internal and external communication.[51]

Imagine that you're Hisperia's deputy city manager. A council member has publicly criticized a member of your staff for recommending an expensive computer system when the city faces grave financial difficulties. This council member has tried to block nearly every change suggested by you or your staff, regardless of cost or benefit. You want to be professional in dealing with any resistance to change. On the other hand, you also want to protect your staff from being openly criticized. Look over Exhibit 13–4 as you consider this ethical challenge and decide which of the following options to choose—and why.

Option A: Using education and cooperation, convince other council members to prohibit any critical remarks except when the criticized employee is present to explain or defend.

Option B: Using negotiation, offer to advance the council member's pet projects in exchange for public silence (if not support) on staff members' decisions and actions.

Option C: Using participation, ask for periodic, private meetings during which council members can air concerns for you and your staff to address.

Case Application

Electronic Arts

The video game industry is serious business. For two years straight, U.S. computer and video game revenues surpassed domestic movie box-office receipts. In this industry, where customers are fickle and demanding and competition is intense, one company, Electronic Arts (EA), has prospered. As the number-one video game publisher in the United States, EA lives and dies by its innovations. Its product lineup includes over 100 popular titles such as *Def Jam Vendetta*, *Medal of Honor Frontline*, *Madden NFL 2003*, *SimCity 4*, *The Lord of the Rings: The Two Towers*, and *Harry Potter and the Sorcerer's Stone*, a popular game, which in 2002 accounted for 12 percent of sales. The company has created over 50 best-sellers (each with more than 1 million copies sold) since 1998. Fiscal year 2002 was its best ever. Revenues were $1.7 billion (30 percent higher than 2001) and net income was up by 212 percent. In addition, EA was ninety-first on *Fortune*'s list of best companies to work for. "EA is more than a successful company in a glamorous industry. It's a model of successful management for companies in *any* industry."

With its record of accomplishments, you wouldn't think there'd be much anxiety or stress at EA. Yet, the reality is that paranoia is critical to its success. A top game title takes anywhere from 12 to 36 months to produce and costs between $5 million and $10 million. That's a significant investment risk riding on the company's ability to be innovative. John Riccitello, president and chief operating officer, says, "The forgotten aspect of creativity is discipline." The hard part, and the part that EA pursues relentlessly, "is identifying the right idea, assembling the best development team, solving the inevitable technical problems, creating a game that people want to play, getting all of the work done on schedule, getting it to market at the right time, and knowing how to generate buzz about it in an increasingly crowded market." How does EA get this done?

It starts with the discipline of understanding ideas. Game designers try to identify the creative center of a game—what they call the "creative x"—so they understand what the game is about. Then, it's the discipline of understanding the customers by using focus groups to pinpoint desires and likes and dislikes. And it's the discipline of sharing best practices and technologies through the company's intranet library. As one employee said, "If somebody develops a better blade of grass in one game, that grass will be in somebody else's game the next day." Then, there's the discipline of developing the next generation of creative leaders. The company's "emerging leaders" program gives participants firsthand experience in departments outside their own. And there's the discipline of studying the competition. Employees are encouraged to know the features of competitors' products. Then, it's disciplined project management. Riccitello says, "If you're working on a game and you miss your deadlines, you won't be working here very long." Although the discipline of creativity is important at EA, you can't overlook the passion of the company's game designers. Nearly everyone at EA grew up playing games. They love what they do and are inspired to look for new and creative challenges not only for the hardcore gamers, but for the casual gamers as well.

The pressure of creating constant hits might seem to be an incredible strain on employees. Yet, that doesn't seem to be the case at EA. Sometimes programmers will spend days working on something that takes three seconds in the actual game. But it's that kind of devotion, discipline, and innovation that has served EA well.

DISCUSSION QUESTIONS

1. Do you think EA faces more of a calm waters or white-water rapids environment? Explain. What external and internal forces might create the need for EA to change?

2. Using Exhibit 13-10, describe how EA stimulates innovation.

3. Describe EA's disciplined approach to innovation. What do you think of this approach? Explain.

4. What could other organizations learn about change and innovation from EA?

Sources: Information from company Web site (*www.ea.com*), and Hoover's Online (*www.hoovers.com*), June 11, 2003; C. Salter, "Playing to Win," *Fast Company*, December 2002, pp. 80–91; G.L. Cooper and E.K. Brown, "Video Game Industry Update," *Bank of America Equity Research Brief*, June 7, 2002; and M. Athitakis, "Steve Rechtschaffner, Game Wizard," *Business 2.0*, May 2002, p. 82.

John Riccitello, president and COO of Electronic Arts.

Part 4

You're the Manager: Putting Ethics into Action

As a manager, you'll often face decisions involving ethical questions. How can you learn to identify the ethical dilemma, keep stakeholders in mind, think through the alternatives, and foresee the consequences of your decisions? This unique interactive feature, positioned at the end of Parts Two, Three, Four, Five, and Six, casts you in the role of a manager dealing with hypothetical yet realistic ethical issues. To start, read the preview paragraph below. Then **log on to www.prenhall.com/robbins and go the R.O.L.L.S. Web site** *to consider the decisions you would make in the role of manager.*

General Electric has long been known for the quality of its products and its management. One reason the company continues to be so highly regarded—and so successful—is its careful attention to human resource management. In this hypothetical situation, you play the role of a General Electric executive who must appraise subordinates' performance using a multiperson ranking system. How will you deal ethically with those you rank among the lowest? Log on to *www.prenhall.com/robbins* to put ethics into action!

Passport

Scenario 1

Patrick Hollis, a native of the United Kingdom, is the Corporate Director of Strategic Planning for Grupo Bimbo, SA, Mexico's largest commercial baking company and one of the top baking companies in the world. He transferred from the London office to Bimbo's headquarters in Mexico City nine months ago. In Patrick's previous position as Director of Strategic Planning for the European division, he had developed an annual strategic planning procedure that the European managers had used quite successfully. One of his first goals in his new corporate position was implementing this strategic planning procedure throughout the organization. But the initiative had not gone as smoothly as he had hoped and it needed to be dealt with.

Patrick had a number of other critical strategic projects that his boss, the CEO, had assigned him so he had delegated the assignment of finding out what had happened with the strategic planning initiative to two of his team members, Maria Mendez and Satoshi Okuda. He had also asked Maria and Satoshi to come up with some recommendations for addressing the problem.

Maria, a native of Mexico, had her MBA from the Universidad de Monterrey (University of Monterrey) and had worked in strategic planning at Grupo Bimbo for two years. Satoshi had recently joined the company after completing his studies at Chiba University. Patrick had thought that the unique global perspective of these two would be beneficial to uncovering the problems associated with the implementation of the corporate strategic planning process. However, after two weeks, the two hadn't made any progress and in fact, had expressed to others in the department that they were uncomfortable with being delegated such an important task. What role might cross-cultural differences in delegating tasks be playing here? How can Patrick get Maria and Satoshi to proceed with this important assignment?

To answer these questions, you'll have to do some research on the countries. **Go to www.prenhall.com/robbins, the R.O.L.L.S. Web site, and click on Passport.** *When the map appears, click on the countries you need to research. You'll find background information on the country and general information about the country's economy, population, and workforce. In addition, you'll find specific information on the country's culture and the unique qualities associated with doing business there.*

Scenario 2

After studying the idea for some time, Scott Estes, manager of global marketing research for Reebok International, is convinced that the athletic footwear and apparel company would benefit greatly from a customer-based interactive Web site. Considering that communicating via the Internet is second nature to most teens and young adults and that these age groups are the prime target market for athletic footwear and apparel, Scott believes that good marketing research feedback and information could be obtained from such a site.

Scott manages a great team of marketing research experts—Kerstin Muller from Germany, Antony Liow from Singapore, and Marta Ochoa from Brazil have several years of industry and marketing research experience among them. It's a great resource and knowledge base that Scott relies on as each team member brings a different perspective to the department's marketing research tasks. However, when Scott presented the idea of an interactive customer research Web site at last week's meeting, his globally diverse marketing research team wasn't sold on the idea. However, Scott wants to implement the idea. How can he get his team behind the change? Keeping in mind any cross-cultural differences, what will Scott need to do to overcome their resistance to this new idea? If you were Scott, what would you do?

To answer these questions, you'll have to do some research on the countries. **Go to www.prenhall.com/robbins, the R.O.L.L.S. Web site, and click on Passport.** *When the map appears, click on the countries you need to research. You'll find background information on the country and general* *information about the country's economy, population, and workforce. In addition, you'll find specific information on the country's culture and the unique qualities associated with doing business there.*

Managing Entrepreneurial Ventures

Organizing Issues

Donald Hannon, president of Graphic Laminating Inc., in Solon, Ohio, redesigned his organization's structure by transforming it into an employee-empowered company. He wanted to drive authority down through the organization so that employees were responsible for their own efforts. One way he did this was by creating employee teams to handle specific projects. Employees with less experience were teamed with veteran employees. He says, "I want to build a good team and give people the ability to succeed. Sometimes that means giving them the ability to make mistakes, and I have to keep that in perspective. The more we allow people to become better at what they do, the better they will become—and the better we all will do."[1]

Once the start-up and planning issues for the entrepreneurial venture have been addressed, the entrepreneur is ready to begin organizing the entrepreneurial venture. There are five organizing issues an entrepreneur must address: the legal forms of organization, organizational design and structure, human resource management, stimulating and making changes, and the continuing importance of innovation.

Legal Forms of Organization

The first organizing decision that an entrepreneur must make is a critical one. It's the form of legal ownership for the venture. The two primary factors that affect this decision are taxes and legal liability. An entrepreneur wants to minimize the impact of both of these factors. The right choice can protect the entrepreneur from legal liability as well as save tax dollars, in both the short run and the long run.

What alternatives are available? There are three basic ways to organize an entrepreneurial venture: sole proprietorship, partnership, and corporation. However, when you include the variations of these basic organizational alternatives, you end up with six possible choices, each with its own tax consequences, liability issues, and pros and cons. These six choices are sole proprietorship, general partnership, limited liability partnership (LLP), C corporation, S corporation, and limited liability company (LLC). Let's briefly look at each one with its advantages and drawbacks. (Exhibit P4–1 on page 336 summarizes the basic information about each organizational alternative.)

Sole Proprietorship. A **sole proprietorship** is a form of legal organization in which the owner maintains sole and complete control over the business and is personally liable for business debts. There are no legal requirements for establishing a sole proprietorship other than obtaining necessary local business licenses and permits. In a sole proprietorship, income and losses "pass through" to the owner and are taxed at the owner's personal income tax rate. The biggest drawback, however, is the unlimited personal liability for any and all debts of the business.

General Partnership. A **general partnership** is a form of legal organization in which two or more business owners share the management and risk of the business. Even though a partnership is possible without a written agreement, the potential and inevitable problems that arise in any partnership make a written partnership agreement drafted by legal counsel a highly recommended thing to do.

Can partnerships work? Can best friends in personal life be best friends at work? Gail Tessler and Norma Menkin, longtime best friends, are partners and co-presidents of Gainor Staffing, a staffing firm located in New York City. Each woman brings a particular strength to the business. And even though they have had their disagreements, both women know that they have a rarity in partnerships—an arrangement that has worked successfully for them.[2]

Limited Liability Partnership (LLP). The **limited liability partnership (LLP)** is a form of legal organization in which there are general partner(s) and limited liability partner(s). The general partners actually operate and manage the business. They are the ones who have unlimited liability. There must be at least one general partner in an LLP. However, there can be any number of limited partners. These partners are usually passive investors, although they can make management suggestions to the general partners. They also have the right to inspect the business and make copies of business records. The limited partners are entitled to a share of the business's profits as agreed to in the partnership agreement, and their risk is limited to the amount of their investment in the LLP.

C Corporation. Of the three basic types of ownership, the corporation (also known as a C corporation) is the most complex to form and operate. A **corporation** is a legal business entity that is separate from its owners and managers. Many entrepreneurial ventures are organized as a **closely held corporation**, which, very simply, is a corporation owned by a limited number of people who do not trade the stock publicly. Whereas the sole proprietorship and partnership forms of organization do not exist

Structure	Ownership Requirements	Tax Treatment	Liability	Advantages	Drawbacks
Sole proprietorship	One owner	Income and losses "pass through" to owner and are taxed at personal rate	Unlimited personal liability	*Low start-up costs* Freedom from most regulations *Owner has direct control* All profits go to owner *Easy to exit business*	Unlimited personal liability *Personal finances at risk* Miss out on many business tax deductions *Total responsibility* May be more difficult to raise financing
General partnership	Two or more owners	Income and losses "pass through" to partners and are taxed at personal rate; *flexibility in profit-loss allocations to partners*	Unlimited personal liability	*Ease of formation* Pooled talent *Pooled resources* Somewhat easier access to financing *Some tax benefits*	Unlimited personal liability *Divided authority and decisions* Potential for conflict *Continuity of transfer of ownership*
Limited liability partnership (LLP)	Two or more owners	Income and losses "pass through" to partners and are taxed at personal rate; *flexibility in profit-loss allocations to partners*	Limited, although one partner must retain unlimited liability	*Good way to acquire capital from limited partners*	Cost and complexity of forming can be high *Limited partners cannot participate in management of business without losing liability protection*
C corporation	Unlimited number of shareholders; *no limits on types of stock or voting arrangements*	Dividend income is taxed at corporate and personal shareholder levels; *losses and deductions are corporate*	Limited	*Limited liability* Transferable ownership *Continuous existence* Easier access to resources	Expensive to set up *Closely regulated* Double taxation *Extensive record keeping* Charter restrictions
S corporation	Up to 75 shareholders; *no limits on types of stock or voting arrangements*	Income and losses "pass through" to partners and are taxed at personal rate; *flexibility in profit-loss allocation to partners*	Limited	*Easy to set up* Enjoy limited liability protection and tax benefits of partnership *Can have a tax-exempt entity as a shareholder*	Must meet certain requirements *May limit future financing options*
Limited liability company (LLC)	Unlimited number of "members"; *flexible membership arrangements for voting rights and income*	Income and losses "pass through" to partners and are taxed at personal rate; *flexibility in profit-loss allocations to partners*	Limited	*Greater flexibility* Not constrained by regulations on C and S corporations *Taxed as partnership, not as corporation*	Cost of switching from one form to this can be high *Need legal and financial advice in forming operating agreement*

Exhibit P4–1   **Legal Forms of Business Organization**

separately from the entrepreneur, the corporation does. The corporation functions as a distinct legal entity and, as such, can make contracts, engage in business activities, own property, sue and be sued, and of course, pay taxes. A corporation must operate in accordance with its charter and the laws of the state in which it operates.

S Corporation. The **S corporation** (also called a subchapter S corporation) is a specialized type of corporation that has the regular characteristics of a corporation but is unique in that the owners are taxed as a partnership as long as certain criteria are met. The S corporation has been the classic organizing approach for getting the limited liability of a corporate structure without incurring corporate tax. However, this form of legal organization must meet strict criteria. If any of these criteria are violated, a venture's S status is automatically terminated.

Limited Liability Company (LLC). The limited liability company (LLC) is a relatively new form of business organization that's a hybrid between a partnership and a corporation. The LLC offers the liability protection of a corporation, the tax benefits of a partnership, and fewer restrictions than on an S corporation. However, the main drawback of this approach is that it's quite complex and expensive to set up. Legal and financial advice is an absolute necessity in forming the LLC's **operating agreement**, which is the document that outlines the provisions governing the way the LLC will conduct business.

Summary of Legal Forms of Organization. The organizing decision regarding the legal form of organization is an important one because it can have significant tax and liability consequences. Although the legal form of organization can be changed, it's not an easy thing to do. An entrepreneur needs to think carefully about what's important, especially in the areas of flexibility, taxes, and amount of personal liability in choosing the best form of organization.

Organizational Design and Structure

The choice of an appropriate organizational structure is also an important decision when organizing the entrepreneurial venture. At some point, successful entrepreneurs find that they can't do everything alone. More people are needed. The entrepreneur must then decide on the most appropriate structural arrangement for effectively and efficiently carrying out the organization's activities. Without some suitable type of organizational structure, the entrepreneurial venture may soon find itself in a chaotic situation.

In many small firms, the organizational structure tends to evolve with very little conscious and deliberate planning by the entrepreneur. For the most part, the structure may be very simple—one person who does whatever is needed. As the entrepreneurial venture grows and the entrepreneur finds it increasingly difficult to go it alone, employees are brought onboard to perform certain functions or duties that the entrepreneur can't handle. These individuals tend to keep doing those same functions as the company grows. Then, as the entrepreneurial venture continues to grow, each of these functional areas may require managers and employees.

With the evolution to a more deliberate structure, the entrepreneur faces a whole new set of challenges. All of a sudden, he or she must share decision making and operating responsibilities. This is typically one of the most difficult things for an entrepreneur to do—to let go and allow someone else to make decisions. After all, he or she reasons, how can anyone know this business as well as I do? Also, what might have been a fairly informal, loose, and flexible atmosphere that worked well when the organization was small may no longer be effective. Many entrepreneurs are greatly concerned about keeping that "small company" atmosphere alive even as the venture grows and evolves into a more structured arrangement. But having a structured organization doesn't necessarily mean giving up flexibility, adaptability, and freedom. In fact, the structural design may be as fluid as the entrepreneur feels comfortable with and yet still have the rigidity it needs to operate efficiently.

Organizational design decisions in entrepreneurial ventures revolve around the six key elements of organizational structure that we discussed in Chapter 10: work specialization, departmentalization, chain of command, span of control, amount of centralization-decentralization, and amount of formalization. Decisions about these six elements will determine whether an entrepreneur designs a more mechanistic or a more organic organizational structure (concepts we also discussed in Chapter 10). When would each be preferable? A mechanistic structure would be preferable when cost-efficiencies are critical to the venture's competitive advantage; where more control over employees' work activities is important; if the venture produces standardized products in a routine fashion; and when the external environment is relatively stable and certain. An organic structure would be most appropriate when innovation is critical to the organization's competitive advantage; for smaller organizations where rigid approaches to dividing and coordinating work aren't necessary; if the organization produces customized products in a flexible setting; and where the external environment is dynamic, complex, and uncertain.

Human Resource Management Issues in Entrepreneurial Ventures

As an entrepreneurial venture grows, additional employees will need to be hired to perform the increased workload. As employees are brought on board, the entrepreneur faces certain human resource management issues. Two

HRM issues of particular importance to entrepreneurs are employee recruitment and employee retention.

Employee Recruitment. An entrepreneur wants to ensure that the venture has the people it needs to do the work that's required. And recruiting new employees is one of the biggest challenges that entrepreneurs face. In fact, the ability of small firms to successfully recruit appropriate employees is consistently rated as one of the most important factors influencing organizational success.[3]

Entrepreneurs, particularly, are looking for high-potential people who can perform multiple roles during various stages of venture growth. They look for individuals who "buy into" the venture's entrepreneurial culture—individuals who have a passion for the business.[4] Unlike their corporate counterparts, who often focus on filling a job by matching a person to the job requirements, entrepreneurs look to fill in critical skills gaps. They're looking for people who are exceptionally capable and self-motivated, flexible, multiskilled, and who can help grow the entrepreneurial venture. While corporate managers tend to focus on using traditional HRM practices and techniques, entrepreneurs are more concerned with matching characteristics of the person to the values and culture of the organization; that is, they focus on matching the person to the organization.[5]

Employee Retention. Getting competent and qualified people into the venture is just the first step in effectively managing the human resources. An entrepreneur wants to keep the people he or she has hired and trained. Sabrina Horn, president of The Horn Group, based in San Francisco, understands the importance of having good people on board and keeping them. Her public relations firm employs around 50 employees who create PR for technology firms. In this rough-and-tumble, intensely competitive industry, Sabrina knows that the loss of talented employees could harm client services. To combat this, she offers employees a wide array of desirable benefits such as raises of 6 percent or more each year, profit sharing, trust funds for employees' children, paid sabbaticals, personal development funds, and so forth. But, more importantly, Sabrina recognizes that employees have a life outside the office and treats them accordingly. This type of HRM approach has kept her employees loyal and productive.[6]

A unique and important employee retention issue entrepreneurs must deal with is compensation. Whereas traditional organizations are more likely to view compensation from the perspective of monetary rewards (base pay, benefits, and incentives), smaller entrepreneurial firms are more likely to view compensation from a total rewards perspective. For these firms, compensation encompasses psychological rewards, learning opportunities, and recognition, in addition to monetary rewards (base pay and incentives).[7]

Stimulating and Making Changes

We know from an earlier module that the context facing entrepreneurs is one of dynamic change. Both external and internal forces (see Chapter 13) may bring about the need for making changes in the entrepreneurial venture. Entrepreneurs need to be alert to problems and opportunities that may create the need to change. In fact, of the many hats an entrepreneur wears, that of change agent may be one of the most important.[8] If changes are needed in the entrepreneurial venture, often it is the entrepreneur who first recognizes the need for change and acts as the catalyst, coach and cheerleader, and chief change consultant. Change isn't easy in any organization, but it can be particularly challenging for entrepreneurial ventures. Even if a person is comfortable with taking risks, as entrepreneurs usually are, change can be hard. That's why it's important for an entrepreneur to recognize the critical roles he or she plays in stimulating and implementing change. For instance, Ray Ferguson, CEO, and Ed Moody, vice president, of high-end sunglass manufacturer Costa Del Mar, are well aware of the important roles they play in stimulating and implementing changes. Competing in the tough sunglasses business, they've had to make a number of changes over the years. One change was pulling their sunglasses out of the Totes retail chain. Although having their product in so many retail outlets across the United Sates seemed like a good idea at the time they made the decision, it actually wasn't a good one at all. So, they changed. But their most recent change was the most important. They decided in April 2003 to sell their business to A.T. Cross, the maker of fine pens and other writing instruments.[9]

During any type of organizational change, an entrepreneur also may have to act as chief coach and cheerleader. Since organizational change of any type can be disruptive and scary, the entrepreneur must assume the role of explaining the change and encouraging change efforts by supporting, explaining, getting employees excited about the change, building employees up, and motivating employees to put forth their best efforts.

Finally, the entrepreneur may have to guide the actual change process as changes in strategy, technology, products, structure, or people are being implemented. In this role, the entrepreneur answers questions, makes suggestions, gets needed resources, facilitates conflict, and does whatever else is necessary to get the change(s) implemented.

The Continuing Importance of Innovation

In today's dynamic, chaotic world of global competition, organizations must continually innovate new products and services if they want to compete successfully. We know that innovation is a key characteristic of entrepreneurial ventures. In fact, you can say that innovation is what makes the entrepreneurial venture "entrepreneurial."

What must an entrepreneur do to encourage innovation in the venture? Having an innovation-supportive culture is crucial. What does such a culture look like?[10] It's one in which employees perceive that supervisory support and organizational reward systems are consistent with a commitment to innovation. It's also important in this type of culture that employees not perceive that their workload pressures are excessive or unreasonable. And research has shown that firms with cultures supportive of innovation tend to be smaller, have fewer formalized human resource practices, and less abundant resources.[11]

● ● ● Learning Summary

After reading and studying this material, you should be able to:

- Contrast the six different forms of legal organization.

- Describe the organizational design issues entrepreneurs face as the venture grows.

- Explain when a more mechanistic or a more organic structure would be most desirable.

- Discuss the unique HRM issues entrepreneurs face.

- Explain why the role of change agent is an important one for entrepreneurs.

- Describe what an innovation-supportive culture looks like.

Part FIVE
Leading

Chapter

14

Foundations of Behavior

A **Manager's** *Dilemma*

From the heartland of America comes bread baked with heart.[1] Panera Bread Company, based in a suburb of St. Louis, operates and franchises bakery-cafés in 30 states under the Panera Bread and St. Louis Bread Company brands. Panera was originally formed in March 1981 under the name Au Bon Pain Company, which operated bakery-cafés on the East Coast and internationally.

In late 1993, Au Bon Pain's CEO Ron Shaich (pictured) met the owners of St. Louis Bread Company, which had 19 bakery-cafés doing about $1 million in lunch business a year. Ron sensed an opportunity and bought the business. He saw it as "our gateway into the suburban marketplace and backward into a manufacturing business." Ron and his management team were looking for a concept that combined Au Bon Pain's quality food with the potential for broader appeal. In 1998, after studying the business inside and out, Ron and his management team decided to sell the Au Bon Pain company and build the St. Louis Bread Company concept into a national brand under the Panera Bread name.

A lot of behavioral analyses went into this decision. The team spent numerous hours trying to figure out what this new business should look like.

They looked at restaurants, coffeehouses, and even retailers in an attempt to understand shopping behavior. One thing the team discovered was that consumers were tiring of the boring sameness of dining-out choices. They knew they would have to eliminate that perception by paying careful attention to all the details. They also used what they had learned at Au Bon Pain—quality makes a real difference. In Panera's case, that meant making fresh dough every single day in 14 locations and trucking it into the cafés for baking.

Ron felt another key ingredient to success was the quality of the people he employed. He knew that to get good people he needed a systematic approach to hiring and development. Put yourself in Ron's shoes. You know that emotional intelligence (EI) has been found to be related to employee performance. How might Ron use information on EI to help him attract and retain quality people?

What would **you** do **?**

on Shaich's desire to attract and retain quality employees is something most managers want—they want people who show up and work hard, get along with co-workers and customers, and have good attitudes and exhibit good work behaviors in other ways. But as you well know, people don't always behave like that "ideal" employee. They differ in their behaviors and even the same person can behave one way one day and a completely different way another day. For instance, haven't you seen family members, friends, or co-workers behave in ways that prompted you to wonder: Why did they do that? As the chapter-opening case implies, effective managers need to understand behavior.

WHY LOOK AT INDIVIDUAL BEHAVIOR?

●●● **behavior**
The actions of people.

●●● **organizational behavior**
The actions of people at work.

The material in this and the next three chapters draws heavily on the field of study that's known as *organizational behavior (OB)*. Although it's concerned with the subject of **behavior**—that is, the actions of people—**organizational behavior** is concerned more specifically with the actions of people at work.

One of the challenges in understanding organizational behavior is that it addresses issues that aren't obvious. Like an iceberg, OB has a small visible dimension and a much larger hidden portion. (See Exhibit 14–1.) What we see when we look at organizations is their visible aspects: strategies, goals, policies and procedures, structure, technology, formal authority relationships, and chain of command. But under the surface are other elements that managers need to understand—elements that also influence how employees work. As we'll show, OB provides managers with considerable insights into these important, but hidden, aspects of the organization. (■◻▮▮▮ Go to the Web and check out Q & A 14.1.)

■ **Q & A**
Whenever you see this green square, go to the R.O.L.L.S. Web site (*www.prenhall.com/ robbins*) to the Q & A, your 24/7 educational assistant. These video clips and written material presented by your authors address questions that we have found students frequently ask.

Focus of Organizational Behavior

Organizational behavior focuses on two major areas. First, OB looks at *individual behavior*. Based predominantly on contributions from psychologists, this area includes such topics as attitudes, personality, perception, learning, and motivation. Second, OB is concerned with *group behavior*, which includes norms, roles, team building, leadership, and conflict. Our knowledge about groups comes basically from the work of sociologists and social psychologists. Unfortunately, the behavior of a group of employees can't be understood by merely summing up the actions of the individuals in the group because individuals in a group setting behave differ-

Exhibit 14–1

The Organization as an Iceberg

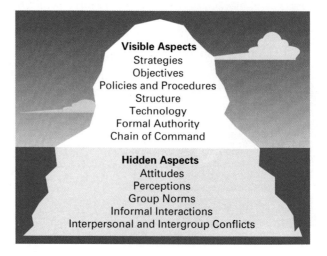

Visible Aspects
Strategies
Objectives
Policies and Procedures
Structure
Technology
Formal Authority
Chain of Command

Hidden Aspects
Attitudes
Perceptions
Group Norms
Informal Interactions
Interpersonal and Intergroup Conflicts

ently from individuals acting alone. Think about yourself and your group of closest friends. Have you done things with your group of friends that you wouldn't ever do on your own? Most of us have. Because employees in an organization are both individuals and members of groups, we need to study them at two levels. In this chapter, we'll provide the foundation for understanding individual behavior. Then, in the next chapter, we'll introduce the basic concepts related to understanding group behavior.

Goals of Organizational Behavior

The goals of OB are to *explain*, *predict*, and *influence* behavior. Why do managers need to be able to do these? Simply, in order to manage their employees' behavior. We know that a manager's success depends on getting things done through people. To do this, the manager needs to be able to *explain* why employees engage in some behaviors rather than others, *predict* how employees will respond to various actions the manager might take, and *influence* how employees behave. (▮▯▮▮ Go to the Web and check out Q & A 14.2.)

What employee behaviors are we specifically concerned about explaining, predicting, and influencing? Five important ones have been identified: employee productivity, absenteeism, turnover, organizational citizenship behavior (OCB), and job satisfaction. **Employee productivity** is a performance measure of both efficiency and effectiveness. Managers want to know what factors will influence the efficiency and effectiveness of employees. **Absenteeism** is the failure to report to work. It's difficult for work to get done if employees don't show up. Although absenteeism can never be totally eliminated, excessive levels will have a direct and immediate impact on the organization's functioning. **Turnover** is the voluntary and involuntary permanent withdrawal from an organization. It can be a problem because of increased recruiting, selection, and training costs and work disruptions. Just like absenteeism, managers can never eliminate turnover, but it is something they want to minimize, especially among high-performing employees and those difficult to replace. **Organizational citizenship behavior** is discretionary behavior that's not part of an employee's formal job requirements, but which promotes the effective functioning of the organization.[2] Examples of good OCB include helping others on one's work team, volunteering for extended job activities, avoiding unnecessary conflicts, and making constructive statements about one's work group and the organization. Organizations need individuals who will do more than their usual job duties, and the evidence indicates that organizations that have such employees outperform those that don't.[3] **Job satisfaction** refers to an individual's general attitude toward his or her job. Although job satisfaction is an attitude rather than a behavior, it's an outcome that concerns many managers because satisfied employees are more likely to show up for work and stay with an organization. In the following pages, we'll address how an understanding of four psychological factors—employee attitudes, personality, perception, and learning—can help us predict and explain employee productivity, absenteeism and turnover rates, organizational citizenship behavior, and job satisfaction.

●●● **employee productivity**
A performance measure of both efficiency and effectiveness.

●●● **absenteeism**
The failure to report to work.

●●● **turnover**
The voluntary and involuntary permanent withdrawal from an organization.

●●● **organizational citizenship behavior**
Discretionary behavior that is not part of an employee's formal job requirements, but that nevertheless promotes the effective functioning of the organization.

●●● **job satisfaction**
An employee's general attitude toward his or her job.

●●● **Learning Review**

- Explain why the concept of an organization as an iceberg is important to understanding organizational behavior.
- Describe the focus and goals of organizational behavior.

- Define the five important employee behaviors that managers want to explain, predict, and influence.

ATTITUDES

Attitudes are evaluative statements—either favorable or unfavorable—concerning objects, people, or events. They reflect how an individual feels about something. When a person says, "I like my job," he or she is expressing an attitude about work.

An attitude is made up of three components: cognition, affect, and behavior.[4] The **cognitive component** of an attitude refers to the beliefs, opinions, knowledge, or information held by a person. The belief that "discrimination is wrong" illustrates a cognition. The **affective component** of an attitude is the emotional or feeling part of an attitude. Using our example, this component would be reflected by the statement, "I don't like Jon because he discriminates against minorities." Finally, affect can lead to behavioral outcomes. The **behavioral component** of an attitude refers to an intention to behave in a certain way toward someone or something. To continue our example, I might choose to avoid Jon because of my feelings about him. Understanding that attitudes are made up of three components—cognition, affect, and behavior—helps show their complexity. (▮▮□▮▮ Check out Passport Scenario 2 on p. 452.) But for the sake of clarity, keep in mind that the term *attitude* usually refers only to the affective component.

Naturally, managers aren't interested in every attitude an employee has. They're especially interested in job-related attitudes. (▮▮□▮▮ Go to the Web and check out Q & A 14.3.) The three most widely known are job satisfaction, job involvement, and organizational commitment, which have been popular topics for organizational researchers.[5]

Job Satisfaction

As we know from our earlier definition, job satisfaction refers to a person's general attitude toward his or her job. (▮▮□▮▮ Go to the Web and check out Q & A 14.4.) A person with a high level of job satisfaction has a positive attitude toward the job, while a person who is dissatisfied with the job has a negative attitude. When people speak of employee attitudes, they usually are referring to job satisfaction. Let's look at some findings about job satisfaction.

Are most people satisfied with their jobs? The answer seems to be a qualified "yes" in the United States and in most developed countries. (▮▮▮□▮ Go to the

Fewer workers want to become CEO these days, and many have explored making the transition from the corporate to the nonprofit world in search of jobs that are personally significant. Barbara Heffernan left Merrill Lynch, where she was co-director of mergers and acquisitions in Chicago, to earn a degree in social work and become a counselor for substance abusers at Project Courage in Connecticut. "By my early 30s," she said, "I really felt like there needed to be something more in my life. One of the things that happens to people on Wall Street is that they are earning so much money they put off their happiness."

Web and check out S.A.L. #11—How Satisfied Am I with My Job?) Independent studies, conducted among U.S. workers over the past 30 years, generally indicate that workers are satisfied with their jobs.[6] While the percentage is pretty wide—from the high 40s to the high 70s—more have reported that they're satisfied than not. In spite of these generally positive results, recent trends aren't encouraging. Since the 1990s, there's been a marked decline in job satisfaction. A Conference Board study in 1995 found that 58.6 percent of Americans were satisfied with their jobs. By 2003, that percentage was down to just 49 percent.[7] Not surprisingly, job satisfaction tends to increase as income increases. Individuals earning less than $15,000 are the least satisfied of all income groups while those earning more than $50,000 are the most satisfied, although satisfaction levels actually have fallen for all income categories since 1995. Does the fact that those with higher incomes have higher levels of job satisfaction mean that money can buy happiness? Not necessarily. While it's possible that higher pay alone translates into higher job satisfaction, an alternative explanation is that higher pay reflects different types of jobs.[8] Higher-paying jobs generally require more advanced skills, give jobholders greater responsibilities, are more stimulating and provide more challenges, and allow workers more control. It's more likely that the reports of higher satisfaction among higher-income levels reflect the greater challenge and freedom they have in their jobs rather than the pay itself.

What effect does job satisfaction have on employee behavior—that is, on productivity, absenteeism, and turnover? (▮▯▮ Go to the Web and check out Q & A 14.5.)

Satisfaction and Productivity For a good part of the twentieth century, managers believed that happy workers were productive workers. As a result of the Hawthorne Studies (discussed in Chapter 2), managers generalized that if their employees were satisfied with their jobs, that satisfaction would translate to working hard. But that belief is generally false. At the individual level, research suggests the reverse to be more accurate—that productivity is likely to lead to satisfaction. However, if we look at the organization level, there's more support for the original satisfaction–productivity relationship.[9] When satisfaction and productivity information is gathered for the organization as a whole, rather than at the individual level, we find that organizations with more satisfied employees tend to be more effective than organizations with fewer satisfied employees. So while we may not be able to say that a happy *worker* is more productive, it might be true that happy *organizations* are more productive.

Satisfaction and Absenteeism Although research shows that satisfied employees have lower levels of absenteeism than do dissatisfied employees, the correlation isn't strong.[10] While it certainly makes sense that dissatisfied employees are more likely to miss work, other factors have an impact on the relationship. For instance, organizations that provide liberal sick leave benefits are encouraging all their employees—including those who are highly satisfied—to take "sick" days. Assuming that your job has some variety in it, you can find work satisfying and yet still take off a "sick" day to enjoy a three-day weekend or tan yourself on a warm summer day if those days come free with no penalties.

Satisfaction and Turnover Research on the relationship between satisfaction and turnover is much stronger. Satisfied employees have lower levels of turnover while dissatisfied employees have higher levels of turnover.[11] Yet, things such as labor-market conditions, expectations about alternative job opportunities, and length of employment with the organization also affect the decision to leave.[12] Research also suggests that an important moderator of the satisfaction–turnover relationship is the employee's level of performance.[13] For superior performers, the level of satisfaction is less important in predicting turnover. Why? The organization typically does everything it can to keep high performers—they get pay raises, praise, recognition, increased promotion opportunities, and so forth.

Consumer researchers have found that customer satisfaction at Wal-Mart Stores has dropped more than 20 percent since 1999, based on ratings of staff courtesy and friendliness. It's now below industry average. Wal-Mart disputes the ratings, but some observers point to the firm's troubles with workers suing for unpaid overtime and sex discrimination as possible sources for the reported drop in service quality.

Job Satisfaction and Customer Satisfaction Is employee satisfaction related to positive customer outcomes? For frontline employees who have regular contact with customers, the answer is "yes." Satisfied employees increase customer satisfaction and loyalty.[14] Why? In service organizations, customer retention and defection are highly dependent on how frontline employees deal with customers. Satisfied employees are more likely to be friendly, upbeat, and responsive, which customers appreciate. And because satisfied employees are less likely to leave their jobs, customers are more likely to encounter familiar faces and receive experienced service. These qualities help build customer satisfaction and loyalty. In addition, the relationship seems to work in reverse: Dissatisfied customers can increase an employee's job dissatisfaction. Employees who have regular contact with customers report that rude, thoughtless, or unreasonably demanding customers adversely affect the employees' job satisfaction.[15]

A number of companies appear to understand this connection. Service-oriented businesses such as FedEx, Southwest Airlines, American Express, and Office Depot obsess about pleasing their customers. Toward that end, they also focus on building employee satisfaction—recognizing that satisfied employees will go a long way toward contributing to their goal of having happy customers. These firms seek to hire upbeat and friendly employees, they train employees in the importance of customer service, they reward customer service, they provide positive work climates, and they regularly track employee satisfaction through attitude surveys.

Although it's important to understand job satisfaction and its impact on employee behavior, there are two other job-related attitudes we need to look at: job involvement and organizational commitment.

Job Involvement and Organizational Commitment

• • • job involvement
The degree to which an employee identifies with his or her job, actively participates in it, and considers his or her job performance to be important to self-worth.

Job involvement is the degree to which an employee identifies with his or her job, actively participates in it, and considers his or her job performance to be important to his or her self-worth.[16] Employees with a high level of job involvement strongly identify with and really care about the kind of work they do. What do we know about the influence of job involvement on employee behavior? High levels have been found to be related to fewer absences and lower resignation rates.[17] (▬▬▬□ Go to the Web and check out S.A.L. #10—How Involved Am I in My Job?)

• • • organizational commitment
An employee's orientation toward the organization in terms of his or her loyalty to, identification with, and involvement in the organization.

Organizational commitment is the degree to which an employee identifies with a particular organization and its goals and wishes to maintain membership in the organization.[18] Whereas job involvement is identifying with your job, organizational commitment is identifying with your employing organization. (▬▬▬□ Go to the Web and check out S.A.L. #43—How Committed Am I to My Organization?) Research suggests that organizational commitment also leads to lower levels of both absenteeism and turnover and, in fact, is a better indicator of turnover than job satisfaction.[19] Why? Probably because it's a more global and enduring response to the organization than is satisfaction with a particular job.[20] However, we need to be careful about drawing conclusions from this research since most of it is almost three decades old and the employee–employer relationship has changed considerably in that time. The notion of an employee staying with a single organization for most of his or her career has become increasingly obsolete. As such, "measures of employee–firm attachment, such as commitment, are problematic."[21] Organizational commitment is probably less important as a work-related attitude than it once was.

• • • perceived organizational support
Employees' general belief that their organization values their contribution and cares about their well-being.

Although the commitment of *an employee to an organization* may not be as important a work-related attitude as it once was, research about **perceived organizational support**—

employees' general belief that their organization values their contribution and cares about their well-being—shows that the commitment of *the organization to the employee* can be beneficial. How? High levels of perceived organizational support have been shown to lead to increased job satisfaction and lowered turnover.[22]

Attitudes and Consistency

Did you ever notice that people change what they say so it doesn't contradict what they do? Perhaps a friend of yours has repeatedly argued that she thinks joining a sorority is an important part of college life. But then she goes through rush and doesn't get accepted. All of a sudden, she's saying that sorority life isn't all that great.

Research has generally concluded that people seek consistency among their attitudes *and* between their attitudes and behavior.[23] This means that individuals try to reconcile differing attitudes and align their attitudes and behavior so they appear rational and consistent. When there is an inconsistency, individuals will take steps to make it consistent either by altering the attitudes or the behavior or by developing a rationalization for the inconsistency.

For example, a campus recruiter for R&S Company, who visits college campuses, identifies qualified job candidates, and sells them on the advantages of R&S as a good place to work, would experience conflict if he personally believed that R&S had poor working conditions and few opportunities for promotion. This recruiter could, over time, find his attitudes toward R&S becoming more positive. He might actually convince himself by continually articulating the merits of working for the company. Another alternative is that the recruiter could become openly negative about R&S and the opportunities within the company for prospective applicants. The original enthusiasm that the recruiter might have shown would dwindle and probably be replaced by outright cynicism toward the company. Finally, the recruiter might acknowledge that R&S is an undesirable place to work, but as a professional recruiter, realize that his obligation is to present the positive aspects of working for the company. He might further rationalize that no workplace is perfect and that his job is not to present both sides of the issue but to present a favorable picture of the company.

Cognitive Dissonance Theory

Can we assume from this consistency principle that an individual's behavior can always be predicted if we know his or her attitude on a subject? The answer, unfortunately, is more complex than merely "yes" or "no." The reason is cognitive dissonance. (▮▮▮▮▮ Go to the Web and check out Q & A 14.6.)

The theory of cognitive dissonance sought to explain the relationship between attitudes and behavior.[24] **Cognitive dissonance** is any incompatibility or inconsistency between attitudes or between behavior and attitudes. The theory argued that any form of inconsistency causes discomfort and that individuals will try to reduce the dissonance and, thus, the discomfort. In other words, individuals seek stability with a minimum of dissonance.

Of course, no one can completely avoid dissonance. You know that cheating on your tax return is wrong, but you "fudge" the numbers a bit every year and hope that you won't be audited. Or you tell your children to floss their teeth every day, but don't do it yourself. In each of these instances, there's an inconsistency between attitude and behavior. How do people cope with cognitive dissonance? The theory proposed that the desire to reduce dissonance is determined by the *importance* of the factors creating the dissonance, the degree of *influence* the individual believes he or she has over those factors, and the *rewards* that may be involved in dissonance.

If the factors creating the dissonance are relatively unimportant, the pressure to correct the inconsistency will be low. For instance, say that a corporate manager—Mrs. Smith—believes strongly that no company should treat assembly-line employees

• • • **cognitive dissonance**
Any incompatibility or inconsistency between attitudes or between behavior and attitudes.

When Brenda Ross-Dulan joined Wells Fargo, the company's idea of community development was somewhat limited. With her background in corporate banking and construction lending at a bank that merged with Wells Fargo, Ross-Dulan changed that attitude with an analytical approach to community development that transformed it from a series of photo opportunities to a $100 million profit center. "The idea that there were business opportunities in low to moderate income communities changed everyone's perspective on community development. It transformed 'community development' into a sustainable business strategy."

unfairly or inhumanely. Unfortunately, because of job requirements Mrs. Smith is placed in the position of having to make decisions that would trade off her company's profitability against her attitudes on compassionate treatment of employees. She knows that running an efficient manufacturing facility is in her company's best interest. What will she do? Clearly, Mrs. Smith will be experiencing a high degree of cognitive dissonance. Because of the *importance* of the issue to Mrs. Smith, we can't expect her to ignore the inconsistency, but there are several paths that she can follow to deal with her discomfort. She can change her behavior by using her authority to order that employees be treated fairly and humanely. Or she can reduce dissonance by concluding that the dissonant behavior isn't so important after all. ("I've got to have a job, and in my role as a corporate decision maker, I often have to place the good of my company above that of society.") A third alternative would be for Mrs. Smith to change her attitude. ("There's nothing wrong with the way our employees are treated. After all, they do have a job.") Still another choice would be for her to identify compatible factors that outweigh the dissonant ones. ("The benefits to society from our giving people jobs more than offset the cost to society of not always treating employees compassionately.")

The degree of *influence* that individuals believe they have over the factors also will affect their reaction to the dissonance. If they perceive the dissonance to be uncontrollable—something about which they have no choice—they're not likely to be receptive to attitude change or to feel a need to do so. If, for example, the dissonance-producing behavior was required as a result of a manager's order, the pressure to reduce dissonance would be less than if the behavior had been performed voluntarily. Although dissonance would exist, it could be rationalized and justified by the need to follow the manager's orders—that is, the individual has no choice or control.

Finally, *rewards* also influence the degree to which individuals are motivated to reduce dissonance. Coupling high dissonance with high rewards tends to reduce the discomfort inherent in the dissonance, by motivating the individual to believe that there is consistency.

These moderating factors suggest that the fact that individuals experience dissonance doesn't mean they will necessarily move to reduce it. If the issues contributing to the dissonance are of minimal importance, if an individual perceives that the dissonance is externally imposed and is substantially uncontrollable by him or her, or if rewards are significant enough to offset the dissonance, the individual will not be pressured to reduce the dissonance.

What are the behavioral implications of cognitive dissonance theory? It can help predict how likely individuals are to change their attitudes and behaviors. For example, if job demands require individuals to say or do things that contradict their personal attitudes, they'll tend to modify their attitudes in order to make them compatible with the belief (cognition) of what they have said or done. In addition, the greater the dissonance—after it has been moderated by importance, influence, and reward factors—the greater the pressure to reduce it.

Attitude Surveys

● ● ● **attitude surveys**
Surveys that elicit responses from employees through questions about how they feel about their jobs, work groups, supervisors, or the organization.

Many organizations regularly survey their employees about their attitudes.[25] Exhibit 14–2 shows what an attitude survey might look like. Typically, **attitude surveys** present the employee with a set of statements or questions eliciting how they feel about their jobs, work groups, supervisors, or the organization. Ideally, the items will be designed to obtain the specific information that managers desire. An attitude score

Exhibit 14–2

Sample Attitude Survey

Please answer each of the following statements using the following rating scale:
5 = Strongly agree
4 = Agree
3 = Undecided
2 = Disagree
1 = Strongly disagree

Statement	**Rating**

1. This company is a pretty good place to work. _____
2. I can get ahead in this company if I make the effort. _____
3. This company's wage rates are competitive with those of other companies. _____
4. Employee promotion decisions are handled fairly. _____
5. I understand the various fringe benefits the company offers. _____
6. My job makes the best use of my abilities. _____
7. My workload is challenging but not burdensome. _____
8. I have trust and confidence in my boss. _____
9. I feel free to tell my boss what I think. _____
10. I know what my boss expects of me. _____

Source: Based on T. Lammers, "The Essential Employee Survey," *Inc.,* December 1992, pp. 159–61.

is achieved by summing up responses to individual questionnaire items. These scores can then be averaged for work groups, departments, divisions, or the organization as a whole. For instance, Trident Precision Manufacturing of Webster, New York, administers a twice-yearly employee satisfaction survey to gauge their employees' overall satisfaction with the company and its practices.[26]

Using attitude surveys on a regular basis provides managers with valuable feedback on how employees perceive their working conditions. Policies and practices that managers view as objective and fair may be seen as inequitable by employees in general or by certain groups of employees. The use of regular attitude surveys can alert managers to potential problems and employees' intentions early so that action can be taken to prevent repercussions.[27]

Implications for Managers

Managers should be interested in their employees' attitudes because attitudes give warnings of potential problems and because they influence behavior. (████████ Go to the Web and check out You're the Manager: Diversity in Action #3.) Satisfied and committed employees, for instance, have lower rates of turnover and absenteeism. Given that managers want to keep resignations and absences down—especially among their more productive employees—they'll want to do the things that will generate positive job attitudes.

The findings about the satisfaction–productivity relationships have important implications for managers. They suggest that the goal of making employees happy on the assumption that their being happy will lead to high productivity is probably misdirected. Managers who follow this strategy could end up with a very content, but very unproductive, group of employees. Managers would get better results by directing their attention primarily to what will help employees become more productive. Then, successful job performance should lead to feelings of accomplishment, increased pay, promotions, and other rewards—all desirable outcomes—which then lead to job satisfaction.

Finally, managers should also recognize that employees will try to reduce dissonance. (████████ Go to the Web and check out Q & A 14.7.) If employees are required to do things that appear inconsistent to them or that are at odds with their attitudes, managers should remember that pressure to reduce the dissonance is minimized when the employee perceives that the dissonance is externally imposed and uncontrollable. The pressure is also decreased if rewards are significant enough to offset the dissonance. So the manager might point to external forces such as competitors, customers, or other factors when explaining the need to perform some work activity the individual may have some dissonance about. Or the manager can provide rewards that an individual desires in order to decrease his or her attempts to eliminate the dissonance.

• • • Learning Review

- Describe the three components of an attitude.
- Explain the three job-related attitudes.
- Describe the impact job satisfaction has on employee behavior.

- Discuss how individuals reconcile inconsistencies between attitudes and behavior.

PERSONALITY

Some people are quiet and passive; others are loud and aggressive. When we describe people using terms such as *quiet, passive, loud, aggressive, ambitious, extroverted, loyal, tense,* or *sociable,* we're describing their personalities. An individual's **personality** is the unique combination of psychological characteristics that affect how a person reacts and interacts with others. (▮▮▮▯▮▮ Go to the Web and check out S.A.L. #1—What's My Basic Personality?) Personality is most often described in terms of measurable traits that a person exhibits. We're interested in looking at personality because, just like attitudes, it too affects how and why people behave the way they do. (▮▯▮▮▮ Go to the Web and check out Q & A 14.8.)

There are hundreds of personality traits. Over the years, researchers have attempted to focus specifically on which traits would best describe personality. Two approaches to classifying personality traits have received the most attention: the Myers Briggs Type Indicator (MBTI) and the Big Five model.

> • • • **personality**
> The unique combination of psychological characteristics that affect how a person reacts and interacts with others.

Joyce Hanson gave up her work uniform of jeans and T-shirt when she left a reporter's job and took time off to write a book for a position as technical writer with Bank One Corporation in Chicago. Hanson found the corporate culture as different from what she was used to as the dress code was, and she learned to adapt to the requirements of her manager who "wanted to make sure that I looked and acted like a banker." But the effort paid off. Says Hanson, "The new job required me to adapt my personality to the new circumstances. But I knew that in making these changes there would be a payoff. I've been able to achieve my personal goals."

MBTI

One of the most popular approaches to classifying personality traits is a general personality assessment called the Myers-Briggs Type Indicator (or MBTI, as it's often called). The MBTI consists of more than 100 questions asking people how they usually act or feel in different situations.[28] (▮▮▮▮□▮ Go to the Web and check out S.A.L. #2—What's My MBTI Personality Type?) The way you respond to these questions puts you at one end or another of four dimensions:

1. *Social interaction:* Extrovert or Introvert (E or I). An extrovert is someone who is outgoing, dominant, and often aggressive and who wants to change the world. Extroverts need a work environment that's varied and action oriented, that lets them be with others, and that gives them a variety of experiences. An individual who's shy and withdrawn and focuses on understanding the world is described as an introvert. Introverts prefer a work environment that is quiet and concentrated, that lets them be alone, and that gives them a chance to explore in depth a limited set of experiences.

2. *Preference for gathering data:* Sensing or Intuitive (S or N). Sensing types dislike new problems unless there are standard ways to solve them; they like an established routine, have a high need for closure, show patience with routine details, and tend to be good at precise work. On the other hand, intuitive types are individuals who like solving new problems, dislike doing the same thing over and over again, jump to conclusions, are impatient with routine details, and dislike taking time for precision.

3. *Preference for decision making:* Feeling or Thinking (F or T). Individuals who are feeling types are aware of other people and their feelings, like harmony, need occasional praise, dislike telling people unpleasant things, tend to be sympathetic, and relate well to most people. Thinking types are unemotional and uninterested in people's feelings, like analysis and putting things into logical order, are able to reprimand people and fire them when necessary, may seem hard-hearted, and tend to relate well only to other thinking types.

4. *Style of making decisions:* Perceptive or Judgmental (P or J). Perceptive types are curious, spontaneous, flexible, adaptable, and tolerant. They focus on starting a task, postpone decisions, and want to find out all about the task before starting it. Judgmental types are decisive, good planners, purposeful, and exacting. They focus on completing a task, make decisions quickly, and want only the information necessary to get a task done. Combining these preferences provides descriptions of 16 personality types. Exhibit 14–3 summarizes a few of them.

Exhibit 14–3

●●●———

Examples of MBTI Personality Types

Type	Description
INFJ (introvert, intuitive, feeling, judgmental)	Quietly forceful, conscientious, and concerned for others. Such people succeed by perseverance, originality, and the desire to do whatever is needed or wanted. They are often highly respected for their uncompromising principles.
ESTP (extrovert, sensing, thinking, perceptive)	Blunt and sometimes insensitive. Such people are matter-of-fact and do not worry or hurry. They enjoy whatever comes along. They work best with real things that can be assembled or disassembled.
ISFP (introvert, sensing, feeling, perceptive)	Sensitive, kind, modest, shy, and quietly friendly. Such people strongly dislike disagreements and will avoid them. They are loyal followers and quite often are relaxed about getting things done.
ENTJ (extrovert, intuitive, thinking, judgmental)	Warm, friendly, candid, and decisive; also usually skilled in anything that requires reasoning and intelligent talk, but may sometimes overestimate what they are capable of doing.

Source: Based on I. Briggs-Myers, *Introduction to Type* (Palo Alto, CA: Consulting Psychologists Press, 1980), pp. 7–8.

More than two million people a year take the MBTI in the United States alone. Organizations using the MBTI include Apple Computer, AT&T, Citigroup, GE, 3M, plus many hospitals, educational institutions, and even the U.S. Armed Forces. What may be somewhat surprising, given its popularity, is that there's no hard evidence that the MBTI is a valid measure of personality. However, that doesn't seem to deter its widespread use in a variety of organizations.

How could the MBTI help managers? Proponents of the assessment believe that it's important to know these personality types because they influence the way people interact and solve problems. For instance, if your boss is an intuitive type and you're a sensing type, you'll gather information in different ways. An intuitive type prefers gut reactions, whereas a sensor prefers facts. To work well with your boss, you would have to present more than just facts about a situation and bring out how you feel about it. Also, the MBTI has been used to help managers select employees who are well matched to certain types of jobs.

The Big Five Model

● ● ● **Big Five Model**
Five-factor model of personality that includes extraversion, agreeableness, conscientiousness, emotional stability, and openness to experience.

Although the MBTI is popular, it lacks evidence to support its validity. The same can not be said about the Big Five Model. In recent years, research has shown that five basic personality dimensions underlie all others and encompass most of the significant variation in human personality.[29] The five personality traits in the **Big Five Model** are:

1. *Extraversion*: The degree to which someone is sociable, talkative, and assertive.
2. *Agreeableness*: The degree to which someone is good-natured, cooperative, and trusting.
3. *Conscientiousness*: The degree to which someone is responsible, dependable, persistent, and achievement oriented.
4. *Emotional stability*: The degree to which someone is calm, enthusiastic, and secure (positive) or tense, nervous, depressed, and insecure (negative).
5. *Openness to experience*: The degree to which someone is imaginative, artistically sensitive, and intellectual.

The Big Five provide more than just a personality framework. Research has shown that important relationships exist between these personality dimensions and job performance. For example, one study examined five categories of occupations: *professionals* (such as engineers, architects, and attorneys), *police*, *managers*, *salespeople*, and *semiskilled and skilled employees*.[30] Job performance was defined in terms of employee performance ratings, training competence, and personnel data such as salary level. The results of the study showed that conscientiousness predicted job performance for all five occupational groups. Predictions for the other personality dimensions depended on the situation and on the occupational group. For example, extraversion predicted performance in managerial and sales positions—occupations in which high social interaction is necessary. Openness to experience was found to be important in predicting training competency. Ironically, emotional security wasn't positively related to job performance. Although one might expect calm and secure workers to perform better than nervous ones, that wasn't the case. Perhaps that result is a function of the likelihood that emotionally stable workers often keep their jobs while emotionally unstable workers often do not. Given that all the people who participated in the study were employed, the variance on that dimension was small and insignificant.

Additional Personality Insights

In addition to the Big Five Model, personality researchers have identified five other personality traits that have proved to be the most powerful in explaining individual behavior in organizations. They are *locus of control*, *Machiavellianism*, *self-esteem*, *self-monitoring*, and *risk propensity*.

Those with an internal locus of control believe they control their own fate. Ursula Burns, president of Xerox Business Group Operations, is such a manager. Colleagues praise her decisiveness and negotiating skills. Says Burns, "My perspective comes in part from being a New York black lady, in part from being an engineer. I know that I'm smart and have opinions that are worth being heard."

• • • **locus of control**
The degree to which people believe they are masters of their own fate.

• • • **Machiavellianism (Mach)**
A measure of the degree to which people are pragmatic, maintain emotional distance, and believe that ends justify means.

• • • **self-esteem (SE)**
An individual's degree of like or dislike for himself or herself.

• • • **self-monitoring**
A personality trait that measures an individual's ability to adjust his or her behavior to external situational factors.

1. *Locus of Control.* Some people believe that they control their own fate. Others see themselves as pawns, believing that what happens to them in their lives is due to luck or chance. The **locus of control** in the first case is *internal*; these people believe that they control their own destiny. The locus of control in the second case is *external*; these people believe that their lives are controlled by outside forces.[31] Research evidence indicates that employees who rate high on externality are less satisfied with their jobs, more alienated from the work setting, and less involved in their jobs than are those who rate high on internality.[32] A manager might also expect externals to blame a poor performance evaluation on their boss's prejudice, their co-workers, or other events outside their control; internals would explain the same evaluation in terms of their own actions. (▬▬▬▭ Go to the Web and check out S.A.L. #3— What's My Locus of Control?)

2. *Machiavellianism.* The second characteristic is called **Machiavellianism (Mach),** named after Niccolo Machiavelli, who wrote in the sixteenth century on how to gain and manipulate power. An individual who is high in Machiavellianism is pragmatic, maintains emotional distance, and believes that ends can justify means.[33] "If it works, use it" is consistent with a high Mach perspective. Do high Machs make good employees? That depends on the type of job and whether you consider ethical factors in evaluating performance. In jobs that require bargaining skills (such as a purchasing manager) or that have substantial rewards for winning (such as a salesperson working on commission), high Machs are productive. In jobs in which ends do not justify the means or that lack absolute measures of performance, it's difficult to predict the performance of high Machs.

3. *Self-Esteem.* People differ in the degree to which they like or dislike themselves. This trait is called **self-esteem (SE)**.[34] The research on self-esteem offers some interesting insights into organizational behavior. For example, self-esteem is directly related to expectations for success. High SEs believe that they possess the ability they need in order to succeed at work. Individuals who are high SEs will take more risks in job selection and are more likely to choose unconventional jobs than are people who are low SEs.
The most common finding on self-esteem is that low SEs are more susceptible to external influence than are high SEs. Low SEs are dependent on receiving positive evaluations from others. As a result, they're more likely to seek approval from others and are more prone to conform to the beliefs and behaviors of those they respect than are high SEs. In managerial positions, low SEs will tend to be concerned with pleasing others and, therefore, will be less likely to take unpopular stands than are high SEs.
Not surprisingly, self-esteem has also been found to be related to job satisfaction. A number of studies confirm that high SEs are more satisfied with their jobs than are low SEs.

4. *Self-Monitoring.* Another personality trait that has received increasing attention is called **self-monitoring**.[35] It refers to an individual's ability to adjust his or her behavior to external, situational factors. Individuals high in self-monitoring show considerable adaptability in adjusting their behavior. They're highly sensitive to external cues and can behave differently in different situations. High self-monitors are capable of presenting striking contradictions between their public persona and their private selves. Low self-monitors can't adjust their behavior. They tend to display their true dispositions and attitudes in every situation, and there's high behavioral consistency between who they are and what they do.

Research on self-monitoring is fairly new, thus predictions are hard to make. However, preliminary evidence suggests that high self-monitors pay closer attention to the behavior of others and are more flexible than are low self-monitors.[36] In addition, high self-monitoring managers tend to be more mobile in their careers, receive more promotions (both internal and cross-organizational), and are more likely to occupy central positions in an organization.[37] We might also hypothesize that high self-monitors will be successful in managerial positions that require them to play multiple, and even contradictory, roles. The high self-monitor is capable of putting on different "faces" for different audiences. (▭ Go to the Web and check out S.A.L. #33—How Well Do I Manage Impressions?)

5. *Risk-Taking.* People differ in their willingness to take chances. Differences in the propensity to assume or to avoid risk have been shown to affect how long it takes managers to make a decision and how much information they require before making their choice. For instance, in one study, a group of managers worked on simulated exercises that required them to make hiring decisions.[38] High risk-taking managers took less time to make decisions and used less information in making their choices than did low risk-taking managers. Interestingly, the decision accuracy was the same for the two groups. To maximize organizational effectiveness, managers should try to align employee risk-taking propensity with specific job demands. For instance, high risk-taking propensity may lead to effective performance for a commodities trader in a brokerage firm because this type of job demands rapid decision making. On the other hand, high risk-taking propensity might prove a major obstacle to accountants auditing financial statements. (▭ Go to the Web and check out S.A.L. #5—How Proactive Am I?)

Personality Types in Different Cultures

Do personality frameworks, like the Big Five Model, transfer across cultures? Are dimensions like locus of control relevant in all cultures? Let's try to answer these questions.

The five personality factors studied in the Big Five Model appear in almost all cross-cultural studies.[39] This includes a wide variety of diverse cultures such as China, Israel, Germany, Japan, Spain, Nigeria, Norway, Pakistan, and the United States. Differences are found in the emphasis on dimensions. The Chinese, for example, use the category of conscientiousness more often and use the category of agreeableness less often than do Americans. But there is a surprisingly high amount of agreement, especially among individuals from developed countries. As a case in point, a comprehensive review of studies covering people from the European Community found that conscientiousness was a valid predictor of performance across jobs and occupational groups.[40] This is exactly what U.S. studies have found.

We know that there are certainly no common personality types for a given country. You can, for instance, find high risk-takers and low risk-takers in almost any culture. Yet a country's culture influences the *dominant* personality characteristics of its people. We can see this effect of national culture by looking at one of the personality traits we just discussed: locus of control.

National cultures differ in terms of the degree to which people believe they control their environment. For instance, North Americans believe that they can dominate their environment; other societies, such as those in Middle Eastern countries, believe that life is essentially predetermined. Notice how closely this distinction parallels the concept of internal and external locus of control. On the basis of this particularly cultural characteristic, we should expect a larger proportion of internals in the U.S. and Canadian workforces than in the workforces of Saudi Arabia or Iran.

As we have seen throughout this section, personality traits influence employees' behavior. For global managers, understanding how personality traits differ takes on added significance when looking at it from the perspective of national culture.

Emotions and Emotional Intelligence

We can't leave the topic of personality without looking at another important behavioral aspect—emotions, especially since how we respond emotionally and how we deal with our emotions can be functions of our personality. **Emotions** are intense feelings that are directed at someone or something. They're object specific; that is, emotions are reactions to an object.[41] For instance, when a work colleague criticizes you for the way you spoke to a client, you might become angry at him. That is, you show emotion (anger) toward a specific object (your colleague). Since employees bring an emotional component with them to work every day, managers need to understand the role that emotions play in employee behavior.[42] (▮▮▮▮ Go to the Web and check out You're the Manager: Diversity in Action #3.)

How many emotions are there? Although you could probably name several dozen, research has identified six universal emotions: anger, fear, sadness, happiness, disgust, and surprise.[43] Do these six basic emotions surface in the workplace? Absolutely! I get *angry* after receiving a poor performance appraisal. I *fear* that I could be laid off as a result of a company cutback. I'm *sad* about one of my co-workers leaving to take a new job in another city. I'm *happy* after being selected as employee-of-the-month. I'm *disgusted* with the way my supervisor treats women on our team. And I'm *surprised* to find out that management plans a complete restructuring of the company's retirement program.

People respond differently to identical emotion-provoking stimuli. In some cases, this can be attributed to the individual's personality, because people vary in their inherent ability to express emotions. For instance, you undoubtedly know people who almost never show their feelings. They rarely get angry. They never show rage. In contrast, you probably also know people who seem to be on an emotional roller coaster. When they're happy, they're ecstatic. When they're sad, they're deeply depressed. And two people can be in the exact same situation—one showing excitement and joy, the other remaining calm and collected.

However, at other times, how people respond is a result of job requirements. Jobs make different demands in terms of what types of emotions and how much emotion needs to be displayed. For instance, air traffic controllers and trial judges are expected to be calm and controlled, even in stressful situations. On the other hand, the effectiveness of public-address announcers at sporting events and lawyers can depend on their ability to alter their emotional intensity as the need arises.

One area of emotions research that's offered new insights into personality is **emotional intelligence (EI)**, which is an assortment of noncognitive skills, capabilities, and competencies that influence a person's ability to succeed in coping with environmental demands and pressures.[44] It's composed of five dimensions:

- *Self-awareness:* The ability to be aware of what you're feeling.
- *Self-management:* The ability to manage one's own emotions and impulses.
- *Self-motivation:* The ability to persist in the face of setbacks and failures.
- *Empathy:* The ability to sense how others are feeling.
- *Social skills:* The ability to handle the emotions of others.

EI has been shown to be positively related to job performance at all levels. For instance, one study looked at the characteristics of Lucent Technologies' engineers who were rated as stars by their peers. The researchers concluded that stars were better at relating to others. That is, it was EI, not academic intelligence, that characterized high performers. A study of Air Force recruiters generated similar findings. Top-performing recruiters exhibited high levels of EI. What can we conclude from these results? EI appears to be especially relevant to success in jobs that demand a high degree of social interaction.

●●● emotions
Intense feelings that are directed at someone or something.

●●● emotional intelligence (EI)
An assortment of noncognitive skills, capabilities, and competencies that influence a person's ability to succeed in coping with environmental demands and pressures.

Implications for Managers

The major value in understanding personality differences probably lies in employee selection. Managers are likely to have higher-performing and more-satisfied employees if consideration is given to matching personalities with jobs. The best-documented personality–job fit theory has been developed by psychologist John Holland.[45] His theory states that an employee's satisfaction with his or her job, as well as his or her likelihood of leaving that job, depend on the degree to which the individual's personality matches the occupational environment. Holland identified six basic personality types. Exhibit 14–4 describes each of the six types, their personality characteristics, and sample occupations.

Holland's theory proposes that satisfaction is highest and turnover lowest when personality and occupation are compatible. Social individuals should be in "people" type jobs, and so forth. A realistic person in a realistic job will be more satisfied than a realistic person in an investigative job. The key points of this theory are that (1) there do appear to be intrinsic differences in personality among individuals; (2) there are different types of jobs; and (3) people in job environments compatible with their personality types should be more satisfied and less likely to resign voluntarily than should people in incongruent jobs.

In addition, there are other benefits to a manager's understanding of personality. By recognizing that people approach problem solving, decision making, and job interactions differently, a manager can better understand why, for instance, an employee is uncomfortable with making quick decisions or why another employee insists on gathering as much information as possible before addressing a problem. Or, for instance, managers can expect that individuals with an external locus of control may be less satisfied with their jobs than internals and also that they may be less willing to accept responsibility for their actions.

Finally, being a successful manager and accomplishing goals means working well with others both inside and outside the organization. In order to work effectively together, you need to understand each other. This understanding comes, at least in part, from recognizing the ways in which people differ from each other—that is, from an appreciation of personality traits and emotions.

Exhibit 14–4

Holland's Typology of Personality and Sample Occupations

Type	Personality Characteristics	Sample Occupations
Realistic. Prefers physical activities that require skill, strength, and coordination.	Shy, genuine, persistent, stable, conforming, practical	Mechanic, drill press operator, assembly-line worker, farmer
Investigative. Prefers activities involving thinking, organizing, and understanding.	Analytical, original, curious, independent	Biologist, economist, mathematician, news reporter
Social. Prefers activities that involve helping and developing others.	Sociable, friendly, cooperative, understanding	Social worker, teacher, counselor clinical psychologist
Conventional. Prefers rule-regulated, orderly, and unambiguous activities.	Conforming, efficient, practical, unimaginative, inflexible	Accountant, corporate manager, bank teller, file clerk
Enterprising. Prefers verbal activities in which there are opportunities to influence others and attain power.	Self-confident, ambitious, energetic, domineering	Lawyer, real estate agent, public relations specialist, small business manager
Artistic. Prefers ambiguous and unsystematic activities that allow creative expression.	Imaginative, disorderly, idealistic, emotional, impractical	Painter, musician, writer, interior decorator

Source: Based on J.L. Holland, *Making Vocational Choices: A Theory of Vocational Personalities and Work Environments* (Odessa, FL: Psychological Assessment Resources, 1997).

● ● ● Learning Review

- Contrast the MBTI and the Big Five Model of personality.
- Describe the five personality traits that have proved to be the most powerful in explaining individual behavior in organizations.

- Explain how emotions and emotional intelligence impact behavior.

PERCEPTION

● ● ● **perception**
The process of organizing and interpreting sensory impressions in order to give meaning to the environment.

Perception is a process by which individuals give meaning to their environment by organizing and interpreting their sensory impressions. Research on perception consistently demonstrates that individuals may look at the same thing yet perceive it differently. (Go to the Web and check out Q & A 14.9.) One manager, for instance, can interpret the fact that her assistant regularly takes several days to make important decisions as evidence that the assistant is slow, disorganized, and afraid to make decisions. Another manager with the same assistant might interpret that tendency as evidence that the assistant is thoughtful, thorough, and deliberate. The first manager would probably evaluate her assistant negatively; the second manager would probably evaluate the person positively. The point is that none of us sees reality. We interpret what we see and call it reality. And, of course, as the example shows, we behave according to our perceptions.

Factors That Influence Perception

How do we explain the fact that people can perceive the same things differently? A number of factors act to shape and sometimes distort perception. These factors can reside in the *perceiver*, in the object, or *target*, being perceived; or in the context of the *situation* in which the perception occurs.

The Perceiver When an individual looks at a target and attempts to interpret what he or she sees, the individual's personal characteristics will heavily influence the interpretation. These personal characteristics include attitudes, personality, motives, interests, experiences, and expectations.

The Target The characteristics of the target being observed can also affect what's perceived. Loud people are more likely to be noticed in a group than quiet people. So, too, are extremely attractive or unattractive individuals. Because targets aren't looked at in isolation, the relationship of a target to its background also influences perception, as does our tendency to group close things and similar things together. You can experience these tendencies by looking at the visual perception examples shown in Exhibit 14–5. Notice how what you see changes as you look differently at each one.

Exhibit 14–5

● ● ● **Perception Challenges: What Do You See?**

Old woman or young woman?   A knight on a horse?

Costco started out much like other warehouse clubs, carrying cut-rate groceries and office supplies in bulk packages amid a spartan environment. But CEO Jim Sinegal has been slowly and steadily changing customers' perceptions of the store by upgrading the merchandise and adopting a "treasure hunt" strategy to raise customers' expectations of what they'll find on any given trip to the store. Right next to crates of toilet paper and stacks of tires you might find a 42-inch plasma TV, a Lalique crystal vase, fresh lobster, wine and champagne, or even a diamond ring. Says one well-heeled shopper, "I find better deals here on high-end stuff than I do at Neiman Marcus or Saks. You don't get the box, but so what?"

● ● ● **attribution theory**
A theory used to explain how we judge people differently depending on the meaning we attribute to a given behavior.

The Situation The context in which we see objects or events is also important. The time at which an object or event is seen can influence attention, as can location, light, heat, color, and any number of other situational factors.

Attribution Theory

Much of the research on perception is directed at inanimate objects. Managers, though, are more concerned with people. Our discussion of perception, therefore, should focus on how we perceive people.

Our perceptions of people differ from our perception of inanimate objects because we make inferences about the behaviors of people that we don't make about objects. Objects don't have beliefs, motives, or intentions; people do. The result is that when we observe people's behavior, we try to develop explanations of why they behave in certain ways. Our perception and judgment of a person's actions, therefore, will be significantly influenced by the assumptions we make about the person. (▭▭▭ Go to the Web and check out You're the Manager: Diversity in Action #2.)

Attribution theory was developed to explain how we judge people differently depending on what meaning we attribute to a given behavior.[46] Basically, the theory suggests that when we observe an individual's behavior, we attempt to determine whether it was internally or externally caused. Internally caused behaviors are those that are believed to be under the personal control of the individual. Externally caused behavior results from outside factors; that is, the person is forced into the behavior by the situation. That determination, however, depends on three factors: distinctiveness, consensus, and consistency.

Distinctiveness refers to whether an individual displays different behaviors in different situations. Is the employee who arrived late today the same person that some employees are complaining is a "goof-off"? What we want to know is whether this behavior is unusual. If it's unusual, the observer is likely to attribute the behavior to external forces, something beyond the control of the person. However, if the behavior isn't unusual, it will probably be judged as internal.

If everyone who's faced with a similar situation responds in the same way, we can say the behavior shows *consensus*. A tardy employee's behavior would meet this criterion if all employees who took the same route to work were also late. From an attribution perspective, if consensus is high, you're likely to give an external attribution to the employee's tardiness; that is, some outside factor—maybe road construction or a traffic accident—caused the behavior. However, if other employees who come the same way to work made it on time, you would conclude that the cause of the late behavior was internal.

Finally, an observer looks for *consistency* in a person's actions. Does the person engage in the behaviors regularly and consistently? Does the person respond the same way over time? Coming in 10 minutes late for work isn't perceived in the same way if, for one employee, it represents an unusual case (she hasn't been late in months), while for another employee, it's part of a routine pattern (she's late two or three times every week). The more consistent the behavior, the more the observer is inclined to attribute it to internal causes. (▭▭▭ Go to the Web and check out Q & A 14.10.)

Exhibit 14–6 summarizes the key elements of attribution theory. It would tell us, for instance, that if an employee—let's call him Mr. Liu—generally performs at or about the same level on other related tasks as he does on his current task (low distinctiveness), if other employees frequently perform differently (better or worse) than Mr. Liu does on that current task (low consensus) and if Mr. Liu's performance on this

Exhibit 14–6

Attribution Theory

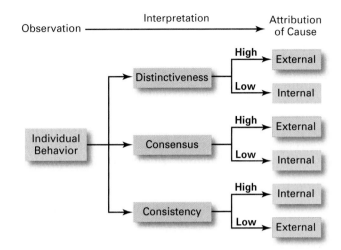

current task is consistent over time (high consistency), his manager or anyone else who is judging Mr. Liu's work is likely to hold him primarily responsible for his task performance (internal attribution).

One of the most interesting findings drawn from attribution theory is that there are errors or biases that distort attributions. For instance, there's substantial evidence to support the fact that when we make judgments about the behavior of other people, we have a tendency to *under*estimate the influence of external factors and to *over*estimate the influence of internal or personal factors.[47] This tendency is called the **fundamental attribution error** and can explain why a sales manager may be prone to attribute the poor performance of her sales representative to laziness rather than to the innovative product line introduced by a competitor. (■□■■■ Go to the Web and check out Q & A 14.11.) There's also a tendency for individuals to attribute their own successes to internal factors such as ability or effort while putting the blame for personal failure on external factors such as luck. This tendency is called the **self-serving bias** and suggests that feedback provided to employees in performance reviews will be predictably distorted by them depending on whether it's positive or negative.

Are these errors or biases that distort attributions universal across different cultures? We can't answer that question definitively, but there is some preliminary evidence that indicates cultural differences.[48] For instance, a study of Korean managers found that, contrary to the self-serving bias, they tended to accept responsibility for group failure "because I was not a capable leader" instead of attributing it to group members.[49] Attribution theory was developed largely based on experiments with Americans and Western Europeans. But the Korean study suggests caution in making attribution theory predictions in non-Western societies, especially in countries with strong collectivist traditions.

Shortcuts Frequently Used in Judging Others

We use a number of shortcuts when we judge others. Perceiving and interpreting what others do is a lot of work. As a result, individuals develop techniques for making the task more manageable. These techniques are frequently valuable; they let us make accurate perceptions rapidly and provide valid data for making predictions. However, they aren't perfect. They can and do get us into trouble. An understanding of these shortcuts can be helpful for recognizing when they can result in significant distortions.

It's easy to judge others if we assume that they're similar to us. In **assumed similarity**, or the "like me" effect, the observer's perception of others is influenced more by the observer's own characteristics than by those of the person observed. For example, if you want challenges and responsibility in your job, you'll assume that others want the same. People who assume that others are like them can, of course, be right, but most of the time they're wrong.

•• • fundamental attribution error
The tendency to underestimate the influence of external factors and overestimate the influence of internal factors when making judgments about the behavior of others.

•• • self-serving bias
The tendency for individuals to attribute their own successes to internal factors while putting the blame for failures on external factors.

•• • assumed similarity
The belief that others are like oneself.

• • • stereotyping
Judging a person on the basis of one's perception of a group to which he or she belongs.

When we judge someone on the basis of our perception of a group he or she is part of, we're using the shortcut called **stereotyping**. For instance, "Married people are more stable employees than single persons" and "Union people expect something for nothing" are examples of stereotyping. To the degree that a stereotype is based on fact, it may produce accurate judgments. However, many stereotypes have no foundation in fact. In such cases, stereotyping distorts judgment.[50]

• • • halo effect
A general impression of an individual based on a single characteristic.

When we form a general impression about a person on the basis of a single characteristic, such as intelligence, sociability, or appearance, we're being influenced by the **halo effect**. This effect frequently occurs when students evaluate their classroom instructor. Students may isolate a single trait such as enthusiasm and allow their entire evaluation to be slanted by the perception of this one trait. An instructor may be quiet, assured, knowledgeable, and highly qualified, but if his classroom teaching style lacks enthusiasm, he might be rated lower on a number of other characteristics.

Implications for Managers

Managers need to recognize that their employees react to perceptions, not to reality. So whether a manager's appraisal of an employee is actually objective and unbiased or whether the organization's wage levels are among the highest in the community is less relevant than what employees perceive them to be. If individuals perceive appraisals to be biased or wage levels as low, they'll behave as if those conditions actually exist. Employees organize and interpret what they see, so there is always the potential for perceptual distortion.

The message to managers should be clear: Pay close attention to how employees perceive both their jobs and management actions. Remember, the valuable employee who quits because of an inaccurate perception is just as great a loss to an organization as the valuable employee who quits for a valid reason.

• • • Learning Review

- Explain how an understanding of perception can help managers better understand individual behavior.
- Describe the key elements of attribution theory.

- Discuss how the fundamental attribution error and self-serving bias can distort attributions.
- Name three shortcuts used in judging others.

LEARNING

The last individual behavior concept we're going to introduce is learning. It's included for the obvious reason that almost all complex behavior is learned. If we want to explain, predict, and influence behavior, we need to understand how people learn.

What is learning? Psychologists' definition of learning is considerably broader than the average person's view that "it's what we do in school." In actuality, each of us is constantly learning. Learning occurs all the time as we continuously learn from our experiences. A workable definition of **learning** is, therefore, any relatively permanent change in behavior that occurs as a result of experience. How do people learn, then? We're going to look at two learning theories relevant to understanding how and why individual behavior occurs: operant conditioning and social learning. Then, we'll discuss how managers can use learning principles to shape employees' behaviors.

• • • learning
Any relatively permanent change in behavior that occurs as a result of experience.

Operant Conditioning

• • • operant conditioning
A type of learning in which desired voluntary behavior leads to a reward or prevents a punishment.

Operant conditioning is the term applied to the theory that behavior is a function of its consequences. People learn to behave to get something they want or to avoid something they don't want. Operant behavior describes voluntary or learned behavior in contrast to reflexive or unlearned behavior. The tendency to repeat learned behavior is influenced by the reinforcement or lack of reinforcement that happens as a result of the behavior. Reinforcement, therefore, strengthens a behavior and increases the likelihood that it will be repeated.

Building on earlier work in the field, B.F. Skinner's research widely expanded our knowledge of operant conditioning.[51] Even his most outspoken critics admit that his operant concepts work.

Behavior is assumed to be determined from without—that is, *learned*—rather than from within—reflexive or unlearned. Skinner argued that creating pleasing and desirable consequences to follow some specific behavior would increase the frequency of that behavior. People will most likely engage in desired behaviors if they are positively reinforced for doing so, and rewards are most effective if they immediately follow the desired response. In addition, behavior that isn't rewarded or is punished, is less likely to be repeated.

You see examples of operant conditioning everywhere. Any situation in which it's either explicitly stated or implicitly suggested that reinforcement (rewards) are contingent on some action on your part is an example of operant conditioning. Your instructor says that if you want a high grade in this course, you must perform well on tests by giving correct answers. A salesperson working on commission knows that earning a sizeable income is contingent upon generating high sales in his or her territory. Of course, the linkage between behavior and reinforcement can also work to teach the individual to behave in ways that work against the best interests of the organization. Assume that your boss tells you that if you'll work overtime during the next three-week busy season, you'll be compensated for it at the next performance appraisal. Then, when performance appraisal time comes, you are given no positive reinforcements (such as being praised for pitching in and helping out when needed). What will you do the next time your boss asks you to work overtime? You'll probably refuse. Your behavior can be explained by operant conditioning: If a behavior isn't positively reinforced, the probability that the behavior will be repeated declines.

Social Learning

Individuals also can learn by observing what happens to other people and just by being told about something as well as by direct experiences. So, for example, much of what we have learned comes from watching others (models)—parents, teachers, peers, television and movie actors, managers, and so forth. (▆▆▆▆▆ Go to the Web and check out PRISM #7—Mentoring.) This view that we can learn through both observation and direct experience is called **social learning theory**.

The influence of others is central to the social learning viewpoint. The amount of influence that these models will have on an individual is determined by four processes:

• • • **social learning theory**
A theory of learning that says people can learn through observation and direct experience.

1. *Attentional processes.* People learn from a model only when they recognize and pay attention to its critical features. We tend to be most influenced by models who are attractive, repeatedly available, thought to be important, or are seen as similar to us.

2. *Retention processes.* A model's influence will depend on how well the individual remembers the model's action, even after the model is no longer readily available.

3. *Motor reproduction processes.* After a person has seen a new behavior by observing the model, the watching must become doing. This process then demonstrates that the individual can actually do the modeled activities.

4. *Reinforcement processes.* Individuals will be motivated to exhibit the modeled behavior if positive incentives or rewards are provided. Behaviors that are reinforced will be given more attention, learned better, and performed more often.

MANAGING YOUR CAREER

Learning to Get Along with Difficult People

We've all been around people who are, to put it nicely, difficult to get along with. These people might be chronic complainers, they might be meddlers who think they know everything about everyone else's job and don't hesitate to tell you so, or they might exhibit any number of other unpleasant interpersonal characteristics. They can make your job as a manager extremely hard and your workday very stressful if you don't know how to deal with them. Being around difficult people tends to bring out the worst in all of us. What can you do? How do you learn to get along with these difficult people?[52]

Getting along with difficult people takes a little bit of patience, planning, and preparation. What you need is an approach that helps you diffuse a lot of the negative aspects of dealing with these individuals. For instance, it helps to write down a detailed description of the person's behavior. Describe what this person does that bothers you. Then, try to understand that behavior. Put yourself in that person's shoes and attempt to see things from his or her perspective. Doing these things initially might help you better understand, predict, and influence behavior.

Unfortunately, trying to understand the person usually isn't enough for getting along. You'll also need some specific strategies for coping with different types of diffi-

cult personalities. Here are some of the most common types of difficult people you'll meet and some strategies for dealing with them.

The Hostile, Aggressive Types. With this type, you need to: stand up for yourself; give them time to run down; don't worry about being polite; just jump in if you need to; get their attention carefully; get them to sit down; speak from your own point of view; avoid a head-on fight; and be ready to be friendly.

The Complainers. With the complainers you need to: listen attentively; acknowledge their concerns; be prepared to interrupt their litany of complaints; don't agree, but do acknowledge what they're saying; state facts without comment or apology; and switch them to problem solving.

The Silent or Nonresponsive Types. With this type, you need to: ask open-ended questions; use the friendly, silent stare; don't fill the silent pauses for them in conversations; comment on what's happening; and help break the tension by making them feel more at ease.

The Know-It-All Experts. The keys to dealing with this type are: be on top of things; listen and acknowledge their comments; question firmly, but don't confront; avoid being a counterexpert; and work with them to channel their energy in positive directions.

Shaping: A Managerial Tool

● ● ● **shaping behavior**
The process of systematically reinforcing each successive step that moves an individual closer to the desired behavior.

Because learning takes place on the job as well as prior to it, managers are concerned with how they can teach employees to behave in ways that most benefit the organization. Thus, managers will often attempt to "mold" individuals by guiding their learning in graduated steps. This process is called **shaping behavior**.

Consider the situation in which an employee's behavior is significantly different from that sought by his or her manager. If the manager reinforced the individual only when he or she showed desirable responses, there might be very little reinforcement taking place. In such a case, shaping offers a logical approach toward achieving the desired behavior.

We shape behavior by systematically reinforcing each successive step that moves the individual closer to the desired behavior. If an employee who has chronically been a half hour late for work comes in only 20 minutes late, we can reinforce the improvement. Reinforcement would increase as an employee gets closer to the desired behavior.

There are four ways to shape behavior: positive reinforcement, negative reinforcement, punishment, or extinction. When a behavior is followed by something pleasant, such as when a manager praises an employee for a job well done, it's called *positive reinforcement*. Positive reinforcement will increase the likelihood of the desired behavior being repeated. Rewarding a response with the elimination

Becoming a Manager

- *Begin paying attention to the behaviors of those around you. Try to use what you've learned about attitudes, personality, perception, and learning to explain how and why they're behaving the ways they do.*
- *Write down some of your own attitudes and try to identify the cognitive, affective, and behavioral components of those attitudes.*
- *Take different personality tests so you have a good feel for your own unique personality.*
- *Notice when you're using shortcuts in judging others and how these shortcuts either helped or hindered your behavior.*
- *Pay attention to how you shape the behaviors of those around you.*
- *There are a number of self-assessments from the (S.A.L.) Self-Assessment Library found on R.O.L.L.S. that are relevant to this chapter. You might want to try the following: #1, #2, #3, #4, #5, #7, #10, #11, #12, and #33.*

or withdrawal of something unpleasant is called *negative reinforcement.* A manager who says "I won't dock your pay if you start getting to work on time" is using negative reinforcement. The desired behavior (getting to work on time) is being encouraged by the withdrawal of something unpleasant (the employee's pay being docked). On the other hand, *punishment* penalizes undesirable behavior and will eliminate it. Suspending an employee for two days without pay for habitually coming to work late is an example of punishment. (Go to the Web and check out Q & A 14.12.) Finally, eliminating any reinforcement that's maintaining a behavior is called *extinction.* When a behavior isn't reinforced, gradually it disappears. In meetings, managers who wish to discourage employees from continually asking irrelevant or distracting questions can eliminate this behavior by ignoring those employees when they raise their hands to speak. Soon this behavior will disappear.

Both positive and negative reinforcement result in learning. They strengthen a desired behavior and increase the probability that the desired behavior will be repeated. Both punishment and extinction also result in learning; however, they weaken an undesired behavior and tend to decrease its frequency.

THINKING CRITICALLY ABOUT ETHICS

Is shaping behavior a form of manipulative control? Animal trainers use rewards to get dogs, porpoises, and whales to perform extraordinary stunts. Behavioral psychologists put rats through thousands of experiments by manipulating their food supply. Trainers and researchers shape the behavior of animals by controlling consequences. Such learning techniques may be appropriate for animals performing in zoos, circuses, or laboratories, but are they appropriate for managing the behavior of people at work?

Suppose an employee does something the organization judges to be wrong but that was motivated by a manager's control of rewards. Say, for instance, an employee inflates the numbers on a sales report because bonuses are based on sales volume. Is that employee any less responsible for his or her actions than if such rewards had not been involved? Explain your position.

Implications for Managers

Employees are going to learn on the job. The only issue is whether managers are going to manage their learning through the rewards they allocate and the examples they set, or allow it to occur haphazardly. If marginal employees are rewarded with pay raises and promotions, they will have little reason to change their behavior. In fact, productive employees, seeing that marginal performance gets rewarded, might change their behavior. If managers want behavior A, but reward behavior B, they shouldn't be surprised to find employees learning to engage in behavior B. Similarly, managers should expect that employees will look to them as models. Managers who are consistently late to work, or take two hours for lunch, or help themselves to company office supplies for personal use should expect employees to read the message they are sending and model their behavior accordingly.

Learning Review

- Explain how operant conditioning helps managers understand, predict, and influence behavior.
- Describe the implications of social learning theory for managing people at work.

- Discuss how managers can shape behavior.

Managers **Respond** to a **Manager's** Dilemma

····**Amanda Ferguson**
Sales Representative, Eli Lilly and Company, Kirkwood, Missouri

Top managers often say their most important organizational asset is their people. Therefore, finding the best people is of utmost priority. Research indicates that emotional intelligence (EI) may be a better predictor of high performance than academic intelligence. Ron needs to use the traits of EI, like self-motivation and social skills, to choose highly effective people for Panera Bread. In order to attract people with EI, the jobs themselves have to be motivating. Once motivating jobs are in place, Ron can apply some principles of EI to fill them with top people. For instance, Ron could determine the self-motivation by asking an applicant a question like, "Tell me about a time when you faced a setback and were able to overcome it." From an interview, Ron could also determine the applicant's social skills, which are particularly important when hiring for positions with high customer interaction.

Barbara Gomes-Beach
Senior Principal, B. G. Beach Associates, Dorchester, Massachusetts

I would definitely utilize emotional intelligence (EI) in my employee hiring and development practices. If I were to rate the five EI qualifications, social skills would be at the top of the list. In order to satisfy customers in a highly competitive industry, Ron will have to pay close attention to this aspect. I would also look at potential employees who want employment opportunities that offer upward mobility and who actually "enjoy" meeting and interacting with people. It might also be helpful to look at applicants who have had some experience as a volunteer working in a service industry. The skills gained from volunteer work often result in patient, empathic individuals who are acutely aware that being pleasant and helpful is a definite plus no matter where one works—but essential in the food industry.

Learning Summary

● ● ●

After reading and studying this chapter, you should be able to:

- Explain why the concept of an organization as an iceberg is important to understanding organizational behavior.

- Describe the focus and the goals of organizational behavior.

- Define the five important employee behaviors that managers want to explain, predict, and influence.

- Describe the three components of an attitude.

- Discuss the three job-related attitudes.

- Explain how individuals reconcile inconsistencies between attitudes and behavior.

- Describe the relationship between job satisfaction and productivity.

- Contrast the MBTI and the Big Five Model of personality.

- Describe the five personality traits that have proved to be the most powerful in explaining individual behavior in organizations.

- Explain how emotions impact behavior and how emotional intelligence plays a role.

- Explain how an understanding of perception can help managers better understand individual behavior.

- Describe the key elements of attribution theory.

- Discuss how the fundamental attribution error and self-serving bias can distort attributions.

- Name three shortcuts used in judging others.

- Explain how operant conditioning helps managers understand, predict, and influence behavior.

- Describe the implications of social learning theory for managing people at work.

- Discuss how managers can shape behavior.

Thinking About Management Issues

● ● ●

1. How, if at all, does the importance of knowledge of OB differ based on a manager's level in the organization? Be specific.

2. "A growing number of companies are now convinced that people's ability to understand and to manage their emotions improves their performance, their collaboration with peers, and their interaction with customers." What are the implications of this statement for managers?

3. What behavioral predictions might you make if you knew that an employee had (a) an external locus of

control, (b) a low Mach score, (c) low self-esteem, or (d) high self-monitoring tendencies?

4. "Managers should never use discipline with a problem employee." Do you agree or disagree? Discuss.

5. A Gallup Organization survey shows that most workers rate having a caring boss even higher than they value money or fringe benefits. How should managers interpret this information? What are the implications?

Working Together: Team-Based Exercise

● ● ●

When we use shortcuts to judge others, are the consequences always negative? Form teams of three to four students. Your instructor will assign each class team either to "yes, the consequences are always negative" or to "no, the consequences

aren't always negative." After these assignments are made, your group should discuss this question. Come up with evidence and examples to support your group's argument. Be prepared to debate your group's position in class.

Ethical Dilemma Exercise

● ● ●

Can too much communication create an ethical dilemma? Companies that demonstrate support by keeping employees fully informed seek to build trust in management, avoid misperceptions, and encourage positive attitudes. Marriott International, for example, is careful to communicate often about a variety of decisions affecting employees, such as downsizing plans. "While there have

been layoffs here in the past," comments Jeff Ecott, a senior systems analyst at Marriott, "we were always informed well ahead of time about what was going on. We have 'town hall' meetings where management talks to us and lets us ask questions. That puts us at ease."

Another example is Avon Products, where information technology managers and employees worried that their jobs would be moved to another country or an outside supplier—until management met the issue head-on. "Avon told us in October that they had looked at outsourcing but didn't feel it met their requirements," states one technology manager. "As a result, I don't think anybody feels right now that the company has any plans to outsource [information technology]." However, would employees maintain their positive attitudes and perceptions if they receive too many or too frequent communications about possible outsourcing or potential layoff plans? How much communication is appropriate to avoid putting additional stress on employees and provoking negative attitudes and perceptions?[53]

Imagine that you're the vice president of information technology for Avon. To save money, you are again exploring the idea of outsourcing some tasks currently handled by your department. Even though outsourcing didn't make sense in previous years, this time could be different. You've just begun to ask suppliers for proposals; a final decision will not be made for six months or more. What should you communicate to your staff and when should you communicate it? Review the section on goals of organizational behavior as you consider this ethical challenge and decide which of the following options to choose—and why.

Option A: Talk with your employees now, so they are prepared for the possibility that some jobs will be eliminated if you eventually decide that outsourcing is the right approach.

Option B: Say nothing to your employees until a decision has been reached to outsource some or all of the department's tasks within a definite time period.

Option C: Mention the possibility of outsourcing only to the managers who report directly to you but have them say nothing to avoid upsetting the entire department.

Case Application

Washington Mutual, Inc.

"More human interest." That's the quirky motto of Seattle-based Washington Mutual. Yet it's quite fitting given how they view their customers and their employees. In business since 1889, WaMu (as it's known) is a financial services retailer, providing a variety of financial products and services to individual consumers and to small and medium-sized businesses. Its key markets are in California, Florida, Oregon, Texas, Washington, and now New York City, a market it entered in 2002. And CEO Kerry Killinger isn't finished yet. He wants to "reinvent how people think about banking." His goal is to have WaMu thought of in the same category as Wal-Mart, Southwest Airlines, Best Buy, and Target. Killinger says, "In every retailing industry, there are category killers who figure out how to have a very low cost structure and pass those advantages on to customers, day in and day out, with better pricing. I think we have a shot at doing that in this segment." With the company's push to keep costs low, you might think that employees would not rank high on the list of priorities. Yet, that impression would be wrong! Killinger knows how important his employees are to the success of the company. WaMu is extremely customer-focused. As the largest savings and loan institution in the United States, WaMu serves more than 7 million customers. And that means taking care of those customers.

With more than 50,000 employees, WaMu's managers see a lot of behaviors—good and not so good. To become the retail powerhouse it wants to be, those employee behaviors must be channeled in an appropriate direction. And the company has done this by focusing on its culture and hiring for attitude.

WaMu's culture is simple: Everyone should be treated with dignity and respect. The company has created a work environment in which *everyone* has the opportunity to thrive, have fun, and succeed. As mentioned earlier, customer service is a high priority. "People don't want conversations with uptight bankers; they want a friendly smile, fast service, and our respect." And the company recognizes that it's not just the frontline employees—the tellers—who service customers. Every WaMu employee has customers, whether they're external or internal. Even for those employees whose only contact is with other employees, the expectations are the same: outstanding service. With the company's continued growth, it's important to maintain that culture. It does this by hiring for attitude—a philosophy first espoused by former Southwest Airlines' CEO Herb Kelleher, who said, "We draft great attitudes. If you don't have a good attitude, we don't want you, no matter how skilled you are. We can change skill level through training. We can't change attitude." And WaMu adheres to that philosophy. Employees can be taught the mechanics of financial services, but to be successful, they must have the right attitude—caring, dynamic, driven, and fair.

DISCUSSION QUESTIONS

1. What type of personality characteristics would best fit into WaMu's culture?

2. Design an employee attitude survey that WaMu's managers might use. If you want, check out information on the company's Web site (*www.wamu.com*).

3. WaMu was named one of the 100 Best Companies to Work For by *Fortune* in 2003. What predictions, if any, could you make about job satisfaction at WaMu? How might job satisfaction affect work outcomes at WaMu?

4. The company's motto is "More human interest." How does it practice this motto?

Sources: Information on company from company Web site (*www.wamu.com*) and Hoover's Online (*www.hoovers.com*), June 15, 2003; L. Tischler, "Bank of (Middle) America," *Fast Company*, March 2003, pp. 104–9; and K. Godsey, "Slow Climb to New Heights: Combine Strict Discipline with Goofy Antics and Make Billions," *Success*, October 1, 1996, p. 20.

Chapter
15

Understanding Groups and Teams

····· A **Manager's** *Dilemma*

BMW has become the hottest car company on the planet.[1] Need proof? 2002 and 2003 were record-breaking sales years. Also, in 2003, BMW ranked number 12 on *Fortune*'s list of the World's Most Admired Companies—the highest-ranked European company. At a time when many global companies were being cautious in their strategies, BMW was pulling out all the stops. A major component of the company's growth strategy has been its continual introduction of striking new cars designed by a team led by Chris Bangle (in picture, seated in BMW Z9).

Bangle, a native of Wisconsin, is BMW's chief of design and works at the technological heart of the BMW Group—*Forschungs und Innovationszentrum* (better known by its German abbreviation FIZ), the company's glass-and-steel R&D center in Munich. Seen from the outside, the honeycomb-shaped FIZ building hints at the work going on inside. Arranged in open modules, the building was designed so employees would be in close proximity to each other and have to walk only short distances to confer with colleagues. But it's not just the building design that has played a key role in the company's ability to innovate and react rapidly to changes; it's also the emphasis on teamwork. The building's design just facilitates the team emphasis.

When Bangle was selected as design chief in 1992, industry analysts were surprised. He was largely unknown in automotive circles and an American on top of that. Bangle says that he was "humbled" to have won the job, but that humility might have been a subtle ploy to win over the company's senior designers. As a newcomer, he looked for ways to counteract the suffocating effects of the company's hierarchical *Festung* (fortress) design culture where lines of authority were rarely crossed and where employees rarely ventured to interact with others outside their own assigned work activities. Although it was his responsibility to safeguard the all-important creative process, he also wanted his designers to build trusting relationships with other designers and with the rest of the company. Since that time, Bangle has built what he calls a *dutzen* culture: an open, informal place where people aren't afraid to say what they really think. His main challenge has been orienting new engineers to the design team's more open culture.

Put yourself in Chris Bangle's position. What can he do to maintain his teams' effectiveness when new designers join?

What would *you* do **?**

ork teams are one of the realities—and challenges—of managing in today's dynamic global environment. Thousands of organizations have made the move to restructure work around teams rather than individuals. Why? What do these teams look like? And, like the challenge facing Chris Bangle, how can managers build effective teams? These are some of the types of questions we'll be answering in this chapter. First, however, let's begin by developing our understanding of group behavior.

UNDERSTANDING GROUPS

Each person in the group had his or her assigned role: The Spotter, The Back Spotter, The Gorilla, and The Big Player. For over 10 years, this group—former MIT students who were members of a secret Black Jack Club—used their extraordinary mathematical abilities, expert training, teamwork, and interpersonal skills to take millions of dollars from some of the major casinos in the United States.[2]

Although most groups aren't formed for such dishonest purposes, the success of this group at its task was impressive. Managers would like their employees to be successful at their tasks also. How can they do so? As we discussed in the previous chapter, managers need to understand the behavior of individuals in organizations. But since most organizational work is done by individuals who are part of a work group, it's important for managers to understand group behavior. And the behavior of a group is not merely the sum total of the behaviors of all the individuals in the group. Why? Because individuals act differently in groups than they do when they are alone. Therefore, if we want to understand organizational behavior more fully, we need to study groups.

What Is a Group?

●●● **group**
Two or more interacting and interdependent individuals who come together to achieve particular goals.

A **group** is defined as two or more interacting and interdependent individuals who come together to achieve particular goals. Groups can be either formal or informal. *Formal groups* are work groups defined by the organization's structure that have designated work assignments and specific tasks. In formal groups, appropriate behaviors are established by and directed toward organizational goals. Exhibit 15–1 provides some examples of different types of formal groups in today's organizations. (Go to the Web and check out You're the Manager: Diversity in Action #3.)

■ **Diversity**
Whenever you see this gold square, go to the R.O.L.L.S. Web site (**www.prenhall.com/ robbins)** and click on "You Be the Manager: Diversity in Action" to find an exercise that puts you in the role of a manager making a decision about diversity.

In contrast, *informal groups* are social. These groups occur naturally in the workplace in response to the need for social contact. For example, three employees from different departments who regularly eat lunch together are an informal group. Informal groups tend to form around friendships and common interests.

Stages of Group Development

Group development is a dynamic process. Most groups are in a continual state of change. Even though groups probably never reach complete stability, there's a general pattern that describes how most groups evolve. Research shows that groups pass

Exhibit 15–1

●●●———

Examples of Formal Groups

- *Command Groups:* Groups that are determined by the organization chart and composed of individuals who report directly to a given manager.
- *Task Groups:* Groups composed of individuals brought together to complete a specific job task; their existence is often temporary because once the task is completed, the group disbands.
- *Cross-functional Teams:* Groups that bring together the knowledge and skills of individuals from various work areas or groups whose members have been trained to do each others' jobs.
- *Self-managed Teams:* Groups that are essentially independent and in addition to their own tasks, take on traditional managerial responsibilities such as hiring, planning and scheduling, and performance evaluations.

Exhibit 15–2

Stages of Group Development

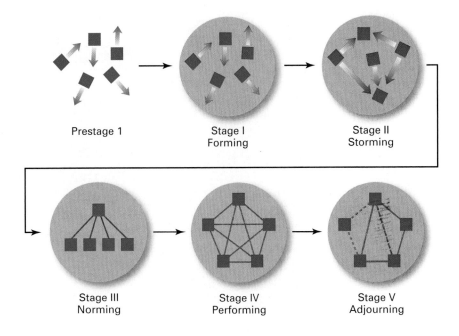

Prestage 1 | Stage I Forming | Stage II Storming

Stage III Norming | Stage IV Performing | Stage V Adjourning

through a standard sequence of five stages.[3] As shown in Exhibit 15–2, these five stages are: *forming, storming, norming, performing,* and *adjourning.*

The first stage, **forming**, has two aspects. First, people join the group either because of a work assignment, in the case of a formal group; or for some other benefit desired (such as status, self-esteem, affiliation, power, or security), in the case of an informal group.

Once the group's membership is in place, the second part of the forming stage begins: the task of defining the group's purpose, structure, and leadership. This phase is characterized by a great deal of uncertainty. Members are "testing the waters" to determine what types of behavior are acceptable. This stage is complete when members begin to think of themselves as part of a group.

The **storming** stage is one of intragroup conflict. Members accept the existence of the group but resist the control that the group imposes on individuality. Further, there is conflict over who will control the group. When this stage is complete, there will be a relatively clear hierarchy of leadership within the group and agreement on the group's direction.

The third stage is one in which close relationships develop and the group demonstrates cohesiveness. There's now a strong sense of group identity and camaraderie. This **norming** stage is complete when the group structure solidifies and the group has assimilated a common set of expectations of what defines correct member behavior. (▮▮▮▮▮ Go to the Web and check out Q & A 15.1.)

The fourth stage is **performing**. The group structure at this point is fully functional and accepted. Group energy has moved from getting to know and understand each other to performing the task at hand.

Performing is the last stage in the development of permanent work groups. Temporary groups—such as project teams, task forces, and similar groups that have a limited task to perform—have a fifth stage, **adjourning**. In this stage, the group prepares to disband. High levels of task performance are no longer the group's top priority. Instead, attention is directed at wrapping up activities. Responses of group members vary at this stage. Some are upbeat, basking in the group's accomplishments. Others may be saddened by the loss of camaraderie and friendships gained during the work group's life.

Many of you have probably experienced each of these stages in working on a class group project. Group members are selected and then meet for the first time. There's a "feeling out" period to assess what the group is going to do and how it's going to do it. This is usually rapidly followed by a battle for control: Who's going to be in charge? Once this issue is resolved and a "hierarchy" agreed on, the group identifies specific aspects of the task, who's going to do them, and dates by which the assigned work needs to be completed. General expectations are established and

forming
The first stage of group development in which people join the group and then define the group's purpose, structure, and leadership.

storming
The second stage of group development which is characterized by intragroup conflict.

norming
The third stage of group development which is characterized by close relationships and cohesiveness.

performing
The fourth stage of group development when the group is fully functional.

adjourning
The final stage of group development for temporary groups during which group members are concerned with wrapping up activities rather than task performance.

Self-managing teams at Toyo Ink in Australia are in the performing stage. There are no more time clocks because team members are responsible for the amount of work they do, and they will soon also be in charge of planning and organizing their own vacation times. Information sharing is more efficient, and communication with management has increased as well.

agreed upon by each member. These decisions form the foundation for what you hope will be a coordinated group effort culminating in a project well done. Once the group project is completed and turned in, the group breaks up. Of course, some groups don't get much beyond the first or second stage; these groups typically have serious interpersonal conflicts, turn in disappointing work, and get lower grades.

Should you assume from the preceding discussion that a group becomes more effective as it progresses through the first four stages? Some researchers argue that effectiveness of work groups increases at advanced stages, but it's not that simple.[4] That assumption may be generally true, but what makes a group effective is a complex issue. Under some conditions, high levels of conflict are conducive to high levels of group performance. We might expect to find situations in which groups in Stage II (storming) outperform those in Stages III (norming) or IV (performing). Similarly, groups don't always proceed clearly from one stage to the next. Sometimes, in fact, several stages may be going on simultaneously, as when groups are storming and performing at the same time. Groups even occasionally regress to previous stages. Therefore, don't always assume that all groups precisely follow this developmental process or that Stage IV (performing) is always the most preferable. It's better to think of this model as a general framework. It underscores the fact that groups are dynamic entities, and it can help you better understand the problems and issues that are most likely to surface during a group's life. (▨▨▨ Go to the Web and check out You're the Manager: Diversity in Action #1.)

● ● ● ● Learning Review

- Define the different types of groups.
- Describe the five stages of group development.

EXPLAINING WORK-GROUP BEHAVIOR

Why are some groups more successful than others? Why do some groups achieve high levels of performance and high levels of member satisfaction and others do not? The answers are complex, but they include variables such as the abilities of the group's members, the size of the group, the level of conflict, and the internal pressures on members to conform to the group's norms. Exhibit 15–3 presents the major components that determine group performance and satisfaction.[5] Let's look at each.

Exhibit 15–3

Group Behavior Model

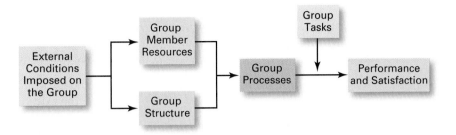

External Conditions Imposed on the Group

To begin understanding the behavior of a work group, you need to recognize it as a subsystem of a larger system.[6] Work groups don't exist in isolation. They're part of a larger organization. For instance, a quality control team at a Kraft Foods plant in Missouri must live within the rules and policies handed down by the division's headquarters in Chicago. As a subset of that larger organizational system, the work group is influenced by external conditions imposed from outside it. These external conditions include the organization's overall strategy, authority structures, formal regulations, availability or absence of organizational resources, employee selection criteria, the organization's performance management system, the organization's culture, and the general physical layout of the group's work space. For instance, some groups will have modern, high-quality tools and equipment to do their jobs while other groups aren't as fortunate. Or the organization might be pursuing a strategy of lowering costs or improving quality, which will affect what a group does and how it does it.

Group Member Resources

A group's potential level of performance depends to a large extent on the resources that its members individually bring to the group. These would include members' knowledge, abilities, and skills; and personality characteristics.

Part of a group's performance can be predicted by looking at the knowledge, abilities, and skills of its individual members. We do occasionally hear about an athletic team composed of mediocre players who, because of excellent coaching, determination, and precision teamwork, beat a far more talented group of players. Such examples make the news precisely because they are unusual. Group performance isn't merely the summation of its individual members' knowledge and abilities. However, they do set parameters for what members can do and how effectively they will perform in a group. In addition, interpersonal skills consistently emerge as important for high performance by work groups.[7] These skills include conflict management and resolution, collaborative problem solving, and communication. For instance, group members need to be able to recognize the type and source of conflict confronting the group and to implement an appropriate conflict-resolution strategy; to identify situations requiring participative group problem solving and to utilize the proper degree and type of participation; and to listen nonevaluatively and to appropriately use active listening techniques.

There has been a great deal of research on the relationship between personality traits and group attitudes and behaviors. The general conclusion is that attributes that tend to be viewed as positive in our culture (such as sociability, self-reliance, and independence) tend to be positively related to group productivity and morale. In contrast, negative personality characteristics such as authoritarianism, dominance, and unconventionality tend to be negatively related to productivity and morale.[8] These personality traits affect group performance by strongly influencing how the individual will interact with other group members.

Group Member Resources in Cross-cultural Groups Understanding the relationship between group performance and group member resources is made more challenging in global organizations in which cross-cultural groups are prevalent. Given these conditions, managers need to clearly understand the cultural characteristics of the groups and the group members they manage.[9]

MANAGING WORKFORCE
DIVERSITY

The Challenge of Managing Diverse Teams

Understanding and managing teams composed of people who are similar can be difficult! Add in diverse members and managing teams can be even more of a challenge. However, the benefits to be gained from the diverse perspectives, skills, and abilities often more than offset the extra effort.[10] How can you meet the challenge of coordinating a diverse work team? It's important to stress four critical interpersonal behaviors: understanding, empathy, tolerance, and communication.

You know that people aren't the same, yet they need to be treated fairly and equitably. And differences (cultural, physical, or other) can cause people to behave in different ways. Team leaders need to understand and accept these differences. Each and every team member should be encouraged to do the same.

Empathy is closely related to understanding. As a team leader, you should try to understand others' perspectives. Put yourself in their place and encourage team members to empathize as well. For instance, suppose an Asian woman joins a team of Caucasian and Hispanic men. They can make her feel more welcome and comfortable by identifying with how she might feel. Is she excited or disappointed about her new work assignment? Has she had any experiences working with male colleagues? How have her cultural experiences shaped her attitudes toward men? By putting themselves in her position, the existing team members can enhance their ability to work together as an effective group.

Tolerance is another important interpersonal behavior in managing diverse teams. The fact that you understand that people are different and you empathize with them doesn't mean that it's any easier to accept different perspectives or behaviors. But it's important to be tolerant in dealing with diverse ages, gender, and cultural backgrounds—to allow team members the freedom to be themselves. Part of being tolerant is being open-minded about different values, attitudes, and behaviors.

Finally, open communication is important to managing a diverse team. Diversity problems may intensify if people are afraid or unwilling to openly discuss issues that concern them. And communication within a diverse team needs to be two-way. If a person wants to know whether a certain behavior is offensive to someone else, it's best to ask. Likewise, a person who is offended by a certain behavior of someone else should explain his or her concerns and ask that person to stop. As long as these communication exchanges are handled in a non-threatening, low-key, and friendly manner, they generally will have a positive outcome. Finally, it helps to have an atmosphere within the team that supports and celebrates diversity.

Group Structure

Work groups aren't unorganized crowds. They have a structure that shapes members' behavior and makes it possible to explain, predict, and influence a large portion of individual behavior within the group as well as the performance of the group itself. This internal structure defines member roles, norms, conformity, status systems, group size, group cohesiveness, and formal leadership positions. Let's look at the first six of these. We'll look at the seventh—leadership—in Chapter 17.

Roles We introduced the concept of roles in Chapter 1 when we discussed what managers do. (Remember Mintzberg's managerial roles.) Of course, managers aren't the only individuals in an organization who play various roles. The concept of roles applies to all employees in organizations and to their lives outside the organization as well. (■■■■■ Go to the Web and check out Q & A 15.2.)

● ● ● **role**
A set of behavior patterns expected of someone occupying a given position in a social unit.

A **role** refers to a set of expected behavior patterns attributed to someone who occupies a given position in a social unit. In a group, individuals are expected to perform certain roles because of their position in the group. These roles tend to be oriented toward either task accomplishment or toward maintaining group member satisfaction.[11] Think about groups that you've been in and the roles that you played. Were you continually trying to keep the group focused on getting its work done? If so, you were filling a task accomplishment role. Or were you more concerned that group members had the opportunity to offer ideas and that they were satisfied with the experience? If so, you were performing a group member satisfaction role. Both roles are important to the ability of a group to function effectively and efficiently.

A general problem that arises in understanding role behavior is that individuals play multiple roles, adjusting their roles to the group to which they belong at the time. They read their job descriptions, get suggestions from their managers, and watch what their co-workers do. When that individual is confronted by different role expectations, he or she experiences *role conflict*. Employees often face role conflicts. For instance, a credit manager expects her credit analysts to process a minimum of 30 applications a week so that everyone has work to do and no one gets laid off. Or a new college instructor's colleagues want him to give very few high grades in order to maintain the department's reputation for having tough standards, but students want him to give out high grades to enhance their grade point averages. To the degree that the instructor wants to satisfy the expectations of both his colleagues and his students, he faces role conflict. (▮▮▮▮▮ Go to the Web and check out Q & A 15.3.)

Norms All groups have established **norms**—acceptable standards or expectations that are shared by the group's members. Norms dictate factors such as work output levels, absenteeism, promptness, and the amount of socializing allowed on the job. (▮▮▮▮▮ Go to the Web and check out Q & A 15.4.)

• • • **norms**
Acceptable standards or expectations shared by a group's members.

Norms, for example, dictate the "arrival ritual" among office assistants at Coleman Trust and Realty. The workday begins at 8:00 A.M. Most employees typically arrive a few minutes before and hang up their coats and put their purses and other personal items on their chairs or desks so everyone knows they're "at work." They then go to the company cafeteria to get coffee and chat. Employees who violate this norm by starting work sharply at eight o'clock are teased and pressured to encourage behavior that conforms to the group's standard.

Although each group will have its own unique set of norms, there are common types of norms in most organizations which focus on effort and performance, dress, and loyalty. Probably the most widespread norms are related to levels of effort and performance. Work groups typically provide their members with explicit cues on how hard to work, what level of output to have, when to look busy, when it's acceptable to goof off, and the like. These norms are very powerful in influencing an individual employee's performance. They're so powerful that performance predictions that are

One of the reasons that norms are so important to groups is that they ensure everyone is working to the same standards. After all, says Robert Falcon, a team leader at this Dana automotive assembly plant in Stockton, California, "Your job is dependent on the person before you, and the person behind you is dependent on you. If one person is not performing, that creates a problem for the others on the team."

based solely on an employee's ability and level of personal motivation often prove to be wrong. And dress norms frequently dictate the kind of clothing that should be worn to work. Of course, what's acceptable dress in one organization may be very different from what's acceptable in another. Finally, loyalty norms will influence whether or not individuals work late, work on weekends, or move to locations they might not want to live in. (◼◻▨▨ Go to the Web and check out Q & A 15.5.)

Conformity Because individuals want to be accepted by groups to which they belong, they're susceptible to conformity pressures. The impact that group pressures for conformity can have on an individual member's judgment and attitudes was demonstrated in research by Solomon Asch.[12] In his conformity experiments, groups of seven or eight people were asked to compare two cards held up by the experimenter. One card had three lines of different lengths and the other had one line which was equal in length to one of the three lines on the other card (see Exhibit 15–4). Each group member was to announce aloud which of the three lines matched the single line. Asch wanted to know what would happen if members began to give incorrect answers. Would the pressures to conform cause individuals to align with the others? The experiment was "fixed" so that all but one of the members (the unsuspecting subject) had been told ahead of time to start giving obviously incorrect answers after one or two rounds of these matching exercises. Over many experiments and trials, the unsuspecting subject conformed over a third of the time; that is, the person gave answers he or she knew were wrong but that were consistent with the replies of other group members.

These conclusions are based on research that's over 50 years old. Are they still valid? And are they generalizable across cultures? More current research suggests that there have been changes in the level of conformity over time and that Asch's findings are culture-bound.[13] Levels of conformity have declined since Asch's studies. In addition, as might be expected, conformity to social norms is higher in collectivist cultures than in individualistic cultures. Nevertheless, even in individualistic countries such as the United States, you should consider conformity to norms to still be a powerful force in groups. (◼◻▨▨ Go to the Web and check out Q & A 15.6.) As group members, we often desire to be one of the group and to avoid being visibly different. So we conform. In addition, when an individual's opinion of objective data differs significantly from that of others in the group, he or she feels extensive pressure to align his or her opinion to conform to others' opinions, a phenomenon known as **groupthink**. As group members, we find it more pleasant to be in agreement and harmony—to be a positive part of the group—than to be a disruptive force, even if disruption is necessary to improve the effectiveness of the group's decisions.

Fortunately, groupthink doesn't appear in all groups. It seems to occur most often when there is a clear group identity, where members hold a positive image of their group that they want to protect, and when the group perceives a collective threat to this positive image.[14]

Status Systems Status is a prestige grading, position, or rank within a group. As far back as researchers have been able to trace groups, they have found status hierarchies. Status systems are an important factor in understanding behavior. Status is a

⦁⦁● **groupthink**
A form of conformity in which group members feel extensive pressure to align their opinions with others' opinions.

⦁⦁● **status**
A prestige grading, position, or rank within a group.

⦁ ⦁ ⦁━━━━━
Exhibit 15–4

Examples of Cards Used in the Asch Study

You've been hired as a summer intern in the auditing section of an accounting firm in Dallas. After working there about a month, you conclude that the attitude in the office is "anything goes." Employees know that supervisors won't discipline them for ignoring company rules. For example, employees have to turn in expense reports, but the process is a joke; nobody submits receipts to verify reimbursement, and nothing is ever said. In fact, when you tried to turn in your receipts with your expense report, you were told, "Nobody else turns in receipts and you don't really need to, either." You know that no expense check has ever been denied because of failure to turn in a receipt, even though the employee handbook says that receipts are required. Also, your co-workers use company phones for personal long distance calls even though that is prohibited by the employee handbook. And one permanent employee told you to "help yourself" to any paper, pens, or pencils you might need here or at home.

What are the norms of this group? Suppose that you were the supervisor in this area. How would you go about changing the norms?

significant motivator and has behavioral consequences when individuals see a disparity between what they perceive their status to be and what others perceive it to be.

Status in a group may be informally conferred by characteristics such as education, age, skill, or experience. Anything can have status value if others in the group evaluate it that way. Of course, the fact that status is informal doesn't mean that it's unimportant or that it's hard to determine who has it or who does not. Members of groups have no problem placing people into status categories, and they usually agree about who has high, middle, or low status.

Status is also formally conferred, and it's important for employees to believe that the organization's formal status system is congruent—that is, there's equity between the perceived ranking of an individual and the status symbols he or she is given by the organization. For instance, status incongruence would occur when a supervisor earns less than his or her subordinates, a desirable office is occupied by a person in a low-ranking position, or paid country club memberships are provided to division managers but not to vice presidents. Employees expect the "things" an individual receives to be congruent with his or her status. When they're not, employees are likely to question the authority of their managers. Also, the motivational potential of promotions declines, and the general pattern of order and consistency in the organization is disturbed.

Before we leave the topic of status, we need to address its cross-cultural transferability. Do cultural differences affect status? Yes! The importance of status does vary between cultures. The French, for example, are extremely status conscious. Also, countries differ on the criteria that confer status. For instance, status for Latin Americans and Asians tends to come from family position and formal roles held in organizations. In contrast, while status is important in countries like the United States and Australia, it tends to be less "in your face." And it tends to be given based on accomplishments rather than on titles and family history.

Our message for managers is to make sure you understand who and what holds status when interacting with people from a culture different from your own. An American manager who doesn't understand that office size isn't a measure of a Japanese executive's position, or who fails to grasp the importance the British place on family genealogy and social class, is likely to unintentionally offend others and lessen his or her interpersonal effectiveness.

Group Size Does the size of a group affect the group's overall behavior? Yes, but the effect depends on which outcomes you're focusing on.[15] The evidence indicates, for instance, that small groups are faster at completing tasks than larger ones. However, if the group is engaged in problem solving, large groups consistently get better results than smaller ones. Translating these findings into specific numbers is a bit more difficult, but we can offer some guidelines. Large groups—those with a dozen or more members—are good for getting diverse input. Thus, if the goal of the group is to find facts, a larger group should be more effective. On the other hand, smaller groups are better at doing something productive with those facts. Groups of approximately seven members tend to be more effective for taking action.

● ● ● **social loafing**
The tendency for individuals to expend less effort when working collectively than when working individually.

One of the more important findings related to group size is **social loafing**, which is the tendency for individuals to expend less effort when working collectively than when working individually.[16] It directly challenges the logic that the group's productivity should at least equal the sum of the productivity of each group member. What causes this social loafing effect? It may be due to a belief that others in the group are not carrying their fair share. If you see others as lazy or inept, you can reestablish equity by reducing your effort. Another explanation is the dispersion of responsibility. Because the results of the group can't be attributed to any one person, the relationship between an individual's input and the group's output is clouded. In such situations, individuals may be tempted to become "free riders" and coast on the group's efforts. In other words, there will be a reduction in efficiency when individuals think that their contribution can't be measured.

The implications of social loafing for managers are significant. When managers use collective work situations to enhance morale and teamwork, they must also have a way to identify individual efforts. If this isn't done, they must weigh the potential losses in productivity from using groups against any possible gains in employee satisfaction.[17] However, this conclusion does have a Western bias. It's consistent with individualistic cultures, like the United States and Canada, that are dominated by self-interest. It's not consistent with collectivistic societies, in which individuals are motivated by in-group goals. For instance, in studies comparing employees from the United States with employees from the People's Republic of China and Israel (both collectivistic societies), the Chinese and Israelis showed no propensity to engage in social loafing. In fact, they actually performed better in a group than when working alone.[18]

Group Cohesiveness Intuitively, it makes sense that groups in which there's a lot of internal disagreement and lack of cooperation are less effective in completing their tasks than are groups in which members generally agree, cooperate, and like each other. Research in this area has focused on **group cohesiveness**, or the degree to which members are attracted to a group and share the group's goals. Cohesiveness is important because it has been found to be related to a group's productivity.[19]

● ● ● **group cohesiveness**
The degree to which group members are attracted to one another and share the group's goals.

Research has generally shown that highly cohesive groups are more effective than are less cohesive ones.[20] However, this relationship between cohesiveness and effectiveness is more complex. (■□▨▨▨▨ Go to the Web and check out Q & A 15.7.) A key moderating variable is the degree to which the group's attitude aligns with its goals or with the goals of the organization.[21] The more cohesive a group is, the more its members will follow its goals. If the goals are desirable (for instance, high output, quality work, cooperation with individuals outside the group), a cohesive group is more productive than a less cohesive group. But if cohesiveness is high and attitudes are unfavorable, productivity decreases. If cohesiveness is low and goals are supported, productivity increases, but not as much as when both cohesiveness and support are high. When cohesiveness is low and goals are not supported, cohesiveness has no significant effect on productivity. These conclusions are illustrated in Exhibit 15–5.

Group Processes

The next component in our group behavior model concerns the processes that go on within a work group—the communication patterns used by members to exchange information, group decision processes, power dynamics, conflict interactions, and the like. Why are processes important to understanding work-group behavior? Because in

Exhibit 15–5

The Relationship Between Cohesiveness and Productivity

		Cohesiveness	
		High	**Low**
Alignment of Group and Organizational Goals	**High**	Strong Increase in Productivity	Moderate Increase in Productivity
	Low	Decrease in Productivity	No Significant Effect on Productivity

groups, one and one don't necessarily add up to two. Every group begins with a potential defined by its constraints, resources, and structure. Then you add in the positive and negative process factors created within the group itself. An example of a positive process factor is the synergy of four people on a marketing research team who are able to generate far more ideas as a group than the members could produce individually. However, the group also may have negative process factors such as social loafing, high levels of conflict, or poor communication, which may hinder group effectiveness. Two group processes that are of particular importance to managers are group decision making and conflict management.

Group Decision Making Many organizational decisions are made by groups. It's a rare organization that doesn't at some time use committees, task forces, review panels, study teams, or similar groups to make decisions. In addition, studies show that managers may spend up to 30 hours a week in group meetings.[22] Undoubtedly, a large portion of that time is spent identifying problems, developing solutions, and determining how to implement the solutions. It's possible, in fact, for groups to be assigned any of the eight steps in the decision-making process. (Refer to Chapter 6 for a review of these steps.) In this section, we'll look at the advantages and disadvantages of group decision making, discuss when groups would be preferred, and review some techniques for improving group decision making.

What advantages do group decisions have over individual decisions?

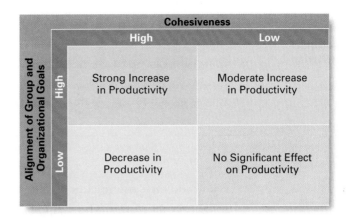

Group decision making is the norm among Google's engineering teams. According to engineering head Wayne Rosing, if something is wrong with a Google product, his teams make a decision to fix it without the need to get anyone's approval. "The teams knew what they had to do. That set a cultural bit in people's heads: You are the boss. Don't wait to take the hill. Don't wait to be managed."

1. *Generate more complete information and knowledge.* A group brings a diversity of experience and perspectives to the decision process that an individual cannot.

2. *Generate more diverse alternatives.* Because groups have a greater amount and diversity of information, they can identify more diverse alternatives than an individual.

3. *Increase acceptance of a solution.* Group members are reluctant to fight or undermine a decision they have helped develop.

4. *Increase legitimacy.* Decisions made by groups may be perceived as more legitimate than decisions made unilaterally by one person.

If groups are so good at making decisions, how did the phrase, "A camel is a horse put together by a committee" become so popular? The answer, of course, is that group decisions also have disadvantages.

Criteria of Effectiveness	Groups	Individuals
Accuracy	√	
Speed		√
Creativity	√	
Degree of acceptance	√	
Efficiency		√

1. *Time-consuming.* Groups almost always take more time to reach a solution than it would take an individual.

2. *Minority domination.* The inequality of group members creates the opportunity for one or more members to dominate others. A dominant and vocal minority frequently can have an excessive influence on the final decision.

3. *Pressures to conform.* As we know from our earlier discussion, there are pressures to conform in groups. This groupthink undermines critical thinking in the group and eventually harms the quality of the final decision.[23]

4. *Ambiguous responsibility.* Group members share responsibility, but the responsibility of any single member is diluted.

Determining whether groups are effective at making decisions depends on the criteria you use to assess effectiveness.[24] Exhibit 15–6 summarizes when groups or individuals are most effective.

Keep in mind, however, that the effectiveness of group decision making is also influenced by the size of the group. Although a larger group provides greater opportunity for diverse representation, it also requires more coordination and more time for members to contribute their ideas. So groups probably should not be too large. Evidence indicates, in fact, that groups of five, and to a lesser extent, seven, are the most effective.[25] Having an odd number in the group helps avoid decision deadlocks. Also, these groups are large enough for members to shift roles and withdraw from unfavorable positions but still small enough for quieter members to participate actively in discussions.

What techniques can managers use to help groups make more creative decisions? Exhibit 15–7 describes three possible techniques.

Conflict Management   Another important group process is how a group manages conflict. As a group performs its assigned tasks, disagreements inevitably arise. When we use the term **conflict**, we're referring to *perceived* incompatible differences resulting in some form of interference or opposition. Whether the differences are real

••• **conflict**
Perceived incompatible differences that result in interference or opposition.

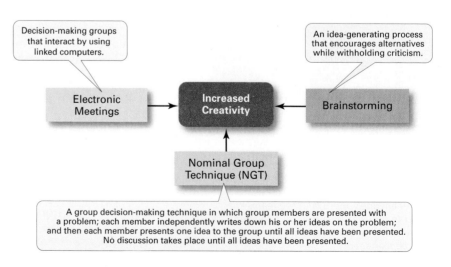

A group decision-making technique in which group members are presented with a problem; each member independently writes down his or her ideas on the problem; and then each member presents one idea to the group until all ideas have been presented. No discussion takes place until all ideas have been presented.

●●● **traditional view of conflict**
The view that all conflict is bad and must be avoided.

●●● **human relations view of conflict**
The view that conflict is a natural and inevitable outcome in any group.

●●● **interactionist view of conflict**
The view that some conflict is necessary for a group to perform effectively.

●●● **functional conflicts**
Conflicts that support a group's goals and improve its performance.

●●● **dysfunctional conflicts**
Conflicts that prevent a group from achieving its goals.

●●● **task conflict**
Conflicts over content and goals of the work.

●●● **relationship conflict**
Conflict based on interpersonal relationships.

●●● **process conflict**
Conflict over how work gets done.

or not is irrelevant. If people in a group perceive that differences exist, then there is conflict. Our definition encompasses the full range of conflict—from subtle, indirect, and highly controlled forms of interferences to overt acts such as strikes, riots, or wars.

Over the years, three different views have evolved regarding conflict.[26] One view argues that conflict must be avoided—that it indicates a problem within the group. We call this the **traditional view of conflict**. (▇▇ Go to the Web and check out Q & A 15.8.) A second view, the **human relations view of conflict**, argues that conflict is a natural and inevitable outcome in any group and need not be negative but, rather, has potential to be a positive force in contributing to a group's performance. The third and most recent perspective proposes that not only can conflict be a positive force in a group but that some conflict is *absolutely necessary* for a group to perform effectively. This third approach is called the **interactionist view of conflict**.

The interactionist view doesn't suggest that all conflicts are good. Some conflicts are seen as supporting the goals of the work group and improving its performance; these are **functional conflicts** of a constructive nature. Other conflicts are destructive and prevent a group from achieving its goals. These are **dysfunctional conflicts**. Exhibit 15–8 illustrates the challenge facing managers. (▇▇ Go to the Web and check out Q & A 15.9.)

What differentiates functional from dysfunctional conflict? (▇▇ Go to the Web and check out You're the Manager: Diversity in Action #2.) The evidence indicates that you need to look at the *type* of conflict.[27] Three types have been identified: task, relationship, and process.

Task conflict relates to the content and goals of the work. **Relationship conflict** focuses on interpersonal relationships. **Process conflict** refers to how the work gets done. Studies demonstrate that relationship conflicts are almost always dysfunctional. Why? It appears that the friction and interpersonal hostilities inherent in relationship conflicts increase personality clashes and decrease mutual understanding, thereby hindering the completion of organizational tasks. On the other hand, low levels of

Exhibit 15–8

●●● **Conflict and Group Performance**

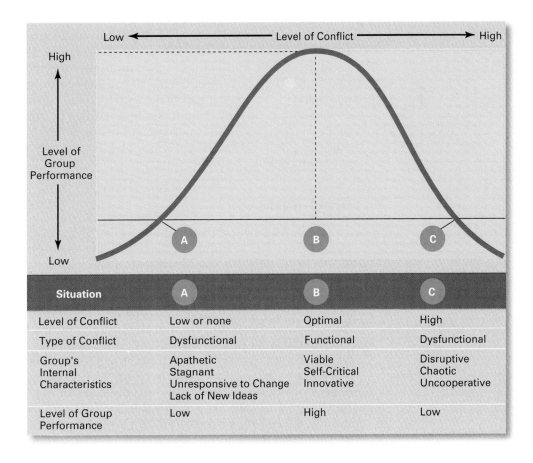

Situation	A	B	C
Level of Conflict	Low or none	Optimal	High
Type of Conflict	Dysfunctional	Functional	Dysfunctional
Group's Internal Characteristics	Apathetic Stagnant Unresponsive to Change Lack of New Ideas	Viable Self-Critical Innovative	Disruptive Chaotic Uncooperative
Level of Group Performance	Low	High	Low

Exhibit 15–9

**Conflict-Resolution
Techniques**

Source: Adapted from K.W.
Thomas, "Conflict and Negotiation
Processes in Organizations," in
M.D. Dunnette and L.M. Hough
(eds.), *Handbook of Industrial and
Organizational Psychology*, vol. 3,
2d ed. (Palo Alto, CA: Consulting
Psychologists Press, 1992), p. 668.
With permission.

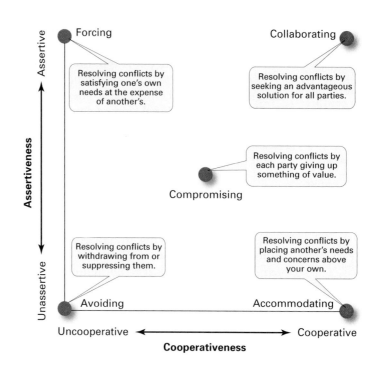

process conflict and low-to-moderate levels of task conflict are functional. For process conflict to be productive, it must be kept minimal. Intense arguments about who should do what become dysfunctional when they create uncertainty about task roles, increase the time taken to complete tasks, and lead to members working at cross-purposes. A low-to-moderate level of task conflict consistently demonstrates a positive effect on group performance because it stimulates discussions of ideas that help groups perform better. Because we have yet to devise a sophisticated measuring instrument for assessing whether a given task, relationship, or process conflict level is optimal, too high, or too low, the manager must make intelligent judgments. (Check out You're the Manager: Putting Ethics into Action on p. 452.)

When group conflict levels are too high, what techniques can managers use to reduce it? They can select from five conflict-resolution options: avoidance, accommodation, forcing, compromise, and collaboration.[28] (See Exhibit 15–9 for a description of each of these techniques.) Keep in mind that no one option is ideal for every situation. Which approach to use depends upon the manager's desire to be more or less cooperative and more or less assertive. (▮▮▮░░░ Go to the Web and check out Q & A 15.10.)

Group Tasks

The final box in our model points out that the impact of group processes on group performance and member satisfaction depends on the task that the group is doing. More specifically, the *complexity* and *interdependence* of tasks influence the group's effectiveness.[29]

Tasks can be generalized as either simple or complex. Simple tasks are routine and standardized. Complex tasks are ones that tend to be novel or nonroutine. We would hypothesize that the more complex the task, the more the group will benefit from discussion among group members about alternative work methods. If the task is simple, group members don't need to discuss such alternatives. They can rely on standard operating procedures. Similarly, if there's a high degree of interdependence among the tasks that group members must perform, they'll need to interact more. Effective communication and controlled conflict should, therefore, be most relevant to group performance when tasks are complex and interdependent.

TURNING GROUPS INTO EFFECTIVE TEAMS

More than 25 years ago when companies like W.L. Gore, Volvo, and Kraft General Foods introduced teams into their production processes, it made news because no one else was doing it. Today, it's just the opposite. It's the organization that *doesn't* use teams that has become newsworthy. Currently, 80 percent of *Fortune* 500 companies have half or more of their employees on teams. And 68 percent of small U.S. manufacturers are using teams in their production.[30] And the popularity of teams is likely to continue. Why? Research evidence suggests that teams typically outperform individuals when the tasks being done require multiple skills, judgment, and experience.[31] As organizations have restructured themselves to compete more effectively and efficiently, they have turned to teams as a way to use employee talents better. Managers have found that teams are more flexible and responsive to changing events than are traditional departments or other permanent work groups. Teams have the ability to quickly assemble, deploy, refocus, and disband. (■□▨▨▨ Go to the Web and check out Q & A 15.11.) In this section, we'll discuss what a work team is, the different types of teams that organizations might use, and how to develop and manage work teams.

What Is a Team?

Most of you are already familiar with teams, especially if you've watched organized sports events. Although a sports team has many of the same characteristics as a work team, work teams *are* different from work groups and have their own unique traits. Work groups interact primarily to share information and to make decisions to help each member do his or her job more efficiently and effectively. These groups have no need or opportunity to engage in collective work that requires joint effort. On the other hand, **work teams** are groups whose members work intensely on a specific, common goal using their positive synergy, individual and mutual accountability, and complementary skills. In a work team, the combined individual efforts of team members result in a level of performance that is greater than the sum of those individual inputs. How? By generating positive synergy through coordinated effort.

• • • • **work teams**
Groups whose members work intensely on a specific, common goal using their positive synergy, individual and mutual accountability, and complementary skills.

Types of Teams

Teams can do a variety of things. They can design products, provide services, negotiate deals, coordinate projects, offer advice, and make decisions.[32] For instance, at Motorola's facility in Austin, Texas, teams are used in work-process optimization projects. At Acxiom Corporation, a team of human resource professionals planned and implemented a cultural change that was focused more on customer service. And every summer weekend at NASCAR races, you can see work teams in action during drivers' pit stops.[33] The four most common types of teams you're likely to find in an organization include problem-solving teams, self-managed work teams, cross-functional teams, and virtual teams.

Teams work toward their goal with an intensity and commitment that General Motors managers understand well. When GM executive Mike DiGiovanni was putting together his Hummer team, the goal was to create a consumer version of the famous military vehicle on a shoestring budget. "I knew Hummer would never get out of the box without a good team," he said. "I needed some cockiness, irreverence, and a belief that you could change the rules. I needed people who would constantly push each other out of their comfort zone."

••• **problem-solving team**
A team of 5 to 12 employees from the same department or functional area who are involved in efforts to improve work activities or to solve specific problems.

••• **self-managed work team**
A type of work team that operates without a manager and is responsible for a complete work process or segment.

••• **cross-functional team**
A type of work team that's a hybrid grouping of individuals who are experts in various specialties and who work together on various tasks.

••• **virtual team**
A type of work team that uses computer technology to link physically dispersed members in order to achieve a common goal.

If we look back at when work teams were just beginning to gain in popularity, most were what we call **problem-solving teams**, which are teams of 5 to 12 employees from the same department or functional area who are involved in efforts to improve work activities or to solve specific problems. In problem-solving teams, members share ideas or offer suggestions on how work processes and methods can be improved. However, these teams are rarely given the authority to unilaterally implement any of their suggested actions.

Although problem-solving teams were on the right track, they didn't go far enough in getting employees involved in work-related decisions and processes. This led to the development of another type of team that could not only solve problems but implement solutions and take full responsibility for outcomes. These teams are called **self-managed work teams**, a formal group of employees who operate without a manager and are responsible for a complete work process or segment. The self-managed team is responsible for getting the work done *and* for managing themselves. This usually includes planning and scheduling of work, assigning tasks to members, collective control over the pace of work, making operating decisions, and taking action on problems. For instance, teams at Corning have no shift supervisors and work closely with other manufacturing divisions to solve production-line problems and coordinate deadlines and deliveries. The teams have the authority to make and implement decisions, finish projects, and address problems.[34] Other organizations such as Xerox, General Motors, Coors Brewing, PepsiCo, Hewlett-Packard, and Industrial Light & Magic use self-managed teams. It's estimated that about 30 percent of U.S. employers now use this form of team; and among large firms, the number is probably closer to 50 percent.[35] How effective are self-managed teams? Most organizations that use them find them to be successful and plan to expand their use in the coming years.[36] However, managers can't forget to consider cultural differences when deciding whether to use self-managed teams. For instance, evidence suggests that these types of teams have not fared well in Mexico largely due to that culture's low tolerance of ambiguity and uncertainty and employees' strong respect for hierarchical authority.[37]

The third type of team we want to discuss is the **cross-functional team**, which we introduced in Chapter 10 and defined as a hybrid grouping of individuals who are experts in various specialties and who work together on various tasks. Many organizations are using cross-functional teams. For example, at the AMS Operations Hillend factory in Fife, Scotland, cross-functional teams manufacture printed circuit boards that are used in military applications.[38] The concept of cross-functional teams is even being applied in health care. For instance, at Suburban Hospital in Bethesda, Maryland, intensive care unit (ICU) teams composed of a doctor trained in intensive care medicine, a pharmacist, a social worker, a nutritionist, the chief ICU nurse, a respiratory therapist, and a chaplain meet daily with every patient's bedside nurse to discuss and debate the best course of treatment. The hospital credits this team care approach with reducing errors, shortening the amount of time patients spent in ICU, and improving communication between families and the medical staff.[39] (▮▭▭▭ Go to the Web and check out Q & A 15.12.)

The final type of team we want to discuss is the **virtual team**. Virtual teams are teams that use computer technology to link physically dispersed members in order to achieve a common goal. For instance, StrawberryFrog, a small advertising agency based in Amsterdam, relies on a global network of more than 50 individuals from 22 countries. These freelancers and their skills are brought in as needed on various projects. By relying on this virtual team, StrawberryFrog is able to exploit a network of talent without unnecessary overhead and complex work arrangements.[40] In a virtual team, members collaborate online with tools such as wide-area networks, videoconferencing, fax, e-mail, or even Web sites where the team can hold online conferences.[41] Virtual teams can do all the things that other teams can—share information, make decisions, and complete tasks; however, they miss the normal give-and-take of face-to-face discussions. Because of this omission, virtual teams tend to be more task-oriented, especially if the team members have never personally met.

Creating Effective Teams

Teams are not automatic productivity enhancers. They can also be disappointments. How can managers create effective teams? (▉▉▉▢▉ Go to the Web and check out PRISM #9—Coaching and Creating Effective Teams.)

Research on teams provides insights into the characteristics associated with effective teams.[42] Let's look more closely at these characteristics, which are listed in Exhibit 15–10. (Check out Passport Scenario 1 on p. 452.)

Clear Goals High-performance teams have a clear understanding of the goal to be achieved. Members are committed to the team's goals; they know what they're expected to accomplish and understand how they will work together to achieve these goals.

Relevant Skills Effective teams are composed of competent individuals who have the necessary technical and interpersonal skills to achieve the desired goals while working well together. This last point is important since not everyone who is technically competent has the interpersonal skills to work well as a team member.

Mutual Trust Effective teams are characterized by high mutual trust among members. That is, members believe in each other's ability, character, and integrity. But as you probably know from personal relationships, trust is fragile. Maintaining this trust requires careful attention by managers. (▉▉▉▢▉ Go to the Web and check out S.A.L. #29—Do Others See Me As Trusting?)

Unified Commitment Unified commitment is characterized by dedication to the team's goals and a willingness to expend extraordinary amounts of energy to achieve them. Members of an effective team exhibit intense loyalty and dedication to the team and are willing to do whatever it takes to help their team succeed.

Good Communication Not surprisingly, effective teams are characterized by good communication. Members convey messages, verbally and nonverbally, to each other in ways that are readily and clearly understood. Also, feedback helps to guide

Exhibit 15–10

Characteristics of Effective Teams

Becoming a Manager

♦ *Use any opportunities that come up to work in a group. Note things such as stages of group development, roles, norms, social loafing, and so forth.*

♦ *When confronted with conflicts, pay attention to how you manage or resolve them.*

♦ *In group projects, try different techniques for improving the group's creativity.*

♦ *When you see a successful team, try to assess what makes it successful.*

♦ ▪▪▪▫▪ *Go to the Web and complete the following exercises from the Self-Assessment Library (S.A.L.) on R.O.L.L.S.: #25—How Good Are My Listening Skills?, #29—Do Others See Me As Trusting?, and #30—How Good Am I at Building and Leading a Team?*

team members and to correct misunderstandings. Like a couple who has been together for many years, members on high-performing teams are able to quickly and efficiently share ideas and feelings. (▪▪▪▫▪ Go to the Web and check out S.A.L. #25—How Good Are My Listening Skills?)

Negotiating Skills Effective teams are continually making adjustments as to whom does what. This flexibility requires team members to possess negotiating skills. Since problems and relationships are regularly changing in teams, members need to be able to confront and reconcile differences.

Appropriate Leadership Effective leaders can motivate a team to follow them through the most difficult situations. How? By clarifying goals, demonstrating that change is possible by overcoming inertia, increasing the self-confidence of team members, and helping members to more fully realize their potential. Increasingly, effective team leaders act as coaches and facilitators. They help guide and support the team, but don't control it. (▪▪▪▫▪ Go to the Web and check out S.A.L. #30—How Good Am I at Building and Leading a Team?)

Internal and External Support The final condition necessary for an effective team is a supportive climate. Internally, the team should have a sound infrastructure which means having proper training, a clear and reasonable measurement system that team members can use to evaluate their overall performance, an incentive program that recognizes and rewards team activities, and a supportive human resource system. The right infrastructure should support members and reinforce behaviors that lead to high levels of performance. Externally, managers should provide the team with the resources needed to get the job done.

A Final Note About Teams

Few trends have influenced employee jobs as much as the massive move to introduce teams into the workplace. The shift from working alone to working in teams requires employees to cooperate with others, share information, confront differences, and sublimate personal interests for the greater good of the team. Like Chris Bangle, the manager highlighted in our chapter opener, managers can build effective teams by understanding their behavior.

● ● ● ● **Learning Review**

- Compare groups and teams.
- Explain why teams have become so popular in organizations.

- Describe the four most common types of teams.
- List the characteristics of effective teams.

Managers **Respond** to a **Manager's** Dilemma

····Joseph Small

Vice President Strategic Sales, Pearson Scott Foresman, Dorchester, Massachusetts

Some suggestions that Chris might use to maintain his team effectiveness when new members join the team include: Establish an annual or quarterly "Get to Know You Day" where different departments are brought together to meet and exchange overviews on their various activities, projects, needs, talents, and so forth; establish a BMW Advisory Council comprised of junior and senior designers brought together to address common goals and issues; establish a new hires program that officially socializes new designers to the desired BMW culture; develop a mentors program that matches designers from different areas with new hires; have some type of recognition program for innovation, trend setting, or being a good team builder; and set up an off-site team building retreat where team members can get to know each other.

Learning Summary

After reading and studying this chapter, you should be able to:

- Define the different types of groups.

- Describe the five stages of group development.

- Explain the major components that determine group performance and satisfaction.

- Discuss how roles, norms, conformity, status systems, group size, and group cohesiveness influence group behavior.

- Explain how group norms can both help and hurt an organization.

- Define groupthink and social loafing.

- Describe the relationships between group cohesiveness and productivity.

- Discuss how conflict management influences group behavior.

- Describe the advantages and disadvantages of group decision making.

- Compare groups and teams.

- Explain why teams have become so popular in organizations.

- Describe the four most common types of teams.

- List the characteristics of effective teams.

Thinking About Management Issues

1. Think of a group to which you belong (or have belonged). Trace its development through the stages of group development shown in Exhibit 15–2. How closely did its development parallel the group development model? How might the group development model have been used to improve the group's effectiveness?

2. How do you think scientific management theorists would react to the increased reliance on teams in organizations? How would the behavioral science theorists react?

3. How do you explain the popularity of work teams in the United States when its culture places such high value on individualism and individual effort?

4. Why might a manager want to stimulate conflict in a group or team? How could conflict be stimulated?

5. Do you think that everyone should be expected to be a team player, given the trends we're seeing in the use of teams? Discuss.

Working Together: Team-Based Exercise

What happens when a group is presented with a task that must be completed within a certain time frame? Does the group exhibit characteristics of the stages of group development? Can the group behavior model (Exhibit 15–3) explain what happens in the group? Your instructor will divide the class into groups and give you instructions about what to do next.

Ethical Dilemma Exercise

What ethical issues arise when representatives of competing companies work in task groups that make decisions affecting the entire industry? Industrywide standards for product performance are often developed by committees of representatives drawn from a number of companies. The idea is to minimize noncompatibility problems (for products such as computers) or meet government-imposed requirements (such as water conservation rules) through one set of widely adopted specifications. However, members of these committees and managers of the companies represented may face role conflict because their decisions have consequences for individual companies as well as the industry as a whole.

For example, chip-maker Rambus once encouraged a standards committee to approve a particular computer memory standard—without disclosing that it owned patents on that design. Management later stated that the company had revealed all the information it was required to disclose. As another example, consider the pressures felt by members of a standards committee grappling with decisions about disk-drive connections within computers. Representatives of companies that made disk drives built to older standards realized that any radical change would hurt their companies. Meanwhile, other companies' representatives were pushing to immediately adopt an aggressive new standard. In the end, the committee compromised by making a group decision to adopt changes in stages rather than switching to a new standard right away.[43]

Imagine that you're a Rambus engineer serving on a multicompany committee to develop more efficient memory standards that will put less strain on power connections. Everyone agrees on the goal, which is to extend the life of batteries that power laptop computers. If the committee adopts an extremely stringent standard, your company will have to invest considerable time and money in altering chips so they meet the standard. On the other hand, your largest competitor's representative has not expressed any concerns about the standard's requirements or schedule. Look back at Exhibit 15–3 as you consider this

ethical challenge and decide which of the following options to choose—and why.

Option A: Vote to adopt the change but insist on flexibility in the standards deadline, to give Rambus more time to make the necessary changes.

Option B: Vote against any radical change because it will hurt Rambus's profitability and could give other companies a short-term competitive edge.

Option C: Before you vote, initiate a group discussion of how the new standards might alter the competitive environment within the industry.

Case Application

BASF

BASF is the world's largest chemical company. In its more than 100 major worldwide manufacturing facilities, the company uses something unusual: Something it calls its "Verbund" philosophy—an idea developed by BASF's founder back in 1865. What is Verbund? It's the idea of linking each production facility with others so that the products and leftover material from one plant serve as raw materials in the next. For instance, all the facilities at the company's manufacturing complex in Ludwigshafen, Germany, are connected to each other by at least one product or process stage; the goal of Verbund—improved global efficiency. This pursuit of global efficiency is important to companies that want to be competitive. For instance, at another of BASF's Verbund plants found in Freeport, Texas, teams have played an important role in making the facility more productive and competitive.

Managers at BASF Freeport—like manufacturing managers everywhere—were searching for ways to make the facility's production process more efficient and effective. Rather than tackling the problems themselves from the top down, they created employee project teams; a move that made sense given the fact that these employ-

ees worked day in and day out with the production processes. The project teams' assignments were to find specific ways to improve operational efficiency and to implement those ideas.

One of the major responsibilities of the teams was applying statistically designed experiments to gather information and test various production factors. For instance, one team tested 13 production factors using 32 different experiments—a process that took two months to complete. How successful were the project teams? Almost $742,000 was trimmed from annual costs and another $750,000 one-time capital purchase was avoided—a total savings of almost $1.5 million.

What factors contributed to the employee teams' successes? One factor that the teams said was critical was management commitment and faith in the effort. Many process improvement efforts fail because they lack such support. These teams had their managers' support. Another factor was the training the teams received. In this situation, employee teams were trained to use statistical tools so they could apply them correctly and effectively. Training was provided by outside experts who also assisted the teams throughout the process. Finally, the managers believed that their decision to use a bottom-up approach was valuable because it involved everyone in the search for possible solutions.

DISCUSSION QUESTIONS

1. What type of team are these BASF teams? Explain your choice.

2. Using Exhibit 15–3, explain the teams' successes.

3. It's your chance to be creative! Think of a team-building exercise that would help a team achieve one of the characteristics of an effective team. (See Exhibit 15.10.) Describe the characteristic you chose and then describe the exercise you'd use to help a team develop or enhance that characteristic.

4. What could other managers learn about managing teams from BASF's successes?

BASF team, Freeport, Texas, plant. (left to right: Tracie Coldiron, Jessier Delmundo, Tony Harris)

Sources: Information from company's Web site *(www.basf.com)* and Hoover's Online *(www.hoovers.com)*, June 19, 2003; and D. Drickhamer, "BASF Breaks Through with Statistics," *Industry Week,* June 2002, pp. 81–82.

● ● ● Learning Outline

Follow this Learning Outline as you read and study this chapter.

What Is Motivation?
- Define motivation.
- Explain motivation as a need-satisfying process.

Early Theories of Motivation
- Describe the five levels in Maslow's hierarchy and how Maslow's hierarchy can be used in motivation efforts.
- Discuss how Theory X and Theory Y managers approach motivation.
- Describe Herzberg's motivation-hygiene theory.
- Explain Herzberg's views of satisfaction and dissatisfaction.

Contemporary Theories of Motivation
- Describe the three needs McClelland proposed as being present in work settings.
- Explain how goal-setting and reinforcement theories explain employee motivation.
- Describe the job characteristics model as a way to design motivating jobs.
- Discuss the motivation implications of equity theory.
- Contrast distributive justice and procedural justice.
- Explain the three key linkages in expectancy theory and their role in motivation.

Current Issues in Motivation
- Describe the cross-cultural challenges of motivation.
- Discuss the challenges managers face in motivating unique groups of workers.
- Describe open-book management and employee recognition, pay-for-performance, and stock option programs.

Motivating Employees

Angel Lorenzo (pictured) is a shift supervisor at Grupo M, the largest private employer in the Dominican Republic.[1] The company's employees make clothes for popular fashion companies such as Abercrombie & Fitch, Hugo Boss, and Tommy Hilfiger. Angel began working at Grupo M as a sewing machine operator and was promoted to a job as a quality control inspector.

Now, he manages 14 teams of machine operators, making sure that jobs are done on time and correctly. He says that his job is to let his employees know that they are the most important people in the factory. If they don't do their jobs well, the business loses customers.

Grupo M defies the stereotypical image of garment manufacturers found in many Third World countries. The company is not a sweatshop and does not employ child labor. Its factories are clean, brightly lit, and nice places to work. The company's founder, Fernando Capellan, envisioned an exemplary business that would be an innovator in the garment industry. Grupo M has earned a reputation as a remarkably progressive company. It has developed a private social security system for employees that covers programs related to health, education, sports, culture, and child care. Also, all employees can participate in a stock ownership plan. In 1999, it earned a corporate conscience award from the U.S.-based Council on Economic Priorities for "empowering employees." Capellan says, "We have proven that you don't have to run a factory like a sweatshop in order to be profitable and to grow. In fact, we believe that we have been able to innovate, to expand, and to do what we have done because of the way that we treat our people. Everything that we give to our workers gets returned to us in terms of efficiency, quality, loyalty, and innovation. It's just smart business."

Although the company's philosophy is admirable, managers such as Angel are challenged to keep employees motivated. Even though Grupo M factories are clean and modern, employees still do fast-paced work. Put yourself in Angel's position. How could you motivate your workers?

What would *you* do **?**

Motivating and rewarding employees is one of the most important, and one of the most challenging, activities that managers perform. Successful managers, like Angel Lorenzo, understand that what motivates them personally may have little or no effect on others. Just because *you're* motivated by being part of a cohesive work team, don't assume everyone is. Or the fact that you're motivated by challenging work doesn't mean everyone is. Effective managers who want their employees to put forth maximum effort recognize that they need to know how and why employees are motivated and to tailor their motivational practices to satisfy the needs and wants of those employees.

WHAT IS MOTIVATION?

As the newly appointed president of Ajilon, a staffing firm based in New Jersey, Neil Lebovits had some serious employee problems.[2] Turnover was high and morale was low. The severity of the situation hit home when he hosted an after-work party and only 5 out of 50 employees bothered to show up. Lebovits wanted to improve employees' spirits, but like many managers, he didn't have the resources to give out big raises. So he tried some different things that wouldn't cost a lot of money. He started in-house training programs on various topics in which employees had expressed interest. He initiated monthly conference calls with every employee to discuss management decisions point by point. He set up an e-mail address where employees could propose ideas and responded to every single one. And he gave every employee three "YDOs" or Your Days Off a year with no questions asked. After implementing these changes, staff morale skyrocketed. Company employees even sent notes to Lebovits enthusing about how they felt reenergized.

Neil Lebovits is a good motivator. Like Neil, all managers need to be able to motivate their employees and that requires understanding what motivation is. To understand what motivation is, let's begin by pointing out what it is not. Why? Because many people incorrectly view motivation as a personal trait—that is, a trait that some people have and others don't. Although, in reality, a manager might describe a certain employee as unmotivated, our knowledge of motivation tells us that we can't label people that way. What we *do* know is that motivation is the result of the interaction between a person and a situation. Certainly, individuals differ in motivational drive, but overall, motivation varies from situation to situation. For instance, your level of motivation probably differs among the various courses you take each term. As we analyze the concept of motivation, keep in mind that the level of motivation varies both between individuals and within individuals at different times. (▮▮▮□ Go to the Web and check out S.A.L. #13—What Motivates Me?)

Motivation refers to the processes that account for an individual's willingness to exert high levels of effort to reach organizational goals, conditioned by the effort's ability to satisfy some individual need. Although, in general, motivation refers to effort exerted toward any goal, we're referring to organizational goals because our focus is on work-related behavior. Three key elements can be seen in this definition: effort, organizational goals, and needs.

The *effort* element is a measure of intensity or drive. A motivated person tries hard. But high levels of effort are unlikely to lead to favorable job performance unless the effort is channeled in a direction that benefits the organization.[3] Therefore, we must consider the quality of the effort as well as its intensity. Effort that is directed toward, and consistent with, *organizational goals* is the kind of effort that we should be seeking. Finally, we'll treat motivation as a *need-satisfying* process, as shown in Exhibit 16–1. (▮▮▮□ Go to the Web and check out You're the Manager: Diversity in Action #1.)

A **need** is an internal state that makes certain outcomes appear attractive. An unsatisfied need creates tension, which an individual reduces by exerting effort. Because we're interested in work behavior, this tension-reduction effort must be directed toward organizational goals. Therefore, inherent in our definition of motivation is the require-

●●● **motivation**
The processes that account for an individual's willingness to exert high levels of effort to reach organizational goals, conditioned by the effort's ability to satisfy some individual need.

▪ **Self-Assessment Library**
Whenever you see this orange square, go to the R.O.L.L.S. Web site *(www.prenhall.com/robbins)* to the Self-Assessment Library (S.A.L.) and complete the suggested self-assessment exercise. These exercises will help you discover things about yourself, your attitudes, and your personal strengths and weaknesses.

●●● **need**
An internal state that makes certain outcomes appear attractive.

Exhibit 16–1

The Motivation Process

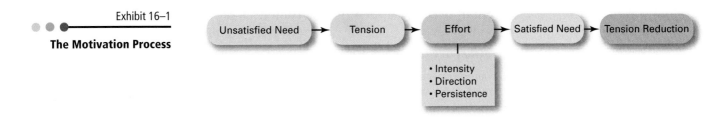

ment that the individual's needs be compatible with the organization's goals. When the two don't match, individuals may exert high levels of effort that run counter to the interests of the organization. Incidentally, this isn't all that unusual. Some employees regularly spend a lot of time talking with friends at work to satisfy their social need. There's a high level of effort, but little being done in the way of work.

Motivating high levels of employee performance is an important organizational problem, and managers keep looking for a solution. For instance, a recent Gallup poll found that a majority of U.S. employees—55 percent to be exact—have no enthusiasm for their work.[4] It's no wonder then that both academic researchers and practicing managers want to understand and explain employee motivation. In this chapter, we're going to first look at some early motivation theories and then at the contemporary theories. We'll finish by looking at some current motivation issues and some practical suggestions managers can use in motivating employees.

Learning Review

- Define motivation.
- Explain motivation as a need-satisfying process.

EARLY THEORIES OF MOTIVATION

We begin by looking at three early theories of motivation that, although questionable in terms of validity, are probably the most widely known approaches to employee motivation. These three theories are *Maslow's hierarchy of needs*, *McGregor's Theories X and Y*, and *Herzberg's motivation-hygiene theory*. Although more valid explanations of motivation have been developed, you should know these early theories because (1) they represent the foundation from which contemporary motivation theories were developed, and (2) practicing managers continue to regularly use these theories and their terminology in explaining employee motivation.

Maslow's Hierarchy of Needs Theory

When Lincoln Hershberger's team was honored for best exemplifying one of his company's (video game company Electronic Arts or EA) important values during a fiscal quarter of 2002, it wasn't the trophy or shaking the CEO's hand that most excited him. It was getting one of the six desirable parking spaces in the front row of the first floor of the indoor parking lot for three months. And he isn't alone in coveting those parking spots—many employees at EA are motivated to win the privilege of parking in those spots.[5] EA's managers obviously understand employee needs and their impact on motivation. The first motivation theory we're going to look at addresses employee needs. (■□■■■ Go to the Web and check out Q & A 16.1.)

The best-known theory of motivation is probably Abraham Maslow's **hierarchy of needs theory**.[6] Maslow was a psychologist who proposed that within every person is a hierarchy of five needs:

1. **Physiological needs**: Food, drink, shelter, sexual satisfaction, and other physical requirements.

• • • hierarchy of needs theory
Maslow's theory that there is a hierarchy of five human needs: physiological, safety, social, esteem, and self-actualization.

• • • physiological needs
A person's need for food, drink, shelter, sexual satisfaction, and other physical needs.

2. **Safety needs**: Security and protection from physical and emotional harm, as well as assurance that physical needs will continue to be met.

3. **Social needs**: Affection, belongingness, acceptance, and friendship.

4. **Esteem needs**: Internal esteem factors such as self-respect, autonomy, and achievement and external esteem factors such as status, recognition, and attention.

5. **Self-actualization needs**: Growth, achieving one's potential, and self-fulfillment; the drive to become what one is capable of becoming.

In terms of motivation, Maslow argued that each level in the needs hierarchy must be substantially satisfied before the next is activated and that once a need is substantially satisfied it no longer motivates behavior. In other words, as each need is substantially satisfied, the next need becomes dominant. In terms of Exhibit 16–2, the individual moves up the needs hierarchy. From the standpoint of motivation, Maslow's theory proposed that, although no need is ever fully satisfied, a substantially satisfied need will no longer motivate an individual. Therefore, according to Maslow, if you want to motivate someone, you need to understand what level that person is on in the hierarchy and focus on satisfying needs at or above that level. Managers who accepted Maslow's hierarchy attempted to change their organizations and management practices so that employees' needs could be satisfied.

In addition, Maslow separated the five needs into higher and lower levels. Physiological and safety needs were considered *lower-order needs*; social, esteem, and self-actualization needs were considered *higher-order needs*. The difference was that higher-order needs are satisfied internally while lower-order needs are predominantly satisfied externally.

Maslow's needs theory received wide recognition, especially among practicing managers during the 1960s and 1970s, probably because of its intuitive logic and ease of understanding. However, Maslow provided no empirical support for his theory, and several studies that sought to validate it could not.[7]

McGregor's Theory X and Theory Y

Douglas McGregor is best known for proposing two sets of assumptions about human nature: Theory X and Theory Y.[8] Very simply, **Theory X** presents an essentially negative view of people. It assumes that workers have little ambition, dislike work, want to avoid responsibility, and need to be closely controlled to work effectively. **Theory Y** offers a positive view. It assumes that workers can exercise self-direction, accept and actually seek out responsibility, and consider work to be a natural activity. McGregor believed that Theory Y assumptions best captured the true nature of workers and should guide management practice. (▓▓□▌ Go to the Web and check out S.A.L. #15—What's My View on the Nature of People?)

Exhibit 16–2

**Maslow's Hierarchy of
Needs**

What did McGregor's analysis imply about motivation? The answer is best expressed in the framework presented by Maslow. Theory X assumed that lower-order needs dominated individuals, and Theory Y assumed that higher-order needs dominated. McGregor himself held to the belief that the assumptions of Theory Y were more valid than those of Theory X. Therefore, he proposed that participation in decision making, responsible and challenging jobs, and good group relations would maximize employee motivation. (███ ▬▬ Go to the Web and check out Q & A 16.2.)

Unfortunately, there's no evidence to confirm that either set of assumptions is valid or that accepting Theory Y assumptions and altering your actions accordingly will make employees more motivated. For instance, Jen-Hsun Huang, founder of Nvidia Corporation, an innovative and successful microchip manufacturer, has been known to use both reassuring hugs and tough love in motivating employees. But he has little tolerance for screw-ups. "In one legendary meeting, he's said to have ripped into a project team for its tendency to repeat mistakes. 'Do you suck?' he asked the stunned employees. 'Because if you suck, just get up and say you suck.'" His message, delivered in classic Theory X style, was that if you need help, ask for it.[9]

Herzberg's Motivation-Hygiene Theory

●●● **motivation-hygiene theory**
The motivation theory that intrinsic factors are related to job satisfaction and motivation, whereas extrinsic factors are associated with job dissatisfaction.

Frederick Herzberg's **motivation-hygiene theory** proposes that intrinsic factors are related to job satisfaction and motivation, whereas extrinsic factors are associated with job dissatisfaction.[10] Believing that individuals' attitudes toward work determined success or failure, Herzberg investigated the question, "What do people want from their jobs?" He asked people for detailed descriptions of situations in which they felt exceptionally good or bad about their jobs. These findings are shown in Exhibit 16–3.

Herzberg concluded from his analysis that the replies people gave when they felt good about their jobs were significantly different from the replies they gave when they felt bad. Certain characteristics were consistently related to job satisfaction (factors on the left side of the exhibit), and others to job dissatisfaction (factors on the right side). Those factors associated with job satisfaction were intrinsic and included things such as achievement, recognition, and responsibility. When people felt good about their work, they tended to attribute these characteristics to themselves. On the other hand, when they were dissatisfied, they tended to cite extrinsic factors such as company policy and administration, supervision, interpersonal relationships, and working conditions.

In addition, Herzberg believed that the data suggested that the opposite of satisfaction was not dissatisfaction, as traditionally had been believed. Removing dissatisfying characteristics from a job would not necessarily make that job more satisfying (or

Exhibit 16–3

●●● **Herzberg's Motivation-Hygiene Theory**

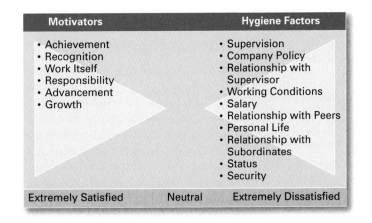

Motivators	Hygiene Factors
• Achievement • Recognition • Work Itself • Responsibility • Advancement • Growth	• Supervision • Company Policy • Relationship with Supervisor • Working Conditions • Salary • Relationship with Peers • Personal Life • Relationship with Subordinates • Status • Security
Extremely Satisfied	Neutral Extremely Dissatisfied

Exhibit 16–4

**Contrasting Views of
Satisfaction-
Dissatisfaction**

Exhibit 16–4

**Contrasting Views of
Satisfaction-
Dissatisfaction**

motivating). As shown in Exhibit 16–4, Herzberg proposed that his findings indicated the existence of a dual continuum: The opposite of "satisfaction" is "no satisfaction," and the opposite of "dissatisfaction" is "no dissatisfaction."

According to Herzberg, the factors that led to job satisfaction were separate and distinct from those that led to job dissatisfaction. Therefore, managers who sought to eliminate factors that created job dissatisfaction could bring about workplace harmony but not necessarily motivation. The extrinsic factors that create job dissatisfaction were called **hygiene factors**. When these factors are adequate, people won't be dissatisfied, but they won't be satisfied (or motivated) either. To motivate people on their jobs, Herzberg suggested emphasizing **motivators**, the intrinsic factors that increase job satisfaction.

Herzberg's theory enjoyed wide popularity from the mid-1960s to the early 1980s, but criticisms arose concerning his procedures and methodology. Although today we say the theory was too simplistic, it has had a strong influence on how we currently design jobs.

● ● ● **hygiene factors**
Factors that eliminate job dissatisfaction, but don't motivate.

● ● ● **motivators**
Factors that increase job satisfaction and motivation.

● ● ● Learning Review

- Describe the five levels in Maslow's hierarchy and how Maslow's hierarchy can be used in motivation efforts.
- Discuss how Theory X and Theory Y managers approach motivation.

- Describe Herzberg's motivation-hygiene theory.
- Explain Herzberg's views of satisfaction and dissatisfaction.

CONTEMPORARY THEORIES OF MOTIVATION

● ● ● **three-needs theory**
The motivation theory that says three acquired (not innate) needs—achievement, power, and affiliation—are major motives in work.

The theories and approaches we're going to look at in this section represent current explanations of employee motivation. Although these may not be as well known as some of the theories we just discussed, they do have reasonable degrees of valid research support.[11] What are these contemporary motivation approaches? We're going to look at six: three-needs theory, goal-setting theory, reinforcement theory, designing motivating jobs, equity theory, and expectancy theory.

Three-Needs Theory

● ● ● **need for achievement (nAch)**
The drive to excel, to achieve in relation to a set of standards, and to strive to succeed.

● ● ● **need for power (nPow)**
The need to make others behave in a way that they would not have behaved otherwise.

● ● ● **need for affiliation (nAff)**
The desire for friendly and close interpersonal relationships.

David McClelland and others have proposed the **three-needs theory**, which says there are three acquired (not innate) needs that are major motives in work.[12] These three needs include the **need for achievement (nAch)**, which is the drive to excel, to achieve in relation to a set of standards, and to strive to succeed; the **need for power (nPow)**, which is the need to make others behave in a way that they would not have behaved otherwise; and the **need for affiliation (nAff)**, which is the desire for friendly and close interpersonal relationships. Of these three needs, the need for achievement has been researched the most. What does this research show?

People with a high need for achievement are striving for personal achievement rather than for the trappings and rewards of success. They have a desire to do something better or more efficiently than it's been done before.[13] They prefer jobs that offer personal responsibility for finding solutions to problems, in which they can receive rapid and unambiguous feedback on their performance in order to tell whether they're improving, and in which they can set moderately challenging goals. High achievers aren't gamblers; they don't like succeeding by chance. They're motivated by and prefer the challenge of working at a problem and accepting the personal responsibility for success or failure. (▣◻▥▥ Go to the Web and check out Q & A 16.3.) An important point is that high achievers avoid what they perceive to be very easy or very difficult tasks. Also, a high need to achieve doesn't necessarily lead to being a good manager, especially in large organizations. A high nAch pharmaceutical salesperson at Merck doesn't necessarily make a good sales manager, and good managers in large organizations such as SBC Communications, Wal-Mart, or Microsoft don't necessarily have a high need to achieve. The reason high achievers don't necessarily make good managers is probably because they focus on their *own* accomplishments while good managers emphasize helping *others* accomplish their goals.[14] However, we do know that employees can be trained to stimulate their achievement need.[15] (▣◻▥▥ Go to the Web and check out Q & A 16.4.)

The other two needs in this theory haven't been researched as extensively as the need for achievement. However, we do know that the needs for affiliation and power are closely related to managerial success.[16] The best managers tend to be high in the need for power and low in the need for affiliation.

How do you determine your levels of these needs? All three are typically measured using a projective test (known as the Thematic Apperception Test or TAT), in which respondents react to a set of pictures. Each picture is briefly shown to a subject who then writes a story based on the picture. (See Exhibit 16–5 for some examples of these pictures.) Trained interpreters then determine an individual's levels of nAch, nPow, and nAff from the stories written.

Exhibit 16–5 **Examples of Pictures Used for Assessing Levels of nAch, nAff, and nPow**

nAch: Indicated by someone in the story wanting to perform or do something better.
nAff: Indicated by someone in the story wanting to be with someone else and enjoy mutual friendship.
nPow: Indicated by someone in the story desiring to have an impact or make an impression on others in the story.

Goal-Setting Theory

Before a big assignment or major class project presentation, has a teacher ever encouraged you to "Just do your best"? What does that vague statement, "do your best" mean? Would your performance on a class project have been higher had that teacher said you needed to score a 93 percent to keep your A in the class? Would you have done better in high school English had your parents said, "You should strive for 85 percent or higher on all your work in English class" rather than telling you to do your best? Research on goal-setting theory addresses these issues, and the findings, as you'll see, are impressive in terms of the effect that goal specificity, challenge, and feedback have on performance.[17]

There is substantial support for the proposition that specific goals increase performance and that difficult goals, when accepted, result in higher performance than do easy goals. This proposition is known as **goal-setting theory**.

Intention to work toward a goal is a major source of job motivation. Studies on goal setting have demonstrated that specific and challenging goals are superior motivating forces.[18] Specific hard goals produce a higher level of output than does the generalized goal of "do your best." The specificity of the goal itself acts as an internal stimulus. For instance, when a sales representative commits to making eight sales calls daily, this intention gives him a specific goal to try to attain. We can say that, all things being equal, the sales representative with a specific goal will outperform someone else operating with no goals or the generalized goal of "do your best."

Is it a contradiction that goal-setting theory says that motivation is maximized by difficult goals, whereas achievement motivation is stimulated by moderately challenging goals? No, and our explanation is twofold.[19] First, goal-setting theory deals with people in general, while the conclusions on achievement motivation are based on people who have a high nAch. Given that no more than 10 to 20 percent of North Americans are naturally high achievers and that that proportion is likely lower in underdeveloped countries, difficult goals are still recommended for the majority of employees. Second, the conclusions of goal-setting theory apply to those who accept and are committed to the goals. Difficult goals will lead to higher performance *only* if they are accepted.

Will employees try harder if they have the opportunity to participate in the setting of goals? (▬▢▬ Go to the Web and check out Q & A 16.5.) Although we can't say that having employees participate in the goal-setting process is *always* desirable, participation is probably preferable to assigning goals when you expect resistance to accepting difficult challenges.[20] In some cases, participatively set goals elicited superior performance; in other cases, individuals performed best when their managers assigned goals.

Finally, people will do better when they get feedback on how well they're progressing toward their goals because feedback helps identify discrepancies between what they have done and what they want to do; that is, feedback acts to guide behavior. But all feedback isn't equally effective. Self-generated feedback—where the employee is able to monitor his or her own progress—has been shown to be a more powerful motivator than externally generated feedback.[21]

Are there any contingencies in goal-setting theory, or we can just assume that difficult and specific goals always lead to higher performance? In addition to feedback, three other factors have been found to influence the goals–performance relationship. These are goal commitment, adequate self-efficacy, and national culture. Goal-setting theory presupposes that an individual is committed to the goal—that is, is determined not to lower or abandon the goal. Commitment is most likely to

• • • goal-setting theory
The proposition that specific goals increase performance and that difficult goals, when accepted, result in higher performance than do easy goals.

Mark Cuban, who made a fortune selling his company Broadcast.com to Yahoo!, and who owns the NBA Dallas Mavericks, appears to believe in the idea that people are motivated by having difficult goals. When all his ticket reps made their sales quotas, he rewarded them by saying, "Good. That's what you're supposed to do."

Exhibit 16–6

Goal-Setting Theory

• • • self-efficacy
An individual's belief that he or she is capable of performing a task.

occur when goals are made public, when the individual has an internal locus of control, and when the goals are self-set rather than assigned.[22] **Self-efficacy** refers to an individual's belief that he or she is capable of performing a task.[23] The higher your self-efficacy, the more confidence you have in your ability to succeed in a task. So, in difficult situations, we find that people with low self-efficacy are likely to reduce their effort or give up altogether, whereas those with high self-efficacy will try harder to master the challenge.[24] In addition, individuals with high self-efficacy seem to respond to negative feedback with increased effort and motivation, whereas those with low self-efficacy are likely to reduce their effort when given negative feedback.[25] Finally, goal-setting theory is culture-bound. It's well adapted to countries like the United States and Canada because its main ideas align reasonably well with North American cultures. It assumes that subordinates will be reasonably independent (not too high a score on power distance), that managers and employees will seek challenging goals (low in uncertainty avoidance), and that performance is considered important by both managers and subordinates (high in quantity of life). So don't expect goal setting to necessarily lead to higher employee performance in countries such as Portugal or Chile, where the cultural characteristics are different.

Exhibit 16–6 summarizes the relationships among goals, motivation, and performance. Our overall conclusion from goal-setting theory is that intentions—as articulated in terms of hard and specific goals—are a powerful motivating force. Under the proper conditions, they can lead to higher performance. (▮▮▯▯▯ Go to the Web and check out Q & A 16.6.) However, there is no evidence that such goals are associated with increased job satisfaction.[26]

Reinforcement Theory

• • • reinforcement theory
The theory that behavior is a function of its consequences.

• • • reinforcers
Any consequence immediately following a response that increases the probability that the behavior will be repeated.

In contrast to goal-setting theory, **reinforcement theory** says that behavior is a function of its consequences. While goal-setting theory proposes that an individual's purpose directs his or her behavior, reinforcement theory argues that behavior is externally caused. What controls behavior are **reinforcers**, consequences that, when given immediately following a behavior, increase the probability that the behavior will be repeated.

The key to reinforcement theory is that it ignores factors such as goals, expectations, and needs. Instead, it focuses solely on what happens to a person when he or she takes some action. This idea helps explain why publishers such as Pearson Education may include incentive clauses in authors' contracts. If every time an author submits a completed chapter, the company sends an advance check against future royalties, the person is motivated to keep submitting chapters.

In Chapter 14 we showed how managers use reinforcers to shape behavior. But the concept of reinforcement is also widely believed to explain motivation. According to

B.F. Skinner, reinforcement theory can be explained as follows: People will most likely engage in desired behaviors if they are rewarded for doing so; these rewards are most effective if they immediately follow a desired behavior, and behavior that isn't rewarded, or is punished, is less likely to be repeated.[27]

Following reinforcement theory, managers can influence employees' behavior by reinforcing actions they deem desirable. However, because the emphasis is on positive reinforcement, not punishment, managers should ignore, not punish, unfavorable behavior. Even though punishment eliminates undesired behavior faster than nonreinforcement does, its effect is often only temporary and may later have unpleasant side effects including dysfunctional behavior such as workplace conflicts, absenteeism, and turnover. Research has shown that reinforcement is an important influence on work behavior, but isn't the only explanation for differences in employee motivation.[28]

Designing Motivating Jobs

• • • **job design**
The way tasks are combined to form complete jobs.

Because managers are primarily interested in how to motivate individuals on the job, we need to look at ways to design motivating jobs. If you look closely at what an organization is and how it works, you'll find that it's composed of thousands of tasks. These tasks, in turn, are aggregated into jobs. We use the term **job design** to refer to the way tasks are combined to form complete jobs. The jobs that people perform in an organization should not evolve by chance. Managers should design jobs deliberately and thoughtfully to reflect the demands of the changing environment, the organization's technology, and its employees' skills, abilities, and preferences.[30] When jobs are designed with those things in mind, employees are motivated to work hard. What are some ways that managers can design motivating jobs?[31]

• • • **job scope**
The number of different tasks required in a job and the frequency with which those tasks are repeated.

• • • **job enlargement**
The horizontal expansion of a job by increasing job scope.

Job Enlargement As we saw earlier, in Chapters 2 and 10, job design historically has concentrated on making jobs smaller and more specialized. Yet, when jobs are narrow in focus and highly specialized, motivating employees is a real challenge. One of the earliest efforts at overcoming the drawbacks of job specialization involved the horizontal expansion of a job through increasing **job scope**—the number of different tasks required in a job and the frequency with which these tasks are repeated. For instance, a dental hygienist's job could be enlarged so that in addition to dental cleaning, he or she is pulling patients' files, re-filing them when finished, and cleaning and storing instruments. This type of job design option is called **job enlargement**.

MANAGING YOUR CAREER

What Do You Want from Your Job?

Since you're reading this textbook, you're likely enrolled in a class that's helping you earn credit toward a college degree. You're probably also taking the courses you need to earn a college degree because you hope to get a good job (or a better job, if you're already working) upon graduating. With all this effort you're putting forth, have you ever stopped to think about what you really want from your job?[29] A high salary? Work that challenges you? Autonomy and flexibility? Perhaps the results of a recent survey of workers will give you some insights into what you might want from your job. The top reasons that employees stay with their jobs are as follows:

Reason	Percentage of Respondents
Like co-workers	71 percent
Pleasant work environment	68 percent
Easy commute	68 percent
Challenging work	65 percent
Flexible work hours	54 percent

Do any of these characteristics describe what you want from your job? Whether they do or don't, you should spend some time reflecting on what you want your job to provide you. Then, when it's time to do that all-important job search, look for situations that will offer what you're looking for.

Efforts at job enlargement that focused solely on increasing the number of tasks have had less-than-exciting results. As one employee who experienced such a job redesign said, "Before I had one lousy job. Now, thanks to job enlargement, I have three lousy jobs!" However, one study that looked at how *knowledge* enlargement activities (expanding the scope of knowledge used in a job) affected workers found benefits such as more satisfaction, enhanced customer service, and fewer errors.[32] Even so, most job enlargement efforts provided few challenges and little meaning to workers' activities, although they addressed the lack of variety in overspecialized jobs.

It is easy to identify the task that Manuela Frank and Erika Seres perform at Audi's headquarters in Ingolstadt, Germany. Their job is to ensure that new cars have no unappealing odors. "You can't smell more than six specimens at a time," says Seres (right), "because after that, you are not discerning. Like wine tasters, we have rules."

Job Enrichment Another approach to designing motivating jobs is the vertical expansion of a job by adding planning and evaluating responsibilities—**job enrichment**. Job enrichment increases **job depth**, which is the degree of control employees have over their work. In other words, employees are empowered to assume some of the tasks typically done by their managers. Thus, the tasks in an enriched job should allow workers to do a complete activity with increased freedom, independence, and responsibility. These tasks should also provide feedback so that individuals can assess and correct their own performance. For instance, in an enriched job, our dental hygienist, in addition to dental cleaning, could schedule appointments and follow up with clients. Although job enrichment can improve the quality of work, employee motivation, and satisfaction, the research evidence on the use of job enrichment programs has been inconclusive.[33]

Job Characteristics Model Even though many organizations have implemented job enlargement and job enrichment programs and experienced mixed results, neither of these job design approaches provided a conceptual framework for analyzing jobs or for guiding managers in designing motivating jobs. The **job characteristics model (JCM)** offers such framework.[34] It identifies five primary job characteristics, their interrelationships, and their impact on employee productivity, motivation, and satisfaction. (■□■■ Go to the Web and check out Q & A 16.7.)

According to the JCM, any job can be described in terms of five core dimensions, defined as follows:

1. **Skill variety**: The degree to which a job requires a variety of activities so that an employee can use a number of different skills and talents.

2. **Task identity**: The degree to which a job requires completion of a whole and identifiable piece of work.

3. **Task significance**: The degree to which a job has a substantial impact on the lives or work of other people.

4. **Autonomy**: The degree to which a job provides substantial freedom, independence, and discretion to the individual in scheduling the work and determining the procedures to be used in carrying it out.

5. **Feedback**: The degree to which carrying out work activities required by a job results in the individual's obtaining direct and clear information about the effectiveness of his or her performance.

Exhibit 16–7 on page 402 presents the model. Notice how the first three dimensions—skill variety, task identity, and task significance—combine to create meaningful work. What we mean is that if these three characteristics exist in a job, we can predict that the person will view his or her job as being important, valuable, and

---

●●● job enrichment
The vertical expansion of a job by adding planning and evaluating responsibilities.

●●● job depth
The degree of control employees have over their work.

●●● job characteristics model (JCM)
A framework for analyzing and designing jobs that identifies five primary job characteristics, their interrelationships, and their impact on outcomes.

●●● skill variety
The degree to which a job requires a variety of activities so that an employee can use a number of different skills and talents.

●●● task identity
The degree to which a job requires completion of a whole and identifiable piece of work.

●●● task significance
The degree to which a job has a substantial impact on the lives or work of other people.

Exhibit 16–7

Job Characteristics Model

Source: J.R. Hackman and J.L. Suttle (eds.). *Improving Life at Work* (Glenview, IL: Scott, Foresman, 1977). With permission of the authors.

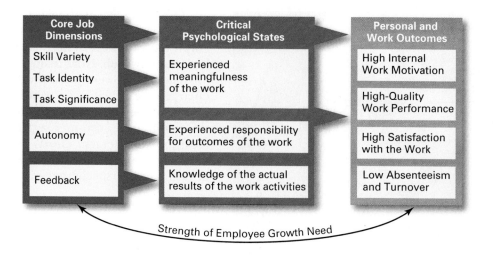

autonomy
The degree to which a job provides substantial freedom, independence, and discretion to the individual in scheduling work and determining the procedures to be used in carrying it out.

feedback
The degree to which carrying out work activities required by a job results in the individual's obtaining direct and clear information about his or her performance effectiveness.

worthwhile. Notice, too, that jobs that possess autonomy give the job incumbent a feeling of personal responsibility for the results, and that if a job provides feedback, the employee will know how effectively he or she is performing.

From a motivational standpoint, the JCM suggests that internal rewards are obtained when an employee *learns* (knowledge of results through feedback) that he or she *personally* (experienced responsibility through autonomy of work) has performed well on a task that he or she *cares about* (experienced meaningfulness through skill variety, task identity, and/or task significance).[35] The more these three conditions characterize a job, the greater the employee's motivation, performance, and satisfaction and the lower his or her absenteeism and likelihood of resigning. As the model shows, the links between the job dimensions and the outcomes are moderated by the strength of the individual's growth need (the person's desire for self-esteem and self-actualization). This means that individuals with a high growth need are more likely to experience the critical psychological states and respond positively when their jobs include the core dimensions than are low-growth-need individuals. This may explain the mixed results with job enrichment: Individuals with low growth need don't tend to achieve high performance or satisfaction by having their jobs enriched. (▪▪▪□▪▪ Go to the Web and check out PRISM #1—Designing Motivating Jobs.)

The JCM provides specific guidance to managers for job design. (See Exhibit 16–8.) The following suggestions, which are based on the JCM, specify the types of changes in jobs that are most likely to lead to improvement in each of the five core job dimensions. You'll notice that two of these suggestions incorporate the earlier job design concepts we discussed (job enlargement and job enrichment), although the other suggestions also involve more than vertically and horizontally expanding jobs.

1. *Combine tasks.* Managers should put fragmented tasks back together to form a new, larger module of work (job enlargement) to increase skill variety and task identity.

Exhibit 16–8

Guidelines for Job Redesign

Source: J.R. Hackman and J.L. Suttle (eds.). *Improving Life at Work* (Glenview, IL: Scott, Foresman, 1977). With permission of the authors.

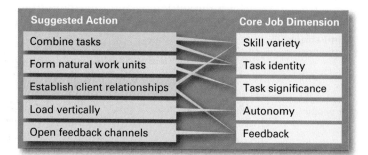

2. *Create natural work units.* Managers should design tasks that form an identifiable and meaningful whole to increase employee "ownership" of the work and encourage employees to view their work as meaningful and important rather than as irrelevant and boring.

3. *Establish client relationships.* The client is the external or internal user of the product or service that the employee works on. Whenever possible, managers should establish direct relationships between workers and their clients to increase skill variety, autonomy, and feedback. For instance, at San Francisco's Parc Fifty Five Hotel, a property of Park Lane Hotels International, guests nominate their favorite staff for awards including Sony televisions and free nights at the hotel.[36]

4. *Expand jobs vertically.* Vertical expansion (job enrichment) gives employees responsibilities and controls that were formerly reserved for managers. It partially closes the gap between the "doing" and the "controlling" aspects of the job and increases employee autonomy.

5. *Open feedback channels.* Feedback lets employees know how well they're performing their jobs and whether their performance is improving, deteriorating, or remaining constant. Ideally, employees should receive performance feedback directly as they do their jobs rather than from managers on an occasional basis. For example, frequent fliers at Continental Airlines bestow Pride in Performance certificates to employees who have been helpful. Employees can then redeem the coupons for valuable merchandise.[37]

Equity Theory

Do you ever wonder what kind of grade the person sitting next to you in class makes on a test or on a major class assignment? Most of us do! Being human, we tend to compare ourselves with others. (▭▭◻ Go to the Web and check out S.A.L. #16—How Sensitive Am I to Equity Differences?) If someone offered you $50,000 a year on your first job after graduating from college, you'd probably jump at the offer and report to work enthusiastic, ready to tackle whatever needed to be done, and certainly satisfied with your pay. How would you react, though, if you found out a month into the job that a co-worker—another recent graduate, your age, with comparable grades from a comparable school, and with comparable work experience—was getting $55,000 a year? You'd probably be upset! Even though in absolute terms, $50,000 is a lot of money for a new graduate to make (and you know it!), that suddenly isn't the issue. You see the issue now as relative rewards and what you believe is *fair*—what is *equitable*. The term *equity* is related to the concept of fairness and equal treatment compared with others who behave in similar ways. There's considerable evidence that employees compare their job inputs and outcomes relative to others' and that inequities influence the degree of effort that employees exert.[38] (▭▭▭ Go to the Web and check out Q & A 16.8.)

● ● ● equity theory
The theory that an employee compares his or her job's input–outcomes ratio with that of relevant others and then corrects any inequity.

Equity theory, developed by J. Stacey Adams, proposes that employees perceive what they get from a job situation (outcomes) in relation to what they put into it (inputs) and then compare their inputs–outcomes ratio with the inputs–outcomes ratios of relevant others (Exhibit 16–9 on page 404). If an employee perceives her ratio to be equal to those of relevant others, a state of equity exists. In other words, she perceives that her situation is fair—that justice prevails. However, if the ratio is unequal, inequity exists and she views herself as underrewarded or overrewarded. When inequities occur, employees attempt to do something about it. What will employees do when they perceive an inequity?

Equity theory proposes that employees might (1) distort either their own or others' inputs or outcomes, (2) behave in some way to induce others to change their inputs or outcomes, (3) behave in some way to change their own inputs or outcomes,

Exhibit 16–9

Equity Theory

Perceived Ratio Comparison[a]	Employee's Assessment
$\dfrac{\text{Outcomes A}}{\text{Inputs A}} < \dfrac{\text{Outcomes B}}{\text{Inputs B}}$	Inequity (underrewarded)
$\dfrac{\text{Outcomes A}}{\text{Inputs A}} = \dfrac{\text{Outcomes B}}{\text{Inputs B}}$	Equity
$\dfrac{\text{Outcomes A}}{\text{Inputs A}} > \dfrac{\text{Outcomes B}}{\text{Inputs B}}$	Inequity (overrewarded)

[a] Person A is the employee, and person B is a relevant other or referent.

(4) choose a different comparison person, or (5) quit their job. These types of employee reactions have generally proved to be correct.[39] A review of the research consistently confirms the equity thesis: Employee motivation is influenced significantly by relative rewards as well as by absolute rewards. Whenever employees perceive inequity, they'll act to correct the situation.[40] The result might be lower or higher productivity, improved or reduced quality of output, increased absenteeism, or voluntary resignation. (▮▮▮▮▮▯ Go to the Web and check out You're the Manager: Diversity in Action #2.)

The other aspect we need to examine in equity theory is who these "others" are against whom people compare themselves. The **referent**—the other persons, systems, or selves individuals compare themselves against in order to assess equity—is an important variable in equity theory.[41] Three referent categories have been defined: other, system, and self. The "other" category includes other individuals with similar jobs in the same organization but also includes friends, neighbors, or professional associates. On the basis of what they hear at work or read about in newspapers or trade journals, employees compare their pay with that of others. The "system" category includes organizational pay policies and procedures and the administration of the system. Whatever precedents have been established by the organization regarding pay allocation are major elements of this category. The "self" category refers to inputs—outcomes ratios that are unique to the individual. It reflects past personal experiences and contacts and is influenced by criteria such as past jobs or family commitments. The choice of a particular set of referents is related to the information available about the referents as well as to their perceived relevance.

Historically, equity theory focused on **distributive justice**, which is the perceived fairness of the amount and allocation of rewards among individuals. Recent equity research has focused on looking at issues of **procedural justice**, which is the perceived fairness of the process used to determine the distribution of rewards. This research shows that distributive justice has a greater influence on employee satisfaction than procedural justice, while procedural justice tends to affect an employee's organizational commitment, trust in his or her boss, and intention to quit.[42] What are the implications of these findings for managers? They should consider openly sharing information on how allocation decisions are made, follow consistent and unbiased procedures, and engage in similar practices to increase the perception of procedural justice. By increasing the perception of procedural justice, employees are likely to view their bosses and the organization as positive even if they're dissatisfied with pay, promotions, and other personal outcomes. (▮▮▮▮▮▯ Check out You're the Manager: Putting Ethics into Action on p. 452.)

In conclusion, equity theory shows that, for most employees, motivation is influenced significantly by relative rewards as well as by absolute rewards, but some key issues are still unclear.[43] For instance, how do employees define inputs and outcomes?

●●● **referents**
The persons, systems, or selves against which individuals compare themselves to assess equity.

●●● **distributive justice**
Perceived fairness of the amount and allocation of rewards among individuals.

●●● **procedural justice**
Perceived fairness of the process used to determine the distribution of rewards.

How do they combine and weigh their inputs and outcomes to arrive at totals? When and how do the factors change over time? And how do people choose referents? Despite these problems, equity theory does have an impressive amount of research support and offers us some important insights into employee motivation.

Expectancy Theory

● ● ● **expectancy theory**
The theory that an individual tends to act in a certain way based on the expectation that the act will be followed by a given outcome and on the attractiveness of that outcome to the individual.

The most comprehensive and widely accepted explanation of employee motivation to date is Victor Vroom's **expectancy theory**.[44] Although the theory has its critics,[45] most research evidence supports it.[46]

Expectancy theory states that an individual tends to act in a certain way based on the expectation that the act will be followed by a given outcome and on the attractiveness of that outcome to the individual. It includes three variables or relationships (see Exhibit 16–10):

1. *Expectancy or effort-performance linkage* is the probability perceived by the individual that exerting a given amount of effort will lead to a certain level of performance.

2. *Instrumentality or performance-reward linkage* is the degree to which the individual believes that performing at a particular level is instrumental in attaining the desired outcome.

3. *Valence or attractiveness of reward* is the importance that the individual places on the potential outcome or reward that can be achieved on the job. Valence considers both the goals and needs of the individual. (▬▬□▬ Go to the Web and check out S.A.L. #14—What Rewards Do I Value Most?)

This explanation of motivation might sound complex, but it really isn't. It can be summed up in the questions: How hard do I have to work to achieve a certain level of performance, and can I actually achieve that level? What reward will performing at that level of performance get me? How attractive is the reward to me, and does it help me achieve my goals? Whether you are motivated to put forth effort (that is, to work) at any given time depends on your particular goals and your perception of whether a certain level of performance is necessary to attain those goals.

The key to expectancy theory is understanding an individual's goal and the linkage between effort and performance, between performance and rewards, and finally, between rewards and individual goal satisfaction. It emphasizes payoffs, or rewards. As a result, we have to believe that the rewards an organization is offering align with what the individual wants. Expectancy theory recognizes that there is no universal principle for explaining what motivates individuals and thus stresses that managers understand why employees view certain outcomes as attractive or unattractive. After all, we want to reward individuals with those things they value positively. Also, expectancy theory emphasizes expected behaviors. Do employees know what is expected of them and how they'll be evaluated? Finally, the theory is concerned with perceptions. Reality is irrelevant. An individual's own perceptions of performance, reward, and goal outcomes, not the outcomes themselves, will determine his or her motivation (level of effort). (▬□▬▬ Go to the Web and check out Q & A 16.9.)

Exhibit 16–10

● ● ●━━━━━━

Simplified Expectancy Model

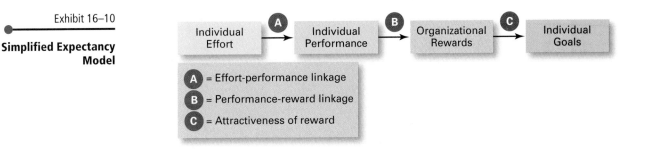

Integrating Contemporary Theories of Motivation

We've presented six contemporary motivation theories. You might be tempted to view them independently, but doing so would be a mistake. Many of the ideas underlying the theories are complementary, and you'll better understand how to motivate people if you see how the theories fit together.[47] Exhibit 16–11 presents a model that integrates much of what we know about motivation. Its basic foundation is the expectancy model shown in Exhibit 16–10. Let's work through this model, starting on the left.

The individual effort box has an arrow leading into it. This arrow flows from the individual's goals. Consistent with goal-setting theory, this goals-effort link is meant to illustrate that goals direct behavior. Expectancy theory predicts that an employee will exert a high level of effort if he or she perceives that there is a strong relationship between effort and performance, performance and rewards, and rewards and satisfaction of personal goals. Each of these relationships is, in turn, influenced by certain factors. You can see from the model that the level of individual performance is determined not only by the level of individual effort but also by the individual's ability to perform and by whether the organization has a fair and objective performance evaluation system. The performance–reward relationship will be strong if the individual perceives that it is performance (rather than seniority, personal favorites, or some other criterion) that is rewarded. The final link in expectancy theory is the rewards–goal relationship. Needs theories come into play at this point. Motivation would be high to the degree that the rewards an individual received for his or her high performance satisfied the dominant needs consistent with his or her individual goals.

Exhibit 16–11

**Integrating Contemporary
Theories of Motivation**

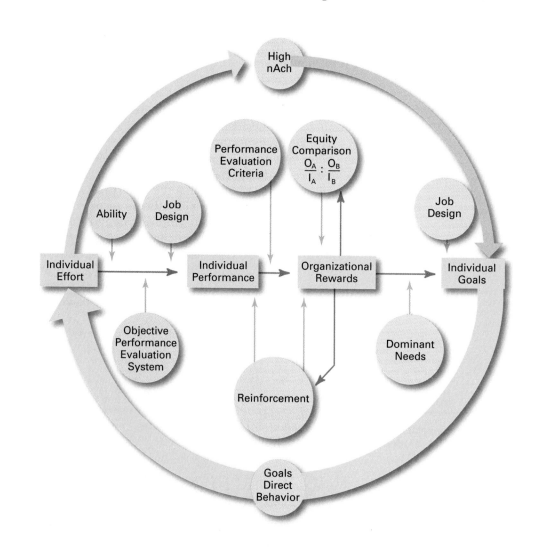

A closer look at the model also shows that it considers the achievement-need, reinforcement, equity, and JCM theories. The high achiever isn't motivated by the organization's assessment of his or her performance or organizational rewards; hence the jump from effort to individual goals for those with a high nAch. Remember that high achievers are internally driven as long as the jobs they're doing provide them with personal responsibility, feedback, and moderate risks. They're not concerned with the effort-performance, performance-reward, or rewards-goals linkages.

Reinforcement theory is seen in the model by recognizing that the organization's rewards reinforce the individual's performance. If managers have designed a reward system that is seen by employees as "paying off" for good performance, the rewards will reinforce and encourage continued good performance. Rewards also play a key part in equity theory. Individuals will compare the rewards (outcomes) they have received from the inputs or efforts they made with the inputs–outcomes ratio of relevant others. If inequities exist, the effort expended may be influenced.

Finally, we can see the JCM in this integrative model. Task characteristics (job design) influence job motivation at two places. First, jobs that are designed around the five job dimensions are likely to lead to higher actual job performance because the individual's motivation will be stimulated by the job itself—that is, they will increase the linkage between effort and performance. Second, jobs that are designed around the five job dimensions also increase an employee's control over key elements in his or her work. Therefore, jobs that offer autonomy, feedback, and similar task characteristics help to satisfy the individual goals of employees who desire greater control over their work.

Learning Review

- Describe the three needs McClelland proposed were present in work settings.
- Explain how goal-setting and reinforcement theories explain employee motivation.
- Describe the job characteristics model as a way to design motivating jobs.

- Discuss the motivation implications of equity theory.
- Contrast distributive justice and procedural justice.
- Explain the three key linkages in expectancy theory and their role in motivation.

CURRENT ISSUES IN MOTIVATION

So far, we've covered a lot of the theoretical bases of employee motivation. Understanding and predicting employee motivation continues to be one of the most popular areas in management research. However, even current studies of employee motivation are influenced by several significant workplace issues—issues such as cross-cultural challenges, motivating unique groups of workers, and designing appropriate rewards programs. Let's take a closer look at each of these issues.

Cross-Cultural Challenges

In today's global business environment, managers can't automatically assume that motivational programs that work in one location are going to work in others. Most current motivation theories were developed in the United States by Americans and about Americans.[48] Maybe the most blatant pro-American characteristic in these theories is the strong emphasis on individualism and quantity-of-life cultural characteristics. For instance, both goal-setting and expectancy theories emphasize goal accomplishment as well as rational and individual thought. Let's look at several theories to see if there's any cross-cultural transferability.

Maslow's needs hierarchy argues that people start at the physiological level and then move progressively up the hierarchy in order. This hierarchy, if it has any

In countries like The Netherlands, where the needs identified in Maslow's famous hierarchy are ranked differently than they are in the United States, quality of life is probably more important to workers like these. Thus they may be more motivated by group work because it meets their social needs to gather and cooperate.

application at all, aligns with American culture. In countries like Japan, Greece, and Mexico, where uncertainty avoidance characteristics are strong, security needs would be on the top of the needs hierarchy. Countries that score high on quality-of-life characteristics—Denmark, Sweden, Norway, the Netherlands, and Finland—would have social needs on top.[49] We would predict, for instance, that group work will motivate employees more when the country's culture scores high on the quality of life criterion.

Another motivation concept that clearly has an American bias is the achievement need. The view that a high achievement need acts as an internal motivator presupposes two cultural characteristics—a willingness to accept a moderate degree of risk (which excludes countries with strong uncertainty avoidance characteristics) and a concern with performance (which applies almost singularly to countries with strong quantity-of-life characteristics). This combination is found in Anglo-American countries like the United States, Canada, and Great Britain.[50] On the other hand, these characteristics are relatively absent in countries such as Chile and Portugal.

Equity theory has a relatively strong following in the United States. That's not surprising given that U.S.-style reward systems are based on the assumption that workers are highly sensitive to equity in reward allocations. And in the United States, equity is meant to closely tie pay to performance. However, recent evidence suggests that in collectivistic cultures, especially in the former socialist countries of Central and Eastern Europe, employees expect rewards to reflect their individual needs as well as their performance.[51] Moreover, consistent with a legacy of communism and centrally planned economies, employees exhibited a greater "entitlement" attitude—that is, they expected outcomes to be greater than their inputs.[52] These findings suggest that U.S.-style pay practices may need modification, especially in Russia and former communist countries, in order to be perceived as fair by employees.

Despite these cross-cultural differences in motivation, don't assume there are no cross-cultural consistencies. For instance, the desire for interesting work seems important to almost all workers, regardless of their national culture. In a study of seven countries, employees in Belgium, Britain, Israel, and the United States ranked "interesting work" number one among 11 work goals. And this factor was ranked either second or third in Japan, the Netherlands, and Germany.[53] Similarly, in a study comparing job-preference outcomes among graduate students in the United States, Canada, Australia, and Singapore, growth, achievement, and responsibility were rated the top three and had identical rankings.[54] Both of these studies suggest some universality to the importance of intrinsic factors identified by Herzberg in his two-factor theory.

Motivating Unique Groups of Workers

Motivating employees has never been easy! Employees come into organizations with very different needs, personalities, skills, abilities, interests, and aptitudes. They have different expectations of their employers and different views of what they think their employer has a right to expect of them. And they vary widely in what they want from their jobs. For instance, some employees get more satisfaction out of their personal interests and pursuits and only want a weekly paycheck—nothing more. They're not interested in making their work more challenging or interesting or in "winning" performance contests. Others derive a great deal of satisfaction in their jobs and are motivated to exert high levels of effort. Given these differences, how can managers do an effective job of motivating the unique groups of employees found in today's workforce? One thing managers must do is to understand the motivational requirements of these groups including diverse employees, professionals, contingent workers, and low-skilled, minimum-wage employees.

Motivating a Diverse Workforce To maximize motivation among today's workforce, managers need to think in terms of *flexibility*. For instance, studies tell us that men place more importance on having autonomy in their jobs than do women. In contrast, the opportunity to learn, convenient and flexible work hours, and good interpersonal relations are more important to women.[55] Managers need to recognize that what motivates a single mother with two dependent children who's working full time to support her family may be very different from the needs of a single part-time employee or an older employee who is working only to supplement his or her retirement income. A diverse array of rewards is needed to motivate employees with such diverse needs. Many of the work–life balance programs (see Chapter 12) that organizations have implemented are a response to the varied needs of a diverse workforce. In addition, many organizations have developed flexible working schedules that recognize different needs. For instance, a **compressed workweek** is a workweek where employees work longer hours per day but fewer days per week. The most common form is four 10-hour days (a 4-40 program). However, organizations could design whatever schedules they wanted to fit employees' needs. Another alternative is **flexible work hours** (also popularly known as **flextime**), which is a scheduling system in which employees are required to work a specific number of hours a week but are free to vary those hours within certain limits. In a flextime schedule, there are certain common core hours when all employees are required to be on the job, but starting, ending, and lunch-hour times are flexible. Flextime is one of the most desired benefits among employees.[56] And employers have responded, as a survey shows that 74 percent of U.S. employers were offering flexible work options in 2002.[57]

Another job scheduling option that can be effective in motivating a diverse workforce is **job sharing**—the practice of having two or more people split a full-time job. This type of job schedule might be attractive to individuals who want to work but do not want the demands and hassles of a full-time position.

Another alternative made possible by information technology is **telecommuting**. Here, employees work at home and are linked to the workplace by computer and modem. Since many jobs can be done at home, this approach might be close to the ideal job for some people as there is no commuting, the hours are flexible, there's freedom to dress as you please, and there are few or no interruptions from colleagues. However, keep in mind that not all employees embrace the idea of telecommuting. Some workers relish the informal interactions at work that satisfy their social needs as well as provide a source of new ideas. (▮▮▮▯▯ Go to the Web and check out Q & A 16.10.)

Lawrence A. Read, founder of the Oil Changers chain of automotive shops, began hiring workers with drug-related criminal records almost from the beginning of his business, after realizing that some of his best-performing managers had prison records. His success with these employees speaks to Read's understanding that people want different things from their work experience. In this case, he says, they want to put the past behind them. "These are men and women with strong personalities and a burning desire to prove something. They don't want to go back to jail. It makes good, solid business sense."

∘•• **compressed workweek**
A workweek where employees work longer hours per day but fewer days per week.

∘•• **flexible work hours (flextime)**
A scheduling system in which employees are required to work a certain number of hours per week, but are free, within limits, to vary the hours of work.

∘•• **job sharing**
The practice of having two or more people split a full-time job.

∘•• **telecommuting**
A job approach where employees work at home and are linked to the workplace by computer and modem.

MANAGING WORKFORCE DIVERSITY

Developing Employee Potential: The Bottom Line of Diversity

One of a manager's more important goals is helping employees develop their potential.[58] This is particularly important in managing talented diverse employees who can bring new perspectives and ideas to the business but who may find that the workplace environment is not as conducive as it could be to accepting and embracing these different perspectives. For instance, managers at Lucent Technologies' distinguished Bell Labs have worked hard to develop an environment in which the ideas of diverse employees are encouraged openly. What can managers do to ensure that their diverse employees have the opportunity to develop their potential? One thing they can do is to make sure that there are diverse role models in leadership positions so that others see that there are opportunities to grow and advance. Giving motivated, talented, hard-working, and enthusiastic diverse employees opportunities to excel in decision-making roles can be a powerful motivator to other diverse employees to work hard to develop their own potential. A mentoring program in which diverse employees are given the opportunity to work closely with organizational leaders can be a powerful tool. At Silicon Graphics, for instance, new employees become part of a mentoring group called "Horizons." Through this mentoring group, diverse employees have the opportunity to observe and learn from key company decision makers.

Another way for managers to develop the potential of their diverse employees is to offer developmental work assignments that provide a variety of learning experiences in different organizational areas. DaimlerChrysler, for example, started its Corporate University, which offers a comprehensive series of learning opportunities for all employees. The company's director of diversity and work/family says that employees who are provided the opportunity to learn new processes and new technology are more likely to excel at their work and to stay with the company. These types of developmental opportunities are particularly important for diverse employees because it empowers them with tools that are critical to professional development.

Motivating Professionals In contrast to a generation ago, the typical employee today is more likely to be a highly trained professional with a college degree than a blue-collar factory worker. What special concerns should managers be aware of when trying to motivate a team of engineers at Intel, software designers at SAS Institute, or a group of consultants at Accenture?

Professionals are typically different from nonprofessionals.[59] They have a strong and long-term commitment to their field of expertise. Their loyalty is more often to their profession than to their employer. To keep current in their field, they need to regularly update their knowledge, and because of their commitment to their profession they rarely define their workweek as 8:00 A.M. to 5:00 P.M. five days a week.

What motivates professionals? Money and promotions typically are low on their priority list. Why? They tend to be well paid and enjoy what they do. In contrast, job challenge tends to be ranked high. They like to tackle problems and find solutions. Their chief reward in their job is the work itself. Professionals also value support. They want others to think that what they are working on is important. That may be true for all employees, but professionals tend to be focused on their work as their central life interest, whereas nonprofessionals typically have other interests outside of work that can compensate for needs not met on the job.

Motivating Contingent Workers The elimination of jobs through downsizing and other organizational restructurings has increased the number of openings for part-time, contract, and other forms of temporary workers. Contingent workers don't have the security or stability that permanent employees have, and they don't identify with the organization or display the commitment that other employees do. Temporary workers also typically get few or no benefits such as health care or pensions.[60]

There's no simple solution for motivating contingent employees. For that small set of individuals who prefer the freedom of their temporary status—for instance, some students, working mothers, retirees—the lack of stability may not be an issue. In addition, temporariness might be preferred by highly compensated physicians, engineers, accountants, or financial planners who don't want the demands of a full-time job. But these are the exceptions. For the most part, temporary employees are not temporary by choice.

What will motivate involuntarily temporary employees? An obvious answer is the opportunity to become a permanent employee. In cases in which permanent employees are selected from a pool of temps, the temps will often work hard in hopes of becoming permanent. A less obvious answer is the opportunity for training. The ability of a temporary employee to find a new job is largely dependent on his or her skills. If the employee sees that the job he or she is doing can help develop marketable skills, then motivation is increased. From an equity standpoint, you should also consider the repercussions of mixing permanent and temporary workers when pay differentials are significant. When temps work alongside permanent employees who earn more, and get benefits, too, for doing the same job, the performance of temps is likely to suffer. Separating such employees or perhaps converting all employees to a variable-pay or skill-based pay plan might help minimize the problems.

Motivating Low-Skilled, Minimum-Wage Employees Suppose that in your first managerial position after graduating, you're responsible for managing a work group composed of low-skilled, minimum-wage employees. Offering more pay to these employees for high levels of performance is out of the question: Your company just can't afford it. In addition, these employees have limited education and skills. What are your motivational options at this point? (▮▮▮▮▮ Go to the Web and check out Q & A 16.11.)

One trap we often fall into is thinking that people are motivated only by money. Although money is important as a motivator, it's not the only reward that people seek and that managers can use. In motivating minimum-wage employees, managers might look at employee recognition programs, which we'll describe later in this chapter. And many managers also recognize the power of praise. However, you need to be sure that these "pats on the back" are sincere and given for the right reasons.

Designing Appropriate Rewards Programs

Blue Cross of California, one of the nation's largest health insurers, pays bonuses to doctors serving its health maintenance organization members based on patient satisfaction and other quality standards. FedEx's drivers are motivated by a pay system that rewards them for timeliness and how much they deliver.[61] Employee rewards programs play a powerful role in motivating appropriate employee behavior. In this section, we want to look at how managers can design appropriate rewards programs by using open-book management, employee recognition programs, pay-for-performance programs, and stock option programs.

Open-Book Management Many organizations of various sizes involve their employees in workplace decisions by opening up the financial statements (the "books"). They share that information so that employees will be motivated to make better decisions about their work and better able to understand the implications of what they do, how they do it, and the ultimate impact on the bottom line. (▮▮▮▮▮ Go to the Web and check out Q & A 16.12.) This approach is called **open-book management**.[62] Who's using it? More than 3,500 organizations, including Springfield Remanufacturing Corporation, Allstate Insurance, Amoco Canada, Rhino Foods, and Sprint's Government Systems division.[63]

• • • **open-book management**
A motivational approach in which an organization's financial statements (the "books") are shared with all employees.

The goal of open-book management is to get employees to think like an owner by seeing the impact their decisions and actions have on financial results. Since most employees don't have the knowledge or background to understand the financials, they have to be taught how to read and understand the organization's financial statements. Once employees have this knowledge, managers need to share the numbers regularly with them. By sharing this information, employees begin to see the link between their efforts, level of performance, and operational results.

Open-book management is growing as a means of motivating employees by sharing with them important information about the way their company works. Sabre, the travel company that operates the Travelocity Web site and a well-known airline reservation system, recently used a board game called Zodiak as a simulation to teach employees about income statements, balance sheets, and return on equity. After playing the game for a fictional fiscal year, during which they refinanced debt, brought out a new product, watched competitors hire away their employees, were sued, and boosted earnings, the four members of each "owner" team came away with a better understanding of Sabre's business and some rudimentary financial skills.

●●● **employee recognition programs**
Personal attention and expressing interest, approval, and appreciation for a job well done.

Employee Recognition Programs **Employee recognition programs** consist of personal attention and expressing interest, approval, and appreciation for a job well done.[64] They can take numerous forms. For instance, Nichols Foods Ltd., a British bottler of soft drinks and syrups, has a comprehensive recognition program.[65] Monthly awards are presented to people who have been nominated by peers for extraordinary effort on the job. And monthly award winners are eligible for further recognition at an off-site meeting for all employees. In contrast, most managers use a far more informal approach. For example, when Julia Stewart, currently the president and CEO of IHOP International, was president of Applebee's Restaurants, she would frequently leave sealed notes on the chairs of employees after everyone had gone home.[66] These notes explained how critical Stewart thought the person's work was or how much she appreciated the completion of a project. Stewart also relied heavily on voice-mail messages left after office hours to tell employees how appreciative she was for a job well done.

A recent survey of organizations found that 84 percent had some type of program to recognize worker achievements.[67] And do employees think these programs are important? You bet! In a survey conducted a few years ago, a wide range of employees was asked what they considered the most powerful workplace motivator. Their response? Recognition, recognition, and more recognition![68]

Consistent with reinforcement theory, rewarding a behavior with recognition immediately following that behavior is likely to encourage its repetition. And recognition can take many forms. You can personally congratulate an employee in private for a good job. You can send a handwritten note or e-mail message acknowledging something positive that the employee has done. For employees with a strong need for social acceptance, you can publicly recognize accomplishments. To enhance group cohesiveness and motivation, you can celebrate team successes. For instance, you can throw a pizza party to celebrate a team's accomplishments.

●●● **pay-for-performance programs**
Variable compensation plans that pay employees on the basis of some performance measure.

Pay-for-Performance **Pay-for-performance programs** are variable compensation plans that pay employees on the basis of some performance measure.[69] Piece-rate pay plans, wage-incentive plans, profit-sharing, and lump-sum bonuses are examples. What differentiates these forms of pay from more traditional compensation plans is that instead of paying a person for time on the job, pay is adjusted to reflect some performance measure. (▮▯▮▮ Go to the Web and check out Q & A 16.13.) These performance measures might include such things as individual productivity, team or work-group productivity, departmental productivity, or the overall organization's profit performance.

Employee recognition plays an important role in motivating the workers at Nichols Foods Ltd, in Merseyside, England, where the average wage is only a little above the norm. The main hallway in the production department is hung with "bragging boards" on which the accomplishments of employee teams are noted. Monthly awards are presented to workers recognized for their efforts by their peers, and plant-floor supervisors make presentations about their results at every annual meeting. "To deliver really great customer service," says operations manager Martin Lee, "you need really great, motivated people."

Pay-for-performance is probably most compatible with expectancy theory. Specifically, individuals should perceive a strong relationship between their performance and the rewards they receive for motivation to be maximized. If rewards are allocated only on nonperformance factors—such as seniority, job title, or across-the-board pay raises—then employees are likely to reduce their efforts. From a motivation perspective, making some or all of an employee's pay conditional on some performance measure focuses his or her attention and effort toward that measure, then reinforces the continuation of the effort with a reward. If the employee, team, or organization's performance declines, so does the reward. Thus, there's an incentive to keep efforts and motivation strong. (◼◻▨ Go to the Web and check out Q & A 16.14.)

Pay-for-performance programs are popular. In 2002, 80 percent of large U.S. companies had some form of variable pay plan.[70] These types of pay plans have also been tried in other countries such as Canada and Japan. About 35 percent of Canadian companies and 22 percent of Japanese companies have company-wide pay-for-performance plans.[71] However, one Japanese company, Fujitsu, dropped its performance-based program after eight years because it proved to be "flawed and a poor fit with Japanese culture."[72] Management found that some employees set goals as low as possible for fear of falling short. Others set extremely short-term goals. As a result, Fujitsu executives felt that ambitious projects that could produce hit products were being avoided.

Do pay-for-performance programs work? For the most part, studies seem to indicate that they do. For instance, one study found that companies that used pay-for-performance programs performed better financially than those that did not.[73] Another study showed that pay-for-performance programs with outcome-based incentives had a positive impact on sales, customer satisfaction, and profits.[74] If the organization uses work teams, managers should consider group-based performance incentives that will reinforce team effort and commitment. But whether these programs are individual based or team based, managers do need to ensure that they're specific about the relationship between an individual's pay and his or her expected level of appropriate performance. Employees must clearly understand exactly how performance—theirs and the organization's—translates into dollars on their paychecks.[75] The sometimes tenuous link between pay

---

THINKING CRITICALLY ABOUT ETHICS

You've been hired as a phone sales representative at World Adventures Travel in Dover, Delaware. In this job, you help customers who have called to book vacations by finding what works best for them and their needs as you check airline flights, times, and fares, and also help with rental car and hotel reservations.

Most car rental firms and hotels run contests for the sales representative who books the most cars or most hotel rooms. The contest winners receive very attractive rewards! For instance, if you book just 50 clients for one rental car company, your name is put in a drawing for $1,000. If you book 100 clients, the drawing is for $2,500. And if you book 200 clients, you receive an all-expenses-paid, one-week Caribbean vacation. So the incentives are attractive enough to encourage you to "steer" customers toward one of those companies even though it might not be the best or cheapest for them. Your manager doesn't discourage participation in these programs.

Do you see anything wrong with this situation? Explain. What ethical issues do you see for (a) the employee, (b) the organization, and (c) the customer? How could an organization design performance incentive programs that encourage high levels of performance without compromising ethics?

and performance is nowhere more evident than in the final type of rewards program we're going to look at—employee stock options.

Stock Option Programs During 2002, Henry R. Silverman, Cendant Corporation's CEO, got $11 million in salary and bonus, a 41 percent increase, while Cendant's total stock return fell 47 percent. And Gary Crittenden, CFO of American Express Company, earned more than $4.5 million, including almost $3 million in stock options, even though the company's stock price declined 31 percent.[76] Such executive bonus and stock option programs have come under fire because they seem to fly in the face of the belief that executive pay aligns with the organization's performance. What are stock option programs, what are they designed to do, and what do managers need to know about designing appropriate ones?

Stock options are financial instruments that give employees the right to purchase shares of stock at a set price. The original idea behind stock options was to turn employees into owners and give them strong incentives to work hard to make the company successful.[77] If the company was successful, the value of the stock went up, making the stock options valuable. In other words, there was a link between performance and reward. The popularity of stock options as a motivation and compensation tool skyrocketed during the dot-com boom in the late 1990s. Because many dot-coms couldn't afford to pay employees the going market-rate salaries, stock options were offered as performance incentives. However, the shakeout among dot-com stocks in 2000 and 2001 illustrated one of the inherent risks of offering stock options. As long as the market was rising, employees were willing to give up a large salary in exchange for stock options. However, when stock prices tanked, many individuals who joined and stayed with a dot-com for the opportunity to get rich through stock options found those stock options had become worthless. And the declining stock market became a powerful demotivator.

Despite the risk of potential lost value and the widespread abuse of stock options, managers might want to consider them as part of their overall motivational program. An appropriately designed stock option program can be a powerful motivational tool for the entire workforce.[78] Exhibit 16–12 lists several recommendations for designing stock options programs.

• • • **stock options**
Financial instruments that give employees the right to purchase shares of stock at a set price.

Exhibit 16–12

Recommendations for Designing Stock Options

Design Question	Choices	Recommendations
Who receives them?	• Broad-based or restricted	• Match company growth prospects, management style, and organizational culture.
How many?	• Large or small percentage of employee income	• Match company growth prospects.
	• Many or few options in previous grants	• Know that large, previous grants may increase recipient risk aversion.
What terms?	• Vesting*	• Should match business cycle.
	• Maturity	• Terms shorter than 10 years can create stronger pay-for-performance relationships.
How often?	• Fixed or variable schedule	• Predictable grants may reduce incentive alignment prospects.
		• Internal equity issues may result from schedules that result in a variety of exercise prices.
What price?	• Fair-market value • Premium • Discounted • Indexed	• Employees must view stock option exercise prices as feasible and believe that chosen benchmarks are appropriate.
What ownership?	• Holding requirements after exercise	• Requiring recipients to hold some of their shares after exercise encourages better incentive alignment.
	• Ownership guidelines	• Clear general ownership guidelines can also increase incentive alignment.

* Vesting refers to the time that must pass before a person can exercise the option.

Source: P. Brandes, R. Dharwadkar, and G.V. Lemesis, "Effective Employee Stock Option Design: Reconciling Stakeholder, Strategic, and Motivational Factors," *Academy of Management Executive*, February 2003, p. 84.

• • • •**Learning Review**

- Describe the cross-cultural challenges of motivation.
- Discuss the challenges managers face in motivating unique groups of workers.

- Describe open-book management and employee recognition, pay-for-performance, and stock option programs.

FROM THEORY TO PRACTICE: SUGGESTIONS FOR MOTIVATING EMPLOYEES

We've covered a lot of information about motivation. If you're a manager concerned with motivating your employees, what specific recommendations can you draw from the theories and issues presented in this chapter? Although there's no simple, all-encompassing set of guidelines, the following suggestions draw on what we know about motivating employees.

- *Recognize Individual Differences.* Almost every contemporary motivation theory recognizes that employees aren't identical. They have different needs, attitudes, personalities, and other important individual variables.

- *Match People to Jobs.* There's a great deal of evidence showing the motivational benefits of carefully matching people to jobs. For example, high achievers should have jobs that allow them to participate in setting moderately challenging goals and that involve autonomy and feedback. Also, keep in mind that not everybody is motivated by jobs that are high in autonomy, variety, and responsibility.

- *Use Goals.* The literature on goal-setting theory suggests that managers should ensure that employees have hard, specific goals and feedback on how well they're doing in achieving those goals. Should the goals be assigned by the manager or should employees participate in setting them? The answer depends on your perception of goal acceptance and the organization's culture. If you expect resistance to goals, participation should increase acceptance. If participation is inconsistent with the culture, use assigned goals.

- *Ensure That Goals Are Perceived as Attainable.* Regardless of whether goals are actually attainable, employees who see goals as unattainable will reduce their effort because they'll be thinking "why bother?" Managers must be sure, therefore, that employees feel confident that increased efforts *can* lead to achieving performance goals.

- *Individualize Rewards.* Because employees have different needs, what acts as a reinforcer for one may not for another. Managers should use their knowledge of employee differences to individualize the rewards they control, such as pay, promotions, recognition, desirable work assignments, autonomy, and participation.

- *Link Rewards to Performance.* Managers need to make rewards contingent on performance. Rewarding factors other than performance will only reinforce those other factors. Important rewards such as pay increases and promotions should be given for the attainment of specific

Andrew Robinson, who runs an information security company in Portland, ME, has taken the idea of matching people to jobs a step further than most by matching future workers to potential jobs. Robinson runs a free after-school program to teach students like these about "ethical hacking," or the fine art of protecting computer systems by hacking them first. Of the 50 students in the program, Robinson says, "They have all the skills that they need to cause trouble, and some of them may have even started doing some of those things just for fun." His point to the students is, "Here's how you can do this legally, within a moral and ethical framework, and make a good amount of money doing it."

Becoming a Manager

- ◆ *Set goals for yourself using the suggestions from goal-setting theory.*
- ◆ *Start paying attention to times when you're highly motivated and times when you're not as motivated. What accounts for the difference?*
- ◆ *When working on teams for class projects or on committees in student organizations, try different approaches to motivating others.*
- ◆ *If you're working, assess your job using the Job Characteristics Model. How might you redesign your job to make it more motivating?*
- ◆ *As you visit various businesses, note what, if any, employee recognition programs these businesses use.*
- ◆ *Talk to practicing managers about their approaches to employee motivation. What have they found works?*
- ◆ ▪▪▪▪◻▪ *Go to the Web and complete any of the following exercises found in the Self-Assessment Library (S.A.L.) on R.O.L.L.S.: #13—What Motivates Me?, #14—What Rewards Do I Value Most?, #15—What's My View on the Nature of People?, and #16—How Sensitive Am I to Equity Differences?*

goals. Managers should also look for ways to increase the visibility of rewards, making them potentially more motivating.

- *Check the System for Equity.* Employees should perceive that rewards or outcomes are equal to the inputs. On a simple level, experience, ability, effort, and other obvious inputs should explain differences in pay, responsibility, and other obvious outcomes. And remember that one person's equity is another's inequity, so an ideal reward system should probably weigh inputs differently in arriving at the proper rewards for each job.

- *Use Recognition.* Recognize the power of recognition. In a stagnant economy where cost-cutting is widespread (like it was from 2001 to 2003), using recognition is a low-cost means to reward employees. And it's a reward that most employees consider valuable.

- *Don't Ignore Money.* It's easy to get so caught up in setting goals, creating interesting jobs, and providing opportunities for participation that you forget that money is a major reason why most people work. Thus, the allocation of performance-based wage increases, piecework bonuses, and other pay incentives is important in determining employee motivation. We're not saying that managers should focus solely on money as a motivational tool. Rather, we're simply stating the obvious—that is, if money is removed as an incentive, people aren't going to show up for work. The same can't be said for removing goals, enriched work, or participation.

Managers **Respond** to a **Manager's** Dilemma

····**Stacey Ficken**

AVP, Banking Center Manager, Allegiant Bank,
St. Louis, Missouri

Motivating employees is perhaps one of the hardest jobs of a manager. Rewarding and recognizing employees is the end result of motivating the employees. In order to do that, you must set goals and give them the tools to meet those goals. Angel could try implementing the following: determining the reward first, making sure it is something employees value; allowing employees to have a part in deciding the production quotas; communicating to employees how their job and department fits in with the company as a whole and how important they are to the entire process; creating a detailed plan on how the goals can be met; making sure employees have necessary tools and training to meet goals; and revisiting the goals on an ongoing basis to monitor progress and make adjustments. Finally, when goals are met, be sure to reward employees in a timely manner and review what could be done better next time.

Mary Hsue

**Business Manager, South Sound Dental Care,
Tacoma, Washington**

I recommend that Angel implement both an employee recognition program and a team recognition program. Recognition, both personal and public, is a powerful motivator. It costs little and helps to build employee esteem and team pride. The recognition could be expressed in terms of acknowledgment and appreciation for meeting or exceeding production goals as well as demonstrating certain desirable behaviors. Some points to consider in developing a recognition program include: communicate to employees how the company's success is dependent upon operating with a firm commitment to the company's mission statement; inform teams of how their group performance has contributed to the company's success; identify performance goals and standards and let employees participate in identifying, if at all possible; make sure performance goals include behaviors that relate to the company's mission; keep employees informed of their progress toward meeting goals; and consider presenting a small reward along with the recognition.

Learning Summary

After reading and studying this chapter, you should be able to:

- Define motivation.
- Explain motivation as a need-satisfying process.
- Describe the five levels in Maslow's hierarchy and how Maslow's hierarchy can be used in motivation efforts.
- Discuss how Theory X and Theory Y managers approach motivation.
- Describe Herzberg's motivation-hygiene theory.
- Explain Herzberg's views of satisfaction and dissatisfaction.
- Describe the three needs McClelland proposed as being present in work settings.

- Explain how goal-setting and reinforcement theories explain employee motivation.
- Describe the job characteristics model as a way to design motivating jobs.
- Discuss the motivation implications of equity theory.
- Contrast distributive justice and procedural justice.
- Explain the three key linkages in expectancy theory and their role in motivation.
- Describe the cross-cultural challenges of motivation.
- Discuss the challenges managers face in motivating unique groups of workers.
- Describe open-book management and employee recognition, pay-for-performance, and stock option programs.

Thinking About Management Issues

1. Most of us have to work for a living, and a job is a central part of our lives. So why do managers have to worry so much about employee motivation issues?

2. Describe a task you have done recently for which you exerted a high level of effort. Explain your behavior using any three of the motivation approaches described in this chapter.

3. If you had to develop an incentive system for a small company that makes tortillas, which elements from which motivation approaches or theories would you

use? Why? Would your choice be the same if it was a software design firm?

4. Could managers use any of the motivation theories or approaches to encourage and support workforce diversity efforts? Explain.

5. Many job design experts who have studied the changing nature of work say that people do their best work when they're motivated by a sense of purpose rather than by the pursuit of money. Do you agree? Explain your position.

Working Together: Team-Based Exercise

List five criteria (for example: pay, recognition, challenging work, friendships, status, the opportunity to do new things, the opportunity to travel, and so forth) that would be most important to you in a job. Rank them by order of

importance. Break into small groups (three or four other class members) and compare your responses. What patterns, if any, did you find?

Ethical Dilemma Exercise

Employees who feel unfairly forced into accepting deep cuts in salary and benefits may not be the most motivated workers. This is the situation facing many major U.S. airlines as they struggle for survival. To stay in business, management at US Airways and other carriers have pressured unionized pilots, mechanics, and flight attendants for concessions on pay and work rules again and again. As a result of lower compensation for the workforce and for management, US Airways was able to slash $1.2 billion (25 percent) from its payroll costs and emerge from bankruptcy protection. Other airlines improved their financial situations by slicing similar percentages from their payroll budgets.

Still, many airline employees are resentful that their compensation would not return to previous levels until the

end of 2008—at the earliest. In fact, the issue of whether cuts in management's compensation will also remain in place until 2008 has hurt relations between managers and employees. Moreover, representatives of the pilots' union announced a vote of "no confidence" in US Airways' top management over disagreements about pension problems and the size of new airplanes. Although keeping US Airways in business saves some 30,000 jobs, many employees are bitter about what they see as inequitable treatment. "We know we had to help the airline," says one flight attendant. "But we think they took more than they needed from us." This sense of inequity could dampen motivation and make a huge difference in the way employees work together and the way they deal with customers.[79]

Imagine that you were just promoted and now manage one of your airline's mechanical maintenance facilities at a regional airport. Your boss just told you that the airline has lost a large number of managers to jobs outside the industry. To stop defections and retain good managers, your company has decided to return managers to full pay and benefits within 12 months. However, employees must wait much longer. You sympathize with your workers' gripes about compensation cuts and you know they have little hope of getting a maintenance job at another airline. Although you like your new job and would welcome full pay, you could easily move to another industry. Look back at this chapter's discussion of equity theory as you consider this ethical challenge and decide which of the following options to choose—and why.

Option A: Leak the news to the local union representative so union leaders can prepare to pressure the airline for equal treatment, and clean up your résumé.

Option B: Call the local newspaper and anonymously tip off a reporter to investigate the situation and publicly expose any inequities between employees and managers.

Option C: Since the decision is out of your hands, look for other ways to reward and encourage your workers, such as bringing in pizza after an especially busy day.

Case Application

Motive Communications, Inc.

"We're not warm and fuzzy, there's not a lot of cheerleading, and we don't give back rubs on Friday." Such is the motivational philosophy of Scott Harmon, CEO and co-founder of Motive Communications, an Austin, Texas, software company. Founded in 1997, Motive provides customer service software that enables companies to offer and manage a variety of services. Some of its customers include such well-known global corporations as Fujitsu, 3Com, British Telecom, AT&T, and Merrill Lynch. The company's mission is: "To enable companies to compete and win with superior service. We believe that service is more than just an obligation, or a necessary expense. Service is our singular focus. From the beginning, Motive has helped its customers revolutionize the way they deliver services to improve profitability and reduce costs."

Although the company is passionate about servicing customers, Harmon doesn't believe in coddling employees. Steven Semelsberger, who oversees the company's business partnerships, says, "If you need a lot of pats on the back, this place is not for you." And Claire Campbell-Seeger, Motive's public relations director, says that during her five years at Motive, she has received only three e-mails from Harmon praising her work. Employees who need more visible and vocal praise and recognition tend to leave the company. Those who stay and succeed tend to be athletes or sports fans who thrive on competition and winning. As the company says on the jobs page on its Web site, "Our culture attracts employees who are not only driven to succeed, but are fueled by technology and share a passion for success."

Harmon's philosophy of people management was shaped by *Atlas Shrugged*, a 1957 novel by Ayn Rand, in which a person's main source of strength is described as thinking and reason. This philosophy can be seen, as well, in the way business decisions are made at Motive. The process is no-nonsense, and to keep emotions from influencing decisions, executives debate an issue and then wait a day to make the final decision. And at meetings, employees better be prepared with the facts. One company story tells of a meeting where an account representative described a customer as "pleasantly content." Harmon shot back, "Did you just make that up? If we aren't measuring it, how do you really know?"

Despite what may seem to be a harsh or uncaring approach to treating its employees, Motive has been successful. In 2002, the privately held company earned a $1.5 million profit on revenues of $59 million. With its acquisition of competitor BroadJump in December 2002, revenues almost doubled.

DISCUSSION QUESTIONS

1. Explain the advantages and disadvantages of Harmon's motivational approach using Maslow's hierarchy of needs theory, reinforcement theory, and expectancy theory.

2. Log onto Motive's Web site (*www.motive.com*) and find the information on Careers. Click on two job titles listed there and assess these jobs according to the job characteristics model.

3. Design an employee recognition program that might fit in with Harmon's motivational philosophy.

4. At a time when most managers are encouraged to be nice to their employees, would you suggest that Harmon change his motivational approach? Explain your answer.

Sources: Information on company from company's Web site (*www.motive.com*) and Hoover's Online (*www.hoovers.com*), June 21, 2003; A.E. Lemen, "Motivated to Grow," *Austin Business Journal*, June 2, 2003, accessed online at (*austin.bizjournals.com*), June 21, 2003; and J. Gordon, "Management by Black Belt," *Forbes*, February 17, 2003, p. 54.

Scott Harmon, CEO of Motive Communications, Austin, Texas.

●●●Learning Outline

Follow this Learning Outline as you read and study this chapter.

Managers Versus Leaders

- Contrast leaders and managers.
- Explain why leadership is an important behavioral topic.

Early Leadership Theories

- Discuss what research has shown about leadership traits.
- Contrast the findings of the four behavioral leadership theories.
- Explain the dual nature of a leader's behavior.

Contingency Theories of Leadership

- Explain how Fiedler's model of leadership is a contingency model.
- Contrast situational leadership theory and the leader participation model.
- Discuss how path-goal theory explains leadership.

Cutting-Edge Approaches to Leadership

- Differentiate between transactional and transformational leaders.
- Describe charismatic and visionary leadership.
- Discuss what team leadership involves.

Leadership Issues in the Twenty-First Century

- Describe the five sources of a leader's power.
- Discuss the issues today's leaders face.
- Explain why leadership is sometimes irrelevant.

Chapter

17

Leadership

United Parcel Service. It's the world's largest integrated package delivery company, with its chocolate-colored trucks traveling thousands of miles every business day, delivering more than 14 million packages throughout the United States and to more than 200 countries and territories.[1] Not only is it the largest in its industry, it's also viewed as one of the best. UPS continues to rack up awards. For instance, for the fifth year in a row, it was rated the "World's Most Admired" company in the delivery industry in *Fortune* magazine's 2003 Most Admired survey. Behind these excellent performance results is an army of over 370,000 employees who sort the packages, load the trucks, drive the trucks, deliver the packages, and do whatever else it takes to retain the trust between UPS and its customers. Trust is also important for UPS managers like Jennifer Shroeger in keeping employees focused on doing their jobs. Shroeger is district manager of the UPS distribution center in Buffalo, New York, and is responsible for 2,300 workers, $225 million in revenue, and 45,000 boxes an hour.

Work in a distribution center is complex and stressful. Every hour or so, a huge brown truck pulls into an unloading bay. Employees unload its packages and place them on a conveyor belt. It's box after box

after box—one every three seconds: 1,200 an hour. It's hard work in an environment that's anything but calm and quiet. Many employees on the night shift are part-timers—college students or people picking up a second job. Needless to say, employee turnover can be a problem. Before Shroeger arrived at the Buffalo center, part-time workers were leaving at the rate of about 50 percent a year. Since part-timers accounted for half of this facility's workforce, the attrition was costly and disruptive. Shroeger believed that resolving this problem was going to require targeted hiring, effective communication, and more empowered employees. As the newly appointed manager, it was also going to require building trust between her and the employees.

Put yourself in Jennifer Shroeger's position. What can she do to create a culture of trust with her employees?

What would *you* do **?**

Jennifer Shroeger is facing a major leadership challenge! It's important that she create this culture of trust and be seen as an effective leader. Why is leadership so important? Because it's the leaders in organizations who make things happen. If leadership is so important, it's only natural to ask: What differentiates leaders from nonleaders? What's the most appropriate style of leadership? And what can you do if you want to be seen as a leader? In this chapter, we'll try to answer these and other questions about leaders.

MANAGERS VERSUS LEADERS

Let's begin by clarifying the distinction between managers and leaders. Authors and practitioners often equate the two, although they're not necessarily the same. Managers are appointed to their positions. Their ability to influence employees is based on the formal authority inherent in that position. In contrast, leaders are appointed or emerge from within a work group and are able to influence others for reasons beyond formal authority.

Should all managers be leaders? Conversely, should all leaders be managers? Because no one yet has shown that leadership ability is a handicap to a manager, we believe that all managers should *ideally* be leaders. However, not all leaders have the capabilities or skills of effective managers, and thus, not all leaders should be managers. The fact that an individual can influence others doesn't mean that he or she can also plan, organize, and control. Given that all managers should be leaders, we'll study leadership from a managerial perspective. Therefore, our definition of a **leader** is someone who can influence others and who has managerial authority. What is **leadership** then? It's the process of influencing a group toward the achievement of goals.

Leadership, like motivation, is an organizational behavior topic that has been heavily researched, and most of that research has been aimed at answering the question: *What is an effective leader?* We'll begin our study of leadership by looking at some early leadership theories.

● ● ● **leader**
Someone who can influence others and who has managerial authority.

● ● ● **leadership**
The process of influencing a group toward the achievement of goals.

● ● ● **Learning Review**

- Contrast leaders and managers.

- Explain why leadership is an important behavioral topic.

EARLY LEADERSHIP THEORIES

Leadership has been of interest since the early days of people gathering together in groups to accomplish goals. However, it wasn't until the early part of the twentieth century that researchers began to study leadership. These early leadership theories focused on the *leader* (trait theories) and how the *leader interacted* with his or her group members (behavioral theories).

Trait Theories

Leadership research in the 1920s and 1930s focused on leader traits—characteristics that might be used to differentiate leaders from nonleaders. (■▭▭▭ Go to the Web and check out Q & A 17.1.) The intent was to isolate traits that leaders possessed and nonleaders did not. Some of the traits studied included physical stature, appearance, social class, emotional stability, fluency of speech, and sociability. Despite the best efforts of researchers, it proved to be impossible to identify a set of traits that would

■ **Q & A**
Whenever you see this green square, go to the R.O.L.L.S. Web site (*www.prenhall.com/ robbins*) to the Q & A, your 24/7 educational assistant. These video clips and written material presented by your authors address questions that we have found students frequently ask.

always differentiate leaders (the person) from nonleaders. Maybe it was a bit optimistic to think that there could be consistent and unique traits that would apply universally to all effective leaders, whether they were in charge of Toyota Motor Corporation, the Moscow Ballet, Ted's Malibu Surf Shop, or Oxford University. However, later attempts to identify traits consistently associated with leadership (the process, not the person) were more successful. Seven traits associated with effective leadership include drive, the desire to lead, honesty and integrity, self-confidence, intelligence, job-relevant knowledge, and extraversion.[2] These traits are briefly described in Exhibit 17–1.

Researchers agreed that traits alone were not sufficient for explaining effective leadership since explanations based solely on traits ignored the interactions of leaders and their group members as well as situational factors. Possessing the appropriate traits only made it more likely that an individual would be an effective leader. (◼◼▢▢▢ Go to the Web and check out Q & A 17.2.) Therefore, leadership research from the late 1940s to the mid-1960s concentrated on the preferred behavioral styles that leaders demonstrated. Researchers wondered whether there was something unique in what effective leaders *did*—in other words, in their *behavior.*

Behavioral Theories

Paul Johnston is president and general manager of Agri-Mark Inc., a successful and growing Massachusetts dairy cooperative that's known for its high-quality dairy products. Johnston is a demanding, autocratic boss who's described as "blunt, sarcastic, tactless, and tough." In contrast, Gerald Chamales, founder and chairman of Rhinotek Computer Products, a California-based manufacturer of inkjet and laser cartridges, has learned to tap into his employees' passions and strengths and get the best out of them. How? By encouraging their participation and letting them figure out how best to do things. Rhinotek's sales have risen 20 percent over the last three years and profits are up by 90 percent.[3] Agri-Mark and Rhinotek are two successful companies but, as you can see, the leaders behave in two very different ways. What do we know about leader behavior and how can it help us in our understanding of what an effective leader is?

Exhibit 17–1

● ● ●───────

Seven Traits Associated with Leadership

1. *Drive.* Leaders exhibit a high effort level. They have a relatively high desire for achievement; they are ambitious; they have a lot of energy; they are tirelessly persistent in their activities; and they show initiative.

2. *Desire to lead.* Leaders have a strong desire to influence and lead others. They demonstrate the willingness to take responsibility.

3. *Honesty and integrity.* Leaders build trusting relationships between themselves and followers by being truthful or nondeceitful and by showing high consistency between word and deed.

4. *Self-confidence.* Followers look to leaders for an absence of self-doubt. Leaders, therefore, need to show self-confidence in order to convince followers of the rightness of their goals and decisions.

5. *Intelligence.* Leaders need to be intelligent enough to gather, synthesize, and interpret large amounts of information, and they need to be able to create visions, solve problems, and make correct decisions.

6. *Job-relevant knowledge.* Effective leaders have a high degree of knowledge about the company, industry, and technical matters. In-depth knowledge allows leaders to make well-informed decisions and to understand the implications of those decisions.

7. *Extraversion.* Leaders are energetic, lively people. They are sociable, assertive, and rarely silent or withdrawn.

Sources: S.A. Kirkpatrick and E.A. Locke, "Leadership: Do Traits Really Matter?" *Academy of Management Executive,* May 1991, pp. 48–60; T.A. Judge, J.E. Bono, R. Ilies, and M.W. Gerhardt, "Personality and Leadership: A Qualitative and Quantitative Review," *Journal of Applied Psychology,* August 2002, pp. 765–80.

Exhibit 17–2

Behavioral Theories of Leadership

	Behavioral Dimension	Conclusion
University of Iowa	*Democratic style:* involving subordinates, delegating authority, and encouraging participation *Autocratic style:* dictating work methods, centralizing decision making, and limiting participation *Laissez-faire style:* giving group freedom to make decisions and complete work	Democratic style of leadership was most effective, although later studies showed mixed results.
Ohio State	*Consideration:* being considerate of followers' ideas and feelings *Initiating structure:* structuring work and work relationships to meet job goals	High-high leader (high in consideration and high in initiating structure) achieved high subordinate performance and satisfaction, but not in all situations.
University of Michigan	*Employee oriented:* emphasized interpersonal relationships and taking care of employees' needs *Production oriented:* emphasized technical or task aspects of job	Employee-oriented leaders were associated with high group productivity and higher job satisfaction.
Managerial Grid	*Concern for people:* measured leader's concern for subordinates on a scale of 1 to 9 (low to high) *Concern for production:* measured leader's concern for getting job done on a scale of 1 to 9 (low to high)	Leaders performed best with a 9.9 style (high concern for production and high concern for people).

behavioral theories
Leadership theories that identified behaviors that differentiated effective leaders from ineffective leaders.

autocratic style
A leader who tended to centralize authority, dictate work methods, make unilateral decisions, and limit employee participation.

democratic style
A leader who tended to involve employees in decision making, delegate authority, encourage participation in deciding work methods and goals, and use feedback as an opportunity for coaching employees.

laissez-faire style
A leader who generally gave the group complete freedom to make decisions and complete the work in whatever way it saw fit.

Researchers hoped that the **behavioral theories** approach would provide more definitive answers about the nature of leadership than did the trait theories. There are four main leader behavior studies we need to look at. (Exhibit 17–2 provides a summary of the major leader behavior dimensions and the conclusions of each of these studies.)

University of Iowa Studies The University of Iowa studies (conducted by Kurt Lewin and his associates) explored three leadership styles.[4] The **autocratic** style described a leader who typically tended to centralize authority, dictate work methods, make unilateral decisions, and limit employee participation. The **democratic** style described a leader who tended to involve employees in decision making, delegate authority, encourage participation in deciding work methods and goals, and use feedback as an opportunity for coaching employees. Finally, the **laissez-faire**-style leader generally gave the group complete freedom to make decisions and complete the work in whatever way it saw fit. Lewin and his associates researched which style was the most effective. Their results seemed to indicate that the democratic style contributed to both good quantity and quality of work. (■□■ Go to the Web and check out Q & A 17.3.) Had the answer to the question of the most effective leadership style been found? Unfortunately, it wasn't that simple. Later studies of the autocratic and democratic styles showed mixed results. For instance, the democratic style sometimes produced higher performance levels than the autocratic style, but at other times, it produced lower or equal performance levels. More consistent results were found, however, when a measure of subordinate satisfaction was used. Group members' satisfaction levels were generally higher under a democratic leader than under an autocratic one.[5] (■□■ Go to the Web and check out S.A.L. #27—What's My Leadership Style?)

Now leaders had a dilemma! Should they focus on achieving higher performance or on achieving higher member satisfaction? This recognition of the dual nature of a leader's behavior—that is, focusing on the task and on the people—was also a key characteristic of the other behavioral studies.

Leaders are often responsible for structuring their roles and the roles of others in the organization. Anthony Bourdain, executive chef at New York's Les Halles restaurant, and his highly disciplined staff thrive on a hierarchical structure that is in some ways at odds with the increasingly flat structures of corporate organizations. Bourdain likens his model to the military, with a rigid chain of command and an us-versus-them psychology that fosters team effort. "Because of its very rigidity and clarity," he says, "the hierarchical system allows you to speak your mind in an environment where there's no ego allowed or needed. . . . Everyone lives and dies by the same rules."

● ● ● **initiating structure**
The extent to which a leader was likely to define and structure his or her role and the roles of group members in the search for goal attainment.

● ● ● **consideration**
The extent to which a leader had job relationships characterized by mutual trust and respect for group members' ideas and feelings.

● ● ● **high-high leader**
A leader high in both initiating structure and consideration behaviors.

● ● ● **managerial grid**
A two-dimensional grid of two leadership behaviors—concern for people and concern for production—which resulted in five different leadership styles.

The Ohio State Studies The Ohio State studies identified two important dimensions of leader behavior.[6] Beginning with a list of more than 1,000 behavioral dimensions, the researchers eventually narrowed it down to just two that accounted for most of the leadership behavior described by group members. The first was called **initiating structure**, which referred to the extent to which a leader was likely to define and structure his or her role and the roles of group members in the search for goal attainment. It included behavior that involved attempts to organize work, work relationships, and goals. The second one was called **consideration**, which was defined as the extent to which a leader had job relationships characterized by mutual trust and respect for group members' ideas and feelings. A leader who was high in consideration helped group members with personal problems, was friendly and approachable, and treated all group members as equals. He or she showed concern for (was considerate of) his or her followers' comfort, well-being, status, and satisfaction.

Were these behavioral dimensions adequate descriptions of leader behavior? Research found that a leader who was high in both initiating structure and consideration (a **high-high leader**) achieved high group task performance and satisfaction more frequently than one who rated low on either dimension or both. However, the high-high style didn't always yield positive results. Enough exceptions were found to indicate that perhaps situational factors needed to be integrated into leadership theory.

University of Michigan Studies Leadership studies conducted at the University of Michigan's Survey Research Center at about the same time as those being done at Ohio State had a similar research objective: Identify behavioral characteristics of leaders that were related to performance effectiveness. The Michigan group also came up with two dimensions of leadership behavior, which they labeled employee oriented and production oriented.[7] Leaders who were *employee oriented* were described as emphasizing interpersonal relationships; they took a personal interest in the needs of their followers and accepted individual differences among group members. The *production-oriented* leaders, in contrast, tended to emphasize the technical or task aspects of the job, were concerned mainly with accomplishing their group's tasks, and regarded group members as a means to that end. The conclusions of the Michigan researchers strongly favored leaders who were employee oriented, as they were associated with high group productivity and high job satisfaction.

The Managerial Grid The behavioral dimensions from these early leadership studies provided the basis for the development of a two-dimensional grid for appraising leadership styles. This **managerial grid** used the behavioral dimensions "concern for people" and "concern for production" and evaluated a leader's use of these behaviors, ranking them on a scale from 1 (low) to 9 (high).[8] Although the grid (shown in Exhibit 17–3 on p. 426) had 81 potential categories into which a leader's behavioral style might fall, emphasis was placed on five: impoverished management (1,1), task management (9,1), middle-of-the-road management (5,5), country club management (1,9), and team management (9,9). Of these five styles, the researchers concluded that managers performed best when using a 9,9 style. Unfortunately, the grid offered no answers to the question of what made a manager an effective leader; it only provided a framework for conceptualizing leadership style. In fact, there's been little substantive evidence to support the conclusion that a 9,9 style is most effective in all situations.[9]

Leadership researchers were discovering that predicting leadership success involved something more complex than isolating a few leader traits or preferable behaviors. They began looking at situational influences. Specifically, which leadership styles might be suitable in different situations and what these different situations were.

● ● ● Exhibit 17–3

The Managerial Grid

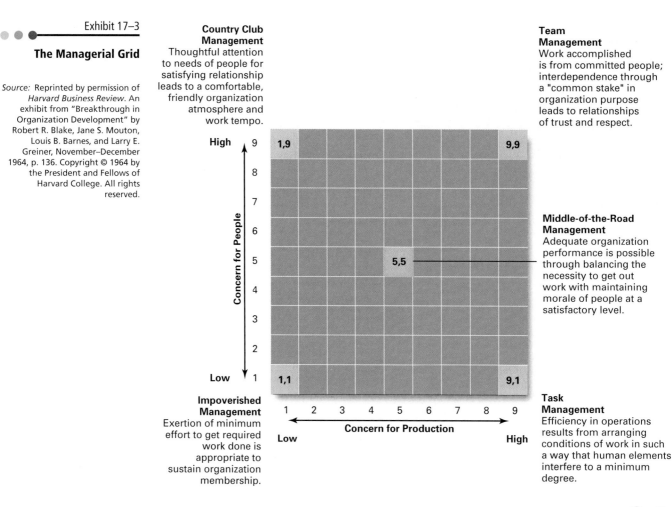

Country Club Management
Thoughtful attention to needs of people for satisfying relationship leads to a comfortable, friendly organization atmosphere and work tempo.

Team Management
Work accomplished is from committed people; interdependence through a "common stake" in organization purpose leads to relationships of trust and respect.

Middle-of-the-Road Management
Adequate organization performance is possible through balancing the necessity to get out work with maintaining morale of people at a satisfactory level.

Impoverished Management
Exertion of minimum effort to get required work done is appropriate to sustain organization membership.

Task Management
Efficiency in operations results from arranging conditions of work in such a way that human elements interfere to a minimum degree.

● ● ● **Learning Review**

- Discuss what research has shown about leadership traits.
- Contrast the findings of the four behavioral leadership theories.
- Explain the dual nature of a leader's behavior.

CONTINGENCY THEORIES OF LEADERSHIP

In this section we examine four contingency theories—Fiedler, Hersey-Blanchard, leader participation, and path-goal. Each looks at defining leadership style and the situation, and attempts to answer the *if-then* contingencies (that is, *if* this is the situation, *then* this is the best leadership style to use).

The Fiedler Model

● ● ● **Fiedler contingency model**
A leadership theory that proposes that effective group performance depends upon the proper match between a leader's style of interacting with his or her followers and the degree to which the situation allows the leader to control and influence.

The first comprehensive contingency model for leadership was developed by Fred Fiedler.[10] The **Fiedler contingency model** proposed that effective group performance depended on the proper match between the leader's style of interacting with his or her followers and the degree to which the situation allowed the leader to control and influence. The model was based on the premise that a certain leadership style would be most effective in different types of situations. The key was to define those leadership styles and the different types of situations and then to identify the appropriate combinations of style and situation.

Fiedler proposed that a key factor in leadership success was an individual's basic leadership style, either task oriented or relationship oriented. To measure a leader's style, Fiedler developed the **least-preferred co-worker (LPC) questionnaire**. This questionnaire contained 18 pairs of contrasting adjectives—for example, pleasant-unpleasant, cold-warm, boring-interesting, and friendly-unfriendly. Respondents were asked to think of all the co-workers they had ever had and to describe that one person they *least enjoyed* working with by rating him or her on a scale of 1 to 8 (the 8 always described the positive adjective out of the pair and the 1 always described the negative adjective out of the pair) for each of the 18 sets of adjectives. Fiedler believed that you could determine a person's basic leadership style on the basis of the responses to the LPC questionnaire.

If the leader described the least-preferred co-worker in relatively positive terms (in other words, a "high" LPC score—a score of 64 or above), then the respondent was primarily interested in good personal relations with co-workers. That is, if you described the person that you least liked to work with in favorable terms, your style would be described as *relationship oriented*. In contrast, if you saw the least-preferred co-worker in relatively unfavorable terms (a low LPC score—a score of 57 or below), you were primarily interested in productivity and getting the job done; thus, your style would be labeled as *task oriented*. Fiedler did acknowledge that there was a small group of people who fell in between these two extremes and who did not have a cut-and-dried leadership personality style. One other point is that Fiedler assumed that a person's leadership style was always the same (fixed) regardless of the situation. (▭ Go to the Web and check out Q & A 17.4.) In other words, if you were a relationship-oriented leader, you'd always be one, and the same for a task-oriented leader.

After an individual's leadership style had been assessed through the LPC, it was necessary to evaluate the situation in order to match the leader with the situation. Fiedler's research uncovered three contingency dimensions that defined the key situational factors for determining leader effectiveness. These were:

- **Leader-member relations**: The degree of confidence, trust, and respect employees had for their leader; rated as either good or poor.
- **Task structure**: The degree to which job assignments were formalized and procedurized; rated as either high or low.
- **Position power**: The degree of influence a leader had over power-based activities such as hiring, firing, discipline, promotions, and salary increases; rated as either strong or weak.

Each leadership situation was evaluated in terms of these three contingency variables, which combined produced eight possible situations in which a leader could find himself or herself (see the bottom of the chart in Exhibit 17–4 on p. 428). Each of these situations was further described in terms of its favorableness for the leader. Situations I, II, and III were classified as very favorable for the leader. Situations IV, V, and VI were moderately favorable for the leader. And, situations VII and VIII were described as very unfavorable for the leader.

Once Fiedler had described the leader variables and the situational variables, he was ready to define the specific contingencies for leadership effectiveness. To do so, he studied 1,200 groups where he compared relationship-oriented with task-oriented leadership styles in each of the eight situational categories. He concluded that task-oriented leaders performed better in very favorable situations and in very unfavorable situations. (See top of Exhibit 17–4 where performance is shown on the vertical axis and situation favorableness is shown on the horizontal axis.) On the other hand, relationship-oriented leaders performed better in moderately favorable situations.

• • • least-preferred co-worker (LPC) questionnaire
A questionnaire that measured whether a leader was task or relationship oriented.

• • • leader-member relations
One of Fiedler's situational contingencies that described the degree of confidence, trust, and respect employees had for their leader.

• • • task structure
One of Fiedler's situational contingencies that described the degree to which job assignments were formalized and procedurized.

• • • position power
One of Fiedler's situational contingencies that described the degree of influence a leader had over power-based activities such as hiring, firing, discipline, promotions, and salary increases.

Many leaders have had to change their management styles during the economic shifts of the last few years. When business was booming, they had to work hard to keep their best employees from accepting better offers from competing firms. Now that firms in many industries are tightening their belts, leaders like Patricia Russo, CEO of Lucent Industries, are more concerned with motivating workers who may feel overworked in the wake of sweeping layoffs and budget cuts. Under Russo, Lucent, which sells telecommunications equipment, has had to change its focus from sales of new products to servicing equipment already sold, and Russo now encourages employees to wait for economic recovery.

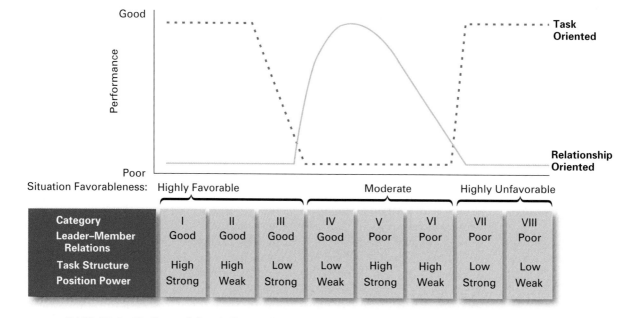

Exhibit 17–4   **Findings of the Fiedler Model**

Since Fiedler treated an individual's leadership style as fixed, there were only two ways to improve leader effectiveness. First, you could bring in a new leader whose style better fit the situation. For instance, if the group situation was rated as highly unfavorable but was led by a relationship-oriented leader, the group's performance could be improved by replacing that person with a task-oriented leader. The second alternative was to change the situation to fit the leader. This could be done by restructuring tasks or increasing or decreasing the power that the leader had over factors such as salary increases, promotions, and disciplinary actions.

Reviews of the major studies undertaken to test the overall validity of Fiedler's model have shown considerable evidence to support the model.[11] However, his theory wasn't without criticisms. For instance, additional variables were probably needed to fill in some gaps in the model. Moreover, there were problems with the LPC, and the practicality of it needed to be addressed. In addition, it's probably unrealistic to assume that a person can't change his or her leadership style to fit the situation. Effective leaders can, and do, change their styles to meet the needs of a particular situation. Finally, the contingency variables were difficult for practitioners to assess.[12] Despite its shortcomings, the Fiedler model showed that effective leadership style needed to reflect situational factors.

Hersey and Blanchard's Situational Leadership Theory

Paul Hersey and Ken Blanchard developed a leadership theory that has gained a strong following among management development specialists.[13] This model, called **situational leadership theory (SLT)**, is a contingency theory that focuses on followers' readiness. Hersey and Blanchard argue that successful leadership is achieved by selecting the right leadership style, which is contingent on the level of the followers' readiness. Before we proceed, there are two points we need to clarify: Why a leadership theory focuses on the followers, and what is meant by the term *readiness*.

The emphasis on the followers in leadership effectiveness reflects the reality that it *is* the followers who accept or reject the leader. Regardless of what the leader does, effectiveness depends on the actions of his or her followers. (■□■■■ Go to the Web and check out Q & A 17.5.) This is an important dimension that has been overlooked or underemphasized in most leadership theories. And **readiness**, as defined by Hersey

●●● **situational leadership theory (SLT)**
A leadership contingency theory that focuses on followers' readiness.

●●● **readiness**
The extent to which people have the ability and willingness to accomplish a specific task.

Exhibit 17–5

Hersey and Blanchard's Situational Leadership Model

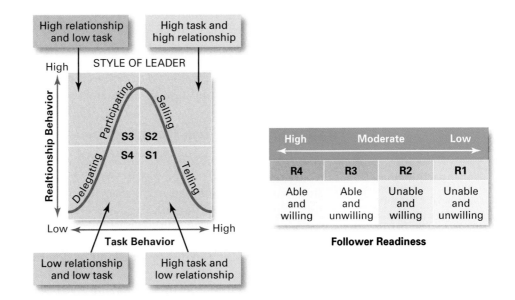

and Blanchard, refers to the extent to which people have the ability and willingness to accomplish a specific task.

SLT uses the same two leadership dimensions that Fiedler identified: task and relationship behaviors. However, Hersey and Blanchard go a step further by considering each as either high or low and then combining them into four specific leadership styles (see Exhibit 17–5), described as follows:

- *Telling* (high task-low relationship): The leader defines roles and tells people what, how, when, and where to do various tasks.
- *Selling* (high task-high relationship): The leader provides both directive and supportive behavior.
- *Participating* (low task-high relationship): The leader and follower share in decision making; the main role of the leader is facilitating and communicating.
- *Delegating* (low task-low relationship): The leader provides little direction or support.

The final component in the model is the four stages of follower readiness:

- *R1:* People are both unable and unwilling to take responsibility for doing something. They're neither competent nor confident.
- *R2:* People are unable but willing to do the necessary job tasks. They're motivated but currently lack the appropriate skills.
- *R3:* People are able but unwilling to do what the leader wants.
- *R4:* People are both able and willing to do what is asked of them.

SLT essentially views the leader–follower relationship as analogous to that of a parent and a child. Just as a parent needs to relinquish control as a child becomes more mature and responsible, so, too, should leaders. As followers reach high levels of readiness, the leader responds not only by continuing to decrease control over their activities, but also by continuing to decrease relationship behavior. The SLT says if followers are *unable* and *unwilling* to do a task, the leader needs to give clear and specific directions; if followers are *unable* and *willing*, the leader needs to display high task orientation to compensate for the followers' lack of ability and high relationship orientation to get followers to "buy into" the leader's desires; if followers are *able* and *unwilling*, the leader needs to use a supportive and participative style; and if employees are both *able* and *willing*, the leader doesn't need to do much.

SLT has intuitive appeal. It acknowledges the importance of followers and builds on the logic that leaders can compensate for ability and motivational limitations in their followers. Yet research efforts to test and support the theory generally have been disappointing.[14] Why? Possible explanations include internal inconsistencies in the model itself as well as problems with research methodology. So despite its appeal and wide popularity, any enthusiastic endorsement should be done with caution.

Leader Participation Model

• • • **leader participation model**
A leadership contingency model that related leadership behavior and participation in decision making.

Another early contingency model, developed by Victor Vroom and Phillip Yetton, was the **leader participation model**, which related leadership behavior and participation to decision making.[15] Developed in the early 1970s, the model argued that leader behavior must adjust to reflect the task structure—whether it was routine, nonroutine, or in between. Vroom and Yetton's model is what we call a *normative* one, because it provided a sequential set of rules (norms) that the leader followed in determining the form and amount of participation in decision making, as determined by the different situations.

The leader participation model has changed as research continues to provide additional insights into effective leadership style.[16] A current model reflects *how* and *with whom* decisions are made and uses variations of the same five leadership styles identified in the original model (see a description of these styles in Exhibit 17–6). It also expands upon the decision-making contingencies leaders look at in determining what leadership style would be most effective.[17] These contingencies—decision significance, importance of commitment, leader expertise, likelihood of commitment, group support, group expertise, and team competence—are either present (H for high) or absent (L for Low). Exhibit 17–7 shows a current leader participation model—the Time-Driven Model, which is short-term in its orientation and concerned with making effective decisions with minimum cost. To use the model, a leader goes from left to right determining whether each contingency factor is high or low. After assessing all these contingencies, the most effective leadership style is identified on the far right-hand side of the model. Another model—the Development-Driven Model—is structured the same way but emphasizes making effective decisions with maximum employee development outcomes and places no value on time.

Path-Goal Model

• • • **path-goal theory**
A leadership theory that says it's the leader's job to assist his or her followers in attaining their goals and to provide the direction or support needed to ensure that their goals are compatible with the overall objectives of the group or organization.

Currently, one of the most respected approaches to understanding leadership is **path-goal theory**, which states that it's the leader's job to assist his or her followers in attaining their goals and to provide the direction or support needed to ensure that their goals are compatible with the overall objectives of the group or organization. Developed by Robert House, path-goal theory is a contingency model of leadership that takes key elements from the expectancy theory of motivation.[18] The term *path-goal* is derived from the belief that effective leaders clarify the path to help their followers get from where they are to the achievement of their work goals and make the journey along the path easier by reducing roadblocks and pitfalls.

Exhibit 17–6
• • •—————

Leadership Styles in the Vroom Leader Participation Model

- *Decide:* Leader makes the decision alone and either announces or sells it to group.
- *Consult Individually:* Leader presents the problem to group members individually, gets their suggestions, and then makes the decision.
- *Consult Group:* Leader presents the problem to group members in a meeting, gets their suggestions, and then makes the decision.
- *Facilitate:* Leader presents the problem to the group in a meeting and, acting as facilitator, defines the problem and the boundaries within which a decision must be made.
- *Delegate:* Leader permits the group to make the decision within prescribed limits.

Source: Based on V. Vroom, "Leadership and the Decision-Making Process," *Organizational Dynamics*, vol. 28, no. 4 (2000), p. 84.

Exhibit 17–7

Time-Driven Model

Source: Adapted from V. Vroom, "Leadership and the Decision-Making Process," *Organizational Dynamics*, vol. 28, no. 4 (2000), p. 87.

PROBLEM STATEMENT

Decision Significance	Importance of Commitment	Leader Expertise	Likelihood of Commitment	Group Support	Group Expertise	Team Competence	
H	H	H	H	–	–	–	Decide
H	H	H	L	H	H	H	Delegate
H	H	H	L	H	H	L	Consult (Group)
H	H	H	L	H	L	–	Consult (Group)
H	H	H	L	L	–	–	Consult (Group)
H	H	L	H	H	H	H	Facilitate
H	H	L	H	H	H	L	Consult (Individually)
H	H	L	H	H	L	–	Consult (Individually)
H	H	L	H	L	–	–	Consult (Individually)
H	H	L	L	H	H	H	Facilitate
H	H	L	L	H	H	L	Consult (Group)
H	H	L	L	H	L	–	Consult (Group)
H	H	L	L	L	–	–	Consult (Group)
H	L	H	–	–	–	–	Decide
H	L	L	–	H	H	H	Facilitate
H	L	L	–	H	H	L	Consult (Individually)
H	L	L	–	H	L	–	Consult (Individually)
H	L	L	–	L	–	–	Consult (Individually)
L	H	–	H	–	–	–	Decide
L	H	–	L	–	–	H	Delegate
L	H	–	L	–	–	L	Facilitate
L	L	–	–	–	–	–	Decide

House identified four leadership behaviors:

- *Directive leader:* Lets subordinates know what's expected of them, schedules work to be done, and gives specific guidance on how to accomplish tasks
- *Supportive leader:* Is friendly and shows concern for the needs of followers
- *Participative leader:* Consults with group members and uses their suggestions before making a decision
- *Achievement-oriented leader:* Sets challenging goals and expects followers to perform at their highest level

In contrast to Fiedler's view that a leader couldn't change his or her behavior, House assumed that leaders are flexible. In other words, path-goal theory assumes that the same leader can display any or all of these leadership styles depending on the situation.

As Exhibit 17–8 on page 432 illustrates, path-goal theory proposes two situational or contingency variables that moderate the leadership behavior–outcome relationship: those in the *environment* that are outside the control of the follower (factors including task structure, formal authority system, and the work group) and those that are part of the personal characteristics of the *follower* (including locus of control, experience, and perceived ability). Environmental factors determine the type of leader

Exhibit 17–8

Path-Goal Theory

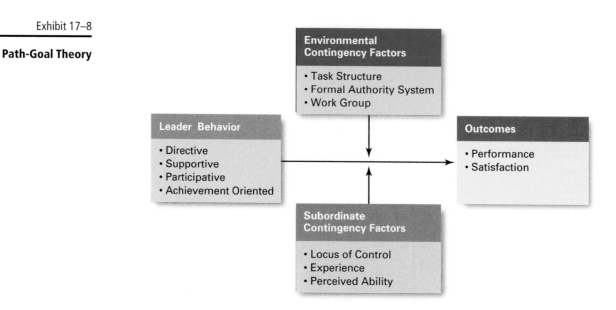

behavior required if subordinate outcomes are to be maximized; personal characteristics of the follower determine how the environment and leader behavior are interpreted. The theory proposes that leader behavior will be ineffective when it's redundant with sources of environmental structure or incongruent with follower characteristics. For example, some predictions from path-goal theory are:

- Directive leadership leads to greater satisfaction when tasks are ambiguous or stressful than when they are highly structured and well laid out.

- Supportive leadership results in high employee performance and satisfaction when subordinates are performing structured tasks.

- Directive leadership is likely to be perceived as redundant among subordinates with high perceived ability or with considerable experience.

- The clearer and more bureaucratic the formal authority relationships, the more leaders should exhibit supportive behavior and deemphasize directive behavior.

- Directive leadership will lead to higher employee satisfaction when there is substantive conflict within a work group.

- Subordinates with an internal locus of control will be more satisfied with a participative style.

- Subordinates with an external locus of control will be more satisfied with a directive style.

- Achievement-oriented leadership will increase subordinates' expectancies that effort will lead to high performance when tasks are ambiguously structured.

Research on the path-goal model is generally encouraging. (■■□■■ Go to the Web and check out Q & A 17.6.) Although not every study has found support, the majority of the evidence supports the logic underlying the theory. [19] In summary, employee performance and satisfaction are likely to be positively influenced when the leader compensates for shortcomings in either the employee or the work setting. However, if the leader spends time explaining tasks that are already clear or when the employee has the ability and experience to handle them without interference, the employee is likely to see such directive behavior as redundant or even insulting.

Learning Review

- Explain how Fiedler's model of leadership is a contingency model.
- Contrast situational leadership theory and the leadership participation model.

- Discuss how path-goal theory explains leadership.

CUTTING-EDGE APPROACHES TO LEADERSHIP

What are the latest views of leadership in organizations? In this section, we want to look at three contemporary approaches to leadership including transformational-transactional leadership, charismatic-visionary leadership, and team leadership.

Transformational-Transactional Leadership

transactional leaders
Leaders who guide or motivate their followers in the direction of established goals by clarifying role and task requirements.

transformational leaders
Leaders who provide individualized consideration and intellectual stimulation, and who possess charisma.

Most of the leadership theories presented so far in this chapter have described **transactional leaders**; that is, leaders who guide or motivate their followers in the direction of established goals by clarifying role and task requirements. (■□■■■ Go to the Web and check out Q & A 17.7.) But there's another type of leader who inspires followers to transcend their own self-interests for the good of the organization, and who is capable of having a profound and extraordinary effect on his or her followers. These are **transformational leaders**, and examples include Jim Goodnight of SAS Institute and Andrea Jung of Avon. They pay attention to the concerns and developmental needs of individual followers; they change followers' awareness of issues by helping those followers look at old problems in new ways; and they are able to excite, arouse, and inspire followers to put out extra effort to achieve group goals.

Transactional and transformational leadership shouldn't be viewed as opposing approaches to getting things done.[20] Transformational leadership is built on top of transactional leadership. Transformational leadership produces levels of employee effort and performance that go beyond what would occur with a transactional approach alone. Moreover, transformational leadership is more than charisma since the transformational leader attempts to instill in followers the ability to question not only established views but those views held by the leader.[21]

The evidence supporting the superiority of transformational leadership over transactional is overwhelmingly impressive. For instance, studies that looked at managers in different settings, including the military and business, found that transformational leaders were evaluated as more effective, higher performers, and more promotable than their transactional counterparts.[22] In addition, evidence indicates that transformational leadership is strongly correlated with lower turnover rates, higher productivity, and higher employee satisfaction.[23]

Charismatic-Visionary Leadership

charismatic leader
An enthusiastic, self-confident leader whose personality and actions influence people to behave in certain ways.

Jeff Bezos, founder and CEO of Amazon.com, is a person who exudes energy, enthusiasm, and drive.[24] He's fun-loving (his legendary laugh has been described as a flock of Canadian geese on nitrous oxide), but has pursued his vision for Amazon with serious intensity and has demonstrated an ability to inspire his employees through the ups and downs of a rapidly growing company. Bezos is what we call a **charismatic leader**—that is, an enthusiastic, self-confident leader whose personality and actions influence people to behave in certain ways.

Several authors have attempted to identify the personal characteristics of a charismatic leader.[25] The most comprehensive analysis identified five such characteristics that differentiate charismatic leaders from noncharismatic ones: They have a vision, are able to articulate that vision, are willing to take risks to achieve that vision, are sensitive to both environmental constraints and follower needs, and exhibit behaviors that are out of the ordinary.[26] (■□▨▨▨▨ Go to the Web and check out Q & A 17.8.)

What can we say about the charismatic leader's effect on his or her followers? There's an increasing body of evidence that shows impressive correlations between charismatic leadership and high performance and satisfaction among followers.[27]

If charisma is desirable, can people learn to be charismatic leaders? Or are charismatic leaders born with their qualities? Although a small number of experts still think that charisma can't be learned, most believe that individuals can be trained to exhibit charismatic behaviors.[28] For example, researchers have succeeded in teaching undergraduate students to "be" charismatic. How? They were taught to articulate a sweeping goal, communicate high performance expectations, exhibit confidence in the ability of subordinates to meet those expectations, and empathize with the needs of their subordinates; they learned to project a powerful, confident, and dynamic presence; and they practiced using a captivating and engaging voice tone. The researchers also trained the student leaders to use charismatic nonverbal behaviors including leaning toward the follower when communicating, maintaining direct eye contact, and having a relaxed posture and animated facial expressions. In groups with these "trained" charismatic leaders, members had higher task performance, higher task adjustment, and better adjustment to the leader and to the group than did group members who worked in groups led by noncharismatic leaders. (■▨▨□▨ Go to the Web and check out S.A.L #28—How Charismatic Am I?)

One last thing we need to say about charismatic leadership is that it may not always be needed to achieve high levels of employee performance. It may be most appropriate when the follower's task has an ideological purpose or when the environment involves a high degree of stress and uncertainty.[29] This may explain why, when charismatic leaders surface, it's more likely to be in politics, religion, or wartime; or when a business firm is starting up or facing a survival crisis. For example, Martin Luther King Jr., used his charisma to bring about social equality through nonviolent means; and Steve Jobs achieved unwavering loyalty and commitment from Apple Computer's technical staff in the early 1980s by articulating a vision of personal computers that would dramatically change the way people lived.

Although the term *vision* is often linked with charismatic leadership, **visionary leadership** goes beyond charisma since it's the ability to create and articulate a realistic, credible, and attractive vision of the future that improves upon the present situation.[30] This vision, if properly selected and implemented, is so energizing that it "in effect jump-starts the future by calling forth the skills, talents, and resources to make it happen."[31]

A vision should offer clear and compelling imagery that taps into people's emotions and inspires enthusiasm to pursue the organization's goals. It should be able to generate possibilities that are inspirational and unique and offer new ways of doing things that are clearly better for the organization and its members. Visions that are clearly articulated and have powerful imagery are easily grasped and accepted. For instance, Michael Dell (Dell Computer) created a vision of a business that sells and delivers a finished PC directly to a customer in less than a week. The late Mary Kay Ash's vision of women as entrepreneurs selling products that improved their self-image gave impetus to her cosmetics company, Mary Kay Cosmetics.

What skills do visionary leaders exhibit? Once the vision is identified, these leaders appear to have three qualities that are related to effectiveness in their visionary roles.[32] First is the *ability to explain the vision to others* by making the vision clear in terms of required goals and actions through clear oral and written communication. The second skill is the *ability to express the vision not just verbally but through behavior*, which requires behaving in ways that continually convey and reinforce the vision. For example, former Southwest Airlines CEO Herb Kelleher continually demonstrated his com-

● ● ● **visionary leadership**
The ability to create and articulate a realistic, credible, and attractive vision of the future that improves upon the present situation.

mitment to customer service. He was legendary within the company for his boundless energy and for jumping in, when needed, to help check in passengers, load baggage, fill in for flight attendants, or do anything else to make the customers' experiences more pleasant and memorable. The third skill visionary leaders need is the *ability to extend or apply the vision to different leadership contexts.* For instance, the vision has to be as meaningful to the people in accounting as it is to those in production, and to employees in Cleveland as it is to those in Sydney.

Team Leadership

Since leadership is increasingly taking place within a team context and more organizations are using work teams, the role of the leader in guiding team members has become increasingly important. The role of team leader *is* different from the traditional leadership role, as J.D. Bryant, a supervisor at Texas Instruments' Forest Lane plant in Dallas, discovered.[33] One day he was contentedly overseeing a staff of 15 circuit-board assemblers. The next day he was told that the company was going to use employee teams and he was to become a "facilitator." He said, "I'm supposed to teach the teams everything I know and then let them make their own decisions." But, confused about his new role, he admitted, "There was no clear plan on what I was supposed to do." What *is* involved in being a team leader? (■□■□ Go to the Web and check out Q & A 17.9.)

Many leaders are not equipped to handle the change to employee teams. As one consultant noted, "Even the most capable managers have trouble making the transition because all the command-and-control type things they were encouraged to do before are no longer appropriate. There's no reason to have any skill or sense of this."[34] This same consultant estimated that "probably 15 percent of managers are natural team leaders; another 15 percent could never lead a team because it runs counter to their personality—that is, they're unable to sublimate their dominating style for the good of the team. Then there's that huge group in the middle: Team leadership doesn't come naturally to them, but they can learn it."[35]

The challenge for many managers is learning how to become an effective team leader. They have to learn skills such as having the patience to share information, being able to trust others and to give up authority, and understanding when to intervene. And effective team leaders have mastered the difficult balancing act of knowing when to leave their teams alone and when to get involved. New team leaders may try to retain too much control at a time when team members need more autonomy, or they may abandon their teams at times when the teams need support and help.[36]

One study of organizations that had reorganized themselves around employee teams found certain common responsibilities of all leaders. These included coaching, facilitating, handling disciplinary problems, reviewing team and individual performance, training, and communication.[37] However, a more meaningful way to describe the team leader's job is to focus on two priorities: (1) managing the team's external boundary and (2) facilitating the team process.[38] These priorities entail four specific leadership roles. (See Exhibit 17–9.)

First, team leaders are *liaisons with external constituencies.* These may include upper management, other organizational work teams, customers, or suppliers. The leader

Dennis Hastings is a visionary leader who hopes to transform his tiny Omaha tribe of 2,500 people from an impoverished people into proud inheritors of a great culture. He has worked tirelessly for many years to recover the Omaha Nation's cultural heritage from institutions like the Smithsonian and Harvard's Peabody Museum, and he wants to enshrine priceless tribal artifacts in a museum overlooking the Missouri River. "It will become a significant spot," Hastings predicts. "Our whole culture will be here."

Exhibit 17–9

Specific Team Leadership Roles

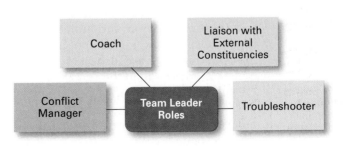

represents the team to other constituencies, secures needed resources, clarifies others' expectations of the team, gathers information from the outside, and shares that information with team members.

Next, team leaders are *troubleshooters*. When the team has problems and asks for assistance, team leaders sit in on meetings and try to help resolve the problems. Troubleshooting rarely involves technical or operational issues because the team members typically know more about the tasks being done than does the team leader. The leader is most likely to contribute by asking penetrating questions, helping the team talk through problems, and getting needed resources to tackle problems.

Third, team leaders are *conflict managers*. They help identify issues such as the source of the conflict, who's involved, the issues, the resolution options available, and the advantages and disadvantages of each. By getting team members to address questions such as these, the leader minimizes the disruptive aspects of intrateam conflicts.

Finally, team leaders are *coaches*. They clarify expectations and roles, teach, offer support, and do whatever else is necessary to help team members keep their work performance high. (▣▣ Go to the Web and check out S.A.L. #30—How Good Am I at Building and Leading a Team?)

● ● ● Learning Review

- Differentiate between transactional and transformational leaders.

- Describe charismatic and visionary leadership.

- Discuss what team leadership involves.

LEADERSHIP ISSUES IN THE TWENTY-FIRST CENTURY

Rudolph Giuliani, former mayor of New York City, probably never dreamed that he would have to assume the leadership role that he did at the end of his term. As shock and fear gripped the nation after the terrorist attacks on 9/11, Giuliani stepped up and led the city and nation through the crisis. Within minutes after the first plane hit, he was on the scene directing operations. And in the weeks that followed he provided effective leadership—being a hardnosed administrator when needed and a caring and emotional leader when needed.[39]

For most leaders, being effective in today's environment is unlikely to involve such dramatic and traumatic circumstances. However, twenty-first-century leaders do face some important leadership issues. In this section, we're going to look at some of these issues including managing power, developing trust, providing moral leadership, providing online leadership, empowering employees, cross-cultural leadership, gender differences in leadership, the demise of heroic leadership, and becoming an effective leader.

Managing Power

Where do leaders get their power—that is, their capacity to influence work actions or decisions? (▣▣ Go to the Web and check out Q & A 17.10.) Five sources of leader power have been identified: legitimate, coercive, reward, expert, and referent.[40]

● ● ● legitimate power
The power a leader has as a result of his or her position in the organization.

Legitimate power and authority are the same. Legitimate power represents the power a leader has as a result of his or her position in the organization. People in positions of authority are also likely to have reward and coercive power, but legitimate power is broader than the power to coerce and reward.

● ● ● coercive power
The power a leader has because of his or her ability to punish or control.

Coercive power is the power that rests on the leader's ability to punish or control. Followers react to this power out of fear of the negative results that might occur if they did not comply. As a manager, you typically have some coercive power, such as being able to suspend or demote employees or to assign them work they find unpleasant or undesirable.

The Ins and Outs of Office Politics

Office politics. You've probably heard the term before and probably have experienced it if you've ever worked in an organization. Office politics is a fact of life in organizations.[41] Since organizations are made up of individuals and groups with different values, goals, and interests, this sets up the potential for conflict over resources such as budgets, space allocations, project responsibilities, and salary adjustments. To gain control over these resources, people exert power. People want to carve out a niche from which to exert influence, to earn awards, and to advance their careers. When employees convert their power into action, we describe them as being engaged in office politics. Those with good political skills effectively use their various sources of power to get what they need and want. Although you may not like the idea of engaging in office politics, it *is* important that you know how to be politically adept. You can use the following suggestions to improve *your* political effectiveness.

1. *Frame arguments in terms of organizational goals.* Effective politicking requires camouflaging your self-interests. People whose actions appear to blatantly further their own interests at the expense of the organization are almost universally denounced, are likely to *lose* influence, and may even be expelled from the organization.

2. *Develop the right image.* Know your organization's culture; understand what the organization wants and values from its employees. Because the assessment of your performance isn't fully objective, you must pay attention to style as well as substance.

3. *Gain control of organizational resources.* The control of scarce and important organizational resources is a source of power. Knowledge and expertise are particularly effective resources to control.

4. *Make yourself appear indispensable.* If the organization's key decision makers believe there is no ready substitute for what you bring to the organization, they are likely to go to great lengths to ensure that your desires are satisfied.

5. *Be visible.* Make your boss and those in power aware of your contributions. Routinely highlight your successes in reports, have satisfied customers express their satisfaction to your managers, be seen at company social functions, be active in your professional associations, and so forth.

6. *Develop powerful allies.* It helps to have powerful people on your side. Cultivate contacts with potentially influential people above you, at your own level, and at lower organizational levels. These allies can speak positively about your accomplishments to others and provide you with important information that might not otherwise be available.

7. *Avoid "tainted" members.* In every organization, there are individuals whose status is questionable. Their performance and loyalty are suspect. Keep your distance from such individuals so that your own effectiveness isn't compromised.

8. *Support your boss.* Your immediate future is in your boss's hands. Since he or she evaluates your performance, try to do whatever is necessary to have your boss on your side. Make every effort to help your boss look good and succeed, support your boss, and find out what criteria will be used to assess your effectiveness. Don't speak negatively of your boss to others and definitely don't undermine your boss.

●●● **reward power**
The power a leader has to give positive benefits or rewards.

●●● **expert power**
Influence that's based on expertise, special skills, or knowledge.

●●● **referent power**
Power that arises because of a person's desirable resources or personal traits.

Reward power is the power to give positive benefits or rewards. These rewards can be anything that another person values. In an organizational context, that might include money, favorable performance appraisals, promotions, interesting work assignments, friendly colleagues, and preferred work shifts or sales territories.

Expert power is influence that's based on expertise, special skills, or knowledge. As jobs have become more specialized, managers have become increasingly dependent on staff "experts" to achieve the organization's goals. If an employee has skills, knowledge, or expertise that's critical to the operation of a work group, that person's expert power is enhanced.

Finally, **referent power** is the power that arises because of a person's desirable resources or personal traits. If I admire and identify with you, you can exercise power over me because I want to please you. Referent power develops out of admiration of another and a desire to be like that person. If you admire someone to the point of modeling your behavior and attitudes after him or her, that person has referent power over you. (▨▨▨▨▨ Go to the Web and check out You're the Manager: Diversity in Action #2.)

Most effective leaders rely on several different forms of power to affect the behavior and performance of their followers. For example, Lieutenant Commander Horden Wiltshire, commanding officer of one of Australia's state-of-the-art submarines, the HMAS *Sheean*, employs different types of power in managing his crew and equipment. He gives orders to the crew (legitimate), praises them (reward), and disciplines those who commit infractions (coercive). As an effective leader, he also strives to have expert power (based on his expertise and knowledge) and referent power (based on his being admired) to influence his crew.[42] (▨▨▨▨▨ Go to the Web and check out PRISM #5—Acquiring Power.)

Developing Trust

After reluctantly agreeing to union contract concessions that they believed were necessary to keep their company from bankruptcy and accepting the fact that their paychecks would be reduced, American Airline's employees were stunned at CEO Don Carty's after-the-fact disclosure of lucrative compensation policies and pension protections designed to retain key executives. Suddenly, Carty's pleas for "shared sacrifice" seemed insincere and false. Any trust that employees had in Carty's ability to lead the airline into the future had completely evaporated. Not long after the disclosure, Carty was forced by American's board to resign.[43]

Carty's behavior illustrates how fragile leader trust can be. In today's uncertain environment, an important consideration for leaders is building trust and credibility. Before we can discuss ways leaders can build trust and credibility, we have to know what trust and credibility are and why they're so important. (▨▨▨▨▨ Go to the Web and check out S.A.L. #29—Do Others See Me As Trusting?)

The main component of credibility is honesty. Surveys show that honesty is consistently singled out as the number-one characteristic of admired leaders. "Honesty is absolutely essential to leadership. If people are going to follow someone willingly, whether it be into battle or into the boardroom, they first want to assure themselves that the person is worthy of their trust." In addition to being honest, credible leaders are competent and inspiring.[44] They are personally able to communicate effectively their confidence and enthusiasm. Thus, followers judge a leader's **credibility** in terms of his or her honesty, competence, and ability to inspire.

Trust is closely entwined with the concept of credibility, and, in fact, the terms are often used interchangeably. **Trust** is defined as the belief in the integrity, character, and ability of a leader. Followers who trust a leader are willing to be vulnerable to the leader's actions because they are confident that their rights and

● ● ● **credibility**
The degree to which followers perceive someone as honest, competent, and able to inspire.

● ● ● **trust**
The belief in the integrity, character, and ability of a leader.

THINKING CRITICALLY ABOUT ETHICS

Your boss isn't satisfied with the way one of your colleagues is handling a project and she reassigns the project to you. She tells you to work with this person to find out what he has done already and to discuss any other necessary information that he might have. She wants your project report by the end of the month. This person is pretty upset and angry over the reassignment and won't give you the information you need to even start, much less complete, the project. You won't be able to meet your deadline unless you get this information.

What type of power does your colleague appear to be using? What type of influence could you possibly use to gain his cooperation? If you were involved in this situation, what could you do to resolve it successfully, yet ethically?

interests will not be abused.[45] Research has identified five dimensions that make up the concept of trust:[46]

Gregg Popovich, head coach of the San Antonio Spurs, has the sixth-best winning percentage of all time in the NBA. Although his manner is unassuming and he describes himself as a "facilitator," he is also clearly in charge of his players, who admire and trust him for his frankness and honesty. "He's straightforward," says retired point guard Steve Kerr. "He's not going to mess with your head, and he isn't going to play mind games."

- *Integrity:* Honesty and truthfulness
- *Competence:* Technical and interpersonal knowledge and skills
- *Consistency:* Reliability, predictability, and good judgment in handling situations
- *Loyalty:* Willingness to protect a person, physically and emotionally
- *Openness:* Willingness to share ideas and information freely

Of these five dimensions, integrity seems to be the most critical when someone assesses another's trustworthiness.[47] However, both integrity and competence were seen in our earlier discussion of leadership traits found to be consistently associated with leadership.

Workplace changes have reinforced why such leadership qualities are so important. For instance, the trend toward empowerment (which we'll discuss later in this chapter) and self-managed work teams has reduced or eliminated many of the traditional control mechanisms used to monitor employees. If a work team is free to schedule its own work, evaluate its own performance, and even make its own hiring decisions, trust becomes critical. Employees have to trust managers to treat them fairly, and managers have to trust employees to conscientiously fulfill their responsibilities.

Also, leaders have to increasingly lead others who may not be in their immediate work group—members of cross-functional teams, individuals who work for suppliers or customers, and perhaps even people who represent other organizations through strategic alliances. These situations don't allow leaders the luxury of falling back on their formal positions for influence. Many of these relationships, in fact, are fluid and fleeting. So the ability to quickly develop trust is crucial to the success of the relationship.

Why is it important that followers trust their leaders? Research has shown that trust in leadership is significantly related to positive job outcomes including job performance, organizational citizenship behavior, job satisfaction, and organizational commitment.[48]

Given the importance of trust in effective leadership, how should leaders build trust? Exhibit 17–10 lists some suggestions, which are explained in the Skills Module on Developing Trust found on pp. 524-525[49] (■ ■□■ Go to the Web and check out PRISM #4—Developing Trust.)

Now, more than ever, managerial and leadership effectiveness depends on the ability to gain the trust of followers.[50] For instance, downsizing, corporate financial misrepresentations, and the increased use of temporary employees have undermined employees' trust in their leaders and shaken the confidence of investors, suppliers, and customers. A recent survey found that only 39 percent of U. S. employees and 51

Exhibit 17–10

● ● ●——

Suggestions for Building Trust

> *Practice openness.*
> *Be fair.*
> *Speak your feelings.*
> *Tell the truth.*
> *Show consistency.*
> *Fulfill your promises.*
> *Maintain confidences.*
> *Demonstrate competence.*

percent of Canadian employees trusted their executive leaders.[51] Today's leaders are faced with the challenge of rebuilding and restoring trust with employees and with other important organizational stakeholders.

Providing Moral Leadership

The topic of leadership and ethics has received surprisingly little attention. Only recently have ethics and leadership researchers begun to consider the ethical implications in leadership.[52] Why now? One reason may be the growing general interest in ethics throughout the field of management. And there's no doubt that recent corporate financial scandals have increased the public's and politicians' concerns about ethical standards in American business. For instance, in June 2003, a federal jury indicted Charles W. McCall, the former chairman of health services company McKesson, alleging he conspired in an accounting fraud that resulted in $9 billion in shareholder losses after it was discovered. Jeffrey Rogers, CEO of Pizza Inn, resigned in 2002 after "the company took a $1.9 million charge to offset the cost of an unpaid loan to Rogers, a write-off that erased the firm's quarterly profit."[53] When people hear about such financial misconduct, it's no wonder they're demanding that today's corporate leaders do a better job of providing moral and ethical leadership.

Ethics are part of leadership in a number of ways. For instance, transformational leaders have been described as fostering moral virtue when they try to change the attitudes and behaviors of followers.[54] We can also see an ethical component to charisma. Unethical leaders may use their charisma to enhance their power over followers and use that power for self-serving purposes. On the other hand, ethical leaders may use their charisma in more socially constructive ways to serve others.[55] We also see a lack of ethics when leaders abuse their power and give themselves large salaries and bonuses while, at the same time, they seek to cut costs by laying off employees. And of course, trust, which is important to ethical behavior, explicitly deals with the leadership traits of honesty and integrity.

As we have seen recently, leadership is not value free. Providing moral leadership involves addressing the *means* that a leader uses in trying to achieve goals as well as the content of those goals. For instance, George David, CEO of United Technologies Corporation (UTC) and *Industry Week*'s 2002 CEO of the year, is very clear about his role in providing ethical leadership. In a meeting of his company's board of directors held at the New York Public Library, he said, "What you see is what you get. The library is among the most truly open institutions in the world and UTC aspires to be held to the same kind of standards and expectations in governance and financial management. We must have a spotless, perfect record. Period." And the company's 16-page code of ethics provides guidance—that is, the *means*—for employees.[56] As a recent study concluded, ethical leadership is more than being ethical; it's reinforcing ethics through organizational mechanisms such as communication and the reward system.[57] Thus, before we judge any leader to be effective, we should consider both the moral content of his or her goals *and* the means used to achieve those goals.

Demonstrating moral leadership is an important role for managers. But it is not always an easy one when the firm is facing difficult challenges. When asked "What gives you a sense of satisfaction in your work?" Charles Schwab's president and CEO David S. Pottruck replied, "We've managed through a 36 percent downsizing, a 25 percent drop in revenue, and an even greater drop in our stock price without losing our moral compass or our culture."

Providing Online Leadership

How do you lead people who are physically separated from you and where interactions are basically reduced to written digital communications? Pat O'Day, manager of a five-person virtual team at KPMG International, understands the challenges of providing online leadership. To help his team be more effective, O'Day says, "We communicate through email and conference calls and meet in person four times a year."[58]

Online leadership encompasses many new tasks, even for managers in firms that have already established themselves in the brick-and-mortar world like Costco Wholesale Corp. has. Costco's four-year-old Internet company, Costco.com, offers shoppers only about 15 percent of the products they can find in one of its warehouse stores. Vice President Susan Castillo has made the site a success with unexpected items like computers and diamond jewelry instead of "safe" items like books and CDs. Castillo likes relying on the Internet to control performance. "We know immediately whether something is successful simply by how many people order it," she says. "That's the joy of the Internet. You can see minute by minute what members are ordering."

What little research has been done in online leadership has focused on managing virtual teams.[59] This research suggests that there are three fundamental challenges in providing online leadership: communication, performance management, and trust.

In a virtual setting, leaders may need to learn new communication skills in order to be seen as effective. To effectively convey online leadership, managers must realize that they have choices in words, structure, tone, and style of their digital communications and be alert to expressions of emotions. For instance, in face-to-face communications, harsh *words* can be softened by nonverbal action. A smile and comforting gestures, for instance, can lessen the blow behind words like *disappointed, unsatisfactory, inadequate,* or *below expectations.* In online interactions, that nonverbal aspect doesn't exist. Also, the *structure* of words in a digital communication has the power to motivate or demotivate the receiver. Is the message made up of full sentences or phrases? The latter, for instance, is likely to be seen as curt and more threatening. Similarly, a message in all caps is the equivalent of shouting. Leaders also need to be sure the *tone* of their message correctly conveys the emotions they want to send. Is the message formal or informal? Does it convey the appropriate level of importance or urgency? And is the leader's writing style consistent with his or her verbal style? If leaders, for instance, make their written communications more formal than their verbal style, it creates confusion for employees and probably hinders their effectiveness. Also, online leaders must choose a *style.* Do they use emoticons, abbreviations, jargon, and the like? Do they adapt their style to their audience? Observation suggests that some managers are having difficulty adjusting to computer-based communications. For instance, they use the same style with their bosses that they use with their staff. Or they selectively use digital communication to "hide" when delivering bad news. Finally, online leaders need to develop the skills of "reading between the lines" in the messages they receive so they can decipher the emotional components.

Another challenge of online leadership is managing performance. How? By defining, facilitating, and encouraging it.[60] As leaders *define* performance, it's important to ensure that all members of a virtual team understand the team's goals, their responsibilities in achieving those goals, and how goal achievement is going to be assessed. There should be no surprises or uncertainties about performance expectations. Although these are important managerial responsibilities in all situations, they're particularly critical in virtual work environments as there are no face-to-face interactions to convey expectations or address performance problems. Online leaders also have a responsibility to *facilitate* performance. This means reducing or eliminating obstacles to successful performance and providing adequate resources to get the job done. This can be particularly challenging, especially if the virtual team is global since the physical distance separating the leader and the team means it's not easy to get team members the resources they may need. Finally, online leaders are responsible for *encouraging* performance by providing sufficient rewards that virtual employees really value. As we know from Chapter 16, motivating employees can be difficult, even in work settings where there's face-to-face interaction. In a virtual setting, the motivational challenge can be even greater because the leader isn't there in person to encourage, support, and guide. So what can online leaders do? They can ask virtual employees what rewards are most important to them—pay, benefits, technology upgrades, opportunities for professional development, or whatever. Then, they can make sure the rewards are provided in a timely manner after major work goals have been achieved. Finally, any rewards program must be perceived as fair. This expectation isn't any different from that of leaders in nonvirtual settings—employees want and expect rewards to be distributed fairly.

The final challenge of providing online leadership is the trust issue. In a virtual setting, there are numerous opportunities to violate trust. One possible trust issue is whether the system is being used to monitor and evaluate employees. The technology is there to do so, but leaders must consider whether that's really the best way to influence employee behavior. For instance, T.J. Rodgers, founder and CEO of Cypress Semiconductor, found out the hard way that it might not be.[61] He built an in-house system that tracked goals and deadlines. If a department missed its target, the software shut down its computers and canceled the manager's next paycheck. After realizing the system encouraged dishonesty, Rodgers ditched it. The experience made him understand that it was more important to create a culture where trust among all participants is expected and required. In fact, the five dimensions of trust we described earlier—integrity, competence, consistency, loyalty, and openness—would be vital to the development of such a culture.

Empowering Employees

Employees at DuPont's facility in Uberaba, Brazil, recently planted trees to commemorate the site's tenth anniversary. Although they had several things to celebrate, one of the most important was the fact that since production began, the facility has had zero environmental incidents and no recordable safety violations. The primary reason for this achievement was the company's STOP (Safety Training Observation Program) program—a program in which empowered employees were responsible for observing one another, correcting improper procedures, and encouraging safe procedures.[62]

● ● ● **empowerment**
Increasing the decision-making discretion of workers.

As we've described in different places throughout the text, managers are increasingly leading by empowering their employees. **Empowerment** involves increasing the

---

Jack Stack
Chairman of the Board and Chief Executive Officer
SRC Holdings Corporation
Springfield, Missouri

Describe your job.

I am presently the chairman of the board and chief executive officer of SRC Holdings Corporation. The company is decentralized so that the employee-owners have as much authority as they can grasp and at the same time are supported by a corporate office that doesn't interfere with the operational details, but is there if needed. In addition to being available to assist each of the divisions, I investigate long-term investments that could have an impact on the future of the company. I also do a lot of traveling around the country speaking to companies and associations about SRC's form of open-book management, which we call The Great Game of Business®. In this process, we teach our people business principles and provide the training necessary to create extraordinary products and services. But most importantly, we teach our people how to create a

great company, and as a result, get great products and services. In my job, there is something new every day. I honestly can say that not one day has ever been the same in twenty-some years.

What types of skills do you think tomorrow's managers will need?

Learning how to evaluate a business. There are three things that need to be measured when determining how strong a company is and whether valuable time should be spent growing the company: understanding the solvency, the profitability, and the efficiency of the company in which you plan on spending a major portion of your life. SRC got to where it is today by initiating a new and radical management design when most of our competition ran their organizations through archaic styles of leadership. We elected to teach our people business principles and to maximize their intellectual capacities in addition to their skills. We appealed to a higher level of thinking with every member of our organization and, as a result, received better than average performances. The ongoing process that we use, The Great Game of Business®, teaches people how to think and act like owners—and in this company, they are.

decision-making discretion of workers. Millions of individual employees and employee teams are making the key operating decisions that directly affect their work. They're developing budgets, scheduling workloads, controlling inventories, solving quality problems, and engaging in similar activities that until very recently were viewed exclusively as part of the manager's job.[63] For instance, at The Container Store, any employee who gets a customer request has permission to take care of it. The company's chairman Garret Boone says, "Everybody we hire, we hire as a leader. Anybody in our store can take an action that you might think of typically being a manager's action."[64]

Why are more and more companies empowering employees? One reason is the need for quick decisions by those people who are most knowledgeable about the issues—often those at lower organizational levels. If organizations are to successfully compete in a dynamic global economy, they have to be able to make decisions and implement changes quickly. (Check out Passport Scenario 2 on p. 452.) Another reason is the reality that organizational downsizings left many managers with larger spans of control. In order to cope with the increased work demands, managers had to empower their people. Although empowerment is not a universal panacea, when employees have the knowledge, skills, and experience to do their jobs competently and when they seek autonomy and possess an internal locus of control, it can be beneficial. (▪■☐■ Go to the Web and check out PRISM #10—Delegating.)

Cross-Cultural Leadership

One general conclusion that surfaces from leadership research is that effective leaders do not use any single style. They adjust their style to the situation. Although not mentioned explicitly, national culture is certainly an important situational variable in determining which leadership style will be most effective. What works in China isn't likely to be effective in France or Canada. For instance, one study of Asian leadership styles revealed that Asian managers preferred leaders who were competent decision makers, effective communicators, and supportive of employees.[65]

National culture affects leadership style because it influences how followers will respond. Leaders can't (and shouldn't) just choose their styles randomly. They're constrained by the cultural conditions their followers have come to expect. Exhibit 17–11 provides some findings from selected examples of cross-cultural leadership studies. Since most leadership theories were developed in the United States, using U.S. subjects, they have an American bias. They emphasize follower responsibilities rather than rights; assume self-gratification rather than commitment to duty or altruistic motivation; assume centrality of work and democratic value orientation; and stress

Exhibit 17–11

● ● ● ━

Selected Cross-Cultural Leadership Findings

- Korean leaders are expected to be paternalistic toward employees.
- Arab leaders who show kindness or generosity without being asked to do so are seen by other Arabs as weak.
- Japanese leaders are expected to be humble and speak frequently.
- Scandinavian and Dutch leaders who single out individuals with public praise are likely to embarrass, not energize, those individuals.
- Effective leaders in Malaysia are expected to show compassion while using more of an autocratic than a participative style.
- Effective German leaders are characterized by high performance orientation, low compassion, low self-protection, low team orientation, high autonomy, and high participation.

Sources: Based on J.C. Kennedy, "Leadership in Malaysia: Traditional Values, International Outlook," *Academy of Management Executive*, August 2002, pp. 15–17; F.C. Brodbeck, M. Frese, and M. Javidan, "Leadership Made in Germany: Low on Compassion, High on Performance," *Academy of Management Executive*, February 2002, pp. 16–29; M.F. Peterson and J.G. Hunt, "International Perspectives on International Leadership," *Leadership Quarterly*, Fall 1997, pp. 203–31; R.J. House and R.N. Aditya, "The Social Scientific Study of Leadership: Quo Vadis?" *Journal of Management*, vol. 23, no. 3, (1997), p. 463; and R.J. House, "Leadership in the Twenty-First Century," in A. Howard (ed.), *The Changing Nature of Work* (San Francisco: Jossey-Bass, 1995), p. 442.

rationality rather than spirituality, religion, or superstition.[66] However, the GLOBE research program, which we first introduced in Chapter 4, is the most extensive and comprehensive cross-cultural study of leadership ever undertaken. One of the results coming from the GLOBE program is that there are some universal aspects to leadership. Specifically, a number of elements of transformational leadership appear to be associated with effective leadership regardless of what country the leader is in.[67] Which elements appear universal? Vision, foresight, providing encouragement, trustworthiness, dynamism, positiveness, and proactiveness. The results led two members of the GLOBE team to conclude that "effective business leaders in any country are expected by their subordinates to provide a powerful and proactive vision to guide the company into the future, strong motivational skills to stimulate all employees to fulfill the vision, and excellent planning skills to assist in implementing the vision."[68] Some people suggest that the universal appeal of these transformational leader characteristics is due to the pressures toward common technologies and management practices, as a result of global competitiveness and multinational influences.

Gender Differences and Leadership

There was a time when the question "Do males and females lead differently?" could be accurately characterized as a purely academic issue—interesting, but not very relevant. That time has certainly passed! Many women now hold senior management positions, and many more around the world will continue to join the management ranks. For instance, more than 21 million women in the United States worked in managerial and professional occupations in 2002—a 30 percent increase in 10 years. And in other economically developed countries, the percentage of female managerial and administrative workers in selected countries included Australia (24 percent), Canada (43 percent), France (10 percent), Germany (19 percent), Japan (9 percent), Poland (66 percent), and Sweden (59 percent).[69] Misconceptions about the relationship between leadership and gender can adversely affect hiring, performance evaluation, promotion, and other human resource decisions for both men and women. For instance, evidence indicates that a "good" manager is still perceived as predominantly masculine.[70]

A warning before we proceed: This topic is controversial. If male and female styles differ, is one inferior? If there is a difference, does labeling leadership styles by gender encourage stereotyping? These are important questions and we'll address them shortly.

A number of studies focusing on gender and leadership style have been conducted in recent years. Their general conclusion is that males and females *do* use different styles. Specifically, women tend to adopt a more democratic or participative style. Women are more likely to encourage participation, share power and information, and attempt to enhance followers' self-worth. They lead through inclusion and rely on their charisma, expertise, contacts, and interpersonal skills to influence others. Women tend to use transformational leadership, motivating others by transforming their self-interest into organizational goals. Men are more likely to use a directive, command-and-control style. They rely on formal position authority for their influence. Men use transactional leadership, handing out rewards for good work and punishment for bad.[71]

There is an interesting qualifier to the above findings. The tendency for female leaders to be more democratic than males declines when women are in male-dominated jobs. Apparently, group norms and male stereotypes influence women and they tend to act more autocratically.[72]

Although it's interesting to see how male and female leadership styles differ, a more important question is whether they differ in effectiveness. Although some researchers have shown that males and females tend to be equally effective as leaders,[73] an increasing number of studies have shown that women executives, when rated by their peers, employees, and bosses, score higher than their male counterparts on a wide variety of measures.[74] (See Exhibit 17–12 for a summary.) Why? One possible explanation is that in today's organizations, flexibility, teamwork and partnering, trust,

Exhibit 17–12

Where Female Managers Do Better: A Scorecard

Source: R. Sharpe, "As Leaders, Women Rule," *BusinessWeek,* November 20, 2000, p. 75.

Where Female Managers Do Better: A Scorecard

None of the five studies set out to find gender differences. They stumbled on them while compiling and analyzing performance evaluations.

Skill (Each check mark denotes which group scored higher on the respective studies)	MEN	WOMEN
Motivating Others		✓✓✓✓
Fostering Communication		✓✓✓*
Producing High-Quality Work		✓✓✓✓
Strategic Planning	✓✓	✓✓*
Listening to Others		✓✓✓✓
Analyzing Issues	✓✓	✓✓*

*In one study, women's and men's scores in these categories were statistically even.
Data: Hagberg Consulting Group, Management Research Group, Lawrence A. Pfaff, Personnel Decisions International Inc., Advanced Teamware Inc.

and information sharing are rapidly replacing rigid structures, competitive individualism, control, and secrecy. In these types of workplaces, effective managers must use more social and interpersonal behaviors. They listen, motivate, and provide support to their people. They inspire and influence rather than control. And women seem to do those things better than men.[75]

Although women seem to rate highly on those leadership skills needed to succeed in today's dynamic global environment, we don't want to fall into the same trap as the early leadership researchers who tried to find the "one best leadership style" for all situations. We know that there is no one *best* style for all situations. Instead, which leadership style is effective will depend on the situation. So even if men and women differ in their leadership styles, we shouldn't assume that one is always preferable to the other.

The Demise of Heroic Leadership

Polls show that just 16 percent of Americans trust business executives. And the number of senior business executives who said they would not want to be a CEO doubled in just one year from 26 percent to 54 percent.[76] Business leaders seem to be losing their luster. When and how did corporate leaders go from visionary, larger-than-life heroes who were almost as popular as rock stars, to being reviled outcasts?

The well-publicized corporate financial scandals obviously contributed to this shift of opinion. In addition, there's been the controversy surrounding executive pay. When the public hears that the average CEO makes 411 more times than the average worker or when you consider that had the minimum wage increased since 1990 at the same rate as executive pay had, it would be $21.41 an hour, not $5.15, it's no wonder that the public is outraged.[77] And there's further resentment when huge management salaries or benefits are given to executives when their company's performance, in fact, has declined. For example, at Cendant Corporation, CEO Henry R. Silverman got $11 million in salary and bonus in 2002, a 41 percent increase, while Cendant's total stock return fell 47 percent.[78]

When corporate boards wanted to better align managers' interests with shareholders' interests, stock options became a popular choice for motivating CEOs. The idea had merit: Instead of just overseeing an organization, managers would become owners. This made sense because individuals would be rewarded for achieving outcomes that benefited the organization. Boards of directors began giving CEOs and other senior executives stock options worth tens and hundreds of millions of dollars. In reality, CEOs began treating the company's stock price as an end in itself instead of it being the outcome of building a successful company. They were motivated to engage in practices—many questionable—whose only purpose was to increase the stock's price in the short run. The executives got rich but often at the expense of their firm's long-term prospects.[79]

Reuben Mark, CEO of Colgate-Palmolive since 1984, is in some ways the opposite of the heroic leader of recent headlines. Mark prefers execution over flashy strategy pronouncements, focuses on quiet but continual improvement, and prefers the role of team member to that of celebrity. He is known for spurning executive privileges and sometimes answers his own phone (with "Hello, Colgate"), yet he has consistently improved the company's profitability and growth throughout his tenure. Market analyst Andrew Shore of Deutsche Bank has studied Colgate for 16 years and says, "Nobody knows Reuben Mark. He just happens to be one of the most successful CEOs in the world."

The public and business press had allowed CEOs to become perceived unrealistically as "gods." The rising stock market of the 1990s reinforced this perception. CEOS began to believe the myth and just as the high-tech bubble burst, so did the CEO bubble, thanks to the high-profile scandals and outrageous executive pay, especially in companies with mediocre performance.

The demise of this "heroic leader" view in the twenty-first century was brought about by arrogance, greed, and hype. But in reality, corporate leaders should never have been anointed as superheroes to begin with.[80] They didn't have all the answers. And they definitely couldn't run companies all by themselves. The myth of the "savior CEO" who could single-handedly expand and enrich a corporation was just that—a myth based on the idea that having a vision and the ability to inspire others to reach that vision were what made CEOs worth the hundreds of millions of dollars they were paid. Although this heroic leader may not be real, it doesn't mean that the CEO is irrelevant. Instead, his or her role as organizational leader needs to change.

Boards of directors need to have a more pragmatic view of what the CEO's job really is and what an appropriate salary should be. And CEOs need to get back to the basics of what it means to be a leader.[81] How? Here are some suggestions: Give people a reason to come to work. Help them develop a passion for their work, a commitment to their colleagues, and a sense of responsibility to the organization's customers. Be loyal to the organization's people. Southwest Airlines, for example, will do whatever it takes to keep from laying off employees because it genuinely believes that its employees are the key to the company's success. This loyalty is a two-way street. When employees feel that their organization is being loyal to them, they work harder, are more productive, and give better service to customers. If financial problems arise, CEOs should show that employees matter by cutting their own (CEOs') salaries and the salaries of top managers first rather than downsizing. Spend time with people who do the real work of the organization—people down at the loading dock, or in the check-out line, or out on sales calls. Finally, today's CEOs need to be more open and more candid about what business practices are acceptable and proper and how the unacceptable ones should be fixed. They should be prepared to take strong decisive action when something wrong is discovered. For instance, when Harvey Kraemer, CEO of Baxter International, discovered that dialysis filters manufactured by a company Baxter had recently acquired had been involved in patients' deaths, he did something. "He took responsibility for the problem. He apologized for it. He directed his team to make sure it never happened again. He took a $189 million hit to the company's books and then he recommended to his own board of directors that it reduce his bonus by 40 percent as a measure of his own responsibility for the problem."[82] Today's CEOs need to show that type of openness, integrity, and accountability.

Becoming an Effective Leader

Organizations need effective leaders. (▮▮▮▯▮ Go to the Web and check out PRISM #2—Choosing an Effective Leadership Style.) Two issues pertinent to becoming an effective leader are leader training and recognizing that sometimes being an effective leader means *not* leading. Let's take a look at these issues.

Leader Training Organizations around the globe spend billions of dollars, yen, and euros on leadership training and development.[83] These efforts take many forms—from $50,000 leadership programs offered by universities such as Harvard to

Becoming a Manager

- ◆ *As you interact with various organizations, note different leadership styles.*
- ◆ *Think of people that you would consider effective leaders and try to determine why they're effective.*
- ◆ *If you have the opportunity, take leadership development courses.*
- ◆ *Practice building trust in relationships that you have with others.*
- ◆ *Read books on great leaders (not just business leaders) and on leadership development topics.*
- ◆ █ ████ *Go to the Web and complete any of the exercises from the Self-Assessment Library (S.A.L.) found on R.O.L.L.S.: #27—What's My Leadership Style?, #28—How Charismatic Am I?, #29—Do Others See Me as Trusting?, and #30—How Good Am I at Building and Leading a Team?*

sailing experiences at the Outward Bound School. Although much of the money spent on training may provide doubtful benefits, our review suggests that there are some things managers can do to get the maximum effect from leadership training.[84]

First, let's recognize the obvious. Some people don't have what it takes to be a leader. For instance, evidence indicates that leadership training is more likely to be successful with individuals who are high self-monitors than with low self-monitors. Such individuals have the flexibility to change their behavior as different situations may require. In addition, organizations may find that individuals with higher levels of a trait called motivation to lead are more receptive to leadership development opportunities.[85]

What kinds of things can individuals learn that might be related to being a more effective leader? It may be a bit optimistic to think that "vision-creation" can be taught, but implementation skills can be taught. People can be trained to develop "an understanding about content themes critical to effective visions."[86] We can also teach skills such as trust building and mentoring. And leaders can be taught situational analysis skills. They can learn how to evaluate situations, how to modify situations to make them fit better with their style, and how to assess which leader behaviors might be most effective in given situations.

Sometimes Leadership Is Irrelevant Despite the belief that some leadership styles will always be effective regardless of the situation, leadership may not always be important! (█ ████ Go to the Web and check out Q & A 17.11.) Research indicates that, in some situations, any behaviors a leader exhibits are irrelevant. In other words, certain individual, job, and organizational variables can act as "substitutes for leadership," negating the influence of the leader.[87]

For instance, follower characteristics such as experience, training, professional orientation, or need for independence can neutralize the effect of leadership. These characteristics can replace the employee's need for a leader's support or ability to create structure and reduce task ambiguity. Similarly, jobs that are inherently unambiguous and routine or that are intrinsically satisfying may place fewer demands on the leadership variable. Finally, such organizational characteristics as explicit formalized goals, rigid rules and procedures, or cohesive work groups can substitute for formal leadership.

●●●●Learning Review

- Explain the five sources of a leader's power.
- Discuss the issues today's leaders face.

- Explain why leadership is sometimes irrelevant.

Managers **Respond** to a **Manager's** Dilemma

....**Sharna Small Borsellino**

Manager of Private Carrier Services, Massachusetts Bay Transportation Authority, Boston, Massachusetts

Jennifer should take the role of a transformational leader and enlist the participation of the workers in establishing a part-time employee retention and support package. Because employee surveys don't usually work, she should form employee focus groups representative of her workforce (such as college students, those working second jobs, etc.). These focus groups would submit several retention and support ideas relevant for their particular group. Whatever ideas come from the focus groups should be evaluated and the selected ones put into effect. Seeing that their input was used and valued will instill a sense of trust among the employees. Whatever ideas are implemented, Jennifer might also want to consider using part-time employee awards for attendance as well as bonuses for each year of service to the company. This might help retention and motivation as well.

Sheila O'Neill

Clinical Research Associate, Sankyo Pharma Inc., New York, New York

Jennifer should actively, openly, and honestly communicate with her employees by: holding group, shift, or one-on-one meetings to find out what people think of the job, why people are leaving, and what ideas they have to help retain workers; letting employees help solve these issues; having a suggestion box for ideas that employees would like to see implemented; continuing to emphasize the company's mission; being out on the floor regularly talking to employees; and always being open and honest with them. Jennifer also should create incentives to stay, such as performance incentives (both individual and team), term incentives based on duration of service; and she might evaluate whether tuition reimbursement programs would work. Finally, Jennifer should make sure she understands each person's job so she can deal with job-specific issues.

Learning Summary

After reading and studying this chapter, you should be able to:

- Contrast leaders and managers.
- Explain why leadership is an important behavioral topic.
- Discuss what research has shown about leadership traits.
- Contrast the findings of the four behavioral leadership theories.
- Explain the dual nature of a leader's behavior.
- Explain how Fiedler's model of leadership is a contingency model.
- Contrast situational leadership theory and the leader participation model.
- Discuss how path-goal theory explains leadership.
- Differentiate between transactional and transformational leaders.
- Describe charismatic and visionary leadership.
- Discuss what team leadership involves.
- Explain the five sources of a leader's power.
- Discuss the issues today's leaders face.
- Explain why leadership is sometimes irrelevant.

Thinking About Management Issues

1. What types of power are available to you? Which ones do you use most? Why?

2. Do you think that most managers in real life use a contingency approach to increase their leadership effectiveness? Discuss.

3. If you ask people why a given individual is a leader, they tend to describe the person in terms such as *competent, consistent, self-assured, inspiring a shared vision,* and *enthusiastic.* How do these descriptions fit in with leadership concepts presented in the chapter?

4. What kinds of campus activities could a full-time college student do that might lead to the perception that he or she is a charismatic leader? In pursuing those activities, what might the student do to enhance this perception of being charismatic?

5. Do you think trust evolves out of an individual's personal characteristics or out of specific situations? Explain.

Working Together: Team-Based Exercise

You're the new manager of customer service operations at Preferred Bank Card, Inc., a credit card issuer with offices throughout California. Your predecessor, who was very popular with the customer service representatives and who is still with the company, concealed from your team how far behind they are on their goals this quarter. As a result, your team members are looking forward to a promised day off that they are not entitled to and will not be getting. It's your job to tell them the bad news. How will you do it?

Form small groups of no more than four people. Discuss this situation and how you would handle it. Then, create a role-playing situation that illustrates your group's proposed approach. Be ready to do your role play in front of the class. Also, be prepared to provide the rest of the class with the specific steps that your group suggested be used in this situation.

Ethical Dilemma Exercise

What happens when a charismatic leader's relentless pursuit of a vision encourages extreme or even ethically questionable behavior? Consider the CEO of a company that hired an investigator to dive into other firms' dumpsters for information about their dealings with a major competitor. The same CEO's company has used precisely timed news releases as strategic weapons against particular rivals. And the same CEO's company once announced a hostile takeover bid for a direct competitor with the stated intention of not actively selling its products but acquiring its best customers and employees. This CEO, described by *The Wall Street Journal* as "a swashbuckling figure in Silicon Valley," is Larry Ellison of Oracle.

Ellison's charismatic leadership has built Oracle into a software powerhouse. Although it is locked in fierce competition with Microsoft and other giants, it doesn't ignore smaller rivals such as Siebel Systems and i2 Technologies. Oracle once issued a news release belittling i2's attempt at developing a certain type of software only minutes before i2's CEO was to meet with influential analysts. Such hardball tactics are hardly random or spontaneous. "We definitely sit down with a calendar and work out which week we're going to pick on Siebel and which week we're going to pick on i2," says Oracle's chief marketing officer. When Oracle pursued an unwelcome acquisition bid for rival PeopleSoft, the two CEOs traded barbed quotes for weeks as the companies battled in courtrooms and in the media. PeopleSoft's CEO, a former Oracle executive, described the situation as "enormously bad behavior from a company that's had a history of it."[88]

Imagine that you are the CEO of i2 Technologies, which makes inventory and supply tracking systems that compete with Oracle's large-scale business software suites. In five minutes, you will be meeting with a roomful of financial analysts who make buy or sell recommendations to investors. Your goal is to showcase your company's accomplishments, outline your vision for its future, and encourage a positive recommendation so your stock price will go even higher. You just heard about Oracle's news release belittling your product in development—and you suspect the analysts also know about it. What will you do? Think about the different types of leadership as you consider this ethical challenge and decide which of the following options to choose—and why.

Option A: Demonstrate your confidence in your company's superiority by boldly predicting, at the end of the meeting, that your new product will be significantly better than Oracle's.

Option B: Enhance your credibility by mentioning the news release at the end of the meeting, offering a few facts to refute Oracle, and inviting the analysts to ask questions.

Option C: Have your public relations director draft a statement to the media quoting you as saying that, according to your sources, Oracle's product is barely "cobbled together."

Case Application

Dale Earnhardt, Inc.

Stock car racing is one of the fastest-growing spectator sports in the United States and attracts fans from all different demographics. One of the most popular NASCAR (National Association for Stock Car Auto Racing) drivers was the late Dale Earnhardt, who died in an accident at the Daytona International racetrack on February 18, 2001. After his death, there were questions about the future of his racing empire, Dale Earnhardt, Inc. (DEI), an organization with annual revenues of over $20 million. However, Earnhardt's widow, Teresa, was determined not to let anything happen to the organization Dale had worked so hard to build. She went from a behind-the-scenes negotiator for Dale Earnhardt merchandising to the CEO of a multimillion-dollar organization with four race teams and an assortment of other business ventures. And in so doing, she had to take on a leader's role.

Teresa Earnhardt isn't a flashy person and doesn't enjoy being the center of attention. She tends to be

Teresa Earnhardt, CEO of Dale Earnhardt Enterprises, with Dale Earnhardt Jr.

more emotionally guarded by nature and she's not comfortable with having to engage in small talk. She says, "I'm not an entertainer. However, I'll do what I need to do." She prefers staying in the background. For instance, on race weekends, while other NASCAR owners make the rounds of the garage area, Teresa negotiates business deals, reads through contracts, and deals with employee issues. She approaches decisions differently from her late husband, as well. While Dale was more adamant, spontaneous, and headstrong—after all, his racing nickname was "The Intimidator"—Teresa makes more calculated decisions. She uses her quiet demeanor and strong determination and character to make DEI even more successful.

DEI's female CEO may be quiet and subdued, but she's no pushover. Soon after assuming control of the company's business decisions, Teresa eliminated some excessive corporate expenses, one of which was Dale's helicopter, a luxury she felt was no longer necessary. Michael Waltrip, one of the drivers for DEI, says, "When it's the gloomiest and the darkest and other people say there's no way, that's when she really shines. She comes in with her style and takes control and fixes things." At the end of the 2002 Winston Cup season after finishing eleventh and fourteenth in the point totals standings, several high-ranking company executives were in a room discussing the pluses and minuses of the season when Teresa said, "How do I tell you guys you did a good job but your results stink?" It was a "subtle reminder that the season wasn't up to the standards she and Dale were used to."

Teresa's leadership style has had to evolve to meet the demands of running a successful business in an industry that's very much male dominated. NASCAR president Mike Helton has talked to her about becoming more visible—something that he thinks is important for her team *and* for the sport in which there are few women in positions of power. Teresa recognizes that there are times when, as the organization's CEO, she needs to be out in front as the company's spokesperson. For instance, in January 2003, Teresa helped Dale Earnhardt Jr., unveil the logo for the shop of his new Busch series team. And she continues her work behind the scenes, as well. Teresa helped sign her other well-known driver, Michael Waltrip, and his primary sponsor, NAPA Auto Parts, to a new contract. So Teresa does what needs to be done. She's using her skills and strengths and working on her weaknesses to be the type of leader that will help her company survive and thrive in the rough-and-tumble racing business.

DISCUSSION QUESTIONS

1. Describe Teresa Earnhardt's leadership style. What do you think the advantages and drawbacks of her style might be?

2. Do you think it's easy for a leader to change his or her preferred style? Explain. What are the implications for leadership training?

3. What challenges does a leader who's replacing a well-known leader of any organization face? How did Teresa Earnhardt deal with these challenges?

4. How might the fact that stock car racing is a male-dominated business affect Teresa Earnhardt's approach to leading her company?

Sources: C. Jenkins, "Teresa Earnhardt Keeps Team on Track," *USA Today*, June 23, 2003 (*www.usatoday.com*); D. Newton, "Teresa Earnhardt: Driving Force Behind a Racing Empire," *The State*, March 18, 2003 (*www.charlotte.com*); and Owner's Profile on NASCAR Web site (*www.nascar.com*).

Part 5

You're the Manager: Putting Ethics into Action

As a manager, you'll often face decisions involving ethical questions. How can you learn to identify the ethical dilemma, keep stakeholders in mind, think through the alternatives, and foresee the consequences of your decisions? This unique interactive feature, positioned at the end of Parts Two, Three, Four, Five, and Six, casts you in the role of a manager dealing with hypothetical yet realistic ethical issues. To start, read the preview paragraph below. Then log on to **www.prenhall.com/robbins** *and go to the R.O.L.L.S. Web site to consider the decisions you would make in the role of manager.*

Avon Products relies on information technology to support a global army of sales representatives selling face powder, fragrances, and hundreds of other personal-care products. The goal of keeping every system running smoothly at all times puts intense pressure on technology managers and employees, however. What happens when an important project falls behind schedule—and the team handling the work can't agree on a solution? As an Avon manager, what could you do to introduce conflict in an ethical way and get the project moving again? Log onto **www.prenhall.com/robbins** to put ethics into action!

Passport

Scenario 1

Robert Mathis grew up just outside of Detroit and had always been in love with cars. So it wasn't surprising that he studied automotive engineering in college and went to work for Chrysler Corporation upon graduation.

Robert spent 17 years working in product development for Chrysler in the Detroit area. Then, in 2002, he was offered a promotion to become a product manager for his firm's parent, DaimlerChrysler, in Germany. He accepted the position. Following a three-month intense Berlitz course in German, Robert, his wife, and two teenage children took off for Stuttgart.

Robert was assigned to direct a new product team. None of the 10 people assigned to his team had worked with each other before. Three were from the United Kingdom, one was from South Africa, and the rest were Germans. All were a bit suspicious of their new American boss. Within a month of starting his new job, Robert realized he had problems. Team members weren't working well together. They seemed reluctant to share information and were looking out more for themselves than for the team. The German members seemed particularly uncomfortable working with Robert. One, in fact, openly said, "You're a fish out of water. You can't possibly understand the way we think and work here in Germany." And his South African team member complained to Robert that he felt isolated from the group. He said he was unhappy and thinking about asking for a transfer to another department. If you were Robert, what would you do?

To answer these questions, you'll have to do some research on the countries. **Go to www.prenhall.com/robbins, the R.O.L.L.S. Web site, and click on Passport.** *When the map appears, click on the countries you need to research. You'll find background information on the country and general information about the country's economy, population, and workforce. In addition, you'll find specific information on the country's culture and the unique qualities associated with doing business there.*

Scenario 2

Mary Chang grew up in Hong Kong. She got her undergraduate degree from the Hong Kong University of Science and Technology and her M.B.A. from UCLA. Upon graduation, she became a technology consultant with a consulting firm in Singapore.

Mary travels a lot in her job. In the past year, she's spent most of her time in Hong Kong and China working with several high tech firms. She's helped them set up quality improvement programs and also helped one firm restructure its employee benefits program. Mary's immediate boss is Japanese. Most of her clients are Chinese. In most cases, she finds herself working as part of a consulting team with colleagues from China, Japan, Singapore, Taiwan, Korea, and Thailand.

Multicultural consulting teams provide challenges for their members. There are communication problems, issues about trust, and concerns about sharing authority and responsibility. Mary, for instance, prefers that her boss leave her alone and let her make independent decisions. On the other hand, her colleagues from Japan—including her boss—prefer to do tasks in small groups and share responsibility. What specific problems do you think Mary will face in working with colleagues and clients? What advice would you give her to help her be more effective in her job?

To answer these questions, you'll have to do some research on the countries. **Go to www.prenhall.com/robbins, the R.O.L.L.S. Web site, and click on Passport.** *When the map appears, click on the countries you need to research. You'll find background information on the country and general information about the country's economy, population, and workforce. In addition, you'll find specific information on the country's culture and the unique qualities associated with doing business there.*

Managing Entrepreneurial Ventures

Leading Issues

In Boise, Idaho, where industry giants like Micron Technology, Inc., and Hewlett-Packard compete for scarce talented employees, Pro-Team Inc., a manufacturer of specialty vacuum cleaners for industrial settings, has an impressive annual turnover rate below 5 percent. How has it achieved such success? President Larry R. Shideler recognizes the importance of leading and focusing the same level of excellence on the venture's human resources as it does on product excellence.[1]

Leading is an important function of entrepreneurs. As an entrepreneurial venture grows and people are brought on board, an entrepreneur takes on a new role—that of a leader. In this section, we want to look at what's involved with the leading function. First, we're going to look at the unique personality characteristics of entrepreneurs. Then we're going to discuss the important role that entrepreneurs play in motivating employees through empowerment and leading the venture and employee teams.

Personality Characteristics of Entrepreneurs

Think of someone you know who is an entrepreneur. Maybe it's someone you know personally or maybe it's someone like Bill Gates of Microsoft, Dineh Mohajer of Hard Candy, or Larry Ellison of Sun Microsystems. How would you describe this person's personality? One of the most researched areas of entrepreneurship has been the search to determine what, if any, psychological characteristics entrepreneurs have in common; what types of personality traits entrepreneurs have that might distinguish them from nonentrepreneurs; and what traits entrepreneurs have that might make it possible to predict who will be a successful entrepreneur.

Is there a classic "entrepreneurial personality"? Although trying to pinpoint specific personality characteristics that all entrepreneurs share has the same problem as the trait theories of leadership—that is, being able to identify specific personality traits that *all* entrepreneurs share—this hasn't stopped entrepreneurship researchers from listing common traits.[2] For instance, one list of personality characteristics included the following: high level of motivation, abundance of self-confidence, ability to be involved for the long term, high energy level, persistent problem solver, high degree of initiative, ability to set goals, and moderate risk-taker.[3] Another list of characteristics of "successful" entrepreneurs included high energy level, great persistence, resourcefulness, the desire and ability to be self-directed, and relatively high need for autonomy. Another development in defining entrepreneurial personality characteristics was the proposed use of a proactive personality scale to predict an individual's likelihood of pursuing entrepreneurial ventures. What is a **proactive personality**? Very simply, it describes those individuals who are more prone to take actions to influence their environment—that is, they're more proactive. Obviously, an entrepreneur is likely to exhibit proactivity as he or she searches for opportunities and acts to take advantage of those opportunities.[4] Various items on the proactive personality scale were found to be good indicators of a person's likelihood of becoming an entrepreneur, including gender, education, having an entrepreneurial parent, and possessing a proactive personality. In addition, studies have shown that entrepreneurs have greater risk propensity than do managers.[5] However, this propensity is moderated by the entrepreneur's primary goal. Risk propensity is greater for entrepreneurs whose primary goal is growth than for those whose focus is on producing family income.

Another perspective on entrepreneurial personality has been suggested—that of Type E personalities. *Is* there a Type E (entrepreneurial) personality? A recent study suggests that entrepreneurs tend to share certain characteristics that set them apart from their corporate counterparts.[6] Exhibit P5–1 describes those characteristics.

Exhibit P5–1

Type E's

1. Aggressively pursues goals; pushes both self and others.
2. Seeks autonomy, independence, and freedom from boundaries; very individualistic.
3. Sends consistent messages; very focused and doesn't deviate from purpose.
4. Acts quickly, often without deliberating.
5. Keeps distance and maintains objectivity; expects others to be self-sufficient and and tough-minded.
6. Pursues simple, practical solutions; able to cut through complexity and find the essential and important issues.
7. Is willing to take risks, comfortable with uncertainty.
8. Exhibits clear opinions and values; makes quick judgments; often finds fault and has high expectations.
9. Impatient regarding results and with others; "just do it" mentality.
10. Positive, upbeat, optimistic; communicates confidence.

Source: Based on J. Chun, "Type E Personality," *Entrepreneur*, January 1997, p. 10.

Motivating Employees Through Empowerment

At Sapient Corporation (creators of Internet and software systems for e-commerce and automating back-office tasks such as billing and inventory), co-founders Jerry Greenberg and J. Stuart Moore recognized that employee motivation was vitally important to their company's ultimate success.[7] They designed their organization so that individual employees are part of an industry-specific team that works on an entire project rather than on one small piece of it. Their rationale was that people often feel frustrated when they're doing a small part of a job and never get to see the whole job from start to finish. They figured people would be more productive if they got the opportunity to participate in all phases of a project.

When you're motivated to do something, don't you find yourself energized and willing to work hard at doing whatever it is you're excited about? Wouldn't it be great if all of a venture's employees were energized, excited, and willing to work hard at their jobs? Having motivated employees is an important goal for any entrepreneur, and employee empowerment is an important motivational tool entrepreneurs can use.

Although it's not easy for entrepreneurs to do, employee empowerment—giving employees the power to make decisions and take actions on their own—is an important motivational approach. Why? Because successful entrepreneurial ventures must be quick and nimble, ready to pursue opportunities and go off in new directions. Empowered employees can provide that flexibility and speed. When employees are empowered, they often display stronger work motivation, better work quality, higher job satisfaction, and lower turnover. For example, employees at Butler International, Inc., a technology consulting services firm based in Montvale, New Jersey, work at client locations. Ed Kopko, president and CEO, recognized that employees had to be empowered to do their jobs if they were going to be successful.[8] Another entrepreneurial venture that has found employee empowerment to be a strong motivational approach is Stryker Instruments in Kalamazoo, Michigan, a division of Stryker Corporation. Each of the company's production units is responsible for its operating budget, cost reduction goals, customer service levels, inventory management, training, production planning and forecasting, purchasing, human resource management, safety, and problem solving. In addition, unit members work closely with marketing, sales, and R&D during new-product introductions and continuous improvement projects. Says one team supervisor, "Stryker lets me do what I do best and rewards me for that privilege."[9]

Empowerment is a philosophical concept that entrepreneurs have to "buy into." This doesn't come easily. In fact, it's hard for many entrepreneurs to do. Their lives are tied up in their ventures. They've built them from the ground up. But continuing to grow the entrepreneurial venture is eventually going to require handing over more responsibilities to employees. How can entrepreneurs empower employees? For many entrepreneurs, it's a gradual process.

They can begin by using participative decision making in which employees provide input into decisions. Although getting employees to participate in decisions isn't quite taking the full plunge into employee empowerment, it, at least, is a way to begin tapping into the collective array of employees' talents, skills, knowledge, and abilities.

Another way to empower employees is through delegation—the process of assigning certain decisions or specific job duties to employees. (See the Skills Module on Delegating in the back of this book to find out how to empower effectively.) By delegating decisions and duties, the entrepreneur is turning over the responsibility for carrying them out.

When an entrepreneur is finally comfortable with the idea of employee empowerment, fully empowering employees means redesigning their jobs so they have discretion over the way they do their work. It's allowing employees to do their work effectively and efficiently by using their creativity, imagination, knowledge, and skills.

If an entrepreneur implements employee empowerment properly—that is, with complete and total commitment to the program and with appropriate employee training—results can be impressive for the entrepreneurial venture and for the empowered employees. The business can enjoy significant productivity gains, quality improvements, more satisfied customers, increased employee motivation, and improved morale. Employees can enjoy the opportunities to do a greater variety of work that is more interesting and challenging. In addition, employees are encouraged to take the initiative in identifying and solving problems and doing their work. For example, at Mine Safety Appliances Company in Pittsburgh, Pennsylvania, employees are empowered to change their work processes in order to meet the organization's challenging quality improvement goals. Getting to this point took an initial 40 hours of classroom instruction per employee in areas such as engineering drawing, statistical process control, quality certifications, and specific work instruction. However, the company's commitment to an empowered workforce has resulted in profitability increasing 57 percent over the last four years and 95 percent of the company's employees achieving multi-skill certifications.[10]

The Entrepreneur as Leader

The last topic we want to discuss in this module is the role of the entrepreneur as a leader. In this role, the entrepreneur has certain responsibilities in leading the venture and in leading employee work teams.

Leading the Venture Today's successful entrepreneur must be like the leader of a jazz ensemble that is known for its improvisation, innovation, and creativity. Max DePree, former head of Herman Miller, Inc., a leading office furniture manufacturer known for its innovative leadership approaches, said it best in his book *Leadership Jazz*:

> Jazz band leaders must choose the music, find the right musicians, and perform—in public. But the effect of the performance depends on so many things—the environment, the volunteers playing in the band, the need for everybody to perform as individuals and as a group, the absolute dependence of the leader on the members of the band, the need for the followers to play well. . . . The leader of the jazz band has the beautiful opportunity to draw the best out of the other musicians. We have much to learn from jazz band leaders, for jazz, like leadership, combines the unpredictability of the future with the gifts of individuals.[11]

The way an entrepreneur leads the venture should be much like the jazz leader—drawing the best out of other individuals despite the unpredictability of the situation. And one way that an entrepreneur does this is through the vision he or she creates for the organization. In fact, the driving force through the early stages of the entrepreneurial venture is often the visionary leadership of the entrepreneur. The entrepreneur's ability to articulate a coherent, inspiring, and attractive vision of the future is a key test of his or her leadership. But if an entrepreneur can do this, the results can be worthwhile. A study contrasting visionary and nonvisionary companies showed that visionary companies outperformed the nonvisionary ones by six times on standard financial criteria, and their stocks outperformed the general market by 15 times.[12]

Leading Employee Work Teams As we know from Chapter 15, many organizations, entrepreneurial and otherwise, are using employee work teams to perform organizational tasks, create new ideas, and resolve problems.

Employee work teams tend to be popular in entrepreneurial ventures. An *Industry Week* Census of Manufacturers showed that nearly 68 percent of survey respondents used teams to varying degrees.[13] The three most common ones respondents said they used (similar to those we discussed in Chapter 15) included empowered teams (teams that have the authority to plan and implement process improvements), self-directed teams (teams that are nearly autonomous and responsible for many managerial activities), and cross-functional teams (teams that include a hybrid grouping of individuals who are experts in various specialties and who work together on various tasks.)

These entrepreneurs also said that developing and using teams is necessary because technology and market demands are forcing them to make their products faster, cheaper, and better. And tapping into the collective wisdom of the venture's employees and empowering them to make decisions just may be one of the best ways to adapt to change. In addition, a team culture can improve the overall workplace environment and morale.

For team efforts to work, however, entrepreneurs must shift from the traditional command-and-control style to a coach-and-collaboration style (look back at the discussion on team leadership in Chapter 17). They must recognize that individual employees can understand the business and can innovate just as effectively as they can. For example, at Marque, Inc., of Goshen, Indiana, CEO Scott Jessup recognized that he wasn't the smartest guy in the company regarding production problems, but he was smart enough to recognize that if his company wanted to expand its market share in manufacturing medical-emergency-squad vehicles, new levels of productivity needed to be reached. He formed a cross-functional team—bringing together people from production, quality assurance, and fabrication—that could spot production bottlenecks and other problems and then gave the team the authority to resolve the constraints.[14]

● ● ● ● Learning Summary

After reading and studying this material, you should be able to:

- Explain what personality research shows about entrepreneurs.
- Explain how the concept of a proactive personality relates to entrepreneurs.

- Describe the characteristics of a Type E personality.
- Discuss how entrepreneurs can empower employees.
- Describe the analogy of an entrepreneur to the leader of a jazz ensemble.
- Explain how entrepreneurs can be effective at leading employee work teams.

Part SIX
Controlling

Chapter

18

Foundations of Control

"Haier and Higher" is the tag line on the Haier Group's Web site—a tag line that epitomizes the ambitious goals of Zhang Ruimin (pictured), CEO and director of the Haier Group.[1] While the United States has General Electric, Germany has Mercedes-Benz, and Japan has Sony, fast-growing China has yet to produce a comparable global competitor. However, with more than $7 billion in annual sales and 13 overseas factories in locations such as Italy, Pakistan, and the United States, Zhang is hoping to change that with the Haier Group. His goals for Haier are to gain worldwide recognition, to build the company into China's first global brand, and to be listed on the *Fortune* Global 500.

The Haier Group started out in 1984 as the Qingdao Refrigerator Factory. When it was founded, the company had only one product and 800 workers. Today, 30,000 employees make over 13,000 products in 86 different categories. Haier is the number-one domestic electrical appliance producer in China and ranks fifth in global appliance sales behind General Electric, Whirlpool, Electrolux, and Siemens. If Haier does develop into a genuine global player, much of the credit will go to Zhang.

Zhang is considered by many to be China's leading corporate executive. In November 2002, he became the first businessman ever elected to the Chinese Communist Party's Central Committee, a major political triumph for the 54-year-old with an M.B.A. from China's University of Science & Technology. He has been described as "a very charismatic business leader and not just in the Chinese perspective. He's emerging as a global business leader." One of the tools Zhang plans to use to build Haier's global brand is benchmarking. He views this as a means to ensure that his products match up against the best of his competitor's products.

Put yourself in Zhang's position. How could he implement benchmarking in his organization in the pursuit of his strategy to create a global brand?

·················**What** would *you* do **?**

n today's competitive global marketplace, managers want their organizations to achieve high levels of performance, and one way they can do that is by searching out the best practices successful organizations are using. By comparing themselves against the best, managers look for specific performance gaps and areas for improvement—areas where better controls over the work being done are needed.

Zhang Ruimin understands the importance of management controls. No matter how thorough the planning, a decision still may be poorly implemented without a satisfactory control system in place. This chapter describes controls and how to create a well-designed organizational control system.

WHAT IS CONTROL?

Both the viewing public and NASA officials were devastated by the tragic *Columbia* shuttle disaster in February 2003. Investigations of the tragedy suggest that organizational safety controls may not have been as thorough as they should have been.[2] When problems were spotted, managers may have been too quick to dismiss them as non-life-threatening, and in this situation that choice may have led to disastrous consequences. Although most managers won't face such tragic consequences if they ignore signs that something may be wrong, the situation does point out the importance of control.

What is **control**? It's the process of monitoring activities to ensure that they are being accomplished as planned, and correcting any significant deviations. All managers should be involved in the control function even if their units are performing as planned. (■□■ Go to the Web and check out Q & A 18.1.) Managers can't really know whether their units are performing properly until they've evaluated what activities have been done and have compared the actual performance with the desired standard.[3] An effective control system ensures that activities are completed in ways that lead to the attainment of the organization's goals. The criterion that determines the effectiveness of a control system is how well it facilitates goal achievement. The more it helps managers achieve their organization's goals, the better the control system.[4]

Ideally, every organization would like to efficiently and effectively reach its goals. Does this mean that the control systems organizations use are identical? In other words, would SAS Institute, Inc., Matsushita, and BP have the same types of control systems? Probably not. Three different approaches to designing control systems have been identified: market, bureaucratic, and clan.[5] (See Exhibit 18–1.)

Market control is an approach to control that emphasizes the use of external market mechanisms, such as price competition and relative market share, to establish the standards used in the control system. Using market control, a company's divisions often are turned into profit centers and evaluated by the percentage of total corporate

---

●●● control
The process of monitoring activities to ensure that they are being accomplished as planned and of correcting any significant deviations.

■ Q & A
Whenever you see this green square, go to the R.O.L.L.S. Web site (*www.prenhall.com/robbins*) to the Q & A, your 24/7 educational assistant. These video clips and written material presented by your authors address questions that we have found students frequently ask.

●●● market control
An approach to control that emphasizes the use of external market mechanisms to establish the standards used in the control system.

Exhibit 18–1

Characteristics of Three Approaches to Control Systems

Type of Control	Characteristics
Market	Uses external market mechanisms, such as price competition and relative market share, to establish standards used in system. Typically used by organizations whose products or services are clearly specified and distinct and that face considerable marketplace competition.
Bureaucratic	Emphasizes organizational authority. Relies on administrative and hierarchical mechanisms, such as rules, regulations, procedures, policies, standardization of activities, well-defined job descriptions, and budgets to ensure that employees exhibit appropriate behaviors and meet performance standards.
Clan	Regulates employee behavior by the shared values, norms, traditions, rituals, beliefs, and other aspects of the organization's culture. Often used by organizations in which teams are common and technology is changing rapidly.

profits each contributes. For instance, at Matsushita, the various divisions (audiovisual and communication networks, components and devices, home appliances, and industrial equipment) are evaluated according to the profits each generates.

Another approach to a control system is **bureaucratic control**, which emphasizes organizational authority and relies on administrative rules, regulations, procedures, and policies. BP provides a good example of bureaucratic control. Although managers at BP's various divisions are allowed considerable autonomy and freedom to run their units as they see fit, they're expected to adhere closely to their budgets and stay within corporate guidelines.

Under **clan control**, employee behaviors are regulated by the shared values, norms, traditions, rituals, beliefs, and other aspects of the organization's culture. Whereas bureaucratic control is based on strict hierarchical mechanisms, clan control is dependent on the individual and the group (or clan) to identify appropriate and expected behaviors and performance measures. For instance, at SAS Institute, individuals are well aware of the expectations regarding appropriate work behavior and performance standards. The organizational culture—through the shared values, norms, and stories about the company's founder, Jim Goodnight—conveys to individual employees "what's important around here" and "what's not important." Rather than relying on prescribed administrative controls, SAS employees are guided and controlled by the clan's culture.

Most organizations don't rely totally on just one of these approaches to designing an appropriate control system. Instead, they choose to emphasize either bureaucratic or clan control, in addition to using some market control measures. The key is designing an appropriate control system that helps the organization efficiently and effectively reach its goals.

> ●●● **bureaucratic control**
> An approach to control that emphasizes organizational authority and relies on administrative rules, regulations, procedures, and policies.

> ●●● **clan control**
> An approach to control in which employee behavior is regulated by the shared values, norms, traditions, rituals, beliefs, and other aspects of the organization's culture.

WHY IS CONTROL IMPORTANT?

Why is control so important? Planning can be done, an organizational structure can be created to efficiently facilitate the achievement of goals, and employees can be motivated through effective leadership. (▮◼▮▮▮ Go to the Web and check out Q & A 18.2.) Still, there's no assurance that activities are going as planned and that the goals managers are seeking are, in fact, being attained. Control is important, therefore, because it's the final link in the management functions. It's the only way managers know whether organizational goals are being met and, if not, the reasons why. The value of the control function lies in its relation to planning, empowering employees, and protecting the workplace.

In Chapter 7, we described goals as the foundation of planning. Goals give specific direction to managers. However, just stating goals or having employees accept your goals is no guarantee that the necessary actions to accomplish those goals have been taken. As the old saying goes, "The best-laid plans often go awry." The effective manager needs to follow up to ensure that what others are supposed to do is, in fact, being done and that their goals are, in fact, being achieved. In reality, managing is an ongoing process, and controlling activities provides the critical link back to planning (Exhibit 18–2 on page 460). If managers didn't control, they'd have no way of knowing whether their goals and plans were on target and what future actions to take.

Another reason controlling is important is employee empowerment. Many managers are reluctant to empower their employees because they fear employees will do something wrong for which the manager would be held responsible. Thus, many managers are tempted to do things themselves and avoid empowering. This reluctance, however, can be reduced if managers develop an effective control system that provides information and feedback on employee performance.

The final reason that managers control is to protect the organization and the physical workplace.[6] Given today's environment with heightened security alerts, the possibility of terrorist attacks, and surprise financial scandals, managers must have

Exhibit 18–2

The Planning–Controlling Link

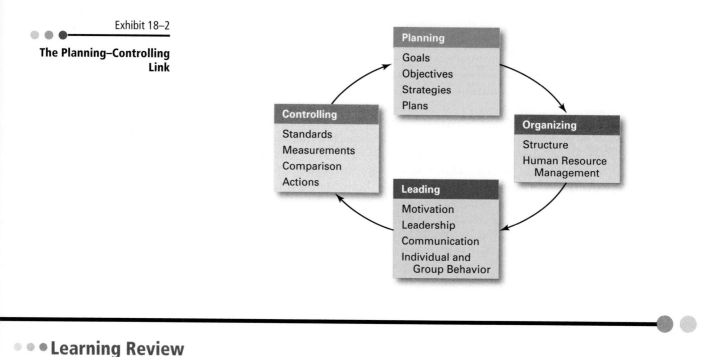

Learning Review

- Define control.
- Contrast the three approaches to designing control systems.
- Discuss the reasons control is important.
- Explain the planning–controlling link.

plans in place to protect the organization's employees, data, and infrastructure. As many organizations discovered in the aftermath of 9/11, those with comprehensive controls and back-up plans encountered minimal disruptions of their ongoing business operations.

THE CONTROL PROCESS

control process
A three-step process including measuring actual performance, comparing actual performance against a standard, and taking managerial action to correct deviations or inadequate standards.

The **control process** is a three-step process: measuring actual performance, comparing actual performance against a standard, and taking managerial action to correct deviations or inadequate standards. (See Exhibit 18–3.) The control process assumes that performance standards already exist. These standards are the specific goals created during the planning process against which performance progress is measured.

Exhibit 18–3

The Control Process

Measuring

To determine what actual performance is, a manager must acquire information about it. The first step in control, then, is measuring. Let's consider how we measure and what we measure.

How We Measure Four sources of information frequently used by managers to measure actual performance are personal observation, statistical reports, oral reports, and written reports. Exhibit 18–4 summarizes the advantages and drawbacks of each approach. (▉▉▉ Go to the Web and check out Q & A 18.3.) For most managers, using a combination of approaches increases both the number of input sources and the probability of getting reliable information.

What We Measure What we measure is probably more critical to the control process than how we measure. Why? (▉▉▉ Go to the Web and check out Q & A 18.4.) The selection of the wrong criteria can result in serious dysfunctional consequences. Besides, what we measure determines, to a great extent, what people in the organization will attempt to excel at.[7]

Some control criteria are applicable to any management situation. For instance, because all managers, by definition, coordinate the work of others, criteria such as employee satisfaction or turnover and absenteeism rates can be measured. Most managers also have budgets set in dollar costs for their area of responsibility. Keeping costs within budget is, therefore, a fairly common control measure. However, any comprehensive control system needs to recognize the diversity of activities that managers do. For instance, a production manager at a paper tablet manufacturer might use measures such as quantity of paper tablets produced per day and per labor-hour, scrap rate, or percent of rejects returned by customers. On the other hand, the manager of an administrative unit in a governmental agency might use number of document pages typed per day, number of client requests processed per hour, or average time required to process paperwork. Marketing managers often use measures such as percentage of market held, average dollar per sale, number of customer visits per salesperson, or number of customer impressions per advertising medium.

Most jobs and activities can be expressed in tangible and measurable terms. However, when a performance indicator can't be stated in quantifiable terms, managers should use subjective measures. Although subjective measures have significant limitations, they're better than having no standards at all and ignoring the control function. If an activity is important, the excuse that it's difficult to measure is unacceptable.

Exhibit 18–4

Common Sources of Information for Measuring Performance

	Advantages	Drawbacks
Personal Observations	• Get firsthand knowledge • Information isn't filtered • Intensive coverage of work activities	• Subject to personal biases • Time-consuming • Obtrusive
Statistical Reports	• Easy to visualize • Effective for showing relationships	• Provide limited information • Ignore subjective factors
Oral Reports	• Fast way to get information • Allow for verbal and nonverbal feedback	• Information is filtered • Information can't be documented
Written Reports	• Comprehensive • Formal • Easy to file and retrieve	• Take more time to prepare

Comparing

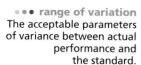

● ● ● **range of variation**
The acceptable parameters
of variance between actual
performance and
the standard.

The comparing step determines the degree of variation between actual performance and the standard. Although some variation in performance can be expected in all activities, it's critical to determine the acceptable **range of variation**. (See Exhibit 18–5.) Deviations that exceed this range become significant and need the manager's attention. In the comparison stage, managers are particularly concerned with the size and direction of the variation. An example can help make this concept clearer.

Chris Tanner is sales manager for Eastern States, a distributor of imported beers in several states on the U.S. East Coast. Chris prepares a report during the first week of each month that describes sales for the previous month, classified by brand name. Exhibit 18–6 displays both the sales goal (standard) and actual sales figures for the month of July.

Should Chris be concerned about July's sales performance? Sales were a bit higher than originally targeted, but does that mean there were no significant deviations? Even though overall performance was generally quite favorable, several brands might need to be examined more closely by Chris. However, the number of brands that deserve attention depends on what Chris believes to be *significant*. How much variation should Chris allow before corrective action is taken?

The deviation on several brands (Molson, Victoria Bitter, and Amstel Light) is very small and doesn't need special attention. On the other hand, are the shortages for Corona and Dos Equis brands significant? That's a judgment Chris must make. Heineken sales were 15 percent below Chris's goal. This deviation is significant and needs attention. Chris should look for a cause. In this instance, Chris attributes the decrease to aggressive advertising and promotion programs by the big domestic producers, Anheuser-Busch and Miller. Because Heineken is his company's number-one selling import, it's most vulnerable to the promotion clout of the big domestic producers. If the decline in sales of Heineken is more than a temporary slump (that is, if it happens again next month), then Chris will need to cut back on inventory stock.

An error in understating sales can be as troublesome as an overstatement. For instance, is the surprising popularity of Tecate (up 68 percent) a one-month aberration, or is this brand becoming more popular with customers? If the brand is increasing in popularity, Chris will want to order more product to meet customer demand, so as not to run short and risk losing customers. Again, Chris will have to interpret the information and make a decision. Our Eastern States' example illustrates that both overvariance and undervariance in any comparison of measures may require managerial attention. (■□■■■■ Go to the Web and check out Q & A 18.5.)

Exhibit 18–5

● ● ●━━━

**Defining the Acceptable
Range of Variation**

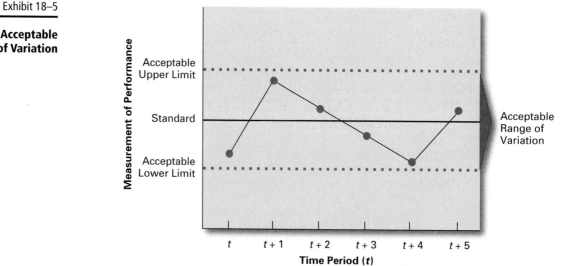

Exhibit 18–6

Sales Performance Figures for July, Eastern States Distributors

Brand	Standard	(hundreds of cases) Actual	Over (Under)
Heineken	1,075	913	(162)
Molson	630	634	4
Irish Amber	800	912	112
Victoria Bitter	620	622	2
Labatt's	540	672	132
Corona	160	140	(20)
Amstel Light	225	220	(5)
Dos Equis	80	65	(15)
Tecate	170	286	116
Total cases	4,300	4,464	164

Taking Managerial Action

immediate corrective action
Corrective action that corrects problems at once to get performance back on track.

basic corrective action
Corrective action that looks at how and why performance deviated and then proceeds to correct the source of deviation.

The third and final step in the control process is taking managerial action. Managers can choose among three possible courses of action: They can do nothing; they can correct the actual performance; or they can revise the standards. Because "doing nothing" is fairly self-explanatory, let's look more closely at the other two.

Correct Actual Performance If the source of the performance variation is unsatisfactory work, the manager will want to take corrective action. Examples of such corrective action might include changing strategy, structure, compensation practices, or training programs; redesigning jobs; or firing employees. (▭▭▭ Check out Passport Scenario 1 on p. 510.)

A manager who decides to correct actual performance has to make another decision: Should immediate or basic corrective action be taken? **Immediate corrective action** corrects problems at once to get performance back on track. **Basic corrective action** looks at how and why performance has deviated and then proceeds to correct the source of deviation. (▭▭▭ Go to the Web and check out Q & A 18.6.) It's not unusual for managers to rationalize that they don't have the time to take basic corrective action and therefore must be content to perpetually "put out fires" with immediate corrective action. Effective managers, however, analyze deviations and, when the benefits justify it, take the time to pinpoint and correct the causes of variance.

To return to our Eastern States example, taking immediate corrective action on the negative variance for Heineken, Chris might contact the company's retailers and have them immediately drop the price on Heineken by 5 percent. However, taking basic corrective action would involve more in-depth analysis by Chris. After assessing how and why sales deviated, Chris might choose to increase in-store promotional efforts, increase the advertising budget for this brand, or reduce future purchases from the breweries. The action Chris takes will depend on the assessment of each brand's potential profitability.

Revise the Standard It's possible that the variance was a result of an unrealistic standard; that is, the goal may have been too high or too low. In such instances, it's the standard that needs corrective attention, not the performance. In our example, Chris might need to raise the sales goal (standard) for Tecate to reflect its growing popularity.

Corrective action can take many forms. On the selling floor of Home Depot stores, where one contractor spent 20 minutes waiting for a Home Depot forklift operator to arrive so he could load some purchased drywall, the need to improve customer service led to changes in the composition of the workforce. CEO Bob Nardelli realized he had allowed stores to hire too many part-time workers, whose commitment to the job and knowledge about the do-it-yourself business sometimes lagged behind those of full-timers. So he scaled back from a 50-50 mix to a new balance of 40 percent part-time and 60 percent full-time workers and says customer service has since improved.

Exhibit 18–7

**Managerial Decisions in
the Control Process**

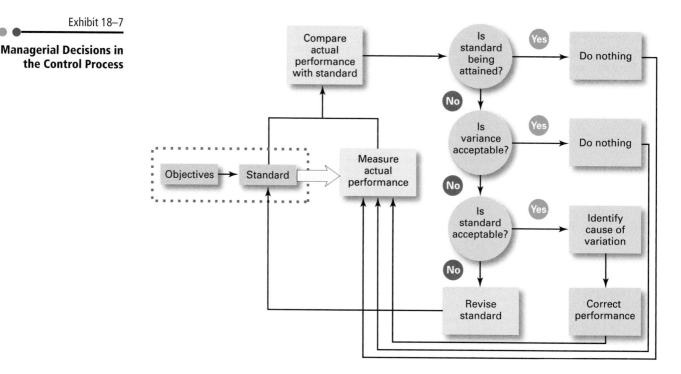

The more troublesome problem is revising a performance standard downward. If an employee, work team, or work unit falls significantly short of reaching its goal, their natural response is to shift the blame for the variance to the goal. For instance, students who make a low grade on a test often attack the grade cutoff standards as too high. Rather than accept the fact that their performance was inadequate, students argue that the standards are unreasonable. Similarly, salespeople who fail to meet their monthly quota may attribute the failure to an unrealistic quota. It may be true that when standards are too high, it can result in a significant variation and may even contribute to demotivating those employees being measured. But keep in mind that if employees or managers don't meet the standard, the first thing they're likely to attack is the standard. If you believe that the standard is realistic, fair, and achievable, hold your ground. Explain your position, reaffirm to the employee, team, or unit that you expect future performance to improve, and then take the necessary corrective action to turn that expectation into reality.

Summary of Managerial Decisions

Exhibit 18–7 summarizes the manager's decisions in the control process. (▮ ◻ ▮▮▮▮ Go to the Web and check out Q & A 18.7.) The standards evolve out of goals which are developed during the planning process. These goals then provide the basis for the control process which is essentially a continuous flow between measuring, comparing, and taking managerial action. Depending on the results of comparing, a manager's decisions about what course of action to take might be to do nothing, revise the standard, or correct the performance.

● ● ● Learning Review

- Describe the three steps in the control process.
- Explain why what is measured is more critical than how it's measured.

- Explain the three courses of action managers can take in controlling.

CONTROLLING FOR ORGANIZATIONAL PERFORMANCE

Available seat miles. Seat-miles flown. Revenue per passenger-miles. Passenger load factors. These are just a few of the important performance indicators that executives in the intensely competitive airline industry measure. Then, of course, there's the Triple Crown—not the famous one awarded for winning three horse races—but the one awarded by the U.S. Department of Transportation's Air Travel Consumer Report for outstanding performance accomplishments in three areas: customer service, on-time performance, and baggage handling. To make good decisions, managers in the airline industry want and need this type of information so they can manage organizational performance. Managers in all types of businesses are responsible for managing organizational performance.

What Is Organizational Performance?

●●● **performance**
The end result of an activity.

When you hear the word *performance* what do you think of? A summer evening concert given by a local community orchestra? An Olympic athlete striving for the finish line in a close race? A Southwest Airlines ramp agent in Tulsa, Oklahoma, loading passengers as quickly and efficiently as possible in order to meet the company's 20-minute gate turnaround goal? A Web site designer at Prentice Hall Publishers creating an online learning site that professors and students will find valuable? **Performance** is all of these. It's the end result of an activity. And whether that activity is hours of intense practice before a concert or race or whether it's carrying out job responsibilities as efficiently and effectively as possible, performance is what results from that activity.

●●● **organizational performance**
The accumulated end results of all the organization's work processes and activities.

Managers are concerned with **organizational performance**—the accumulated end results of all the organization's work processes and activities. It's a complex but important concept. And managers need to understand the factors that contribute to high organizational performance. After all, they don't want (or intend) to manage their way to mediocre performance. They *want* their organizations, work units, or work groups to achieve high levels of performance, no matter what mission, strategies, or goals are being pursued. (▇▇▇▇ Go to the Web and check out Q & A 18.8.)

Measures of Organizational Performance

Theo Epstein, general manager of the Boston Red Sox, is using some unusual statistics to evaluate his baseball players' performance rather than the century-old standards like batting average, home runs, and runs batted in. These "new" performance measures include on-base percentage, pitches per plate appearance, at-bats per home run, and on-base plus slugging percentage.[8] Also, by using these statistics to predict future performance, Epstein has been able to identify some potential star players in both the major and minor leagues and sign them for a fraction of the cost of a big name player. His management team is already working on new statistics that will measure the impact of a player's defensive skills. Epstein has identified the performance measures that are most important to his organizational decisions.

Like Epstein, all managers must know what organizational performance measures will give them the information they need. The most frequently used organizational performance measures include organizational productivity, organizational effectiveness, and industry rankings.

●●● **productivity**
The overall output of goods or services produced divided by the inputs needed to generate that output.

Organizational Productivity **Productivity** is the overall output of goods or services produced divided by the inputs needed to generate that output. Organizations strive to be productive. They want the most goods and services produced using the least amount of inputs. Output is measured by the sales revenue an organization receives when those goods and services are sold (selling price × number sold). Input is measured by the costs of acquiring and transforming the organizational resources into the outputs.

Fred Eintracht is director of organizational development for Lennox Industries, Inc., which manufactures heating and air conditioning equipment in Texas. His firm measures intangibles like communication, leadership, and employee involvement with a "vitality metric." Says Eintracht, "Making the metrics more visible to everyone is as important as having the metric itself," and he believes that such visibility also motivates employees to reach their performance goals.

It's management's job to increase this ratio. The easiest way to do this, of course, would be to raise the selling price of the outputs, but today's competitive environment makes this a risky choice which may, in fact, decrease the total output sold. The only other viable option for increasing productivity, then, is to decrease the input part of ratio—that is, the organization's expenses. Doing this means being more efficient in performing the organization's work activities. So, organizational productivity becomes a measure of how efficiently employees do their work. (■□▨▨ Go to the Web and check out Q & A 18.9)

Organizational Effectiveness In Chapter 1, we defined managerial effectiveness as goal attainment. Can the same interpretation apply to organizational effectiveness? Yes, it can. **Organizational effectiveness** is a measure of how appropriate organizational goals are and how well an organization is achieving those goals. It's a common performance measure used by managers.

Other descriptions of organizational effectiveness have been suggested by management researchers.[9] For instance, the systems resource model of organizational effectiveness proposes that effectiveness is measured by the organization's ability to exploit its environment in acquiring scarce and valued resources. The process model emphasizes the transformation processes of the organization and how well the organization converts inputs into desired outputs. And the multiple constituencies model says that several different effectiveness measures should be used, reflecting the different criteria of the organization's constituencies. For example, customers, advocacy groups, suppliers, and security analysts each would have their own measures of how well the organization was performing. Although each of these different effectiveness models may have merit in measuring certain aspects of organizational effectiveness, the bottom line for managers continues to be how

●●● **organizational effectiveness**
A measure of how appropriate organizational goals are and how well an organization is achieving those goals.

MANAGING WORKFORCE DIVERSITY

Diversity Success Stories

U.S. companies are making progress in their diversity programs. Although many still have a long way to go, some companies are doing their best to make employees of all races into full and active participants in their businesses.[10] Every year, *Fortune* identifies America's 50 Best Companies for Minorities. Each of the companies on this list has made a strong commitment to diversity at every organizational level and in every aspect—from new hires to suppliers, and even to the charitable causes supported. Who are some of these diversity champions and what are they doing? Let's look at a few examples.

McDonald's Corporation is number one on the list. More than 20 percent of the company's officers and 24

percent of middle managers are members of minorities. The company also has the largest number of minority franchises in the quick-service industry.

Number 12 on the list is Wyndham International, whose CEO created an external diversity advisory board and a diversity officer position. The company's career-management program was changed to focus on helping minorities advance.

Finally, PepsiCo is number nine on the list for its community partnerships. For instance, with money it raised from special Pepsi promotions, the Greater Grace Chapel in Detroit was able to purchase a van which it uses to haul elderly citizens for shopping and banking trips, medical and social appointments, and other needs.

Exhibit 18–8

Popular Industry and Company Rankings

Fortune (www.fortune.com)	*Industry Week* (www.industryweek.com)
100 Best Companies to Work For	World's Best Plants
Fortune 1000	Technology and Innovation Awards of the Year
Fortune 1000 Top Performing Companies	Census of Manufacturers
Global 500	25 Fastest Growing Companies
America's Most Admired Companies	*Industry Week* 1000
World's Most Admired Companies	
America's Best Wealth Creators	*Customer Satisfaction Indexes*
America's Best and Worst Boards of Directors	American Customer Satisfaction Index—
e50 Companies	University of Michigan Business School
America's 50 Best for Minorities	Customer Satisfaction Measurement
	Association
BusinessWeek (www.businessweek.com)	
Standard & Poor's 500	
Global 1000	
Forbes (www.forbes.com)	
Forbes 500	
Forbes International 500	
500 Top Private Companies	
200 Best Small Companies	

well the organization meets its goals. That's what guides managerial decisions in designing strategies, work processes, and work activities, and in coordinating the work of employees.

Industry Rankings There's no shortage of different types of industry and company rankings. Exhibit 18–8 lists some of the more popular rankings used to measure organizational performance. (▪◻▪▪▪ Go to the Web and check out Q & A 18.10) The rankings for each list are determined by specific performance measures. For instance, *Fortune*'s Top Performing Companies of the *Fortune* 500 are determined by financial results including, for example, profits, return on revenue, and return on shareholders' equity; growth in profits for 1 year, 5 years, and 10 years; and revenues per employee, revenues per dollar of assets, and revenues per dollar of equity.[11] *Fortune*'s 100 Best Companies to Work For are chosen by answers given by thousands of randomly selected employees on a questionnaire called the Great Place to Work Trust Index, and on materials filled out by thousands of company managers, including a corporate culture audit created by the Great Place to Work Institute and a human resources questionnaire designed by Hewitt Associates, a compensation and benefits consultant.[12] *Industry Week*'s Best Managed Plants are determined by organizational accomplishments and demonstrations of superior management skills in the areas of financial performance, innovation, leadership, globalization, alliances and partnerships, employee benefits and education, and community involvement.[13] The American Customer Satisfaction Index (ACSI) measures customer satisfaction with the quality of goods and services available to household consumers in the United States and then links the results to financial returns.[14] Each of the other rankings listed in Exhibit 18.8 is compiled from specific performance measures chosen by the organization doing the ranking. (▪◻▪▪▪ Go to the Web and check out Q & A 18.11.)

Learning Review

- Define organizational performance.

- Describe the most frequently used measures of organizational performance.

TOOLS FOR CONTROLLING ORGANIZATIONAL PERFORMANCE

Managers at Applebee's Neighborhood Grill & Bar restaurant chain play by their own rules. They're applying cutting-edge ideas to a traditional industry. Rather than carefully locating restaurants so that the sales of one don't eat into another's sales, Applebee's floods an area with stores in order to gain brand recognition and market dominance. For instance, in Kansas City, where its corporate headquarters are located, the company has 10 restaurants. In contrast, Chili's, its biggest competitor, only has 4 units. Appleby's philosophy: Faster is better. Get into a neighborhood before the competition. Keep things moving by giving customers a convenient experience.[15] Given its approach to business, what kinds of tools would Applebee's managers need for monitoring and measuring performance?

At Murata Manufacturing Company of Kyoto, Japan, managers know that performance will be measured against a challenging goal set by Yasutaka Murata, the company's chairman. That goal? Thirty percent of annual sales should come from new products. Since Murata manufactures components for information-age devices such as cellular phones, personal digital assistants, and so forth, measures of new-product innovation are key indicators.[16]

As these examples illustrate, managers need appropriate tools for monitoring and measuring organizational performance. Before describing some specific types of organizational performance control tools managers might use, let's look at the concept of feedforward, concurrent, and feedback control.

Feedforward/Concurrent/Feedback Controls

Managers can implement controls *before* an activity begins, *during* the time the activity is going on, and *after* the activity has been completed. The first type is called *feedforward control*, the second is *concurrent control*, and the last is *feedback control*. (See Exhibit 18–9.)

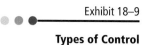
••• feedforward control
A type of control that focuses on preventing anticipated problems since it takes place in advance of the actual work activity.

Feedforward Control The most desirable type of control—**feedforward control**—prevents anticipated problems since it takes place before the actual activity.[17] Let's look at some examples of feedforward control.

When McDonald's opened its first restaurant in Moscow, it sent company quality control experts to help Russian farmers learn techniques for growing high-quality potatoes and bakers to learn processes for baking high-quality breads. Why? Because McDonald's strongly emphasizes product quality no matter what the geographical location. It wants a cheeseburger in Moscow to taste like one in Omaha. Still another example of feedforward control is the scheduled preventive maintenance programs on aircraft done by the major airlines. These are designed to detect and, it is hoped, to prevent structural damage that might lead to an accident. And at the Collins & Aikman automotive instrument panels plant, employees follow the rule of "a place for

Exhibit 18–9

Types of Control

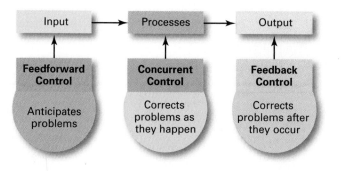

everything and everything in its place." That way, they can find what they need when they need it with no disruption to work flow.[18]

The key to feedforward controls is taking managerial action *before* a problem occurs. Feedforward controls are desirable because they allow managers to prevent problems rather than having to correct them later after the damage (such as poor-quality products, lost customers, lost revenue, and so forth) has already been done. Unfortunately, these controls require timely and accurate information that often is difficult to get. As a result, managers frequently end up using the other two types of controls.

• • • **concurrent control**
A type of control that takes place while a work activity is in progress.

• • • **management by walking around**
A term used to describe a manager being out in the work area, interacting directly with employees.

• • • **feedback control**
A type of control that takes place after a work activity is done.

Concurrent Control **Concurrent control**, as its name implies, takes place while an activity is in progress. When control is enacted while the work is being performed, management can correct problems before they become too costly.

The best-known form of concurrent control is direct supervision. When managers use **management by walking around**, which is a term used to describe a manager being out in the work area, interacting directly with employees, they're using concurrent control. When a manager directly oversees the actions of employees, he or she can monitor their actions and correct problems as they occur. Although, obviously, there's some delay between the activity and the manager's corrective response, the delay is minimal. Problems usually can be addressed before much resource waste or damage has been done. Also, technical equipment (computers, computerized machine controls, and so forth) can be programmed for concurrent controls. For instance, you may have experienced concurrent control when using a computer program such as word processing software which alerts you to misspelled words or incorrect grammatical usage. In addition, many organizational quality programs rely on concurrent controls to inform workers if their work output is of sufficient quality to meet standards.

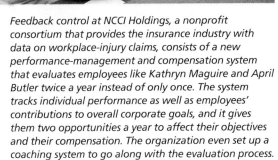

Feedback control at NCCI Holdings, a nonprofit consortium that provides the insurance industry with data on workplace-injury claims, consists of a new performance-management and compensation system that evaluates employees like Kathryn Maguire and April Butler twice a year instead of only once. The system tracks individual performance as well as employees' contributions to overall corporate goals, and it gives them two opportunities a year to affect their objectives and their compensation. The organization even set up a coaching system to go along with the evaluation process.

Feedback Control The most popular type of control relies on feedback. In **feedback control**, the control takes place *after* the activity is done. For instance, when McDonald's executives learned that a suspected criminal ring had allegedly stolen millions of dollars in top prizes in their customer games, it was discovered with feedback control.[19] Even though the company took corrective action once it was discovered, the damage had already occurred.

As the McDonald's example shows, the major drawback of this type of control is that by the time the manager has the information, the problems have already occurred—leading to waste or damage. But for many activities, feedback is the only viable type of control available. For instance, financial statements are an example of feedback controls. If, for example, the income statement shows that sales revenues are declining, the decline has already occurred. So at this point, the manager's only option is to try to determine why sales have decreased and to correct the situation.

Feedback controls do have two advantages.[20] First, feedback provides managers with meaningful information on how effective their planning efforts were. Feedback that indicates little variance between standard and actual performance is evidence that the planning was generally on target. If the deviation is significant, a manager can use that information when formulating new plans to make them more effective. Second, feedback control can enhance employee motivation. People want information on how well they have performed and feedback control provides that information.

Financial Controls

One of the primary purposes of every business firm is to earn a profit. To achieve this goal, managers need financial controls. Managers might, for instance, carefully analyze quarterly income statements for excessive expenses. They might also perform several financial ratio tests to ensure that sufficient cash is available to pay ongoing expenses, that debt levels haven't become too high, or that assets are being used productively. Or, they might look at some newer financial control tools such as EVA (economic value added) to see if the company is creating economic value.

Traditional Financial Control Measures Traditional financial measures include ratio analysis and budget analysis. (■◼▨▨▨ Go to the Web and check out Q & A 18.12) Exhibit 18–10 summarizes some of the most popular financial ratios used in organizations. The liquidity ratios measure an organization's ability to meet its current debt obligations. Leverage ratios examine the organization's use of debt to finance its assets and whether it's able to meet the interest payments on the debt. The activity ratios assess how efficiently the firm is using its assets. Finally, the profitability ratios measure how efficiently and effectively the firm is using its assets to generate profits. These are calculated using information from the organization's two primary financial statements (the balance sheet and the income statement); they compare two figures and express them as a percentage or ratio. Because you've undoubtedly

Exhibit 18–10

Popular Financial Ratios

Objective	Ratio	Calculation	Meaning
Liquidity	Current ratio	$\dfrac{\text{Current assets}}{\text{Current liabilities}}$	Tests the organization's ability to meet short-term obligations
	Acid test	$\dfrac{\text{Current assets less inventories}}{\text{Current liabilities}}$	Tests liquidity more accurately when inventories turn over slowly or are difficult to sell
Leverage	Debt to assets	$\dfrac{\text{Total debt}}{\text{Total assets}}$	The higher the ratio, the more leveraged the organization
	Times interest earned	$\dfrac{\text{Profits before interest and taxes}}{\text{Total interest charges}}$	Measures how far profits can decline before the organization is unable to meet its interest expenses
Activity	Inventory turnover	$\dfrac{\text{Sales}}{\text{Inventory}}$	The higher the ratio, the more efficiently inventory assets are being used.
	Total asset turnover	$\dfrac{\text{Sales}}{\text{Total assets}}$	The fewer assets used to achieve a given level of sales, the more efficiently management is using the organization's total assets
Profitability	Profit margin on sales	$\dfrac{\text{Net profit after taxes}}{\text{Total sales}}$	Identifies the profits that various products are generating
	Return on investment	$\dfrac{\text{Net profit after taxes}}{\text{Total assets}}$	Measures the efficiency of assets to generate profits

discussed these ratios in introductory accounting and finance courses, or you will in the near future, we aren't going to elaborate on how they're calculated. Instead, we mention these ratios only briefly here to remind you that managers use such ratios as internal control devices for monitoring how efficiently and profitably the organization uses its assets, debt, inventories, and the like.

We discussed budgets as a planning tool in Chapter 9. When a budget is formulated, it's a planning tool because it gives direction to work activities. It indicates what activities are important and how much resources should be allocated to each activity. But budgets are also used for controlling.

Budgets provide managers with quantitative standards against which to measure and compare resource consumption. By pointing out deviations between standard and actual consumption, they become control tools. If the deviations are judged to be significant enough to require action, the manager will want to examine what has happened and try to uncover the reasons behind the deviations. With this information, he or she can take whatever action is necessary. For example, if you use a personal budget for monitoring and controlling your monthly expenses, you might find one month that your miscellaneous expenses were higher than you had budgeted for. At that point, you might cut back spending in another area or work extra hours to try to get more income.

Other Financial Control Measures In addition to the traditional financial tools, managers are using measures such as EVA (economic value added) and MVA (market value added). The fundamental concept behind these financial tools is that companies are supposed to take in capital from investors and make it worth more. When managers do that, they've created wealth. When they take in capital and make it worth less, they've destroyed wealth.

> ● ● ● **economic value added (EVA)**
> A financial tool for measuring corporate and divisional performance, calculated by taking after-tax operating profit minus the total annual cost of capital.

Economic value added (EVA) is a tool for measuring corporate and divisional performance. It's calculated by taking after-tax operating profit minus the total annual cost of capital.[21] EVA is a measure of how much economic value is being created by what a company does with its assets, less any capital investments the company has made in its assets. As a performance control tool, EVA focuses managers' attention on earning a rate of return over and above the cost of capital. Companies such as Hewlett-Packard, Equifax, Boise Cascade Corporation, and even the U.S. Postal Service have integrated EVA measures into their organizations and improved their performance as a result.[22] When EVA is used as a performance measure, employees soon learn that they can improve their organization's or business unit's EVA by either using less capital or by investing capital in high-return projects.

> ● ● ● **market value added (MVA)**
> A financial tool that measures the stock market's estimate of the value of a firm's past and expected investment projects.

Market value added (MVA) adds a market dimension since it measures the stock market's estimate of the value of a firm's past and expected capital investment projects. If the company's market value (value of all outstanding stock plus company's debt) is greater than all the capital invested in it (from shareholders, bondholders, and retained earnings), it has a positive MVA, indicating that managers have created wealth. If the company's market value is less than all the capital invested in it, the MVA will be negative, indicating that managers have destroyed wealth. Studies have shown that EVA is a predictor of MVA and that consecutive years of positive EVA generally lead to a high MVA.[23] (▮▮▮▮▮ Go to the Web and check out Q & A 18.13.)

The Practice of Managing Earnings A financial practice that has come under increased scrutiny recently is the management of earnings. When organizations "manage" earnings, they "time" income and expenses to enhance current financial performance, which gives an unrealistic picture of the organization's financial performance. For instance, many organizations have deferred compensation programs for their top executives. They don't have to account for these expenses now—although there's usually a short reference to them buried in footnotes in the annual report. As such they make earnings look better in the present. The problem is they can add up to a large future corporate liability. For example, at Wyeth (a pharmaceutical company), chairman John Stafford participates in a retirement program that allows company executives to set aside, pretax, as much as 100 percent of their cash compensation.[24] Wyeth guarantees these executives a 10 percent return on this deferred pay. In 2002 alone, that amounted to $3.8 million in interest credited to Stafford's account. At some point, these amounts are going to have to be paid out to the recipients. Needless to say, these types of financial manipulations raise serious ethical questions.

The Sarbanes-Oxley Act, passed by the U.S. Congress in 2002, requires more financial disclosure by organizations and even goes so far as to have senior managers certify the financial statements. But some companies are doing more. For instance, at Krispy Kreme Doughnuts, new details are being added to financial statement footnotes that explain specific loan guarantees to franchisees. Prior to 2002, the amounts involved were reported only in aggregate. Now, the company specifies the amount of each guarantee.[25]

Balanced Scorecard

● ● ● **balanced scorecard**
A performance measurement tool that looks at four areas—financial, customer, internal processes, and people/innovation/growth assets—that contribute to a company's performance.

The balanced scorecard approach to performance measurement was introduced as a way to evaluate organizational performance from more than just the financial perspective.[26] The **balanced scorecard** is a performance measurement tool that looks at four areas—financial, customer, internal processes, and people/innovation/growth assets—that contribute to a company's performance. According to this approach, managers should develop goals in each of the four areas and measures to determine if these goals are being met. (■◻■■ Go to the Web and check out Q & A 18.14.) For instance, a company might include cash flow, quarterly sales growth, and ROI as measures for success in the financial area. Or, it might include percentage of sales coming from new products as a measure of customer goals. The intent of the balanced scorecard is to emphasize that all of these areas are important to an organization's success and that there should be a balance among them.

Although a balanced scorecard makes sense, unfortunately, managers still tend to focus on areas that drive their organization's success.[27] Their scorecards reflect their strategies. If those strategies center on the customer, for example, then the customer area is likely to get more attention than the other three areas. Yet, managers need to recognize that you really can't focus on one performance area without affecting the others. For instance, at IBM Global Services in Houston, managers developed a scorecard around an overriding strategy of customer satisfaction. However, the other areas (financial, internal processes, and people/innovation/growth) are intended to support that central strategy. The division manager described the approach as follows, "The internal processes part of our business is directly related to responding to our customers in a timely manner, and the learning and innovation aspect is critical for us since what we're selling to our customers above all is our expertise. Of course, how successful we are with those things will affect our financial component."[28] And in Canada, the Ontario Hospital Association developed a scorecard for 89 hospitals designed to evaluate four main areas: clinical utilization and outcomes, financial performance and financial condition of the hospital, patient satisfaction, and how the hospital was investing for the future. The scorecard was purposefully designed to recognize the synergies among each of these measures. After hospitals were evaluated on the scorecard measures, the results of the scorecard evaluations were made available to patients giving them an objective basis for choosing a hospital.[29]

Information Controls

Information is critical to monitoring and measuring an organization's performance. Managers need the right information at the right time and in the right amount. Inaccurate, incomplete, excessive, or delayed information will seriously impede performance. How can managers use information for control? (■■■■ Check out You're the Manager: Putting Ethics into Action on p. 510.)

DST Output prints and mails over 100 million customized billing statements a month for its corporate clients, so in addition to operating a vast array of highspeed printing and insertion equipment, it must also manage a tidal wave of information. At the Data Control Center in El Dorado Hills (California), staff members rely on management information systems not only to monitor plant operations but also to receive massive streams of client data in virtually every format. Adding to the complexity of its operations, DST Output also allows its clients to split their data streams and send some customer statements through the mail and others over the Internet. "It is a finely orchestrated symphony of people, processes and technology," says director of business operations Bob Logue.

●●● **management information system (MIS)**
A system used to provide management with needed information on a regular basis.

●●● **data**
Raw, unanalyzed facts.

●●● **information**
Processed and analyzed data.

Management Information Systems Although there's no universally agreed-upon definition of a **management information system (MIS)**, we'll define it as a system used to provide management with needed information on a regular basis. In theory, this system can be manual or computer-based, although all current discussions focus on computer-supported applications. The term *system* in MIS implies order, arrangement, and purpose. Further, an MIS focuses specifically on providing managers with *information*, not merely *data*. These two points are important and require elaboration.

A library provides a good analogy. Although it can contain millions of volumes, a library doesn't do users much good if they can't find what they want quickly. That's why librarians spend a great deal of time cataloging a library's collections and ensuring that materials are returned to their proper locations. Organizations today are like well-stocked libraries. There's no lack of data. There is, however, an inability to process that data so that the right information is available to the right person when he or she needs it. Likewise, a library is almost useless if it has the book you need immediately, but either you can't find it or the library takes a week to retrieve it from storage. An MIS, on the other hand, has organized data in some meaningful way and can access the information in a reasonable amount of time. **Data** are raw, unanalyzed facts, such as numbers, names, or quantities. Raw, unanalyzed facts are relatively useless to managers. When data are analyzed and processed, they become **information**. An MIS collects data and turns them into relevant information for managers to use.

How Are Information Systems Used in Controlling?

Managers need information to monitor organizational performance and to control organizational activities. Without information, they would find it difficult to measure, compare, and take action as part of the controlling process. For instance, in measuring actual performance, managers need information about what is, in fact, happening within their area of responsibility, about what the standards are in order to be able to compare actual performance with the standard, and to help them determine acceptable ranges of variation within these comparisons. And they rely on information to help them develop appropriate courses of action if there are or are not significant deviations between actual and standard. As you can see, information is an important tool in monitoring and measuring organizational performance.

Benchmarking of Best Practices

Much like Zhang Ruimin in our chapter-opening dilemma, managers in diverse industries from medical and educational to financial services and information technology are discovering the benefits of benchmarking. For instance, when the first

THINKING CRITICALLY ABOUT ETHICS

Duplicating software for co-workers and friends is a widespread practice, but software in the United States is protected by copyright laws. Copying it is punishable by fines of up to $100,000 and five years in jail.

Is reproducing copyrighted software ever an acceptable practice? Explain. Is it wrong for employees of a business to pirate software but permissible for struggling college students who can't afford to buy their own software? As a manager, what types of ethical guidelines could you establish for software use? What if you were a manager in another country where software piracy was an accepted practice?

SYSCO Corporation is a food-services firm, headquartered in Houston, that operates more than 120 subsidiary companies around the country. A recent innovation developed by its human resources department is the Innovation Key Metrics Benchmark System, which provides executives at all SYSCO's regional offices with scorecards showing how well their company has performed against others in the SYSCO family. A database of its business practices also lets SYSCO executives look up subsidiary companies of similar size and learn about what has made them strong in particular areas. Site visits to these benchmark firms are encouraged.

••• **benchmarking**
The search for the best practices among competitors or noncompetitors that lead to their superior performance.

••• **benchmark**
The standard of excellence against which to measure and compare.

Chrysler Sebring convertible rolled off the assembly line at DaimlerChrysler's assembly plant, the company was able to avoid $100 million in production costs because it was built using manufacturing best practices shared by Mercedes-Benz, Chrysler's German owner.[30]

We first introduced the concept of benchmarking in Chapter 9. Remember that **benchmarking** is the search for the best practices among competitors or noncompetitors that lead to their superior performance. The **benchmark** is the standard of excellence against which to measure and compare.[31] At its most fundamental level, benchmarking means learning from others.[32] As a tool for monitoring and measuring organizational performance, benchmarking can be used to help identify specific performance gaps and potential areas of improvement.[33] (■□▨▨▨ Go to the Web and check out Q & A 18.15.) But managers shouldn't just look at external organizations for best practices. It's also important for them to look inside their organization for best practices that can be shared.

Did you ever work somewhere that had an employee suggestion box on a wall in an office or in the plant? When an employee had an idea about a new way of doing something—such as reducing costs, improving delivery time, and so forth—it went into the suggestion box where it usually sat until someone decided to empty the box. Businesspeople frequently joked about the suggestion box and cartoons lambasted the futility of putting ideas in the employee suggestion box.

Unfortunately, this attitude about suggestion boxes still persists in many organizations, and it shouldn't. Research shows that best practices frequently already exist within an organization but usually go unidentified and unused.[34] In today's environment, organizations striving for high performance levels can't afford to ignore such potentially valuable information. Some companies already have recognized the potential of internally benchmarking best practices as a tool for monitoring and measuring performance. For example, Toyota Motor Corporation developed a suggestion-screening system to prioritize best practices based on potential impact, benefits, and difficulty of implementation. Ameren Corporation's power plant managers use internal benchmarking to help identify performance gaps and opportunities. And, General Motors Corporation sends employees—from upper management to line employees—to different plants where they learn about internal and external best practices.[35]

Exhibit 18–11 provides a summary of what managers must do to implement an internal benchmarking best practices program.

Exhibit 18–11

••• •————

Steps to Successfully Implement an Internal Benchmarking Best Practices Program

1. *Connect best practices to strategies and goals.* The organization's strategies and goals should dictate what types of best practices might be most valuable to others in the organization.
2. *Identify best practices throughout the organization.* Organizations must have a way to find out what practices have been successful in different work areas and units.
3. *Develop best practices reward and recognition systems.* Individuals must be given an incentive to share their knowledge. The reward system should be built into the organization's culture.
4. *Communicate best practices throughout the organization.* Once best practices have been identified, that information needs to be shared with others in the organization.
5. *Create a best practices knowledge-sharing system.* There needs to be a formal mechanism for organizational members to continue sharing their ideas and best practices.
6. *Nurture best practices on an ongoing basis.* Create an organizational culture that reinforces a "we can learn from everyone" attitude and emphasizes sharing information.

Source: Based on T. Leahy, "Extracting Diamonds in the Rough," *Business Finance*, August 2000, pp. 33–37.

● ● ● ●**Learning Review**

- Contrast feedforward, concurrent, and feedback controls.
- Explain the types of financial and information controls managers can use.
- Describe how balanced scorecards and benchmarking are used in controlling.

CONTEMPORARY ISSUES IN CONTROL

The employees of Tempe, Arizona-based Integrated Information Systems Inc., thought there was nothing wrong with exchanging copyrighted digital music over a dedicated office server they had set up. Like office betting on college basketball games, it was technically illegal, but harmless, or so they thought. But after the company had to pay a $1 million settlement to the Recording Industry Association of America, managers wished they had controlled the situation better.[36]

Control is an important managerial function. What types of control issues do today's managers face? We're going to look at four: cross-cultural differences, workplace concerns, customer interactions, and corporate governance.

Adjusting Controls for Cross-Cultural Differences

The concepts of control that we've been discussing are appropriate for an organization whose units are not geographically separated or culturally distinct. But what about global organizations? Will control systems be different, and what should managers know about adjusting controls for national differences?

Methods of controlling people and work can be quite different in different countries. The differences we see in organizational control systems of global organizations are primarily in the measurement and corrective action steps of the control process. In a global corporation, managers of foreign operations tend to be less directly controlled by the home office, if for no other reason than that distance keeps managers from being able to observe work directly. Because distance creates a tendency to formalize controls, the home office of a global company often relies on extensive formal reports for control. The global company also may use the power of information technology to control work activities. For instance, the Japanese retailer Ito-Yokado, which owns the 7-Eleven convenience store chain, uses automated cash registers not only to record sales and monitor inventory, but also to schedule tasks for store managers and to track managers' use of the built-in analytical graphs and forecasts. If managers don't use them enough, they're told to increase their activities.[37]

Technology's impact on control also can be seen when comparing technologically advanced nations with those that are less technologically advanced. In countries such as the United States, Japan, Canada, Great Britain, Germany, and Australia, global managers use indirect control devices—especially computer-generated reports and analyses—in addition to standardized rules and direct supervision to ensure that work activities are going as planned. In less technologically advanced countries, managers tend to rely more on direct supervision and highly centralized decision making for control.

Also, constraints on what corrective actions managers can take may affect managers in foreign countries because laws in some countries do not allow managers the option of closing facilities, laying off employees, taking money out of the country, or bringing in a new management team from outside the country.

Finally, another challenge for global companies in collecting data for measurement and comparison is comparability. For instance, a company's manufacturing facility in Mexico might produce the same products as a facility in Scotland. However, the Mexican facility might be much more labor intensive than its Scottish counterpart (to take strategic advantage of lower labor costs in Mexico). If the top-level executives were to control costs by, for example, calculating labor costs per unit or output per worker, the figures would not be comparable. Global managers must address these types of control challenges.

Workplace Concerns

Today's workplace presents considerable control challenges for managers. (▮▮□▮ Go to the Web and check out PRISM # 8—Disciplining.) From monitoring employees' computer usage at work to protecting the workplace against disgruntled employees or even possible terrorist attacks, managers must control the workplace to ensure that the organization's work can be carried out efficiently and effectively as planned. In this section we want to look at three main workplace concerns: workplace privacy, employee theft, and workplace security.

Workplace Privacy If you work, do you think you have a right to privacy at your workplace? What can your employer find out about you and your work? You might be surprised by the answers! Employers can (and do), among other things, read your e-mail (even those marked "personal or confidential"), tap your telephone, monitor your work by computer, store and review computer files, and monitor you in an employee bathroom or dressing room. And these actions aren't all that uncommon. Today, 70 percent of all companies with 1,000 or more employees use electronic monitoring systems.[38] Exhibit 18–12 summarizes the percentage of employers engaging in different forms of workplace monitoring.

Why do managers feel they must monitor what employees are doing? A big reason is that employees are hired to work, not to surf the Web checking stock prices, placing bets at online casinos, or shopping for presents for family or friends. Recreational on-the-job Web surfing is thought to cost a billion dollars in wasted computer resources and billions of dollars in lost work productivity annually. In fact, a recent survey of U.S. employers said that workers spend an average of 8.3 hours a week—more than one entire workday—looking at non-work-related Web sites.[39] That's a significant cost to businesses.

Another reason that managers monitor employee e-mail and computer usage is that they don't want to risk being sued for creating a hostile workplace environment because of offensive messages or an inappropriate image displayed on a co-worker's computer screen. Concern about racial or sexual harassment is one of the reasons why companies might want to monitor or keep back-up copies of all e-mail. This electronic record can help establish what actually happened and can help managers react quickly.[40]

Finally, managers want to ensure that company secrets aren't being leaked.[41] Although protecting intellectual property is important for all businesses, it's especially important in high-tech industries. Managers need to be certain that employees are not, even inadvertently, passing information on to others who could use that information to harm the company.

Even with the workplace monitoring that managers can do, U.S. employees do have some protection through the federal Electronic Communications Privacy Act, which prohibits unauthorized interception of electronic communication. Although

Exhibit 18–12

● ● ●━━━━━━

Types of Workplace Monitoring by Employers

• Internet use	54.7%
• Telephone use	44%
• E-mail messages	38.1%
• Computer files	30.8%
• Job performance using video cameras	14.6%
• Phone conversations	11.5%
• Voice mail messages	6.8%

Source: Based on S. McElvoy, "E-Mail and Internet Monitoring and the Workplace: Do Employees Have a Right to Privacy?" *Communications and the Law*, June 2002, p. 69.

Julian E. Montoya, founder of the Burrito King chain of restaurants, has seen his once-thriving business falter as a result of fierce competition. Employee theft was sometimes a problem as well. Montoya recalls the difficulty of monitoring the performance of all his stores at the height of expansion. One night he went to one of his restaurants unannounced, donned an apron, and went up front to cover the cash register. "The cook took me aside," Montoya remembers, "and said, 'Here's how it works: You take the order; you take the cash and don't put it in the register. At the end of the night we split it.'"

● ● ● **employee theft**
Any unauthorized taking of company property by employees for their personal use.

this law gives employees some privacy protection, it doesn't make workplace electronic monitoring illegal, as employers are allowed to monitor communications for business reasons or when employees have been notified of the practice.[42] Although employees may think that it's unfair for a company to monitor their work electronically and to fire them for what they feel are minor infractions, the courts have ruled that since the computer belongs to the company, managers have a right to view everything on it.[43]

Because of the potentially serious costs, and given the fact that many jobs now entail work that involves using a computer, many companies are developing and enforcing workplace monitoring policies. The responsibility for this falls on managers. It's important to develop some type of viable workplace monitoring policy. What can managers do to maintain control but do so in a way that isn't demeaning to employees? They should develop an unambiguous computer usage policy and make sure that every employee knows about it. Tell employees up front that their computer use may be monitored at any time and provide clear and specific guidelines as to what constitutes acceptable use of company e-mail systems and the Web.

Employee Theft Would you be surprised to find out that up to 85 percent of all organizational theft and fraud is committed by employees, not outsiders?[44] And, it's a costly problem—estimated to be around $4,500 per U.S. worker each year.[45]

Employee theft is defined as any unauthorized taking of company property by employees for their personal use.[46] It can range from embezzlement to fraudulent filing of expense reports to removing equipment, parts, software, and office supplies from company premises. While retail businesses have long faced serious potential losses from employee theft, loose financial controls at start-ups and small companies and the ready availability of information technology have made employee stealing an escalating problem in all kinds and sizes of organizations. It's a control issue that managers need to educate themselves about and with which they must be prepared to deal.[47]

Why do employees steal? The answer depends on whom you ask.[48] Experts in various fields—industrial security, criminology, clinical psychology—all have different perspectives. The industrial security people propose that people steal because the opportunity presents itself through lax controls and favorable circumstances. Criminologists say that it's because people have financial-based pressures (such as personal financial problems) or vice-based pressures (such as gambling debts). And the clinical psychologists suggest that people steal because they can rationalize whatever they're doing as being correct and appropriate behavior ("everyone does it," "they had it coming," "this company makes enough money and they'll never miss anything this small," "I deserve this for all that I put up with," and so forth).[49] Although each of these approaches provides compelling insights into employee theft and has been instrumental in program designs to deter it, unfortunately, employees continue to steal. So what can managers do? Let's look at some suggestions for managing employee theft.

We can use the concept of feedforward, concurrent, and feedback control to identify measures for deterring or reducing employee theft.[50] Exhibit 18–13 on p. 478 summarizes several possible managerial actions.

Workplace Violence

During April 2003, in Indianapolis, a manager of a Boston Market restaurant was killed by a fellow employee after the restaurant closed because the manager had refused the employee's sexual advances. In July 2003, an employee at an aircraft assembly plant in Meridian, Mississippi, walked out of a mandatory class on ethics and respect in the workplace, returned with firearms and ammunition, and shot 14 of his co-workers, killing

Feedforward	Concurrent	Feedback
Careful prehiring screening.	Treat employees with respect and dignity	Make sure employees know when theft or fraud has occurred—not naming names but letting people know this is not acceptable.
Establish specific policies defining theft and fraud and discipline procedures.	Openly communicate the costs of stealing.	Use the services of professional investigators.
Involve employees in writing policies.	Let employees know on a regular basis about their successes in preventing theft and fraud.	Redesign control measures.
Educate and train employees about the polices.	Use video surveillance equipment if conditions warrant.	Evaluate your organization's culture and the relationships of managers and employees.
Have professionals review your internal security controls.	Install "lock-out" options on computers, telephones, and e-mail.	
	Use corporate hot lines for reporting incidences. Set a good example.	

Sources: Based on A.H. Bell and D.M. Smith. "Protecting the Company Against Theft and Fraud," *Workforce Online* (*www.workforce.com*) December 3, 2000; J.D. Hansen. "To Catch a Thief," *Journal of Accountancy*, March 2000, pp. 43–46; and J. Greenberg, "The Cognitive Geometry of Employee Theft," in *Dysfunctional Behavior in Organizations: Nonviolent and Deviant Behavior*, eds. S.B. Bacharach, A. O'Leary-Kelly, J.M. Collins, and R.W. Griffin (Stamford, CT: JAI Press, 1998), pp. 147–93.

five and himself.[51] Is workplace violence really an issue with which managers might have to deal? Yes. Despite the earlier examples we described, the number of workplace homicides is decreasing.[52] However, the U.S. National Institute of Occupational Safety and Health says that each week, an average of 18,000 workers are assaulted at work.[53] Exhibit 18–14 describes the results from a survey of workers and their experiences with office rage. Anger, rage, and violence in the workplace are intimidating to co-workers and adversely affect their productivity. The annual cost to U.S. businesses is estimated at between $20 and $35 billion.[54]

What factors are believed to be contributing to workplace violence? Undoubtedly, employee stress caused by rising layoffs, declining value of retirement accounts, long hours, information overload, other daily interruptions, unrealistic deadlines, and uncaring managers play a role. Even office layout designs with small cubicles where employees work amidst the noise and commotion from those around them have been cited as contributing to the problem.[55] Other experts have described dangerously dysfunctional work environments characterized by the following as primary contributors to the problem:[56]

- Employee work driven by TNC (time, numbers, and crises).
- Rapid and unpredictable change where instability and uncertainty plague employees.
- Destructive communication style where managers communicate in excessively aggressive, condescending, explosive, or passive-aggressive styles; excessive workplace teasing or scapegoating.

Exhibit 18–14

Workplace Violence

• Witnessed yelling or other verbal abuse	42%
• Yelled at co-workers themselves	29%
• Cried over work-related issues	23%
• Seen someone purposely damage machines or furniture	14%
• Seen physical violence in the workplace	10%
• Struck a co-worker	2%

Source: Integra Realty Resources, October-November Survey of Adults 18 and Over, in "Desk Rage." *BusinessWeek*, November 20, 2000, p. 12.

- Authoritarian leadership with a rigid, militaristic mind-set of managers versus employees; employees aren't allowed to challenge ideas, participate in decision making, or engage in team-building efforts.
- Defensive attitude where little or no performance feedback is given; only numbers count; and yelling, intimidation, or avoidance are the preferred ways of handling conflict.
- Double standards in terms of policies, procedures, and training opportunities for managers and employees.
- Unresolved grievances because there are no mechanisms or only adversarial ones in place for resolving them; dysfunctional individuals may be protected or ignored because of long-standing rules, union contract provisions, or reluctance to take care of problems.
- Emotionally troubled employees and no attempt by managers to get help for these people.
- Repetitive, boring work where there's no chance of doing something else or of new people coming in.
- Faulty or unsafe equipment or deficient training which keeps employees from being able to work efficiently or effectively.
- Hazardous work environment in terms of temperature, air quality, repetitive motions, overcrowded spaces, noise levels, excessive overtime, and so forth. To minimize costs, no additional employees are hired when workload becomes excessive, leading to potentially dangerous work expectations and conditions.
- Culture of violence where there's a history of individual violence or abuse; violent or explosive role models; or tolerance of on-the-job alcohol or drug abuse.

Reading through this list, you may feel that workplaces where you'll spend your professional life won't be anything like this. However, the competitive demands of succeeding in a 24/7 global economy do put pressure on organizations and employees in many ways.

What can managers do to deter or reduce possible workplace violence? Once again, we can use the concept of feedforward, concurrent, and feedback control to identify actions that managers can take.[57] Exhibit 18–15 on page 480 summarizes several suggestions.

Controlling Customer Interactions

Every month, every local branch of Enterprise Rent-a-Car conducts telephone surveys with customers.[58] Each branch earns a ranking based on the percentage of its customers who say they were "completely satisfied" with their last Enterprise experience—a level of satisfaction referred to as "top box." Top box performance is important to Enterprise because completely satisfied customers are far more likely to be repeat customers. And by using this service quality index measure, employees' careers and financial aspirations are linked with the organizational goal of providing consistently superior service to each and every customer. Managers at Enterprise Rent-a-Car understand the connection between employees and customers and the importance of controlling these interactions.

There's probably no better area to see the link between planning and controlling than in customer service. If a company proclaims customer service as one of its goals, it quickly and clearly becomes apparent whether or not that goal is being achieved by seeing how satisfied customers are with their service! How can managers control the interactions between the goal and the outcome when it comes to customers? The concept of a service profit chain can help. (See Exhibit 18–16 on page 480.)

● ● ● **service profit chain**
The service sequence from employees to customers to profit.

The **service profit chain** is the service sequence from employees to customers to profit.[59] According to this concept, the company's strategy and service delivery system influences how employees service customers—their attitudes, behaviors, and service capability. Service capability, in turn, enhances how productive employees are in providing service and the quality of that service. The level of employee service productivity and service quality influences customer perceptions of service value. When service value is high, it has a positive impact on customer satisfaction which leads to customer loyalty. And customer loyalty improves organizational revenue growth and profitability.

Exhibit 18–15

Control Measures for Deterring or Reducing Workplace Violence

Feedforward	Concurrent	Feedback
Management commitment to functional not dysfunctional, work environments.	MBWA (managing by walking around) to identify potential problems; observe how employees treat and interact with each other.	Communicate openly about incidences and what's being done.
Employee assistance programs (EAP) to help employees with serious behavioral problems.	Allow employees or work groups to "grieve" during periods of major organizational change.	Investigate incidences and take appropriate action.
Organizational policy that any workplace rage, aggression, or violence will not be tolerated.	Be a good role model in how you treat others.	Review company policies and change, if necessary.
Careful prehiring screening.	Use corporate hot lines or some mechanism for reporting and investigating incidences.	
Never ignore threats. Train employees about how to avoid danger if situation arises.	Use quick and decisive intervention. Get expert professional assistance if violence erupts.	
Clearly communicate policies to employees.	Provide necessary equipment or procedures for dealing with violent situations (cell phones, alarm systems, code names or phrases, and so forth).	

Sources: Based on M. Gorkin, "Five Strategies and Structures for Reducing Workplace Violence," *Workforce Online* (*www.workforce.com*), December 3, 2000; "Investigating Workplace Violence: Where Do You Start?" *Workforce Online* (*www.forceforce.com*), December 3, 2000; "Ten Tips on Recognizing and Minimizing Violence," *Workforce Online* (*www.workforce.com*), December 3, 2000; and "Points to Cover in a Workplace Violence Policy," *Workforce Online* (*www.workforce.com*), December 3, 2000.

Exhibit 18–16   **The Service Profit Chain**

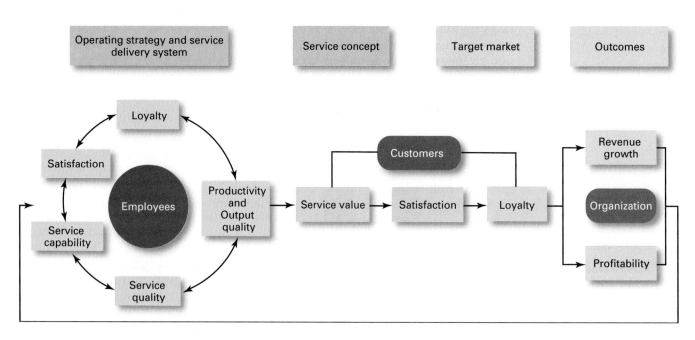

Source: Adapted and reprinted by permission of *Harvard Business Review*. An exhibit from "Putting the Service Profit Chain to Work," by J.L. Heskett, T.O. Jones, G.W. Loveman, W.E. Sasser, Jr., and L.A. Schlesinger. March–April 1994: 166. Copyright (C) by the President and Fellows of Harvard College. All rights reserved. See also J.L. Heskett, W.E. Sasser, and L.A. Schlesinger, *The Service Profit Chain* (New York: Free Press, 1997).

Ted V. Schaefer, Partner
PricewaterhouseCoopers
Denver, Colorado

Describe your job.

I am a partner in PricewaterhouseCoopers' Denver office and I work in the Global Risk Management Solutions group. I provide our clients with internal control and process improvement advisory services. I also lead our West Region Information & Communications industry advisory group.

Why are controls important to your organization?

Controls are critical to the quality delivery of PricewaterhouseCoopers' audit, tax, and advisory services. We have many professional, regulatory, and internal controls that help to ensure that we meet our goals. Controls provide staff a clear road map to follow for client service delivery, human resources, career development, client independence, code of conduct, and regulatory and professional rules. Our industry is based on controls that provide staff the ability to carry out their jobs in an orderly fashion.

What control issues do you think are particularly important to managers today?

Recent business scandals have raised the bar for strong internal controls. The government has taken a major step in regulating internal control through the enactment of the Sarbanes-Oxley legislation requiring public companies to implement an effective internal control structure that must be externally audited. Regardless of this legislation, internal controls are just good business for several reasons. Controls allow companies to manage regulatory compliance and financial and operational activities to meet business goals. They also provide for an orderly environment so management can focus their time on strategic issues. Companies with poor controls are constantly putting out fires, taking away from more important activities. Companies need to align controls with the goals of the organization and ensure that they provide a cost benefit.

What skills do you think managers need to be effective?

Due to the fast-paced business environment, managers must be lifelong learners. Soft skills like communication, creativity, and the ability to motivate and challenge employees are equally important for success. Knowing when employees need help or when to stay out of their way is a skill necessary to manage people.

So what does the concept of a service profit chain mean for managers? Managers who want to control customer interactions should work to create long-term and mutually beneficial relationships among the company, employees, and customers. How? By creating a work environment that not only enables employees to deliver high levels of quality service, but makes them feel they're capable of delivering top-quality service. In such a service climate, employees are motivated to deliver superior service. These employee efforts to satisfy customers, coupled with the service value provided by the organization, improve customer satisfaction. And when customers receive high service value, they're loyal and they come back, which ultimately improves the company's growth and profitability.

There's no better example of the service profit chain in action than Southwest Airlines. Southwest is the most consistently profitable U.S. airline and its customers are fiercely loyal. This is because the company's operating strategy (hiring, training, rewards and recognition, teamwork, and so forth) is built around customer service. Employees consistently deliver outstanding service value to customers. And Southwest's customers reward the company by coming back. It's through efficiently and effectively controlling these customer interactions that companies like Southwest and Enterprise have succeeded.

Corporate Governance

Although Andrew Fastow, Enron's former chief financial officer, had an engaging and persuasive personality, that still doesn't explain why Enron's board of directors failed to raise even minimal concerns about management's questionable accounting

Becoming a Manager

♦ *Identify the types of controls you use in your own personal life and whether they're feedforward, concurrent, or feedback controls.*

♦ *When preparing for major class projects, identify some performance measures that you can use to help you determine whether or not the project is going as planned.*

♦ *Try to come up with some ways to improve your personal efficiency and effectiveness.*

♦ ▮▮▮ ☐ *Go to the Web and complete any of the following exercises from the Self-Assessment Library (S.A.L.) found on R.O.L.L.S: #5—How Proactive Am I?; #21—What Time of Day Am I Most Productive?, and #36—How Heavy Is My Workload?*

••• corporate
governance
The system used to govern a
corporation so that the
interests of corporate
owners are protected.

practices. The board even allowed Fastow to set up off-balance-sheet partnerships for his own profit at the expense of Enron's shareholders.

Corporate governance, the system used to govern a corporation so that the interests of corporate owners are protected, failed abysmally at Enron, as it did at many of the other companies caught in the recent financial scandals. In the aftermath of these scandals, there have been increased calls for better corporate governance. Two areas in which corporate governance is being reformed are the role of boards of directors and financial reporting. And these improvements aren't limited to U.S. corporations. The problem of corporate governance is a global one.[60] A full 75 percent of senior executives at U.S. and western European corporations expect their boards of directors to take a more active role.[61]

The Role of Boards of Directors The original purpose of a board of directors was to have a group, independent from management, looking out for the interests of shareholders who, because of the corporate structure, were not involved in the day-to-day management of the organization. However, it doesn't always work that way in practice. Board members often enjoy a cozy relationship with managers in which board members "take care" of the CEO and the CEO "takes care" of the board members.

This "quid pro quo" arrangement is changing. Since the passage of the Sarbanes-Oxley Act of 2002, demands on board members of publicly traded companies in the United States have increased considerably.[62] To help boards do their job better, researchers at the Corporate Governance Center at Kennesaw State University developed 10 governance principles for U.S. public companies that have been endorsed by the Institute of Internal Auditors. (See Exhibit 18–17 for a list of these principles.)

Financial Reporting In addition to expanding the role of boards of directors, the previously mentioned Sarbanes-Oxley Act also called for more disclosure and transparency of corporate financial information. In fact, senior managers in the United States are now required to certify their companies' financial results. These types of changes should lead to better information—that is, information that is more accurate and reflective of the firm's financial condition. In fulfilling their financial reporting responsibilities, managers might want to follow the financial reporting principles, also developed by the researchers at the Corporate Governance Center at Kennesaw State University. These seven principles are explained in Exhibit 18–18.

••• **Learning Review**

- Explain how managers may have to adjust controls for cross-cultural differences.
- Discuss the types of workplace concerns managers face and how they can address those concerns.

- Explain why control is important to customer interactions.
- Discuss what corporate governance is and how it's changing.

Exhibit 18–17

21st Century *Governance* Principles for U.S. Public Companies

1. *Interaction*: Sound governance requires effective interaction among the board, management, the external auditor, and the internal auditor.
2. *Board Purpose*: The board of directors should understand that its purpose is to protect the interests of the corporation's stockholders, while considering the interests of other stakeholders (e.g., creditors, employees, etc.).
3. *Board Responsibilities*: The board's major areas of responsibility should be monitoring the CEO, overseeing the corporation's strategy, and monitoring risks and the corporation's control system. Directors should employ healthy skepticism in meeting these responsibilities.
4. *Independence*: The major stock exchanges should define an "independent" director as one who has no professional or personal ties (either current or former) to the corporation or its management other than service as a director. The vast majority of the directors should be independent in both fact and appearance so as to promote arms-length oversight.
5. *Expertise*: The directors should possess relevant industry, company, functional area, and governance expertise. The directors should reflect a mix of backgrounds and perspectives. All directors should receive detailed orientation and continuing education to assure they achieve and maintain the necessary level of expertise.
6. *Meetings and Information*: The board should meet frequently for extended periods of time and should have access to the information and personnel it needs to perform its duties.
7. *Leadership*: The roles of Board Chair and CEO should be separate.
8. *Disclosure*: Proxy statements and other board communications should reflect board activities and transactions (e.g., insider trades) in a transparent and timely manner.
9. *Committees*: The nominating, compensation, and audit committees of the board should be composed only of independent directors.
10. *Internal Audit*: All public companies should maintain an effective, full-time internal audit function that reports directly to the audit committee.

Source: Corporate Governance Center, Kennesaw State University, March 26, 2002.

Exhibit 18–18

21st Century *Financial Reporting* Principles for U.S. Public Companies

1. *Reporting Model*: The current GAAP financial reporting model is becoming increasingly less appropriate for U.S. public companies. The industrial-age model currently used should be replaced or enhanced so that tangible and intangible resources, risks, and performance of information-age companies can be effectively and efficiently communicated to financial statement users. The new model should be developed and implemented as soon as possible.
2. *Philosophy and Culture*: Financial statements and supporting disclosures should reflect economic substance and should be prepared with the goal of maximum informativeness and transparency. A legalistic view of accounting and auditing (e.g., "can we get away with recording it this way?") is not appropriate. Management integrity and a strong control environment are critical to reliable financial reporting.
3. *Audit Committees*: The audit committee of the board of directors should be composed of independent directors with financial, auditing, company, and industry expertise. These members must have the will, authority, and resources to provide diligent oversight of the financial reporting process. The board should consider the risks of audit committee member stock/stock option holdings and should set audit committee member compensation at an appropriate level given the expanded duties and risks faced by audit committee members. The audit committee should select the external auditor, evaluate external and internal auditor performance, and approve the audit fee.
4. *Fraud*: Corporate management should face strict criminal penalties in fraudulent financial reporting cases. The Securities and Exchange Commission should be given the resources it needs to effectively combat financial statement fraud. The board, management, and auditors all should perform fraud risk assessments.
5. *Audit Firms*: Audit firms should focus primarily on providing high-quality audit and assurance services and should perform no consulting for audit clients. Audit firm personnel should be selected, evaluated, compensated, and promoted primarily based on technical competence, not on their ability to generate new business. Audit fees should reflect engagements' scope of work and risk.
6. *External Auditing Profession*: Auditors should view public accounting as a noble profession focused on the public interest, not as a competitive business. The profession should carefully consider expanding audit reports beyond the current "clean" versus modified dichotomy so as to enhance communication to financial report users.
7. *Analysts*: Analysts should not be compensated (directly or indirectly) based on the investment banking activities of their firms. Analysts should not hold stock in the companies they follow, and they should disclose any business relationships between the companies they follow and their firms.

Source: Corporate Governance Center, Kennesaw State University, March 26, 2002.

Managers Respond to a Manager's Dilemma

····Craig Lizotte

**Senior Project Manager, ESS Group, Inc.,
Wellesley, Massachusetts**

I would start by carefully defining the market or markets I planned to target. Then I'd set clear and quantifiable goals with which to measure my progress. To say you want to be China's first global brand is great, but what does that mean? How long should it take to get there? What is the first step? Then, Zhang should develop an individual sales plan for each market with sales and profit targets that will, if attained, result in achieving his goals. Zhang will want to use benchmarking throughout this process to compare actual progress to targets developed during the planning process. In some cases, the benchmarks might be internal, such as sales volume or profit. Or they may be external, such as market share or brand recognition. If he's to be successful, Zhang will need to continuously match his progress against his defined benchmarks.

Wendy Moran

**Production Manager, Higher Education, Pearson Education Canada,
Don Mills, Ontario, Canada**

There are several things Zhang can do to benchmark. First, he should conduct thorough research on the competition—how these companies started, what their product lines are, how they market their products, what makes them special. Then he should establish focus groups of potential customers to get their input into what they look for in electric appliances. Next he should study the advertising techniques used by the competition in foreign markets. With all this information, he should establish a group that can work to pinpoint three key issues: the product, global marketing, and profitability. Next, he should track successes and areas of improvement of his own products. Finally, in his own company, Zhang should develop and communicate best practices awards and recognition.

Learning Summary

After reading and studying this chapter, you should be able to:

- Define control.
- Contrast the three approaches to designing control systems.
- Discuss the reasons why control is important.
- Explain the planning–controlling link.
- Describe the three steps in the control process.
- Explain why what is measured is more critical than how it's measured.
- Explain the three courses of action managers can take in controlling.
- Define organizational performance.

- Describe the most frequently used measures of organizational performance.
- Contrast feedforward, concurrent, and feedback controls.
- Explain the types of financial and information controls managers can use.
- Describe how balanced scorecards and benchmarking are used in controlling.
- Describe how managers may have to adjust controls for cross-cultural differences.
- Discuss the types of workplace concerns managers face and how they can address those concerns.
- Explain why control is important to customer interactions.
- Discuss what corporate governance is and how it's changing.

Thinking About Management Issues

1. What would an organization have to do to change its dominant control approach from bureaucratic to clan? From clan to bureaucratic?

2. In Chapter 13 we discussed the white-water rapids view of change. Do you think it's possible to establish and maintain effective standards and controls in this type of environment? Explain.

3. How could you use the concept of control in your own personal life? Be specific. (Think in terms of feedforward, concurrent, and feedback controls as well as controls for the different areas of your life.)

4. When do electronic surveillance devices such as computers, video cameras, and telephone monitoring step over the line from "effective management controls" to "intrusions on employee rights"?

5. "Every individual employee in the organization plays a role in controlling work activities." Do you agree, or do you think control is something that only managers are responsible for? Explain.

Working Together: Team-Based Exercise

You're a professor in the School of Accountancy at Collins State College. Several of your colleagues have expressed an interest in developing some specific controls to minimize opportunities for students to cheat on homework assignments and exams. You and some other faculty members have volunteered to write a report outlining some suggestions that might be used.

Form teams of three or four and discuss this topic. Write a bulleted list of your suggestions from the perspective of controlling possible cheating (1) before it happens, (2) while in-class exams or assignments are being completed, and (3) after it has happened. Please keep the report brief (no more than two pages). Be prepared to present your suggestions before the rest of the class.

Ethical Dilemma Exercise

Pornography and offensive e-mail are two major reasons why many companies establish strict policies and monitor their employees' use of the Internet. Citing legal and ethical concerns, managers are determined to keep inappropriate images and messages out of the workplace. "As a company, if we don't make some effort to keep offensive material off our network, we could end up on the wrong end of a sexual harassment lawsuit or other legal action that could cost the company hundreds of thousands of dollars," says the technology manager at one small business. "To a company our size, that would be devastating." Another reason is cost. Unauthorized Internet activity not only wastes valuable work time, it ties up network resources. Thus, many companies have installed electronic systems to screen e-mail messages and monitor what employees do online. In some companies, one person is designated to review incoming e-mails and delete offensive messages.

Having a clear policy and a monitoring system are only first steps. Management must be sure that employees are aware of the rules—and understand that the company is serious about cleaning up any ethics violations. British Telecom (BT), for example, twice sent e-mails to remind all its employees that looking at online pornography was grounds for dismissal. Despite the warnings, management had to fire 200 employees in an 18-month period. Going further, the company told police about ten employees'

activities, and one has already been sentenced to prison. "We took this decision for the good of BT," explained a spokesperson, "and since we have taken this action the problem has reduced dramatically.[63]

Imagine that you are the administrative assistant for a high-ranking executive at British Telecom. One afternoon you receive an urgent phone call for your boss. You knock on his office door but get no answer, so you open the door, thinking you'll leave a note on his desk. Then you notice that your boss is absorbed in watching a very graphic adult Web site on his personal laptop. As you quietly back out of the office, you wonder how to handle this situation. Review this chapter's section on workplace concerns as you consider this ethical challenge and decide which of the following options to choose—and why.

Option A: Say nothing but anonymously report what you saw by calling BT's ethics hotline as soon as possible.

Option B: Go back in, interrupt your boss, and explain why you entered. Look pointedly at the laptop screen to show that you're aware of what's been going on.

Option C: Knock more loudly to get your boss's attention, wait a moment, and go in and deliver the message without mentioning what you saw.

Case Application

Niku Corporation

Without information, managers can't make good decisions. In order to make good decisions, then, companies need to protect their information. And executives at Niku Corporation, a Silicon Valley software company, thought they had. However, managers were shocked when they discovered that outsiders had penetrated their Web site to steal data. Their experience raises some troubling questions about the security of company information in the Internet age.

Warren Leggett, Niku's chief information officer, had just returned from a relaxing holiday weekend playing golf with his brother-in-law Jay Berlin, who was a mid-level technical manager at Nike Corporation. Jay had agreed to view a demonstration of Niku's project management software. On the morning of the meeting, Jay checked his phone messages and had a voice mail from a salesperson at Business Engine Software Corporation, one of Niku's main competitors. Jay thought that it was quite odd that he'd be getting a message from these people, especially since he didn't

even know the firm and he wouldn't be his company's software contact person anyway. So he told Warren about the message.

Warren also thought that Jay's receipt of such a message was rather unusual and decided to go through Niku's Web access logs. What he discovered shocked him! He found that someone using Internet addresses owned by Business Engine had used Niku passwords to access Niku's network more than 6,000 times, downloading more than 1,000 documents—including one Warren had written about the planned demonstration for Jay.

On August 12, 2002, Niku founder and former CEO Farzad Dibachi filed a lawsuit against Business Engine alleging corporate espionage. Although the lawsuit was settled in December 2002 with a $5 million payment to Niku and additional terms intended to ensure that Business Engine products releases did not incorporate Niku's trade secrets, the whole incident points out a serious problem in today's networked corporations—potential holes in corporate security. "Passwords, which can be easily guessed or tricked out of employees, are becoming the Achilles heel of computer security." An

April 2002 survey of corporations found that 80 percent had their computer systems broken into, resulting in losses of $455 million.

DISCUSSION QUESTIONS

1. Which type of control—feedforward, concurrent, or feedback—do you think would be most important in preventing corporate data theft? Explain your choice.

2. As chief information officer, what might Warren Leggett do to ensure that this situation doesn't happen again?

3. Which would be more important in protecting a company's information or other valuable resources—employees, equipment, or a written procedure? Explain your choice.

Sources: "Niku and Business Engine Announce Settlement of Lawsuit," Niku Press Release, December 4, 2002 (*www.niku.com*); and J. Kerstetter, "You're Only as Good as Your Password," *BusinessWeek*, September 2, 2002, pp. 78–80.

●●●**Learning Outline**

Follow this Learning Outline as you read and study this chapter.

What Is Operations Management and Why Is It Important?

- Explain what operations management is.
- Contrast manufacturing and service organizations.
- Describe managers' roles in improving productivity.
- Discuss the strategic role of operations management.

Value Chain Management

- Define value chain and value chain management.
- Describe the goal of value chain management.
- Discuss the requirements for successful value chain management.
- Describe the benefits that result from value chain management.
- Explain the obstacles to value chain management.

Current Issues in Operations Management

- Discuss technology's role in manufacturing.
- Describe some of the various quality dimensions.
- Explain ISO 9000 and Six Sigma.
- Describe mass customization and how operations management contributes to it.

Chapter

19

Operations and Value Chain Management

..... **A Manager's** *Dilemma*

A *renaissance exceptionnelle*. Even if your knowledge of the French language isn't so good, you'd still be able to ascertain from this description of Bombardier, Inc.'s Sturtevant, Wisconsin, manufacturing facility that something pretty special must be taking place there.[1] Bombardier is a Montreal-based firm best known for its business jets (Learjet), railcars, snowmobiles (Ski Doo), and watercraft (Sea Doo). In early 2001, the company bought the manufacturing operations of Outboard Marine Corporation (OMC), the makers of Evinrude and Johnson outboard engines. And what a mess they got!

OMC had stumbled badly in its manufacturing operations. The quality of its engines had declined and customers were upset. The company's dealers were bailing out in droves. OMC's share of the outboard engine market had dropped from 55 percent in 1995 to 23 percent by 2000. Production facilities were scattered around the United States, Mexico, and China, and component parts often spent three weeks in transit—slowing production and driving up costs. When Bombardier took over the struggling OMC, it brought in Roch Lambert (seated in picture), a manufacturing executive who was already working in Bombardier's pleasure-boat division, to turn things around. Roch immediately put together a team of talented specialists in plant maintenance, finance, marketing, and quality control from Bombardier's Canadian headquarters and together they started working on a highly detailed plan to reorganize manufacturing. They set a lofty goal: "to start producing the highest-quality Evinrude and Johnson engines ever made, as soon as possible, without waiting a year or two before reentering the market."

One of the first decisions they made was to center all manufacturing operations in the Sturtevant plant, a building with $9\frac{1}{2}$ acres under one roof that had formerly housed a book publishing operation. Their decision to consolidate operations drastically shortened transit time. The team also totally reorganized the manufacturing process from beginning to end. An important part of their transformation was carefully selecting employees with problem-solving skills who could be "team players."

Roch wants to ensure that quality drives all aspects of the business. Put yourself in his position. What can he do to successfully implement a quality program?

What would *you* do **?**

This chapter focuses on the importance of operations management to the organization. Operations management encompasses such topics as productivity, value chain management, e-manufacturing, and quality. As our chapter-opening "Manager's Dilemma" points out, it's important for managers everywhere to have well-thought-out and well-designed operating systems, organizational control systems, and quality programs in order to survive in the increasingly competitive global environment. If managers, like Roch Lambert, have these, their organizations will be able to produce high-quality products and services at prices that meet or beat those of their competitors.

WHAT IS OPERATIONS MANAGEMENT AND WHY IS IT IMPORTANT?

Inside Intel's factory in New Mexico, employee Trish Roughgarden is known as a "seed"—an unofficial title for technicians who transfer manufacturing know-how from one Intel facility to another.[2] Her job is to make sure that this new factory works just like an identical one that opened eight months earlier in Oregon. Then, in 2003, when a third plant opened in Ireland, several hundred other seeds copied the same techniques. What the seeds do is part of a major Intel strategy known as "Copy Exactly," which the company implemented after frustrating variations between factories in the early 1980s hurt productivity and product quality. In the intensely competitive chip-making industry, Intel knows that decisions it makes about operations management issues will determine its likelihood of success.

••• operations management
The design, operation, and control of the transformation process that converts resources into finished goods or services.

What is **operations management**? The term refers to the design, operation, and control of the transformation process that converts such resources as labor and raw materials into goods and services that are sold to customers. Exhibit 19–1 portrays, in a very simplified fashion, the fact that every organization has an operations system that creates value by transforming inputs into outputs. The system takes in inputs—people, technology, capital, equipment, materials, and information—and transforms them through various processes, procedures, work activities, and so forth, into finished goods and services. (▓▓▓▓ Go to the Web and check out Q & A 19.1.) And just as every organization produces something, every unit in an organization also produces something. Marketing, finance, research and development, human resources, and accounting convert inputs into outputs such as sales, increased market share, high rates of return on capital, new and innovative products, motivated and committed employees, and accounting reports. As a manager, you'll need to be familiar with operations management concepts, regardless of the area you manage, in order to achieve your goals efficiently and effectively.

▪ Q & A
Whenever you see this green square, go to the R.O.L.L.S. Web site (*www.prenhall.com/robbins*) to the Q & A, your 24/7 educational assistant. These video clips and written material presented by your authors address questions that we have found students frequently ask.

Why is operations management so important to organizations and managers? There are three reasons: It encompasses both services and manufacturing, it's important in effectively and efficiently managing productivity, and it plays a strategic role in an organization's competitive success.

Exhibit 19–1

The Operations System

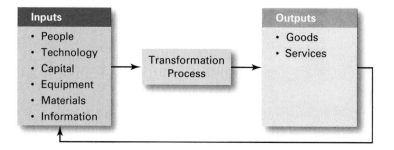

Services and Manufacturing

Every organization produces something. Unfortunately, this fact is often overlooked except in obvious cases such as in the manufacturing of cars, cell phones, or outboard engines. After all, **manufacturing organizations** produce physical goods. It's easy to see the operations management (transformation) process at work in these types of organizations because raw materials are turned into recognizable physical products. But that transformation process isn't as readily evident in **service organizations** because they produce nonphysical outputs in the form of services. For instance, hospitals provide medical and health care services that help people manage their personal health, airlines provide transportation services that move people from one location to another, a cruise line provides a vacation and entertainment service, military forces provide defense capabilities, and the list goes on and on. All of these service organizations transform inputs into outputs. Take a university, for example. University administrators bring together inputs—professors, books, academic journals, audiovisual materials, computers, classrooms, and similar resources—to transform "unenlightened" students into educated and skilled individuals.

The reason we're making this point is that the U.S. economy has gone from being dominated by the creation and sale of manufactured goods to the creation and sale of services. In fact, most of the world's industrialized nations are predominantly service economies. In the United States, for instance, approximately 80 percent of all economic activity is services.[3] Most industrialized countries are over 50 percent; for example, United Kingdom—74 percent; Japan—68 percent; Chile—55 percent; Germany—68 percent; Canada—71 percent; Australia—71 percent; and Mexico—69 percent.[4]

Managing Productivity

At the Evans Findings Company in East Providence, Rhode Island, which makes the tiny cutting devices on dental floss containers, one production shift each day is run without people.[5] The company's goal is to do as much as possible with no labor. And it's not because they don't care about their employees. Instead, like many U.S. manufacturers, Evans needed to raise productivity in order to survive, especially against low-cost competitors. So they turned to "lights-out" manufacturing where machines are designed to be so reliable that they make flawless parts on their own, without people operating them.

Although most organizations can't operate without people, improving productivity has become a major goal in virtually every organization. By **productivity** we mean the overall output of goods or services produced divided by the inputs needed to generate that output. For countries, high productivity can lead to economic growth and development. Employees can receive higher wages and company profits can increase without causing inflation. For individual organizations, increased productivity gives them a more competitive cost structure and the ability to offer more competitive prices. (▮▮▯▯▯ Go to the Web and check out Q & A 19.2.)

Over the past decade, U.S. businesses have made dramatic improvements to increase their efficiency. For example, at Latex Foam International's state-of-the-art digital facility in Shelton, Connecticut, engineers can monitor all of the factory's operations. The new facility boosted capacity by 50 percent in a smaller space but with a 30 percent efficiency gain.[6] And it's not just in manufacturing that companies are pursuing productivity gains. At Pella Corporation in Iowa, the purchasing office improved productivity by reducing purchase order entry times anywhere from 50 percent to 86 percent, decreasing voucher processing by 27 percent, and eliminating 14 financial systems. Its information technology department slashed e-mail traffic in half and implemented work design improvements for heavy PC users such as call center users. The human resources department cut the time to process benefit enrollment by 156.5 days. And the finance department now takes two days, instead of six, to do its end-of-month closeout.[7]

Improving productivity is a major task in operations management. At BJ's Wholesale Club, managers use high-speed wireless Internet technology, known as "wi-fi," to send voice messages among far-flung departments in the huge retail stores. "We looked at it more from a productivity standpoint than a cost-savings standpoint," says the firm's vice president of system services.

Organizations that hope to succeed globally are looking for ways to improve productivity. For example, McDonald's Corporation drastically reduced the amount of time it takes to cook its french fries—now only 65 seconds as compared to the 210 seconds it once took, saving time and other resources.[8] The Canadian Imperial Bank of Commerce, based in Toronto, automated its purchasing function, saving several million dollars annually.[9] And Skoda, the Czech car company owned by Germany's Volkswagen AG, improved its productivity through an intensive restructuring of its manufacturing process, and now produces 500 cars per day, almost doubling the number it used to make.[10]

Productivity is a composite of people and operations variables. (▨▨▨▨ Go to the Web and check out S.A.L. #21—What Time of Day Am I Most Productive?) To improve productivity, managers must focus on both. W. Edwards Deming, the management consultant and quality expert, believed that managers, not workers, were the primary source of increased productivity. He outlined 14 points for improving management's productivity. (See Exhibit 19–2.) A close look at these suggestions reveals Deming's understanding of the interplay between people and operations. High productivity can't come solely from good "people management." The truly effective organization will maximize productivity by successfully integrating people into the overall operations system. For instance, at Simplex Nails Manufacturing in Americus, Georgia, employees were an integral part of the company's much-needed turnaround effort.[11] Some production workers were redeployed on a plant-wide clean-up and organization effort, which freed up floor space. The company's sales force was retrained and refocused to sell what customers wanted rather than what was in inventory. The results were dramatic. Inventory was reduced by more than 50 percent, the plant had 20 percent more floor space, orders were more consistent, and employee morale improved. Here's a company that recognized the important interplay between people and the operations system.

● ● ●─────────
Exhibit 19–2

Deming's 14 Points for Improving Management's Productivity

1. Plan for the long-term future.
2. Never be complacent concerning the quality of your product.
3. Establish statistical control over your production processes and require your suppliers to do so as well.
4. Deal with the best and fewest number of suppliers.
5. Find out whether your problems are confined to particular parts of the production process or stem from the overall process itself.
6. Train workers for the job that you are asking them to perform.
7. Raise the quality of your line supervisors.
8. Drive out fear.
9. Encourage departments to work closely together rather than to concentrate on departmental or divisional distinctions.
10. Do not adopt strictly numerical goals.
11. Require your workers to do quality work.
12. Train your employees to understand statistical methods.
13. Train your employees in new skills as the need arises.
14. Make top managers responsible for implementing these principles.

Source: W.E. Deming, "Improvement of Quality and Productivity Through Action by Management," *National Productivity Review,* Winter 1981–1982, pp. 12–22. With permission. Copyright 1981 by Executive Enterprises, Inc., 22 West 21st St., New York, NY 10010-6904. All rights reserved.

Strategic Role of Operations Management

The era of modern manufacturing originated over 100 years ago in the United States, primarily in Detroit's automobile factories. The success that U.S. manufacturers experienced during World War II led manufacturing executives to believe that troublesome production problems had been conquered. These executives focused, instead, on improving other functional areas such as finance and marketing and gave manufacturing little attention.

However, as U.S. executives neglected production, managers in Japan, Germany, and other countries took the opportunity to develop modern, computer-based, and technologically advanced facilities that fully integrated manufacturing operations into strategic planning decisions. The competition's success realigned world manufacturing leadership. U.S. manufacturers soon discovered that foreign goods were being made not only less expensively but also with better quality. Finally, by the late 1970s, U.S. executives recognized that they were facing a true crisis, and they responded. They invested heavily in improving manufacturing technology, increased the corporate authority and visibility of manufacturing executives, and began incorporating existing and future production requirements into the organization's overall strategic plan. Today, successful organizations recognize the crucial role that operations management plays as part of the overall organizational strategy to establish and maintain global leadership.[12] (▬▭▬▬ Go to the Web and check out Q & A 19.3.)

The strategic role that operations management plays in successful organizational performance can be seen clearly as more organizations move toward managing their operations from a value chain perspective, which we're going to discuss next.

●●●● Learning Review

- Explain what operations management is.
- Contrast manufacturing and service organizations.

- Describe managers' roles in improving productivity.
- Discuss the strategic role of operations management.

VALUE CHAIN MANAGEMENT

It's 11:00 P.M., and you're listening to a voice mail from your parents saying they want to buy you a computer for your birthday this year and to go ahead and order it. You log on to Dell's Web site and configure your dream machine that will serve even your most demanding computing needs for the remainder of your college years. You hit the order button and within three or four days, your dream computer is delivered to your front door, built to your exact specifications, ready to set up and use immediately to finish that management assignment due tomorrow. Or consider Siemens AG's Computed Tomography manufacturing plant in Forcheim, Germany, which has established partnerships with about 30 suppliers. These suppliers are partners in the truest sense as they share responsibility with the plant for overall process performance. This arrangement has allowed Siemens to eliminate all inventory warehousing and has streamlined the number of times paper changes hands to order parts from 18 to one. At the Timken Company's plant in Canton, Ohio, electronic purchase orders are sent across the street to an adjacent "Supplier City" where many of its key suppliers have set up shop. The process takes milliseconds and costs less than 50 cents per purchase order. And when Black & Decker wanted to extend its line of handheld tools to include a glue gun, it chose to totally outsource the entire design and production to the leading glue gun manufacturer. Why? Because it understood that glue guns don't require motors, which was Black & Decker's strong point.[13]

As these examples show, closely integrated work activities among many different players are possible. How? The answer lies in value chain management. The concepts of value chain management are transforming operations management strategies and turning organizations around the world into finely tuned models of efficiency and effectiveness strategically positioned to exploit competitive opportunities as they arise.

What Is Value Chain Management?

Every organization needs customers if it's going to survive and prosper. Even not-for-profit organizations must have "customers" who use its services or purchase its products. Customers want some type of value from the goods and services they purchase or use, and these end users determine what has value. Organizations must provide that value to attract and keep customers. **Value** is the performance characteristics, features and attributes, and any other aspects of goods and services for which customers are willing to give up resources (usually money). For example, when you purchase Ashanti's new CD at Best Buy, a new pair of Australian sheepskin Ugg boots online at the company's Web site, a Wendy's bacon cheeseburger at the drive-through location on campus, or a haircut from your local hair salon, you're exchanging (giving up) money in return for the value you need or desire from these products—providing music during your evening study time, keeping your feet warm *and* fashionable during winter's cold weather, alleviating the lunchtime hunger pangs quickly since your next class starts in 15 minutes, or looking professionally groomed for the job interview you've got next week. Or, using one of our earlier examples, even Siemens AG willingly exchanges money for the value of having reliable supplier relationships. (■■■ Go to the Web and check out Q & A 19.4.)

How *is* value provided to customers? Through the transformation of raw materials and other resources into some product or service that end users need or desire where, when, and how they want it. However, that seemingly simple act of turning a variety of resources into something that customers value and are willing to pay for involves a vast array of interrelated work activities performed by different participants (suppliers, manufacturers, and even customers)—that is, it involves the value chain. The **value chain** is the entire series of organizational work activities that add value at each step beginning with the processing of raw materials and ending with the finished product in the hands of end users. In its entirety, the value chain can encompass everything from the supplier's suppliers to the customer's customer.[14] (■■■ Go to the Web and check out Q & A 19.5.)

Value chain management is the process of managing the entire sequence of integrated activities and information about product flows along the entire value chain. (■■■ Go to the Web and check out Q & A 19.6.) In contrast to supply chain management, which is internally oriented and focuses on efficient flow of incoming materials (resources) to the organization, value chain management is externally oriented and focuses on both incoming materials and outgoing products and services. And while supply chain management is efficiency oriented (its goal is to reduce costs and make the organization more productive), value chain management is effectiveness oriented and aims to create the highest value for customers.[15]

Goal of Value Chain Management

Who has the power in the value chain? Is it the suppliers providing needed resources and materials? After all, they have the ability to dictate prices and quality. Is it the manufacturer who assembles those resources into a valuable product or service? Their contribution in creating a product or service is quite obvious. Is it the distributor that makes sure the product or service is available where and when the customer needs it? Actually, it's none of these! In value chain management, ultimately customers are the ones with power.[16] They're the ones who define what value is and how it's created and provided. Using value chain management, managers hope to find that unique combination where customers are offered solutions that truly meet their unique needs incredibly fast and at a price that can't be

• • ● **value**
The performance characteristics, features and attributes, and any other aspects of goods and services for which customers are willing to give up resources.

• • ● **value chain**
The entire series of organizational work activities that add value at each step beginning with the processing of raw materials and ending with finished product in the hands of end users.

• • ● **value chain management**
The process of managing the entire sequence of integrated activities and information about product flows along the entire value chain.

matched by competitors. For example, in an effort to better anticipate customer demand and replenish customer stocks, Shell Chemical Company developed a supplier inventory management order network. The software used in this network allows managers to track shipment status, calculate appropriate inventory stock levels, and prepare re-supply schedules.

With this in mind then, the goal of value chain management is to create a value chain strategy that meets and exceeds customers' needs and desires and allows for full and seamless integration among all members of the chain. A good value chain is one in which a sequence of participants work together as a team, each adding some component of value—such as faster assembly, more accurate information, better customer response and service, and so forth—to the overall process.[17] The better the collaboration among the various chain participants, the better the customer solutions. When value is created for customers and their needs and desires are satisfied, everyone along the chain benefits. For example, at automotive interior supplier Johnson Controls Inc., managing the value chain started first with improved relationships with internal suppliers, then expanded out to external suppliers and customers. As the company's experience with value chain management intensified and improved, so did its connection with its customers, which ultimately will pay off for all its value chain partners.[18]

Requirements for Value Chain Management

Managing an organization from a value chain perspective isn't easy. (■■■■■■ Go to the Web and check out Q & A 19.7.) Approaches to giving customers what they want that may have worked in the past are likely no longer efficient or effective. Today's dynamic competitive environment facing global organizations demands new solutions. Understanding how and why value is determined by the marketplace has led some organizations to experiment with a new **business model**—that is, a strategic design for how a company intends to profit from its broad array of strategies, processes, and activities. (■■■■■■ Go to the Web and check out Q & A 19.8.) For example, IKEA, the home furnishings manufacturer, transformed itself from a small Swedish mail-order furniture operation into the world's largest retailer of home furnishings by reinventing the value chain in the home furnishings industry. The company offers customers well-designed products at substantially lower prices in return for their willingness to take on certain key tasks traditionally done by manufacturers and retailers—assembling furniture and getting it home.[19] The company's definition of a new business model and willingness to abandon old methods and processes has worked well.

Exhibit 19–3 summarizes the six main requirements of successful value chain management: coordination and collaboration, technology investment, organizational processes, leadership, employees, and organizational culture and attitudes.

● ● ● **business model**
A strategic design for how a company intends to profit from its broad array of strategies, processes, and activities.

Exhibit 19–3

Six Requirements for Successful Value Chain Management

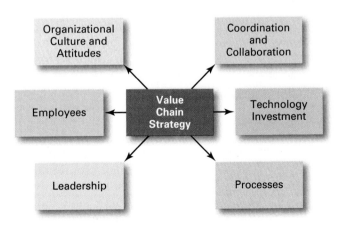

Coordination and Collaboration For the value chain to achieve its goal of meeting and exceeding customers' needs and desires, comprehensive and seamless integration among all members of the chain is absolutely necessary. Collaborative relationships must be developed. Each partner in the value chain must identify things they may not value but that customers do. And sharing information and being flexible as far as who does what in the value chain are important steps in building coordination and collaboration. This sharing of information and analysis requires more open communication among the various value chain partners. For example, Kraft Foods, the number-one U.S. food manufacturer, believes that better communication with customers and with suppliers has facilitated timely delivery of goods and services.[20]

Technology Investment Successful value chain management isn't possible without a significant investment in information technology. The payoff from this investment, however, is that information technology can be used to restructure the value chain to better serve end users. For example, Rollerblade Inc., invested significant dollars in developing a Web site and uses it to educate customers about its products. Although the company has chosen not to sell its products over the Web for fear of antagonizing its dealer network, managers remain flexible about the issue and would reconsider if they felt that value could be better delivered to customers by doing so.

●●● **organizational processes**
The ways that organizational work is done.

Organizational Processes Value chain management radically changes **organizational processes**—that is, the ways that organizational work is done. When managers decide to manage operations using value chain management, old processes are no longer appropriate. Managers must critically evaluate all organizational processes from beginning to end by looking at core competencies—the organization's major skills, capabilities, and resources—to determine where value is being added. Non-value-adding activities should be eliminated. Questions such as "Where can internal knowledge be leveraged to improve the flow of material and information?" "How can we better configure our product to satisfy both customers and suppliers?" "How can the flow of material and information be improved?" and "How can we improve customer service?" should be asked for each and every process. For example, when managers at Deere and Company implemented value chain management, a thorough process evaluation revealed that work activities needed to be better synchronized and interrelationships between multiple links in the value chain better managed. They changed numerous work processes division-wide in order to do this.[21]

We can make three important conclusions about organizational processes. First, better demand forecasting is necessary *and* possible because of closer ties with customers and suppliers. For example, in an effort to make sure that Listerine was on the store shelves when customers wanted it (known in the retail industry as product replenishment rates), Wal-Mart and Pfizer's Consumer Healthcare Group collaborated on improving product demand forecast information. Through their mutual efforts, the partners boosted Wal-Mart's sales of Listerine by $6.5 million, an excellent outcome for supplier and retailer. Customers also benefited because they were able to purchase the product when and where they wanted it.

Second, selected functions may need to be done collaboratively with other partners in the value chain. This collaboration may even extend to sharing employees. For instance, Saint-Gobain Performance Plastics places its own employees in customer sites and brings in employees of suppliers and customers to work on its premises.[22]

Collaboration between value chain partners can also benefit the larger community. At Ford Motor Company's revived assembly plant at the Ford Rouge Center south of Detroit, a partnership between the automaker and Michigan State University is creating a living roof of vegetation to rid the soil of contaminants, absorb carbon dioxide and produce oxygen, and insulate the interior while controlling storm water runoff.

Finally, new measures are needed for evaluating performance of various activities along the value chain. Because the goal in value chain management is meeting and exceeding customers' needs and desires, managers need a better picture of how well this value is being created and delivered to customers. For example, when Nestlé USA implemented a value chain management approach, it redesigned its metrics system to focus on one consistent set of measurements—including, among other measures, accuracy of demand forecasts and production plans, on-time delivery, and customer service levels—that allowed them to more quickly identify problem areas and take actions to resolve them.[23]

Leadership Successful value chain management isn't possible without strong and committed leadership. From top organizational levels to lower levels, managers must support, facilitate, and promote the implementation and ongoing practice of value chain management. Managers must make a serious commitment to identifying what value is, how that value can best be provided, and how successful those efforts have been. That type of organizational atmosphere or culture where all efforts are focused on delivering superb customer value isn't possible without a serious commitment on the part of the organization's leaders.

Also, it's important that managers outline expectations for what's involved in the organization's pursuit of value chain management. Ideally, this should start with a vision or mission statement that expresses the organization's commitment to identifying, capturing, and providing the highest possible value to customers. For instance, when American Standard (the plumbing fixtures company), began its pursuit of value chain management, the CEO held dozens of meetings across the United States to explain the new competitive environment and why the company needed to create better working relationships with its value chain partners in order to better serve the needs of its customers.[24]

Then, managers should clarify expectations regarding each employee's role in the value chain. But clear expectations aren't just important for internal partners. Being clear about expectations also extends to external partners. For example, managers at American Standard identified clear requirements for suppliers and were prepared to drop any that couldn't meet them. The company was so serious about its expectations that it did cut hundreds of suppliers from its plumbing, air conditioning, and automotive businesses. The upside, though, was that those suppliers that met the expectations benefited from more business and American Standard had partners willing to work with them in delivering better value to customers.

THINKING CRITICALLY ABOUT ETHICS

What happens when one partner in the value chain wields its power like a bully? That seems to be an apt description of what some large retailers are doing in the e-commerce arena. Manufacturers are learning that the big retailers—the companies they've always depended on to sell most of their products—can be e-commerce bullies. Instead of the manufacturers using their Web sites to sell products and risking the wrath of their customers (that is, the retailers), most choose to refer potential online buyers to the "dealer nearest you." For example, Newell Rubbermaid had sold an array of its products online. However, its Web site has been stripped of its e-commerce capability. Why? Because of a letter sent by Home Depot to most of its suppliers "suggesting" that they not sell their products to consumers over the Web.

Do you consider such "bully" behavior ethical? Why or why not? Would successful value chain management even be possible given the nature of the relationships here? Explain.

Employees/Human Resources We know from our discussions of management theories throughout this textbook that employees are the organization's most important resource. Without employees, there would be no products produced or services delivered—in fact, there would be no organized efforts in the pursuit of common goals. So, not surprisingly, employees play an important role in value chain management. The three main human resource requirements for value chain management are flexible approaches to job design, an effective hiring process, and ongoing training.

Flexibility is the key to job design in a value chain management organization. Traditional functional job roles—such as marketing, sales, accounts payable, customer service, and so forth—are inadequate in a value chain management environment. Instead, jobs need to be designed around work processes that link all functions involved in creating and providing value to customers. Since the focus needs to be on how each activity performed by an employee can best contribute to the creation and delivery of customer value, employees need to be flexible in what they do and how they do it.

The fact that jobs in a value chain management organization must be flexible contributes to the second requirement as far as employees—that is, flexible jobs require employees who are flexible. In a value chain organization, employees may be assigned to work teams that tackle a given process and are often asked to do different things on different days depending on need. In such an environment where customer value is best delivered through focusing on collaborative relationships that may change as customer needs change and where there are no standardized processes or job descriptions, an employee's ability to be flexible is critical. Therefore, the organization's hiring process must be designed to identify those employees who have the ability to learn and adapt.

Finally, the need for flexibility also requires that there be a significant investment in continual and ongoing employee training. Whether the training involves learning how to use information technology software, how to improve the flow of materials throughout the chain, how to identify activities that add value, how to make better decisions faster, or how to improve any other number of potential work activities, managers must see to it that employees have the knowledge and tools they need to do their jobs efficiently and effectively. That means providing them with training opportunities. For example, at Alenia Marconi Systems, a defense contractor based in Portsmouth, England, ongoing training is part of the company's commitment to efficiently and effectively meeting the needs of customers. Employees continually receive technical training as well as training in strategic issues including the importance of emphasizing people and customers, not just sales and profits.[25]

To cope with the change that flexible jobs can bring, employees like these may participate in simulations, games, and other kinds of training to learn about and role-play other jobs within their firms. That knowledge in turn makes people more open to adapting their own roles when value chain management practices require it.

Exhibit 19–4

Value Chain Benefits

Value chain survey respondents indicated the following are a "major benefit" from sharing information with partners:

	% of companies in excellent or very good chains	% of companies in poor chains	% of all companies
Increased sales	41%	14%	26%
Cost savings	62%	22%	40%
Increased market share	32%	12%	20%
Inventory reductions	51%	18%	35%
Improved quality	60%	28%	39%
Accelerated delivery times	54%	27%	40%
Improved logistics management	43%	15%	27%
Improved customer service	66%	22%	44%

Source: G. Taninecz, "Forging the Chain," *Industry Week*, May 15, 2000, p. 44.

Organizational Culture and Attitudes The last requirement for value chain management that we need to discuss is the importance of having supportive organizational culture and attitudes. From our extensive description of value chain management, you could probably guess the type of organizational culture and attitudes that are going to support its successful implementation! Those cultural attitudes include sharing, collaborating, openness, flexibility, mutual respect, and trust. And these attitudes encompass not only the internal partners in the value chain, but extend to external partners as well.

Benefits of Value Chain Management

Collaborating with external and internal partners in creating and managing a successful value chain strategy requires significant investments in time, energy, and other resources, and a serious commitment by all chain partners. Given this, why would managers ever choose to implement value chain management? Exhibit 19–4 highlights the results of a survey of manufacturers who had embarked on value chain management initiatives and the benefits they perceived.[26] As you can see, the major benefit that companies reported was improved customer service.

Obstacles to Value Chain Management

As desirable as these benefits may be, managers must deal with several obstacles in managing the value chain, including: organizational barriers, cultural attitudes, required capabilities, and people. (See Exhibit 19–5.)

Exhibit 19–5

Obstacles to Successful Value Chain Management

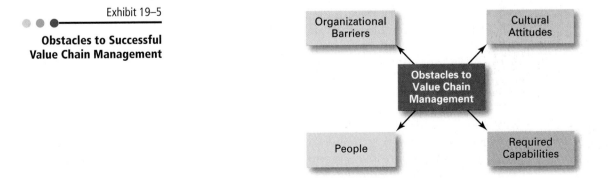

Organizational Barriers Organizational barriers are among the most difficult obstacles managers handle. These barriers include refusal or reluctance to share information, reluctance to shake up the status quo, and security issues. Without shared information, close coordination and collaboration are impossible. And, the reluctance or refusal of employees to disturb the status quo can impede efforts toward value chain management and prevent its successful implementation. Finally, because value chain management relies heavily on a substantial information technology infrastructure, system security and Internet security breaches are issues that need to be addressed.

Cultural Attitudes Unsupportive cultural attitudes—especially trust and control—also can be obstacles to value chain management. The trust issue is a critical one, both lack of trust and too much trust. To be effective, partners in a value chain must trust each other. There must be a mutual respect for, and honesty about, each partner's activities all along the chain. When that trust doesn't exist, the partners will be reluctant to share information, capabilities, and processes. But too much trust also can be a problem. Just about any organization is vulnerable to theft of **intellectual property**—that is, proprietary company information that's critical to its efficient and effective functioning and competitiveness. And today's increased terrorist threats further illustrate the importance of being able to trust your value chain partners so that you don't compromise your organization's valuable assets.[27] Although value chain partners need to trust each other, the potential for theft can be minimized by better understanding each others' operations and by being careful with proprietary intellectual property.

Another cultural attitude that can be an obstacle to successful value chain management is the belief that when an organization collaborates with external and internal partners, it no longer controls its own destiny. However, this just isn't the case. Even with the intense collaboration that must take place, organizations still control critical decisions including what customers value, how much value they desire, and what distribution channels are important.[28]

Required Capabilities We know from our earlier discussion of requirements for successful implementation of value chain management that there are a number of capabilities that value chain partners must have. Several of these, including coordination and collaboration, the ability to configure products to satisfy customers and suppliers, and the ability to educate internal and external partners, aren't easy to do. But they're essential to capturing and exploiting the value chain. Many of the companies we've described throughout this section endured critical, and oftentimes difficult, self-evaluations of their capabilities and processes in order to become more effective and efficient at managing their value chains.

People The final obstacles to successful value chain management can be an organization's members. Without their unwavering commitment to do whatever it takes, value chain management isn't going to be successful. If employees refuse to be flexible, it's going to be difficult to make the necessary changes to meet changing situational demands. After all, it's the employees who do the work. If they're not willing to be flexible in what work they do, and how and with whom they work, collaboration and cooperation throughout the value chain will be hard to achieve.

In addition, value chain management takes an incredible amount of time and energy by an organization's employees. Managers must motivate those high levels of effort from employees, which isn't easy to do.

Finally, a major human resource problem faced by organizations pursuing value chain management is the lack of experienced managers who are able to lead value chain management initiatives. Since it's a relatively new approach to managing operations, there aren't a lot of managers who've done it successfully. However, this obstacle hasn't prevented progressive organizations from pursuing the benefits to be gained from value chain management.

• • • **intellectual property**
Proprietary company information that's critical to its efficient and effective functioning and competitiveness.

Learning Review

- Define value chain and value chain management.
- Describe the goal of value chain management.
- Discuss the requirements for successful value chain management.
- Describe the benefits that result from value chain management.
- Explain the obstacles to value chain management.

CURRENT ISSUES IN OPERATIONS MANAGEMENT

England Inc., a furniture manufacturer owned by La-Z Boy Inc., and based in Tennessee, is pursuing an ambitious goal unheard of in the upholstered furniture industry—making and delivering a custom upholstered couch in three weeks. England's managers responded when customers started turning to importers because they couldn't get the products they wanted in a reasonable time frame. Reaching that goal, however, would require revamping its operations management process to exploit technology while maintaining quality.[29] England's experience illustrates three of today's most important operations management issues: technology, quality, and mass customization.

Technology's Role in Manufacturing

As we know from our previous discussion of value chain management, today's competitive marketplace has put tremendous pressure on organizations to deliver products and services that customers value in a timely manner. Smart companies are looking at ways to harness technology to improve operations management. For example, Schneider Automation Inc., of North Andover, Massachusetts, implemented its Transparent Factory initiative—a framework for linking plant-floor automation with enterprise-wide business network systems. With millions of device sensors and actuators on its factory floors running on stand-alone software but with no way to connect to the factory's system network, managers saw prime opportunities to capitalize on information technology solutions to manage its operations more effectively and efficiently.[30]

Although manufacturing is being driven by the recognition that the customer is king, managers still need to realize that the organization's production activities must be more responsive. For instance, operations managers need systems that can reveal available capacity, status of orders, and product quality while products are in the process of being manufactured, not just after the fact. To connect more closely with customers, operations across the enterprise, including manufacturing, must be synchronized. To avoid production and delivery bottlenecks, the manufacturing function must be a full partner in the entire business system.

What's making this type of extensive involvement and collaboration possible is technology. Technology is also allowing manufacturing plants to control costs, particularly in the areas of predictive maintenance, remote diagnostics, and utility cost savings. For instance, let's look at how technology is affecting the equipment maintenance function—an important operations management activity. New generations of Internet-compatible equipment contain embedded Web servers that can communicate proactively—that is, if a piece of equipment breaks or reaches certain preset parameters that it's about to break, it can ask for help. But technology can do more than sound an alarm or light up an indicator button. For instance, some devices have the ability to initiate e-mail or signal a pager at a supplier, the maintenance department, or contractor describing the specific problem and requesting parts and service. How much is such e-enabled maintenance control worth? It can be worth quite a lot if it prevents equipment breakdowns and subsequent production downtime.

Technology continues to have enormous impact on improving operations management. This revamped and expanded UPS distribution center in Louisville, Kentucky, was the most expensive project in the company's nearly 100-year history and contains a 63-mile long labyrinth of conveyor belts that carries over 300,000 packages through the building every hour. Jack Blaisdell, project manager, says, "The visual of it all is pretty impressive. But I also marvel at the unseen: Many pieces of technology making so many decisions to make it all happen."

●●● **quality**
The ability of a product or service to reliably do what it's supposed to do and to satisfy customer expectations.

Managers who understand the power of technology to contribute to more effective and efficient performance know that managing operations is more than the traditional view of manufacturing's role in producing the product. Instead, the emphasis is on working together with all the organization's business functions to find solutions to customers' business problems.

Quality Initiatives

Quality problems are expensive. For example, it cost Toshiba Corporation $2.1 billion to settle a lawsuit over defects in its laptop computers. Palm, Inc., the leading manufacturer of personal digital assistants (PDAs), revealed that its first model with a color screen had a tendency to crack. It offered customers free replacements for cracked units. At Schering-Plough, problems with inhalers and other pharmaceuticals were traced to chronic quality control shortcomings, for which the company eventually paid a $500 million fine.[31]

Many experts believe that organizations unable to produce high-quality products won't be able to compete successfully in the global marketplace. Look back at the chapter-opening "Manager's Dilemma." Managers at Bombardier knew they would have to produce quality products in order to be a strong competitor in the intensely competitive global engines market. (▮▮▯▯▯▯ Go to the Web and check out Q & A 19.9.)

What is quality? When you consider a product or service to have quality, what does that mean? Does it mean that the product doesn't break or quit working—that is, that it's reliable? Does it mean that the service is delivered in a way that you intended? Does it mean that the product does what it's supposed to do? Or does quality mean something else? Exhibit 19–6 provides a description of several quality dimensions. We're going to define **quality** as the ability of a product or service to reliably do what it's supposed to do and to satisfy customer expectations.

Exhibit 19–6

●●●──────
Quality Dimensions of Goods and Services

Product Quality Dimensions

1. Performance—Operating characteristics
2. Features—Important special characteristics
3. Flexibility—Meeting operating specifications over some period of time
4. Durability—Amount of use before performance deteriorates
5. Conformance—Match with preestablished standards
6. Serviceability—Ease and speed of repair or normal service
7. Aesthetics—How a product looks and feels
8. Perceived quality—Subjective assessment of characteristics (product image)

Service Quality Dimensions

1. Timeliness—Performed in promised period of time
2. Courtesy—Performed cheerfully
3. Consistency—Giving all customers similar experiences each time
4. Convenience—Accessibility to customers
5. Completeness—Fully serviced, as required
6. Accuracy—Performed correctly each time

Source: Adapted from J.W. Dean, Jr., and J.R. Evans, *Total Quality: Management, Organization and Society* (St. Paul, MN: West Publishing Company, 1994); H.V. Roberts and B.F. Sergesketter, *Quality Is Personal* (New York: The Free Press, 1993); D. Garvin, *Managed Quality: The Strategic and Competitive Edge* (New York: The Free Press, 1988); and M.A. Hitt, R.D. Ireland, and R.E. Hoskisson, *Strategic Management*, 4th ed. (Cincinnati, OH: SouthWestern, 2001), p. 211.

How is quality achieved? That's the issue managers must address. A good way to address quality initiatives is to think in terms of the management functions—planning, organizing and leading, and controlling—that need to take place. (▪▫▪ Check out Passport Scenario 2 on p. 510.)

Planning for Quality Managers must have quality improvement goals and strategies and plans formulated to achieve those goals. Goals can help focus everyone's attention toward some objective quality standard. For instance, at the Rockwell Collins avionics plant based in Decorah, Iowa (where Rockwell International's communications and navigation equipment are made), a quality goal being pursued by employees over the next four years is a 30 percent reduction in defects.[32] Although this goal is specific and challenging, managers and employees are partnering together to pursue well-designed strategies to achieve the goals, and are confident they can do so.

Organizing and Leading for Quality Since quality improvement initiatives are carried out by organizational employees, it's important for managers to look at how they can best organize and lead them. For instance, at the Rockwell Collins avionics plant, every employee participates in process improvement workshops. A Rockwell executive says, "The spirit within that plant is high. They do seem to be excited about what they have accomplished. This is not something we are doing to them. This is something they are doing with us."[33]

Organizations with extensive and successful quality improvement programs tend to rely on two important people approaches: cross-functional work teams and self-directed or empowered work teams. Because achieving product quality is something that all employees from upper levels to lower levels must participate in, it's not surprising that quality-driven organizations rely on well-trained, flexible, and empowered employees.

Controlling for Quality Quality improvement initiatives aren't possible without having some way to monitor and evaluate their progress. (▪▪▪▫ Check out You're The Manager: Putting Ethics into Action on p. 510.) Whether it involves standards for inventory control, defect rate, raw materials procurement, or any other operations management area, controlling for quality is important. For instance, at the Aeroquip-Inoac Company (AIC) (an automotive exterior trim plant in Livingston, Tennessee), a closely knit group of employees is dedicated to continuous improvement. They use employee suggestions, benchmarking visits, and other numerous quality initiatives and have built a reputation for delivering high-quality products. The company wasn't always this efficient or effective. Prior to 1992, its quality control was performed mainly by employees in the quality control department. However, when a new plant manager was hired, he wanted to see ownership of quality turned over to employees on the manufacturing floor. It wasn't an easy transformation as employees initially resisted any changes. However, the company's current quality assurance environment supports defect prevention rather than defect detection. Quality became the responsibility of all employees. Today, employees and managers work together to solve problems and provide customers with the quality products they value.[34]

If this man does not look familiar, it's probably because Scott Siegel has never won an Academy Award; he owns the company that manufactures the coveted golden statuettes. Each Oscar takes more than a day to make, using the alloy britannia and an electroplated layer of copper, nickel, and silver topped with a hand-dipped finish of 24-karat gold. Quality controls at the plant are stringent. Even the smallest blemish or flaw requires the statuette to be melted down and begun anew.

These types of quality improvement success stories aren't limited to U.S. operations. For example, at a Delphi Automotive Systems Corporation assembly plant in Matamoros, Mexico, employees have worked hard to improve quality and have made significant strides. The customer reject rate on shipped products is now 10 ppm (parts per million), down from 3,000 ppm just five years ago—an improvement of almost 300 percent.[35] Quality initiatives at several Australian companies, including Alcoa of Australia, Wormald Security, and Carlton and United Breweries, have led to significant quality improvements.[36] And at Valeo Klimasystemme GmbH of Bad Rodach, Germany, assembly teams build different climate-control systems for high-end German cars including the Mercedes E-Class, BMW 5 Series, and Opel Omega/Cadillac Catera. Quality initiatives by Valeo's employee teams have led to significant improvements in various quality standards.[37]

Quality Goals

To publicly demonstrate their quality commitment, many organizations worldwide have pursued challenging quality goals—the two best known being ISO 9000 and Six Sigma. (■□■■■■ Go to the Web and check out Q & A 19.10.)

• • • **ISO 9000**
A series of international quality management standards that set uniform guidelines for processes to ensure that products conform to customer requirements.

ISO 9000 ISO 9000 is a series of international quality management standards established by the International Organization for Standardization (**www.iso.ch**), which set uniform guidelines for processes to ensure that products conform to customer requirements. These standards cover everything from contract review to product design to product delivery. The ISO 9000 standards have become the internationally recognized standard for evaluating and comparing companies in the global marketplace. In fact, this type of certification is becoming a prerequisite for doing business globally. Gaining ISO 9000 certification provides proof that a quality operations system is in place.

The 2002 survey of ISO 9000 certificates showed that the number of registered sites worldwide exceeded 561,000, an increase of almost 10 percent from the previous year.[38] And these certificates had been awarded in 159 countries.

• • • **Six Sigma**
A quality standard that establishes a goal of no more than 3.4 defects per million parts or procedures.

Six Sigma Motorola popularized the use of stringent quality standards more than 30 years ago through a trademarked quality improvement program called Six Sigma.[39] Very simply, **Six Sigma** is a quality standard that establishes a goal of no more than 3.4 defects per million units or procedures. What does the name mean? Sigma is the Greek letter that statisticians use to define a standard deviation from a bell curve. The higher the sigma, the fewer the deviations from the norm—that is, the fewer the defects. At One Sigma, two-thirds of whatever is being measured falls within the curve. Two Sigma covers about 95 percent. At Six Sigma, you're about as close to defect-free as you can get.[40] It's an ambitious quality goal! Although it may be an extremely high standard to achieve, many quality-driven businesses are using it and benefiting from it. For instance, General Electric realized approximately $8 billion in savings through its Six Sigma program from 1999 to 2002, according to company executives.[41] Other well-known companies pursuing Six Sigma include ITT Industries, Dow Chemical, 3M Company, American Express, Sony Corporation, Nokia Corporation, and Johnson & Johnson. Although manufacturers seem to make up the bulk of Six Sigma users, service companies such as financial institutions, retailers, and health care organizations are beginning to apply it. What impact can Six Sigma have? Let's look at an example.

Becoming a Manager

- ◆ *As you interact with various businesses, think about the value chain of each.*
- ◆ *Read about quality management techniques.*
- ◆ *Think of ways that you could (1) be more productive and (2) have higher-quality output.*
- ◆ *Take advantage of mass-customization opportunities and assess what was positive and negative about the experience.*
- ◆ ■■■□■ *Go to the Web and complete the following exercise from the Self-Assessment Library (S.A.L.) found on R.O.L.L.S: #21—What Time of Day Am I Most Productive?*

It used to take Wellmark Inc., a managed-care health care company, 65 days or more to add a new doctor to its Blue Cross & Blue Shield Association medical plans. Now, thanks to Six Sigma, the company discovered that half the processes it used were redundant. With those unnecessary steps gone, the job now gets done in 30 days or less and with reduced staff. The company also has been able to reduce its administrative expenses by $3 million per year, an amount passed on to consumers through lower health insurance premiums.[42]

Summary Although it's important for managers to recognize that many positive benefits can accrue from obtaining ISO 9000 certification or Six Sigma, the key benefit comes from the quality improvement journey itself. In other words, the goal of quality certification should be having work processes and an operations system in place that enable organizations to meet customers' needs and employees to perform their jobs in a consistently high-quality way.

Mass Customization

● ● ● **mass customization**
Providing consumers with a product when, where, and how they want it.

The term "mass customization" seems an oxymoron. However, the design-to-order concept is becoming an important operations management issue for today's managers. **Mass customization** provides consumers with a product when, where, and how they want it.[43] Companies as diverse as BMW, Levi Strauss, Wells Fargo, Mattel, and Dell Computer are adopting mass customization to maintain or attain a competitive advantage.

Mass customization requires flexible manufacturing techniques and continual dialogue with customers.[44] Technology plays an important role in both.

With flexible manufacturing, companies have the ability to quickly readjust assembly lines to make products to order. Using technology such as computer-controlled factory equipment, intranets, industrial robots, bar-code scanners, digital printers, and logistics software, companies can manufacture, assemble, and ship customized products with customized packaging to customers in incredibly short time frames. Dell is a good example of a company that uses flexible manufacturing techniques and technology to custom-build computers to customers' specifications.

Technology also is important in the continual dialogue with customers. Using extensive databases, companies can keep track of customers' likes and dislikes. And

Mass customization requires superior technology as well as ample feedback from customers. E-businesses like Amazon.com make use of customers' orders and inquiries to customize the greetings that top its Web site's homepage and to tailor recommendations of books and other products its customers might want to buy.

the Internet has made it possible for companies to have ongoing dialogues with customers to learn about and respond to their exact preferences. For instance, on Levi Strauss's Web site, customers can create their own virtual model to get a custom-fitted pair of jeans. And Procter & Gamble uses its Reflect.com Web site to customize beauty products for customers. The ability to customize a product to a customer's exact specifications starts an important relationship between the organization and the customer. If the customer likes the product and it provides value, he or she is more likely to be a repeat customer. And, Levi Strauss has found that customers who design their own jeans are a good source of information that can be used in designing its jeans for mass production.

•••• Learning Review

- Discuss technology's role in manufacturing.
- Describe some of the various quality dimensions.
- Explain ISO 9000 and Six Sigma.
- Describe mass customization and how operations management contributes to it.

Managers **Respond** to a **Manager's** Dilemma

····Debra Barnhart

Director, Network Medical Management Support,
St. John's Health System, Springfield, Missouri

For Bombardier and Mr. Lambert to be successful, they must incorporate a culture of quality with a continuous focus on the manufacturing process (including external suppliers) and take steps to reestablish confidence of dealers, former customers, and future customers. He has taken the first steps, but next he needs to: communicate the quality program to all managers, employees, and dealers; provide initial and ongoing quality training; conduct focus groups with dissatisfied dealers to identify critical issues; ensure supplier commitment to quality specifications; establish management and employee incentives tied to key quality measures; implement an internal and external communication program that reports quality performance achievements; and recognize and celebrate successes by managers and employees as they achieve quality goals.

James O'Neill

Marketing Campaign Director, Pearson Prentice Hall,
Minneapolis, Minnesota

Losing half their market share is devastating for any company. I would recommend that Roch Lambert take the following actions: Move toward just-in-time and lean manufacturing, which should help eliminate waste and reduce costs; be more flexible to meet customer preferences; implement a total quality manufacturing process such as Six Sigma; train employees and managers in total quality manufacturing; align employees' and managers' economic incentives with quality; invest heavily in advanced information systems technology so he can best manage the value chain; and he might consider a team-based manufacturing approach since this seems to work well for companies pursuing quality initiatives.

Learning Summary

After reading and studying this chapter, you should be able to:

- Explain what operations management is.
- Contrast manufacturing and service organizations.
- Describe managers' roles in improving productivity.
- Discuss the strategic role of operations management.
- Define value chain and value chain management.
- Describe the goal of value chain management.

- Discuss the requirements for successful value chain management.
- Describe the benefits that result from value chain management.
- Explain the obstacles to value chain management.
- Discuss technology's role in manufacturing.
- Describe some of the various quality dimensions.
- Explain ISO 9000 and Six Sigma.
- Describe mass customization and how operations management contributes to it.

Thinking About Management Issues

1. Do you think that manufacturing or service organizations have the greater need for operations management? Explain.

2. How might operations management apply to other managerial functions besides control?

3. How could you use value chain management concepts in your everyday life?

4. Which is more critical for success in organizations: continuous improvement or quality control? Support your position.

5. Choose some large organization that you're interested in studying. Research this company to find out what types of operations management strategies it is using. Focus on describing what it's doing that's unusual or effective or both.

Working Together: Team-Based Exercise

Break into groups of four to five students. Your team's task is to assess how you believe technology will change the way your college disseminates information to students a decade from now. Specifically, what do you believe the typical college's teaching technologies will look like in the year 2015? Here are some questions to consider:

1. Will there still be a need for a college campus spanning several hundred acres?

2. Do you believe every student will be required to have a laptop for classes?

3. How, if at all, will technology change the classroom?

4. Do you believe students will be required to physically come to campus for their classes?

5. What role will distance learning and telecommuting play in classroom activities? You have 30 minutes to discuss these issues and develop your responses. Appoint someone on your team to present your team's findings to the class.

Ethical Dilemma Exercise

What is a company's responsibility to notify customers of a potential quality problem? Sun Microsystems posed this question to managers in an ethics "boot camp" training program set up by David Farrell, chief compliance officer. Like many corporations, Sun is using a multipronged approach to translating its ethical values and policies into ethical decisions and actions. The company has circulated ethical guidelines to executives for years. It also established a business conduct office to coordinate and supervise all ethics activities. But training is at the heart of Sun's initiatives. All employees must complete an online ethics course. In addition, all managers must attend concentrated boot camp training. Although they hear presenta-

tions from the CEO and other officials, attendees spend most of their time in teams, grappling with realistic ethical issues.

The chief competitive officer describes one particularly difficult scenario his team faced: "We had to pretend a customer was having a problem with a brand-new product. Our mission was to decide whether to immediately scare all customers who had purchased the product by issuing a wide-scale red alert" or wait until Sun's engineers had investigated the problem. "It wasn't easy. There was no correct answer we could look up in some guidebook," the executive commented. David Farrell acknowledges the challenge. "You just can't immunize a company with thousands of managers around the world against [ethical] problems," he says. "But you can make sure that they're better prepared to deal with such issues when they arise."[45]

Imagine that you are at ethics boot camp along with other Sun managers. Your team must decide how to respond to the scenario in which one customer reports a problem with a new product. You can see good arguments for and against quickly communicating with all the customers who own that product. Review Exhibit 19.6 as you consider this ethical challenge and decide which of the following options to choose—and why.

Option A: Don't contact any customers until Sun's engineers have definitely determined the cause and come up with a good solution.

Option B: Reassure any customers who complain that Sun is moving quickly to find the cause; also halt sales of the product until the problem has been resolved.

Option C: Informing customers who bought the product that one problem has been reported and Sun is investigating to determine the cause.

Case Application

DaimlerChrysler

At DaimlerChrysler's three-plant manufacturing complex in Toledo, Ohio, manager Edward Mercer runs the oldest auto plant in the world and also the newest, most high-tech plant in the company. The oldest facility dates back to 1910 and houses the body and paint shops for the Jeep Wrangler, which is assembled in the second facility. However, it's the third facility, the new $700 million factory where DaimlerChrysler has brought together the latest ideas and equipment to manufacture the Jeep Liberty, that most excites Mercer. And it's not that the techniques and technologies being used at the plant are unique to DaimlerChrysler, but it is the first time that all of these have been gathered under one roof. And the payoff—it takes fewer worker-hours to assemble a Liberty than any other Chrysler vehicle, approximately 26.11 production and control worker-hours. Although that's good for Chrysler, it still isn't as good as competitors—Ford builds its Escape SUV in 22.54 worker-hours and Nissan requires only 18.63 for its Xterra.

Unfinished Jeep Liberty at DaimlerChrysler plant in Toledo, Ohio.

One of the first things DaimlerChrysler did in this new plant was to install equipment similar to what was used at its Mercedes facilities, including a pallet system that lifts and lowers the Jeep body from one assembly station to the next. It took the design of a paint shop first used in a truck plant in Delaware. And the facility also does what other auto industry competitors are doing—it outsources large components of the Liberty and receives these components not only exactly when they're needed (just-in-time inventory), but exactly in the correct production line sequence. Many of these suppliers don't even start building the parts until they get electronic notification that the body of the Jeep for which they're intended is heading to the first assembly line workstation.

There is little inventory of components, modules, or parts. Among the daily deliveries for the facility are 199 trailers from eight companies including Johnson Controls and TRW. If any deliveries are delayed, it can stop the assembly line. The company's procurement director says, "If there's a disruption in the supply base anywhere, the plant sees it in a hurry." So far, that hasn't happened. Maybe that's because suppliers are subject to a heavy penalty if they stop the production line. In fact, TRW has twice hired a helicopter to deliver needed bolts.

DISCUSSION QUESTIONS

1. What advantages and drawbacks do you see to DaimlerChrysler's approach at this Jeep plant?

2. Is DaimlerChrysler's new facility an example of value chain management? Explain.

3. How do technology, quality, and mass customization affect this facility's operations management?

Source: P. Siekman, "Jeep Builds a New Kind of Plant," *Fortune,* November 11, 2002, pp. T168B-T168L.

Part 6

● ● ●

You're the Manager: Putting Ethics into Action

As a manager, you'll often face decisions involving ethical questions. How can you learn to identify the ethical dilemma, keep stakeholders in mind, think through the alternatives, and foresee the consequences of your decisions? This unique interactive feature, positioned at the end of Parts Two, Three, Four, Five, and Six, casts you in the role of a manager dealing with hypothetical yet realistic ethical issues. To start, read the preview paragraph below. Then log on to www.prenhall.com/robbins and go to the R.O.L.L.S. Web site to consider the decisions you would make in the role of manager.

Product flaws are never good news—but they're especially unwelcome in sophisticated business software. If you were a Sun Microsystems manager, how would you cope with the news that one of your programs had a security flaw? Suppose the flaw allowed hackers who penetrated the vulnerable part of this software to get into any file stored on the affected computer. Would you want customers to hear about the flaw from news reports, not from you or one of your employees? What ethical issues would be raised by talking to reporters or competitors about the flaw? Log onto www.prenhall.com/robbins to put ethics into action!

Passport

● ● ●

Scenario 1

Nelson Naidoo is vice president of logistics for Diamonds International, a global exporter of high-quality colored diamonds based in Johannesburg, South Africa. Nelson oversees the company's shipping and transportation to the company's other facilities in Rio de Janeiro, New York, Lisbon, and Moscow. It's the Rio facility where Nelson is currently having a problem.

Tatiana Mercado is the logistics manager in Rio and has been employed by Diamonds International for a year. The company's top managers believe strongly in employee job training and Tatiana has been well trained in the company's procedures for accepting and checking in new inventory. But for the last two shipments, Tatiana's paperwork has been missing some key pieces of information. Because of the dollar value involved in the product shipments, Nelson flies to Rio tomorrow to discuss the problems with Tatiana. What will be the best approach for Nelson to handle this situation? He doesn't really want to fire Tatiana as her previous job performance had been good. But how can he ensure that the problems get resolved and don't happen again?

To answer these questions, you'll have to do some research on the countries. Go to www.prenhall.com/robbins, the R.O.L.L.S. Web site, and click on Passport. When the map appears, click on the countries you need to research. You'll find background information on the country and general information about the country's economy, population, and workforce. In addition, you'll find specific information on the country's culture and the unique qualities associated with doing business there.

Scenario 2

Kristen Mesicek is the product quality manager for Global One Cellular, a cell phone distributor based in San Diego, California. Global One imports cellular phone components from China and assembles them at a facility in Guadalajara, Mexico. Once assembled, the cell phones are shipped to customers around the world. Global One's phones are known for their reliability and durability, a reputation that isn't easy to get in this intensely competitive market.

Carlos Lopez, the operations manager in Guadalajara, had alerted Kristen last week that the last seven shipments of cell phone components from the Chinese manufacturer had serious quality problems and 15 percent of the product components had to be discarded. Because of the cost involved, Kristen knew she needed to attend to the problem immediately.

Kristen has scheduled a videoconference for tomorrow with Carlos and with the Chinese plant manager, Dai Tan, to get the problems resolved. What cross-cultural issues might Kristen run into as she attempts to get this quality control problem fixed? How can she make sure the problem is fixed and minimize the potential of the problem reoccurring?

To answer these questions, you'll have to do some research on the countries. Go to www.prenhall.com/robbins, the R.O.L.L.S. Web site, and click on Passport. When the map appears, click on the countries you need to research. You'll find background information on the country and general information about the country's economy, population, and workforce. In addition, you'll find specific information on the country's culture and the unique qualities associated with doing business there.

Managing Entrepreneurial Ventures

Controlling Issues

Entrepreneurs must look at controlling their venture's operations in order to survive and prosper in both the short run and long run. Those unique control issues that face entrepreneurs include managing growth, managing downturns, exiting the venture, and managing personal life choices and challenges.

Managing Growth

Glory Foods has taken an unusual approach to managing growth. The Columbus, Ohio, company sells "down-home-tasting" Southern specialties that are quick and easy to prepare, an alternative to the traditional Southern cooking that takes hours. Glory Foods has successfully cornered a market niche by following a conservative path to growth. The founders decided to move slowly because they didn't want to dilute their equity positions in order to acquire the increased financing needed to grow. Although the slow growth approach may have taken more time, the partners felt it was worth it because they had total control over what happened to the company.[1] Hot Topic, the trendy retail store for teens, has taken a different growth approach. It continues to open new stores and revenues have grown an average of 37 percent over the last three years. CEO Betsy McLaughlin is focused on keeping the company growing at its "hot" pace.[2]

Growth is a natural and desirable outcome for entrepreneurial ventures; it is what distinguishes an entrepreneurial venture. In fact, it's part of our definition of entrepreneurship. Entrepreneurial ventures pursue growth.[3] Growing slowly can be successful, as Glory Foods discovered. But so can rapid growth, as Hot Topic shows.

Growing successfully doesn't just occur randomly or by luck. Successfully pursuing growth typically requires an entrepreneur to manage all the challenges associated with growing. This entails planning, organizing, and controlling for growth.

Planning for Growth Although it may seem we've reverted back to discussing planning issues instead of controlling issues, actually controlling is tied closely to planning, as we know from our discussion in Chapter 18 (see Exhibit 18–2). And the best growth strategy is a well-planned one.[4] Ideally, the decision to grow doesn't come about spontaneously, but instead is part of the venture's overall business goals and plan. Rapid growth without planning can be disastrous. Entrepreneurs need to address growth strategies as part of their business planning but shouldn't be overly rigid in that planning. The plans should be flexible enough to exploit unexpected opportunities that arise. With plans in place, the successful entrepreneur must then organize for growth.

Organizing for Growth The key challenges for an entrepreneur in organizing for growth include finding capital, finding people, and strengthening the organizational culture.

Having enough capital is a major challenge facing growing entrepreneurial ventures. The money issue never seems to go away, does it? It does take capital to expand.

The processes of finding capital to fund growth are much like going through the initial financing of the venture. However, at this time, hopefully, the venture has a successful track record to back up the request. If it doesn't, it may be extremely difficult to acquire the necessary capital. That's why we said earlier that the best growth strategy is a planned one. Part of that planning should be how growth will be financed. For example, the Boston Beer Company, which produces Samuel Adams beer, grew rapidly by focusing almost exclusively on increasing its top-selling product line. However, the company was so focused on increasing market share that it had few financial controls and an inadequate financial infrastructure. During periods of growth, cash flow difficulties would force company president and brewmaster Jim Koch to tap into a pool of unused venture capital funding. However, when a chief financial officer joined the company, he developed a financial structure that enabled it to manage its growth more efficiently and effectively by setting up a plan for funding growth.[5]

Another important issue that a growing entrepreneurial venture needs to address is finding people. If the venture is growing quickly, this challenge may be intensified because of the time constraints. It's important to plan, as much as possible, the numbers and types of employees needed to support the increasing workload as the venture grows. Also, it may be necessary to provide additional training and support to employees to help them handle the increased pressures associated with a growing organization.

Finally, when a venture is growing, it's important to create a positive, growth-oriented culture that enhances the opportunities to achieve success, both organizationally and individually. This sometimes can be difficult to do, particularly when changes are occurring rapidly. However, the values, attitudes, and beliefs that are established and reinforced during these times are critical to the entrepreneurial venture's continued and future success. Exhibit P6–1 lists some suggestions that entrepreneurs might use to ensure that their venture's culture is one that embraces and supports a climate in which organizational growth is viewed as desirable and important. Keeping employees focused and committed to what the venture is doing is critical to the ultimate success of its growth strategies. If employees don't "buy into" the direction in which the entrepreneurial venture is headed, it's unlikely the growth strategies will be successful.

Controlling for Growth Another challenge that growing entrepreneurial ventures face is reinforcing already established organizational controls. Maintaining good financial records and financial controls over cash flow, inventory, customer data, sales orders, receivables, payables, and costs should be a priority of every entrepreneur—whether pursuing growth or not. However, it's particularly important to reinforce these controls when the entrepreneurial venture is expanding. It's all too easy to let things "get away" or to put off doing them when there's an unrelenting urgency to get things done. Rapid growth—or even slow

● ● ●

Exhibit P6–1

Suggestions for Achieving a Supportive Growth-Oriented Culture

- Keep the lines of communication open—inform employees about major issues.
- Establish trust by being honest, open, and forthright about the challenges and rewards of being a growing organization.
- Be a good listener—find out what employees are thinking and facing.
- Be willing to delegate duties.
- Be flexible—be willing to change your plans if necessary.
- Provide consistent and regular feedback by letting employees know the outcomes—good and bad.
- Reinforce the contributions of each person by recognizing employees' efforts.
- Continually train employees to enhance their capabilities and skills.
- Maintain the focus on the venture's mission even as it grows.
- Establish and reinforce a "we" spirit since a successful growing venture takes the coordinated efforts of all the employees.

growth—does not diminish the need to have effective controls in place. In fact, it's particularly important to have established procedures, protocols, and processes and to use them. Even though mistakes and inefficiencies can never be eliminated entirely, at least an entrepreneur should ensure that every effort is being made to achieve high levels of productivity and organizational effectiveness. For example, at Green Gear Cycling, co-founder Alan Scholz recognized the importance of controlling for growth. How? By following a "Customers for Life" strategy, which means continually monitoring customer relationships and orienting organizational work decisions around their possible impacts on customers. Through this type of strategy, Green Gear hopes to keep customers for life. That's significant because it figured that if it could keep a customer for life, the value would range from $10,000 to $25,000 per lifetime customer.[6]

Managing Downturns

Although organizational growth is a desirable and important goal for entrepreneurial ventures, what happens when things don't go as planned—when the growth strategies don't result in the intended outcomes and, in fact, result in a decline in performance? There are challenges, as well, in managing the downturns.

Nobody likes to fail, especially entrepreneurs. However, when an entrepreneurial venture faces times of trouble, what can be done? How can downturns be managed successfully? The first step is recognizing that a crisis is brewing.

Recognizing Crisis Situations An entrepreneur should be alert to the warning signs of a business in trouble. Some signals of potential performance decline include inadequate or negative cash flow, excess number of employees, unnecessary and cumbersome administrative procedures, fear of conflict and taking risks, tolerance of work incompetence, lack of a clear mission or goals, and ineffective or poor communication within the organization.[7]

Another perspective on recognizing performance declines revolves around what is known as the "**boiled frog**" phenomenon.[8] The "boiled frog" is a classic psychological response experiment. In one case, a live frog that's dropped into a pan of boiling water reacts instantaneously and jumps out of the pan. But, in the second case, a live frog that's dropped into a pan of cold water that is gradually heated to the boiling point, fails to react and dies. A small firm may be particularly vulnerable to the boiled frog phenomenon because the

entrepreneur may not recognize the "water heating up"—that is, the subtly declining situation. When changes in performance are gradual, a serious response may never be triggered or may happen too late to do anything about the situation. So what does the boiled frog phenomenon teach us? That entrepreneurs need to be alert to the signals that the venture's performance may be worsening. Don't wait until the water has reached the boiling point to react.

Dealing with Downturns, Declines, and Crises Although an entrepreneur hopes never to have to deal with organizational downturns, declines, or crises, there may come a time when he or she must do just that. After all, nobody likes to think about things going bad or taking a turn for the worse. But that's exactly what the entrepreneur should do—think about it *before* it happens (remember feedforward control from Chapter 18).[9] It's important to have an up-to-date plan for covering crises. It's like mapping exit routes from your home in case of a fire. An entrepreneur wants to be prepared before an emergency hits. This plan should focus on providing specific details for controlling the most fundamental and critical aspects of running the venture—cash flow, accounts receivable, costs, and debt. Beyond having a plan for controlling the venture's critical inflows and outflows, other actions would involve identifying specific strategies for cutting costs and restructuring the venture.

Exiting the Venture

Getting out of an entrepreneurial venture might seem a strange thing for entrepreneurs to do. However, there may come a point when the entrepreneur decides it's time to move on. That decision may be based on the fact that the entrepreneur hopes to capitalize financially on the investment in the venture—called **harvesting**—or that the entrepreneur is facing serious organizational performance problems and wants to get out, or even on the entrepreneur's desire to focus on other pursuits (personal or business). The issues involved with exiting the venture include choosing a proper business valuation method and knowing what's involved in the process of selling a business.

Business Valuation Methods Valuation techniques generally fall into three categories: (1) asset valuations, (2) earnings valuations, and (3) cash flow valuations.[10] Setting a value on a business can be a little tricky. In many cases, the entrepreneur has sacrificed much for the business and sees it as his or her "baby." Calculating the value of the baby

Exhibit P6–2

**Issues in Exiting the
Entrepreneurial Venture**

Be prepared.

Decide who will sell the business.

Consider the tax implications.

Screen potential buyers.

Decide whether to tell employees before or after selling.

based on objective standards such as cash flow or some multiple of net profits can sometimes be a shock. That's why it's important for an entrepreneur who wishes to exit the venture to get a comprehensive business valuation prepared by professionals.

Other Important Considerations in Exiting the Venture
Although the hardest part of preparing to exit a venture is valuing it, other factors also should be considered.[11] Exhibit P6–2 lists these issues. The process of exiting the entrepreneurial venture should be approached as carefully as the process of launching it. If the entrepreneur is selling the venture on a positive note, he or she wants to realize the value built up in the business. If the venture is being exited because of declining performance, the entrepreneur wants to maximize the potential return.

Managing Personal Life Choices and Challenges

Being an entrepreneur is extremely exciting and fulfilling, yet extremely demanding. There are long hours, difficult demands, and high stress. Yet, there are many rewards to being an entrepreneur, as well. In this section, we want to look at how entrepreneurs can make it work—that is, how can they be successful and effectively balance the demands of their work and personal lives?[12]

Entrepreneurs are a special group. They are focused and persistent, hardworking, and intelligent. Because they put so much of themselves into launching and growing their entrepreneurial ventures, many may neglect their personal lives. Entrepreneurs often have to make sacrifices to pursue their entrepreneurial dreams. However, they can make it work. They can balance their work and personal lives. How?

One of the most important things an entrepreneur can do is to *become a good time manager*. Prioritize what needs to be done. Use a planner (daily, weekly, monthly) to help schedule priorities. Some entrepreneurs don't like taking the time to plan or prioritize or think it's a ridiculous waste of time. Yet, identifying the important duties and distinguishing them from those that aren't so impor-

tant actually makes an entrepreneur more efficient and effective. In addition, part of being a good time manager is delegating to trusted employees those decisions and actions that the entrepreneur doesn't have to be involved in personally. Although it may be hard to let go of some of the things they've always done, entrepreneurs who delegate effectively will see their personal productivity levels rise. Another suggestion for finding that balance is to *seek professional advice* in those areas of business where it's needed. Although entrepreneurs may be reluctant to spend scarce cash, the time, energy, and potential problems saved in the long run are well worth the investment. Competent professional advisers can provide entrepreneurs with information to make more intelligent decisions. Also, it's important to *deal with conflicts* as they arise. This includes both workplace and family conflicts. If an entrepreneur doesn't deal with conflicts, negative feelings are likely to crop up and lead to communication breakdowns. When communication falls apart, vital information may get lost and people (employees *and* family members) may start assuming the worst. It can turn into a nightmare situation that feeds upon itself. So, the best strategy is to deal with conflicts as they come up. Talk, discuss, argue (if you must), but an entrepreneur shouldn't avoid the conflict or pretend it doesn't exist. Another suggestion for achieving that balance between work and personal life is to *develop a network of trusted friends and peers*. Having a group of people to talk to is a good way for an entrepreneur to think through problems and issues. The support and encouragement offered by these groups of people can be an invaluable source of strength for an entrepreneur. Finally, *recognize when your stress levels are too high*. Entrepreneurs *are* achievers. They like to make things happen. They thrive on working hard. Yet, too much stress can lead to significant physical and emotional problems (as we discussed in Chapter 13). Entrepreneurs have to learn when stress is overwhelming them and to do something about it. After all, what's the point of growing and building a thriving entrepreneurial venture if you're not around to enjoy it?

• • • Learning Summary

After reading and studying this material, you should be able to:

- Describe how entrepreneurs should plan for growth.

- Discuss the key issues in organizing for growth.

- Explain why controlling for growth is important.

- Describe the boiled frog phenomenon and why it's useful for entrepreneurs.

- Discuss the issues an entrepreneur needs to consider when deciding to exit the entrepreneurial venture.

- Explain how an entrepreneur can balance the demands of his or her personal and work lives.

Skill-Building Modules

In this section of the textbook, you will have the opportunity to learn about, practice, and reinforce specific management skills. We have included 21 skills that encompass the 4 functions of management: planning, organizing, leading, and controlling. (See the matrix that follows.)

For each of the skills, we provide the following: (1) A short introduction discusses some basic facts about the skill and defines it, if necessary. (2) A section called "Learning About" describes the suggested behaviors for doing that skill. These behaviors are presented in numbered lists in order to illustrate the specific actions associated with that skill. (3) A section entitled "Practice" presents a short scenario designed to provide you with an opportunity to practice the behaviors associated with the skill. Your professor may have you do different things with the practice scenarios. (4) A section entitled "Reinforcement" is designed to present additional activities that you could do to practice and reinforce the behaviors associated with the skill.

Management Skills and Management Functions Matrix

| | Function | | | |
Skill	Planning	Organizing	Leading	Controlling
1. Acquiring power		✓	✓	
2. Active listening			✓	✓
3. Budgeting	✓			✓
4. Choosing an effective leadership style			✓	
5. Coaching			✓	
6. Creating effective teams		✓	✓	
7. Delegating (empowerment)		✓	✓	
8. Designing motivating jobs		✓	✓	
9. Developing trust			✓	
10. Disciplining			✓	✓
11. Interviewing		✓	✓	
12. Managing conflict			✓	✓
13. Managing resistance to change		✓	✓	✓
14. Mentoring			✓	
15. Negotiating			✓	
16. Providing feedback			✓	✓
17. Reading an organization's culture		✓	✓	
18. Scanning the environment	✓			✓
19. Setting goals	✓			✓
20. Solving problems creatively	✓	✓	✓	✓
21. Valuing diversity	✓	✓	✓	✓

1 • ACQUIRING POWER

Power is a natural process in any group or organization, and to perform their jobs effectively, managers need to know how to acquire and use **power**—the capacity of a leader to influence work actions or decisions. We discussed the concept of power in Chapter 17 and identified five different sources of power for leaders including legitimate, coercive, reward, expert, and referent. Why is having power important? Because power makes you less dependent on others. When a manager has power, he or she is not as dependent on others for critical resources. And if the resources a manager controls are important, scarce, and nonsubstitutable, her power will increase because others will be more dependent on her for those resources.

Learning About: Acquiring Power

You can be more effective at acquiring and using power if you use the following eight behaviors.

1. *Frame arguments in terms of organizational goals.* To be effective at acquiring power means camouflaging your self-interests. Discussions over who controls what resources should be framed in terms of the benefits that will accrue to the organization; do not point out how you personally will benefit.

2. *Develop the right image.* If you know your organization's culture, you already understand what the organization wants and values from its employees in terms of dress, associates to cultivate and those to avoid, whether to appear risk taking or risk aversive, the preferred leadership style, the importance placed on getting along well with others, and so forth. With this knowledge, you're equipped to project the appropriate image. Because the assessment of your performance isn't always a fully objective process, you need to pay attention to style as well as substance.

3. *Gain control of organizational resources.* Controlling organizational resources that are scarce *and* important is a source of power. Knowledge and expertise are particularly effective resources to control. They make you more valuable to the organization and, therefore, more likely to have job security, chances for advancement, and a receptive audience for your ideas.

4. *Make yourself appear indispensable.* Because we're dealing with appearances rather than objective facts, you can enhance your power by appearing to be indispensable. You don't really have *to be* indispensable as long as key people in the organization believe that you are.

5. *Be visible.* If you have a job that brings your accomplishments to the attention of others, that's great. However, if you don't have such a job, you'll want to find ways to let others in the organization know what you're doing by highlighting successes in routine reports, having satisfied customers relay their appreciation to senior executives, being seen at social functions, being active in your professional associations, and developing powerful allies who speak positively about your accomplishments. Of course, you'll want to be on the lookout for those projects that will increase your visibility.

6. *Develop powerful allies.* To get power, it helps to have powerful people on your side. Cultivate contacts with potentially influential people above you, at your own level, and at lower organizational levels. These allies often can provide you with information that's otherwise not readily available. In addition, having allies can provide you with a coalition of support if and when you need it.

7. *Avoid "tainted" members.* In almost every organization, there are fringe members whose status is questionable. Their performance and/or loyalty may be suspect. Keep your distance from such individuals.

8. *Support your boss.* Your immediate future is in the hands of your current boss. Because he or she evaluates your performance, you'll typically want to do whatever is necessary to have your boss on your side. You should make every effort to help your boss succeed, make her look good, support her if she is under siege, and spend the time to find out the criteria she will use to assess your effectiveness. Don't undermine your boss. And don't speak negatively of her to others.

Source: Based on H. Mintzberg, *Power In and Around Organizations* (Upper Saddle River, NJ: Prentice Hall, 1983), p. 24; and P.L. Hunsaker, *Training in Management Skills* (Upper Saddle River, NJ: Prentice Hall, 2001), pp. 339–364.

Practice: Acquiring Power

Read through the following scenario. Write down some notes about how you would handle the situation described. Be sure to refer to the eight behaviors described for acquiring power. Your professor will then tell you what to do next.

SCENARIO

You used to be the star marketing manager for Hilton Electronics Corporation. But for the past year, you've been outpaced again and again by Conor, a new manager in the design department, who has been accomplishing everything expected of her and more. Meanwhile, your best efforts to do your job well have been sabotaged and undercut by Leonila—your and Conor's manager. For example, prior to last year's international consumer electronics show, Leonila moved $30,000 from your budget to Conor's. Despite your best efforts, your marketing team couldn't complete all the marketing materials normally developed to showcase all of your organization's new products at this important industry show. And Leonila has chipped away at your staff and budget ever since. Although you've been able to meet most of your goals with less staff and budget, Leonila has continued to slice away resources of your group. Just last week, she eliminated two positions in your team of eight marketing specialists to make room for a new designer and some extra equipment for Conor. Leonila is clearly taking away your resources while giving Conor whatever she wants and more. You think it's time to do something or soon you won't have any team or resources left.

Reinforcement: Acquiring Power

The following suggestions are activities you can do to practice and reinforce the behaviors associated with acquiring power.

1. Keep a one-week journal of your behavior describing incidences when you tried to influence others around you. Assess each incident by asking: Were you successful at these attempts to influence them? Why or why not? What could you have done differently?

2. Review recent issues of a business periodical (such as *Business Week, Fortune, Forbes, Fast Company, Industry Week,* or the *Wall Street Journal*). Look for articles on reorganizations, promotions, or departures from management positions. Find at least two articles where you believe power issues are involved. Relate the content of the articles to the concepts introduced in this skill module.

2 • ACTIVE LISTENING

The ability to be an effective listener is often taken for granted. Hearing is often confused with listening, but hearing is merely recognizing sound vibrations. Listening is making sense of what we hear and requires paying attention, interpreting, and remembering. Effective listening is active rather than passive. Active listening is hard work and requires you to "get inside" the speaker's head in order to understand the communication from his or her point of view.

Learning About: Active Listening

We can identify eight specific behaviors that effective active listeners demonstrate. You can be more effective at active listening if you use these behaviors.

1. *Make eye contact.* Making eye contact with the speaker focuses your attention, reduces the likelihood that you'll be distracted, and encourages the speaker.

2. *Exhibit affirmative nods and appropriate facial expressions.* The effective active listener shows interest in what's being said through nonverbal signals. Affirmative nods and appropriate facial expressions that signal interest in what's being said, when added to eye contact, convey to the speaker that you're really listening.

3. *Avoid distracting actions or gestures.* The other side of showing interest is avoiding actions that suggest your mind is elsewhere. When listening, don't look at your watch, shuffle papers, play with your pencil, or engage in similar distractions.

4. *Ask questions.* The serious active listener analyzes what he or she hears and asks questions. This behavior provides clarification, ensures understanding, and assures the speaker you're really listening.

5. *Paraphrase.* Restate *in your own words* what the speaker has said. The effective active listener uses phrases such as "What I hear you saying is ..." or "Do you mean ... ?" Paraphrasing is an excellent control device to check whether or not you're listening carefully and is also a control for accuracy of understanding.

6. *Avoid interrupting the speaker.* Let the speaker complete his or her thoughts before you try to respond. Don't try to second-guess where the speaker's thoughts are going. When the speaker is finished, you'll know it.

7. *Don't overtalk.* Most of us would rather speak our own ideas than listen to what others say. While talking might be more fun and silence might be uncomfortable, you can't talk and listen at the same time. The good active listener recognizes this fact and doesn't overtalk.

8. *Make smooth transitions between the roles of speaker and listener.* In most work situations, you're continually shifting back and forth between the roles of speaker and listener. The effective active listener makes transitions smoothly from speaker to listener and back to speaker.

Source: Based on C.R. Rogers and R.E. Farson, *Active Listening* (Chicago: Industrial Relations Center of the University of Chicago, 1976); and P.L. Hunsaker, *Training in Management Skills* (Upper Saddle River, NJ: Prentice Hall, 2001), pp. 61–62.

Practice: Active Listening

Read through the following scenario. Write down some notes about how you would handle the situation described. Be sure to refer to the eight behaviors described for active listening. Your professor will tell you what to do next.

SCENARIO

Ben Lummis has always been one of the most reliable technicians at the car stereo shop you manage. Even on days when the frantic pace stressed most other employees, Ben was calm and finished his work efficiently and effectively. You don't know much about his personal life except that he liked to read books about model railroading during his lunch break and he asked to listen to his favorite light jazz station on the shop radio for part of the day. Because his work has always been top-notch, you were happy to let him maintain his somewhat aloof attitude. But over the past month, you wish you knew Ben better. He's been averaging about an absence a week and he no longer spends his lunch break reading in the break room. When he returns from wherever it is he goes, he seems even more remote than when he left. You strongly suspect that something is wrong. Even his normally reliable work has changed. Several irate customers have returned with sound systems he installed improperly. At the time of these complaints, you reviewed each problem with him carefully and each time he promised to be more careful. In addition, you checked the company's work absence records and found that Ben has enough time saved up to take seven more sick days this year. But things don't seem to be improving. Just this week Ben took another suspicious sick day and another angry customer has demanded that his improperly installed system be fixed.

Reinforcement: Active Listening

The following suggestions are activities you can do to practice and reinforce the active listening behaviors.

1. In another lecture-format class, practice active listening for one day. Then ask yourself: Was this harder for me than a normal lecture? Did it affect my note taking? Did I ask more questions? Did it improve my understanding of the lecture's content?

2. For one week, practice active-listening behaviors during phone conversations that you have with others. Keep a journal of whether listening actively was easy or difficult, what distractions there were, how you dealt with those distractions, and your assessment of whether or not active listening allowed you to get more out of the conversations.

3 • BUDGETING

Managers do not have unlimited resources to do their jobs. Most managers will have to deal with a **budget**, a numerical plan for allocating resources to specific activities. As planning tools, they indicate what activities are important and how many resources should be allocated to each activity. However, budgets aren't used just in planning. They're also used in controlling. As control tools, budgets provide managers with quantitative standards against which to measure and compare resource consumption. By pointing out deviations between standard and actual consumption, managers can use the budget for control purposes.

Learning About: Budgeting

You can develop your skills at budgeting if you use the following seven suggestions.

1. *Determine which work activities are going to be pursued during the coming time period.* An organization's work activities are a result of the goals that have been established. Your control over which work activities your unit will be pursuing during a specific time period will depend on how much control you normally exercise over the work that must be done in order to meet those goals. In addition, the amount of control you have often depends on your managerial level in the organization.

2. *Decide which resources will be necessary to accomplish the desired work activities; that is, those that will ensure goals are met.* Although there are different types of budgets used for allocating resources, the most common ones involve monetary resources. However, you also may have to budget time, space, material resources, human resources, capacity utilization, or units of production.

3. *Gather cost information.* You'll need accurate cost estimates of those resources you need. Old budgets may be of some help, but you'll also want to talk with your manager, colleagues, and key employees, and to use other contacts you have developed inside and outside your organization.

4. *Once you know which resources will be available to you, assign the resources as needed to accomplish the desired work activities.* In many organizations, managers are given a monthly, quarterly, or annual budget to work with. The budget will detail which resources are available during the time period. As the manager, you have to assign the resources in an efficient and effective manner to ensure that your unit goals are met.

5. *It's wise to review the budget periodically.* Don't wait until the end of the time period to monitor whether you're over or under budget.

6. *Take action if you find that you're not within your budget.* Remember that a budget also serves as a control tool. If resources are being consumed more quickly than budgeted, you may need to determine why and take corrective action.

7. *Use past experience as a guide when developing your budget for the next time period.* Although every budgeted time period will be different, it is possible to use past experience to pinpoint trends and potential problems. This knowledge can help you prepare for any circumstances that may arise.

Source: Based on R.N. Anthony, J. Dearden, and N.M. Bedford, *Management Control Systems*, 5th ed. (Homewood, IL: Irwin, 1984), Chapters 5–7.

Practice: Budgeting

Read through the following scenario and complete the assigned questions. Be sure to refer to the seven behaviors described for budgeting. Your professor will tell you what to do next.

SCENARIO

You have recently been appointed as advertising manager for a new monthly health and lifestyle magazine, *Global Living for Life*, being developed by the magazine division of LifeTime Publications. You were previously an advertising manager on one of the company's established magazines. In this new position, you will report to the new magazine's publisher, Molly Tymon.

Estimates of first-year subscription sales for *Global Living for Life* are 125,000 copies. Newsstand sales should add another 5,000 copies a month to that number, but your concern is with developing advertising revenue for the magazine. You and Molly have set a goal of selling advertising space totaling $6 million during the magazine's first year. You think you can do this with a staff of 10 people. Because this is a completely new publication, there is no previous budget for your advertising group. You've been asked by Molly to submit a preliminary budget for your group.

Write up a report (no longer than two pages in length) that describes in detail how you would go about fulfilling this request by Molly. For example, where would you get budget categories? Whom would you contact? Present your best ideas for creating this budget for your department.

Reinforcement: Budgeting

The following suggestions are activities you can do to practice and reinforce the budgeting skill behaviors.

1. Create a personal budget for the next month. Be sure to identify sources of income and planned expenditures. At the end of the month, answer the following questions: (a) Did your budget help you plan what you could and could not do this month? (b) Did unexpected situations arise that weren't included in the budget? How did you handle those? (c) How is a personal budget similar to and different from a budget that a manager might be responsible for?

2. Interview three managers from different organizations. Ask them about their budgeting responsibilities and the "lessons" they've learned about budgeting.

4 • CHOOSING AN EFFECTIVE LEADERSHIP STYLE

Effective leaders are skillful at helping the groups they lead be successful as the group goes through various stages of development. There is no leadership style that is consistently effective. Situational factors, including follower characteristics, must be taken into consideration in the selection of an effective leadership style. The key situational factors that determine leadership effectiveness include stage of group development, task structure, position power, leader–member relations, the work group, employee characteristics, organizational culture, and national culture.

Learning About: Choosing an Effective Leadership Style

You can choose an effective leadership style if you use the following six suggestions:

1. *Determine the stage in which your group or team is operating: forming, storming, norming, or performing.* Because each team stage involves specific and different issues and behaviors, it's important to know in which stage your team is. **Forming** is the first stage of group development, during which people join a group and then help define the group's purpose, structure, and leadership. **Storming** is the second stage, characterized by intragroup conflict. **Norming** is the third stage, characterized by close relationships and cohesiveness. **Performing** is the fourth stage, when the group is fully functional.

2. *If your team is in the forming stage, there are certain leader behaviors you want to exhibit.* These include making certain that all team members are introduced to one another, answering member questions, working to establish a foundation of trust and openness, modeling the behaviors you expect from the team members, and clarifying the team's goals, procedures, and expectations.

3. *If your team is in the storming stage, there are certain leader behaviors you want to exhibit.* These behaviors include identifying sources of conflict and adopting a mediator role, encouraging a win-win philosophy, restating the team's vision and its core values and goals, encouraging open discussion, encouraging an analysis of team processes in order to identify ways to improve, enhancing team cohesion and commitment, and providing recognition to individual team members as well as the team.

4. *If your team is in the norming stage, there are certain leader behaviors you want to exhibit.* These include clarifying the team's goals and expectations, providing performance feedback to individual team members and the team, encouraging the team to articulate a vision for the future, and finding ways to publicly and openly communicate the team's vision.

5. *If your team is in the performing stage, there are certain leader behaviors you want to exhibit.* These behav-

iors include providing regular and ongoing performance feedback, fostering innovation and innovative behavior, encouraging the team to capitalize on its strengths, celebrating achievements (large and small), and providing the team whatever support it needs to continue doing its work.

6. *Monitor the group for changes in behavior and adjust your leadership style accordingly.* Because a group is not a static entity, it will go through up periods and down periods. You should adjust your leadership style to the needs of the situation. If the group appears to need more direction from you, provide it. If it appears to be functioning at a high level on its own, provide whatever support is necessary to keep it functioning at that level.

Source: Based on D.A. Whetten and K.S. Cameron, *Developing Management Skills*, 4th ed. (Upper Saddle River, NJ: Prentice Hall, 1998), Chapter 9.

Practice: Choosing an Effective Leadership Style

Read through the following scenario. Write down some notes about how you would handle the situation described. Be sure to refer to the six suggestions given for choosing an effective leadership style. Your professor will then tell you what to do.

SCENARIO

You've been put in charge of a three-person team working on the implementation of a central accounting function for all training done by your *Fortune* 500 company. This project is new and your position is a new one. Two team members, Tony and Maria, used to be supervisors themselves but, due to an ongoing corporate reorganization, now find themselves reporting to you. You feel like the only way to get them to do anything is to stay on them all the time. The other team member, Corbett, typically has very good ideas but he's becoming quite reluctant to share them, particularly because Tony and Maria glare at him if he says anything. This situation is proving to be a real test of your leadership skills, but you've got a six-month deadline to complete this project, and one month is already over. You've got to figure out a way to lead this team to a successful completion of the project.

Reinforcement: Choosing an Effective Leadership Style

The following suggestions are activities you can do to practice and reinforce the behaviors in choosing an effective leadership style.

1. Think of a group or team to which you currently belong or of which you have been a part. What type of leadership

style did the leader of this group appear to exhibit? Give some specific examples of the types of leadership behaviors he or she used. Evaluate the leadership style. Was it appropriate for the group? Why or why not? What would you have done differently? Why?

2. Observe a sports team (either college or professional) that you consider extremely successful and one that you would consider not successful. What leadership styles appear to be used in these team situations? Give some specific examples of the types

of leadership behaviors you observe. How would you evaluate the leadership style? Was it appropriate for the team? Why or why not? To what degree do you think leadership style influenced the team's outcomes?

3. Interview three different managers about the leadership styles they use. Ask for specific examples of how they use their leadership style. Ask the managers how they chose the style they're using and how they know if they need to change their style.

---

5 • COACHING

Effective managers are increasingly being described as *coaches* rather than as *bosses.* Just like coaches, they're expected to provide instruction, guidance, advice, and encouragement to help employees improve their job performance.

Learning About: Coaching

There are three general skills that managers should exhibit if they are to help their employees generate performance breakthroughs. You can be more effective at coaching if you use these skills and practice the following specific behaviors associated with each.

1. *Analyze ways to improve an employee's performance and capabilities.* A coach looks for opportunities for an employee to expand his or her capabilities and improve performance. How? By using the following behaviors: Observe your employee's behavior on a daily basis. Ask questions of the employee: Why do you do a task this way? Can it be improved? What other approaches might be used? Show genuine interest in the employee as an individual, not merely as an employee. Respect his or her individuality. Listen to the employee.

2. *Create a supportive climate.* It's the coach's responsibility to reduce barriers to development and to facilitate a climate that encourages personal performance improvement. How? By using the following behaviors: Create a climate that contributes to a free and open exchange of ideas. Offer help and assistance. Give guidance and advice when asked. Encourage your employees. Be positive and upbeat. Don't use threats. Focus on mistakes as learning opportunities. Ask: "What did we learn from this that can help us in the future?" Reduce obstacles. Express to the employee that you value his or her contribution to the unit's goals. Take personal responsibility for the outcome, but don't rob employees of their full responsibility. Validate the employees' efforts when they succeed. Point to what was missing when they fail. Never blame the employees for poor results.

3. *Influence employees to change their behavior.* The ultimate test of coaching effectiveness is whether or not an employee's performance improves. The concern is with ongoing growth and development. How can you do this? By using the following behaviors: Encourage

continual improvement. Recognize and reward small improvements and treat coaching as a way of helping employees to continually work toward improvement. Use a collaborative style by allowing employees to participate in identifying and choosing among improvement ideas. Break difficult tasks down into simpler ones. Model the qualities that you expect from your employees. If you want openness, dedication, commitment, and responsibility from your employees, you must demonstrate these qualities yourself.

Source: Based on C.D. Orth, H.E. Wilkinson, and R.C. Benfari, "The Managers' Role as Coach and Mentor," *Organizational Dynamics,* Spring 1987, p. 67.

Practice: Coaching

Read through the following scenario. Write down some notes about how you would handle the situation described. Be sure to refer to the three general coaching skills and the specific behaviors associated with each. Your professor will then tell you what to do next.

SCENARIO

Store manager Ian McCormick was thrilled with Barbara Kim's work. She was simply the best assistant department manager he had ever seen. Barbara made friends with everyone who came into the store and customers would often bring their items over to her and wait in line just for a chance to visit with her. When a department manager position opened up, Ian was glad to give Barbara the promotion. And Barbara was even happier! She told Ian, "I can't tell you how much this means to me. I'll do anything to make this work."

As a department manager, Barbara was just as friendly as ever—too friendly, in fact. She seemed incapable of saying "no" to her former coworkers. She let them off nearly every time they asked, throwing the work schedule into disarray and leaving checkout lines open. Customers who were once happy about Barbara were now complaining. Transaction error rates also increased. Ian brought this to Barbara's attention several times, and each time Barbara said she would talk to the clerks about being more careful. But mistakes continued. Ian knows that Barbara has potential but he's not sure what to do about this situation now. Something definitely needs to be done.

Reinforcement: Coaching

The following suggestions are activities you can do to practice and reinforce the coaching behaviors.

1. Talk to several instructors about ways that they deal with a student whose performance is not at the level it should be. What kinds of techniques do they use? Which, if any, of the coaching behaviors described do the instructors use?

2. Most of us are aware of coaches and what they do in an athletic team setting. Observe different coaches (on television or firsthand) and how they deal with individuals on their team. What types of behaviors do they exhibit? Based on what you see, what coaching advice could you use as a manager?

---

6 • CREATING EFFECTIVE TEAMS

What differentiates a *team* from a group is that members are committed to a common purpose, have a set of specific performance goals, and hold themselves mutually accountable for the team's results. Teams can produce outputs that are greater than the sum of their individual contributions. The primary force that makes a work group an effective team—that is, a real high-performing team—is its emphasis on performance.

Learning About: Creating Effective Teams

Managers and team leaders have a significant impact on a team's effectiveness. As a result, they need to be able to create effective teams. You can be more effective at creating effective teams if you use the following nine behaviors.

1. *Establish a common purpose.* An effective team needs a common purpose to which all members aspire. This purpose is a vision. It's broader than any specific goals. This common purpose provides direction, momentum, and commitment for team members.

2. *Assess team strengths and weaknesses.* Team members will have different strengths and weaknesses. Knowing these strengths and weaknesses can help the team leader build upon the strengths and compensate for the weaknesses.

3. *Develop specific individual goals.* Specific individual goals help lead team members to achieve higher performance. In addition, specific goals facilitate clear communication and help maintain the focus on getting results.

4. *Get agreement on a common approach for achieving goals.* Goals are the ends a team strives to attain. Defining and agreeing upon a common approach ensures that the team is unified on the *means* for achieving those ends.

5. *Encourage acceptance of responsibility for both individual and team performance.* Successful teams make members individually and jointly accountable for the team's purpose, goals, and approach. Members understand what they are individually responsible for and what they are jointly responsible for.

6. *Build mutual trust among members.* When there is *trust,* team members believe in the integrity, character, and ability of each other. When trust is lacking, members are unable to depend on each other. Teams that lack trust tend to be short-lived.

7. *Maintain an appropriate mix of team member skills and personalities.* Team members come to the team with different skills and personalities. To perform effectively, teams need three types of skills. First, teams need people with technical expertise. Next, they need people with problem-solving and decision-making skills to identify problems, generate alternatives, evaluate those alternatives, and make competent choices. Finally, teams need people with good interpersonal skills.

8. *Provide needed training and resources.* Team leaders need to make sure that their teams have both the training and the resources they need to accomplish their goals.

9. *Create opportunities for small achievements.* Building an effective team takes time. Team members have to learn to think and work as a team. New teams can't be expected to hit home runs every time they come to bat, especially at the beginning. Instead, team members should be encouraged to try for small achievements at the beginning.

Source: Based on P.L. Hunsaker, *Training in Management Skills* (Upper Saddle River, NJ: Prentice Hall, 2001), Chapter 12.

Practice: Creating Effective Teams

Read through the following scenario. Write down some notes about how you would handle the situation described. Be sure to refer to the nine behaviors given for creating effective teams. Your professor will then tell you what to do next.

SCENARIO

You're the leader of a five-member project team that's been assigned the task of moving your engineering firm into the new booming area of high-speed rail construction. You and your team members have been researching the field, identifying specific business opportunities, negotiating alliances with equipment vendors, and evaluating high-speed rail experts and consultants from around the world. Throughout the process, Tonya, a highly qualified and respected engineer, has challenged everything you say during team meetings and in the workplace. For example, at a meeting two weeks ago, you presented the team with a list of 10 possible high-speed rail projects that had been identified by the team and started evaluating your organization's ability to compete for them. Tonya contradicted virtually all your comments, questioned your statistics, and was quite pessimistic about the possibility of contracts. After this latest display of displeasure, two other group members, Liam and Ahmed, came to you and complained that Tonya's actions were damaging the team's effectiveness. You originally put Tonya on the team for her unique expertise and insight. You'd like to find a way to reach her and get the team on the right track to its fullest potential.

Reinforcement: Creating Effective Teams

The following suggestions are activities you can do to practice and reinforce the skills in creating effective teams.

1. Interview three managers at different organizations. Ask them about their experiences in managing teams. What behaviors have they found that have been successful in creating an effective team? What about those behaviors that have not been successful in creating an effective team?

2. After completing a team project for one of your classes, assess the team's effectiveness by answering the following questions: Did everyone on the team know exactly why the team did what it did? Did team members have a significant amount of input into or influence on decisions that affected them? Did team members have open, honest, timely, and two-way communications? Did everyone on the team know and understand the team's priorities? Did the team members work together to resolve destructive conflicts? Was everyone on the team working toward accomplishing the same thing? Did team members understand the team's unwritten rules of how to behave within the group?

---

7 • DELEGATING

Managers get things done through other people. Because there are limits to any manager's time and knowledge, effective managers need to understand how to delegate. **Delegation** is the assignment of authority to another person to carry out specific duties. It allows an employee to make decisions. Delegation should not be confused with participation. In participative decision making, there's a sharing of authority. In delegation, employees make decisions on their own.

Learning About: Delegation

A number of actions differentiate the effective delegator from the ineffective delegator. There are five behaviors that effective delegators will use.

1. *Clarify the assignment.* Determine *what* is to be delegated and *to whom.* You need to identify the person who's most capable of doing the task and then determine whether or not he or she has the time and motivation to do the task. If you have a willing and able employee, it's your responsibility to provide clear information on what is being delegated, the results you expect, and any time or performance expectations you may have. Unless there's an overriding need to adhere to specific methods, you should delegate only the results expected. Get agreement on what is to be done and the results expected, but let the employee decide the best way to complete the task.

2. *Specify the employee's range of discretion.* Every situation of delegation comes with constraints. Although you're delegating to an employee the authority to perform some task or tasks, you're not delegating unlimited authority. You are delegating authority to act on certain issues within certain parameters. You

need to specify what those parameters are so that employees know, without any doubt, the range of their discretion.

3. *Allow the employee to participate.* One of the best ways to decide how much authority will be necessary to accomplish a task is to allow the employee who will be held accountable for that task to participate in that decision. Be aware, however, that allowing employees to participate can present its own set of potential problems as a result of employees' self-interests and biases in evaluating their own abilities.

4. *Inform others that delegation has occurred.* Delegation shouldn't take place behind the scenes. Not only do the manager and employee need to know specifically what has been delegated and how much authority has been given, but so does anyone else who's likely to be affected by the employee's decisions and actions. This includes people inside and outside the organization. Essentially, you need to communicate what has been delegated (the task and amount of authority) and to whom.

5. *Establish feedback channels.* To delegate without establishing feedback controls is inviting problems. The establishment of controls to monitor the employee's performance increases the likelihood that important problems will be identified and that the task will be completed on time and to the desired specifications. Ideally, these controls should be determined at the time of the initial assignment. Agree on a specific time for the completion of the task and then set progress dates when the employee will report back on how well he or she is doing and any major problems that may have arisen. These controls can be supplemented with periodic checks to ensure that authority guidelines aren't being abused, organizational policies are being followed, proper procedures are being met, and the like.

Source: Based on P.L. Hunsaker, *Training in Management Skills* (Upper Saddle River, NJ: Prentice Hall, 2001), pp. 135–36 and 430–32; R.T. Noel, "What You Say to Your Employees When You Delegate," *Supervisory Management*, December 1993, p. 13; and S. Caudron, "Delegate for Results," *Industry Week*, February 6, 1995, pp. 27–30.

Practice: Delegating

Read through the following scenario. Write down some notes about how you would handle the situation described. Be sure to refer to the five behaviors described for delegating. Your professor will then tell you what to do next.

SCENARIO

Ricky Lee is the manager of the contracts group of a large regional office supply distributor. His boss, Anne Zumwalt, has asked him to prepare by the end of the month the department's new procedures manual that will outline the steps followed in negotiating contracts with office products manufac-turers who supply the organization's products. Because Ricky has another major project he's working on, he went to Anne and asked her if it would be possible to assign the rewriting of the procedures manual to Bill Harmon, one of his employees who's worked in the contracts group for about three years. Anne said she had no problems with Ricky reassigning the project as long as Bill knew the parameters and the expectations for the completion of the project. Ricky is preparing for his meeting in the morning with Bill regarding this assignment.

Reinforcement: Delegating

The following suggestions are activities you can do to practice and reinforce the behaviors in delegating.

1. Interview a manager regarding his or her delegation skills. What activities doesn't he or she delegate? Why?

2. Teach someone else how to delegate effectively. Be sure to identify to this person the behaviors needed in delegating effectively as well as explaining why these behaviors are important.

---

8 • DESIGNING MOTIVATING JOBS

As a manager, it's likely you're going to have to design or redesign jobs at some point. How will you ensure that these jobs are motivating? What can you do regarding job design that will maximize your employees' motivation and performance? The job characteristics model, which defines five core job dimensions (skill variety, task identity, task significance, autonomy, and feedback) and their relationships to employee motivation, provides a basis for designing motivating jobs.

Learning About: Designing Motivating Jobs

The following five suggestions, based on the job characteristics model, specify the types of changes in jobs that are most likely to lead to improving the motivating potential for employees.

1. *Combine tasks.* As a manager, you should put existing specialized and divided tasks back together to form a new, larger module of work. This step will increase skill variety and task identity.

2. *Create natural work units.* You should design work tasks that form an identifiable and meaningful whole. This step will increase "ownership" of the work and will encourage employees to view their work as meaningful and important rather than as irrelevant and boring.

3. *Establish client relationships.* The client is the user of the product or service that is the basis for an employee's work. Whenever possible, you should establish direct relationships between your workers and your clients. This step increases skill variety, autonomy, and feedback for the employees.

4. *Expand jobs vertically.* Vertical expansion of a job means giving employees responsibilities and controls that were formerly the manager's. It partially closes the gap between the "doing" and "controlling" aspects of the job. This step increases employee autonomy.

5. *Open feedback channels.* By increasing feedback, employees not only learn how well they are performing their jobs but also whether their performance is improving, deteriorating, or remaining at a constant level. Ideally, this feedback should be received directly as the employee does the job, rather than from his or her manager on an occasional basis.

Source: Based on J.R. Hackman, "Work Design," in J.R. Hackman and J.L. Suttle (eds.), *Improving Life at Work* (Santa Monica, CA: Goodyear, 1977), pp. 132–33.

Practice: Designing Motivating Jobs

Read through the following scenario. Write down some notes about how you would handle the situation described. Be sure to refer to the five suggestions described for designing motivating jobs. Your professor will tell you what to do next.

SCENARIO

You work for Sunrise Deliveries, a freight transportation company that makes local deliveries of products for your customers. In your position, you supervise Sunrise's six delivery drivers. Each morning your drivers drive their preloaded trucks to their destinations and wait for the products to be unloaded. There's a high turnover rate in the job. In fact, most of your drivers don't stay longer than six months. Not only is this employee turnover getting expensive, it's been hard to develop a quality customer service program when you've constantly got new faces. You've also heard complaints from the drivers that "all they do is drive." You know that you're going to have to do something to solve this problem.

Reinforcement: Designing Motivating Jobs

The following suggestions are activities you can do to practice and reinforce the behaviors associated with designing motivating jobs:

1. Think of the worst job you have ever had. Analyze the job according to the five dimensions identified in the job characteristics model. Redesign the job in order to make it more satisfying and motivating.

2. Interview two people in two different job positions on your campus. Ask them questions about their jobs using the job characteristics model as a guide. Using the information provided, list recommendations for making the jobs more motivating.

---

9 • DEVELOPING TRUST

Trust plays an important role in the manager's relationships with his or her employees. Given the importance of trust, today's managers should actively seek to develop it within their work group.

Learning About: Developing Trust

You can be more effective at developing trust among your employees if you use the following eight suggestions:

1. *Practice openness.* Mistrust comes as much from what people don't know as from what they do. Being open with employees leads to confidence and trust. Keep people informed. Make clear the criteria you use in making decisions. Explain the rationale for your decisions. Be forthright and candid about problems. Fully disclose all relevant information.

2. *Be fair.* Before making decisions or taking actions, consider how others will perceive them in terms of objectivity and fairness. Give credit where credit is due. Be objective and impartial in performance appraisals. Pay attention to equity perceptions in distributing rewards.

3. *Speak your feelings.* Managers who convey only hard facts come across as cold, distant, and unfeeling. When you share your feelings, others will see that you are real and human. They will know you for who you are and their respect for you is likely to increase.

4. *Tell the truth.* Being trustworthy means being credible. If honesty is critical to credibility, then you must be perceived as someone who tells the truth. Employees are more tolerant of hearing something "they don't want to hear" than of finding out that their manager lied to them.

5. *Be consistent.* People want predictability. Mistrust comes from not knowing what to expect. Take the time to think about your values and beliefs and let those values and beliefs consistently guide your decisions. When you know what's important to you, your actions will follow, and you will project a consistency that earns trust.

6. *Fulfill your promises.* Trust requires that people believe that you are dependable. You need to ensure that you keep your word. Promises made must be promises kept.

7. *Maintain confidences.* You trust those whom you believe to be discreet and those on whom you can rely. If people open up to you and make themselves vulnerable by telling you something in confidence, they need to feel assured you won't discuss it with others or betray that confidence. If people perceive you as someone who leaks personal confidences or someone who can't be depended on, you've lost their trust.

8. *Demonstrate competence.* Develop the admiration and respect of others by demonstrating technical and professional ability. Pay particular attention to developing and displaying your communication, negotiation, and other interpersonal skills.

Source: Based on F. Bartolome, "Nobody Trusts the Boss Completely—Now What?" *Harvard Business Review*, March–April 1989, pp. 135–42; and J.K. Butler Jr., "Toward Understanding and Measuring Conditions of Trust: Evolution of a Condition of Trust Inventory," *Journal of Management*, September 1991, pp. 643–63.

Practice: Developing Trust

Read through the following scenario. Write down some notes about how you would handle the situation. Be sure to refer to the eight behaviors described for developing trust. Your professor will tell you what to do next.

SCENARIO

Donna Romines is the shipping department manager at Tastefully Tempting, a gourmet candy company based in Phoenix. Orders for the company's candy come from around the world. Your six-member team processes these orders. Needless to say, the two months before Christmas are quite hectic. Everybody counts the days until December 24th when the phones finally stop ringing off the wall, at least for a couple of days. You and all of your team members breathe a sigh of relief as the last box of candy is sent on its way out the door.

When the company was first founded five years ago, after the holiday rush, the owners would shut down Tastefully Tempting for two weeks after Christmas. However, as the business has grown and moved into Internet sales, that practice has become too costly. There's too much business to be able to afford that luxury. And the rush for Valentine's Day orders start pouring in the week after Christmas. Although the two-week post-holiday companywide shutdown has been phased out formally, some departments have found it difficult to get employees to gear up once again after the Christmas break. The employees who come to work after Christmas usually accomplish little. This year, though, things have got to change. You know that the cultural "tradition" won't be easy to overcome, but your shipping team needs to be ready to tackle the orders that have piled up. After all, Tastefully Tempting's customers want their orders filled promptly and correctly!

Reinforcement: Developing Trust

The following suggestions are activities you can do to practice and reinforce the behaviors associated with developing trust:

1. Keep a one-week log describing ways that your daily decisions and actions encouraged people to trust you or to not trust you. What things did you do that led to trust? What things did you do that may have led to distrust? How could you have changed your behavior so that the situations of distrust could have been situations of trust?

2. Review recent issues of a business periodical (such as *Business Week, Fortune, Forbes, Fast Company, Industry Week*, or the *Wall Street Journal*) for articles where trust (or lack of trust) may have played a role. Find two articles and describe the situation. Explain how the person(s) involved might have used skills at developing trust to handle the situation.

---

10 • DISCIPLINING

If an employee's performance regularly isn't up to par or if an employee consistently ignores the organization's standards and regulations, the manager may have to use discipline as a way to control behavior. What exactly is **discipline**? It's actions taken by a manager to enforce the organization's expectations, standards, and rules. The most common types of discipline problems managers have to deal with include attendance (absenteeism, tardiness, abuse of sick leave), on-the-job behaviors (failure to meet performance goals, disobedience, failure to use safety devices, alcohol or drug abuse), and dishonesty (theft, lying to managers).

Learning About: Disciplining

You can be more effective at disciplining employees if you use the following eight behaviors.

1. *Respond immediately.* The more quickly a disciplinary action follows a behavior that requires disciplining, the more likely it is that the employee will associate the discipline with the behavior rather than with you as the disciplinarian. It's best to begin the disciplinary process as soon as possible after you notice a violation.

2. *Provide a warning.* You have an obligation to warn an employee before initiating disciplinary action. This means that the employee must be aware of and accept the organization's rules and standards of behavior and performance. Disciplinary action is more likely to be seen as fair when employees have received a warning that a given behavior will lead to discipline and when they know what that disciplinary action will be.

3. *State the problem specifically.* Give the date, time, place, individuals involved, and any extenuating circumstances surrounding the problem behavior. Be sure to define the problem behavior in exact terms instead of just reciting company regulations. Explain why the behavior isn't acceptable by showing how it specifically affects the employee's job performance, the work unit's effectiveness, and the employee's colleagues.

4. *Allow the employee to explain his or her position.* Regardless of the facts you have, due process demands that an employee be given the opportunity to explain his or her position. From the employee's perspective, what happened? Why did it happen? What was his or her perception of the expectations, rules, regulations, and circumstances?

5. *Keep discussion impersonal.* Make sure that the discipline is directed at what the employee has done (or failed to do) and not at the employee personally.

6. *Be consistent.* Fair treatment of employees demands that disciplinary action be consistent. This doesn't mean, however, treating everyone exactly alike. Be sure to clearly justify disciplinary actions that might appear inconsistent to employees.

7. *Take progressive action.* Choose a disciplinary action that's appropriate to the problem behavior. Penalties should get progressively stronger if, or when, the problem is repeated. For example, you may start with an oral warning, then move progressively to a written warning, a suspension, and then, if the problem behavior warrants, dismissal. Keep in mind, however, that there may be some behaviors that warrant immediate dismissal, and these should be made clear to employees.

8. *Obtain agreement on change.* Disciplining should include guidance and direction for correcting the problem behavior. Let the employee state what he or she plans to do in the future to ensure that the problem won't be repeated.

Source: Based on A. Belohlav, *The Art of Disciplining Your Employees* (Upper Saddle River, NJ: Prentice Hall, 1985); and R.H. Lussier, "A Discipline Model for Increasing Performance," *Supervisory Management*, August 1990, pp. 6–7.

Practice: Disciplining

Read through the following scenario. Write down some notes about how you would handle the disciplinary situation described. Be sure to refer to the eight behaviors suggested for effective disciplining. Your professor will then tell you what to do next.

SCENARIO

You're a team leader in the customer services department at Mountain View Microbrewery. Carla is the newest member of your 10-person team, having been there only 6 weeks. She came to Mountain View with good recommendations from her previous job as a customer support representative at a car dealership. However, not long after joining your team, she was late in issuing an important purchasing order. When you talked to her about it, she said it was "lost." But you discovered it in her in-box where it had been properly placed. Then, just last week, she failed to make an immediate return call to an unhappy customer who could easily have been satisfied at that point. Instead the customer worked himself into an unhappy rage and vented his unhappiness in a letter to the company's CEO. Now the latest incident with Carla came up just yesterday. As part of your company's continual quality improvement program, your team members prepare periodic reports on the service they provide to each customer and turn these reports over to an upper management team that evaluates them. Carla didn't meet the deadline for getting her report into this evalua-

tion group and you received a call from one of the team members wanting to know where this report was. Because Carla is still on probation for another six weeks, it appears that the time has come for you to talk to her about her failure to meet expected work performance goals.

Reinforcement: Disciplining

The following suggestions are activities you can do to practice and reinforce the disciplining behaviors:

1. Talk with a manager at three different organizations. Ask them what guidance they've received from their organizations in disciplining employees. Have them describe specific employee discipline problems they've faced and how they've handled them.

2. Interview three of your current or past instructors. Ask them about their approaches to discipline. How do they handle late papers, cheating, excessive absenteeism, or other disciplinary problems?

---

11 • INTERVIEWING

The interview is used almost universally as part of the employee selection process. Not many of us have ever gotten a job without having gone through one or more interviews. Interviews can be valid and reliable selection tools, but they need to be structured and well organized.

Learning About: Interviewing

You can be an effective interviewer if you use the following seven suggestions for interviewing job candidates:

1. *Review the job description and job specification.* Be sure that prior to the interview, you have reviewed pertinent information about the job. Why? Because this will provide you with valuable information on which to assess the job candidate. Furthermore, knowing the relevant job requirements will help eliminate interview bias.

2. *Prepare a structured set of questions you want to ask all job applicants.* By having a set of prepared questions, you ensure that you'll get the information you want. Furthermore, by asking similar questions, you're able to better compare all candidates' answers against a common base.

3. *Before meeting a candidate, review his or her application form and résumé.* By doing this you'll be able to create a complete picture of the candidate in terms of what is represented on the résumé or application and what the job requires. You can also begin to identify areas to explore during the interview. That is, areas that are not clearly defined on the résumé or application but that are essential to the job can be come a focal point in your discussion with the candidate.

4. *Open the interview by putting the applicant at ease and by providing a brief preview of the topics to be discussed.*

Interviews are stressful for job candidates. Opening the discussion with small talk, such as the weather, can give the candidate time to adjust to the interview setting. By providing a preview of topics to come, you are giving the candidate an agenda. This helps the candidate begin framing what he or she will say in response to your questions.

5. *Ask your questions and listen carefully to the candidate's answers.* Select follow-up questions that flow naturally from the answers given. Focus on the candidate's responses as they relate to information you need to ensure that the person meets your job requirements. If you're still uncertain, use a follow-up question to further probe for information.

6. *Close the interview by telling the applicant what is going to happen next.* Applicants are anxious about the status of your hiring decision. Be up-front with candidates regarding others who will be interviewed and the remaining steps in the hiring process. Let the person know your time frame for making a decision. In addition, tell the applicant how you will notify him or her about your decision.

7. *Write your evaluation of the applicant while the interview is still fresh in your mind.* Don't wait until the end of the day, after interviewing several people, to write your analysis of each person. Memory can (and often will) fail you! The sooner you write your impressions after an interview, the better chance you have of accurately noting what occurred in the interview and your perceptions of the candidate.

Source: Based on S.P. Robbins and D.A. DeCenzo, *Fundamentals of Management,* 4th ed. (Upper Saddle River, NJ: Prentice Hall, 2004), p. 194.

Practice: Interviewing

Read through the following list and do the actions. Be sure to refer to the seven suggestions for conducting effective interviews. Your professor will then tell you what to do next.

1. Break into groups of three.

2. Take up to 10 minutes to compose 5 challenging job interview questions that you think should be relevant in the hiring of new college graduates for a sales-management training program at Kraft Foods. Each hiree will spend 18 to 24 months as a sales representative calling on retail grocery and restaurant accounts. After this training period, successful performers can be expected to be promoted to the position of district sales supervisor.

3. Exchange your 5 questions with another group.

4. Each group should allocate one of the following roles to their 3 members: interviewer, applicant, and observer. The person playing the applicant should rough out a brief résumé of his or her background and experience and then give it to the interviewer.

5. Role-play a job interview. The interviewer should include, but not be limited to, the 5 questions provided by the other group.

6. After the interview, the observer should evaluate the interviewer's behaviors in terms of the effective interview suggestions.

Reinforcement: Interviewing

The following suggestions are activities you can do to practice and reinforce the interviewing skill:

1. On your campus, there's probably a job and career placement service provided for graduating seniors. If possible, talk to two or three graduating seniors who have been interviewed by organizations through this campus service. Ask them to share what happened during their interviews. Then write a brief report describing what you found out and comparing the students' experiences with the suggestions for effective interviewing.

2. Interview a manager about the interview process he or she uses in hiring new employees. What types of information does the manager try to get during an interview? (Be sure that as you interview this manager that you're using the suggestions for good interviewing! Although you're not "hiring" this person, you are looking for information, which is exactly what managers are looking for during a job interview.)

12 • MANAGING CONFLICT

Conflict is a natural byproduct of people's interactions in organizations and can't be—nor should it be—eliminated. Conflict arises because organizational members have different goals and organizations have scarce resources. In addition, contemporary management practices such as empowerment and self-managed work teams where people's work is interdependent and must be coordinated create the potential for conflict. The ability to manage conflict is, therefore, one of the most important skills a manager needs. In fact, when human resource managers of *Fortune* 1000 companies were asked to rank the importance of certain management skills, conflict management was in the top ten.

Learning About Managing Conflict

You can develop your skills at managing conflict if you use the following six behaviors.

1. *Assess the nature of the conflict.* The first thing you should do is assess the source of the conflict. Has the conflict arisen because of communication differences (semantic difficulties, misunderstandings, or noise in the communication channel)? Is the conflict the result of job or organizational structural differentiation such as disagreements over goals, decision alternatives, performance criteria, or resource allocations? Or is the conflict due to personal differences (individual idiosyncrasies or personal value systems)? Also, are there any positive aspects to the conflict that make it more functional than dysfunctional?

2. *Decide if this is a conflict that needs to be handled.* Some conflicts don't justify the manager's attention. Some aren't worth the effort and others might be unmanageable. Try to avoid trivial conflicts and focus on the ones that need attention.

3. *Evaluate the persons involved in the conflict.* It's important that you identify and be familiar with all individuals involved with the conflict. What interests or concerns does each person have? What's important to them? Who has power? What's at stake? What's their time frame? What are their personalities, feelings, and resources? You're likely to manage a conflict better if you're able to view the conflict situation from the perspective of the conflicting parties.

4. *Know your options for handling the conflict.* Managers can choose from five conflict management options: avoidance, accommodation, forcing, compromise, and collaboration. Here's a short description of each:

   Avoidance: Withdrawing from or suppressing the conflict. Most appropriate when conflict is trivial, when emotions are running high and time is needed for the conflicting parties to cool down, or when the potential disruption from a more assertive action outweighs the benefits of resolution.

   Accommodation: Maintaining harmonious relationships by placing others' needs and concerns above your own. Most viable when the issue under dispute isn't that important to you or when you want to "build up credits" for later issues.

Forcing: Satisfying one's own needs at the expense of another's. Works well when you need a quick resolution on important issues where unpopular actions must be taken and when commitment by others to your solution isn't crucial.

Compromise: A solution to conflict in which each party gives up something of value. Can be an optimum strategy when conflicting parties are about equal in power, when it's desirable to achieve a temporary solution to a complex issue, or when time pressures demand an expedient solution.

Collaboration: The ultimate win-win situation in which all parties to a conflict seek to satisfy their interests. It's the best conflict option when time pressures are minimal, when all parties seriously want a win-win solution, and when the issue is too important to be compromised.

5. *Deal with the emotional aspects of conflict.* During conflict, emotions (anger, fear, resentment, etc.) tend to run high. Therefore, it's usually better to deal with those aspects rather than trying to settle the substantive aspects of the conflict. This typically involves three steps. First, treat the other person with respect by being aware of your own emotions and keeping them under control. Next, listen to the other person's point of view and make that person feel understood. Finally, briefly state your own views, needs, and feelings.

6. *Select the best option.* Start by looking at your own preferred conflict-handling style. You can assess this using the self-assessment exercise "What's My Preferred Conflict Handling Style?" found on the Self-Assessment Library on R.O.L.L.S. (*www.prenhall.com/robbins*). Then, look at your goals for resolving the conflict: What is the importance of the conflict issue? How concerned are you about maintaining long-term supportive interpersonal relations? And how quickly does the conflict need to be resolved?

All other things being equal, if the issue is critical to the organization's or unit's success, collaboration is preferred. If sustaining relationships is important, the best strategies in order of preference are accommodation, collaboration, compromise, and avoidance. If it's crucial to resolve the conflict as quickly as possible, the best options are forcing, accommodation, and compromise, in that order.

Finally, knowing the source of the conflict can help you decide the best option. Communication-based conflicts that revolve around misinformation and misunderstandings are best resolved by collaboration. Conflicts based on personal differences, however, arise out of dissimilarities in values and personalities. These types of conflicts are susceptible to avoidance because these differences are often deeply rooted. However, managers who have to resolve these types of conflicts frequently rely on forcing, not so much because it's best for the parties, but because it works. Finally, structural conflicts can be resolved by choosing to use most of the conflict resolution options.

Source: Based on S. P. Robbins and P. L. Hunsaker, *Training in InterPersonal Skills,* 3rd ed. (Upper Saddle River, NJ: Prentice Hall, 2003), pp. 223–226; P. L. Hunsaker, *Training in Management Skills* (Upper Saddle River, NJ: Prentice Hall, 2001); S. Caudron, "On the Contrary: Productive Conflict Has Value," *Workforce,* February 1999, pp. 25–27; and C. Luporter, "Improving Managers' Interpersonal Skills," *Luporter Report,* January 14, 1999.

Practice: Managing Conflict

Read through the following scenario. Write down some notes about how you would handle the situation described. Be sure to refer to the six behaviors described for managing conflict. Your professor will tell you what to do next.

SCENARIO

Shannon Walter has been the sales manager at Super Sports, a Midwestern sporting goods distributor, for four years. During that time, he has seen sales grow steadily. Now, however, he feels that his accomplishments are being overshadowed by one of his own account reps, Maria Hampton.

Yesterday, at one of the quarterly organizationwide brainstorming sessions introduced recently by CEO Reid Sommers, Maria suggested that Super Sports change its focus drastically by going after a specialized market rather than being a full-line distributor. She argued that, "Right now our numbers are okay, but we sell too little of too much. I think we can do so much more by focusing on the children's market that's clamoring for new sporting goods all year round."

Shannon was quite surprised at Maria's suggestion since she had brought up the subject with him last week and after discussing it, had concluded that it wasn't a good idea. He immediately replied, "We've talked about that idea already, Maria, and as we discussed, Good Sports has been very successful with a full product line."

"Wait a second," Reid interrupted. "This is just a brainstorming session, Shannon. Let's get all the ideas out before we rip them to shreds."

Shannon sighed. He knew Reid meant well with her open management style, but frequently he felt it meant wasting a lot of time. And he was also irritated at Maria for bringing up a subject he thought they had already dealt with sufficiently in private.

His irritation increased considerably when Reid decided to explore Maria's proposal after the brainstorming session. She asked Maria to put together an analysis of why she believed a focus on children's products could potentially outperform the full line that Super Sports carried now. "Whatever happened to Maria being my employee?" Shannon wondered. Although he feels that the proposed strategy will not be good for the company, he also gets the feeling that if he doesn't go along with it, it will only make things worse.

Reinforcement: Managing Conflict

The following suggestions are activities you can do to practice and reinforce the behaviors associated with managing conflict:

1. Think of a recent conflict you've had with a friend, colleague, or family member. What was the source of the

conflict? How did you handle the conflict? Was the conflict resolved consistently with your goals? The other person's goals? What other ways of handling the conflict might have been more effective?

2. Interview three managers at different organizations. Ask them about their experiences in managing conflict. What behaviors have they found that have been successful in managing conflict? What have they found doesn't work?

13 • MANAGING RESISTANCE TO CHANGE

Managers play an important role in organizational change—that is, they often serve as change agents. However, managers may find that change is resisted by employees. After all, change represents ambiguity and uncertainty, or it threatens the status quo. How can this resistance to change be effectively managed?

Learning About: Managing Resistance to Change

You can be more effective at managing resistance to change if you use the following suggestions:

1. *Assess the climate for change.* One major factor why some changes succeed and others fail is the readiness for change. Assessing the climate for change involves asking several questions. The more affirmative answers you get, the more likely it is that change efforts will succeed.

   - Is the sponsor of the change high enough in the hierarchy to have power to effectively deal with resistance?
   - Is senior management supportive of the change and committed to it?
   - Is there a strong sense of urgency from senior managers about the need for change, and is this feeling shared by others in the organization?
   - Do managers have a clear vision of how the future will look after the change?
   - Are there objective measures in place to evaluate the change effort, and have reward systems been explicitly designed to reinforce them?
   - Is the specific change effort consistent with other changes going on in the organization?
   - Are managers willing to sacrifice their personal self-interests for the good of the organization as a whole?
   - Do managers pride themselves on closely monitoring changes and actions by competitors?
   - Are managers and employees rewarded for taking risks, being innovative, and looking for new and better solutions?
   - Is the organizational structure flexible?
   - Does communication flow both down *and* up in the organization?
   - Has the organization successfully implemented changes in the recent past?

   - Are employee satisfaction with and trust in management high?
   - Is there a high degree of interaction and cooperation between organizational work units?
   - Are decisions made quickly, and do decisions take into account a wide variety of suggestions?

2. *Choose an appropriate approach for managing the resistance to change.* There are six tactics that have been suggested for dealing with resistance to change. Each is designed to be appropriate for different conditions of resistance. These include *education and communication* (used when resistance comes from lack of information or inaccurate information), *participation* (used when resistance stems from people not having all the information they need or when they have the power to resist), *facilitation and support* (used when those with power will lose out in a change), *manipulation and cooptation* (used when any other tactic will not work or is too expensive), and *coercion* (used when speed is essential and change agents possess considerable power). Which one of these approaches will be most effective depends on the source of the resistance to the change.

3. *During the time the change is being implemented and after the change is completed, communicate with employees regarding what support you may be able to provide.* Your employees need to know that you are there to support them during change efforts. Be prepared to offer the assistance that may be necessary to help your employees enact the change.

Based on J.P. Kotter and L.A. Schlesinger, "Choosing Strategies for Change," *Harvard Business Review*, March–April 1979, pp. 106–14; and T.A. Stewart, "Rate Your Readiness to Change," *Fortune*, February 7, 1994, pp. 106–10.

Practice: Managing Resistance to Change

Read through the following scenario. Write down some notes about how you would handle the situation described. Be sure to refer to the three suggestions for managing resistance to change. Your professor will tell you what to do next.

SCENARIO

You're the nursing supervisor at a community hospital employing both emergency room and floor nurses. Each of these teams of nurses tends to work almost exclusively with others doing the same job. In your professional reading, you've come across the concept of cross-training nursing teams and giving them more varied responsibilities, which in turn has been shown to improve patient care while lowering costs. You call the two team leaders, Sue and Scott, into your office to explain that you want the nursing teams to move to this approach. To your surprise, they're both opposed to the idea. Sue says she and the other emergency room nurses feel they're needed in the ER where they fill the most vital role in the hospital. They work special hours when needed, do whatever tasks are required, and often work in difficult and stressful circumstances. They think the floor nurses have relatively easy jobs for the pay they receive. Scott, leader of the floor nurse team, tells you that his group believes the ER nurses lack the special training and extra experience that the floor nurses bring to the hospital. The floor nurses claim they have the heaviest responsibilities and do the most exacting work. Because they have ongoing contact with patients and families, they believe they shouldn't be called away from vital floor duties to help the ER nurses complete their tasks.

Reinforcement: Managing Resistance to Change

The following suggestions are activities you can do to practice and reinforce the behaviors associated with effectively managing resistance to change.

1. Think about changes (major and minor) that you have dealt with over the last year. Perhaps these changes involved other people and perhaps they were personal. Did you resist the change? Did others resist the change? How did you overcome your resistance or the resistance of others to the change?

2. Interview a manager at three different organizations about changes they have implemented. What was their experience in implementing the change? How did they manage resistance to the change?

---

14 • MENTORING

A **mentor** is someone in the organization, usually older, more experienced, and in a higher-level position, who sponsors or supports another employee (a protégé) who is in a lower-level position in the organization. A mentor can teach, guide, and encourage. Some organizations have formal mentoring programs, but even if your organization does not, mentoring should be an important skill for you to develop.

Learning About: Mentoring

You can be more effective at mentoring if you use the following six suggestions as you mentor another person:

1. *Communicate honestly and openly with your protégé.* If your protégé is going to learn from you and benefit from your experience and knowledge, you're going to have to be open and honest as you talk about what you've done. Bring up the failures as well as the successes. Remember that mentoring is a learning process, and in order for learning to take place, you're going to have to be open and honest in "telling it like it is."

2. *Encourage honest and open communication from your protégé.* You need to know as the mentor what your protégé hopes to gain from this relationship. You should encourage the protégé to ask for information and to be specific about what he or she wants to gain.

3. *Treat the relationship with the protégé as a learning opportunity.* Don't pretend to have all the answers and all the knowledge, but do share what you've learned through your experiences. And in your conversations and interactions with your protégé, you may be able to learn as much from that person as he or she does from you. So be open to listening to what your protégé is saying.

4. *Take the time to get to know your protégé.* As a mentor, you should be willing to take the time to get to know your protégé and his or her interests. If you're

not willing to spend that extra time, you should probably not embark on a mentoring relationship.

5. *Remind your protégé that there is no substitute for effective work performance.* In any job, effective work performance is absolutely essential for success. It doesn't matter how much information you provide as a mentor if the protégé isn't willing to strive for effective work performance.

6. *Know when it's time to let go.* Successful mentors know when it's time to let the protégé begin standing on his or her own. If the mentoring relationship has been effective, the protégé will be comfortable and confident in handling new and increasing work responsibilities. And just because the mentoring relationship is over doesn't mean that you never have contact with your protégé. It just means that the relationship becomes one of equals, not one of teacher and student.

Source: Based on H. Rothman, "The Boss As Mentor," *Nation's Business*, April 1993, pp. 66–67; J.B. Cunningham and T. Eberle, "Characteristics of the Mentoring Experience: A Qualitative Study," *Personnel Review*, June 1993, pp. 54–66; S. Crandell, "The Joys of Mentoring," *Executive Female*, March–April 1994, pp. 38–42; and W. Heery, "Corporate Mentoring Can Break the Glass Ceiling," *HRFocus*, May 1994, pp. 17–18.

Practice: Mentoring

Read through the following scenario. Write down some notes about how you would handle the situation described. Be sure to refer to the six behaviors for mentoring. Your professor will then tell you what to do next.

SCENARIO

Lora Slovinsky has worked for your department in a software design firm longer than any other of your employees. You value her skills and commitment and you frequently ask for her judgment on difficult issues. Very often, her ideas have been better than yours and you've let her know through both praise and pay increases how much you appreciate her contributions. Recently, though, you've begun to question Lora's judgment. The fundamental problem is in the distinct difference in the ways you both approach your work. Your strengths lie in getting things done on time and under budget. Although Lora is aware of these constraints, her creativity and perfectionism sometimes make her prolong projects, continually looking for the best approaches. On her most recent assignment, Lora seemed more intent than ever on doing things her way. Despite what you felt were clear guidelines, she was two weeks late in meeting an important customer deadline. And while her product quality was high, as always, the software design was far more elaborate than what was needed at this stage of development. Looking over her work in your office, you feel more than a little frustrated and certain that you need to address matters with Lora.

Reinforcement: Mentoring

The following suggestions are activities you can do to practice and reinforce the behaviors needed in mentoring:

1. If there are individuals on your campus who act as mentors (or advisors) to first-time students, make an appointment to talk to one of these mentors. These mentors may be upper-division students or they may be professors or college staff employees. Ask them about their role as a mentor and the skills they think it takes to be an effective mentor. How do the skills they mention relate to the behaviors described here?

2. Athletic coaches often act as mentors to their younger assistant coaches. Interview a coach about her or his role as a mentor. What types of things do coaches do to instruct, teach, advise, and encourage their assistant coaches? Could any of these activities be transferred to an organizational setting? Explain.

15 • NEGOTIATING

Negotiating is another interpersonal skill that managers use. For instance, they may have to negotiate salaries for incoming employees, negotiate for resources from their managers, work out differences with associates, or resolve conflicts with subordinates. **Negotiation** is a process of bargaining in which two or more parties who have different preferences must make joint decisions and come to an agreement.

Learning About: Negotiation

You can be more effective at negotiating if you use the following six recommended behaviors:

1. *Research the individual with whom you will be negotiating.* Acquire as much information as you can about the person with whom you'll be negotiating. What are this individual's interests and goals? Understanding this person's position will help you to better understand his or her behavior, predict his or her responses to your offers, and frame solutions in terms of his or her interests.

2. *Begin with a positive overture.* Research shows that concessions tend to be reciprocated and lead to agreements. Therefore, begin bargaining with a positive overture and then reciprocate the other party's concessions.

3. *Address problems, not personalities.* Concentrate on the negotiation issues, not on the personal characteristics of the individual with whom you're negotiating. When negotiations get tough, avoid the tendency to attack this person. Remember it's that person's ideas or position that you disagree with, not him or her personally.

4. *Pay little attention to initial offers.* Treat an initial offer as merely a point of departure. Everyone must have an initial position. Such positions tend to be extreme and idealistic. Treat them as such.

5. *Emphasize win-win solutions.* If conditions are supportive, look for an integrative solution. Frame options in terms of the other party's interests and look for solutions that can allow this person, as well as yourself, to declare a victory.

6. *Create an open and trusting climate.* Skilled negotiators are better listeners, ask more questions, focus their arguments more directly, are less defensive, and have learned to avoid words or phrases that can irritate the person with whom they're negotiating (such as "generous offer," "fair price," or "reasonable arrangement"). In other words, they are better at creating the open and trusting climate that is necessary for reaching a win-win settlement.

Source: Based on M.H. Bazerman and M.A. Neale, *Negotiating Rationally* (New York: The Free Press, 1992); and J.A. Wall, Jr. and M.W. Blum, "Negotiations," *Journal of Management*, June 1991, pp. 278–82.

Practice: Negotiating

Read through the following scenario. Write down some notes about how you would handle the situation. Be sure to refer to the six behaviors described for negotiating. Your professor will then tell you what to do next.

SCENARIO

As marketing director for Done Right, a regional home repair chain, you've come up with a plan you believe has significant potential for future sales. Your plan involves a customer information service designed to help people make their homes more environmentally sensitive. Then, based upon homeowners' assessments of their homes' environmental impact, your firm will be prepared to help them deal with problems or concerns they may uncover. You're really excited about the competitive potential of this new service. You envision pamphlets, in-store appearances by environmental experts, as well as contests for consumers and school kids. After several weeks of preparations, you make your pitch to your boss, Patrick Wong. You point out how the market for environmentally sensitive products is growing and how this growing demand represents the perfect opportunity for Done Right. Patrick seems impressed by your presentation, but he's expressed one major concern. He thinks your workload is already too heavy. He doesn't see how you're going to have enough time to start this new service *and* still be able to look after all of your other assigned marketing duties.

Reinforcement: Negotiating

The following suggestions are activities you can do to practice and reinforce the negotiating behaviors:

1. Find three people who recently have purchased new or used cars. Interview each to learn which tactics, if any, they used to get a better deal (lower price, more car features, and so forth). Write a short paper comparing your findings and relating it to the negotiating behaviors presented in this section.

2. Research current business periodicals for two examples of negotiations. The negotiations might be labor–management negotiations or they might be negotiations over buying and selling real estate or a business. What did the article say about the negotiation process? Write down specific questions that each party to the negotiation might have had. Pretend that you were a consultant to one of the parties in the negotiation. What recommendations would you have made?

---

16 • PROVIDING FEEDBACK

Ask a manager about the feedback he or she gives employees and you're likely to get an answer followed by a qualifier! If the feedback is positive, it's likely to be given promptly and enthusiastically. However, negative feedback is often treated very differently. Like most of us, managers don't particularly enjoy communicating bad news. They fear offending the other person or having to deal with the recipient's defensiveness. The result is that negative feedback is often avoided, delayed, or substantially distorted. However, it is important for managers to provide both positive and negative feedback.

Learning About: Providing Feedback

You can be more effective at providing feedback if you use the following six specific suggestions:

1. *Focus on specific behaviors.* Feedback should be specific rather than general. Avoid such statements as "You have a bad attitude" or "I'm really impressed with the good job you did." They're vague and although they provide information, they don't tell the recipient enough to correct the "bad attitude" or on what basis you concluded that a "good job" had been done so the person knows what behaviors to repeat or to avoid.

2. *Keep feedback impersonal.* Feedback, particularly the negative kind, should be descriptive rather than judgmental or evaluative. No matter how upset you are, keep the feedback focused on job-related behaviors and never criticize someone personally because of an inappropriate action.

3. *Keep feedback goal oriented.* Feedback should not be given primarily to "unload" on another person. If you have to say something negative, make sure it's directed toward the recipient's goals. Ask yourself whom the feedback is supposed to help. If the answer is *you*, bite your tongue and hold the comment. Such feedback undermines your credibility and lessens the meaning and influence of future feedback.

4. *Make feedback well timed.* Feedback is most meaningful to a recipient when there's a very short interval between his or her behavior and the receipt of feedback about that behavior. Moreover, if you're particularly concerned with changing behavior, delays in providing feedback on the undesirable actions lessen the likelihood that the feedback will be effective in bringing about the desired change. Of course, making feedback prompt merely for the sake of promptness can backfire if you have insufficient information, if you're angry, or if you're otherwise emotionally upset. In such instances, "well timed" could mean "somewhat delayed."

5. *Ensure understanding.* Make sure your feedback is concise and complete so that the recipient clearly and fully understands your communication. It may help to have the recipient rephrase the content of your feedback to find out whether or not it fully captured the meaning you intended.

6. *Direct negative feedback toward behavior that the recipient can control.* There's little value in reminding a person of some shortcoming over which he or she has no control. Negative feedback should be directed at behavior that the recipient can do something about. In addition, when negative feedback is given concerning something that the recipient can control, it might be a good idea to indicate specifically what can be done to improve the situation.

Source: Based on P.L. Hunsaker, *Training in Management Skills* (Upper Saddle River, NJ: Prentice Hall, 2001), pp. 60–61.

Practice: Providing Feedback

Read through the following scenario. Write down some notes about how you would handle the situation. Be sure to refer to the six behaviors described for providing feedback. Your professor will tell you what to do next.

SCENARIO

Craig is an excellent employee whose expertise and productivity have always met or exceeded your expectations. But recently he's been making work difficult for other members of your advertising team. Like his co-workers, Craig researches and computes the costs of media coverage for your advertising agency's clients. The work requires laboriously leafing through several large reference books to find the correct base price and add-on charges for each radio or television station and time slot, calculating each actual cost, and compiling the results in a computerized spreadsheet. To make things more efficient and convenient, you've always allowed your team members to bring the reference books they're using to their desks while they're using them. Lately, however, Craig has been piling books around him for days and sometimes weeks at a time. The books interfere with the flow of traffic past his desk and other people have to go out of their way to retrieve the books from Craig's pile. It's time for you to have a talk with Craig.

Reinforcement: Providing Feedback

The following suggestions are activities you can do to practice and reinforce the behaviors in providing feedback:

1. Think of three things that a friend or family member did well recently. Did you praise the person at the time? If not, why? The next time someone close to you does something well, give him or her positive feedback.

2. You have a good friend who has a mannerism (for instance, speech, body movement, style of dress, or whatever) that you think is inappropriate and detracts from the overall impression that he or she makes. Come up with a plan for talking with this person. What will you say? When will you talk with your friend? How will you handle his or her reaction?

---

17 • READING AN ORGANIZATION'S CULTURE

The ability to read an organization's culture can be a valuable skill. For instance, if you're looking for a job, you'll want to choose an employer whose culture is compatible with your values and in which you'll feel comfortable. If you can accurately assess a potential employer's culture before you make your job decision, you may be able to save yourself a lot of anxiety and reduce the likelihood of making a poor choice. Similarly, you'll undoubtedly have business transactions with numerous organizations during your professional career, such as selling a product or service, negotiating a contract, arranging a joint work project, or merely seeking out who controls certain decisions in an organization. The ability to assess another organization's culture can be a definite plus in successfully performing those pursuits.

Learning About: Reading an Organization's Culture

You can be more effective at reading an organization's culture if you use the following behaviors. For the sake of simplicity, we're going to look at this skill from the perspective of a job applicant. We'll assume that you're interviewing for a job, although these skills can be generalized to many situations. Here's a list of things you can do to help learn about an organization's culture.

1. *Observe the physical surroundings.* Pay attention to signs, posters, pictures, photos, style of dress, length of hair, degree of openness between offices, and office furnishings and arrangements.

2. *Make note of those with whom you met.* Was it the person who would be your immediate supervisor? Or did you meet with potential colleagues, managers from other departments, or senior executives? Based on what they revealed, to what degree do people interact with others who may not be in their particular work area or at their particular organizational level?

3. *How would you characterize the style of the people you met?* Are they formal? Casual? Serious? Laid-back? Open? Not willing to provide information?

4. *Look at the organization's human resources manual.* Are formal rules and regulations printed there? If so, how detailed are these policies?

5. *Ask questions of the people with whom you meet.* The most valid and reliable information tends to come from asking the same questions of many people (to see how closely their responses align) and by talking with individuals whose jobs link them to the outside environment. Questions that will give you insights into organizational processes and practices might include: What is the background of the founders? What is the background of current senior managers? What are their functional specialties? Were they promoted from within or hired from outside? How does the organization integrate new employees? Is there a formal orientation program? Are there formal employee training programs? How does your boss define his or her job success? How would you define fairness in terms of reward allocations? Can you identify some people here who are on the "fast track"? What do you think has put them on the fast track? Can you identify someone in the organization who seems to be considered an oddball or deviant? How has the organization responded to this person? Can you describe a decision that someone made that was well received? Can you describe a decision that didn't work out well? What were the consequences for the decision maker? Could you describe a crisis or critical

event that has occurred recently in the organization? How did top management respond? What was learned from this experience?

Source: Based on S.P. Robbins, *Organizational Behavior*, 9th ed. (Upper Saddle River, NJ: Prentice Hall, 2001), p. 513.

Practice: Reading an Organization's Culture

Read through the following scenario. Write down some notes about how you would handle the situation. Be sure to refer to the suggested behaviors for reading an organization's culture. Your professor will tell you what to do next.

SCENARIO

After spending your first three years after college graduation as a freelance graphic designer, you're looking at pursuing a job as an account executive at a graphic design firm. You feel that the scope of assignments and potential for technical training far exceed what you'd be able to do on your own and you're looking to expand your skills and meet a brand-new set of challenges. However, you want to make sure you "fit" into the organization where you're going to be spending more than eight hours every workday. What's the best way for you to find a place where you'll be happy and where your style and personality will be appreciated?

Reinforcement: Reading an Organization's Culture

The following suggestions are activities you can do to practice and reinforce the behaviors associated with reading an organization's culture.

1. If you're taking more than one course, assess the culture of the various classes in which you're enrolled. How do the classroom cultures differ? Which culture(s) do you seem to prefer? Why?

2. Do some comparisons of the atmosphere or feeling you get from various organizations. Because of the number and wide variety that you'll find, it will probably be easiest for you to do this exercise using restaurants, retail stores, or banks. Based on the atmosphere that you observe, what type of organizational culture do you think these organizations might have? On what did you base your decision? Which type of culture do you prefer? Why? If you can, interview three employees at this organization for their descriptions of the organization's culture. Did their descriptions support your interpretation? Why or why not?

---

18 • SCANNING THE ENVIRONMENT

Anticipating and interpreting changes that are taking place in the environment is an important skill that managers need. Information that comes from scanning the environment can be used in making decisions and taking actions. And managers at all levels of an organization need to know how to scan the environment for important information and trends.

Learning About: Scanning the Environment

You can be more effective at scanning the environment if you use the following suggestions:

1. *Decide which type of environmental information is important to your work.* Perhaps you need to know changes in customers' needs and desires or perhaps you need to know what your competitors are doing. Once you know the type of information that you'd like to have, you can look at the best ways to get that information.

2. *Regularly read and monitor pertinent information.* There is no scarcity of information to scan, but what you need to do is read those information sources that are pertinent. How do you know information sources are pertinent? They're pertinent if they provide you with the information that you identified as important.

3. *Incorporate the information that you get from your environmental scanning into your decisions and actions.* Unless you use the information you're getting, you're wasting your time getting it. Also, the more that you find you're using information from your environmental scanning, the more likely it is that you'll want to continue to invest time and other resources into gathering it. You'll see that this information is important to your being able to manage effectively and efficiently.

4. *Regularly review your environmental scanning activities.* If you find that you're spending too much time getting nonuseful information or if you're not using the pertinent information that you've gathered, you need to make some adjustments.

5. *Encourage your subordinates to be alert to information that is important.* Your employees can be your "eyes and ears" as well. Emphasize to them the importance of gathering and sharing information that may affect your work unit's performance.

Source: Based on L.M. Fuld, *Monitoring the Competition* (New York: Wiley, 1988); E.H. Burack and N.J. Mathys, "Environmental Scanning Improves Strategic Planning," *Personnel Administrator*, 1989, pp. 82–87; and R. Subramanian, N. Fernandes, and E. Harper, "Environmental Scanning in U.S. Companies: Their Nature and Their Relationship to Performance," *Management International Review*, July 1993, pp. 271–86.

Practice: Scanning the Environment

Read through the following scenario. Write down some notes about how you would handle the situation described. Be sure to refer to the suggestions for scanning the environment. Your professor will then tell you what to do next.

SCENARIO

You're the assistant to the president at your college. You've been asked to prepare a report outlining the external information that you think is important for her to monitor. Think of the types of information that the president would need in order to do an effective job of managing the college right now and over the next three years. Be as specific as you can in describing this information. Also, identify where this information could be found.

Reinforcement: Scanning the Environment

The following suggestions are activities you can do to practice and reinforce the behaviors associated with scanning the environment.

1. Select an organization with which you're familiar either as an employee or perhaps as a frequent customer. Assume that you're the top manager in this organization. What types of information from environmental scanning do you think would be important to you? Where would you find this information? Now assume that you're a first-level manager in this organization. Would the types of information you'd get from environmental scanning change? Explain.

2. Assume you're a regional manager for a large bookstore chain. Using the Internet, what types of environmental and competitive information were you able to identify? For each source, what information did you find that might help you do your job better?

---

19 • SETTING GOALS

Employees should have a clear understanding of what they're attempting to accomplish. In addition, managers have the responsibility for seeing that this is done by helping employees set work goals. Setting goals is a skill every manager needs to develop.

Learning About: Setting Goals

You can be more effective at setting goals if you use the following eight suggestions.

1. *Identify an employee's key job tasks.* Goal setting begins by defining what it is that you want your employees to accomplish. The best source for this information is each employee's job description.

2. *Establish specific and challenging goals for each key task.* Identify the level of performance expected of each employee. Specify the target toward which the employee is working.

3. *Specify the deadlines for each goal.* Putting deadlines on each goal reduces ambiguity. Deadlines, however, should not be set arbitrarily. Rather, they need to be realistic given the tasks to be completed.

4. *Allow the employee to actively participate.* When employees participate in goal setting, they're more likely to accept the goals. However, it must be sincere participation. That is, employees must perceive that you are truly seeking their input, not just going through the motions.

5. *Prioritize goals.* When you give someone more than one goal, it's important for you to rank the goals in order of importance. The purpose of prioritizing is to encourage the employee to take action and expend effort on each goal in proportion to its importance.

6. *Rate goals for difficulty and importance.* Goal setting should not encourage people to choose easy goals. Instead, goals should be rated for their difficulty and importance. When goals are rated, individuals can be given credit for trying difficult goals, even if they don't fully achieve them.

7. *Build in feedback mechanisms to assess goal progress.* Feedback lets employees know whether their level of effort is sufficient to attain the goal. Feedback should be both self-generated and supervisor generated. In either case, feedback should be frequent and recurring.

8. *Link rewards to goal attainment.* It's natural for employees to ask, "What's in it for me?" Linking rewards to the achievement of goals will help answer that question.

Source: Based on S.P. Robbins and D.A. DeCenzo, *Fundamentals of Management*, 4th ed. (Upper Saddle River, NJ: Prentice Hall, 2004), p. 85.

Practice: Setting Goals

Read through the following scenario. Write down some notes about how you would handle the situation described. Be sure to refer to the eight suggestions for setting goals. Your professor will then tell you what to do next.

SCENARIO

You worked your way through college while holding down a part-time job bagging groceries at Food Town supermarket chain. You like working in the food industry and when you graduated, you accepted a position with Food Town as a management trainee. Three years have passed and you've gained experience in the grocery store industry and in operating a large supermarket. About a year ago, you received a promotion to store manager at one of the chain's locations. One of the things you've liked about Food Town is that it gives store managers a great deal of autonomy in running their stores. The company provided very general guidelines to its managers. The concern was with the bottom line; for the most part, how you got there was up to you. Now that you're finally a store manager, you want to establish an MBO-type program in your store. You like the idea that everyone should have clear goals to work toward and then is evaluated against those goals.

Your store employs 90 people, although, except for the managers, most work only 20 to 30 hours per week. You have six people reporting to you: an assistant manager; a week-end manager; and grocery, produce, meat, and bakery managers. The only highly skilled jobs belong to the butchers, who have strict training and regulatory guidelines.

Other less skilled jobs include cashier, shelf stocker, cleanup, and grocery bagger.

Specifically describe how you would go about setting goals in your new position. Include examples of goals for the jobs of butcher, cashier, and bakery manager.

Reinforcement: Setting Goals

The following suggestions are activities you can do to practice and reinforce the behaviors in setting goals:

1. Where do you want to be in five years? Do you have specific five-year goals? Establish three goals you want to achieve in five years. Make sure these goals are specific, challenging, and measurable.

2. Set personal and academic goals you want to achieve by the end of this college term. Prioritize and rate them for difficulty.

20 • SOLVING PROBLEMS CREATIVELY

In a global business environment, where changes are fast and furious, organizations desperately need creative people. The uniqueness and variety of problems that managers face demand that they be able to solve problems creatively. Creativity is a frame of mind. You need to expand your mind's capabilities—that is, open up your mind to new ideas. Every individual has the ability to improve his or her creativity, but many people simply don't try to develop that ability.

Learning About: Solving Problems Creatively

You can be more effective at solving problems creatively if you use the following 10 suggestions:

1. *Think of yourself as creative.* Although this may be a simple suggestion, research shows that if you think you can't be creative, you won't be. Believing in your ability to be creative is the first step in becoming more creative.

2. *Pay attention to your intuition.* Every individual has a subconscious mind that works well. Sometimes answers will come to you when you least expect them. Listen to that "inner voice." In fact, most creative people will keep a notepad near their bed and write down ideas when the thoughts come to them. That way, they don't forget them.

3. *Move away from your comfort zone.* Every individual has a comfort zone in which certainty exists. But creativity and the known often do not mix. To be creative, you need to move away from the status quo and focus your mind on something new.

4. *Determine what you want to do.* This includes such things as taking time to understand a problem before

beginning to try to resolve it, getting all the facts in mind, and trying to identify the most important facts.

5. *Look for ways to tackle the problem.* This can be accomplished by setting aside a block of time to focus on it; working out a plan for attacking it; establishing subgoals; imagining or actually using analogies wherever possible (for example, could you approach your problem like a fish out of water and look at what the fish does to cope? or can you use the things you have to do to find your way when it's foggy to help you solve your problem?); using different problem-solving strategies such as verbal, visual, mathematical, theatrical (for instance, you might draw a diagram of the decision or problem to help you visualize it better or you might talk to yourself out loud about the problem, telling it as you would tell a story to someone); trusting your intuition; and playing with possible ideas and approaches (for example, look at your problem from a different perspective or ask yourself what someone else, like your grandmother, might do if faced with the same situation).

6. *Look for ways to do things better.* This may involve trying consciously to be original, not worrying about looking foolish, eliminating cultural taboos (like gender stereotypes) that might influence your possible solutions, keeping an open mind, being alert to odd or puzzling facts, thinking of unconventional ways to use objects and the environment (for instance, thinking about how you could use newspaper or magazine headlines to help you be a better problem solver), discarding usual or habitual ways of doing things, and striving for objectivity by being as critical of your own ideas as you would those of someone else.

7. *Find several right answers.* Being creative means continuing to look for other solutions even when you think you have solved the problem. A better, more creative solution just might be found.

8. *Believe in finding a workable solution.* Like believing in yourself, you also need to believe in your ideas. If you don't think you can find a solution, you probably won't.

9. *Brainstorm with others.* Creativity is not an isolated activity. Bouncing ideas off of others creates a synergistic effect.

10. *Turn creative ideas into action.* Coming up with creative ideas is only part of the process. Once the ideas are generated, they must be implemented. Keeping great ideas in your mind, or on papers that no one will read, does little to expand your creative abilities.

Source: Based on J. Calano and J. Salzman, "Ten Ways to Fire Up Your Creativity," *Working Woman*, July 1989, p. 94; J.V. Anderson, "Mind Mapping: A Tool for Creative Thinking," *Business Horizons*, January-February 1993, pp. 42–46; M. Loeb, "Ten Commandments for Managing Creative People," *Fortune*, January 16, 1995, pp. 135–36; and M. Henricks, "Good Thinking," *Entrepreneur*, May 1996, pp. 70–73.

Practice: Solving Problems Creatively

Read through the following scenario. Write down some notes about how you would handle the situation. Be sure to refer to the 10 suggestions for solving problems creatively. Your professor will then tell you what to do next.

Scenario

Every time the phone rings, your stomach clenches and your palms start to sweat. And it's no wonder! As sales manager for Brinkers, a machine tool parts manufacturer, you're besieged by calls from customers who are upset about late deliveries. Your boss, Carter Hererra, acts as both production manager and scheduler. Every time your sales representa-

tives negotiate a sale, it's up to Carter to determine whether or not production can actually meet the delivery date the customer specifies. And Carter invariably says, "No problem." The good thing about this is that you make a lot of initial sales. The bad news is that production hardly ever meets the shipment dates that Carter authorizes. And he doesn't seem to be all that concerned about the aftermath of late deliveries. He says, "Our customers know they're getting outstanding quality at a great price. Just let them try to match that anywhere. It can't be done. So even if they have to wait a couple of extra days or weeks, they're still getting the best deal they can." Somehow the customers don't see it that way, however. And they let you know about their unhappiness. Then it's up to you to try to soothe the relationship. You know this problem has to be taken care of, but what possible solutions are there? After all, how are you going to keep from making your manager mad or making the customers mad?

Reinforcement: Solving Problems Creatively

The following suggestions are activities you can do to practice and reinforce the behaviors associated with solving problems creatively:

1. Take out a couple of sheets of paper. You have 20 minutes to list as many medical or health-care-related jobs as you can that begin with the letter *r* (for instance, radiologist, registered nurse). If you run out of listings before time is up, it's OK to quit early. But, try to be as creative as you can.

2. List on a piece of paper some common terms that apply to both water and finance. How many were you able to come up with?

---

21 • VALUING DIVERSITY

"Understanding and managing people who are similar to us are challenges—but understanding and managing those *who are dissimilar from us and from each other* can be even tougher." The increasing diversity of workplaces around the world means that managers need to recognize that not all employees want the same thing, will act in the same manner, and thus can't be managed the same way. What is a diverse workforce? It's one that's more heterogeneous in terms of gender, race, ethnicity, age, and other characteristics that reflect differences. The ability to value diversity and help a diverse workforce achieve its maximum potential is a skill that managers increasingly will find is needed.

Learning About Valuing Diversity

The diversity issues an individual manager might face are many. They might include issues such as communicating with employees whose familiarity with the language might be limited; creating career development programs that fit the skills, needs, and values of a particular group; helping a diverse team

cope with a conflict over goals or work assignments; or learning which rewards are valued by different groups. You can improve your handling of diversity issues by following these eight behaviors.

1. *Fully accept diversity.* Successfully valuing diversity starts with each individual accepting the principle of multiculturalism. Accept the value of diversity for its own sake—not simply because you have to. Accepting and valuing diversity is important because it's the right thing to do. And it's important that you reflect your acceptance in all you say and do.

2. *Recruit broadly.* When you have job openings, work to get a diverse applicant pool. Although referrals from current employees can be a good source of applicants, that tends to produce candidates similar to the present workforce.

3. *Select fairly.* Make sure that the selection process doesn't discriminate. One suggestion is to use job-specific tests rather than general aptitude or knowledge tests. Such tests measure specific skills, not subjective characteristics.

4. *Provide orientation and training for minorities.* Making the transition from outsider to insider can be particularly difficult for a diverse employee. Provide support either through a group or through a mentoring arrangement.

5. *Sensitize non-minorities.* Not only do you personally need to accept and value diversity, as a manager you need to encourage all your employees to do so. Many organizations do this through diversity training programs. For example, Digital Equipment Corporation (DEC), has a "Valuing Differences" program in which employees go through training programs designed to help them understand workplace diversity by examining the cultural norms of different employee groups. In addition, employees can also be part of ongoing discussion groups whose members meet monthly to discuss stereotypes and ways of improving diversity relationships. And, as mentioned above, the most important thing a manager can do is show by his or her actions that diversity is valued.

6. *Strive to be flexible.* Part of valuing diversity is recognizing that different groups have different needs and values. Be flexible in accommodating employee requests.

7. *Seek to motivate individually.* Motivating employees is an important skill for any manager; motivating a diverse workforce has its own special challenges. Managers must be more in tune with the background, cultures, and values of employees. What motivates a single mother with two young children and who is working full time to support her family is likely to be different from the needs of a young, single, part-time employee or an older employee who's working to supplement his or her retirement income.

8. *Reinforce employee differences.* Encourage individuals to embrace and value diverse views. Create traditions and ceremonies that promote diversity. Celebrate diversity by accentuating its positive aspects. However, also be prepared to deal with the challenges of diversity such as mistrust, miscommunication, lack of cohesiveness, attitudinal differences, and stress.

Source: C. Harvey and M. J. Allard, *Understanding and Managing Diversity: Readings, Cases, and Exercises,* 2nd ed. (Upper Saddle River, NJ: Prentice Hall, 2002); P. L. Hunsaker, *Training in Management Skills* (Upper Saddle River, NJ: Prentice Hall, 2001); and J. Greenberg, *Managing Behavior in Organizations: Science in Service to Practice*, 2nd ed. (Upper Saddle River, NJ: Prentice Hall, 1999).

Practice: Valuing Diversity

Read through the following scenario. Write down some notes about how you would handle the situation described. Be sure to refer to the eight behaviors described for valuing diversity. Your professor will tell you what to do next.

SCENARIO

Read through the descriptions of the following employees who work for the same organization. After reading each description, write a short paragraph describing what you think the goals and priorities of each employee might be. With what types of employee issues might the manager of each employee have to deal? How could these managers exhibit the value of diversity?

LESTER Lester is 57 years old, a college graduate, and a vice president of the firm. His two children are married and he is a grandparent of three beautiful grandchildren. He lives in a condo with his wife who does volunteer work and is active in their church. Marvin is healthy and likes to stay active, both physically and mentally.

SANJYOT Sanjyot is a thirty-year-old clerical worker who came to the United States from Indonesia ten years ago. She completed high school after moving to the United States and has begun to attend evening classes at a local community college. Sanjyot is a single parent with two children under the age of eight. Although her health is excellent, one of her children suffers from a severe learning disability.

YURI Yuri is a recent immigrant from one of the former Soviet republics. He is 42 years old and his English communication skills are quite limited. He has an engineering degree from his country but since he's not licensed to practice in the United States, he works as a parts clerk. He is unmarried and has no children but feels an obligation to his relatives back in his home country. He sends much of his paycheck to them.

Reinforcement: Valuing Diversity

The following suggestions are activities you can do to practice and reinforce the behaviors associated with valuing diversity.

1. Indicate which employees (age, gender, ethnicity, family status, and so forth) you think might be motivated by the following additional employee benefits: on-site day care, fitness center, tuition reimbursement, job sharing, English classes, having a mentor, being a mentor, performance bonus plan, more time off, flextime, enhanced retirement benefits, supervisory training, subsidized dependent care, discounts on company products, religious holidays, free candy and snacks in employee break room, on-site physician, country club membership, and on-site dry cleaning services. Looking at your responses, what are the implications for a manager?

2. Ask your minority friends what kinds of biases they perceive in school or at work. Think about how you, as a manager, might deal with instances of these types of biases.

3. Come up with a list of suggestions that you personally can use to improve your sensitivity to diversity issues.

●●●●Notes

CHAPTER 1

1. Information from company Web site (*www.tiresplus.com*) and Hoover's Online (*www.hoovers.com*), January 5, 2003; and K. Dobbs, "Tires Plus Takes the Training High Road," *Training*, April 2000, pp. 56–63.

2. Information from Catalyst Web page (*www.catalystwomen.org*), January 27, 2003.

3. T. Schwartz, "The Greatest Sources of Satisfaction in the Workplace Are Internal and Emotional," *Fast Company*, November 2000, pp. 398–402; and K. Dobbs, "Plagued by Turnover? Train Your Managers," *Training*, August 2000, pp. 62–65.

4. "Human Capital Index: 2001/2002 Survey Report," Watson Wyatt Worldwide, Washington, DC.

5. D. J. Campbell, "The Proactive Employee: Managing Workplace Initiative," *Academy of Management Executive,* August 2000, pp. 52–66.

6. Information from company Web site (*www.medtronic.com*) and Hoover's Online (*www.hoovers.com*), March 10, 2003; and D. Whitford, "A Human Place to Work," *Fortune*, January 8, 2001, pp. 108–120.

7. "Industry Week's Best Plants," *Industry Week* Web site (*www.industryweek. com*), March 10, 2003.

8. H. Fayol, *Industrial and General Administration* (Paris: Dunod, 1916).

9. For a comprehensive review of this question, see C.P. Hales, "What Do Managers Do? A Critical Review of the Evidence," *Journal of Management*, January 1986, pp. 88–115.

10. H. Mintzberg, *The Nature of Managerial Work* (New York: Harper & Row, 1973); and J. T. Straub, "Put on Your Manager's Hat," *USA Today Online* (*www.usatoday.com*), October 29, 2002.

11. H. Mintzberg and J. Gosling, "Educating Managers Beyond Borders," *Academy of Management Learning and Education*, September 2002, pp. 64–76.

12. See, for example, L.D. Alexander, "The Effect Level in the Hierarchy and Functional Area Have on the Extent Mintzberg's Roles Are Required by Managerial Jobs," *Academy of Management Proceedings* (San Francisco, 1979), pp. 186–89; A.W. Lau and C.M. Pavett, "The Nature of Managerial Work: A Comparison of Public and Private Sector Managers," *Group and Organization Studies*, December 1980, pp. 453–66; M.W. McCall Jr. and C.A. Segrist, "In Pursuit of the Manager's Job: Building on Mintzberg," *Technical Report No. 14* (Greensboro, NC: Center for Creative Leadership, 1980); C.M. Pavett and A.W. Lau, "Managerial Work: The Influence of Hierarchical Level and Functional Specialty," *Academy of Management Journal*, March 1983, pp. 170–77; Hales, "What Do Managers Do?" A.I. Kraut, P.R. Pedigo, D.D. McKenna, and M.D. Dunnette, "The Role of the Manager: What's Really Important in Different Management Jobs," *Academy of Management Executive*, November 1989, pp. 286–93; and M.J. Martinko and W.L. Gardner, "Structured Observation of Managerial Work: A Replication and Synthesis," *Journal of Management Studies*, May 1990, pp. 330–57.

13. Pavett and Lau, "Managerial Work."

14. S.J. Carroll and D.A. Gillen, "Are the Classical Management Functions Useful in Describing Managerial Work?," *Academy of Management Review*, January 1987, p. 48.

15. H. Koontz, "Commentary on the Management Theory Jungle—Nearly Two Decades Later," in H. Koontz, C. O'Donnell, and H. Weihrich (eds.), *Management: A Book of Readings*, 6th ed. (New York: McGraw-Hill, 1984); Carroll and Gillen, "Are the Classical Management Functions Useful in Describing Managerial Work?"; and P. Allan, "Managers at Work: A Large-Scale Study of the Managerial Job in New York City Government," *Academy of Management Journal*, September 1981, pp. 613–19.

16. R.L. Katz, "Skills of an Effective Administrator," *Harvard Business Review*, September–October 1974, pp. 90–102.

17. American Management Association Survey of Managerial Skills and Competence: March/April 2000, found on American Management Association Online (*www.amanet.org*), October 30, 2002.

18. C. Ansberry, "What's My Line?" *Wall Street Journal*, March 22, 2002, pp. A1+.

19. F. F. Reichheld, "Lead for Loyalty," *Harvard Business Review*, July–August 2001, p. 76.

20. Cited in E. Naumann and D. W. Jackson, Jr., "One More Time: How Do You Satisfy Customers?" *Business Horizons*, May–June 1999, p. 73.

21. K. A. Eddleston, D. L. Kidder, and B. E. Litzky, "Who's the Boss? Contending with Competing Expectations from Customers and Management," *Academy of Management Executive*, November 2002, pp. 85–95.

22. See, for instance, M. D. Hartline and O. C. Ferrell, "The Management of Customer-Contact Service Employees: An Empirical Investigation," *Journal of Marketing*, October 1996, pp. 52–70; Naumann and Jackson, Jr., "One More Time: How Do You Satisfy Customers?"; W.C. Tsai, "Determinants and Consequences of Employee Displayed Positive Emotions," *Journal of Management*, vol. 27, no. 4 (2001), pp. 497–512; S. D. Pugh, "Service with a Smile: Emotional Contagion in the Service Encounter," *Academy of Management Journal*, October 2001, pp. 1018–27; S. D. Pugh, J. Dietz, J.W. Wiley, and S.M. Brooks, "Driving Service Effectiveness Through Employee-Customer Linkages," *Academy of Management Executive*, November 2002, pp. 73–84; Eddleston, Kidder, and Litzky, "Who's the Boss? Contending with Competing Expectations from Customers and Management"; and B.A. Gutek, M. Groth, and B. Cherry, "Achieving Service Success Through Relationships and Enhanced Encounters," *Academy of Management Executive*, November 2002, pp. 132–144.

23. R.A. Hattori and J. Wycoff, "Innovation DNA," *Training and Development*, January 2002, p. 24.

24. R.A. Hattori, "Sometimes Innovation Starts with a Relationship," found on the Innovation Network (*www. thinksmart.com*), March 14, 2003.

25. H.G. Barkema, J.A.C. Baum, and E.A. Mannix, "Management Challenges in a New Time," *Academy of Management Journal*, October 2002, pp. 916–930; M.A. Hitt, "Transformation of Management for the New Millennium," *Organizational Dynamics*, Winter 2000, pp. 7–17; T. Aeppel, "Power Generation," *Wall Street Journal*, April 7, 2000, pp. A1+; "Rethinking Work," *Fast Company*, April 2000, p. 253; "Workplace Trends Shifting over Time," *Springfield News Leader*, January 2, 2000; p. 7B+; "Expectations: The State of the New Economy," *Fast Com-*

pany, September 1999, pp. 251–64; T.J. Tetenbaum, "Shifting Paradigms: From Newton to Chaos," *Organizational Dynamics,* Spring 1998, pp. 21–33; T.A. Stewart, "Brain Power: Who Owns It … How They Profit from It,"*Fortune,* March 17, 1997, pp. 105–10; G.P. Zachary, "The Right Mix," *Wall Street Journal,* March 13, 1997, pp. A1+; W.H. Miller, "Leadership at a Crossroads," *Industry Week,* August 19, 1996, pp. 42–56; M. Scott, "Interview with Dee Hock," *Business Ethics,* May/June 1996, pp. 37–41; and J. O. C. Hamilton, S. Baker, and B. Vlasic, "The New Workplace," *BusinessWeek,* April 29, 1996, pp. 106–17.

26. Headlines from *USA Today,* April 10, 2003, April 6, 2003, and March 10, 2003.

27. *Occupational Outlook Handbook, 2002–03 Edition,* U.S. Department of Labor, Bureau of Labor Statistics available online at (*www.bls.gov/oco*), March 15, 2003; and M. A. Verespej, "A Dearth of Good Managers," *Industry Week,* April 2, 2001, pp. 35–36.

CHAPTER 2

1. Information from company Web site (*www.mattel.com*) and Hoover's Online (*www.hoovers.com*), January 5, 2003; C. Salter, "Ivy Ross Is Not Playing Around," *Fast Company,* November 2002, pp. 104–110; and T. Howard, "Mattel Counts on Innovation for '03 Success," *USA Today Online* (*www.usatoday.com*), February 14, 2003.

2. C.S. George Jr., *The History of Management Thought,* 2d ed. (Upper Saddle River, NJ: Prentice Hall, 1972), p. 4.

3. Ibid., pp. 35–41.

4. F.W. Taylor, *Principles of Scientific Management* (New York: Harper, 1911), p. 44. For other information on F.W. Taylor, see M. Banta, *Taylored Lives: Narrative Productions in the Age of Taylor, Veblen, and Ford* (Chicago: University of Chicago Press, 1993); and R. Kanigel, *The One Best Way: Frederick Winslow Taylor and the Enigma of Efficiency* (New York: Viking, 1997).

5. See, for example, F.B. Gilbreth, *Motion Study* (New York: Van Nostrand, 1911); and F.B. Gilbreth and L.M. Gilbreth, *Fatigue Study* (New York: Sturgis and Walton, 1916).

6. G. Colvin, "Managing in the Info Era," *Fortune,* March 6, 2000, pp. F6–F9; and A. Harrington, "The Big Ideas," *Fortune,* November 22, 1999, pp. 152–153.

7. H. Fayol, *Industrial and General Administration* (Paris: Dunod, 1916).

8. M. Weber, *The Theory of Social and Economic Organizations,* ed. T. Parsons, trans. A.M. Henderson and T. Parsons (New York: Free Press, 1947).

9. E. Mayo, *The Human Problems of an Industrial Civilization* (New York: Macmillan, 1933); and F.J. Roethlisberger and W.J. Dickson, *Management and the Worker* (Cambridge, MA: Harvard University Press, 1939).

10. See, for example, A. Carey, "The Hawthorne Studies: A Radical Criticism," *American Sociological Review,* June 1967, pp. 403–16; R.H. Franke and J. Kaul, "The Hawthorne Experiments: First Statistical Interpretations," *American Sociological Review,* October 1978, pp. 623–43; B. Rice, "The Hawthorne Defect: Persistence of a Flawed Theory," *Psychology Today,* February 1982, pp. 70–74; J.A. Sonnenfeld, "Shedding Light on the Hawthorne Studies," *Journal of Occupational Behavior,* April 1985, pp. 111–30; and S.R.G. Jones, "Worker Interdependence and Output: The Hawthorne Studies Reevaluated," *American Sociological Review,* April 1990, pp. 176–90; S.R. Jones, "Was There a Hawthorne Effect?" *American Sociological Review,* November 1992, pp. 451–68; and G.W. Yunker, "An Explanation of Positive and Negative Hawthorne Effects: Evidence from the Relay Assembly Test Room and Bank Wiring Observation Room Studies," paper presented at Academy of Management annual meeting, August 1993, Atlanta, Georgia.

11. K. B. DeGreene, *Sociotechnical Systems: Factors in Analysis, Design, and Management* (Englewood Cliff, NJ: Prentice Hall, 1973), p. 13.

12. J.E. Garten, "Globalism without Tears," *Strategy & Business,* Fourth Quarter 2002, pp. 36–45; and L.L. Bierema, J.W. Bing, and T.J. Carter, "The Global Pendulum," *Training and Development,* May 2002, pp. 70–78; C. Taylor, "Whatever Happened to Globalization?," *Fast Company,* September 1999, pp. 228–36; and S. Zahra, "The Changing Rules of Global Competitiveness in the 21st Century," *Academy of Management Executive,* February 1999, pp. 36–42.

13. K. Yourish, "Corporate America's New Math," *Newsweek,* July 22, 2002, p. 30.

14. R.W. Judy and Carol D'Amico, *Workforce 2020* (Indianapolis: Hudson Institute, August 1999).

15. "Hispanics Now Top Minority," *Hispanic Business,* March 2003, p. 16.

16. G. Naik, L. Chang, and J. Slater, "Leveraging the Age Gap," *Wall Street Journal,* February 27, 2003, pp. B1+.

17. G.W. Loveman and J.J. Gabarro, "The Managerial Implications of Changing Work Force Demographics: A Scoping Study," *Human Resource Management,* Spring 1991, pp. 7–29.

18. J. Hickman, "America's 50 Best Companies for Minorities," *Fortune,* July 8, 2002, pp. 110–20.

19. "The Third Millennium: Small Business and Entrepreneurship in the 21st Century," Office of Advocacy, U.S. Small Business Administration, accessed on U.S. Small Business Administration Web site (*www.sba.gov*), February 15, 2002; "Economic Growth Linked to Levels of Business Start-Ups," GEM 2000 Report available at *www.entreworld.org*; and "On the Continent, On the Cusp," *New York Times,* May 14, 2000, pp. BU1+.

20. T.J. Mullaney, H. Green, M. Arndt, R. D. Hof, and L. Himelstein, "The E-Biz Surprise," *Business Week,* May 12, 2003, pp. 60–68; R. D. Hof and S. Hamm, "How E-Biz Rose, Fell, and Will Rise Anew," *Business Week,* May 13, 2002, pp. 64–72; and "Companies Leading Online," *IQ Magazine,* November–December 2001, pp. 54–63.

21. D.A. Menace and V.A.F. Almeida, *Scaling for E-Business* (Upper Saddle River, NJ: Prentice Hall PTR, 2000).

22. Menace and Almeida, *Scaling for E-Business;* M. Lewis, "Boom or Bust," *Business 2.0,* April 2000, pp. 192–205; J. Davis, "How It Works," *Business 2.0,* February 2000, pp. 112–15; and S. Alsop, "e or Be Eaten," *Fortune,* November 8, 1999, pp. 86–98.

23. D. Pottruck and T. Pearce, *Clicks and Mortar* (San Francisco: Jossey-Bass, 2000).

24. J.S. Brown and P. Duguid, "Balancing Act: How to Capture Knowledge without Killing It," *Harvard Business Review,* May–June 2000, pp. 73–80; J. Torsilieri and C. Lucier, "How to Change the World," *Strategy and Business,* Second Quarter 2000, pp. 17–20; E.C. Wenger and W.M. Snyder, "Communities of Practice: The Organizational Frontier," *Harvard Business Review,* January–February 2000, pp. 139–145; S.R. Fisher and M.A. White, "Downsizing in a Learning Organization: Are There Hidden Costs?" *Academy of Management Review,* January 2000, pp. 244–51; R. Myers, "Who Knows?" *CFO,* December 1999, pp. 83–87; and M.T. Hansen, N. Nohria, and T. Tierney, "What's Your Strategy for Managing Knowledge?" *Harvard Business Review,* March–April 1999, pp. 106–16.

25. See, for example, B. Krone, "Total Quality Management: An American

Odyssey," *The Bureaucrat*, Fall 1990, pp. 35–38; A. Gabor, *The Man Who Discovered Quality* (New York: Random House, 1990); J.W. Dean Jr. and D.E. Bowen, "Management Theory and Total Quality: Improving Research and Practice through Theory Development," *Academy of Management Review*, July 1994, pp. 392–418; C.A. Reeves and D.A. Bednar, "Defining Quality: Alternatives and Implications," *Academy of Management Review*, July 1994, pp. 419–45; R.K. Reger, L.T. Gustafson, S.M. Demarie, and J.V. Mullane, "Reframing the Organization: Why Implementing Total Quality Is Easier Said Than Done," *Academy of Management Review*, July 1994, pp. 565–84; T.C. Powell, "Total Quality Management as Competitive Advantage: A Review and Empirical Study," *Strategic Management Journal*, January 1995, pp. 15–37; J.R. Hackman and R. Wageman, "Total Quality Management: Empirical, Conceptual, and Practical Issues," *Administrative Science Quarterly*, June 1995, pp. 309–42; T.A. Stewart, "A Conversation with Joseph Juran," *Fortune*, January 11, 1999, pp. 168–70; and J. Jusko, "Tried and True," *IW*, December 6, 1999, pp. 78–84.

CHAPTER 3

1. Information from company Web site (*www.athleta.com*), January 5, 2003; and "A Study in Retention," *Workforce*, April 2001, p. 59.

2. For insights into the symbolic view, see J. Pfeffer, "Management as Symbolic Action: The Creation and Maintenance of Organizational Paradigms," in L.L. Cummings and B.M. Staw (eds.), *Research in Organizational Behavior*, vol. 3 (Greenwich, CT: JAI Press, 1981), pp. 1–52; D.C. Hambrick and S. Finkelstein, "Managerial Discretion: A Bridge between Polar Views of Organizational Outcomes," in L.L. Cummings and B.M. Staw (eds.), *Research in Organizational Behavior*, vol. 9 (Greenwich, CT: JAI Press, 1987), pp. 369–406; J.A. Byrne, "The Limits of Power," *BusinessWeek*, October 23, 1987, pp. 33–35; J.R. Meindl and S.B. Ehrlich, "The Romance of Leadership and the Evaluation of Organizational Performance," *Academy of Management Journal*, March 1987, pp. 91–109; C.R. Schwenk, "Illusions of Management Control? Effects of Self-Serving Attributions on Resource Commitments and Confidence in Management," *Human Relations*, April 1990, pp. 333–47; S.M. Puffer and J.B. Weintrop, "Corporate Performance and CEO Turnover: The Role of Performance Expectations," *Administrative Science Quarterly*,

March 1991, pp. 1–19; "Why CEO Churn is Healthy," *BusinessWeek*, November 13, 2000, p. 230.

3. T.M. Hout, "Are Managers Obsolete?," *Harvard Business Review*, March–April 1999, pp. 161–68; and Pfeffer, "Management as Symbolic Action."

4. "Fun and Feel-Good ROI," *Workforce*, December 2000, p. 38.

5. L. Smircich, "Concepts of Culture and Organizational Analysis," *Administrative Science Quarterly*, September 1983, p. 339; D.R. Denison, "What Is the Difference between Organizational Culture and Organizational Climate? A Native's Point of View on a Decade of Paradigm Wars," paper presented at Academy of Management Annual Meeting, 1993, Atlanta, Georgia; and M.J. Hatch, "The Dynamics of Organizational Culture," *Academy of Management Review*, October 1993, pp. 657–93.

6. K. Shadur and M.A. Kienzle, "The Relationship Between Organizational Climate and Employee Perceptions of Involvement," *Group & Organization Management*, December 1999, pp. 479–503; and A.M. Sapienza, "Believing Is Seeing: How Culture Influences the Decisions Top Managers Make," in R.H. Kilmann et al. (eds.), *Gaining Control of the Corporate Culture* (San Francisco: Jossey-Bass, 1985), p. 68.

7. C.A. O'Reilly III, J. Chatman, and D.F. Caldwell, "People and Organizational Culture: A Profile Comparison Approach to Assessing Person-Organization Fit," *Academy of Management Journal*, September 1991, pp. 487–516; and J.A. Chatman and K.A. Jehn, "Assessing the Relationship between Industry Characteristics and Organizational Culture: How Different Can You Be?" *Academy of Management Journal*, June 1994, pp. 522–53.

8. A.E.M. Va Vianen, "Person-Organization Fit: The Match Between Newcomers' and Recruiters' Preferences for Organizational Cultures," *Personnel Psychology*, Spring 2000, pp. 113–149; K. Shadur and M.A. Kienzle, "The Relationship Between Organizational Climate and Employee Perceptions of Involvement," *Group & Organization Management*, December 1999, pp. 479–503; P. Lok and J. Crawford, "The Relationship Between Commitment and Organizational Culture, Subculture, and Leadership Style," *Leadership & Organization Development Journal*, vol. 20, nos. 6/7 (1999), pp. 365–74; C. Vandenberghe, "Organizational Culture, Person-Culture Fit, and Turnover: A Replication in the

Health Care Industry," *Journal of Organizational Behavior*, March 1999, pp. 175–84; and C. Orphen, "The Effect of Organizational Cultural Norms on the Relationships between Personnel Practices and Employee Commitment," *Journal of Psychology*, September 1993, pp. 577–79.

9. See, for example, D.R. Denison, *Corporate Culture and Organizational Effectiveness* (New York: Wiley, 1990); G.G. Gordon and N. DiTomaso, "Predicting Corporate Performance from Organizational Culture," *Journal of Management Studies*, November 1992, pp. 793–98; J.P. Kotter and J.L. Heskett, *Corporate Culture and Performance* (New York: Free Press, 1992), pp. 15–27; J.C. Collins and J.I. Porras, *Built to Last* (New York: HarperBusiness, 1994); Collins and Porras, "Building Your Company's Vision," *Harvard Business Review*, September–October 1996, pp. 65–77; R. Goffee and G. Jones, "What Holds the Modern Company Together?" *Harvard Business Review*, November–December 1996, pp. 133–48; and J. B. Sorensen, "The Strength of Corporate Culture and the Reliability of Firm Performance," *Administrative Science Quarterly*, vol. 47, no. 1 (2002), pp. 70–91.

10. Sorensen, pp. 70–91.

11. E. H. Schien, *Organizational Culture and Leadership* (San Francisco: Jossey-Bass, 1985), pp. 314–15.

12. This box is based on D.W. Brown, "Searching for Clues," *Black Enterprise*, November 2002, pp. 114–20; L. Bower, "Weigh Values to Decide if Working for 'Beasts' Worthwhile," *Springfield Business Journal*, November 4, 2002, p. 73; S. Shellenbarger, "How to Find Out if You're Going to Hate a New Job Before You Agree to Take It," *Wall Street Journal*, June 13, 2002, p. D1; and M. Boyle, "Just Right," *Fortune*, June 10, 2002, pp. 207–8.

13. S. E. Ante, "The New Blue," *BusinessWeek*, March 17, 2003, p. 82.

14. B. Filipczak, "Trained by Starbucks," *Training*, June 1995, pp. 73–79; and S. Gruner, "Lasting Impressions," *Inc.*, July 1998, p. 126.

15. J. Forman, "When Stories Create an Organization's Future," *Strategy & Business*, Second Quarter 1999, pp. 6–9; D.M. Boje, "The Storytelling Organization: A Study of Story Performance in an Office-Supply Firm," *Administrative Science Quarterly*, March 1991, pp. 106–26; C.H. Deutsch, "The Parables of Corporate Culture," *New York Times*, October 13, 1991, p. F25; and T. Terez, "The Business of Storytelling," *Workforce*, May 2002, pp. 22–24.

16. E. Ransdell, "The Nike Story? Just Tell It!" *Fast Company*, January–February 2000, pp. 44–46.

17. J. Useem, "Jim McNerney Thinks He Can Turn 3M from a Good Company into a Great One—With a Little Help from His Former Employer, General Electric," *Fortune*, August 12, 2002, pp. 127–32.

18. A.M. Pettigrew, "On Studying Organizational Cultures," *Administrative Science Quarterly*, December 1979, p. 576.

19. Ibid.

20. Cited in J.M. Beyer and H.M. Trice, "How an Organization's Rites Reveal Its Culture," *Organizational Dynamics*, Spring 1987, p. 15.

21. M. Zagorski, "Here's the Drill," *Fast Company*, February 2001, p. 58.

22. A. Bryant, "The New Power Breakfast," *Newsweek*, May 15, 2000, p. 52.

23. G. Anders, "AOL's True Believers," *Fast Company*, July 2002, p. 101.

24. This box is based on "Diversity at the Forefront," *BusinessWeek*, November 4, 2002, pp. 27–38; "Talking to Diversity Experts: Where Do We Go from Here?" *Fortune*, September 30, 2002; pp. 157–72; "Keeping Your Edge: Managing a Diverse Corporate Culture," *Fortune*, June 11, 2001, pp. S1–S18; "Diversity Today," *Fortune*, June 12, 2000, pp. S1–S24; O.C. Richard, "Racial Diversity, Business Strategy, and Firm Performance: A Resource-Based View," *Academy of Management Journal*, April 2000, pp. 164–177; A. Markels, "How One Hotel Manages Staff's Diversity," *Wall Street Journal*, November 20, 1996, pp. B1+; C.A. Deutsch, "Corporate Diversity in Practice," *New York Times*, November 20, 1996, pp. C1+; and D.A. Thomas and R.J. Ely, "Making Differences Matter: A New Paradigm for Managing Diversity," *Harvard Business Review*, September–October 1996, pp. 79–90.

25. P. LaBarre, "Success: Here's the Inside Story," *Fast Company*, November 1999, pp. 128–32; and A. Law, *Creative Company: How St. Luke's Became "the Ad Agency to End all Ad Agencies,"* (New York: Wiley, 1999).

26. A. Raghavan, K. Kranhold, and A. Barrionuevo, "Full Speed Ahead: How Enron Bosses Created a Culture of Pushing Limits," *Wall Street Journal*, August 26, 2002, pp. A1+

27. J.A. Byrne and others, "How to Fix Corporate Governance," *BusinessWeek*, May 6, 2002, pp. 68–78.

28. See B. Victor and J.B. Cullen, "The Organizational Bases of Ethical Work Climates," *Administrative Science Quarterly*, March 1988, pp. 101–25; L.K. Trevino, "A Cultural Perspective on Changing and Developing Organizational Ethics," in W.A. Pasmore and R.W. Woodman (eds.), *Research in Organizational Change and Development*, vol. 4 (Greenwich, CT: JAI Press, 1990); and M. W. Dickson, D.B. Smith, M.W. Grojean, and M. Ehrhart, "An Organizational Climate Regarding Ethics: The Outcome of Leader Values and the Practices that Reflect Them," *Leadership Quarterly*, Summer 2001, pp. 197–217.

29. J.A. Byrne, "After Enron: The Ideal Corporation," *BusinessWeek*, August 26, 2002, p. 74.

30. C. Fredman, "The IDEO Difference," *Hemispheres*, August 2002, pp. 52–57.

31. "Cirque du Soleil: Creating a Culture of Extraordinary Creativity," available on the Innovation Network Web site *(www.thinksmart.com)*, March 14, 2003.

32. L. Simpson, "Fostering Creativity," *Training*, December 2001, p. 56.

33. L. Gary, "Simplify and Execute: Words to Live By in Times of Turbulence," *Harvard Management Update*, January 2003, p. 12.

34. Based on M.J. Bitner, B.H. Booms, and L.A. Mohr, "Critical Service Encounters: The Employee's Viewpoint," *Journal of Marketing*, October 1994, pp. 95–106; M.D. Hartline and O.C. Ferrell, "The Management of Customer-Contact Service Employees: An Empirical Investigation," *Journal of Marketing*, October 1996, pp. 52–70; M.L. Lengnick-Hall and C.A. Lengnick-Hall, "Expanding Customer Orientation in the HR Function," *Human Resource Management*, Fall 1999, pp. 201–14; B. Schneider, D.E. Bowen, M.G. Ehrhart, and K.M. Holcombe, "The Climate for Service: Evolution of a Construct," in N.M. Ashkanasy, C.P.M. Wilderom, and M.F. Peterson (eds.), *Handbook of Organizational Culture and Climate* (Thousand Oaks, CA: Sage, 2000), pp. 21–36; M.D. Hartline, J.G. Maxham III, and D.O. McKee, "Corridors of Influence in the Dissemination of Customer-Oriented Strategy to Customer Contact Service Employees," *Journal of Marketing*, April 2000, pp. 35–50; L.A. Bettencourt, K.P. Gwinner, and M.L. Mueter, "A Comparison of Attitude, Personality, and Knowledge Predictors of Service-Oriented Organizational Citizenship Behaviors," *Journal of Applied Psychology*, February 2001, pp. 29–41; R.C. Ford and C.P. Heaton, "Lessons from Hospitality that Can Serve Anyone," *Organizational Dynamics*, Summer 2001, pp. 30–47; S.D. Pugh, J. Dietz, J.W. Wiley, and S.M. Brooks, "Driving Service Effectiveness Through Employee-Customer Linkages," *Academy of Management Executive*, November 2002, pp. 73–84; K.A. Eddleston, D.L. Kidder, and B.E. Litzky, "Who's the Boss? Contending with Competing Expectations from Customers and Management," *Academy of Management Executive*, November 2002, pp. 85–95; and B.A. Gutek, M. Groth, and B. Cherry, "Achieving Service Success Through Relationships and Enhanced Encounters," *Academy of Management Executive*, November 2002, pp. 132–144.

35. D.P. Ashmos and D. Duchon, "Spirituality at Work: A Conceptualization and Measure," *Journal of Management Inquiry*, June 2000, p. 139.

36. This section is based on I.A. Mitroff and E.A. Denton, *A Spiritual Audit of CorporateAmerica: A Hard Look at Spirituality, Religion, and Values in the Workplace* (San Francisco: Jossey-Bass, 1999); J. Milliman, J. Ferguson, D. Trickett, and B. Condemi, "Spirit and Community at Southwest Airlines: An Investigation of a Spiritual Values-Based Model," *Journal of Organizational Change Management*, vol. 12, no. 3 (1999), pp. 221–33; E.H. Burack, "Spirituality in the Workplace," *Journal of Organizational Change Management*, vol. 12, no. 3 (1999), pp. 280–91; F. Wagner-Marsh and J. Conley, "The Fourth Wave: The Spiritually-Based Firm," *Journal of Organizational Change Management*, vol. 12, no. 3 (1999), pp. 292–302; and K.C. Cash and G.R. Gray, "A Framework for Accommodating Religion and Spirituality in the Workplace," *Academy of Management Executive*, August 2000, pp. 124–33.

37. Cited in F. Wagner-Marsh and J. Conley, "The Fourth Wave," p. 295.

38. M. Conlin, "Religion in the Workplace: The Growing Presence of Spirituality in Corporate America," *BusinessWeek*, November 1, 1999, pp. 151–58; and P. Paul, "A Holier Holiday Season," *American Demographics*, December 2001, pp. 41–45.

39. Cited in M. Conlin, "Religion in the Workplace," p. 153.

40. C.P. Neck and J.F. Milliman, "Thought Self-Leadership: Finding Spiritual Fulfillment in Organizational Life," *Journal of Managerial Psychology*, vol. 9, no. 8 (1994), p. 9.

41. D.W. McCormick, "Spirituality and Management," *Journal of Managerial Psychology*, vol. 9, no. 6 (1994), p. 5; E. Brandt, "Corporate Pioneers Explore Spiritual Peace," *HRMagazine*, vol. 41, no. 4 (1996), p. 82; P. Leigh, "The New Spirit at Work," *Training and Develop-

ment, vol. 51, no. 3 (1997), p. 26; P.H. Mirvis, "Soul Work in Organizations," *Organization Science*, vol. 8, no. 2 (1997), p. 193; and J. Millman, A. Czaplewski, and J. Ferguson, "An Exploratory Empirical Assessment of the Relationship Between Spirituality and Employee Work Attitudes," paper presented at the National Academy of Management meeting, Washington, DC, August 2001.

42. T.S. Mescon and G.S. Vozikis, "Federal Regulation—What Are the Costs?" *Business*, January–March 1982, pp. 33–39.

43. See, for instance, A.S. Hayes, "Layoffs Take Careful Planning to Avoid Losing the Suits That Are Apt to Follow," *Wall Street Journal*, November 2, 1990, p. B1.

44. B. McKay, "Fit to Eat?" *Wall Street Journal*, September 23, 2002, pp. A1+.

45. F. Hansen, "Mega Shifts Remake Marketing," *Business Finance*, March 2003, p. 9.

46. T. Donaldson and L.E. Preston, "The Stakeholder Theory of the Corporation: Concepts, Evidence, and Implications," *Academy of Management Review*, January 1995, pp. 65–91.

47. J.S. Harrison and C.H. St. John, "Managing and Partnering with External Stakeholders," *Academy of Management Executive*, May 1996, pp. 46–60.

48. A.J. Hillman and G.D. Keim, "Shareholder Value, Stakeholder Management, and Social Issues: What's the Bottom Line?" *Strategic Management Journal*, March 2001, pp. 125–39; and J. Kotter and J. Heskett, *Corporate Culture and Performance* (New York: The Free Press, 1992).

49. Harrison and St. John, 1996.

CHAPTER 4

1. Information from company Web site (*www.inditex.com*), January 5, 2003; and M. Helft, "Fashion Fast-Forward," *Business 2.0*, May 2002, pp. 60–66.

2. G. Koretz, "Things Go Better with Multinationals—Except Jobs," *Business Week*, May 2, 1994, p. 20.

3. The idea for this quiz was adapted from R.M. Hodgetts and F. Luthans, *International Management*, 2nd ed. (New York: McGraw-Hill, 1994).

4. N. Adler, *International Dimensions of Organizational Behavior*, 3rd ed. (Cincinnati, OH: South-Western, 1996).

5. M.R.F. Kets De Vries and E. Florent-Treacy, "Global Leadership from A to Z: Creating High Commitment Organizations," *Organizational Dynamics*, Spring 2002, pp. 295–309; P.R. Harris and R.T. Moran, *Managing Cultural Differences*, 4th ed. (Houston: Gulf Publishing Co., 1996); R.T. Moran, P.R. Harris, and W.G. Stripp, *Developing the Global Organization: Strategies for Human Resource Professionals* (Houston, TX: Gulf Publishing Co., 1993); Y. Wind, S.P. Douglas, and H.V. Perlmutter, "Guidelines for Developing International Marketing Strategies," *Journal of Marketing*, April 1973, pp. 14–23; and H.V. Perlmutter, "The Tortuous Evolution of the Multinational Corporation," *Columbia Journal of World Business*, January–February 1969, pp. 9–18.

6. A.K. Gupta and V. Govindarajan, "Cultivating a Global Mindset," *Academy of Management Executive*, February 2002, pp. 117–18.

7. *WTO Policy Issues for Parliamentarians*, document published by the World Trade Organization, available on the World Trade Organization Web site (*www.wto.org*), p. 1.

8. B. Mitchener, "Ten New Members to Weigh In on Future of EU," *Wall Street Journal*, April 16, 2003, p. A16; C. Taylor, "Go East, Young Man," *Smart Money*, January 2003, p. 25; and S. Miller and B. Grow, "A Bigger Europe? Not So Fast," *Wall Street Journal*, December 12, 2002, p. A15.

9. B. Mitchener, "A New EU, but No Operating Manual," *Wall Street Journal*, December 16, 2002, p. A10.

10. H. Cooper, "The Euro: What You Need to Know," *Wall Street Journal*, January 4, 1999, pp. A5+; The Associated Press, "Exit Polls Show Swedes Reject Euro", USA Today, September 14, 2003, P. 6A.

11. D.T. Griswold and W.R. Hawkins, "Symposium: Free Trade Agreement, 1991, United States-Canada-Mexico," *Insight on the News*, January 21, 2003, pp. 46–49.

12. "Ministerial Declaration," Web site of the Free Trade Area of the Americas (*www.ftaa-alca.org*), April 4, 2003; and "NAFTA: Five-Year Anniversary," *Latin Trade*, January 1999, pp. 44–45.

13. J. Epstein, "The Bell Tolls for Mercosur's," *Latin Trade*, January 2002, p. 20; and R. Colitt, "Rain on Mercosur's Parade," *Latin Trade*, March 2001, pp. 42–45; and C. Sims, "Chile Will Enter a Big South American Free-Trade Bloc," *New York Times*, June 26, 1996, p. C2.

14. D. Kraft, "Leaders Question, Praise African Union," *Springfield News-Leader*, July 10, 2002, p. 8A.

15. This section is based on materials from the World Trade Organization Web site (*www.wto.org*).

16. These examples are taken from L. Chang, "McDonald's Still Plans Growth in China, Despite Cuts in U.S.," *Wall Street Journal*, November 14, 2002, p. B10; C. Belton, "To Russia with Love: The Multinationals' Song," *BusinessWeek*, September 16, 2002, pp. 44–46; and P.J. Kiger, "How Deloitte Builds Global Expertise," *Workforce*, June 2002, p. 62.

17. D.A. Aaker, *Developing Business Strategies*, 5th ed. (New York: John Wiley & Sons, 1998); and J.A. Byrne et al., "Borderless Management," *BusinessWeek*, May 23, 1994, pp. 24–26.

18. J. Teresko, "United Plastics Picks China's Silicon Valley," *Industry Week*, January 2003, p. 58.

19. "Emerging Economies are Following the Global Trend of Disinflation," *The Economist*, October 19, 2002, p. 36.

20. These examples taken from L. Khosla, "You Say Tomato," *Forbes*, May 21, 2001, p. 36; and T. Raphael, "Savvy Companies Build Bonds with Hispanic Employees," *Workforce*, September 2001, p. 19.

21. See G. Hofstede, *Culture's Consequences: International Differences in Work-Related Values*, 2nd ed. (Thousand Oaks, CA: Sage Publications, 2001), pp. 9–15.

22. G. Hofstede, *Culture's Consequences*; and G. Hofstede, "The Cultural Relativity of Organizational Practices and Theories," *Journal of International Business Studies*, Fall 1983, pp. 75–89.

23. Hofstede called the fourth dimension "masculinity versus femininity," but we have changed it because of the strong sexist connotation in his choice of terms.

24. R. House, M. Javidan, P. Hanges, and P. Dorfman, "Understanding Cultures and Implicit Leadership Theories Across the Globe: An Introduction to Project GLOBE," *Journal of World Business*, vol. 37 (2002), pp. 3–10; R. House, M. Javidan, and P. Dorfman, "Project GLOBE: An Introduction," *Applied Psychology: An International Review*, October 2001, pp. 489–505; and M. Javidan and R.J. House, "Cultural Acumen for the Global Manager: Lessons from Project GLOBE," *Organizational Dynamics*, Spring 2001, pp. 289–305.

25. S. Holmes, "Boeing's High-Speed Flight," *BusinessWeek*, August 12, 2002, pp. 74–75; and J. Slater, "GE Takes Advantage of India's Talented Research Pool," *Wall Street Journal*, March 26, 2003, p. A10.

26. A. Kreamer, "America's Yang Has a Yen for Asia's Yin," *Fast Company*, July 2003, p. 58; D. Yergin, "Globalization Opens Door to New Dangers," *USA*

Today, May 28, 2003, p. 11A; K. Lowrey Miller, "Is It Globaloney?" *Newsweek*, December 16, 2002, pp. E4–E8; L. Gomes, "Globalization Is Now a Two-Way Street—Good News for the U.S.," *Wall Street Journal*, December 9, 2002, p. B1; J. Kurlantzick and J.T. Allen, "The Trouble with Globalism," *U.S. News and World Report*, February 11, 2002, pp. 38–41; and J. Guyon, "The American Way," *Fortune*, November 26, 2001, pp. 114–120.

27. Guyon, "The American Way," p. 114.

28. Situation adapted from information in: Rachel Miller, "Licensing: Unlock the Equity Within Your Brand," *Marketing*, April 24, 2003, pp. 21+; Gabriel Kahn, "Factory Fight: A Sneaker Maker Says China Partner Became Its Rival," *Wall Street Journal*, December 19, 2002, pp. A1+.

CHAPTER 5

1. Information from company Web site (*www.coco-mat.com*) January 5, 2003; and T. Mudd, "Sleeping Beauty," *Industry Week*, August 2002, pp. 64–65.

2. A.B. Carroll, "A Three-Dimensional Conceptual Model of Corporate Performance," *Academy of Management Review*, October 1979, p. 499.

3. M. Friedman, *Capitalism and Freedom* (Chicago: University of Chicago Press, 1962); and Friedman, "The Social Responsibility of Business Is to Increase Profits," *New York Times Magazine*, September 13, 1970, p. 33.

4. Information from Avon's Web site (*www.avoncrusade.com*), April 9, 2003.

5. E.P. Lima, "Seeding a World of Transformation," *IW*, September 6, 1999, pp. 30–31.

6. E. White, "PR Firms Advise Corporations on Social Responsibility Issues," *Wall Street Journal*, November 13, 2002, p. B10.

7. See, for example, A.B. Carroll, "The Pyramid of Corporate Social Responsibility: Toward the Moral Management of Organizational Stakeholders," *Business Horizons*, July–August 1991, pp. 39–48.

8. This section has been influenced by K.B. Boal and N. Peery, "The Cognitive Structure of Social Responsibility," *Journal of Management*, Fall–Winter 1985, pp. 71–82.

9. This section is based on R.J. Monsen Jr., "The Social Attitudes of Management," in J.M. McGuire (ed.), *Contemporary Management: Issues and Views* (Upper Saddle River, NJ: Prentice Hall, 1974), p. 616; and K. Davis and W.C. Frederick, *Business and Society: Management, Public Policy,*

Ethics, 5th ed. (New York: McGraw-Hill, 1984), pp. 28–41.

10. See S.P. Sethi, "A Conceptual Framework for Environmental Analysis of Social Issues and Evaluation of Business Response Patterns," *Academy of Management Review*, January 1979, pp. 68–74.

11. See, for example, D.J. Wood, "Corporate Social Performance Revisited," *Academy of Management Review*, October 1991, pp. 703–8.

12. Information from *Philanthropy at American Express*, found on American Express Web site (*www.americanexpress.com*), April 9, 2003.

13. See, for example, R.A. Buccholz, *Essentials of Public Policy for Management*, 2d ed. (Upper Saddle River, NJ: Prentice Hall, 1990).

14. A. Schendler, "Where's the Green in Green Business?" *Harvard Business Review*, June 2002, p. 28.

15. S.L. Wartick and P.L. Cochran, "The Evolution of the Corporate Social Performance Model," *Academy of Management Review*, October 1985, p. 763.

16. See, for instance, P. Cochran and R.A. Wood, "Corporate Social Responsibility and Financial Performance," *Academy of Management Journal*, March 1984, pp. 42–56; K. Aupperle, A.B. Carroll, and J.D. Hatfield, "An Empirical Examination of the Relationship between Corporate Social Responsibility and Profitability," *Academy of Management Journal*, June 1985, pp. 446–63; J.B. McGuire, A. Sundgren, and T. Schneeweis, "Corporate Social Responsibility and Firm Financial Performance," *Academy of Management Journal*, December 1988, pp. 854–72; D.M. Georgoff and J. Ross, "Corporate Social Responsibility and Management Performance," paper presented at the National Academy of Management Conference, Miami, Florida, August 1991; S.A. Zahra, B.M. Oviatt, and K. Minyard, "Effects of Corporate Ownership and Board Structure on Corporate Social Responsibility and Financial Performance," paper presented at the National Academy of Management Conference, Atlanta, Georgia, August 1993; "Social Responsibility and the Bottom Line," *Business Ethics*, July–August, 1994, p. 11; D.B. Turban and D.W. Greening, "Corporate Social Performance and Organizational Attractiveness to Prospective Employees," *Academy of Management Journal*, June 1996, pp. 658–72; S.A. Waddock and S.B. Graves, "The Corporate Social Performance–Financial Performance Link," *Strategic Management*

Journal, April 1997, pp. 303–19; and S.L. Berman and others, "Does Stakeholder Orientation Matter? The Relationship Between Stakeholder Management Models and Firm Financial Performance, *Academy of Management Journal*, October 1999, pp. 488–506.

17. D.J. Wood and R.E. Jones, "Stakeholder Mismatching: A Theoretical Problem in Empirical Research on Corporate Social Performance," *International Journal of Organizational Analysis* (1995), pp. 229–67.

18. See A.A. Ullmann, "Data in Search of a Theory: A Critical Examination of the Relationships among Social Performance, Social Disclosure, and Economic Performance of U.S. Firms," *Academy of Management Review*, July 1985, pp. 540–57; R.E. Wokutch and B.A. Spencer, "Corporate Saints and Sinners: The Effects of Philanthropic and Illegal Activity on Organizational Performance," *California Management Review*, Winter 1987, pp. 62–77; R. Wolfe and K. Aupperle, "Introduction to Corporate Social Performance: Methods for Evaluating an Elusive Construct," pp. 265–68, in J.E. Post (ed.), *Research in Corporate Social Performance and Policy*, vol. 12 (1991); and Wood and Jones, "Stakeholder Mismatching: A Theoretical Problem in Empirical Research on Corporate Social Performance."

19. McGuire, Sundgren, and Schneeweis, "Corporate Social Responsibility and Firm Financial Performance."

20. A. McWilliams and D. Siegel, "Corporate Social Responsibility and Financial Performance: Correlation or Misspecification?" *Strategic Management Journal*, June 2000, pp. 603–9.

21. A.J. Hillman and G.D. Keim, "Shareholder Value, Stakeholder Management, and Social Issues: What's the Bottom Line?" *Strategic Management Journal*, vol. 22, (2001), pp. 125–39.

22. Information from Domini Social Investments Web site (*www.domini.com*), August 1, 2000; R. Wherry, "The Cleans & The Greens," *Forbes*, June 12, 2000, p. 412; S. Scherreik, "A Conscience Doesn't Have to Make You Poor," *BusinessWeek*, May 1, 2000, pp. 204–8; and P. Keating, "Know What You Own," *Money*, November 1999, pp. 79–81.

23. R.W. Ahrens, "How Socially Responsible Funds Work," *USA Today*, March 31, 2003, p. 8B.

24. This section is based on P. Shrivastava, "Environmental Technologies and Competitive Advantage," *Strategic Management Journal*, Summer 1995, pp. 183–200; S.L. Hart, "A Natural-Resource-Based View of the Firm,"

Academy of Management Review, December 1995, pp. 986–1014; S.L. Hart, "Beyond Greening: Strategies for a Sustainable World," *Harvard Business Review*, January–February 1997, pp. 66–76; M. Stark and A.A. Marcus, "Introduction to the Special Research Forum on the Management of Organizations in the Natural Environment: A Field Emerging from Multiple Paths, with Many Challenges Ahead," *Academy of Management Journal*, August 2000, pp. 539–46; P. Bansal and K. Roth, "Why Companies Go Green: A Model of Ecological Responsiveness," *Academy of Management Journal*, August 2000, pp. 717–36; P. Bansal, "The Corporate Challenges of Sustainable Development," *Academy of Management Executive*, May 2002, pp. 122–31; P. Christmann and G. Taylor, "Globalization and the Environment: Strategies for International Voluntary Environmental Initiatives," *Academy of Management Executive*, August 2002, pp. 121–35; J. Alberto Aragon-Correa and S. Sharma, "A Contingent Resource-Based View of Proactive Corporate Environmental Strategy," *Academy of Management Review*, January 2003, pp. 71–88; D.A. Rondinelli and T. London, "How Corporations and Environmental Groups Cooperate: Assessing Cross-Sector Alliances and Collaborations," *Academy of Management Executive*, February 2003, pp. 61–76; and K. Buysse and A. Verbeke, "Proactive Environmental Strategies: A Stakeholder Management Perspective," *Strategic Management Journal*, May 2003, pp. 453–70.

25. These examples come from P. LaBarre, "How to Lead a Rich Life," *Fast Company*, March 2003, p. 74; J. Ball and J.J. Fialka, "Global Warming Spurs Companies," *Wall Street Journal*, November 8, 2002, p. A7; and M. Conlin and P. Raeburn, "Industrial Evolution," *BusinessWeek*, April 8, 2002, pp. 70–72.

26. J.L. Seglin, "It's Not That Easy Going Green," *Inc.*, May 1999, pp. 28–32; W.H. Miller, "What's Ahead in Environmental Policy?" *IW*, April 19, 1999, pp. 19–24; and Shrivastava, "Environmental Technologies and Competitive Advantage," p. 183.

27. Hart, "Beyond Greening," p. 68.

28. J. Kluger and A. Dorfman, "The Challenges We Face," *Time*, August 26, 2002, pp. A6–A12; Worldwatch Institute, "Earth Day 2000: What Humanity Can Do Now to Turn the Tide," Web site for Worldwatch Institute (*www.worldwatch.org*), August 2, 2000; and L. Brown and Staff of the Worldwatch Institute, *State of the World* (New York: Norton, 1987–1996).

29. C. Marsden, "The New Corporate Citizenship of Big Business: Part of the Solution to Sustainability?" *Business & Society Review*, Spring 2000, pp. 9–25; R.D. Klassen and D.C. Whybark, "The Impact of Environmental Technologies on Manufacturing Performance," *Academy of Management Journal*, December 1999, pp. 599–615; H. Bradbury and J.A. Clair, "Promoting Sustainable Organizations with Sweden's Natural Step," *Academy of Management Executive*, October 1999, pp. 63–73; F.L. Reinhardt, "Bringing the Environment Down to Earth," *Harvard Business Review*, July–August 1999, pp. 149–57; I. Henriques and P. Sadorsky, "The Relationship Between Environmental Commitment and Managerial Perceptions of Stakeholder Importance," *Academy of Management Journal*, February 1999, pp. 87–99; and M.A. Berry and D.A. Rondinelli, "Proactive Corporate Environmental Management: A New Industrial Revolution," *Academy of Management Executive*, May 1998, pp. 38–50.

30. The concept of shades of green can be found in R.E. Freeman, J. Pierce, and R. Dodd, *Shades of Green: Business Ethics and the Environment* (New York: Oxford University Press, 1995).

31. W.G. Bliss, "Why is Corporate Culture Important?" *Workforce*, February 1999, pp. W8–W9; E.J. Giblin and L.E. Amuso, "Putting Meaning into Corporate Values," *Business Forum*, Winter 1997, pp. 14–18; R. Barrett, "Liberating the Corporate Soul," *HR Focus*, April 1997, pp. 15–16; K. Blanchard and M. O'Connor, *Managing By Values* (San Francisco: Berrett-Koehler Publishers, 1997); and G.P. Alexander, "Establishing Shared Values through Management Training Programs," *Training and Development Journal*, February 1987, pp. 45–47.

32. Ibid.; J.L. Badaracco Jr. and R.R. Ellsworth, *Leadership and the Quest for Integrity* (Boston: Harvard Business School Press, 1989); and T. Chappell, *Managing Upside Down: The Seven Intentions of Values-Centered Leadership* (New York: William Morrow, 1999).

33. Information from Tom's of Maine Web site (*www.tomsofmaine.com*), April 11, 2003.

34. Information from Herman Miller Web site (*www.hermanmiller.com*), April 11, 2003.

35. R. Kamen, "Values: For Show or for Real?" *Working Woman*, August 1993, p. 10.

36. "AMA 2002 Corporate Values Survey," American Management Association Web site (*www.amanet.org*), October 30, 2002.

37. C. Hymowitz, "Companies Experience Major Power Shifts as Crises Continue," *Wall Street Journal*, October 9, 2001, p. B1.

38. J.A. Byrne and others, "How to Fix Corporate Governance," *BusinessWeek*, May 6, 2002, pp. 68–78.

39. J.L. Roberts and E. Thomas, "Enron's Dirty Laundry," *Newsweek*, March 11, 2002, pp. 22–28.

40. Davis and Frederick, *Business and Society*, p. 76.

41. F.D. Sturdivant, *Business and Society: A Managerial Approach*, 3rd ed. (Homewood, IL: Richard D. Irwin, 1985), p. 128.

42. G.F. Cavanagh, D.J. Moberg, and M. Valasquez, "The Ethics of Organizational Politics," *Academy of Management Journal*, June 1981, pp. 363–74. See F.N. Brady, "Rules for Making Exceptions to Rules," *Academy of Management Review*, July 1987, pp. 436–44 for an argument that the theory of justice is redundant with the prior two theories. See T. Donaldson and T.W. Dunfee, "Toward a Unified Conception of Business Ethics: Integrative Social Contracts Theory," *Academy of Management Review*, April 1994, pp. 252–84; M. Douglas, "Integrative Social Contracts Theory: Hype Over Hypernorms," *Journal of Business Ethics*, July 2000, pp. 101–10; and E. Soule, "Managerial Moral Strategies—In Search of a Few Good Principles," *Academy of Management Review*, January 2002, pp. 114–24 for discussions of integrative social contracts theory.

43. Soule, "Managerial Moral Strategies—In Search of a Few Good Principles," p. 117.

44. D.J. Fritzsche and H. Becker, "Linking Management Behavior to Ethical Philosophy—An Empirical Investigation," *Academy of Management Journal*, March 1984, pp. 166–75.

45. L. Kohlberg, *Essays in Moral Development: The Philosophy of Moral Development*, vol. 1 (New York: Harper & Row, 1981); L. Kohlberg, *Essays in Moral Development: The Psychology of Moral Development*, vol. 2 (New York: Harper & Row, 1984); J.W. Graham, "Leadership, Moral Development, and Citizenship Behavior," *Business Ethics Quarterly*, January 1995, pp. 43–54; and T. Kelley, "To Do Right or Just To Be Legal," *New York Times*, February 8, 1998, p. BU12.

46. See, for example, J. Weber, "Managers' Moral Reasoning: Assessing Their Responses to Three Moral Dilemmas," *Human Relations*, July 1990, pp. 687–702.

47. J.H. Barnett and M.J. Karson, "Personal Values and Business Decisions: An Exploratory Investigation," *Journal of Business Ethics*, July 1987, pp. 371–82; and W.C. Frederick and J. Weber, "The Value of Corporate Managers and Their Critics: An Empirical Description and Normative Implications," in W.C. Frederick and L.E. Preston (eds.), *Business Ethics: Research Issues and Empirical Studies* (Greenwich, CT: JAI Press, 1990), pp. 123–44.

48. L.K. Trevino and S.A. Youngblood, "Bad Apples in Bad Barrels: A Causal Analysis of Ethical Decision-Making Behavior," *Journal of Applied Psychology*, August 1990, pp. 378–85; and M.E. Baehr, J.W. Jones, and A.J. Nerad, "Psychological Correlates of Business Ethics Orientation in Executives," *Journal of Business and Psychology*, Spring 1993, pp. 291–308.

49. R.L. Cardy and T.T. Selvarajan, "Assessing Ethical Behavior Revisited: The Impact of Outcomes on Judgment Bias," paper presented at the Annual Meeting of the Academy of Management, Toronto, Canada, 2000.

50. B.Z. Posner and W.H. Schmidt, "Values and the American Manager: An Update," *California Management Review*, Spring 1984, pp. 202–16; R.B. Morgan, "Self- and Co-Worker Perceptions of Ethics and Their Relationships to Leadership and Salary," *Academy of Management Journal*, February 1993, pp. 200–14; G.R. Weaver, L.K. Trevino, and P.L. Cochran, "Corporate Ethics Programs as Control Systems: Influences of Executive Commitment and Environmental Factors," *Academy of Management Journal*, February 1999, pp. 41–57; and G.R. Weaver, L.K. Trevino, and P.L. Cochran, "Integrated and Decoupled Corporate Social Performance: Management Commitments, External Pressures, and Corporate Ethics Practices," *Academy of Management Journal*, October 1999, pp. 539–52.

51. B. Victor and J.B. Cullen, "The Organizational Bases of Ethical Work Climates," *Administrative Science Quarterly*, March 1988, pp. 101–25; J.B. Cullen, B. Victor, and C. Stephens, "An Ethical Weather Report: Assessing the Organization's Ethical Climate," *Organizational Dynamics*, Autumn 1989, pp. 50–62; Victor and Cullen, "A Theory and Measure of Ethical Climate in Organizations," in Frederick and Preston (eds.), *Business Ethics*, pp. 77–97; R.R. Sims, "The Challenge of Ethical Behavior in Organizations," *Journal of Business Ethics*, July 1992, pp. 505–13; and V. Arnold and J.C. Lampe, "Understanding the Factors Underlying Ethical Organizations: Enabling Continuous Ethical Improve-

ment," *Journal of Applied Business Research*, Summer 1999, pp. 1–19.

52. T.M. Jones, "Ethical Decision Making by Individuals in Organizations: An Issue-Contingent Model," *Academy of Management Review*, April 1991, pp. 366–95; and T. Barnett, "Dimensions of Moral Intensity and Ethical Decision Making: An Empirical Study," *Journal of Applied Social Psychology*, May 2001, pp. 1038–57.

53. Ibid., pp. 374–78.

54. C.J. Robertson and W.F. Crittenden, "Mapping Moral Philosophies: Strategic Implications for Multinational Firms," *Strategic Management Journal*, April 2003, pp. 385–92.

55. Information from The Global Compact Web site (*www.unglobalcompact.org*), April 12, 2003; J. Cohen, "Socially Responsible Business Goes Global," *In Business*, March/April 2000, p. 22; and C.M. Solomon, "Put Your Ethics to a Global Test," *Personnel Journal*, January 1996, pp. 66–74.

56. Sears example taken from series of posters called "Sears Ethics and Business Practices: A Century of Tradition," in *Business Ethics*, May/June 1999, pp. 12–13; and B.J. Feder, "The Harder Side of Sears," *New York Times*, July 20, 1997, pp. BU1+ Enron example taken from P.M. Lencioni, "Make Your Values Mean Something," *Harvard Business Review*, July 2002, p. 113.

57. Trevino and Youngblood, "Bad Apples in Bad Barrels," p. 384.

58. J.S. McClenahen, "UTC's Master of Principle," *Industry Week*, January 2003, pp. 30–36.

59. "Global Ethics Codes Gain Importance As a Tool To Avoid Litigation and Fines," *Wall Street Journal*, August 19, 1999, p. A1; and J. Alexander, "On the Right Side," *World Business*, January/February 1997, pp. 38–41.

60. P. Richter, "Big Business Puts Ethics in Spotlight," *Los Angeles Times*, June 19, 1986, p. 29.

61. F.R. David, "An Empirical Study of Codes of Business Ethics: A Strategic Perspective," paper presented at the 48th Annual Academy of Management Conference; Anaheim, California, August 1988.

62. "Ethics Programs Aren't Stemming Employee Misconduct," *Wall Street Journal*, May 11, 2000, p. A1.

63. A.K. Reichert and M.S. Webb, "Corporate Support for Ethical and Environmental Policies: A Financial Management Perspective," *Journal of Business Ethics*, May 2000; Weaver, Trevino, and Cochran, "Corporate Ethics Programs

as Control Systems"; Weaver, Trevino, and Cochran, "Integrated and Decoupled Corporate Social Performance"; Morgan, "Self- and Co-Worker Perceptions of Ethics and Their Relationships to Leadership and Salary"; and Posner and Schmidt, "Values and the American Manager: An Update."

64. L. Nash, "Ethics without the Sermon," *Harvard Business Review*, November–December 1981, p. 81.

65. V. Wessler, "Integrity and Clogged Plumbing," *Straight to the Point*, newsletter of VisionPoint Corporation, Fall 2002, pp. 1–2.

66. Associated Press, "Cheating Rampant in Workplace, Study Says," *Springfield News Leader*, April 5, 1997, p. A5.

67. T.A. Gavin, "Ethics Education," *Internal Auditor*, April 1989, pp. 54–57.

68. L. Myyry and K. Helkama, "The Role of Value Priorities and Professional Ethics Training in Moral Sensitivity," *Journal of Moral Education*, vol. 31, no. 1 (2002), pp. 35–50; W. Penn and B.D. Collier, "Current Research in Moral Development as a Decision Support System," *Journal of Business Ethics*, January 1985, pp. 131–36.

69. J.A. Byrne, "After Enron: The Ideal Corporation," *BusinessWeek*, August 19, 2002, pp. 68–71; D. Rice and C. Dreilinger, "Rights and Wrongs of Ethics Training," *Training & Development Journal*, May 1990, pp. 103–09; and J. Weber, "Measuring the Impact of Teaching Ethics to Future Managers: A Review, Assessment, and Recommendations," *Journal of Business Ethics*, April 1990, pp. 182–90.

70. T. Kelley, "Charting a Course to Ethical Profits," *New York Times*, February 28, 1998, pp. BU1+.

71. See, for instance, A. Wheat, "Keeping an Eye on Corporate America," *Fortune*, November 25, 2002, pp. 44–46; R.B. Schmitt, "Companies Add Ethics Training: Will It Work?" *Wall Street Journal*, November 4, 2002, pp. B1+; and P.F. Miller and W.T. Coady, "Teaching Work Ethics," *Education Digest*, February 1990, pp. 54–55.

72. Ethics Officer Association web site (*www.eoa.org*), April 12, 2003; and Schmitt, "Companies Add Ethics Training: Will It Work?"

73. See, for example, A. Stark, "What's the Matter with Business Ethics?" *Harvard Business Review*, May–June 1993, pp. 38–48; "More Big Businesses Set Up Ethics Offices," *Wall Street Journal*, May 10, 1993, p. B1; W.D. Hall, *Making the Right Decision: Ethics for Managers* (New York: John Wiley & Sons, 1993); S. Gaines, "Handing Out Halos," *Business*

Ethics, March–April 1994, pp. 20–24; and L.S. Paine, "Managing for Organizational Integrity," *Harvard Business Review*, March–April 1994, pp. 106–17.

74. Associated Press, "Cheating Rampant in Workplace, Study Says"; and H. Fountain, "Of White Lies and Yellow Pads," *New York Times*, July 6, 1997, p. F7.

75. "High School Students Show Ethical Decline," *USA Today*, October 22, 2002, p.7D.

76. "Students Aren't Squealers," *USA Today*, March 27, 2003, p. 1D; and J. Merritt, "You Mean Cheating is Wrong?" *BusinessWeek*, December 9, 2002, p. 8.

77. "Trust Busters," *CFO*, August 2002, p. 17.

78. D. Jones, "Do You Trust Your CEO?" *USA Today*, February 12, 2003, p. 7B.

79. C. Hymowitz, "Managers Must Respond to Employees' Concerns about Honest Business," *Wall Street Journal*, February 19, 2002, p. B1.

80. W. Zellner and others, "A Hero—And a Smoking-Gun Letter," *BusinessWeek*, January 28, 2002, pp. 34–35.

81. R. Lacayo and A. Ripley, "Persons of the Year," *Time*, December 30, 2002–January 5, 2003, pp. 30–33.

82. E. Krell, "Corporate Whistleblowers: How to Stop Wrongdoing Dead in Its Tracks," *Business Finance*, September 2002, p. 20.

83. S. Armour, "More Companies Urge Workers to Blow the Whistle," *USA Today*, December 16, 2002, p. 1B.

84. J. Wiscombe, "Don't Fear Whistleblowers," *Workforce*, July 2002, pp. 26–27.

85. T. Reason, "Whistle Blowers: The Untouchables," *CFO*, March 2003, p. 18; and C. Lachnit, "Muting the Whistle-blower?" *Workforce*, September 2002, p. 18.

86. M.C. Gentile, "Social Impact Management: A Definition," a discussion paper of the Aspen Institute's Initiative for Social Innovation through Business, available on the Aspen Institute Web site (*www.aspeninstitute.org*), April 12, 2003, p. 5.

87. Ibid., p. 3.

88. Situation adapted from information in: Claudia H. Deutsch, "Green Marketing: Label with a Cause," *New York Times*, June 15, 2003, sec. 3, p. 6; Brenda Lloy, "Sierra Club Hits the Apparel Trail," *Daily News Record*, February 17, 2003, p. 104.

PART 2

1. C. Dugas, "Hip-hop Legend Far Surpassed Financial Goals," *USA Today*, May 15, 2003, p. 6B.

2. P. Burrows, "Ringing Off the Hook in China," *BusinessWeek*, June 9, 2003, pp. 80–82.

3. J.W. Carland, F. Hoy, W.R. Boulton, and J.C. Carland, "Differentiating Entrepreneurs from Small Business Owners: A Conceptualization," *Academy of Management Review*, vol. 9, no. 2 (1984), pp. 354–59.

4. "Small Business Statistics," U.S. Small Business Administration, found at (*www.sba.gov*), July 4, 2003.

5. P. Almeida and B. Kogut, "The Exploration of Technological Diversity and Geographic Localization in Innovation: Start-Up Firms in the Semiconductor Industry," *Small Business Economics*, vol. 9, no. 1 (1997), pp. 21–31.

6. R.J. Arend, "Emergence of Entrepreneurs Following Exogenous Technological Change," *Strategic Management Journal*, vol. 20, no. 1 (1999), pp. 31–47.

7. J. McDowell, "New Study Confirms Small Businesses' Power as Innovators," *SBA Office of Advocacy*, February 2003, available online at (*www.sba.gov/advo*).

8. "Small Business Statistics."

9. Ibid.

10. "GEM 2002 Executive Summary," available at (*www.gemconsortium.org*), p. 6.

11. P.F. Drucker, *Innovation and Entrepreneurship: Practice and Principles* (New York: Harper & Row), 1985.

12. W. Royal, "Real Expectations," *Industry Week*, September 4, 2000, pp. 31–34.

13. M.A. Verespej, "25 Growing Companies," *Industry Week*, November 20, 2000, p. 70.

14. T. Purdum, "25 Growing Companies," *Industry Week*, November 20, 2000, p. 82.

15. C. Sandlund, "Trust Is a Must," *Entrepreneur*, October 2002, pp. 70–75.

CHAPTER 6

1. S. Alleyne, "A World Leader," *Black Enterprise*, June 2002, p. 74.

2. I. Wylie, "Who Runs This Team Anyway?" *Fast Company*, April 2002, pp. 32–33.

3. D.A. Garvin and M.A. Roberto, "What You Don't Know about Making Decisions," *Harvard Business Review*, September 2001, pp. 108–116.

4. W. Pounds, "The Process of Problem Finding," *Industrial Management Review*, Fall 1969, pp. 1–19.

5. R.J. Volkema, "Problem Formulation: Its Portrayal in the Texts," *Organizational Behavior Teaching Review*, 11, No. 3 (1986–87), pp. 113–26.

6. M.W. McCall Jr. and R.E. Kaplan, *Whatever It Takes: Decision Makers at Work* (Upper Saddle River, NJ: Prentice Hall, 1985), pp. 36–38.

7. H.A. Simon, *The New Science of Management Decision* (New York: Harper & Row, 1960), p. 1.

8. See H.A. Simon, "Rationality in Psychology and Economics," *Journal of Business*, October 1986, pp. 209–24; and A. Langley, "In Search of Rationality: The Purposes behind the Use of Formal Analysis in Organizations," *Administrative Science Quarterly*, December 1989, pp. 598–631.

9. F.A. Shull Jr., A.L. Delbecq, and L.L. Cummings, *Organizational Decision Making* (New York: McGraw-Hill, 1970), p. 151.

10. See, for example, J.G. March, *A Primer on Decision Making* (New York: Free Press, 1994), pp. 8–25; and A. Langley, H. Mintzberg, P. Pitcher, E. Posada, and J. Saint-Macary, "Opening Up Decision Making: The View from the Black Stool," *Organization Science*, May–June 1995, pp. 260–79.

11. J.G. March, "Decision-Making Perspective: Decisions in Organizations and Theories of Choice," in A.H. Van de Ven and W.F. Joyce (eds.), *Perspectives on Organization Design and Behavior* (New York: Wiley-Interscience, 1981), pp. 232–33.

12. See N.McK. Agnew and J.L. Brown, "Bounded Rationality: Fallible Decisions in Unbounded Decision Space," *Behavioral Science*, July 1986, pp. 148–61; B.E. Kaufman, "A New Theory of Satisficing," *Journal of Behavioral Economics*, Spring 1990, pp. 35–51; and D.R.A. Skidd, "Revisiting Bounded Rationality," *Journal of Management Inquiry*, December 1992, pp. 343–47.

13. See, for example, B.M. Staw, "The Escalation of Commitment to a Course of Action," *Academy of Management Review*, October 1981, pp. 577–87; D.R. Bobocel and J.P. Meyer, "Escalating Commitment to a Failing Course of Action: Separating the Roles of Choice and Justification," *Journal of Applied Psychology*, June 1994, pp. 360–63; C.F. Camerer and R.A. Weber, "The Econometrics and Behavioral Economics of Escalation of Commitment: A Re-examination of Staw's Theory," *Journal of Economic Behavior and Organization*, May 1999, pp. 59–82; V.S. Rao and A. Monk, "The Effects of Individual Differences and Anonymity on Commitment to Decisions," *Journal of Social Psychology*, August 1999, pp. 496–515; and G. McNamara, H. Moon, and P. Bromiley, "Banking on Commitment: Intended and Unintended Consequences of an Organization's Attempt to Attenuate Escalation of Commitment,"

Academy of Management Journal, April 2002, pp. 443–52.

14. T.A. Stewart, "How to Think with Your Gut," *Business 2.0*, November 2002, p. 102.

15. See K.R. Hammond, R.M. Hamm, J. Grassia, and T. Pearson, "Direct Comparison of the Efficacy of Intuitive and Analytical Cognition in Expert Judgment," in *IEEE Transactions on Systems, Man, and Cybernetics SMC-17*, (1987), pp. 753–70; W. H. Agor (ed.), *Intuition in Organizations* (Newbury Park, CA: Sage Publications, 1989); O. Behling and N.L. Eckel, "Making Sense Out of Intuition," *The Executive*, February 1991, pp. 46–47; L.A. Burke and M.K. Miller, "Taking the Mystery Out of Intuitive Decision Making," *Academy of Management Executive*, October 1999, pp. 91–99; A.L. Tesolin, "How to Develop the Habit of Intuition," *Training & Development*, March 2000, p. 76; and Stewart, "How to Think with Your Gut," pp. 98–104.

16. V. Pospisil, "Gut Feeling or Skilled Reasoning?" *IW*, March 3, 1997, p. 12.

17. Information for this box came from S. Caudron, "Some New Rules for the New World of Work," *Business Finance*, October 2001, p. 24; C. Kanchier, *Dare to Change Your Job and Your Life*, 2d ed. (Indianapolis, IN: Jist Publishing, 2000); and S. Hagevik, "Responsible Risk Taking," *Journal of Environmental Health*, November 1999, pp. 29+.

18. A.J. Rowe, J.D. Boulgarides, and M.R. McGrath, *Managerial Decision Making, Modules in Management Series* (Chicago: SRA, 1984), pp. 18–22.

19. D. Kahneman and A. Tversky, "Judgment under Uncertainty: Heuristics and Biases," *Science*, vol. 185 (1974), pp. 1124–31.

20. Information for this section taken from S.P. Robbins, *Decide & Conquer* (Upper Saddle River, NJ: Financial Times/Prentice Hall, 2004).

21. Information for this box came from B.C. McDonald and D. Hutcheson, "Dealing with Diversity Is Key to Tapping Talent," *Atlanta Business Chronicle*, December 18, 1998, pp. 45A+; P.M. Elsass and L.M. Graves, "Demographic Diversity in Decision-Making Groups: The Experience of Women and People of Color," *Academy of Management Review*, October 1997, pp. 946–73; and N.J. Adler (ed.), *International Dimensions of Organizational Behavior*, 4th ed. (Cincinnati: South-Western College Publishing, 2001).

22. L. Margonelli, "How IKEA Designs Its Sexy Price Tags," *Business 2.0*, October 2002, p. 108.

23. "Hurry Up and Decide!" *Business Week*, May 14, 2001, p. 16.

24. J. Klayman, R.P. Larrick, and C. Heath, "Organizational Repairs," *Across the Board*, February 2000, pp. 26–31.

25. J.S. Hammond, R.L. Keeney, and H. Raiffa, *Smart Choices: A Practical Guide to Making Better Decisions* (Boston: Harvard Business School Press, 1999), p. 4.

26. This discussion is based on K.H. Hammonds, "5 Habits of Highly Reliable Organizations: An Interview with Karl Weick," *Fast Company*, May 2002, pp. 124–28.

27. Situation adapted from information in: Neil Weinberg, "Holier Than Whom?" *Forbes*, June 23, 2003, pp. 71+; Eric Baum, "Schwab Campaign Bundles Controversy, Consistency," *Fund Marketing Alert*, March 10, 2003, p. 10.

28. Information from C.F. Martin's Web site (*www.cfmartin.com*), April 24, 2003; D. Lieberman, "Guitar Sales Jam Despite Music Woes," *USA Today*, December 16, 2002, p. 2B; and S. Fitch, "Stringing Them Along," *Forbes*, July 26, 1999, pp. 90–91.)

CHAPTER 7

1. Information from company Web site (*www.ubsag.com*), January 5, 2003; and S. Greengard, "Dr. Gabriela Payer Fruithof," *IQ Magazine*, November/December 2002, p. 48.

2. K.J. Lamiman, "Leader of the Pack: Harley-Davidson, Inc.," *Better Investing* May 2003, pp. 42–44; and E. Eldridge, "Investors Fear Harley's Thunder Grows Faint," *USA Today*, April 8, 2003, p. 3B.

3. See, for example, J.A. Pearce II, K.K. Robbins, and R.B. Robinson, Jr., "The Impact of Grand Strategy and Planning Formality on Financial Performance," *Strategic Management Journal*, March–April 1987, pp. 125–34; L.C. Rhyne, "Contrasting Planning Systems in High, Medium, and Low Performance Companies," *Journal of Management Studies*, July 1987, pp. 363–85; J.A. Pearce II, E.B. Freeman, and R.B. Robinson Jr., "The Tenuous Link between Formal Strategic Planning and Financial Performance," *Academy of Management Review*, October 1987, pp. 658–75; D.K. Sinha, "The Contribution of Formal Planning to Decisions," *Strategic Management Journal*, October 1990, pp. 479–92; N. Capon, J.U. Farley, and J.M. Hulbert, "Strategic Planning and Financial Performance: More Evidence," *Journal of Management Studies*, January 1994, pp. 22–38; C.C. Miller and L.B. Cardinal, "Strategic Planning and Firm Performance: A Syn-

thesis of More Than Two Decades of Research," *Academy of Management Journal*, March 1994, pp. 1649–85; and P.J. Brews and M.R. Hunt, "Learning to Plan and Planning to Learn: Resolving the Planning School/Learning School Debate," *Strategic Management Journal*, December 1999, pp. 889–913.

4. R. Molz, "How Leaders Use Goals," *Long Range Planning*, October 1987, p. 91.

5. A. Taylor III, "Getting Ford in Gear," *Fortune*, April 28, 2003, pp. 44–47; B. Morris, "Can Ford Save Ford?" *Fortune*, November 18, 2002, pp. 52–64; K. Naughton, "Ford Goes for the Green," *Newsweek*, August 7, 2000, p. 62; J. Ball, "Ford Contacts Environmentalists Behind Scenes," *Wall Street Journal*, May 15, 2000, p. B2; and B. Morris, "This Ford Is Different," *Fortune*, April 3, 2000, pp. 122–36.

6. Annual reports from Claire's Stores (2002), Nike (2001), Winnebago (2002), and Revlon (2002).

7. See, for instance, C.K. Warriner, "The Problem of Organizational Purpose," *Sociological Quarterly*, Spring 1965, pp. 139–46; and J. Pfeffer, *Organizational Design* (Arlington Heights, IL: AHM Publishing, 1978), pp. 5–12.

8. J.D. Hunger and T.L. Wheelen, *Strategic Management*, 7th ed. (Upper Saddle River, NJ: Prentice Hall, 2000).

9. P.N. Romani, "MBO by Any Other Name Is Still MBO," *Supervision*, December 1997, pp. 6–8; and A.W. Schrader and G.T. Seward, "MBO Makes Dollar Sense," *Personnel Journal*, July 1989, pp. 32–37.

10. Romani, "MBO by Any Other Name is Still MBO," pp. 6–8; and R. Rodgers and J.E. Hunter, "Impact of Management by Objectives on Organizational Productivity," *Journal of Applied Psychology*, April 1991, pp. 322–36.

11. For additional information on goals, see, for instance, P. Drucker, *The Executive in Action* (New York: HarperCollins Books, 1996), pp. 207–14; and E.A. Locke and G.P. Latham, *A Theory of Goal Setting and Task Performance* (Upper Saddle River, NJ: Prentice Hall, 1990).

12. Several of these factors were suggested by J.S. Armstrong, "The Value of Formal Planning for Strategic Decisions: Review of Empirical Research," *Strategic Management Journal*, July–September 1982, pp. 197–211; and R.K. Bresser and R.C. Bishop, "Dysfunctional Effects of Formal Planning: Two Theoretical Explanations," *Academy of Management Review*, October 1983, pp. 588–99.

13. Brews and Hunt, "Learning to Plan and Planning to Learn: Resolving the Planning School/Learning School Debate."

14. Ibid.

15. Information on the building project found on MoMA's Web site (*www.moma.org*), May 9, 2003; C. McGuigan, "MoMA Cops Street Cred," *Newsweek*, July 1, 2002; and D. Costello, "Museum of Modern Art's Ambitious Expansion Plan Faces Trouble," *Wall Street Journal*, June 7, 2000, pp. B1+.

16. A. Campbell, "Tailored, Not Benchmarked: A Fresh Look at Corporate Planning," *Harvard Business Review*, March–April 1999, pp. 41–50.

17. J.H. Sheridan, "Focused on Flow," *IW*, October 18, 1999, pp. 46–51.

18. H. Mintzberg, *The Rise and Fall of Strategic Planning* (New York: Free Press, 1994).

19. Ibid.

20. Ibid.

21. G. Hamel and C.K. Prahalad, *Competing for the Future* (Boston: Harvard Business School Press, 1994).

22. D. Miller, "The Architecture of Simplicity," *Academy of Management Review*, January 1993, pp. 116–38.

23. Brews and Hunt, "Learning to Plan and Planning to Learn: Resolving the Planning School/Learning School Debate."

24. Information on Wipro Limited from Hoover's Online (*www.hoovers.com*), June 4, 2003; and K.H. Hammonds, "Smart, Determined, Ambitious, Cheap. The New Face of Global Competition," *Fast Company*, February 2003, pp. 90–97.

25. Situation adapted from information in: Scott Leith, "Coke Faces Damage Control," *Atlanta Journal-Constitution*, June 19, 2003, p. C1; Chad Terhume, "Coke Employees Acted Improperly in Marketing Test," *Wall Street Journal*, June 18, 2003, pp. A3, A6; Theresa Howard, "Burger King, Coke May Face Off in Frozen Coke Suit," *USA Today*, June 6, 2003, *www.usatoday.com/money/industries/food/2003-06-04.bk_x.htm*.

CHAPTER 8

1. Information from company Web site (*www.okemo.com*), and Ski Vermont Web site (*www.skivermont.com*), January 5, 2003, and S. Kirsner, "Moguls with a Mission," *Fast Company*, January 2003, pp. 108–111.

2. J.W. Dean Jr. and M.P. Sharfman, "Does Decision Process Matter? A Study of Strategic Decision-Making Effectiveness," *Academy of Management Journal*, April 1996, pp. 368–96.

3. T.L. Wheelen and J.D. Hunger, *Strategic Management and Business Policy*, 7th ed. (Upper Saddle River, NJ: Prentice Hall, 2000), p. 3.

4. E.H. Bowman and C.E. Helfat, "Does Corporate Strategy Matter?" *Strategic Management Journal*, 22 (2001), pp. 1–23; P.J. Brews and M.R. Hunt, "Learning to Plan and Planning to Learn: Resolving the Planning School—Learning School Debate," *Strategic Management Journal*, 20 (1999), pp. 889–913; D.J. Ketchen Jr., J.B. Thomas, and R.R. McDaniel Jr., "Process, Content and Context; Synergistic Effects on Performance," *Journal of Management*, 22, no. 2 (1996), pp. 231–57; C.C. Miller and L.B. Cardinal, "Strategic Planning and Firm Performance: A Synthesis of More than Two Decades of Research," *Academy of Management Journal*, December 1994, pp. 1649–65; and N. Capon, J.U. Farley, and J.M. Hulbert, "Strategic Planning and Financial Performance: More Evidence," *Journal of Management Studies*, January 1994, pp. 105–10.

5. "A Solid Strategy Helps Companies' Growth," *Nation's Business*, October 1990, p. 10.

6. See, for example, H. Mintzberg, *The Rise and Fall of Strategic Planning* (New York: Free Press, 1994); S.J. Wall and S.R. Wall, "The Evolution (Not the Death) of Strategy," *Organizational Dynamics*, Autumn 1995, pp. 7–19; and J.A. Byrne, "Strategic Planning: It's Back!" *BusinessWeek*, August 26, 1996, pp. 46–52.

7. "Sports Sales Get Extreme," *Springfield News Leader*, February 12, 2000, p. 7A.

8. C.K. Prahalad and G. Hamel, "The Core Competence of the Corporation," *Harvard Business Review*, May–June 1990, pp. 79–91.

9. I.M. Kunii, C. Dawson, and C. Palmeri, "Toyota Is Way Ahead of the Hybrid Pack," *BusinessWeek*, May 5, 2003, p. 48; S. Spear and H.K. Bowen, "Decoding the DNA of the Toyota Production System," *Harvard Business Review*, September–October 1999, pp. 96–106.

10. See, for example, J.B. Barney, "Organizational Culture: Can It Be a Source of Sustained Competitive Advantage?" *Academy of Management Review*, July 1986, pp. 656–65; C. Scholz, "Corporate Culture and Strategy—The Problem of Strategic Fit," *Long Range Planning*, August 1987, pp. 78–87; S. Green, "Understanding Corporate Culture and Its Relation to Strategy," *International Studies of Management and Organization*, Summer 1988, pp. 6–28; T. Kono, "Corporate Culture and Long-Range Planning," *Long Range Planning*, August 1990, pp. 9–19; and C.M. Fiol, "Managing Culture as a Competitive Resource: An Identity-Based View of Sustainable Competitive Advantage,"

Journal of Management, March 1991, pp. 191–211.

11. J.P. Kotter and J.L. Heskett, *Corporate Culture and Performance* (New York: Free Press, 1992).

12. T. Mucha, "The Payoff for Trying Harder," *Business 2.0*, July 2002, pp. 84–85.

13. Box based on R.J. Lewicki, D.D. Bowen, D.T. Hall, and F.S. Hall, *Experiences in Management and Organizational Behavior*, 3rd ed. (New York: John Wiley & Sons, 1988), pp. 261–67; A. Williams, "Career Planning: Build on Strengths, Strengthen Weaknesses," *The Black Collegian*, September–October 1993, pp. 78–86; C.C. Campbell-Rock, "Career Planning Strategies That Really Work," *The Black Collegian*, September–October 1993, pp. 88–93; B. Kaye, "Career Development—Anytime, Anyplace," *Training and Development*, December 1993, pp. 46–49; W. Wooten, "Using Knowledge, Skill, and Ability (KSA) Data to Identify Career Pathing Oportunities," *Public Personnel Management*, Winter 1993, pp. 551–63; C. Mossop, "Values Assessment: Key to Managing Careers," *CMA—The Management Accounting Magazine*, March 1994, p. 33; and A.D. Pinkney, "Winning in the Workplace," *Essence*, March 1994, pp. 79–80.

14. P. Haspeslagh, "Portfolio Planning: Uses and Limits," *Harvard Business Review*, January–February 1982, pp. 58–73.

15. *Perspective on Experience* (Boston: Boston Consulting Group, 1970).

16. R. Rumelt, "Towards a Strategic Theory of the Firm," in R. Lamb (ed.), *Competitive Strategic Management* (Upper Saddle River, NJ: Prentice Hall, 1984), pp. 556–70; M.E. Porter, *Competitive Advantage: Creating and Sustaining Superior Performance* (New York: Free Press, 1985); J. Barney, "Firm Resources and Sustained Competitive Advantage," *Journal of Management* 17, no. 1 (1991), pp. 99–120; M.A. Peteraf, "The Cornerstones of Competitive Advantage: A Resource-Based View," *Strategic Management Journal*, March 1993, pp. 179–91; and J.B. Barney, "Looking Inside for Competitive Advantage," *Academy of Management Executive*, November 1995, pp. 49–61.

17. T.C. Powell, "Total Quality Management as Competitive Advantage: A Review and Empirical Study," *Strategic Management Journal*, January 1995, pp. 15–37.

18. See R.J. Schonenberger, "Is Strategy Strategic? Impact of Total Quality Management on Strategy," *Academy of Management Executive*, August 1992, pp. 80–87; C.A. Barclay, "Quality Strategy and TQM Policies: Empirical Evidence," *Management International Review*, Special Issue 1993, pp. 87–98; T.E. Benson, "A Business Strategy Comes of Age," *Industry Week*, May 3, 1993, pp. 40–44; R. Jacob, "TQM: More Than a Dying Fad?" *Fortune*, October 18, 1993, pp. 66–72; R. Krishnan, A.B. Shani, R.M. Grant, and R. Baer, "In Search of Quality Improvement Problems of Design and Implementation," *Academy of Management Executive*, November 1993, pp. 7–20; B. Voss, "Quality's Second Coming," *Journal of Business Strategy*, March–April 1994, pp. 42–46; M. Barrier, "Raising TQM Consciousness," *Nation's Business*, April 1994, pp. 62–64; and special issue of *Academy of Management Review* devoted to TQM, July 1994, pp. 390–584.

19. See, for example, M.E. Porter, *Competitive Strategy: Techniques for Analyzing Industries and Competitors* (New York: Free Press, 1980); Porter, *Competitive Advantage: Creating and Sustaining Superior Performance*; G.G. Dess and P.S. Davis, "Porter's (1980) Generic Strategies as Determinants of Strategic Group Membership and Organizational Performance," *Academy of Management Journal*, September 1984, pp. 467–88; Dess and Davis, "Porter's (1980) Generic Strategies and Performance: An Empirical Examination with American Data—Part I: Testing Porter," *Organization Studies*, no. 1 (1986), pp. 37–55; Dess and Davis, "Porter's (1980) Generic Strategies and Performance: An Empirical Examination with American Data—Part II: Performance Implications," *Organization Studies*, no. 3 (1986), pp. 255–61; M.E. Porter, "From Competitive Advantage to Corporate Strategy," *Harvard Business Review*, May–June 1987, pp. 43–59; A.I. Murray, "A Contingency View of Porter's 'Generic Strategies'," *Academy of Management Review*, July 1988, pp. 390–400; C.W.L. Hill, "Differentiation versus Low Cost or Differentiation and Low Cost: A Contingency Framework," *Academy of Management Review*, July 1988, pp. 401–12; I. Bamberger, "Developing Competitive Advantage in Small and Medium-Sized Firms," *Long Range Planning*, October 1989, pp. 80–88; D.F. Jennings and J.R. Lumpkin, "Insights between Environmental Scanning Activities and Porter's Generic Strategies: An Empirical Analysis," *Strategic Management Journal*, 18, no. 4 (1992), pp. 791–803; N. Argyres and A. M. McGahan, "An Interview with Michael Porter," *Academy of Management Executive*, May 2002, pp. 43–52; and A. Brandenburger, "Porter's Added Value: High

Indeed!" *Academy of Management Executive*, May 2002, pp. 58–60.

20. D. Miller and J. Toulouse, "Strategy, Structure, CEO Personality, and Performance in Small Firms," *American Journal of Small Business*, Winter 1986, pp. 47–62.

21. Hill, "Differentiation versus Low Cost or Differentiation and Low Cost"; R.E. White, "Organizing to Make Business Unit Strategies Work," in H.E. Glass (ed.), *Handbook of Business Strategy*, 2d ed. (Boston: Warren Gorham and Lamont, 1991), pp. 24.1–24.14; D. Miller, "The Generic Strategy Trap," *Journal of Business Strategy*, January–February 1991, pp. 37–41; S. Cappel, P. Wright, M. Kroll, and D. Wyld, "Competitive Strategies and Business Performance: An Empirical Study of Select Service Businesses," *International Journal of Management*, March 1992, pp. 1–11; and J.W. Bachmann, "Competitive Strategy: It's O.K. to Be Different," *Academy of Management Executive*, May 2002, pp. 61–65.

22. D. Leonard, "Songs in the Key of Steve," *Fortune*, May 12, 2003, pp. 52–62; L. Grossman, "It's All Free!" *Time*, May 5, 2003, pp. 60–67; and "Everybody Hurts: Music Sales Fall 7.2 %," *USA Today*, April 9, 2003, p. 1B.

23. This section based on work by J.N. Sheth and R.S. Sisodia in "Competitive Markets and the Rule of Three," *Ivey Business Journal*, September/October 2002, pp. 1–5; and *The Rule of Three: Surviving and Thriving in Competitive Markets* (New York: The Free Press, 2002).

24. D. Lyons, "Mommy Doesn't Carry Cash," *Forbes*, September 16, 2002, p. 81.

25. G.T. Lumpkin, S.B. Droege, and G.G. Dess, "E-Commerce Strategies: Achieving Sustainable Competitive Advantage and Avoiding Pitfalls," *Organizational Dynamics*, Spring 2002, pp. 325–40.

26. J. Gaffney, "Shoe Fetish," *Business 2.0*, March 2002, pp. 98–99.

27. M. Boyle, "Rapid Growth in Tough Times," *Fortune*, September 2, 2002, p. 150.

28. M.P. Walker, "Going for Customer Service Gold," *Training and Development*, May 2002, pp. 62–69.

29. S. Ellison, "P&G to Unleash Dental Adult-Pet Food," *Wall Street Journal*, December 12, 2002, p. B4.

30. Situation adapted from information in: Jim Frederick, "War of Words," *Time International*, February 17, 2003, p. 33; Keith Regan, "Bugging Out Over Bezos' Bargain Book Bin," *E-Commerce Times*, April 17, 2002, *www.ecommercetimes.com*.

CHAPTER 9

1. Information from company Web site (*www.hepmc.com*), January 5, 2003; "Winning in China," *Business Week Online* (*www.businessweek.com*), January 27, 2003; E.J. Adams, "Junjie Li," *IQ Magazine*, November/December, 2002, p. 50; and B. Powell, "China's Great Step Forward," *Fortune*, September 17, 2001, pp. 128–142.

2. D. McGray, "Translating Sony into English," *Fast Company*, January 2003, p. 38.

3. S.C. Jain, "Environmental Scanning in U.S. Corporations," *Long Range Planning*, April 1984, pp. 117–28; see also L.M. Fuld, *Monitoring the Competition* (New York: John Wiley & Sons, 1988); E.H. Burack and N.J. Mathys, "Environmental Scanning Improves Strategic Planning," *Personnel Administrator*, April 1989, pp. 82–87; R. Subramanian, N. Fernandes, and E. Harper, "Environmental Scanning in U.S. Companies: Their Nature and Their Relationship to Performance," *Management International Review*, July 1993, pp. 271–86; B.K. Boyd and J. Fulk, "Executive Scanning and Perceived Uncertainty: A Multidimensional Model," *Journal of Management*, 22, No. 1 (1996) pp. 1–21; D.S. Elkenov, "Strategic Uncertainty and Environmental Scanning: The Case for Institutional Influences on Scanning Behavior," *Strategic Management Journal*, vol. 18 (1997), pp. 287–302; K. Kumar, R. Subramanian, and K. Strandholm, "Competitive Strategy, Environmental Scanning and Performance: A Context Specific Analysis of Their Relationship," *International Journal of Commerce and Management*, Spring 2001, pp. 1–18; and C.G. Wagner, "Top 10 Reasons to Watch Trends," *The Futurist*, March–April 2002, pp. 68–69.

4. T.L. Wheelen and J.D. Hunger, *Strategic Management*, 8th ed. (Upper Saddle River, NJ: Prentice Hall, 2001), pp. 52–53.

5. B. Gilad, "The Role of Organized Competitive Intelligence in Corporate Strategy," *Columbia Journal of World Business*, Winter 1989, pp. 29–35; L. Fuld, "A Recipe for Business Intelligence," *Journal of Business Strategy*, January–February 1991, pp. 12–17; J.P. Herring, "The Role of Intelligence in Formulating Strategy," *Journal of Business Strategy*, September–October 1992, pp. 54–60; K. Western, "Ethical Spying," *Business Ethics*, September–October 1995, pp. 22–23; D. Kinard, "Raising Your Competitive IQ: The Payoff of Paying Attention to Potential Competitors," *Association Management*, February 2003, pp. 40–44; and K. Girard,

"Snooping on a Shoestring," *Business 2.0*, May 2003, pp. 64–66.

6. C. Davis, "Get Smart," *Executive Edge*, October/November 1999, pp. 46–50.

7. B. Ettore, "Managing Competitive Intelligence," *Management Review*, October 1995, pp. 15–19.

8. A. Serwer, "P&G's Covert Operation," *Fortune*, September 17, 2001, pp. 42–44.

9. B. Rosner, "HR Should Get a Clue: Corporate Spying Is Real," *Workforce*, April 2001, pp. 72–75.

10. Western, "Ethical Spying."

11. W.H. Davidson, "The Role of Global Scanning in Business Planning," *Organizational Dynamics*, Winter 1991, pp. 5–16.

12. Wheelen and Hunger, *Strategic Management*, p. 67.

13. Collaborative, Planning, Forecasting, and Replenishment Committee Web site (*www.cpfr.org*), May 20, 2003; and J.W. Verity, "Clearing the Cobwebs from the Stockroom," *BusinessWeek*, October 21, 1996, p. 140.

14. T. Leahy, "Turning Managers into Forecasters," *Business Finance*, August 2002, pp. 37–40.

15. See A.B. Fisher, "Is Long-Range Planning Worth It?" *Fortune*, April 23, 1990, pp. 281–84; J.A. Fraser, "On Target," *Inc.*, April 1991, pp. 113–14; P. Schwartz, *The Art of the Long View* (New York: Doubleday/Currency, 1991); G. Hamel and C.K. Prahalad, "Competing for the Future," *Harvard Business Review*, July–August 1994, pp. 122–28; F. Elikai and W. Hall, Jr., "Managing and Improving the Forecasting Process," *Journal of Business Forecasting Methods & Systems*, Spring 1999, pp. 15–19; L. Lapide, "New Developments in Business Forecasting," *Journal of Business Forecasting Methods & Systems*, Summer 1999, pp. 13–14; and T. Leahy, "Building Better Forecasts," *Business Finance*, December 1999, pp. 10–12.

16. P.N. Pant and W.H. Starbuck, "Innocents in the Forest: Forecasting and Research Methods," *Journal of Management*, June 1990, pp. 433–60; Elikai and Hall, "Managing and Improving the Forecasting Process"; M.A. Giullian, Marcus D. Odom, and M.W. Totaro, "Developing Essential Skills for Success in the Business World: A Look at Forecasting," *Journal of Applied Business Research*, Summer 2000, pp. 51–65; and T. Leahy, "Turning Managers into Forecasters."

17. This section is based on Y.K. Shetty, "Benchmarking for Superior Performance," *Long Range Planning*, 1 (April 1993) pp. 39–44; G.H. Watson, "How Process Benchmarking Supports Corpo-

rate Strategy," *Planning Review*, January–February 1993, pp. 12–15; S. Greengard, "Discover Best Practices," *Personnel Journal*, November 1995, pp. 62–73; J. Martin, "Are You as Good as You Think You Are?" *Fortune*, September 30, 1996, pp. 142–52; R.L. Ackoff, "The Trouble with Benchmarking," *Across the Board*, January 2000, p. 13; V. Prabhu, D. Yarrow, and G. Gordon-Hart, "Best Practice and Performance within Northeast Manufacturing," *Total Quality Management*, January 2000, pp. 113–121; "E-Benchmarking: The Latest E-Trend," *CFO*, March 2000, p. 7; and E. Krell, "Now Read This," *Business Finance*, May 2000, pp. 97–103.

18. "Newswatch," *CFO*, July 2002, p. 26.

19. Benchmarking examples were found in the following: "Benchmarkers Make Strange Bedfellows," *IW*, November 15, 1993, p. 8; G. Fuchsberg, "Here's Help in Finding Corporate Role Models," *Wall Street Journal*, June 1, 1993, p. B1; and A. Tanzer, "Studying at the Feet of the Masters," *Forbes*, May 10, 1993, pp. 43–44.

20. This section is based on T. Gutner, "Better Your Business, Benchmark It," *BusinessWeek*, April 27, 1998, pp. ENT4–6; and J.A. Berk, "The Six Benchmarking Steps You Need," *Workforce*, accessed on (*www.workforce.com*), March 13, 2001.

21. J. Hope and R. Fraser, "Who Needs Budgets?" *Harvard Business Review*, February 2003, pp. 108–115; T. Leahy, "The Top 10 Traps of Budgeting," *Business Finance*, November 2001, pp. 20–16; T. Leahy, "Necessary Evil," *Business Finance*, November 1999, pp. 41–45; J. Fanning, "Businesses Languishing in a Budget Comfort Zone?" *Management Accounting*, July/August 1999, p. 8; "Budgeting Processes: Inefficiency or Inadequate?" *Management Accounting*, February 1999, p. 5; A. Kennedy and D. Dugdale, "Getting the Most From Budgeting," *Management Accounting*, February 1999, pp. 22–24; G.J. Nolan, "The End of Traditional Budgeting," *Bank Accounting & Finance*, Summer 1998, pp. 29–36; and J. Mariotti, "Surviving the Dreaded Budget Process," *IW*, August 17, 1998, p. 150.

22. See, for example, S. Stiansen, "Breaking Even," *Success*, November 1988, p. 16.

23. S.E. Barndt and D.W. Carvey, *Essentials of Operations Management* (Upper Saddle River, NJ: Prentice Hall, 1982), p. 134.

24. E.E. Adam Jr. and R.J. Ebert, *Production and Operations Management*, 5th ed. (Upper Saddle River, NJ: Prentice Hall, 1992), p. 333.

25. See, for instance, C. Benko and F.W. McFarlan, *Connecting the Dots: Aligning Projects with Objectives in Unpre-

dictable Times* (Boston, Harvard Business School Press, 2003); M.W. Lewis, M.A. Welsh, G.E. Dehler, and S.G. Green, "Product Development Tensions: Exploring Contrasting Styles of Project Management," *Academy of Management Journal*, June 2002, pp. 546–64; C.E. Gray and E.W. Larsen, *Project Management: The Managerial Process* (Columbus, OH: McGraw-Hill Higher Education, 2000); J. Davidson Frame, *Project Management Competence: Building Key Skills for Individuals, Teams, and Organizations* (San Francisco: Jossey-Bass, 1999).

26. For more information, see *www.project-management-software.org*; and P. Gordon, "Track Projects on the Web," *Information Week*, May 22, 2000, pp. 88–89.

27. S. Greengard, "The Project Management Advantage," *Business Finance*, November 2002, pp. 36–40.

28. L. Fahey, "Scenario Learning," *Management Review*, March 2000, pp. 29–34; S. Caudron, "Frontview Mirror," *Business Finance*, December 1999, pp. 24–30; and J.R. Garber, "What if…?," *Forbes*, November 2, 1998, pp. 76–79.

29. S. Caudron, "Frontview Mirror," p. 30.

30. Situation adapted from information in: John Helyar, "The Bizarre Reign of King Richard," *Fortune*, July 7, 2002, pp. 76–86; Reed Abelson, "Scrushy Chided Staff About Profits, Tape Reveals," *New York Times*, May 22, 2003, p. C1.

PART THREE

1. M. Arndt, "Zimmer: Growing Older Gracefully," *BusinessWeek*, June 9, 2003, pp. 82–84.

2. G.B. Knight, "How Wall Street Whiz Found a Niche Selling Books on the Internet," *Wall Street Journal*, May 15, 1996, pp. A1+.

3. N.F. Krueger, Jr., "The Cognitive Infrastructure of Opportunity Emergence," *Entrepreneurship Theory and Practice*, Spring 2000, p. 6.

4. P. Drucker, *Innovation and Entrepreneurship* (New York: Harper & Row, 1985).

5. B. McClean, "This Entrepreneur Is Changing Underwear," *Fortune*, September 18, 2000, p. 60.

6. Latest figures on registered users from Hoover's Online (*www.hoovers.com*), July 7, 2003; and A. Cohen, "eBay's Bid to Conquer All," *Time*, February 5, 2001, pp. 48–51.

7. S. McFarland, "Cambodia's Internet Service Is in Kids' Hands," *Wall Street Journal*, May 15, 2000, p. A9A.

8. Information on Whole Foods Market from Hoover's Online (*www.hoovers.com*), July 7, 2003.

9. A. Eisenberg, "What's Next: New Fabrics Can Keep Wearers Healthy and Smelling Good," *New York Times*, February 3, 2000, pp. D1+.

10. S. Greco, "The Start-Up Years," *Inc. 500*, October 21, 1997, p. 57.

11. T. Stevens, "Master of His Universe," *Industry Week*, January 15, 2001, pp. 76–80; and R. Grover, "Back from a Black Hole," *BusinessWeek*, May 29, 2000, p. 186.

12. E. Neuborne, "Hey, Good-Looking," *BusinessWeek*, May 29, 2000, p. 192.

CHAPTER 10

1. Information from company Web site (*www.handelsbanken.se*), January 5, 2003; and N. George, "Counting on the Spirit of Independent Branches," *Financial Times*, November 5, 2001, p. 10.

2. C. Fishman, "Boomtown, U.S.A.," *Fast Company*, June 2002, pp. 106–14.

3. T. Starner, "Room for Improvement," *IQ Magazine*, March/April 2003, pp. 36–37.

4. See, for example, R.L. Daft, *Organization Theory and Design*, 6th ed. (St. Paul, MN: West Publishing, 1998).

5. D. Drickhamer, "Moving Man," *IW*, December 2002, pp. 44–46.

6. For a discussion of authority, see W.A. Kahn and K.E. Kram, "Authority at Work: Internal Models and Their Organizational Consequences," *Academy of Management Review*, January 1994, pp. 17–50.

7. E.P. Gunn, "Who's the Boss?" *Smart Money*, April 2003, p. 121.

8. D. Van Fleet, "Span of Management Research and Issues," *Academy of Management Journal*, September 1983, pp. 546–52.

9. R. Gibson, "Interstate Bakeries Is Able to Mine Profit from a Golden Cake," *Wall Street Journal*, January 31, 1997, pp. A1+.

10. C. Tohurst, "Companies March on the Morale of Their Workers," *Australian Financial Review*, November 13, 1998, p. SP2.

11. A. Ross, "BMO's Big Bang," *Canadian Business*, January 1994, pp. 58–63; and information on company from Hoover's Online (*www.hoovers.com*), May 25, 2003.

12. See, for example, H. Mintzberg, *Power In and Around Organizations* (Upper Saddle River, NJ: Prentice Hall, 1983); J. Child, *Organization: A Guide to Prob-*

lems and Practices (London: Kaiser & Row, 1984).

13. T. Burns and G.M. Stalker, *The Management of Innovation* (London: Tavistock, 1961); and D.A. Morand, "The Role of Behavioral Formality and Informality in the Enactment of Bureaucratic versus Organic Organizations," *Academy of Management Review*, October 1995, pp. 831–72.

14. C. Fishman, "Isolating the Leadership Gene," *Fast Company*, March 2002, p. 90.

15. A.D. Chandler, Jr., *Strategy and Structure: Chapters in the History of the Industrial Enterprise* (Cambridge, MA: MIT Press, 1962).

16. See, for instance, R.E. Miles and C.C. Snow, *Organizational Strategy, Structure, and Process* (New York: McGraw-Hill, 1978); D. Miller, "The Structural and Environmental Correlates of Business Strategy," *Strategic Management Journal*, January–February 1987, pp. 55–76; H.L. Boschken, "Strategy and Structure: Reconceiving the Relationship," *Journal of Management*, March 1990, pp. 135–50; H.A. Simon, "Strategy and Organizational Evolution," *Strategic Management Journal*, January 1993, pp. 131–42; R. Parthasarthy and S.P. Sethi, "Relating Strategy and Structure to Flexible Automation: A Test of Fit and Performance Implications," *Strategic Management Journal*, 14, no. 6 (1993), pp. 529–49; D.C. Galunic and K.M. Eisenhardt, "Renewing the Strategy-Structure-Performance Paradigm," in B.M. Staw and L.L. Cummings (eds.), *Research in Organizational Behavior*, vol. 16 (Greenwich, CT: JAI Press, 1994), pp. 215–55; and D. Jennings and S. Seaman, "High and Low Levels of Organizational Adaptation: An Empirical Analysis of Strategy, Structure, and Performance," *Strategic Management Journal*, July 1994, pp. 459–75.

17. See, for instance, P.M. Blau and R.A. Schoenherr, *The Structure of Organizations* (New York: Basic Books, 1971); D.S. Pugh, "The Aston Program of Research: Retrospect and Prospect," in A.H. Van de Ven and W.F. Joyce (eds.), *Perspectives on Organization Design and Behavior* (New York: John Wiley, 1981), pp. 135–66; and R.Z. Gooding and J.A. Wagner III, "A Meta-Analytic Review of the Relationship between Size and Performance: The Productivity and Efficiency of Organizations and Their Subunits," *Administrative Science Quarterly*, December 1985, pp. 462–81.

18. J. Woodward, *Industrial Organization: Theory and Practice* (London: Oxford University Press, 1965).

19. See, for instance, C. Perrow, "A Framework for the Comparative Analysis of Organizations," *American Sociological Review*, April 1967, pp. 194–208; J.D. Thompson, *Organizations in Action* (New York: McGraw-Hill, 1967); J. Hage and M. Aiken, "Routine Technology, Social Structure, and Organizational Goals," *Administrative Science Quarterly*, September 1969, pp. 366–77; C.C. Miller, W.H. Glick, Y.D. Wang, and G. Huber, "Understanding Technology-Structure Relationships: Theory Development and Meta-Ánalytic Theory Testing," *Academy of Management Journal*, June 1991, pp. 370–399.

20. D. Gerwin, "Relationships between Structure and Technology," in P.C. Nystrom and W.H. Starbuck (eds.), *Handbook of Organizational Design*, vol. 2 (New York: Oxford University Press, 1981), pp. 3–38; and D.M. Rousseau and R.A. Cooke, "Technology and Structure: The Concrete, Abstract, and Activity Systems of Organizations," *Journal of Management*, Fall–Winter 1984, pp. 345–61.

21. F.E. Emery and E. Trist, "The Causal Texture of Organizational Environments," *Human Relations*, February 1965, pp. 21–32; P. Lawrence and J.W. Lorsch, *Organization and Environment: Managing Differentiation and Integration* (Boston: Harvard Business School, Division of Research, 1967); and M. Yasai-Ardekani, "Structural Adaptations to Environments," *Academy of Management Review*, January 1986, pp. 9–21.

22. H. Mintzberg, *Structure in Fives: Designing Effective Organizations* (Upper Saddle River, NJ: Prentice Hall, 1983), p. 157.

23. R.J. Williams, J.J. Hoffman, and B.T. Lamont, "The Influence of Top Management Team Characteristics on M-Form Implementation Time," *Journal of Managerial Issues*, Winter 1995, pp. 466–80.

24. See, for example, R.E. Hoskisson, C.W.L. Hill, and H. Kim, "The Multidivisional Structure: Organizational Fossil or Source of Value?" *Journal of Management*, 19, no. 2 (1993) pp. 269–98; I.I. Mitroff, R.O. Mason, and C.M. Pearson, "Radical Surgery: What Will Tomorrow's Organizations Look Like?" *Academy of Management Executive*, February 1994, pp. 11–21; T. Clancy, "Radical Surgery: A View from the Operating Theater," *Academy of Management Executive*, February 1994, pp. 73–78; M. Hammer, "Processed Change: Michael Hammer Sees Process as 'the Clark Kent of Business Ideas'—A Concept That Has the Power to Change a Company's Organizational Design," *Journal of Business Strategy*, November–December 2001, pp. 11–15; D.F.

Twomey, "Leadership, Organizational Design, and Competitiveness for the 21st Century," *Global Competitiveness*, Annual 2002, pp. S31–S40; and G.J. Castrogiovanni, "Organization Task Environments: Have They Changed Fundamentally over Time?" *Journal of Management*, vol. 28, no. 2 (2002), pp. 129–50.

25. See, for example, H. Rothman, "The Power of Empowerment," *Nation's Business*, June 1993, pp. 49–52; B. Dumaine, "Payoff from the New Management"; *Fortune*, December 13, 1993, pp. 103–110; J.A. Byrne, "The Horizontal Corporation," *Business Week*, December 20, 1993, pp. 76–81; J.R. Katzenbach and D.K. Smith, *The Wisdom of Teams* (Boston: Harvard Business School Press, 1993); L. Grant, "New Jewel in the Crown," *U.S. News & World Report*, February 28, 1994, pp. 55–57; D. Ray and H. Bronstein, *Teaming Up: Making the Transition to a Self-Directed Team-Based Organization* (New York: McGraw Hill, 1995); and D.R. Denison, S.L. Hart, and J.A. Kahn, "From Chimneys to Cross-Functional Teams: Developing and Validating a Diagnostic Model," *Academy of Management Journal*, December 1996, pp. 1005–23.

26. C. Fishman, "Whole Foods Is All Teams," *Fast Company*, Greatest Hits, vol. 1, 1997, pp. 102–13.

27. P. LaBarre, "This Organization is Dis-Organization," *Fast Company* Web site (*www.fastcompany.com*), April 16, 1997.

28. See, for example, G.G. Dess, A.M.A. Rasheed, K.J. McLaughlin, and R.L. Priem, "The New Corporate Architecture," *Academy of Management Executive*, August 1995, pp. 7–20.

29. For additional readings on boundaryless organizations, see M. Hammer and S. Stanton, "How Process Enterprises Really Work," *Harvard Business Review*, November–December 1999, pp. 108–18; T. Zenger and W. Hesterly, "The Disaggregation of Corporations: Selective Intervention, High-Powered Incentives, and Modular Units," *Organization Science*, vol. 8 (1997), pp. 209–22; R. Ashkenas, D. Ulrich, T. Jick, and S. Kerr, *The Boundaryless Organization: Breaking the Chains of Organizational Structure* (San Francisco: Jossey-Bass, 1997); R.M. Hodgetts, "A Conversation with Steve Kerr," *Organizational Dynamics*, Spring 1996, pp. 68–79; and J. Gebhardt, "The Boundaryless Organization," *Sloan Management Review*, Winter 1996, pp. 117–19. For another view of boundaryless organizations, see B. Victor, "The Dark Side of the New Organizational Forms: An Editorial Essay," *Organization Science*, November 1994, pp. 479–82.

30. See, for instance, W.H. Davidow and M.S. Malone, *The Virtual Corporation* (New York: HarperCollins, 1992); H. Chesbrough and D. Teece, "When Is Virtual Virtuous: Organizing for Innovation," *Harvard Business Review*, January–February 1996, pp. 65–73; Dess, Rasheed, McLaughlin, and Priem, "The New Corporate Architecture"; M. Sawhney and D. Parikh, "Break Your Boundaries," *Business 2.0*, May 2000, pp. 198–207; D. Pescovitz, "The Company Where Everybody's a Temp," *New York Times Magazine*, June 11, 2000, pp. 94–96; W.F. Cascio, "Managing a Virtual Workplace," *Academy of Management Executive*, August 2000, pp. 81–90; and D. Lyons, "Smart and Smarter," *Forbes*, March 18, 2002, pp. 40–41.

31. R.E. Miles and C.C. Snow, "Causes of Failures in Network Organizations," *California Management Review*, vol. 34, no. 4 (1992), pp. 53–72; R.E. Miles and C. C. Snow, "The New Network Firm: A Spherical Structure Built on Human Investment Philosophy," *Organizational Dynamics*, Spring 1995, pp. 5–18; C. Jones, W. Hesterly, and S. Borgatti, "A General Theory of Network Governance: Exchange Conditions and Social Mechanisms," *Academy of Management Review*, October 1997, pp. 911–45; and R.E. Miles, C.C. Snow, J.A. Matthews, G. Miles, and H.J. Coleman, Jr., "Organizing in the Knowledge Age: Anticipating the Cellular Form," *Academy of Management Executive*, November 1997, pp. 7–24.

32. S. Reed, A. Reinhardt, and A. Sains, "Saving Ericsson," *BusinessWeek*, November 11, 2002, pp. 64–68.

33. D.A. Ketchen, Jr. and G.T.M. Hult, "To Be Modular or Not to Be? Some Answers to the Question," *Academy of Management Executive*, May 2002, pp. 166–67; M.A. Schilling, "The Use of Modular Organizational Forms: An Industry-Level Analysis," *Academy of Management Journal*, December 2001, pp. 1149–68; D. Lei, M.A. Hitt, and J.D. Goldhar, "Advanced Manufacturing Technology: Organizational Design and Strategic Flexibility," *Organization Studies*, vol. 17 (1996), pp. 501–23; R. Sanchez and J. Mahoney, "Modularity Flexibility and Knowledge Management in Product and Organization Design," *Strategic Management Journal*, vol. 17 (1996), pp. 63–76; and R. Sanchez, "Strategic Flexibility in Product Competition," *Strategic Management Journal*, vol. 16 (1995), pp. 135–59.

34. Ketchen and Hult, "To Be Modular or Not to Be? Some Answers to the Question."

35. K. Kerwin, "GM: Modular Plants Won't be a Snap," *BusinessWeek*, November 9, 1998, pp. 168+.

36. P.M. Senge, *The Fifth Discipline: The Art and Practice of Learning Organizations* (New York: Doubleday, 1990).

37. J.M. Liedtka, "Collaborating across Lines of Business for Competitive Advantage," *Academy of Management Executive*, April 1996, pp. 20–37; G. Szulanski, "Exploring Internal Stickiness: Impediments to the Transfer of Best Practice within the Firm," *Strategic Management Journal*, Winter Special Issue 1996, pp. 27–43; D. Zell, "Overcoming Barriers to Work Innovations: Lessons Learned at Hewlett-Packard," *Organizational Dynamics*, Summer 2001, pp. 77–86; M. Schulz, "The Uncertain Relevance of Newness: Organizational Learning and Knowledge Flows," *Academy of Management Journal*, August 2001, pp. 661–81; R. Cross, A. Parker, L. Prusak, and S. P. Borgati, "Supporting Knowledge Creation and Sharing in Social Networks," *Organizational Dynamics*, Fall 2001, pp. 100–120; and B. Marr, "How to Knowledge Management," *Financial Management*, February 2003, pp. 26–27.

38. Situation adapted from information in: "HR Pressured to Breach Ethics Policies, Says Survey," *HR Briefing*, June 1, 2003, p. 1; Susan Pulliam, "A Staffer Ordered to Commit Fraud Balked, Then Caved," *Wall Street Journal*, June 23, 2003, pp. A1, A6; Jennifer Gilbert, "A Matter of "Trust," *Sales & Marketing Management*, March 2003, pp. 30+.

CHAPTER 11

1. Information on company from Progressive Baker Web site (*www.progressivebaker.com*), January 5, 2003; and M. Hofman, "Lost in the Translation," *Inc.*, May 2000, pp. 161–62.

2. T. Dixon, *Communication, Organization, and Performance* (Norwood, NJ: Ablex Publishing Corporation, 1996), p. 281; P.G. Clampitt, *Communicating for Managerial Effectiveness* (Newbury Park, CA: Sage Publications, 1991); and L.E. Penley, E.R. Alexander, I. Edward Jernigan, and C.I. Henwood, "Communication Abilities of Managers: The Relationship to Performance," *Journal of Management*, March 1991, pp. 57–76.

3. "Electronic Invective Backfires," *Workforce*, June 2001, p. 20; and E. Wong, "A Stinging Office Memo Boomerangs," *New York Times*, April 5, 2001, pp. C1+.

4. C.O. Kursh, "The Benefits of Poor Communication," *Psychoanalytic Review*, Summer–Fall 1971, pp. 189–208.

5. W.G. Scott and T.R. Mitchell, *Organization Theory: A Structural and Behavioral Analysis* (Homewood, IL: Richard D. Irwin, 1976).

6. D.K. Berlo, *The Process of Communication* (New York: Holt, Rinehart & Winston, 1960), pp. 30–32.

7. Clampitt, *Communicating for Managerial Effectiveness*.

8. A. Warfield, "Do You Speak Body Language?" *Training & Development*, April 2001, pp. 60–61; D. Zielinski, "Body Language Myths," *Presentations*, April 2001, pp. 36–42; and "Visual Cues Speak Loudly in Workplace," *Springfield News-Leader*, January 21, 2001, p. 8B.

9. J. Langdon, "Differences Between Males and Females at Work," *USA Today*, (*www.usatoday.com*), February 5, 2001; J. Manion, "He Said, She Said," *Materials Management in Health Care*, November 1998, pp. 52–62; G. Franzwa and C. Lockhart, "The Social Origins and Maintenance of Gender Communication Styles, Personality Types, and Grid-Group Theory," *Sociological Perspectives*, vol. 41, no. 1 (1998), pp. 185–208; and D. Tannen, *Talking From 9 to 5: Women and Men in the Workplace* (New York: Avon Books, 1995).

10. V. Murphy, "You've Got Expertise," *Forbes*, February 5, 2001, p. 134; and "Fast Fact," *Fast Company*, November 2000, p. 104.

11. Berlo, *The Process of Communication*, p. 103.

12. A. Mehrabian, "Communication without Words," *Psychology Today*, September 1968, pp. 53–55.

13. L. Haggerman, "Strong, Efficient Leadership Minimizes Employee Problems," *Springfield Business Journal*, December 9–15, 2002, p. 23.

14. See, for instance, S.P. Robbins and P.L. Hunsaker, *Training in InterPersonal Skills*, 3d ed. (Upper Saddle River, NJ: Prentice Hall, 2003); M. Young and J.E. Post, "Managing to Communicate, Communicating to Manage: How Leading Companies Communicate with Employees," *Organizational Dynamics*, Summer 1993, pp. 31–43; J.A. DeVito, *The Interpersonal Communication Book*, 6th ed. (New York: HarperCollins, 1992); and A.G. Athos and J.J. Gabarro, *Interpersonal Behavior* (Upper Saddle River, NJ: Prentice Hall, 1978).

15. A. Overholt, "Power Up the People," *Fast Company*, January 2003, p. 50.

16. Cited in "Heard It Through the Grapevine," *Forbes*, February 10, 1997, p. 22.

17. See, for instance, A. Bruzzese, "What To Do about Toxic Gossip," *USA Today*, (*www.usatoday.com*), March 14, 2001; N.B. Kurland and L.H. Pelled, "Passing the Word: Toward a Model of Gossip and Power in the Workplace," *Academy of Management Review*,

April 2000, pp. 428–38; N. DiFonzo, P. Bordia, and R.L. Rosnow, "Reining in Rumors," *Organizational Dynamics*, Summer 1994, pp. 47–62; M. Noon and R. Delbridge, "News from Behind My Hand: Gossip in Organizations," *Organization Studies*, vol. 14, no. 1 (1993), pp. 23–26; and J.G. March and G. Sevon, "Gossip, Information and Decision Making," in J.G. March (ed.), *Decisions and Organizations* (Oxford: Blackwell, 1988), pp. 429–42.

18. "Human Capital Index: 2001/2002 Survey Report," Watson Wyatt Worldwide, Washington, DC.

19. J. Rohwer, "Today, Tokyo. Tomorrow, the World," *Fortune*, September 18, 2000, pp. 140–52; J. McCullam and L. Torres, "Instant Enterprising," *Forbes*, September 11, 2000, p. 28; J. Guyon, "The World Is Your Office," *Fortune*, June 12, 2000, pp. 227–34; S. Baker and others, "The Wireless Internet," *BusinessWeek*, May 29, 2000, pp. 136–44; and R. Lieber, "Information is Everything…" *Fast Company*, November 1999, pp. 246–54.

20. Based on P. Sloan, "New Ways to Goof Off at Work," *U.S. News & World Report*, September 4, 2000, p. 42; and M. Conlin, "Workers, Surf at Your Own Risk," *BusinessWeek*, June 12, 2000, pp. 105–6.

21. C.Y. Chen, "The IM Invasion," *Fortune*, May 26, 2003, pp. 135–138; and K. Blakeley, "Instant Headache," *Forbes*, November 25, 2002, pp. 118+.

22. K.C. Laudon and J.P. Laudon, *Essentials of Management Information Systems* (Upper Saddle River, NJ: Prentice Hall, 1995), p. 234.

23. M. Kessler, "Making Decisions by Long-Distance," *USA Today*, May 1, 2003, p. 3B.

24. J. Karaian, "Where Wireless Works," *CFO*, May 2003, pp. 81–83.

25. M. Boyle, "The Really Really Messy Wi-Fi Revolution," *Fortune*, May 12, 2003, pp. 86–92.

26. Statistics on "Worldwide Number of Mobile Users and Consumers, 2001," available on (*epaynews.com/statistics*), May 28, 2003.

27. K. Hafner, "For the Well Connected, All the World's an Office," *New York Times*, March 30, 2000, pp. D1+.

28. S. Luh, "Pulse Lunches at Asian Citibanks Feed Workers' Morale, Lower Job Turnover," *Wall Street Journal*, May 22, 2001, p. B11.

29. J. Simons, "Stop Moaning about Gripe Sites and Log On," *Fortune*, April 2, 2001, pp. 181–82.

30. "Internet Gripe Sites a Tool for Management," University of Melbourne Web site,

(*www.uninews.unimelb.edu.au/*), May 28, 2003.

31. J. Scanlon, "Woman of Substance," *Wired*, July 2002, p. 027.

32. H. Dolezalek, "Collaborating in Cyberspace," *Training*, April 2003, p. 33.

33. E. Wenger, R. McDermott, and W. Snyder, *Cultivating Communities of Practice: A Guide to Managing Knowledge* (Boston: Harvard Business School Press, 2002), p. 4.

34. Ibid., p. 39.

35. B.A. Gutek, M. Groth, and B. Cherry, "Achieving Service Success Through Relationship and Enhanced Encounters," *Academy of Management Executive*, November 2002, pp. 132–44.

36. R.C. Ford and C.P. Heaton, "Lessons from Hospitality That Can Serve Anyone," *Organizational Dynamics*, Summer 2001, pp. 30–47.

37. M.J. Bitner, B.H. Booms, and L.A. Mohr, "Critical Service Encounters: The Employee's Viewpoint," *Journal of Marketing*, October 1994, pp. 95–106.

38. S.D. Pugh, J. Dietz, J.W. Wiley, and S.M. Brooks, "Driving Service Effectiveness Through Employee-Customer Linkages," *Academy of Management Executive*, November 2002, pp. 73–84.

39. "Assisting Customers with Disabilities: A Summary of Policies and Guidelines Regarding the Assistance of Customers with Disabilities for the Sears Family of Companies," pamphlet from Sears, Roebuck and Company, obtained at Springfield, Missouri, Sears store, May 28, 2003.

40. M.L. LaGanga, "Are There Words That Neither Offend Nor Bore?" *Los Angeles Times*, May 18, 1994, pp. 11–27; and J. Leo, "Language in the Dumps," *U.S. News & World Report*, July 27, 1998, p. 16.

41. Situation adapted from information in: Thom Weidlich, "The Corporate Blog Is Catching On," *New York Times*, June 22, 2003, sec. 3, p. 12; "CNN Shuts Down Correspondent's Blog," *EuropeMedia*, March 24, 2003, *www.vandusseldorp.com*.

CHAPTER 12

1. Information from company Web site (*www.national.com.au*), January 5, 2003; and S. Greengard, "Brett Ellison," *IQ Magazine*, November–December 2002, p. 52.

2. P.M. Wright and G.C. McMahan, "Theoretical Perspectives for Strategic Human Resource Management," *Journal of Management* 18, no. 1 (1992), pp. 295–320; A.A. Lado and M.C. Wilson, "Human Resource Systems and Sustained Competitive Advantage," *Academy of Management Review*, October 1994, pp. 699–727; J. Pfeffer,

Competitive Advantage Through People (Boston: Harvard Business School Press, 1994); and J. Pfeffer, *The Human Equation* (Boston: Harvard Business School Press, 1998).

3. "Human Capital Index," Watson Wyatt Worldwide Web site (*www.watsonwyattcom/hci*), May 30, 2003.

4. See, for example, M.A. Huselid, "The Impact of Human Resource Management Practices on Turnover, Productivity, and Corporate Financial Performance," *Academy of Management Journal*, June 1995, pp. 635–72; M.J. Koch and R.G. McGrath, "Improving Labor Productivity: Human Resource Management Policies Do Matter," *Strategic Management Journal*, May 1996, pp. 335–54; B. Becker and B. Gerhart, "The Impact of Human Resource Management on Organizational Performance: Progress and Prospects," *Academy of Management Journal*, August 1996, pp. 779–801; J.T. Delaney and M.A. Huselid, "The Impact of Human Resource Management Practices on Perceptions of Organizational Performance," *Academy of Management Journal*, August 1996, pp. 949–69; M.A. Huselid, S.E. Jackson, and R.S. Schuler, "Technical and Strategic Human Resource Management Effectiveness as Determinants of Firm Performance," *Academy of Management Journal*, January 1997, pp. 171–88; A.S. Tsui, J.L. Pearce, L.W. Porter, and A.M. Tripoli, "Alternative Approaches to the Employee–Organization Relationship: Does Investment in Employees Pay Off?," *Academy of Management Journal*, October 1997, pp. 1089–1121; and R. Batt, "Managing Customer Services: Human Resource Practices, Quit Rates, and Sales Growth," *Academy of Management Journal*, June 2002, pp. 587–97.

5. "Human Capital a Key to Higher Market Value," *Business Finance*, December 1999, p. 15.

6. C. Tejada, "In Weak Economy, Management Has Advantage in U.S.," *Wall Street Journal*, December 17, 2002, pp. A2+; "Foreign Labor Trends–Germany," U.S. Department of Labor, 1999; "Foreign Labor Trends–Japan," U.S. Department of Labor, 2002; and "Foreign Labor Trends–Mexico," U.S. Department of Labor, 2002.

7. P. Digh, "Religion in the Workplace," *HRMagazine*, December 1998, p. 88.

8. S. Armour, "Lawsuits Pin Target on Managers," *USA Today* (*www.usatoday.com*), October 1, 2002.

9. J.S. McClenahen, "The Next Crisis: Too Few Workers," *IW*, May 2003, pp. 40–45; J. McCafferty, "Washington Weighs In," *CFO*, September 2002, p. 19.

10. "John Deere Lays the Foundation," *Training*, April 2001, p. 56.

11. J. Sullivan, "Workforce Planning: Why to Start Now," *Workforce*, September 2002, pp. 46–50.

12. T.J. Bergmann and M.S. Taylor, "College Recruitment: What Attracts Students to Organizations?" *Personnel*, May–June 1984, pp. 34–46; and A.S. Bargerstock and G. Swanson, "Four Ways to Build Cooperative Recruitment Alliances," *HRMagazine*, March 1991, p. 49.

13. J.R. Gordon, *Human Resource Management: A Practical Approach* (Boston: Allyn and Bacon, 1986), p. 170.

14. J. Hitt, "Are Brands Out of Hand?" *Fast Company*, November 2000, p. 52.

15. C. Lachnit, "Going for Generation Y," *Workforce*, April 2002, p. 16.

16. S. Burton and D. Warner, "The Future of Hiring—Top 5 Sources for Recruitment Today," *Workforce Vendor Directory 2002*, p. 75.

17. "FlipDog Flips Online Recruiting on End," *Workforce*, December 2002, p. 60.

18. See, for example, J.P. Kirnan, J.E. Farley, and K.F. Geisinger, "The Relationship between Recruiting Source, Applicant Quality, and Hire Performance: An Analysis by Sex, Ethnicity, and Age," *Personnel Psychology*, Summer 1989, pp. 293–308; and R.W. Griffeth, P.W. Hom, L.S. Fink, and D.J. Cohen, "Comparative Tests of Multivariate Models of Recruiting Sources Effects," *Journal of Management*, vol. 23, no. 1 (1997), pp. 19–36.

19. S. Caudron, "Who Are You Really Hiring?" *Workforce*, November 2002, pp. 28–32; and "Short Tenure," *Sports Illustrated* (*www.si.com*), December 15, 2001.

20. G.W. England, *Development and Use of Weighted Application Blanks*, rev. ed. (Minneapolis: Industrial Relations Center, University of Minnesota, 1971); J.J. Asher, "The Biographical Item: Can It Be Improved?" *Personnel Psychology*, Summer 1972, p. 266; G. Grimsley and H.F. Jarrett, "The Relation of Managerial Achievement to Test Measures Obtained in the Employment Situation: Methodology and Results," *Personnel Psychology*, Spring 1973, pp. 31–48; E.E. Ghiselli, "The Validity of Aptitude Tests in Personnel Selection," *Personnel Psychology*, Winter 1973, p. 475; I.T. Robertson and R.S. Kandola, "Work Sample Tests: Validity, Adverse Impact, and Applicant Reaction," *Journal of Occupational Psychology*, 55, no. 3 (1982), pp. 171–83; A.K. Korman, "The Prediction of Managerial Performance: A Review," *Personnel Psychology*, Summer 1986, pp. 295–

322; G.C. Thornton, *Assessment Centers in Human Resource Management* (Reading, MA: Addison-Wesley, 1992); C. Fernandez-Araoz, "Hiring without Firing," *Harvard Business Review*, July–August, 1999, pp. 108–20; and A.M. Ryan and R.E. Ployhart, "Applicants' Perceptions of Selection Procedures and Decisions: A Critical Review and Agenda for the Future," *Journal of Management*, vol. 26, no. 3 (2000), pp. 565–606.

21. G. Flynn, "A Legal Examination of Testing," *Workforce*, June 2002, pp. 92–94; S. Randall, "An Overview of Personality Testing in the Workforce," *Workforce* Online (*www.workforce.com*), December 13, 2000; S. Randall, "Legal Challenges to Personality Tests," *Workforce* Online (*www.workforce.com*), December 13, 2000; Gilbert Nicholson, "Tests and the Law," *Workforce*, October 2000, p. 73.

22. D.J. Woehr and W. Arthur Jr., "The Construct-Related Validity of Assessment Center Ratings: A Review and Meta-Analysis of the Role of Methodological Factors," *Journal of Management*, vol. 29, no. 2 (2003), pp. 231–58; and P.G.W. Jansen, and B.A.M. Stoop, "The Dynamics of Assessment Center Validity: Results of a 7-Year Study," *Journal of Applied Psychology*, August 2001, pp. 741–53.

23. R.L. Dipboye, *Selection Interviews: Process Perspectives* (Cincinnati: South-Western Publishing, 1992), p. 6.

24. See, for instance, R.D. Arveny and J.E. Campion, "The Employment Interview: A Summary and Review of Recent Research," *Personnel Psychology*, Summer 1982, pp. 281–322; and M.M. Harris, "Reconsidering the Employment Interview: A Review of Recent Literature and Suggestions for Future Research," *Personnel Psychology*, Winter 1989, pp. 691–726.

25. J. Merritt, "Improv at the Interview," *BusinessWeek*, February 3, 2003, p. 63.

26. S. Caudron, "Who Are You Really Hiring?"

27. P. Johnson, "Fibbing Applicants Filtered Out," *Springfield News Leader*, August 4, 2002, p. 6E.

28. See, for example, S.L. Premack and J.P. Wanous, "A Meta-Analysis of Realistic Job Preview Experiments," *Journal of Applied Psychology*, November 1985, pp. 706–20; J.A. Breaugh and M. Starke, "Research on Employee Recruitment: So Many Studies, So Many Remaining Questions," *Journal of Management*, vol. 26, no. 3 (2000), pp. 405–34; B.M. Meglino, E.C. Ravlin, A.S. DeNisi, "A Meta-Analytic Examination of Realistic Job Preview Effectiveness: A Test of Three Counterintuitive Propositions," *Human Resource Management Review*, vol. 10, no. 4 (2000), pp. 407–34; and Y.

Ganzach, A. Pazy, Y. Ohayun, and E. Brainin, "Social Exchange and Organizational Commitment: Decision-Making Training for Job Choice as an Alternative to the Realistic Job Preview," *Personnel Psychology*, Autumn 2002, pp. 613–37.

29. Information from company's Web site (*www.trilogy.com*), May 31, 2003; and N. M. Tichy, "No Ordinary Boot Camp," *Harvard Business Review*, April 2001, pp. 63–70.

30. C.L. Cooper, "The Changing Psychological Contract at Work: Revisiting the Job Demands-Control Model," *Occupational and Environmental Medicine*, June 2002, p. 355; D.M. Rousseau and S.A. Tijoriwala, "Assessing Psychological Contracts: Issues, Alternatives and Measures," *Journal of Organizational Behavior*, vol. 19 (1998), pp. 679–95; S.L. Robinson, M.S. Kraatz, and D.M. Rousseau, "Changing Obligations and the Psychological Contract: A Longitudinal Study," *Academy of Management Journal*, February 1994, pp. 137–52.

31. T. Raphael, "It's All in the Cards," *Workforce*, September 2002, p. 18.

32. T. Galvin, "2002 Industry Report," *Training*, October 2002, pp. 24–33.

33. J. Schettler, "Training Top 100: Top Five Profile and Ranking," *Training*, March 2003, pp. 40–41.

34. B. Hall, "The Top Training Priorities for 2003," *Training*, February 2003, p. 40; and T. Galvin, "2002 Industry Report."

35. B. Hall, "The Top Training Priorities for 2003."

36. U. Boser, "Gaming the System, One Click at a Time," *U.S. News & World Report*, October 28, 2002, p. 60.

37. S. Leibs, "Class Struggle," *CFO*, May 2002, pp. 31–32.

38. K. Clark, "Judgment Day," *U.S. News and World Report*, January 13, 2003, pp. 31–32; E.E. Lawler III, "The Folly of Forced Ranking," *Strategy & Business*, Third Quarter 2002, pp. 28–32; K. Cross, "The Weakest Links," *Business2.Com*, June 26, 2001, pp. 36–37; J. Greenwald, "Rank and Fire," *Time*, June 18, 2001, pp. 38–39; D. Jones, "More Firms Cut Workers Ranked at Bottom to Make Way for Talent," *USA Today*, May 30, 2001, pp. B1+; and M. Boyle, "Performance Reviews: Perilous Curves Ahead," *Fortune*, May 28, 2001, pp. 187–88.

39. K. Clark, "Judgment Day."

40. R.D. Bretz, Jr., G.T. Milkovich, and W. Read, "The Current State of Performance Appraisal Research and Practice: Concerns, Directions, and Implications," *Journal of Management*, June 1992, p. 331.

41. J.L. Seglin, "Reviewing Your Boss," *Fortune*, June 11, 2001, p. 248.

42. J.D. Glater, "Seasoning Compensation Stew," *New York Times*, March 7, 2001, pp. C1+.

43. This section based on R.I. Henderson, *Compensation Management in a Knowledge-Based World*, 9th ed. (Upper Saddle River, NJ: Prentice Hall, 2003).

44. L.R. Gomez-Mejia, "Structure and Process of Diversification, Compensation Strategy, and Firm Performance," *Strategic Management Journal*, 13 (1992), pp. 381–97; and E. Montemayor, "Congruence between Pay Policy and Competitive Strategy in High-Performing Firms," *Journal of Management*, 22, no. 6 (1996), pp. 889–908.

45. E.E. Lawler III, G.E. Ledford Jr., and L. Chang, "Who Uses Skill-Based Pay and Why," *Compensation and Benefits Review*, March–April 1993, p. 22; G.E. Ledford, "Paying for the Skills, Knowledge and Competencies of Knowledge Workers," *Compensation and Benefits Review*, July–August 1995, pp. 55–62; and C. Lee, K.S. Law, and P. Bobko, "The Importance of Justice Perceptions on Pay Effectiveness: A Two-Year Study of a Skill-Based Pay Plan," *Journal of Management*, vol. 26, no. 6 (1999), pp. 851–73.

46. M. Rowland, "It's What You Can Do That Counts," *New York Times*, June 6, 1993, p. F17.

47. D.E. Super and D.T. Hall, "Career Development: Exploration and Planning," in M.R. Rosenzweig and L.W. Porter (eds.), *Annual Review of Psychology*, vol. 29 (Palo Alto, CA: Annual Reviews, 1978), p. 334.

48. A.K. Smith, "Charting Your Own Course," *U.S. News & World Report*, November 6, 2000, pp. 56–65; S.E. Sullivan, "The Changing Nature of Careers: A Review and Research Agenda," *Journal of Management*, vol. 25, no. 3 (1999), pp. 457–84; D.T. Hall, "Protean Careers of the 21st Century," *Academy of Management Executive*, November 1996, pp. 8–16; M.B. Arthur and D.M. Rousseau, "A Career Lexicon for the 21st Century," *Academy of Management Executive*, November 1996, pp. 28–39; N. Nicholson, "Career Systems in Crisis: Change and Opportunity in the Information Age," *Academy of Management Executive*, November 1996, pp. 40–51; and K.R. Brousseau, M.J. Driver, K. Enertoh, and R. Larsson, "Career Pandemonium: Realigning Organizations and Individuals," *Academy of Management Executive*, November 1996, pp. 52–66.

49. Smith, "Charting Your Own Course"; and Hall, "Protean Careers of the 21st Century."

50. M.B. Arthur and D.M. Rousseau, *The Boundaryless Career: A New Employment Principle for a New Organizational Era* (New York: Oxford University Press, 1996).

51. M. Cianni and D. Wnuck, "Individual Growth and Team Enhancement: Moving toward a New Model of Career Development," *Academy of Management Executive*, February 1997, pp. 105–15.

52. D.E. Super, "A Life-Span Life Space Approach to Career Development," *Journal of Vocational Behavior*, Spring 1980, pp. 282–98; see also E.P. Cook and M. Arthur, *Career Theory Handbook* (Upper Saddle River, NJ: Prentice Hall, 1991), pp. 99–131; and L.S. Richman, "The New Worker Elite," *Fortune*, August 22, 1994, pp. 56–66.

53. R. Henkoff, "Winning the New Career Game," *Fortune*, July 12, 1993, pp. 46–49; "10 Tips for Managing Your Career," *Personnel Journal*, October 1995, p. 106; A. Fisher, "Six Ways to Supercharge Your Career," *Fortune*, January 13, 1997, pp. 46–48; A.K. Smith, "Charting Your Own Course;" and D.D. Dubois, "The 7 Stages of One's Career," *Training & Development*, December 2000, pp. 45–50.

54. L.T. Cullen, "Where Did Everyone Go?" *Time*, November 18, 2002, pp. 64–66.

55. S. Alleyne, "Stiff Upper Lips," *Black Enterprise*, April 2002, p. 59; C. Hymowitz, "Getting a Lean Staff to Do 'Ghost Work' of Departed Colleagues," *Wall Street Journal*, October 22, 2002, p. B1; and E. Krell, "Defusing Downsizing," *Business Finance*, December 2002, pp. 55–57.

56. Interview with Bill Gates, "Bill Gates on Rewiring the Power Structure," *Working Woman*, April 1994, p. 62; F. Moody, "Wonder Women in the Rude Boys' Paradise," *Fast Company* Web Page (*www.fastcompany.com*), April 17, 1997.

57. R. Leger, "Linked by Differences," *Springfield News Leader*, December 31, 1993, pp. B6+.

58. J. Hickman, "America's 50 Best Companies for Minorities," *Fortune*, July 8, 2002, pp. 110–20; and J. Kahn, "Diversity Trumps the Downturn," *Fortune*, July 9, 2001, pp. 114–16.

59. "Sexual Harassment Charges FY 1992–FY2002," *The U.S. Equal Employment Opportunity Commission* (*www.eeoc.gov*), June 1, 2003.

60. A.B. Fisher, "Sexual Harassment, What to Do," *Fortune*, August 23, 1993, pp. 84–88.

61. P.M. Buhler, "The Manager's Role in Preventing Sexual Harassment," *Supervision*, April 1999, p. 18; and "Cost of Sexual Harassment in the

U.S.," *The Webb Report: A Newsletter on Sexual Harassment* (Seattle, WA: Premier Publishing, Ltd.), January 1994, pp. 4–7 and April 1994, pp. 2–5.

62. "U.S. Leads Way in Sex Harassment Laws, Study Says," *Evening Sun*, November 30, 1992, pp. A1+; and W. Hardman and J. Heidelberg, "When Sexual Harassment Is a Foreign Affair," *Personnel Journal*, April 1996, pp. 91–97.

63. Although the male gender was referred to in this case, it is important to note that sexual harassment may involve persons of either sex sexually harassing others or a person of the same sex harassing another individual. (See, for instance, *Oncale v. Sundowner Offshore Service Inc.*, 118 S. Ct. 998.)

64. "Facts About Sexual Harassment," *The U.S. Equal Employment Opportunity Commission* (www.eeoc.gov), June 1, 2003.

65. Ibid.

66. A. Fisher, "After All This Time, Why Don't People Know What Sexual Harassment Means?" *Fortune*, January 12, 1998, p. 68; and A.R. Karr, "Companies Crack Down on the Increasing Sexual Harassment by E-Mail," *Wall Street Journal*, September 21, 1999, p. A1.

67. See T.S. Bland and S.S. Stalcup, "Managing Harassment," *Human Resource Management*, Spring 2001, pp. 51–61; K.A. Hess and D.R.M. Ehrens, "Sexual Harassment—Affirmative Defense to Employer Liability," *Benefits Quarterly*, Second Quarter 1999, p. 57; J.A. Segal, "The Catch-22s of Remedying Sexual Harassment Complaints," *HRMagazine*, October 1997, pp. 111–17; S.C. Bahls and J.E. Bahls, "Hands-Off Policy," *Entrepreneur*, July 1997, pp. 74–76; J.A. Segal, "Where Are We Now?" *HRMagazine*, October 1996, pp. 69–73; B. McAfee and D.L. Deadrick, "Teach Employees to Just Say No," *HRMagazine*, February 1996, pp. 86–89; G.D. Block, "Avoiding Liability for Sexual Harassment," *HRMagazine*, April 1995, pp. 91–97; and J.A. Segal, "Stop Making Plaintiffs' Lawyers Rich," *HRMagazine*, April 1995, pp. 31–35. Also, it should be noted here that under the Title VII and the Civil Rights Act of 1991, the maximum award that can be given, under the Federal Act, is $300,000. However, many cases are tried under state laws that permit unlimited punitive damages, such as the $7.1 million that Rena Weeks received in her trial based on California statutes.

68. C. Oglesby, "More Options for Moms Seeking Work–Family Balance," (www.cnn.com), May 10, 2001.

69. "On the Daddy Track," *Wall Street Journal*, May 11, 2000, pp. A1+.

70. F. Hansen, "Truths and Myths about Work/Life Balance," *Workforce*, December 2002, pp. 34–39.

71. S.D. Friedman and J.H. Greenhaus, *Work and Family—Allies or Enemies?* (New York: Oxford University Press, 2000).

72. N.P. Rothbard, T.L. Dumas, and K.W. Phillips, "The Long Arm of the Organization: Work-Family Policies and Employee Preferences for Segmentation," paper presented at the 61st Annual Academy of Management meeting, Washington, DC, August 2001.

73. Situation adapted from information in: John Russell, "Older Goodyear Workers Who Say Age Played into Evaluations Get Day in Court," *Akron Beacon Journal*, July 3, 2003, www.ohio.com/bj; Kim Clark, "Judgment Day," *U.S. News and World Report*, January 13, 2003, pp. 31–32.

CHAPTER 13

1. Information from company Web site (www.rrdonnelley.com), and Hoover's Online (www.hoovers.com), January 5, 2003; and S. Fitch, "Pressing for Change," *Forbes*, November 25, 2002, pp. 82–87.

2. J.S. McClenahen, "Waking Up to a New World," *Industry Week*, June 2003, pp. 22–26.

3. C.R. Leana and B. Barry, "Stability and Change as Simultaneous Experiences in Organizational Life," *Academy of Management Review*, October 2000, pp. 753–759.

4. E. Nee, "The Hottest CEO in Tech," *Business 2.0*, June 2003, p. 86.

5. The idea for these metaphors came from J.E. Dutton, S.J. Ashford, R.M. O'Neill, and K.A. Lawrence, "Moves that Matter: Issue Selling and Organizational Change," *Academy of Management Journal*, August 2001, pp. 716–36; B.H. Kemelgor, S.D. Johnson, and S. Srinivasan, "Forces Driving Organizational Change: A Business School Perspective," *Journal of Education for Business*, January/February 2000, pp. 133–37; G. Colvin, "When It Comes to Turbulence, CEOs Could Learn a Lot from Sailors," *Fortune*, March 29, 1999, pp. 194–96; and P.B. Vaill, *Managing as a Performing Art: New Ideas for a World of Chaotic Change* (San Francisco: Jossey-Bass, 1989).

6. K. Lewin, *Field Theory in Social Science* (New York: Harper & Row, 1951).

7. G. Hamel, "Take It Higher," *Fortune*, February 5, 2001, pp. 169–70.

8. Information on company from Web site (www.converse.com) and Hoover's Online (www.hoovers.com), June 6, 2003; and M. Davids, "Wanted: Strategic Planners," *Journal of Business Strategy*, May–June 1995, pp. 30–38.

9. "Hallmark Spots Emerging Trends for 2003 and Beyond," Hallmark Web site (www.hallmark.com), June 6, 2003.

10. S. Crock, J. Carey, P. Magnusson, G. Smith, and O. Port, "Storming the Streets of Baghdad," *BusinessWeek*, October 21, 2002, pp. 46–47.

11. J. Jesitus, "Change Management: Energy to the People," *IW*, September 1, 1997, pp. 37, 40.

12. D. Lavin, "European Business Rushes to Automate," *Wall Street Journal*, July 23, 1997, p. A14.

13. See, for example, T.C. Head and P.F. Sorensen, "Cultural Values and Organizational Development: A Seven-Country Study," *Leadership & Organization Development Journal*, March 1993, pp. 3–7; A.H. Church, W.W. Burke, and D.F. Van Eynde, "Values, Motives, and Interventions of Organization Development Practitioners," *Group & Organization Management*, March 1994, pp. 5–50; W.L. French and C.H. Bell Jr., *Organization Development: Behavioral Science Interventions for Organization Improvement*, 6th ed. (Upper Saddle River, NJ: Prentice Hall, 1998); N.A. Worren, K. Ruddle, and K. Moore, "From Organizational Development to Change Management," *Journal of Applied Behavioral Science*, September 1999, pp. 273–86; G. Farias, "Organizational Development and Change Management," *Journal of Applied Behavioral Science*, September 2000, pp. 376–79; W. Nicolay, "Response to Farias and Johnson's Commentary," *Journal of Applied Behavioral Science*, September 2000, p. 380–81; S. Hicks, "What Is Organization Development?" *Training & Development*, August 2000, p. 65.

14. T. White, "Supporting Change: How Communicators at Scotiabank Turned Ideas Into Action," *Communication World*, April 2002, pp. 22–24.

15. See, for example, B.M. Staw, "Counterforces to Change," in P.S. Goodman and Associates (eds.), *Change in Organizations* (San Francisco: Jossey-Bass, 1982), pp. 87–121; A.A. Armenakis and A.G. Bedeian, "Organizational Change: A Review of Theory and Research in the 1990s," *Journal of Management*, vol. 25, no. 3 (1999), pp. 293–315; C.R. Wanberg and J.T. Banas, "Predictors and Outcomes of Openness to Changes in a Reorganizing Workplace," *Journal of Applied Psychology*, February 2000, pp. 132–42; S.K. Piderit, "Rethinking Resistance and Recognizing Ambivalence: A Multidimensional

View of Attitudes Toward an Organizational Change," *Academy of Management Review*, October 2000, pp. 783–794; R. Kegan and L.L. Lahey, "The Real Reason People Won't Change," *Harvard Business Review*, November 2001, pp. 85–92; M.A. Korsgaard, H.J. Sapienza, and D.M. Schweiger, "Beaten Before Begun: The Role of Procedural Justice in Planning Change," *Journal of Management*, vol. 28, no. 4 (2002), pp. 497–516; and C.E. Cunningham, C.A. Woodward, H.S. Shannon, J. MacIntosh, B. Lendrum, D. Rosenbloom, and J. Brown, "Readiness for Organizational Change: A Longitudinal Study of Workplace, Psychological and Behavioral Correlates," *Journal of Occupational and Organizational Psychology*, December 2002, pp. 377–92.

16. J.P. Kotter and L.A. Schlesinger, "Choosing Strategies for Change," *Harvard Business Review*, March–April 1979, pp. 107–9; P. Strebel, "Why Do Employees Resist Change?" *Harvard Business Review*, May–June 1996, pp. 86–92; J. Mariotti, "Troubled by Resistance to Change," *IW*, October 7, 1996, p. 30; and A. Reichers, J.P. Wanous, and J.T. Austin, "Understanding and Managing Cynicism about Organizational Change," *Academy of Management Executive*, February 1997, pp. 48–57.

17. Kotter and Schlesinger, "Choosing Strategies for Change," pp. 106–11; K. Matejka and R. Julian, "Resistance to Change Is Natural," *Supervisory Management*, October 1993, p. 10; C. O'Connor, "Resistance: The Repercussions of Change," *Leadership & Organization Development Journal*, October 1993, pp. 30–36; J. Landau, "Organizational Change and Barriers to Innovation: A Case Study in the Italian Public Sector," *Human Relations*, December 1993, pp. 1411–29; A. Sagie and M. Koslowsky, "Organizational Attitudes and Behaviors as a Function of Participation in Strategic and Tactical Change Decisions: An Application of Path-Goal Theory," *Journal of Organizational Behavior*, January 1994, pp. 37–47; V.D. Miller, J.R. Johnson, and J. Grau, "Antecedents to Willingness to Participate in a Planned Organizational Change," *Journal of Applied Communication Research*, February 1994, pp. 59–80; P. Pritchett and R. Pound, *The Employee Handbook for Organizational Change* (Dallas: Pritchett Publishing, 1994); R. Maurer, *Beyond the Wall of Resistance: Unconventional Strategies That Build Support for Change* (Austin: TX Bard Books, 1996); D. Harrison, "Assess and Remove Barriers to Change," *HR Focus*, July 1999, pp. 9–10; L.K. Lewis, "Disseminating Information and Soliciting Input During Planned Organizational Change," *Management

Communication Quarterly*, August 1999, pp. 43–75; J.P. Wanous, A.E. Reichers, and J.T. Austin, "Cynicism about Organizational Change," *Group & Organization Management*, June 2000, pp. 132–53; K.W. Mossholder, R.P. Settoon, A.A. Armenakis, and S.G. Harris, "Emotion During Organizational Transformations," *Group & Organization Management*, September 2000, pp. 220–43; and Piderit, "Rethinking Resistance and Recognizing Ambivalence."

18. Based on H. Ibarra, "How to Stay Stuck in the Wrong Career," *Harvard Business Review*, December 2002, pp. 40–47; "Before Uprooting Your Career," *BusinessWeek*, October 22, 2001, p. 131; N.G. Carr, "Being Virtual: Character and the New Economy," *Harvard Business Review*, May–June 1999, pp. 181–90; B. Kaye, "Career Development—Anytime, Anyplace," *Training & Development*, December 1993, pp. 46–49; A.D. Pinkney, "Winning in the Workplace," *Essence*, March 1994, pp. 79–80; C.B. Bardwell, "Career Planning & Job Search Guide 1994," *The Black Collegian*, March–April 1994, pp. 59–64; and W. Kiechel III, "A Manager's Career in the New Economy," *Fortune*, April 4, 1994, pp. 68–72.

19. C. Hymowitz, "How Leader at 3M Got His Employees to Back Big Changes," *Wall Street Journal*, April 23, 2002, p. B1; and J. Useem, "Jim McNerney Thinks He Can Turn 3M from a Good Company into a Great One—With a Little Help from his Former Employer; General Electric," *Fortune*, August 12, 2002, pp. 127–32.

20. See T.H. Fitzgerald, "Can Change in Organizational Culture Really Be Managed?" *Organizational Dynamics*, Autumn 1988, pp. 5–15; B. Dumaine, "Creating a New Company Culture," *Fortune*, January 15, 1990, pp. 127–31; P.F. Drucker, "Don't Change Corporate Culture—Use It!" *Wall Street Journal*, March 28, 1991, p. A14; J. Martin, *Cultures in Organizations: Three Perspectives* (New York: Oxford University Press, 1992); D.C. Pheysey, *Organizational Cultures: Types and Transformations* (London: Routledge, 1993); C.G. Smith and R.P. Vecchio, "Organizational Culture and Strategic Management: Issues in the Strategic Management of Change," *Journal of Managerial Issues*, Spring 1993, pp. 53–70; P. Bate, *Strategies for Cultural Change* (Boston: Butterworth-Heinemann, 1994); and P. Anthony, *Managing Culture* (Philadelphia: Open University Press, 1994).

21. K. Maney, "Famously Gruff Gerstner Leaves IBM a Changed Man," *USA Today*, November 11, 2002, pp. 1B+; and Louis V. Gerstner, *Who Says Ele-

phants Can't Dance: Inside IBM's Historic Turnaround* (New York: Harper Business, 2002).

22. See, for example, R.H. Kilmann, M.J. Saxton, and R. Serpa (eds.), *Gaining Control of the Corporate Culture* (San Francisco: Jossey-Bass, 1985); and D.C. Hambrick and S. Finkelstein, "Managerial Discretion: A Bridge between Polar Views of Organizational Outcomes," in L.L. Cummings and B.M. Staw (eds.), *Research in Organizational Behavior*, vol. 9 (Greenwich, CT: JAI Press, 1987), p. 384.

23. Based on C. Lindsay, "Paradoxes of Organizational Diversity: Living within the Paradoxes," in L.R. Jauch and J.L. Wall (eds.), *Proceedings of the 50th Academy of Management Conference*, San Francisco, 1990, pp. 374–78.

24. M.A. Cavanaugh, W.R. Boswell, M.V. Roehling, and J.W. Boudreau, "An Empirical Examination of Self-Reported Work Stress among U.S. Managers," *Journal of Applied Psychology*, February 2000, pp. 65–74; M.A. Verespej, "Stressed Out," *IW*, February 21, 2000, pp. 30–34; J. Laabs, "Time-Starved Workers Rebel," *Workforce*, October 2000, pp. 26–28; and C. Daniels, "The Last Taboo," *Fortune*, October 28, 2002, pp. 137–44.

25. "Too Much Work, Too Little Time," *BusinessWeek*, July 16, 2001, p. 12.

26. Adapted from R.S. Schuler, "Definition and Conceptualization of Stress in Organizations," *Organizational Behavior and Human Performance*, April 1980, p. 189. For an updated review of definitions, see R.L. Kahn and P. Byosiere, "Stress in Organizations," in M.D. Dunnette and L.J. Hough (eds.), *Handbook of Industrial and Organizational Psychology* vol. 3, 2d ed. (Palo Alto, CA: Consulting Psychologists Press, 1992), pp. 573–80.

27. Schuler, "Definition and Conceptualization of Stress in Organizations," p. 191.

28. S.E. Jackson, "Participation in Decision Making as a Strategy for Reducing Job-Related Strain," *Journal of Applied Psychology*, February 1983, pp. 3–19; C.D. Fisher, "Boredom at Work: A Neglected Concept," *Human Relations*, March 1993, pp. 395–417; C.A. Heaney et al., "Industrial Relations, Worksite Stress Reduction and Employee Well-Being: A Participatory Action Research Investigation," *Journal of Organizational Behavior*, September 1993, pp. 495–510; P. Froiland, "What Cures Job Stress?" *Training*, December 1993, pp. 32–36; C.L. Cooper and S. Cartwright, "Healthy Mind, Healthy Organization—A Proactive Approach to Occupational Stress," *Human Relations*, April 1994, pp. 455–71; A.A. Brott, "New Approaches to Job

Stress," *Nation's Business*, May 1994, pp. 81–82; and Daniels, "The Last Taboo."

29. See R.S. Schuler, "Time Management: A Stress Management Technique," *Personnel Journal*, December 1979, pp. 851–55; and M.E. Haynes, *Practical Time Management: How to Make the Most of Your Most Perishable Resource* (Tulsa, OK: Penn Well Books, 1985).

30. P.J. Kiger, "Optimas Award Innovation: Healthy, Wealthy, and Wise," *Workforce*, July 2003, pp. 41–42; Well Workplace Award Executive Summaries, Coors Brewing Company and Lab Safety Supply, available on Wellness Councils of America Web site (*www.welcoa.org*).

31. S.F. Gale, "Seminars and Wills on Wheels," *Workforce*, May 2002, pp. 68–69.

32. P.A. McLagan, "Change Leadership Today," *T & D*, November 2002, pp. 27–31.

33. Ibid., p. 29.

34. C. Haddad, "UPS: Can It Keep Delivering?" *Business Week Online Extra* (*www.businessweek.com*), Spring 2003.

35. W. Pietersen, "The Mark Twain Dilemma: The Theory and Practice for Change Leadership," *Journal of Business Strategy*, September–October 2002, pp. 32–37; C. Hymowitz, "To Maintain Success, Managers Must Learn How to Direct Change," *Wall Street Journal*, August 13, 2002, p. B1; and J.E. Dutton, S.J. Ashford, R.M. O'Neill, and K.A. Lawrence, "Moves That Matter: Issue Selling and Organizational Change," *Academy of Management Journal*, August 2001, pp. 716–736.

36. W. Pietersen, "The Mark Twain Dilemma: The Theory and Practice for Change Leadership," p. 35.

37. P.A. McLagan, "The Change-Capable Organization," *T & D*, January 2003, pp. 50–58.

38. R.M. Kanter, "From Spare Change to Real Change: The Social Sector as Beta Site for Business Innovation," *Harvard Business Review*, May–June 1999, pp. 122–132.

39. J.E. Perry-Smith and C.E. Shalley, "The Social Side of Creativity: A Static and Dynamic Social Network Perspective," *Academy of Management Review*, January 2003, pp. 89–106; and P.K. Jagersma, "Innovate or Die: It's Not Easy, but It Is Possible to Enhance Your Organization's Ability to Innovate," *Journal of Business Strategy*, January–February 2003, pp. 25–28.

40. These definitions are based on T.M. Amabile, *Creativity in Context* (Boulder, CO: Westview Press, 1996).

41. R.W. Woodman, J.E. Sawyer, and R.W. Griffin, "Toward a Theory of Organizational Creativity," *Academy of Management Review*, April 1993, pp. 293–321.

42. F. Damanpour, "Organizational Innovation: A Meta-Analysis of Effects of Determinants and Moderators," *Academy of Management Journal*, September 1991, pp. 555–90; S.D. Saleh and C.K. Wang, "The Management of Innovation: Strategy, Structure, and Organizational Climate," *IEEE Transactions on Engineering Management*, February 1993, pp. 14–22; G.R. Oldham and A. Cummings, "Employee Creativity: Personal and Contextual Factors at Work," *Academy of Management Journal*, June 1996, pp. 607–34; J.B. Sorensen and T.E. Stuart, "Aging, Obsolescence, and Organizational Innovation," *Administrative Science Quarterly*, March 2000, pp. 81–112; T.M. Amabile, C.N. Hadley, and S.J. Kramer, "Creativity under the Gun," *Harvard Business Review*, August 2002, pp. 52–61; and N. Madjar, G.R. Oldham, and M. G. Pratt, "There's No Place Like Home? The Contributions of Work and Nonwork Creativity Support to Employees' Creative Performance," *Academy of Management Journal*, August 2002, pp. 757–67.

43. P.R. Monge, M.D. Cozzens, and N.S. Contractor, "Communication and Motivational Predictors of the Dynamics of Organizational Innovations," *Organization Science*, May 1992, pp. 250–74.

44. Amabile, Hadley, and Kramer, "Creativity under the Gun."

45. Madjar, Oldham, and Pratt, "There's No Place Like Home?"

46. For more information on 3M's innovation efforts, check out its Web site (*www.3m.com*); and E. von Hippel, S. Thomke, and M. Sonnack, "Creating Breakthroughs at 3M," *Harvard Business Review*, September–October 1999, pp. 47–57.

47. C. Salter, "Mattel Learns to 'Throw the Bunny,'" *Fast Company*, November 2002, p. 22.

48. See, for instance, Amabile, *Creativity in Context*, M. Tushman and D. Nadler, "Organizing for Innovation," *California Management Review*, Spring 1986, pp. 74–92; R. Moss Kanter, "When a Thousand Flowers Bloom: Structural, Collective, and Social Conditions for Innovation in Organization," in B.M. Staw and L.L. Cummings (eds.), *Research in Organizational Behavior*, vol. 10 (Greenwich, CT: JAI Press, 1988), pp. 169–211; G. Morgan, "Endangered Species: New Ideas," *Business Month*, April 1989, pp. 75–77; S.G. Scott and R.A. Bruce, "Determinants of Innovative People: A Path Model of Individual Innovation in the Workplace," *Academy of Management Journal*, June 1994, pp. 580–607; T.M. Amabile, R. Conti, H. Coon, J. Lazenby, and M. Herron, "Assessing the Work Environment for Creativity," *Academy of Management Journal*, October 1996, pp. 1154–84; A. deGues, "The Living Company," *Harvard Business Review*, March–April 1997, pp. 51–59; J. Zhou, "Feedback Valence, Feedback Style, Task Autonomy, and Achievement Orientation: Interactive Effects on Creative Behavior," *Journal of Applied Psychology*, vol. 83 (1998), pp. 261–276; G. Hamel, "Reinvent Your Company," *Fortune*, June 12, 2000, pp. 98–118; J.M. George and J. Zhou, "When Openness to Experience and Conscientiousness are Related to Creative Behavior: An Interactional Approach," *Journal of Applied Psychology*, June 2001, pp. 513–24; and Perry-Smith and Shalley, "The Social Side of Creativity: A Static and Dynamic Social Network Perspective."

49. J.M. Howell and C.A. Higgins, "Champions of Change," *Business Quarterly*, Spring 1990, pp. 31–32; P.A. Carrow-Moffett, "Change Agent Skills: Creating Leadership for School Renewal," *NASSP Bulletin*, April 1993, pp. 57–62; T. Stjernberg and A. Philips, "Organizational Innovations in a Long-Term Perspective: Legitimacy and Souls-of-Fire as Critical Factors of Change and Viability," *Human Relations*, October 1993, pp. 1193–2023; and J. Ramos, "Producing Change That Lasts," *Across the Board*, March 1994, pp. 29–33.

50. The Associated Press, "Mars Rover is Launched on Voyage to Look for Water," *USA Today*, (*www.usatoday.com*), June 11, 2003; NASA's Web site (*www.nasa.gov*), June 11, 2003; and W.J. Broad, "A Tiny Rover, Built on the Cheap, Is Ready to Explore Distant Mars," *New York Times*, July 5, 1997, p. 9.

51. Situation adapted from information in: "The Intrusive Elected Official," *Public Management*, May 2003, pp. 2+; Robb Quincey and Rod Foster, "A Turnaround Story of Success," *Public Management*, March 2003, pp. 12+.

PART FOUR

1. J. Hovey, "25 Growing Companies," *Industry Week*, November 20, 2000, p. 66.

2. R.D. Schatz, "A Perfect Blendship," *Business Week Enterprise*, March 1, 1999, p. ENT 20.

3. I.O. Williamson, "Employer Legitimacy and Recruitment Success in Small Businesses," *Entrepreneurship Theory and Practice*, Fall 2000, pp. 27–42.

4. R.L. Heneman, J.W. Tansky, and S.M. Camp, "Human Resource Management Practices in Small and Medium-Sized Enterprises: Unanswered Questions and Future Research Perspectives," *Entrepreneurship Theory and Practice*, Fall 2000, pp. 11–26.

5. Ibid.

6. "Best Employer," *Working Woman*, May 1999, p. 54.

7. Heneman, Tansky, and Camp, "Human Resource Management Practices in Small and Medium-Sized Enterprises: Unanswered Questions and Future Research Perspectives."

8. Based on G. Fuchsberg, "Small Firms Struggle with Latest Management Trends," *Wall Street Journal*, August 26, 1993, p. B2; M. Barrier, "Re-engineering Your Company," *Nation's Business*, February 1994, pp. 16–22; J. Weiss, "Reengineering the Small Business," *Small Business Reports*, May 1994, pp. 37–43; and K.D. Godsey, "Back on Track," *Success*, May 1997, pp. 52–54.

9. Company information from Hoover's Online (*www.hoovers.com*), July 7, 2003; and R. Wherry, "Full Speed Ahead," *Forbes*, January 7, 2002, p. 142.

10. G.N. Chandler, C. Keller, and D.W. Lyon, "Unraveling the Determinants and Consequences of an Innovation-Supportive Organizational Culture," *Entrepreneurship Theory and Practice*, Fall 2000, pp. 59–76.

11. Ibid.

CHAPTER 14

1. Information from company Web site (*www.panerabread.com*), January 5, 2003; C. Hymowitz, "Panera CEO's Recipe: Learn from the Past, Anticipate the Trends," *Wall Street Journal*, June 10, 2003, p. B1; J. Suhr, "Panera Knows How to Make the Dough," *Springfield News-Leader*, March 29, 2003, p. 5B; and L. Tischler, "Vote of Confidence," *Fast Company*, December 2002, pp. 110–12.

2. D.W. Organ, *Organizational Citizenship Behavior: The Good Soldier Syndrome* (Lexington, MA: Lexington Books, 1988), p. 4. See also J.A. LePine, A. Erez, and D. E. Johnson, "The Nature and Dimensionality of Organizational Citizenship Behavior: A Critical Review and Meta-Analysis," *Journal of Applied Psychology*, February 2002, pp. 52–65.

3. P.M. Podsakoff, S.B. MacKenzie, J.B. Paine, and D.G. Bachrach, "Organizational Citizenship Behaviors: A Critical Review of the Theoretical and Empirical Literature and Suggestions for Future Research," *Journal of Management*, vol. 26, no. 3 (2000), pp. 543–48.

4. S.J. Breckler, "Empirical Validation of Affect, Behavior, and Cognition as Distinct Components of Attitude," *Journal of Personality and Social Psychology*, May 1984, pp. 1191–1205; and S.L. Crites, Jr., L.R. Fabrigar, and R.E. Petty, "Measuring the Affective and Cognitive Properties of Attitudes: Conceptual and Methodological Issues," *Personality and Social Psychology Bulletin*, December 1994, pp. 619–34.

5. P.P. Brooke, Jr., D.W. Russell, and J.L. Price, "Discriminant Validation of Measures of Job Satisfaction, Job Involvement, and Organizational Commitment," *Journal of Applied Psychology*, May 1988, pp. 139–45; and R.T. Keller, "Job Involvement and Organizational Commitment as Longitudinal Predictors of Job Performance: A Study of Scientists and Engineers," *Journal of Applied Psychology*, August 1997, pp. 539–45.

6. A.F. Chelte, J. Wright, and C. Tausky, "Did Job Satisfaction Really Drop During the 1970s?" *Monthly Labor Review*, November 19, 1982, pp. 33–36; "Job Satisfaction High in America, Says Conference Board Study," *Monthly Labor Review*, February 1985, p. 52; C. Hartman and S. Pearlstein, "The Job of Working," *Inc.*, November 1987, pp. 61–66; E. Graham, "Work May Be a Rat Race, but It's Not a Daily Grind," *Wall Street Journal*, September 19, 1997, p. R1; and J.L. Seglin, "Americans @ Work," *Inc.*, June 1998, pp. 91–94.

7. G. Koretz, "Hate your Job? Join the Club", *Business Week*, October, 6, 2003, pp. 40.

8. R. Gardyn, "Happiness Grows on Trees," *American Demographics*, May 2001, pp. 18–21.

9. C. Ostroff, "The Relationship Between Satisfaction, Attitudes, and Performance: An Organizational Level Analysis," *Journal of Applied Psychology*, December 1992, pp. 963–74; and A.M. Ryan, M.J. Schmit, and R. Johnson, "Attitudes and Effectiveness: Examining Relations at an Organizational Level," *Personnel Psychology*, Winter 1996, pp. 853–82.

10. E.A. Locke, "The Nature and Causes of Job Satisfaction," in M.D. Dunnette (ed.), *Handbook of Industrial and Organizational Psychology* (Chicago: Rand McNally, 1976), p. 1331; S.L. McShane, "Job Satisfaction and Absenteeism: A Meta-Analytic Re-Examination," *Canadian Journal of Administrative Science*, June 1984, pp. 61–77; R.D. Hackett and R.M. Guion, "A Reevaluation of the Absenteeism–Job Satisfaction Relationship," *Organizational Behavior and Human Decision Processes*, June 1985, pp. 340–81; K.D.

Scott and G.S. Taylor, "An Examination of Conflicting Findings on the Relationship Between Job Satisfaction and Absenteeism: A Meta-Analysis," *Academy of Management Journal*, September 1985, pp. 599–612; R.D. Hackett, "Work Attitudes and Employee Absenteeism: A Synthesis of the Literature," paper presented at the 1988 National Academy of Management Meeting, Anaheim, California, August 1988; and R. Steel and J.R. Rentsch, "Influence of Cumulation Strategies on the Long-Range Prediction of Absenteeism," *Academy of Management Journal*, December 1995, pp. 1616–34.

11. W. Hom and R.W. Griffeth, *Employee Turnover* (Cincinnati, OH: Southwestern, 1995); R.W. Griffth, P.W. Hom, and S. Gaertner, "A Meta-Analysis of Antecedents and Correlates of Employee Turnover: Update, Moderator Tests, and Research Implications for the Next Millennium," *Journal of Management*, vol. 26, no. 3 (2000), p. 479; P.W. Hom and A.J. Kinicki, "Toward a Greater Understanding of How Dissatisfaction Drives Employee Turnover," *Academy of Management Journal*, October 2001, pp. 975–87.

12. See, for example, C.L. Hulin, M. Roznowski, and D. Hachiya, "Alternative Opportunities and Withdrawal Decisions: Empirical and Theoretical Discrepancies and an Integration," *Psychological Bulletin*, July 1985, pp. 233–50; and J.M. Carsten and P.E. Spector, "Unemployment, Job Satisfaction, and Employee Turnover: A Meta-Analytic Test of the Muchinsky Model," *Journal of Applied Psychology*, August 1987, pp. 374–81.

13. D.G. Spencer and R.M. Steers, "Performance as a Moderator of the Job Satisfaction–Turnover Relationship," *Journal of Applied Psychology*, August 1981, pp. 511–14.

14. See, for instance, B. Schneider and D.E. Bowen, "Employee and Customer Perceptions of Service in Banks: Replication and Extension," *Journal of Applied Psychology*, August 1985, pp. 423–33; W.W. Tornow and J.W. Wiley, "Service Quality and Management Practices: A Look at Employee Attitudes, Customer Satisfaction, and Bottom-line Consequences," *Human Resource Planning*, vol. 4, no. 2 (1991), pp. 105–16; E. Naumann and D.W. Jackson, Jr., "One More Time: How Do You Satisfy Customers?" *Business Horizons*, May–June 1999, pp. 71–76; D.J. Koys, "The Effects of Employee Satisfaction, Organizational Citizenship Behavior, and Turnover on Organizational Effectiveness: A Unit-Level, Longitudinal Study," *Personnel Psychology*, Spring 2001, pp. 101–14; J.

Griffith, "Do Satisfied Employees Satisfy Customers? Support-Services Staff Morale and Satisfaction among Public School Administrators, Students, and Parents," *Journal of Applied Social Psychology*, August 2001, pp. 1627–58; and J.K. Harter, F.L. Schmidt, and T.L. Hayes, "Business-Unit-Level Relationship Between Employee Satisfaction, Employee Engagement, and Business Outcomes: A Meta-Analysis," *Journal of Applied Psychology*, April 2002, pp. 268–79.

15. M.J. Bittner, B.H. Blooms, and L.A. Mohr, "Critical Service Encounters: The Employees' Viewpoint," *Journal of Marketing*, October 1994, pp. 95–106.

16. See, for example, S. Rabinowitz and D.T. Hall, "Organizational Research in Job Involvement," *Psychological Bulletin*, March 1977, pp. 265–88; G.J. Blau, "A Multiple Study Investigation of the Dimensionality of Job Involvement," *Journal of Vocational Behavior*, August 1985, pp. 19–36; and N.A. Jans, "Organizational Factors and Work Involvement," *Organizational Behavior and Human Decision Processes*, June 1985, pp. 382–96.

17. G.J. Blau, "Job Involvement and Organizational Commitment as Interactive Predictors of Tardiness and Absenteeism," *Journal of Management*, Winter 1986, pp. 577–84; and K. Boal and R. Cidambi, "Attitudinal Correlates of Turnover and Absenteeism: A Meta-Analysis," paper presented at the meeting of the American Psychological Association, Toronto, Canada, 1984.

18. G.J. Blau and K. Boal, "Conceptualizing How Job Involvement and Organizational Commitment Affect Turnover and Absenteeism," *Academy of Management Review*, April 1987, p. 290.

19. See, for instance, W. Hom, R. Katerberg, and C.L. Hulin, "Comparative Examination of Three Approaches to the Prediction of Turnover," *Journal of Applied Psychology*, June 1979, pp. 280–90; R.T. Mowday, L.W. Porter, and R.M. Steers, *Employee Organization Linkages: The Psychology of Commitment, Absenteeism, and Turnover* (New York: Academic Press, 1982); H. Angle and J. Perry, "Organizational Commitment: Individual and Organizational Influence," *Work and Occupations*, May 1983, pp. 123–45; and J.L. Pierce and R.B. Dunham, "Organizational Commitment: Pre-Employment Propensity and Initial Work Experiences," *Journal of Management*, Spring 1987, pp. 163–78.

20. L.W. Porter, R.M. Steers, R.T. Mowday, and V. Boulian, "Organizational Commitment, Job Satisfaction, and Turnover among Psychiatric Techni-

cians," *Journal of Applied Psychology*, October 1974, pp. 603–9.

21. D.M. Rousseau, "Organizational Behavior in the New Organizational Era," in J.T. Spence, J.M. Darley, and D.J. Foss (eds.), *Annual Review of Psychology*, vol. 48 (Palo Alto, CA: Annual Reviews, 1997), p. 523.

22. R. Eisenberger, F. Stinglhamber, C. Vandenberghe, I.L. Sucharski, and L. Rhoades, "Perceived Supervisor Support: Contributions to Perceived Organizational Support and Employee Retention," *Journal of Applied Psychology*, June 2002, pp. 565–73; and L. Rhoades and R. Eisenberger, "Perceived Organizational Support: A Review of the Literature," *Journal of Applied Psychology*, August 2002, pp. 698–714.

23. A.J. Elliott and P.G. Devine, "On the Motivational Nature of Cognitive Dissonance: Dissonance as Psychological Discomfort," *Journal of Personality and Social Psychology*, September 1994, pp. 382–94.

24. L. Festinger, *A Theory of Cognitive Dissonance* (Stanford, CA: Stanford University Press, 1957).

25. See, for example, B. Fishel, "A New Perspective: How to Get the Real Story from Attitude Surveys," *Training*, February 1998, pp. 91–94.

26. "Trident's Employee Satisfaction Survey," *Workforce Online* (*www.workforce.com*), August 9, 2000.

27. See S. Shellenbarger, "Companies Are Finding It Really Pays to Be Nice to Employees," *Wall Street Journal*, July 22, 1998, p. B1.

28. I. Briggs-Myers, *Introduction to Type* (Palo Alto, CA: Consulting Psychologists Press, 1980); W.L. Gardner and M.J. Martinko, "Using the Myers-Briggs Type Indicator to Study Managers: A Literature Review and Research Agenda," *Journal of Management*, vol. 22, no. 1 (1996), pp. 45–83; and N.L. Quenk, *Essentials of Myers-Briggs Type Indicator Assessment* (New York: Wiley, 2000).

29. J.M. Digman, "Personality Structure: Emergence of the Five-Factor Model," in M.R. Rosenweig and L.W. Porter (eds.), *Annual Review of Psychology*, vol. 41 (Palo Alto, CA: Annual Review, 1990), pp. 417–40; O.P. John, "The Big Five Factor Taxonomy: Dimensions of Personality in the Natural Language and in Questionnaires," in L.A. Pervin (ed.), *Handbook of Personality Theory and Research* (New York: Guilford Press, 1990), pp. 66–100; M.K. Mount, M.R. Barrick, and J.P. Strauss, "Validity of Observer Ratings of the Big Five Personality Factors," *Journal of Applied Psychology*, April 1996, pp. 272–80;

G.M. Hurtz and J.J. Donovan, "Personality and Job Performance: The Big Five Revisited," *Journal of Applied Psychology*, December 2000, pp. 869–79; and T.A. Judge, D. Heller, and M.K. Mount, "Five-Factor Model of Personality and Job Satisfaction: A Meta-Analysis," *Journal of Applied Psychology*, June 2002, pp. 530–41.

30. M.R. Barrick and M.K. Mount, "The Big Five Personality Dimensions and Job Performance: A Meta-Analysis," *Personnel Psychology* 44 (1991), pp. 1–26; A.J. Vinchur, J.S. Schippmann, F.S. Switzer III, and P.L. Roth, "A Meta-Analytic Review of Predictors of Job Performance for Salespeople," *Journal of Applied Psychology*, August 1998, pp. 586–97; G.M. Hurtz and J.J. Donovan, "Personality and Job Performance Revisited," *Journal of Applied Psychology*, December 2000, pp. 869–79; T.A. Judge and J.E. Bono, "Relationship of Core Self-Evaluations Traits—Self-Esteem, Generalized Self-Efficacy, Locus of Control, and Emotional Stability—With Job Satisfaction and Job Performance: A Meta-Analysis," *Journal of Applied Psychology*, February 2001, pp. 80–92; and Judge, Heller, and Mount, "Five-Factor Model of Personality and Job Satisfaction: A Meta-Analysis."

31. J.B. Rotter, "Generalized Expectancies for Internal versus External Control of Reinforcement," *Psychological Monographs* 80, no. 609 (1966).

32. See, for instance, D.W. Organ and C.N. Greene, "Role Ambiguity, Locus of Control, and Work Satisfaction," *Journal of Applied Psychology*, February 1974, pp. 101–2; and T.R. Mitchell, C.M. Smyser, and S.E. Weed, "Locus of Control: Supervision and Work Satisfaction," *Academy of Management Journal*, September 1975, pp. 623–31.

33. R.G. Vleeming, "Machiavellianism: A Preliminary Review," *Psychological Reports*, February 1979, pp. 295–310.

34. See J. Brockner, *Self-Esteem at Work: Research, Theory, and Practice* (Lexington, MA: Lexington Books, 1988), chapters 1–4; and N. Branden, *Self-Esteem at Work* (San Francisco: Jossey-Bass, 1998).

35. See M. Snyder, *Public Appearances/Private Realities: The Psychology of Self-Monitoring* (New York: W.H. Freeman, 1987); and D.V. Day, D.J. Schleicher, A.L. Unckless, and N.J. Hiller, "Self-Monitoring Personality at Work: A Meta-Analytic Investigation of Construct Validity," *Journal of Applied Psychology*, April 2002, pp. 390–401.

36. Snyder, *Public Appearances/Private Realities*; and J.M. Jenkins, "Self-Monitoring and Turnover: The Impact of Personality on Intent to Leave,"

Journal of Organizational Behavior, January 1993, pp. 83–90.

37. M. Kilduff and D.V. Day, "Do Chameleons Get Ahead? The Effects of Self-Monitoring on Managerial Careers," *Academy of Management Journal*, August 1994, pp. 1047–60; and A. Mehra, M. Kilduff, and D.J. Brass, "The Social Networks of High and Low Self-Monitors: Implications for Workplace Performance," *Administrative Science Quarterly*, March 2001, pp. 121–146.

38. N. Kogan and M.A. Wallach, "Group Risk Taking as a Function of Members' Anxiety and Defensiveness," *Journal of Personality*, March 1967, pp. 50–63; and J.M. Howell and C.A. Higgins, "Champions of Technological Innovation," *Administrative Science Quarterly*, June 1990, pp. 317–41.

39. See, for instance, G.W.M. Ip and M.H. Bond, "Culture, Values, and the Spontaneous Self-Concept," *Asian Journal of Psychology*, vol. 1 (1995), pp. 30–36; J.E. Williams, J.L. Saiz, D.L. FormyDuval, M.L. Munick, E.E. Fogle, A. Adom, A. Haque, F. Neto, and J. Yu, "Cross-Cultural Variation in the Importance of Psychological Characteristics: A Seven-Year Country Study," *International Journal of Psychology*, October 1995, pp. 529–50; V. Benet and N.G. Walker, "The Big Seven Factor Model of Personality Description: Evidence for Its Cross-Cultural Generalizability in a Spanish Sample," *Journal of Personality and Social Psychology*, October 1995, pp. 701–18; R.R. McCrae and P.T. Costa Jr., "Personality Trait Structure as a Human Universal," *American Psychologist* (1997), pp. 509–16; and M.J. Schmit, J.A. Kihm, and C. Robie, "Development of a Global Measure of Personality," *Personnel Psychology*, Spring 2000, pp. 153–93.

40. J.F. Salgado, "The Five Factor Model of Personality and Job Performance in the European Community," *Journal of Applied Psychology*, February 1997, pp. 30–43. Note: This study covered the 15-nation European community and did not include the 10 countries that joined in 2004.

41. N.H. Frijda, "Moods, Emotion Episodes, and Emotions," in M. Lewis and J.M. Havilland (eds.), *Handbook of Emotions* (New York: Guilford Press, 1993), pp. 381–403.

42. N.M. Ashkanasy and C.S. Daus, "Emotion in the Workplace: The New Challenge for Managers," *Academy of Management Executive*, February 2002, pp. 76–86; and N.M. Ashkanasy, C.E.J. Hartel, and C.S. Daus, "Diversity and Emotions: The New Frontiers in Organizational Behavior Research," *Journal of Management*, vol. 28, no. 3, (2002), pp. 307–38.

43. H.M. Weiss and R. Cropanzano, "Affective Events Theory," in B.M. Staw and L.L. Cummings, *Research in Organizational Behavior*, vol. 18 (Greenwich, CT: JAI Press, 1996), pp. 20–22.

44. This section is based on D. Goleman, *Emotional Intelligence* (New York: Bantam, 1995); M. Davies, L. Stankov, and R.D. Roberts, "Emotional Intelligence: In Search of an Elusive Construct," *Journal of Personality and Social Psychology*, October 1998, pp. 989–1015; D. Goleman, *Working with Emotional Intelligence* (New York: Bantam, 1999); R. Bar-On and J.D.A. Parker, eds., *The Handbook of Emotional Intelligence: Theory, Development, Assessment, and Application at Home, School, and in the Workplace* (San Francisco: Jossey-Bass, 2000); and P.J. Jordan, N.M. Ashkanasy, and C.E.J. Hartel, "Emotional Intelligence as a Moderator of Emotional and Behavioral Reactions to Job Insecurity," *Academy of Management Review*, July 2002, pp. 361–72.

45. J.L. Holland, *Making Vocational Choices: A Theory of Vocational Personalities and Work Environments* (Odessa, FL: Psychological Assessment Resources, 1997).

46. See, for instance, M.J. Martinko (ed.), *Attribution Theory: An Organizational Perspective* (Delray Beach, FL: St. Lucie Press, 1995); and H.H. Kelley, "Attribution in Social Interaction," in E. Jones et al. (eds.), *Attribution: Perceiving the Causes of Behavior* (Morristown, NJ: General Learning Press, 1972).

47. See A.G. Miller and T. Lawson, "The Effect of an Informational Option on the Fundamental Attribution Error," *Personality and Social Psychology Bulletin*, June 1989, pp. 194–204.

48. See, for instance, G.R. Semin, "A Gloss on Attribution Theory," *British Journal of Social and Clinical Psychology*, November 1980, pp. 291–330; and M.W. Morris and K. Peng, "Culture and Cause: American and Chinese Attributions for Social and Physical Events," *Journal of Personality and Social Psychology*, December 1994, pp. 949–71.

49. S. Nam, "Cultural and Managerial Attributions for Group Performance," unpublished doctoral dissertation, University of Oregon. Cited in R.M. Steers, S.J. Bischoff, and L.H. Higgins, "Cross-Cultural Management Research," *Journal of Management Inquiry*, December 1992, pp. 325–26.

50. See, for example, S.T. Fiske, "Social Cognition and Social Perception," *Annual Review of Psychology* (1993), pp. 155–94; G.N. Powell and Y. Kido, "Managerial Stereotypes in a Global Economy: A Comparative Study of Japanese and American Business Students' Perspectives," *Psychological Reports*, February 1994, pp. 219–26; and J.L. Hilton and W. von Hippel, "Stereotypes," in J.T. Spence, J.M. Darley, and D.J. Foss (eds.), *Annual Review of Psychology*, vol. 47 (Palo Alto, CA: Annual Reviews Inc., 1996), pp. 237–71.

51. B.F. Skinner, *Contingencies of Reinforcement* (East Norwalk, CT: Appleton-Century-Crofts, 1971).

52. Based on R.M. Bramson, *Coping with Difficult People* (Garden City, NY: Anchor Press/Doubleday, 1981); J.D. O'Brian, "De-Clawing the Chronic Complainer," *Supervisory Management*, June 1993, pp. 1–2; R. Cooper, "Dealing Effectively with Difficult People," *Nursing*, September 1993, pp. 97–100; A. Urbaniak, "How to Supervise Problem Employees," *Supervision*, September 1993, pp. 10–13; K. Mannering, *Managing Difficult People: Proven Strategies to Deal with Awkwardness in Business Situations* (Philadelphia: Trans-Atlantic Publications, Inc., 2000); J. Langdon, "Do You Have a Negative Personality?" *USA Today* (www.usatoday.com), March 14, 2001; R.D. Clarke, "Nix the Negativity," *Black Enterprise*, May 2001, p. 67; R.D. Clarke, "Solve the Pessimist Problem," *Black Enterprise*, June 2001, p. 85; M. Gaskill, "Bigger Bullies," *American Way*, August 2001, pp. 92–96; and M. Solomon, *Working with Difficult People* (Upper Saddle River, NJ: Prentice Hall, 2002).

53. Situation adapted from information in: Peter W. Lilienthal, "Should Companies Offer Employees a Lifeline?" *USA Today (Magazine)*, July 2003, pp. 68+; Steve Alexander, "Stress-Busters," *Computerworld*, June 9, 2003, p. 50.

CHAPTER 15

1. Information from company Web site (www.bmw.com), *Fortune Online* (www.fortune.com), and Hoover's Online (www.hoovers.com), January 5, 2003; B. Breen, "BMW: Driven by Design," *Fast Company*, September 2002, pp. 122–36; and J. Tayman, "Different by Design," *Business 2.0*, March 2003, pp. 124–25.

2. B. Mezrich, *Bringing Down the House: The Inside Story of Six MIT Students Who Took Vegas for Millions* (New York: Free Press, 2002).

3. B.W. Tuckman and M.C. Jensen, "Stages of Small-Group Development Revisited," *Group and Organizational Studies*, December 1977, pp. 419–27; and M.F. Maples, "Group Development: Extending Tuckman's Theory," *Journal for Specialists in Group Work*, Fall 1988, pp. 17–23.

4. L.N. Jewell and H.J. Reitz, *Group Effectiveness in Organizations* (Glenview, IL: Scott, Foresman, 1981); and M. Kaeter, "Repotting Mature Work Teams," *Training*, April 1994, pp. 54–56.

5. This model is based on the work of P.S. Goodman, E. Ravlin, and M. Schminke, "Understanding Groups in Organizations," in L.L. Cummings and B.M. Staw (eds.), *Research in Organizational Behavior*, vol. 9 (Greenwich, CT: JAI Press, 1987), pp. 124–28; J.R. Hackman, "The Design of Work Teams," in J.W. Lorsch (ed.), *Handbook of Organizational Behavior* (Upper Saddle River, NJ: Prentice Hall, 1987), pp. 315–42; G.R. Bushe and A.L. Johnson, "Contextual and Internal Variables Affecting Task Group Outcomes in Organizations," *Group and Organization Studies*, December 1989, pp. 462–82; M.A. Campion, C.J. Medsker, and A.C. Higgs, "Relations Between Work Group Characteristics and Effectiveness: Implications for Designing Effective Work Groups," *Personnel Psychology*, Winter 1993, pp. 823–50; D.E. Hyatt and T.M. Ruddy, "An Examination of the Relationship Between Work Group Characteristics and Performance: Once More into the Breach," *Personnel Psychology*, Autumn 1997, pp. 553–85; and P.E. Tesluk and J.E. Mathieu, "Overcoming Roadblocks to Effectiveness: Incorporating Management of Performance Barriers into Models of Work Group Effectiveness," *Journal of Applied Psychology*, April 1999, pp. 200–217.

6. F. Friedlander, "The Ecology of Work Groups," in Lorsch (ed.), *Handbook of Organizational Behavior*, pp. 301–14.

7. M.J. Stevens and M.A. Campion, "The Knowledge, Skill, and Ability Requirements for Teamwork: Implications for Human Resource Management," *Journal of Management*, Summer 1994, pp. 503–30.

8. V.U. Druskat and S.B. Wolff, "The Link between Emotions and Team Effectiveness: How Teams Engage Members and Build Effective Task Processes," *Academy of Management Proceedings*, on CD-ROM, 1999; D.C. Kinlaw, *Developing Superior Work Teams: Building Quality and the Competitive Edge* (San Diego, CA: Lexington, 1991); and M.E. Shaw, *Contemporary Topics in Social Psychology* (Morristown, NJ: General Learning Press, 1976), pp. 350–51.

9. B.L. Kirkman, C.B. Gibson, and D.L. Shapiro, "Exporting Teams: Enhancing the Implementation and Effectiveness of Work Teams in Global Affiliates," *Organizational Dynamics*, Summer 2001, pp. 12–29; J.W. Bing and C.M. Bing, "Helping Global Teams Compete," *Training & Development*, March 2001, pp. 70–71; C.G. Andrews, "Factors That Impact Multi-Cultural Team Performance," Center for the Study of Work Teams, University of North Texas (*www.workteams.unt.edu/reports/*), November 3, 2000; P. Christopher Earley and E. Mosakowski, "Creating Hybrid Team Cultures: An Empirical Test of Transnational Team Functioning," *Academy of Management Journal*, February 2000, pp. 26–49; J. Tata, "The Cultural Context of Teams: An Integrative Model of National Culture, Work Team Characteristics, and Team Effectiveness," *Academy of Management Proceedings*, on CD-ROM, 1999; D.I. Jung, K.B. Baik, and J.J. Sosik, "A Longitudinal Investigation of Group Characteristics and Work Group Performance: A Cross-Cultural Comparison," *Academy of Management Proceedings*, on CD-ROM, 1999; and C.B. Gibson, "They Do What They Believe They Can? Group-Efficacy Beliefs and Group Performance across Tasks and Cultures," *Academy of Management Proceedings* on CD-ROM, 1996.

10. Based on L. Copeland, "Making the Most of Cultural Differences at the Workplace," *Personnel*, June 1988, pp. 52–60; C.R. Bantz, "Cultural Diversity and Group Cross-Cultural Team Research," *Journal of Applied Communication Research*, February 1993, pp. 1–19; L. Strach and L. Wicander, "Fitting In: Issues of Tokenism and Conformity for Minority Women," *SAM Advanced Management Journal*, Summer 1993, pp. 22–25; M.L. Maznevski, "Understanding Our Differences: Performance in Decision-Making Groups with Diverse Members," *Human Relations*, May 1994, pp. 531–52; F. Rice, "How to Make Diversity Pay," *Fortune*, August 8, 1994, pp. 78–86; J. Jusko, "Diversity Enhances Decision Making," *Industry Week*, April 2, 2001, p. 9; and K. Lovelace, D.L. Shapiro, and L.R. Weingart, "Maximizing Cross-Functional New Product Teams' Innovativeness and Constraint Adherence: A Conflict Communications Perspective," *Academy of Management Journal*, August 2002, pp. 779–93.

11. G. Prince, "Recognizing Genuine Teamwork," *Supervisory Management*, April 1989, pp. 25–36; R.F. Bales, *SYMLOG Case Study Kit* (New York: Free Press, 1980); and K.D. Benne and P. Sheats, "Functional Roles of Group Members," *Journal of Social Issues*, vol. 4 (1948), pp. 41–49.

12. S.E. Asch, "Effects of Group Pressure upon the Modification and Distortion of Judgments," in H. Guetzkow (ed.), *Groups, Leadership and Men* (Pittsburgh: Carnegie Press, 1951), pp. 177–90; and S.E. Asch, "Studies of Independence and Conformity: A Minority of One Against a Unanimous Majority," *Psychological Monographs: General and Applied*, vol. 70, no. 9 (1956), pp. 1–70.

13. R. Bond and P.B. Smith, "Culture and Conformity: A Meta-Analysis of Studies Using Asch's [1952, 1956] Line Judgment Task," *Psychological Bulletin*, January 1996, pp. 111–37.

14. M.E. Turner and A.R. Pratkanis, "Mitigating Groupthink by Stimulating Constructive Conflict," in C. DeDreu and E. Van deVliert (eds.), *Using Conflict in Organizations* (London: Sage, 1997), pp. 53–71.

15. See, for instance, E.J. Thomas and C.F. Fink, "Effects of Group Size," *Psychological Bulletin*, July 1963, pp. 371–84; and M.E. Shaw, *Group Dynamics: The Psychology of Small Group Behavior*, 3rd ed. (New York: McGraw-Hill, 1981).

16. See D.R. Comer, "A Model of Social Loafing in Real Work Groups," *Human Relations*, June 1995, pp. 647–67.

17. S.G. Harkins and K. Szymanski, "Social Loafing and Group Evaluation," *Journal of Personality and Social Psychology*, December 1989, pp. 934–41.

18. See P.C. Earley, "Social Loafing and Collectivism: A Comparison of the United States and the People's Republic of China," *Administrative Science Quarterly*, December 1989, pp. 565–81; and P.C. Earley, "East Meets West Meets Mideast: Further Explorations of Collectivistic and Individualistic Work Groups," *Academy of Management Journal*, April 1993, pp. 319–48.

19. C.R. Evans and K.L. Dion, "Group Cohesion and Performance: A Meta-Analysis," *Small Group Research*, May 1991, pp. 175–86; B. Mullen and C. Copper, "The Relation between Group Cohesiveness and Performance: An Integration," *Psychological Bulletin*, March 1994, pp. 210–27; and P.M. Podsakoff, S.B. MacKenzie, and M. Ahearne, "Moderating Effects of Goal Acceptance on the Relationship between Group Cohesiveness and Productivity," *Journal of Applied Psychology*, December 1997, pp. 974–83.

20. See, for example, L. Berkowitz, "Group Standards, Cohesiveness, and Productivity," *Human Relations*, November 1954, pp. 509–19; and Mullen and Copper, "The Relation between Group Cohesiveness and Performance: An Integration."

21. S.E. Seashore, *Group Cohesiveness in the Industrial Work Group* (Ann Arbor: University of Michigan, Survey Research Center, 1954).

22. C. Shaffran, "Mind Your Meeting: How to Become the Catalyst for Culture

Change," *Communication World*, February–March 2003, pp. 26–29.

23. I.L. Janis, *Victims of Groupthink* (Boston: Houghton Mifflin, 1972); R.J. Aldag and S. Riggs Fuller, "Beyond Fiasco: A Reappraisal of the Groupthink Phenomenon and a New Model of Group Decision Processes," *Psychological Bulletin*, May 1993, pp. 533–52; and T. Kameda and S. Sugimori, "Psychological Entrapment in Group Decision Making: An Assigned Decision Rule and a Groupthink Phenomenon," *Journal of Personality and Social Psychology*, August 1993, pp. 282–92.

24. See, for example, L.K. Michaelson, W.E. Watson, and R.H. Black, "A Realistic Test of Individual vs. Group Consensus Decision Making," *Journal of Applied Psychology*, 74, no. 5 (1989), pp. 834–39; R.A. Henry, "Group Judgment Accuracy: Reliability and Validity of Postdiscussion Confidence Judgments," *Organizational Behavior and Human Decision Processes*, October 1993, pp. 11–27; P.W. Paese, M. Bieser, and M.E. Tubbs, "Framing Effects and Choice Shifts in Group Decision Making," *Organizational Behavior and Human Decision Processes*, October 1993, pp. 149–65; N.J. Castellan Jr. (ed.), *Individual and Group Decision Making* (Hillsdale, NJ: Lawrence Erlbaum Associates, 1993); and S.G. Straus and J.E. McGrath, "Does the Medium Matter? The Interaction of Task Type and Technology on Group Performance and Member Reactions," *Journal of Applied Psychology*, February 1994, pp. 87–97.

25. E.J. Thomas and C.F. Fink, "Effects of Group Size," *Psychological Bulletin*, July 1963, pp. 371–84; F.A. Shull, A.L. Delbecq, and L.L. Cummings, *Organizational Decision Making* (New York: McGraw-Hill, 1970), p. 151; A.P. Hare, *Handbook of Small Group Research* (New York: Free Press, 1976); Shaw, *Group Dynamics: The Psychology of Small Group Behavior*; and P. Yetton and P. Bottger, "The Relationships among Group Size, Member Ability, Social Decision Schemes, and Performance," *Organizational Behavior and Human Performance*, October 1983, pp. 145–59.

26. This section is adapted from S.P. Robbins, *Managing Organizational Conflict: A Nontraditional Approach* (Upper Saddle River, NJ: Prentice Hall, 1974), pp. 11–14. Also, see D. Wagner-Johnson, "Managing Work Team Conflict: Assessment and Preventative Strategies," Center for the Study of Work Teams, University of North Texas (*www.workteams.unt.edu/reports*), November 3, 2000; and M. Kennedy, "Managing Conflict in Work Teams," Center for the Study of Work Teams, University of North Texas

(*www.workteams.unt.edu/reports*), November 3, 2000.

27. See K.A. Jehn, "A Multimethod Examination of the Benefits and Detriments of Intragroup Conflict," *Administrative Science Quarterly*, June 1995, pp. 256–82; K.A. Jehn, "A Qualitative Analysis of Conflict Type and Dimensions in Organizational Groups," *Administrative Science Quarterly*, September 1997, pp. 530–57; K.A. Jehn, "Affective and Cognitive Conflict in Work Groups: Increasing Performance Through Value-Based Intragroup Conflict," in DeDreu and Van deVliert (eds.), *Using Conflict in Organizations*, pp. 87–100; K.A. Jehn and E. A. Mannix, "The Dynamic Nature of Conflict: A Longitudinal Study of Intragroup Conflict and Group Performance," *Academy of Management Journal*, April 2001, pp. 238–51; and C.K.W. DeDreu and A.E.M. Van Vianen, "Managing Relationship Conflict and the Effectiveness of Organizational Teams," *Journal of Organizational Behavior*, May 2001, pp. 309–28.

28. K.W. Thomas, "Conflict and Negotiation Processes in Organizations," in M.D. Dunnette and L.M. Hough (eds.), *Handbook of Industrial and Organizational Psychology*, vol. 3, 2d ed. (Palo Alto, CA: Consulting Psychologists Press, 1992), pp. 651–717.

29. See, for example, J.R. Hackman and C.G. Morris, "Group Tasks, Group Interaction Process, and Group Performance Effectiveness: A Review and Proposed Integration," in L. Berkowitz (ed.), *Advances in Experimental Social Psychology* (New York: Academic Press, 1975), pp. 45–99; R. Saavedra, P.C. Earley, and L. Van Dyne, "Complex Interdependence in Task-Performing Groups," *Journal of Applied Psychology*, February 1993, pp. 61–72; M.J. Waller, "Multiple-Task Performance in Groups," *Academy of Management Proceedings*, on Disk, 1996; and K.A. Jehn, G.B. Northcraft, and M.A. Neale, "Why Differences Make a Difference: A Field Study of Diversity, Conflict, and Performance in Workgroups," *Administrative Science Quarterly*, December 1999, pp. 741–63.

30. Cited in C. Joinson, "Teams at Work," *HRMagazine*, May 1999, p. 30; and P. Strozniak, "Teams at Work," *Industry Week*, September 18, 2000, p. 47.

31. See, for example, S.A. Mohrman, S.G. Cohen, and A.M. Mohrman, Jr., *Designing Team-Based Organizations* (San Francisco: Jossey-Bass, 1995); P. MacMillan, *The Performance Factor: Unlocking the Secrets of Teamwork* (Nashville, TN: Broadman & Holman, 2001); and E. Salas, C.A. Bowers, and E.

Eden (eds.), *Improving Teamwork in Organizations: Applications of Resource Management Training* (Mahwah, NJ: Lawrence Erlbaum, 2002).

32. See, for instance, E. Sunstrom, K. DeMeuse, and D. Futrell, "Work Teams: Applications and Effectiveness," *American Psychologist*, February 1990, pp. 120–33.

33. P.J. Kiger, "Acxiom Rebuilds from Scratch," *Workforce*, December 2002, pp. 52–55; T. Boles, "Viewpoint—Leadership Lessons from NASCAR," *Industry Week*, May 21, 2002 (*www.industryweek.com*); and C. Rance, "Doing the Team Thing," *The Age*, November 28, 1998, pp. E1–2.

34. M. Cianni and D. Wanuck, "Individual Growth and Team Enhancement: Moving Toward a New Model of Career Development," *Academy of Management Executive*, February 1997, pp. 105–15.

35. "Teams," *Training*, October 1996, p. 69; and Joinson "Teams at Work," p. 30.

36. G.M. Spreitzer, S.G. Cohen, and G.E. Ledford, Jr., "Developing Effective Self-Managing Work Teams in Service Organizations," *Group & Organization Management*, September 1999, pp. 340–66.

37. C.E. Nicholls, H.W. Lane, and M. Brehm Brechu, "Taking Self-Managed Teams to Mexico," *Academy of Management Executive*, August 1999, pp. 15–27.

38. D. Drickhamer, "Mission Critical," *Industry Week*, March 2002, pp. 45–46.

39. J. Appleby and R. Davis, "Teamwork Used to Save Money; Now It Saves Lives," *USA Today* (*www.usatoday.com*), March 1, 2001.

40. Information from company Web site (*www.strawberryfrog.com*), June 18, 2003; E. White and M. Rozenman, "Some Ads in Europe Refer to the War," *Wall Street Journal*, March 26, 2003, p. B4; and S. Ellison, "Ad Firm StrawberryFrog in Amsterdam Thinks Big but Wants to Stay Small," *Wall Street Journal*, April 3, 2000, pp. A43D+.

41. F. Keenan and S.E. Ante, "The New Teamwork," *Business-Week e.biz*, February 18, 2002, pp. EB12–EB16; and G. Imperato, "Real Tools for Virtual Teams" *Fast Company*, July 2000, pp. 378–87.

42. G.R. Jones and G.M. George, "The Experience and Evolution of Trust: Implications for Cooperation and Teamwork," *Academy of Management Review*, July 1998, pp. 531–46; A.R. Jassawalla and H.C. Sashittal, "Building Collaborative Cross-Functional New Product Teams," *Academy of Management Executive*, August 1999, pp. 50–63; R. Forrester and A.B. Drexler, "A Model for Team-Based Organization Performance," *Academy of Management*

Executive, August 1999, pp. 36–49; Druskat and Wolff, "The Link Between Emotions and Team Effectiveness: How Teams Engage Members and Build Effective Task Processes"; M. Mattson, T. Mumford, and G.S. Sintay, "Taking Teams to Task: A Normative Model for Designing or Recalibrating Work Teams," *Academy of Management Proceedings*, on CD-ROM, 1999; J.D. Shaw, M.K. Duffy, and E.M. Stark, "Interdependence and Preference for Group Work: Main and Congruence Effects on the Satisfaction and Performance of Group Members," *Journal of Management*, vol. 26, no. 2 (2000), pp. 259–79; G.L. Stewart and M.R. Barrick, "Team Structure and Performance: Assessing the Mediating Role of Intrateam Process and the Moderating Role of Task Type," *Academy of Management Journal*, April 2000, pp. 135–48; J.E. Mathieu, T.S. Heffner, G.F. Goodwin, E. Salas, and J.A. Cannon-Bowers, "The Influence of Shared Mental Models on Team Process and Performance," *Journal of Applied Psychology*, April 2000, pp. 273–83; J.M. Phillips and E.A. Douthitt, "The Role of Justice in Team Member Satisfaction with the Leader and Attachment to the Team," *Journal of Applied Psychology*, April 2001, pp. 316–25; J.A. Colquitt, R.A. Noe, and C.L. Jackson, "Justice in Teams: Antecedents and Consequences of Procedural Justice Climate," *Personnel Psychology*, vol. 55 (2002), pp. 83–100; M.A. Marks, M.J. Sabella, C.S. Burke, and S.J. Zaccaro, "The Impact of Cross-Training on Team Effectiveness," *Journal of Applied Psychology*, February 2002, pp. 3–13; and S.W. Lester, B.W. Meglino, and M.A. Korsgaard, "The Antecedents and Consequences of Group Potency: A Longitudinal Investigation of Newly Formed Work Groups," *Academy of Management Journal*, April 2002, pp. 352–68.

43. Situation adapted from information in: Lee Gomes, "Committees Are Useful and Very Efficient—Well, in the Tech World," *Wall Street Journal*, July 7, 2003, p. A9; John Swaffield, "Code Committees—Gatekeepers or Pathfinders?" *PM Engineer*, January 2003, pp. 25+.

CHAPTER 16

1. Information from company Web site (*www.grupom.com.do*), January 5, 2003; and C. Dahle, "The New Fabric of Success," *Fast Company*, June 2000, pp. 252–70.

2. C. Taylor, "Rallying the Troops," *SmartMoney*, February 2003, pp. 105–6.

3. See, for instance, T.R. Mitchell, "Matching Motivational Strategies with Organizational Contexts," in L.L. Cummings and B.M. Staw (eds.), *Research in Organizational Behavior*, vol. 19 (Greenwich, CT: JAI Press, 1997), pp. 60–62;

and R. Katerberg and G.J. Blau, "An Examination of Level and Direction of Effort and Job Performance," *Academy of Management Journal*, June 1983, pp. 249–57.

4. Cited in D. Jones, "Firms Spend Billions to Fire UP Workers—With Little Luck," *USA Today*, May 10, 2001, p. 1A.

5. S.L. Hwang, "For Some Employees, Great Parking Spaces Fulfill a Primal Need," *Wall Street Journal*, June 26, 2002, p. B1.

6. A. Maslow, *Motivation and Personality* (New York: McGraw-Hill, 1954); A. Maslow, D.C. Stephens, and G. Heil, *Maslow on Management* (New York: John Wiley & Sons, 1998); M.L. Ambrose and C.T. Kulik, "Old Friends, New Faces: Motivation Research in the 1990s," *Journal of Management*, vol. 25, no. 3 (1999), pp. 231–92; and "Dialogue," *Academy of Management Review*, October 2000, pp. 696–701.

7. See, for example, D.T. Hall and K.E. Nongaim, "An Examination of Maslow's Need Hierarchy in an Organizational Setting," *Organizational Behavior and Human Performance*, February 1968, pp. 12–35; E.E. Lawler III and J.L. Suttle, "A Causal Correlational Test of the Need Hierarchy Concept," *Organizational Behavior and Human Performance*, April 1972, pp. 265–87; R.M. Creech, "Employee Motivation," *Management Quarterly*, Summer 1995, pp. 33–39; J. Rowan, "Maslow Amended," *Journal of Humanistic Psychology*, Winter 1998, pp. 81–92; J. Rowan, "Ascent and Descent in Maslow's Theory," *Journal of Humanistic Psychology*, Summer 1999, pp. 125–33.; and Ambrose and Kulik, "Old Friends, New Faces: Motivation Research in the 1990s."

8. D. McGregor, *The Human Side of Enterprise* (New York: McGraw-Hill, 1960). For an updated analysis of Theories X and Y, see R.J. Summers and S.F. Conshaw, "A Study of McGregor's Theory X, Theory Y and the Influence of Theory X, Theory Y Assumptions on Causal Attributions for Instances of Worker Poor Performance," in S.L. McShane (ed.), *Organizational Behavior, ASAC 1988 Conference Proceedings*, vol. 9, Part 5. Halifax, Nova Scotia, 1988, pp. 115–23.

9. J.M. O'Brien, "The Next Intel," *Wired*, July 2002, pp. 100–107.

10. F. Herzberg, B. Mausner, and B. Snyderman, *The Motivation to Work* (New York: John Wiley, 1959); F. Herzberg, *The Managerial Choice: To Be Effective or To Be Human*, rev. ed. (Salt Lake City: Olympus, 1982); Creech, "Employee Motivation;" and Ambrose

and Kulik, "Old Friends, New Faces: Motivation Research in the 1990s."

11. Ambrose and Kulik, "Old Friends, New Faces: Motivation Research in the 1990s."

12. D.C. McClelland, *The Achieving Society* (New York: Van Nostrand Reinhold, 1961); J.W. Atkinson and J.O. Raynor, *Motivation and Achievement* (Washington, DC: Winston, 1974); D.C. McClelland, *Power: The Inner Experience* (New York: Irvington, 1975); and M.J. Stahl, *Managerial and Technical Motivation: Assessing Needs for Achievement, Power, and Affiliation* (New York: Praeger, 1986).

13. McClelland, *The Achieving Society*.

14. McClelland, *Power*; D.C. McClelland and D.H. Burnham, "Power Is the Great Motivator," *Harvard Business Review*, March–April 1976, pp. 100–110.

15. D. Miron and D.C. McClelland, "The Impact of Achievement Motivation Training on Small Businesses," *California Management Review*, Summer 1979, pp. 13–28.

16. "McClelland: An Advocate of Power," *International Management*, July 1975, pp. 27–29.

17. Ambrose and Kulik, "Old Friends, New Faces: Motivation Research in the 1990s."

18. J.C. Naylor and D.R. Ilgen, "Goal Setting: A Theoretical Analysis of a Motivational Technique," in Staw and Cummings (eds.), *Research in Organizational Behavior*, vol. 6, pp. 95–140; A.R. Pell, "Energize Your People," *Managers Magazine*, December 1992, pp. 28–29; E.A. Locke, "Facts and Fallacies about Goal Theory: Reply to Deci," *Psychological Science*, January 1993, pp. 63–64; M.E. Tubbs, "Commitment as a Moderator of the Goal-Performance Relation: A Case for Clearer Construct Definition," *Journal of Applied Psychology*, February 1993, pp. 86–97; M.P. Collingwood, "Why Don't You Use the Research?" *Management Decision*, May 1993, pp. 48–54; M.E. Tubbs, D.M. Boehne, and J.S. Dahl, "Expectancy, Valence, and Motivational Force Functions in Goal-Setting Research: An Empirical Test," *Journal of Applied Psychology*, June 1993, pp. 361–73; E.A. Locke, "Motivation through Conscious Goal Setting," *Applied and Preventive Psychology*, vol. 5 (1996), pp. 117–24; and Ambrose and Kulik, "Old Friends, New Faces: Motivation Research in the 1990s."

19. J.B. Miner, *Theories of Organizational Behavior* (Hinsdale, IL: Dryden Press, 1980), p. 65.

20. J.A. Wagner III, "Participation's Effects on Performance and Satisfaction: A Reconsideration of Research and Evidence," *Academy of Management*

Review, April 1994, pp. 312–30; J. George-Falvey, "Effects of Task Complexity and Learning Stage on the Relationship between Participation in Goal Setting and Task Performance," *Academy of Management Proceedings*, on Disk, 1996; T.D. Ludwig and E.S. Geller, "Assigned versus Participative Goal Setting and Response Generalization: Managing Injury Control among Professional Pizza Deliverers," *Journal of Applied Psychology*, April 1997, pp. 253–61; and S.G. Harkins and M.D. Lowe, "The Effects of Self-Set Goals on Task Performance," *Journal of Applied Social Psychology*, January 2000, pp. 1–40.

21. J.M. Ivancevich and J.T. McMahon, "The Effects of Goal Setting, External Feedback, and Self-Generated Feedback on Outcome Variables: A Field Experiment," *Academy of Management Journal*, June 1982, pp. 359–72; and Locke, "Motivation through Conscious Goal Setting."

22. J.R. Hollenbeck, C.R. Williams, and H.J. Klein, "An Empirical Examination of the Antecedents of Commitment to Difficult Goals," *Journal of Applied Psychology*, February 1989, pp. 18–23; see also J.C. Wofford, V.L. Goodwin, and S. Premack, "Meta-Analysis of the Antecedents of Personal Goal Level and of the Antecedents and Consequences of Goal Commitment," *Journal of Management*, September 1992, pp. 595–615; and Tubbs, "Commitment as a Moderator of the Goal-Performance Relation."

23. M.E. Gist, "Self-Efficacy: Implications for Organizational Behavior and Human Resource Management," *Academy of Management Review*, July 1987, pp. 472–85; and A. Bandura, *Self-Efficacy: The Exercise of Control* (New York: Freeman, 1997).

24. E.A. Locke, E. Frederick, C. Lee, and P. Bobko, "Effect of Self-Efficacy, Goals, and Task Strategies on Task Performance," *Journal of Applied Psychology*, May 1984, pp. 241–51; M.E. Gist and T.R. Mitchell, "Self-Efficacy: A Theoretical Analysis of Its Determinants and Malleability," *Academy of Management Review*, April 1992, pp. 183–211; and A.D. Stajkovic and F. Luthans, "Self-Efficacy and Work-Related Performance: A Meta-Analysis," *Psychological Bulletin*, September 1998, pp. 240–61.

25. A. Bandura and D. Cervone, "Differential Engagement in Self-Reactive Influences in Cognitively-Based Motivation," *Organizational Behavior and Human Decision Processes*, August 1986, pp. 92–113.

26. See J.C. Anderson and C.A. O'Reilly, "Effects of an Organizational Control System on Managerial Satisfaction and Performance," *Human Relations*, June 1981, pp. 491–501; and J.P. Meyer, B. Schacht-Cole, and I.R. Gellatly, "An Examination of the Cognitive Mechanisms by Which Assigned Goals Affect Task Performance and Reactions to Performance," *Journal of Applied Social Psychology*, 18, no. 5 (1988), pp. 390–408.

27. B.F. Skinner, *Science and Human Behavior* (New York: Free Press, 1953); and Skinner, *Beyond Freedom and Dignity* (New York: Knopf, 1972).

28. The same data, for instance, can be interpreted in either goal-setting or reinforcement terms, as shown in E.A. Locke, "Latham vs. Komaki: A Tale of Two Paradigms," *Journal of Applied Psychology*, February 1980, pp. 16–23. Also, see Ambrose and Kulik, "Old Friends, New Faces: Motivation Research in the 1990s."

29. This box based on R. McNatt, "The Young and the Restless," *BusinessWeek*, May 22, 2000, p. 12; "On the Job," *Wall Street Journal*, April 11, 2000, p. B18; P. Kruger, "Does Your Job Work?" *Fast Company*, November 1999, pp. 181–96; and M.A. Verespej, "What Each Generation Wants," *Industry Week*, October 18, 1999, pp. 14–15.

30. See, for example, R.W. Griffin, "Toward an Integrated Theory of Task Design," in Cummings and Staw (eds.), *Research in Organizational Behavior*, vol. 9, pp. 79–120; and M. Campion, "Interdisciplinary Approaches to Job Design: A Constructive Replication with Extensions," *Journal of Applied Psychology*, August 1988, pp. 467–81.

31. S. Caudron, "The De-Jobbing of America," *Industry Week*, September 5, 1994, pp. 31–36; W. Bridges, "The End of the Job," *Fortune*, September 19, 1994, pp. 62–74; and K.H. Hammonds, K. Kelly, and K. Thurston, "Rethinking Work," *BusinessWeek*, October 12, 1994, pp. 75–87.

32. M.A. Campion and C.L. McClelland, "Follow-Up and Extension of the Interdisciplinary Costs and Benefits of Enlarged Jobs," *Journal of Applied Psychology*, June 1993, pp. 339–51; and Ambrose and Kulik, "Old Friends, New Faces: Motivation Research in the 1990s."

33. See, for example, J.R. Hackman and G.R. Oldham, *Work Redesign* (Reading, MA: Addison-Wesley, 1980); and Miner, *Theories of Organizational Behavior*, pp. 231–66; R.W. Griffin, "Effects of Work Redesign on Employee Perceptions, Attitudes, and Behaviors: A Long-Term Investigation," *Academy of*

Management Journal, June 1991, pp. 425–35; J.L. Cotton, *Employee Involvement* (Newbury Park, CA: Sage, 1993), pp. 141–72; and Ambrose and Kulik, "Old Friends, New Faces: Motivation Research in the 1990s."

34. J.R. Hackman and G.R. Oldham, "Development of the Job Diagnostic Survey," *Journal of Applied Psychology*, April 1975, pp. 159–70; and J.R. Hackman and G.R. Oldham, "Motivation through the Design of Work: Test of a Theory," *Organizational Behavior and Human Performance*, August 1976, pp. 250–79.

35. J.R. Hackman, "Work Design," in J.R. Hackman and J.L. Suttle (eds.), *Improving Life at Work* (Glenview, IL: Scott, Foresman, 1977), p. 129; and Ambrose and Kulik, "Old Friends, New Faces: Motivation Research in the 1990s."

36. "Involve Your Customers," *Success*, October 1995, p. 28.

37. Ibid.

38. J.S. Adams, "Inequity in Social Exchanges," in L. Berkowitz (ed.), *Advances in Experimental Social Psychology*, vol. 2 (New York: Academic Press, 1965), pp. 267–300; and Ambrose and Kulik, "Old Friends, New Faces: Motivation Research in the 1990s."

39. See, for example, P.S. Goodman and A. Friedman, "An Examination of Adams' Theory of Inequity," *Administrative Science Quarterly*, September 1971, pp. 271–88; E. Walster, G.W. Walster, and W.G. Scott, *Equity: Theory and Research* (Boston: Allyn & Bacon, 1978); and J. Greenberg, "Cognitive Reevaluation of Outcomes in Response to Underpayment Inequity," *Academy of Management Journal*, March 1989, pp. 174–84.

40. See, for example, M.R. Carrell, "A Longitudinal Field Assessment of Employee Perceptions of Equitable Treatment," *Organizational Behavior and Human Performance*, February 1978, pp. 108–18; R.G. Lord and J.A. Hohenfeld, "Longitudinal Field Assessment of Equity Effects on the Performance of Major League Baseball Players," *Journal of Applied Psychology*, February 1979, pp. 19–26; and J.E. Dittrich and M.R. Carrell, "Organizational Equity Perceptions, Employee Job Satisfaction, and Departmental Absence and Turnover Rates," *Organizational Behavior and Human Performance*, August 1979, pp. 29–40.

41. P.S. Goodman, "An Examination of Referents Used in the Evaluation of Pay," *Organizational Behavior and Human Performance*, October 1974, pp. 170–95; S. Ronen, "Equity Perception in Multiple Comparisons: A Field Study," *Human*

Relations, April 1986, pp. 333–46; R.W. Scholl, E.A. Cooper, and J.F. McKenna, "Referent Selection in Determining Equity Perception: Differential Effects on Behavioral and Attitudinal Outcomes," *Personnel Psychology*, Spring 1987 pp. 113–27; and C.T. Kulik and M.L. Ambrose, "Personal and Situational Determinants of Referent Choice," *Academy of Management Review*, April 1992, pp. 212–37.

42. See, for example, R.C. Dailey and D.J. Kirk, "Distributive and Procedural Justice as Antecedents of Job Dissatisfaction and Intent to Turnover," *Human Relations*, March 1992, pp. 305–16; D.B. McFarlin and P.D. Sweeney, "Distributive and Procedural Justice as Predictors of Satisfaction with Personal and Organizational Outcomes," *Academy of Management Journal*, August 1992, pp. 626–37; and M.A. Konovsky, "Understanding Procedural Justice and Its Impact on Business Organizations," *Journal of Management*, vol. 26, no. 3 (2000), pp. 489–511.

43. P.S. Goodman, "Social Comparison Process in Organizations," in B.M. Staw and G.R. Salancik (eds.), *New Directions in Organizational Behavior* (Chicago: St. Clair, 1977), pp. 97–132; and J. Greenberg, "A Taxonomy of Organizational Justice Theories," *Academy of Management Review*, January 1987, pp. 9–22.

44. V.H. Vroom, *Work and Motivation* (New York: John Wiley, 1964).

45. See, for example, H.G. Heneman III and D.P. Schwab, "Evaluation of Research on Expectancy Theory Prediction of Employee Performance," *Psychological Bulletin*, July 1972, pp. 1–9; and L. Reinharth and M. Wahba, "Expectancy Theory as a Predictor of Work Motivation, Effort Expenditure, and Job Performance," *Academy of Management Journal*, September 1975, pp. 502–37.

46. See, for example, V.H. Vroom, "Organizational Choice: A Study of Pre- and Postdecision Processes," *Organizational Behavior and Human Performance*, April 1966, pp. 212–25; L.W. Porter and E.E. Lawler III, *Managerial Attitudes and Performance* (Homewood, IL: Richard D. Irwin, 1968); W. Van Eerde and H. Thierry, "Vroom's Expectancy Models and Work-Related Criteria: A Meta-Analysis," *Journal of Applied Psychology*, October 1996, pp. 575–86; and Ambrose and Kulik, "Old Friends, New Faces: Motivation Research in the 1990s."

47. See, for instance, M. Siegall, "The Simplistic Five: An Integrative Framework for Teaching Motivation," *The Organizational Behavior Teaching Review*, 12, no. 4 (1987–88), pp. 141–43.

48. N.J. Adler, *International Dimensions of Organizational Behavior*, 4th ed. (Cincinnati: South-Western, 2002), p. 174.

49. G. Hofstede, "Motivation, Leadership and Organization: Do American Theories Apply Abroad?" *Organizational Dynamics*, Summer 1980, p. 55.

50. Ibid.

51. J.K. Giacobbe-Miller, D.J. Miller, and V.I. Victorov, "A Comparison of Russian and U.S. Pay Allocation Decisions, Distributive Justice Judgments and Productivity under Different Payment Conditions," *Personnel Psychology*, Spring 1998, pp. 137–63.

52. S.L. Mueller and L.D. Clarke, "Political-Economic Context and Sensitivity to Equity: Differences between the United States and the Transition Economies of Central and Eastern Europe," *Academy of Management Journal*, June 1998, pp. 319–29.

53. I. Harpaz, "The Importance of Work Goals: An International Perspective," *Journal of International Business Studies*, First Quarter 1990, pp. 75–93.

54. G.E. Popp, H.J. Davis, and T.T. Herbert, "An International Study of Intrinsic Motivation Composition," *Management International Review*, January 1986, pp. 28–35.

55. J.R. Billings and D.L. Sharpe, "Factors Influencing Flextime Usage Among Employed Married Women," *Consumer Interests Annual* (1999), pp. 89–94; and I. Harpaz, "The Importance of Work Goals: An International Perspective," *Journal of International Business Studies*, First Quarter 1990, pp. 75–93.

56. "Health Club Membership, Flextime Are Most Desired Perks," *Business West*, September 1999, p. 75.

57. Hewitt Associates, "2002 Survey of Work/Life Benefits and Work/Life Scheduling," (*www.hewitt.com*), May 13, 2002.

58. This box based on D. Jones, "Ford, Fannie Mae Tops in Diversity," *USA Today*, May 7, 2003 (*www.usatoday.com*); S.N. Mehta, "What Minority Employees Really Want," *Fortune*, July 10, 2000, pp. 180–86; K.H. Hammonds, "Difference is Power," *Fast Company*, July 2000, pp. 258–66; "Building a Competitive Workforce: Diversity, the Bottom Line," *Forbes*, April 3, 2000, pp. 181–94; and "Diversity: Developing Tomorrow's Leadership Talent Today," *BusinessWeek*, December 20, 1999, pp. 85–100.

59. See, for instance, M. Alpert, "The Care and Feeding of Engineers," *Fortune*, September 21, 1992, pp. 86–95; G. Poole, "How to Manage Your Nerds," *Forbes ASAP*, December 1994, pp. 132–36; and T.J. Allen and R. Katz, "Managing Technical Professionals and

Organizations: Improving and Sustaining the Performance of Organizations, Project Teams, and Individual Contributors," *Sloan Management Review*, Summer 2002, pp. S4–S5.

60. R.J. Bohner, Jr. and E.R. Salasko, "Beware the Legal Risks of Hiring Temps," *Workforce*, October 2002, pp. 50–57.

61. C. Haddad, "FedEx: Gaining on the Ground," *BusinessWeek*, December 16, 2002, pp. 126–28; and M. Freudenheim, "In a Shift, an H.M.O. Rewards Doctors for Quality Care," *New York Times*, July 11, 2001, pp. C1+.

62. J. Case, "The Open-Book Revolution," *Inc.*, June 1995, pp. 26–50; J.P. Schuster, J. Carpenter, and M.P. Kane, *The Power of Open-Book Management* (New York: John Wiley, 1996); J. Case, "Opening the Books," *Harvard Business Review*, March–April 1997, pp. 118–27; and D. Drickhamer, "Open Books to Elevate Performance," *Industry Week*, November 2002, p. 16.

63. Schuster, Carpenter, and Kane, *The Power of Open-Book Management*; and B.J. Simkins, "Open Book Management—Optimizing Human Capital," *Business Horizons*, September–October 2001, pp. 5–13.

64. F. Luthans and A.D. Stajkovic, "Provide Recognition for Performance Improvement," in E.A. Locke (ed.), *Principles of Organizational Behavior* (Oxford, England: Blackwell, 2000), pp. 166–80.

65. D. Drickhamer, "Best Plant Winners: Nichols Foods Ltd.," *Industry Week*, October 1, 2001, pp. 17–19.

66. M. Littman, "Best Bosses Tell All," *Working Woman*, October 2000, p. 54; and Hoover's Online (*www.hoovers.com*), June 20, 2003.

67. K.J. Dunham, "Amid Sinking Workplace Morale, Employers Turn to Recognition," *Wall Street Journal*, November 19, 2002, p. B8.

68. Cited in S. Caudron, "The Top 20 Ways to Motivate Employees," *Industry Week*, April 3, 1995, pp. 15–16. See also B. Nelson, "Try Praise," *Inc.*, September 1996, p. 115; and J. Wiscombe, "Rewards Get Results," *Workforce*, April 2002, pp. 42–48.

69. R.K. Abbott, "Performance-Based Flex: A Tool for Managing Total Compensation Costs," *Compensation and Benefits Review*, March–April 1993, pp. 18–21; J.R. Schuster and P.K. Zingheim, "The New Variable Pay: Key Design Issues," *Compensation and Benefits Review*, March–April 1993, pp. 27–34; C.R. Williams and L.P. Livingstone, "Another Look at the Relationship between Performance and Voluntary Turnover," *Academy of Management*

Journal, April 1994, pp. 269–98; and A.M. Dickinson and K.L. Gillette, "A Comparison of the Effects of Two Individual Monetary Incentive Systems on Productivity: Piece Rate Pay versus Base Pay Plus Incentives," *Journal of Organizational Behavior Management*, Spring 1994, pp. 3–82.

70. Cited in S. Armour, "Bigger Bonuses Hint of Better Times Ahead," *USA Today*, November 25, 2002, p. 1A.

71. "More Than 20 Percent of Japanese Firms Use Pay Systems Based on Performance," *Manpower Argus*, May 1998, p. 7; and "Bonus Pay in Canada," *Manpower Argus*, September 1996, p. 5.

72. M. Tanikawa, "Fujitsu Decides to Backtrack on Performance-Based Pay," *New York Times*, March 22, 2001, p.W1.

73. H. Rheem, "Performance Management Programs," *Harvard Business Review*, September–October 1996, pp. 8–9; G. Sprinkle, "The Effect of Incentive Contracts on Learning and Performance," *Accounting Review*, July 2000, pp. 299–326; and "Do Incentive Awards Work?" *HRFocus*, October 2000, pp. 1–3.

74. R.D. Banker, S.Y. Lee, G. Potter, and D. Srinivasan, "Contextual Analysis of Performance Impacts on Outcome-Based Incentive Compensation," *Academy of Management Journal*, August 1996, pp. 920–48.

75. T. Reason, "Why Bonus Plans Fail," *CFO*, January 2003, p. 53; and "Has Pay for Performance Had Its Day?" *The McKinsey Quarterly*, no. 4 (2002), accessed on Forbes Web site (*www.forbes.com*).

76. J. McCafferty, "For Richer or for Poorer," *CFO*, August 2002, p. 20; J. Useem, "CEO Pay: Have They No Shame?" *Fortune*, April 14, 2003, accessed on Fortune's Web site (*www.fortune.com*); and Hoover's Online (*www.hoovers.com*), June 20, 2003.

77. W.J. Duncan, "Stock Ownership and Work Motivation," *Organizational Dynamics*, Summer 2001, pp. 1–11.

78. P. Brandes, R. Dharwadkar, and G.V. Lemesis, "Effective Employee Stock Option Design: Reconciling Stakeholder, Strategic, and Motivational Factors," *Academy of Management Executive*, February 2003, pp. 77–95; and J. Blasi, D. Kruse, and A. Bernstein, *In the Company of Owners: The Truth about Stock Options* (New York: Basic Books, 2003).

79. Situation adapted from information in: Wendy Zellner, "'They Took More Than They Needed from Us,'" *Business Week*, June 2, 2003, p. 58; "Coffee, Tea, or Bile?" *Business Week*, June 2, 2003, p. 56; "US Airways Pilots' Stand on Management," *New York Times*,

May 24, 2003, p. C2; "US Airways Flight Attendants Delay Concession Talks," *New York Times*, December 4, 2002, p. C4.

CHAPTER 17

1. Information from company Web site (*www.ups.com*) and Hoover's Online (*www.hoovers.com*), January 5, 2003; and K.H. Hammonds, "Handle with Care," *Fast Company*, August 2002, pp. 102–8.

2. See S.A. Kirkpatrick and E.A. Locke, "Leadership: Do Traits Matter?" *Academy of Management Executive*, May 1991, pp. 48–60; and T.A. Judge, J.E. Bono, R. Ilies, and M.W. Gerhardt, "Personality and Leadership: A Qualitative and Quantitative Review," *Journal of Applied Psychology*, August 2002, pp. 765–80.

3. C. Hymowitz, "Bosses Need to Learn Whether They Inspire, or Just Drive, Staffers," *Wall Street Journal*, August 14, 2001, p. B1; and P.C. Judge, "From Country Boys to Big Cheese," *Fast Company*, December 2001, pp. 38–40.

4. K. Lewin and R. Lippitt, "An Experimental Approach to the Study of Autocracy and Democracy: A Preliminary Note," *Sociometry*, 1 (1938), pp. 292–300; K. Lewin, "Field Theory and Experiment in Social Psychology: Concepts and Methods," *American Journal of Sociology*, 44 (1939), pp. 868–96; K. Lewin, R. Lippitt, and R.K. White, "Patterns of Aggressive Behavior in Experimentally Created Social Climates," *Journal of Social Psychology*, 10 (1939), pp. 271–301; and R. Lippitt, "An Experimental Study of the Effect of Democratic and Authoritarian Group Atmospheres," *University of Iowa Studies in Child Welfare*, 16 (1940), pp. 43–95.

5. B.M. Bass, *Stogdill's Handbook of Leadership* (New York: Free Press, 1981), pp. 289–99.

6. R.M. Stogdill and A.E. Coons (eds.), *Leader Behavior: Its Description and Measurement*, Research Monograph No. 88 (Columbus: Ohio State University, Bureau of Business Research, 1951). For an updated literature review of Ohio State research, see S. Kerr, C.A. Schriesheim, C.J. Murphy, and R.M. Stogdill, "Toward a Contingency Theory of Leadership Based upon the Consideration and Initiating Structure Literature," *Organizational Behavior and Human Performance*, August 1974, pp. 62–82; and B.M. Fisher, "Consideration and Initiating Structure and Their Relationships with Leader Effectiveness: A Meta-Analysis," in F. Hoy (ed.), *Proceedings of the 48th Annual Academy of Management Con-*

ference, Anaheim, California, 1988, pp. 201–5.

7. R. Kahn and D. Katz, "Leadership Practices in Relation to Productivity and Morale," in D. Cartwright and A. Zander (eds.), *Group Dynamics: Research and Theory*, 2d ed. (Elmsford, NY: Row, Paterson, 1960).

8. R.R. Blake and J.S. Mouton, *The Managerial Grid III* (Houston, TX: Gulf Publishing, 1984).

9. L.L. Larson, J.G. Hunt, and R.N. Osborn, "The Great Hi-Hi Leader Behavior Myth: A Lesson from Occam's Razor," *Academy of Management Journal*, December 1976, pp. 628–41; and P.C. Nystrom, "Managers and the Hi-Hi Leader Myth," *Academy of Management Journal*, June 1978, pp. 325–31.

10. F.E. Fiedler, *A Theory of Leadership Effectiveness* (New York: McGraw-Hill, 1967).

11. L.H. Peters, D.D. Hartke, and J.T. Pholmann, "Fiedler's Contingency Theory of Leadership: An Application of the Meta-Analysis Procedures of Schmidt and Hunter," *Psychological Bulletin*, March 1985, pp. 274–85; C.A. Schriesheim, B.J. Tepper, and L.A. Tetrault, "Lease Preferred Co-Worker Score, Situational Control, and Leadership Effectiveness: A Meta-Analysis of Contingency Model Performance Predictions," *Journal of Applied Psychology*, August 1994, pp. 561–73; and R. Ayman, M.M. Chemers, and F. Fiedler, "The Contingency Model of Leadership Effectiveness: Its Levels of Analysis," *Leadership Quarterly*, Summer 1995, pp. 147–67.

12. See E.H. Schein, *Organizational Psychology*, 3rd ed. (Upper Saddle River, NJ: Prentice Hall, 1980), pp. 116–17; and B. Kabanoff, "A Critique of Leader Match and Its Implications for Leadership Research," *Personnel Psychology*, Winter 1981, pp. 749–64.

13. P. Hersey and K. Blanchard, "So You Want to Know Your Leadership Style?" *Training and Development Journal*, February 1974, pp. 1–15; and P. Hersey and K.H. Blanchard, *Management of Organizational Behavior: Leading Human Resources*, 8th ed. (Englewood Cliffs, NJ: Prentice Hall, 2001).

14. See, for instance, C.F. Fernandez and R.P. Vecchio, "Situational Leadership Theory Revisited: A Test of an Across-Jobs Perspective," *Leadership Quarterly*, vol. 8, no. 1 (1997), pp. 67–84; and C.L. Graeff, "Evolution of Situational Leadership Theory: A Critical Review," *Leadership Quarterly*, vol. 8, no. 2 (1997), pp. 153–70.

15. V.H. Vroom and P.W. Yetton, *Leadership and Decision-Making* (Pitts-

burgh, PA: University of Pittsburgh Press, 1973).

16. V.H. Vroom and A.G. Jago, *The New Leadership: Managing Participation in Organizations* (Upper Saddle River, NJ: Prentice Hall, 1988). See especially Chapter 8.

17. V.H. Vroom, "Leadership and the Decision-Making Process," *Organizational Dynamics*, vol. 18, no. 4 (2000), pp. 82–94.

18. R.J. House, "A Path-Goal Theory of Leader Effectiveness," *Administrative Science Quarterly*, September 1971, pp. 321–38; R.J. House and T.R. Mitchell, "Path-Goal Theory of Leadership," *Journal of Contemporary Business*, Autumn 1974, p. 86; and R.J. House, "Path-Goal Theory of Leadership: Lessons, Legacy, and a Reformulated Theory," *Leadership Quarterly*, Fall 1996, pp. 323–52.

19. J.C. Wofford and L.Z. Liska, "Path-Goal Theories of Leadership: A Meta-Analysis," *Journal of Management*, Winter 1993, pp. 857–76; and A. Sagie and M. Koslowsky, "Organizational Attitudes and Behaviors as a Function of Participation in Strategic and Tactical Change Decisions: An Application of Path-Goal Theory," *Journal of Organizational Behavior*, January 1994, pp. 37–47.

20. B.M. Bass, "Leadership: Good, Better, Best," *Organizational Dynamics*, Winter 1985, pp. 26–40; and J. Seltzer and B.M. Bass, "Transformational Leadership: Beyond Initiation and Consideration," *Journal of Management*, December 1990, pp. 693–703.

21. B.J. Avolio and B.M. Bass, "Transformational Leadership, Charisma, and Beyond." Working paper, School of Management, State University of New York, Binghamton, 1985, p. 14.

22. J.J. Hater and B.M. Bass, "Supervisors' Evaluation and Subordinates' Perceptions of Transformational and Transactional Leadership," *Journal of Applied Psychology*, November 1988, pp. 695–702; and B.M. Bass and B.J. Avolio, "Developing Transformational Leadership: 1992 and Beyond," *Journal of European Industrial Training*, January 1990, p. 23.

23. Bass and Avolio, "Developing Transformational Leadership"; R.T. Keller, "Transformational Leadership and the Performance of Research and Development Project Groups," *Journal of Management*, September 1992, pp. 489–501; J.M. Howell and B.J. Avolio, "Transformational Leadership, Transactional Leadership, Locus of Control, and Support for Innovation: Key Predictors of Consolidated-Business-Unit Performance," *Journal of Applied Psychology*, December 1993, pp. 891–911; and T.A. Judge and J.E. Bono, "Five-Factor Model of Personality and Transformational Leadership," *Journal of Applied Psychology*, October 2000, pp. 751–65; N. Sivasubramaniam, W.D. Murry, B.J. Avolio, and D.I. Jung, "A Longitudinal Model of the Effects of Team Leadership and Group Potency on Group Performance," *Group and Organization Management*, March 2002, pp. 66–96; and T. Dvir, D. Eden, B.J. Avolio, and B. Shamir, "Impact of Transformational Leadership on Follower Development and Performance: A Field Experiment," *Academy of Management Journal*, August 2002, pp. 735–44.

24. F. Vogelstein, "Mighty Amazon," *Fortune*, May 26, 2003, pp. 60–74.

25. J.A. Conger and R.N. Kanungo, "Behavioral Dimensions of Charismatic Leadership," in J.A. Conger, R.N. Kanungo and Associates, *Charismatic Leadership* (San Francisco: Jossey-Bass, 1988), pp. 78–97; G. Yukl and J.M. Howell, "Organizational and Contextual Influences on the Emergence and Effectiveness of Charismatic Leadership," *Leadership Quarterly*, Summer 1999, pp. 257–83; and J.M. Crant and T.S. Bateman, "Charismatic Leadership Viewed from Above: The Impact of Proactive Personality," *Journal of Organizational Behavior*, February 2000, pp. 63–75.

26. J.A. Conger and R.N. Kanungo, *Charismatic Leadership in Organizations* (Thousand Oaks, CA: Sage, 1998).

27. R.J. House, J. Woycke, and E.M. Fodor, "Charismatic and Noncharismatic Leaders: Differences in Behavior and Effectiveness," in Conger and Kanungo, *Charismatic Leadership*, pp. 103–4; D.A. Waldman, B.M. Bass, and F.J. Yammarino, "Adding to Contingent-Reward Behavior: The Augmenting Effect of Charismatic Leadership," *Group & Organization Studies*, December 1990, pp. 381–94; S.A. Kirkpatrick and E.A. Locke, "Direct and Indirect Effects of Three Core Charismatic Leadership Components on Performance and Attitudes," *Journal of Applied Psychology*, February 1996, pp. 36–51; G.P. Shea and C.M. Howell, "Charismatic Leadership and Task Feedback: A Laboratory Study of Their Effects on Self-Efficacy," *Leadership Quarterly*, Fall 1999, pp. 375–96; R.W. Rowden, "The Relationship Between Charismatic Leadership Behaviors and Organizational Commitment," *Leadership & Organization Development Journal*, January 2000, pp. 30–35; J.A. Conger, R.N. Kanungo, and S.T. Menon, "Charismatic Leadership and Follower Effects," *Journal of Organizational Behavior*, vol. 21 (2000), pp. 747–67; and J. Paul, D.L. Costley, J.P. Howell, P.W. Dorfman, and D. Trafimow, "The Effects of Charismatic Leadership on Followers' Self-Concept Accessibility," *Journal of Applied Social Psychology*, September 2001, pp. 1821–44.

28. J.A. Conger and R.N. Kanungo, "Training Charismatic Leadership: A Risky and Critical Task," in Conger and Kanungo, *Charismatic Leadership*, pp. 309–23; S. Caudron, "Growing Charisma," *Industry Week*, May 4, 1998, pp. 54–55; and R. Birchfield, "Creating Charismatic Leaders," *Management*, June 2000, pp. 30–31.

29. House, "A 1976 Theory of Charismatic Leadership"; R.J. House and R.N. Aditya, "The Social Scientific Study of Leadership: Quo Vadis?" *Journal of Management*, vol. 23, no. 3 (1997), pp. 316–23; and J.G. Hunt and others, "The Effects of Visionary and Crisis-Responsive Charisma on Followers: An Experimental Examination," *Leadership Quarterly*, Fall 1999, pp. 423–48.

30. This definition is based on M. Sashkin, "The Visionary Leader," in Conger and Kanungo, *Charismatic Leadership*, pp. 124–25; B. Nanus, *Visionary Leadership* (New York: Free Press, 1992), p. 8; N.H. Snyder and M. Graves, "Leadership and Vision," *Business Horizons*, January–February 1994, p. 1; and J.R. Lucas, "Anatomy of a Vision Statement," *Management Review*, February 1998, pp. 22–26.

31. Nanus, *Visionary Leadership*, p. 8.

32. Based on Sashkin, "The Visionary Leader," pp. 128–30; and J.R. Baum, E.A. Locke, and S.A. Kirkpatrick, "A Longitudinal Study of the Relation of Vision and Vision Communication to Venture Growth in Entrepreneurial Firms," *Journal of Applied Psychology*, February 1998, pp. 43–54.

33. S. Caminiti, "What Team Leaders Need to Know," *Fortune*, February 20, 1995, pp. 93–100.

34. Ibid., p. 93.

35. Ibid., p. 100.

36. N. Steckler and N. Fondas, "Building Team Leader Effectiveness: A Diagnostic Tool," *Organizational Dynamics*, Winter 1995, p. 20.

37. R.S. Wellins, W.C. Byham, and G.R. Dixon, *Inside Teams* (San Francisco: Jossey-Bass, 1994), p. 318.

38. Steckler and Fondas, "Building Team Leader Effectiveness," p. 21.

39. J. Steinhauer, "In Crisis, Giuliani's Popularity Overflows City," *New York Times*, September 20, 2001, p. A1; C. Jones, "Giuliani Exits as National Icon," *USA Today*, December 28, 2001, p 3A; D. Barry, "A Man Who Became More Than Mayor," *New York Times*, December 31, 2001, p. A1; and E. Pooley, "Mayor of the World," *Time*, December 31, 2001–January 7, 2002.

40. See J.R.P. French Jr. and B. Raven, "The Bases of Social Power," in D. Cartwright and A.F. Zander (eds.), *Group Dynamics: Research and Theory* (New York: Harper & Row, 1960), pp. 607–23; P.M. Podsakoff and C.A. Schriesheim, "Field Studies of French and Raven's Bases of Power: Critique, Reanalysis, and Suggestions for Future Research," *Psychological Bulletin*, May 1985, pp. 387–411; R.K. Shukla, "Influence of Power Bases in Organizational Decision Making: A Contingency Model," *Decision Sciences*, July 1982, pp. 450–70; D.E. Frost and A.J. Stahelski, "The Systematic Measurement of French and Raven's Bases of Social Power in Workgroups," *Journal of Applied Social Psychology*, April 1988, pp. 375–89; and T.R. Hinkin and C.A. Schriesheim, "Development and Application of New Scales to Measure the French and Raven (1959) Bases of Social Power," *Journal of Applied Psychology*, August 1989, pp. 561–67.

41. This box based on S.A. Culbert and J.J. McDonough, *The Invisible War: Pursuing Self-Interest at Work* (New York: John Wiley, 1980); J. Pfeffer, *Power in Organizations* (Marshfield, MA: Pitman, 1981); H. Mintzberg, *Power In and Around Organizations* (Upper Saddle River, NJ: Prentice Hall, 1983); and S.P. Robbins and P.L. Hunsaker, *Training in InterPersonal Skills: TIPS for Managing People at Work*, 3rd ed. (Upper Saddle River, NJ: Prentice Hall, 2003).

42. See Australian Navy Web site (*www.navy.gov.au*).

43. D. Reed, "Sorry Doesn't Sway AMR Workers," *USA Today*, April 22, 2003, p. 1B; D. Reed, "Carty Faces Crisis," *USA Today*, April 23, 2003, p. 3B; D. Reed, "Carty Resigns as 2 Unions Agree to New Concessions," *USA Today*, April 25, 2003, p. 1B; M. Adams and D. Reed, "Workers in Limbo, Morale Horrible," *USA Today*, April 25, 2003, p. 3B; and W. Zellner, "What Was Don Carty Thinking?" *BusinessWeek*, May 5, 2003, p. 32.

44. J.M. Kouzes and B.Z. Posner, *Credibility: How Leaders Gain and Lose It, and Why People Demand It* (San Francisco: Jossey-Bass, 1993), p. 14.

45. Based on L.T. Hosmer, "Trust: The Connecting Link between Organizational Theory and Philosophical Ethics," *Academy of Management Review*, April 1995, p. 393; R.C. Mayer, J.H. Davis, and F.D. Schoorman, "An Integrative Model of Organizational Trust," *Academy of Management Review*, July 1995, p. 712; and G.M.

Spreitzer and A.K. Mishra, "Giving Up Control without Losing Control," *Group & Organization Management*, June 1999, pp. 155–87.

46. P.L. Schindler and C.C. Thomas, "The Structure of Interpersonal Trust in the Workplace," *Psychological Reports*, October 1993, pp. 563–73.

47. H.H. Tan and C.S.F. Tan, "Toward the Differentiation of Trust in Supervisor and Trust in Organization," *Genetic, Social, and General Psychology Monographs*, May 2000, pp. 241–60.

48. K.T. Dirks and D.L. Ferrin, "Trust in Leadership: Meta-Analytic Findings and Implications for Research and Practice," *Journal of Applied Psychology*, August 2002, pp. 611–28.

49. This section is based on F. Bartolome, "Nobody Trusts the Boss Completely—Now What?" *Harvard Business Review*, March–April 1989, pp. 135–42; J.K. Butler Jr., "Toward Understanding and Measuring Conditions of Trust: Evolution of a Conditions of Trust Inventory," *Journal of Management*, September 1991, pp. 643–63; and Dirks and Ferrin, "Trust in Leadership: Meta-Analytic Findings and Implications for Research and Practice."

50. J. Brockner, P.A. Siegel, J.P. Daly, T. Tyler, and C. Martin, "When Trust Matters: The Moderating Effect of Outcome Favorability," *Administrative Science Quarterly*, September 1997, p. 558; S. Armour, "Employees' New Motto: Trust No One," *USA Today*, February 5, 2002, p. 1B; J. Scott, "Once Bitten, Twice Shy: A World of Eroding Trust," *New York Times*, April 21, 2002, p. WK5; and J.A. Byrne, "Restoring Trust in Corporate America," *BusinessWeek*, June 24, 2002, pp. 30–35.

51. "Weathering the Storm: A Study of Employee Attitudes and Opinions," *WorkUSA 2002 Study*, Watson Wyatt (*www.watsonwyatt.com*).

52. This section is based on R.B. Morgan, "Self- and Co-Worker Perceptions of Ethics and Their Relationships to Leadership and Salary," *Academy of Management Journal*, February 1993, pp. 200–14; E.P. Hollander, "Ethical Challenges in the Leader–Follower Relationship," *Business Ethics Quarterly*, January 1995, pp. 55–65; J.C. Rost, "Leadership: A Discussion about Ethics," *Business Ethics Quarterly*, January 1995, pp. 129–42; R.N. Kanungo and M. Mendonca, *Ethical Dimensions of Leadership* (Thousand Oaks, CA: Sage Publications, 1996); J.B. Ciulla (ed.), *Ethics: The Heart of Leadership* (New York: Praeger Publications, 1998); J.D. Costa, *The Ethical Imperative: Why Moral Leadership Is Good Business*

(Cambridge, MA: Perseus Press, 1999); and N.M. Tichy and A. McGill (eds.), *The Ethical Challenge: How to Build Honest Business Leaders* (New York: John Wiley & Sons, 2003).

53. "Former McKesson Chairman Indicted for Alleged Fraud," *USA Today*, June 5, 2003 (*www.usatoday.com*); and M. Benjamin, "Risky Business," *U.S. News & World Report*, September 9, 2002, pp. 34–37.

54. J.M. Burns, *Leadership* (New York: Harper & Row, 1978).

55. J.M. Avolio, S. Kahai, and G.E. Dodge, "The Ethics of Charismatic Leadership: Submission or Liberation?" *Academy of Management Executive*, May 1992, pp. 43–55.

56. J.S. McClenahen, "UTC's Master of Principle," *Industry Week*, January 2003, pp. 30–33.

57. L.K. Trevino, M. Brown, and L.P. Hartman, "A Qualitative Investigation of Perceived Executive Ethical Leadership: Perceptions from Inside and Outside the Executive Suite," *Human Relations*, January 2003, pp. 5–37.

58. C. Kleiman, "Virtual Teams Make Loyalty More Realistic," *Chicago Tribune*, January 23, 2001, p. Business 1.

59. B.J. Alge, C. Wiethoff, and H.J. Klein, "When Does the Medium Matter? Knowledge-building Experiences and Opportunities in Decision-making Teams," *Organizational Behavior and Human Decision Processes*, 2003, forthcoming; C.O. Grosse, "Managing Communication within Virtual Intercultural Teams," *Business Communication Quarterly*, December 2002, pp. 22–38; M.M. Montoya-Weiss, A.P. Massey, and M. Song, "Getting It Together: Temporal Coordination and Conflict Management in Global Virtual Teams," *Academy of Management Journal*, December 2001, pp. 1251–62; M.L. Maznevski and K.M. Chudoba, "Bridging Space over Time: Global Virtual-Team Dynamics and Effectiveness," *Organization Science*, vol. 11 (2000), pp. 473–92; W.F. Cascio, "Managing a Virtual Workplace," *Academy of Management Executive*, August 2000, pp. 81–90; and A.M. Townsend, S.M. DeMarie, and A.R. Hendrickson, " 'Virtual Teams' Technology and the Workplace of the Future," *Academy of Management Executive*, August 1998, pp. 17–29.

60. Cascio, "Managing a Virtual Workplace," pp. 88–89.

61. N. Desmond, "The CEO Dashboard," *Business 2.0*, August 2002, p. 34.

62. T. Vinas, "DuPont: Safety Starts at the Top," *Industry Week*, July 2002, p. 55.

63. W.A. Randolph, "Navigating the Journey to Empowerment," *Organizational Dynamics*, Spring 1995, pp. 19–32; R.C. Ford and M.D. Fottler, "Empowerment: A Matter of Degree," *Academy of Management Executive*, August 1995, pp. 21–31; R.C. Herrenkohl, G.T. Judson, and J.A. Heffner, "Defining and Measuring Employee Empowerment," *Journal of Applied Behavioral Science*, September 1999, p. 373; and C. Robert and T.M. Probst, "Empowerment and Continuous Improvement in the United States, Mexico, Poland, and India," *Journal of Applied Psychology*, October 2000, pp. 643–58; C. Gomez and B. Rosen, "The Leader-Member Link Between Managerial Trust and Employee Empowerment," *Group & Organization Management*, March 2001, pp. 53–69; W. Alan Rudolph and M. Sashkin, "Can Organizational Empowerment Work in Multinational Settings?" *Academy of Management Executive*, February 2002, pp. 102–15; and P.K. Mills and G.R. Ungson, "Reassessing the Limits of Structural Empowerment: Organizational Constitution and Trust as Controls," *Academy of Management Review*, January 2003, pp. 143–53.

64. T.A. Stewart, "Just Think: No Permission Needed," *Fortune*, January 8, 2001, pp. 190–92.

65. F.W. Swierczek, "Leadership and Culture: Comparing Asian Managers," *Leadership & Organization Development Journal*, December 1991, pp. 3–10.

66. House, "Leadership in the Twenty-First Century," p. 443; M.F. Peterson and J.G. Hunt, "International Perspectives on International Leadership," *Leadership Quarterly*, Fall 1997, pp. 203–31; and J.R. Schermerhorn and M.H. Bond, "Cross-cultural Leadership in Collectivism and High Power Distance Settings," *Leadership & Organization Development Journal*, vol. 18, nos. 4/5 (1997), pp. 187–93.

67. R.J. House, P.J. Hanges, S.A. Ruiz-Quintanilla, P.W. Dorfman and Associates, "Culture Specific and Cross-Culturally Generalizable Implicit Leadership Theories: Are the Attributes of Charismatic/Transformational Leadership Universally Endorsed?" *Leadership Quarterly*, Summer 1999, pp. 219–56; and D.E. Carl and M. Javidan, "Universality of Charismatic Leadership: A Multi-Nation Study," paper presented at the National Academy of Management Conference, Washington, DC, August 2001.

68. D.E. Carl and M. Javidan, "Universality of Charismatic Leadership," p. 29.

69. S. Armour, "More Women Cruise to the Top," *USA Today*, June 25, 2003 (*www.usatoday.com*); and "The World's Women 2000: Trends and Statistics: Table 5.F," United Nation's Statistics Division (*unstats.un.org/demographic*).

70. G.N. Powell, D.A. Butterfield, and J.D. Parent, "Gender and Managerial Stereotypes: Have the Times Changed?" *Journal of Management*, vol. 28, no. 2 (2002), pp. 177–93.

71. See F.J. Yammarino, A.J. Dubinsky, L.B. Comer, and M.A. Jolson, "Women and Transformational and Contingent Reward Leadership: A Multiple-Levels-of-Analysis Perspective," *Academy of Management Journal*, February 1997, pp. 205–22; M. Gardiner and M. Tiggemann, "Gender Differences in Leadership Style, Job Stress and Mental Health in Male- and Female-Dominated Industries," *Journal of Occupational and Organizational Psychology*, September 1999, pp. 301–15; C.L. Ridgeway, "Gender, Status, and Leadership," *Journal of Social Issues*, Winter 2001, pp. 637–55; W.H. Decker and D.M. Rotondo, "Relationships among Gender, Type of Humor, and Perceived Leader Effectiveness," *Journal of Managerial Issues*, Winter 2001, pp. 450–65; J.M. Norvilitis and H.M. Reid, "Evidence for an Association Between Gender-Role Identity and a Measure of Executive Function," *Psychological Reports*, February 2002, pp. 35–45; N.Z. Selter, "Gender Differences in Leadership: Current Social Issues and Future Organizational Implications," *Journal of Leadership Studies*, Spring 2002, pp. 88–99; J. Becker, R.A. Ayman, and K. Korabik, "Discrepancies in Self/Subordinates' Perceptions of Leadership Behavior: Leader's Gender, Organizational Context, and Leader's Self-Monitoring," *Group & Organization Management*, June 2002, pp. 226–44; A.H. Eagly and S.J. Karau, "Role Congruity Theory of Prejudice Toward Female Leaders," *Psychological Review*, July 2002, pp. 573–98; and K.M. Bartol, D.C. Martin, and J.A. Kromkowski, "Leadership and the Glass Ceiling: Gender and Ethnic Influences on Leader Behaviors at Middle and Executive Managerial Levels," *Journal of Leadership & Organizational Studies*, Winter 2003, pp. 8–19.

72. Gardiner and Tiggemann, "Gender Differences in Leadership Style, Job Stress and Mental Health in Male- and Female-Dominated Industries."

73. Norvilitis and Reid, "Evidence for an Association Between Gender-Role Identity and a Measure of Executive Function"; W.H. Decker and D.M. Rotondo, "Relationships among Gender, Type of Humor, and Perceived Leader Effectiveness"; H. Aguinis and S.K.R. Adams, "Social-role Versus Structural Models of Gender and Influence Use in Organizations: A Strong Inference Approach," *Group & Organization Management*, December 1998, pp. 414–46; and A.H. Eagly, S.J. Karau, and M.G. Makhijani, "Gender and the Effectiveness of Leaders: A Meta-Analysis," *Psychological Bulletin*, vol. 117 (1995), pp. 125–45.

74. Bartol, Martin, and Kromkowski, "Leadership and the Glass Ceiling: Gender and Ethnic Group Influences on Leader Behaviors at Middle and Executive Managerial Levels"; and R. Sharpe, "As Leaders, Women Rule," *BusinessWeek*, November 20, 2000, pp. 74–84.

75. Bartol, Martin, and Kromkowski, "Leadership and the Glass Ceiling: Gender and Ethnic Group Influences on Leader Behaviors at Middle and Executive Managerial Levels."

76. J. Useem, "From Heroes to Goats and Back Again?" *Fortune*, November 18, 2002, pp. 40–48.

77. N. Minow, "Show Some Real Leadership, CEOs," *USA Today*, November 25, 2002, p. 13A.

78. J. Useem, "CEO Pay: Have They No Shame?" *Fortune*, April 14, 2003, accessed on *Fortune*'s Web site (*www.fortune.com*).

79. Useem, "From Heroes to Goats and Back Again?"

80. A. Webber, "CEO Bashing Has Gone too Far," *USA Today*, June 3, 2003, p. 15A; Minow, "Show Some Real Leadership, CEOs"; Useem, "From Heroes to Goats and Back Again?" and B. Horovitz, "Scandals Grow Out of CEOs' Warped Mind-Set," *USA Today*, October 11, 2002, p. B1.

81. A. Webber, "Above-it-all CEOs Forget Workers," *USA Today*, November 11, 2002, p. 13A.

82. Ibid.

83. See, for instance, R. Lofthouse, "Herding the Cats," *EuroBusiness*, February 2001, pp. 64–65; and M. Delahoussaye, "Leadership in the 21st Century," *Training*, September 2001, pp. 60–72.

84. See, for instance, A.A. Vicere, "Executive Education: The Leading Edge," *Organizational Dynamics*, Autumn 1996, pp. 67–81; J. Barling, T. Weber, and E.K. Kelloway, "Effects of Transformational Leadership Training on Attitudinal and Financial Outcomes: A Field Experiment," *Journal of Applied Psychology*, December 1996, pp. 827–32; and D.V. Day, "Leadership Development: A Review in Context," *Leadership Quarterly*, Winter 2000, pp. 581–613.

85. K.Y. Chan and F. Drasgow, "Toward a Theory of Individual Differences and Leadership: Understanding the Motivation to Lead," *Journal of Applied Psychology*, June 2001, pp. 481–98.

86. Sashkin, "The Visionary Leader," p. 150.

87. S. Kerr and J.M. Jermier, "Substitutes for Leadership: Their Meaning and Measurement," *Organizational Behavior and Human Performance*, December 1978, pp. 375–403; J.P. Howell, P.W. Dorfman, and S. Kerr, "Leadership and Substitutes for Leadership," *Journal of Applied Behavioral Science* 22, no. 1 (1986), pp. 29–46; J.P. Howell, D.E. Bowen, P.W. Dorfman, S. Kerr, and P.M. Podsakoff, "Substitutes for Leadership: Effective Alternatives to Ineffective Leadership," *Organizational Dynamics*, Summer 1990, pp. 21–38; and P.M. Podsakoff, B.P. Niehoff, S.B. MacKenzie, and M.L. Williams, "Do Substitutes for Leadership Really Substitute for Leadership? An Empirical Examination of Kerr and Jermier's Situational Leadership Model," *Organizational Behavior and Human Decision Processes*, February 1993, pp. 1–44.

88. Situation adapted from information in: Joseph Menn, "Ellison Talks Tough on Bid for PeopleSoft," *Los Angeles Times*, July 10, 2003, p. C-1+; Mylene Mangalindan, Don Clark, and Robin Sidel, "Hostile Move Augurs High-Tech Consolidation," *Wall Street Journal*, June 9, 2003, pp. A1+; Alex Pham, "Oracle's Merger Hurdles Get Higher," *Los Angeles Times*, June 30, 2003, pp. C-1+; Shelley Pannill, "Smashmouth PR Meets High Tech," *Forbes*, May 28, 2001, p. 9; Fred Vogelstein, "Oracle's Ellison Turns Hostile," *Fortune*, June 23, 2003, p. 28.

PART FIVE

1. S. Greengard, "25 Growing Companies," *Industry Week*, November 20, 2000, p. 76.

2. P.B. Robinson, D.V. Simpson, J.C. Huefner, and H.K. Hunt, "An Attitude Approach to the Prediction of Entrepreneurship," *Entrepreneurship Theory and Practice*, Summer 1991, pp. 13–31.

3. B.M. Davis, "Role of Venture Capital in the Economic Renaissance of an Area," in R.D. Hisrich (ed.), *Entrepreneurship, Intrapreneurship, and Venture Capital* (Lexington, MA: Lexington Books, 1986), pp. 107–18.

4. J.M. Crant, "The Proactive Personality Scale as Predictor of Entrepreneurial Intentions," *Journal of Small Business Management*, July 1996, pp. 42–49.

5. W.H. Stewart, "Risk Propensity Differences between Entrepreneurs and Managers: A Meta-Analytic Review," *Journal of Applied Psychology*, February 2001, pp. 145–53.

6. J. Chun, "Type E Personality," *Entrepreneur*, January 1997, p. 10.

7. Information from company's Web site (*www.sapient.com*), July 7, 2003; and S. Herrera, "People Power," *Forbes*, November 2, 1998, p. 212.

8. "Saluting the Global Awards Recipients of Arthur Andersen's Best Practices Awards 2000," *Fortune Olivine* (*www.fortune.com*), January 16, 2001.

9. T. Purdum, "Winning with Empowerment," *Industry Week*, October 16, 2000, pp. 109–10.

10. Company financial information from Hoover's Online (*www.hoovers.com*), July 8, 2003; and P. Strozniak, "Rescue Operation," *Industry Week*, October 16, 2000, pp. 103–4.

11. M. DePree, *Leadership Jazz* (New York: Currency Doubleday, 1992), pp. 8–9.

12. J.C. Collins and J.I. Porras, *Built to Last: Successful Habits of Visionary Companies* (New York: HarperBusiness, 1994).

13. P. Strozniak, "Teams at Work," *Industry Week*, September 18, 2000, pp. 47–50.

14. Ibid.

CHAPTER 18

1. Information from company Web site (*www.haier.com*) and Hoover's Online (*www.hoovers.com*), January 5, 2003; D.J. Lynch, "CEO Pushes China's Haier as Global Brand," *USA Today*, January 3, 2003, pp. 1B+; and G. Khermouch, B. Einhorn, and D. Roberts, "Breaking into the Name Game," *BusinessWeek*, April 7, 2003, p. 54.

2. J. Kluger and B. Liston, "A Columbia Culprit?" *Time*, February 24, 2003, p. 13.

3. K.A. Merchant, "The Control Function of Management," *Sloan Management Review*, Summer 1982, pp. 43–55.

4. E. Flamholtz, "Organizational Control Systems as a Managerial Tool," *California Management Review*, Winter 1979, p. 55.

5. W.G. Ouchi, "A Conceptual Framework for the Design of Organizational Control Mechanisms," *Management Science*, August 1979, pp. 833–38; and W.G. Ouchi, "Markets, Bureaucracies, and Clans," *Administrative Science Quarterly*, March 1980, pp. 129–41.

6. P. Magnusson, "Your Jitters Are Their Lifeblood," *BusinessWeek*, April 14, 2003, p. 41; S. Williams, Company Crisis: CEO under Fire," *Hispanic Business*, March 2003, pp. 54–56; T. Purdum, "Preparing for the Worst," *Industry Week*, January 2003, pp. 53–55; and S. Leibs, "Lesson from 9/11: It's Not about Data," *CFO*, September 2002, pp. 31–32.

7. S. Kerr, "On the Folly of Rewarding A, While Hoping for B," *Academy of Management Journal*, December 1975, pp. 769–83.

8. M. Starr, "State-of-the Art Stats," *Newsweek*, March 24, 2003, pp. 47–49.

9. A.M. Ristow, T.L. Amos, and G.E. Staude, "Transformational Leadership and Organizational Effectiveness in the Administration of Cricket in South Africa," *South African Journal of Business Management*, March 1999, pp. 1–5.

10. This box based on J. Hickman, C. Tkaczyk, E. Florian, and J. Stemple, "50 Best Companies for Minorities," *Fortune*, July 7, 2003, pp. 103–20; and S.M. Mehta, "What Minority Employees Really Want," *Fortune*, July 10, 2000, pp. 180–86.

11. "*Fortune 500* Top Performers," *Fortune*, April 17, 2003 (*www.fortune.com*).

12. R. Levering and M. Moskowitz, "100 Best Companies to Work for: How We Pick the 100 Best," *Fortune*, January 7, 2003 (*www.fortune.com*).

13. G. Tanincez, "Road to Excellence," *Industry Week*, July 2003 (*www.industryweek.com*).

14. "ACSI Methodology," American Customer Satisfaction Index, found online at (*www.theacsi.org/model.htm*), June 29, 2003.

15. Information from company Web site (*www.applebees.com*), June 29, 2003; and J. Rosenfeld, "Down-Home Food, Cutting-Edge Business," *Fast Company*, April 2000, pp. 56–58.

16. P. Landers, "Japan Tech Star Sticks to Manufacturing," *Wall Street Journal*, April 24, 2000, p. A22.

17. H. Koontz and R.W. Bradspies, "Managing through Feedforward Control," *Business Horizons*, June 1972, pp. 25–36.

18. T. Purdum, "Lean and Clean," *Industry Week*, October 2002, pp. 47–48.

19. "An Open Letter to McDonald's Customers," *Wall Street Journal*, August 22, 2001, p. A5.

20. W.H. Newman, *Constructive Control: Design and Use of Control Systems* (Upper Saddle River, NJ: Prentice Hall, 1975), p. 33.

21. F. Hansen, "The Value-Based Management Commitment," *Business Finance*, September 2001, pp. 2–5.

22. T. Leahy, "Capitalizing on Economic Value Added," *Business Finance*, July 2000, pp. 83–86.

23. K. Lehn and A.K. Makhija, "EVA and MVA as Performance Measures and Signals for Strategic Change," *Strategy & Leadership*, May/June 1996, pp. 34–38.

24. E.E. Schultz and T. Francis, "Buried Treasure: Well-Hidden Perk Means Big Money for Top Executives," *Wall Street Journal*, October 11, 2002, pp. A1+.

25. R. Fink, "No More Holes," *CFO*, August 2002, p. 42.

26. Balanced Scorecard Collaborative (*www.bscol.com*), June 29, 2003; K. Graham, "Balanced Scorecard," *New Zealand Management*, March 2003, pp. 32–34; K. Ellis, "A Ticket to Ride: Balanced Scorecard," *Training*, April 2001, p. 50; and Leahy, "Tailoring the Balanced Scorecard," *Business Finance*, August 2000, pp. 53–56.

27. Leahy, "Tailoring the Balanced Scorecard."

28. Ibid.

29. Ibid.

30. "Mercedes-Benz Benchmarking Saves DaimlerChrysler $100 Million," *Industry Week*, October 27, 2000 (*www.industryweek.com*).

31. Y.F. Jarrar and M. Zairi, "Future Trends in Benchmarking for Competitive Advantage: A Global Survey," *Total Quality Management*, December 2001, pp. 906–12.

32. M. Simpson and D. Kondouli, "A Practical Approach to Benchmarking in Three Service Industries," *Total Quality Management*, July 2000, pp. S623–S630.

33. K.N. Dervitsiotis, "Benchmarking and Paradigm Shifts," *Total Quality Management*, July 2000, pp. S641–S646.

34. T. Leahy, "Extracting Diamonds in the Rough," *Business Finance*, August 2000, pp. 33–37.

35. B. Bruzina, B. Jessop, R. Plourde, B. Whitlock, and L. Rubin, "Ameren Embraces Benchmarking as a Core Business Strategy," *Power Engineering*, November 2002, pp. 121–24; and Leahy, "Extracting Diamonds in the Rough."

36. J. Yaukey and C.L. Romero, "Arizona Firm Pays Big for Workers' Digital Downloads," *Springfield News-Leader*, May 6, 2002, p. 6B.

37. N. Shirouzu and J. Bigness, "7-Eleven Operators Resist System to Monitor Managers," *Wall Street Journal*, June 16, 1997, p. B1.

38. E. Zimmerman, "When Employee Surveillance Crosses the Line," *Workforce*, February 2002, pp. 38–45.

39. B. Stone, "Is the Boss Watching?" *Newsweek*, September 2002, p. 38.

40. D. Hawkins, "Lawsuits Spur Rise in Employee Monitoring," *U.S. News & World Report*, August 13, 2001, p. 53; L. Guernsey, "You've Got Inappropriate Mail," *New York Times*, April 5, 2000, pp. C1+; and R. Karaim, "Setting E-Privacy Rules," *Cnnfn Online*, December 15, 1999 (*www.cnnfn.com*).

41. E. Bott, "Are You Safe? Privacy Special Report," *PC Computing*, March 2000, pp. 87–88.

42. Karaim, "Setting E-Privacy Rules."

43. K. Naughton, "CyberSlacking," *Newsweek*, November 29, 1999, pp. 62–65.

44. A.M. Bell and D.M. Smith, "Theft and Fraud May Be an Inside Job," *Workforce Online*, (*www.workforce.com*), December 3, 2000.

45. C.C. Verschoor, "New Evidence of Benefits from Effective Ethics Systems," *Strategic Finance*, May 2003, pp. 20–21; and E. Krell, "Will Forensic Accounting Go Mainstream?" *Business Finance*, October 2002, pp. 30–34.

46. J. Greenberg, "The STEAL Motive: Managing the Social Determinants of Employee Theft," in R. Giacalone and J. Greenberg (eds.), *Antisocial Behavior in Organizations* (Newbury Park, CA: Sage, 1997), pp. 85–108.

47. "Crime Spree," *BusinessWeek*, September 9, 2002, p. 8; B.P. Niehoff and R.J. Paul, "Causes of Employee Theft and Strategies that HR Managers Can Use for Prevention," *Human Resource Management*, Spring 2000, pp. 51–64; and G. Winter, "Taking at the Office Reaches New Heights: Employee Larceny Is Bigger and Bolder," *New York Times*, July 12, 2000, pp. C1+.

48. This section is based on J. Greenberg, *Behavior in Organizations: Understanding and Managing the Human Side of Work*, 8th ed. (Upper Saddle River, NJ: Prentice Hall, 2003), pp. 329–30.

49. A.H. Bell and D.M. Smith, "Why Some Employees Bite the Hand that Feeds Them," *Workforce Online* (*www.workforce.com*), December 3, 2000.

50. A.H. Bell and D.M. Smith, "Protecting the Company Against Theft and Fraud," *Workforce Online* (*www.workforce.com*), December 3, 2000; J.D. Hansen, "To Catch a Thief," *Journal of Accountancy*, March 2000, pp. 43–46; and J. Greenberg, "The Cognitive Geometry of Employee Theft," in *Dysfunctional Behavior in Organizations: Nonviolent and Deviant Behavior*, eds. S.B. Bacharach, A. O'Leary-Kelly, J.M. Collins, and R.W. Griffin (Stamford, CT: JAI Press, 1998), pp. 147–93.

51. D. Sharp, "Gunman Just Hated a Lot of People," *USA Today*, July 10, 2003, p. 3A; and M. Prince, "Violence in the Workplace on the Rise; Training, Zero Tolerance Can Prevent Aggression," *Business Insurance*, May 12, 2003, p. 1.

52. E.F. Sygnatur and G.A Tuscano, "Work-related Homicides: The Facts," *Bureau of Labor Statistics Online Report* (*www.bls.gov*), June 29, 2003; and P. Temple, "Real Danger and 'Postal' Mythology," *Workforce*, October 2000, p. 8.

53. G.O. Ginn and L.J. Henry, "Addressing Workplace Violence from a Health Management Perspective," *SAM Advanced Management Journal*, Autumn 2002, pp. 4–11.

54. "Ten Tips on Recognizing and Minimizing Violence," *Workforce Online* (*www.workforce.com*), December 3, 2000.

55. R. McNatt, "Desk Rage," *BusinessWeek*, November 27, 2000, p. 12.

56. M. Gorkin, "Key Components of a Dangerously Dysfunctional Work Environment," *Workforce Online* (*www.workforce.com*), December 3, 2000.

57. "Ten Tips on Recognizing and Minimizing Violence"; M Gorkin, "Five Strategies and Structures for Reducing Workplace Violence"; "Investigating Workplace Violence: Where Do You Start?" and "Points to Cover In a Workplace Violence Policy" all articles from *Workforce Online* (*www.workforce.com*), December 3, 2000.

58. Information from company's Web site (*www.enterprise.com*), June 29, 2003; and A. Taylor, "Driving Customer Satisfaction," *Harvard Business Review*, July 2002, pp. 24–25.

59. S.D. Pugh, J. Dietz, J.W. Wiley, and S.M. Brooks, "Driving Service Effectiveness through Employee-Customer Linkages," *Academy of Management Executive*, November 2002, pp. 73–84.

60. "A Revolution Where Everyone Wins: Worldwide Movement to Improve Corporate-Governance Standards," *BusinessWeek*, May 19, 2003, p. 72.

61. J.S. McClenahen, "Executives Expect More Board Input," *Industry Week*, October 2002, p. 12.

62. D. Salierno, "Boards Face Increased Responsibility," *Internal Auditor*, June 2003, pp. 14–15.

63. Situation adapted from information in: Karl Cushing, "E-Mail Policy," *Computer Weekly*, June 24, 2003, p. 8; "Spam Leads to Lawsuit Fears, Lost Time," *InternetWeek*, June 23, 2003, *www.internetweek.com*.

CHAPTER 19

1. Information from company Web site (*www.bombardier.com*) and Hoover's Online (*www.hoovers.com*), January 5, 2003; and G. Bylinsky, "Elite Factories," *Fortune*, September 2, 2002, pp. 172 (D)–172 (H).

2. D. Clark, "Inside Intel, It's All Copying," *Wall Street Journal*, October 28, 2002, pp. B1+.

3. *World Fact Book 2003*, available online at (*www.odci.gov/cia/publications*).

4. Ibid.

5. T. Aeppel, "Workers Not Included," *Wall Street Journal*, November 19, 2002, pp. B1+.

6. A. Aston and M. Arndt, "The Flexible Factory," *BusinessWeek*, May 5, 2003, pp. 90–91.

7. P. Panchak, "Pella Drives Lean Throughout the Enterprise," *Industry Week*, June 2003, pp. 74–77.

8. J. Ordonez, "McDonald's to Cut the Cooking Time of Its French Fries," *Wall Street Journal*, May 19, 2000, p. B2.

9. C. Fredman, "The Devil in the Details," *Executive Edge*, April–May, 1999, pp. 36–39.

10. T. Mudd, "The Last Laugh," *Industry Week*, September 18, 2000, pp. 38–44.

11. T. Vinas, "Little Things Mean a Lot," *Industry Week*, November 2002, p. 55.

12. S. Levy, "The Connected Company," *Newsweek*, April 28, 2003, pp. 40–48; and J. Teresko, "Plant Floor Strategy," *Industry Week*, July 2002, pp. 26–32.

13. T. Laseter, K. Ramdas, and D. Swerdlow, "The Supply Side of Design and Development," *Strategy & Business*, Summer 2003, p. 23; J. Jusko, "Not All Dollars and Cents," *Industry Week*, April 2002, p. 58; and D. Drickhamer, "Medical Marvel," *Industry Week*, March 2002, pp. 47–49.

14. J.H. Sheridan, "Managing the Value Chain," *Industry Week*, September 6, 1999, available online at (*www.industryweek.com*).

15. Ibid., p. 3.

16. D. Sharma, C. Lucier, and R. Molloy, "From Solutions to Symbiosis: Blending with Your Customers," *Strategy & Business*, Second Quarter 2002, pp. 38–48; and S. Leibs, "Getting Ready: Your Suppliers," *Industry Week*, September 6, 1999, available online at (*www.industryweek.com*).

17. D. Bartholomew, "The Infrastructure," *Industry Week*, September 6, 1999, p. 1, available online at (*www.industryweek.com*).

18. T. Stevens, "Integrated Product Development," *Industry Week*, June 2002, pp. 21–28.

19. R. Normann and R. Ramirez, "From Value Chain to Value Constellation," *Harvard Business Review on Managing the Value Chain* (Boston: Harvard Business School Press, 2000), pp. 185–219.

20. D. Drickhamer, "Looking for Value," *Industry Week*, December 2002, pp. 41–43.

21. Sheridan, "Managing the Value Chain," p. 3.

22. S. Leibs, "Getting Ready: Your Customers," *Industry Week*, September 6, 1999, p. 1, available online at (*www.industryweek.com*).

23. G. Taninecz, "Forging the Chain," *Industry Week*, May 15, 2000, pp. 40–46.

24. Leibs, "Getting Ready: Your Customers."

25. D. Drickhamer, "On Target," *Industry Week*, October 16, 2000, pp. 111–12.

26. Taninecz, "Forging the Chain," p. 44.

27. "Top Security Threats and Management Issues Facing Corporate America: 2003 Survey of *Fortune* 1000 Companies," ASIS International and Pinkerton, available at (*www.asisonline.org*).

28. Sheridan, "Managing the Value Chain," p. 4.

29. D. Morse, "Fast Furniture," *Wall Street Journal*, November 19, 2002, pp. A1+.

30. J. Teresko, "The Dawn of E-Manufacturing," *Industry Week*, October 2, 2000, pp. 55–60.

31. A. Barrett, "Schering's Dr. Feelbetter?" *BusinessWeek*, June 23, 2003, pp. 55–56; J. Simons, "Bitter Medicine," *Fortune*, October 14, 2002, pp. 169–74; and D. Bartholomew, "E-Business Commentary—Quality Is Still Job One," *Industry Week*, September 4, 2000, available online at (*www.industryweek.com*).

32. G. Hasek, "Merger Marries Quality Efforts," *Industry Week*, August 21, 2000, pp. 89–92.

33. Ibid.

34. G. Hasek, "Extraordinary Excursions," *Industry Week*, October 16, 2000, pp. 79–80.

35. W. Royal, "Spotlight Shines on Maquiladora," *Industry Week*, October 16, 2000, pp. 91–92.

36. See B. Whitford and R. Andrew (eds.), *The Pursuit of Quality* (Perth, Australia: Beaumont Publishing, 1994).

37. D. Drickhamer, "Road to Excellence," *Industry Week*, October 16, 2000, pp. 117–18.

38. *ISO Annual Report 2002*, available at (*www.iso.ch*).

39. Hasek, "Merger Marries Quality Efforts."

40. M. Arndt, "Quality Isn't Just for Widgets," *BusinessWeek*, July 22, 2002, pp. 72–73.

41. Ibid.

42. Ibid.

43. "Made-to-Fit Clothes Are on the Way," *USA Today*, July 2002, pp. 8–9; and L. Elliott, "Mass Customization Comes a Step Closer," *Design News*, February 18, 2002, p. 21.

44. E. Schonfeld, "The Customized, Digitized, Have-it-your-way Economy," *Fortune*, October 28, 1998, pp. 114–20.

45. Situation adapted from information in: "How to Help Reinvigorate Your Organization's Ethics Program," *HR Focus*, June 2003, pp. 6+; Melinda Ligos, "Boot Camps on Ethics Ask the 'What Ifs?'" *New York Times*, January 5, 2003, p. 12.

PART SIX

1. Information from company's Web site (*www.gloryfoods.com*), July 8, 2003; and C. Shook, "Making Haste Slowly," *Forbes*, September 22, 1997, pp. 220–22.

2. A. Weintraub, "Hotter than a Pair of Vinyl Jeans," *BusinessWeek*, June 9, 2003, pp. 84–86.

3. G.R. Merz, P.B. Weber, and V.B. Laetz, "Linking Small Business Management with Entrepreneurial Growth," *Journal of Small Business Management*, October 1994, pp. 48–60.

4. J. Bailey, "Growth Needs a Plan or Only Losses May Build," *Wall Street Journal*, October 29, 2002, p. B9; and L. Beresford, "Growing Up," *Entrepreneur*, July 1995, pp. 124–28.

5. J. Summer, "More, Please!" *Business Finance*, July 2000, pp. 57–61.

6. T. Stevens, "Pedal Pushers," *Industry Week*, July 17, 2000, pp. 46–52.

7. P. Lorange and R.T. Nelson, "How to Recognize—and Avoid—Organizational Decline," *Sloan Management Review*, Spring 1987, pp. 41–48.

8. S.D. Chowdhury and J.R. Lange, "Crisis, Decline, and Turnaround: A Test of Competing Hypotheses for Short-Term Performance Improvement in Small Firms," *Journal of Small Business Management*, October 1993, pp. 8–17.

9. C. Farrell, "How to Survive a Downturn," *BusinessWeek*, April 28, 1997, pp. ENT4–ENT6.

10. R.W. Pricer and A.C. Johnson, "The Accuracy of Valuation Methods in Predicting the Selling Price of Small Firms," *Journal of Small Business Management*, October 1997, pp. 24–35.

11. J. Bailey, "Selling the Firm and Letting Go of the Dream," *Wall Street Journal*, December 10, 2002, p. B6; P. Hernan, "Finding the Exit," *Industry Week*, July 17, 2000, pp. 55–61; D. Rodkin, "For Sale by Owner," *Entrepreneur*, January 1998, pp. 148–53; A. Livingston, "Avoiding Pitfalls when Selling a Business," *Nation's Business*, July 1998, pp. 25–26; and G. Gibbs Marullo, "Selling Your Business: A Preview of the Process," *Nation's Business*, August 1998, pp. 25–26.

12. K. Stringer, "Time Out," *Wall Street Journal*, March 27, 2002, p. R14; T. Stevens, "Striking a Balance," *Industry Week*, November 20, 2000, pp. 26–36; and S. Caudron, "Fit to Lead," *Industry Week*, July 17, 2000, pp. 63–68.

● ● ● Photo Credits

CHAPTER 1

page 3: Gegax Consulting & Keynotes; page 6: Michael Quan/The New York Times; page 7: UPPA / Topham/The Image Works;page 10: Robin Nelson; page 12: Timothy Archibald; page 15: World Energy Alternatives; page 21: courtesy of Rita Warner; page 21: courtesy of Lucy Kawaihalau; page 23: Jeff Sciortino Photography.

CHAPTER 2

page 25: Amanda Friedman; page 28: Courtesy S. C. Williams Library, Stevens Institute of Technology, Hoboken, NJ; page 29: UPI/CORBIS BETTMANN; page 32: Diana Koenigsberg Photography; page 37: AP/Wide World Photos; page 40: Gerard Burkhart/The New York Times; page 44: Fred R. Conrad/The New York Times; page 45: courtesy of Jan Coughtrey; page 45: courtesy of Martin Shova; page 47: Butler Photography.

CHAPTER 3

page 49: Athleta Corporation; page 54: K. Dooher Photography; page 56: Keefe, Bruyette & Woods; page 62: Schneider National, Inc.; page 65: Baerbel Schmidt Photography; page 68: The Image Works; page 70: REFORMA-ENRED/NEWSCOM; page 73: courtesy of Dana Murray; page 73: courtesy of Ann M. Kelly; page 75: AP/Wide World Photos.

CHAPTER 4

page 77: Dan Burn-Forti; page 79: CPA/Topham/The Image Works; page 87: Munshi Ahmed Photography; page 88: Bloomberg News; page 94: courtesy of Stuart Silk; page 96: Reuters NewMedia Inc./Landov LLC.

CHAPTER 5

page 99:Courtesy of Coco-Mat, Athens, Greece; page 101: Asia Kepka Photography; page 104: Stephen Webster; page 106: Larry Ford Foto; page 111: The New York Times; page 113: Patrice Tanaka & Company, Inc.; page 113: courtesy of Boeing Aircraft Company; page 121: AP/Wide World Photos; page 123: courtesy of Amanda Ferguson; page 123: courtesy of Steve Literati; page 125: AP/Wide World Photos.

CHAPTER 6

page 133: GVA Worldwide; page 136: Thor Swift Photography; page 138: © 2005 Michael Girard Photography; page 141: Gerard Burkhart/The New York Times; page 143: Beige Jones/Ripple Resort Media; page 148: © 2002 Brian Smith; page 153: courtesy of Jeffrey Sears; page 153: courtesy of Cindy Brewer; page 155: Photo courtesy of C. F. Martin & Co., Inc., Nazareth, PA.

CHAPTER 7

page 157: UBS AG; page 158: Meredith Heuer/J Group Photo; page 160: Don Hogan Charles/The New York Times; page 162: AP/Wide World Photos; page 166: Ethan Hill; page 170: Blake Little Photography; page 167: courtesy of Rodney K. G. Goodwin; page 173: courtesy of Steve Hidy; page 173: courtesy of Daniel K. Borden; pages 175–76: Lend Lease Corporation.

CHAPTER 8

page 179: Ethan Hill; page 181: AP/Wide World Photos; page 188: Matthew Gilson; page 189: AP/Wide World Photos; page 191: AP/Wide World Photos; page 194: AP/Wide World Photos; page 198: courtesy of Amit Shah; page 200: Mike Morrow Photography.

CHAPTER 9

page 205: AP/Wide World Photos; page 206: © Wyman IRA/CORBIS SYGMA; page 207: © Dennis MacDonald/PhotoEdit; page 208: Courtesy of James Leynse; page 212: James Estrin/The New York Times; page 213: Xurxo Lobato/Cover/International Cover; page 221: Cherry Kim Photography; page 223: courtesy of Martha E. Barkman; page 225: Jerry Jack/Ken Barboza Associates, Inc.

CHAPTER 10

page 233: © Claudio Bresciani/SCANPIX/RETNA; page 235: Photo by Michuel Mendez Photography; page 239: Thomas McDonald; page 242: Photo by Terrence Meehan, NIMA College.; page 246: Acxiom Corporation; page 248: © REUTERS/Shannon Stapleton/CORBIS; page 251: courtesy of Peter Crombie; page 251: courtesy of Clare Carter; page 253: AP/Wide World Photos.

CHAPTER 11

page 255: Kathrin Miller; page 257: Scogin Mayo Photography; page 259: Jenny Schulder; page 262: Ann States; page 267: David Deal; page 271: British Petroleum p.l.c.; page 272: Kim Christensen Photography; page 274: John Mabanglo; page 277: courtesy of John Emerman; page 277: courtesy of Chuck Pick; page 279: Jeffrey Lowe Photography;

CHAPTER 12

page 281: Courtesy of Brett Ellison/ National Australia Bank; page 282: The Container Store; page 287: courtesy of PricewaterhouseCoopers; page 294: Health Partners; page 297: Studio 321 Inc.; page 302: Xerox Corporation; page 304: David Carmack Photography; page 305: courtesy of Sandra M. Steiner; page 305: courtesy of David Jolliffe; page 308: John Zich Photography.

CHAPTER 13

page 311: Bob Stefko Photography; page 313: John W. Clark; page 315: Debra McClinton Photography; page 318: © 2002 Robert Houser (roberthouser.com); page 322: AP/Wide World Photos; page 328: Dennis Kleiman Photography; page 331: courtesy of Pauline Thomas; page 333: Electronic Arts.

CHAPTER 14

page 341: AP/Wide World Photos; page 344: Douglas Healey; page 346: AP/Wide World Photos; page 348: Wells Fargo/Community Development; page 350: Banc One Capital Markets Inc.; page 353: Douglas Healey; page 358: Chris Mueller/Redux Pictures; page 365: courtesy of Amanda Ferguson; page 365: courtesy of Barbara Gomes-Beach.

CHAPTER 15

page 369: AP/Wide World Photos; page 372: courtesy of Toyo Inc.; page 375: David Toerge Photograpy; page 379: Google; page 384: AP/Wide World Photos; page 387: courtesy of Joseph Small; page 389: BASF Corporation.

CHAPTER 16

page 391: Mary Ellen Mark; page 398: AFP PHOTO/Paul Buck/Getty Images, Inc.; page 401: Burkhard Schittny; page 408: © John Garrett/CORBIS; page 409: Oil Changers, Inc.; page 412: Nancy Newberry; page 413: Nichols Foods, Ltd.; page 415: Joel Page/The New York Times; page 417: courtesy of Stacey Ficken; page 417: courtesy of Mary Hsue; page 419: Michael O'Brien/Mud Island, Inc.

CHAPTER 17

page 421: David Butow/CORBIS BETTMANN; page 425: AP/Wide World Photos; page 427: AP/Wide World Photos; page 435: Julian Richards Agency; page 439: AP/Wide World Photos; page 440: Anne Hamersky; page 441: Randall Scott; page 442: Photo provided by Jack Stack; page 446: Richard Alcorn/Colgate-Palmolive Company; page 448: courtesy of Sharna Small Borsellina; page 448: courtesy of Sheila O'Neill; page 450: Reuter NewMedia Inc./CORBIS BETTMANN.

CHAPTER 18

page 457: Haier Group; page 463: REUTERS/Win McNamee/Landov LLC; page 466: Christopher Mann; page 469: NCCI; page 473: DST Output; page 474: SYSCO Corporation; page 477: J. Emilio Flores/The New York Times; page 481: courtesy of Ted V. Schaefer; page 484: Craig C. Lizotte, P.E.; page 484: courtesy of Wendy Moran.

CHAPTER 19

page 489: © 2005 Steven Ahlgren; page 492: Jenny Schulder; page 496: Ford Motor Company; page 498: Value Innovation Partners, Ltd.; page 502: Michael Vaughn/Janet C. Bugher; page 503: © 2005 Michael Girard Photography; page 505: courtesy of amazon.com; page 507: courtesy of Debra M. Barnhart; page 507: courtesy of James O'Neill; page 509: Paxton.

●●● ●Name Index

•••• Organization Index

•••Glindex

●●●Notes

● ● ●**Notes**